Business as Ethical and Business as Usual

The Jones and Bartlett Series in Philosophy

Robert Ginsberg, General Editor

Ayer, A. J., *Metaphysics and Common Sense*, 1994 reissue with corrections and new introduction by Thomas Magnell, Drew University

Beckwith, Francis J., University of Nevada, Las Vegas, Editor, *Do the Right Thing: A Philosophical Dialogue on the Moral and Social Issues of Our Time*

Bishop, Anne H. and John R. Scudder, Jr., Lynchburg College, *Nursing Ethics: Therapeutic Caring Presence*

Caws, Peter, The George Washington University, *Ethics from Experience*

DeMarco, Joseph P., Cleveland State University, *Moral Theory: A Contemporary Overview*

Gert, Bernard et al., Dartmouth College, *Morality and the New Genetics: A Guide for Students and Health Care Providers*

Gorr, Michael, Illinois State University, and Sterling Harwood, San Jose State University, Editors, *Crime and Punishment: Philosophic Explorations*

Haber, Joram Graf, Bergen Community College, Interviewer, *Ethics in the '90s*, a 26-part Video Series

Harwood, Sterling, San Jose State University, Editor, *Business as Ethical and Business as Usual: Text, Readings, and Cases*

Heil, John, Davidson College, *First-Order Logic: A Concise Introduction*

Jason, Gary, San Diego State University, *Introduction to Logic*

Minogue, Brendan, Youngstown State University, *Bioethics: A Committee Approach*

Moriarty, Marilyn, Hollins College, *Writing Science through Critical Thinking*

Pauling, Linus, and Daisaku, Ikeda, *A Lifelong Quest for Peace, A Dialogue*, Translator and Editor, Richard L. Gage

Pojman, Louis P., The University of Mississippi, and Francis Beckwith, University of Nevada Las Vegas, Editors, *The Abortion Controversy: A Reader*

Pojman, Louis P., The University of Mississippi, Editor, *Environmental Ethics: Readings in Theory and Application*

Pojman, Louis P., The University of Mississippi, *Life and Death: Grappling with the Moral Dilemmas of Our Time*

Pojman, Louis P., The University of Mississippi, Editor, *Life and Death: A Reader in Moral Problems*

Rolston III, Holmes, Colorado State University, Editor, *Biology, Ethics, and the Origins of Life*

Townsend, Dabney, The University of Texas at Arlington, Editor, *Aesthetics: Classic Readings from the Western Tradition*

Veatch, Robert M., The Kennedy Institute of Ethics, Georgetown University, Editor, *Cross-Cultural Perspectives in Medical Ethics: Readings*

Veatch, Robert M., The Kennedy Institute of Ethics, Georgetown University, Editor, *Medical Ethics, Second Edition*

Verene, D. P., Emory University, Editor, *Sexual Love and Western Morality: A Philosophical Anthology, Second Edition*

Williams, Clifford, Trinity University, Illinois, Editor, *On Love and Friendship: Philosophical Readings*

Business as Ethical and Business as Usual

Text, Readings, and Cases

Sterling Harwood
San Jose State University
San Jose, California

Jones and Bartlett Publishers
Sudbury, Massachusetts

Boston   London   Singapore

Editorial, Sales, and Customer Service Offices
Jones and Bartlett Publishers
40 Tall Pine Drive
Sudbury, MA 01776
1-800-832-0034

Jones and Bartlett Publishers International
7 Melrose Terrace
London W6 7RL
England

Library of Congress Cataloging-in-Publication Data
Harwood, Sterling, 1958–
    Business as ethical and business as usual : text, readings, and cases / Sterling Harwood.--
        p.   cm. -- (The Jones and Bartlett series in philosophy)
    Includes bibliographical references and index.
    ISBN 0-86720-971-2
    1. Business ethics.   2. Corporate culture.   3. Social
responsibility of business.   4. Business ethics--Case studies.
    I. Title.   II. Series.
HF5387.H377   1995
174'.4--dc20   95-39105
                                                                     CIP

Acquisitions Editors: Arthur C. Bartlett and Nancy E. Bartlett
Production Administrator: Anne S. Noonan
Manufacturing Buyer: Dana L. Cerrito
Editorial Production Service: Seahorse Prepress/Book 1
Typesetting: Seahorse Prepress/Book 1
Printing and Binding: Hamilton Printing Company
Cover Printing: New England Book Components, Inc.
Cover Designer: Marshall Henrichs

 This book is printed on acid-free, recycled paper.

Printed in the United States of America
99 98 97 96 95   10 9 8 7 6 5 4 3 2 1

"The maxim of the British people is 'Business as usual.'"

— Winston Churchill

"You can tell the ideals of a nation by its advertisements."

— Norman Douglas

"Bad philosophers are like slum landlords. It's my job to put them out of business!"

— Ludwig Wittgenstein

"The conjunction of an immense military establishment and a large arms industry is new in the American experience. The total influence—economic, political, even spiritual—is felt in every city. . . . In the councils of government we must guard against the acquisition of unwarranted influence, whether sought or unsought, by the military industrial complex. The potential for the disastrous rise of misplaced power exists and will persist. . . . We must never let the weight of this combination endanger our liberties or democratic processes. We should take nothing for granted. . . ."

— President Dwight Eisenhower

For Elizabeth Navarro, the love of my life

CONTENTS

PREFACE

Thales, the first Western philosopher, and a thinker who became rich by following his theories, thought that business and ethics were related in showing the practical value of philosophical theories. But business ethics as a separate study is still quite a new field that is full of challenges. So it is quite fitting to experiment with new ways of thinking about issues in this field.

This entry into the field was edited to address challenging issues with four equally important goals in mind. I wanted selections that (1) had informative arguments about the key areas in business ethics; (2) were written clearly; (3) could be seen by students as relevant to their lives and the lives of people they know; (4) strike a good balance of moral and political views. Each of these goals makes the book stimulating and fascinating enough to engage the interests of students as they read it. Here are examples of how I have tried to meet these four goals.

1. I have included the classics, such as the Ford Pinto case, the infant formula case involving Nestlé, the Baby M case, the Johnson Controls case, and the Exxon Valdez oil spill case. I have made room for such sensitive and timely issues as affirmative action and the debate between capitalism and socialism.

I have also included valuable yet often neglected topics. For example, what determines the price of food is usually not treated in business ethics textbooks. But it's not simply a matter of supply and demand. So I have included a selection from Farmers for an Orderly Market. Now students can figure out what business ethics has to do with the price of peas in Peoria.

2. Though each scholarly selection is notable for its clear writing, I have introduced several other selections from nonacademic sources in my search for the clearest writing on significant issues. These range from Michael Kinsley on the left wing of politics to Rush Limbaugh III on the right wing. They might be clearly right or clearly wrong, but they are surely clear!

3. The old campus joke about college life is that while the students want sex, the alumni want football and the faculty want parking. Sex is a basic part of human life, including the lives of people active in business, but you would not know that from reading the widely used textbooks in business ethics. The truth is: sex sells. This book's discussion of sexual topics, including selling breast implants that enhance sex appeal, sexual harassment, feminism, and homosexuality, will surely interest students as persons.

In addition to the relevance of sex to their lives, students in college can also see the relevance of the price of textbooks. So I have included an essay on the ethics of that subject. Years of experience in the classroom at Cornell University and San Jose State University have taught me that students are also fascinated by the topics of inheritance, surrogate motherhood, and affirmative action. I have added selections on these topics and others with special appeal to students. Good teachers know that their students have more incentive to learn about a topic that they consider important and in which they have an interest.

4. Selections in this book not only represent left-wing and right-wing sources, but also in some cases transcend these labels by discussing post–Cold War eco-

nomics. Environmentalists and feminists are included, as well as critics of environmentalism and feminism. Part II is devoted to a variety of moral theories, including egalitarianism, libertarianism, utilitarianism, perfectionism (virtue ethics), and humanism. I take perfectionism more seriously than do editors of other business ethics texts; for instance, I include Michael Kinsley's evaluation of key characters in business, ranging from Ralph Nader to Lee Iacocca.

The generous size of this book allows a good balance of views on many subjects. A text that never takes a stand makes for bland reading. So I have made sure that wherever a stand is taken in the text, differing views are offered next—or nearby. If any reader would like to see other selections added to strike an even better balance in a future edition of the book, I would heartily welcome such suggestions.

I am grateful to students, faculty, staff, and administrators at Cornell University and San Jose State University for all the help I received in my academic experience with business ethics and related fields. I thank Arthur and Nancy Bartlett of Jones and Bartlett Publishers for their many forms of help with this project. Nancy was especially helpful with her volunteered efforts in the arduous task of acquiring permissions for reprinting materials. I gratefully acknowledge the keen attention to detail of Anne Noonan at Jones and Bartlett. I thank Robert Ginsberg, the general editor of philosophy for Jones and Bartlett, especially for his early and thorough comments on the manuscript. I am grateful for the prepublication evaluation of many reviewers, in particular, Louis P. Pojman, Joseph Betz, Ronald Green, and Bob Rafalko. I am grateful to my colleague, Peter Hadreas, for allowing me to publish, for the first time, his paper on the famous Ford Pinto case. I thank Gregory Stock for permitting some of his questions to be reprinted from *The Book of Questions: Business, Politics, Ethics* (Workman Publishing, 1991).

Finally, my most heartfelt thanks go to Elizabeth Navarro for her inspiration.

"Have you noticed ethics creeping into
some of these deals lately?"

Drawing by H. Martin; © 1992, The New Yorker Magazine, Inc.

PART I

Introduction to Business Ethics:
From Oxymoron to Logic

1

Introduction: Taking Ethics Seriously—Moral Relativism versus Moral Realism

Sterling Harwood

Many people joke that "business ethics" is an oxymoron—a contradiction in terms. They claim that books like this, which take ethics (that is, the principles or study of morality) seriously, are therefore about a nonexistent subject, since no contradiction can exist. Despite the amazing variety of issues arising in business, as the table of contents in this book indicates, these critics of business ethics suggest that ethics is relevant to none of these issues. The view of these critics is so extreme that it can hardly be true. They stress that businesspeople are tough, apparently assuming that ethics incorporates only caring and compassion, not toughness. These critics evidently think that cold, hard business practices are, by their very nature, incompatible with the caring or altruism that all ethical theories require. To prove their point, they often cite sayings such as "Business is business," "A deal is a deal," and "The law is the law." These slogans are intended to indicate that business is isolated from other areas of life and that business somehow has some special finality to it. But these slogans are empty; they lack intellectual content. They are what logicians call tautologies, sayings that go around and around in a circle. Being tough is one thing; it surely has its proper place. But being tough and dumb is an especially poor combination, since the tough and dumb do much damage to people by lashing out harshly and ignorantly. The two articles in this chapter try to show how being ethical is also a key part of being smart and logical. For example, it is illogical to accept uncritically whatever the authorities in one's community claim to be moral. Indeed, questioning authority in one's own community often requires toughness as well as intelligence. The text discusses communitarianism, which claims that the community determines right and wrong, and also discusses the pros and cons of

moral relativism and its alternative, moral realism, which are defined below.

Taking Morality Seriously: The Pros and Cons of Moral Relativism

A. Key Definitions

Many students already have adopted an extreme philosophy about morality even before they enter their first college course in philosophy or morality. This extreme philosophy is moral relativism. The point of this reading is to give students reasons to take morality more seriously and reasons to doubt moral relativism. Students who accept moral relativism tend not to take morality as seriously as they should, since they tend to think that any moral argument is just as good as any other moral argument because morality is all purely subjective opinion. Students who think that all moral arguments are created equal will tend not to strive in developing and pursuing moral arguments in philosophy papers or in classroom discussions. Following are key definitions of moral relativism and its alternative, moral realism. Examples of views in moral realism include ones where facts such as how much suffering and death an alternative would probably cause help determine that alternative's rightness or wrongness, regardless of what a group or individual deemed relevant merely believes about that alternative's rightness or wrongness. The doctrine is named *moral realism* because it emphasizes reality over mere belief, and because it emphasizes the real properties actions have in fact rather than mere opinion. Moral realism insists that, when it comes to morality, merely believing it does not make it so.

Moral relativism: What is right (or wrong) is determined exclusively by what the relevant entity (group or individual) believes is right (or wrong).

Moral realism: What is right (or wrong) is not determined exclusively by what any relevant entity (group or individual) believes is right (or wrong).

B. Four Arguments for Moral Relativism (the Pros)

1. There is a suspiciously large amount of moral disagreement. Reasonable people disagree about moral issues. So there's no right answer to questions of

morality. Morality seems more like a matter of taste, and there's no disputing matters of taste.

Reply: There is much transcultural moral agreement about the basic particular evils of rape, murder, theft, and lying. And there's even much agreement on such general moral principles as The Golden Rule. There is much more agreement about political morality now that communism has fallen in the Soviet bloc, South Africa has made major reforms moving toward a multiracial democracy, and Israel and the Palestine Liberation Organization have signed a historic peace treaty. Northern Ireland has more peace.

2. Relativism promotes tolerance, which is good.
Reply: Argument 2 is self-contradictory because it accepts relativism and the idea that tolerance is good transculturally or independent of culture.

3. Relativism is fairer to historical figures, which is good. For example, Lincoln wanted to repatriate all American blacks to Africa. We now think this would be immoral, but Lincoln was a great man and it is unfair to judge him as immoral and require The Great Emancipator to be further ahead of his time than he already was.

Reply: Argument 3 is self-contradictory because it accepts relativism and the idea that fairness is good transculturally or independent of culture. Also, one need not be ahead of one's time to see the contradictions in racism, sexism, etc. As an example, racists inconsistently believe blacks are filthy, lazy, and untrustworthy yet believe blacks are naturally suited to cook, clean, and handle the children while white parents are away. Sexists believe women are dull, passive, and poor entrepreneurs yet believe women are scheming manipulators with great verbal skills. Puritans believe sex is a dirty, disgusting, degrading act we share only with someone we love. Nazis believed Jews were generally bankers or rich and that Jews were generally revolutionary communists. Nazis believed that Jews were mentally and physically inferior yet controlled Germany.

4. Relativity is true even in hard, objective science. So it must be true in squishy-soft subjects like art and morality.

Reply: First, not everything goes in art. Beauty is not in the eye of the beholder. For example, two computer-generated paintings identical in microscopic detail cannot rationally be judged to have different aesthetic value by the naked eye. Second, Pro 4 equivocates on 'relativity,' since 'relativity' does not mean the same thing in physics and in morality.

C. Five Arguments against Moral Relativism (the Cons)

1. Relativism cannot rationally specify which group's beliefs determine right and wrong. Each of us is a member of many different groups (an age group, an ethnic group, a family, a nation, a gender). And these groups will, as relativists admit in Pro 1 above, disagree about what we should do. So it is relativism's burden to argue for a specific group as relevant.

2. If relativists try to specify the majority of people in a group as the relevant entity whose beliefs determine right and wrong, then relativism will be too intolerant since it will then dismiss moral reformers, minorities, and dissidents within that group has hopelessly and automatically wrong.

3. Majoritarian relativism commits the *ad populum* fallacy. Most believe *X* is moral. Therefore, *X* is moral.

4. Relativism commits the fallacy of equivocation by ignoring the distinction between critical morality and conventional morality. For example, consider "What is right for America?" The question has two different meanings. One meaning involves what Americans happen to believe to be right. The other involves what really is right for America independently of what Americans happen to believe to be right. The first meaning of moral rightness is called conventional, customary, or prevailing morality. The second meaning of moral rightness is called critical, reflective, or enlightened morality. Philosophy requires us to go beyond conventional morality to critical morality, since philosophy requires us to think critically about moral customs and traditions.

5. "No absolutes exist" contradicts itself.

Duska, in the second article in this chapter, also criticizes moral relativism and moral skepticism. Many students who accept moral relativism ask, "Who is to decide the answers to moral questions?" In an episode of the famous science fiction television series *Star Trek*, "The Conscience of the King," Captain Kirk responded to such a question, "Who are you to decide?," by asking, "Who do I have to be?" "Who is to decide?" seems to search for some authoritarian figure who is to decide all moral questions. Of course, we have no such person available. But that fails to prove that moral relativism is true. It merely shows that we should think for ourselves.

A more enlightening question is "On what basis should we decide answers to moral questions?" The most straightforward answer is that moral questions should be decided on facts and logic. If we use this insight to answer "Who is to decide?," we should note that the person with the best argument has, in a valuable way, decided the issue until someone presents a better argument. But how do we decide who has the best argument? We must argue with each other. These are intellectual arguments, not bickering. From the process of arguing itself some arguments will emerge as better than others. Not all arguments are equal when it comes to being factual or logical. For example, if an argument says we should avoid doing some act because that act will cause much death and destruction, we are entitled to reject that argument when we discover that the act in question is in fact harmless. Further, elementary rationality requires that we avoid logical fallacies, errors in reasoning.

None of this means that everyone will agree at the end of the process, or that we should physically force our views on whoever disagrees. But, as a practical matter, the law often forces us to obey. And in democracies the law is usually shaped somewhat by moral arguments about what the law should be. The legal cases in this book show how practical it is even for hard-nosed business types who emphasize the bottom line to develop a moral awareness that will help them distinguish between moral arguments that are logical and moral arguments that are not. To be unaware of the moral values that the law often tries to promote is to risk the costs of losing a lawsuit, getting a poor reputation, and losing a business. This book is designed to help businesspeople stay ahead of the moral curve that shapes the law and the expectations of many consumers. This will enable businesspeople to improve the ethics of their business practices in ways that are good for business.

Later chapters will discuss specific issues. Here we are primarily discussing how to discover moral truths generally, not how to apply these truths to a particular issue. But if we required a process to yield unanimous agreement before we trusted it to help us discover the truth, then we would always be paralyzed. For in a world with so many different people, some will always disagree even with the best argument because they are illogical, ignorant, intolerant, dogmatic, stubborn, or impatient, or because they have yet to develop a counterargument but have an unproven faith that they will develop one later.

Until a counterargument arises, we are justified in treating the best argument as leading us closer to the truth than any of the alternative arguments currently available. This approach does not assume that we must answer all moral questions starkly in absolute terms. This approach is entirely consistent with seeing arguments as leading us closer to the truth. How close we are to discovering the truth is a matter of degree, with shades of gray, not an absolute matter that one must see in black and white. Business ethics is not a Western movie cliché. The good guys will not always wear white hats. The bad guys will not always wear black hats. Many good and bad guys will wear the gray flannel suit of business.

2

Against MacIntyre's Relativistic Communitarianism

Sterling Harwood

Author's abstract: This reading tries to show why elementary logic and rationality require us to take morality seriously. It attempts to expose many fallacies, errors of logic, in the views of moral relativism and communitarianism. It tries to provide a logical defense of moral realism.

1. Introduction

Some have rightly raised the issue of whether communitarianism gives too much support to moral relativism (relativism for short) to be true.[1] I wish to broaden and strengthen objections to communitarianism's relativism. And since communitarianism developed largely out of dissatisfaction with liberalism, I wish to help explain why relativism might appeal to misguided liberals. Then I shall argue that the relativistic communitarianism of Alasdair MacIntyre is both defective, due to its relativism, and unsuccessful in attacking liberalism, due to MacIntyre's irrelevant and contradictory remarks. Let me make it clear that the relativism I attack is not one of the most sophisticated versions of relativism developed. Rather, I attack the rather crude relativism that myself and others think plagues MacIntyre's communitarianism.[2] Finally, I shall not attempt to give a full definition of communitarianism, which is perhaps still too inchoate to define adequately. Rather, I shall assume that, whatever communitarianism is, MacIntyre's views in his recent books count as one form of communitarianism. I shall also briefly dis-

cuss some views of Michael Sandel. I think I am safe in assuming that MacIntyre and Sandel are leading exponents of communitarianism. My defense of liberalism is a somewhat indirect attack on communitarianism, which was developed as an alternative to liberalism. I take communitarianism to imply that communities are intrinsically valuable and are the source of our reasons for accepting other things as valuable. I take MacIntyre to accept this communitarian implication, which I think endorses too crude a form of relativism to be true. So I shall argue that MacIntyre's relativistic communitarianism is false.

I shall discuss four arguments for relativism, showing how some of them might appeal to misguided liberals but also showing how none of them should appeal to liberals. I shall give three arguments for moral realism (realism, for short). Realism, as I define it, is simply the denial of relativism. Realism states there are at least some values that are objective, that is, rationally defensible and applicable transculturally and independently of moral beliefs. Relativism states that all moral values are subjective, that is, determined exclusively by the moral beliefs of a group (for example, cultural traditions).

2. Four Basic Arguments for Relativism—and Realist Replies

First, relativists often stress that there is much moral disagreement generally. Relativists argue that there is so much disagreement about morality that there must be something wrong with the very idea of an objectively true morality (that is, a morality that is applicable transculturally and that is true at least largely independent of any culture). I agree that if people generally held their moral views no more strongly or uniformly than they hold their views on fashion, or if basic moral beliefs were generally held and then disregarded on a minute-by-minute or even a monthly basis (a morality of the month club!), then that would be good evidence that something was subjective or wrong with morality.[3] But there is a huge amount of longstanding moral agreement across otherwise diverse cultures. Moral opinion against basic evils such as murder, rape, assault, and theft is transculturally widespread. Even an abstract and basic moral rule, the golden rule, is found in Buddhism, Christianity, Confucianism, Hinduism, Islam, Judaism, and others.[4] Agreement on political morality has greatly increased with the recent reforms in

Reprinted from *Liberalism and Community*, ed. R. Moffat, C. Murphy and N. Reynolds (New York: New York University Press, 1995).

Eastern Europe and the Soviet Union. And even South Africa has recently made reforms significantly reducing the still fundamental moral differences between it and industrial democracies.

Relativists might try to revive their argument from moral disagreement by arguing that, even if the sheer amount of moral disagreement is not problematic, since reasonable people disagree about morality there is no objectively right answer to the moral questions these reasonable people disagree about. For example, Eskimos have something of a tradition of letting their terminally ill and aged people die passively by abandoning them on ice floes. The relativist expects us to shudder at the thought of such a practice. But we do much the same thing. The Eskimos have not traditionally had the technology that we use in letting our terminally ill and aged people die passively. But we nonetheless do the functional equivalent by letting such people die in nursing homes or hospices. Nursing homes, are, in a functional sense, technologically souped-up ice floes![5] A second example the relativist might stress is homosexuality. The ancient Greeks permitted it, and the ancient Hebrews prohibited it. The relativist then tries to make us say which, the ancient Greeks or the ancient Hebrews, is an unreasonable group. But this example poses a false dilemma. Perhaps the groups were both pursuing a reasonable policy of trying to get a balanced population. The Greeks may have been overpopulated, allowing homosexuality as a nonreproductive outlet for sexual passion, while the Hebrews may have been underpopulated, condemning homosexuality as a wasting of the seed. So, once again, we see there can be underlying agreement that makes the superficial disagreement inadequate to support relativism.

Further, even if we grant that reasonable people can disagree, it scarcely follows that there is no objective or logical basis on which to side with one against the other; for reasonableness is a matter of degree. For example, two people may be generally reasonable, except that one of them is unreasonable—refusing even to listen to argument or evidence—on one issue. Thus, while both disputants are reasonable, if that one issue is the issue in question, we may logically side with the more open-minded of the two people on the issue. For the more open-minded person is the more reasonable person and thus more likely to be right. After all, the more open-minded person has at least heard opposing arguments and tried earnestly to respond to them rationally. The other person has refused to do so. Indeed, relativism cannot adequately account for reasonable disagreement over so many years; for it seems unreasonable to disagree continually on a question with no right answer.

Finally, the relativist's suggestion that moral agreement between people would establish objective moral truth, and that moral disagreement between people prevents objective moral truth, commits the *ad populum* fallacy. We shall return to this below.

Second, relativists argue that relativism leads to more tolerance, which is good. This argument appeals to many liberals, who endorse the value of tolerance. Relativists argue that realism, by supporting moral values of transcultural applicability, is too absolute and rigid. Realism is sometimes even called moral absolution. But this argument is self-contradictory; for the argument is meant to apply to the transcultural truth of relativism. But then the goodness of relativism's promotion of tolerance would also be transcultural. Thus a transcultural, objective value would exist after all, and so realism would be true. Further, utilitarianism is extremely flexible and sensitive to special conditions, yet it is compatible with and supportive of realism. So realism can avoid being rigid or absolute.

Third, relativists may argue that realism requires too much hindsight. Second-guessing historical figures who act on what they sincerely believe is moral at the time requires them to be ahead of their time, which is overly and unfairly demanding. Relativism allegedly avoids this hindsight, and so is fairer. Again, this argument is self-contradictory; for the argument is meant to apply to the transcultural truth of relativism. But then the goodness of relativism's fairness would also be transcultural. Thus a transcultural, objective value would exist after all, and so realism would be true. Further, many historical figures should have known better. Realism is not unfair to expect them to have seen obvious contradictions in their views. For example, bigots in the antebellum South should have seen their contradiction in believing that blacks are by nature (1) filthy, lazy, and untrustworthy; and (2) just the sort to cook and clean for whites and to handle all the children while the whites are away. Similarly, Nazis should have seen their contradiction in believing the propaganda that Jews were generally revolutionary communists and that Jews were generally bankers and other rich people. Further, sexists should see their contradiction in believing that women by nature are (1) stupid and passive and (2) clever and scheming manipulators with great verbal skills who are naturally suited to teach the complex fundamentals of life even to children. Finally, puritanical Victorians should have realized the contradiction in their view that, as one comedienne has put it, sex is a dirty, disgusting, and degrading act that we reserve for someone we love!

Fourth, some argue that since relativity is true even in the so-called hard sciences (for example, physics), relativity must be true in squishy-soft subjects such as art and morality.[6] For example, the American Council of Learned Societies claims,

> As the most powerful modern philosophies and theories have been demonstrating, claims of disinterest, objectivity, and universality are not to be trusted and themselves tend to reflect local historical conditions
>
> The challenge to [such] claims of intellectual authority . . . issue from almost all areas of modern thought—science, psychology, feminism, linguistics, semiotics, and anthropology.[7]

As John Searle notes, those in the council:

> confidently quote "relativity and quantum mechanics" as supporting their new conception of the humanities. One wishes they had told us in some detail how the study of, say, inertial frames in relativity theory or the collapse of the wave function in quantum mechanics support their peculiar conception . . .[8]

I suppose the council has the general rather than the special theory of relativity in mind.

But arguments such as the council's commit the fallacies of equivocation and false analogy; for the relativity or relativism in physics does not imply that truths in physics are relative to cultural beliefs. Rather, the relativity of velocity, for example, is relative to which physical object one focuses on. And even in so-called squishy-soft subjects like art, not anything goes. Beauty is not merely in the eye of the beholder; for one who believed that two identical objects had different aesthetic values can rationally be criticized on an objective basis.[9]

Further, Searle notes how the council fallaciously makes:

> constant appeals to authority. Typical passages claim support from "the most distinguished philosophers of science of our time," or tell us that "the consensus of most of the dominant theories is . . ."[10]

Searle states that:

> whatever [Thomas] Kuhn's intentions, the effect has been to demythologize science in the eyes of people in literary studies, many of whom think that the claim of science to represent any independently existing reality has been discredited. . . . [T]hey . . . clearly have Kuhn in mind.[11]

3. Three Basic Arguments for Realism against Relativism

First, which group does relativism think determines what is right (and wrong) for a given individual? Any individual is a member of many groups. And the prevailing moral beliefs in these groups differ significantly. For example, one is a member of a sex, an ethnic group, a nationality, a geographic group, a religious group (or the group of the nonreligious), an age group, an occupation, and so forth. So relativism leaves morality radically ambiguous or indeterminate, given the disparities between the prevailing beliefs of these many groups. The moral disagreements the relativists stress in the first argument in section 2 above *for* relativism lead to this strong argument *against* relativism.

Second, at least *elementary* logic gives us an objective basis on which to criticize moral views. Alasdair MacIntyre misses this point in getting bogged down in differences between quite sophisticated versions of rationality.[12] One part of elementary logic is the rejection of *ad populum* arguments as fallacious. Realism always allows the possibility that the majority's moral beliefs, or even unanimous moral beliefs, are wrong. This is required by treating *ad populum* arguments as fallacious—specifically, as invalid. But relativism requires us to accept *ad populum* arguments as valid; for relativism insists that if a belief prevails among a group of people, then that belief is true (in their situation).

Third, relativism makes the idea of moral reform self-contradictory. Since relativism defines morality based on what prevails as the status quo, relativism implies that it is a contradiction in terms to speak of morally requiring reform of the status quo. This will lead to intolerance of moral reformers, such as Martin Luther King, Jr., or Gandhi; for relativism implies that moral reformers are talking gibberish when they morally demand reform. The relativist must regard the idea of moral reform of a group's practices and beliefs as just as nonsensical as the idea of a square triangle.

4. MacIntyre's Relativistic Communitarianism

MacIntyre's communitarianism is relativistic. His *Whose Justice? Which Rationality?* concludes that "there are no tradition-independent standards of argument by appeal to which [rival traditions] can be shown to be in error."[13] So the arguments against relativism found in sections 2 and 3 generally apply to MacIntyre's view.

One may object that MacIntyre is not a relativist. For Nussbaum notes:

> The reader of [MacIntyre's] *After Virtue* might easily have concluded from MacIntyre's references to local communities that the solution he favored would lie in some form of cultural relativism ... MacIntyre's [*Whose Justice? Which Rationality?*] shows us that such a conclusion would have been a serious error. He now announces his deep opposition to cultural relativism and his determination to follow ... Aristotle by providing a historically sensitive account of the way in which people should go about justifying their ethical ideas, especially their ideas of justice.[14]

Even if Nussbaum has correctly interpreted MacIntyre's latest announcement as a deep opposition to relativism, and note that she cites no textual evidence for support, the announcement still fails to eliminate his relativistic appeals to communities in *After Virtue* or in *Whose Justice? Which Rationality?* Rather, it merely creates a crisis in interpretation of his work. We shall see below that he contradicts himself repeatedly. So, especially given his conclusion I quoted at the outset of this section, MacIntyre contradicts himself on, or at least expresses ambivalence about, relativism. He makes one conditional criticism of relativism and then, after making two concessions to relativism, concludes that no one can show that relativism is *absolutely* true, which of course relativists see as irrelevant anyway.[15]

More to the point here, MacIntyre's arguments—whether he is a relativist or not—fail to refute liberalism. Much of his argument is in support of platitudes posing no threat to liberalism. For example, MacIntyre insists—against whom I can't fathom—that "Doctrines, theses, and arguments all have to be understood in terms of historical context."[16] And he concludes:

> So theories of justice and practical rationality confront us as aspects of traditions, allegiance to which requires the living out of some more or less systematically embodied form of human life, each with its own spe-

cific modes of social relationship, each with its own canons of interpretation and explanation in respect of the behavior of others, each with its own evaluative practices.[17]

MacIntyre fails to show why liberalism must deny any of this. Indeed, liberalism insists on it, too. MacIntyre has established no more than that justice and practical rationality are essentially contested concepts. Hart, Rawls, and Dworkin, who MacIntyre admits are liberals, have emphasized Gallie's idea of competing conceptions of the same essentially contested contest.[18] MacIntyre seems to make the relativist's mistaken assumption that disagreement implies the disputants are talking about different things, and so are talking at cross-purposes. For MacIntyre says the apparently differing claims are culture-bound:

> it is only insofar as those features of the *polis* which provide an *essential* context for the exercise of Aristotelian justice and for the action-guiding and interpretative uses of the Aristotelian schema of practical reasoning can be reembodied in one's own life and that of one's time and place that one can be an Aristotelian. And it is likewise only insofar as those features of the social order in terms of which Hume framed his accounts of justice and of action can be reproduced that one can actually be a Humean. So also and correspondingly with other traditions of enquiry.[19]

MacIntyre implies that if people from two groups with different prevailing moral beliefs disagree, the relativist seems to interpret them as simply reporting (1) "My group believes X is immoral" and (2) "My group believes X is moral." And of course there is no contradiction between these two claims. But of course that is hardly what is going on in moral arguments between different groups.[20]

Even when MacIntyre's criticisms seem relevant they also seem contradictory. Martha Nussbaum exposes at least six of MacIntyre's contradictions, stating that MacIntyre's *Whose Justice? Which Rationality?*

> is full of maddening inconsistencies. MacIntyre attacks England for attempting to influence the local traditions of Scotland, but he praises the Pope for exercising moral authority over the recalcitrant bishops of Ireland ... Hume is a traitor because he left his native Scottish traditions behind and moved to London, but no account is taken of the local traditions of Thrace, which Aristotle left to come to Athens; or those of Northern Africa, which Augustine left to come to Rome; or those of Southern Italy, which Aquinas left (much against the will of his family, who tried to kid-

nap him) to join the Dominicans in Paris. No moral system has exterminated local traditions more relentlessly and more successfully than Christianity, especially in its Roman Catholic version. And yet, even while continuing to defend the integrity and authority of local traditions, MacIntyre gives his allegiance to Catholic Christianity. Again, he dismisses the English language as a rootless, traditionless, "internationalized" language, because it is used to translate from and to so many local languages; but the Latin of the Church receives no similar criticism. Furthermore, the same criteria that supposedly show liberalism to be an ignominious failure are taken, where Aquinas' view is concerned, as evidence that it is a tradition as yet "incomplete" and evolving.[21]

Another contradiction crops up when he says, "The attempted professionalization of serious and systematic thinking has had a disastrous effect upon our culture."[22] But then he says, "One of the most striking facts about modern political orders is that they lack institutionalized forms within which . . . fundamental disagreements can be systematically explored and charted, let alone there being any attempt made to resolve them."[23] Our culture is a modern political order. And attempted professionalization of serious and systematic thinking involves having some institutionalized forums within which people systematically explore fundamental disagreements and sometimes attempt to resolve them.

Finally, stepping back from the arguments should make us see how curious MacIntyre's general position is. He attacks liberalism for lacking a dominant tradition of values. But stepping back we see that America has the oldest constitutional tradition, with the liberal values of the Bill of Rights growing out of the Enlightenment. And even our party politics has much tradition. The Democratic Party, clearly the party that has the more liberal values of the two main American parties, is the oldest political party in the world. MacIntyre seeks a dominant tradition. While the Democrats have trouble winning one significant office (the Presidency) when they choose not to run a Southern Democrat, Democrats have generally dominated electoral offices for over fifty years. And between the two parties, which share many liberal values (speaking broadly to include libertarianism as classical liberalism), the political domination is almost complete. Indeed, many make the joke, with a serious undertone, that our political choices are generally between tweedledum and tweedledee.[24] But the joke is overstated in seeing no difference between McGovern and Nixon, Mark Green and Al D'Amato, Mario Cuomo and Lew Lehrman, Jesse

Helms and his Democratic opponents, David Duke and his Democratic opponents, et al. But more generally there is enough agreement to constitute the sort of dominant and conclusive tradition MacIntyre seeks.[25] MacIntyre admits, "So-called conservatism and so-called radicalism in these contemporary guises are in general mere stalking-horses for liberalism: the contemporary debates within modern political systems are almost exclusively between conservative liberals, liberal liberals, and radical liberals."[26] So I don't see why he thinks we are in an awful state of "inability to resolve radical disagreement."[27] He suggests that "our society is one not of consensus, but of division and conflict, at least so far as the nature of [political] justice is concerned . . ."[28] Again, MacIntyre seems to make contradictory claims.

In conclusion, MacIntyre's position strikes me as somewhat similar to Alexander Bickel's more than fifteen years ago. Bickel's last book lapsed into relativism and (Burkean) traditionalism.[29] Some plausibly suggest this was a dismal conclusion of a distinguished career.[30] I fear the same may be true of MacIntyre's latest conclusions.

Study Questions

1. If moral relativism were true, why would anyone bother to give a serious or detailed argument to defend his or her ethical views? Doesn't moral relativism imply that the most we could say would be something quite dogmatic like "We believe it, so that settles the ethical issue for us," or "My group says it, I believe it, that settles it!"?

2. What is your assessment of Harwood's suggestion that unethical views tend to be illogical or ignorant in overlooking the well-being of others?

3. What is communitarianism? What was Harwood's weakest point in attacking communitarianism? Can communitarianism be revised or supplemented to better withstand Harwood's arguments?

4. What is your elaluation of Harwood's argument that moral relativism commits the *ad populum* fallacy when the people are specified as the relevant entity?

5. What is your assessment of Harwood's argument that moral relativism commits the fallacy of equivocation by treating the word "morality" as if it has only one sense instead of two?

6. What is your evaluation of Harwood's argument that moral relativists commit the fallacy of equivocation when they argue that because relativity is true in hard sciences like physics, relativism must be true in softer subjects such as morality?

Notes

1. See, for example, John T. Sanders, "The Value of Freedom," elsewhere in this volume.

2. Others who see MacIntyre as embracing a crude relativism, involving narrow ethnocentrism and obscurantism, include Bernard Baumrin, 24 *Nous* 774–782 (1990), especially pp. 779 and 782. But more refined relativism still seems mistaken. For example, the flaws in Gilbert Harman's relativism are summarized well in C. E. Harris, Jr., *Applying Moral Theories*, 2nd ed. (Belmont, Calif.: Wadsworth, 1992), pp. 27–33.

3. For an excellent and recent argument that moral disagreement fails to entail relativism, see Judith Wagner DeCew, "Moral Conflicts and Ethical Relativism," 101 *Ethics* 27–41 (1990). For an anti-relativist argument discussing some of Alasdair MacIntyre's views on patriotism and attacking the value of ethnocentric agreements about the good life, see Paul Gomberg, "Patriotism Is Like Racism," 101 *Ethics* 144–150 (1990).

4. See, e.g., William H. Shaw and Vincent Barry, *Moral Issues in Business*, 5th ed. (Belmont, Calif.: Wadsworth Publishing, 1992), pp. 9–10.

5. Relativists often pick the Eskimos as an example of cultural diversity because of the persistent myth that Eskimos have 38 words for snow. See, for example, the introduction in Martin Hollis and Steven Lukes, eds., *Rationality and Relativism* (Cambridge: MIT Press, 1982), p. 11. In fact, the Eskimos have only two words for snow. And, indeed, English also seems to have two words for snow, namely "snow" and "slush." So, again, cultural diversity is not as great or as fundamental as many relativists assume.

6. One might suspect that the relativist is equivocating simply by switching back and forth between "relativism" and "relativity." But these are not different senses of the same word (or cognates of the same word), since some have in fact called moral relativism "moral relativity" or "ethical relativity." See, for example, David B. Wong, *Moral Relativity* (Berkeley, Calif.: University of California Press, 1984); Clyde Kluckhohn, "Ethical Relativity: *Sic et Non*," 52 *Journal of Philosophy* 663–677 (1955); and Edward Westermarck, *Ethical Relativity* (London: Routledge and Kegan Paul, 1932). Still, some try to draw the following distinction between moral relativism and moral relativity:

The most familiar form of relativism . . . is moral relativism. Distinct from mere moral *diversity* or variation, and from moral *relativity* (that is the relativity of such variation to independent variables, such as cultural and social factors), this is the denial of more than local standing to the grounds of moral belief and practice.

See Hollis and Lukes, *Rationality and Relativism*, pp. 5–6. So, if there is a distinction, then the relativist may well be equivocating.

7. John Searle, "The Storm over the University," 37 *The New York Review of Books* 34–42 (Dec. 6, 1990), p. 39.

8. Searle, p. 40.

9. See, R. M. Hare, *The Language of Morals* (Oxford, 1952), pp. 80–81.

10. Searle, p. 40.

11. Searle, p. 40.

12. See Alasdair MacIntyre, *Whose Justice? Which Rationality?* (Notre Dame, 1988). All citations of MacIntyre below are to this work unless otherwise stated.

13. MacIntyre, p. 9.

14. Martha Craven Nussbaum, "Recoiling from Reason," 36 *The New York Review of Books* 36–41 (Dec. 7, 1989), p. 36

15. MacIntyre, pp. 364 and 366–367.

16. MacIntyre, p. 403.

17. MacIntyre, p. 391.

18. MacIntyre lists these three as liberals on p. 344. See W. B. Gallie, "Essentially Contested Concepts," 56 *Proc. of the Arist. Soc.* 167 (1955–56; H. L. A. Hart, *The Concept of Law* (Oxford, 1961), pp. 155–59; John Rawls, *A Theory of Justice* (Harvard, 1971), p. 5; Ronald Dworkin, *Taking Rights Seriously* (Harvard, 1977), p. 103n. and Chs. 10 & 13; and Ronald Dworkin, *Law's Empire* (Harvard, 1986), pp. 70–74.

19. MacIntyre, p. 391.

20. David Lyons explains this using the example of debating abortion in "Ethical Relativism and the Problem of Incoherence," 86 *Ethics* 107–21 (1976).

21. Nussbaum, p. 38.

22. MacIntyre, p. x.

23. MacIntyre, p. 2.

24. See, e.g., David Lyons, "Substance, Process, and Outcome in Constitutional Theory," 72 *Cornell Law Review* 74–5 (1988).

25. See, e.g., MacIntyre, p. 400.

26. MacIntyre, p. 392.

27. MacIntyre, p. 9.

28. MacIntyre, pp. 1–2.

29. Alexander M. Bickel, *The Morality of Consent* (Yale, 1975), Ch. 1.

30. John Hart Ely, *Democracy and Distrust: A Theory of Judicial Review* (Harvard, 1980), Ch. 3, esp. pp. 43, 71–72.

3

What's the Point of a Business Ethics Course?

Ronald F. Duska

Author's abstract: The paper argues that the point of a business ethics course is to *improve* behavior in business, and that an essential ingredient in that improved behavior is *knowing* what's right or wrong. To make that claim, the paper attempts to dispose of three arguments that support the contrary claim, that business ethics courses are useless. First, it is argued that morals can't be taught, since they only result from training. Second, it is argued that such courses are unnecessary because business executives already know right from wrong. Third, it is argued that ethical knowledge is impossible, so there is nothing to teach. The first two arguments are dealt with briefly, and the third is addressed extensively. The paper argues that the skepticism about ethical knowledge is part of a pervasive "relativism" in our society, but shows that such a relativism/skepticism is untenable and indicates how ethical knowledge is possible. If, then, knowledge of right and wrong is an essential ingredient for improving business behavior, and such knowledge can be imparted in an ethics course, there is some point to teaching business ethics.

Disreputable business practices, ranging from the merely questionable to the wholly indefensible, have become commonplace. Defective pacemakers are sold to unsuspecting medical teams; sugar water is sold as pure apple juice for babies; oil spills are half-heartedly cleaned up; rivers are deliberately polluted when unscrupulous companies find they can dump waste without being detected; entrepreneurs buy out healthy productive companies simply to make a quick buck . . . and the list continues.

To combat this apparent spread of unethical business behavior, society turns, among other places, to teachers of business ethics. The anticipation is that somehow a business ethics course will help improve unethical business behavior. Business ethicists respond by offering more and more courses, producing more and more texts, and a new industry of business ethics is created. But how good is its product?

As the number of courses increases, so does serious criticism of them. *The New York Times* recently carried an op-ed piece by Michael Levin titled "Ethics Courses: Useless." As the title indicates Levin argues that business ethics courses are practically useless (Levin, 1990). Similarly, in a *Wall Street Journal* article entitled "Ethics Anyone? Or Morals?" Irving Kristol asserts that business ethics courses will not help improve the behavior of business people and it is naive to think they will.

At the risk of appearing naive, I will argue in this paper that somehow business ethics courses *can* and *should* improve business behavior, and if they don't there's not much point to them.

But why do Levin, Kristol, and others think business ethics courses cannot improve behavior? Basically, three reasons are given. One reason is that people already know right from wrong so ethics courses are superfluous. A second reason is that moral behavior is the result of training and can't be improved by giving courses in ethics. A third reason, directly in conflict with the first, is a sceptical reason, which claims that no one can "know" right from wrong, so there's no ethical knowledge to be taught.

What these three approaches have in common is that they maintain that ethics courses are useless due to the very nature of ethics, even though they disagree with what the nature is. I propose to show that ethics courses might be "useless," but that uselessness is not due to the very nature of ethics, rather that uselessness is due to *the way ethics courses are taught*. Thus, the futility of ethics courses is not due to ethics being either (1) already known, (2) unteachable, or (3) unknowable, but rather due to the way ethics is taught.

Let's briefly critique the reasons given why business ethics courses are useless. The first reason, that ethics courses are superfluous because people already

Reprinted from Ronald F. Duska, "What's the Point of a Business Ethics?" *Business Ethics Quarterly*, vol. 1, issue A (1991), pp. 335–352. Reprinted by permission. The footnotes have been omitted.

know right from wrong, is found in Kristol's op-ed piece. There he claims that business ethics courses are unnecessary because

... most corporate executives *know*, without prior instruction, the fundamentals of what is right and what is wrong in the conduct of their affairs (Kristol 1987).

Let's assume that what Kristol has in mind is that most executives already know that it is unethical to do something like sell defective pacemakers. One hopes that is the case. Nevertheless, even though executives know that some actions are wrong, that does not mean they know about the ethical implications of all their possible actions. As a matter of fact, the existence of difficult case studies, about which sincere executives disagree, belies Kristol's claim. There are many areas where executives do not know what is right or wrong. Thus it may not be useless to examine the fundamentals that business executives know to see how those fundamentals are or are not in harmony, or how they come to be modified in application. Many of the issues in business ethics are fairly complex, and assuming we can gain some knowledge about ethical issues, analysis of them would seem somewhat useful. So even though some executives might know what's right in some cases, it seems presumptuous to claim they always "know." Hence, some ethical instruction might make them see more ethically viable alternatives to some of their usual courses of action.

The second reason given for the uselessness of ethics courses is articulated by Michael Levin. Levin claims that improved behavior is a matter of training and not of teaching. Thus, even if we *knew* what was morally correct behavior, and could be taught that, it wouldn't improve our behavior.

Our response to Levin will be brief, for he raises the age-old question of whether and how virtue can be taught and to respond fully to that question would lead us too far. Within the constraints of space, we can merely hint why it is tenable to assume there is more to becoming ethical than mere training.

To insist that teaching ethics cannot affect behavior, only training can, seems to go too far. Even Aristotle, the chief proponent of the theory that ethical education was mostly training, who clearly distinguished between the artist who can use his "know-how" to subvert good ends without becoming less of an artist and the ethical person who must direct his skills of living to right ends to remain virtuous, still recognized that one didn't reach the ethical level simply by loving and doing the good. Even Aristotle

insists that the truly virtuous person *knows* the good. Human beings might incidentally do good things, but if they don't *know* why what they are doing is good, they are not fully virtuous.

Thus, though Levin seems right to insist that "moral behavior is the product of training," he fails to see it can also be influenced by theoretical "reflection." Studies of developmental psychologists such as Kohlberg and Piaget indicate that there is cognitive moral development which can be taught as well as moral development acquired through training. Further, training alone does not seem able to explain phenomena such as changing one's mind about moral issues. Isn't it possible to imagine that one can teach another to see other people as ourselves? If education other than training has no effect, how can one explain such phenomena as an ante-bellum southerner, raised to defend slavery, changing his mind? New reasons and new considerations certainly cause him to see things differently and have different attitudes toward those things. Ethics, taught by examining and evaluating moral beliefs, causes people to examine their views of what's right and wrong, their views about the equality of all people, their views of what actions are justified and why, and a host of other matters. To examine one's views, and to critically evaluate one's reasons for holding a position, certainly opens one to the possibility of changing one's *mind*, and it is simply far-fetched to think that a serious change of *mind* will not affect one's attitudes and hence one's behavior. Intellectual reflection can affect behavior. To see that one's reasons for holding a position are inadequate is, then, a way, though admittedly not the only way, to achieve moral improvement.

Let's sum up the response to Levin's contention that ethical courses are useless, because moral improvement only comes through training. We have seen that even though someone like Aristotle insists that moral education involves training, training is not the only way to improve ethical behavior. It is helpful to remember that to be ethical involves three activities: (1) knowing the good, (2) loving the good, and (3) doing the good. Any behavior, to be moral, must be deliberate and involve knowing. Otherwise it is simply reflex behavior. Thus, if knowledge of the good can be taught, and knowing the good is an essential part of ethical behavior, we can see how improvement in ethical behavior is tied to learning what is good.

But the assumption that knowledge of the good can be taught, moves us to a third consideration, the consideration of the moral sceptics, who say ethical knowledge is impossible. Is our assumption of the possibility, not to mention the teachability, of ethical knowledge justified? Having responded to the claims that ethics courses are useless either because people already know the good, or because ethics is something we can only be trained into, we need to turn to the claim that ethics courses are useless, because there is no such thing as ethical knowledge, the claim of the moral sceptics.

The existence, importance, and pervasiveness of this problem is articulated by H. Tristam Englehardt, Jr.

> Given the substantial arguments in the 20th century against the possibility of rationally establishing any particular moral philosophy as intellectually canonical, the broad cultural success of applied philosophy and the continued interest in theories of justice are incongruous at best. At some point the power of sceptical arguments will undermine the universalistic claims of much of contemporary applied philosophy. Yet the contemporary cultural needs that promote interest in applied philosophy are likely to become more intense rather than abate. For these reasons, the significance of applied philosophy will need to be reconsidered (Tristam Englehardt, 1989).

The intent of a major part of this paper is to address Tristam Englehardt's concern and to "reconsider" the "significance of applied philosophy" in the light of the scepticism about ethical knowledge. For, as we have seen, if moral sceptics are correct, business ethics courses are useless because there is no knowledge to teach.

Scepticism as a Pervasive Attitude

Kristol echoes Tristam Englehardt and goes even further, finding the scepticism that affects the teaching of ethics not only in purveyors of ethical theory but throughout our universities among academics who ". . . cheerfully allow that they are much too sophisticated to know right from wrong, and regard claims to such knowledge with disdain" (Kristol, 1987). But along with the scepticism in the heart of ethical theory and the scepticism that pervades academia, there is a derivative scepticism which has spread beyond academia into the general culture.

In that general culture, one finds the sceptical attitude expressed in the use of such phrases as "Who's to say?"; "Everyone's entitled to their own opinion"; "There are no absolutes"; "It's all subjec-

tive"; "It's all relative"; "If you believe it, it's true for you"; "Don't judge"; or any number of other related phrases. I would claim that these phrases are the symptomatic expression of a pervasive sceptical attitude that is found in several closely related forms such as (1) *subjectivism*, which denies objective ethical knowledge and maintains that everyone's moral opinion is "true for them"; (2) *emotivism*, which denies ethical knowledge by insisting that ethical assertions are merely expressions of pro or con attitudes that simply reflect subjective preferences; or (3) *relativism*, which holds that every group has its own set of moral beliefs that are "true for that group."

Allan Bloom in *The Closing of the American Mind* notes the pervasiveness of this sceptical attitude in the general culture which he finds expressed in a form of what he calls "relativism."

> This relativism . . . is necessary to openness; and this is the virtue, the only virtue, which all primary education for more than fifty years has dedicated itself to inculcating . . . the students, of course, cannot defend their opinion. It is something with which they have been indoctrinated. The best they can do is point out all the opinions and cultures there are and have been. What right, they ask, do I or any one else have to say one is better than the others (Bloom, 1987, pp. 25–26)?

My experience as a teacher of ethics concurs with Bloom's. This relativism/scepticism is constantly reiterated in the phrases mentioned above, which I take to be evidence that the relativism has become a prevailing attitude of many if not most students, and at least some faculty. For evidence of the assertion that this relativism has taken hold among faculty, one need only reflect on the struggle of philosophers with post-Nietzchean relativism and the adoption of the theories of Paul DeMan and Jacques Derrida in that brand of literary criticism known as deconstructionist critique.

In short, there is a scepticism which takes the form of relativism pervading society and influencing the teaching of ethics. What is more, even if most teachers of business ethics are not relativists/sceptics, a number of the business ethics textbooks they use reflect Tristam Englehardt's ethical-theoretical scepticism. Rather than taking a position on issues the texts judiciously present both sides of an issue, with no attempt at resolution for the students. This approach is undoubtedly well-intentioned, taken in the name of tolerance and an attempt to be fair to all sides. But failure to resolve issues may turn ethics classes into eristic exercises of *sic et non*, i.e., on the one hand position "A" seems correct, but then on the other hand, the contrary position, position "not-A," seems correct.

Now, an approach which involves looking at both sides of an issue can be fruitful if it is circumscribed by an agreed set of dogmas. Such was the *sic et non* approach of the medieval scholastics. But as Englehardt notes, today, there is no canonical set of dogmas that are agreed on. Thus the *sic et non* approach of 20th century ethics is a logical exercise presumably leading nowhere, since it is not circumscribed by such an agreed-upon set of dogmas. Rather, it seems that today, the reason for looking at all sides is the presumption that every opinion is self-validating for the person or group holding it. In short, the sceptical attitude, in a pluralistic, tolerant society, where there are two or more sides to every story, requires that every side be presented because every side has "its own truth."

In such an atmosphere the sceptic asks, "Who are ethics teachers to teach or promote their own views—views which after all are only their own subjective opinions?" Or: "Who are ethics teachers to say what's right or wrong? Whence their authority? Wouldn't they, after all, only be presenting the views of their society? Is that not ethnocentricism?" In the presence of such an attitude, the only acceptable approach is the detached, noncommittal approach. Judging from the textbooks we use, one could conclude that even if we do not agree with the above, we succumb to the pressure of the reigning relativism.

Our contention is that such a noncommittal approach which reflects the pervasive relativism/scepticism is not only not necessary, but also is not acceptable. It is not necessary because ethical knowledge is possible, and further it is not acceptable because it undermines the very teaching of ethics. But before we show how we take ethical knowledge to be possible and show why a relativistic/sceptical approach is unacceptable, we need to flesh out our claim that relativism is an expression of scepticism.

Relativism as Scepticism

While there is a *descriptive* relativism that maintains the truism that every group has its own set of moral beliefs, and is not necessarily sceptical about ethics, there is an *ethical* relativism that goes further and asserts not only that every group has its own moral beliefs, but that those beliefs are correct (true) for that group. As John Hospers puts it,

> According to ethical relativism, if there are two tribes or societies, and in one of them it is believed that acts of a certain kind are wrong while in the other it is believed that acts of that same kind are right, both beliefs are true: in the first society acts of that kind are wrong and in the other society they are right. Polygamy is right in polygamous societies but not in monogamous societies. Thus there is no overall standard of right and wrong—what is right and what is wrong depends on the society of which you are a member (Hospers, *Human Conduct*, p. 36).

If Hospers' description of relativism is correct it is simple to see why it is a form of scepticism. If what is right or wrong depends on the society of which you are a member, then the only thing that validates your belief is your group's holding it. Thus, two groups can hold contradictory beliefs. But if two contradictory beliefs are true, then logically every proposition is true or none are true. Hence there is no truth, and if a condition of knowledge is that a belief be true, then where there is no truth, there is no knowledge. Hence, the scepticism of relativism. Still, there are those who would claim that Hospers' and my characterization of relativism is too simplistic.

According to that characterization ethical relativists would maintain that for a belief to be true two things are necessary: first, as we said, the group holds the belief. But the second condition, the one that allows truth, is the requirement that the belief coheres with the other beliefs of the group. Thus every belief coherent with the other beliefs held by a group is true, i.e., justified and legitimized because of being held and cohering with the other beliefs. In the phrase, "true for the group," then, the word "true" means nothing more than *held* and *consistent* with other beliefs held by the group. In this way knowledge is reduced to mere internal consistency.

But does not knowledge require more than mere internal consistency? For example, if a group believes that the sun has a god and the sun god demands infant sacrifice for the preservation of the tribe, then infant sacrifice would be "justified" if all that is required for a belief to be justified is that the belief be held and be consistent with the other beliefs of the group. But, surely, justification requires us to look at several other factors. In the first place, the group of sun fearers seems to agree with other groups about the truth of the general principle that the common good of a group ought to be served. (Though they might not articulate it in those terms, their attitude of benevolence toward their group resembles ours.) We would suggest that such a general principle is universally recognized and can serve as an objective standard. But even if the sun fearer group's very general principle is justified or justifiable, the particular application of that principle, which requires infant sacrifice for the common good, is not justified. It is not justified, because, in spite of the fact that the view might be coherent given the beliefs of the group, the beliefs, e.g., that there is a sun god and that the sun god demands infant sacrifice, are not true.

A thorough-going ethical relativist, of course, could maintain that it is possible for there to be a group that did not accept the principle of pursuing the common good. But that means they hold morality, as we envision it, to be just that, simply our society's view of what morality is. In that case if they were talking about "moral" matters they couldn't be talking in a language we understand, and what they did say would be incommensurable. Whereas, what we mean by morality has to do with the needs and goods for human beings as they are societally, and the justice among those human beings, and whereas, those human goods provide us with standards, the thorough-going relativist would deny those standards are objective. They are merely the standards our culture chooses to uphold. Hence the thorough-going relativist is a sceptic who continually denies any objective standard other than coherence can be used to justify a moral belief.

Herein, then, lies the scepticism. A set of beliefs must, at some point, be tied to the way things are. The sun god must be real. Or the fear must somehow be justified. Otherwise the set of beliefs, though coherent, is built on no solid ground. Hence a defense of relativism based only on an appeal to coherence constitutes a scepticism about knowing an objective world, where there is right or wrong. In the absence of any objective standard to justify a belief we are dealing with either scepticism or knowledge not worth calling knowledge. Since ethical knowledge involves more than just coherence of beliefs, a relativism which entails that ethical knowledge is impossible can only be a scepticism.

Still, to show that relativism is a scepticism doesn't refute either relativism or scepticism. What we need to ask further are two questions. First, what if anything can be said in criticism of relativism, and second, how is ethical knowledge possible? We turn to the critique of relativism.

Critiques of Relativism

There are three standard ways to show the difficulties with relativism. One involves showing that the phrase "true for me" trivializes the meaning of true. A second objection involves a *reductio* argument which shows that if relativism or subjectivism were true then one would have to admit that Nazi beliefs about the moral probity of the holocaust would be correct at least for the Nazis, or, on an individual level, Hitler's subjective beliefs about the holocaust would be correct, at least for Hitler. A third objection asks how we are to determine what constitutes a group, how many members are necessary to have a group, or how members of several groups are to reconcile the different conflicting beliefs between groups. But there are objections to relativism as a theoretical scepticism.

Of course, these standard objections to relativism need not deter the serious theoretical relativist, for she can argue: first, that any use of "true" applied to moral beliefs is of course trivial, since there is no criterion of truth except coherence; second, that relativism exactly commits one to accepting Hitler's view as "true" for Hitler, but that just means Hitler holds that view, and, though we can be appalled by Hitler's beliefs, we really can't "know" whether he is right or wrong; and third, the question of what constitutes a group, although interesting, is not decisive, for if by a group we mean a set of those having similar beliefs, nothing precludes a null set, a group with no members, or, paradoxical as it sounds, a group of one. So we don't seem to be able to decisively refute theoretical relativism.

But even if one cannot refute theoretical relativism, there is an argument which bears investigation. It is an argument that maintains that whatever the status of theoretical relativism, it is impossible to live as a relativist.

This argument, that it is existentially impossible to live as a relativist, is effectively presented by Mary Midgley in her book *Heart and Mind*. Midgley shows that relativism involves moral isolationism, a position impossible to live by. Midgley maintains that if each group's moral beliefs are self-validating, as relativism maintains, no person from any other group has any grounds for criticizing the beliefs of any other group. But it is simply a fact that no one can refrain from making moral judgments and that includes judgments about the adequacy of others' beliefs.

The power of moral judgment is, in fact, not a luxury, not a perverse indulgence of the self-righteous. It is a necessity . . . (But) moral isolationism forbids us to form any opinions on moral matters . . . Moral isolationism would lay down a general ban on moral reasoning . . . This is essentially a program of immoralism and it carries a distressing logical difficulty. Immoralists like Nietzsche are actually a rather specialized sect of moralists. [They are parasitic on morality.] They can no more afford to abolish morality than smugglers can abolish customs regulations (Midgley, 1981, p. 71–2).

Midgley continues, showing ironically how the attitude of moral isolationism arose from taking a moral position seriously.

Our involvement in moral isolationism [relativism/subjectivism] does not flow from apathy, but from a rather acute concern about human hypocrisy and other forms of wickedness. But we polarize that concern around a few selected moral truths. WE ARE RIGHTLY ANGRY WITH THOSE WHO DESPISE, OPPRESS OR STEAMROLL OTHER CULTURES. WE THINK THAT DOING THESE THINGS IS ACTUALLY *WRONG*. But this is itself a moral judgment. We could not condemn oppression and insolence if we thought that all our condemnations were just a trivial local quirk of our own culture. We could still less do it if we tried to stop judging altogether. Real moral scepticism, in fact, could lead only to inaction, to our losing all interest in moral questions . . . We cannot avoid judging. What we must avoid are crude judgments (Midgley, 1987, p. 72).

Midgley effectively shows that one cannot really be a relativist or sceptic. One can play at it intellectually, but at some point a person needs to make a judgment, which involves assuming the truth of that judgment, for what else is it to judge, but to assume one's position is correct? If that is so, people can only be sceptical or relativistic about beliefs they do not take seriously. Further, if people think they are right about their beliefs, they logically must think others who disagree with them are wrong about their beliefs and acting on those beliefs will effect harm or injustice. In other words, if they are concerned about preventing harm they must be ready at least to admonish the wrong doer.

Jonathan Bennett outlines this problem quite well.

I imagine that we agree in our rejection of slavery and genocide . . . But then we can say this because we can say that all those are bad moralities, whereas we cannot look at our own moralities (read: set of moral beliefs) and declare them bad. This is not arrogance. It is obviously incoherent for someone to declare the system of moral principles that he accepts to be bad, just

as one cannot coherently say of anything that one believes it but it is false (Bennett, 1974, p. 134).

If all this is the case then one cannot be a relativist. One can only play at it by adopting some sort of methodological scepticism. One cannot live as a relativist because one must make moral judgments and perforce find oneself in disagreement with others, and be "rightly angry" about some beliefs or behavior.

Very well! Suppose we have succeeded in showing that one cannot live as a relativist. Where does that leave us? For to say one cannot help but believe that one's beliefs are true certainly does not show that those beliefs are indeed true. So to show that one cannot live as a relativist still does not show that ethical knowledge is possible. Thus we still need to show how moral knowledge might be possible or, what we take to be the equivalent, how we can have justified true moral beliefs.

The Possibility of Moral Knowledge

To show, in any adequate fashion, that moral knowledge is possible would require a longer excursion into moral epistemology than is possible within the scope of this paper. However, we will attempt to sketch the route a defense of the possibility of moral knowledge might take.

Whether one thinks ethical knowledge, that is, justified moral belief, is possible or not depends to a large extent on one's starting point in addressing the issue. Does one start by adopting a methodic doubt and doubt every belief like Descartes or does one start by assuming that what one thinks is correct and doubt only those beliefs one has good reason to doubt? To doubt only when one has good reason to is congenial to an Aristotelian type of approach toward knowledge which starts with common opinion (doxa) and an assumption that the opinion is probably correct, but allows the possibility of questioning that opinion if reasons to do so arise. From this approach doubt makes sense only if knowledge is possible. Such a starting point offers a solution to the problem of knowledge not available to the sceptics who come out of the modern Cartesian framework.

One does not have to start with radical doubt. I remember a distinction I once learned from a critic of Descartes. He distinguished between "moral certitude" and "metaphysical certitude." On the critic's account, an example of metaphysical certitude is the certitude of the mother who, having stayed conscious through labor and now cradling the child in her arms, knows that the child is hers. An example of "moral" certitude is that of the father who knows the child is his. I have several children I "know" are mine. Why? *Because there is no good reason to think otherwise.* Thus "moral" certitude is the kind of sureness we have when there is no reason to doubt. I "know" my house is still standing because there is no reason to think otherwise and I live on such assured beliefs. I know I shouldn't lie, because in this case at least, there are no legitimate reasons to support the lying. This is moral certitude. Certainly the sceptic could imagine (*pace* Hume) the opposite . . . that the children are not mine, that my house has disappeared, that lying is justifiable. But, aside from the Quixotic Cartesian search for absolute certitude or a Platonic search for a world of forms, why side with the sceptic? What's the point of such radical doubt? We can *imagine* almost anything. But ethics needs to be grounded in *real* possibilities, not possibilities merely dreamed about.

If, then, we get rid of "methodic" doubt and examine the moral beliefs we have *no good reason* to doubt, we realize that we have some pretty good reasons to accept a great deal of our moral beliefs. Take, for example, the case of a person proposing to attend school. On examining that proposed course of action the person realizes that if she goes to school it will (1) benefit her as an individual, (2) benefit society, and (3) will not be unfair to others or violate her other commitments. In such an instance there is a *prima facie* case for the person to attend school, because there is every reason to attend and no good reason not to. On the other hand, activities such as abusing certain substances harm the individual, harm society, and most likely lead to the abuser's failing to meet obligations and commitments. With so many reasons against substance abuse, we can be fairly certain we are justified in condemning it as a practice. Thus, we "know" some actions are wrong by any sane sense of the word "know," and if anyone says they don't "know" such actions are wrong we are at a loss as to what to say to them. They speak a different language.

Incidentally, examination of the reasons we just gave show they are the reasons which provide the basis for the current categorization of ethical theories into Egoistic, Utilitarian, and Deontological, each of which gives primacy to one of the reasons we generally have for believing whether an action or practice is acceptable.

For example, the education case is a clear case of an action which benefits the agent (an egoistic consideration), benefits society (a utilitarian consideration), and meets the demands of obligations arising from promises and commitments and the concerns of justice and fairness (all deontological considerations). Similarly, the drug abuse case is a clear case where the practice is (1) harmful to self, (2) harmful to society, (3) unfaithful to promises and commitments, and (4) unfair and unjust.

Of course the examples we gave do not present us with moral dilemmas. But that is because moral dilemmas are precisely those cases where there are good reasons *for* doing things, as well as good reasons *for not* doing them. For example, an action which benefits society might not be fair, or vice versa, an action which is fair might harm society. Or some action which benefits me harms society or vice versa. Or it may not be clear whether some actions will be harmful or not to me or to society. Or, finally, there may be some actions which fulfill one obligation I have but violate another, i.e., I might be faced with a conflict of duties. But these dilemmas are precisely the tough cases where one doesn't know quite what to do because one is "damned if he does and damned if he doesn't." But the fact that such difficult cases and doubts exist doesn't mean that every case is difficult or needs to engender doubt.

This, then, is the direction my epistemology would take. We would claim it is possible to have justified moral beliefs, based on good reasons of benefit and fairness and justice, beliefs we have not reason to doubt. That, in ethics, is as close as we get to moral "knowledge." Within such an epistemological framework, one would only question those moral beliefs there is some *real*, not methodological, reason to doubt.

Implications for Teaching Business Ethics Courses

Assuming, then, that moral knowledge is sometimes possible, but not always easy, and that gaining knowledge is to some extent important for improving moral behavior, we can see that the reasons given to show that ethics courses are useless are not decisive. Hence the usefulness of ethics courses is not due to the nature of ethics as something unteachable. Rather the futility of ethics courses is more than likely due to the way courses are taught.

What we propose to do now is attempt to defend the claim that ethics courses are useless because of the way they are taught, a way which adopts a method we shall call "methodological relativism." It would seem this method is adopted because of the pervasive attitude of relativism we talked about. Further, we would claim that the adoption of such a method not only makes ethics courses useless, but also may do harm to the student, which makes the method unacceptable.

Why does such an approach, which starts ethical debate from a sceptical stance, even if only a methodological one, have undesirable consequences? Levin mentions, correctly, that such courses cause loss of faith by the student in the effectiveness of ethical reasoning and *a fortiori* in the use of ethics courses (Levin, 1989).

Kristol notes that

> At worst, they (ethics teachers) can provoke severe moral disorientation among the young and immature. At the least, they encourage a superficial cynicism about moral beliefs that gradually pervades our culture and our society as a whole and makes the general task of moral education all the more difficult (Kristol, 1987).

But why would such a loss of faith or disorientation or cynicism develop in the student? For one reason, because the student cannot take the teacher seriously. Consider two possibilities.

A. If on the one hand, the professor actually takes the relativistic approach seriously, the professor is committed to holding that:
   1. no opinion is better than any other;
   2. reasoning and being reasonable are a waste of time; and
   3. ethics as justificatory evaluation is impossible.

In that case, the student is right to ask, "Why bother?"

B. If, on the other hand, the teacher does not take relativism seriously and is simply adopting relativism as a method, she is adopting a stance that she doesn't believe in. The student, in that case, encounters a professor who does not seem to *care* for any position enough to defend it and consequently seems to treat them all cavalierly.

In either case, why should a student bother with something the professor does not appear to take seriously?

In short, teachers who adopt a relativistic stance either show that they don't take what they think seriously, or show that what they think should not be taken seriously, since no position can be judged better than any other. At best a teacher reverts to descriptive ethics where the teacher merely presents the world's best—on what ground we judge them "best" forever remains a mystery—but benighted (benighted because they really thought they were instructing in true beliefs) thinkers, whose speculations are aesthetically pleasing and psychologically interesting, but ultimately useless curiosity pieces from the museum of ideas past. To the extent, then, that teachers adopt this relativistic method, they appear as thinkers unwilling to take a stand in public on what they believe, and subject it to analysis. In this way they appear to lack the courage of their convictions. Such an approach, taken in the name of fairness to all sides, effectively trivializes what they are doing, and at best they appear to be fatuous blow-hards.

Is There a Solution?

What should be done? How teach an ethics course so that it has a chance to make students better? I suggest adopting Socrates as a model. He believed there was knowledge of the good, which he passionately pursued, while maintaining a healthy scepticism about false coin. Further, I suggest adding to the Socratic quest the Aristotelian method of beginning any ethical investigation by examining the common experience of humankind, what Aristotle calle *doxa*, what Wittgenstein designates as "forms of life" we all agree on. But that is only the starting point. To paraphrase J. L. Austin, ordinary opinion is not the last opinion on the subject, but it certainly should be the first opinion.

Why common opinion? Because however independent we take our thinking to be, in reality it is not, for most of us agree on a large body of moral issues, simply because we share our "form of life." Too much emphasis on individualism, plurality, and diversity, the characteristics of an individual who stands out from the crowd, make us forget that for the most part we share a form of life with its communal and agreed-on moral beliefs. So much so, that even the most idiosyncratic individual stands out on just a few moral issues while agreeing with the majority on most (*pace Nietzsche*).

There is a further point to be made about this starting point in common experience. The reason this common experience is common experience is that a good deal of it is probably true. This point is made by Christina Sommers, who, like Kristol and Levin, shows a concern about the bad effects of a sceptical approach to ethics.

> ... moral philosophers should be paying far more attention to the social consequences of their views than they are. It is as concrete as taking care that what one says will not effect adversely the students whom one is addressing. If what students learn from us encourages social disintegration, then we are responsible for the effects this may have on their lives and on the lives of their children ... This then is a grave responsibility, even graver than the responsibility we take in being for or against something serious as euthanasia or capital punishment—since most of our students will never face these questions in a practical way ... (Sommers, 1989).

Sommers, to avoid the scepticism, suggests common experience as a starting point, because if one learns from experience, one usually gets a good deal of things correct. Sommers cites William James' defense of common opinion as a starting point. As James said,

> [Experience] has proved that the laws and usages of the land are what yield the maximum of satisfaction . . . The presumption in cases of conflict must always be in favor of the conventionally recognized good. The philosopher must be a conservative, and in the construction of his casuistic scale must put things most in accordance with the customs of the community on top (James, 1948).

In line with this passage of James, Sommers concludes:

> A moral philosophy that does not give proper weight to the customs and opinions of the community is presumptuous in its attitude and pernicious in its consequences. In an important sense it is not a moral philosophy at all. For it is humanly irrelevant (Sommers, 1989).

What Ethics Courses Need to Add to Common Opinion

But, of course, simply beginning with common opinion is not enough to have ethics. As we said, common opinion is not to be the last word. What does ethics add to common opinion? Here our appeal to the Socratic method comes into play. Ethics and ethics courses should involve us in the self-conscious analysis and evaluation of our commonly held, agreed-upon moral beliefs and principles. If we follow Socrates' lead, doing ethics is really just the examining of our life, for in a real sense, our human life, the life of ours that involves more than our unintended animal activities, is our life directed by our aims and values, in short, our life directed by our moral beliefs.

Clearly, every human being has moral beliefs, i.e., mental attitudes or dispositions about whether certain activities or life styles or character traits are good or fair. Further, every society or group has moral beliefs which it teaches to its members. The ethicist's task, then, is to begin with ordinary beliefs, and critically analyze and evaluate them, seeing if and why they are justified, and if not, to revise or abandon them.

We assume if ethics were done this way, Kristol would then see some use for it, for he spoke approvingly of the way it was taught before the 20th century.

> Moral philosophy, as once taught ... consisted mainly of the intellectual effort to justify by philosophical analysis alone and without reference to divine revelation, the main tenets of our traditional Judaeo-Christian moral code ... But they (the ethicists) took it for granted that a moral code was a necessary and desirable enforcement of any human community—and, moreover, that our moral code, elaborated over two millennia of Western civilization ... was in most respects superior to any other ... One knew right from wrong, even if one went about knowing it in a different way (Kristol, 1987).

From this perspective, the point of any ethics course is to present the commonly accepted moral beliefs to show how, or if, they can be justified ... in short, to seek moral knowledge where knowledge means *justified belief*.

A Final Difficulty: "Who Are You to Say?": Teaching One's Values

But there is a final difficulty we must address. Given the possibility that some of my beliefs are wrong, and that is a very real possibility, dare I teach them as if they are right? If we stay open to the possibility of being wrong, we can dispel that concern.

Consider the following. In reality, as we have seen, one cannot teach without taking some stand even if it is only the stand that a sceptical attitude is desirable, that tolerance is a virtue, that ethnocentrism is wrong, or that ethics is not a respectable intellectual discipline. These are not only second order, epistemological, or meta-ethical positions. They are themselves ethical positions about the proper attitude human beings should have toward truth, knowledge, others' beliefs, and the role of the quest for truth in the fulfilled human life. Since we cannot help teaching positions, even if only inadvertently, why not straightforwardly teach what one believes from where one stands. Since everyone has moral beliefs, why not teach them, instead of acting as if one were neutral? My suspicion is that more good would follow from teaching one's beliefs than from hiding where one stands in the name of impartiality.

Take anyone's ethical belief (this includes your own) which is seriously held. If the belief is presented in an ethics course by a *responsible* ethicist (remember ethics and the profession of ethicist is a human invention with its own standards of acceptable behavior), the presentation will involve analysis and evaluation of those values. If one's position agrees with society's then an *apologia* will take place, and if one's position disagrees with society's then reasons against society's position and for one's own will be forthcoming.

What are the worst consequences of an approach where ethicists teach positions they believe in? Take two worst-case scenarios. Suppose that someone were a Nazi teaching ethics. If we agree that a Nazi shouldn't be allowed to teach his position, then we already condemn Naziism as a bad morality and consequently must hold that Nazi values are unreasonable and unacceptable. But then the ethicist, being reasonable, will either not be a Nazi, or if he is a Nazi, what he is teaching will not withstand rational critique. (I assume those of us who think Naziism was evil have reasons for so thinking.)

Take a second scenario. Suppose someone teaches the value of apartheid. Note again the objection is made by citing a worst-case scenario of what most of us already agree is a "bad" morality. The very act of objecting to defenders of Naziism or apartheid supporters shows that we at least at times believe that teaching certain values might be unacceptable and unreasonable and should not be done. But that would entail that we believe there are correct positions which should be taught. Since people are going to argue surreptitiously for their values in any case, what undesirable consequences arise from the conscious articulation and defense of them, even those we think are misguided? If the positions are incorrect and unreasonable, public profession should

show that unreasonableness and if the positions are not incorrect, then they involve rationally defensible values.

But isn't teaching our own values different from starting with common opinion? Only to an extent, and not in all cases. We might have some idiosyncratic values different from society's, but by and large no one's position is radically different from, in the sense of totally incompatible with or incommensurable with, the position of their society. For example, Nietzsche, the great "transvaluer of values," recognizes that what makes human beings distinctive is their being the "promising" animal. Thus even the radical "immoralist" such as Nietzsche agrees with common experience that expects promises to be kept and, by his very actions of teaching and writing, implicitly commits to valuing communication, integrity, truth, the good of self-assertion, etc. In short, most of an ethicist's values will be in accord with his society's.

Further, ethics teachers are teachers, which means they are service oriented, and have committed to the obligations of a teacher as defined by their society. Thus, even in the case where the values of the teacher differ from those of the society, the action of presenting and defending values is approved of and the presentation and defense of values the teacher takes "seriously" will be done in the value framework of her society. This presentation and defense will enable students to experience what is involved in a serious, responsible critique of society. In such a situation, students will also be exposed to a lived example of "the examined life," an example which should help develop the students' autonomy by coaxing them to examine and understand what implicit agreements (forms of life) move them. Such prodding should help students articulate their own positions.

Finally, it is helpful to remember that the evaluation or transvaluation of society's values and moral beliefs only occurs with respect to those beliefs where some disagreement already exists or arises. That about which all agree is rarely, if ever, challenged. Hence for a critical evaluation of a position, an opposing perspective must be presented, otherwise there is no dilemma, and chances are there is no problem to arise. If no problem arises, it could be none exists and the raising of one is simply superfluous or eristic. Since there are enough real problems to go around, eristic arguments seem a wasteful superfluity.

In summary, not to teach and defend one's position, to act as if one is value neutral, as we saw, leads to either treating ethical issues eristically or creates scepticism or cynicism. If teachers and their students agree on most issues, the teachers can show the students what reasons ground their positions. If teachers and students disagree they can engage in a dialogue. In that dialogue, if the teacher's reasons are sound, students are provided with tools (reasons) to use in the examination and critique of their moral beliefs; or if, as sometimes happens, the student's challenge to the teacher's reasons is sound, the teacher if honest (a value intrinsic to the teacher's role) should rethink her position and that position will be improved. In either case, a method which presents a position one holds seriously and attempts to justify seems a better approach than a method of adopting a detached neutral perspective.

Conclusion

In a sense we *are* our moral beliefs. They constitute our distinctly human projects. They indicate what we are. If that means we need to get our life in order to teach ethics, so be it. Ours is a profession, and professionals have responsibilities. Teaching ethics as we do in the United States is a luxury. Not so in El Salvador and other countries, or recently and still, in Communist bloc countries. But since it is a luxury, we tend not to take it seriously, and it gets treated as a frivolity, not having much point.

To sum up, if we firmly believe in (and think we have good reasons in support of) a course of action, why wouldn't we or shouldn't we try to persuade others to adopt such an attitude? In this way we can lead our students to know the good by insisting on justified beliefs while giving them an example of a person who cares about the good and within limits is committed to do it. Ethics courses taught in this way become more than a mere eristic exercise and have a point. Society and business would have to start taking such courses seriously. To the objection, this is an unwarranted use of power, the answer is, it is an honest one.

Study Questions

1. Were the Nazis so clearly evil that they are a counterexample to moral relativism and moral scepticism?

2. Are any other individuals or groups, besides the Nazis, so clearly evil that you would consider them to be counterexamples to moral relativism and moral scepticism?

3. Who had the better arguments, Duska or Levin?

4. What is your evaluation of Kristol's argument that business ethics is unnecessary because enough people already know right and wrong well enough?

PART II

Five Ethical Theories to Apply to
Usual Business Practices: From Secular Saints to
Experience Machines

4

Introduction: Basic Definitions of Five Major Moral Theories

Sterling Harwood

Egalitarianism (Often Called Fairness or Justice)

The basic value of egalitarianism is equality (often called fairness or justice). The basic idea of egalitarianism is that good people should fare well and bad people should fare badly.

The definition of egalitarianism includes the following principles:

1. Treat relevantly similar cases similarly, and relevantly different cases differently.
2. Discrimination (e.g., racism and sexism) is wrong. Discrimination is failing to treat relevantly similar cases similarly or failing to treat relevantly different cases differently.
3. We should prevent innocent people from suffering through no fault of their own.
4. Exploitation—taking unfair advantage of an innocent person's predicament—is wrong.
5. We should regularly give significant amounts to charity.
6. No one should profit from his or her own wrong.
7. The punishment should fit (be proportional to) the crime.
8. Promises should be kept.
9. Merit should be rewarded.
10. Reciprocity is important.
11. Gratitude is important.

Libertarianism

The basic value of libertarianism is liberty (also called freedom). But libertarianism does *not* support always maximizing liberty, since it generally does not allow violating one person's liberty to increase the liberty

of others. The definition of libertarianism includes the following principles:

1. Anything between consenting adults is morally permissible. (Note that this does not mean that doing some things to an adult without his consent [e.g., punishment] is immoral.)
2. Laissez-faire capitalism is morally required. This includes *caveat emptor* (let the buyer beware) rather than government safety or health regulations. There would be no welfare state or government food stamps to save the poor. Private property is important.
3. Coercion (the deprivation of liberty) is wrong except to punish criminals, to defend against an immoral attack, and to supervise the mentally incompetent (e.g., children, the senile, the retarded, and the insane). Paternalism against mentally competent adults is wrong.
4. Promises must be kept, and fraud is wrong.
5. Government should be minimal; it should be as a nightwatchperson limited to peacekeeping functions (the police and the military) enforcing principles 1–4 above with as little force as possible.

Utilitarianism

The basic and only value of utilitarianism is utility (also called happiness, welfare, well-being or flourishing). Since this is the only value utilitarianism has, utilitarianism has only one principle in its definition, namely, to maximize net happiness for all in the long run. Utilitarianism has two slogans: (1) Promote the greatest happiness for the greatest number of people; and (2) Each person counts for one and only one in calculating the maximum amount of happiness. Note that (1) does *not* mean that we should do whatever most people want to do. The minority might be made so unhappy, for example, that the majority's happiness cannot outweigh it. Utilitarianism also does *not* require merely that you produce some more happiness than unhappiness. It requires each person to produce the *greatest* net balance of happiness over unhappiness for everyone in the long run. Slogan (2) means that each person's happiness counts the same, so it would be wrong, for example, to count a particular amount of happiness for a white person as more important (or less important) than the same amount of happiness for a black person.

Prima Facie Moral Principles

The basic idea of these principles is that there is more than one basic moral value. The principles below will often conflict, and so some will outweigh others depending on the circumstances. We cannot say in advance which ones will outweigh which others. We must take each moral situation as it comes and judge, based on the totality of its particular circumstances, which principle is more important in that case. *Prima facie* moral principles are moral factors that can be outweighed by other moral factors (i.e., by other *prima facie* moral principles). The main *prima facie* moral principles are:

1. Fidelity: Avoid breaking promises.
2. Veracity: Avoid telling lies.
3. Fair play: Avoid exploiting, cheating, or freeloading.
4. Gratitude: Return favors and appreciate the good others do for you.
5. Nonmaleficence: Avoid causing pain or suffering. (Note this is not the same as nonmalevolence, which concerns only motivation rather than causation.)
6. Beneficence: Benefit others and cause them to be happier. (Note this is not the same as benevolence, which concerns only motivation rather than causation.)
7. Reparation: Right your wrongs; repair the damage that's your fault.
8. Avoid killing except when necessary to defend against an immoral attack.
9. Avoid stealing.
10. Oppose injustices at least when this involves no great sacrifice.
11. Promote just institutions and work for their establishment, maintenance, and improvement.

Perfectionism (Often Called Virtue Ethics)

The basic value of perfectionism is having a good character. One has a duty to perfect one's own character. The following are the main character traits that are virtues (forms of excellence tending to constitute a good character), or vices (character flaws tending to constitute a bad character):

1. Courage is a virtue and cowardice is a vice.
2. Honesty is a virtue and dishonesty is a vice.
3. Kindness is a virtue and unkindness is a vice.
4. Loyalty is a virtue and disloyalty is a vice.
5. Gratitude is a virtue and ingratitude is a vice.
6. Charity is a virtue and uncharitableness is a vice.
7. Being forgiving exhibits a virtue and being unforgiving exhibits a vice.

See the two accompanying tables about virtues and vices.

Table 4-1 Summary of the Virtues and Vices as Discussed by Aristotle

Sphere of Action; Kind of Situation	Types of Emotion, Desire, Attitude	Vice of Too Much (Excess)	Virtue (Mean)	Vice of Too Little (Deficiency or Defect)
Responses to danger	Fear, confidence	Foolhardiness	Courage	Cowardice
Satisfying appetites	Physical pleasure	Overindulgence	Temperance	Inhibition
Giving gifts	Desire to help	Extravagance	Generosity	Miserliness
Pursuing accomplishments	Desire to succeed	Vaulting ambition	Proper ambition	Unambitiousness
Appraising oneself	Self-affirmation	Vanity	Proper pride	Sense of inferiority
Self-expression	Desire to be recognized	Boastfulness	Truthfulness	False modesty
Responding to insults	Anger	Irascibility	Patience	Apathy
Social conduct	Attitudes to others	Obsequiousness	Friendliness	Rudeness
Indignation at others' undeserved good fortune*	Distress	Envy	Righteous indignation	Malicious enjoyment
Awareness of one's flaws	Shame	Shyness	Modesty	Shamelessness
Conversation, humor	Amusement	Buffoonery	Wittiness	Boorishness

*This entry may seem puzzling. Aristotle writes: "Righteous Indignation is a mean between Envy and Spite [or malicious enjoyment], and they are all concerned with feelings of pain or pleasure at the experiences of our neighbors. The man who feels righteous indignation is distressed at instances of undeserved good fortune but the envious man goes further and is distressed at *any* good fortune, while the spiteful man is so far from feeling distress that he actually rejoices [at others' misfortune]."

SOURCE: M. W. Martin, *Everyday Morality* (Wadsworth, 1989), p. 42.

Table 4-2 Jones's Table of Classic Virtues and Vices

Activity	Vice (Excess)	Virtue (Mean)	Vice (Deficit)
Facing death	Too much fear (i.e., cowardice)	Right amount of fear (i.e., courage)	Too little fear (i.e., foolhardiness)
Bodily actions (eating, drinking, sex, etc.)	Profligacy	Temperance	No name for this state, but it may be called "insensitivity"
Giving money	Prodigality	Liberality	Illiberality
Large-scale giving	Vulgarity	Magnificence	Meanness
Claiming honors	Vanity	Pride	Humility
Social intercourse	Obsequiousness	Friendliness	Sulkiness
According honors	Injustice	Justice	Injustice
Retribution for wrong-doing	Injustice	Justice	Injustice

SOURCE: W. T. Jones. *The Classical Mind* (New York: Harcourt, Brace, & World, 1952, 1969), p. 268.

"IT APPEALS TO GREED, LUST, PRIDE, SLOTH AND ENVY, BUT WE'RE OVERLOOKING GLUTTONY AND AVARICE."

5

Saint Ralph

Michael Kinsley

Editor's note: Kinsley once worked for Ralph Nader. Kinsley was one of the so-called "Nader's Raiders." Kinsley, though he admires Nader as America's foremost consumer advocate, notes how extreme some of Nader's views seem to be. Nader is often denounced as a socialist, but in a recent interview (with David Frost) Nader emphasized his rejection of socialism, which is defined as government ownership of the means of production (for example, factories and farms).

Henry James captured Ralph Nader in his 1886 novel, *The Bostonians*. James called the character Miss Birdseye.

> She always dressed in the same way: she wore a loose black jacket, with deep pockets, which were stuffed with papers. . . . She belonged to the Short-Skirts League, as a matter of course; for she belonged to any and every league that had been founded for almost any purpose whatsoever. [Yet she] knew less about her fellow-creatures, if possible, after fifty years of humanitary zeal, than on the day she had gone into the field to testify against the iniquity of most arrangements. . . . No one had an idea how she lived; whenever money was given her she gave it away. . . . There was a legend that an Hungarian had once possessed himself of her affections, [but] it was open to grave doubt that she could have entertained a sentiment so personal. She was in love . . . only with causes.

Thus the social reformer, skewered. I worked several years for Ralph Nader, and he's actually quite warm and funny in person. Nevertheless, his is the classic zealot's worldview, paranoid and humorless, and his vision of the ideal society—regulations for all contingencies of life, warning labels on every French fry, and a citizenry on hair-trigger alert for violations of its personal space—is not one many others would care to share with him.

But reasonable people don't move the world. On the twentieth anniversary of *Unsafe at Any Speed*, his tract against dangerous automobiles, no living American is responsible for more concrete improvements in the society we actually do inhabit than Ralph Nader.

In all statistical probability, at least several dozen of you who are reading this would be dead today if Nader hadn't single-handedly invented the issue of auto safety. His long campaign for mandatory air bags may bore most people and enrage a few. But would even these people want cars without seat belts, padded dashboards, collapsible steering wheels, and shatter-resistant glass? On matters ranging from the Occupational Safety and Health Administration to the Freedom of Information Act (just two of his monuments), Nader stands accused—sometimes justly—of going "too far." But without the people who go too far, we wouldn't go far enough.

Although Nader's personal popularity has diminished, and the causes he favors are out of fashion, his achievements are as immutable as FDR's. President Reagan may inveigh against burdensome government regulation, just as he inveighs against government spending. He may attempt changes at the margin. But he would no more get the government out of the business of protecting consumers, workers, and the environment than he would dismantle Social Security. Americans like clean air and water, safe transportation, open government, honest advertisements, uncontaminated meat. No electable politician would attempt to push back the clock by twenty years.

I wonder how many conservative businessmen, even, would care to return to the days when anyone could light up a cigarette next to you on a long airplane flight, and when an airline could overbook and bump you with no explanation or compensation. No-smoking sections and airline bumping rules—minor bits of Naderism—seemed like quixotic obsessions when first proposed. Now they are taken for granted.

Like James's Miss Birdseye, Nader knows little of ordinary human appetites. This gives him his fanatic's strength of purpose. But it also sometimes leads him astray by blinding him to the benefits that come with the risks he campaigns against. The pleasure of a hot dog means nothing to Ralph. He tastes only the nitrite. If everyone lived like Ralph Nader, we could dispense with nuclear power and not worry

---

Reprinted from "Saint Ralph," *The New Republic* (December 9, 1985). Reprinted by permission.

about replacing the energy. In this world of sinners, though, not everyone wants to live on raw vegetables and set the thermostat at 60. Intelligent public policy requires trade-offs that the fanatic is ill equipped and indisposed to make.

Nader's other great weakness as a reformer is that he's a prisoner of the legal mind-set. He believes in the infinite power of lawyers to achieve both bad and good. "The ultimate goal of this movement," says a recent Nader press release, "is to give all citizens more rights and remedies for resolving their grievances and for achieving a better society." But it's open to doubt, to say the least, whether the better society is one where all grievances are thought of as a matter of legal rights and remedies, to be enforced by lawyers and judges.

These days Ralph Nader is something less than a colossus bestriding American society, but still something more than another colorful Washington character. Over two decades he and his ever replenished band of disciples have operated out of a series of ratty offices, generally moving in shortly before the developers arrive to tear the place down and put up another fancy building for fancy lawyers (some of them, no doubt, getting rich off the very laws and agencies Ralph created).

He still wears those awful suits and lives in that same studio apartment. Some cynics think the asceticism is an act. And it's true that his story about wearing shoes bought at the Army PX in 1959 is wearing as thin as those shoes must be. But if a good marketing sense were a bar to canonization, there would be few saints.

At age fifty-two, Nader may be softening a little. He sometimes shows up at those business parties that pass for social life in Washington. I even think I saw him eating a piece of cheese at one a few weeks ago. His narrow lapels, pointy shoes, and skinny ties are now the height of fashion, offering some hope that the day will come when his clothes will be out again and his politics will be back.

For twenty years Washington has been wondering, Where's the catch? Will he sell out for money, or will he run for office? Those are the normal options. But Ralph Nader is not a normal person. Operating on the mental fringe where self-abnegation blurs into self-obsession, Ralph is living proof that there isn't much difference between a fanatic and a saint. I'll bet you Mother Teresa is impossible to deal with, too.

Study Questions

1. Even if Nader's views are sometimes too extreme, should we be thankful that he makes such extreme points because they pull the rest of us further in the right direction?

2. Do you think Kinsley's remark that Nader wants warning labels on every french fry was a cheap shot, or just a bit of exaggerated but acceptable humor?

3. If you rejected Kinsley's praise of Nader just because Kinsley used to work for Nader, then wouldn't you commit the *ad hominem* fallacy? One commits the *ad hominem* fallacy when one attacks the arguer, rather than the argument, but considers the attack on the arguer decisive. The *ad hominem* fallacy fits the following form: Person A argues that X is true. Person A has defect B. Therefore, X is false.

6

Arguments for Utilitarianism

John Stuart Mill

Editor's note: Mill, one of the founders of utilitarianism in Western philosophy, gives what he considers the only kind of proof that can be given for utilitarianism, which is his first principle of morality. He compares 'desirable' with 'visible' and argues by analogy that utilitarianism is proven to be acceptable by the desires of people, just as we would prove that a thing was visible by showing that people viewed it. Mill also argues that since each person's happiness is good to that person, the general happiness is therefore the general good to all.

It has already been remarked, that questions of ultimate ends do not admit of proof, in the ordinary acceptation of the term. To be incapable of proof by reasoning is common to all first principles; to the first premises of our knowledge, as well as to those of our conduct. But the former, being matters of fact, may be the subject of a direct appeal to the faculties which judge of fact—namely, our senses, and our internal consciousness. Can an appeal be made to the same faculties on questions of practical ends? Or by what other faculty is cognisance taken of them?

Questions about ends are, in other words, questions about what things are desirable. The utilitarian doctrine is, that happiness is desirable, and the only thing desirable, as an end; all other things being only desirable as means to that end. What ought to be required of this doctrine—what conditions is it requisite that the doctrine should fulfil—to make good its claim to be believed?

The only proof capable of being given that an object is visible, is that people actually see it. The only

proof that a sound is audible, is that people hear it; and so of the other sources of our experience. In like manner, I apprehend, the sole evidence it is possible to produce that anything is desirable, is that people do actually desire it. If the end which the utilitarian doctrine proposes to itself were not, in theory and in practice, acknowledged to be an end, nothing could ever convince any person that it was so. No reason can be given why the general according to the utilitarian doctrine, is not naturally and originally part of the end, but it is capable of becoming so, and in those who love it disinterestedly it has become so, and is desired and cherished, not as a means to happiness, but as a part of their happiness.

To illustrate this farther, we may remember that virtue is not the only thing, originally a means, and which if it were not a means to anything else, would be and remain indifferent, but which by association with what it is a means to, comes to be desired for itself, and that too with the utmost intensity. What, for example, shall we say of the love of money? There is nothing originally more desirable about money than about any heap of glittering pebbles. Its worth is solely that of the things which it will buy; the desires for other things than itself, which it is a means of gratifying. Yet the love of money is not only one of the strongest moving forces of human life, but money is, in many cases, desired in and for itself; the desire to possess it is often stronger than the desire to use it, and goes on increasing when all the desires which point to ends beyond it, to be compassed by it, are falling off. It may, then, be said truly, that money is desired not for the sake of an end, but as part of the end. From being a means to happiness, it has come to be itself a principal ingredient of the individual's conception of happiness. The same may be said of the majority of the great objects of human life—power, for example, or fame; except that to each of these there is a certain amount of immediate pleasure annexed, which has at least the semblance of being naturally inherent of fame, is the immense aid they give to the attainment of in them; a thing which cannot be said of money. Still, however, the strongest natural attraction, both of power and our other wishes; and it is the strong association thus generated between them and all our objects of desire, which gives to the direct desire of them the intensity it often assumes, so as in some characters to surpass in strength all other desires. In these cases the means have become a part of the end, and a more important part of it than any of the things which they are means to. What was once desired as an instrument

Reprinted from John Stuart Mill, *Utilitarianism*, Chapter 4.

for the attainment of happiness, has come to be desired for its own sake. In being desired for its own sake it is, however, desired as *part* of happiness. The person is made, or thinks he would be made, happy by its mere possession; and is made unhappy by failure to obtain it. The desire of it is not a different thing from the desire of happiness, any more than the love of music, or the desire of health. They are included in happiness. They are some of the elements of which the desire of happiness is made up. Happiness is not an abstract idea, but a concrete whole, and these are some of its parts. And the utilitarian standard sanctions and approves their being so. Life would be a poor thing, very ill provided with sources of happiness, if there were not this provision of nature, by which things originally indifferent, but conducive to, or otherwise associated with, the satisfaction of our primitive desires, become in themselves sources of pleasure more valuable than the primitive pleasures, both in permanency, in the space of human existence that they are capable of covering, and even in intensity.

Virtue, according to the utilitarian conception, is a good of this description. There was no original desire of it, or motive to it, save its conduciveness to pleasure, and especially to protection from pain. But through the association thus formed, it may be felt a good in itself, and desired as such with as great intensity as any other good; and with this difference between it and the love of money, of power, or of fame, that all of these may, and often do, render the individual noxious to the other members of the society to which he belongs, whereas there is nothing which makes him so much a blessing to them as the cultivation of the disinterested love of virtue. And consequently, the utilitarian standard, while it tolerates and approves those other acquired desires, up to the point beyond which they would be more injurious to the general happiness than promotive of it, enjoins and requires the cultivation of the love of virtue up to the greatest strength possible, as being above all things important to the general happiness.

It results from the preceding considerations, that there is in reality nothing desired except happiness. Whatever is desired otherwise than as a means to some end beyond itself, and ultimately to happiness, is desired as itself a part of happiness, and is not desired for itself until it has become so. Those who desire virtue for its own sake, desire it either because the consciousness of it is a pleasure, or because the consciousness of being without it is a pain, or for both reasons united; as in truth the pleasure and pain seldom exist separately, but almost always together, the same person feeling pleasure in the degree of virtue attained, and pain in not having attained more. If one of these gave him no pleasure, and the other no pain, he would not love or desire virtue, or would desire it only for the other benefits which it might produce to himself or to persons whom he cared for.

We have now, then, an answer to the question, of what sort of proof the principle of utility is susceptible. If the opinion which I have now stated is psychologically true—if human nature is so constituted as to desire nothing which is not either a part of happiness or a means of happiness, we can have no other proof, and we require no other, that these are the only things desirable. If so, happiness is the sole end of human action, and the promotion of it the test by which to judge of all human conduct; from whence it necessarily follows that it must be the criterion of morality, since a part is included in the whole.

And now to decide whether this is really so, whether mankind does desire nothing for itself but that which is a pleasure to them, or of which the absence is a pain; we have evidently arrived at a question of fact and experience, dependent, like all similar questions, upon evidence. It can only be determined by practised self-consciousness and self-observation, assisted by observation of others. I believe that these sources of evidence, impartially consulted, will declare that desiring a thing and finding it pleasant, aversion to it and thinking of it as painful, are phenomena entirely inseparable, or rather two parts of the same phenomenon; in strictness of language, two different modes of naming the same psychological fact: that to think of an object as desirable (unless for the sake of its consequences), and to think of it as pleasant, are one and the same thing; and that to desire anything, except in proportion as the idea of it is pleasant, is a physical and metaphysical impossibility.

So obvious does this appear to me, that I expect it will hardly be disputed: and the objection made will be, not that desire can possibly be directed to anything ultimately except pleasure and exemption from pain, but that the will is a different thing from desire; that a person of confirmed virtue, or any other person whose purposes are fixed, carries out his purposes without any thought of the pleasure he has in contemplating them, or expects to derive from their fulfilment; and persists in acting on them, even though these pleasures are much diminished, by changes in his character or decay of his passive sensibilities, or are out-weighed by the pains which the pursuit of the purposes may bring upon him. All this I fully admit, and have stated it elsewhere, as positively and emphatically as any one. Will, the active phenomenon, is a different thing from desire, the state of passive sensibility, and though originally an offshoot from it, may in time take root and detach itself from the parent stock; so much so, that in the case of an habitual purpose, instead of willing the thing because we desire it, we often desire it only because we will it. This, however, is but an instance of that familiar fact, the power of habit, and is nowise confined to the case of virtuous actions. Many indifferent things, which men originally did from a motive of some sort, they continue to do from habit. Sometimes this is done unconsciously, the consciousness coming only after the action; at other times with conscious volition, but volition which has become habitual, and is put in operation by the force of habit, in opposition perhaps to the deliberate preference, as often happens with those who have contracted habits of vicious or hurtful indulgence. Third and last comes the case in which the habitual act of will in the individual instance is not in contradiction to the general intention prevailing at other times, but in fulfilment of it; as in the case of the person of confirmed virtue, and of all who pursue deliberately and consistently any determinate end. The distinction between will and desire thus understood is an authentic and highly important psychological fact; but the fact consists solely in this—that will, like all other parts of our constitution, is amenable to habit, and that we may will from habit what we no longer desire for itself, or desire only because we will it. It is not the less true that will, in the beginning, is entirely produced by desire, including in that term the repelling influence of pain as well as the attractive one of pleasure. Let us take into consideration, no longer the person who has a confirmed will to do right, but him in whom that virtuous will is still feeble, conquerable by temptation, and not to be fully relied on; by what means can it be strengthened? How can the will to be virtuous, where it does not exist in sufficient force, be implanted or awakened? Only by making the person *desire* virtue—by making him think of it in a pleasurable light, or of its absence in a painful one. It is by associating the doing right with pleasure, or the doing wrong with pain, or by eliciting and impressing and bringing home to the person's experience the pleasure naturally involved in the one or the pain in the other, that it is possible to call forth that will to be virtuous, which, when

confirmed, acts without any thought of either pleasure or pain. Will is the child of desire, and passes out of the dominion of its parent only to come under that of habit. That which is the result of habit affords no presumption of being intrinsically good, and there would be no reason for wishing that the purpose of virtue should become independent of pleasure and pain, were it not that the influence of the pleasurable and painful associations which prompt to virtue is not sufficiently to be depended on for unerring constancy of action until it has acquired the support of habit. Both in feeling and in conduct, habit is the only thing which imparts certainty; and it is because of the importance to others of being able to rely absolutely on one's feelings and conduct, and to oneself of being able to rely on one's own, that the will to do right ought to be cultivated into this habitual independence. In other words, this state of the will is a means to good, not intrinsically a good; and does not contradict the doctrine that nothing is a good to human beings but in so far as it is either itself pleasurable, or a means of attaining pleasure or averting pain.

But if this doctrine be true, the principle of utility is proved. Whether it is or not must now be left to the consideration of the thoughtful reader.

Study Questions

1. When Mill moves from what is rational for the individual, pursuing happiness, to what is rational for a group, pursuing happiness, does Mill commit the fallacy of composition? One commits the fallacy of composition when one assumes that whatever is true of each part of the whole is also true of the whole.

2. Does Mill commit the fallacy of equivocation on the suffixes 'ible' and 'able', since he uses 'desirable' to mean able to be desired, as he uses 'visible' to mean able to be viewed? Or is it a better criticism to claim that Mill is making a false analogy by comparing 'desirable' with 'visible'?

3. Does Mill commit the *ad populum* fallacy when he implies that if enough people want something badly enough, then that makes it good?

4. Even if first principles cannot be proven, why can't we offer an indefinitely long series of justifications? Because we are finite beings, we could never question each step in an infinitely long chain of justifications in a proof. But that does not mean that the steps are missing or that the proof fails, only that we

fail to appreciate all of it. Even if there is an infinite regress, as a practical matter, won't we reasonably lose or suspend our skepticism once we see a substantially long series of justified steps in a proof? Wouldn't there be some principles that we wouldn't bother to question seriously because they seem obvious enough in practice—even if they aren't first principles? If this obviousness faded away, then couldn't we still move another step further along an indefinitely long chain of reasoning to follow?

© 1995 by Sidney Harris.

7

Eleven Objections to Utilitarianism

Sterling Harwood

Author's abstract: This essay examines 11 criticisms of various forms of utilitarianism (it mentions 12 forms), arguing that the most plausible form of utilitarianism is act-utilitarianism as opposed to rule-utilitarianism. However, act-utilitarianism is still subject to severe criticisms, including the criticisms that utilitarianism is unjust, fails to grant sufficient weight to promise keeping, enjoins going into an experience machine, and gives undue weight to animals.

A. Introduction

I will discuss 11 significant objections to utilitarianism, though I will not accept all 11. My purpose is not to bury utilitarianism once and for all but to survey a large number of objections and provoke further discussion, although I may perhaps put a few more nails in utilitarianism's coffin. I start by trying to clarify the nature of utilitarianism since it has so many versions both drawing criticism and developing as responses to criticism. Here is a list of 12 versions I will at least mention below (though some of these can be combined to form still more versions): motive-utilitarianism, act-utilitarianism, rule-utilitarianism, average utilitarianism, total utilitarianism, hedonistic utilitarianism, eudaimonistic utilitarianism, negative utilitarianism, welfare-utilitarianism, preference-satisfaction utilitarianism, felt-satisfaction utilitarianism, and ideal utilitarianism. Of course these 12 versions of utilitarianism do not

Reprinted from Louis P. Pojman, ed., *Moral Philosophy: A Reader* (Indianapolis: Hackett Publishing Co., Inc., 1993), pp. 141–154.

correspond to the 11 objections to utilitarianism I consider, but many of these versions were developed to deal with objections to other versions of utilitarianism. Indeed, many critics who thought they had finally driven a stake through the heart of utilitarianism have only seen utilitarianism live on by being transformed into another version.

Utilitarianism is a consequentialist (that is, teleological) moral principle. As a moral principle, utilitarianism tells us how we should act. Consequentialism is not itself a moral principle but a category into which some moral principles fit. Consequentialism insists that an act is determined to be morally right (or morally wrong) exclusively by particular consequences of doing that act. (Consequentialism and utilitarianism can go beyond acts to include evaluations of institutions, policies, motives, and persons, but for simplicity I shall focus on acts and deemphasize versions of utilitarianism such as motive-utilitarianism.) Some include the maximizing theory of the right as a definition of consequentialism, but this would make the definition of consequentialism under-inclusive because we can imagine moral principles that value consequences alone but do not require maximizing good consequences (because, for example, there could be two different kinds of consequences to maximize and no rule for trading off between them). The particular consequences determining the rightness (or wrongness) of the act in question are specified not by consequentialism itself but by a particular consequentialist principle. Utilitarianism is the particular consequentialist principle that specifically concerns utility. Utility is psychological satisfaction (for example, pleasure, happiness, and well-being). Since utility is utilitarianism's only value, utilitarianism is a monistic rather than a pluralistic moral principle. And it is utilitarianism's monism rather than its consequentialism that explains why utilitarianism requires maximizing utility. Because utility is the only value, there is no other value to check or limit the logical approach of requiring the gain of more and more of the only value.

Many versions of utilitarianism differ primarily according to which psychological satisfaction they emphasize. For example, hedonistic utilitarianism stresses pleasure; preference-satisfaction utilitarianism stresses satisfaction of preferences; ideal utilitarianism stresses what would be desired under ideal conditions; negative utilitarianism stresses that avoiding dissatisfaction is more important than gaining satisfaction; and welfare-utilitarianism stresses what is in the best interests of those whose well-being is in question. And of course, many of these psychological satisfactions interrelate and overlap with one another. Disutility—psychological dissatisfaction (for example, pain and unhappiness)—is the opposite of utility.

Utilitarianism essentially specifies that the consequences that determine an act's rightness (or wrongness) are the psychological satisfactions that the act causes. Utilitarianism is a monistic moral principle, since it implies that there is only one thing that has moral value, namely, psychological satisfaction. Since there is no other moral value to check or limit the value of psychological satisfaction, utilitarianism says an act is right only to the extent that it maximizes these satisfactions, that is, produces the greatest balance of satisfaction over dissatisfaction for all in the long run. If only dissatisfaction is available, then utilitarianism says an act is right to the extent that it minimizes dissatisfaction. This is not a second or separate value in utilitarianism; for we can represent utilitarianism as claiming that an act is right to the extent that its expected consequences fall as far to the right as possible on the following scale. The far left ranges to an infinite amount of dissatisfaction, the 0 represents where the amount of satisfaction equals the amount of dissatisfaction, and the far right ranges to an infinite amount of satisfaction.

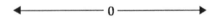

The left and right directions on the scale should not be confused with the political left or political right. Indeed, utilitarians have historically promoted governmental reforms (for example, abolishing slavery, improving prisons, and feeding, clothing, and housing the poor) that the political left has also endorsed.

B. The 11 Objections

1. Utilitarianism Is Overly Demanding

Perhaps the first objection that occurs to students is that utilitarianism appears to demand an extreme amount of self-sacrifice from us. This stems from utilitarianism's monism, its insistence that only one thing has moral value, and its insistence that we obtain more and more of that thing without limit; for there is no other value to counterbalance or limit it. Must we really sell all of our nonessential material

goods (for example, musical recordings and baseball cards) and give the money to worthy charitable causes (for example, relief of famine)? Further, must we be ready to sacrifice friends and loved ones by acting impartially to maximize satisfaction? Bentham stated the utilitarianism formula "Everybody to count for one and nobody to count for more than one."[1] Utilitarianism's impartiality stems from its counting everyone's satisfaction as equally valuable (so long as the amount of satisfaction is the same). Later, we will see that eudaimonistic utilitarianism seems to depart from Bentham's statement, and we will see an objection to the statement from those who believe that interpersonal comparisons of utility are impossible. Alleged counterexamples often hurled at utilitarianism include: 1) the instance where utilitarianism requires that the least useful person in a lifeboat lost at sea be killed and eaten whenever necessary to keep the other persons in the lifeboat alive long enough to be rescued; and 2) the instance where a healthy and innocent person comes in for a checkup, but his doctor can maximize satisfaction by killing him and using his organs to save the lives of five or more other people. Indeed, if the person in charge of the lifeboat or the doctor, respectively, can make these facts clear enough to us, then utilitarianism requires us to submit to being killed rather than to resist.

So we can see why a version of Objection 1, called the "objection from integrity," says that utilitarianism requires us to have a psychologically impossible (or nearly impossible) impartiality and detachment from our own lives, projects, friends, and loved ones. Of course, utilitarianism scarcely requires us to attempt the impossible, since that would be futile and would fail to maximize *expected* satisfaction; for the satisfaction expected from an act known to be impossible must be nil. The objection thus seems to be merely a complaint that morality is sometimes or oftentimes difficult to live up to. But this is hardly a conclusive objection. Nobody ever said it was going to be easy to be moral. Indeed, all or almost all moral principles require us to give up our lives under some scenarios. Even the most self-centered of moral principles, ethical egoism, which commands each person to maximize his or her own satisfaction, requires us to commit suicide the moment when the satisfaction we can expect in the rest of our lives is outweighed—even slightly—by the dissatisfaction we can expect in the rest of our lives. Every moral principle seems to require extreme actions under some scenario or other. And it would also be extreme to require this alternative: "*Never* do any extreme acts." So the objection that utilitarianism sometimes leads to extreme self-sacrifice or extreme acts is inconclusive.

Moreover, I suspect that utilitarianism is not as extremely demanding in everyday life as many think. Here is how a utilitarian could argue that utilitarianism is easy enough to pursue in everyday life. All indications are that overpopulation and depletion of needed natural resources will get worse. Therefore, rather than give almost all of one's wealth away now, one ought to invest one's wealth wisely, probably making more wealth, and hold one's wealth in reserve for these more troubled times ahead, when charity will be needed more than ever and when the stakes will be even greater. In the meantime, one can gain satisfaction from the security of having wise investments (and from the knowledge that one is self-sufficient and not a charity case oneself. Indeed, some investment activities (for example, following the business news) and investments (for example, collectibles such as baseball cards, rare musical recordings, and other art) are intrinsically satisfying for many investors. As long as the population explosion continues and needed natural resources continue to be depleted faster than they are replaced, one can maximize satisfaction by wisely investing his or her wealth to make more wealth and by holding it in reserve to help with the greater calamity likely to occur in the foreseeable future. If these trends continue through the rest of one's life, with a greater calamity always likely to occur in the foreseeable future, then one can then leave all of his or her amassed wealth to the charity one believes will maximize satisfaction. One's leaving wealth to others at one's death is no personal sacrifice at all, since "you can't take it with you when you die." But one's legal will must sacrifice some satisfaction of one's relatives if they are not needy enough. Some critics of utilitarianism will doubtless say, "How convenient!" But that misses the point here, which is that at least utilitarianism would dodge Objection 1, which claims utilitarianism is not convenient for individuals but overly demanding.

Finally, in case one thinks that utilitarianism will still be overly demanding in too many cases, consider these two arguments by Kurt Baier:

> Surely, in the absence of any *special* reasons for preferring someone else's interests, *everyone's* interests are best served if *everyone* puts his own interests first. For, by and large, everyone is himself the best judge of what is in his own best interests, since everyone usually knows best what his plans, aims, ambitions, or aspirations are. Moreover, everyone is more diligent in the promotion of his own interests than that of others.[2]

2. Utilitarianism Eliminates Supererogation

Some have argued that since utilitarianism leaves no room for supererogation (that is, self-sacrifice above and beyond the call of duty), utilitarianism objectionably flies in the face of commonsense morality, which recognizes supererogation. For example, during a hasty retreat a soldier might stop to pick up and carry a fellow soldier many hazardous yards to safety, and endure being wounded. There seems to be nothing *above* or *beyond* the call of utilitarian duty, since utilitarianism says our duty is to *maximize* satisfaction. Of course, one cannot cause an amount of satisfaction above or beyond the maximum amount. So we seem to face a dilemma. Either we reject utilitarianism, or else we reject supererogation.

But this is a false dilemma, since ties are overlooked. Utilitarianism allows that the expected satisfaction of two (or even more) alternatives can be tied for the maximal amount. One of these alternatives can involve more sacrifice (dissatisfaction) for us than that expected from the other alternatives tied for the maximal amount of satisfaction. Utilitarianism cannot *require* us to make this sacrifice by choosing this alternative among those that are tied, since all of those alternatives are equally acceptable, but utilitarianism *permits* us to choose the alternative that sacrifices more of our satisfaction than the other alternatives do. So utilitarianism does allow for moral self-sacrifice that is not morally required (that is, moral self-sacrifice beyond the call of duty).

One may object that ties are so uncommon that utilitarianism still leaves too little room for supererogation, which is the main point of Objection 2. But ties are probably more common than many of us think. For example, Raymond D. Gastil interprets James Q. Wilson's research as pointing out:

> that almost all recent major American studies testing hypotheses that major long-term behavior changes result from particular social policy or educational inputs have provided inconclusive or negative findings. Thus, studies have shown that the type of school or educational method makes no difference (Coleman report). . . . [Wilson] suggests, and it is probably true, that in real-life situations there is too much going on, too many cycles of reinforcement stretched over too many years, for particular interventions to get up out of the noise.[3]

This feature of ties is notorious in the so-called dismal science, economics, the social science utilitarianism has perhaps influenced most. Some joke that one can lay all the economists from end to end and never reach a definite conclusion. And some joke that the search continues for the one-armed economist, the one who cannot say "On the other han . . ." The serious undertone to these jokes is that utilitarianism all too often has us consider two or more alternatives which, as far as we can tell, are tied in the amount of satisfaction they will produce. Perhaps this is why some joke that economists know the price of everything but the value of nothing.

3. Utilitarianism Is Unjust

Utilitarianism is often criticized for failing to treat retributive justice (giving the guilty and only the guilty the punishment they deserve in fair proportion to the severity of their respective crimes) as having intrinsic moral importance. Familiar counterexamples to utilitarianism here include: 1) a case where a scientific genius murders his wife just as he is about to develop a cure for cancer, and giving him the punishment he justly deserves will delay the development of the cure for years or decades; 2) a case involving racial violence, where a local woman has been raped and murdered, and angry mobs are about to take the law into their own hands by executing people of the opposite race whom they suspect of being involved in the crime. The sheriff can easily prevent all this violence, which is likely to kill innocent people, by framing the useless town drunk who remembers nothing about the night in question and who has no alibi. The sheriff alone knows that he is innocent because he locked the drunk up for public drunkenness at the same time the crime was committed in the middle of the night; and 3) a case where parking offenders (or other minor offenders) are punished way out of proportion to the severity of their offenses whenever the deterrent effect of the unjustly severe punishment produces so much satisfaction from a nearly perfectly obeyed law that it maximizes satisfaction even while leading to the torture and execution of that one driver in a million or more who is foolish enough to break the law. Critics object that utilitarianism would unjustly: 1) fail to give the scientist the severe punishment he deserves; 2) frame the innocent town drunk; and 3) sometimes torture and execute people for merely parking illegally.

Critics also charge that utilitarianism violates distributive justice (giving each person his or her fair share of benefits and burdens in society). Familiar counterexamples to utilitarianism here include: 1) the

case where, instead of fairly and randomly determining who should bear the burden of dying by casting lots, the occupants of a lifeboat lost at sea kill and eat the least useful occupant as a last resort to keep all others alive long enough to be rescued; 2) a case of secretly killing a healthy man just in for a routine checkup in order to maximize satisfaction by using his various organs in a number of life-saving operations; and 3) a case of neglecting to give ordinary people their fair share of benefits and instead indulging so-called utility monsters, people with nearly insatiable appetites for wealth and for whom the general economic law of diminishing marginal utility of wealth does not apply because they are so miserly and greedy that each new unit of wealth obtained causes far more satisfaction for the utility monster than it would for those with normal human psychologies.

Utilitarians often dismiss such examples as unrealistic and thus irrelevant to our real world of troubles. Utilitarians say they have done enough to develop a moral principle that deals with the problems of real life, and need not develop a moral principle that covers every imaginable problem in every fantasy land. But the utilitarian defense that these cases are unrealistic misses the point. How realistic or unrealistic a case is surely is a matter of degree. These cases are realistic enough that some of them can and will eventually occur in real life, and when they do utilitarianism will be refuted, refutation we can know in advance by thinking ahead.

Indeed, there have been, after all, some lifeboat cases where cannibalism has been a last resort to survive. And there have been some awfully greedy people in the history of our world. Perhaps they were utility monsters. And some would say that at least one of these situations recently occurred in California, and even one of these counterexamples is enough to refute utilitarianism. The nearly all-white jury that acquitted the police officers of nearly all criminal charges in the famous videotaped beating of motorist Rodney King has been called the jury from another planet! But of course it was a real jury. Suppose you were one of these jurors who believed there was a reasonable doubt on almost all the charges against the policemen but who also predicted, as many others did, that rioting would occur if almost all the policemen were acquitted of these charges. So, you could realistically change your vote from "not guilty beyond a reasonable doubt" to "guilty beyond a reasonable doubt" on every charge and create a mistrial, preventing the policemen from being acquitted on any charge, allowing a new trial, and probably preventing enough violence to maximize satisfaction with your vote of "guilty beyond a reasonable doubt."

I conclude that at least some of these counter-examples concerning retributive and distributive justice seem realistic enough to refute utilitarianism, especially since truth is often stranger than fiction.

4. Utilitarianism Fails to Take Promises Seriously Enough

Utilitarianism implies that keeping one's promises has no intrinsic moral value apart from any satisfaction it causes but has only instrumental and contingent moral value. Objection 4 pits utilitarianism squarely against commonsense morality, which recognizes the intrinsic moral importance of keeping promises. For example, one promises his or her dying mother to beautify her grave by always putting fresh and gorgeous flowers on her grave when her birthday arrives each year. But since an afterlife with a dissatisfied mother is unexpected, utilitarianism requires one to completely discount one's solemn pledge. After all, she will never know the difference. So utilitarianism emphasizes that life is for the living, and that one should spend his or her time, energy, and money, not putting flowers on a grave, but doing what will maximize satisfaction.

Utilitarians reply that we should not uncritically accept whatever commonsense morality dictates. Sometimes commonsense morality is wrong (for example, racist and sexist views that used to be considered commonsensical). But this reply will go only so far, for the commonsense belief in the intrinsic importance of keeping promises survives critical scrutiny that racist and sexist views cannot.

The example also seems to commit the appeal to pity. It is surely pitiful that the dying mother has such a son. But the mere fact that something is pitiful is not a conclusive reason against it. For example, it is pitiful to amputate a child's leg, but this is all too often medically necessary and for the best.

Further, some forms of utilitarianism would count the mother's preference as something to satisfy. Felt-satisfaction utilitarianism would not count her preference, since she will never feel the satisfaction. But preference-satisfaction utilitarianism can count it. Yet as Robert E. Goodin has said in objecting to a somewhat different form of utilitarianism, the closer a version of utilitarianism comes to embracing an "aesthetic ideal regardless of whether or not that is good for any living being, the less credible this analysis is as an ethical theory."[4] Keeping the promise to beautify one's mother's grave each year does seem to be a matter of aesthetics, which is presumably distinct from ethics.

There is a further problem with this type of utilitarian defense. Where do we draw the line in respecting the preferences of the dead? It seems arbitrary to limit it to those covered by promises. The other preferences were just as real and important to those now dead. Sometimes it is a fluke that one preference was covered by a promise and another was not. For example, suppose our mother is struck by lightning before we can make another promise to her. But surely we cannot cater to all the preferences the dead had. We cannot cater to all the preferences that those now dead had to live longer. Otherwise, we might have to exhaust our resources trying to put them in cryogenic freeze so that they can be thawed later when science might be able to revive them. But this seems absurd. Drawing the line at death, when preferences and satisfactions and all other psychological states presumably cease, seems less arbitrary than trying to distinguish between which preferences of the dead we will try to satisfy.

Utilitarianism cannot completely dismiss Objection 4 as requiring the impossible, namely, the satisfaction of a dead person's preference. One might think that death prevents the preference from being satisfied. But this is to assume that felt-satisfactions are the only satisfactions, which seems false. For example, a man prefers that his wife not commit adultery. But his wife is clever and decides while he is on submarine duty for months to have a secret affair with a sexually inexperienced bookworm who is a leading specialist in prevention of sexually transmitted diseases and who shyly wants only a few months more of secret sexual experience. The wife rightly expects, let us suppose, that her husband will never know the difference. He will have no felt-dissatisfaction of his preference that she not commit adultery.

Felt-satisfaction utilitarianism requires the wife to have the affair she and the bookworm want, but preference-satisfaction utilitarianism would at least count her husband's preference that she not do so (though whether there is an affair or not will make no difference to how he feels). Some critics charge that this is enough to refute felt-satisfaction utilitarianism. But again we should be concerned about whether the alleged counterexample commits the fallacy of appealing to pity. It may seem a pity that this dutiful submariner is deceived by his wife, who has broken her marriage vows (that is, promises). But mere pity is not decisive.

The error utilitarianism makes about promises is exposed by another example, though. You promise to meet me for an ordinary lunch. On your way to meet me you spot victims just emerging from a car accident in a remote area. They need your medical help immediately. So you stop to help them at the cost of making me dissatisfied with your lateness to lunch. Utilitarianism clearly requires this, and so does commonsense morality. Where they differ is in the reply you give when you come to lunch late. Commonsense morality implies, rightly I think, that you *owe* me an explanation and an expression of regret that you were sidetracked. A utilitarian cannot *simply* express sincere regret here. Once your dissatisfaction was outweighed by the prevention of more serious dissatisfaction for the accident victims, there was either nothing to be regretted or at least the expression of regret is viewed as a completely separate act, whose rightness or wrongness is determined exclusively by a separate calculation of its consequences rather than on a backward-looking expression of a genuinely felt emotion. Utilitarianism's unnecessarily complex conceptual separation of these conceptually, emotionally, and simply linked acts seems mistaken.

5. Average and Total Utilitarianism Produce Absurdities

Average utilitarianism states that an act is morally right only to the extent that it maximizes the amount of satisfaction per person in existence (that is, maximizes the mean of utility). Total utilitarianism states that an act is morally right only to the extent that it maximizes the aggregate amount of satisfaction (that is, maximizes the sum of satisfaction). These two forms of utilitarianism lead to different results only when population policy is involved; for, if the population is held constant, then average satisfaction and total satisfaction must rise or fall together.

Critics charge that average utilitarianism degenerates into number worship that squanders satisfaction, whereas total utilitarianism will lead us to reduce the standard of living too much and make the world barely livable. Either way, utilitarianism seems objectionable.

First, here is a counterexample to average utilitarianism. Suppose we have a person who is quite satisfied in his life but whose level of satisfaction is always consistently and predictably below the average amount of satisfaction people have. And suppose that from our experience trying to help him we know that there is no way to raise his level of satisfaction without lowering the overall average amount of satisfaction. Now, if we can raise the average of satisfaction for all by painlessly killing and disposing of this fellow who is below average, then average utilitarianism requires us to do so. But this seems absurd and contrary to a key point of utilitarianism, which is that satisfaction is the only value. Here, average utilitarianism requires us to squander an amount of net satisfaction just to raise a mere number, an average level of satisfaction. We can suppose that not one more unit of satisfaction is gained, but that the average is raised only by subtracting the below-average fellow from the population. (This would be a rather extreme case of what baseball genius Branch Rickey called "addition by subtraction"!) So average utilitarianism seems unacceptable, even to many utilitarians.

But total utilitarianism seems to err on an even more massive scale; for it requires us to bring more and more people into the world—even if this lowers the average level of satisfaction—so long as adding another person to the world adds more net satisfaction to the world than any other alternative. The worry here is that total utilitarianism will be too tolerant of the population explosion and will lead to a world where standards of living are drastically lowered and almost all of us eke out a life just barely worth living because our planet is filled to capacity. Because there will be so many of us, this will make up for the extremely low average satisfaction we will have and will maximize total satisfaction. Total satisfaction is figured by adding the amount of satisfaction each person has. Making the world barely satisfactory for everyone seems to miss a key point of utilitarianism, which is that we should try to improve the lives of everyone as much as possible. So total utilitarianism seems unacceptable, even to many utilitarians.

Since utilitarianism must take a stand on population policy, and since both its alternatives—average and total utilitarianism—seem absurd, is utilitarianism *obviously* unacceptable here? No, because total utilitarianism *might* survive. In real life, we cannot jam the planet full of people and expect to retain enough control of the situation to maximize total satisfaction. First, the more people there are to satisfy, the harder it is likely to be to satisfy them. Second, a world where everyone ekes out a life barely worth living is likely to be unstable, presenting a great danger of disease and a chain reaction of catastrophes going through the population. Given these empirically contingent facts, it is unlikely that pushing population to such extreme limits will maximize expected total satisfaction, since the catastrophes would involve so much dissatisfaction and since the chances of them occurring would be so high.

In conclusion, utilitarianism's best prospect for surviving Objection 5 is the endorsement of total utilitarianism and the rejection of average utilitarianism. But even this strategy will probably fail, since we saw in the previous section (section 4) that utilitarianism should avoid overreliance on contingent empirical facts and avoid dismissal of hypothetical counterexamples. A world where we can maximize total satisfaction by increasing the population explosion and lowering average satisfaction is possible. It might be, for example, that our technology will improve to allow us to control the weather and the entire planet and that the more people we have the more labor power we have to enable us to keep the low average satisfaction stable and to avoid catastrophes. So utilitarianism seems unacceptable because it is woefully unprepared for this eventuality. It will yield unacceptable requirements whenever that day arrives. But we are entitled to think ahead and find utilitarianism unacceptable now.

6. Rule-Utilitarianism Is Incoherent or Redundant

Rule-utilitarianism (sometimes called restricted or indirect utilitarianism) is often distinguished from act-utilitarianism (sometimes called extreme or direct utilitarianism). R. M. Hare says:

> Act-utilitarianism is the view that we have to apply the so-called 'principle of utility' [that is, maximize satisfaction] directly to individual acts. . . . Rule-utilitarianism . . . is the view that this test is not to be applied to individual actions, but to *kinds* of action. . . . Actions are to be assessed by asking whether they are forbidden or enjoined by certain moral rules or principles; and it is only when we start to ask which moral rules or principles we are to adopt for assessing actions, that we apply the utilitarian test.[5]

Rule-utilitarianism was developed to try to save utilitarianism from the sort of counterexamples we have seen from commonsense morality (for example, "do not hang the innocent," and "keep promises"). Utilitarianism recognizes that commonsense moral rules such as "keep promises" and "do not kill" are generally useful in gaining satisfaction.

Jonathan Harrison, however, gives at least three good reasons for rejecting rule-utilitarianism. First, "It is not the case that I ought to obey a rule which has good consequences, however bad the consequences of my obeying it are."[6] For example, "do not steal" is a rule which, if generally adopted, would seem to maximize satisfaction, but we can easily imagine a scenario where stealing a radio is necessary to warn people to evacuate before a dam bursts and kills thousands of people. If the rule-utilitarian makes an exception to the rules to cover such cases, then rule-utilitarianism would seem redundant; for it would contain rules such as "do not kill, except to maximize satisfaction"; "do not steal, except to maximize satisfaction"; and "keep promises, but only if it maximizes satisfaction." These rules tell us nothing more than utilitarianism's fundamental rule "maximize satisfaction for all in the long run."

Second, following J. J. C. Smart, Harrison argues that "rule-utilitarianism is a manifestation of rule-worship."[7] Act-utilitarianism and rule-utilitarianism lead to different conclusions only if rule-utilitarianism sometimes forbids us from breaking a rule by doing an act that maximizes satisfaction. So rule-utilitarianism seems more a form of rule-worship than a form of utilitarianism, which says satisfaction—not rule following—is the only value.

Third, rule-utilitarians fail to distinguish three types of rule: 1) an actually operating social rule; 2) "a general moral *belief*, which most people in most societies have, *about* this (social) rule, to the effect that it usually or always ought to be acted upon"; and 3) "the *fact* about the social rule that it ought usually to be obeyed, whether most members of the society which has it think that it ought to be obeyed or not."[8] If rule-utilitarianism means (1) then it is still subject to the other objections above, but at least it is coherent. But if rule-utilitarianism means either (2) or (3), then it will end up referring to itself—for it is also a rule—in such a viciously circular way that it will be incoherent.

Finally, there is a fourth objection to rule-utilitarianism that Harrison does not explore. This objection uses the concept of *extensional equivalence*. Two moralities are extensionally equivalent if they always agree about what we should do in any case. Some critics argue that rule-utilitarianism is extensionally equivalent to act-utilitarianism and thus cannot coherently defend utilitarianism from familiar objections using plausible examples from commonsense morality (for example, "do not hang the innocent") as counterexamples to utilitarianism.[9] As R. M. Hare says, "The merit of rule-utilitarianism has been said to be that it is more in accord with our common moral beliefs than is act-utilitarianism. . . ."[10] But if the two are extensionally equivalent, then rule-utilitarianism has no more merit than act-utilitarianism. Act- and rule-utilitarianism do seem to be extensionally equivalent, because if rule-utilitarianism ever disagreed with act-utilitarianism and required us to follow a rule by doing an act that failed to maximize satisfaction, then rule-utilitarianism would be rejecting the lone value of utilitarianism, satisfaction (not mere obedience to rules). Further, act- and rule-utilitarianism seem to agree and converge because the adoption of a rule is itself an act. So if a rule really were so useful that its adoption would maximize satisfaction, then act-utilitarianism would require us to do the act of adopting that rule and taking that rule to heart.

In conclusion, the best prospect for utilitarianism's surviving Objection 6 is to reject rule-utilitarianism and emphasize the strength and flexibility of act-utilitarianism, which still has its own problems, as we have seen.

7. Utilitarianism Requires Us to Enter the Experience Machine

I suspect that all of us are intrigued by the experimental new technology called *virtual reality*. Some models are already used as flight simulators to train pilots. But imagine programming one's own artificial universe! What wonders would it contain?! With utilitarianism, however, it seems we will be forced to have too much of a good thing here. Robert Nozick has theorized about what he calls the *experience machine*, which resembles virtual reality, though he fails to apply his example of the experience machine directly to refuting utilitarianism.[11]

We can use the experience machine to object to utilitarianism because utilitarianism will require us to spend our entire lives in the machine if that will maximize satisfaction, as it might very well do. A life spent inside the experience machine seems like one of mental masturbation, an unreal and degraded life unworthy of us, though it will seem perfectly real and satisfying to us as long as we stay inside the machine. Utilitarianism's monism, its insistence that satisfaction is the only moral value, prevents utilitarians from placing greater moral value on genuine, veridical experiences than on artificial yet credible simulations. Utilitarianism is objectionable because its monism leaves no room to place any intrinsic value on truth, knowledge, or reality, with which we lose touch once we enter the experience machine. Moreover, independent of utilitarianism's monism, utilitarianism is also objectionable because the subjective character of what utilitarianism counts as valuable—namely, the subjects' feelings or satisfactions—allows value to be radically and objectionably disconnected from how things are in the world external to the subjects.

8. Utilitarianism Wildly Overstates Our Duties to Animals

One might conceive of Objection 8 as a version of Objection 1, since animals (I use 'animals' to mean 'nonhuman animals') outnumber humans by so much that humans will be swamped with duties to maximize the satisfactions animals are psychologically capable of having. (Of course, some living things evidently have no psychology.) But Objection 8 can be made by those who refuse to object to utilitarianism as overly demanding; for they can object that what is wrong with utilitarianism here is not how much it demands but what utilitarianism is demanding of us, namely, the satisfaction of mere nonhuman animals. Utilitarians from Bentham to Mill to Singer have insisted on considering animals in moral deliberations. But critics charge that utilitarianism will all too often require debased or beastly satisfaction. The critics charge that utilitarianism implies that it is better to be a pig satisfied than to be Socrates dissatisfied.

In response to such criticisms, John Stuart Mill tried to develop eudaimonistic utilitarianism, which would distinguish qualities of happiness, with some types of satisfaction having more moral value than other types present in the same quantity but of lower quality. But eudaimonistic utilitarianism is incompatible with utilitarianism's monism. Since utilitarianism insists that there is only one moral value, satisfaction, there is no other value to which a utilitarian can consistently appeal in claiming that one type of satisfaction is morally better than another type of satisfaction.[12]

9. Utilitarianism Panders to Bigots and Sadists

Critics charge that utilitarianism is fundamentally mistaken in treating racist, sexist, bigoted, and sadistic satisfaction as intrinsically valuable. Since satisfaction is utilitarianism's only value, utilitarianism has no other value enabling the utilitarian to distinguish between better and worse satisfactions. Only the amount of satisfaction (or dissatisfaction) caused makes an act right (or wrong), not whether the satisfaction is noble or unbiased. Critics charge that some motivations ought not to be satisfied because they are intrinsically wrong and their satisfaction is morally bankrupt and completely without value.

But Tom L. Beauchamp and LeRoy Walters suggest that utilitarianism can dodge this objection:

> because 'perverse' [for example, extremely sadistic] desires have been determined on the basis of past experience to cut against the objectives of utilitarianism by creating conditions productive of unhappiness, the desires (preferences) could never even be permitted to count. We discount preferences to rape children. . . . Preferences that serve merely to frustrate the preferences of others are thus ruled out by the goal of utilitarianism. As Mill himself argued, the cultivation of certain kinds of desires is built into the 'ideal' of utilitarianism.[13]

But this defense of utilitarianism is unconvincing, since we saw in section 8 that Mill's eudaimonistic utilitarianism was developed to handle similar objections to the kinds of satisfactions utilitarianism would respect, and we saw that eudaimonistic utilitarianism seems inconsistent because it abandons utilitarianism's monism, its insistence that there is only one value, namely, satisfaction. As Hare suggested, "Mill's mistake was perhaps to try to incorporate ideals into a utilitarian theory, which cannot really absorb them."[14] Utilitarianism's single-minded pursuit of the maximization of only one value leaves no room for other ideals. Further, unfortunately some preferences to rape children do not serve merely to frustrate the preferences of others but also serve to satisfy the rapists. The problem for utilitarianism is not the general prohibition of rape; it surely does condemn almost all rapes. Rather, Objection 9 claims utilitarianism is pandering to sadists and bigots by counting their sadistic and bigoted satisfactions as morally valuable *at all*—even if their satisfactions are readily overridden by the dissatisfactions of others.

10. Utilitarianism Makes Interpersonal Comparisons of Utility

> I am a child.
> I last awhile.
> You can't conceive of the pleasure in my smile.
> —The Buffalo Springfield[15]

Utilitarianism requires interpersonal comparisons of utility (that is, satisfaction), because it requires us to maximize satisfaction for all in the long run. Thus, we must consider trade-offs, promoting the satisfaction of some at the expense of allowing the dissatisfaction of others in order to maximize the net satisfaction for everyone over the long haul. But how can we compare one person's pleasure, for example, with another's pain? Are not pleasure and pain subjective experiences? Are not thresholds and tolerances for pain highly idiosyncratic and unpredictable? Being stuck with a needle, for example, seems to bother some people much more than others. And even though sugar presumably tastes the same to everyone, some seem to have more of a sweet tooth than others and enjoy sweets immeasurably more than others. After all, critics charge, it is a well-recognized maxim that there is no accounting for or disputing matters of taste (that is, *De gustibus non est disputandum*).

Objection 10 is flashy, but there is less here than meets the eye. Objection 10 relies on what it takes to be commonsensical, namely, that people enjoy and value the same psychological experiences differently. This is true even for basic psychological experiences such as pain. Masochists sometimes seem to enjoy significant levels of pain. But there is an equivocation in Objection 10 that is illustrated by the following joke: A masochist goes up to a sadist and says, "Hit me"; the sadist prepares to hit the masochist but then, realizing the masochist will enjoy being hit, says, "No." These mind games take some surprising twists and turns for which human psychology is notorious. But the point is that pain or sweet taste should not be equated with satisfaction. Utilitarianism is fully capable of allowing individual differences in what brings about satisfaction, not any particular experience we might misidentify as satisfaction.

Moreover, we commonsensically make interpersonal comparisons every day. For example, we build freeways even though we know that it is just a matter of time before an innocent baby who would not have died nearly so soon had the freeway never been built gets crushed in an automobile accident on the freeway. But the great convenience of the freeway and the other lives saved by allowing ambulances and other emergency vehicles to use the new freeway to speed to emergencies outweighs the harm caused to the crushed baby. So, whatever plausibility Objection 10 gains by relying on common sense is blunted by the commonsensical way we make interpersonal comparisons of satisfaction everyday.

Further, *inter*personal comparisons of satisfaction

seem no more problematic than *intra*personal comparisons of satisfaction. All the same arguments for Objection 10 could be made against intrapersonal comparisons of satisfaction. After all, Objection 10 must allow that I might become a masochist or an old man with satisfactions incommensurable with those I can now have. Yet we still think that it makes good common sense to trade off some satisfaction at one stage of life (for example, exercising hard rather than enjoying more sleep) for more satisfaction later in life (for example, living longer and with fewer illnesses).

Furthermore, Objection 10 strikes me as being mathematically suspect. Even if satisfaction was as wildly unpredictable from person to person as Objection 10 states, which I doubt, would it not minimize our margin of error if we assumed that each person's satisfactions were comparable? It seems so. For if we started giving preference or extra weight to persons whose satisfaction was assumed to be weightier, then the wildly unpredictable nature of satisfaction, which Objection 10 insists upon, would imply that we are as apt to be preferring and weighing the satisfactions of the right persons (those whose satisfaction is more satisfying than others' satisfactions) as those of the wrong persons. If we chose the wrong person and thus gave extra weight, in deciding what to do, to the satisfactions of a person whose satisfactions are actually *less* satisfying than the satisfactions of others, then we have compounded any mistake we would have made by considering all satisfactions comparable, and we have extended the margin of error further than it was. For example, suppose we expect to get ten percent more satisfaction by satisfying Pojman slightly than by satisfying Harwood slightly, but Pojman actually gets ten percent less satisfaction from being slightly satisfied than Harwood does from being slightly satisfied. Our margin of error is then twenty percent rather than the ten percent margin of error present in treating the satisfactions of Harwood and Pojman as comparable, only to learn that we could have obtained ten percent more satisfaction by satisfying Harwood slightly rather than satisfying Pojman slightly.

Finally, how can Objection 10 make sense of its claims such as, "Interpersonal comparisons of satisfaction are impossible because a slightly satisfied Harwood has immeasurably more satisfaction than a very satisfied Pojman. That's just the kind of guy Harwood is." How could we ever know such a thing unless interpersonal comparisons of satisfaction were not only possible but actually known? This very claim seems to make an interpersonal comparison of the satisfactions of Harwood and Pojman. The contradiction in claiming to know that interpersonal comparisons of satisfaction are impossible is similar to that of claiming, "My experience was impossible to describe; it was simply indescribable." Our making this very claim describes the experience. In calling our satisfactions incommensurable we make a comparison among them, namely, that they all have in common the feature for which we lack a scale by which we can accurately measure them all in the same units. But—and this is my main point—this common lack of a scale would also prevent anyone from knowing if we made a mistake in treating the satisfactions as comparable.

I conclude that rough-and-ready, short-and-snappy interpersonal comparisons of satisfaction are justified enough. Some interpersonal comparisons of utility are clearly much more plausible and defensible than others. For example, do we really have any doubt that the following claim is false: "Each time I lose a penny from my pocket change it causes me more dissatisfaction than all the dissatisfactions in human history combined"? The implications of Objection 10 are too extreme and absurd to accept.

11. Utilitarianism Is Too Secretive, Undemocratic, and Elitist

Since moral principles conceptually must concern how each person should live, we might think that any acceptable moral principle must be public and available for all to use in our thinking. But utilitarians often think that it would be a mistake to let most or all people directly pursue maximizing satisfaction, since too many will show bias or incompetence in calculating what will maximize satisfaction, thereby leading to too much dissatisfaction. Many critics find utilitarianism's restriction of the direct pursuit of maximizing satisfaction to a trusted utilitarian elite objectionably secretive, undemocratic, and elitist.

Utilitarians might reply that rule-utilitarianism can be more public than act-utilitarianism, since the people can be trusted as competent to follow basic and straightforward rules such as "do not kill" and "keep your promises." But we have already seen (in section 6) numerous reasons to doubt that rule-utilitarianism can ultimately remain distinct enough from act-utilitarianism, or to doubt that rule-utilitarianism is acceptable.

But Objection 11 fails because it accepts too uncritically the commonsense morality of public notification and use of moral rules. Indeed, it seems uncertain whether this is a requirement of commonsense morality at all. No less a champion of democracy than Winston Churchill insisted that "democracy is the worst form of Government except all those other forms that have been tried from time to time."[16] And Churchill's wisdom here is commonly quoted and accepted. So perhaps a utilitarian form of government would improve upon democracy and all the other forms of government tried so far.

C. Conclusion

In conclusion, though I reject some of the objections to utilitarianism that I still found to be worth presenting (Objections 1, 2, 10, and 11), the remaining objections collectively have enough force to convince me and many others to reject utilitarianism. But I can hardly rule out the development of a new version of utilitarianism that will dodge or withstand any silver bullets fired at utilitarianism here. I encourage those who wish to try to develop a new and improved utilitarianism.[17]

Study Questions

1. Who has the better of this debate, Mill or Harwood? Is utilitarianism true?

2. Can you develop another version of utilitarianism that is more defensible than the one Harwood attacks?

3. What is your evaluation of Harwood's argument about the experience machine? Is Harwood right to conclude that utilitarianism should not morally require people to enter the experience machine even if doing so would produce more happiness for everyone involved than any alternative?

4. Would you enter the experience machine and never return from it?

5. Even if you would enter the experience machine, is it your moral duty to enter it? Is it your moral duty never to leave it so long as staying in it will maximize utility?

Notes

1. Quoted in J. S. Mill, *Utilitarianism* (many editions), Chapter 5.

2. Kurt Baier, *The Moral Point of View: A Rational Basis of Ethics*, abr. ed. (New York: Random House, 1965), p. 147; unabridged edition (Ithaca, N.Y.: Cornell University Press, 1958), p. 307.

3. Raymond D. Gastil, "The Moral Right of the Majority to Restrict Obscenity and Pornography through Law," 86 *Ethics* (1976): 231–40; reprinted in John Arthur and William H. Shaw, eds., *Readings in Philosophy off Law* (Englewood Cliffs, N.J.: Prentice Hall, 1984), p. 572.

4. Robert E. Goodin, "Utility and the Good," in Peter Singer, ed., *A Companion to Ethics* (Oxford: Basil Blackwell, 1991), p. 243.

5. Richard Mervyn Hare, *Freedom and Reason* (Oxford: Oxford University Press, 1963), p. 130.

6. Jonathan Harrison, "Rule-Utilitarianism and Cumulative-Effect Utilitarianism," in Wesley E. Cooper, Kai Nielsen, and Steven C. Patten, eds., *New Essays on John Stuart Mill and Utilitarianism* (Guelph, Ont.: Canadian Association for Publishing in Philosophy, 1979), p. 22.

7. Harrison, "Rule-Utilitarianism and Cumulative-Effect Utilitarianism," p. 24.

8. Ibid., p. 25.

9. Hare was apparently the first in print to argue that act- and rule-utilitarianism are extensionally equivalent, though David Lyons shortly thereafter published a similar argument with much more detail and logical rigor. See Hare, *Freedom and Reason*, p. 131, and David Lyons, *The Forms and Limits of Utilitarianism* (Oxford: Oxford University Press, 1965).

10. Hare, *Freedom and Reason*, p. 130.

11. Robert Nozick, *Anarchy, State & Utopia* (Cambridge: Harvard University Press, 1974), pp. 42–45. Compare the idea of the experience machine with Woody Allen's 'orgasmitron' in his film *Sleeper* from 1973 and with the 'Holodeck' on the current television program *Star Trek: The Next Generation*.

12. For a recent attempt to rescue Mill's utilitarianism from this type of objection, see David O. Brink, "Mill's Deliberative Utilitarianism," *Philosophy & Public Affairs* 21 (1992): 67–103.

13. Tom L. Beauchamp and LeRoy Walters, eds., *Contemporary Issues in Bioethics*, 2d ed. (Belmont, Calif.: Wadsworth Publishing Co., 1982), p. 15.

14. Hare, *Freedom and Reason*, p. 121.

15. From "I Am a Child," written by Neil Young for The Buffalo Springfield, Springalo Toones/Cotillion Music, Inc.—BMI (Atco Records, 1967).

16. Winston Churchill, quoted in *The Oxford Dictionary of Quotations*, 3d ed., s.v. "Winston Churchill."

17. I thank Louis Pojman and an anonymous reviewer for comments.

"YOU MUST REALIZE THAT DESIRE IS THE CAUSE OF ALMOST ALL UNHAPPINESS — BUT, JUST OUT OF CURIOSITY, WHERE COULD I GET A SUIT LIKE THAT?"

© 1995 by Sidney Harris.

8

Arguments for Libertarianism

John Hospers

Editor's note: Hospers, a professor of philosophy at the University of Southern California, was the Libertarian Party's presidential candidate in 1972. Though he lost, he helped set the stage for Ed Clark, who received over a million votes as the Libertarian candidate for president in 1980. Clark also fell far short of winning, but American election laws tend to discourage third parties (that is, parties other than the Democratic and the Republican) and work against them. The Libertarian Party has generally been the strongest third party since 1972. Ross Perot's United We Stand America has the potential to become an even stronger third party than the Libertarian Party is now. In what follows, taken from the book published when he was running for president, Hospers gives the basic arguments for why the libertarian philosophy should be the basis of government.

Liberty and Government

Everyone is in favor of liberty—at least everyone pays it lip service. Yet many of those who pose as eager champions of liberty agitate for measures that would destroy it in one segment of man's life after another. In the name of liberty, social reformers have supported legislation which has led to totalitarian dictatorships. Sometimes they have done this knowingly, being so anxious to interfere forcibly in the lives of other people that they have advocated the most harebrained utopias (to be managed by themselves or those friendly to their ideas) and called the bastions

Reprinted from John Hospers, "Liberty and Government" and "Economic Liberty" in *Libertarianism* (Santa Barbara, Calif.: Reason Press, 1971), pp. 9–17, 100–116. Reprinted by permission. The footnotes have been omitted.

of freedom. But more often they have done it unknowingly, with a real interest in justice and motivated by various kinds of idealism and humanitarianism; but nonetheless they have advocated policies which, not by their intention but by the operation of natural laws, have led to the very negation of liberty. In this book, I shall endeavor to show the lines of connection between these policies and their ultimate results.

What, then, is liberty? In its most fundamental sense, the sense from which the other senses stem, and the sense which is also historically the earliest, liberty (or freedom) is the *absence of coercion by other human beings*. To the extent that a person is forced against his will to do something, he is not free. A slave is not free, for the activities of his life are undertaken at the whim of others who are his masters. A person who is being robbed by a gunman is not free in that episode of his life, for he is forced to surrender his money against his will, though of course he is free in other aspects of his life. A people under the grip of a tyrannical dictator and secret police are not free in most of the activities of their lives, for they are forced by threat of death or loss of livelihood to do things they would not willingly do and to refrain from countless activities in which they would prefer to engage.

This sense of liberty should be distinguished from a second one that is dependent on it. A compulsive gambler may say in a reflective moment, "I am a slave to my desire to gamble." In one sense he is not free, because he cannot control his desires—it is just *as if* some inner demon were forcing him to gamble, even knowing that obeying the demon's dictates will lead to his own destruction. This sense of freedom or liberty is of great importance for the therapeutic psychologist, who attempts to remove the psychological stumbling-blocks to the realization of the person's rational desires. Nevertheless, it *is* a different sense: the word "slave" here is a metaphor. The literal slave has his life and work subject to the commands of another human being, external to himself; such a person is not free in the first and fundamental sense, no matter how psychologically well-adjusted he may be. The "slave to his own desires" need be no slave in this first sense at all; he just can't make himself stop doing things he knows will injure him, and the outcome may be much the same as if someone else were forcing him to do them. This similarity of outcome, plus the inner sense of "feeling enslaved and powerless," probably accounts for the use of the same word for both situations. But the second sense is a metaphor only; the victim of powerful destructive inner drives is not a literal slave such as existed on Southern plantations before the Civil War. And it is this literal sense which concerns us in political philosophy. Southern Negroes were quite literally slaves; the compulsive gambler who flies to Las Vegas every weekend is not, for no *other* human will intervenes to prevent him from acting in accordance with his voluntary choices. Whatever problem he may have in altering the trend of his choices is a problem between him and his psychiatrist, and does not affect his enjoyment of political freedom or rights.

There is still a third sense of the term "liberty" which is much more easily confused with the first and original sense: liberty, or freedom, in the sense of *power* or *ability*. I am free to walk; that is, I can do so if I choose; but I am not free to fly in the air like a bird, or to make myself fifty feet tall, or to change myself into an ostrich. Doubtless the range of my choices is limited because I cannot do all these things; but I am still free in the first sense as long as no one is coercing me. Similarly, I may have few choices open to me, or even just one at a given time; if I have undertaken a dangerous river trip and find myself in the rapids, I may be quite helpless to do anything and have no choice but to continue downstream, but I am still free in the first sense as long as I voluntarily decided to embark on the journey and no one forced me to make it. My finding myself in this position, as well as my failure to fly, is not the result of the imposition of any other human will upon mine. The distinction is an important one because much confusion results from the failure to observe it: those who say, for example, that "a poor man is not free" may be speaking truly in the third sense, in that the range of a poor man's choices is much more limited than that of a wealthy man: but he is not speaking truly if he is using the word "free" in the first sense, for a man may be poor and yet coerced by no one (a humble fisherman, for example). For the sake of clarity, the word "liberty" will be used in this book in the first and fundamental sense, the sense with which political philosophy is primarily concerned.

Now, what shall we say of freedom in this first sense? One's first thought might well be that the ideal of liberty would be that there should be no coercion whatever by anyone on anyone else—no limitation through the use of force on anyone's actions. And if no one ever used force against anyone else, this would indeed be true: there would be no interference by anyone with anyone else's choices, hence no need to defend one's liberty against the one who would take it away. But people do sometimes use force against others, and hence one must be permitted to retaliate. Suppose, for example, that I commit multiple murders, or hold up others at gunpoint and take away their possessions. I would then be using my freedom to deprive other people of theirs. If I were permitted to do this, my freedom to act thus would be bought at the price of the freedom of others, indeed of their very lives. My freedom would be considered so valuable that the extinction of the freedom of others would weigh nothing against it. But if *everyone* should have freedom, then the freedom of one person to violate the freedom of others must be inhibited, in order to preserve the equal freedom of those others.

If everyone were permitted the liberty to infringe on the liberty of others, some people would soon be murdered, and countless others would be the slaves of the strongest. Clearly in such a situation the freedom of the victims would be violated. If each human being is to have liberty, he cannot also have the liberty to deprive others of *their* liberty.

It appears reasonable, then, to conclude that in any society there must be a set of rules in operation, designed to protect people from infringement on their freedom. The prohibition of killing, robbing, assaulting, maiming, and otherwise inflicting damage on others, including taking away by force the products of their labor, would be rules of first importance, for only if such rules are operative can citizens live free from coercive acts or attempts.

Not only do such rules have to be conceived of, they must be enforced. And here government enters the picture. If no one ever attempted to interfere with the liberty of another, government would not be necessary. But once some individual or group does interfere, or attempts to do so, government comes in to punish the offender after a trial according to prescribed rules.

Why not leave it up to the individual? For one thing, an individual who had to be constantly protecting himself would be unable to engage in many more activities than self-defense; when the government takes over that function for him, he is to a large measure relieved of this responsibility. Secondly, a criminal is also entitled to protection of his rights by impartial judgment. A theft of ten dollars, for example, is not justly punishable by death. When government exists, and its laws are enforced by uncorrupted officials, the punishments attaching to various offenses are known in advance and carried out according to previously enacted laws.

Most of the social relations into which we enter, and the organizations to which we belong, are voluntary: clubs, churches, fraternities, professional societies. We choose to join them, and we can pull out if we no longer wish to be associated with them. The exception to this is government. If we are born in a certain country, we are subject to its laws and restrictions even though we did not consent to be, or ever choose to live in that nation. We can, if we live in the United States (but not as a rule if we live in Soviet Russia), emigrate to another country—but then of course we are subject to *its* laws and restrictions.

Nor can we plausibly say that our continued residence in a country implies consent to its laws. It would be perfectly absurd to say that a person born into a dictatorship, whose life is beset by harsh laws at every turn, who is hounded by the secret police and shot if he tries to leave the country, has tacitly consented to live under its government. Membership in such a government is far from a matter of choice; and, if the government under which we live is one under which we would have chosen to live in any case, we can consider ourselves fabulously fortunate.

The feature that distinguishes government from all other institutions, which is obvious on reflection but comes as a surprise to those who have not considered the matter, is that *it operates by the use of force and threat of force*—that is, by coercion, and that this system of coercion includes everyone in the land. (It is, of course, legalized coercion: the Mafia also operates by force, but illegal force—and one is not compelled to belong to the Mafia.) The government of a nation has a *monopoly of legalized physical force* within the defined boundaries of that nation. (A nation in which there are two competing armies within the same nation is in a state of civil war.) Government's distinctive function, within the geographical boundaries of the nation, is to pass laws that will be binding on everyone and to enforce them.

The use of force by government is not always obvious to everyone because the threat usually lies in the background: but it is always ready to be used if the citizen does not conform. If you receive a letter "advising" you to pay your income tax, and you write back to Washington that you have thought the matter over and decided not to accept the advice, you will soon see the iron fist which lies concealed under the velvet glove. The government does not operate through advisement, preachment, moralizing, persuasion, or exhortation; it operates through coercion. Therein lies its power and its efficacy—and also its tremendous danger.

The only government tolerated by libertarians is one that exercises only *retaliatory* use of force on anyone who initiates the use of force against anyone else within its borders. Such a government removes the need for the individual to provide his own defense by taking to itself the protection of the individual's "inalienable right of self-defense." The danger of government is that it may exceed this function—that instead of (or in addition to) the exercise of retaliatory force it itself will initiate force against its own citizens. The former government is a protector of the individual: the citizen is free to engage in his chosen activities without constantly having to defend himself, for the government takes over that function. The latter government is not a protector, but an aggressor—an aggressor far worse than any criminal or even a band of criminals; for the criminal at least wishes to escape detection and the law is constantly working against him, whereas if the government becomes the initiator of force against you, there is nowhere else to turn: for it has the guns and you are the disarmed victim. Unfortunately most of the governments in the history of the world have belonged to the latter class.

Should an individual or a government use force at all, even in retaliation? Clearly yes; complete pacifism is self-defeating. If a person were not permitted to protect himself against those who would harm him, he would be a victim at the hands of any aggressor; and an announced policy of not resisting would be an open invitation to anyone who wanted to harm him. If such a policy were known in advance, the peaceful people would soon be eliminated in favor of the aggressive ones. It is surely a deterrent to the use of force for the aggressor to know that his efforts will be resisted. "It is only as retaliation that force may be used and only against the man who starts its use. No, I do not share his evil or sink to his concept of morality: I merely grant him his choice, destruction, the only destruction he had the right to choose: his own. He uses force to seize a value; I use it only to destroy destruction. A holdup man seeks to gain wealth by killing me; I do not grow richer by killing a holdup man."

If each individual had constantly to defend himself against possible aggressors, he would have to spend a considerable portion of his life in target practice, karate exercises, and other means of self-defense, and even so he would probably be helpless against groups of individuals who might try to kill, maim, or rob him. He would have little time for cultivating those qualities which are essential to civilized life, nor would improvements in science, medicine, and the arts be likely to occur. The function of government is to take this responsibility off his shoulders: the government undertakes to defend him against aggressors and to punish them if they attack him. When the government is effective in doing this, it enables the citizen to go about his business unmolested and without constant fear for his life. To do this, of course, government must have physical power—the police, to protect the citizen from aggression within its borders, and the armed forces, to protect him from aggressors outside. Beyond that, the government should not intrude upon his life, either to run his business, or adjust his daily activities, or prescribe his personal moral code.

Government, then, undertakes to be the individual's protector; but historically governments have gone far beyond this function. Since they already have the physical power, they have not hesitated to use it for purposes far beyond that which was entrusted to them in the first place. Undertaking initially to protect its citizens against aggression, it has often itself become an aggressor—a far greater aggressor, indeed, than the criminals against whom it was supposed to protect its citizens. Governments have done what no private citizens can do: arrest and imprison individuals without a trial and send them to slave labor camps. Government must have power in order to be effective—and yet the very means by which alone it can be effective make it vulnerable to the abuse of power, leading to managing the lives of individuals and even inflicting terror upon them.

Governments would not exist everywhere if they did not answer to some need. But since they do possess the physical force to implement their commands, it is all too easy for them to get out of hand and to aim the force they have garnered for legitimate purposes toward illegitimate purposes. Since they have the force at their disposal anyway, who is to stop them? The signs we see on bumper stickers are tragically true: "Beware: the Government Is Armed and Dangerous."

Economic Liberty

It is true that life was grim in the early stages of the Industrial Revolution. Hours were long and wages small—they could be nothing else, for the employers in the new factories had so little reserve against disaster that if they had doubled the wages they paid they would have had to close down. Yet grim as conditions were then, people voluntarily came in large numbers from the farms to the factories because they could make a better living in the factories. Young children labored in these factories, true; but parents made them do this to earn extra money to keep the family ahead. It was not legislation which put an end to these conditions, but the gradually increasing *capital accumulation* of the employers' enterprises; year by year, decade by decade, the reserve of capital increased, labor-saving machinery was devised, and it was possible to pay higher wages—higher not merely in money but in the things that the money would buy. And gradually a life became possible even for the most humble worker, which while poor by the standards of twentieth-century America, was paradise compared with what it had been in centuries past.

In all centuries prior to the Industrial Revolution, the population of the world increased very little. It is not that people had sexual relations less frequently than now; it is simply that many more people were born than could survive. The excess people born died through disease, malnutrition, and starvation. There was not enough production of life's essential goods to support them, so they died—it was as simple as that. But between the beginning of the nineteenth century and the end of it, the population of the world doubled; and it has doubled again since that time. How was this enormous increase possible? How could they live, these thousands who in every preceding generation would have died? Only because more production was achieved per man-hour of labor, thanks to the machine; only because of the gains in production made possible by the Industrial Revolution, and which continue to this day. There are more American Indians today than there were when the first settlers came. But with fewer than a million Indians in the seventeenth century, there was already an overpopulation problem. They had no machinery, of course, and in many cases no agricultural production at all. Most of them survived by hunting with simple weapons, and the vast land mass of the United States could sustain only that small population. Consider any metropolitan area in the U.S. today, such as Los Angeles. Here are millions of people in a few square miles. If they had to scrounge off the land, which is a desert, almost all of them would starve, if they did not first die of thirst from the lack of water in the area. Those today who scoff at our present economy and repudiate all these advances would be not only dead wrong, but dead. In a pre-industrial economy, the entire area of the United States would be insufficient to keep a million people alive.

It is enlarged production, then, that is the key, providing people with the vast quantity of produce they want and need, and which relieves life of much of its drudgery. But now let us go back a step further: how did this vast production by machines come about? Obviously someone had to invent the machines; invention is required before we can enjoy the benefits of mass production. And invention is something that takes place only in the minds of creative men.

Now as long as mankind has existed there have been creative men. There has been no lack of human inventiveness. But in most ages of mankind's history the genius of these men has fallen on barren soil. The conditions required for bringing about an improvement in man's life did not prevail. What were these conditions?

First an atmosphere of *liberty* was essential, in which people could investigate any areas they wished—to work, experiment, and compare notes with other men, without interference from their governments or the Church, when the Church was identical with the government. During the time that the Church permitted no dissection of cadavers, very little advance in medical science was possible. Untold millions of lives were lost through pestilence, plague, and disease, until such time as men could devote their inventive talents to a study of the body. Similarly, modern engineering would have been impossible without the prior development of physics. And this occurred through the creative thinking of men such as Galileo, who usually suffered condemnation, excommunication, sometimes torture and death for their efforts. But slowly, through a handful of men, working in an increasing atmosphere of freedom to think and to experiment, modern science and its resultant technology became a reality.

But it is one thing to invent something, and another to make it available to masses of men. Between the invention of the steam engine, and the existence of railroads spanning a continent, there is an enormous gap. Between the invention of a process for the manufacture of steel, and the actual use of that process in factories around the world, there is a gap. The gap is filled by many hundreds or thousands of men who (though perhaps not geniuses) are inventive and productive in other ways—those who can take the ideas of others and put them to commercial use through the facilities of mass-production. After someone has devised a method for extracting aluminum

from bauxite, someone else starts a factory for the mass-production of aluminum products and millions of people consequently can buy aluminum products. After Eli Whitney invented the cotton gin, thousands of them were manufactured, and the cost of cotton goods came within reach of even the poorest individuals in the land.

But to start a factory and to install large and complex machines takes much planning and a great deal of capital. It may be years before the man who initiates these moves is out of debt, and still more years before he turns a penny of profit. Besides, countless things may go wrong: the demand for the product may not be what he anticipated, or someone else may think of it first and outsell him, or the process of mass-producing the item may not be as foolproof as he thought, so that the products cannot be made, or made as cheaply, as he thought. The entrepreneur who undertakes these jobs is the *risk-taker* of a society, laying all his capital on the line and borrowing more in the hopes that the enterprise will succeed. Moreover, once factories are built they cannot easily be moved; so before he will take such risks, of course, he wants to be quite sure that he will not be taxed to death once he breaks even, and that his property will not be expropriated by the government after all his capital expenditures and years of planning.

If the risks are to be worth taking, the entrepreneur must live in a country that is politically stable; his property rights must be secure, so that he can start a major enterprise without fear of losing all he has through nationalization or excessive taxation. Only then can he go ahead with confidence and begin to be economically productive. Then he can borrow money with some fair chance of his enterprise turning a profit so that he can return the money with interest; then he can start up a factory or a processing plant or a chain of stores. Then he can produce steel for buildings and mechanical equipment, or wood for houses and paper, or any of a million other products. Then he can mass-produce his products so that thousands or millions of them can come into existence where few or none existed before—lowering the prices through mass-production, so that great masses of people can afford to buy them. The person who sells the product uses the money he gets from this transaction to buy other things from other individuals, and this in turn requires the work of other producers similar to himself in other areas of productive activity. Each producer—both managers and workers—trades his goods or services on the free market, that is, the market regulated not by bureaucratic decisions but by the natural law of supply and demand. Thus the free-enterprise system, or capitalism, is born.

Capitalism is the economic system of freedom to produce and freedom to trade the products of one's labor on the free (open) market. Freedom of *production* and *trade* is the essence of the capitalistic system. Equally important is the freedom of individuals to keep the fruits of their labor: if people were free to produce and trade, but not free to keep what they had earned, there would be no incentive to produce and the system of economic liberty (capitalism) would not function.

In the capitalist system, the supply of a product tends to meet the demand. If there is not enough of product X to meet the demand for it, those who are producing X will expand their facilities and hire additional workers; and other would-be producers would enter the arena and produce it as well. Once they are competing with each other, the supply of the product increases and the price comes down, which usually means that more people will buy product X. When the demand is satisfied and more of X is produced than the buying public wants, the price comes down below the point at which it is profitable to produce it, and production of it tapers off until the demand and the supply are in equilibrium.

Capitalism might also be called a system of *economic democracy*. Every time a housewife goes to the supermarket and buys, let us say, twenty products from the shelves, she is casting a vote for these products. The plebiscite is going on every day in every store in the land. The products that receive the most votes are the ones whose producers reap the most profits with the result that more of these products get produced in order to meet the demand. Competitors who are less efficient either make less profit or are forced to get out of the business entirely for lack of profit. And thus inefficient production gives way to efficient production.

The efficient producer is the gainer in all this, of course, but so is the *consumer*, but because of this efficiency the manufacturer can get the product to him at a lower price (or a higher price for one of higher quality). In the free market the consumer is king. This does not mean that the manufacturer is his slave, for the manufacturer freely undertakes to go into his enterprise with a hope of turning a profit, but that the consumer is the *final arbiter* of what products get produced and in what quantity. If enough Mrs. Joneses don't like Drudge Soap, they won't buy it, and for lack of profit Drudge Soap will no longer be made; but if enough Mrs. Joneses prefer Sludge Soap to any other, more of it will get made in order to meet the demand and turn a profit for the Sludge Soap Company. The manufacturer cannot make a profit without the cooperation of the consumer, for it is the consumer who lays down the money from which the manufacturer must glean his profit. If most of them do not want product X, in vain will the manufacturer remonstrate that product X is the best one. Even if X is really superior to Y, but Y is more attractively packaged or more convincingly sold, the manufacturers of X will give way to the manufacturers of Y. In an economic democracy there is no appeal from the decision of the consumers.

Under the conditions of peace that would prevail if government performed its proper offices, every consumer is a king, of sorts. All those who have anything to sell court his favor; each vies with the other to give greater quantity and higher quality at lower cost. The legend that the customer is always right might well be rendered "the consumer is always right," for the great cater to his whims, and the mighty are brought low by his adverse decisions. There is daily evidence of this in our lives in America. The daily mail brings its catalogs or circulars describing a vast variety of merchandise available at my command; the merchants have stocked their shelves in anticipation of my wishes; the salesmen may even beset me with persuasive arguments, so eager are they to satisfy my desires and have my custom. Indeed, advertisers wax poetic in the description of their wares thinking by some means to lure my trade their way. The business which does not serve the desires of its customers will lose out and fail, no matter how great the name of its founder, how far-flung its establishments, or how numerous its salesmen. If men may not use fraud and violence, the consumer is king.

There is a great deal of misunderstanding about this point. People often talk as if there were some conspiracy among manufacturers to sell one kind of product while the consumers want a different kind. At the present moment consumers are busy blaming automobile manufacturers for not providing them with safer cars. But the fact is that car buyers get pretty much what they are willing to pay for. If most consumers wanted safer cars, and were willing to pay a somewhat higher price to get them (since it costs more to make them), that is what the car manufacturers would produce. People sometimes talk as if the manufacturers could make enormous amounts of money manufacturing safer cars but that out of sheer perversity they refuse to do so. But this is a delusion. If cars now are not as safe as they could be made, this is because the vast majority of the buying public does not want them safer—when the chips are down they prefer the lower price and less safety. In fact, for many years the sales have gone to the fastest cars with the highest horsepower and the most streamlined design rather than the ones with more safety features—and the car manufacturers, responding to the public demand, make them the way the public wants them.

There are many kinds and qualities of cars, some cheaper, some less so; some more safe, some less safe; some with much chrome, some with little or none, and so on—each one appealing to a different segment of the market. When the market is as huge as it is in America, the manufacturer can mass-produce each of these kinds and still make a profit on them. But when he miscalculates the public taste, as with the Edsel, he loses heavily, for once again, the consumer is king. If most buyers wanted their cars yellow, manufacturers would make them yellow; and if most consumers wanted collapsible steering-wheels and non-protruding dashboards, the manufacturers would do this also. If it is technically possible for the manufacturer to produce a specific product, and there is good reason to believe that enough people will buy it, there is no reason for the manufacturer *not* to produce it.

The situation is, of course, quite different in government-controlled economies where factories are government-owned and the decision as to what products are to be made is determined not by market conditions but by government-employed bureaucrats. The bureaucrats need pay no attention to the consumers' demands at all. Most consumers may want product A, and yet it may not be made; and product B, which they don't much care for, will be made instead—and since they are prohibited from entering into production themselves, there is nothing they can do about it. Since no manufacturer in such an economy stands to lose his own money if his product doesn't sell, it doesn't matter if the product doesn't meet with consumer approval; the consumer is just out of luck; there is no competing producer to whom he can turn, for the government controls all production and has a monopoly on it. If the product is shoddily made and falls apart after a few uses (as is typically the case in a government-controlled economy), again it is no skin off the producer's back—the product is financed by the government, that is, by increased taxation upon everyone. And thus the consumer pays twice over—once for a shoddy product that he wouldn't have chosen to buy

on the free market in the first place, and again, in taxes to help recoup the losses to the government in making it.

On the free market, by contrast, any manufacturer who offers a shoddy product is in danger. He may deceive his customers for a while, particularly if he has developed a good reputation in the past, but as more and more customers become dissatisfied with his product they will cease to buy it. The manufacturers and store-owners who fare best in the long run are those who offer the best products at the lowest price, and who are willing to stand by the products that they sell, repairing or replacing them if they are defective. Only in this way can they develop a reputation that will endure through the years, and keep customers coming back again and again to buy. How, for example, could Sears Roebuck have grown into a multi-billion-dollar company if it regularly sold shoddy or defective products and refused to replace them? The company has doubtless short-changed some customers and left others unsatisfied, but if it had done this on a large scale in comparison with other companies, it would gradually have lost out to them in competition, even if it had established a good reputation at the beginning.

We have, then, in the capitalistic system of production and trade, a marvelous automatic machine for causing supply to meet demand.

> The private enterprise system might be compared to thousands of machines, each regulated by its own quasi-automatic governor, yet with these machines and their governors all interconnected and influencing each other, so that they act in effect like one great machine. Most of us must have noticed the automatic "governor" on a steam engine. It usually consists of two balls or weights which work by centrifugal force. As the speed of the engine increases, these balls fly away from the rod to which they are attached and so automatically narrow or close off a throttle valve which regulates the intake of steam and thus slows down the engine. If the engine goes too slowly, on the other hand, the balls drop, widen the throttle valve, and increase the engine's speed. Thus every departure from the desired speed itself sets in motion the forces that tend to correct that departure.
>
> It is precisely in this way that the relative supply of thousands of different commodities is regulated under the system of competitive private enterprise. When people want more of the commodity, their competitive bidding raises its price. This increases the profits of the producers who make that product. This stimulates them to increase their production. It leads others to stop making some of the products they previously made, and turn to making the product that offers them

the better return. But this increases the supply of that commodity at the same time that it reduces the supply of some other commodities. The price of that product therefore falls in relation to the price of other products, and the stimulus to the relative increase in its production disappears.

The free market—freedom in exchange, with prices freely responsive to changing supply and demand—is, in fact, an enormous computer, far superior to any electronic computer man has ever devised or ever will. Data from all over the world, of the most varied and complex nature—only fragments of which any one man or set of men can even be aware of, let alone assemble and feed into it—are automatically and quickly processed, answers coming out as prices. These prices are, in effect, stop and go signals which clearly say to all would-be enterprisers: "Go into this activity at once, the supply is comparatively short now, and the demand is comparatively heavy" or "Get out of this activity now, the supply is comparatively bountiful and the demand is comparatively negligible. . . ."

Tomatoes, let us say, are suddenly in "short supply." Millions of people relish this fruit, and, thus, the demand continues high. The few growers fortunate enough to have escaped the destructive blight discover that they can sell their small supply for two dollars per pound—and they do! Salad lovers who cannot afford to pay this "exorbitant" price are inclined to think unfavorably of these growers: Why, they're highway robbers." Yet these fortunate few are only adhering closely to the computer's instructions; they are behaving precisely as you and I act when we accept an increase in our wages. . . .

Assuming the market to be free, what would happen in this situation? Several corrective forces would automatically and immediately go to work. First, the high price, with promises of exceptional profit, would entice others to grow tomatoes; and even more important, it would lead to the development of blight-resistant strains. In the shortest possible time, there would be tomatoes galore, perhaps at a dollar a bushel—within reach of all.

For contrast, imagine the other extreme: a law to keep the price at its old level. What would be the probable results? At that price there would be little incentive for new tomato growers to enter the field. And, thus, *favoritism* instead of prices would necessarily determine the allocation of the reduced supply of tomatoes.

The price of products on the free market is not the result of an arbitrary decision by bureaucrats. It is the result of the laws of supply and demand, which operate impersonally and to the benefit of consumers, supplying them with the products they want, or at least the products they want most, given their ability to buy. It is the only economic system geared to the satisfaction of men's wants.

To read most newspapers these days, one would think that the history of the United States is nothing but a series of dismal failures. We are constantly reminded of our failures at home—many of which, of course, stem from the very government intervention which these same editorial writers advocate.

Failure at home indeed. Is it failure to have converted an empty continent in two centuries into the most prosperous and thriving area in the world? Is it failure to have absorbed the "poor" of Europe by the teeming millions and to have converted them into affluent middle-class citizens? Is it failure to have produced the most extensive network of private eleemosynary [charitable] institutions in the world? The most extensive system of higher education? To have a larger fraction of the population go to college than any other nation?

Seldom if ever has there been a success story like ours. Consider the third of a century from 1880 to 1914. Population doubled from 50 million to 100 million, as more than 22 million immigrants came to our shores. Most came with little besides the clothes on their backs—plus two hands and the urge to improve their lot and the lot of their children. Not only were they absorbed but their level of living as well as that of the rest of the population rose by leaps and bounds. And all this—let present-day liberals note—without any governmental wars on poverty, graduated income taxes, and burgeoning bureaucracies. This was a triumph of participatory democracy—the right kind, voluntary cooperation coordinated by a free market.

Capitalism and Selfishness

But capitalism, it is said, is an economic system dedicated to selfishness. This charge, more than anything else, is the reason for the opprobrium popularly attached to it, and the reason why "social engineers" get by with dismissing it so casually without ever going into specific detail about how it functions.

The word "selfish" is popularly employed as a term of abuse, in which the evil of selfishness is something taken for granted without question. The present work is on political philosophy and not on moral philosophy; nevertheless it is worth pointing out that the person who hurls the charge very seldom considers what forms or kinds of selfishness there may be. If being selfish is being concerned with the needs and interests of one's self, then no one who is *not* thus concerned could remain alive for a single day, unless he could count on others to minister to his interests as well as their own. Normally a person must see to it that *he* has food and clothing and shelter, and such of the other goods of life as he is able to procure; once this is done, it is difficult or impossible for him to provide for the needs of others beyond a very limited few, such as his family, unless, like the owner of a business enterprise with hundreds of employees, he receives some return (profits from the industry) for providing them with a livelihood. Unlimited beneficence, even the attempt to care for (without a return) a large number of others, must inevitably result in the poverty or bankruptcy of the benefactor. Each person's concern is and must be first and foremost a selfish one—one whose goal is the continued existence and well-being of himself and his family—if he and his family are to remain alive; this is simply a fact of reality, the nature of the "human condition." People who advocate anything other than this are living in a realm of floating abstractions unconnected with man's actual situation on this planet and the choices actually open to him in real-life situations.

Capitalism is a selfish system in the sense that it is the one socio-economic system that recognizes each individual's right to pursue his own self-interest. To produce for profit, and trade one's product or service non-coercively on a free market, is the means to greater wealth than any other economic system ever designed by man—this is a lesson that history teaches beyond the slightest shadow of a doubt. Nor is it true that capitalism is necessarily "materialistic": an individual is free to spend the money he has earned on symphony concerts just as much as on yachts; he can even build and sustain a concert hall or a cathedral if he has the money. What he does with the money he earns is up to him; it can be put to a "spiritual" as well as "material" use if he so chooses.

But the most important point, one that is constantly ignored by capitalism's critics, is that he cannot obtain his money on the free market unless he has a product or service that other people will pay for because the product serves *their* needs or desires. If he amassed a million dollars by inventing a beauty aid for aging women, well, then he served them in providing for them what they wanted—they wouldn't have given him the money for just doing nothing; he clearly provided them with something they were willing to pay for. Maybe they *shouldn't* have wanted it, but what bureaucrat has the right to dictate what they *should* want? Anyway, they *did* want it, and they wanted it enough to pay him for the product he offered them. There is all the difference in the

world between the robber who takes property from people by force, and the entrepreneur who exchanges goods and services for money on the free market—and who stands to lose his skin if people don't buy the product he may have spent a fortune producing. Yet both of these men are popularly lumped together under the heading of "selfish."

Very well, we say, the entrepreneur is selfish—he wants to making a living—he *has* to make a living—and his concept of how to do it involves much expenditure of time, effort, and money, and, incidentally, the employment of numerous other people, who earn their living as a result. If he fails, he loses everything; if he succeeds, he makes a profit; and if he succeed spectacularly, he makes a spectacular profit. And why not? It was his time, his money, his effort—so who has the right to take it away from him? He is entitled to every bit of his selfish reward. But he doesn't get one penny of this selfish reward unless he has placed on the market a product or service for which the consuming public will pay. He cannot earn a dime without their voluntary purchase of whatever it is he has to offer. In other words, on the free market he cannot serve himself without first serving others.

What I say applies to the man who obtains his fortunes on the free (uncoerced) market—without any help from the government. The businessman who can't make it on his own, who lobbies or bribes the legislature into subsidizing him, is forcing every taxpayer in the land to give up a portion of his income to pay for something that he wouldn't willingly buy on the open market. To the extent that a businessman does this, he is morally no different from the gunman who steals your wallet or your jewelry. Both have taken from you a portion of your earnings which you would not have given them voluntarily.

But now suppose you are not an egoist, but an ethical altruist, believing you should live entirely to serve others. The altruist typically despises the man who has a large income; but in all consistency he shouldn't. It isn't merely that the man with a large income has more than he can give to others (if he earned nothing, he would have nothing to give, so the chances of the needy are greater with him if he earns a lot). The main point is that in order to get the large income on a free market, he has already had to serve the interests of others. If Vanderbilt earned a million dollars by building his railroad, he had to serve others in order to get the million dollars: they would have paid him nothing if he had provided no service. His possession of the million is already evidence of his socially important deed—not necessarily intention, but deed. In fact, as Murray Rothbard has pointed out, if a well-paid coal-miner decides to take a lower-paying but more pleasant job as a grocery clerk, the consistent altruist ought to condemn him for depriving his fellow men of the benefit he was conferring on them by mining coal. The fact that he got more money for mining coal shows that his services as a coal miner were worth more to consumers than are his present services as a grocery clerk. And his purpose in life is to serve others in the best possible way, isn't it?

Capitalism and the Jungle

The free market, many critics claim, is "the rule of the jungle," where "the survival of the fittest" is the only law.

But the free market is the very opposite of the "jungle." When not involved with government, it is characterized by peaceful competition. If a man miscalculates and starts a second grocery store in a village where one grocery store is all that the market will bear, the second one goes under—that is true. The failure is a result of the man's miscalculation, based on his own free decision. Either he must bear the consequences of the failure himself (as capitalism requires), or every taxpayer in the land must be called upon to pay a few cents more in taxes to protect him against the loss (as the welfare state requires—and if a man is thus cushioned against loss, there will be many more losing enterprises). In the real, literal jungle, there is a struggle for survival in which the stronger crushes his weaker foe, but in the free market one man gains wealth only through serving the consumers best, as determined by the opinion of those very consumers themselves.

"Survival of the fittest." Is this equivocation to be foisted on us forever? Fitness for what? "The 'fit' in the jungle are those [who are] most adept at the exercise of brute force. The 'fit' on the market are those most adept in the service of society [consumers]." In the jungle, "some seize from others and all live at the starvation level; the market is a peaceful and productive place where all serve themselves *and* others at the same time and live at infinitely higher levels of consumption. On the market, the charitable can provide a luxury that cannot exist in the jungle.

> The free market . . . transmutes the jungle's destructive competition for meager subsistence into a peaceful *cooperative* competition in the service of one's self

and others. In the jungle, some gain only at the expense of others. On the market, everyone gains. It is the market—the contractual society—that wrests order out of chaos, that subdues natures and *eradicates* the jungle, that permits the "weak" to live productively, or out of gifts from production, and in a regal style compared to the life of the "strong" in the jungle. Furthermore, the market, by raising living standards, permits man the leisure to cultivate the very qualities of civilization that distinguish him from the brutes.

No, it is the rise of government control over ever increasing sectors of the lives of individuals that is bringing back the jungle.

Study Questions

1. Can libertarianism consistently condemn fraud and yet endorse *caveat emptor*, "let the buyer beware"? Why not keep government even more minimal by letting the buyer beware of fraud, too, just as libertarianism lets the buyer beware of so many other hazards? Why does libertarianism make an exception to allow the government to punish fraud but not to let government make other regulations that would encourage honesty and safety?

2. What if an eccentric millionaire bought up all the land around your house as you slept one night, and then refused to let you onto his land to escape your house to get food? There would be no access to a public street, since libertarianism would require private toll roads wherever possible rather than publicly owned roads. What if you starved because the millionaire wouldn't let anyone else cross his land to give you food and because in a libertarian country the government would provide no food to those in need? Would a libertarian consider this morally acceptable? If so, wouldn't this be a counterexample to libertarianism, since it would accept murder without any adequate justification? Is this example murder or merely a rich person vigorously exercising his property rights to his land?

*3. If no foreign military threat existed, what would you want our government to do beyond maintaining society's legal and economic framework? Would a libertarian allow the government to maintain society's economic framework? Would the free market maintain itself if government just left it alone? Or do we need government to maintain a free mar-

---

*From *The Book of Questions: Business, Politics and Ethics*, by Gregory Stock.

ket by preventing monopolies, oligopolies, price-fixing, and other practices that tend to undermine the free market by undermining competition? For example, should the government have a small business loan department to foster more competition by helping smaller companies compete with larger ones? And should the government maintain the market by providing a stable currency that is generally trusted to be valuable? Doesn't providing the stable currency and stable legal system that capitalism needs to succeed require much regulation to prevent poverty, crime, and real estate or stock market speculation of the sort that was the catalyst for America's Great Depression?

9

Why Libertarianism Is Mistaken

Hugh LaFollette

Editor's note: LaFollette, a professor of philosophy at East Tennessee State University, offers many criticisms of libertarianism, including the surprising argument that, ironically, libertarianism limits liberty. La Follette is most concerned to rebut the separate libertarian arguments of F. A. Hayek, Nobel Prize–winning economist Milton Friedman, and Harvard professor of philosophy Robert Nozick.

Taxing the income of some people to provide goods or services to others, even those with urgent needs, is unjust. It is a violation of the wage earner's rights, a restriction of his freedom. At least that is what the libertarian tells us. I disagree. Not all redistribution of income is unjust; or so I shall argue.

Libertarianism has experienced a noticeable reemergence in the past few years. F. A. Hayek, Milton Friedman, and Robert Nozick have given new intellectual impetus to the movement[1] while a growing concern for personal autonomy has provided personal ground for the sowing of the idea. Yet even though this theory is prima facie plausible and demands serious reassessment of the concepts of liberty and property, it ultimately fails. Once we admit, as the libertarian does, that the state justifiably takes on certain functions, for example, police protection of persons and property, there is no rational basis for believing that the state is unjustified in redistributing tax revenue. We cannot stop, as the libertarian suggests, with the minimal state of classical liberal

Reprinted from Hugh LaFollette, "Why Libertarianism Is Mistaken," in John Arthur and William H. Shaw, eds., *Justice and Economic Distribution*, first ed. (Englewood Cliffs, N.J.: Prentice-Hall, 1978), pp. 194–206. Reprinted by permission.

philosophy. I will not, in this paper, say exactly how far beyond the minimal state we should go. I only argue that libertarianism is not a moral option. On the surface this conclusion seems meager, yet its implications are far-reaching. By eliminating a previously plausible and popular conception of distributive justice, we will narrow the alternatives. By identifying a major flaw in libertarianism, we will secure direction in our search for an adequate theory.

After briefly describing libertarianism I will argue that the theory is guilty of internal incoherence; the theory falls prey to the very objection it offers against competing theories. Then I will consider four possible libertarian replies to my argument. Each, I will claim, fails to disarm my internal objection. After concluding my argument, I will speculate on the roles freedom and property should play in an adequate theory of distributive justice.

A Description of Libertarianism

Central to libertarianism is the claim that individuals should be free from the interference of others. Personal liberty is the supreme moral good. Hence, one's liberty can justifiably be restricted only if he consents to the restriction. Any other restriction, including taxing incomes for purposes of redistribution, is unjust. Or the libertarian may couch his theory in the language of rights: each individual has natural negative rights[2] to at least life, liberty, and property. No one can justifiably harm him, restrict his freedom, or take his property—that is, no one can violate his rights—without his consent. Moreover, these are general (*in rem*) rights; they apply, so to speak, against the whole world. And since rights invariably have correlative duties, all the people in the world have the duty not to interfere with the right holder's life, liberty, and property. Each person possesses these rights simply in virtue of his humanity—he does not have to *do* anything to obtain this moral protection. The possession of rights does not depend upon the consent of others. They are essential moral constituents of personhood.

However, we should note that these two ways of speaking seem to amount to the same thing for the libertarian. Libertarian theorists often move back and forth between talk of negative rights and talk of liberty. I suspect that is because they ultimately see rights and liberty as equivalent or because they hold a theory of rights which is grounded in personal liberty. That is, the libertarian might say, the *reason* we have all and only libertarian rights (absolute negative rights to life, liberty, property, etc.) is that these rights protect individual liberty. Hence, on both models liberty is fundamental.

Libertarianism also contends that in certain prescribed circumstances there can be positive *in personam* rights, that is, that individual X has a positive right to, say, $1,000 and someone else Y has a positive duty to give X that money. These positive rights, however, are not natural rights; they are not possessed by all persons just because they are persons. They can arise only consensually. For example, if A promises B that he will serve as a lifeguard at B's swimming pool, then B has a right against A and A has a duty to B—a duty to guard those in B's pool. But unless A so consents, he has no positive duties to B, or to anyone else for that matter. Consequently, for the libertarian, there are no general positive duties and no general positive rights. There are only *alleged* general positive rights; claims to such rights (or of such duties) are mistaken. For if there were positive general duties we would have to violate negative general rights to satisfy them. For example, suppose everyone had a positive general right to life; then everyone would have rights (entitlements) *to* those goods necessary to stay alive, e.g., food to eat. But food, or the money to buy it, doesn't grow on trees (or, if it does, the trees are owned). Those who own the food or the money have negative rights protecting their possession of these things. And negative general rights, for the libertarian, are absolute.[3] There are no circumstances in which these rights can be justifiably overridden, in which one's liberty can be justifiably limited without his consent. Hence, X's rights to property (or life or liberty) can never be overridden for the benefit of others (to satisfy the alleged positive rights of others). X can choose to charitably give his property to someone, or he can voluntarily give someone a positive right to his property. Nevertheless, morally he cannot be forced—either by legal sanctions or moral rules—to give up his life, liberty, or property. This moral/legal prohibition insures that an individual's liberty cannot be restricted in any way without his consent.

Thus we see two important features of libertarianism. First, the primary purpose of negative general rights is the protection of individual liberty, to insure that no one's life is restricted without his consent. Or as Nozick puts it: "Side constraints [which are equivalent to negative general rights] upon action reflect the underlying Kantian principle that individuals are ends and not merely means; they can

not be sacrificed or used for the achieving of other ends without their consent. . . . [These constraints] reflect the fact of our separate existences. They reflect the fact that no moral balancing act can take place among us."[4] Secondly, the libertarian holds that a sufficient reason to reject any alleged moral rule or principle of distributive justice is that that rule or principle restricts someone's freedom without his consent. Hayek, for example, argues that we should reject plans to expand governmental roles since such expansion necessarily undermines individual liberty.[5] And Nozick's primary objection to Rawls is that Rawls's two principles restrict individual liberty without consent.

Libertarianism, though morally austere, has a certain plausibility. Each of us wants to be able to live his own life, to be free from the unnecessary interference of others. We want, in Kant's words, to be ends in ourselves and not merely means for others.[6] But just because a theory is plausible does not mean that it is correct. Libertarianism, I think, can be shown to be mistaken. I will argue that negative general rights fail to protect individual liberty the way the libertarian suggests. Since the protection of liberty is the express purpose of these libertarian rights, the theory fails. My argument will also show that even the libertarian must hold that one should not reject a moral rule or principle of distributive justice simply because it permits (or requires) non-consensual limitations on freedom. Once this failure is exposed there appears to be no good reason for denying that there are at least some positive general duties and probably some positive general rights. How many and how extensive these duties or rights are is another question.

Libertarianism Limits Liberty

The problem with libertarianism can be seen once we recognize the limitations that negative rights (libertarian constraints) themselves place on individual liberty. Suppose, for example, that I am the biggest and strongest guy on the block. My size is a natural asset, a physical trait I inherited and then developed. But can I use my strength and size any way I please? No! At least not morally. Though I am physically capable of pummeling the peasants, pillaging property, and ravishing women, I am not morally justified in doing so. My freedom is restricted without my consent. I didn't make a contract with the property owners or the women; I didn't promise not to rap, rob, or rape. Just the same, morally I cannot perform these actions and others can justifiably prohibit me from performing them.

Consequently, everyone's life is not, given the presence of negative general rights and negative general duties, free from the interference of others. The "mere" presence of others imposes duties on each of us; it limits everyone's freedom. In fact, these restrictions are frequently extensive. For example, in the previously described case I could have all of the goods I wanted; I could take what I wanted, when I wanted. To say that such actions are morally or legally impermissible significantly limits my freedom, and my "happiness," without my consent. Of course I am not saying these restrictions are bad. Obviously they aren't. But it does show that the libertarian fails to achieve his major objective, namely, to insure that an individual's freedom cannot be limited without his consent. The libertarian's own moral constraints limit each person's freedom without consent.[7]

This is even more vividly seen when we look at an actual historical occurrence. In the nineteenth century American slaveholders were finally legally coerced into doing what they were already morally required to do: free their slaves. In many cases this led to the slave owners' financial and social ruin: they lost their farms, their money, and their power. Of course they didn't agree to their personal ruin; they didn't agree to this restriction on their freedom. Morally they didn't have to consent; it was a remedy long overdue. Even the libertarian would agree. The slaveholders' freedom was justifiably restricted by the presence of other people; the fact that there were other persons limited their acceptable alternatives. But that is exactly what the libertarian denies. Freedom, he claims, cannot be justifiably restricted without consent. In short, the difficulty is this: the libertarian talks as if there can be no legitimate non-consensual limitations on freedom, yet his very theory involves just such limitations. Not only does this appear to be blatantly inconsistent, but even if he could avoid this inconsistency, there appears to be no principled way in which he can justify only his theory's non-consensual limitations on freedom.

This theoretical difficulty is extremely important. First, the libertarian objections against redistribution programs (like those practiced in the welfare state) are weakened, if not totally disarmed. His ever-present objection to these programs has always been that they are unjust because they are non-consensual limitations on freedom. However, as I have shown,

libertarian constraints themselves demand such limitations. Therefore, that cannot be a compelling reason for rejecting welfare statism unless it is also a compelling reason for rejecting libertarianism.

Secondly, once we see that justice demands certain non-consensual limitations on someone's (X's) freedom, there seems to be no good reason for concluding (and good reason not to conclude) that X's freedom can be limited only by negative general duties. There seems to be no reason, for example, for concluding that X's freedom to make $1 million should not be restricted to aid other people, e.g., to give some workers enough funds to help them escape the de facto slavery in which they find themselves.

Think of it this way. Liberty, for the libertarian, is negative in nature. An individual's liberty is restricted whenever (and only if) his potential actions are restricted. This is essentially a Hobbesian view of liberty. So imagine with Hobbes and some libertarians that individuals are seen as initially being in a state of perfect freedom. In such a state, Hobbes claims, "nothing can be just. Right and wrong have there no place."[8] To introduce right and wrong of any sort is to put moral limitations on individual freedom. To that extent, everyone's freedom is restricted. Each person has an external impediment—a moral rule which can be coercively enforced—against doing some action A (and actions relevantly like A). Therefore, to introduce negative general rights and duties, as the libertarian does, is to admit that there are non-consensual limitations on freedom. And these limits—as I argued—are sometimes significant and far-reaching. They arise—and this is crucial—without consent; each person has them simply because he is a person. Now if one's freedom can be limited without consent by negative rights, then it is unreasonable to hold that these are the only limitations on freedom which can legitimately arise without consent. This is particularly apparent when we realize duties are more—even much more—than limitations which would be imposed if some claims of positive rights or duties were recognized. For example, forcing a slaveholder to free his slaves would limit his freedom more than would a law forcing him to pay ten percent of his salary to educate and provide health care for his slaves. Or forcing Hitler to not take over the world (in other words, forcing him to recognize others' negative rights) would limit his freedom more extensively than would forcing him to support, by his taxes, some governmental welfare program. Yet the libertarian concludes that redistribution of income is unjust since it limits the taxed person's liberty without his consent. If redistribution is unjust for that reason, then so are libertarian constraints. Libertarian constraints also limit personal liberty without consent.

The libertarian might attempt to immediately avoid my conclusion by claiming that there is a principled difference between redistribution of income and libertarian constraints such that the former is *never* a justified restriction of liberty while the latter is always justified. For although both do limit personal liberty without consent, he might argue, libertarian constraints only restrict liberty in order to protect individual rights. And it is the protection of personal rights which justifies these, and only these, non-consensual restrictions on liberty.

However, this reply won't do. For as I have stated, any libertarian conception of rights is itself grounded in—justified by reference to—personal liberty. Or, as Eric Mack puts it, they are grounded in the right not to be coerced.[9] Hence, given my preceding argument, there is no principled way that concerns for personal liberty could generate *only* libertarian rights and duties, since negative rights restrict liberty as much as, or more than, would some positive rights or duties. Consequently, appeals to personal rights cannot provide the libertarian with a principled basis for distinguishing between types of non-consensual limitations on liberty.

We have uncovered a very telling incoherence. We have taken the main libertarian weapon against welfare statism and turned it on itself. The once-so-sharp sword is seen to have two sides. Instead of menacing the enemy, the sword only frustrates its wielder. As everyone knows, two-edged swords cut both ways. The libertarian is unable to support his conception of the minimal state. At least some redistribution of tax monies is justified.

Possible Libertarian Replies

"Liberty" Is Normative, Not Descriptive

The libertarian might object to this argument by claiming that I have misunderstood his use of the word "liberty." "Liberty" is not, he might argue, a purely descriptive term. On a purely descriptive model of liberty, anything which restricts an individual's options would be a restriction of his liberty. Hence, negative rights would be a restriction of

individual liberty. But not just any restriction of someone's option is a restriction of his liberty. Prohibitions of unjust actions are surely not limitations of freedom. For example, a person does not have the liberty to knife someone even though he physically might be able to do it. In short, individuals have liberty to do only those things which are just. Consequently, "liberty" should be seen as a normative term such that if A has the liberty to do X then not only is no one prohibiting him from doing it, but it is also morally permissible that he do it. "Therefore," the libertarian might conclude, "your objection fails since negative duties do not really limit individual liberty. It is not just that people kill each other, so prohibitions against killing are not limitations of freedom."

This linguistic proposal is intriguing since "liberty" clearly does have a positive emotive force which suggests ethical overtones. My own hunch, though, is that "liberty" should be maintained as a descriptive term. That is, "liberty" is, and should be maintained as, a value-neutral term which merely states that there are limitations, without any judgment as to their propriety. For although we all have some tendencies to vacillate between the descriptive and normative senses of the term,[10] it seems clear that its basic sense is descriptive. It is only after we identify liberty descriptively that we are able to distinguish between just and unjust restrictions on it. For the purposes of this paper, however, I need not belabor the point. For even the acceptance of this linguistic proposal cannot patch up the libertarian's deflated case. For if "liberty" is a normative term in the way proposed, then we could not know if something is a restriction of liberty until we knew if the restrained action is just. For example, we would not know that taxing a millionaire's money and distributing it to the needy was a violation of the millionaire's liberty until we knew if it was just to so tax him. Hence, the claim that A has the liberty to do X (spend his millions any way he pleases) could not be a *reason* for believing that some action (taxing his millions) is unjust. The justificatory relationship on this model would be exactly opposite. We would have reason to believe that A had the liberty to do X only if we already knew that it was just that he do it. Consequently, the protection of individual liberty cannot be the purpose of (or consequence of) negative rights since the determination that someone had the liberty to do X depends upon the determination that he has the right to do it. For example, one would have the liberty to bequeath property P to Z only if he had the right of bequeathal. Yet the libertarian wants to ground such rights in personal liberty. Therefore, even if this linguistic proposal were acceptable, the libertarian's stated purpose of negative rights would be undermined. He would no longer be able to argue for stringent negative rights on the grounds that they protect individual liberties. Nor would he be able to reject other principles of distributive justice on grounds that they limited individual liberty without consent.

Liberty Should Be Maximized

The libertarian might attempt another tack. "Admittedly negative rights limit individual freedom. There has never been any doubt about that. What the libertarian demands is that everyone have maximum personal liberty with equal liberty consistent for all." However, this popular statement of libertarianism fails to soften my objection. The maximum amount of liberty with equal liberty for all is absolute liberty—a state in which there are no legal or moral prohibitions of any kind. (Notice that this is a Hobbesian state of nature.) In such state there are no prohibitions and everyone is equally free from prohibitions. The libertarian, I suspect, would disagree. Although in such a state people would *ideally* have equal liberty, the libertarian would probably contend that because some people would take advantage of the situation and deprive others of their liberty, people so situated would not, in fact, have equal liberty. In other words, though liberty is ideally maximal, it would not be prudentially maximal.

There are three problems with this reply. First, on this view there would be no longer be absolute prohibitions against restriction of liberty. Liberty could be justifiably restricted; it would not be an absolute good. True, it is only liberty which overrides liberty. Nevertheless, to say that one species of liberty overrides another is to say that there is something about one of them (liberty$_1$) which makes it morally more potent than the other (liberty$_2$). This something—e.g., good consequences following the action—which makes liberty$_1$ more potent, must be something other than liberty. Otherwise, there would be no rational basis for preferring liberty$_1$ over liberty$_2$. This implies that this other feature (e.g., good consequences) is more important than liberty or that liberty is morally good only when it has this (or some other) specific feature.[11] Thus, liberty would be neither absolute nor supreme.

Secondly, if the libertarian concern *is* with maximizing liberty, then there would no longer be absolute rights to liberty. Instead, liberty would be a goal, an end-state to be maximized. And, as Robert Nozick realizes (he makes his point in the language of rights), "This ... would require us to violate someone's rights when doing so minimizes the total (weighted) amount of violations of rights in the society."[12] That is why he rejects such an option. An individual's liberty could be justifiably protected only if certain empirical statements (about whether the requisite action maximized liberty) were true. Hence, negative rights would be neither theoretically nor practically absolute. And to deny that they are absolute is to deny libertarianism.

Thirdly, if liberty must be *exactly* equal, as the rebuttal suggests, then we would have to have an extremely repressive government (a police state with constant electronic surveillance, etc.). Otherwise some people's (but not all people's) rights would be violated by murders, muggers, etc. Consequently, if the demand were on maximizing liberty, a Hobbesian state of liberty would be chosen; if the emphasis were on equality of liberty, then something like a police state would be chosen.

In other words, any reference to maximal or equal liberty indicates only a formal criterion of justice which fails to distinguish between alternative determinations of what counts as maximal or equal liberty.

Individuals Tacitly Consent to Libertarianism

The libertarian could attempt another reply by appealing to the notion of implied or tacit consent. "You have correctly identified my criterion for justifiably restricting personal freedom," he might say. "An individual must consent to any restriction. Consent, however, need not be explicitly offered. An individual can, merely by his action, tacitly consent to some limitations of his freedom."[13] The libertarian then might go on to conjecture that by seeking interaction with others, all individuals tacitly agree to respect others' liberty in certain specified ways, namely, those ways protected by negative general rights.

There are, however, several difficulties with this reply. Initially there is the difficult question of how to adequately describe some action(s) such that it does indicate tacit consent. And no matter how one describes such an action, undoubtedly someone in the world would fail to perform it—yet the libertarian would still assume that that person had a duty not to violate libertarian constraints. We could also note that the notion of tacit consent normally implies that such consent is like explicit consent, it is just that it is not verbally offered. That suggests that A cannot be said to have tacitly consented to X, if, when he is explicitly asked if he so consents, he (A) denies it. Yet surely there would be at least one person in the world who would vehemently deny that he had consented to the presence of all and only negative general rights. Hence, there would be no basis for claiming that A is morally or legally required to do X. Still the libertarian would want to contend that A could not justifiably kill others, steal their property, etc.

Secondly, it is highly implausible to think that all people would consent—explicitly or implicitly—to all and only libertarian constraints. Robert Nozick, for example, recognizes this when he emphatically rejects the principle of fairness.[14] If a rule of tacit consent could undergird negative general rights, then it could also justify at least some governmental redistribution programs. We don't, however, need to cite Nozick here; we can simply make the obvious claim that people would choose something other than libertarianism. They would at least opt for a system which also gave them sufficient goods (or the ready opportunity to obtain them) to stay alive. Finally, we could also note John Rawls's argument in *A Theory of Justice*[15] which shows that *if* one works from a consent model, a more-than-minimal state would emerge. The rebuttal fails.

Libertarianism Is Grounded in Immediate Intuition

Libertarianism is beginning to flounder. So the libertarian might attempt to salvage his theory by arguing that his view of morality, and its emphasis on negative general rights, is established by immediate intuition. "Rights are not grounded in liberty," he might say; "hence your arguments just miss the mark. I intuitively recognize that we have these and only these rights." Or he might offer a slightly more sophisticated intuitionist model: he claims to immediately intuit some fundamental moral "fact" which justifies all and only libertarian rights. For example, he might claim that he intuitively knows that people can *never* be used as a means for others' ends (à la

Kant), and that this truth strictly implies his account of rights.

There are two questions to be raised about this proposal. First, even if the suggested intuition about the Kantian imperative were true, would it imply the truth of libertarianism? Secondly, are *any* intuitions singularly sufficient to ground particular moral principles? The answer to both, I will argue, is: "No."

Let us imagine for a moment that the proposed intuition is indubitably true: "(I)ndividuals are ends and not merely means; they cannot be sacrificed or used for the achieving of other ends without their consent."[16] Why must we suppose, as this reply suggests, that the only way people are used as a means for others is if libertarian rights are violated? Why, for example, isn't a poor worker being used by a rich factory owner as a means for his making a million dollars? I, for one, think he clearly is.[17]

Besides, I could also point out, following my argument in the second section, that libertarian restraints themselves involve using some individuals as means for others. For example, the slaveholder is used against his will as a means for achieving the freedom of the slaves; he is forced to do something just to benefit others. In fact, all libertarian constraints use us to benefit others. They force us to do (or not do) certain actions as a means of allowing individuals to do other actions—actions which are deemed more important than the prohibited ones. The presence of other individuals uses each of us by limiting our range of permissible alternatives. Admittedly, we may sometimes not see ourselves as being used under these circumstances; but if we don't, I suspect it is because we don't desire (for the most part) to kill other people, enslave them, etc., or because we have been so ingrained with the view that such restrictions are morally required. But when the cost is significant, people often do, in fact, see this. The slaveholders, for example, argued that since they didn't agree to abolition, they shouldn't have to set their slaves free—to force them to was a non-consensual limitation of their freedom. And they're right: it was a violation of their descriptive liberty. It is just that it was a just violation. The libertarian, it seems, must agree. But, of course, that implies that there are no absolute prohibitions against using people.[18]

In fact, this argument helps focus on an underlying difficulty with libertarianism. Libertarians seem to desire a totally individualistic system in which one's interests never have to be weighed against anyone (or everyone) else's. But that is impossible.

People's interests inevitably will conflict in any society in which there is limited space and resources. The purpose of law and morality is just to provide a rational procedure for settling such conflicts. For example, on this view X's enslaving someone to increase his (X's) income, is clearly a worse "using" than is prohibiting X from enslaving others. That is why we prohibit slavery. One person's interest (not to be enslaved) is weighed against another person's interest (to enslave) and the former is clearly superior. Surely this is a more plausible understanding of negative rights. Therefore, even if we grant the suggested intuition, the libertarian view of rights is not established.

However, there is still the general question concerning the role of intuition in moral argument. I would contend that intuitions *may* play some legitimate role in moral argument. But if they do, these intuitions must be revisable in the face of cogent argument; they must also be sensitive to opposing intuitions. Yet I have shown that there appears to be no principled basis for the absolute emphasis on negative general rights. So if the libertarian does found his theory only on intuitions, particularly when basic distinctions within the theory (the emphasis on libertarian constraints rather than positive duties) seem *ad hoc* and even counter-intuitive, then the theory crumbles in the sands of weak intuitions. In short, since the claim that there are no general positive duties or rights is unprincipled, we just reject it. Therefore, even *if* the suggested intuitions did strictly imply a libertarian conception of rights, libertarianism would still not be established since the intuitions themselves would be highly questionable.

Conclusion and Speculation

My argument is completed. I have argued that libertarianism is untenable.[19] I have challenged four possible replies to my argument. I would like to end with some rather brief speculation on the direction an adequate theory of justice must go. My speculation emerges from the previous arguments. I have shown that neither property nor liberty (as defined by the libertarian) should be seen as the only social good; singling these out as the only social values is unreasonable. Instead, these should be seen as two values among many, all competing for recognition.

Property, as I have said, is important. But how important? Well, it should be apparent that an individual cannot be alive without some property, or at least some goods to use; neither can a person have any real options without goods to work on. In addition, there is some force to the Hegelian claim that individuals need property with which to "identify" themselves, and there is the Jeffersonian point that property seems to be necessary for the protection of civil liberty. These might suggest that everyone is entitled to some minimum of goods, and that that minimum is protected by negative rights. Beyond this minimum? That's a difficult question.

And what of liberty? Surely it is important. Just as surely it is not all-important. But in some societies, say, rather affluent ones, it (e.g., political and civil liberties) may be the highest (but even here not the only) value. The libertarian's claim that it is is mistaken.

Study Questions

1. Who has the better of this debate, Hospers or La Follette? Is libertarianism true?

2. Do you agree with La Follette in accepting Hegel's point that people need property to enhance their sense of identity? Do many people invest their personalities and identities in being the owner of a home, a dog, a particular car, baseball cards of a particular team, or the like? Does each person have a moral right to a solid sense of identity? Even if there were no right involved, would it not be a morally good thing for each person to have a solid sense of his or her own identity? Does Hegel's point support some redistribution of property?

3. Should there be laws to regulate the behavior of consenting adults? If so, what—if anything—do you feel should be the punishment for a prostitute and her client? For two friends who insist on betting with each other on football? Is libertarianism right to allow *anything* between consenting adults, even a suicide pact with the famous Dr. Kevorkian, playing Russian roulette, creating and buying the most pornographic material imaginable, and using the most dangerous, harmful, and addictive drugs in the world? Does libertarianism contradict itself when it allows the use of most addictive drugs in the name of freedom? Is a drug addict, especially when he or she is in desperate need of a fix, really free?

4. Libertarianism allows anything between consenting adults. But is anything between them only, given the numerous and subtle interconnections among people who all live on the same planet? For

example, in a planetary emergency, due to environmental catastrophe or extraterrestrial invasion for example, might we not need everyone to do his or her best in the effort to keep our species alive? If so, then why must we wait for such an extreme emergency before calling upon consenting adults to limit the damage they do to each other? Can't we reasonably see people as human resources on call at least for emergencies, and limit their self-destructive or harmful behavior accordingly in order to conserve our resources?

Notes

1. F. A. Hayek, *The Constitution of Liberty* (Chicago: Henry Regnery Company, 1960) and *Individualism and Economic Order* (Chicago: Henry Regnery Company, 1948); Milton Friedman, *Capitalism and Freedom* (Chicago: The University of Chicago Press, 1958); Robert Nozick, *Anarchy, State, and Utopia* (New York: Basic Books, Inc., 1974).

2. These rights are natural, inasmuch as they exist prior to the existence of the state and set limits within which the state can justifiably act. They are negative since they prohibit external, other-agent interference.

3. E.g., Nozick, particularly pp. 28–32.

4. Although Nozick equates liberties and negative rights, there are good reasons to separate the concepts. See, e.g., W. N. Hohfeld's analysis, *Some Fundamental Legal Conceptions as Applied in Judicial Reasoning* (New Haven, Conn.: Yale University Press, 1953). Still, since Nozick does identify them—in fact, many theorists do—I will, in this paper, adhere to that identification.

5. Hayek, *The Road to Serfdom* (Chicago: The University of Chicago Press, 1944).

6. There is serious question whether Kant would want his "slogan" appropriated by libertarianism. Still, it is easy to understand why they gravitate toward Kant.

7. Some libertarians might object: Negative rights are not limitations of liberty. You have simply misunderstood, they might say, the very nature of libertarianism. One does not have the liberty to kill others. However, it seems to me that such rights are restrictions of liberty and hence my objections go through. Nonetheless, I will consider this suggestion in some detail in the next section.

8. Thomas Hobbes, *Leviathan*, ed. Michael Oakeshott (New York: Collier Books, 1973 edition), p. 101.

9. Eric Mack, "Natural and Contractual Rights," *Ethics*, 87, no. 2 (1977), pp. 153ff.

10. Actually, I think it is the libertarian's vacillation in his use of this term that makes his case so initially compelling.

11. See Joel Feinberg, *Social Philosophy* (Englewood Cliffs, N. J.: Prentice-Hall, Inc. 1973), p. 19.

12. Nozick, p. 28.

13. For two discussions of tacit consent see R. P. Wolff's *In Defense of Anarchism* (New York: Harper & Row, 1970), and P. Singer's *Democracy and Disobedience* (Oxford: Oxford University Press, 1972).

14. Nozick, pp. 90–95.

15. John Rawls, *A Theory of Justice* (Cambridge: Harvard University Press, 1971).

16. Nozick, p. 31.

17. It won't do for the libertarian to argue that this is a just "using" while violations of negative rights are unjust "usings." Such a distinction (between just and unjust "usings") presupposes that the Kantian ends/means principle is not the fundamental building block of libertarianism. Hence, such a response would undermine the very ground of this objection.

18. A similar argument could be developed against any libertarian attempt to use the act/omission distinction to undergird his theory of rights. Let me explain: occasionally the libertarian will claim that there is an unbridgeable moral gulf between actively harming someone and "merely" letting harm happen to him. Active harms are always wrong while omissions (failures to act) are never wrong. This explains why all general rights are only negative, the libertarian might say. Violations of negative rights are active harms while omissions never violate negative rights.

I have three comments about such a reply. First, though this distinction apparently has some service—there is, in many cases, some moral difference between omissions and commissions—it does not seem, even to most supporters of this distinction, that the moral difference is so vast that omissions are *never* wrong. Secondly, the libertarian has never tried, as far as I know, to defend his use of the distinction. Thirdly, and probably more to the point, my main argument first aired in the second section spells trouble for the distinction's utility as a grounding for the libertarian view of rights. Libertarian constraints themselves actively intrude into individuals' lives. They justify coercively prohibiting individuals from doing actions they may want to do and rarely are able to do. So by his own account, active intrusions are not always wrong. The act/omission distinction cannot undergird the libertarian conception of rights. And it won't do for the libertarian to argue that active intrusions to stop active intrusions are permissible since there is no non-question-begging way in which such an analysis would support the libertarian view of rights. The slaveholder, for example, could claim that by enslaving others he was actively intruding to stop the state from actively intruding on him.

Therefore, I would again want to argue that the libertarian is overlooking the obvious reason why the slaveholder's activities are curtailed: an individual's interest in not being enslaved is more fundamental and more extensive than his (or anyone else's) interest in enslaving another. One need not resort to mysterious talk of either intrusions to stop intrusions or acts and omissions. In fact, I suspect that if the act/omission distinction is morally significant it is because it describes part of our moral life—not because it proscribes that life.

19. There is one possible variety of libertarianism that I have not examined here. Someone might offer a distinctly consequentialist argument for libertarianism. They might argue, for example, that a society which recognized only negative general rights would be freer, happier, etc. However, this certainly does appear to violate the spirit as well as the letter of libertarianism. Libertarianism involves the claim that violations of negative general rights are always wrong, come what may, and it is difficult to envision how such a theory could be compatible with anything but a deontological justification.

Secondly, it is wildly implausible to think that any traditional consequentialist principle could generate libertarian claims—or even something closely approximating them. Classical utilitarianism, for example, would at least insure that each individual has the basic goods necessary for survival (given the truth of the principle of diminishing utility).

Still, I suppose someone might develop such a theory, and if he did, then further argument would be required to demonstrate its inadequacies.

10

Quotations Concerning
Libertarianism (Often Called
Classical Liberalism)

Compiled by Quee Nelson

To the intellectual, the social device of capitalism offers a displeasing picture. Why? In his own terms, here
are self-seeking men in quest of personal aggrandizement. How? By providing consumers with things they
want or can be induced to want. The same intellectual, puzzlingly, is not shocked by the workings of hedonistic democracy; here also self-seeking men accomplish their aggrandizement by promising to other men
things they want or are induced to demand. The difference seems to lie mainly in that the capitalist delivers the goods.

— Bertrand de Jouvenal, classical liberal, 1954[1]

Socialism, like the ancient ideas from which it springs,
confuses the distinction between government and society. As a result of this, every time we object to a thing
being done by government, the socialists conclude that
we object to its being done at all. We disapprove of
state education. Then the socialists say that we are
opposed to any education. We object to a state religion. Then the socialists say that we want no religion
at all. We object to a state-enforced equality. Then they
say that we are against equality. And so on, and so on.
It is as if the socialists were to accuse us of not wanting persons to eat because we do not want the state to
raise grain.

— Frederic Bastiat,[2] classical liberal, 1850

Against individualism, the fascist conception is for the
State; and it is for the individual in so far as he coincides with the state . . . It is opposed to classical liberalism, which arose as a reaction to absolutism and exhausted its historical function when the State became
the expression of the conscience and will of the people.

— Benito Mussolini,[3] 1932

Private property, as conceived under the liberalistic
economic order . . . represented the right of the individual to manage and to speculate with inherited or
acquired property as he pleased, without regard for

the general interests . . . German socialism had to overcome this "private," that is, unrestrained and irresponsible view of property. All property is common property. The owner is bound by the people and the Reich
to the responsible management of his goods. His legal position is only justified when he satisfies this responsibility to the community.

— Ernst Rudolf Huber,[4] official
Nazi spokesperson, 1939

I have, truly, no property in that which another can by
right take from me when he pleases, against my consent. Hence it is a mistake to think that the supreme
or legislative power of any commonwealth can do
what it will, and dispose of the estates of the subject
arbitrarily or take any part of them at pleasure.

— John Locke,[5] classical liberal, 1690

Notes

1. Jouvenal, "The Treatment of Capitalism by Continental Intellectuals," in *Capitalism and the Historians*, ed. F.
A. Hayek (Chicago: University of Chicago Press, 1954), pp.
95–96.

2. Bastiat, *The Law*, originally published as a pamphlet, June 1850 (reprinted New York: Foundation for
Economic Education, 1984), pp. 32–33.

3. Mussolini, "The Doctrine of Fascism: Fundamental
Ideas," *Enciclopedia Italiana*, 1932. See Charles F. Delzell,
ed., *Mediterranean Fascism: 1919–1945* (New York: Harper &
Row, 1970), pp. 94, 101–102.

4. Huber, *Verfassungsrecht des grossdeutschen Reiches*
(Hamburg, 1939), in Raymond E. Murphy, et al., ed., *National Socialism: Basic Principles*, reprinted in *Readings on
Fascism and National Socialism*, selected by Dept. of Philosophy, University of Colorado (Denver: Swallow Press, 1952),
p. 91.

5. Locke, *Second Treatise on Government*, Chapter XI,
138.

11

Arguments for Egalitarianism

Joel Feinberg

Editor's note: Feinberg, a leading philosopher who teaches at the University of Arizona, associates egalitarianism with human rights, that is, rights all humans have just because of human nature or what it means to be human. Feinberg notes that egalitarianism is a revolutionary idea in the history of thought. He searches for a rational basis on which to ground human rights that are at least somewhat independent of merit. He suggests that the real point of the view that all persons are equal is that each person has his or her own view, a unique perspective and experience. Feinberg thinks a more egalitarian world would be more civilized and less dangerous.

Despite its current popularity, the theory that there are rights held equally by all human beings continues to trouble philosophers. It is natural for them to imagine skeptics asking: "Why *all* human beings *equally*, and not only, or primarily, the deserving ones?" The skeptical question still has great force. To appreciate this we have only to consider that the theory of human rights requires that in certain basic ways we treat even congenital idiots and convicted mass murderers the same as everyone else.

To appreciate fully how revolutionary the idea of equal human rights was, recall how European society was organized during the centuries preceding the revolutionary period. The feudal system recognized distinct hereditary castes, each with its peculiar and irreducible legal status defined by elaborate sets of rights and duties. A legal *status* in the relevant

Reprinted from Joel Feinberg, *Social Philosophy* (Englewood Cliffs, N.J.: Prentice-Hall, 1973), pp. 88–94. Reprinted by permission.

sense differs from mere social roles like father, promiser, and farmer, in part because it is entirely hereditary and unmodifiable by voluntary arrangements. The rights men had as a matter of status were theirs as royalty, nobility, clergy.

To be sincere, reliable, fair, kind, tolerant, unintrusive, modest in my relations with my fellows is not due them because they have made brilliant or even passing moral grades, but simply because they happen to be members of the moral community. It is not necessary to add "members in good standing": the moral community is not a club from which members may be dropped for delinquency. Our morality does not provide for moral outcastes or half-castes. It does provide for punishment. But this takes place *within* the moral community and under its rules. It is for this reason that, for example, one has no right to be cruel to a cruel person. His offense against the moral law has not put him outside the law. He is still protected by its prohibition of cruelty—as much so as are kind persons. The pain inflicted on him as punishment for his offense does not close out the great reserve of good will on the part of others which is his birthright as a human being; it is a limited withdrawal from it. Capital punishment even is no exception. The fact that a man has been condemned to death does not license his jailors to beat him or virtuous citizens to lynch him.[1]

A society based on human rights is actually closer to the old fixed status idea (except that it has but a single status) than to the society in which all basic rights are distributed in proportion to merit. *Some* rights in any society, of course, will have to be based on merit, but the ones that are independent of merit define the class in which human rights are located.

Why treat all people equally in any respect in the face of manifest inequalities of merit among them? The skeptic's challenge has not been met, and is certainly not disposed of by the reply that all humans are equal in "moral worth," whatever their other differences. No skeptic who denies equal rights will be easily convinced that there is equal human worth. Whatever kind of value "human worth" may be, if it is generically like every other kind of worth it is a *supervenient* property,[2] i.e., a property possessed by something in virtue of some other property or properties it possesses. It is impossible that two things should be alike in every other respect and have different degrees of worth, for degree of worth is determined by other characteristics. If one is more worthy than the other it must be *because* they have different properties. Similarly, if two things or two persons have the same worth (any kind of worth), they must have in common some other characteristic—a nonvalue characteristic—that is the basis of their equal worth. But what might this common characteristic be? Philosophical champions of human rights have replied to this legitimate query with a bewildering variety of answers, almost all of them inadequate.

Most philosophers agree with their skeptical challengers that if there are certain rights possessed by all men independently of their merits, this must be because, despite their many inequalities, all men are equal in some one respect that is of supreme moral importance. In attempting to identify this respect, some mention other *value characteristics*; some opt for certain *natural capacities*, no matter how fully realized, such as "rationality," or for *natural vulnerabilities*, such as the liability to pain and suffering; others leave the empirical world altogether in search of *transcendental properties*, an intrinsic dignity attaching to all human beings as "ends in themselves."

None of this has proved very satisfactory. The intrinsically moral qualities invoked to explain equal human worth must rest, as moral qualities, on some common nonvalue characteristics which are *their* bases or determinants; the question about the nature of the common characteristic arises all over again about them. If human beings have human worth *because* of their "intrinsic pricelessness" or "infinite value," asks the skeptic, where do those extravagantly dimensioned endowments come from? In virtue of what other traits can *they* be properly ascribed? These questions seem even more appropriate and difficult to answer than the question that was their occasion. Worse still, the "moral property" approach often involves, in the words of A. I. Melden, "the radical muddle that if one could somehow see. . .into the very depths of person's being, one would somehow find a quality of sheer preciousness in itself that endows a person with his status as the possessor of a right."[3] Part of the muddle consists in treating the mysterious value property "preciousness" as if it were not supervenient upon other characteristics, and hence not a genuine value characteristic at all. Surely to "see" a person as precious is to see him *as he is* and *therefore* precious. It is not to see the preciousness directly, as one might see a dab of paint on a wall. Preciousness is not "a kind of mystic moral badge" worn on the wall of the soul; it is a way of valuing something based on an awareness of the kind of thing it is.

Empirical characteristics, especially natural capabilities and vulnerabilities, are somewhat more plausible candidates for grounds of human worth,

since their candidacies do not involve regresses or logical muddles. But very little more than that can be said for them. The capability most commonly favored for this role is man's unique *rationality*. Some men are more rational than others, however, and we do not want it to follow that the more rational are the more worthy, for that would be to make variable merit a ground for invariant worth. It might be said that all men, even the most irrational, have the potential to be rational, but again it would seem that even these universal potentials are unequal. Perhaps what is meant is that all men have the potential to be at least minimally rational, that is, to measure up to a modest standard that exceeds anything lower animals can reach. That may be true in some extremely weak sense of "potential" (in which even an irreparably brain-damaged idiot still has the "potential" to be rational), but it is difficult to discern any intuitive connection between such weak potentiality and human worth. In more familiar sense of "potential," many possessors of human rights are not even potentially rational.

The natural vulnerability most commonly favored as a ground of human worth is liability to pain and suffering. This criterion would also permit entry of lower animals into the moral community, but we needn't cavil over that. It does have difficulties of a more serious kind. Some of these stem from the fact that liabilities to pain and suffering can vary from person to person. Some people are naturally more sensitive than others; does this make them more worthy? Moreover, drugs and other artificial devices might be used to accentuate these natural differences. The most serious difficulty, however, is that certain forms of treatment presumably violative of human rights might cause no pain or suffering at all, such as the sudden painless murder of an innocent man who has no family or friends to grieve for him.

Various terms from the metaphysical vocabulary "explain" human worth only by renaming that which is to be explained. Thus, without further explanation, the fact that all human beings are "persons, not things" or the claim that "men are ends in themselves" do not clearly account for the equality of human worth. Similarly, that men are "sacred" or of "infinite value"[4] are other (and perhaps better) ways of putting the claim of equal worth, but not descriptions of the grounds of that worth. If "sacred" (like "precious") is best defined as being the proper object of a certain kind of attitude, then the fact of a man's sacredness cannot be invoked in justification of that attitude without a kind of trivializing circularity. It would be like telling a man he ought to be amused by a joke, and then justifying that claim by asserting that the joke is amusing. That would give the unamused no insight into the basis of the joke he is unable to appreciate, and leave his "skepticism" untouched. Finally, it will not do, for similar reasons, to rest the case for equal and universal human worth on "our common humanity," for we wish to know precisely what it is about our common humanity that makes it so worthy of our respect.

It may well be that universal "respect" for human beings is, in a sense, "groundless"—a kind of ultimate attitude not itself justifiable in more ultimate terms. This is what might be said, after all, about parental (and other) love. The parent's unshaken love for the child who has gone bad may not be a response to any merit of the child (he may have none), or to any of his observable qualities (he may be a repulsive brute). In such a case, no quality of the child can be cited as a "reason" in justification of the parent's love. "I am his father after all" might be said to *explain* to others an affection that might otherwise seem wholly unintelligible, but that does not state a *ground* for the affection so much as indicate that it is "groundless" (but not irrational or mysterious for that). The "respect" said by Kant and many others to be owed to every human being by his fellows is not the same as affection or love, but it may well share this logical feature of ultimacy and "groundlessness" with it.

We are generally not puzzled by the fact that parents can love their children in a "groundless" and ultimate way, because we assume that normal human beings are equipped by their biological natures with the disposition to react in just that way to their own children. Respect for the human worth of strangers and villains, however, is a more mysterious phenomenon. It may well be, however, that most normal people are disposed to fall into that attitude whenever their attention is drawn to certain traits of all humans, or when they acquire the habit of looking at (or conceiving) their fellows in a certain way. The traits thus attended to may not constitute logically coercive reasons in support of the attitude of Kantian respect (that may be too much to hope for), but a thorough awareness of them can make the attitude seem less mysterious and actually lead people to acquire it—a result almost as good! We can think of our fellows simply as wise or entertaining, threatening or helpful, sexually attractive, authorities, physicians, or cooks, and adopt the attitude appropriate to the category. Bernard Williams contrasts these narrowly personal or technical attitudes toward another

with what he calls the "human point of view," which is "concerned primarily with what it is for *him* to live that life and do those actions in that character."[5] When we look at a person from that perspective, we do not simply regard him as "the surface to which a certain label can be applied"; rather we "try to see the world (including the label) from *his* point of view."[6] The real point of a maxim that all men are equal may be simply that all men equally have a point of view of their own, a unique angle from which they view the world. They are all equally centers of experience, foci of subjectivity. This implies that they are all capable of being viewed by others imaginatively from their own point of view. They "have shoes" into which we can always try to put ourselves; this is not true of mere things. It may follow (causally, not logically) from this way of so regarding them that we come to *respect* them in the sense tied to the idea of "human worth."

"Human worth" itself is best understood to name no property in the way that "strength" names strength and "redness" redness. In attributing human worth to everyone we may be ascribing no property or set of qualities, but rather expressing an attitude—the attitude of respect—toward the humanity in each man's person. That attitude follows naturally from regarding everyone from the "human point of view," but it is not grounded on anything more ultimate than itself, and it is not demonstrably justifiable.

It can be argued further against skeptics that a world with equal human rights is a *more just* world, a way of organizing society for which we would all opt if we were designing our institutions afresh in ignorance of the roles we might one day have to play in them. It is also a *less dangerous* world generally, and one with a *more elevated and civilized* tone. If none of this convinces the skeptic, we should turn our backs on him to examine more important problems.

Study Questions

1. In struggling to find a basis for human rights independent of merit, is Feinberg neglecting the aspect of egalitarianism that requires us to treat unequals unequally, that is, differently (as well as to treat equals equally)?

2. All the moral principles we apply in these study questions, including egalitarianism, assume moral realism. But does Feinberg's claim, that egalitarianism means that each person is equal in having a unique perspective and experience, suggest that

egalitarianism is well positioned to gain support from those who reluctantly reject moral relativism?

*3. Do you believe that government services such as education, health care, and police protection should be equally good everywhere, or that wealthier communities should have better services because they pay more taxes?

Notes

1. Vlastos, "Justice and Equality," p. 47.

2. R. M. Hare, *The Language of Morals* (Oxford: Oxford University Press, 1952), pp. 80 ff.

3. A. I. Melden, *Rights and Right Conduct* (Oxford: Basil Blackwell, 1959), p. 80.

4. The metaphor of infinitude has its point. An infinite set is defined as one that contains a proper subset such that there is a one-to-one correspondence between the members of the set and those of its own subset. Thus, the class of all cardinal integers is infinite since it contains a proper subset (the class of all odd numbers) that has as many members as it does! In transfinite arithmetic, the (infinite) number of all cardinal numbers is called "aleph-null" (after the Hebrew letter), and it can be shown that aleph-null plus any finite number equals aleph-null; aleph-null minus any finite number equals aleph-null; aleph-null plus or times itself, or taken to any finite power of itself, still equals aleph-null! Hence the laws of transfinite arithmetic are quite different from those of ordinary arithmetic. This should sober the hasty "rationalists" in politics who would murder finite numbers of human beings for the sake of many millions of other human beings, including those unborn. If *each* life is of "infinite" value, that kind of political arithmetic doesn't work, as each life is the equal of all the others combined. For a simple statement of the basic notions of transfinite arithmetic presupposing no more mathematics than elementary arithmetic, see Edward Kasner and James Newman, *Mathematics and the Imagination* (New York: Simon and Schuster, Inc., 1940), Chapter II. For a perceptive critique of the misuse of "moral arithmetic" in Stalinist Russia, see Arthur Koestler, *Darkness at Noon* (New York: The Macmillan Company, 1941).

5. Bernard Williams, "The Idea of Equality," in *Philosophy, Politics, and Society* (second series), ed. P. Laslett and W. G. Runciman (New York: Barnes & Noble, Inc., 1962), p. 115.

6. Williams, "The Idea of Equality," p. 116.

---

*From *The Book of Questions: Business, Politics and Ethics*, by Gregory Stock.

12

Why Egalitarianism Is Mistaken

Louis P. Pojman

Editor's note: Pojman counterargues against ten different arguments for equality, including Feinberg's. Pojman concludes that, despite historic commitments to equality in America and internationally, egalitarianism is one of the shallowest assumptions of our time. He defends fired gambler Jimmy the Greek's claim that blacks have some natural peculiarities that make them significantly different from whites. Pojman calls the main critics of Jimmy the Greek persecutors or liars. Pojman seeks to use scientific observations to establish a presumption of inequality against certain people. He is very skeptical of humanism and secular (nonreligious) arguments.

> All human beings are born free and equal in dignity and rights. They are endowed with reason and conscience and should act towards one another in a spirit of brotherhood.
> —*United Nations' Universal Declaration of Human Rights*, 1948

The rhetoric of human rights and theories of equal human rights have experienced an exponential growth during the past thirty or forty years. From declarations of human rights, such as the United Nations' Universal Declaration of Human Rights, to arguments about the rights of fetuses versus the rights of women, to claims and counter-claims about the rights of minorities to preferential hiring, to assertions of the rights of animals to life and well-being and the rights of trees to be cherished and pre-

Reprinted from Louis P. Pojman, "Are Human Rights Based on Equal Human Worth?" *Philosophy and Phenomenological Research*, vol. LII (1992), pp. 605–622. Reprinted by permission.

served, the proliferation of rights affects every phase of our socio-political discourse. Hardly a month goes by without a new book appearing on the subject.[1]

As J. L. Mackie used to say, "Rights are pleasant. They allow us to make claims of others. Duties are onerous. They obligate us to others." Rights threaten to replace responsibility as the central focus point of moral theory. But this need not be the case. A rights theory balanced by a strong sense of the social good and individual responsibility may well be the best kind of moral-political theory we can have.

Virtually the only candidate for a rights theory today is egalitarianism, at least with regard to rational human beings. While there are differences between contemporary egalitarian arguments, they all accept what Ronald Dworkin calls the "egalitarian plateau," the "deepest moral assumption" of our time, that each person is of equal intrinsic value or "dignity" and thus ought to be treated with equal respect and be given equal rights.[2] The phrase, 'dignity of the human person', signifies in the words of Jacques Maritain, that 'the human person has the right to be respected, is the subject of rights, possesses rights. These are things which are owned to [a person] because of the very fact that he is a [person]."[3]

Ronald Green says that egalitarianism is the presupposition for morality itself, the "precondition of moral discourse and the necessary first assumption of any moral system, whatever its resultant values."[4] Systems as diverse as Robert Nozick's Libertarianism, John Rawls' Liberalism and Kai Nielsen's Marxism all share this notion that each person matters equally.

What distinguishes most contemporary egalitarianism from earlier natural law models is its self-conscious secularism. There is no appeal to a God or a transcendental realm. Although Kant's doctrine of Ends ("Human beings qua rational have an inherent dignity and so ought to treat each other as ends and never merely as means") is the touchstone of most egalitarians, they generally distance themselves from the metaphysical grounding of Kant's doctrine. In the words of Dworkin, contemporary egalitarianism is "metaphysically unambitious."[5] Yet it may well be that without some deeper metaphysical underpinnings equal rights theories fail to persuade thoughtful persons.

If a deconstructed Kant is the father of contemporary egalitarians, their enemies are Aristotle and Thomas Hobbes. Aristotle thought that humans were essentially unequal, depending on their ability to reason. Hobbes rejected the notion of humans having any intrinsic worth at all. "The *value* or worth of a man is, as of all other things, his price—that is to say, so much as would be given for the use of his power—and therefore is not absolute but a thing dependent on the need and judgment of another."[6]

In this paper I outline and examine the principal arguments for equal human rights given by contemporary egalitarians. I argue that in their present form none of them is compelling and that there are reasons to give up egalitarianism altogether.

Contemporary Secular Arguments for Equal Human Worth

Ten arguments (or strategies) for equal human rights based on equal human worth appear in current philosophical literature. They are: (1) The Presumption Argument; (2) The Properly Basic Belief Strategy; (3) The Existential Strategy; (4) The Libertarian Argument; (5) The Family Argument; (6) The Pragmatic Argument; (7) The Utilitarian Argument; (8) The Coherentist Argument; (9) The Rational Agency Argument; and (10) The Argument from Moral Personality. Let me briefly describe them and point out their deficiencies. I regret the cursory treatment of important theories, but my purpose is simply to show that little attention has been paid to justifying the egalitarian plateau. As someone who has always considered himself an egalitarian, I am now puzzled by this theory and wonder whether it is simply a leftover from a religious world view now rejected by all of the philosophers examined in this paper. At any rate, my discussion is meant to be exploratory and provocative, not the final word on the subject.

1. The Presumption of Equality Argument

R. S. Peters, Stanley Benn, Monroe Beardsley, E. F. Carritt, and James Rachels interpret equal worth in terms of equal consideration or impartiality and argue that there is a presumption in favor of treating people equally. "All persons are to be treated alike, unless there are good reasons for treating them differently."[7] This type of egalitarianism seems unduly formal. One might as well say that "all sentient beings should be treated alike, unless there are good reasons for treating them differently." The formula only shifts the focus onto *good reasons*. We need to

know by virtue of what material criterion people are to be treated equally or differently. What are the material criteria? Need, effort, contribution, intelligence, sentience, self-consciousness? And if there is more than one, how do we weight them in various circumstances? As far as I know, the problem of material criteria has not been solved.

Aristotle's aristocratic views could accommodate this formal notion of equal worth, so could the slave owner who believed his slaves less intelligent than himself and more suited to hard labor. Educational elitists could accept it as they deny advanced education to the poor or those with IQs less than 110. Inegalitarians simply claim that there is a good reason for unequal treatment of human beings. They are unequal in the relevant aspect.

The presumption of equality argument reduces to the notion of impartiality (what R. M. Hare calls "universalizability") and is not really an egalitarian argument at all. It prescribes that we not act arbitrarily, but consistently. We should make our discriminations according to a relevant standard, but doing so does not commit us to egalitarianism.

Furthermore, there seems something arbitrary about the Presumption Argument. Why should we start off with a bias towards equality and not inequality? Why don't we have a principle presuming unequal treatment: "All persons are to be treated unequally unless there is some reason for treating them equally"? Neither a presumption of equality nor one of inequality is necessary, though there may be pragmatic or utilitarian considerations that incline us to opt for a presumption of equality rather than inequality. We will consider that strategy later.

2. The Properly Basic Belief Strategy

Sometimes, no argument at all is given for the claim of equal human worth and the equal human rights that flow from it. Ronald Dworkin begins his book *Taking Rights Seriously* with a rejection of metaphysical assumptions.

> Individual rights are political trumps held by individuals. Individuals have rights when, for *some reason*, a collective goal is not a sufficient justification for denying them what they wish, as individuals, to have or to do, or not a sufficient justification for imposing some loss or injury upon them. That characterization of a right is, of course, formal in the sense that it does not indicate what rights people have or guarantee, indeed, that they have any. But it does not suppose that

rights have some special metaphysical character, and the theory defended in these essays therefore departs from older theories of rights that do rely on that supposition (p. xi, italics mine).

Nowhere in his book does Dworkin parse out the notion of "some reasons" to override "collective goals." It is a given, something intuitively self-evident. The notion of equal natural rights based on equal human worth simply becomes the assumption that replaces earlier religious or Kantian metaphysical assumptions. Every plausible political theory is egalitarian in that it holds that all members of the community have a right to equal concern and respect. "The Deepest Moral Assumption: the assumption of a natural right of all men and women to an equality of concern and respect, a right they possess not in virtue of birth or characteristic or merit or excellence but simply as human beings with the capacity to make plans and give justice."[8] In other words, we don't need to argue for this thesis.

Dworkins' view seems similar to what Alvin Plantinga calls "a properly basic belief," a foundational belief which doesn't need any further justification. But whatever merits this strategy has for religious beliefs, it seems unsatisfactory when employed to justify moral and political equality. At the very least, we should want to know why the capacity to "make plans and give justice" grants all and only humans equal concern and respect.

3. The Existential Strategy

Closely related to Dworkin's view is the view that equal human worth is something we simply, arbitrarily choose. The Marxist philosopher, Kai Nielsen, admits that the egalitarian posit is without foundation. His allegiance to "Radical Egalitarianism" is an existential commitment.

> I do not know how anyone could show this belief to be true—to say nothing of showing it to be self-evident—or in any way prove it or show that if one is through and through rational, one must accept it . . . A Nietzschean, a Benthamite, or even a classist amoralist who rejects it cannot thereby be shown to be irrational or even in any way necessarily to be diminished in his reason. It is a moral belief that I am committed to . . . [and which leads] to some . . . form of radical egalitarianism.[9]

In other words, equal human worth is a posit of secular faith, but a faith that seems to suffer from counter-examples: the apparent inequalities of abili-

ties of every sort. We will look at Nielsen's later argument below.

The first three types of egalitarianism which we have examined can hardly be called arguments at all. Presumption arguments simply presume, properly basic beliefs stipulate, and existential choices do not claim rational justification. These theories already suppose egalitarian foundations. We turn to more substantive efforts.

4. The Libertarian Argument

At the other end of the political spectrum from Nielsen's Socialism with a rich panoply of positive welfare rights is the Libertarian idea that there is only one natural right, the negative equal right not to be interfered with. In *Anarchy, State and Utopia*, Robert Nozick, like Dworkin, simply assumes such a natural right. "Individuals have rights, and there are things no persons or groups may do to them (without violating their rights)." But unlike Dworkin, Nozick believes that only the minimal state, which protects the individual "against force, theft, fraud, [the breaking] of contracts, and so on, is justified." Drawing on the Kantian notion that "individuals are ends and not merely means; they may not be sacrificed or used for achieving of other ends without their consent," Nozick argues that individuals possess an equal and absolute right to self-ownership which gives them an absolute right to their justly acquired property.[10] Similarly, Tibor Machan formulates the Libertarian position in this way. "In short, a just human community is one that first and foremost protects the individual's right to life and liberty—the sovereignty of human individuals to act without *aggressive* intrusion from other human beings."[11]

On the face of it, after the rhetoric of absolute rights to property is deflated (Nozick wrongly supposes that the notion of self-ownership entails an absolute rather than prima facie right to property), Libertarian arguments come down to little more than the back side of an ultra-minimalist morality, one which sets up its single principle: Do not interfere with the liberty of another. But this by itself doesn't even distinguish humans from animals, for it doesn't tell us what is so special about human beings which gives them but not animals dignity. We shouldn't interfere with the liberty of any purposive creature without moral justification.

Machan separates himself both from Libertarians like Nozick, who does not offer arguments for natural rights, and from metaphysical determinists like John Hospers, and grounds his political Libertarianism in metaphysical Libertarianism. It is our ability to act freely (contra-causally) that separates humans from other animals and gives us value.

This seems a promising move, a departure from the mainstream rejection of metaphysics, but it has problems. The first is that the Libertarian (contra-causal) notion of freedom seems mysterious and hard to argue for. It seems to presuppose a notion of the self that is metaphysically richer than the physicalist version held by most compatibilists, though if we grant a transcendent notion of agency, the Libertarian notion will be more promising. However it will probably not be secular in the usual meaning of that term (as disclaiming a notion of the spiritual or transcendent).

Secondly, even if we grant the property of libertarian free will: if freedom is intrinsically valuable, it would seem that we should *positively* promote it—by increasing a person's opportunities (through non-Libertarian institutions like public education and welfare economics) to use it. Thirdly, it seems that people are unequally free. Some people deliberate and choose more rationally than others who seem driven by circumstances, short term goals, and emotion. So Libertarianism is not obviously egalitarian.

There seems no reason on Libertarian premises to value all humans equally. Here David Gauthier's Libertarian theory of "morals by agreement" seems more consistent with a secular world view. People do not have inherent moral value. Indeed, there are no objective values. Values are simply subjective preferences of different individuals, and the "moral artifice" is merely a convention which is mutually advantageous. We refrain from coercing or harming, not because people have inherent equal dignity, but because it is not mutually advantageous to do so.[12]

5. The Family Metaphor Argument

Gregory Vlastos in his celebrated article "Justice and Equality" appeals to the metaphor of a 'loving family" to defend his egalitarianism. If we are asked why we hold to equal human rights, Vlastos replies, "Because the human worth of all persons is equal, however unequal may be their merit."[13]

> The moral community is not a club from which members may be dropped for delinquency. Our morality does not provide for moral outcasts or half-castes. It does provide for punishment. But this takes place *within* the moral community and under its rules. It is for this reason that, for example, one has no right to be cruel to a cruel person. His offence against the moral law has not put him outside the law. . . . The pain inflicted on him as punishment for his offence does not close out the reserve of goodwill on the part of all others which is his birthright as a human being; it is limited withdrawal for it. . . . [The] only justification [of human rights is] the value which persons have simply because they are person: their 'intrinsic value as individual human beings,' as Frankena calls it; the 'infinite value' or the 'sacredness' of their individuality, as others have called it (p. 55).

Vlastos distinguishes *gradable* or meritorious traits from *nongradable* but valuable traits and says that talents, skills, character and personality belong to the gradable sort, but that our humanity is a nongradable value. Regarding human worth all humans get equal grades. In this regard, human worth is like love. "Constancy of affection in the face of variations of merit is one of the surest tests of whether a parent does love a child." But the family metaphor, which is the closest Vlastos come to providing an argument for his position, needs further support. It is not obvious that all humans are related to each other as members of a family. If we're all brothers and sisters, who's the parent? By virtue of what property in human beings do we obtain value? Vlastos doesn't tell us.

Nor does the *gradable-nongradable* distinction make a difference here. There are nongradable properties. All members of the set of books or cats may be equally books or cats, but we can still grade members with respect to specific interests or standards and say from the point of view of aesthetic value some books and cats are better than others. Likewise, we may agree that all homo sapiens equally are homo sapiens but insist that within that type there are important differences which include differences in value (e.g., fetal homo sapiens, retarded homo sapiens, and highly productive homo sapiens may have different value). The point is that Vlastos has not grounded his claim of *equal* worth, or any *worth* for that matter, and until he does, his idea of the family connection remains a mere metaphor.

6. The Pragmatic (or Useful Attitude) Argument

Joel Feinberg, who rejects Vlastos' essentialist position as unpromising, concedes that the notion of human worth is "not demonstrably justifiable." His support for the principle of equal human worth seems based on a combination of existential commitment and pragmatic concerns.

"Human worth" itself is best understood to name no property in the way that "strength" names strength and "redness" names redness. In attributing human worth to everyone we may be ascribing no property or set of qualities, but rather expressing an attitude—the attitude of respect—towards the humanity in each man's person. That attitude follows naturally from regarding everyone from the 'human point of view', but it is not grounded on anything more ultimate than itself, and it is not demonstrably justifiable.

It can be argued further against the skeptics that a world with equal human rights is a *more just* world, a way of organizing society for which we would all opt if we were designing our institutions afresh in ignorance of the roles we might one day have to play in them. It is also a *less dangerous* world generally, and one with a *more elevated and civilized* tone. If none of this convinces the skeptic, we should turn our backs on him to examine more important problems.[14]

Feinberg may be correct in seeking to disentangle the concept of *human worth* from a property-view, but his own position seems to have its own problems. He needs to tell us why we should take the *attitude* of regarding every one as equally worthy. What is this peculiar "human point of view" which supposedly grounds the notion of equal human worth? His pragmatic justification (i.e., that it will result in a less dangerous world and a more elevated and civilized world) simply needs to be argued out, for it's not obvious that acting as if everyone were of equal worth would result in a less dangerous world than one in which we treated people according to some other criteria.

Feinberg's claim that a world with equal human rights based on equal worth "is a more just world" is simply question-begging, since it is exactly the notion of equal worth that is contested in the idea of justice. Formally, we are to treat equals equally and unequals unequally. Feinberg seems to be saying that justice consists in treating everyone as though they were equal whether or not they are.

But supposing that there were good utilitarian reasons to treat people as though they were of equal worth, we would still want to know whether we really were of equal worth. If the evidence is not forthcoming, then the thesis of equal worth would have all the ear-marks of Plato's *Noble Lie*, ironically, asserting the very contrary of the original. Whereas for Plato the Noble Lie specified that we are to teach people that they are really unequal in order to pro-

duce social stability in an aristocratic society, in Feinberg's version of the *Noble Lie* we are to teach people that they are all equal in order to bring social stability to a democratic society.

One might argue that this is exactly what is happening in the severe censure and persecution of scholars like Linda Gottfredson and Philippe Rushton, who are engaged in studies of innate racial differences, in the dismissal of Jimmy the Greek from CBS for his assertion that blacks had certain innate athletic abilities that whites lacked, and even in the dismissal of the Malverne, Long Island, black eighth grade teacher, Janet Morgan, for assigning her class an essay on whether or not Jimmy the Greek should have been fired.[15]

Feinberg's final comment, "If none of this convinces the skeptic, we should turn our backs on him to examine more important problems," signals a flight from the battle, an admission that the Emperor has no clothes, for what could be more important than setting the foundations of socio-political philosophy?

7. The Utilitarian Argument for Human Equality

A slightly different argument for equal treatment of human beings is given by Peter Singer in his ground breaking book, *Animal Liberation* (1975). After admitting that the notion of equality is problematic and that there doesn't seem to be any way in which people are equal, Singer tries to justify the ideal from a utilitarian point of view.

Fortunately there is no need to pin the case for equality to one particular outcome of a scientific investigation. The appropriate response to those who claim to have found evidence of genetically based differences in ability between the races or sexes is not to stick to the belief that the genetic explanation must be wrong, whatever the evidence to the contrary may turn up: instead we should make it quite clear that the claim to equality does not depend on intelligence, moral capacity, physical strength, or similar matters of fact. Equality is a moral idea, not an assertion of fact. There is no logically compelling reason for assuming that a factual difference in ability between two people justifies any difference in the amount of consideration we give to their needs and interests. *The principle of the equality of human beings is not a description of an alleged actual equality among humans: it is a prescription of how we should treat humans* (p. 5).

Singer quotes Bentham, "Each to count for one and none for more than one," and Sidgwick, "The good of any one individual is of no more importance, from the point of view (if I may say so) of the Universe, than the good of any other." Singer calls on the growing consensus in moral philosophy. "More recently the leading figures in contemporary moral philosophy have shown a great deal of agreement in specifying as a fundamental presupposition of their moral theories some similar requirement which operates so as to give everyone's interest equal consideration" (p. 5f). "Concern for a child growing up in America would require that we teach him to read; concern for the well-being of a pig may require no more than that we leave him alone with other pigs in a place where there is adequate food and room to run freely" (p. 6). The application of equal consideration of interests is meant to apply to animals as well as humans. Here again Singer quotes Bentham in saying that we have duties to animals on the same level as those to humans. "The question is not, Can they *reason*? nor Can they *talk*? but *Can they suffer*? (p. 8).

Later in the book Singer agrees that higher beings have more complex needs and interests than animals. Because an animal doesn't have the concept of death, it may be justified to kill an animal when it wouldn't be justified to kill a human, but when it comes to suffering, it may well be that if an animal suffers more pain than a human is also suffering, we have a duty to give the only pain reliever to the animal!

The problem comes in when we apply Singer's utilitarian calculus to competing interests. Suppose Aristotle needs slaves to do his manual labor so that he can carry on his philosophical contemplation. It is not in the slaves' interest to be slaves to Aristotle, but if we can maximize utility by subjugating the interests of the slaves to the interests of the whole group (treating the slaves kindly, of course), what becomes of Singer's equal consideration of interests? Does he say to the slaves, "We considered your interests along with Aristotle's and the rest of society and concluded that on balance it's in all our interest that you stay slaves." Perhaps the same logic can be used to justify some of the harmful animal experiments that Singer condemns in his book. If this is so, it turns out that equal consideration of interests is simply a gloss for total utilitarian calculations in which individual rights are sacrificed for the good of the whole. We can still do the animal experiments if we anesthetize them first, so that they don't feel pain. But we may kill them and *anyone else* where net utility is expected.

8. The Coherentist Argument

In a recent article, "On Not Needing to Justify Equality," Kai Nielsen derives a defense of egalitarianism from John Rawls' and Norman Daniels' method of wide reflective equilibrium—a method which aims at providing a fit between our moral theory and particular moral judgments, which results in an overall coherent account of morality. Nielsen claims that the method can be used to show that the principle of equal human worth and equal treatment are justified as part of an overall coherent account of morality.[16]

If an egalitarianism rights theory is to succeed, my guess is that it will be a coherentist theory of the kind that Nielsen adumbrates. But, as things stand, there are two criticisms of Nielsen's argument. First, at best we have only a promissory note for a coherent secular system where equal worth plays a legitimate role. That is, no one has set forth a naturalistic account of morality where human worth, let alone equal human worth, doesn't have an unduly ad hoc appearance. Secondly, Coherentist justifications in general are subject to the criticism of not tying into reality. A Nazi world view, a religious fundamentalist theology, and Nielsen's Marxist egalitarianism, not to mention fairy tales, are all coherent and internally consistent, but no more than one of these mutually incompatible world views can be correct. Coherence is a necessary but not sufficient condition for justification. We want to know by which criteria we can distinguish between coherent theories. In scientific theory building empirical observation and other theoretical constraints do this sort of work. But it would seem that the empirical and theoretical data we have count against the notion of equal worth, so that the kind of justification needed for secular egalitarianism is wanting.

9. The Rational Agency Argument

An attempt at getting a deeper argument for equal rights based on equal worth is found in the work of Alan Gewirth. In his book *Reason and Morality*, his essay, "Epistemology of Human Rights," and elsewhere, Gewirth argues that we can infer equal human rights to freedom and well-being from the notion of rational agency.[17] A broad outline of the argument is as follows: Each rational agent must recognize that a measure of freedom and well-being is necessary for his or her exercise of rational agency.

That is, each rational agent must will, if he is to will at all, that he possess that measure of freedom and well-being. Therefore anyone who holds that freedom and well-being are necessary for his exercise of rational agency is logically committed to holding that he has a prudential right to these goods. By the principle of universalizability we obtain the conclusion that all rational agents have a prima facie equal right to freedom and well-being. Gewirth formalizes this in his Principle of Generic Consistency (PGC): "Act in accord with the generic rights of your recipients as well as yourself."

But I think that Gewirth's argument is invalid. The notion of a prudential right is problematic. From the premise that I need freedom and well-being in order to exercise my will nothing follows by itself concerning a right to freedom and well-being. From the fact that I assert a prudential right to some x does not give anyone else a sufficient reason to grant me that x.

But even if we could make sense of Gewirth's argument, contrary to Gewirth's claim that he has given us an-all encompassing principle (an ethical monism), this wouldn't give us a notion of equal human worth, but merely *minimal* equal prima facie rights to freedom and well-being, which could be overridden for other reasons. For example, Aristotle might say that the freedom and well-being of the mentally superior aristocrat overrides that of the man or woman of low intelligence or that the prima facie right to minimal freedom of action should be overridden either when the actions are irrational or when a hierarchically structured society has need of slaves, in which case those who were best suited to this role would have their prima facie right to free action suitably constrained. In like manner Utilitarians could accept Gewirthian equal prima facie rights and override them whenever greater utility was at stake.

Furthermore, I don't see why the PGC doesn't apply to animals as well as humans, thus making them equal recipients of our attention. Cats and rats implicitly act on the principles of needing freedom and well-being, even if they cannot articulate them or bring them consciously to mind (remember, Gewirth's argument stipulates that these qualities are necessary conditions for purposive action). This would seem to push him towards viewing animals as equal to humans.

If my critique is near target, Gewirthian equal rights, rather than offering an all-encompassing absolute system, reduce to little more than recognizing that non-interference and well-being are values which we have a prima facie moral duty to promote

whether in animals or angels, humans or Galacticans. They don't give us a set of thick natural rights.

Tom Nagel has set forth a version of Gewirth's Rational Agency Argument in his book *A View from Nowhere* and other places which may be more promising than Gewirth's own version in that it centers not on free action but on essential value. A typical passage is the following:

> You cannot sustain an impersonal indifference to the things in your life which matter to you personally ... But since the impersonal standpoint does not single you out from anyone else, the same must be true of the values arising in other lives. If you matter impersonally, so does everyone. We can usefully think of the values that go into the construction of a political theory as being revealed in a series of four stages, each of which depends on a moral response to an issue posed by what was revealed at the previous stage. At the first stage, the basic insight that appears from the impersonal standpoint is that everyone's life matters, and no one is more important than anyone else. This does not mean that some people may not be more important in virtue of their greater value for others. But at the baseline of value in the lives of individuals, from which all higher-order inequalities of value must derive, everyone counts the same. For a given quality of whatever it is that's good or bad—suffering or happiness or fulfillment or frustration—its intrinsic impersonal value doesn't depend on whose it is.[18]

The argument goes like this.

1. I cannot help but value myself as a subject of positive and negative experiences (e.g., suffering, happiness, fulfillment or frustration).
2. All other humans are relevantly similar to me, subjects of positive and negative experiences.
3. Therefore, I must, on pain of contradiction, ascribe equal value to all other human beings.

Although this looks more promising than Gewirth's argument, I think that it too is defective. First of all, it is not necessary to value oneself primarily as a possessor of the capacity for positive and negative experiences. Why cannot I value myself because of a complex of specific properties: excellence of skill, discipline, rationality, high integrity, athletic ability, artistic talent, or quickness of wit without which I would not deem living worth the effort? Perhaps it is a combination of such traits that gives life value and that without these life would lose all value for me. I would just as soon be dead.

Hence I may value all those who are suitably like myself—or like what I aspire to be, but I am under no rational obligation "on pain of contradiction" to esteem the child molester, the foolish, the sick, the Philistine and so forth. They might just as well be slaves under a benevolent master.

There is a second problem with Nagel's argument. It rests too heavily on the agent's judgment about himself. "If you matter impersonally, so does everyone." There are two ways to invalidate this conditional. The conditional won't go through if you don't value yourself. If I am sick of life and believe that I don't matter, then, on Nagel's premises, I have no reason to value anyone else. Secondly, I may deny the consequent and thereby reject the antecedent. I may come to believe that no one else does matter and then be forced to acknowledge that I don't matter either. We're all equal—equally worthless.

Thirdly, note the consequentialist tone of the last two sentences of Nagel's statement: ". . . at the baseline of value in the lives of individuals, from which all higher order inequalities of value must derive, everyone counts the same. For a given quantity of whatever it is that's good or bad—suffering or happiness or fulfillment or frustration—its intrinsic impersonal value doesn't depend on whose it is." We hear the echo of Bentham's "each one to count for one and no one for more than one" in this passage. But Nagel, like Bentham before him, cannot be both a maximizer and an egalitarian. If it is the suffering or happiness that really is the good to be maximized, then individuals are mere place holders for these qualities, so that if we can maximize happiness by subordinating some individuals to others, we should do so.

If it is the properties of happiness or pleasure or non-suffering that are important, then it doesn't really matter who has them, so long as they are had. If A can derive 10 hedons by eliminating B and C who together can only obtain 8 hedons, it would be a good thing for A to kill B and C. If it turns out that a pig satisfied really is happier than Socrates dissatisfied, then we ought to value the pig's life more than Socrates, and if a lot of people are miserable and are making others miserable, we would improve the total happiness of the world by killing them.

10. The Argument from Moral Personality

No exposition of egalitarianism has had a greater influence on our generation than John Rawls' *A*

Theory of Justice, which Robert Nisbet has called "the long awaited successor to Rousseau's *Social Contract* . . . the Rock on which the Church of Equality can properly be founded in our time."[19] Rawls sets forth a hypothetical contract theory in which the bargainers go behind a veil of ignorance in order to devise a set of fundamental agreements that are fair.

> First of all no one knows his place in society, his class position or social status; nor does he know his fortune in the distribution of natural assets and abilities, his intelligence and the like. Nor, again, does anyone know his conception of the good, the particulars of his rational plan of life, or even the special features of his psychology such as his aversion to risk or liability to optimism or pessimism. More than this, I assume that the parties do not know the particular circumstances of their own society. That is, they do not know its economic or political situation, or the level of civilization and culture it has been able to achieve. The persons in the original position have no information as to which generation they belong (p. 137).

By denying individuals knowledge of their natural assets and social position Rawls prevents them from exploiting their advantages, thus transforming a decision under risk (where probabilities of outcomes are known) to a decision under uncertainty (where probabilities are not known). To the question, why should the individual acknowledge the principles chosen as morally binding? Rawls would answer, "We should abide by these principles because we all chose them under fair conditions." That is, the rules and rights chosen by fair procedures are themselves fair, since these procedures take full account of our moral nature as equally capable of "doing justice." The two principles that would be chosen, Rawls argues, are (1) everyone will have an equal right to equal basic liberties and (2) social and economic inequalities must satisfy two conditions: (a) they are to attach to positions open to all under conditions of fair equality of opportunity; and (b) they must serve the greatest advantage of the least advantaged members of society (the difference principle).

Rawls has been criticized by Michael Sandel for failing to accord humans intrinsic worth. "Rawls' principles do not mention moral desert because, strictly speaking, no one can be said to deserve anything . . . On Rawls' view *people have no intrinsic worth*, no worth that is intrinsic in the sense that it is theirs prior to or independent of . . . what just institutions attribute to them."[20]

While Rawls sometimes lays himself open to this kind of charge, I think that Sandel is wrong here.

Rawls' social contract is grounded in Kantian humanism.

> Each person possesses an inviolability founded on justice that even the welfare of society as a whole cannot override. For this reason justice denies that the loss of freedom for some is made right by a greater good shared by others. It does not allow that the sacrifices imposed on a few are outweighed by the larger sum of advantages enjoyed by the many. Therefore, in a just society the liberties of equal citizenship are taken as settled; the rights secured by justice are not subject to political bargaining or the calculus of social interest (p. 3f).

At the center of Rawls' project is a respect for the individual as "inviolable," sacred, whose essential rights are inalienable. In section 77 of Rawls' book this *inviolability* is grounded in our having "the capacity for moral personality," that is, the ability to enter into moral deliberation. "It is precisely the moral persons who are entitled to equal justice. Moral persons are distinguished by two features: first they are capable of having . . . a conception of the good; and second they are capable of having . . . a sense of justice. . . . One should observe that moral personality is here defined as a potentiality that is ordinarily realized in due course. It is this potentiality which brings the claims of justice into play" (p. 505).

Members in the original position are not mere utilitarian containers of the good but Kantian "ends in themselves," who are worthy of "equal concern and respect." Rawls already presupposes equal and positive worth at the very beginning of his project. The question is, is this assumption reasonable? Is Rawls' egalitarian starting point justified? I think not. Given the framework in which Rawls writes there is no reason to suppose that we have intrinsic and equal value. Let me explain.

A standard criticism of *A Theory of Justice* is that it fails to take into account the conservative who, as is a gambler, would rather take his chances on a meritocratic or hierarchical society and so reject part or all of Rawls' second principle. I think that this objection is even stronger than has been made out, for it is not simply as a *gambler* that the conservative will self-interestedly choose meritocracy, but rather because he or she deems it the essence of justice.

This point becomes highlighted when we examine Rawls' *threshold* principle. "Once a certain minimum is met, a person is entitled to equal liberty on a par with everyone else" (p. 506). This move seems *ad hoc*. There is no obvious reason why we should opt for tacit equal status (let alone *inviolability*) rather than

an Aristotelian hierarchial structure based on differential ability to reason or deliberate. Even as some life plans are objectively better than others, so some people might well be considered more worthy than others and treated accordingly.

Why would it be wrong to weight the votes behind the veil of ignorance according to criteria of assessment? For example, the deeply reflective with low time preferences would be given more votes than the less reflective with high time preference. Those with high grades might get four or five votes whereas the minimally reflective might get only one vote. Why have only one threshold between those who pass and those who fail the rationality test, as Rawls proposes? Why not have five or six thresholds?

With different layers of weighted votes one would still expect a benevolent society, but the difference principle might well be replaced by Harsanyi's average utility principle or Frankfurt's sufficiency principle, permitting hierarchical arrangements.[21] Rawls' first principle (maximum liberty) and the first half of the second principle (equal opportunity) would very likely result in a hierarchical, elitist society.

What would Rawls say to these criticisms? Why does he hold on to a principle of equal intrinsic worth? The closest Rawls comes to addressing this question gets us back to his self-respect argument, discussed in section 8. Self-respect, according to Rawls, is a fundamental human need which his theory satisfies and which hierarchical arrangements fail to satisfy. But we have already seen that this is severely problematic.

Counter-Evidence to Egalitarianism: The Empirical Consideration

Contrary to egalitarians, and in spite of the widespread acceptance of the "egalitarian plateau," there is good reason to believe that humans are not of equal worth. Given the empirical observation, it is hard to see that humans are equal in any way at all. We all seem to have vastly different levels of abilities. Some, like Aristotle, Newton, Shakespeare, Gödel, and Einstein, are geniuses; others are imbeciles and idiots; the rest at various places along the intelligence continuum. Some are wise like Socrates and Abraham Lincoln; others are very foolish. Some have great powers of foresight and are able to defer gratification, while others can hardly assess their present circumstances, gamble away their future, succumb to immediate gratification and generally go through life as through a fog. Empirically, it looks like Churchill, Gandhi and Mother Teresa have more value than Jack-the-Ripper or Adolf Hitler. While all members of a community may be equally parts of that body, some members are more indispensable than others. Just as the brain is more important than the little toe or appendix, people vary in functional value.

Take any capacity or ability you like: reason, a good will, self-control, industry, the capacity to suffer, the capacity for pleasure, the ability to deliberate and choose freely, the ability to make moral decisions and carry them out, and it seems that humans (not to mention animals) differ in the degree to which they have those capacities and abilities.

Furthermore, given the purely secular version of the theory of evolution, there doesn't seem to be any reason to believe that the family metaphor, supposed by philosophers like Vlastos and the *United Nations' Declaration on Human Rights* (see the beginning of this paper), has much evidence in its favor. If we're simply a product of blind evolutionary chance and necessity, it is hard to see where the family connection comes in. Who is the parent? In fact, given a naturalistic account of the origins of homo sapiens, it is hard to see that humans have *intrinsic* value at all. If we are simply physicalist constructions, where does intrinsic value emerge?

No doubt, most, if not all, of the egalitarians discussed above recognize this empirical consideration. They seem to find inegalitarianism so unacceptable that even bad arguments or intuitions are to be preferred to settling for what is contrary to the democratic tradition. But philosophers must do better than that. The empirical problem seems to place its own burden of proof on any theory that would claim that equal rights are based on equal human worth. As far as I can see, none have countered the presumption of inequality.

Dworkin calls the principle of equality the "deepest moral assumption" of our time. If what I have said is correct, quite the reverse is true. It is one of the shallowest assumptions of our times. Secular egalitarian arguments for equal rights seem, at best, to be based on a posit of faith that all humans are of equal worth or that it is useful to regard them as such. They have not offered plausible reasons for their thesis, and, given the empirical consideration, inegalitarianism seems plausible. I suggest in closing that secular egalitarians have inherited a notion of inviolability or intrinsic human worth from a religious tradition which they no longer espouse. The question is whether the kind of democratic ideals that egalitarians espouse can do without a religious tradition. If it cannot, then egalitarians may be living off the borrowed interest of a religious metaphysic, which (in their eyes) has gone bankrupt.[22]

Study Questions

1. Who has the better of this debate, Feinberg or Pojman? Is egalitarianism true?

2. Is Pojman right to criticize the end of Feinberg's essay for making an illegitimate retreat from the person who, in the face of all the considerations Feinberg presents (e.g., that uncivilized danger should generally be avoided), remains completely skeptical about the value of equality? Or is Feinberg just being practical to part company at the end of his essay with those who are still completely skeptical about the practical value of equality?

3. If you dismissed Pojman's ideas just because he is from Mississippi, the only state until 1995 never to ratify the Constitution's Thirteenth Amendment banning slavery and a state that still has the Confederate flag as part of its state flag, would you commit the *ad hominem* fallacy? Even if you do not dismiss Pojman's ideas entirely, would it be logical or scientific to discount his ideas somewhat given the many observations of racism in Mississippi over many years? Could this discounting establish a rebuttable presumption against Pojman's ideas? Is the Confederate flag a racist symbol of inequality similar to the Nazi swastika?

*4. Pojman defends Jimmy the Greek. If you knew that the innate abilities of different ethnic groups were unequal, how, if at all, would it change your attitudes about discrimination? What if you knew that all groups were essentially the same? Keep the following in mind. On October 23, 1994, the *San Jose Mercury-News* reported that the average difference in IQ scores between blacks and whites is 15 percent and that the average difference in IQ scores between identical twins is 15 percent (p. 12A). Since identical twins are obviously genetically equal to each other, a 15 percent difference in IQ scores is perfectly compatible with genetic equality (that is, innate equality). Indeed, studies show that the range of difference in the IQ scores of blacks and whites is only 10 percent to 15 percent, and the environmental (noninnate) differences between blacks and whites are much greater than the environmental differences between identical twins. For example, the average environment of whites includes more educational and economic advantages than blacks have, and identical twins usually grow up in the same household with similar educational and economic advantages.

5. Does Pojman even mention equality of opportunity? Isn't equality of opportunity what many of the egalitarians seem to argue for, and what America has stood for? Does Pojman miss the point of egalitarianism by ignoring equality of opportunity?

Notes

1. Among the most prominent recent works on equal human rights are: John Baker, *Arguing for Equality* (Verso, 1987); Maurice Cranston, *What Are Human Rights?* (Taplinger, 1973); J. Finnis, *Natural Law and Natural Rights* (Clarendon Press, 1980); Alan Gewirth, *Human Rights* (University of Chicago, 1982); Ronald Dworkin, *Taking Rights Seriously* (Harvard University, 1977); Will Kymlicka, *Contemporary Political Philosophy: An Introduction* (Oxford University, 1990); Rex Martin, *Rawls and Rights* (University of Kansas, 1985); Tibor Machan, *Individual Rights* (Open Court, 1989); James Nickel, *Making Sense of Human Rights* (University of California, 1987); Ellen Frankl Paul, Fred Miller, and Jeffrey Paul, eds., *Human Rights* (Basil Blackwell, 1984); Robert Nozick, *Anarchy, State and Utopia* (Basic Books, 1974); John Rawls, *A Theory of Justice* (Harvard, 1971); Jeremy Waldron, ed., *Theories of Rights* (Oxford University, 1984); Carl Wellman, *A Theory of Rights* (Rowman and Allenheld, 1985) and Morton E. Winston, ed., *The Philosophy of Human Rights* (Wadsworth, 1989). One of the few philosophers to recognize the problems inherent in egalitarianism is Joseph Raz in Chapter 9 of *The Morality of Freedom* (Clarendon Press, 1986).

2. Ronald Dworkin, *Taking Rights Seriously* (Harvard, 1977), pp.179–83).

3. Jacques Maritain, *The Rights of Man* (London, 1944) p. 37. For a good introduction to the significance of human rights see the introduction and readings in *The Philosophies of Human Rights*, ed. Morton Winston (Wadsworth, 1989). Mortimer Adler's statement is representative of contemporary egalitarians: "All human beings are equal as human. Being equal as humans, they are equal in the rights that arise from needs inherent in their common human nature. A constitution is not just if it does not treat equals equally. Nor is it just if it does not recognize the equal right of all to freedom—to be ruled as human beings should be ruled, as citizens, not as slaves or subjects." *Aristotle for Everybody* (Bantam, 1978), p. 114.

4. Ronald Green, *Morality and Religion* (Oxford University Press, 1988), pp. 140f. Green continues, "If we regard morality in minimal terms as a rational means of arbitrating social disputes, a means whose principal alternative is coercion or force, then it is axiomatic that an equal role in the choice of moral principles must be accorded to all parties capable of this means of settlement." In response to Green it should be pointed out that his notion of morality is too narrow. Although resolving conflicts of interest is one goal of morality, it is not the only one. The amelioration of suffering, the promotion of flourishing, and the assignment of praise and blame are also functions of morality. But even if he were correct, that wouldn't give him the conclusion he wants—an equal voice for all parties, for some negotiators might bring more to the bargaining table. Furthermore, equal voice or role does not in itself entail equal worth. I may agree that everyone may have an equal say in a matter, especially if I know I can persuade them to see things my way.

5. Dworkin, "The Original Position," *University of Chicago Law Review*, 40, no. 3 (Spring 1973):532.

6. Thomas Hobbes, *Leviathan* (Bobbs-Merrill, 1958), chapter 10, pp. 79f.

7. R. S. Peters and S. I. Benn, *Social Principles and the Democratic State* (George Allen and Unwin, 1959), chap. 5; R. S. Peters, "Equality and Education," S. I. Benn and R. S. Peters, "Justice and Equality," and Monroe Beardsley, "Equality and Obedience to Law," all in *The Concept of Equality*, W. T. Blackstone, ed. (Burgess Publishing Company, 1960). Benn and Peters recognize the negative character of their definition and appeal to the principle of relevance to fill in the positive content (*Social Principles and the Democratic State*, pp. 111f). E. F. Carritt in *Ethical and Political Thinking* (Oxford, 1947), pp. 156f, writes, "Equality of consideration is the only thing to the whole of which men have a right, [and] it is just to treat men as equal until some reason, other than preference, such as need, capacity, or desert, has been shown to the contrary." James Rachels, *Created from Animals* (Oxford, 1990) also holds this position, and Bruce Ackerman in Chapter I of *Social Justice in the Liberal State* (Yale, 1980) seems to hold a version of it. Some of the points made in this section and sections 3 and 6 were made in "A Critique of Contemporary Egalitarianism," *Faith and Philosophy* (October, 1991).

8. Ronald Dworkin, *Taking Rights Seriously*, p. 184.

9. Kai Nielsen, *Equality and Liberty* (Rowman and Allenheld, 1985), p. 95.

10. Nozick in *Anarchy, State and Utopia* (Blackwell, 1874), pp. ix, 30f.

11. Tibor Machan, *Individuals and Their Rights* (Open Court, 1989), xxiv. For Machan's views on freedom of the will, see pp. 14f.

12. David Gauthier, *Morals by Agreement* (Oxford University Press, 1986), pp. 14; 55ff; 222. Even Gauthier finds himself pushed onto the egalitarian plateau, holding the Hobbesian idea that people are more or less equal in their ability to harm others, in their vulnerability to being harmed, and in their bargaining power, but I doubt this very much. The strong and clever can do more damage to others and

have more to bring to the bargaining table. Gauthier's theory could work in an inegalitarian framework.

13. Gregory Vlastos, "Justice and Equality," *Theories of Rights*, ed. Jeremy Waldron (Oxford, 1984), p. 51. Cf. note 16. I have taken the next few paragraphs from my article "Egalitarianism: Secular and Religious" (*Faith and Philosophy*, forthcoming).

14. Joel Feinberg, *Social Philosophy* (Prentice-Hall, 1973), pp. 93f.

15. See Barry Gross, "The Case of Philippe Rushton," *Academic Questions* vol. 3:4 (1990).

16. Kai Nielsen, "On Not Needing to Justify Equality," *International Studies in Philosophy*, vol. XX/3 (1988), pp. 55–71.

17. Alan Gewirth, *Reason and Morality* (University of Chicago, 1978), "Epistemology of Human Rights" in *Human Rights*, ed. Ellen Paul, Fred Miller, and Jeffrey Paul (Blackwell, 1984), and *Human Rights: Essays on Justification and Applications* (University of Chicago, 1982).

18. Tom Nagel, *A View from Nowhere* (Oxford University Press, 1986) and *Equality and Impartiality* (Oxford University Press, 1991), p. 11.

19. Robert Nisbet, "The Pursuit of Equality" *The Public Interest* vol. 35 (1974), 103–20.

20. Michael Sandel, *Liberalism and the Limits of Justice* (Cambridge University Press, 1982), p. 88.

21. John Harsanyi, *Essays in Ethics, Social Behavior and Scientific Explanation* (Reidel, 1976), and Harry Frankfurt, "Equality as a Moral Ideal" *Ethics* vol. 98:1 (Oct. 1987).

22. Versions of this paper were read to the Graduate Philosophy Colloquium at the City of New York University and at the Pacific Division of the American Philosophical Association. The commentator Donald Blackeley provided excellent comments which led to an improved paper. I am also indebted to Sterling Harwood, Tziporah Kasachkoff, Michael Levin, Peter Simpson, Robert Westmoreland, and an anonymous reviewer for this journal for comments on previous drafts of this paper.

13

Why Be Moral?: A Definition and Defense of Humanism

Sterling Harwood

Author's abstract: This article tries to go beyond what was said in the introduction to Part I to show more reasons why one should be moral.

Whatever new world order or chaos is underway seems to allow some room for humanism. Humanitarian military operations (for example, in Bosnia and Somalia) are the order of the day. But what is humanism and why should we do—or defend—humanist acts? Everyone from Karl Marx to Daisaku Ikeda to Jean-Paul Sartre to Ted Turner to Martin Buber to Bill Clinton has been termed a humanist. No doubt Phil, Oprah, and Geraldo also have claims to be humanists, given their concern to expose the wide variety of human suffering. Any philosophy encompassing such a diverse group of people will be hard to define precisely. But humanism and humanitarianism seem interchangeable. And humanism, true to its name, stresses the importance of humans. So is humanism an indefensible form of discriminatory anthropocentrism, a species chauvinism analogous to racism and sexism? Consider this exchange from the film *Star Trek VI*:

Chekov: We do believe all planets have a sovereign claim to inalienable human rights.

Klingon: "Inalien" . . . if you could only hear yourselves. "Human rights" . . . why, the very name is racist. The Federation is no more than a *homo sapiens*–only club.

Humanism needs a new name to avoid connotations of discrimination against nonhuman species. But humanism's main idea seems to require caring about

the well-being of others. "Others" is broad enough to include other species. After all, *humane* societies are on the frontlines preventing mistreatment of (non-human) animals. And if you won't believe me about how inclusive humanism can be, then consider these words of wisdom from Captain Kirk in *Star Trek VI*:

Kirk: Human beings . . .

Spock: But Captain, we both know I am not human.

Kirk: Spock, you wanna know something: everybody's human.

Humanism may sound, as many philosophies do initially, too abstract. As John Lennon quipped, "You wanna save humanity, but it's people that you just can't stand." But the relevant literature makes clear that humanists often emphasize the individual. Thus, humanism seems to strike a balance between individuals and abstract humanity, and does so at least as well as feminism's ethics of care (based on Carol Gilligan's views). This form of feminism wants to distinguish itself sharply from liberalism's individualism yet to insist—as W. D. Ross did long ago—that all moral judgments must avoid absolute general rules and instead stress caring about the particulars that pertain to the individual facing a moral choice. This feminism seeks to stress the individual's social context rather than rules, but this poses a false dichotomy since the social context of nearly all individuals consists largely of rules. Feminists might embrace the balance as a contradiction while left/liberal humanists embrace it as an egalitarian leveling of the scales of justice. But I see precious little difference between the best versions of feminism or humanism. So perhaps we have found a better name for humanism: care ethics. (OK, "care ethics" is not a real "ism," but give me a break, at least it's better than "give-a-damn ethics"! And what's in a name anyway?) Humanism and feminism could converge. Lennon, for example, made a fascinating try to embrace both. Compare Lennon's humanist "Imagine" and his feminist "Woman Is the Nigger of the World." Lennon also mocked the sexist saying "Women should be seen and not heard" when he ridiculed the view as "Women should be obscene and not heard."

Humanism still needs a defense. Why care about others enough to act morally? It won't do to try to ground a morality in human capacities per se, since there are morally bad human capacities—for example, the capacity for cruelty. (I'm not illogically appealing to the authority of The King, but Elvis did command "Don't be cruel," at least to a love that's true.) Nicholas Rescher addresses morality's key question: "Why be moral?" "Why should I act morally?" puts the matter more clearly and concretely. Rescher believes that H. A. Prichard correctly answered this question. Rescher says, "It makes no real sense to ask 'Why should I be moral?' For once an act is recognized as being the morally appropriate thing to do, there is really no room for any further question . . ." Rescher suggests the question resembles "Why believe the true?," to which one should answer, simply, "Because it *is* true." The truth is always inherently worthy of belief. No further reason for belief is needed. One may object that Rescher commits the fallacy of false analogy, since belief is so involuntary and since voluntariness is the hallmark of actions for which we are morally responsible. But I think the question "Why should I act morally?" can be answered after trying to understand its component question "Should I act morally?" "Should I act morally?," which we can rephrase as "Should I do the moral act?," is analogous to "Could I do the moral act?" Once an act is admitted to be possible, the question answers itself: yes, of course you could do the possible act. Similarly, once an act is admitted to be moral, "Should I act morally?" answers itself: yes, of course you should do the moral act. So, the answer to "Why should I act morally?" is that the self-answering "Should I act morally?" shows how it is the very meaning of a moral act that it should be done. Rescher dismisses Prichard's analysis as perfectly correct but unpersuasive to those who are already moral skeptics. Yet persuasiveness is overrated; it's enough for Prichard to be, as Rescher says he is, "perfectly correct." Further, correctness is underrated, as shown by the antihumanist smear campaign against "political correctness" and anti-intellectual smears of "egghead" and "know-it-all." As Lennon sang, "They hate you if you're clever and they despise a fool." How we discover what's humanist or moral in a particular case is a question for another day, but scientifically or empirically discovering the factors rational and clever people use to decide is obviously a logical and intelligent start toward an answer.

Study Questions

1. Some think that humanism, by definition, must be antireligious or nonreligious. But if this were so, wouldn't the common phrase "secular humanist" be redundant?

2. Is humanism a moral philosophy that essentially accepts the *prima facie* principles of beneficence and nonmaleficence?

3. Is the following another reason to be moral? One way to ground morality on rationality is to see what rational people care about. Rational people care about their happiness, liberty, and getting their fair share and not being discriminated against. A person who cared about none of these things would be considered irrational. Such people would be a danger to themselves or others, since they would not care about walking out in front of a car, for example. Science is at least somewhat objective. And psychology is a science, although not an exact one. Psychology tells us that people who lose interest in life and their own happiness suffer from the mental illness of depression. There is a clinical definition of depression that is associated with irrational behavior. So utilitarianism, which promotes happiness, libertarianism, which promotes liberty, and egalitarianism, which promotes fairness and fights discrimination, must each be at least plausible starting points for any rational person in deciding what he or she should do.

4. Whose views on humanism are more plausible, Harwood's or Pojman's?

*5. What do you feel society owes you simply because you are a citizen and a human being? What do you feel you owe in return?

14

Benevolence

Sterling Harwood

Type of ethics: Theory of ethics.

Date: Coined 1384.

Associated with: Thomas Aquinas, Richard Cumberland, Jonathan Edwards, Carol Gilligan, William Goodwin, Johann Friedrich Herbart, humanitarians, David Hume, Francis Hutcheson, Earl of Shaftesbury, Henry Sidgwick, and virtue ethicists.

Definition: Benevolence is a motivation to act sympathetically and altruistically.

Significance: Hume considered benevolence the foundation of ethics, and many people believe that the central task of ethics is encouraging benevolence, but ethical egoism and Friedrich Nietzsche consider benevolence unethical.

Thomas Aquinas, David Hume, and many others consider benevolence or altruism a key virtue. As Mike W. Martin acutely observes, "Hume makes [benevolence] the supreme virtue, and of all virtue ethicists Hume most deserves to be called the philosopher of benevolence." Jonathan Edwards considers benevolence the supreme virtue in Christianity. Hume believes that benevolent acts are natural products of two features of human nature: sympathy and imagination. Sympathy generates altruistic desires, while imagination enables one to see oneself in the shoes of others in need and conclude, "There but for the grace of God or good fortune go I."

Charity is a virtue that involves benevolence. Martin reports some hard data on charity: (1) rich people and wealthy foundations account for only 10

percent of private donations; (2) the remaining 90 percent comes from individuals, half of them in families whose income is under $39,000; (3) about half of Americans older than thirteen volunteer an average of 3.5 hours of their time each week. Horace Mann used the concept of benevolence to try to distinguish between the ethical value of generosity during the prime of life (for example, teenage volunteers) and deathbed generosity. He said, "Generosity during life is a very different thing from generosity in the hour of death; one proceeds from genuine liberality and benevolence, the other from pride or fear."

In law, mortmain statutes forbid deathbed gifts, apparently out of concern that the gift may be motivated by desperate fear rather than genuine benevolence. Law often encourages benevolence by providing tax deductions for charitable donations, but traditional Anglo-American law (unlike Islamic law, for example) imposes no general duty to rescue strangers and thus fails to require much benevolence.

Regarding political and business ethics, some people argue that the welfare state institutionalizes benevolence and charity. They contend that welfare state programs such as those that mandate minimum wages and relief payments smooth some of the rough edges of laissez-faire capitalism, which is notorious for its cutthroat competition. The alternative of relying on private donations to charity, they believe, will tend to fail precisely when charity is needed most, during an economic recession or depression. During such hard times, people will have less to give for charity and will be less willing to give what they do have as a result of economic insecurity. These trends will intensify as the number of charity cases grows and the need for charitable giving grows with them.

In political ethics and in debates on sex and gender issues, benevolence plays a crucial role. While many feminists try to debunk stereotypes of women as the more emotional and illogical sex, other feminists support the idea that women have a special ethical outlook called Care Ethics. The latter feminists follow Carol Gilligan in suggesting that women are generally more cooperative and less confrontational than men. Care Ethics claims that women are generally less interested in dealing with abstract rules and impersonal ideals such as justice and impartiality and are more interested in nurturing personal relationships by attending to the specifics of the backgrounds or surroundings of particular people. This view seems self-contradictory, however, since so much of the specific backgrounds of particular people consists of rules, which Care Ethics was designed to

Reprinted from Sterling Harwood, "Benevolence," in *Ready Reference: Ethics* (Pasadena, Calif.: Salem Press, 1994). Reprinted by permission.

deemphasize. Such contradictions do not deter some feminists, who openly embrace inconsistency while criticizing traditional ethics for being male-dominated and logocentric. Unfortunately, aside from its obvious illogic, this view has the defect of playing into the hands of those who would stereotype women as more prone to hysteria and inconsistent mood swings between emotional extremes (for example, the view that it is a woman's prerogative to change her mind). Some feminists thus regard Care Ethics as making a retrograde step in the women's movement.

Ethical egoism and the thinking of Friedrich Nietzsche condemn benevolence. Ethical egoists, such as Ayn Rand, think that each person should always act only in his or her own self-interest. In contrast, Johann Friedrich Herbart argued that benevolence involves the harmonization of one's will with others' wills. Nietzsche's concept of the will to power rejects such harmony between wills. One's will to power involves one's domination of the weak.

In conclusion, it would be appropriate to ponder Walter Bagehot's view that "The most melancholy of human reflections, perhaps, is that, on the whole, it is a question whether the benevolence of mankind does most good or harm."

Study Questions

1. If we added a requirement to maximize benevolence, would that give us the same requirement as utilitarianism?

2. What is the difference between benevolence and beneficence?

*3. If you had to make a difficult sacrifice in either your career or your marriage, which would you choose? For example, what if you had to either forgo a long-sought promotion or move overseas for two years, uprooting your whole family against their wishes?

*4. Do you behave as a "good citizen" even when you know your small action will make no real difference—for example, do you ever pick up other people's litter?

*5. If you knew that famine and disease brought about by overpopulation would claim a quarter of the babies born in this decade, how much of the defense budget would you divert to programs to reduce the birth rate? Assume there is *no* other source of money. Many refuse to be benevolent to help with

problems of overpopulation because they think that would subsidize self-indulgent sexual behavior. But having a larger family is not self-indulgent or a luxury but logical and a practical necessity in the Third World. For example, Third World countries generally have no social security programs. People have larger families so they will have a child to support them in their old age. This is especially important because so many of their children die before the parents reach old age. Further, many in the Third World need cheap labor to farm food, and so they need to put more of their own children to work in the field.

*6. To what extent are others responsible for taking care of you when you suffer calamity? Obviously, the better the care provided to relieve such suffering, the more it costs; what percentage of your income would you be willing to spend to provide a safety net for everyone? In your opinion, what care should such a safety net include—regardless of cost?

Bibliography

Broad, C. D., *Five Types of Ethical Theory* (London: Routledge & Kegan Paul, 1956).

Gauthier, David P., ed., *Morality and Rational Self-interest* (Englewood Cliffs, N.J.: Prentice-Hall, 1970).

Gilligan, Carol, *In a Different Voice: Psychological Theory and Women's Development* (Cambridge: Harvard University Press, 1982).

Kaufmann, Harry, *Aggression and Altruism* (New York: Holt, Rinehart and Winston, 1970).

Martin, Mike W., *Everyday Morality: An Introduction to Applied Ethics* (Belmont, Calif: Wadsworth, 1989).

Nagel, Thomas, *The Possibility of Altruism* (Oxford: Clarendon Press, 1970).

Peters, R. S., *The Concept of Motivation*, 2d ed. (New York: Huntington Press, 1967).

Pojman, Louis P., *Ethics: Discovering Right and Wrong* (Belmont, Calif.: Wadsworth, 1990).

Prichard, H. A., *Duty and Interest* (Oxford: Clarendon Press, 1928).

Rand, Ayn, *The Virtue of Selfishness: A New Concept of Egoism* (New York: New American Library, 1964).

Rescher, Nicholas, *Unselfishness: The Role of the Vicarious Affects in Moral Philosophy and Social Theory* (Pittsburgh: University of Pittsburgh Press, 1975).

Singer, Peter, *The Expanding Circle: Ethics and Sociobiology* (New York: Farrar, Straus & Giroux, 1981).

Wilson, Edward O., *On Human Nature* (Cambridge: Harvard University Press, 1978).

15

Accountability

Sterling Harwood

Type of ethics: Theory of ethics.

Date: Coined 1794; the relevant sense of "account" dates back to 1340.

Associated with: Compatibilism and metaphysical libertarianism.

Definition: The state of being responsible, liable, answerable, or obligated.

Significance: Moralities generally require accountability, either individual or collective, before ethical evaluations can assign praise or blame.

Accountability can be either individual or collective, but the latter has been much more controversial (for example, the alleged collective responsibility of Germans for Nazi atrocities). Ethicists usually believe that individual accountability applies to any free or voluntary act. Accountability is thus a key concept in morality and metaphysics.

One key doctrine that is related to accountability is compatibilism, the view that the causal determination of actions is consistent with moral responsibility for those actions. For example, a compatibilist holds that one would still be accountable for one's actions even if a scientist or god could predict all of those actions in detail. Compatibilism is a metaphysical doctrine that is relevant to ethics. Incompatibilists claim that the causal determination of one's acts would prevent one from having the freedom necessary for having moral accountability for one's acts. Metaphysical libertarianism (which is completely

distinct from political libertarianism) endorses incompatibilism but allows for accountability by denying that acts are causally determined. Another key doctrine here is the idea that "ought" implies "can," which denies that an agent can be accountable for failing to do the impossible. Accountability assumes that there is a duty (that is, a responsibility or obligation) that one is to discharge. One can generally be held to account for failure to do one's duty. As Joseph F. Newton wrote, "A duty dodged is like a debt unpaid; it is only deferred, and we must come back and settle the account at last."

Accountability is a key concept in law, where ethical issues are often discussed in terms of liability. Strict liability implies that one is responsible even if one is not at fault. Thus, strict liability seems to be inconsistent with the doctrine that ought implies can. Vicarious liability is responsibility for harm done by another (for example, one's child). Product liability is a field of law that holds manufacturers and merchants accountable for defective goods that they sell. Legal liability is the most general term for exposure to being held to account by a court or other legal institution. To be legally liable is to be subject to punishment or to an order to provide compensation to at least help make up for one's infraction.

Accountability is a key concept in politics. The Left (liberals, socialists, and communists) often calls for increased social responsibility for corporations and social elites, and often criticizes the allegedly unaccountable power that corporations and elites wield. The Right (conservatives, traditionalists, and fascists) often calls for people to take more responsibility for their own actions, and often criticizes individuals for allegedly shirking their duties by claiming to be victims of circumstance or of society. The importance of accountability is thus something about which the political moralities of the Left and the Right seem to agree.

Some people argue that corporations cannot be accountable, because, first, they are not persons or agents that are distinct from corporate employees, and, second, praise and blame can apply only to distinct agents. Others argue that corporations are agents, since they have internal decisio-making structures, which arguably provide enough of a chain of command for ethicists to attribute acts to corporations as distinct from merely attributing the acts to some individual or some subset of the corporation's employees. Some argue that the whole is greater than the sum of its parts in this case. Even if no single employee were held accountable for a bad result, for

Reprinted from Sterling Harwood, "Accountability," in *Ready Reference: Ethics* (Pasadena, Calif.: Salem Press, 1994). Reprinted by permission.

example, the corporation could still be held accountable. Synergistic effects of individual acts of employees can produce corporate accountability for an immoral outcome. To deny this possibility would seem to be to commit the fallacy of composition, which assumes that whatever is true of each part of a whole (in this case, unaccountability) must be true of the whole as well.

Study Questions

*1. Do you believe that collective responsibility and guilt are possible? Do you have any examples of them?

*2. How can a corporation be responsible or accountable as an entity, over and above the responsibility and accountability of its individual employees?

*3. What financial transaction of yours would be most difficult to justify to others if it became public knowledge?

*4. If someone you had just hired wasn't doing a very good job, would you be more inclined to get rid of the person or try to help him or her improve?

*5. If you were cheated by a business but didn't have the resources to pursue a court battle, what would you do?

*6. Should corporations try to behave as "moral" creatures, or is any sacrifice of profit a betrayal of the interests of the shareholders? Many parties are affected by any corporation: shareholders, employees, customers, suppliers, the surrounding community. Whose interests should be of primary concern to upper management? How strongly should the interests of others be considered? Should we judge corporations just as we do people, on the basis of not only their success but also their integrity?

*7. Imagine you lost your thumb because of your own carelessness with a power saw. If you knew you could collect a lot of money even though the accident was your fault, would you sue the manufacturer? What if you knew that to win the suit you would have to lie under oath?

*8. In what ways—if any—do you apply looser ethical standards when you deal with large companies rather than individuals? For example, would you consider it theft to take a few tablets of paper home from an office at a big corporation? What about from a friend's house? If you do apply looser standards, does this mean that the increasing presence in your

life of large corporations has made your overall behavior less ethical?

*9. If you accidentally damaged merchandise in a store, would you tell someone or try to hide what you had done? What if the damage were so subtle you knew it would go unnoticed until someone bought the item and tried to use it? Would you ever buy something, use it, and return it just because you grew tired of it?

*10. When managers foster an environment that tolerates questionable methods of achieving goals, to what extent should they be held accountable for resultant excesses, even if they are unaware of them?

*11. If late one night you left a door at work unlocked and someone vandalized the place, would you admit your carelessness? Assume that no one knows you were there.

Bibliography

Adkins, Arthur W., *Merit and Responsibility: A Study in Greek Values* (New York: Oxford University Press, 1960).

Erikson, Erik H., *Insight and Responsibility* (New York: Norton, 1964).

Fischer, John Martin, ed., *Moral Responsibility* (Ithaca, N.Y.: Cornell University Press, 1984).

French, Peter, *Individual and Collective Responsibility: Massacre at My Lai* (Cambridge, Mass.: Schenkman, 1972).

————, *The Spectrum of Responsibility* (New York: St. Martin's Press, 1991).

Glover, Jonathan, *Responsibility* (Atlantic Highlands, N.J.: Humanitarian Press, 1970).

Gorr, Michael J., and Sterling Harwood, eds., *Controversies in Criminal Law: Philosophical Essays on Liability and Procedure* (Boulder, Colo.: Westview Press, 1992).

Hart, Herbert L., *Punishment and Responsibility: Essays in the Philosophy of Law* (New York: Oxford University Press, 1968).

Kenny, Anthony, *Freewill and Responsibility* (Boston: Routledge & Kegan Paul, 1978).

May, Larry, and Stacey Hoffman, eds., *Collective Responsibility: Five Decades of Debate in Theoretical and Applied Ethics* (Savage, Md.: Rowman & Littlefield, 1991).

Morris, Herbert, *Guilt and Shame* (Belmont, Calif.: Wadsworth, 1971).

Nadel, Mark V., *Corporations and Political Accountability* (Lexington, Mass.: D.C. Heath, 1976).

Walton, Clarence C., *Corporate Social Responsibilities* (Belmont, Calif.: Wadsworth, 1967).

16

Prescriptivism

Sterling Harwood

Type of ethics: Theory of ethics.

Date: Coined in 1952 by Richard Mervyn Hare.

Associated with: Richard Mervyn Hare.

Definition: The theory that the main meaning and purpose of moral language is to prescribe or command.

Significance: Prescriptivism implies that ethical knowledge as such does not exist.

Hare's view has received at least five important criticisms. First, his view that morality consists only of commands implies that ethical knowledge is impossible, since a command, unlike an indicative statement, cannot be true. Second, his view that anyone who accepts a moral statement and can act on it will obey the command has counterexamples in apathetic and evil people who knowingly refuse to do what they admit is ethically required. Third, the great variety of uses of moral claims makes it unlikely that they can all be reduced to imperatives. Fourth, F. E. Sparshott believes that Hare neglects the fact that any morality must incorporate "those rules of conduct that seem necessary for communal living." Fifth, P. H. Nowell-Smith reduces Hare's theory to the absurd by exposing its implication that "Nothing that we discover about the nature of moral judgments entails that it is wrong to put all Jews in gas-chambers."

In ethics and religion, prescriptivism sometimes refers not to Hare's theory but to the theory that the only justifications for moral claims are the commands of some authority (such as God). Socrates criticized this view in Plato's *Euthyphro*, where he suggested that an act was not good only because God commanded it but that God commanded the act because it was independently good.

Study Questions

1. Do you think the criticisms offered of Hare's view are sound?

2. Hare is a utilitarian. Is this consistent with his prescriptivism? Is utilitarianism a form of moral realism while prescriptivism is a form of moral relativism or skepticism?

*3. If you knew that when you died you would immediately be reincarnated as the next baby born in the world, how—if at all—would your attitudes change about foreign aid, international politics, and birth control? (Note that 90 percent of all births now are in the poorer regions of the world.)

*4. When doing business with strangers, do you generally approach a deal more with suspicion or with trust? Do you begin a new romance any differently?

*5. Generally do you work harder to earn praise and regard or to avoid criticism and punishment? All told, have you yourself dispensed more criticism or praise?

*6. If everyone would follow your lead, would you adjust your life so as to sharply reduce the mileage you drive? If the price of gasoline doubled, would you use your car much less than you do now?

Reprinted from Sterling Harwood, "Prescriptivism," in *Ready Reference: Ethics* (Pasadena, Calif.: Salem Press, 1994). Reprinted by permission.

17

Needs

Sterling Harwood

A need is commonly conceived in either of two ways: (1) as a means required for some end, or (2) as a biological or psychological requirement of an organism that, if unmet, will damage that organism. The first sense of the word is often called the "relative conception" of needs, since it understands the existence of any need as depending on its relation to some particular end. The second sense of need is often called the "absolute conception," since it commonly concerns basics such as food, water, shelter, and health care, which are unconditionally required for survival.

Some have tried to reduce all needs to either one or the other of these two conceptions, but there is no consensus that anyone has achieved either goal. But there is a significant consensus that needs can be not only natural (e.g., food) but also conventional. For example, philosophers as different as Adam Smith and Karl Marx each wrote that a shirt was a need in society. Smith wrote: "By necessaries I understand, not only the commodities which are indispensably necessary for the support of life, but whatever the custom of the country renders it indecent for creditable people, even of the lowest order, to be without." Further, Marx discussed the conventional swelling of needs in "keeping up with the Joneses" by suggesting that many will feel a need for a bigger house once the house next to theirs is expanded.

This capacity of needs to swell so quickly and easily has led many libertarians and other capitalists to have ambivalent, inconsistent, or even hostile attitudes toward emphatic efforts to meet needs. On one hand, capitalists often emphasize the greatness of capitalism in using the profit motive to give producers a driving incentive to meet consumers' needs more efficiently than any other economic system known. On the other hand, facing massive starvation and poverty in a world largely dominated by capitalism, capitalists often deny that emphasizing meeting needs per se is useful or even tolerable. For

example, Antony Flew states, "An emphasis upon needs as opposed to wants cannot but appeal to those who would like to see themselves as experts qualified both to determine what the needs of others are, and to prescribe and enforce the means appropriate to the satisfaction of those needs." Capitalists fear demands for the right to realize Marx's requirement "From each according to ability, to each according to need." In short, these capitalists praise ambition but condemn envy, though both seem fundamentally similar, if not identical, needs to outdo others.

To escape this ambivalence about needs, some try to reduce needs to mere preferences (wants or desires). Economists often clash with psychologists here, because many economists want to reduce the urgency and rhetorical force of meeting needs to merely some preferences among many others while many psychologists follow Abraham Maslow in accepting a hierarchy of needs, ranked in order of importance. For example, the longer one can go undamaged without an item, the less likely that item is to be a high-ranking need. Further, the greater the damage incurred without an item, the more likely it is to be a high-ranking need. David Braybrooke argues against reducing all needs to preferences. He writes: "There is no contradiction between a person having a set of needs and her preferring not to have any of them met; people can and do prefer on occasion not to go on living, and they act on that preference by disregarding their needs . . . " But his example fails, since he overlooks the needs to relieve suffering or save money for one's family, assuming the case he has in mind is rational euthanasia rather than irrational suicide, which would be an irrational foundation for understanding needs.

Reducing needs to preferences seems more feasible with the relative conception than with the absolute conception of needs. Preferences serve as ends, and the required means to that end are needs in the relative sense. But absolute needs often seem irreducible to preferences. For example, a baby or an unconscious adult often needs medical care, but do they prefer the medical care? It seems not, unless one counts hypothetical preferences, what one would prefer under certain ideal conditions. But explaining needs in terms of hypothetical preferences seems unsatisfactory, since hypothetical preferences are much more inexplicable, abstract, and speculative than needs were in the first place. Everything hinges on the technical arguments over what conditions are deemed ideal. An explanation should not be more inexplicable than what it seeks to explain. Complicating analysis here is that needs and preferences are matters of degree. For example, we can sensibly ask, "How badly do you need a new car?" or "How great is your need to buy that?" Absolute needs are often more urgent than mere preferences, but even they will often shade off by degrees into actual preferences.

At the most fundamental level, needs are equalizers, since even though some people have special needs or even embarrassing needs, we all have many basic needs in common. For example, a tycoon in a palace or limousine who is seemingly without a need or care in the world one moment can the next moment easily be reduced (e.g., by an earthquake) to a charity case in dire need of medical care. Our common needs make many reflect on the old saying "There but for the grace of God or good fortune go I." Some emerge from this reflection optimistically, or perhaps idealistically, in resolving to try to reduce dramatically the role of luck in meeting needs. Others emerge pessimistically, or perhaps realistically, by fatalistically resigning themselves to the prospect that, without a lot of luck, needs will not be met. These are two ends of a spectrum along which many approaches appear in business ethics, which surely has room for both idealism and realism about needs.

Study Questions

1. Which conception of needs is the best, the relative conception or the absolute conception?

2. Does each conception of needs capture part of the truth?

3. Can all needs be reduced to mere desires? Can most needs be reduced to mere desires? Which, if any, needs cannot be reduced to mere desires?

4. Do all innocent people have a moral right that their most basic needs (for example, for food, simple clothing, shelter, and necessary medicine) be met somehow in society? If not, why not? If so, which moral principles would best support such a right?

5. Since the world is largely dominated by capitalism, does your inspection of the world show that capitalism has done an adequate job providing for the basic needs of the world's people? What single change would most increase the meeting of people's basic needs?

6. Can most people who are well off see how lucky they are? Can they understand that "There but

for the grace of God or good fortune go I" applies to them? Or is there an inevitable tendency in those who are well off to think that tragic things only happen to somebody else?

Bibliography

Braybrooke, David, *Meeting Needs* (Princeton, N.J.: Princeton University Press, 1987). [criticizes all definitions of need]

Heller, Agnes, *The Theory of Need in Marx* (Alison & Busby, 1976).

Ignatieff, Michael, *The Needs of Strangers* (Chatto & Windus, 1984).

Katz, Leo, "The Defense of Necessity," in Michael J. Gorr and Sterling Harwood, eds., *Controversies in Criminal Law: Philosophical Essays on Responsibility and Procedure* (Boulder, Colo.: Westview Press, 1992).

Leiss, William, *The Limits of Satisfaction: An Essay on the Problem of Needs and Commodities* (University of Toronto Press, 1976).

Martin, Rex, "Poverty and Welfare in Rawls's Theory of Justice: On the Just Response to Needs," in Kenneth Kipnis and Diana T. Meyers, eds., *Economic Justice: Private Rights and Public Responsibilities* (Rowman and Allanheld, 1985), pp. 161–175.

Marx, Karl, *Capital*, Vol. 1 (1867). Many editions. [a classic of socialism]

Maslow, Abraham, *Dominance, Self-Esteem, Self-Actualization: Germinal Papers of A. H. Maslow*, ed. Richard J. Lowry (Brooks/Cole Publishers, 1973). [classic work in psychology]

Maslow, Abraham, *Motivation and Personality* (New York: Harper & Row, 1970). [classic work in psychology]

McCloskey, H. J., "Human Needs, Rights and Political Values," *American Philosophical Quarterly* 13 (1976), pp. 1–11.

Miller, David, *Social Justice* (The Clarendon Press, 1976).

Smith, Adam, *The Wealth of Nations* (1776). Many editions. [a classic of capitalism]

Soper, Kate, *On Human Needs: Open and Closed Theories in a Marxist Perspective* (Harvester Press, 1981).

Springborg, Patricia, *The Problem of Human Needs and the Critique of Civilization* (Allen & Unwin, 1981).

White, Alan, *Modal Thinking* (Ithaca, N.Y.: Cornell University Press, 1975).

Wiggins, David, "Claims of Need," in Ted Honderich, ed., *Morality and Objectivity: A Tribute to J. L. Mackie* (Routledge & Kegan Paul, 1985).

Wollheim, Richard, "Needs, Desires and Moral Turpitude," in R. S. Peters, ed., *Nature and Conduct* (New York: Macmillan, 1975), pp. 162–180.

PART III

Cultural Challenges to Business as Usual:
From Racism to the Rat Race

18

Introduction: The Pros and Cons of Affirmative Action (AA)

Sterling Harwood

PROS

1. Compensatory justice: reparations remedying past injustice of racial discrimination. Analogy: If I steal your watch and give it to my innocent son before I die, you or your son are justified in repossessing the watch.
2. Diversity in education and employment. Powell's reason in the Bakke case.
3. Many more role models, which provide greater motivation for blacks to achieve in school.
4. Greater competition and a larger pool to draw from.
5. Preventing or offsetting capitalism's magnification of disadvantage. The rich get richer and the poor get poorer.
6. Replacing diminishing marginal utility of jobs for richer whites with greater utility for poorer blacks. Average black family income is only 56 percent of average white family income.

CONS

1. AA is an unjust means used for a just end. Discrimination is inherently bad, even if used to discriminate against those guilty of racism.
   Rebuttal: Discrimination is failing to treat relevantly like cases alike and relevantly different cases differently. So-called reverse discrimination does not fit that definition, since there is a relevant difference between blacks and whites, namely, that only blacks have been victims of such severe and systematic racial discrimination. Only blacks deserve so much compensation. There is less, or nothing, to compensate whites for.
2. Innocent whites are hurt for the sins of their fathers, which is unjust.
   Rebuttal: The hurting is merely the absence of the unfair advantage that the father had. Suppose a black person has been handicapped by past racism, and a white person has been neither helped nor handicapped by past racism. There's nothing wrong with using AA to remove the black's handicap so that the black and the white can compete on an equal and fair basis. The white's innocence does not entitle him to the same unfair advantage that other whites had.
3. AA accepts lower quality applicants.
   Rebuttal: Scores are skewed to begin with. Tests are often class-biased. A lower score under adverse circumstances often shows more ability that does a higher score under nearly optimum conditions. And AA can even be a mere tiebreaker.
4. AA reinforces racial resentment and the stereotype that blacks are inferior and need help to be equal to whites.
   Rebuttals: (a) Without AA the absence of blacks will reinforce the same stereotype of inferiority; (b) exposure to blacks will give white people direct experience on which they can conclude that blacks are not inferior; and (c) not all racial resentment should be respected, since some of it is racist (e.g., the KKK will resent AA no matter what).
5. Women don't deserve AA as much as blacks do, since women usually marry, and so the disadvantages of sexism are rarely passed on to offspring, since the man's sexist advantages roughly cancel out the woman's sexist disadvantages.
   Rebuttal: Con 5 has a point, but the point is at least greatly weakened by the following: (a) Many mothers are unwed, divorced, or widowed; (b) AA combats current sexism; (c) Con 5 would reinforce and perpetuate old stereotypes by financially encouraging women to become financially dependent on men, in order to cancel out the effects of sexism; and (d) sexist roles of parents pass sexism to kids.

19

The Justice of Affirmative Action

Sterling Harwood

I. Introduction

Recent decisions suggest the Supreme Court is retreating somewhat from a vigorous defense and application of affirmative action (AA, for short). Some liberals advocate legislative action to restore the vigor of AA. So this essay's look as the legislative, policy grounds for AA is timely.

It is becoming accepted that "No single development of the past fifteen years [or so] has turned more liberals into former liberals than" AA.[1] The familial autonomy I discuss concerns inheritance. I will primarily provide a liberal defense of AA and, secondarily, in doing so suggest a (partial, at least) reconciliation of the triad. Liberalism's definition is a subject unto itself, and so I will not explore it here, especially since AA is independently important. I assume that liberalism involves justice.[2] I will focus on AA for blacks, though one can make parallel arguments for other racial or ethnic minorities. I will briefly discuss some differences in the case for AA for women. I will rebut arguments that AA is unjust, and argue that, on the contrary, justice *requires* AA.

II. Compensatory Justice Requires AA

Discussions of AA often begin badly. Many start off on the wrong foot by misleadingly defining or labeling AA. It is not neutral to talk of AA as *preferential* treatment that *favors* blacks, since such talk misleadingly suggests that AA is merely doing blacks a favor rather than giving blacks their just deserts.[3] Call-

Reprinted from Yeager Hudson and Creighton Peden, eds., *The Bill of Right s: Bicentennial Reflections* (Lewiston, N. Y.: Edwin Mellen Press, 1993), pp. 77–89.

ing AA preferential treatment suggests unfair favoritism based on mere preferences rather than deserved restitution based on justice.

Similarly, R. Fullinwider defines AA in hiring as: "where a person is hired *because* he or she is a black, a woman . . . etc., and where these characteristics are irrelevant to job performance."[4] The word that makes his definition misleading is "because." The reason AA selects more blacks is not that blackness per se is preferred. Rather, AA selects blacks because blacks have been traditionally, systematically, and profoundly discriminated against, and thus justice entitles blacks to compensation. The justification I offer for AA claims that AA is required by compensatory justice, which involves reparations remedying the current, unfair effects of past racism. Such AA does not select someone because he is black, but because he is a victim. His blackness is merely very strong evidence that he is a victim of racism. AA is perfectly compatible with a system that generally selects more blacks, except blacks who are shown never to have been victims of racism, and who thus deserve no compensation for suffering the injustice of racism.

Some would place on blacks the burden of proving that they are victims of racism. But racism against blacks has been so thoroughgoing, systematic, and pervasive throughout America's history, that history more than establishes a strong presumption of any American black's victimization. Since any black is presumably a victim, and since proving racism is usually hard, the fair and efficient procedure would be to put the burden of proof of non-discrimination on those who oppose AA. One may object that AA is unjust because some blacks who are not victims of racism will undeservedly receive compensation. But the objection violates "'ought' implies 'can,'" since any administrative procedure dealing with millions of people will imperfectly identify who deserve aid. The alternatives of banning AA or placing on blacks the burden of proof of discrimination would result in far more cases of people not getting what they deserve.[5]

To understand the argument from compensatory justice, consider this analogy. If I steal your watch and give it to my innocent son before I die, you or your children are justified in repossessing the watch. A child's innocence does not entitle him to keep the watch stolen by his father. Since the watch was unearned, the child does not, in justice, deserve the watch. And the watch can be kept only at the expense of victims who are equally innocent. Returning the watch helps restore the situation to what it would have been had there been no injustice. Refusing to acknowledge a duty to compensate in this example commits one to the following *extreme* claim. By giving the watch to one's innocent son one launders the stolen goods to the point where they are so squeaky clean as to eliminate *entirely any* taint which would require *any* compensation. Since the thief's child does not deserve the watch, and since the victim's child is just as innocent as the thief's child, it is implausible to claim that such a *complete* laundering can be so *easily* achieved.

Similarly, suppose you receive too much change back from a teller at a Ma & Pa grocery. Justice requires you to return the excess change, which in effect compensates for the mistake—even though you are innocent of the mistake. Indeed, this example puts the case for AA too weakly, since the teller made the mistake, and since there was no analogous mistake blacks made leading to their victimization. But even in this example, justice requires (*ceteris paribus*, at least) returning the excess change.

But Fullinwider gives this alleged counter-example, which even its harshest critic so far, B. Boxill, calls "ingenious."[6]

> My neighbor contracts to have his driveway repaved while he is out of town. Having paid the contractor in advance, he leaves a set of directions in his mailbox, indicating which driveway to pave. An enemy of my neighbor takes the directions from the mailbox and replaces them with others which describe my driveway to the contractor. The contractor arrives while I am out . . . and, following the directions . . . resurfaces my driveway.[7]

Further, the example assumes the enemy is unidentifiable and that the contractor won't absorb the cost. Fullinwider says

> Compensating my neighbor means I must pay the cost of the contractor . . . but if I must pay the cost of the contractor, I am left worse off than I was. Presumably I valued other things more dearly than having my own driveway repaved; otherwise I would have had it done myself.[8]

I doubt this last presumption, since repaving one's driveway is just the sort of thing one puts off even if one wants it done. But Fullinwider can stipulate that repaving was not valuable enough to warrant hiring the contractor. So Fullinwider concluded, "Given . . . that the undeserved benefit cannot be taken from me and my neighbor cannot be compensated by me

without my incurring a loss, am I under an obligation to pay compensation? I do not see that I am."[9]

But AA differs from this example in that AA need not involve paying the entire cost of compensation in one step, or putting the compensator in a worse situation than he was before he received the undeserved benefits. The proper test for whether some form of AA is justified is to ask, "Should the beneficiary of the mistakenly repaved driveway pay *anything* to compensate his neighbor?" If he should pay even a penny, then some form of AA is justified. And the more he should pay, the stronger the form of AA may justifiably be. I think it is clear that the beneficiary should pay at least *something* to his neighbor to help compensate him for the loss. Of course, the beneficiary might be surprised by the benefit, and be unable to raise money to compensate without causing himself an even greater loss. But this possibility fails to show that the beneficiary has no *prima facie* obligation to compensate. Rather, it shows merely that the *prima facie* obligation to compensate is overrideable or postponable.

Further, intuitions about this case are too apt to be improperly skewed against AA, for some might have the intuition that the beneficiary need pay nothing because they might 1) blame the victim for failing to prevent his easily preventable victimization by simply phoning the directions rather than leaving them in his mailbox unattended; and 2) tacitly assume the contractor is richer and better able to absorb the cost or file a claim with an insurer. 1) gains extra purchase on intuitions if the intuiter suspects that the victim knew he had an enemy to avoid. 1) and 2) involve facts that are not analogous to AA, and so basing one's intuitions on them would be improper in arguing by analogy against AA. But if we forget the contractor, etc., and focus on the essential issue of whether innocent beneficiaries of injustice should compensate victims of that injustice at all, then I think it becomes clear that the beneficiaries should give something back to the victims. For presumably the amount to give back should be the amount of value the beneficiary received, since the beneficiary would then be no worse off than he was at the start, and the victim would be at least partially compensated. Since the beneficiary would be no worse off, he could not complain that he was wronged. And partially compensating the victim helps right the situation.

Another factor may improperly skew intuitions against compensation here. Fullinwider asks if the beneficiary is *obligated* to compensate the victim. But since we generally have the intuition that stronger arguments and needs are required to show an obligation rather than a *permission*, perhaps it would be better to ask if an impartial third party may *permissibly* redistribute some wealth from the beneficiary to compensate the victim.[10] The government could, e.g., tax windfall profits (i.e., unearned benefits) and use the taxes collected to help compensate those victimized by the windfall (i.e., the unfair events). Further, it seems likely that a government may sometimes *permissibly* tax its citizens in order to fund worthy (supererogatory) projects which the citizens would not otherwise strictly be *obligated* to fund. So even if Fullinwider showed that beneficiaries are free of an obligation to compensate, it would scarcely follow that the government has no permission to compensate with windfall profit taxes from the beneficiaries. But windfall taxes on unfair inheritances are inferior to traditional AA. As J. Thomson argues,

> the wrongs done . . . make jobs the best . . . form of compensation. [B]lacks and women were denied . . . full membership in the community; and nothing can more appropriately make amends . . . than precisely what will make them feel they now finally have it. And that means jobs. Financial compensation . . . slips through the fingers; having a job, and discovering you do it well, yield—perhaps better than anything else—that very self-respect which blacks and women have had to do without.[11]

One may object that stare decisis provides another argument by analogy against AA, since stare decisis promotes reasonable reliance and legitimate expectation. And, arguably, whites have come to expect their inherited advantages over blacks, and rely on the continuance of those advantages. But the alleged counter-example is disanalogous, since there is no *reasonable* reliance or *legitimate* expectation to keep ill-gotten gains due to America's *notoriously* deep and widespread racism. Expecting or relying on the unfair advantages from past racism to be perpetuated is unreasonable and illegitimate. Further, we cannot assume that the party winning on precedent received any unfair or unearned gain. In AA, however, America's history and traditional, familial relations show that whites presumably have inherited unfair and unearned gains from past racism.

One may object that AA is an unjust means used for a just end. The end doesn't always justify the means. Discrimination is inherently bad, even if used to discriminate against those benefiting from racism. But discrimination is standardly defined as "failing to treat relevantly like cases alike and relevantly dif-

ferent cases differently."[12] So-called reverse discrimination (AA) does not fit that definition, since there is a morally relevant difference between blacks and whites, namely, that only blacks have been victims of such severe and systematic racial discrimination. Only blacks deserve so much compensation. There is nothing remotely comparable for which to compensate whites.

Some call this definition of unjust discrimination "the formal principle of justice" and criticize the principle as too vague.[13] They claim the formal justice of treating like cases alike fails to specify what differences and similarities are morally relevant. But elementary justice does specify them. Racism is obviously unjust. Using irrelevant information (e.g., race) as the basis for an important decision affecting others (e.g., job placement) is arbitrary and therefore unjust. And regardless of any alleged badness of being black, excluding an entire race is unjust because it violates the principle of "'ought' implies 'can,'" which concerns fault. Regardless of whether blackness is bad, as the racist alleges, since blackness is an immutable trait determined by an accident of birth over which blacks have no control, they are not at fault for any undesirable features of their blackness.

One may also object that AA hurts or punishes innocent whites for the sins of their fathers, which is unjust. But the hurting is merely the absence of the unfair advantage that the father had. Suppose a black has been handicapped by past racism, and a white has been neither helped nor handicapped by past racism. There's nothing wrong with using AA to remove the black's handicap so that the black and white can compete on an equal and fair basis. The white's innocence does not entitle him to inherit the same unfair advantage previous whites had. Similarly, as we saw above, a child's innocence does not entitle him to keep a watch stolen by his father and left to the child.

Further, there is an important sense in which whites who never practiced racism, but who continue to benefit from racism, are not utterly innocent. By knowingly keeping such ill-gotten gains (e.g., in unearned inheritances), those whites are knowingly perpetuating the unjust effects of past racism. Whites benefiting from racism know, or should know, that the gains are ill-gotten, since America's racism against blacks is so notorious. Knowingly receiving stolen goods is not utterly innocent. Still, AA's goal is not punishment (or hurting whites) but compensation.

When will it all end? When will AA stop compensating blacks? As soon as the unfair advantage is gone, AA will stop. The elimination of the unfair advantage can be determined by showing that the percentage of blacks hired and admitted at least roughly equaled the percentage of blacks in the population. Either can suffice to end AA.

One may object that we cannot so use such statistics. For there may be other sociological factors, besides racism, that explain why blakcs are underrepresented in various fields. And given this ignorance, arguably we cannot assume that only racism is responsible for the under representation of blacks. But given our ignorance, it is only fair to presume (rebuttably) that blacks would, over time, be represented roughly proportionately in the major fields. There is no evidence of racial inferiority to support a presumption of less representation. And to presume less representation based on sheer ignorance smacks of putting a racist brand of inferiority on blacks. Even assuming, based on sheer ignorance, that blacks must have different *values* that explain underrepresentation seems not only unwarranted but dangerous or insulting.[14]

One may also object that laws and the bureaucracies administering them take on lives of their own.[15] So, arguably, we will be unable to stop legalized AA from outliving its usefulness as a program compensating blacks and from eventually becoming a program punishing whites. But this slippery slope argument poses a false dilemma. For one alternative, to the dilemma of having no more AA or having too much AA, is a standard technique for nipping a law in the bud, namely, making laws which create or allow AA sunset laws which will automatically expire in a few years and will need full passage again to continue (which can be blocked by a minority, e.g., half of either house in Congress).

Moreover, the real danger is not that AA will become too well-entrenched and last too long, fostering more injustice than justice in the long run. The worry is premature. Given the colossal amounts of injustice that must be rectified, and given the relatively mild forms of AA we have now and that are likely to pass in a democracy like America with a white population of 86%, we should continue what AA we have started.

Indeed, we should embark on more now before getting even further behind in the amount of injustice to rectify. Part of our reason for doing so stems from how capitalism magnifies the effects of past injustices, and thus magnifies the unjust effects AA must rectify. Racism has made whites disproportionately rich and blacks disproportionately poor. The rich get richer and the poor get poorer, since the rich use their competitive advantages (e.g., greater credit and more efficient machines) to survive bad luck (e.g., poor weather for a harvest) and to drive their less fortunate competitors out of business. Capitalism, by stressing economic competition, continuously magnifies the effects of past injustices, and thus magnifies and multiplies the unjust effects AA must rectify. Further, there is a significant chance that our time is not the start of an overlong period of AA, but only a narrow window in history where we can make substantial restitution. We cannot assume the long-term survival of AA, given how white and self-interested America is. These factors more than outweigh any influence of bureaucratic turf-fighting, even if we have no sunset law to regulate the length of AA.

One may object that I fail even to mention whites who have not benefited at *all* from current or past racism. If AA selects blacks over such whites, then AA discriminates against whites in the sense of discrimination accepted above. I have yet to account for such whites because I consider them pretty rare birds—about as rare as the Horatio Alger bird. Centuries of deep and systematic racism against blacks, which continues today, show that such whites are rare. This becomes even clearer when we recall that one can extend the arguments for AA for blacks to other racial or ethnic minorities, including American Indian and Hispanics. Almost all whites have benefited from racism against blacks, Indians, or Hispanics (e.g., arguably, profiting off land unjustly conquered or swindled from Indians, purchasing clothes at our national market's artificially low prices due to Hispanic labor in illegal sweat-shops). Given the rarity of such whites, AA should allow such whites to avoid unjust harm from AA by showing that they never benefited from racism. But the burden of proof should be on them. After all it is the white's case, and they should know more about it and have the incentive to show what they know. And since they are so rare, rather than expensively searching them out to ask their views, they should come to us if they object to AA. Similarly, as I said above, administrators may permissibly exclude from AA, or at least de-emphasize the selection of, individual blacks upon showing that they have never been victims of racism, and thus have no loss for which they can or should be compensated. But, again, there the burden of proof should be on the administrators of AA, since proving racism in individual cases is usually hard, and since centuries of American racism establish an extremely strong (but rebuttable) presumption that any American black has been hurt by racism.

One may object that AA based on compensatory justice should exclude blacks from families which have over some high amount of yearly family income, or at least tend to select blacks from families which make less. The high amount (e.g., $100,000) is strong evidence that the black family in question has already overcome discrimination, and so does not need AA to do so. Further, excluding such blacks would create more opportunities for poorer blacks whose poverty is evidence of both greater likelihood and greater severity of victimization from discrimination. This is a reasonable and measured modification to AA. I can accept it. But I wish to present four considerations which might justify even forms of AA without such ceilings. First, the modification seeks to avoid using resources unnecessarily to try to help those who have already overcome their victimization. But there are two senses of "overcome." Suppose you shoot me, but I heal myself to the point where I no longer have any dysfunction. In one sense I have overcome your victimization of me. But in another important sense I have not. I am still uncompensated for my pain and suffering, and for any lost wages due to the injury. We can hardly assume richer blacks do not deserve to be richer still. So outright exclusion of rich blacks from AA seems questionable. But the modification tending to select blacks from poorer families over blacks from richer families is still reasonable.

Second, B. Boxill helps us see how all blacks, even those who have fared well, can still be victims of racism by living in well-founded fear:

> Nozick, certainly no radical egalitarian, . . . pointed out that [people] have a right not to reasonably fear that their other rights will be violated, and I submit that the right is violated even if they respond courageously to threats of transgression [and fare well].[16]

Third, failing to select richer blacks over poorer blacks tends to rob AA of benefits not directly related to compensatory justice. One benefit of AA, which I will discuss a bit more later, is the production of role models for blacks. Richer blacks would tend (*ceteris paribus*) to make better role models, since wealth is so commonly seen in America as a measure of achievement and prestige. Role models are especially important to blacks, since the black family provides disproportionately few good role models. Richer blacks would also tend (*ceteris paribus*) to debunk racial stereotypes better than would poorer blacks, which is another benefit of AA which I will discuss more later.

Fourth, even if a black has not yet been victimized by racism, stopping current and future discrimi-nation against him are still reasons to keep that black in an AA program. If he has *completely* escaped racism so far, this is in all probability due to his isolation from many whites. But AA helps end the isolation of blacks from whites. So AA is justified in helping the black as it ends his isolation and places him among whites, some of whom will very probably discriminate against him. Since racism is rare and much less harmful than it used to be (e.g., during American slavery), and since centuries of the more common and harmful racism have accumulated so much injustice, the primary justification for AA is compensatory justice rather than stopping current discrimination. Thus there is a danger of neglecting the comparatively much less, but still very serious injustice of present (or future) discrimination. Technically, current (or future) injustice is probably a matter of distributive justice, since a present instance of racism would create an unfair and unequal distribution that distributive justice requires us to prevent. But current injustice is also linked extremely closely to compensatory justice, since any current injustice will immediately become a past injustice requiring compensation.[17] Despite these four drawbacks, the modification of AA to tend to select poorer blacks over richer blacks (*ceteris paribus*), or even to exclude very rich blacks from AA, seems permissible and advisable. For it is calculated to further compensatory justice. And it would release AA from the burden of arguing for what many would seize upon as absurd, namely, that even Bill Cosby, a multimillioniare with a doctoral degree, must receive help from AA if he applies for another degree. Even if Cosby has yet to overcome fully the effects of racism, presumably the distance he must travel to overcome these effects fully is small enough that we may justifiably focus our attention on other victims of racism who have much farther to go.

One may object that AA reinforces racial resentment and the stereotype that blacks are inferior and need help to be equal to whites. So instead of compensating blacks, AA merely maintains or even increases the degree of unjust treatment of blacks. I have four responses to this objection. First, without AA, the absence of blacks will reinforce the same stereotype of inferiority. Second, exposure to blacks will give people direct experience on which they can conclude that blacks are not inferior. Third, not all racial resentment is to be respected. Some racial resentment is racist resentment. For example, the KKK will resent AA no matter what. But we should hardly pander to racists in developing plans to compensate victims of racism. Fourth, AA helps relieve the guilt some whites feel, offsetting somewhat any increase in white resentment.

Finally, L. Katzner objects that women do not deserve AA as much as blacks do, since the husband's benefits from sexism roughly cancel out the wife's harm from sexism.[18] And even if the disadvantages were passed on to offspring, half of the offspring will be male, and so will be directly hurt by AA for females.

I have four replies. First, the objection is increasingly undermined by the increase in the number of unmarried mothers. Second, sexism is often passed on to daughters, for the mother's role in the family or workplace will be a role model for the daughter and perpetuate sexist roles. Sons will tend to expect these roles, leading to difficulties with those who reject them. And sons will share in the social benefits of AA, as we will see in section III below. Third, the objection reinforces the sexist structure of single women needing to become financially dependent on men to get their fair share (to get their costs canceled out). Fourth, marriages with a husband who is of a racial minority would tend not to cancel out a wife's harm from sexism, since the husband would have suffered comparable harm from racism.

III. A Brief Conclusion

Many may be unsympathetic to AA because they assume that being born into a white family, and thus getting certain advantages, is just a matter of good luck which comes with no responsibilities toward those who are less fortunate. Many may not adequately realize that the family is a multigenerational institution which has great, cumulative effects on the advantages a member of the family will enjoy over members of other families. While one's race is obviously an accident of birth and luck, it is no accident or stroke of luck that explains why whites traditionally enjoy advantages over blacks. Our economic and social structure—including the family finances of inheritance and the traditional method of hiring—systematically perpetuate racism and its harmful effects. I hope I have shown that with the "good luck" of being born into a white family generally comes the responsibility to compensate those who are not so "lucky." AA achieves such compensation. And by stressing the compensatory nature of AA I hope I have shown that AA is not a handout but a hand up.[19]

Study Questions

1. Does Harwood defend quotas? If so, how limited are they? Would you accept as moral quotas that just added extra positions reserved for women and minorities? Such quotas would also help white males, because some women and minorities would be assigned to the extra positions rather than competing with the white males for the original number of positions.

2. Are quotas the only form of affirmative action?

3. On March 13, 1994, the PBS public affairs show *To the Contrary* reported that the number of black women holding jobs in the professions has increased by 125 percent in the last ten years. Does this statistic show that affirmative action works well?

4. Black women are often called "twofers," meaning that a company can get credit for hiring in two affirmative action categories (women and blacks) for the price of only one job. Is branding black women as twofers a form of bigotry, since it assumes that there is a "price" of one job that one must pay to hire a black woman? Is thinking of black women as twofers a form of cynical and bigoted tokenism?

5. On the television program *To the Contrary*, Linda Chavez, a conservative member of the media and unsuccessful Republican congressional candidate in Maryland, noted that white women are the single largest group of people who have benefitted by receiving jobs and positions from affirmative action. Given this fact, would it be better to see affirmative action primarily as a feminist issue rather than a racial issue, an issue involving integrating the races into all parts of American culture? Do the news media usually portray affirmative action as primarily a racial issue or as primarily a feminist issue? Why do you think the news media classify affirmative action as they do? Hispanics are another affirmative action category, yet the U.S. Census notes that Hispanics may be of any race. So is this further evidence that affirmative action should not be seen primarily in racial terms, which tend to provoke much emotion?

6. Marriages between blacks and whites have increased by 33 percent since 1977, 27 percent of Americans believe interracial marriage should be legally banned, and 58 percent of Americans say blacks "should not push themselves where they are not wanted."[20] Do these statistics show a serious need for affirmative action programs to combat racist attitudes?

Notes

1. Michael Kinsley, "Equal Lack of Opportunity," *Harper's* (June 1983), p. 8. See also Bernard R. Boxill, *Blacks and Social Justice* (Rowman & Allanheld, 1984), p. 147.

2. See, e.g., Ronald M. Dworkin, *A Matter of Principle* (Harvard, 1985), Ch. 8.

3. See, e.g., Louis Katzner, "Is Favoring of Women and Blacks in Employment and Educational Opportunities Justified?," in Joel Feinberg and Hyman Gross, eds., *The Philosophy of Law*, 3rd ed. (Wadsworth, 1986), pp. 450–55 and Marshall Cohen, Thomas Nagel and Thomas Scanlon, eds., *Equality and Preferential Treatment* (Princeton, 1977).

4. Robert K. Fullinwider, *The Reverse Discrimination Controversy: A Moral and Legal Analysis* (Rowman & Littlefield, 1980), p. 13.

5. For a brief and effective argument that each alternative involves a trade-off of justice, see George Sher, "Right Violations and Injustices: Can We Always Avoid Trade-offs?," 94 *Ethics* 212–24 (1984), p. 213.

6. Boxill, p. 166.

7. Fullinwider, pp. 38–39.

8. Ibid., p. 39.

9. Ibid.

10. On the moral force of voluntary programs of AA, and democratic government imposing AA on itself, see, e.g., Richard Lempert, "The Force of Irony: On The Morality of Affirmative Action and *United Steelworkers v. Weber*," 95 *Ethics* 86–89 (1985).

11. Judith Jarvis Thomson, "Preferential Hiring," 2 *Philosophy & Public Affairs* 364 (1973), p. 383. Thomson effectively presents the quoted argument to counter the objection that we should make amends "in some way in which the costs could be shared by everyone, and not imposed entirely on the young white male job applicants . . ." But her argument also counters the objection that "If blacks and females know that they have been given jobs because of their groups membership and that they have been chosen over better-qualified individuals, they may suffer severe losses of self-respect." See Hardy E. Jones, "On the Justificabilty of Reverse Discrimination," in Barry R. Gross, ed., *Reverse Discrimination* (Prometheus, 1977), p. 356. In section 5 of his paper Jones argues against this objection. The objection appears, e.g., in Thomas Nagel, "A Defense of Affirmative Action," *Report From the Center for Philosophy & Public Policy* 6 (1981), p. 7. The objection is paternalistic and forgets that blacks have the options of applying without specifying their race, reapplying specifying their race, and refusing acceptance if they fear a loss of self-respect makes admission on balance undesirable. Given these options, deciding how to deal with a highly individualized reaction such as loss of self-respect should be left to the individual.

12. See, e.g., Katzner, p. 450, and Fullinwider, p. 13.

13. Fullinwider, pp. 13f.

14. See, Boxill, pp. 157–58. Another argument for a presumption of equality appears in Theodore M. Benditt, "The Demands of Justice," 95 *Ethics* 224–32 (1985), pp. 230–32. As we have seen, the presumption of *racial* equality is material, not merely formal, principle. See Joel Feinberg, *Social Philosophy* (Prentice-Hall, 1973), Ch. 7, sect. 2.

15. For a very different and much more controversial suggestion that any law at any time depends for its life on serving the interests of the ruling class, see Karl Marx and Frederick Engels, *The German Ideology*, C. J. Arthur, ed. (International Publishers, 1978), p. 81.

16. Boxill, p. 165 and p. 151, exposes this type of *fatal* error underestimating the number of black victims of racism.

17. While present racism also seems to be a violation of meritocractic justice, I think all of the same cases can be handled under distributive justice. Fullinwider, pp. 93–94, admits that compensatory justice, which I primarily rely on, is less controversial than distributive justice.

18. Katzner, pp. 454–55.

19. I thank David Lyons, Laurence Thomas, Michael Gorr, Shelley Stillwell, Steve Maitzen, Georgette Sinkler, Max O'Connor, Theo Correl, and Jill Frank for their comments on this paper.

20. Lewis H. Lapham, Michael Pollan, and Eric Etheridge, eds., *The Harper's Index Book* (New York: Henry Holt, 1987), p. 10.

20

Against Affirmative Action: The Price of Preference

Shelby Steele

Editor's note: Steele is a professor of English at San Jose State University and the winner of the National Book Critics' Circle Award for the best nonfiction book *The Content of Our Character*, from which this essay is drawn. He argues that the price of affirmative action, what some call preferential treatment, is too high. On page 17 Steele has summed up his view of the situation thus: "Whites gain superiority by not knowing blacks; blacks gain entitlement by not seeing their own responsibility for bettering themselves." Steele is highly critical of this situation, though he is on record as supporting some forms of affirmative action.

In a few short years, when my two children will be applying to college, the affirmative action policies by which most universities offer black students some form of preferential treatment will present me with a dilemma. I am a middle-class black, a college professor, far from wealthy, but also well-removed from the kind of deprivation that would qualify my children for the label "disadvantaged." Both of them have endured racial insensitivity from whites. They have been called names, have suffered slights, and have experienced firsthand the peculiar malevolence that racism brings out in people. Yet, they have never experienced racial discrimination, have never been stopped by their race on any path they have chosen to follow. Still, their society now tells them that if they will only designate themselves as black on their col-

lege applications, they will likely do better in the college lottery than if they conceal this fact. I think there is something of a Faustian bargain in this.

Of course, many blacks and a considerable number of whites would say that I was sanctimoniously making affirmative action into a test of character. They would say that this small preference is the meagerest recompense for centuries of unrelieved oppression. And to these arguments other very obvious facts must be added. In America, many marginally competent or flatly incompetent whites are hired everyday—some because their white skin suits the conscious or unconscious racial preference of their employer. The white children of alumni are often grandfathered into elite universities in what can only be seen as a residual benefit of historic white privilege. Worse, white incompetence is always an individual matter, while for blacks it is often confirmation of ugly stereotypes. The Peter Principle was not conceived with only blacks in mind. Given that unfairness cuts both ways, doesn't it only balance the scales of history that my children now receive a slight preference over whites? Doesn't this repay, in a small way, the systematic denial under which their grandfather lived out his days?

So, in theory, affirmative action certainly has all the moral symmetry that fairness requires—the injustice of historical and even contemporary white advantage is offset with black advantage; preference replaces prejudice, inclusion answers exclusion. It is reformist and corrective, even repentant and redemptive. And I would never sneer at these good intentions. Born in the late forties in Chicago, I started my education (a charitable term in this case) in a segregated school and suffered all the indignities that come to blacks in a segregated society. My father, born in the South, only made it to the third grade before the white man's fields took permanent priority over his formal education. And though he educated himself into an advanced reader with an almost professorial authority, he could only drive a truck for a living and never earned more than ninety dollars a week in his entire life. So yes, it is crucial to my sense of citizenship, to my ability to identify with the spirit and the interests of America, to know that this country, however imperfectly, recognizes its past sins and wishes to correct them.

Yet good intentions, because of the opportunity for innocence they offer us, are very seductive and can blind us to the effects they generate when implemented. In our society, affirmative action is, among other things, a testament to white goodwill and to black power, and in the midst of these heavy investments, its effects can be hard to see. But after 20 years of implementation, I think affirmative action has shown itself to be more bad than good and that blacks—whom I will focus on in this essay—now stand to lose more from it than they gain.

In talking with affirmative action administrators and with blacks and whites in general, it is clear that supporters of affirmative action focus on its good intentions while detractors emphasize its negative effects. Proponents talk about "diversity" and "pluralism"; opponents speak of "reverse discrimination," the unfairness of quotas and set-asides. It was virtually impossible to find people outside either camp. The closest I came was a white male manager at a large computer company who said, "I think it amounts to reverse discrimination, but I'll put up with a little of that for a little more diversity." I'll live with a little of the effect to gain a little of the intention, he seemed to be saying. But this only makes him a halfhearted supporter of affirmative action. I think many people who don't really like affirmative action support it to one degree or another anyway.

I believe they do this because of what happened to white and black Americans in the crucible of the sixties when whites were confronted with their racial guilt and blacks tasted their first real power. In this stormy time white absolution and black power coalesced into virtual mandates for society. Affirmative action became a meeting ground for these mandates in the law, and in the late sixties and early seventies it underwent a remarkable escalation of its mission from simple anti-discrimination enforcement to social engineering by means of quotas, goals, timetables, set-asides, and other forms of preferential treatment.

Legally, this was achieved through a series of executive orders and EEOC guidelines that allowed racial imbalances in the workplace to stand as proof of racial discrimination. Once it could be assumed that discrimination explained racial imbalances, it became easy to justify group remedies to presumed discrimination, rather than the normal case-by-case redress for proven discrimination. Preferential treatment through quotas, goals, and so on is designed to correct imbalances based on the assumption that they always indicate discrimination. This expansion of what constitutes discrimination allowed affirmative action to escalate into the business of social engineering in the name of anti-discrimination, to push society toward statistically proportionate racial representation, without any obligation of proving actual discrimination.

What accounted for this shift, I believe, was the white mandate to achieve a new racial innocence and the black mandate to gain power. Even though blacks had made great advances during the sixties without quotas, these mandates, which came to a head in the very late sixties, could no longer be satisfied by anything less than racial preferences. I don't think these mandates in themselves were wrong, since whites clearly needed to do better by blacks and blacks needed more real power in society. But, as they came together in affirmative action, their effect was to distort our understanding of racial discrimination in a way that allowed us to offer the remediation of preference on the basis of mere color rather than actual injury. By making black the color of preference, these mandates have reburdened society with the very marriage of color and preference (in reverse) that we set out to eradicate. The old sin is reaffirmed in a new guise.

But the essential problem with this form of affirmative action is the way it leaps over the hard business of developing a formerly oppressed people to the point where they can achieve proportionate representation on their own (given equal opportunity) and goes straight for the proportionate representation. This may satisfy some whites of their innocence and some blacks of their power, but it does very little to truly uplift blacks.

A white female affirmative action officer at an Ivy League university told me what many supporters of affirmative action now say: "We're after diversity. We ideally want a student body where racial and ethnic groups are represented according to their proportion in society." When affirmative action escalated into social engineering, diversity became a golden word. It grants whites an egalitarian fairness (innocence) and blacks an entitlement to proportionate representation (power). *Diversity* is a term that applies democratic principles to races and cultures rather than to citizens, despite the fact that there is nothing to indicate that real diversity is the same thing as proportionate representation. Too often the result of this on campuses (for example) has been a democracy of colors rather than of people, an artificial diversity that gives the appearance of an educational parity between black and white students that has not yet been achieved in reality. Here again, racial preferences allow society to leapfrog over the difficult problem of developing blacks to parity with whites and into a cosmetic diversity that covers the blemish of disparity—a full six years after admission, only about 26 percent of black students graduate from college.

Racial representation is not the same thing as racial development, yet affirmative action fosters a confusion of these very different needs. Representation can be manufactured; development is always hard-earned. However, it is the music of innocence and power that we hear in affirmative action that causes us to cling to it and to its distracting emphasis on representation. The fact is that after 20 years of racial preferences, the gap between white and black median income is greater than it was in the seventies. None of this is to say that blacks don't need policies that ensure our right to equal opportunity, but what we need more is the development that will let us take advantage of society's efforts to include us.

I think that one of the most troubling effects of racial preferences for blacks is a kind of demoralization, or put another way, an enlargement of self-doubt. Under affirmative action the quality that earns us preferential treatment is an implied inferiority. However this inferiority is explained—and it is easily enough explained by the myriad deprivations that grew out of our oppression—it is still inferiority. There are explanations, and then there is the fact. And the fact must be borne by the individual as a condition apart from the explanation, apart even from the fact that others like himself also bear this condition. In integrated situations where blacks must compete with whites who may be better prepared, these explanations may quickly wear thin and expose the individual to racial as well as personal self-doubt.

All of this is compounded by the cultural myth of black inferiority that blacks have always lived with. What this means in practical terms is that when blacks deliver themselves into integrated situations, they encounter a nasty little reflex in whites, a mindless, atavistic reflex that responds to the color black with alarm. Attributions may follow this alarm if the white cares to indulge them, and if they do, they will most likely be negative—one such attribution is intellectual ineptness. I think this reflex and the attributions that may follow it embarrass most whites today, therefore, it is usually quickly repressed. Nevertheless, on an equally atavistic level, the black will be aware of the reflex his color triggers and will feel a stab of horror at seeing himself reflected in this way. He, too, will do a quick repression, but a lifetime of such stabbings is what constitutes his inner realm of racial doubt.

The effects of this may be a subject for another essay. The point here is that the implication of inferiority that racial preferences engender in both the white and black mind expands rather than contracts this doubt. Even when the black sees no implication of inferiority in racial preferences, he knows that whites do, so that—consciously or unconsciously—the result is virtually the same. The effect of preferential treatment—the lowering of normal standards to increase black representation—puts blacks at war with an expanded realm of debilitating doubt, so that the doubt itself becomes an unrecognized preoccupation that undermines their ability to perform, especially in integrated situations. On largely white campuses, blacks are five times more likely to drop out than whites. Preferential treatment, no matter how it is justified in the light of day, subjects blacks to a midnight of self-doubt, and so often transforms their advantage into a revolving door.

Another liability of affirmative action comes from the fact that it indirectly encourages blacks to exploit their own past victimization as a source of power and privilege. Victimization, like implied inferiority, is what justifies preference, so that to receive the benefits of preferential treatment one must to some extent become invested in the view of one's self as a victim. In this way, affirmative action nurtures a victim-focused identity in blacks. The obvious irony here is that we become inadvertently invested in the very condition we are trying to overcome. Racial preferences send us the message that there is more power in our past suffering than our present achievements—none of which could bring a *preference* over others.

When power itself grows out of suffering, then blacks are encouraged to expand the boundaries of what qualifies as racial oppression, a situation that can lead us to paint our victimization in vivid colors, even as we receive the benefits of preference. The same corporations and institutions that give us preference are also seen as our oppressors. At Stanford University minority students—some of whom enjoy as much as $15,000 a year in financial aid—recently took over the president's office demanding, among other things, more financial aid. The power to be found in victimization, like any power, is intoxicating and can lend itself to the creation of a new class of super-victims who can feel the pea of victimization under 20 mattresses. Preferential treatment rewards us for being underdogs rather than for moving beyond that status—a misplacement of incentives that, along with its deepening of our doubt, is more a yoke than a spur.

But, I think, one of the worst prices that blacks pay for preference has to do with an illusion. I saw this illusion at work recently in the mother of a middle-class black student who was going off to his first semester at college. "They owe us this, so don't think for a minute that you don't belong there." This is the logic by which many blacks, and some whites, justify affirmative action—it is something "owed," a form of reparation. But this logic overlooks a much harder and less digestible reality, that it is impossible to repay blacks living today for the historic suffering of the race. If all blacks were given a million dollars tomorrow morning, it would not amount to a dime on the dollar of three centuries of oppression, nor would it obviate the residues of that oppression that we still carry today. The concept of historic reparation grows out of man's need to impose a degree of justice on the world that simply does not exist. Suffering can be endured and overcome, it cannot be repaid. Blacks cannot be repaid for the injustice done to the race, but we can be corrupted by society's guilty gestures of repayment.

Affirmative action is such a gesture. It tells us that racial preferences can do for us what we cannot do for ourselves. The corruption here is in the hidden incentive *not* to do what we believe preferences will do. This is an incentive to be reliant on others just as we are struggling for self-reliance. And it keeps alive the illusion that we can find some deliverance in repayment. The hardest thing for any sufferer to accept is that his suffering excuses him from very little and never has enough currency to restore him. To think otherwise is to prolong the suffering.

Several blacks I spoke with said they were still in favor of affirmative action because of the "subtle" discrimination blacks were subject to once on the job. One photojournalist said, "They have ways of ignoring you." A black female television producer said, "You can't file a lawsuit when your boss doesn't invite you to the insider meetings without ruining your career. So we still need affirmative action." Others mentioned the infamous "glass ceiling" through which blacks can see the top positions of authority but never each them. But I don't think racial preferences are a protection against this subtle discrimination; I think they contribute to it.

In any workplace, racial preferences will always create two-tiered populations composed of preferreds and unpreferreds. This division makes automatic a perception of enhanced competence for the unpreferreds and of questionable competence for the preferreds—the former earned his way, even though

others were given preference, while the latter made it by color as much as by competence. Racial preferences implicitly mark whites with an exaggerated superiority just as they mark blacks with an exaggerated inferiority. They not only reinforce America's oldest racial myth but, for blacks, they have the effect of stigmatizing the already stigmatized.

I think that much of the "subtle" discrimination that blacks talk about is often (not always) discrimination against the stigma of questionable competence that affirmative action delivers to blacks. In this sense, preferences scapegoat the very people they seek to help. And it may be that at a certain level employers impose a glass ceiling, but this may not be against the race so much as against the race's reputation for having advanced by color as much as by competence. Affirmative action makes a glass ceiling virtually necessary as a protection against the corruptions of preferential treatment. This ceiling is the point at which corporations shift the emphasis from color to competency and stop playing the affirmative action game. Here preference backfires for blacks and becomes a taint that holds them back. Of course, one could argue that this taint, which is, after all, in the minds of whites, becomes nothing more than an excuse to discriminate against blacks. And certainly the result is the same in either case—blacks don't get past the glass ceiling. But this argument does not get around the fact that racial preferences now taint this color with a new theme of suspicion that makes it even more vulnerable to the impulse in others to discriminate. In this crucial yet gray area of perceived competence, preferences make whites look better than they are and blacks worse, while doing nothing whatever to stop the very real discrimination that blacks may encounter. I don't wish to justify the glass ceiling here, but only to suggest the very subtle ways that affirmative action revives rather than extinguishes the old rationalizations for racial discrimination.

In education, a revolving door; in employment, a glass ceiling.

I believe affirmative action is problematic in our society because it tries to function like a social program. Rather than ask it to ensure equal opportunity we have demanded that it create parity between the races. But preferential treatment does not teach skills, or educate, or instill motivation. It only passes out entitlement by color, a situation that in my profession has created an unrealistically high demand for black professors. The social engineer's assumption is that this high demand will inspire more blacks to earn Ph.D.'s and join the profession. In fact, the number of blacks earning Ph.D.'s has declined in recent years. A Ph.D. must be developed from preschool on. He requires family and community support. He must acquire an entire system of values that enables him to work hard while delaying gratification. There are social programs, I believe, that can (and should) help blacks *develop* in all these areas, but entitlement by color is not a social program; it is a dubious reward for being black.

It now seems clear that the Supreme Court, in a series of recent decisions, is moving away from racial preferences. It has disallowed preferences except in instances of "identified discrimination," eroded the precedent that statistical racial imbalances are *prima facie* evidence of discrimination, and in effect granted white males the right to challenge consent degrees that use preference to achieve racial balances in the workplace. One civil rights leader said, "Night has fallen on civil rights." But I am not so sure. The effect of these decisions is to protect the constitutional rights of everyone rather than take rights away from blacks. What they do take away from blacks is the special entitlement to more rights than others that preferences always grant. Night has fallen on racial preferences, not on the fundamental rights of black Americans. The reason for this shift, I believe, is that the white mandate for absolution from past racial sins has weakened considerably during the eighties. Whites are now less willing to endure unfairness to themselves in order to grant special entitlements to blacks, even when these entitlements are justified in the name of past suffering. Yet the black mandate for more power in society has remained unchanged. And I think part of the anxiety that many blacks feel over these decisions has to do with the loss of black power they may signal. We had won a certain specialness and now we are losing it.

But the power we've lost by these decisions is really only the power that grows out of our victimization—the power to claim special entitlements under the law because of past oppression. This is not a very substantial or reliable power, and it is important that we know this so we can focus more exclusively on the kind of development that will bring enduring power. There is talk now that Congress will pass new legislation to compensate for these new limits on affirmative action. If this happens, I hope that their focus will be on development and anti-discrimination rather than entitlement, on achieving racial parity rather than jerry-building racial diversity.

I would also like to see affirmative action go back to its original purpose of enforcing equal opportunity—a purpose that in itself disallows racial preferences. We cannot be sure that the discriminatory impulse in America has yet been slammed into extinction, and I believe affirmative action can make its greatest contribution by providing a rigorous vigilance in this area. It can guard constitutional rather than racial rights, and help institutions evolve standards of merit and selection that are appropriate to the institution's needs yet as free of racial bias as possible (again, with the understanding that racial imbalances are not always an indication of racial bias). One of the most important things affirmative action can do is to define exactly what racial discrimination is and how it might manifest itself within a specific institution. The impulse to discriminate *is* subtle and cannot be ferreted out unless its many guises are made clear to people. Along with this there should be monitoring of institutions and heavy sanctions brought to bear when actual discrimination is found. This is the sort of affirmative action that America owes to blacks and to itself. It goes after the evil of discrimination itself, while preferences only sidestep the evil and grant entitlement to its *presumed* victims.

But if not preferences, then what? I think we need social policies that are committed to two goals: the educational and economic development of disadvantaged people, regardless of race, and the eradication from our society—through close monitoring and severe sanctions—of racial, ethnic, or gender discrimination. Preferences will not deliver us to either of these goals, since they tend to benefit those who are not disadvantaged—middle-class white women and middle-class blacks—and attack one form of discrimination with another. Preferences are inexpensive and carry the glamour of good intentions—change the numbers and the good deed is done. To be against them is to be unkind. But I think the unkindest cut is to bestow on children like my own an undeserved advantage while neglecting the development of those disadvantaged children on the East Side of my city who will likely never be in a position to benefit from a preference. Give my children fairness; give disadvantaged children a better shot at development— better elementary and secondary schools, job training, safer neighborhoods, better financial assistance for college, and so on. Fewer blacks go to college today than ten years ago; more black males of college age are in prison or under the control of the criminal justice system than in college. This despite racial preferences.

The mandates of black power and white absolution out of which preferences emerged were not wrong in themselves. What was wrong was that both races focused more on the goals of these mandates than on the means to the goals. Blacks can have no real power without taking responsibility for their own educational and economic development. Whites can have no racial innocence without earning it by eradicating discrimination and helping the disadvantaged to develop. Because we ignored the means, the goals have not been reached, and the real work remains to be done.

Study Questions

1. Is Steele's claim that whites gain superiority by not knowing blacks true? Isn't such segregation or ignorance a loss to whites and blacks, who could learn and benefit from knowing each other? Is Steele's claim that blacks gain from neglecting responsibilities true? Since Steele criticizes victims for trying to end their victimization, isn't Steele guilty of the fallacy of blaming the victim for his or her own victimization?

2. Does Steele give any statistics to support his views? If not, does he need to do so? Since affirmative action affects millions of people directly, is Steele's reliance on anecdotes to reject affirmative action a form of hasty generalization? A hasty generalization occurs when one draws a general conclusion from a sample that one has not taken the time to make big enough or random enough to control for variables involved in rival explanations of whatever is at issue.

3. Does Steele pose a false dilemma in suggesting that affirmative action is incompatible with accepting high quality applicants?

4. Is Steele paternalistic in suggesting that we end affirmative action as an option for blacks in order to try to help blacks? Aren't individual applicants in the best position to decide if they want to list their race on the application form, which is always optional, and receive the benefits of affirmative action?

5. Is Steele right to conclude that, given affirmative action, the prize is not worth the price? Shouldn't that determination be left to each individual rather than eliminating affirmative action altogether?

21

Affirmative Action Is Justified: A Reply to Newton

Sterling Harwood

Author's abstract: This article argues that Newton commits several fallacies in her analysis of affirmative action. For example, Newton poses a false dilemma in suggesting that affirmative action will turn into a pushing and shoving match in the political process. The article notes that this was the case before affirmative action and that it is inherent in the nature of a democratic political process.

Lisa Newton's "Reverse Discrimination As Unjustified" may well be the most widely reprinted and widely read philosophical essay on affirmative action (AA).[1] Yet, Newton's essay has been neglected in that it has so far received, I believe, no direct and sustained rebuttal. I aim to defend AA against Newton's attacks.

Newton's First Argument

Newton's first argument rejects AA because AA allegedly will lead to increased injustice by turning playing by the legal rules into a shoving match between self-interested groups. She says:

> eventually, the WASPs will have to form their own lobby, for they too are a minority. The point is . . .: there is no "majority" in America who will not mind giving up just a bit of their rights to make room for a favored minority. There are only other minorities, each of which is discriminated against by the favoring. The initial injustice is then repeated dozens of times, and if each

Reprinted from *Contemporary Philosophy* XIII, no. 2 (1990), pp. 14–17.

minority is granted the same right of restitution as the others, an entire area of rule governance is dissolved into a . . . shoving match between self-interested groups.[2]

Three errors plague Newton's analysis here. First, the mere fact that there is no majority that will not mind AA is inconclusive. For, if one treated lack of majority acceptance of AA as a conclusive reason to reject AA, one would commit the *ad populum* fallacy.

Second, in the relevant senses, whites form a majority in America, and blacks form a discrete and insular minority.[3] WASPs, or whites generally, are not a minority in the relevant sense of being discrete and insular. Many have discriminated against Irish or Italian Americans or other whites. But because whites in these sub-groups can readily assimilate, the effects of this discrimination are much more avoidable and haphazard, and much less systematically passed on to offspring. Discrimination against blacks is much more systematic and harmful, and is systematically passed on to black offspring. Those in white sub-groups don't even have to pass for white—they are white, a fact stressed by millions of racists. Further, how systematic something is must be a matter of degree, and that degree is profoundly higher with blacks, since they are a profoundly more discrete and insular minority that is much less able to assimilate and thereby dodge discrimination. At some point the difference in degree becomes a difference in kind that allows AA for blacks but not for the other groups—especially if, as almost all opponents of AA would admit, the case for AA for any group is at best a very close case, and thus the sort of case in which even a slight difference in degree is more likely to be a decisive difference.

Third, Newton also errs in overlooking that our government is *already* involved in lobbying and pushing and shoving between self-interested groups. Pluralism in a democracy is a sort of shoving match. This has been so from the start. *The Federalist* No. 10 shows how factions operate in a democracy.[4] Indeed, it details how the framers' design of the Constitution *counted* on self-interested factions to act as a moderating force to encourage the building and shifting of coalitions rather than the development of a permanent underclass. So, Newton poses a false dilemma in suggesting that we either reject AA or else we will fall into this democratic pushing and shoving match. Further, Newton fails to show that such democracy must be unjust. The shoving match Newton fears is fair play under the legal rules in a pluralistic democracy. Democracy is fair to whites as such in distributing the vote equally, "one person, one vote." Indeed, since money talks in politics, unfairness here would favor whites, who are disproportionately richer than blacks. The annual income of the average black family is only 56% of the annual income of the average white family.[5] So Newton's fears of whites unfairly losing in a democratic shoving match are unfounded.

Newton's Second Argument

Newton's second main argument against AA is: "[R]emedial rights exist only where there is law: primary human rights are useful guides to legislation but cannot stand as reasons for awarding remedies for injuries sustained."[6] Here Newton is targeting the argument for AA based on compensatory justice. But she gives no further support for her view that law is the exclusive source of compensatory rights. Thus, she seems merely to commit the fallacy of appealing to the authority of law. Or perhaps she is equivocating on "right" by trading on the ambiguity between *legal* rights and *moral* rights. But, in either case, whether equivocation or appeal to authority, her argument is fallacious. Further, she has failed to show that advocates of AA must claim that remedial *rights* demand AA. Another alternative would be merely to stress that compensatory justice gives enough *reasons* to permit AA even if AA is not strictly speaking required as a matter of one's *rights*. At least for all Newton has shown, reasons need not be translated into rights in order to justify. Finally, since AA *is* well-entrenched in the law of both legislation and executive orders, her emphasis on the supposed problem of the legal grounding of AA is misplaced.[7]

Newton's Third Argument

Newton's third argument against AA is:

> all discrimination is wrong prima facie because it violates justice, and that goes for [AA] too. No violation of justice among the citizens may be justified . . . by appeal to the ideal of equality, for that ideal is logically dependent upon the notion of justice. [AA], then, which attempts no other justification than an appeal to equality, is wrong.[8]

Newton assumes that justice is simple and monolithic. But, in fact, justice is so complex that we can distinguish types of justice, which can conflict. So

Newton's argument is unsound. She errs in using a process of elimination to conclude that since all discrimination—including the allegedly reverse discrimination of AA—is (at least prima facie) unjust, no argument from justice can save AA. She overlooks the realistic possibility of clashing forms of justice.

Three Types of Justice

I now examine some forms of justice that can clash. Moreover, I will show that AA is not unjust and that AA is even supported by compensatory justice. Three types of justice seem to be meritocratic justice, distributive justice, and compensatory justice. Meritocratic justice requires that we hire only the most qualified for the job. Distributive justice requires us, prima facie, to minimize serious inequalities in well-being. Compensatory justice is distinct from distributive justice in that the former requires (even innocent) beneficiaries in particular to give up their unearned advantages over innocents unjustly deprived or disadvantaged.

Robert K. Fullinwider gives an example that undermines the decisiveness and exclusivity of meritocratic justice. He says meritocracy is "too rigid and specific" and would condemn acts that "seem unobjectionable."[9] His example is:

> Suppose . . . an employer had two well-qualified applicants for a position, the slightly better qualified applicant already having a good, secure job, the other being unemployed. If the employer hired the unemployed applicant, would he have violated a . . . moral principle? To suggest [so] is . . . strongly counterintuitive.[10]

The distributive justice of hiring the unemployed seems to outweigh the problem with meritocratic justice. So Newton's argument is invalid, since it fails to rule out the realistic possibility of meritocratic justice clashing with distributive justice, as it does here.[11]

Moreover, Norman Daniels shows how the argument from meritocracy is *not* an argument from justice. Daniels considers the following example:

> Jack and Jill both want jobs A and B and each much prefers A to B. Jill can do either A or B better than Jack. But the situation S in which Jill performs B and Jack A is more productive than Jack doing B and Jill A (S'), even when we include the effects on productivity of Jill's lesser satisfaction. [Meritocracy] selects S, not S', because it is attuned to macroproductivity, not microproductivity. . . . It says, "Select people for jobs so that *overall* job performance is maximized."[12]

Daniels anticipates the objection that meritocracy would select S', not S, because meritocracy implies that "a person should get a job if he or she is the best available person for *that* job."[13] He admits this objection appears based on the point of justice "that it seems *unfair* to Jill that she gets the job she wants less even though she can do the job Jack gets better than he can." But Daniels thinks the seeming unfairness derives from "inessential features of our economic system," namely, that promoting microproductivity *happens* to be "the best rule of thumb" to follow to achieve macroproductivity.[14] He says favoring microproductivity (S') over macroproductivity (S) because S seems unfair is relying on an intuition that is "just a by-product of our existing institutions" rather than based on justice.[15] The *happenstance* that we have a mere rule of thumb in our existing institutions is too superficial and arbitrary to be a fundamental consideration of justice. Once we realize the basis of meritocracy is macroproductivity, meritocracy will not support the intuition that Jill, in justice, deserves her favorite job A, or the claim that justice requires S'. That the "inessential features of our economic system" are irrelevant to justice undermines the standing of meritocracy—when conceived of as microproductivity—as a principle of justice. Meritocracy as macroproductivity survives.

Indeed, once we focus on the distinction between macroproductivity and microproductivity, we see numerous cases where favoring macroproductivity in hiring is *not* unfair.[16] In the game of baseball, sluggers should not use every time up at bat to pursue only raising their own individual statistics. The purpose of the game—including the slugger's purpose—is winning, which requires teamwork. A slugger should not threaten to quit the team if the manager wants a sacrifice bunt or a pinch-hitter who is better at bunting. A slugger should not complain if moved (for instance, to third base) from a favorite fielding position (such as first base) to make room for a new player (at first) who is better than the replaced player (at third). This is true even if the slugger moved is far better at either position than either the new player (at first base) or the replaced player (at third base). Fairness requires doing what is good for the team. Individual statistics or preferences should not be pursued at the expense of the team effort. On the contrary, fairness *requires* macroproductivity. Sluggers who complain or quit are not willing to do their fair share, which is sacrificing for the good of the team.

Further, Ronald Dworkin gives the following argument that supports Daniels' claim that there is no merit abstracted from macroproductivity. Dworkin says:

> There is no combination of abilities and skills and traits that constitutes "merit" in the abstract; if quick hands count as "merit" in the case of a prospective surgeon, this is because quick hands will enable him to serve the public better and for no other reason. If a black skin will, as a matter of regrettable fact [e.g., the need for black role models], enable another doctor to do a different medical job better, then that black skin is by the same token "merit" as well. That argument may strike some as dangerous; but only because they confuse its conclusion—that black skin may be a socially useful trait in particular circumstances—with the very different and despicable idea that one race may be *inherently* more worthy than another.[17]

One may object that black skin cannot count as merit, since pigmentation is an inherited accident of birth rather than a matter of choice and achievement. But, as Dworkin argues,

> It is also true that those who score low in aptitude or admissions tests do not choose their levels of intelligence. Nor do those denied admission because they are too old, or because they do not come from a part of the country underrepresented in the school, or because they cannot play basketball well, choose not to have the qualities that made the difference.[18]

I must stress that the argument against AA based on meritocratic justice is entirely dependent on the *false* assumption that AA must involve hiring blacks with less merit. Tests allegedly measuring merit are often biased.[19] Further, a lower score under inferior conditions often shows more ability than does a higher score under superior conditions. And blacks tend to take the tests under conditions (poverty, reduced parental supervision, and reduced incentives due to bleaker prospects caused by racism, and so on) which are dramatically inferior to the conditions under which whites take such tests. For example, consider the dramatic differences between the best group and the worst group of American public high schools. The best group will generally give its students at least the following advantages over the students in the worst group: (1) better teachers, (2) better equipment, (3) more programs (for example, extracurricular activities), (4) better atmospheres in which to learn (such as less crime, noise, and disorder), (5) better role models, and (6) more peer pressure to achieve. It is a familiar set of facts. Blacks are disproportionately assigned to the worst group of schools, since high schools are generally funded by local property taxes. White flight from inner cities has reduced property values there and undermined the schools, creating disparities between predominantly white, suburban schools and schools in the inner cities.

One may object that many whites attend such inferior public schools. I agree. But this provides a reason for *more* AA, not less. Some programs of AA select disadvantaged white groups such as Cajuns and Appalachian Mountain whites. I advocate extending AA to cover all students from inferior public schools and disadvantaged environments. But helping blacks with AA does a major part of this job. Half a loaf is better than none. We should extend AA to cover as many disadvantaged people as is administratively possible rather than ban AA. Using race as a classification is an administratively easy way to target generally relevant groups. But targeting the relevant schools and neighborhoods would be more accurate.

As Peter Singer notes, "taking into account a student's race would merely be a way of correcting for the failure of standard tests to allow for the disadvantages that face blacks in competing with whites on such tests."[20] Such disadvantages include less ability to afford preparation courses, which whites commonly take and which the free market has specifically designed to boost scores on such standard tests as the SAT.[21] Similarly, Richard Wasserstrom argues:

> Most of what are regarded as the decisive characteristics for higher education have a great deal to do with things over which the individual has neither control nor responsibility: such things as home environment, socioeconomic class of parents, and of course, the quality of the primary and secondary schools attended. Since individuals do not deserve having had any of these things vis-à-vis other individuals, they do not, for the most part, deserve their qualifications.[22]

Wasserstrom's argument sums up both why AA is needed as compensation for undeserved disadvantages and why AA need not admit genuinely inferior candidates. Finally, there is a clear check on inferior candidates, since any who fall below acceptable standards once admitted can easily be barred from returning. AA could go so far as to involve hiring those with less merit, but AA clearly need not do so. For example, the most modest form of AA would be to use race only as a tiebreaker to select blacks. Much bolder forms of AA can avoid generally hiring those with significantly less merit, since the aforementioned, overall competitive advantage whites generally have is dramatic and itself unrelated to merit under any definition, since it is determined by race and an accident of birth unrelated to productivity.

So, meritocracy not only is compatible with but demands AA unskewing scores to show true merit.

Further, if, as Daniels and I argue, meritocracy is a matter of macroproductivity rather than justice, then there would seem to be more room for compromise in trading off macroproductivity (if necessary) in exchange for AA's benefits (that is, AA's benefits in terms of justice and productivity). As Daniels notes, "Many will feel less concerned about such compromises of productivity than they would if a claim to merit a job was really a claim of right, a claim of justice."[23]

Conclusion

I conclude that each of Lisa Newton's three main arguments against AA contains some fatal flaws. I have shown that each of her arguments commits some well-recognized logical fallacies or relies heavily on some false assumptions. Newton's flawed arguments fail to rebut the familiar, positive arguments for AA based on compensatory justice and the utilitarian (or humanitarian) considerations that AA promotes: (1) role models to motivate harder work by encouraging blacks that their prospects are not so bleak; (2) encouragement of more blacks to apply, thus increasing competition by increasing the pool of competitors; (3) diversity in education; (4) replacing diminishing marginal utility of richer whites with more utility for poorer blacks; and (5) unskewing biased tests of merit. These arguments for AA are familiar enough that I need not discuss them further, especially since I have above detailed how AA unskews biased and significantly incomplete tests of merit.

Study Questions

1. Newton later wrote that she supported much affirmative action but not reverse discrimination, which she defined (only at this later date, but not in her original article) as deceptive affirmative action. Newton complained that Harwood never informed the reader that she was using the term "reverse discrimination." How many places in Harwood's essay can you find him referring to Newton's use of "reverse discrimination"?

2. Do you think Newton's use of "reverse discrimination" begs the question of whether affirmative action discriminates at all? Harwood denies that all programs of affirmative action discriminate. And the official name of the program is affirmative ac-

tion. Nowhere will you find a university with an Office of Reverse Discrimination. So there is at least a question about whether affirmative action is reverse discrimination.

*3. Do you believe it is more important to give ethnic groups equal opportunity in different fields or to ensure that they achieve equal levels of success in those fields? Under what circumstances, if any, do you believe that government should regulate the ethnic diversity of a particular profession? How, if at all, would you compensate individuals for past discrimination against them or their ancestors?

*4. If you and your family emigrated to Spain, how long would it be before you spoke Spanish in your home? Do you think you would lose your cultural identity if you had to give up your native tongue?

Notes

I wish to thank the following for their comments on this paper: Arthur Cody, Theo Correl, Michael Gorr, Peter Hadreas, Thomas Leddy, David Lyons, Steven Maitzen, Max O'Connor, Georgette Sinkler, Calvin Stewart, Shelley Stillwell, and Laurence Thomas.

1. Lisa H. Newton, "Reverse Discrimination as Unjustified," *Ethics* 83 (1973): 308–312; reprinted in Barry R. Gross, ed., *Reverse Discrimination* (Buffalo, N.Y.: Prometheus Books, 1977), 373–378; reprinted in Thomas A. Mappes and Jane S. Zembaty, eds., *Social Ethics: Morality and Social Policy* (New York: McGraw-Hill, 1977), 173–177; reprinted in Jan Narveson, ed., *Moral Issues* (New York: Oxford University Press, 1983), 388–392; reprinted in Joel Feinberg and Hyman Gross, eds., *The Philosophy of Law*, 3rd ed. (Belmont, Calif.: Wadsworth, 1986), 456–458; reprinted as "Against Affirmative Action," in Raziel Abelson and Marie-Louise Friquegnon, eds., *Ethics for Modern Life*, 3rd ed. (New York: St. Martin's Press, 1987), 236–241; reprinted in Jeffrey Olen and Vincent Barry, eds., *Applying Ethics*, 3rd ed. (Belmont, Calif.: Wadsworth, 1989), 316–319; reprinted in David Appelbaum and Sarah Verone Lawton, eds., *Ethics and the Professions* (Englewood Cliffs, N.J.: Prentice-Hall, 1990), 178–181; reprinted in Joseph R. DesJardins and John J. McCall, eds., *Contemporary Issues In Business Ethics*, 2nd ed. (Belmont, Calif.: Wadsworth, 1990), 384–387; reprinted in Stephen Satris, ed., *Taking Sides: Clashing Views on Controversial Moral Issues*, 2nd ed. (Guilford, Conn.: Dushkin, 1990), 262–266; and reprinted in Lisa H. Newton and Maureen M. Ford, eds., *Taking Sides: Clashing Views on Controversial Issues in Business Ethics and Society* (Guilford, Conn.: Dushkin, 1990), 94–98. All citations below are to the original.

2. Newton, 311.

3. See *United States v. Carolene Products Co.*, 304 U.S. 144 (1938), note 4.

4. On this aspect of *Federalist* No. 10, see my "Madisonian Democracy and Marxist Analysis," in Christopher B. Gray, ed., *Philosophical Reflections on the United States Constitution: A Collection of Bicentennial Essays* (Lewiston, NY: Edwin Mellen Press, 1989), 29–36.

5. U.S. Dept. of Commerce, Bureau of the Census, Statistical Abstract of the U.S. (U.S. Government Printing Office, 1985), 446.

6. Newton, 312.

7. See Thomas Sowell, *Civil Rights: Rhetoric or Reality?* (New York: Quill, 1984), 39–41.

8. Newton, 310.

9. Robert K. Fullinwider, *The Reverse Discrimination Controversy: A Moral and Legal Analysis* (Totowa, N.J.: Rowman and Littlefield, 1980), 234. What I call meritocracy Fullinwider calls the "right to equal consideration for a job" or "RTEC."

10. Fullinwider, 234.

11. AA further serves distributive justice by helping prevent inequality from increasing due to capitalism's magnification of unfair disadvantages, as we saw above. See also D. W. Haslett, "Is Inheritance Justified?" *Philosophy & Public Affairs* 15 (1986): 122, especially section II. Haslett's otherwise excellent case for increasing inheritance taxes suffers from underemphasizing arguments that *workers earn* the right to improve the destinies of their children (simpliciter) even if—as Haslett emphasizes—the *children* do not independently deserve to have their destinies improved (vis-à-vis other children). For another evaluation of the morality of inheritance, see my "Is Inheritance Immoral?," *The Barrister* 1 (1989): 11–12.

12. Norman Daniels, "Merit and Meritocracy," *Philosophy & Public Affairs* 7 (1978): 210.

13. Daniels, 210.

14. Daniels, 211–212.

15. Daniels, 212.

16. See Robert S. Summers, *Lon L. Fuller* (Stanford, Calif.: Stanford University Press, 1984), 87 and 99–100, on polycentricity.

17. Ronald M. Dworkin, *A Matter of Principle* (Cambridge: Harvard University Press, 1985), 299 (emphasis added). On the occasional relevance of race for merit, see Alan Wertheimer, "Jobs, Qualifications and Preferences," *Ethics* 94 (1983): 99–112; and Peter Singer, "Is Racial Discrimination Arbitrary?" in Narveson, 308–324.

18. Dworkin, 301.

19. See Stephen Jay Gould, *The Mismeasure of Man* (Cambridge: Harvard University Press, 1983); and N. J. Block and Gerald Dworkin, eds., *The I.Q. Controversy* (New York: Pantheon, 1976).

20. Singer, 322.

21. Recall that the average black family's income is only 56% of the average white family's income. See note 5, above, and the accompanying text.

22. Richard Wasserstrom, "A Defense of Programs of Preferential Treatment," in Narveson, 397.

23. Daniels, 215.

22

City of Richmond v.
J. A. Croson Company

Supreme Court of the United States

In this case we confront once again the tension between the Fourteenth Amendment's guarantee of equal treatment to all citizens, and the use of race-based measures to ameliorate the effects of past discrimination on the opportunities enjoyed by members of minority groups in our society.

I

On April 11, 1983, the Richmond City Council adopted the Minority Business Utilization Plan (the Plan). The Plan required prime contractors to whom the city awarded construction contracts to subcontract at least 30% of the dollar amount of the contract to one or more Minority Business Enterprises (MBEs), Ordinance No. 83-69-59, codified in Richmond, Va., City Code, § 12-156(a) (1985). The 30% set-aside did not apply to city contracts awarded to minority-owned prime contractors. *Ibid.*

The Plan defined an MBE as "[a] business at least fifty-one (51) percent of which is owned and controlled ... by minority group members." "Minority group members" were defined as "[c]itizens of the United States who are Blacks, Spanish-speaking, Orientals, Indians, Eskimos, or Aleuts." There was no geographic limit to the Plan; an otherwise qualified MBE from anywhere in the United States could avail itself of the 30% set-aside. The Plan declared that it was "remedial" in nature, and enacted "for the purpose of promoting wider participation by minority business enterprises in the construction of public projects." § 12-158(1). The Plan expired on June 30, 1988, and was in effect for approximately five years.

Reprinted from Supreme Court of the United States, 488 U.S. 469 (1989).

The Plan authorized the Director of the Department of General Services to promulgate rules which "shall allow waivers in those individual situations where a contractor can prove to the satisfaction of the director that the requirements herein cannot be achieved." To this end, the Director promulgated Contract Clauses, Minority Business Utilization Plan (Contract Clauses). Section D of these rules provided: "No partial or complete waiver of the foregoing requirement shall be granted by the city other than in exceptional circumstances. To justify a waiver, it must be shown that every feasible attempt has been made to comply, and it must be demonstrated that sufficient, relevant, qualified Minority Business Enterprises ... are unavailable or unwilling to participate in the contract to enable meeting the 30% MBE goal."
. . .

The Plan was adopted by the Richmond City Council after a public hearing. App. 9-50. Seven members of the public spoke to the merits of the ordinance; five were in opposition, two in favor. Proponents of the set-aside provision relied on a study which indicated that, while the general population of Richmond was 50% black, only .67% of the city's prime construction contracts had been awarded to minority businesses in the 5-year period from 1978 to 1983. . . .

There was no direct evidence of race discrimination on the part of the city in letting contracts or any evidence that the city's prime contractors had discriminated against minority-owned subcontractors.
. . .

. . . On September 6, 1983, the city of Richmond issued an invitation to bid on a project for the provision and installation of certain plumbing fixtures at the city jail. On September 30, 1983, Eugene Bonn, the regional manager of J. A. Croson Company (Croson), a mechanical plumbing and heating contractor, received the bid forms. The project involved the installations of stainless steel urinals and water closets in the city jail. Products of either of two manufacturers were specified, Acorn Engineering Company (Acorn) or Bradley Manufacturing Company (Bradley). Bonn determined that to meet the 30% set-aside requirement, a minority contractor would have to supply the fixtures. The provision of the fixtures amounted to 75% of the total contract price. . . .

Bonn subsequently began a search for potential MBE suppliers. The only potential MBE fixture supplier was Melvin Brown, president of Continental Metal Hose, hereafter referred to as "Continental." However, because of Continental's inability to obtain credit approval, Continental was unable to submit a bid by the due date of October 13, 1983. Shortly thereafter and as a direct result, Croson submitted a request for a waiver of the 30% set-aside. Croson's waiver request indicated that Continental was "unqualified" and that the other MBEs contacted had been unresponsive or unable to quote. Upon learning of Croson's waiver request, Brown contacted an agent of Acorn, the other fixture manufacturer specified by the city. Based upon his discussions with Acorn, Brown subsequently submitted a bid on the fixtures to Croson. Continental's bid was $6,183.29 higher than the price Croson had included for the fixtures in its bid to the city. This constituted a 7% increase over the market price for the fixtures. With added bonding and insurance, using Continental would have raised the cost of the project by $7,663.16. On the same day that Brown contacted Acorn, he also called city procurement officials and told them that Continental, an MBE, could supply the fixtures specified in the city jail contract. On November 2, 1983, the city denied Croson's waiver request, indicating that Croson had 10 days to submit an MBE Utilization Commitment Form, and warned that failure to do so could result in its bid being considered unresponsive.

Croson wrote the city on November 8, 1983. In the letter Bonn indicated that Continental was not an authorized supplier for either Acorn or Bradley fixtures. He also noted that Acorn's quotation to Brown was subject to credit approval and in any case was substantially higher than any other quotation Croson had received. Finally, Bonn noted that Continental's bid had been submitted some 21 days after the prime bids were due. In a second letter, Croson laid out the additional costs that using Continental to supply the fixtures would entail, and asked that it be allowed to raise the overall contract price accordingly. The city denied both Croson's request for a waiver and its suggestion that the contract price be raised. The city informed Croson that it had decided to rebid the project. On December 9, 1983, counsel for Croson wrote the city asking for a review of the waiver denial. The city's attorney responded that the city had elected to rebid the project, and that there is no appeal of such a decision. Shortly thereafter Croson brought this action under 42 U.S.C. § 1983 in the Federal District Court for the Eastern District of Virginia, arguing that the Richmond ordinance was unconstitutional on its face and as applied in this case.

The District Court upheld the Plan in all respects ... [and held that] the 30% figure was "reasonable in light of the undisputed fact that minorities consti-

tute 50% of the population of Richmond." *Ibid.*

Croson sought certiorari from this Court. We granted the writ, vacated the opinion of the Court of Appeals, and remanded the case for further consideration in light of our intervening decision in *Wygant v. Jackson Board of Education* (1986). . . .

On remand, a divided panel of the Court of Appeals struck down the Richmond set-aside program as violating both prongs of strict scrutiny under the Equal Protection Clause of the Fourteenth Amendment. *J. A. Croson Co. v. Richmond (Croson II).*

In this case, the debate at the city council meeting "revealed no record of prior discrimination by the city in awarding public contracts. . . ." *Croson II.* Moreover, the statistics comparing the minority population of Richmond to the percentage of *prime* contracts awarded to minority firms had little or no probative value in establishing prior discrimination in the relevant market, and actually suggested "more of a political than a remedial basis for the racial preference." 822 F.2d, at 1359. The court concluded that, "[i]f this plan is supported by a compelling governmental interest, so is every other plan that has been enacted in the past or that will be enacted in the future."

The Court of Appeals went on to hold that even if the city had demonstrated a compelling interest in the use of a race-based quota, the 30% set-aside was not narrowly tailored to accomplish a remedial purpose. The court found that the 30% figure was "chosen arbitrarily" and was not tied to the number of minority subcontractors in Richmond or to any other relevant number. *Ibid.* The dissenting judge argued that the majority had "misconstrue[d] and misapplie[d]" our decision in *Wygant,* 822 F.2d, at 1362. We noted probable jurisdiction of the city's appeal, . . . and we now affirm the judgment.

II

. . . Congress, unlike any State or political subdivision, has a specific constitutional mandate to enforce the dictates of the Fourteenth Amendment. The power to "enforce" may at times also include the power to define situations which *Congress* determines threaten principles of equality and to adopt prophylactic rules to deal with those situations. . . .

That Congress may identify and redress the effects of society-wide discrimination does not mean that, *a fortiori,* the States and the political subdivisions are free to decide that such remedies are appropriate. Section I of the Fourteenth Amendment is an explicit *constraint* on state power, and the States must undertake any remedial efforts in accordance with that provision. To hold otherwise would be to cede control over the content of the Equal Protection Clause to the 50 state legislatures and their myriad political subdivisions. The mere recitation of a benign or compensatory purpose for the use of a racial classification would essentially entitle the States to exercise the full power of Congress under § 5 of the Fourteenth Amendment and insulate any racial classification from judicial scrutiny under § 1. We believe that such a result would be contrary to the intentions of the Framers of the Fourteenth Amendment, who desired to place clear limits on the States' use of race as a criterion for legislative action, and to have the federal courts enforce those limitations. . . .

It would seem equally clear, however, that a state or local subdivision (if delegated the authority from the State) has the authority to eradicate the effects of private discrimination within its own legislative jurisdiction. This authority must, of course, be exercised within the constraints of § 1 of the Fourteenth Amendment. . . . As a matter of state law, the city of Richmond has legislative authority over its procurement policies, and can use its spending powers to remedy private discrimination, if it identifies that discrimination with the particularity required by the Fourteenth Amendment. . . .

Thus, if the city could show that it had essentially become a "passive participant" in a system of racial exclusion practiced by elements of the local construction industry, we think it clear that the city could take affirmative steps to dismantle such a system. It is beyond dispute that any public entity, state or federal, has a compelling interest in assuring that public dollars, drawn from the tax contributions of all citizens, do not serve to finance the evil of private prejudice. . . .

IIIA

The Equal Protection Clause of the Fourteenth Amendment provides that "[N]o State shall . . . deny to *any person* within its jurisdiction the equal protection of the laws" (emphasis added). As this Court has noted in the past, the "rights created by the first section of the Fourteenth Amendment are, by its terms, guaranteed to the individual. The rights es-

tablished are personal rights." *Shelley v. Kraemer* (1948). The Richmond Plan denies certain citizens the opportunity to compete for a fixed percentage of public contracts based solely upon their race. To whatever racial group these citizens belong, their "personal rights" to be treated with equal dignity and respect are implicated by a rigid rule erecting race as the sole criterion in an aspect of public decision making. . . .

Classifications based on race carry a danger of stigmatic harm. Unless they are strictly reserved for remedial settings, they may in fact promote notions of racial inferiority and lead to a politics of racial hostility. . . .

IIIB

The District Court found the city council's "findings sufficient to ensure that, in adopting the Plan, it was remedying the present effects of past discrimination in the *construction industry*." Supp. App. (emphasis added). Like the "role model" theory employed in *Wygant*, a generalized assertion that there has been past discrimination in an entire industry provides no guidance for a legislative body to determine the precise scope of the injury it seeks to remedy. It "has no logical stopping point." *Wygant* (plurality opinion). "Relief" for such an ill-defined wrong could extend until the percentage of public contracts awarded to MBEs in Richmond mirrored the percentage of minorities in the population as a whole.

Appellant argues that it is attempting to remedy various forms of past discrimination that are alleged to be responsible for the small number of minority businesses in the local contracting industry. Among these the city cites the exclusion of blacks from skilled construction trade unions and training programs. This past discrimination has prevented them "from following the traditional path from laborer to entrepreneur." Brief for Appellant 23-24. The city also lists a host of nonracial factors which would seem to face a member of any racial group attempting to establish a new business enterprise, such as deficiencies in working capital, inability to meet bonding requirements, unfamiliarity with bidding procedures, and disability caused by an inadequate track record. *Id.*, at 25-26, and n. 41.

While there is no doubt that the sorry history of both private and public discrimination in this country has contributed to a lack of opportunities for black entrepreneurs, this observation, standing alone, cannot justify a rigid racial quota in the awarding of public contracts in Richmond, Virginia. Like the claim that discrimination in primary and secondary schooling justifies a rigid racial preference in medical school admissions, an amorphous claim that there has been past discrimination in a particular industry cannot justify the use of an unyielding racial quota.

It is sheer speculation how many minority firms there would be in Richmond absent past societal discrimination, just as it was sheer speculation how many minority medical students would have been admitted to the medical school at Davis absent past discrimination in educational opportunities. Defining these sorts of injuries as "identified discrimination" would give local governments license to create a patchwork of racial preferences based on statistical generalizations about any particular field of endeavor.

These defects are readily apparent in this case. The 30% quota cannot in any realistic sense be tied to any injury suffered by anyone. . . .

There is nothing approaching a prima facie case of a constitutional or statutory violation by *anyone* in the Richmond construction industry. . . .

The District Court accorded great weight to the fact that the city council designated the Plan as "remedial." But the mere recitation of a "benign" or legitimate purpose for a racial classification, is entitled to little or no weight. . . . Racial classifications are suspect, and that means that simple legislative assurances of good intention cannot suffice. . . .

In this case, the city does not even know how many MBEs in the relevant market are qualified to undertake prime or subcontracting work in public construction projects. . . . Nor does the city know what percentage of total city construction dollars minority firms now receive as subcontractors on prime contracts let by the city.

To a large extent, the set-aside of sub-contracting dollars seems to rest on the unsupported assumption that white prime contractors simply will not hire minority firms. . . . Without any information on minority participation in subcontracting, it is quite simply impossible to evaluate overall minority representation in the city's construction expenditures.

The city and the District Court also relied on evidence that MBE membership in local contractors' associations was extremely low. Again, standing alone this evidence is not probative of any discrimination in the local construction industry. There are numerous explanations for this dearth of minority

participation, including past societal discrimination in education and economic opportunities as well as both black and white career and entrepreneurial choices. Blacks may be disproportionately attracted to industries other than construction. . . . The mere fact that black membership in these trade organizations is low, standing alone, cannot establish a prima facie case of discrimination. . . .

While the States and their subdivisions may take remedial action when they possess evidence that their own spending practices are exacerbating a pattern of prior discrimination, they must identify that discrimination, public or private, with some specificity before they may use race-conscious relief. . . .

In sum, none of the evidence presented by the city points to any identified discrimination in the Richmond construction industry. We, therefore, hold that the city has failed to demonstrate a compelling interest in apportioning public contracting opportunities on the basis of race. To accept Richmond's claim that past societal discrimination alone can serve as the basis for rigid race preferences would be to open the door to competing claims for "remedial relief" for every disadvantaged group. The dream of a Nation of equal citizens in a society where race is irrelevant to personal opportunity and achievement would be lost in a mosaic of shifting preferences based on inherently unmeasurable claims of past wrongs. . . .

IV

Since the city must already consider bids and waivers on a case-by-case basis, it is difficult to see the need for a rigid numerical quota. . . .

Given the existence of an individualized procedure, the city's only interest in maintaining a quota system rather than investigating the need for remedial action in particular cases would seem to be simple administrative convenience. But the interest in avoiding the bureaucratic effort necessary to tailor remedial relief to those who truly have suffered the effects of prior discrimination cannot justify a rigid line drawn on the basis of a suspect classification. . . . Under Richmond's scheme, a successful black, Hispanic, or Oriental entrepreneur from anywhere in the country enjoys an absolute preference over other citizens based solely on their race. We think it obvious that such a program is not narrowly tailored to remedy the effects of prior discrimination.

V

... Because the city of Richmond has failed to identify the need for remedial action in the awarding of its public construction contracts, its treatment of its citizens on a racial basis violates the dictates of the Equal Protection Clause. Accordingly, the judgment of the Court of Appeals for the Fourth Circuit is Affirmed.

Study Questions

1. Does the court rule that quotas are legal here?

2. How many other types of affirmative action are there besides quotas?

3. Should the majority of the court have combined the historical fact that Richmond was the capital of the Confederacy with the statistical disparity between the races in Richmond to get a more comprehensive picture of whether there was racism in the case that would allow minority set-asides? Even if the statistical disparity alone is not decisive evidence of racism, doesn't a long history of much racism in the relevant area help make the evidence of racism decisive or much closer to decisive?

23

The Case of Racism in the 1990s

Associated Press

Women and blacks who bargain for a new car are given higher final prices than white men, according to a study surveying hundreds of car dealerships in the Chicago area.

Black women were offered the highest prices, averaging $875 a car more than white men, the study found.

Ian Ayres, a law professor at Northwestern University who led the research, said yesterday that the results may be attributable to car dealers trying to concentrate profits by targeting a relatively few "suckers" who will pay higher markups.

That may not be bigotry, but it's definitely discrimination, Ayres said. "Treating black people differently in order to increase your revenues runs afoul of our traditional civil-rights norms," he said.

An official with the National Automobile Dealers Association said that no responsible salesman would target a person by race or sex, especially because most people go to several dealers and play one off another while shopping. And although he hadn't seen the study, NADA vice president Frank McCarthy said that the premise was not valid.

The study began three years ago and involved 90 Chicago-area dealerships. A follow-up survey of 275 to 300 dealerships was conducted during the past year.

In the first study, three white male researchers divided among themselves dealerships selling the same brand of domestic car, then tried to get the best deal on a new car. Each dealership also was visited at about the same time by one of three other researchers—a white woman, a black woman, and a black man—who bargained over the same car. The researchers were prepared with carefully rehearsed negotiating tactics to get the best deal.

The make and model of the car was not disclosed, but researchers estimated the dealers' cost at about $11,000.

The study found that white men received final offers that averaged about $11,362 on a new car with a sticker price of $13,465.

The white woman was given an average final price of $11,504, the black man an average final price of $11,783 and the black woman an average price of $12,237. No cars were actually purchased.

Study Questions

1. Do you think this study refutes the view of William F. Buckley, Jr., and Robert Bork (which they argued in 1994 on the PBS television show *Firing Line*) that racism is not a serious problem in the United States today?

2. Sen. Warren G. Magnuson and Jean Carper have argued as follows: "The plight of the poverty-stricken consumer is all the more poignant when it is realized that his pursuit of goods and credit, which in turn makes him so vulnerable to callous exploitation, is in reality what has been called 'compensatory consumption,' a desire to infuse his existence with dignity denied him elsewhere by accumulating material goods." Does it make any sense for poor people to feel a need to spend more of their scarce money just because they are poor? When you feel down and out, do you tend to spend money to cheer yourself up? Many middle-class people resent seeing poor people driving a dignified car such as a Cadillac, but do Magnuson and Carper help explain why such a sight makes some sense?

3. Magnuson and Caper[1] write that some studies "demonstrated how costly the color of your skin can be. . . . a racial price differential of 60 percent! Shopping surveys in Boston, Philadelphia, Chicago, and San Francisco reveal the same pattern: the poor are paying exorbitant prices, usually 75 to 100 percent more for goods from stores in low-income areas as compared with those in 'ethical' stores patronized by the middle class." Is it ethical for companies to take advantage of such needs of the poor and of racial minorities? As former Federal Trade Commissioner Mary Gardiner Jones writes: "Like [the rest of] us they are the recipients of the daily advertising messages of the necessities of life which we should

buy, of the constant urgings to buy now and pay later ... The social pressure on them to consume is almost irresistible, not simply because of their actual physical needs for many of these possessions, but also because of their deep psychological needs for self-respect, for dignity, for a feeling of belonging and for approval from their neighbors ... The only sense of status which is in any way available to them is through a possession of the material accoutrements of our economy ... [for example] an automobile ..."

4. Are the poor and minorities victims of circumstances largely beyond their control?

Notes

1. Magnuson, Warren G. and Jean Carper, *The Dark Side of the Marketplace: The Plight of the American Consumer* (Englewood Cliffs, N.J.: Prentice-Hall, 1968), pp. 33–34.

24

Learning to Love Your Corporate Culture

Michael Lewis

Editor's note: Lewis takes us on a tour inside one of the biggest investment firms. After experiencing the rude and the crude, Lewis ends up leaving the firm and doubting the value of such work. Lewis even comes to doubt such basic commonsensical ideas as "supply and demand determine price (or wages)," and "merit is rewarded since you can't keep a good man or good woman down" and "the cream always rises to the top."

He who makes a beast of himself gets rid of the pain of being a man.

—Samuel Johnson

I remember almost exactly how I felt and what I saw my first day at Salomon Brothers. There was a cold shiver doing laps around my body, which, softened and coddled by the regime of a professional student, was imagining it was still asleep. With reason. I wasn't due at work until 7:00 A.M., but I rose early to walk around Wall Street before going to the office. I had never seen the place before. There *was* a river at one end and a graveyard at the other. In between was vintage Manhattan: a deep, narrow canyon in which yellow cabs smacked into raised sewer lids, potholes, and garbage. Armies of worried men in suits stormed off the Lexington Avenue subway line and marched down the crooked pavements. For rich people, they didn't look very happy. They seemed serious, at least compared with how I felt. I had only a few jitters that accompany any new beginning. Oddly enough,

I didn't really imagine I was going to work, more as if I were going to collect lottery winnings.

Salomon Brothers had written me in London to announce that it would pay me an M.B.A.'s wage—though I had no M.B.A.—of forty-two thousand dollars plus a bonus after the first six months of six thousand more. At that time I hadn't had the education required to feel poor on forty-eight thousand dollars (then equivalent to forty-five thousand British pounds) a year. Receiving the news in England, the land of limp paychecks, accentuated the generosity of Salomon's purse. A chaired professor of the London School of Economics, who took a keen interest in material affairs, stared at me bug-eyed and gurgled when he heard what I was to be paid. It was twice what he earned. He was in his mid-forties and at the top of his profession. I was twenty-four years old and at the bottom of mine. There was no justice in the world, and thank goodness for that.

Perhaps it is worth explaining where this money was coming from, not that I gave it much thought at the time. Man for man Salomon Brothers was, in 1985, the world's most profitable corporation. At least that is what I was repeatedly told. I never bothered to check it because it seemed so obviously true. Wall Street was hot. And we were Wall Street's most profitable firm.

Wall Street trafficks in stocks and bonds. At the end of the 1970s, and the beginning of both super indulgent American politics and modern financial history, Salomon Brothers knew more about bonds than any firm on Wall Street: how to value them, how to trade them, and how to sell them. The sole chink in its complete dominance of the bond markets in 1979 was in junk bonds, which we shall return to later and which were the specialty of another firm, similar to us in many ways: Drexel Burnham. But in the late 1970s and early 1980s, junk bonds were such a tiny fraction of the market that Salomon effectively dominated the entire bond market. The rest of Wall Street had been content to let Salomon Brothers be the best bond traders because the occupation was neither terribly profitable nor prestigious. What was prestigious was raising capital (equity) for corporations. What was prestigious was knowing lots of corporate CEOs. Salomon was a social and financial outlier.

That, anyway, is what I was told. It was hard to prove any of it because the only evidence was oral. But consider the kickoff chuckle to a speech given to the Wharton School in March 1977 by Sidney Homer of Salomon Brothers, the leading bond analyst on

Wall Street from the mid-1940s right through to the late 1970s. "I felt frustrated," said Homer about his job. "At cocktail parties lovely ladies would corner me and ask my opinion of the market, but alas, when they learned I was a bond man, they would quietly drift away."

Or consider the very lack of evidence itself. There are 287 books about bonds in the New York Public Library, and most of them are about chemistry. The ones that aren't contain lots of ugly numbers and bear titles such as *All Quiet on the Bond Front*, and *Low-Risk Strategies for the Investor*. In other words, they aren't the sort of page turners that moisten your palms and glue you to your seat. People who believe themselves of social consequence tend to leave more of a paper trail, in the form of memoirs and anecdotiana. But while there are dozens of anecdotes and several memoirs from the stock markets, the bond markets are officially silent. Bond people pose the same problem to a cultural anthropologist as a nonliterate tribe deep in the Amazon.

In part this is due to the absence from the bond market of the educated classes, which in turn reinforces the point about how unfashionable bonds once were. In 1968, the last time a degree count was taken at Salomon Brothers, thirteen of the twenty-eight partners hadn't been to college, and one hadn't graduated from the eighth grade. John Gutfreund was, in this crowd, an intellectual; though he was rejected by Harvard, he did finally graduate (without distinction) from Oberlin.

The biggest myth about bond traders, and therefore the greatest misunderstanding about the unprecedented prosperity on Wall Street in the 1980s, are that they make their money by taking large risks. A few do. And all traders take small risks. But most traders act simply as toll takers. The source of their fortune has been nicely summarized by Kurt Vonnegut (who, oddly, was describing lawyers): "There is a magic moment, during which a man has surrendered a treasure, and during which the man who is about to receive it has not yet done so. An alert lawyer [read bond trader] will make that moment his own, possessing the treasure for a magic microsecond, taking a little of it, passing it on."

In other words, Salomon carved a tiny fraction out of each financial transaction. This adds up. The Salomon salesman sells $50 million worth of new IBM bonds to pension fund X. The Salomon trader, who provides the salesman with the bonds, takes for himself an eighth (of a percentage point), or $62,500. He may, if he wishes, take more. In the bond market, unlike in the stock market, commissions are not openly stated.

Now the fun begins. Once the trader knows the location of the IBM bonds and the temperament of their owner, he doesn't have to be outstandingly clever to make the bonds (the treasure) move again. He can generate his own magic microseconds. He can, for example, pressure one of his salesmen to persuade insurance company Y that IBM bonds are worth more than pension fund X paid for them initially. Whether it is true is irrelevant. The trader buys the bonds from X and sells them to Y and takes out another eighth, and the pension fund is happy to make a small profit in such a short time.

In this process, it helps if neither of the parties on either side of the middleman knows the value of the treasure. The men on the trading floor may not have been to school, but they have Ph.D.'s in man's ignorance. In any market, as in any poker game there is a fool. The astute investor Warren Buffett is fond of saying that any player unaware of the fool in the market probably *is* the fool in the market. In 1980, when the bond market emerged from a long dormancy, many investors and even Wall Street banks did not have a clue who was the fool in the new game. Salomon bond traders knew about fools because that was their job. Knowing about markets is knowing about other people's weaknesses. And a fool, they would say, was a person who was willing to sell a bond for less or buy a bond for more than it was worth. A bond was worth only as much as the person who valued it properly was willing to pay. And Salomon, to complete the circle, was the firm that valued the bonds properly.

But none of this explains why Salomon Brothers was particularly profitable in the 1980s. Making profits on Wall Street is a bit like eating the stuffing from a turkey. Some higher authority must first put the stuffing into the turkey. The turkey was stuffed more generously in the 1980s than ever before. And Salomon Brothers, because of its expertise, had second and third helpings before other firms even knew that supper was on.

One of the benevolent hands doing the stuffing belonged to the Federal Reserve. That is ironic, since no one disapproved of the excesses of Wall Street in the 1980s so much as the chairman of the Fed, Paul Volcker. At a rare Saturday press conference, on October 6, 1979, Volcker announced that the money supply would cease to fluctuate with the business cycle; money supply would be fixed, and interest rates would float. The event, I think, marks the beginning of the golden age of the bond man. Had Volcker never pushed through his radical change in policy, the world would be many bond traders and one memoir the poorer. For in practice, the shift in the focus of monetary policy meant that interest rates would swing wildly. Bond prices move inversely, lockstep, to rates of interest. Allowing interest rates to swing wildly meant allowing bond prices to swing wildly. Before Volcker's speech, bonds had been conservative investments, into which investors put their savings when they didn't fancy a gamble in the stock market. After Volcker's speech, bonds became objects of speculation, a means of creating wealth rather than merely storing it. Overnight the bond market was transformed from a backwater into a casino. Turnover boomed at Salomon. Many more people were hired to handle the new business, on starting salaries of forty-eight grand.

Once Volcker had set interest rates free, the other hand stuffing the turkey went to work: America's borrowers. American governments, consumers, and corporations borrowed money at a faster clip during the 1980s than ever before; this meant the volume of bonds exploded (another way to look at this is that investors were lending money more freely than ever before). The combined indebtedness of the three groups in 1977 was $323 billion, much of which wasn't bonds but loans made by commercial banks. By 1985 the three groups had borrowed $7 *trillion*. What is more, thanks to financial entrepreneurs at places like Salomon and the shakiness of commercial banks, a much greater percentage of the debt was cast in the form of bonds than before.

So not only were bond prices more volatile, but the number of bonds to trade increased. Nothing changed within Salomon Brothers that made the traders more able. Now, however, trades exploded in both size and frequency. A Salomon salesman who had in the past moved five million dollars' worth of merchandise through the traders' books each week was now moving three hundred million dollars through each *day*. He, the trader, and the firm began to get rich. And they decided for reasons best known to themselves to invest some of their winnings in buying people like me.

Classes at Salomon Brothers were held on the twenty-third floor of its building on the southeastern tip of Manhattan. I made my way there to begin, at last, my career. At first blush my prospects looked bleak. The other trainees appeared to have been in the office for hours. In fact, to get an edge on their colleagues, most had been there for weeks. As I

walked into the training area, they were gathered in packs in the hallways or in the foyer behind the classroom, chattering. It was a family reunion. Everyone knew everyone else. Cliques had gelled. All the best lockers had been taken. Newcomers were regarded with suspicion. Already opinions had formed of who was "good," meaning who was cut out for the Salomon trading floor, and who was a loser.

One group of men stood in a circle in a corner of the foyer playing a game I didn't recognize but now know to be Liar's Poker. They were laughing, cursing, eyeing each other sideways, and generally behaving in a brotherly, traderly manner. They wore belts. I think I gave up the idea of feeling immediately at home at Salomon Brothers when I saw the belts. I had taken the opportunity to break out a pair of bright red suspenders with large gold dollar signs running down them. Time to play investment banker, I had thought. Wrong. Later a well-meaning fellow trainee gave me a piece of advice. "Don't let them see you on the trading floor in those things," he said. "Managing directors are the only guys who can get away with wearing suspenders. They'll take one look at you and say, `Who the fuck does he think he is anyway?'"

I remember also that as I walked into the foyer that first morning, a female trainee was shouting into what must have been a fuzzy phone connection. In the midst of a scorching July, the pudgy woman on the phone was stuffed into a three-piece tweed suit with an oversize white boy tie, which I probably would not have given a second thought had she not herself called attention to it. She placed one hand over the receiver and declared to a tiny group of women: "Look, I can do six full suits for seven hundred and fifty bucks. *These* are quality. And *that* is a good price. You can't get them any cheaper."

That explained it. She wearing tweed only because she was *selling* tweed. She guessed rightly that her training class represented a market in itself: people with money to burn, eyes for a bargain, and space in their closets for the executive look. She had persuaded an Oriental sweatshop to supply her with winter wear in bulk. When she saw me watching her, she said that given a bit of time, she could "do men too." She did not mean this as a bawdy joke. Thus the first words spoken to me by a fellow trainee were by someone trying to sell me something. It was a fitting welcome to Salomon Brothers.

From the foyer's darkest corner came a tiny ray of hope, the first sign that there was more than one perspective on life at Salomon Brothers. A fat young man lay spread-eagled on the floor. He was, as far as I could determine, asleep. His shirt was untucked and badly wrinkled; his white belly pushed through like a whale's hump where the buttons had come undone. His mouth was opened wide as if awaiting a bunch of grapes. He was an Englishman. He was predestined for the London office, I later learned, and not terribly worried about his career. Compared with most trainees, he was a man of the world. He complained incessantly of being treated like a child by the firm. He had been in the markets in the City of London for two full years and found the whole idea of a training program absurd. So he turned Manhattan into his sporting ground at night. He convalesced during the day. He drank pots of coffee and slept on the training class floor, from which he made his first, indelible impression on many of his new colleagues.

The 127 unholy members of the Class of 1985 were one of a series of human waves to wash over what was then the world's most profitable trading floor. At the time we were by far the largest training class in Salomon's history, and the class after us was nearly twice as large again. The ratio of support staff to professional (we were, believe or not, the "professionals") was 5:1 so 127 of us meant 635 more support staff. The increase in numbers was dramatic in a firm of slightly more than 3,000 people. The hypergrowth would eventually cripple the firm and, even to us, seemed unnatural, like dumping too much fertilizer on a plant. For some strange reason management did not share our insight.

In retrospect it is clear to me that my arrival at Salomon marked the beginning of the end of that hallowed institution. Wherever I went, I couldn't help noticing, the place fell apart. Not that I was ever a big enough wheel in the machine to precipitate its destruction on my own. But that they let me—and other drifters like me—in the door at all was an early warning signal. Alarm bells should have rung. They were losing touch with their identity. They had once been shrewd traders of horseflesh. Now they were taking in the all the wrong kinds of people. Even my more commercially minded peers—no, especially my more commercially minded peers, such as the woman selling the suits—did not plan to devote their lives to Salomon Brothers. And neither did I.

Nothing bound us to the firm but what had enticed many of us to apply: money and a strange belief that no other jobs in the world were worth doing. Not exactly the stuff of deep and abiding loyalties. Inside of three years 75 percent of us would be gone (compared with previous years when after three years, on average, 85 percent of the class was still with the firm). After this large infusion of strangers intent on keeping their distance the firm went into convulsions, just as when any body ingests large quantities of an alien substance.

We were a paradox. We had been hired to deal in a market, to be more shrewd than the next guy, to be, in short, traders. Ask any astute trader and he'll tell you that his best work cuts against the conventional wisdom. Good traders tend to do the unexpected. We, as a group, were painfully predictable. By coming to Salomon Brothers, we were doing only what every sane money-hungry person would do. If we were unable to buck convention in our lives, would we be likely to buck convention in the market? After all, the job market is a *market*.

We were as civil to the big man addressing the class as we had been to anyone, which wasn't saying much. He was the speaker for the entire afternoon. That meant he was trapped for three hours to the ten-yard trench in the floor at the front of the room with a long table, a podium, and a blackboard. The man paced back and forth in the channel like a coach on the sidelines, sometimes staring at the floor, other times menacingly at us. We sat in rows of interconnected school chairs—twenty-two rows of white male trainees in white shirts punctuated by the occasional female in a blue blazer, two blacks, and a cluster of Japanese. The dull New England clam chowder color of the training room walls and floor set the mood of the room. One wall had long, narrow slits for windows with a sweeping view of New York Harbor and the Statue of Liberty, but you had to be sitting right beside them to see anything, and even then you were not supposed to soak in the view.

It was, all in all, more like a prison than an office. The room was hot and stuffy. The seat cushions were an unpleasant Astroturf green; the seat of your trousers stuck both to it and to you as you rose at the end of each day. Having swallowed a large and greasy cheeseburger at lunch, and having only a mild sociological interest in the speaker, I was overcome with drowsiness. We were only one week into our five-month training program, and I was already exhausted. I sank in my chair.

The speaker was a leading bond salesman at Salomon. On the table in the front of the room was a telephone, which rang whenever the bond market went berserk. As the big man walked, he held his arms tight to his body to hide the half-moons of sweat that were growing under his armpits. Effort or nerves? Probably nerves. You couldn't blame him. He was airing his heartfelt beliefs and in so doing making himself more vulnerable than any speaker yet. I was in the minority in finding him a bit tedious. He was doing well with the crowd. People in the back row listened. All around the room, trainees put down their *New York Times* crossword puzzles. The man was telling us how to survive. "You've got to think of Salomon Brothers as like a jungle," he said. Except it didn't come out that way. It came out: "Ya gotta tink a Salomon Bruddahs as like a jungle."

"The trading floor is a jungle," he went on, "and the guy you end up working for is your jungle leader. Whether you succeed here or not depends on knowing how to survive in the jungle. You've got to learn from your boss. He's key. Imagine if I take two people and I put them in the middle of the jungle and I give one person a jungle guide and the other person nothing. Inside the jungle there's a lot of bad shit going down. Outside the jungle there's a TV that's got the NCAA finals on and a huge fridge full of Bud. . . ."

The speaker had found the secret to managing the Salomon Brothers Class of 1985: Win the hearts and minds of the back row. The back row, from about the third day of classes on, teetered on the brink of chaos. Even when they felt merely ambivalent about a speaker, back-row people slept or chucked paper wads at the wimps in the front row. But if the back-row people for some reason didn't care for a speaker, all hell broke loose. Not now. Primitive revelation swept through the back of the classroom at the sound of the jungle drums; it was as if a hunting party of Cro-Magnon men had stumbled upon a new tool. The guys in the back row were leaning forward in their seats for the first time all day. Oooooooo. Aaaahhhhh.

With the back row neutralized, the speaker effectively controlled the entire audience, for the people sitting in the front row were on automatic pilot. They were the same as front-row people all over the world, only more so. Most graduates of Harvard Business School sat in the front row. One of them greeted each new speaker by drawing an organization chart. The chart resembled a Christmas tree, with John Gutfreund on the top and us at the bottom. In between were lots of little boxes, like ornaments. His way of controlling the situation was to identify the rank of the speaker, visualize his position in the hierarchy, and confine him to his proper box.

They were odd, these charts, and more like black magic than business. Rank wasn't terribly important on the trading floor. Organizational structure at Salomon Brothers was something of a joke. Making

money was mostly what mattered. But the front row was less confident than the back that the firm was a meritocracy of money-makers. They were hedging their bets—just in case Salomon Brothers after all bore some relation to the businesses they had learned about in school.

". . . a huge fridge of Bud," said the speaker, a second time. "And chances are good that the guy with the jungle guide is gonna be the first one through the jungle to the TV and the beer. Not to say the other guy won't eventually get there too. But"—here he stopped pacing and even gave the audience a little sly look—"he'll be *reeeaaal* thirsty and there's not going to be any beer left when he arrives."

This was the punch line. Beer. The guys in the back row liked it. They fell all over each other slapping palms, and looked as silly as white men in suits do when they pretend to be black soul brothers. They were relieved as much as excited. When not listening to this sort of speech, we faced a much smaller man with a row of Bic fine points in a plastic case in his breast pocket—otherwise known as a nerd pack—explaining to us how to convert a semiannual bond yield to an annual bond yield. The guys in the back row didn't like that. Fuck the fuckin' bond math, man, they said. Tell us about the jungle.

That the back row was more like a postgame shower than a repository for the future leadership of Wall Street's most profitable investment bank troubled and puzzled the more thoughtful executives who appeared before the training class. As much time and effort had gone into recruiting the back row as the front, and the class, in theory, should have been uniformly attentive and well behaved, like an army. The curious feature of the breakdown in discipline was that it was random, uncorrelated with anything outside itself and, therefore, uncontrollable. Although most of the graduates from Harvard Business School sat in the front, a few sat in the back. And right beside them were graduates from Yale, Stanford, and Penn. The back had its share of expensively educated people. It had at least its fair share of brains. So why were these people behaving like this?

And why Salomon let it happen, I still don't understand. The firm's management created the training program, filled it to the brim, then walked away. In the ensuing anarchy the bad drove out the good, the big drove out the small, and the brawn drove out the brains. There was a single trait common to denizens of the back row, though I doubt it ever occurred to anyone: They sensed that they needed to shed whatever refinements of personality and intellect they had brought with them to Salomon Brothers. This wasn't a conscious act, more a reflex. They were the victims of the myth, especially popular at Salomon Brothers, that a trader is a savage, and a great trader a great savage. This wasn't exactly correct. The trading floor held evidence to that effect. But it also held evidence to the contrary. People believed whatever they wanted to.

There was another cause for hooliganism. Life as a Salomon trainee was like being beaten up every day by the neighborhood bully. Eventually you grew mean and surly. The odds of making it into the Salomon training program in spite of my own fluky good luck, had been 60:1 against. You beat those odds and you felt you deserved some relief. There wasn't any. The firm never took you aside and rubbed you on the back to let you know that everything was going to be fine. Just the opposite, the firm built a system around the belief that trainees should wriggle and squirm. The winners of the Salomon interviewing process were pitted against one another in the classroom. In short, the baddest of the bad were competing for jobs.

Jobs were doled out at the end of the program on a blackboard beside the trading floor. Contrary to what we expected when we arrived, we were not assured of employment. "Look to your left and look to your right," more than one speaker said. "In a year one of those people will be out on the street." Across the top of the job placement blackboard appeared the name of each department on the trading floor: municipal bonds; corporate bonds; government bonds; etc. Along the side of the board was each office in the firm: Atlanta; Dallas; New York; etc. The thought that he might land somewhere awful in the matrix—or nowhere at all—drove the trainee to despair. He lost all perspective on the relative merits of the jobs. He did not count himself lucky just to be at Salomon Brothers; anyone who thought that way would never have got in in the first place. The Salomon trainee saw only the extremes of failure and success. Selling municipal bonds in Atlanta was unthinkably wretched. Trading mortgages in New York was mouthwateringly good.

Within weeks after our arrival the managers of each department had begun to debate our relative merits. But the managers were traders at heart. They couldn't discuss a person, place, or thing without also trading it. So they began to trade trainees, like slaves. One day you'd see three of them leaning over the fat blue binder that held our photographs and résumés. The next day you'd hear that you had been swapped for one front-row person and one draft choice from the next training program.

The pressure mounted. Who was overheard speaking of whom? Which trainees had cut deals for themselves? Where were jobs left? Like any selection process, this one had its winners and losers. But this selection process was wildly subjective. Since there was no objective measure of ability, landing a good job was one part luck, one part "presence," and one part knowing how and when to place your lips firmly to the rear end of some important person. There wasn't much you could do about the first two, so you tended to focus on the third. You needed a sponsor. Befriending one of the 112 managing directors was not enough; you had to befriend trainees. After all, what was in it for them?

A managing director grew interested only if he believed you were widely desired. Then there *was* a lot in you for him. A managing director won points when he spirited away a popular trainee from other managing directors. The approach of many a trainee, therefore, was to create the illusion of desirability. Then bosses wanted him not for any sound reason but simply because other bosses wanted him. The end result was a sort of Ponzi scheme of personal popularity that had its parallels in the markets. To build it required a great deal of self-confidence and faith in the gullibility of others; this was my chosen solution to the job problem. A few weeks into the training program I made a friend on the trading floor, though not in the area in which I wanted to work. That friend pressed for me to join his department. I let other trainees know I was pursued. They told their friends on the trading floor, who in turn became curious. Eventually the man I wanted to work for overheard others talking about me and asked me to breakfast.

If that sounds calculating and devious, consider the alternatives. Either I left my fate in the hands of management, which, as far as I could tell, did not show a great deal of mercy toward anyone foolish enough to trust it, or I appealed directly to the ego of the managing director of my choice. I had friends who tried this tactic. They threw themselves at their dream boss's feet, like a vassal before a lord, and said something unctuous and serflike, such as "I am your humble and devoted servant. Hire me, oh, Great One, and I will do anything you ask." They hoped that the managing director would respond favorably, perhaps say something like "Raise yourself up, young man, you've no need to fear. If you are true to me, I shall protect you from the forces of evil and unemployment." Sometimes this happened. But if it didn't you'd shot your wad. You were remaindered goods. Within the training class a dispute arose over whether, under the circumstances, groveling was acceptable. As if the whole point of the Salomon system were simply to see who wilted under the pressure and who did not.

Each trainee had to decide for himself. Thus was born the Great Divide. Those who chose to put on a full-court grovel from the opening buzzer found seats in the front of the classroom, where they sat, lips puckered, through the entire five-month program. Those who treasured their pride—or perhaps thought it best to remain aloof—feigned cool indifference by sitting in the back row and hurling paper wads at managing directors.

Of course, there were exceptions to these patterns of behavior. A handful of people fell between the cracks of the Great Divide. Two or three people cut deals with managing directors at the start of the program that ensured them jobs of their choice. They floated unpredictably, like freemen among slaves, and were widely thought to be management's spies. A few trainees had back-row hearts, but also wives and children to support. They had no loyalty. They remained aloof from the front row out of disdain and from the back row out of a sense of responsibility.

I considered myself an exception, of course. I was accused by some of being a front-row person because I liked to sit next to the man from the Harvard Business School and watch him draw organization charts. I wondered if he would succeed (he didn't). Also, I asked too many questions. It was assumed that I did this to ingratiate myself with the speakers, like a front-row person. This was untrue. But try telling that to the back row. I lamely compensated for my curiosity by hurling a few paper wads at important traders. And my stock rose dramatically in the back row when I was thrown out of class for reading the newspaper while a trader spoke. But I was never the intimate of those in the back row.

Of all exceptions, however, the Japanese were the greatest. The Japanese undermined any analysis of our classroom culture. All six of them sat in the front row and slept. Their heads rocked back and forth and on occasion fell over to one side, so that their cheeks ran parallel to the floor. So it was hard to argue that they were just listening with their eyes shut, as Japanese businessmen are inclined to do. The most charitable explanation for their apathy was that they could not understand English. They kept to themselves, however, and you could never be sure of either their language skills or their motives. Their leader was a man named Yoshi. Each morning and afternoon the back-row boys made bets on how many minutes it would take Yoshi to fall asleep. They liked to think that Yoshi was a calculating troublemaker. Yoshi was their hero. A small cheer would go up in the back row when Yoshi crashed, partly because someone had just won a pile of money, but also in appreciation of any man with the balls to fall asleep in the front row.

The Japanese were a protected species, and I think they knew it. Their homeland, as a result of its trade surpluses, was accumulating an enormous pile of dollars. A great deal of money could be made shepherding these dollars from Tokyo back into U.S. government bonds and other dollar investments. Salomon was trying to expand its office in Tokyo by employing experienced locals. Here was the catch. Japanese tend to spend their lives with one Japanese company, and the more able ones normally wouldn't dream of working for an American firm. In joining Salomon Brothers, they traded in sushi and job security for cheeseburgers and yuppie disease, which few were willing to do. The rare Japanese whom Salomon had been able to snatch away were worth many times their weight in gold and treated like the family china. The traders who spoke to us never uttered so much as a peep against them. In addition, while Salomon Brothers was otherwise insensitive to foreign cultures, it was strangely aware that the Japanese were different. Not that there was a generally accepted view of *how* they might be different. The Japanese could have rubbed noses and practiced the Kiwanis Club handshake each morning, and I'll bet no one would have thought it out of character.

Still, in the end, the Japanese were reduced to nothing more than a bizarre distraction. The back row set the tone of the class because it acted throughout as one, indivisible, incredibly noisy unit. The back-row people moved in herds, for safety and for comfort, from the training class in the morning and early afternoon, to the trading floor at the end of the day, to the Surf Club at night, and back to the training program the next morning. They were united by their likes as well as their dislikes. They rewarded the speakers of whom they approved by standing and doing the Wave across the back of the class.

And they approved wholeheartedly of the man at the front of the room now. The speaker paused, as if lost in thought, which was unlikely. "You know," he finally said, "you think you're hot shit, but when you start out on the trading floor, you're going to be at the bottom."

Was that really necessary? He was playing so well by telling the hooligans what they liked to hear: Being a winner at Salomon meant being a he-man in a jungle. Now he risked retaliation by telling the hooligans what they didn't like to hear: In the jungle their native talents didn't mean squat. I checked around for spitballs and paper wads. Nothing. The speaker had built sufficient momentum to survive his mistake. Heads in the back nodded right along. It is possible that they assumed the speaker intended that remark for the front row.

In any case, on this point the speaker was surely wrong. A trainee didn't have to stay on the bottom for more than a couple of months. Bond traders and salesmen age like dogs. Each year on the trading floor counts for seven in any other corporation. At the end of his year a trader or salesman had stature. Who cared for tenure? The whole beauty of the trading floor was its complete disregard for tenure.

A new employee, once he reached the trading floor, was handed a pair of telephones. He went online almost immediately. If he could make millions of dollars come out of those phones, he became the most revered of all species: A Big Swinging Dick. After the sale of a big block of bonds and the deposit of a few hundred thousand dollars into the Salomon till, a managing director called whoever was responsible to confirm his identity: "Hey, you Big Swinging Dick, way to be." To this day the phrase brings to my mind the image of an elephant's trunk swaying from side to side. Swish. Swash. Nothing in the jungle got in the way of a Big Swinging Dick.

That was the prize we coveted. Perhaps the phrase didn't stick in everyone's mind the way it did in mine; the name was less important than the ambition, which was common to us all. And of course, no one actually said, "When I get out onto the trading floor, I'm going to be a Big Swinging Dick." It was more of a private thing. But everyone wanted to be a Big Swinging Dick, even the women. Big Swinging Dickettes. Christ, even front-row people hoped to be Big Swinging Dicks once they had learned what it meant. Their problem, as far as the back row was concerned, was that they didn't know how to act the part. Big Swinging Dicks showed more grace under pressure than front-row people did.

A hand shot up (typically) in the front row. It belonged to a woman. She sat high in her regular seat, right in front of the speaker. The speaker had momentum. The back-row people were coming out of their chairs to honor him with the Wave. The speaker didn't want to stop now, especially for a front-row person. He looked pained, but he could hardly ignore a hand in his face. He called her name, Sally Findlay.

"I was just wondering," said Findlay, "if you could tell us what you think has been the key to your success."

This was too much. Had she asked a dry technical question, she might have pulled it off. But even the speaker started to smile. He knew he could abuse the front row as much as he wanted. His grin spoke volumes to the back row. It said, "Hey, I remember what these brown-nosers were like when I went through the training program, and I remember how much I despised speakers who let them kiss butt, so I'm going to let this woman hang out and dry for a minute, heh, heh, heh." The back row broke out in its loudest laughter yet. Someone cruelly mimed Findlay in a high-pitched voice, "Yes, do tell us why you're sooooo successful." Someone else shouted, "Down, boy!" as if scolding an overheated poodle. A third man cupped his hands together around his mouth and hollered, "Equities in Dallas."

Poor Sally. There were many bad places your name could land on the job placement blackboard in 1985, but the absolute worst was in the slot marked "Equities in Dallas." We could not imagine anything less successful in our small world than an equity salesman in Dallas; the equity department was powerless in our firm, and Dallas was, well, a long way from New York. Thus, "Equities in Dallas" became training program shorthand for "Just bury that lowest form of human scum where it will never be seen again." Bury Sally, they shouted from the back of the room.

The speaker didn't bother with an answer. He raced to a close before the mob he had incited became uncontrollable. "You spend a lot of time asking yourself questions: Are munis right for me? Are govys right for me? Are corporates right for me? You spend a lot of time thinking about that. And you should. But think about this: *It might be more important to choose a jungle guide than to choose your product.* Thank you."

The room emptied immediately. There was a fifteen-minute break until the next speaker began, and two separate crowds rushed as usual for the two doors out of the classroom. Front-row people exited front, back-row people exited back in a footrace to the four telephones with the free WATS lines.

The powers of Salomon Brothers relied on the training program to make us more like them. What did it mean to be more like them? For most of its life Salomon had been a scrappy bond trading house distinguished mainly by its ability and willingness to take big risks. Salomon had had to accept risk to make money because it had no list of fee-paying corporate clients, unlike, say, the genteel gentiles of Morgan Stanley. The image Salomon had projected to the public was a firm of clannish Jews, social nonentities, shrewd but honest, sinking its nose more deeply into the bond markets than any other firm cared to. This was a caricature, of course, but it roughly captured the flavor of the place as it once was.

Now Salomon wanted to change. The leading indicator of the shift in the collective personality of our firm was the social life of our chairman and CEO, John Gutfreund. He had married a woman with burning social ambition, twenty years his junior. She threw parties and invited gossip columnists. Her invitations, the value of which seemed to rise and fall with our share price, were wrapped in a tiny bow and delivered by hand. She employed a consultant to ensure she and her husband received the right sort of coverage. And though she did not go so far as to insist that the employees of Salomon Brothers were made as presentable as her husband (whom she stuffed into a new wardrobe), it was impossible in our company for some of this indulgence and posturing not to trickle down.

Despite the nouveau fluctuation in our corporate identity, the training program was without a doubt the finest start to a career on Wall Street. Upon completion a trainee could take his experience and cash it in for twice the salary on any other Wall Street trading floor. He had achieved, by the standards of Wall Street, technical mastery of his subject. It was an education in itself to see how quickly one became an "expert" on Wall Street. Many other banks had no training program. Drexel Burnham, in what I admit is an extreme example, even told one applicant to befriend someone at Salomon just to get hold of the Salomon training program handouts. Then, materials in hand, he should work for Drexel.

But the materials were the least significant aspect of our training. The relevant bits, the ones I would recall two years later, were the war stories, the passing on of the oral tradition of Salomon Brothers. Over three months leading salesmen, traders, and financiers shared their experiences with the class. They trafficked in unrefined street wisdom: how money travels around the world (any way it wants), how a trader feels and behaves (any way he wants), and how to schmooze a customer. After three months

in the class trainees circulated wearily around the trading floor for two months more. Then they went to work. All the while there was a hidden agenda: to Salomonize the trainee. The trainee was made to understand, first, that inside Salomon Brothers he was, as a trader once described us, lower than whale shit on the bottom of the ocean floor and, second, that lying under whale shit at Salomon Bothers was like rolling in clover compared with not being at Salomon at all.

In the short term the brainwashing nearly worked. (In the long term it didn't. For people to accept the yoke, they must believe they have no choice. As we shall see, we newcomers had both an exalted sense of our market value and no permanent loyalties.) A few investment banks had training programs, but with the possible exception of Goldman Sachs's, none was so replete with firm propaganda. A woman from *The New York Times* who interviewed us three months into our program was so impressed by the uniformity in our attitudes toward the firm that she called her subsequent article "The Boot Camp for Top MBA's." Like all newspaper articles about Salomon Brothers, it was quickly dismissed. *"The bitch don' know what she's talking about,"* said the back row. The class Boy Scouts were mercilessly hounded for saying in print things like "They—Salomon—don't need to give us a pep talk, we're pumped up," which, you had to admit, was a little much.

The article was revealing for another reason. It was the only time someone from the outside was let in and permitted to ask the most obvious question: Why were we so well paid? A back-row person, who had just taken an M.B.A. from the University of Chicago explained to the readers of the *Times*, "It's supply and demand," he said. "My sister teaches kids with learning disabilities. She enjoys her work as much as I do, but earns much less. If nobody else wanted to teach, she'd make more money." Say what you will about the analysis. The *Times* readers certainly did. The same article had mentioned more than 6,000 people had applied for the 127 places in the program. Paychecks at Salomon Brothers spiraled higher in spite of the willingness of others who would, no doubt, do the same job for less. There was something fishy about the way supply met demand in an investment bank.

But there was also something refreshing about any attempt to explain the money we were about to be paid. I thought it admirable that my colleague had given it the old business school try. No one else ever did. The money was just there. Why did investment banking pay so many people with so little experience so much money? Answer: When attached to a telephone, they could produce even more money. How could they produce money without experience? Answer: Producing in an investment bank was less a matter of skill and more a matter of intangibles—flair, persistence, and luck. Were the qualities found in a producer so rare that they could be purchased only at great expense? Answer: yes and no. That was the question of questions. The ultimate expression of our dumb compliance was in not asking at the outset why the money flowed so freely and how long it would last. The answer could be found on the Salomon Brothers trading floor, perhaps more easily than anywhere on Wall Street, but many never bothered to work it out.

Each day after class, around about three or four or five o'clock we were pressured to move from the training class on the twenty-third floor to the trading floor on the forty-first. You could get away with not going for a few days, but if not seen on the floor occasionally, you were forgotten. Forgotten at Salomon meant unemployed. Getting hired was a positive act. A manager had to request you for his unit. Three people were fired at the end of our training program. One was assigned to Dallas and refused to go. A second disappeared mysteriously, amid rumors that he had invited a senior female Salomon executive into a *ménage à trois* (the firm tolerated sexual harassment but not sexual deviance). And a third, by far the most interesting, couldn't bear to step off the elevator and onto the trading floor. He rode up and down in the rear of the elevator every afternoon. He meant to get off, I think, but was petrified. Word of his handicap spread. It reached the woman in charge of the training program. She went to see for herself. She stood outside the elevator banks on the forty-first floor and watched with her own eyes the doors open and shut for an hour on one very spooked trainee. One day he was gone.

On braver days you cruised the trading floor to find a manager who would take you under his wing, a mentor, better known to us as a rabbi. You also went to the trading floor to learn. Your first impulse was to step into the fray, select a likely teacher, and present yourself for instruction. Unfortunately it wasn't so easy. First, a trainee by definition had nothing of merit to say. And, second, the trading floor was a minefield of large men on short fuses just waiting to explode if you so much as breathed in their direction. You didn't just walk up and say hello. Actually that's not fair.

Many, many traders were instinctively polite, and if you said hello they'd just ignore you. But if you happened to step on a mine, then the conversation went something like this:

Me:	Hello.
Trader:	What fucking rock did you crawl out from under? Hey, Joe, hey, Bob, check out this guy's suspenders.
Me:	(reddening) I just wanted to ask you a couple of questions.
Joe:	Who the fuck does he think he is?
Trader:	Joe, let's give this guy a little test! When interest rates go up, which way do bond prices go?
Me:	Down.
Trader:	Terrific. You get an A. Now I gotta work.
Me:	When would you have some time—
Trader:	What the fuck do you think this is, a charity? I'm busy.
Me:	Can I help in any way?
Trader:	Get me a burger. With ketchup.

So I watched my step. There were a million little rules to obey; I knew none of them. Salesmen, traders, and managers swarmed over the floor, and at first I could not tell them apart. Sure, I knew the basic differences. Salesmen talked to investors, traders made bets, and managers smoked cigars. But other than that I was lost. Most of the men were on two phones at once. Most of the men stared at small green screens full of numbers. They'd shout into one phone, then into the other, then at someone across the row of trading desks, then back into the phones, then point to the screen and scream, "*Fuck!*" Thirty seconds was considered a long attention span. As a trainee, a plebe, a young man lying under all that whale shit, I did what every trainee did: I sidled up to some busy person without saying a word and became the Invisible Man.

That it was perfectly humiliating was, of course, precisely the point. Sometimes I'd wait for an hour before my existence was formally acknowledged; other times, a few minutes. Even that seemed like forever. *Who is watching me in my current debased condition?* I'd wonder. *Will I ever recover from such total neglect? Will someone please notice that the Invisible Man has arrived?* The contrast between me standing motionless and the trader's frenetic movements made the scene particularly unbearable. It underlined my uselessness. But once I'd sidled up, it was difficult to leave without first being officially recognized. To leave was to admit defeat in this peculiar ritual of making myself known.

Anyway, there wasn't really any place else to go. The trading room was about a third the length of a football field and was lined with connected desks. Traders sitting elbow to elbow formed a human chain. Between the rows of desks there was not enough space for two people to pass each other without first turning sideways. Once he started wandering aimlessly, a trainee risked disturbing the gods at play. All the senior people, from Chairman Gutfreund down, stalked the trading floor. It was not a normal corporation, in which trainees were smiled benevolently upon by middle-aged executives because they represented the future of the organization. Salomon trainees were freeloaders, guilty until proven innocent. With this rap on your head, you were not particularly eager to meet the boss. Sadly you had no choice. The boss was everywhere. He saw you in your red suspenders with gold dollar signs and knew instantly who you were. A cost center.

Even if you shed your red suspenders and adopted protective coloration, you were easily identifiable as a trainee. Trainees were impossibly out of step with the rhythm of the place. The movements of the trading floor respond to the movements of the markets as if roped together. The American bond market, for example, lurches whenever important economic data are released by the U.S. Department of Commerce. The bond trading floor lurches with it. The markets decide what are important data and what are not. One month it is the U.S. trade deficit, the next month the consumer price index. The point is that the traders know what economic number is the flavor of the month and the trainees don't. The entire Salomon Brothers trading floor might be poised for a number at 8:30 A.M., gripped by suspense and a great deal of hope, ready to leap and shout, to buy or sell billions of dollars' worth of bonds, to make or lose millions of dollars for the firm, when a trainee arrives, suspecting nothing, and says, "Excuse me, I'm going to the cafeteria, does anybody want anything?" Trainees, in short, were idiots.

One lucky trainee was spared the rite of passage. His name was Myron Samuels, and he had cut such a deal with the head of municipal bond trading that by the time I arrived at Salomon Brothers, he was carpooling to work with two managing directors and a senior trader. He was rumored to have family connections in the higher reaches of the firm; the alternative explanation is that he was a genius. Anyway, he did not fail to exploit his exalted status. He walked around the trading floor with a confidence seen in few of the people who were actually working. Since Samuels didn't work, he could enjoy himself, like a kid who had been let into Daddy's office. He would make his way to the municipal bond desk, take a seat, call for the shoeshine man, phone a friend long distance, light up a cigar, and put the shoe that wasn't being shined up on the desk. He'd holler at passing managing directors like old friends. No one but no one dreamed of doing this—except Samuels. In general, the more senior the figure, the more amusing he found Samuels; I think this was because the more senior people were more aware of Samuels's connections. Nevertheless, a few were furious. But on the municipal trading desk Samuels could not be touched. I walked by once and overheard two vice-presidents whispering about him. "I can't stand that fuckin' guy," said one to the other. "Yeah," said the other, "but what are you going to do about it?"

To avoid being squashed on my visits to the floor, I tried to keep still, preferably in some corner. Except for Gutfreund, whom I knew from magazine pictures and thought of as more a celebrity than a businessman, the faces were foreign to me. That made it hard to know whom to avoid. Many of them looked the same, in that most were white, most were male, and all wore the same all-cotton button-down shirts (one of our Japanese told me he couldn't for the life of him tell them apart). The forty-first floor of Salomon New York was Power Central, holding not just the current senior management of the firm but its future management as well. You had to go by their strut to distinguish between who should be approached and who avoided.

Did I grow more comfortable on the trading floor over time? I suppose. But even when I had established myself within the firm, I got the creepy crawlies each time I walked out onto 41. I could see certain developments in myself, however. One day I was out playing the Invisible Man, feeling the warmth of the whale shit and thinking that no one in life was lower than I. Onto the floor rushed a member of the corporate finance department wearing his jacket like a badge of dishonor. Nobody wore a jacket on the floor. It must have been his first trip down from his glass box office, and he looked one way and then the other in the midst of the bedlam. Someone bumped into him and sharply told him to watch his step. Watch his step? But he was just standing there. You could see him thinking that the gaze of the whole world was on him. And he started to panic, like a stage actor who had forgotten his lines. He'd probably forgotten why he'd come in the first place. And he left. Then I thought a nasty thought. A terrible thought. A truly unforgivable thought. But it showed I was coming along. *What a wimp,* I thought. *He doesn't have a fucking clue.*

* * *

I left Salomon Brothers in the beginning of 1988, but not for any of the obvious reasons. I didn't think the firm was doomed. I didn't think that Wall Street would collapse. I wasn't even suffering from growing disillusionment (it grew to a point, still bearable, then stopped). Although there were many perfectly plausible reasons to jump ship, I left, I think, more because I didn't need to stay any longer.

My father's generation grew up with certain beliefs. One of those beliefs is that the amount of money one earns is a rough guide to one's contribution to the welfare and prosperity of our society. I grew up unusually close to my father. Each evening I would plop into a chair near him, sweaty from a game of baseball in the front yard, and listen to him explain why such and such was true and such and such was not. One thing that was almost always true was that people who made a lot of money were neat. Horatio Alger and all that. It took watching his son being paid 225 grand at the age of twenty-seven, after two years on the job, to shake his faith in money. He has only recently recovered from the shock.

I haven't. When you sit, as I did, at the center of what has been possibly the most absurd money game ever and benefit out of all proportion to your value to society (as much as I'd like to think I got only what I deserved, I don't), when hundreds of equally undeserving people around you are all raking it in faster than they can count it, what happens to the money belief? Well, that depends. For some, good fortune simply reinforces the belief. They take the funny money seriously, as evidence that they are worthy citizens of the Republic. It becomes their guiding assumption—for it couldn't possibly be clearly thought out—that a talent for making money come out of a telephone is a reflection of merit on a grander scale. It is tempting to believe that people who think this way eventually suffer their comeuppance. They don't. They just get richer. I'm sure most of them die fat and happy.

For me, however, the belief in the meaning of making dollars crumbled; the proposition that the more money you earn, the better the life you are leading was refuted by too much hard evidence to the contrary. And without that belief, I lost the need to make huge sums of money. The funny thing is that I was largely unaware how heavily influenced I was by the money belief until it had vanished.

It is a small piece of education, but still the most useful thing I picked up at Salomon Brothers. Almost everything else I learned I left behind. I became fairly handy with a few hundred million dollars, but I'm still lost when I have to decide what to do with a few thousand. I learned humility briefly in the training program but forgot it as soon as I was given a chance. And I learned that people can be corrupted by organizations, but since I remain willing to join organizations and even to be corrupted by them (mildly, please), I'm not sure what practical benefit will come from this lesson. All in all, it seems, I didn't learn much of practical value.

Perhaps the best was yet to come and I left too soon. But having lost my need to stay at Salomon Brothers, I discovered a need to leave. My job became nothing more than showing up every morning to do what I had already done, the reward for which was simply more of the same. I disliked the lack of adventure. You might say that I left the trading floor of Salomon Brothers in search of risk, which was as stupid a financial decision as I hope I'll ever make. In the markets you don't take risk without being paid hard cash at the same time. Even in the job market it's a handy rule, and I have broken it. I am now both poorer and more exposed than I would have been had I remained on the trading floor.

So, on the face of it, my decision to leave was an almost suicidal trade, the sort of thing a customer might do if he fell into the hands of a geek salesman at Salomon. I believe I walked away from the clearest shot I'll ever have at being a millionaire. Sure, Salomon Brothers had fallen on hard times, but there was still plenty of gravy on the tray for a good middleman; that is the nature of the game. And if Salomon turns itself around, the money will flow even more freely. As it happens, I still own shares in Salomon Brothers because I believe it will eventually recover. The strength of the firm lies in the raw instincts of people like John Meriwether, the Liar's Poker champion of the world. People with those instincts, including Meriwether and his boys, are still trading bonds for Salomon. Anyway, business at Salomon simply couldn't get much worse. The captains have done their level best to sink the ship, and the ship insists on floating. In leaving, I was sure I was making the beginner's mistake of selling at the bottom, which I could only partially offset by buying a few shares in the company as I walked out the door.

If I made a bad trade, it's because I wasn't making a trade. I was given pause, however, after I had decided to vamoose, to think that maybe what I was doing wasn't so foolish after all. Alexander insisted at our farewell dinner that I was making a great move. The best decisions he has made in his life, he said, were completely unexpected, the ones that cut against convention. Then he went even farther. He said that *every* decision he has forced himself to make *because* it was unexpected has been a good one. It was refreshing to hear a case for unpredictability in this age of careful career planning. It would be nice if it were true.

Study Questions

1. Is Lewis right to question the accuracy of the basic economic law that states that price (in his case, his wage) is determined by supply and demand? Consider another example. Many claim that the United States has too many lawyers. But many of those who complain also complain that the price of hiring a lawyer is clearly too high. But if there is an oversupply of lawyers, shouldn't the price be reasonably low, if the law of supply and demand determines price? Similarly, many complain that there is too much medical care available to those who can afford it. Often too many tests and procedures are done. But many of those who complain also complain that the price of this medical care is clearly too high and increasing in price faster than inflation in general. But if there is an oversupply of medical care available to those who can afford it, shouldn't the price be reasonably low if the law of supply and demand determines price?

2. Is Lewis right to question the correspondence between merit and high wages?

"Your honor, my client would like to explain how a financial incentive differs from a bribe."

25

Bribery: It Is Accepted Cross-Culturally Yet Is Wrong

John T. Noonan, Jr.

Editor's note: Noonan evaluates the following arguments supporting the moral permissibility of bribery: (1) every culture bribes; (2) bribery is a practical necessity; (3) acceptable reciprocities are formally indistinguishable from bribes; (4) bans on bribes are enforced immorally; and (5) the evil effects of common bribes are either trivial or unshown.

The Nonmoral Nature of Exchanges with Officeholders

By bribery is meant improper reciprocation with an officeholder for an act intended by society to be gratuitous. To approach the matter neutrally, "exchange with an officeholder" will be substituted for "bribery." Five arguments exist why such exchanges should not now be subject to predominantly moral judgments. These arguments are directed at the oral nature of bribery today. When reference is made to history it is to be understood that the argument is by analogy, to analogous not identical concepts of bribery.

1. *Everybody does it.* Wherever one looks, whatever time or place or country, exchanges with officeholders are found. From the mayors of Nippur and Nuzi in 1500 B.C. to the mayor of Lansing, Illinois, in 1976, payoffs have been made. From the Roman Curia under Innocent III to the Supreme Court of the United States under Earl Warren such exchanges have

been arranged. In religious representations as ancient as *The Book of the Dead* and in secular reporting as recent as the *Wall Street Journal* such exchanges are commemorated. No religion has banned exchanges with the divine officeholder. No government has ever ruled without exchanges by and with the rulers.

"All sects, all ages smack of this vice." This observation, made apropos fornication in *Measure for Measure*, is equally apt here. Women, it is true, appear to smack of it less than men, for in the case of bribery, special opportunities must be conjoined to appetite. Only officeholders can be the objects of bribes, and women have been officeholders less frequently than men. The sex differential apart, there is no common denominator isolating those who do participate in bribery and those who do not. Romans and Visigoths, Englishmen and Africans, Catholics and Jews, pagans and Protestants, capitalists and Communists, imperialists and patriots have engaged in these exchanges. It was done by officeholders in the England of Edward I and in the England of James I and in the England of George III. It was done in the America of Lincoln and the America of Teddy Roosevelt. It has been a way of life in Iran and Indonesia, Italy and Japan, our state houses and our national capital.

What has been done everywhere at every time cannot be contrary to human nature or destructive of the human pursuit of the Good. Universal, vast, ineradicable, bribery is a practice that accompanies the human condition.

2. *It is necessary to do it.* Such a practice cannot be counter to basic human needs; rather, it must itself meet human needs. The second argument builds on the observation underlying the first argument: what is commonly done must be done if one is to live and act in the world.

To take one example, from the life of an illustrious philosopher, when Germany annexed Austria, Ludwig Wittgenstein was in England; his two sisters lived in Vienna; they became subject to the Nazi laws on race. Wittgenstein went to Germany, negotiated with the Nazi authorities, and made an arrangement whereby for a certain sum put at the disposal of the Reichsbank from the family fortune in Switzerland, the two sisters would remain undisturbed. In short, the Germans were bribed not to apply the racial code. But does it make moral sense to put this foresighted and courageous action of Wittgenstein in a morally reprehensible category? Generally speaking, is it not true that all payments made to prevent the application of unjust laws are justified? Wittgenstein's case is, indeed, an example of the class covered generally by the scholastics' phrase *redimere vexationem*—to buy back harassment. When you have a right to a civil good—property, fair treatment, peace—you have a right to prevent its unjust denial. To use effective and necessary means of securing the right is not unjust. These means include an exchange with the powerholder who is unjustly denying you your due.

The same reasoning holds true of the removal of unjust laws. The classic case is the passage of the Thirteenth Amendment. Let us take it as proved that Abraham Lincoln through his agents did use presidential patronage to obtain the necessary Democratic votes or abstentions. Did not his pure purpose justify his trading? Would it really have been morally preferable for him to have acquiesced in the continued enslavement of the blacks until he could get the amendment enacted without the use of any quid pro quo? A great human need for liberty had to be met. Lincoln took the means necessary to meet the need.

What holds as to political necessity holds as to commercial necessity. There is no reason to rank lower the exigencies of economics. "Was it really possible, from the standpoint of reality, to say, 'I refuse to pay'?" Carl Kotchian asks and knows the answer is No if he is to sell his company's planes. As Daniel Haughton puts it, payments were "necessary in order to compete against U.S. and foreign competitors." Kotchian and Haughton are representative reciprocators with officeholders. They reciprocated not out of desire to violate the law or malice toward anyone, but because they had to be reciprocators if they were to stay in business. Business necessity was their motivation. Business necessity was their justification.

The necessity that binds the donor, it may be objected, is not a necessity that binds the recipient. True, the recipient is bound by different necessities—the necessity of obtaining campaign contributions, the necessity of finding funds for his party, the necessity of maintaining a standard of living congruent with his office. The officeholder is a needy man, nearly everywhere not officially compensated in a way commensurate with his responsibilities and power. His acceptance of reciprocities is itself token and evidence of his needs.

Anthropologists who have found exchanges the rule in the societies they have investigated do not describe one group of recipients as more grasping than another: the exchanges represent an equilibrium of needs. American political scientists who have studied Third World countries have found reciprocation with official officeholders playing a part in the tran-

sition of the countries from colonies to democratic nations. They have discovered an important truth. Such exchanges help to build nascent political parties. Such exchanges lessen the impersonality of government. Such exchanges overcome the inertia of bureaucracy. Such exchanges, in short, make the country run. They are a functional necessity in the new nations. Is not as much now admitted of the city and state machines once so scored for their reliance on reciprocities? In the period of the vigorous expansion of the United States, in the building of the strongest nation in the world, did not the reciprocal exchanges in every American city from New York to San Francisco function to provide the necessary capital construction? Did they not function in Washington to provide the necessary railroad connections? We should not condemn with moral judgment what has been needed to make other systems, and our own, work.

3. *Reciprocities are formally indistinguishable.* The usury prohibition known to medieval Europe broke down because at home it became impossible in practice to distinguish unlawful usury ("profit on a loan") from lawful interest, lawful profit on foreign exchange, and lawful partnership income. A similar phenomenon can be observed here and is indeed implicit in the two preceding arguments that reciprocity with an officeholder is normal and necessary. A multitude of reciprocal exchanges are generally accepted as legitimate. No satisfactory criteria exist by which these exchanges can be distinguished from what bribery prohibitions classify as bribes.

To begin with, there are gifts. The difficulty of distinguishing bribes from gifts was signaled in antiquity by the language. *Shohadh, döron, munus*—are they to be translated gift or bribe? Wise ambiguity. We hesitate because the Hebrews, Greeks, and Romans hesitated. Who could be certain that the gift was a corrupt gift? The Greeks had a word for it, runs the proverb. The Greeks did not have a word for bribes because all gifts are bribes. All gifts are given by way of reciprocation for favors past or to come.

The difference between a bribe and a gift lies, for some, in the nonspecific and tacit character of the request for reciprocity that accompanies a gift. Consider Kotchian's response to Senator Church's question as to what Lockheed got for its $1 million to Prince Bernhard. Kotchian replied, "It was from a great good will and helpfulness in various programs that were going on in that area. . . . My understanding of a bribe is quid pro quo for a specific item in return, and I would categorize this more as a gift.

But I don't want to quibble with you, sir." Quibbling indeed is the right term to describe the attempt to segregate bribes from gifts; or (a *reductio ad absurdum* of the moral argument) shall we distinguish by size—one million dollars is a bribe, one hundred is a gift? As in the prince's case, a gift is not made out of the air but with an appreciation of who the donee is and what he has done or will do. Dealing with intelligent donees, the donor may reasonably expect a better return if he is not specific. The essence of the transaction remains reciprocal.

Gifts overlap with another subdivision of reciprocities, tips, which are equally hard to tell from bribes. The paradigm of a tip, it will be said, is a payment whose minimum amount is set by custom, given a waiter after he has provided service; the waiter has no legal right to even the minimum; the waiter's employer is aware of the practice and takes it into account in setting the waiter's salary. Nothing distinguishes the paradigm from the practice of Christmas gifts to mailmen. Yet such gifts to mailmen and any other tips to federal employees are by law classified as bribes. The law is not peculiarly arbitrary in this instance. Any attempt to isolate one set of reciprocities and stigmatize them as illegal or immoral must be arbitrary.

Throughout much of the world, low-level government officials depend on tips to supplement their salaries. They are exactly like waiters, poorly paid because their governmental employers know they will be compensated by those who use their services. The Foreign Corrupt Practices Act distinguishes the grease that goes to them from the bribes it condemns. The distinction discloses the arbitrariness in classifying reciprocities.

The tip to the official is excused because the official is said to be underpaid. Will this distinction hold? The cabinet minister in many countries is underpaid, considering his responsibilities and comparing his government salary with that paid by the private sector. If the low-level official is entitled to a kind of "occult compensation," designed to give him an income commensurate with his work, the same logic holds for the cabinet minister: he is entitled to a gift to bring his income up to a proper standard. The rationale for the tip destroys any effort to stigmatize the larger payment to the minister.

The tip, it might be said, is only for the execution of a nondiscretionary task; and it is only for the proper performance of a task not its perversion. But surely many of the acts tipped are precisely for the exercise of discretion—for putting one application ahead of another, for not examining every article of luggage, for overlooking minor failures to meet the regulations. As for being tipped only for doing the job the right way, the high-level donee may make the same claim: "I selected the airplane our country needed most. I am being rewarded for an act which was beneficial to the country and fair to all competitors."

The only difference between what is jocularly called "lubrication" and a bribe appears to be the amount. Even a difference in magnitude is not always suggested. "Machinery stuck for lack of grease," wired a Lockheed representative in Saudi Arabia where Lockheed payments were by the thousand and the million. What would be one man's bribe in terms of amount would be a more affluent man's tip. Such a varying yardstick is insufficient to show that bribes and tips to officials are different.

Gifts, tips, and campaign contributions! [I examined] these "donations of democracy," these gifts without which the whole electoral system would disappear or become dependent on the dole of a central government agency. Nothing in that [examination] established a functional difference between campaign contribution and bribes. All that was shown were governmental efforts, usually clumsy, half-baked and ineffective, to channel contributions, publicize them, and limit their amounts and origins. Lines were drawn between contributions and bribes. Each line was arbitrary—corporations could not give; corporations could give only by arranging for a committee; contributors could give only so much to one committee, etc. No line reflected a substantial moral distinction. The system presently in force—lawful contributions through PACs—is simply one of licensed bribery.

Look again at a federal court of appeals trying to distinguish bribes and subvarieties of bribes such as illegal gratuities and campaign contributions in the cases of Anderson and Brewster. The court entangles itself in verbiage. The distinctions are not intelligible. Reason does not know how to distinguish. The only discernible lines are those arbitrarily drawn by election statutes.

Did any functional difference exist between bribes and the campaign contributions made so widely by the Gulf Oil Corporation? When Gulf's lobbyist disbursed cash to Lyndon Johnson and other leaders of the Congress, did he have to say, "Vote for Gulf on such and such an issue"? The recipients knew who the donor was and for what company he worked. Whether the amounts delivered were called gifts, bribes, or contributions, they accomplished the same objective. They induced and rewarded gratitude and reciprocal response in the recipients.

Campaign contributions may be considered a subspecies of a larger class—access payments. "I'm not paying for my congressman's vote," the large contributor will say. "I simply want to be sure he will listen to my side of the case." In *The Book of the Dead* Ani's gift to the gods is for access. Bailiffs of imperial judges and clerks of Roman cardinals took money on their masters' behalf, that they should give time to the case. If everyone gave the same amount, as is done when court fees are paid, no particular reciprocity would be set up between the receiver of an access payment and its maker. But in every age the maker has had the opportunity of making his case appear particularly attractive by what he gives. Ani's platter for the gods was put together to be pleasing. The access money received by Roman bailiffs was perceived as a common way of influencing the court. The access money taken by curial clerks was seen to be symptomatic of a Roman Curia where everything was for sale. Access payments in the form of campaign contributions are not uniform. The access bought by the large donor is the same as influence. In most contested matters the ear of an official is needed to obtain the result desired. The access payment in fact and function, if not in hairsplitting theory, is a payment to establish reciprocity with the officeholder.

Access payments, campaign contributions, tips, gifts—the ways in which exchanges with an officeholder may be made are so many that no exhaustive list can be made. Need one catalogue the forbearances, the appointments, the promotions, the kindnesses to siblings and in-laws, the sexual favors paid for or voluntarily given, or the business opportunities afforded, which constitute the common coin of reciprocity as much as cash and which, escaping legal condemnation, are morally indistinguishable as returns to officeholders? The perfect impossibility of making any but arbitrary definitions of what is morally acceptable and what is "bribery" is evident.

4. *It is immorally enforced.* A moral idea that lives by immoralities is a contradiction in terms. Such is the notion of the bribe. When certain exchanges are categorized as bribes, enforcement of their condemnation is inconsistent; intemperate; hypocritical; an expression of envy. The idea is made effective by technicalities, lies, and bribes.

When the antibribery ideal is invoked it is inconsistently applied. At the level of law, the great unevenness has been demonstrated. The crime of bribery needs two for completion; in its inception in Israel the Law (like the Prophets and Wisdom) only condemned the bribetaker—the first fatal inconsistency. A second inconsistency—the crime is the more dangerous the higher the official from ancient Israel to America, the general rule has been, the higher the official, the greater his immunity from prosecution for bribery. If the bribetaker has been high enough—the lawmakers of Israel, the Senate of Rome—he has been completely immune.

When a law has existed and been applied, it has been applied fitfully. Warren Hastings suffered shame; his predecessors, surely little different in their rule of Bengal, received honor. Oakes Ames and James Brooks were disciplined and died in disgrace; James Garfield and James Blaine, their partners, became, respectively, President and Secretary of State. Richard Nixon was forced out of office for planning certain condemned exchanges; Lyndon Johnson rose to the presidency on the back of such exchanges. Such a hit-or-miss notion as bribery can be the convenient weapon of journalists and politicians as simony once was of preachers and religious reformers. Neither bribery nor its subspecies simony have today the consistency, the stability, the exigency of a true moral concept.

From Cicero to Caro the haters of bribery have been driven to create "Hogs," caricatures of human beings, devoid of redeeming characteristics, so that in pillorying the caricature they can express their devotion to the antibribery ethic. Their devotion has led them to reduce human beings to objects. Their devotion, as in Burke's case, has put them in the unchristian posture of unforgiving hatred of the bribetaker.

Hypocrisy in the enforcement of the antibribery ethic is common. Cicero, the great foe of bribery, will not subject his clients, the knights, to the bribery law. Richard Nixon, whose administration creates federal "common law" bribery to bring down the Kenny machine, plots to give bribes. The Watergate Committee, nearly all of whose members took money from Gulf, judges Nixon.

Often enough, popular dislike of a bribetaker reflects a sense that he is getting something the critics would like to have themselves. How much the monastic complaints about the Roman Curia incorporate ill-natured envy! How much the impotence of the Adamses inspires ill-will in the portraits of the powerful in *Democracy!* How often is the journalist a man of action *manqué* revenging his frustrations! Just as a large ingredient of sexual Puritanism is the malice of the sexually deprived toward the sexually content, so the desire to repress bribery conceals the desire to share the fruits of office. Small wonder that accusations of bribery can be fruitfully analogized to accusations of witchcraft. Accusations of either practice satisfy the deep resentments of the accusers.

Their dispositions are uncharitable and hypocritical; their motivation jealous, and their means are typically foul. They catch a briber on a technicality—William Tweed is skewered on an accounting statute. Spiro Agnew trips on a tax law. They do not blush to manipulate statutes to punish crimes that the statutes were not meant to prevent. They exploit illegal leaks of government information as William Lambert did to topple Abe Fortas. They encourage treachery by a man's associates or employees, as Coke must have done to catch Bacon. They set up hoaxes such as Abscam which depend on sustained deception and lying by agents of the government. They capture bribeable congressmen by having the government furnish the bribe money.

The antibribery ethic is supposed to encourage trust. Enforcement of the antibribery ethic is destructive of trust. Dante's insight in the *Inferno* was profound: those who pursue bribees are themselves diabolical in their pursuit. They pretend to defend a moral ideal. They express hatred and envy, they practice immoral duplicity.

5. *The material effect of the exchanges commonly condemned is either trivial or undemonstrated.* At best, the bribery rules, which have been so extravagantly expanded, are like the taboos on sexual intercourse, which were so extravagantly expanded by elaborate biblical provisions about certain classes of kin, virgins, and the menstruous, all of whom were shielded from sexual encounters. Purity rules of this kind, designed to impose order on chaos and prevent national catastrophe, rest on no rational basis and prevent no substantive harm. Taboos, they should be discarded when no actual injury which they avert can be identified.

The work of the world is concerned with the distribution of goods and services. What matters first is how much there is to distribute and next that the distribution be fair. But fairness is notoriously difficult to determine *a priori*, and in practice circumstances that appear accidental such as inherited wealth have as much to do with distribution as factors that might appear more fundamental (to philosophers anyway) such as inherited brains. The effect of reciprocal exchanges with officeholders upon fair distribution is minuscule compared with the effect of the inheritance of property. The effect of such exchanges upon the production of goods and services is undemonstrable.

In the typical case of such an exchange in connection with the purchase or sale of a government asset, the payment to the official is calculated as a percentage like the 3% of Dasaad Musim. It is true that middlemen enjoying great influence and a quasi-monopoly position such as Khashoggi have asked more, but it is reasonable to regard a Khashoggi as extraordinary. If one puts the average at between 5% and 10% of the price, it is not unrealistic. An increase of this sort in the cost of goods, inflationary though it may be, cannot be called substantial. If 90 to 95 percent of what a government spends is being paid for actual goods and services, the cost of a payment built into the purchase price is *de minimis*.

Lex non curat de minimis, "The law pays no attention to trifles," runs the old adage. What is true of law is *a fortiori* true of morality. Morals are concerned with what aids or impedes the fulfillment of basic human needs. A small increase in the cost of government, an increase probably less than what is due to sheer waste and inefficiency, is not the sort of thing with which morality concerns itself.

It will be said that the receipt of a favor encourages an official to accept shoddy work or to order a product the government does not need. Let the official be condemned then for the cheating which is the gravemen of the offense. But if, like Samuel Pepys, he buys the best quality work and contracts for only what is necessary, what substantial injury is done the government if he is enriched at the same time? By the same token the commissioner who votes for what he believes to be a reasonable rate of return deprives no one of anything if he is rewarded by the regulated utility for his reasonableness. The commissioner who selects the best qualified applicant for a television license or a redevelopment project or a liquor permit and pockets remuneration from the company selected has inflicted no material harm. The governor who helps a racetrack get dates for racing determines a schedule indifferent in itself. The judge who takes money voluntarily offered by the litigant he thinks is right has taken nothing from the loser and nothing unwillingly from the winner.

The modern American cases, it is true, say that bribery defrauds the people of honest government. Honest government, however, has no cash value. Intangible ideals such as justice, trust, honor have no place in the calculation of material harm. To bring in the ideals is to smuggle in the moral idea, much as though such ideals as chastity, virginity, and fidelity were brought into a frank discussion of the material harm in sexual promiscuity. If we stick to what can be measured by any material standard no one has ever demonstrated that a country with all kinds of reciprocal exchanges with officeholders, such as the United States, has had less goods and service distributed than a country such as _____. But who can say which country has fewer reciprocal exchanges? A comprehensive comparative study of all the forms of reciprocities with officeholders, which is the necessary predicate to any judgment of harm done, has never been made. In the absence of such a study, the harm is undemonstrated. Given the probability that no study could isolate the effect of reciprocity from other factors such as the political maturity of the country, the state of its economy, the degree of personal freedom of its citizens, their intelligence and character, the existing distribution of wealth, and a dozen other interacting sociopolitical conditions, the harm is undemonstrable.

The foregoing arguments show that reciprocal exchanges with officeholders are engaged in everywhere; that as far as is known no time or country is free of them; that they have been a way of life as much in the United States as in Saudi Arabia; that they are necessary to the conduct of business; that no intelligible moral line distinguishes one type of reciprocity from another; and that in themselves, apart from separable effects such as cheating and deception, the material harm done by them cannot be known and falls, for want of demonstration, into the category of trifles ruled by etiquette, convention, and purity taboo, not morality.

The Arguments Evaluated

1. The first argument has shown illustratively, but not exhaustively, that bribery has been practiced by some persons of every country, race, or creed. It is essentially a quantitative argument, and its failure to produce quantitative data is its first deficiency. As the final argument on the same side contends, bribery has never been quantified. We have no statistics showing how many do take bribes or have taken them. The argument is unproved.

The argument suffers from a second deficiency, the assumption on which it rests—that what should be done is what is done. This assumption, particularly prominent in recent arguments on sexual mor-

als, has no validity. Many common practices—torture, religious persecution, the denial of rights to those born out of wedlock—are known to be wrong. Slavery was once "a way of life" in almost every country in the world. Its ubiquity did not change its moral character. The very question being examined is whether bribery is in the same category once occupied by slavery as a general but detestable custom.

2. The second argument does not show that bribery is necessary but that it has been thought necessary, just as the maintenance of slavery was thought necessary even by such critics of the system as Jefferson. What is perceived to be necessary is often a function of what risks one is willing to run. No absolute constraint compels a business to bribe, just as no force made anyone a slaveholder. Many persons doing business in America and abroad assert that they have prospered without bribery. Only a fraction of American companies—less than 4 percent of those registered with the Securities and Exchange Commission—have confessed to paying bribes abroad; so that even in circumstances where confession was solicited without penalties and even as to business in countries where bribery statutes were weakly enforced, it was seen that only a small number of corporations actually found it necessary to bribe. Companies such as Gulf and Lockheed, which have repented of their corrupt ways, are as prosperous as when they were the paymasters of politicians throughout the world. If, as has been asserted, business has been lost in certain countries because it is now an American crime to bribe abroad, the loss has not been shown to be as much as 5 percent of the American total for the country. It was argued earlier that even 5 percent was *de minimis*. Surely, a drop of less than 5 percent is an index that bribes are not necessary for most businesses. Necessity, it seems, is not only the tyrant's plea but also the plea of those too used to taking the easy course. When required to reform, businesses discover that what looks like inexorable reality is a mirage generated by their fears.

The plea of necessity is restated by those who insist that bribery has a social function. Functional observations prove too much if they are translated into moral argument. Tweed's New York, Ruef's San Francisco functioned by bribery. Railroads were constructed, traction lines laid, airplanes manufactured because bribes worked to diminish the capital risks of the corporations involved. Thailand and Haiti run because officials are paid off. Bribes have a function. Every persistent practice has a function, else why would it persist?

Cannibalism had a social function. Child sacrifice had a social function. Child marriage had a social function. Racial segregation had a social function. To convert observation into argument, an assumption is added: that human beings always know their own needs and the right way to meet them. On this assumption, it follows that every functional practice, since it fulfills a human need, is moral. Few believe the assumption. When Haiti is pronounced "more corrupt" than Thailand, the implicit judgment is made that, however functional, bribes interfere with the fulfillment of basic human needs, otherwise why speak of corruption?

The great maxim, "Whatever is, is right," makes moral judgment vacuous by depriving it of any criterion. Moral judgment must always be comparing what is done to satisfy human needs with what could be done, and it must always be scrutinizing the needs themselves. Functionally useful, bribes sometimes satisfy the wrong needs—for example, the need to make several million dollars without risk—and they do so by a method always destructive of trust. The social purpose a bribe serves does not make the breach of trust disappear.

One kind of necessity remains, the necessity to bribe to prevent oppression. It is a necessity alleged only on behalf of the bribepayer. It is no defense at all for the bribetaker. He must bear the full moral weight of being a bribee. As to bribers, relief of oppression is urged in mitigation or excuse. Not merely the victim of extortion because he is the initiator actively seeking to pay, a Wittgenstein or a Lincoln urges superior moral obligations that outweigh the obligation not to bribe.

Where the right of war exists, so does the right of usury, ran a scholastic maxim. A similar rule holds of bribery. In actual warfare, bribery is a weapon, less lethal than a bomb, which may justly be employed. Social orders may exist where the bonds of civic friendship have been so far dissolved that the state of society approaches warfare, at least as to the oppressed. The Germany in which Wittgenstein acted was in such a state. In such conditions it is necessary to "buy back harassment."

The existence of exceptions does not disprove a moral rule. Exceptions subvert a moral rule only if they are easily admitted and widely extended. General social trust must have disintegrated if war, or a state approximating war, has come into being. The excuse of buying off harassment cannot be evoked in a merely individual situation; the damage to the common good is too great. The case as to Lincoln's

supposed bribery is unproved. Judged as a hypothetical case, it must be condemned: it did occur in the course of an unfinished war, but it did not involve a measure taken against the enemy; it did, as hypothetically admitted, subvert the democratic process. It is not like Wittgenstein's action. The exception is admissible only when the social order and attendant trust are seriously impaired.

3. The third argument pretends that no distinction can be drawn between bribes and other reciprocities. All are reciprocities; they must be either all good or all bad. In structure the argument is like those of ultra-Puritans or ultra-libertarians who say there is no difference between marital and other sex. For the ultra-Puritan, all sex is condemned; for the ultra-libertarian, all sex is permissible. The distinctions on which civilized conduct depends disappear in a raw reductionism.

Defensible definitions, not dependent on the lines drawn by legal statutes, can be drawn. To draw them it is necessary to go beyond the words "gift," "tip," "contribution," and "bribe" and not to accept the use of the first three words to conceal bribery. It is necessary to sketch the salient characteristics of the transactions these words denote as types.

A gift—I speak of our developed sense of the term—is meant as an expression of personal affection, of some degree of love. It is given in a context created by personal relations to convey a personal feeling. The more it reflects the donee's interests and the donor's tastes the better. The more completely it is a gift the more completely it declares an identification of the giver with the recipient. In modesty or shyness gifts may sometimes be made in secret; but secrecy is not their necessary concomitant. The donee is glad to acknowledge the donor. The size of what is given is irrelevant. What counts is how much the donor expresses identification with the recipient. The gift once given is wholly the donee's and no one else's—it is with this donee and not someone else that the donor identifies. Sacrifice is a supreme gift: the donor identifies wholly with the donee.

It would be ideal to pretend that donors are usually not responding to favors given or hoping for favors to come. The donor, however, does not give by way of compensation or by way of purchase. No equivalence exists between what the donee has done and what is given. No obligation is imposed which the donee must fulfill. The donee's thanks are but the ghost of a reciprocal bond. That the gift should operate coercively is indeed repugnant and painful to the donor, destructive of the liberality that is intended. Freely given, the gift leaves the donee free. When the love the gift conveys is total, donor and donee are one, so the donor has no one to whom to respond. Every gift tries to approximate this ideal case. A present of any amount is a gift when it conveys love.

At the center of the Western tradition, endlessly instructive on the difference between gift and bribe, is the transaction known as the redemption—a term which as late as Shakespeare could be used ambiguously. But,

> Lawful mercy is nothing kin to foul redemption.

By a bold capture of language, Christian thought changed the meaning of the word redemption from payoff to liberation, achieved by a gift. The gift is of Christ, made by Christ, to us:

> The giver gives Himself.

God identifies with us to the point of being able to divinize us:

> He who became a participant in our nature [makes] us co-sharers in His divinity.

A chasm separates this uncoerced and uncoercive, loving, exemplary action from the manipulatively motivated, exploitative, secret exchange we call a bribe.

Between the polar opposites of bribe and gift lie a variety of transactions like tips and contributions. The tip is remuneration for the work of an employee, given according to a custom known and consented to by the employer. Given for service, it is intended to create no identification between tipper and tippee. The service has been given in expectation of the tip. Proportionality exists between the two. Size is significant. A very large tip is either a gift or a bribe.

The tip is meant to reward past acts and influence future ones. It affects the employee's exercise of discretion. The employee is faster, more attentive, more imaginative in expectation of the tip. As the employer knows and consents to the custom and its impact on the employee's discretion, no conflict exists between the employee's loyalty to the employer and the employee's response to the remuneration. Only low-level employees, however, receive tips. High-level employees make too many discretionary decisions where single-minded loyalty to the employer is important for the employer to consent that his agents be distracted by the tip's influence.

Campaign contributions are imperfect gifts because they are usually not set in a context of personal relations; they are intended to express a limited love—an identification with a cause. They are not wholly the recipient's—their purpose is restricted. They are not tips because they are not given to low-level employees but to those who if elected must exercise discretion in public affairs. They do not express or create overriding obligations, that is, there is no absolute obligation on the part of the contributor to recognize past work by the candidate; and there is no absolute obligation on the part of the candidate to do the work the contributor expects. Absence of absolute obligation creates one difference between contributions and bribes. Size is thus a relevant characteristic. A large contribution can create an overriding obligation; its proper name becomes bribe.

Contributions normally differ from bribes in a second way. They are not secret. They are given openly. They are recorded and reported. Above a very small amount, they are given in a traceable form, not in cash. They are not disguised or laundered. The difference between secrecy and nonsecrecy bears on accountability. The contributor acknowledges that he stands with this candidate. The candidate acknowledges that he takes this contributor's money. Voters know with whom the candidate identifies. Political accountability is preserved.

A bribe is not an expression of love. The briber seeks to move the bribee to serve the briber's interest. The more impersonal the medium, as Simmel observed, the better; if sex is used, it is as a commodity. The bribe never belongs to the bribee but in equity and morals to the principal for whom the bribee had a duty to act. The bribe is necessarily secret. If it becomes known the bribee is damaged, disgraced, incapacitated from delivering on the bribe. Deceit and lies are the bribe's normal accompaniment, necessary to protect its secrecy. The accountability of the briber and the bribee is not to the public but to each other. Equivalence and hence size are important. The larger the amount relative to the recipient, the greater the pressure created.

The bribe is intended to reflect or to create an overriding obligation. The briber pays because he feels he must reciprocate or must have reciprocation. The bribee delivers because he must. Angelo is double-damned because he takes a bribe and does not act upon it; so is Hog in Cicero's classic indictment. In the obligation created by the bribe, moral paradox abounds. Reciprocity is basic to human society. To violate the trust put in reciprocity is, generally speaking, immoral. The briber relies on the general trust put in reciprocity to impose an obligation contrary to the special trust placed in the officeholder. The bribe creates a conflict of duties nonexistent in the case of the tip; a secret, absolute obligation different from the contribution; a loveless compulsion unknown to the gift.

"Bribe" is used today not only in its primary sense of an exchange with an officeholder but in the sense of any inducement given to alter conduct that would naturally be otherwise. In this derivative usage some of the differences between a bribe and a gift disappear. In their primary senses, a bribe expresses self-interest; a gift conveys love. A bribe subordinates the recipient to the donor, a gift identifies the donor with the recipient. A gift brings no shame, a bribe must be secret. A gift may be disclosed, a bribe must be concealed. The size of a gift is irrelevant; the size of a bribe, decisive. A gift does not oblige; a bribe coerces. A gift belongs to the donee; a bribe belongs to those to whom the bribee is accountable. When a parent gives something to a child to get him to do something, is it a gift or a bribe? Normally what is given belongs to the child; it is disclosed; no shame attaches; sometimes love is expressed. At the same time the child is subordinated to the donor; size is not irrelevant; coercive obligation is imposed. If we make no objection to what is given, we say gift. If we disapprove morally, we say bribe.

Difficulties in discerning differences in the derivative usage do not change the main question, the moral distinguishability of gifts, tips, contributions, and bribes to officeholders. These can be masked as one another; but the masks are removable. The one million dollars paid by Lockheed to Prince Bernhard was no gift. It was paid in secret. Its size was decisive. It was meant to bind. We cannot be misled by Kotchian's quibble. The half-million dollars loaned by Nelson Rockefeller to a New York public official was too big for a tip, and its recipient was not low-level. It was too big for a gift. Its size created an obligation to the lender going beyond repayment of the loan. Uncondemned by New York law, its moral status is evident. The ten dollars given at Christmas to the mailman—literally a bribe by federal law—is a classic tip and its inclusion within the law an error. Campaign contributions can be bribes, as successful prosecutions have established. Cash and secrecy are today the normal badges of criminality. But contributions can also be distinct from bribes meant not to manipulate an officeholder but to identify with him and the cause he supports. No doubt in close cases the motivations of contributor and candidate are morally significant; it is not surprising that moral

lines should depend on motivation. The entire set of laws on campaign contributions can be read as an effort, clumsy surely but persistent also, to reinforce the moral line already in existence between bribes and contributions.

The access payment, too, may be readily classified. If the payment is small, open, and uniform for all, it will of course be no more than an entrance fee, as morally legitimate as any fee charged for the use of a court. Large, secret, variable, it bears the marks of what is given in expectation of official action. The pretense is then made that only attention is purchased. The pretense is transparent. In its ancient form of a price paid to a judge's servants, or in its modern form of a substantial campaign contribution, it is accompanied by the tacit understanding that the attention bought will be favorable. Access payments of this sort are bribes.

Intermediate cases, borderline cases exist. What moral concept is free of them? Gray depends on black and white. The most difficult area is that of employment. Is a person given a job as a payoff or on the merits? Motives may be mixed when the President makes an appointment or when a private corporation hires a former government employee. Double effect can often be found—choice of a responsible appointee, reciprocation of an official favor. As in countless other situations of double effect, a moral judgment is required to determine the predominant motive and consequences. The difficulty of the judgment does not destroy the moral nature of the concept being employed. If sexual favors are used, are they predominantly expressions of simple lust or affection, or are they intended chiefly to influence official action? If banking favors are extended, do they reflect business judgment or are they benefits conferred to obtain official responses? The existence of a second effect other than the obtaining of governmental action cannot obscure or disguise a real purpose of bribery. At the same time there will be cases where bribery is neither intended nor effected. Close cases, the necessary weighing of complex elements, accentuate the moral character of the judgments needed.

Convention plays a large part in the development of any area of morals. Convention will mark off areas where reciprocities are tolerable, acceptable, desirable from those areas, extending beyond the hardcore central case of cash for official actions, where immoral payoffs are present. The necessary appeal of moral judgment to conventional guidelines does not mean that the basic principles are merely conventionally related to the moral good; the conventions are always subject to criticism and revision in the light of basic principles.

4. The fourth argument is a species of familiar gamesmanship. It involves an objection applicable to all moral ideas, and uses it to attack a particular moral idea as if no other moral idea were open to it. If the objections were sound, no moral idea would survive. Yet the argument itself, to succeed at all, appeals to morality. It is self-destructive.

What moral idea has not been exploited by the envious and the hypocritical? What moral idea has not been treated to rhetorical overkill? Patriotism, piety, purity—all positive moral concepts—and negative moral concepts such as avarice, pride, and usury all have been used extravagantly. Bribery is not special in the abuse made of the basic idea.

What moral idea has ever been consistently enforced by Law? From anger to xenophobia, many sins have never been punished by law. As to such moral notions as fraud which the law does undertake to incorporate, the law acts spottily and with indifferent success. The moral character of bribery does not depend on its thorough application by statutes or by prosecutors. The objection, however, is particularly ill taken today, when the moral idea animates an immense expansion of the criminal law of bribery, so that the law includes commerce and sports as well as politics, is applied to congressmen and governors as well as to sheriffs and mayors, and is made a measure for American conduct in every country.

Unlike some vicious actions, bribetaking is the peculiar vice of a distinct class. To be a bribee one must hold a position of trust. To expose bribery is ordinarily to go against those who have, or recently had, power. Special efforts not necessary for the correction of humbler vices are required. Add that reciprocal exchange is the natural form of relationship with strangers and enforcement of the antibribery ethic goes against the grain. It is not surprising, and it is not disastrous to the moral concept, if extraordinary measures need to be taken to assert the duty not to receive a bribe.

A moral government will not resort to foul means to enforce the ethic. Abscam went too far: the government that touches pitch is also stained. But no injury is done a bribetaker when his co-conspirator is led to confess their common crime. No injury is done a bribee photographed in the act. No injustice is done when bribers or bribees are punished for other crimes they have committed although their participation in unpunished bribery is the reason for their prosecution. Next to tyranny, corruption is the great

disease of government. Skillful surgeons need more than a single way of curing the disease.

5. The fifth argument invites morality to overlook bribery as too trivial for its high concerns. Joined to the first three arguments it is hypocritical, pretending on the one hand that bribery is universal and necessary and, on the other hand, that it is too small to notice. Isolated and taken on its merits, the argument is morally obtuse. Using a quantitative measure, it doubts the effect of bribery on material goods. But the common good of any society consists not only in its material possessions but in its shared ideals. When these ideals are betrayed, as they are betrayed when bribery is practiced, the common good, intangible though it be, suffers injury.

The quantitative argument further overlooks the effect upon individual persons of engaging in behavior everywhere felt as shameful and contrary to social ideals. To take a bribe is commonly understood as a prostitution of one's office. To pay a bribe is to play the part of a professional seducer. Secrecy and deceit are the common badges of the bribe and must be practiced by the parties to it. To accept a bribe is to take on the necessity of lying. Human beings do not engage in such acts without affecting their characters, their view of themselves, their integrity.

Finally, the quantitative argument innocently ignores the massive popular discontent that can be ignited by corruption. No doubt, there is an element of envy in this discontent. No doubt, the discontent is often politically fanned and exploited. But the envy stirred and the political passions manipulated get their strength from the shared perception that a real evil is being perpetuated by the corrupt officials. In relatively stable countries such as Japan and Italy, revelations of corruption have affected the electoral strength of the ruling parties. In less stable African nations, corruption has been an invitation to coups and revolution. In the noncommunist world, capitalist corruption has been effectively used to attract disillusioned youth to Communism. In the Soviet Union and Eastern Europe, corruption has prevented the realization of the announced ideological objectives. West or East, bribery has a political impact corresponding to the moral magnitude of the issue.

The question was asked if bribery as a moral concept was more like usury or slavery. The answer is that today it is like neither. Usury has little vigor as a moral concept; bribery has much. Slavery is indisputably immoral; the morality of bribery is debated.

The closest parallel is furnished by sexual morality. That genital intercourse is primarily for procreation and permitted only in marriage; that intercourse with another's spouse is wicked and with a person of the same sex worse; that faithful, free, marital intercourse is significantly set apart from random sexual acts—these propositions constituted the proclaimed Western sexual ethic from A.D. 500 to the mid-twentieth century. Buttressed by auxiliary rules of lesser importance such as the ban on contraception, the main lines went unchallenged. They were incorporated into the law of every Western nation. Adultery and homosexual acts were crimes. Marriage was a state with multiple legal privileges.

This ethic had its foundation in religious belief, and with the erosion of belief, it crumbled within Western society in general; within a religious tradition the ethic may still hold. Against it in the twentieth century was urged the universality of practice. Abroad, in many parts of the world, it was not honored. At home, as the Kinsey studies were cited to show, it was not observed. What was generally done, it was then argued, must be necessarily done; and what was generally and necessarily done could not be wrong.

Intrinsically, the sexual act was the same whatever its context. Harm in the act was undemonstrated, undemonstrable, at most trivial. The distinction between the conjugal intercourse of sterile spouses and the intercourse of homosexuals became blurred. The auxiliary rules were discarded. Then the laws protecting marriage were either left unenforced or actually repealed. The legal privileges of the married shrank to almost none. The distinction between living together and marriage became almost invisible. Rape and the exploitation of children remained condemned. Between consenting adults any sexual act appeared acceptable.

Could the bribery ethic undergo the same decline so that only extortion and the exploitation of great disparities in bargaining power would remain condemned? The question, put now at the height or near the height of the embodiment of the bribery ethic in law, seems preposterous. Does not the bribery ethic assure an essential condition of government, while sexual sins are merely private acts? But sexual morals once were thought to speak to issues more central to society than government. Privatization is only a symptom of their fall. If the bribery ethic were to be regarded as obsolete, it too would be privatized.

Historically, the tie between the ethics of bribery and sexual ethics are close. It is not simply that they were formed in the same religious milieu and taught by the same religious tradition and depended on the command of the same God. They have shared the same language. "Corruption" is a state of civic graft or sexual depravity. Bribed judges are "whores," who have "prostituted" their office. Francis Bacon, as he said in self-defense, was at least a virgin in the king's affairs. "Fig-leaves" covered his shameful acts of bribetaking. Even cynical rejections of the two ethics are alike in implying that true "virility" cannot be confined by the feminine virtues the ethical standards incorporate.

The parallelism of language and metaphor points to an analogy deeper than the linguistic. At the core of each ethic are two moral concepts—fidelity and gratuitousness. Genital acts and official acts must be faithful, and they must be unpaid. Neither kind of act is in the realm of commerce. Both require loyalty. The Western ethic as to each draws lines that distinguish purchased action from free action, lines that depend on the special status of a gift. The Western ethic as to each teaches that human fidelity is possible and in one case is the foundation of the human family, in the other of the social enterprise. The usual sanction as to each is internal, the judgment of conscience, sometimes reinforced by public shame.

Intention, context, ceremony set off one sexual act from another. Reductionists look at the physiological process and find adultery, prostitution, and conjugal intercourse indistinguishable. Ceremony marks off the marital setting, and marriage provides the context in which the intention to express faithful love governs intercourse. In the same way intent and context distinguish campaign contributions, gifts, and tips from bribes. In each case the physical act of payment is the same. Nothing in the physical action itself, everything in the relational aspects makes the moral difference.

Alike by the analogical values at their center, relying on the same metaphors and the same sanctions, rooted in the same religions, the sexual ethic and the bribery ethic carve out of common reciprocities a special realm of sacred gratuitousness and insist on creating distinctiveness by context. If the sexual ethic has been abandoned, the bribery ethic is likely to have a similar fate. It is already presaged by the kind of arguments just summarized, now available in the literature of social science.

Against this future is not only the obvious fact that the two ethics deal with different sets of acts alike only metaphorically. There is the observable phenomenon that as public recognition of the sexual ethic has declined in America, public recognition and reinforcement of the bribery ethic have increased.

Whether or not the movement is compensatory, it is evident that the bribery ethic is not narrowly tied to the sexual ethic, and that a society for substantial periods can promote one and not the other. Considerations other than analogy will decide the future of the bribe.

Conclusions

There are four reasons why bribery is likely to continue to be morally condemned:

1. *Bribery is universally shameful*. There is not a country in the world which does not treat bribery as criminal on its lawbooks. There are some laws such as those on gambling that are constantly broken without any particular sense of shame attaching to the offense. Bribery law is not among them. In no country do bribetakers speak publicly of their bribes, or bribegivers announce the bribes they pay. No newspaper lists them. No one advertises that they can arrange a bribe. No one is honored precisely because he is a big briber or a big bribee. No one writes an autobiography in which he recalls the bribes he has taken or the bribes he has paid. Pepys's diary is for himself. Kotchian's accounting to a foreign nation is an anomaly. Not merely the criminal law—for the transaction could have happened long ago and prosecution be barred by time—but an innate fear of being considered disgusting restrains briber and bribee from parading their exchange. Significantly, it is often the Westerner with ethnocentric prejudice who supposes that a modern Asian or African society does not regard the act of bribery as shameful in the way Westerners regard it.

The shame affects even those caught with little more than fig leaves to protect their modesty. For Francis Bacon what he received as chancellor from litigants were "gifts" not bribes. For Chairman Haughton of Lockheed what Lockheed paid constituted not bribes but "kickbacks." In the files of the great corporation engaged in bribery on a world scale the term "bribe" itself is not the usual description for a payment; euphemism is essential.

Shame and hypocrisy in the use of language are vice's tribute to virtue. Shame may be culturally conditioned. Shame so strong and so general is acknowledgment that there is something objectionable in the conduct that goes beyond the impolite and the merely illegal. Shame does not conclusively establish but it points to the moral nature of the matter.

2. *Bribery is a sellout to the rich*. In any situation ruled only by money or its equivalent, the deeper pocket will prevail. If judicial judgments could be bought and paid for, there would be a market in judgments as there is in soybeans and potatoes. The same holds true of the decisions of regulatory agencies, of public authorities, of government procurement officers, of legislators. If bribes were not morally objectionable, we would live in a world of pure plutocracy where wealth would be the measure of all things.

Only in caricature or jeremiad is there such a predominance of wealth over all other values. Our culture, and the culture of every nation, cultivates values other than wealth. Part of the cultivation is resistance to the encroachment of money into every sphere, and part of the resistance depends on the moral condemnation of bribery.

In judicial proceedings, efforts not totally useless are made to make factors other than money determine the outcome: the skill of the lawyers and the prudence of the judge as well as more general ideals such as fairness and truth are given a weight that would be reduced to zero if bribery were acceptable and money alone counted. In legislative proceedings, the security of the country, the welfare of particular groups, the success of an administration are all values that work against the dominance of money and make its employment through bribery a repugnant intrusion. Regulatory agencies and public authorities have the well-being of rich and middle class and poor before them; if money buys their decisions the interests of all but a few are injured. In each of these forums where public policy is made, if bribery were regarded as an inconsequential matter, wealth would swallow up the other values. To claim "The rich usually have it their way anyway" is not responsive to this observation, in part because it fails to acknowledge the accommodations the rich must usually make to "have it their way," in part because it blurs the difference between a society in which money talks and a society in which money would rule. It is not, I should suppose, the experience of anyone familiar with any of the governmental processes of the United States that success in them is a direct correlative of money. But if bribery were to be cynically put behind moral censure, there would be no bounds to the triumph of wealth. Such a triumph would be contrary to the pursuit of basic human needs, and what is necessary to prevent it is a moral matter.

The advocate of the acceptance of bribery as a nonmoral matter may say he does not go so far. His position is that bribery, like pornography, may be restrained if it thrusts itself too boldly on the citizenry, if it flaunts itself in public areas where decent conventions prevent its acknowledgment, if it fails to pay rhetorical tribute to other values a society honors. To accept bribery is to accept the way things are, not to proclaim a regime where mammon is publicly enthroned as a sole monarch.

This rejoinder is unconvincing. Once it is accepted that decisions may be paid for, a market is introduced. The bribery ethic gradually extended its sway from courts to high-level administration to legislatures. The process could be reversed. Old markets in legislatures, government procurement, and public employment could by degrees be restored. Once the restraint of conscience accepting the moral ideal is removed, there is no obvious or convenient point where it would be wrong to bribe. The democratic commitment to equality before the law, however haltingly realized, is too great to permit such a regression.

3. *Bribery is a betrayal of trust.* Trust, that is, the expectation that one will do what one is relied on to do, is a precious necessity of every social enterprise. The notion of fidelity in office, as old as Cicero, is inextricably bound to the concept of public interest distinct from private advantage. It is beyond debate that officials of the government are relied upon to act for the public interest not their own enrichment. When they take bribes they divide their loyalty. Whether or not they consciously act against the public interest, they have adopted a second criterion of action, the proper reciprocation of the bribe. Their resultant conflict of interest is always a dilution of loyalty, always a betrayal of trust.

A trust cannot be betrayed if a trust is not imposed, cynics may say. Everyone knows that leaders act for their political advantage. No one trusts them to act always selflessly for the public good. The cynical objection fails to note that action motivated by political expediency carries with it political accountability. The trust, although tempered, is that officeholders will act accountably. It is supposed, not unreasonably, that perceptions of political advantage by the accountable officeholder will often coincide with what is the public good. For a bribe there is no accountability but to the briber.

The social injury inflicted by breaches of trust goes beyond any material measurement. When government officials act to enrich themselves they act against the fabric on which they depend, for what else does government rest upon except the expectation that those chosen to act for the public welfare will serve that welfare? The trust comes with the office. A person is no mere powerholder but an officer of government because he is invested with this trust. The trust cannot be repudiated without denying the responsibility inherent in the role and thereby denying the role itself. As the trust reposed in a mother is central to the family, so the trust reposed in the officeholder is central to government. To preserve this trust, to keep it from betrayal, is to protect what reason requires in the pursuit of the Good. The condemnation of bribery functions to this end and in so doing functions as the command of morality.

4. *Bribery violates a divine paradigm.* The imitation of God lies at the root of the bribery prohibition. God "does not take *shohadh,*" the Book of Deuteronomy proclaims. The God of Israel is not turned from the widow and the orphan by the wealth of their opponent. The God of Israel judges impartially. No human gift can blind God's eye or bind His judgment. Nothing, as the Book of Job teaches, can compel the Creator to reciprocate. Fixed in the biblical basis of Western culture is the model of the Ruler-Judge who is above all attempts to bribe Him. We are to be like Him. Fixed in the Christian tradition which has been recurrently invoked to reform our civilization are the image of what cannot be bought, the paradigm of the Donor who identifies with the donees, and the teaching that what is freely received must be freely given. Generous gift and base bribe are demarcated forever by religious example and instruction.

The argument, it will be urged, is too nationalistic and too religious. It is too nationalistic because it appeals to a tradition nurtured in the West and fully accepted only in the American commitment to recurrent reformation. It will not work in a world in which Western or American values cannot dictate morality. It is too religious because it depends on a belief in God and belief in a nonbribeable, giftgiving God. It will not work with those who believe God is bribeable or bribegiving. It will not work in a secularist society where belief in God is either not admitted or not acknowledged to have consequences.

Nonetheless for those who believe in God and who believing in Him believe that He is the source of morality, the argument works. "Be holy because I the Lord Your God am holy" is the law of Israel (Lv 19:2). "Be you therefore perfect even as your Father in heaven is perfect" is the law given by Jesus (Mt 5:48). Jews and Christians are called to this imitation of God. It is a moral call, based on religious command; for one of the great human needs is for divine example; for, as Plato says, God is the measure of all things. As the God of Job and Jesus does not take or give bribes, so cannot those who imitate Him.

One's origins, one's experiences, one's existing balance of values go into the perception of one's ends; at the same time the ends chosen affect the person one becomes. The dynamism of movement to ends determines what one regards as human needs and affects one's choice of the means necessary to satisfy them.

From the perspective taken here, the shame of the briber and the bribee are true indicia of violation of the human good; the acceptance in practice of plutocratic rule is abhorrent; the trust reposed in government is inherent in public office, which becomes raw power without it; and the divine paradigm is real. Personal and social needs are frustrated by the act of bribery, which violates the basic need to honor by action not mere words values other than wealth, the basic need to trust one's government, the basic need to be like one's heavenly Father. The nature of bribery is contrary to the nature of the human person in its full development.

Going beyond the data, I venture a prediction: as slavery was once a way of life and now, whatever analogues in economic duress remain, has become obsolete and incomprehensible, so the practice of bribery in the central form of the exchange of payment for official action will become obsolete. The movement to restrict by law many forms of reciprocal exchange with officeholders incorporates the thrust of a dominant moral idea. The conventions that give concreteness to the idea of the bribe will be refined and made responsive to the needs satisfied by human trust and human conformity to God's example.

Study Questions

1. Does the first argument listed in the headnote commit the *ad populum* fallacy?

2. Does it pose a false dilemma to assume that bans on bribes must be enforced immorally?

*3. If you took a job in a country where bribery was an accepted business practice, would you refuse to arrange such payments and thereby risk losing business? If so, what would you do if you learned that a local employee of yours was still paying the customary bribes?

*4. Have you ever given a "gift" in the hope of gaining someone's help on a project of yours? What—if any—is the distinction between such gift giving and bribery?

*5. In some hospitals it is common for physicians to use gifts and favors to buy patient referrals from the emergency-room staff. If you became director of such a hospital, would you ignore the practice or try to stop it?

*6. If all public officials found guilty of accepting bribes were to suffer the same punishment and you could set that punishment, what would it be?

*7. If is said (for example, by psychological egoism) that everyone has his price. If you were responsible for awarding a huge building contract and a construction firm wanted to influence your decision, what would be *your* price? Assume you were convinced you'd never be discovered.

8. Should Wittgenstein have bribed the Nazis? Did paying the Nazis make Wittgenstein a collaborator with the Nazis?

26

Confucian Ethics and Japanese Management Practices

Marc J. Dollinger

Author's abstract: This paper proposes that an important method for understanding the ethics of Japanese management is the systematic study of its Confucian traditions and the writing of Confucius. Inconsistencies and dysfunction in Japanese ethical and managerial behavior can be attributed to contradictions in Confucius' writings and inconsistencies between the Confucian code and modern realities. Attention needs to be directed to modern Confucian philosophy since, historically, Confucian thought has been an early warning system for impending change.

There seems to be little doubt that the management practices of Japanese corporations will have, and are having an important impact on management thinking and practice in the United States and the rest of the world (Abegglen and Stalk, 1986). In the academic arena, papers are being published and research programs launched to determine the nature and efficacy of the phenomenon. A major portion of the curricula development effort in "International business" is directed toward the study of, and contact with, the Japanese firm and trading company. Japanese firms and the Japanese government have established academic centers within the university environment to help foster cooperative projects and mutual understanding.

Questions have naturally arisen concerning the adoption of Japanese ways and whether or not non-Japanese firms can successfully implement techniques which have been proved in another culture (e.g., Tsurumi, 1978; Buckley and Mirza, 1985; Dillon, 1983; Sethi *et al.*, 1984). The debate over the issues of convergence and divergence places the question in an academic framework and the evidence is thoroughly mixed (Dunphy, 1987). It is unclear from both theoretical development and empirical findings whether or not the Japanese (and therefore other East Asian economies) are becoming more like the West or vice versa.

Even though references to culture as a factor in the convergence debate are ubiquitous, a gap exists in our understanding of the ethics of Japanese culture. Most Westerners, including business academics, have had little or no exposure to original source materials (in translation). There has been considerable reliance on secondary sources for interpretations and representations of the cultural phenomena. For example, Ouchi (1981) offers a set of managerial prescriptions and concludes that both East and West are converging on a Z form of organization which is not dependent on Japanese culture for its existence. Abegglen and Stalk (1985) briefly summarize the theory that Japanese managerial and industrial practices are embedded in the culture, and then discount the theory's influence. Hamada (1985) rejects Theory Z and attempts to build a model of the corporation which integrates corporate practices, Japanese culture and the economic environment. Jaeger and Baliga (1985) attribute the effectiveness of control systems in Japanese organizations to the shared values and culture. All of these authors, and others (see Dunphy, 1987, for a voluminous review), offer their interpretation of the culture of Japan and their enactment of it. Since most Western readers have no direct experience of Japanese ethics and society, its philosophical and historical roots, the reader is forced to accept reconstructions of Japanese culture rather than the logic-in-use (Kaplan, 1964).

The purposes of this paper are twofold. One design is to offer original material from one of the major sources of Japanese ethical tradition, the *Analects* of Confucius, and illustrate its contributions in the context of Japanese managerial and industrial practices. The *Analects* are regarded as the most reliable source of Confucius' writings. In the *Analects*, Confucius set the tone and introduced the major themes of Chinese philosophy. The most important of these themes is humanism. Confucius wrote of the importance of the individual, the character of human nature, and the value of developing oneself through learning. He wrote of the perfectibility of human beings and the need for constant renovation of the spirit in order to achieve that perfection.

The second purpose is to offer the hypothesis that much of the contradictory results obtained in researching the convergency-divergence question can be explained by the contradictory nature of Japanese tradition. This approach may be termed an exercise in hermeneutics. Hermeneutical method relies on textual interpretation and emphasizes the historical dimension of research. The researcher interprets first level-constructs found in the text material and translates these into symbolic representations (Steffy and Grimes, 1986). Hermeneutical exegesis is one of a number of methodologies that fall into the general classification of subjective, qualitative research, emphasizing an idiographic perspective (Morey and Luthans, 1984).

Japan is a complex society combining Buddhism, Shintoism, and Confucianism with the artifacts of modernization. The contributions of Confucian thought are directed at the ethical aspects of human interaction, leading some to call Japan a Confucian society (Adler *et al.*, 1986; MacFarquhar, 1980). Japanese Confucianism has at its core four distinct, though not mutually exclusive (or consistent) themes. First, in its most essential form, Confucianism is a humanistic philosophy and the human being is regarded with dignity and respect. Second, Confucianism inculcates the values of harmony with its concurrent emphasis on loyalty, group and family identification, and the submergence of the individual. Righteousness and the acts of righteous individuals within the framework of loyalty provide a third dimension. Lastly, there is the integrating theme of the morally superior person, the Chun-Tzu, who leads by example and is devoted to the other Confucian values. It is through the Chun-Tzu that the ethical system comes alive and is actuated. The Chun-Tzu is the leader of the Confucian society.

Before beginning, a note of caution is offered. The purposes here are not to subsume all managerial phenomena under a cultural imperative model. Culture is not the only determinant of managerial behavior. Models which posit culture as the single cause of managerial behavior and practice have been critiqued by Kagono et al. (1985), and these are seen as insufficient to explain all Japanese business phenomena. Indeed the empirical question of whether or not Confucian societies differ more among themselves than with the West has not been settled. There is no suggestion that societies cannot change in some ways

while maintaining underlying traditions. This is in fact exactly the Japanese experience, reflected in one of Japan's most famous slogans of the modernization era, "Eastern ethics, Western science" (*toyo no do toku, seiyo no gei*). However, although causality cannot be proved, two of the three criteria of causality are present: covariance and time precedence (Selltiz *et al.*, 1976). Only the elimination of alternative explanations, e.g., materialism, is missing.

Confucianism in Japan

Confucius was born in 551 or 552 B.C. in the state of Lu in modern Shantung. His career was devoted almost exclusively to teaching and education. He gathered around him a group of scholars as he made his way, serving in minor administrative posts. At the age of 56, finding that his superiors were unwilling to adopt his teachings as policy, he began a 13-year journey pushing for social reforms. He returned to Lu at the age of 68 and for the next five years he wrote and taught. Among the writings thought to have been produced during this period are the *Analects*. He died at age 73 (see Chan, 1963, for a good historical accounting).

Confucianism spread out from China throughout Asia in spite of the fact that Confucianism had no missionaries. The bearers of the message of Confucius were Buddhist monks, who while proselytizing for Buddha, carried the day-to-day values of Confucius with them. Since Confucianism is not native to Japan, having been imported from China, in order to understand the divergent route that Japanese Confucianism has taken, it is necessary to trace the history of Confucian thought in Japan.

The course of Confucian philosophy has changed many times since Confucius wrote and lived. A detailed historical perspective of Confucianism is beyond the scope of this paper. However, due to the influence of Chu Hsi (1130–1200), the philosophy of Confucius was re-established as the fundamental philosophy of Chinese civilization. Chu Hsi's Neo-Confucianism remains a pervasive influence throughout East Asia and has shaped behavior there for hundreds of years (Chan, 1986). It was among Chu Hsi' accomplishments to select the four books that became known as the Classics: the *Analects*, the *Book of Mencius*, the *Great Learning*, and the *Doctrine of the Mean*. These four Classics preserved Confucian thought intact down through the twentieth century. The Classics and Chu Hsi's commentaries on them were adopted in 1313 as the official texts for the civil service examinations and remained so, unchanged, until 1905.

The earliest record of Confucianism in Japan occurs somewhere between the sixth and seventh centuries A.D. (de Bary, 1938). The more important wave of Confucian influence arrived in Japan in the sixteenth century with Zen Buddhist monks. This Confucianism, the Sung Neo-Confucianism of Chu Hsi, was quickly adopted by the early Tokugawa rulers (1600–1868) to help them justify and solidify their reign. The Shogun was the military and political ruler of Japan under Tokugawa rule. Confucianism provided the focus for precisely the problem that the Shogun faced: the creation and maintenance of a stable political and social order on the basis of a firm ethical code (Reischauer and Fairbank, 1960). Conversely, Confucian scholars used the peace and unity created by the Tokugawa's military government as an opportunity to rid themselves of the clerical dominance of Chinese-style mandarins and to unite Confucian thinking with statism.

The Tokugawa Confucianists had a different thrust than the Manchu Chinese although the orthodoxy was, in principle, the same. Jansen (1965) sees the Japanese Confucianist of the time as a forerunner of administrative innovation and experiment. The political organization of the decentralized daimyo (the local clan chief) provided many opportunities for heterodoxy and allowed Confucianism to interact with local political conditions. (The Manchu thrust was on administrative control of a large central state.)

Thus there began a mutual dependency between the state as represented by the Tokugawa Shogunate, the baku-han system (the decentralized political-military network), and the Neo-Confucianists. Much of the Chu Hsi orthodoxy was adopted intact; the natural hierarchy of classes (elite and samurai, farmer, artisan, merchant), the four themes described previously, and the shedding of Buddhist and Taoist philosophical tenets (Hall, 1970). Basic education in Japan was Chinese Confucian by the mid 1700s; its purpose was to develop the individual's moral character both as an absolute human duty and in order to better fulfill the samurai's function (Dore, 1965).

In the Japanese setting, Confucian teachings served to reinforce values of duty, self-discipline, loyalty and achievement—in honor to one's name and gratitude and respect to one's superiors ... (Jansen, 1965, p. 96).

Later on in Tokugawa rule, during the late seventeenth and early eighteenth centuries, some distinctly Japanese elements of Confucianism began to emerge. These Japanese elements helped to tighten the bonds between the philosophy and the secular needs of the ruling elite. Two of the more important aspects of this new heterodoxy were the development of bushido (the code of ethics and behavior for the samurai) and the increasing respectability of commercial activities (Hall, 1970). These two developments were not unrelated. As a means of regulating society and controlling the social order, each class of people was given its own Tao (do), or code of behavior. The samurai's code was the bushido, the warrior's way. The merchant's code was chonindo, the merchant's way. There could be righteousness, humanity, and principle for each class in a Confucian scheme, and each class could perform its duties according to the ethical principles of its do without shame.

The elements of bushido were devotion to duty, cultivation of the martial arts, austerity, temperance, self-discipline, and the readiness to die immediately for their superiors. The chonin, or merchants, attempted to imitate the more highly esteemed samurai. Their code demanded loyalty (to the trading house or firm), frugality (re-investment of profits, renovation of equipment and machines) as well as harmony and righteousness. In fact, the class barriers that prevented wealthy merchants from changing their status made them even richer by forcing them to re-invest their wealth in commercial activities (Reischauer and Fairbank, 1960). Over time class lines began to blur but were never completely eliminated. Warriors, deeply in debt to merchants, commonly had their debts cancelled by the merchants in exchange for higher status (Borton, 1970). And even though original Confucian thought denigrated money and profit, it was possible for a seventeenth century Confucian, Muro Kyuso to write,

To rejoice when one makes a profitable transaction or buys valuable merchandise cheaply is part of a merchant's trade, but it is unpardonable in a samurai ... (de Bary, 1938, p. 430).

By the nineteenth century it was possible to argue from the very Confucian manner of historical reflection that human society rested on the twin pillars of labor and the exchange of merchandise. De Bary quotes Kaiho Seiyo,

... it is a ridiculous thing that the aristocracy and the military class in Japan should disdain profit, or that they should say that they disdain profit. When a man does not disdain profit, he is called a bad person. Such is the perverse practice of the times ... Rice is li (principle), gold is li, li is the commodity ... buying, selling and paying interest are all part of li ... the Law of the Universe ... (de Bary, 1958, p. 491).

In 1868 the Tokugawa rule of over 250 years came to an end with the restoration of the Emperor Meiji. This was essentially a peaceful revolution designed to begin Japan on the road to modernization. The lessons drawn from the Chinese experience in the Opium Wars (1842) and the Perry Expedition of 1854 demonstrated to the Japanese that change was needed to preserve their nation's independence. At the time of the Meiji Restoration there were a number of exceptional individuals (like Iwasaki of Mitsubishi) who straddled samurai and merchant traditions and helped lead Japan through this revolutionary time. There even emerged a group of peasant entrepreneurs who possessed capital, skill and the technology necessary to form large business organizations (Fairbank et al., 1965). The guiding philosophy of the Restoration, epitomized by Sakuma Shozan's slogan "Eastern ethics, Western science" (Passin, 1965), was characterized by an easy blend of Confucianism, which taught the perfectibility of society through the proper ethical/political organization and leadership (Fairbank et al., 1965). Many Japanese recognized that their Confucianism was on the fringe of Chinese Confucianism; however, it was clear that this Confucian philosophy contributed to the development of a strong sense of nationalism, and promoted education and ambition as fundamental values in the general population (Jansen, 1965a).

The modernization brought on by the Meiji Restoration and the opening of Japan succeeded in creating a strong military and economic state, capable of resisting Western pressures. However, much of the culture of Confucian Japan persisted. Although social classes were formally abolished, strong class distinctions remained. The Confucian concept of superior/inferior was ingrained. By 1890, as a part of the Meiji Constitution, the Imperial Rescript of Education made Confucian education mandatory and universal (Borton, 1970).

In the late twentieth century Confucianism as a philosophy has been weakened by emerging patterns of individuation (Maruyama, 1965), but as a moral and ethical code it is still dominant.

Japanese Management Practices

The survival from feudal times of a sense of personal relationship between employer and employee in industry [is] paralleled by a strong sense of personal or corporate loyalty within management itself (Reischauer and Fairbank, 1960, p. 511).

There is no single homogeneous set of managerial behaviors that can safely be labeled as "Japanese." Within Japan there is a good deal of variance in managerial practice, especially between the larger trading company/financial center firm and the smaller firms. Variation surely exists within these two groups as well. Additionally, as Ouchi (1981) observes, there are a number of American firms that appear to use similar practices (labeled Theory Z) and therefore these managerial behaviors may be deemed acultural. Another interpretation however is that the practices are pan-cultural; that is, there are multiple cultures and ethical systems capable of producing very similar management practices (equi-finality). However, a great deal has been written about Japanese management and many authors agree on its major components (Pascale, 1978; Tsurumi, 1978; Munchus, 1983; Nonaka and Johansson, 1985; Kagono et al., 1985).

Keys and Miller (1984) review and attempt to integrate what they refer to as the "Japanese management theory jungle." Their review encompasses Japanese manufacturing practices, human resource policies, and decision-making modes. Through a subjective review of the literature, they reduce a myriad of observable managerial practices to three underlying factors: a long-run planning horizon, a commitment to lifetime employment, and the Japanese sense of collective responsibility. All three underlying factors have bases in Confucian thought.

The practices which underline the first factor in their integration, the long run planning horizon, include a commitment to sufficient time to manage, diligence in implementation, discipline in work, and the development and the articulation of an organizational philosophy. These are all consistent with the Confucian goal of the search for perfection and the development of a righteous character.

It is in the fulfillment of these obligations that the Chun-Tzu is expected to make his contribution. Writing on these subjects, (all quotes from Chan, 1963).

Confucius said, "A ruler who governs his state by virtue is like the north polar star, which remains in place while the others revolve around it."

Confucius said, "Lead the people with governmental measures and regulate then by law and punishment, and they will avoid wrong-doing but have no sense of honor or shame. Lead them by virtue and regulate them by the rules of propriety and they will have a sense of shame, and moreover, set themselves right."

Confucius said, "The superior man brings the good things of others to completion and does not bring the bad things of others to completion. The inferior man does just the opposite."

These three Analects help describe what could be characterized as the "preferred leadership style" in Confucian society. Leaders are constant, steady, and this behavior provides guidance for subordinates. Leaders must act with magnanimity, compassion, vision, and wisdom (Sethi *et al.*, 1984). Also, the Confucian leader does not resort to rules and laws to lead, but instead trusts that the shared virtue of propriety will enable the people to accomplish their tasks. The one exception to this in Chinese history was the Legalist School of the Ch'in dynasty (221-206 B.C.) which rejected Confucian doctrine in favor of a legalistic society based upon power. The Legalists succeeded in unifying China but their violence and brutality led to their overthrow (Chan, 1963). Even now in Japan, there is a decided preference for shared values over legalisms.

Following are four additional Analects commenting on the character of the Chun-Tzu:

Confucius said, "The superior man does not seek fulfillment of his appetite nor comfort in his lodging. He is diligent in his duties and careful in his speech. He associates with men of moral principles and thereby realizes himself. Such a person may be said to love learning."

Confucius said, "The superior man thinks of virtue; the inferior man thinks of possessions . . ."

Confucius said, "The superior man wants to be slow in word but diligent in action."

Confucius was completely free from four things. He had no arbitrariness of opinion, no dogmatism, no obstinacy and no egotism.

The tasks of achieving perfection cannot be accomplished overnight, require a patient attention to detail, and encourage Japanese workers to "pursue the last grain of rice in the corner of their lunch box" (Hayes, 1981). The Confucian ideal of renovation and renewal enables the Japanese to renew each day the commitment to the long-term goals of the organization, and a search for perfection without the pressure for immediate results. From the book, the *Great Learning* (Chan, 1963) comes this description.

The inscription on the bath tub of King Tang read, "If you can renovate yourself one day, then you can do so everyday, and keep doing so everyday, and keep doing so day after day."

and

Confucius said, "Is it not a pleasure to learn and to repeat or practice from time to time what has been learned? . . ."

Confucius said, "A man who reviews the old so as to find out the new is qualified to teach others."

The second underlying factor identified by Keys and Miller (1984) was the commitment, albeit by a minority of firms, to lifetime employment. This factor manifested itself by high levels of investment in employee development, training, and socialization, reduced turnover, non-specialized career paths, and the development of internal labor markets. The Confucian emphasis on the family, which has been redirected to the firm, and the groupism that dominates the Confucian ethos serve as a foundation for these practices. Abegglen and Stalk (1985), who also identify career employment as one of the signature characteristics of Japanese corporation, note that new recruits are selected for the general characteristics of their character, as opposed to their skills. The characteristics that are valued are, of course, the Confucian ones of loyalty, diligence, and the submergence of individual needs. Writing on these subjects, Confucius said,

. . . The superior man is not an implement.

This saying expresses the fundamental view that people are good, they have inherent value, they exist as total organisms, not to be treated as tools.

Originally, the Confucian ethic of group was most often applied to relationships in the family and to government. These are traditionally lifetime relationships. In Japan, the group concept was extended first to the clan, around which agriculture was organized, and then, in the industrial era, to the firm.

Yu Tzu [a student of Confucius] said, "Few of those who are filial and respectful brothers will show disrespect to superiors, and there has never been a man who is not disrespectful to superiors, yet creates disorder. A superior man is devoted to the fundamentals (roots). When the root is firmly established, the moral law (Tao) will grow. Filial piety and brotherly respect are the root of humanity (jen)."

Confucius said, "[A good man] does not worry about being known by others but rather worries about not knowing them."

On loyalty:

> Tseng-Tsu [a student] said, "Everyday I examine myself on three points; whether in counseling others I have not been loyal; whether in intercourse with my friends I have not been faithful; and whether I have not repeated again and again and practiced the instructions of my teacher."

When Japanese are offered lifetime employment, they are expected to stay as well. Job hopping is not a positive value in Japan (Browning, 1986). The leaders of the kaisha speak of entry into the company as "being born again into another family" (Abegglen and Stalk, 1985, p. 200).

The third factor that emerges from the Key and Miller study (1984) is that of collective responsibility. This value and its practice may trace its roots to the necessities of rice cultivation which requires the whole village to cooperate at planting and harvest time. (Since rice cultivation pre-dates Confucianism, a materialist explanation is a plausible alternative.)

This collectivism finds its values in the group-centered nature of Confucian thought. Such practices as consensus decision-making (ringi), participative management (nemawashi), and quality circles all use the group as the basis for action. Concomitant with the group values are the personal values that are required to make the group work. Ouchi (1981) describes these in his Theory Z as trust, subtlety, intimacy, and loyalty. These are all components of the current worker's bushido.

> Meng I Tzu asked about filial piety. Confucius said, "Never disobey . . ."
>
> . . . Confucius said, "A ruler should employ his ministers according to the principles of propriety, and ministers should serve their ruler with loyalty."
>
> . . . Hold loyalty and faithfulness to be fundamental. Have no friends who are not as good as yourself. When you make mistakes, don't be afraid to correct them.
>
> Meng Wu-po asked about filial piety. Confucius said, "Especially be anxious lest parents should be sick."

The quotations above reflect the character of Confucian loyalty, and it is readily apparent that if the dicta are expanded from family to firm, this is a powerful tool of social control (Abegglen and Stalk, 1986). It requires the submergence of the individual to achieve perfection. Self-promotion is more than egotism, it is disloyal and immoral.

> Confucius said, "A man with clever words and an ingratiating appearance is seldom a man of humanity."

Ethical Contradictions in Japanese Management

In addition to the positive values and practices detailed above, negative and contradictory aspects of the Confucian tradition have been noted. Contradictions can be classified into two types: internal contradictions of Confucian thought and contradictions between Confucian ethics and the realities of modern democratic capitalism. Each of these types helps to explain the disparate results obtained by researchers investigating the convergence/divergence issue.

Internal Contradictions

The core themes of humanity and harmony produce major stress for the modern Japanese. The importance of the human being is emphasized throughout, yet for the sake of harmony individuals are to submerge desires and needs. In the West, there is a bias which values the individual above the need for harmony. In the East the bias is generally reversed (Maruyama, 1965). The Japanese have consciously attempted to avoid Westernization as they achieved modernization through "Western science, Eastern ethics." For example, when the Japanese ruling elite after the Meiji Restoration went searching for a constitution on which to model their new one, they chose the German model of Bismarck because it played down individual freedoms. This made it more attractive to the Confucian ethic. However, once the country was opened it was inevitable that Western elements and ideas would seep into the Japanese consciousness.

Another source of internal conflict in the Confucian value system is the need for rigid hierarchy and the full development of humanity (jen). Clearly, the hierarchical barriers prevent each person from reaching full potential. The integration of Confucianism with the Taoist concept of the Way helps alleviate some of the stress by enabling people, within their strata, to develop fully while never leaving that level. However there remains in Japan great resistance to an egalitarian ethic that would allow full personal rights for all. For example, Japanese of Korean ancestry are discriminated against and kept segregated from Japanese of native ancestry, and women are discriminated against in almost all forms of economic life. Irish (1986) describes an experience he had while working in a Japanese firm, in which he is reprimanded for showing sympathy with a woman manager who has been passed over for promotion many times and is treated as the lowest ranking member of the group, even though she is senior to a number of the men. As Confucius said (Chan, 1963),

> ... Women and servants are most difficult to deal with. If you are familiar with them, they will cease to be humble. If you keep them at a distance they will resent it.

A third internal contradiction concerns the emergence of the superior person as leader. From where is this individual to come? If individuality is to be suppressed, and self-promotion abhorred, how will the superior person be known? The difference between a true Chun-Tzu standing calmly amidst confusion and chaos while his trusty subordinates accomplish superior things, and a do-nothing, know-nothing, over-promoted senior official who silently stands by while better educated juniors solve problems can be very difficult to determine by unobtrusive observation. Confucius himself faced a similar problem. As a virtuous but minor administrator he was unable, within his own lifetime, to exert any leadership other than among his disciples.

External Contradictions

Confucian ethics and teachings occasionally clash with the realities of the modern and complex business world. For example, the emphasis on renovation and the values of ritualizing behavior seem inconsistent with the need for change and innovation. The Japanese mitigate this contradiction by focusing their rituals on interpersonal behavior and concentrating their efforts in technological innovation.

Similarly, the Confucian distaste for profit and the corresponding suspicion of ill-gotten gain have been reconciled as well. Japanese companies prefer to emphasize growth and their contributions to the national policy instead of profit. And while all are aware that profits are necessary for future investment, they are made to appear a by-product of virtuous behavior. This puts enormous pressure on Japanese executives to be both pure and productive at the same time. When profits are obtained in inferior ways, by inferior people, the consequences for those individuals are severe.

> Confucius said, "Wealth and honor are what every man desires. But if they have been obtained in violation of moral principles (li), they must not be kept ..."

> Confucius said, "If one's acts are motivated by profit, he will have many enemies."

> Confucius said, "The superior man understands righteousness, the inferior man understands profit."

A legitimate question would be, "If Confucius disdained wealth, how do Confucian societies maintain capitalism?" This is not unlike the question Weber asked and answered in his critique of the Chinese mandarin system (Weber, 1951). His point was to show that Protestantism was conducive and supportive of capitalism while Confucianism was not. The answer for Japan is different from the one Weber construed for China. Japanese Confucianism developed differently and the merchant was encouraged to follow his Way (Tao), and to seek perfection in commercial transactions. For example, according to the Mitsui house laws, the chonin (merchants) were inferior to the samurai, yet within the chonin's world, he was master (Hall, 1970).

Chief executive resignations at Kikkoman, Japan Airlines, and most recently Toshiba are significant because the executives surrender authority but not responsibility for corporate mistakes (Passin, cited in the *Wall Street Journal*, 7/10/1987, p. 19).

> Within Japanese corporate culture and social ethics, the whole notion is that the leader can delegate the authority to anyone he or she wishes, but not the responsibility. In the U.S. (leaders) delegate authority and responsibility (Yoshi Tsurumi, cited in the *Wall Street Journal*, 7/10/1987, p. 19).

The potential for unreconciled inconsistency exists between human perfectibility, endless renovation and the economic realities of failed policies. What does failure mean to a Japanese Confucian? Failure to a Confucian is shame and dishonor, and is not immediately grasped in economic terms. The executive resignations above were not as an immediate consequence of economic failure. The Kikkoman incident was over tainted wine, the JAL incident over a crash which killed over 500 people, the Toshiba scandal concerned selling top-secret American technology to the Soviets. While each case has secondary financial repercussions, the primary cause of the resignations was the reality of imperfectability.

> Confucius said, "The superior man seeks [room for improvement or occasion to blame] in himself; the inferior man seeks it in others."

The Japanese's dedication to hierarchical systems, following the Confucian model, and to extreme loyalty within the hierarchy, can be seen as dysfunctional. Bresler (1986) blames Japan's group-centered, hierarchical social mores for interfering with the free play of market forces. He claims that loyalty to a firm or a family of related firms is more important than price and quality in many purchasing decisions. He also claims that the special emphasis that Japanese culture places on long-term relationships and social harmony results in massive distribution inefficiencies. Layers of middlemen and small stores are protected from the development of more efficient distribution policies because of their long service to larger firms.

Sullivan (1983) has suggested that the Theory Z mentality produces minimally competent managers chosen for their characteristics and not their abilities. He adds that the rigidity of the strict adherence to hierarchical relationships, which emanate from the earlier industrial clan, are stifling and counterproductive. Ouchi (1981) also recognized the negative aspects of a Confucian-dominated organizational culture. He noted that xenophobia and racism are byproducts of this intense group loyalty as well.

Confucian values also have occasional negative consequences for the industrial organization of Japan. Morgan (1985), in his observations of the just-in-time (kanban) inventory practices, calls the relationships between the larger assemblers and the smaller manufacturers "incestuous." Arm's-length contracting is not common in Japan. The hierarchical structure of industrial organization puts smaller, lower-class firms at a severe economic disadvantage. Similarly, lower-class workers, women, the retired elderly, and part-time workers are often shabbily treated.

Popper, Janow, and Wheeler (1985) suggest another consequence of the Confucian tendency to order by hierarchy.

> In societies with Confucian traditions . . . concepts of obligation are generally based upon unequal relationships in a vertical hierarchy. Equal rights in a Western sense are not part of the traditional system (p. 10).

Pyle, discussing the status of freedom in Confucian Asia (cited in the *Wall Street Journal*, 3/27/87, p. 15), illustrates the differences between Western and Eastern conceptions of equality:

> . . . In particular there seems to be in Asia greater tolerance for governmental guidance, less value placed on individualism, greater respect for community interests, far less reliance on legal guarantees, and more stress upon the need for morality on the part of the leaders and the masses. Dissent remains suspect in most of the Asian countries . . . (from *Freedom at Issue*, Jan.-Feb. 1987).

Conclusions

This paper was designed to enable the reader to examine the writings of Confucius and the Confucian tradition, and the managerial practices found in the Japanese corporation. There is abundant evidence that the ethos of the Confucian tradition continues to contribute to interpersonal and organizational practices in Japanese firms.

In terms of the evidence on convergence versus divergence, it seems that the Japanese have adopted and implemented a voluntarist mode (Dunphy, 1987). They have consciously chosen to diverge and maintain their traditions on matters social and interpersonal. On technological issues, they have adopted Western science and practice when it is in their best interests. When the issue has been the adoption or design of a socio-technical system, the Japanese have chosen system harmony over individual rights.

Whether or not this will continue indefinitely in the face of contradictions and inconsistencies is problematic. If the contradictions and inconsistencies are conceived of by the Japanese as superficial, no change will be forthcoming. If the problems are serious, dissonance theory predicts that the Japanese will either change their behavior or their attitudes. The historical evidence suggests that, in Japan, Confucian thought was an instrument of political elites who consciously interpreted it to give priority to modernization. A forecaster of trends in Japanese management practices would monitor the proceedings and papers of Confucian scholars and philosophers. A conservative or fundamentalist trend would indicate a call for the Japanese way of management to be maintained. Liberal re-interpretations and trends would portend the legitimizing of new behaviors and practices. The "collective mental programming" known as culture (Hofstede, 1983) is too entrenched to be abandoned but malleable enough to promote continuity during change.

Study Questions

1. Is there any way to avoid the confusion over Confucian ethics by reconciling the apparent inconsistencies that Dollinger notes in Confucianism?

2. Are some aspects of Confucianism outdated, as Dollinger claims?

3. *The Economist* argues that since Confucianism is "elevating the welfare of the community over the individual, it could provide a convenient cloak for the authoritarian actions of a ruling party that claims to speak for 'the people.'"[1] Is this a serious threat or merely a remote possibility?

4. *The Economist* notes that Confucius said, "If one is guided by profit in one's actions, one will incur much ill-will." *The Economist* concludes that, "The ideal Confucian gentleman is a scholar bureaucrat." Does this conclusion fit with what Dollinger says about Confucianism?

5. *The Economist* claims "Confucianism" has "become a codeword for a set of 'Asian' values: commitment to education and family loyalty, and a quiescent attitude to authoritarian rule, where they government assumes the role of the father in a family." Would libertarianism support this role for government?

6. Is Singapore's former prime minister Lee Kuan Yew right to say that Confucianism is "the exact opposite of the American rights of the individual"? Note that *The Economist* reports that the Chinese Communist Party has embraced Confucianism.

7. *The Economist* concludes that since "people often turn back to old beliefs in times of rapid change" and since "divorce rates and delinquency rise in Asia, as voters become less acquiescent," "[m]aybe, then, Confucianism is in fashion because the way of life it prescribes is in decline." Is this a serious threat or merely a remote possibility?

Notes

1. This and subsequent quotations are from *The Economist*, January 21, 1995, p. 39.

References

Abegglen, J. C. and Stalk, G., 1985, *Kaisha*, New York: Basic Books.

Abegglen, J. C. and Stalk, G., 1986, "The Japanese corporation as competitor," *California Management Review* 28, 9–27.

Adler, N. J., Doktor, R., and Redding, S. G., 1986, "From the Atlantic to the Pacific Century: Cross-cultural management reviewed," *Journal of Management* 12, 295–318.

Borton, H., 1970, *Japan's Modern Century*. New York: Roland Press.

Bresler, L., 1986, "You won't find a bargain in Tokyo," *Wall Street Journal*, October 20, p. 21.

Browning, E. S., 1986, "Job-hopping in Japan," *Wall Street Journal*, September 9, p. 1.

Buckley, P. J. and Mirza, H., 1985, "The wit and wisdom of Japanese management: An iconoclastic analysis." *Management International Review* 25, 16–29.

Chan, W. T., 1963. *Source Book in Chinese Philosophy*, Princeton, N. J.: University Press.

Chan, W. T. (ed.), 1986, *Chu Hsi and Neo-Confucianism*, Honolulu: University of Hawaii Press.

de Bary, W. T., 1958: *Sources of Japanese Tradition: Volume 1*, New York: Columbia University Press.

Dillon, L. S., 1983. "Adapting Japanese management: Some cultural stumbling blocks," *Personnel*, July–August, 73–77.

Dore, R. P., 1965, "The legacy of Tokugawa education," in M. Jansen (ed.), *Changing Japanese Attitudes toward Modernization*, pp. 99–133, Princeton, N. J.: University Press.

Dunphy, D., 1987, "Convergence/divergence: A temporal review of the Japanese enterprise and its management," *Academy of Management Review*, 12, 445–459.

Fairbank, J. K., Reischauer, E. O., and Craig, A., 1965, *East Asia: The Great Tradition, Volume 2*, Boston: Houghton, Mifflin.

Hall, J. W., 1970, *Japan: From Pre-History to Modern Times*. New York: Dell.

Hamada, T., 1985, "Corporation, culture and environment: The Japanese model," *Asian Survey*, 25, 1215–1228.

Hayes, R. H., 1981, "Why Japanese factories work," *Harvard Business Review*, July–August, 56–66.

Hofstede, G., 1983, "The cultural relativity of organizational practices and theories," *Journal of International Business Studies*, Fall, 75–90.

Irish, J. S., 1986, "A Yankee learns to bow," *New York Times Magazine Part II*, June 8, p. 38.

Jaeger, A. M. and Baliga, B. R., 1985, "Control systems and strategic adaptation: Lessons from the Japanese experience," *Strategic Management Journal* 6, 115–134.

Jansen, M. B., 1965, "Changing Japanese attitudes toward modernization," in M. B. Jansen (ed.), *Changing Japanese Attitudes toward Modernization*, pp. 43–97, Princeton, N.J.: University Press.

Jansen, M. B., 1965a, "Tokugawa and modern Japan," in J. W. Hall and M. B. Jansen (eds.), *Studies in the Institutional History of Early Modern Japan*, pp. 317–330, Princeton, N. J.: University Press.

Kagono, T., Nonaka, I., Sakakibara, K., and Okumura, A., 1985, *Strategic versus Evolutionary Management: A U.S.-*

Japan Comparison of Strategy and Organization, Amsterdam, Holland: Elsevier.

Kaplan, A., 1964, *The Conduct of Inquiry,* New York: Harper and Row.

Keys, J. B. and Miller, J. R., 1984, "The Japanese management theory jungle," *Academy of Management Review* 9, 342–353.

MacFarquhar, R., 1980, "The post-Confucian challenge," *The Economist,* February 9, p. 74.

Maruyama, M., 1965, "Patterns of individuation and the case of Japan," in M. B. Jansen (ed.), *Changing Japanese Attitudes toward Modernization,* pp. 489–532, Princeton, N. J.: University Press.

Morey, N. C. and Luthans, E., 1984, "An ethnic perspective and ethnoscience methods for organizational research," *Academy of Management Review* 9, 27–36.

Morgan, J. P., 1985, "The facts about just-in-time, Japan, and Japanese business," *Purchasing,* December 19, pp. 43–50.

Munchus, G., 1983, "Employer-employee based quality circles in Japan: Human resource policy implications for American firms," *Academy of Management Review* 8, 255–261.

Nonaka, I. and Johansson, J. K., 1985, "Japanese management: What about the hard skills?," *Academy of Management Review,* 10, 181–191.

Ouchi, W. G., 1981, *Theory Z,* Reading, Mass: Addison-Wesley.

Pascale, R. T., 1978, "Zen and the art of management," *Harvard Business Review,* April–May, 153–162.

Passin, H., 1965, "Modernization and the Japanese intellectual: Some comparative observations," in M. B. Jansen (ed.), *Changing Japanese Attitudes towards Modernization,* pp. 447–487, Princeton, N. J.: University Press.

Popper, T., Janow, M. E., and Wheeler, J. W., 1985, *The Competition.* New York: Praeger.

Reischauer, E. O. and Fairbank, J. K., 1960. *East Asia: The Great Tradition,* Boston: Houghton, Mifflin.

Selltiz, C., Wrightsman, L., and Cook, S., 1976, *Research Methods in Social Relations,* New York: Holt, Rinehart and Winston.

Sethi, S. P., Namiki, N., and Swanson, C. L., 1984, *The False Promise of the Japanese Miracle,* Boston: Pittman Press.

Steffy, B. D. and Grimes, A. J., 1986, "A critical theory of organization science," *Academy of Management Review* 11, 322–336.

Sullivan, J. J., 1983, "A critique of Theory Z," *Academy of Management Review* 8, 132–142.

Tsurumi, Y., 1978, "The best of times and the worst of times: Japanese management in America," *Columbia Journal of World Business* 13, 56–61.

Wall Street Journal, 1987, March 27, p. 15.

Weber, M., 1951, *The Religion of China: Confucianism and Taoism.* H. H. Gerth (tr. and ed.), New York: Free Press.

27

The Case of Boycotting the Beatles

Nicholas Schaffner

Editor's note: Schaffner tells us about one insightful episode with the Beatles at the height of Beatlemania. The episode shows the great cultural influence the Beatles have had even beyond rock music. The boycott concerns business ethics because it is a weapon in what some (for example, presidential candidate Pat Buchanan) have called the culture wars. Those supporting the boycott claimed the Beatles were an unethical influence in the music business. Of course, many of the millions of Beatles fans interpreted the Beatles' music very differently, as spreading the message for peace, love, and freedom.

Poor Brian Epstein—he had gotten the Beatles to shed their black leather and clean up their act, but nothing would ever keep John Lennon from shooting his mouth off in the presence of reporters. And, as John later complained, when you're famous you can be held accountable for the sort of off-the-cuff remarks ordinary mortals get to tell their buddies over a pint of lager.

By mid 1966 the Beatles had managed to air quite a few flamboyant opinions in the press (sample: "Show business belongs to the Jews, it's part of the Jewish religion"). Reporters always in search of a good story egged them on. In mid 1965, *Playboy* ran a lengthy interview with the Beatles, plying them with queries about their religious beliefs and the "homosexual problem" in England. They came out for agnosticism, and George informed *Playboy*'s readers that the U.S. was full of homosexuals, only "they've got crewcuts in America. You can't spot 'em."

Reprinted from Nicholas Schaffner, *The Beatles Forever* (Harrisburg, Pa.: Stackpole Books).

But nothing caused quite the flap of these observations of John's: "Christianity will go. It will vanish and shrink. I needn't argue about that, I'm right and will be proved right. We're more popular than Jesus Christ now. I don't know which will go first, rock 'n' roll or Christianity. Jesus was all right, but his disciples were thick and ordinary. It's them twisting it that ruins it for me." Actually these comments were made back in February for the *London Evening Standard*, whose readers evidently shrugged them off as just another Lennonism. But when *Datebook*, an American teen-age magazine, chose to reprint them just prior to the boys' visit, Lennon's five-month-old comments became a hot news flash, and God-fearing disk jockeys, church leaders, and right-wing politicians across the old Confederacy decided the time had come to stamp the Beatles out for good.

Throughout the first two weeks of August, papers carried lurid reports that read like scenes from Ray Bradbury's *Fahrenheit 451*, of rallies around bonfires into which were dumped large quantities of Beatle records and memorabilia, and sometimes even effigies of the Fab Four. Birmingham's WAQY hired a giant tree-grinding machine with which to pulverize its listeners' Beatle albums to dust. Another station donated garbage cans that bore the legend "place Beatle trash here." Although one anti-Beatle station—KLUE of Longview, Texas—was struck by lightning and knocked off the air for the night, its disc jockeys refused to take that as a message from heaven and resumed the crusade the following morning.

A flu-smitten Epstein rose from his sickbed and jetted to the States nearly two weeks before his clients were due, in order to "clarify" Lennon's statement. John, Brian insisted, was only expressing his "deep concern " at the decline of interest in religion.

Nonetheless, the fever rapidly spread from the Bible Belt to the Midwest, and even to Spain and that citadel of Christian morality South Africa, where the Beatles were banned from the airwaves for the next five years (when the group split in 1970, local fans could once again be serenaded by the voices of Paul, George, and Ringo—but not John). The Vatican mouthpiece *L'Osservatore Romano* warned that "some subjects must not be dealt with profanely, not even in the world of beatniks." Even the stock market was affected: the value of a share in the Beatles' Northern Songs slumped from $1.64 to $1.26 in a week.

Some stations, however, came to the Beatles' defense and played more of their music than before, in one case to "show contempt for hypocrisy." Back in London, *Melody Maker* ran a rare editorial to say that "much of the fantastically unreasoned reaction to Lennon merely adds weight to his statement that some of Jesus' followers are a bit thick." For most fans, the attacks on John merely served to strengthen their loyalty, and record sales weren't harmed any: the butcherless *Yesterday and Today* clung to *Billboard*'s number one slot throughout August.

Actually, John's comments, which seemed so off-the-wall in 1966, soon proved to be almost prophetic. The seriousness with which fans took the Beatles was about to increase dramatically, at a time when traditional religious, moral, and patriotic values were being discarded wholesale. For young people left with little to believe in, infatuation with rock stars in the late '60s—especially Dylan and the Beatles—often assumed the characteristics of a mystical cult. Little over two years after the John-Jesus flap, Timothy Leary would tell his thousands of followers the Beatles were nothing less than "Divine Messiahs," and Charlie Manson's singularly warped interpretation of the gospel according to the "four angels" would lead to the most bizarre and gruesome murder case in the Sixties.

When the Beatles themselves arrived in Chicago on August 12, a rather pale and nervous Lennon found a great many microphones and T.V. cameras aimed in his direction, and did his best to apologize without selling himself out: "I suppose if I had said television was more popular than Jesus, I would have gotten away with it. I'm sorry I opened my mouth. I'm not anti-God, anti-Christ, or anti-religion. I was not knocking it. I was not saying we are greater or better."

In the Vatican, the *Osservatore* editorially accepted Lennon's apology. An editorial in the staid *New York Times* declared the case closed, adding that "the wonder is that such an articulate young man could have expressed himself imprecisely in the first place."

Despite a unanimous vote of the Memphis city council requesting the Beatles to stay away, and a demonstration by the Ku Klux Klan when the Beatles played there anyway, the tour proceeded on schedule and without mishap. The Beatles even courted further controversy at their New York City press con-

ference when they all defied their manager's instructions and denounced the Vietnam war as "wrong"—an opinion not shared by 90 per cent of the American population at that time.

Later that afternoon midtown traffic was tied up by the spectacle of two somewhat over-zealous Beatlemaniacs poised precariously on a 22nd-story ledge. Their plan was to hurl themselves into Sixth Avenue if the Beatles wouldn't pay them a visit. Police managed to rescue the young ladies and commit them to a hospital.

Meanwhile, outside the Beatles' digs at the Warwick Hotel, Christian demonstrators jostled with screaming fans: both sides were liberally armed with placards, *Beatles 4-Ever* vs. *Stamp Out The Beatles*. Aloof from the holy war, a young man stood on the street corner, solemnly holding up a sign that read "John Is A Lesbian."

At the Beatles' return to Shea Stadium that night there were, unlike the year before, a few vacant rows in the back rafters. Still, the Beatles had managed to sell nearly 50,000 tickets to one performance, a feat nobody else at the time could have come near to duplicating.

Study Questions

1. Do you think it is unethical to burn the work of an artist just because he disagrees with some of your religious views? John Lennon was assassinated in 1980. Would the violence against property in burning art create a climate of hostility that would tend to lead to more violence against people?

2. Were some of the Beatles' remarks anti-Semitic or homophobic?

3. Do you think that what John Lennon said about Jesus was false, or did Lennon accurately state the amount of cultural influence the music business has?

4. Was someone sending a message when radio station KLUE was knocked off the air with a lightning bolt, or was it just a coincidence? Did KLUE have a clue?

28

Profiting from Evil: The Case of Charles Manson and Axl Rose

Phil Rosenthal

Editor's note: This brief case raises questions about the limits of artistic license and bad taste as well as the moral issue of sending money to the notorious Charles Manson, who was convicted of conspiracy to commit mass murder. Another issue raised is deception of or withholding of information from contractual partners.

When you see him on TV today at age 59, some 25 years later, he comes across as no more menacing than the disheveled drunk who hassles the passersby outside the local liquor store. But he is worse. Much worse.

Charles Manson is a sick, twisted horror. His crimes and those of his "family" tapped into the darkest fears of 1969 mainstream America. Here was a messianic, drug-addled freak who convinced his disciples that evil was good, leading them on a senseless killing spree that left several dead, many mourning and a nation unnerved.

Maybe Axl Rose of Guns N' Roses is too young to remember. Maybe he is too jaded to care.

A Bad Joke

His puzzling decision to include Manson's "Look at Your Game, Girl," a song the cult leader wrote in prison about an insane woman, on GNR's just-released "The Spaghetti Incident?" can be construed only as a bad joke, bad politics or both.

This article originally appeared as "No One Should Profit from Evil," *Los Angeles Daily News* (Friday, December 3, 1993).

Sung by Rose, who is accompanied by an acoustic guitar, Manson's song is not officially listed on the album and was not included on review cassettes sent to critics. Its inclusion, discovered by the public shortly after the recording went on sale last week, seemed to surprise many Geffen Records executives and even some of Rose's band mates.

* * *

In a statement through Geffen, Rose, whose wardrobe of late often has included a Manson T-shirt, mouthed something about how he felt the song "was ironic," and how "Manson is a dark part of American culture and history . . . the subject of fear and fascination."

Tell it to the survivors.

No one is denying Rose and his group their artistic license, even if it sometimes seems as though Rose's idea of art is not falling off the stage in a stupor. His voice is a shriek as distinctive as his sense of fashion, health and hygiene. On the other hand, no one ever has accused Guns N' Roses of being overly sensitive, either. GNR's work has, at various times, been derided as misogynistic, homophobic, racist, you name it.

Rose and others have explained away much of that criticism, but this is less easy to dismiss.

But, then, maybe we no longer recognize Manson as such a demon. Maybe we're no longer so young or so innocent. Maybe we've been desensitized.

Perhaps it has gotten to the point where he's just another nut case ranting and raving on "Geraldo." Someone else with something to sell.

Study Questions

1. Which moral principle states "No one should profit from his or her own wrong"? Note that this moral principle is found in Alexander Hamilton's writings in *The Federalist Papers* in the 18th century, in court cases such as *Riggs v. Palmer* (115 N.Y. 506, 22 N.E. 188 [1889]) in New York in the 19th century, and in the writing of leading legal, moral, and political philosophers such as Ronald Dworkin in the 20th century.

2. Would libertarianism condemn Axl Rose for including Manson's song on the album?

3. Would utilitarianism require Axl Rose to include Manson's song on the album? Would utilitarianism condemn Rose for including it?

4. Did Rose act immorally toward his bandmates if he kept the song's inclusion on the group's album secret from the rest of the band?

29

The Myth That Merit Is Always Recognized

Ronald Duncan

Editor's note: Duncan tries to debunk the common notion that merit is always or almost always recognized. He gives several interesting examples of meritorious work that could easily have been overlooked, since they were discovered largely by chance. Duncan has a problem with mob education, mass media, and popular culture, too.

My target is the current and persistent notion that merit is inevitably, eventually recognised. This absurd belief is generally applied to creative work in the arts or sciences.

The reason why this fallacy persists is, of course, it removes any burden from the social conscience for failing to recognise and removes from people any guilt for their inability to distinguish between taste and fashion.

Of course it is true that Joseph Haydn has perforated St. Dunstans. But what happened to Michael, his father, who also wrote several dozen elegant symphonies? How many, even amongst musicians, have heard of him?

True, we kneel to Mozart now—but even he had to wait a century before London heard one of his operas and would have waited another if it hadn't been for the eccentric enthusiasm of Tommy Beecham.

And where would Schubert's Leider be had it not been for that accident when Sullivan put his hat on the top of a cupboard at a Vienna publishers and,

This article originally appeared as "Merit Is Always Recognized," in Ronald Duncan et al., eds., *The Encyclopedia of Delusions* (New York: Wallaby Books, 1979), pp. 12–15.

in retrieving his bowler, brought down a sheaf of forgotten masterpieces?

'To buried merit raise the tardy bust. . . .' 'Tardy' is putting it mildly. Schubert wrote fourteen operas. Not one has yet received a professional performance in this country. Why? Would it be likely that Schubert could not write vocal music? His libretti are poor—it's true that one or two such as *Alphonso and Estrella* and *Fierabras* are little better dramatically than say *The Magic Flute*; but when in *The War of the Sexes* he used Aristophanes' story that charge is hardly valid. If a Schubert after a century and a half cannot get a toe into the Union dominated Coliseum or Royal Opera House, how many other unknown, unnamed composers endure his oblivion never to be unearthed, heard?

The myth that merit must inevitably be recognised does not bear the most casual scrutiny. Indeed the opposite is more likely to be true: mediocrity is sure of its applause and recognition while great merit will, because of its capacity to disturb, generally be overlooked.

I recall Brancusi asking me to try to get a gallery in London to show his work. I went to the Marlborough. Not interested.

In 1937 in Rapallo, Ezra Pound showed me Henri Gaudier-Brezka's notebook. It was a children's autograph album. Gaudier had kept it in the trenches in Flanders and filled it with notes and drawings. I told Pound that I thought the book should be reproduced exactly as it was. I took it to London. I showed it to Eliot. Uninterested. Still unpublished, fifty years after Gaudier's death. More interesting, to my eye, than Henry Moore's excellent Tube notebook.

Nor did my brush with Stravinsky's publishers, Boosey and Hawkes, exactly help me to believe in the recognition of merit. Stravinsky told me he would be willing to write a piece especially for a concert at the Queen's Hall. When I informed Ralph Hawkes he said: 'Stravinsky hasn't written anything interesting since *Firebird*'. This dictum of idiocy was in 1938. I then wrote to the Royal Philharmonic Orchestra. They replied. Not interested either. A question of fashion, not taste. Perhaps it is not irrelevant to recall that in Latin 'fama' means fashion or fame. Indeed, Latin identifies them.

And where would Gerard Manley Hopkins be? Still no doubt unpublished in Robert Bridge's bottom drawer if it had not been for accident rather than the Poet Laureate's recognition. The same applies to the poet, Isaac Rosenberg, still hardly known in spite of Leavis's comments. He lies beneath the rubble of

Wilfred Owen and Rupert Brooke. Just as Sir Walter Raleigh, and the Earls of Rochester and Dorset were passed by.

Perhaps it takes genius alone to recognise merit in another? Certainly that was the case with Pound, when he unearthed several dozen Vivaldi concertos in a box where they had lain forgotten in the Vatican Library. Even then it took a Count Chigi to do anything about it and get this music played.

When Bach was appointed Kappelmeister at Leipzig they wrote: 'We couldn't get the composer we wanted, so we've taken on a composer called Bach'. The man they wanted, and whom Bach himself looked up to, was called Frohberger. Who plays him?

We hear of Purcell, Boyce and Morley. But Jenkins, and a dozen more Elizabethan thrushes, where are they? At the taxidermists?

I remember going round Leopold Survage's studio, or rather crawling between his thousand stacked canvasses. Survage used to share a studio with Picasso. Survage, the better painter, not draughtsman. But fashion has decreed he should remain almost totally unknown because he lacked his colleague's gift for self-publicity.

What do these bitter comments amount to? The resentment that merit goes unrecognised except by accident, circumstances little to do with the work's worth. And it is my conviction that there is more good music, or if you stake me, great music entirely unknown than there is known. My hunch is that the same applies to painting and poetry too.

How could it be otherwise when you consider the level of criticism which greets any new work? To assume that merit is recognised is the assumption that we have perceptive critics, or to give them their correct title, journalists. Turn back to the pages: read their comments on *Peter Grimes*'s first performance, on *Sacre du Printemps*, on Jacob Epstein's first exhibition; on T. S. Eliot's *Waste Land*; on Verdi's *Otello*. A review of our reviews reveals that they could ignore a Rembrandt as they did a Van Gogh; that even if a 10th Beethoven Symphony were discovered they wouldn't know from the notes. To them: one criterion: the name that is known whether that is in soap flakes or contraceptives.

The fact that Brancusi and Stravinsky are now accepted does not disprove my thesis. I am concerned with the Brancusi who remain unknown, the Stravinsky who will never be heard.

One gloomy day Hermann Bondi listed the names of people to me whose scientific discoveries when submitted to the Royal Society had been ignored. They were too soon. One young man had the effrontery to describe the Heaverside Layer and its effects thirty years before it was recognised. There have been others, too many others.

Can anything be done to rectify? Possibly some sort of sieve to focus on specific eras, to re-examine some of the submitted operas, re-read some of the unpublished unperformed plays.

Mob education and mass media which lower standards and criteria perceptibly every decade only get the known names more widely known. They do nothing to assist discrimination, the ability to tell chalk from cheese. Indeed the more educated we become and the more mass media we suffer, the less chance there is of talent being recognised because the printers of textbooks, their teachers too and the compilers of T.V. programmes for the many dare not risk promoting the unknown. 'We cannot televise one of your plays', they wrote recently to an unknown dramatist, 'until you have had one televised.'

So I am sure there are still more strawberries in the hedge than ever reached a plate. We equate fashion with taste. And our worst artistic fallacy is the notion that people have any of the latter at all. Fashion is other people's bad taste.

Study Questions

1. If merit often goes unrecognized, does that undermine the plausibility of libertarianism's support of free markets?

2. Do you think there are many more meritorious pieces of art yet to be discovered, as Duncan suggests?

3. Should Duncan's essay change the conventional thinking that "You can't keep a good man or woman down" and "The cream always rises to the top"? This conventional thinking does claim that merit will inevitably be rewarded. So Duncan is not attacking a straw person.

4. Are you part of what Duncan calls "mob education"?

5. Have your biggest professional successes resulted from following well-thought-out plans or from taking advantage of unanticipated opportunities? If your answer is unanticipated opportunities, then is the success really a matter of merit or luck? How large a role does serendipity play in making discoveries?

*6. If you knew you were destined to never achieve anything of real importance, how would it change your goals and attitudes?

*7. If someone working for you made a costly mistake and you realized that your instructions should have been clearer, would you be more likely ...perior in a way ... a way that pro-... yourself, then ... that the merit of ...gnized?

*8. Would you rather work with people who are less or more talented than you? If you prefer the less talented, then won't merit go unrecognized? Is this preference for working with less talented people prevalent enough to be a major cause of the problem of merit going unrecognized?

PART IV

Feminist Challenges to Business as Usual:
From Sexism to Gender Benders

30

Introduction:
A Statistical Portrait

Sterling Harwood

Philosopher Christina Hoff Sommers, in her book *Who Stole Feminism?: How Women Have Betrayed Women*, exposes several significant statistical errors that have helped to shape the landscape of this area of thinking about women. So in introducing this chapter, using statistics to paint a more accurate picture of this landscape is valuable. Sommers notes how some of these inaccurate statistics have made it into the press and even into college textbooks.[1]

The first erroneous statistic that Sommers corrects is Gloria Steinem's claim that in America about 150,000 females die of anorexia each year. Anorexia is an eating disorder in which a person takes dieting to an extreme and eats and digests too little to remain healthy. The death from anorexia of Karen Carpenter, of the famous pop duo the Carpenters, made the general public much more aware of the disorder. To put this statistic into perspective, Sommers notes that it is more than triple the annual number of deaths from traffic accidents in the United States.[2] Sommers discovers from the American Anorexia and Bulimia Association that the correct statistic is that in America 150,000 to 200,000 females suffer from anorexia nervosa, but of course not all who suffer from the disorder die from it. In fact, Sommers reports that, according to the National Center for Health Statistics, 101 died from anorexia nervosa in 1983 and 67 died from it in 1988.[3] This statistic is politically important to feminism, since many feminists analyze anorexia as a symptom of something wrong not just with the many thousands who suffer from it but with American society, which puts cultural pressure on women to rely on a slim body to attract a man. Society also puts pressure on women to be financially dependent on men and psychologically dependent on gaining self-esteem from being the wife or mate of a man. In short, many feminists see anorexia as a symptom of America's sexism. Anorexia shows that

American culture's old saying "You can never be too rich or too thin" is a dangerous lie. The key point, however, which Sommers seems to underemphasize, is that even the corrected statistic is a scandal. Far too many women suffer from this serious disorder that concerns a fundamental part of everyday living, namely, eating.

Another erroneous statistic that Sommers exposes is the claim that domestic violence or battery against pregnant women is the number one (that is, single largest) cause of birth defects. Indeed, some claim that domestic violence causes more birth defects than all other causes combined.[4] Sommers discovered that the mix-up was due to misunderstanding a claim that more women are screened for birth defects than are ever screened for domestic battery. Again, although we should be grateful to Sommers for getting to the bottom of this matter and correcting the statistic, Sommers fails to emphasize sufficiently that even the corrected claim exposes quite a scandal. Society's stress on screening women for birth defects more often than for battery fits the sexist pattern of seeing women as primarily valuable for having babies rather than in their own right. It fits the sexist thinking of women having bodies that are expendable in the service of society in general or men in particular.

Further, there is something suspicious about Sommers' attempts to minimize the feminist case here, since she makes a rather telling error herself. She calls the National Organization *for* Women the National Organization *of* Women.[5] Conservatives and antifeminists often try to minimize, or at least wind up minimizing, the importance of the National Organization *for* Women (NOW) by calling it the National Organization *of* Women, as if no men were members. But of course many men are members of NOW and men are freely invited to join the group. Calling NOW, a group having many tens of thousands of members, the National Organization *of* Women seems to be an attempt to make NOW seem sexist, hypocritical, fanatical, and out of the mainstream by falsely implying that it excludes men simply based on their sex. Conservative writers such as William F. Buckley, Jr., on the PBS show *Firing Line*, make this error. And highly publicized writers vociferously opposing affirmative action (a program for women as well as minorities) such as Shelby Steele (in the magazine *Harper's*) make this error of calling NOW the National Organization *of* Women. Of course accidents will happen. But a reviewer of Steele's book thought the fact that Steele misspelled *both* names of the famous Supreme Court case *Plessy v. Ferguson* was a telltale sign of Steele's sloppy thinking. So using the wrong preposition, "of" instead of "for," could just be sloppiness in typing or thinking, but that all three of these major opponents of programs for women would make the same error seems to go beyond pure coincidence. The slip seems to be at least a symptom of their thinking of NOW as a fanatical group rather than one in the mainstream of political thought. In this sense at least, it seems to be a politically motivated typo!

Another statistic Sommers challenges is the claim that the incidence of domestic battery tends to rise by 40 percent on Super Bowl Sunday.[6] Sommers notes that only one reporter, Ken Ringle of the *Washington Post*, checked the statistic and found that it had no basis in fact. Again, however, although Sommers is right to note Ringle's correction of factual record, her emphasis seems skewed. She asks why so many people found this false statistic so plausible, and she comes up with the conspiracy theory that there is an organized effort in the media, which many criticize for being left-wing or liberal, to put out misinformation or disinformation to make men look bad. But the statistic's falsity was exposed by a reporter for the *Washington Post*, which is one of the two newspapers (along with the *New York Times*) most often criticized for having a bias in favor of liberalism (which includes feminism). And Sommers also underemphasizes the commonsense plausibility of the claim. Men often bet large amounts of money on the Super Bowl, especially given the game's importance in determining the football champion and given that each gambler is confident that he has had all season to learn who the superior team is and how superior they are to their Super Bowl opponent. Both Super Bowl teams are very highly publicized by the time the game starts. Obviously, for every winner betting on the Super Bowl, there is a loser. So half the men in this large group of at least thousands and probably millions of men who bet on the Super Bowl are in a worse mood after the game because they lost their bet. Obviously,

couples often argue over finances. Obviously, arguments often escalate into pushing, shoving, and fighting. So why does Sommers see it as so odd that people should find the claim about domestic violence on Super Bowl Sunday so easy to believe? Indeed, the scandal is that sexism is so bad in our society that even such a false or baseless statistic is so easy for so many to believe. Sommers unwittingly documents the prevalence of sexism by chronicling how so many believed this statistic so quickly and easily, since she emphasized that only one reporter in a country with thousands of reporters—generally an informed and skeptical group—even challenged the statistic by checking it. That in itself shows that people in the know realize that sexism against women is a bigger problem than Sommers would have us believe. Sommers ridicules feminists for being "constantly on the lookout for proof, for the smoking gun, the telling fact that will drive home to the public how profoundly the system is rigged against women."[7] Ironically, by showing how believable even a false statistic about Super Bowl Sunday is, it was Sommers who unwittingly discovered the smoking gun. And in any event, why should Sommers ridicule anyone for being "constantly on the lookout for proof"? Isn't that diligence the hallmark of the good scientist or scholar? In her attempt to make NOW seem fanatical, Sommers has implied that we should close our eyes somewhat to the violence against women and just not look at the facts so hard.

Notes

1. Christina Hoff Sommers, *Who Stole Feminism?* (New York: Simon & Schuster, 1994), pp. 12-13.
2. Ibid., p. 11.
3. Ibid., p. 12.
4. Ibid., pp. 12–13.
5. Ibid, p. 13.
6. Ibid., p. 15.
7. Ibid., p. 16.

31

Gender Benders:
How Many Sexes Are There?

Anne Fausto-Sterling

Editor's note: Fausto-Sterling suggests that there are more than two sexes, and that there is a continuum or spectrum of genders. She details some startling cases that challenge our usual ways of thinking.

Western culture is committed to the idea that there are only two sexes. For the situations described in this essay, I have to invent conventions—s/he and his/her—to denote someone who is neither male nor female or who is perhaps both sexes at once. Legally, too, every adult is either man or woman, and the difference is not trivial. It means being available for, or exempt from draft registration, as well as being subject to laws governing marriage, the family and human intimacy.

But if the state and the legal system have an interest in maintaining a two-party sexual system, they are defying nature. For biologically speaking, there are many gradations running from female to male; along that spectrum lie at least five sexes—perhaps even more.

Medical investigators recognize the concept of the intersexual body. But medicine uses the term "intersex" as a catch-all for three major subgroups with some mixture of male and female characteristics: the so-called true hermaphrodites, whom I call herms, who possess one testis and one ovary (the sperm and egg-producing vessels, or gonads); male pseudo-hermaphrodites ("merms"), who have testes and some aspects of female genitalia but no ovaries; and

female pseudo-hermaphrodites ("ferms"), who have ovaries and some aspects of the male genitalia but lack testes.

It is difficult to estimate the frequency of intersexuality; it's not the sort of information one volunteers on a job application. John Money of Johns Hopkins University, a specialist in the study of congenital sexual-organ defects, suggests that intersexuals may constitute as many as four percent of births.

However, few intersexuals maintain their natural sexuality. Medical advances enable physicians to catch most at birth. Such infants are entered into a program of hormonal and surgical management so that they can slip quietly into society as "normal" heterosexual males or females. The aims of the policy are humanitarian, reflecting the wish that people fit in. In the medical community, however, the assumptions behind that wish—that there be only two sexes, that heterosexuality alone is normal—have gone virtually unexamined.

The word "hermaphrodite" comes from the Greek names Hermes and Aphrodite. According to Greek mythology, the gods parented Hermaphroditus, who at 15 become half male and half female when his body fused with the body of a nymph he fell in love with. In some true hermaphrodites, the testis and the ovary grow separately but bilaterally; in others, they grow together within the same organ, forming an ova-testis. Not infrequently, at least one of the gonads functions well, producing either sperm cells or eggs, as well as functional levels of the sex hormones: androgens or estrogens.

In contrast with true hermaphrodites, pseudo-hermaphrodites possess two gonads of the same kind along with the usual male (XY) or female (XX) chromosomal makeup. But their external genitalia and secondary sex characteristics do not match their chromosomes. Thus, merms have testes and XY chromosomes, yet they also have a vagina and a clitoris, and at puberty they often develop breasts. They do not menstruate, however. Ferms have ovaries, XX chromosomes and sometimes a uterus, but they also have at least partly masculine external genitalia.

No classification scheme could more than suggest the variety of sexual anatomy encountered in clinical practice. In 1969, Paul Guinet of the Endocrine Clinic in Lyons, France, and Jacques Decourt of the Endocrine Clinic in Paris, classified 98 cases of true hermaphroditism solely according to the appearance of the external genitalia and the accompanying ducts.

Reprinted from Anne Fausto-Sterling, "How Many Sexes Are There?" *The New York Times* (March 12, 1993), op-ed. Copyright © The New York Times.

In some cases, the people exhibited strongly feminine development. They had separate openings for the vagina and the urethra, a cleft vulva defined by both the large and the small labia, or vaginal lips, and at puberty they developed breasts and usually began to menstruate. It was the oversize and sexually alert clitoris, which threatened sometimes to grow into a penis, that usually impelled them to seek medical attention.

Members of another group also had breasts and a feminine body type, and they menstruated. But their labia were at least partly fused, forming an incomplete scrotum. The phallus (here an embryological term for a structure that during usual fetal development goes on to form either a clitoris or a penis) was between 1.5 and 2.8 inches long; nevertheless, they urinated through a urethra that opened into or near the vagina.

The most frequent form of true hermaphrodite encountered by the French doctors—55 percent—appeared to have a more masculine physique. In such people the urethra runs either through or near the phallus, which looks more like a penis than a clitoris. Any menstrual blood exits during urination. But in spite of the relatively male appearance of the genitalia, breasts appear at puberty.

Intersexuality itself is old news. Early biblical scholars believed Adam began life as a hermaphrodite and later divided into two people—a male and female—after falling from grace. According to Plato there once were three sexes—male, female and hermaphrodite—but the third sex was lost with time. The Talmud lists regulations for people of mixed sex.

In Europe, a pattern emerged by the end of the Middle Ages that, in a sense, has lasted to the present day: hermaphrodites were compelled to choose an established gender role and stick with it. The penalty for transgression was often death. In the 1600's, a Scottish hermaphrodite living as a woman was buried alive after impregnating his/her master's daughter.

To determine questions of inheritance, legitimacy, paternity, succession to title and eligibility for certain professions, modern Anglo-Saxon legal systems require that newborns be registered as either male or female. In the U.S., sex determination is governed by state laws. Illinois permits adults to change the sex recorded on their birth certificates if a doctor attests to having performed the appropriate surgery.

The New York Academy of Medicine takes an opposite view. In spite of surgical alterations of the external genitalia, the academy argued in 1966, the chromosomal sex remains the same. By that measure, a person's wish to conceal his or her original sex cannot outweigh the public interest in protection against fraud.

Ironically, a more sophisticated knowledge of sexuality led to the repression of intersexuality.

In 1937, Hugh H. Young, a urologist at Johns Hopkins, published "Genital Abnormalities, Hermaphroditism and Related Adrenal Diseases." In this unusually evenhanded study, Dr. Young drew together case histories to demonstrate and study the medical treatment of such "accidents of birth."

One of his cases was a hermaphrodite named Emma who had grown up as a female. Emma had a penis-size clitoris and a vagina, which made it possible for him to have "normal" heterosexual sex with men or women. As a teenager, Emma had had sex with a number of girls to whom s/he was attracted, but at 19 s/he married a man. He gave Emma little sexual pleasure, and so throughout that marriage and subsequent ones s/he kept girlfriends on the side.

Though Dr. Young told Emma it would be relatively easy to turn him/her into a man, the patient's reply struck a heroic blow for self-interest. "Would you have to remove that vagina? I don't know about that because that's my meal ticket. If you did that, I would have to quit my husband and go to work, so I think I'll keep it and stay as I am."

Yet even as Dr. Young was illuminating intersexuality with the light of scientific reason, he was beginning its suppression. His book is also a treatise on surgical and hormonal methods of changing intersexuals into either males or females.

Dr. Young may have differed from his successors in being less judgmental and controlling of the patients and their families, but he nonetheless supplied the foundation on which current intervention practices were built.

By 1969, when Christopher J. Dewhurst and Ronald R. Gordon wrote "The Intersexual Disorders," medical approaches had neared a state of rigid uniformity: intersexual infants were almost always subject to surgery and hormonal treatment. The condition, they wrote, "is a tragic event which immediately conjures up visions of a hopeless psychological misfit doomed to live always as a sexual freak in loneliness and frustration." Though there are few empirical studies to back up such near-hysterical assertions, scientific dogma has held fast to the theory that without medical care hermaphrodites are doomed to a life of misery.

The treatment of intersexuality in this century

demands scrutiny. Why should we care if there are people whose biological equipment enables them to have sex "naturally" with both men and women? The answers seem to lie in a need to maintain clear distinctions between the sexes. Society mandates the control of intersexual bodies because they blur and bridge the great divide; they challenge traditional beliefs about sexual difference. Hermaphrodites have unruly bodies. They do not fall into a binary classification: only a surgical shoehorn can put them there.

What if things were different? Imagine a world in which medical knowledge used to intervene in the management of intersexual patients had been placed at their service. Medicine's central mission would be to preserve life. Thus hermaphrodites would be concerned primarily not about whether they conform to society but about whether they might develop the life-threatening conditions that sometimes accompany their development: hernias, gonadal tumors, adrenal malfunction. Medical intervention would take place only rarely before the age of reason; subsequent treatment would be a cooperative venture between physician, patient, and, perhaps, a gender advisor.

I do not pretend that the transition to my utopia would be smooth. Sex, even the supposedly "normal," heterosexual kind, causes untold anxieties in Western society. And certainly a culture that has yet to come to grips with the ancient and relatively uncomplicated reality of homosexual love will not readily embrace intersexuality.

No doubt the most troublesome arena would be the rearing of children. Parents, at least since the Victorian era, have fretted over the fact that their children are sexual beings. But would rearing children as intersexuals be that fraught with peril? Modern investigators tend to overlook numerous case histories, such as those collected by Dr. Young, that describe children who grew up knowing they were intersexual and adjusted to their status.

With remarkable unanimity, the scientific community has avoided contemplating the alternative route of unimpeded intersexuality. Perhaps it will begin now.

Study Questions

1. Well, after reading this article, how many sexes do you think there are?

2 Consider the case of Emma. Does his/her refusal to change her sex to male because she would lose her "meal ticket" give us insight into the financially dependent role many women find themselves in? Or is Emma just an isolated and freakish case?

3. Has conventional thinking about the sexes posed a false dilemma: either you are male or you are female?

4. If the science of how many sexes there are is so unclear, then how can the business world be ethical in so rigidly imposing particular roles on each sex?

32

10 Million Dead Babies a Year: The Case of Breast-Feeding versus Bottle-Feeding in the Third World

Associated Press

Editor's note: This case involves a shocking amount of death and suffering. Doug Clement writes: "A typical Nestle radio advertisement tells listeners: 'When mother's milk is not enough, baby needs a special milk . . .' That message reinforced the unproven notion that breast-feeding will not be sufficient. Furthermore, such words can become a self-fulfilling prophecy. By stimulating doubts about breast-feeding ability, the sales pitches create anxiety. Doctors have long recognized that anxiety and lack of confidence strongly inhibit the 'let-down reflex' which allows milk to flow successfully. Thus unsuccessful lactation [would occur] and a 'need' for formula [would be created]."[1] Despite such radio ads, Nestle won a foreign libel case against the authors of a book called *Nestle Kills Babies*. Many boycotted Nestle for years, but the boycott ended after Nestle substantially changed its marketing practices. To celebrate, one of those in the boycott ate a Nestle candy bar at the press conference announcing the end of the boycott. Still, R. G. Hendrickse, a prominent physician, calls the switch from breast-feeding to bottle-feeding "probably the most significant change in human behavior in recorded history."[2]

Alleging that one million babies die each year in underdeveloped countries from diseases brought on by bottlefeeding, two senior U.S. government officials said yesterday they will resign when the administration of President Ronald Reagan votes against an in-

ternational code favoring mothers' milk.

Dr. Stephen Joseph and Eugene Babb, both senior executives of the Agency for International Development (AID), issues their resignation threat during a news conference at the American Public Health Association.

The resignations would make the two men the first top officials to quit over Reagan administration policies. Both went to work for AID during the Jimmy Carter administration.

Joseph, a pediatrician who is the highest ranking health professional at AID, alleged that the administration "has been swayed by the self-interested arguments of the infant formula lobby."

Joseph said that one child in ten born in developing countries dies in infancy, a total of 10 million a year. While precise figures are not available, "the best estimates ascribe up to one million of these infant deaths to diarrhea and under-nutrition associated with artificial formula feeding," he said.

The voluntary code is an attempt to stop advertising and selling tactics designed to convince parents in poor countries that infant formula is critical to child health. It would bar, for example, the practice of sending women dressed as nurses to rural villages—or paying local health workers—to recommend formulas.

Administration officials do not dispute that breast-feeding is preferable, but contend the code represents an unwarranted attempt by the United Nations to regulate how private businesses promote their products.

Meanwhile, a bipartisan group of ten congressmen called on Reagan to personally intervene to reverse the decision to vote against the milk code.

"The United States' vote pits America against every other nation in the World Health Organization," said the congressmen in a letter to Reagan.

"We cannot believe that the U.S. stands for the death of millions of children from hunger and disease."

Several prominent physicians joined Joseph and Babb in deploring the administration plan to cast what is expected to be a solitary vote against the code at the World Health Assembly in Geneva.

At AID, administrator M. Peter McPherson criticized the two men for going public with their opposition. He said they intend to submit their resignations when the vote is cast. "Naturally I will accept them effective immediately," he said.

At the White House, deputy press secretary Larry Speakes said the U.S. decision to vote against the code resulted from a consensus of several federal agencies that "we did not want to make the World Health Organization an international Federal Trade Commission."

Study Questions

1. Did the officials in President Reagan's administration do the right thing to resign in protest over policies that allowed the death of millions each year?

2. Should President Reagan have done something to try to prevent the millions of deaths? What more should he have done? Would libertarianism require President Reagan to do nothing in this case?

3. Should Nestle have won the libel case? Is the chain of causation from the radio ad to the dead babies too indirect or unproven to be killing, or is the chain of causation direct enough to count as killing? Some companies also used so-called mothercraft nurses, dressed in white uniforms, to market infant formula to mothers still in the hospital. Once a mother uses infant formula instead of breast-feeding, her ability to breast-feed starts to atrophy and disappear. After trying free samples and giving up breast-feeding for a while, many mothers no longer have the option to go back to breast-feeding. Many also lack the money and refrigeration to keep enough infant formula safe for use. So babies go unfed and their resistance to disease is lowered. And the formula becomes infected with germs causing life-threatening disease. Though many of these mothers are poor, they are tempted to try the formula to gain social status, since breast-feeding is often seen as a sign of poverty or lower status. Is this marketing of formula ethical?

Notes

1. Doug Clement, "Infant Formula Malnutrition: Threat to the Third World," *The Christian Century* (1978).
2. Quoted in Clement.

33

Bigger Breasts:
The Great Implant Lie

Robert Scheer

Editor's note: Major manufacturers of breast implants (for example, Dow Corning) have set aside $4.2 billion as a part of a class-action settlement with many women who have suffered as a result of using the implants. Manufacturers recently announced that they had set aside hundreds of millions of dollars more for those women who refuse to be a part of the $4.2 billion settlement. Scheer, however, tries to use scientific findings to accuse the Food and Drug Administration (FDA) of unwarranted gloom and doom on the issue of the safety of breast implants.

Two years ago the Food and Drug Administration frightened the daylights out of the 2 million American women who have had breast implants. The FDA imperiously banned the sale of silicone gel implants, suggesting that silicone may be carcinogenic and pose serious risks to a woman's health.

Now comes a report from the American Medical Association, published in that organization's journal and endorsed by its governing house of delegates, stating categorically that the anxiety over breast implants is "not warranted based on current scientific evidence."

The AMA study states unequivocally that "no clinical data are available that definitively prove that an increased incidence of breast cancer or any other type of cancer is associated with silicone-gel breast implants." It also dismisses any connection between

silicone-gel breast implants and immune disorders, as alleged in some lawsuits. This same conclusion was reached by the FDA's own medical advisory panel.

That's all good news for the women with implants, but the FDA is doing its darndest to ensure that they never hear those reassuring words. Instead of welcoming the AMA report, the FDA has attacked the messenger.

I had been covering this issue for the *Los Angeles Times* for a series on cosmetic surgery. My original intention was to write an investigative piece on the explosion of cosmetic surgery, some of which is quite risky. My assumption, I confess, was that this was all a terrible example of life imitating art, particularly the art of fashion and cosmetics, and that people should be content with their own noses, breasts and thighs. How could a new look be worth the risk?

I was disabused of this notion by a student of mine at the University of California who, after asking me what I was working on, said she hoped I wouldn't dump on implants. She had had them put in four years before and they made a major difference in her life; clothes fit better and her social life had improved dramatically. For her, breast implants were a matter of choice, a means of taking control of her own body.

Her response was typical of the hundreds of women I interviewed. It was also the opinion of most women and physicians who testified before the FDA and Congress. For that reason, I was startled when the FDA acted so abruptly on the basis of fragmented and mostly anecdotal evidence that suggested implants could be bad for women.

Until the FDA's decision, the women I had met at various hospital briefings had been quite satisfied with their implants. With the stroke of a pen, the FDA made those women feel they have a time bomb ticking inside their bodies. It took away the right of women to weigh the risks and choose silicone implants for cosmetic purposes. As the AMA report put it, "The AMA supports the position that women have the right to choose silicone-gel-filled or saline-filled breast implants for both augmentation and reconstruction after being fully informed about the risks and benefits."

This is the real issue. Is it the individual or the FDA who should ultimately be responsible for an individual's health care when the evidence regarding risk is not clear-cut? For an answer, just look at the FDA's hysterical crusade against nutritional supplements and homeopathic medicine. As it has done with its treatment of both garlic tablets and breast implants, the FDA shoots first with regulations and asks questions later. The FDA specializes in gloom and doom, forgetting that anxiety in patients is itself a major health risk.

My own conclusion, after spending a year poring over records of lawsuits and state medical malpractice hearings, was that breast implants are safer than most other cosmetic surgery procedures. The innocent-sounding "tummy tucks" and face-lifts carry higher risks of infection and disfigurement. Fact is, anyone with a medical license can perform any operation, whether trained in that procedure or not. Cosmetic surgery is elective and mostly performed in private clinics. Since insurance companies and hospitals are not involved, that means less regulation than there is for other surgeries. The main risk of cosmetic surgery is that less qualified doctors may perform these procedures because they are lucrative. The main risks in breast augmentation lie in the imperfect skills of the doctor and the equipment rather than in the implants themselves.

The dirty secret of health regulation in this country is that there is little supervision by the states—and none by the federal government—of what doctors do. The FDA lacks the authority to regulate doctors' procedures and can deal only with health products, which is the reason that the silicone implants became the target.

Silicone has been used for decades in thousands of medical procedures, from coating needles to penile implants. Has the breast implant been singled out because it esthetically or morally offends those running the FDA? The hypocrisy of the ban on breast implants was underlined by the fact that the FDA permits their use for reconstructive purposes after a mastectomy. If silicone implants threaten a woman's health, why expose women recovering from breast cancer? Maybe it's because the FDA doesn't really find the risk all that alarming.

In his reply to the AMA report, FDA chairman David Kessler doesn't even claim that there is evidence that the implants cause cancer. Instead, he argues that the drug companies that manufactured the implants did not adequately prove their safety. What he's really doing is covering his own behind and, more broadly, the sorry record of the FDA in this and other regulatory matters. Now, in a fitful lunge at catching up with its responsibilities, the agency has gone way too far. Instead of rationally applying existing regulations to the drug companies to obtain more solid data on implant safety, the FDA arrived at a more self-serving conclusion.

The overkill of the FDA bureaucrats in this matter, as in so many others, smells of a fear and vindictiveness that mandate a congressional overhaul of the agency. The FDA is out of control. It is a bureaucratic monstrosity that, as the breast-implant controversy shows, is contemptuous of the views of consumers as well as the medical community. The FDA seems determined to demonstrate that the agency is far more dangerous to our health than are the products it seeks to monitor.

Study Questions

1. Would libertarianism agree with Scheer?

2. Does Scheer suggest a bigger role for government when it comes to licensing doctors? If so, is this consistent with what he says about the role of the Food and Drug Administration?

3. If Scheer is even close to being right, why would corporations such as Dow Corning pay so many billions of dollars to settle these cases against them? But if Scheer is not close to being right, how could he find so much support from the American Medical Association?

4. Is there a moral distinction between a woman using implants to reconstruct her breasts after injuring them in an accident and an uninjured, healthy woman using implants only to enhance her sex appeal? If so, what is the moral basis of this distinction? If not, why do many people make this distinction? Are they committing what we might call "the Unnatural Fallacy," which is to assume that whatever is unnatural is worse than any natural alternative to it? In this case, the argument would refer to a woman's natural endowment of breasts and would refer to the breast implants as unnatural. Many examples show that the Unnatural Fallacy is indeed a fallacy, that is, an error in reasoning. For example, many artificial or synthetic drugs and medical procedures are better than the alternative of letting a disease run its natural course, causing pain, dysfunction, and death. Further, chairs are often better to sit on than the natural terrain, houses are usually better homes than caves are, etc.

34

The Money of Playboy Magazine

Catherine A. MacKinnon

Editor's note: MacKinnon, a professor of law at Harvard Law School, criticizes *Playboy*'s treatment of women as products to be bought and sold. Some have called this the commodification of women. MacKinnon asks whether *Playboy*'s claim that it is a feminist publication has any truth. She explores whether feminists should reject the money that *Playboy* gives to feminist charities or organizations. She also analyzes the defense of pornography based on the First Amendment to the U.S. Constitution and the moral values on which that amendment is based.

They are able to distort the pictures or do anything that they want to with them . . . for example, I was a puzzle. I was a deck of playing cards. This is what they call Playboy products . . . By the way, a Playmate is a product. The term "Playmate" is a trademark of Playboy.
—Miki Garcia ("Miss January 1973"), Hearings of the National Commission on Pornography, Los Angeles, October 17, 1985

Playboy, the magazine, sells women's sexuality as "entertainment for men." It is socially accepted. Playboy, the foundation, gives a fair amount of the money the magazine makes this way to some kinds of feminist work and brags about it more than a fair amount. I want to think through the connections between

Reprinted by permission of the publishers from *Feminism Unmodified: Discourses on Life and Law* by Catharine A. MacKinnon (Cambridge, Mass.: Harvard University Press). Copyright © 1987 by the President and Fellows of Harvard College. The footnotes have been omitted.

these facts, focusing on how feminists' acceptance of money from Playboy, the foundation, helps make acceptable what *Playboy*, the magazine, does to women. This is a preliminary report on some research. I am just beginning to get a handle on what I think Playboy is, what they are doing, what their views of themselves are, and how they are socially regarded.

Among feminists I see two views of Playboy's money. One is that it is really our money. Playboy took and sold women's sexuality to make it in the first place, so we should use it in the interests of women to cushion or change the system that extracts it from us. If feminism is at all about transforming the sexuality-for-survival dynamic, the reparations theory could make Playboy's money look like part of a feminist strategy for change.

The other view is not that Playboy's money is dirty money; the objection is not a moral one, that Playboy is dirty in some sense in which other things are clean. The objection is not from the standpoint of any kind of purity. It is a political objection. By this I mean it is not about good and evil or virtue and perversity but about power and powerlessness. From this standpoint, the axrgument against taking Playboy's money is: if we think we are going to use their money to undercut the system of power that extracts it, we think we are more powerful than we are and Playboy is less powerful than it is, which is a dangerous delusion. Even more, if much of *Playboy*'s power against women derives from its legitimacy, and what its legitimacy in turn makes legitimate, we become part of their legitimacy support system when we accept their financial help. Taking their money, in this view, digs us deeper into the system we are fighting. The issue then becomes not whether we are pure, or even whether we can afford not to take their money and still survive, but whether taking their money hurts us more than the money helps us, although it comes as an influx of often desperately needed resources. Can feminists survive *taking* their money? What do we survive *as*?

Those are the positions in their most difficult postures, for me. If their analysis of women's situation is not identical, at least their senses of feminist goals overlap. On one level of theory, the question of Playboy's money can be seen as an example of the marxism-feminism problematic, because it connects materiality in the money sense with male power in the sexual sense. What follows is one attempt to work through that tension, understanding that money and sexuality are *both* material and gendered.

Playboy's money, considered from a feminist perspective, requires answering three questions: what is feminism? what is Playboy? what is money? I will bring in facts about who Playboy gives money to and, to the extent we have been able to determine empirically, how much is involved, under what conditions it is given, and with what results.

Playboy asserts it is a feminist publication; at least both Hugh Hefner and Christie Hefner say that they are feminists and that the magazine liberates women. I am less interested in what is utterly ludicrous about this claim than in the sense in which it might have some truth. If you ask, is there anything that goes around calling itself feminist that *Playboy* has anything in common with, the answer is yes. For that reason I need to discuss what feminism is before I can evaluate Playboy in its terms. I will also say I am real tired of people calling things feminist that come from quite other traditions. Applying other traditions to women doesn't make them feminist.

I believe that thought is systematic, socially speaking, even when it is not particularly consistent or coherent, logically or philosophically speaking. It always occupies a place in society's material/consciousness context, which is a context that gives some people power over other people. When Playboy says it is feminist, the substance of the positions it refers to is systematically—formally, historically, and philosophically—liberal, period.

Liberalism applied to the sex question provides a critique of gender differentiation in which the sexes are imagined as fundamentally different, so inequality means inaccurate or irrational differentiation. Why inequality happens is never very clear. No one is ever actively doing it, everybody has it done to them, and no one benefits from it. It sort of just comes from the stork. Liberal feminism seeks to solve this version of the sex problem, which is this imperfect fit between gender differentiation—social sex—and sexual dimorphism—biological sex. The resulting liberal feminist position on sexuality, like its position on most else, is that women should be able to get what men have had access to, so long as biological differentiation is not altered as a bottom line. On this view of equality, what you get is the sixties' "liberated woman," that is, the woman who initiates sex with lots of men ("partners") and regards it as an indoor or spectator sport (like men have) and has lots of (biologically female) orgasms.

Playboy certainly presents the biological differences between the sexes on its pages, if a difference can be shown by displaying only half of it. What are

thought as women's *gender* characteristics are what the magazine sells as *sexuality*. To say that *Playboy* presents the natural beauty of women's bodies and promotes the sexual liberation of women—here I draw on *Playboy* itself, which says it does these things—reveals a liberal concept of the relation between nature and freedom. It starts with the idea that people, even people who as a group are poor and powerless, do what they do voluntarily, so that women who pose for *Playboy* are there by their own free will. Forget the realities of womens' sexual/economic situation. When women express our free will, we spread our legs for a camera.

Implicit here, too, is the idea that a natural physical body exists, prior to its social construction through being viewed, which can be captured and photographed, even, or especially, when "attractively posed"—that's a quote from the Playboy Philosophy. Then we are told that to *criticize* this is to criticize "ideas," not what is being *done* either to the women in the magazine or to women in society as a whole. Any critique of what is done is then cast as moral critique, which, as liberals know, can involve only opinions or ideas, not facts about life. This entire defensive edifice, illogical as it may seem, relies utterly coherently on the five cardinal dimensions of liberalism: individualism, naturalism, voluntarism, idealism, and moralism. I mean: members of groups who have no choice but to live life *as* members of groups are taken as if they are unique individuals; their social characteristics are then reduced to natural characteristics; preclusion of choices becomes free will; material reality is turned into "ideas about" reality; and concrete positions of power and powerlessness are transformed into relative value judgments, as to which reasonable people can form different but equally valid preferences.

What I have just described is the ideological defense of pornography. Given the consequences for women of this formal theoretical structure, consequences that we live out daily as social inequality (not to mention its *inherent* blame-the-victim posture), I do not think it can be said that liberal feminism is feminist. What it is, is liberalism applied to women. If the sexes are equally different but not equally socially powerful, "differences" in the liberal sense are irrelevant to the politics of our situation, which is one of inequality. Radical feminism, as I understand it, is against gender hierarchy. Since such a critique *does* address the situation of women as I understand it, I term it simply feminism.

One's position, then, on whether feminists

should accept Playboy's money depends on one's analysis of the situation of women: where it comes from, what makes it move, how to change it. It means one thing to take their money in the situation of women is forced—specifically, if the situation is one of forced sex—and quite another if women's problem is, say, that selling our sexuality is illegal. I think that gender defines the status of women, that forced sex defines gender, that pornography eroticizes and thereby legitimizes forced sex, and that *Playboy* is pornography and makes pornography legitimate. Playboy is, in part and in turn, legitimized through its articles, which include some by putative feminists, and its intensive and very successful public relations, of which its financial contributions to the women's movement are a real part. Playboy uses its contributions to our work (among other things) to transform its position as active oppressors of women into the appearance of being standard bearers of women's equality.

Playboy's legitimacy I term "the *Playboy* standard." The way it works is that anything that might hurt *Playboy*, meaning anything real addressing pornography, can't be done. According to this standard, *Playboy* isn't "really" pornography, but it is indistinguishable from it; since nothing can be done about pornography that wouldn't also hurt *Playboy*, nothing can be done about pornography. *Playboy* is so much a standard that people may even be against what they call the violence in pornography yet think *Playboy* is fine. Either they miss or don't mind the force in and behind *Playboy*; or if they do see it, they don't feel they can take a stand against the more expressly violent pornography, because that might do something to *Playboy*. I'm saying, the first premise is "*Playboy* is OK"; everything else, including what *Playboy* does to women, has to be measured against the standard *Playboy* sets, rather than measuring *Playboy* by some other standard of how women should be treated.

From a feminist perspective, what exactly does *Playboy* do? It takes a woman and makes her sexuality something any man who wants to can buy and hold in his hand for three dollars and fifty cents. His access to her sexuality is called freedom—his *and hers*. She becomes something to be used by him, specifically, an object for his sexual use. Think of it this way. A cup is part of the object world, valued according to its looks and for how it can be used. If someone breaks it, maybe that is considered an abuse, or maybe it is briefly mourned and then replaced. But using it does not violate anything, because that is

what it is for. *Playboy* as a standard means that to use a woman sexually does not violate her nature because it expresses her nature; it is what she is *for*. To criticize *Playboy* as a standard for how a woman should be treated is to say something very simple: a woman is not a cup, and her sexuality isn't, either.

What *Playboy* does to women is very carefully legitimized, both inside and outside the magazine. *Playboy's* articles push their views, including their views of the First Amendment, in an expressly sexualized context, and at the same time those articles serve to legitimize what their pictures do to women. Masturbating over the positions taken by the women's bodies associates male orgasm with the positions expressed in the articles. Ever wonder why men are so passionate about the First Amendment? At the same time the articles help make it seem legitimate to treat women the way *Playboy* does, because the articles are so legitimate. The sex contextualizes the articles and the articles contextualize the sex.

Playboy defends itself against the charge of being merely a skin magazine by pointing to having published many people it calls feminists, some we might call feminists, women like Gloria Emerson, Susan Sontag, Doris Lessing, Joyce Carol Oates, Pearl Buck, and Mary McCarthy. And interviews with Germaine Greer, Jane Fonda, Betty Friedan, Mary Calderone, Bernadette Devlin, Shere Hite, and Virginia Johnson. Under the legal doctrine of obscenity, courts may not take materials apart. They have to take them "as a whole." *Playboy's* format, like that of much pornography, is designed around obscenity law so that its sexual objectification of women is legalized as well as legitimized through being surrounded by legitimate articles. In one recent case the Supreme Court said that people who are having sex on a street corner cannot protect that as speech even if they are the same time engaging in valid political dialogue. On the level of publications, this is what *Playboy* does. It gets itself off the hook for pimping women under the "taken as a whole" rule by simultaneously publishing works that are unquestionably protected speech.

Another way Playboy legitimizes itself is by its research grants. Playboy has funded particular research items; say you need a videotape machine to do an experiment on pornography, they'll send you a check for $2,500. What do we make of this? Perhaps Playboy *is* interested in figuring out if there is a relation between explicit sex, their version, and rape or force or violence and all those things they say they are so much against and don't do. Maybe Playboy wants the people who are asking these questions to be friendly to them. When people claim that the brutalization of women is a recurring theme and reality of and in *Playboy* and its imitators, *Playboy* responds, "We can infer that they are referring to psychological or social brutalizations because we never lay a hand on a female except in passion or self-defense." As if passion is never violent, as if women can't wait to jump on playboys. Psychic or social brutality they own up to only to trivialize. How sincere or cynical their rejection of rape is, I don't know. I do know that breaking a cup, accidentally or on purpose, is made less wrenching by the availability of glue and replacements and that the line between use and abuse of women, a line *Playboy* insists on to defend itself, does not exist in practice.

As I see it, the cornerstone of *Playboy*'s principled civil libertarianism comes from the bedrock of their material self-interest: "publishing sex." Forget for the moment that what they "publish" is women; that *is* sex. The freer the access to sex in print, the more freedom there is, the sexier the sex is, and the more money they make. Any critique of this is seen as the forces of darkness moving in to have the government restrict existing freedom. The term freedom in the phrase "freedom of speech" here means free sexual access to women. Freedom is freedom of *access* to us. Listen, I want to increase women's power over sexuality, hence over our social definition and treatment. I think that means decreasing the pornographers' power over it. I have no particular interest in increasing the power of the *state* over sexuality or speech. I do not have that kind of faith in the government. It has largely operated from the same perspective that Playboy does—that is, the male point of view. At least, no one has yet convinced me that extending the obscenity prohibition, liberalizing its application, would do anything but further eroticize pornography. Suppressing obscenity criminally has enhanced its value, made it more attractive and more expensive and a violation to get, therefore more valuable and more sexually exciting. Censoring pornography has not delegitimized it; I want to delegitimize it. What would do that is unclear to me at this time. Maybe there is a way. There needs to be. It is not that I think the state can't do anything for women in this area. I think making sexual harassment sex discrimination has helped delegitimize sexual harassment. That is as far as I have gotten with the problem at this time.

The First Amendment absolutist position is very different from this position. Absolutism supposes that we all have an equal interest in the marketplace of ideas it supposedly guarantees. This is not the case for women. First of all, the marketplace of ideas is literal: those with the most money can buy the most speech, and women are poor. Second, protecting pornographers, as the First Amendment now does, does not promote the freedom of speech of women. It *has* not done so. Pornography terrorizes women into silence. Pornography is therefore not in the interest of our speech. We do not, as women, have a stake in the existing system we have been said to have. The First Amendment has also been interpreted to support the speech of Nazis, as if that would promote the rights of Jews. I doubt that, too, although the issues are specific to each case. Jews are not lying down for anti-Semitism any more than women are lying down for misogyny. But that isn't a victory for the First Amendment; it's a victory for Jews and women against odds that the First Amendment has been used to stack. What I think is that people who are absolutely interested in the First Amendment should turn their efforts to getting speech for people, like women, who have been denied that speech almost entirely, who have not been able to speak or to get themselves heard. Understanding free speech as an abstract system is a liberal position. Understanding how speech also exists within a substantive system of power relations is a feminist position.

On the basis of the First Amendment values I have just criticized, Playboy selects people who epitomize them, people who will give Playboy legitimacy, and calls them First Amendment Awards judges and gives them First Amendment Awards. They make a major public event of it. In one situation some students objected to the participation of one of their professors as a judge. Discussing this issue with the students, the professor said that his association with Playboy went back to 1971, when it was the only organization willing to fund his draft counseling activities. He was very impressed with it—as many people who deal with only the foundation often are, by the way. They feel that the foundation is socially concerned, that it funds many highly important activities, and that it is, as they put it, "totally unrelated to the magazine." (When asked where they think it gets its money, they demur.) The students asked the professor whether he really understood their concern with lending his name to legitimizing the use of women's bodies to make money. He assured them that he did understand but did not agree that that was what was going on. They spoke about laundering money and pointed out that he could object strongly to that laundering, and especially to the exploitation that originally made that money, without denigrating the worth of the projects the money was spent on. His bottom line was that he had taken lots of Hefner's money for lots of very good causes and was not about to turn on him now. Soon after, however, he withdrew.

I learned a lot from this, because it never would have occurred to me that the professor's original position was a takeable one, even in the abstract. What does money buy? I mean, if someone gives you ten dollars to do something good, does that mean you are loyal to that person for life? If someone who helped you when you were a starving student rapes a child, are you obligated to defend him in court? Is there nothing that breaks the loyalty of money, or is it only an issue of what does or how much money? I had imagined that one could take the money—for draft counseling if it is needed and no one else would pay for it—and that would be that. We have found projects in which people said that no one other than Playboy would pay for the work, like rape victim assistance kits, for instance. So you take the money and you use it in good ways, in ways that support your opposition to sexism, knowing *Playboy* is sexist and that other women paid for that money. Then I come across someone who took such money and felt that it bought extended loyalty, that is, *he* was bought, not just his project. There is something about money as a social relation that I was not taking seriously enough when I thought that people could take the money and do good things with it and then have no further ties with or loyalty to Playboy.

Audience: Why can't we take the money and continue to say *Playboy* is not okay without delegitimizing our work?

C. M.: In theory, we could take the money and continue to say, "*Playboy*'s not okay." But even if we do, *Playboy* uses us to make themselves appear okay to the world, by saying that they fund us. This legitimizes *them* and everything they do, which undermines our work. We legitimize them more than our delegitimizing of them ever takes away—which is part of what powerlessness means. The dilemma, of course, is that it is also delegitimizing not to be able to do feminist work.

To think about whether the question you just asked is a hypothetical one or a question in the real world, I want to ask about the feminism of the projects and the funding relations that are said *not* to be undermined when Playboy says they funded it. The pattern of who Playboy funds and how they do

it makes my analysis of their funding consistent with Playboy's real function in male supremacy. Playboy's contributions seem typically to be not especially large but very well targeted. Often they are absolutely crucial to small projects. The amounts are $1,000, $2,000, $5,000, which is a lot to us, but in the foundation world it is not a lot. A contribution often goes to a group that is midstream in a project when it is hit by a postage increase or needs a printed document or pilot leaflet or mailing, or if they can get this document out maybe other people will give them more money, or an ongoing community organization suddenly needs to do a single event. Discrete, crucial events that begin and end, Playboy tends to fund: little newspapers, documents to get conferences off the ground, things like that. A lot of them. The Playboy Foundation gives money to feminists the way a pimp does a prostitute: at desperate moments, just enough to keep you hooked and in line, never enough so you don't need to crawl back for more, never enough so you don't have to worry all the time about how he will see who you are and what you do, buying gratitude and loyalty way out of proportion to the amount of money, in part *because* so little is involved that the relation that money maintains is dependence. You are doing the work, and he isn't, but you never get enough money not to need him anymore.

This parallel raises the question of whether the specific *work* Playboy funds is in their interest in any way. What Playboy has funded is a little different from what they will fund in the immediate future, because they don't have as much money as they have had. But their history with sexology research and the abortion movement is revealing. Playboy funds Masters and Johnson. This makes sense. Not that Masters and Johnson have not discovered some truth. But their research, like *Playboy*, revolves around the search for the perfect fuck, the modern equivalent of the holy grail. It is about the science, the technology, of how to produce the same sexuality the pornography eroticizes without facing the fact that women's unequal social status is the precondition for their definition of sexual adjustment. Playboy funded Masters and Johnson's sex therapist training. This is so perfect for *Playboy*'s "achiever" philosophy. There is a way to fuck right, and if you can't manage it, Playboy is there to help you. Beneath this "how to" is a sexual politics. Technique is never pure means.

Some say that sexology has been monopolized or taken over by Playboy funding. To ask what it means to take something over is to need to ask whether the sexologists' sexuality is all that different from *Playboy*'s sexuality in the first place. *Playboy*'s operative definition of sexuality, like that of most sexology, essentially derives from neo-Freudian derepression theory, even when Freud is superficially repudiated as inadequately empirically based. (The same basic view of sexuality can be found in most marxist feminism and in liberalism, as well as in a lot of behavioral work, such as the 1970 President's Commission report on obscenity.) This view underlies what has been called the movement for sexual liberation. A feminist critique of it suggest that this definition of sexuality frees male sexual aggression. Making the penis work and getting women to go with that is what sex research perfects. In other words, saying that *Playboy* is feminist means that *Playboy* furthers the sexual liberation of women, meaning it frees women for sexual access by men. That *is* female sexuality, hence freedom for women, according to them. They will take away whatever inhibitions we "frigid" ones have had when we say we are not moved, we don't want "it," *you* we don't want. Our resistance is taken as our repression, something we need sex therapy and pornography for.

It is interesting that censorship of speech is discussed in the same terms that this purported sexual restriction is discussed: as "suppression." Censorship excites men a lot. It is as if they make an analogy from the Freudian view of the individual experience of sexual intercourse to the public experience of sex in words and pictures, so that censorship is a form of sexual repression. It seems that what they *do* to us sexually is their speech. Freedom of sexual explicitness derepresses the public in the same way that an individual's freedom is actuated by more intercourse. In other words, the more sex an individual or a society has, in print or in life interchangeably, the more sexually free and healthy he/she/it is.

Without launching into a full critique of Freudian derepression theory, I will say that I think feminism is developing a non-Freudian theory of sexuality. Repressed in the Freudian sense is not exactly what has been done to women's sexuality. We *have* experienced deadening and silence and subordination. Male sexuality has not exactly been repressed either. Men have eroticized the idea that their sexuality has been denied, but their sexuality has been nothing but expressed and expressed and expressed. Sexual liberation, from this perspective, looks like a male rationalization for forcing sex on women. Intellectually, it derives from Freud, including Freud's (in the end) disbelief of women's accounts of victimiza-

tion through sexual abuse as children. When women reported what happened to them, Freud couldn't finally believe it was real, so he invented fantasy to explain the inexplicable and put it in the unconscious. That's where you keep things you repress; repression is how you keep them there. All this presupposes that what women said happened *didn't*. Check it out: these parts of Freud's *formal* theory are based on his substantive belief that women who told him about childhood sexual abuse were lying.

That Playboy would fund abortion rights—which, as they never tire of pointing out, they have done from its beginning—also makes sense in this context. Abortion allows women to have sex on the same terms as men have had it: "no consequences." The entire right wing, and men in general, know that abortion has been fought as an issue of sexual liberation in the sense I mentioned. When women need abortion, it is often so that, since we cannot stop the sex being forced on us, we can at least stop being stuck with the reproductive consequences for the rest of our lives. If women's sexuality means our being able to have sex initiated by men, or our initiating sex with men when men want us to, then freeing *that* sexuality includes separating it from reproduction, so that we don't have to stay pregnant as a result of it. *That* is the liberation of women: women equaling heterosexual intercourse, liberation equaling lack of restraints on men getting it. Abortion offers women the liberal feminist dream of being real women—that is, available to be freely fucked—while still being able to live out a socially male biography—not having to be responsible for children. This is the "equality" it offers us. I hope this makes clear why liberal so-called feminists and the pornographers wind up on the same side of things.

What I really want to know is how much of the women's movement the pornographers own. I wonder if there is a relationship between the money Playboy gives the women's movement and the fact that we have not yet been able to establish—or as a movement even to begin—a real critique of pornography. It is very difficult to think certain thoughts, to get beyond certain ways of thinking, if you have a material investment in not letting your thinking lead in certain directions. Playboy funded one sexual harassment conference proposal that did not even mention sexuality as part of the problem—it was entirely an economic analysis. *Playboy* regularly celebrates what is essentially sexual harassment in its pages, but it's presented as fun., as consensual, as sex. Maybe the conference organizers would have had the same analysis of sexual harassment whether or not they were looking to Playboy for funding. But I doubt that Playboy would have funded a conference to explore sexual harassment as integral to male supremacist *sexuality*.

Some might see feminists' material interest in pornography as similar to our material interest in the family or the workplace, like prostitutes' interest in pimps: we can't afford to destroy them, we need them, we are dependent on them, they help us get from one day to the next. But they also destroy us. Any system of power gives an interest in the status quo to those it keeps powerless. Our stake in *this* family structure, *this* workplace organization, *this* sexuality, *this* protection racket. This makes me wonder, if taking Playboy's money is okay, is anybody's money too damaging to take? How about directly from Hefner? What about Larry Flynt? Al Goldstein? La Cosa Nostra? How about cosmetic companies? Is there a difference—say, the famous difference be-

tween cause and effect—between those who create the system and those who pander to it? Or is it just two ways of getting through another day?

I know it matters how much room we have, but how can a feminism worthy of the name live off something women are paying for? If it is Playboy's money that is allowing us to survive, and *Playboy* is what I have said it is, is this survival killing us?

Study Questions

1. Is *Playboy*'s claim that it is a feminist publication true?

2. Must publishing photographs of nude women for entertainment, which *Playboy* does, be pornographic?

3. Does the fact that no one is forced to look at *Playboy* make the magazine harmless?

"WE SAID, MADAM, THAT YOU MAY VIEW PORNOGRAPHY IN THE PRIVACY OF YOUR HOME. WE DIDN'T SAY YOU HAD TO!"

35

A Defense of Pornography

F. M. Christensen

[T]he belief that pornography is evil in itself is simply wrong. This leaves open the important question of whether it has effects on the user's attitudes or behavior that are harmful to anyone. Charges that this is so are continually being made, so . . . we will explore that issue.

One particularly profound problem involves the issue of human agency. Now, some people are logically inconsistent in regard to this issue. In response to the suggestion that a violent criminal was made that way by a traumatic childhood, they invoke the notion of absolute free will: "His circumstances are not to blame; he *chose* to let them affect him!" But let the subject be something as comparatively minor as exposure to words or pictures, and suddenly the same people insist on a causal influence. The perennial debate over freedom of the will can hardly be discussed here. But one thing is perfectly clear from all the evidence: heredity and environment have a powerful influence on human behavior. The only room for rational debate is over whether that influence is total (deterministic) or not—and, once more, over just how much effect different types of causal factor exert. . . .*

The first of the claims we will discuss is usually expressed in vague generalities; it is basically the charge that use of pornography tends to produce all sorts of wrongful behavior. From the rhetoric some of its proponents employ, one would swear they believe sexual thoughts that are not strictly confined will create a desire to rush out and break windows and steal cars. It is as if they retained the primitive belief that individuals are motivated by only two

basic desires—to do good or to do evil—rather than by a complex panoply of needs and emotions. In the minds of some, this idea seems to rest on the conviction that one sort of corruption just naturally leads to others. Few, if any, scientists take such ideas seriously today; "degeneracy theory," with its concept that physical, psychological, and moral defects are all bound together, was popular in the last century but died with the rise of psychology and scientific medicine. In the rest of the population, unfortunately, notions like this one linger on.

The more specific suggestion is sometimes made that "losing self-control" in regard to sex—as allegedly might be precipitated by the use of pornography—produces a general lack of self-discipline, hence a tendency toward selfish libertinism or worse. This sort of thinking has a long history. In Victorian times, married couples were advised to limit the frequency of their sexual activities strictly lest they lead to a weakening of the will and of general character. And the myth that sexual excess brought about the decline and fall of Rome has been around for centuries, having come down to us with those old suspicions about bodily pleasure. (Never mind the gladiators and slavery and brutal imperialism; sexual pleasure was Rome's real failing.) Part of what is involved in the thinking, evidently, is an inability to distinguish between the very specific matter of sexual "permissiveness" and the rejection of *all* restraints on behavior. Alternatively, it is a confusion between a strong interest in sex and a failure to care about any other sources of happiness, or else a tendency to be concerned only with one's own happiness or with the pleasures of the moment. Such tendencies are certainly bad; for example, a person or nation fixated on momentary satisfactions will lack the discipline to plan for and protect future happiness. But there is no reason to suppose that sexual desires are any more apt to have such consequences than are other strong desires.

. . . [I]t is revealing to point out the inconsistency between these concerns and the lack of fears associated with other needs and pleasures, say, those involving food, love, religious devotion, or the arts. How many are alarmed that our lack of eating taboos—so common in other cultures—will lead to a general obsession with the happiness of the moment? Perhaps we should ban the Wednesday food section in the newspaper, with its seductive pictures and emphasis on the pleasure of eating over its utilitarian function. How many suppose that getting great enjoyment from music or dance will lead to a general lack of self-discipline, or to a disregard for the welfare of others (say, of those who perform them)? The rhetoric about the perils of "pleasure-seeking" is remarkably selective in regard to which pleasures it notices. The real source of this belief, it seems clear, is the sexual anxiety with which so many are raised; it produces the fear that something terrible will happen if one should ever "let go."

The most important response to such charges, however, is that those who make them do not have a shred of genuine evidence. They have been accepted and repeated endlessly, like so many other cultural beliefs, without critical examination. In earlier times, when racism was more socially acceptable than it is now, mixing of the races was often alleged to have brought about the decline of Rome and other civilizations—on the basis of the same worthless *post hoc* reasoning . . . . Certain commentators have claimed to have evidence from one or two studies that reported finding a statistical association between exposure to sexual materials and juvenile delinquency in the United States. It could well be true that in this society, there has been a tendency for those who lack the traditional sexual attitudes to reject other social standards as well. The former is easily explained as a result of the latter, however: those who have been less well socialized into or have rebelled against the system as a whole will naturally be among the ones whose sexual behavior is less constrained. Alternatively, those whose needs have led them to break one social taboo will feel less threatened by other societal rules . . .

Of course, that a belief is held for bad reasons does not mean there are no good reasons for it. Nonetheless, it can be said without hesitation that the evidence available is strongly against the "domino theory" of character. One has only to consider the cross-cultural picture to begin to realize this, say, the promiscuous children and youth of Mangaia or the Trobriand Islands or the Muria villages, who grow up into hard-working adults who have internalized all of their society's moral standards. More generally, there is no indication that sexually positive cultures have greater amounts of antisocial behavior. In fact, one cross-cultural survey found significantly more personal crime in groups where premarital sex is strongly punished than in others. (The fact that the crime rate in permissive Northern Europe is much lower than that in the United States may already be known to the reader—but beware of *post hoc* thinking.) The belief that gratifying sexual feelings tends somehow to turn into a general state of moral cor-

ruption, or even to damage one's capacity for self-discipline, is sheer superstition . . . .

A second variety of claim that pornography has ill effects is that its use tends to damage personal relationships between men and women. This charge takes several different forms, including some that are bizarre (e.g., the idea that many men prefer it to real women and hence will avoid relationships with them if given that option). The simplest of these allegations, however, just points out that numerous women are upset by their partners' interest in pornography, so that it becomes a source of conflict. Part of the problem here is jealousy: the mere biologically normal fact that the partner is attracted to other persons is threatening to some, even when it is all fantasy. But that is evidently not the main difficulty. Few men feel upset over their partners' interest in love stories, say, in soap operas, with their romantic hunks and adulterous love affairs. The real problem seems to be the woman's aversion to nudity and sexual openness.

That being so, this argument presupposes that pornography is hurtful rather than proving it. For it could equally well be said that it is the woman's prudishness, rather than the man's interest in pornography, that is "the real" source of the trouble; which it is would have to be argued for rather than just assumed. Mention to the feminists and religionists who employ this objection that women's liberation or religious devotion has broken up many relationships, and they will make the same basic point . . . . [M]oreover, it seems clear which one is the real culprit. In earlier years, the attitude that explicit sex is offensive to women led men to go off by themselves to watch "stag films"; what could have been an enjoyable shared experience became a source of alienation. Although female interest in such things might never approach that of males, the ones who divide the sexes are those who say, "My desires are noble and yours are nasty," not those who believe in the equal worth and dignity of the needs of both.

One special argument of this kind alleges that pornography harms relationships by its overemphasis on sex, and also by its underemphasis on companionship or romantic love. It is said to "teach men" to value the former too much and the latter too little. with its culture-bound and egocentric notions of how much emphasis is too much or too little, this claim ignores the possibility of keeping the sexes in harmony by teaching women to want sex in the same way. Its biggest error, however, lies in assigning to media depictions far more power to influence basic desires than is at all justified. As usual, those who make this claim express no similar beliefs about the persuasive powers of the constant barrage of love songs and love stories in all the entertainment media. Is such exposure were really so effective, one would think, we would all be incurable love-junkies by now. In any case, there is certainly no lack of publicity promoting love and companionship in our society. Moreover, male sexuality is not detectably different in cultures without appreciable amounts of pornography; indeed, it is evidently very much the same the world over.

What really underlies this claim is an old problem: the unfortunate fact that, on average, men's and women's needs in regard to love/commitment and sex are not well matched. Unable—or perhaps just unwilling—to believe men could ultimately have such different needs than they themselves do, some women suppose it must be the different amount of stress on sex or love among men that does it. One common sense response is simply to deny that men are really different. For example, these women say men just *think* they have a strong need for sex because advertisers keep telling them they do. Others grant the reality of male sexual responses but do not want to believe they are natural. (Among feminists, this is just part of the wider conviction that there are *no* innate differences between the sexes except anatomical ones.) Yet those who make both claims insist it is men who have been most affected by culture in this regard. Over and again, without offering any argument as to which is cause and which effect, they assert that men would not be so interested in sex, or so attracted to female bodies, if only there were not so much emphasis on those things in this society. Besides projecting their own responses onto male nature—responses that are themselves largely culture-conditioned—the women (and sometimes men) who make such claims are somehow blind to all the societal efforts to suppress male sexuality and promote female needs.

What is true is that a double standard is still taught to adolescents in our culture. But it is glaringly false to say that it encourages males to be sexual; it merely discourages them less. Consider the common charge that "this society" teaches young males they have to "score" to be real men, for example. In fact, you will not find this preached by any of the major socializing institutions, not by church, government, school, family, *or* the media. Even that small segment of the latter that celebrates sex overtly cannot really be said to do this—and it is standardly

maligned and even banned by the society at large. The one place where such a thing is taught is in the peer groups of some young men as they themselves rebel against society's teaching on the subject, trying to justify their own needs and feelings. However all this may be, the point remains that pornography is not the cause of male sexuality. It has again become a scapegoat in connection with the male-female conflicts whose real causes lie in biology, or at least much deeper in the socialization of men—or of women. . . .

Some have claimed there is scientific evidence that standard pornography causes misperception of other people's sexual desires. In a certain type of experiment, volunteers are exposed to a presentation of some kind and then asked questions about their beliefs or attitudes. (A subterfuge is used to keep them from realizing the true purpose of the test.) In one version of this test, subjects who have been shown sexual materials indicated they regarded women (as well as men) as somewhat more sexually liberal than did subjects who had not been shown the materials. In itself, this is no evidence of misperception; the former might have been closer to the truth than the latter. In any case, the result is not in the least remarkable. A recent or extended experience of *any* kind looms large in one's consciousness. Hence just about any book or movie, *or* real person that one has recently met, would have a similar influence on one's other judgments, temporarily. For a more striking example, one who has just seen a scary movie is much more likely to look under the bed before retiring at night. The effect soon fades, however; it is swamped by that of subsequently encountered books or movies or real people. And most of the latter tend to promote the culture's current party line on sex, just as they do on other subjects. Except in unusual circumstances, the conclusion remains: sexual entertainment will have little effect on perceptions of reality.

A variant of this objection says that the ecstatic pleasure often portrayed in pornography will tend to make the readers or viewers disappointed with their own sexual experience and, hence, with their partners or their partners' performance. (Although it is women who standardly complain about the latter, this new claim is usually framed in terms of male dissatisfaction.) It is not always clear whether those who present the argument believe ordinary tepid sex is really all that possible—the half-hour orgasms of the Mangaian women argue otherwise—or whether for some reason they just think it unwise to aspire to greater enjoyment. In any case, few people would be misled even by genuine exaggeration, which is an extremely common part of life. Does the hysterical euphoria of the consumers in commercials for hamburgers and soft drinks make anyone seriously expect them to taste different? Once again, the only reason for possibly being misled in the special case of sex is societally imposed ignorance. And it is people who use arguments like this one who often want to keep young people in that vulnerable state. . . .

Most of the . . . claims about pornography's "effects" assume that too much stress on sex is dangerous to an intimate relationship. That can certainly be true, but the proper balance of emphasis between sex and other needs in that context is one that requires sensitive exploration, not dogma. In fact, those who give these fallacious arguments typically overlook the opposite problem. Surveys and clinical experience have long revealed that a high percentage of couples have unsatisfying sex lives. That is a major destroyer of relationships in itself. There are many reasons for this, but a serious one continues to be the sexual inhibition this society inculcates, with its *negative* stress on sex. Conversely, . . . countless women have discovered that sex can be a joy rather than a burden, and they have done so precisely by learning to become more sexually assertive and more adventurous in bed.

What is especially relevant to our purposes about the latter fact is that pornography has often aided in the process. Large numbers of people have reported that it has helped their sex lives and hence their relationships. In one survey of couples who went to sex movies together, for example, 42 percent made that claim. In her beautiful little book on female sexuality, *For Yourself*, Dr. Lonnie Barbach tells how women have overcome difficulty in getting sexually aroused, or in having orgasms, by learning to use fantasy and pornography. Indeed, it has become standard practice for therapists to use sex films to treat the sexual disabilities of individuals and couples. The ways in which they help are very revealing in light of what has just been discussed: they aid in overcoming inhibition, enhance arousal in preparation for sex, and introduce ideas and techniques that bring freshness to a stale routine. So far from harming intimate personal relationships, pornography can have the very opposite effect.

A third general charge of social harm from pornography has been put forth, mostly by traditionalists. Its use is seen as a threat, not to love and personal relationship as such, but to marriage and the family. The basic claim is that by celebrating sex for its own sake, pornography entices people to leave or refrain from entering committed relationships—"Why be married if you can get sex without it?"—or else leads to their breakup by encouraging extramarital adventures that result in jealous conflicts. This is a serious charge indeed. The legalistic concern some have with marriage ceremonies is highly questionable; but the family, in its role of raising children, is of crucial importance. And divorce, with its adverse effects on children, has become increasingly common in recent decades. Such a large and complex topic can hardly be explored adequately here, but we can address two relevant questions: Is a positive attitude toward sex for its own sake necessarily a threat to marriage? And is pornography an appreciable factor in promoting that sort of attitude, hence itself such a threat?

The answer to the first question seems to be negative. For one thing, there have been many cultures with a stable family life and also an accepting attitude toward nonmarital nd the empires that spread them, socially sanctioned premarital sex may well have been the cross-cultural norm. It has even been suggested that such behavior contributes to later marital stability by providing young people with experience on which to base a wiser choice of mate. In any case, it does not speak very well of marriage to suggest that, given a choice, people will reject it. As a matter of fact, most do have a strong inclination toward pair-bonding. Since they do not marry just for sex in the first place (and *shouldn't* do so), liberal sexual attitudes are not likely to dissuade them; only the timing is apt to be affected. In addition, there are many good reasons for not forcing young people to rush into marriage by making it the only way they can get sex.

As for the case of *extra*marital sex, where it has been socially sanctioned and controlled, it too has not been a serious threat to the stability of the family. It is true that jealousy is a powerful emotion. But it is also true that humans are far from being strictly monogamous in their feelings. Although our culture has traditionally taken jealousy as morally justified and condemned extramarital desires, others have done just the reverse: they have sought to mitigate the conflict between the two emotions by controlling the former more than the latter. And the anthropological reports indicate that they succeed rather well. It just may be, for all we know, that their system works better than ours in this respect. In fact, it can be argued that our unbending attitude toward sexual exclusivity contributes to marital breakup by creating unrealistic expectations. The offending party may not want such a break but feel it is necessary to satisfy other desires; and the offended one may fear loss of face in not avenging the act, or else think there must be something wrong with one of them or with the marriage for such a thing to have happened.

However all this may be, it is not the immediate question here. For us the issue is whether pornography is in any of the ways suggested a threat to the family in our culture. In spite of what many assume, it is far from obvious that it is. Indeed, it may be more likely to act as a "safety valve" for preventing marital breakup by providing a substitute way to satisfy nonmonogamous desires. Many cultures of the world have had special festival times and special locations in which the usual sexual taboos could be broken. (For just one example, consider the temple "prostitution" of the ancient Near East, in which all men and women took part.) The seeming value of such institutions in maintaining both monogamy and mental health has been noted by many students of the subject. The fact that such large numbers of strictly monogamous couples in the present time have come to use sexual entertainment together hints that it can serve the same purpose. Given the strong biological urge to have more than one sex partner, this may be an extremely important consideration.

Furthermore, pornography can help to preserve marriages by means of the positive effects listed earlier. As for the chance that it can also have the opposite effect, it might be suggested that romantic love stories present more of a danger to long-term pairing by awakening desires that many a marriage gone stale cannot satisfy. After all, falling in love with someone else is more likely to produce the wish for divorce than is a one-night stand. In any case, factors other than sexual fantasies have been vastly more influential in creating marital instability. The data indicate that such things as the following have been responsible for increasing divorce rates: greater independence for women (most female advocates of long-term commitment do not assail *this* causal factor), changes in laws and attitudes regarding divorce, unemployment and other financial troubles, and the greater mobility of the population, which has led to a loss of controls by the extended family and the community.

To really answer the question before us, however, we must consider the possible dynamics. Exactly how might pornography produce the allegedly destabilizing desires? Those who make the charge sometimes talk as if it is just a matter of arousing feelings that would not otherwise exist. But that is *their* fantasy, for biology can quite adequately do so. It does not take "outside agitators" like pornography to produce lust and wandering eyes. There is one thing, however, that pornography certainly can do, and that is to thwart attempts to suppress such feelings. Efforts to promote one moral point of view are indeed apt to be hampered when people are allowed to become aware of other views as genuine alternatives. This is just to say, however, that freedom and knowledge are an obstacle to attempts at thought control. "How're you gonna keep 'em down on the farm, after they've seen Paris?" asks an old song. It was not only the pill, but the loosening of restraints on sexual content in the media, that launched the reassessment of traditional sexual attitudes that occurred in the 1960s.

So there is a much broader point here that is very important. It is clear that formal and informal education—learning more about the world—tends to make people more tolerant and liberal in their views. For just one apparent example, surveys have revealed that half the readers of sex magazines are college educated, in contrast to a third of the readers of magazines in general. Ideologues, however, do not like such tolerance; what they are opposed to at bottom is the right of other people to make up their own minds. (From Moscow to Washington, they answer, "Don't *let* 'em see Paris.") But it cannot easily be argued that keeping people in ignorance of different ideas is best for them. As Carl Sagan pointed out in *Cosmos*, science has flourished at those times and places in history where there have been the greatest social openness and freedom. So it is for good reasons that we have our tradition of freedom of expression; aside from the great value of liberty itself, we have a better chance of discovering truth in a "free marketplace of ideas" than in conditions where only certain beliefs and attitudes may be extolled.

In particular, our best hope of working out the most viable social arrangement concerning sex and the family is to allow an open dialogue in which all human needs are given consideration. It is just as wrong to censor portrayals of alternative sexual lifestyles as it is to suppress those of different political or religious systems. In all likelihood, given the large range of human differences that exists, the best system in the present regard is a pluralistic one that allows individuals to discover the different modes of living that maximize their fulfillment. To rigidly impose the same kinds of relationships upon everyone (on homosexual and heterosexual, pair-bonder and non-pair-bonder and so forth) surely does not serve the best interests of individual people. And the common assumption that it is best for society as a whole is the product, not of a careful study of alternatives, but of the very prejudice that censors consideration of alternatives. Socially enforced error is self-perpetuating.

Study Questions

1. Who has the better of this debate, MacKinnon or Christensen? Do magazines that are often called pornographic, such as *Playboy*, do more harm than good?

2. Pornography is at least an $8 billion industry in the United States. Is it an ethical business? If not, which moral principles does creating and selling pornography violate?

3. Would banning pornography nationwide create a huge black market and a dangerous underworld of outlaws to profit from it?

4. Does it pose a false dilemma to make a slippery slope argument that banning pornography will make us slip down the slope and inevitably lead to banning artistic, political, scientific, or other expressions that should not be banned?

5. Christensen defends pornography by denying that it causes harm and by claiming that the open marketplace of ideas that permits pornography produces many benefits. The marketplace of ideas is a concept many scholars use in offering a moral foundation for the legal right to freedom of expression in the First Amendment of the U.S. Constitution. Is this moral foundation adequate, or are there major cracks in the foundation?

6. Scandinavia and Japan have fewer restrictions on pornography than the United States does, but the United States has far more crimes per capita against women than these other countries do. Do these facts refute the argument that pornography causes too much harm?

7. There is far more pornography in America in 1995 than there was in 1895; there are thousands of pornographic films and video today, for example. Yet women are much closer to equality in 1995 than they were in 1895. Do these facts refute the argument that pornography oppresses women and leads to more discrimination against women?

"...THIS STATION RECENTLY BROADCAST AN EDITORIAL AGAINST SURROGATE MOTHERHOOD...TONIGHT WE PRESENT AN OPPOSING VIEW....."

BILL SCHORR reprinted by permission of United Feature Syndicate, Inc.

36

Womb for Rent: Surrogate Motherhood and the Case of Baby M

Anita Silvers
Sterling Harwood

The famous Baby M case involves both moral and legal issues that arise when one person contracts with another to use the latter person's body for surrogate motherhood (that is, for creation of a baby who will become solely the former person's child). This is a real case that will enable us to practice using the moral concepts we've learned to recognize. If this case seems distant from your lives, you might be interested to know that surrogate motherhood is now a not uncommon reproductive practice, although it rarely attracts as much publicity as the case of Baby M. In the future, you might find yourself considering whether to become or to employ a surrogate mother or advising a friend or relative about doing so.

As you read the facts of the case, keep track of which facts trigger the application of any of the moral positions or derivative principles we've discussed. Be prepared to use these facts in constructing well-considered evaluations of the actions in the case. Also, of course, keep track of the actions you think are morally questionable, based on your knowledge of the moral positions you have just learned. Here are the basic but dramatic facts of the case:

In 1985, Mary Beth Whitehead agreed to become impregnated by artificial insemination with the sperm of William Stern and to give up the resulting child to Stern: that is, Whitehead agreed to become a surrogate mother. When she agreed to this, she was twenty-

nine years old and married, with two children of her own, a boy and a girl. Two of her motivations for becoming a surrogate mother, she said, were that giving Stern the child was "the most loving gift of happiness" and that the ten thousand dollars she was to earn would help pay for her children's college education.

William Stern was a forty-year-old biochemist, and his wife, Elizabeth, was a pediatrician. Both wanted very much to have their own children. However, doctors diagnosed Elizabeth Stern as suffering from a mild case of multiple sclerosis. The Sterns decided that becoming pregnant would therefore be too risky for Elizabeth. The Sterns considered adopting a child. But there is a so-called shortage of healthy, white babies available for adoption. The Sterns also learned that many adoption agencies viewed them as too old to adopt. Besides, Mr. Stern wanted a child of his own flesh and blood.

Mr. Stern hired Noel Keane, a lawyer who specialized in writing contracts hiring surrogate mothers. Mr. Stern and Mrs. Whitehead signed a lengthy contract Keane wrote. The contract specified that Whitehead's payment of ten thousand dollars was to be held in trust until she delivered the baby to Mr. Stern. Mr. Stern paid more than ten thousand dollars to Keane. The contract specified that Stern would have all legal responsibilities for the baby, even if it was born with serious defects or was stillborn. Mrs. Whitehead, the contract stated, was required to submit to amniocentesis, a test checking on the health of the fetus. Whitehead agreed in the contract to have an abortion if Mr. Stern simply requested it. The contract stated that the child would be conceived "for the sole purpose of giving said child to William Stern."

After Mrs. Whitehead had been given standard psychological tests, Keane thought there was little or no reason to expect difficulties, especially because only two of his firm's more than 150 surrogate mothers had changed their minds about meeting the contractual terms.

Mrs. Whitehead gave birth to a healthy little girl. Mrs. Whitehead turned over the baby to the Sterns. But the next day, she implored the Sterns to let her have the child for just one week, and the Sterns agreed. At the end of the week, however, Whitehead refused to return the baby and asked if the Sterns would agree to giving her the child for one weekend each month and two weeks each summer. The Sterns went to court to enforce the contract.

To help protect the anonymity of the girl, the court called her "Baby M." Mrs. Whitehead stated, "Seeing her, holding her . . . . she was my child . . . . It overpowered me. I had not control. I had to keep her." After Mrs. Whitehead had refused to give up the child, the Sterns taped some of their telephone conversations with Whitehead. In at least one of these conversations,

Reprinted from Anita Silvers and Sterling Harwood, "Moral Reasoning," chapter 13 in Brooke Noel Moore and Richard Parker, eds., *Critical Thinking*, 3rd ed. (Mountain View, Calif.: Mayfield Press, 1992), pp. 371–378. Reprinted by permission.

Mrs. Whitehead stated that she would rather kill the child than give it up to the Sterns.

A judge awarded temporary custody of Baby M to the Sterns, but Mrs. Whitehead ran away with her the next day. The Sterns paid over twenty thousand dollars for a private investigator, who spent more than three months tracing Mrs. Whitehead to the house of her mother in Florida. The FBI and the private eye came to that house, took Baby M, and returned her to the Sterns.

Another judge decided just after Baby M's first birthday that Mr. Stern had legal custody of her. Mrs. Whitehead then appealed this decision and lost, but she appealed again to the Supreme Court of New Jersey, which ruled that the contract was "illegal, perhaps criminal, and potentially degrading to women." The court awarded custody of Baby M to Mr. Stern and granted Mrs. Whitehead the right to visit Baby M. The court nullified Mrs. Stern's adoption of Baby M and stripped her of any parental rights.

The court's decision settles the case of Baby M, but it fails to settle the moral or even the legal controversies surrounding the case. In New Jersey, the legislature or a future ruling by the Supreme Court of New Jersey can change the law, and, of course, the court's decision is binding precedent only in New Jersey. The moral questions were not settled by the court's decision, since we cannot automatically conclude that whatever is legal is moral (remember, buying and selling slaves in pre–Civil War American and the Nazi extermination of millions of Jews were technically legal acts).

Here are some of the questions that your study of the five moral positions described earlier should have raised in your mind as you read this case:

1. Was the making of the surrogate motherhood contract immoral?
2. Was the breaking of the surrogate motherhood contract immoral?
3. Should Mr. and Mrs. Whitehead have run away with the baby, and should Mrs. Whitehead have threatened to kill it rather than give it to the Sterns?
4. Did the Supreme Court of New Jersey reach a morally justifiable decision?

Study Question

List five other moral questions raised by the Baby M case.

Was It Immoral to Make the Contract?

Here are some facts and considerations that trigger the application of the moral positions we have studied. Let us begin with the first moral question we raised above, Was the making of the surrogate motherhood contract immoral? Notice that a moral position sometimes can generate reasons both for and against an action. So, moral disagreements are not always due to differences in fundamental values, but instead are sometimes caused by the complexities of applying a fundamental moral position to an intricate, many-sided case.

Egalitarianism can argue against making the contract on the basis that the Sterns were wrong to insist on either getting a white baby for adoption or else employing a surrogate mother to obtain a child of Mr. Stern's own flesh and blood. This action seems to discriminate unfairly against some orphans on the basis of their race, a trait beyond their control that does not prevent a happy adoption if the prospective adoptive parents are fair-minded.

Egalitarianism can also argue against the contract's morality on the basis that the contract exploits Mrs. Whitehead. The wealthier Sterns were arguably taking unfair advantage of the poorer Whiteheads by using their wealth to pressure or draw Mrs. Whitehead into such a risky enterprise with such high stakes. The Sterns took advantage of the fact that the Whiteheads, through no fault of their own, lacked enough money to pay for the college education of their two children.

Perfectionism also can prescribe that the contract is immoral, reasoning that the Sterns should have exhibited the virtue of courage by trying to have their own baby naturally, which involved only some extra risk because Mrs. Stern was older and had a mild case of multiple sclerosis. At least, a courageous attempt should have been made; the fetus could have been aborted at the first sign of medical trouble or if medical complications warranted. Contracting to give the poorer Mrs. Whitehead ten thousand dollars does not seem to count as charity, since the money was payment for a job performed, which is quite different from charity. So perfectionism can criticize the contract as diverting the Sterns from more charitable and courageous courses of action.

But perfectionism also can *condemn* the contract as an expression of Mrs. Whitehead's charity in helping the Sterns by giving to them and sharing with them "the most loving gift of happiness" that Mrs. Whitehead was already enjoying. Perfectionism also can praise Mrs. Whitehead for her courage in undergoing another pregnancy to earn money for the education of her children, an act that also exhibits toward her children the virtue of benevolence.

Notice that from the same moral position we may find ourselves having to weigh considerations both for and against the moral correctness of any particular action. On balance, what do you think perfectionism advises us about the morality of the contract? In considering this question, you might wish to review whether other virtues and vices of character are or should be exhibited by the persons involved in the Baby M case. This is the central concern of perfectionism in supporting moral evaluations.

Study Question

You have just seen how the question of the morality of the surrogate motherhood contract might be treated from the moral positions of egalitarianism and perfectionism. Take each of the other three moral positions—utilitarianism, libertarianism, and prima facie principles—and write brief paragraphs showing how the facts of the Baby M case trigger the application of these three moral positions to answer this question. Complete three paragraphs, one for each position. You need not offer both a pro and a con for each moral position.

Was It Immoral to Break the Contract?

Was it immoral to break the surrogate motherhood contract? Perfectionism can argue against Mrs. Whitehead's breaking the contract on the basis that doing so was dishonest and disloyal to people she had encouraged to count on her. Egalitarianism and libertarianism argue in general against breaking promises and contracts, which Mrs. Whitehead did here. The prima facie moral principles of fidelity, fair play, and nonmaleficence also argue for her abiding by the contract. Utilitarians think the decisive issue is whether breaking the contract will cause more happiness or unhappiness, on balance, than will fulfilling the contract.

To make a utilitarian decision about the morality of breaking the contract, we must weight (1) the probable happiness of Mrs. Whitehead in keeping the child and the probable unhappiness of the Sterns in losing the baby against (2) the alternative outcome, the happiness of the childless Sterns in having the child against the biological mother's unhappiness at losing her. Utilitarianism also requires us to consider the effects of each alternative on the children involved, both on Baby M and on Mrs. Whitehead's other two children, as well as on their relatives and friends and on persons whose happiness may be even less directly affected by the outcome of this case.

Study Questions

Sometimes moral evaluation is complicated by fallacious reasoning. Identify the fallacy involved in each of these arguments.

1. Since making the surrogate motherhood contract was morally wrong, breaking the contract made everything all right again.

2 . If Mrs. Whitehead is allowed to free herself of her obligations under this contract, then no other contract for surrogate motherhood will be secure, and finally the entire practice will be destroyed despite its having proved highly satisfactory to all parties in most cases.

3. Breaking the surrogate motherhood contract is wrong because surrogate motherhood is an increasingly popular and accepted practice.

4. Mrs. Whitehead was right to break the contract because if she didn't raise the child herself, she would never know what happened to the child.

5. If we refuse to believe Mrs. Whitehead's claim that motherly love for the baby compelled her to break the contract, we abandon our respect for the sanctity of motherhood.

6. Because a child is an extension of a mother's very person and life, depriving a mother of her baby is tantamount to depriving her of her life, and no one can contract to do away with her own life; so, to insist that Mrs. Whitehead honor the contract is like insisting she kill herself.

Was the Court's Decision Moral?

Did the Supreme Court of New Jersey reach a moral decision? Libertarianism argues that the original contract should be enforced as it was written. Since that agreement gives Mrs. Whitehead no rights of visitation, the justice system should not meddle in the private affairs of consenting adults by granting Mrs.

Whitehead visitation rights, nor should it coerce the Sterns into agreeing.

Moral Deliberation

Perhaps you have been asking yourself throughout whether moral reasoning can bring about agreement, since there are many different moral positions from which to consider any question of right or wrong conduct. After all, as we have seen, different people may come to different, but apparently equally justifiable, conclusions about the morality of a particular action—simply because they belong to different schools of moral thought. While this is so, it would be too hasty to relegate morality to the domain of chaotic feeling. Of course, no absolute decision-making procedure for all moral action exists, nor is there a guaranteed method for determining beyond doubt who is right and who is wrong in every particular moral disagreement. But reasoned deliberation can be powerfully effective in advancing agreement about moral conduct.

You may have noticed that on many matters, most or all of the fundamental moral positions tend to converge. So, to deliberate with each other, drawing reasoned conclusions about what actions each position recommends, enhances our prospects for consensus. Equally effective is the understanding achieved when persons with different basic approaches to morality consider a disputed case from each other's moral point of view. In recognizing how each other's decisions arise out of thoughtful moral deliberation, guided by serious commitment to reasonable standards, persons who might otherwise be angry adversaries instead can appreciate where their differences lie. Consequently, they can try to minimize their differences or, at least, disagree without hard feelings. Thus, engaging in moral reasoning is valuable to our interpersonal relations.

Practicing moral reasoning is also beneficial from the perspective of personal development. To reason from your acknowledged moral principle(s) to decisions that motivate your actions is to empower yourself as a self-determining, self-respecting moral agent. Thus, to guide your conduct by moral reasoning is a sign of self-control—it is also a source of self-satisfaction and self-esteem.

Recap

Factual claims are descriptive, whereas evaluative claims are prescriptive and assign values to objects, actions, agents, or situations. The reasoning used to support evaluations is in principle no different from the reasoning that justifies factual claims. Five moral positions—egalitarianism, utilitarianism, prima facie principles, libertarianism, and perfectionism—provide ways to approach moral evaluation. Often, these different approaches converge to produce similar conclusions about an issue; sometimes, however, they diverge.

37

Automobile Workers v. Johnson Controls, Inc.

Supreme Court of the United States

In this case we are concerned with an employer's gender-based fetal-protection policy. May an employer exclude a fertile female employee from certain jobs because of its concern for the health of the fetus the woman might conceive?

I

Respondent Johnson Controls, Inc., manufactures batteries. In the manufacturing process, the element lead is a primary ingredient. Occupational exposure to lead entails health risks, including the risk of harm to any fetus carried by a female employee.

Before the Civil Rights Act of 1964 became law, Johnson Controls did not employ any woman in a battery-manufacturing job. In June 1977, however, it announced its first official policy concerning its employment of women in lead-exposure work. . . .

Johnson Controls "stopped short of excluding women capable of bearing children from lead exposure," but emphasized that a woman who expected to have a child should not choose a job in which she would have such exposure. The company also required a woman who wished to be considered for employment to sign a statement that she had been advised of the risk of having a child while she was exposed to lead. . . .

Five years later, in 1982, Johnson Controls shifted from a policy of warning to a policy of exclusion. Between 1979 and 1983, eight employees became pregnant while maintaining blood lead levels in excess of 30 micrograms per deciliter. This appeared to be the critical level noted by the Occupational Safety

and Health Administration (OSHA) for a worker who was planning to have a family. The company responded by announcing a broad exclusion of women from jobs that exposed them to lead:

> ". . . [I]t is [Johnson Controls'] policy that women who are pregnant or who are capable of bearing children will not be placed into jobs involving lead exposure or which could expose them to lead through the exercise of job bidding, bumping, transfer or promotion rights." App. 85 86.

The policy defined "women . . . capable of bearing children" as "[a]ll women except those whose inability to bear children is medically documented." It further stated that an unacceptable work station was one where, "over the past year," an employee had recorded a blood lead level of more than 30 micrograms per deciliter or the work site had yielded an air sample containing a lead level in excess of 30 micrograms per cubic meter. *Ibid.*

II

In April 1984, petitioners filed in the United States District Court for the Eastern District of Wisconsin a class action challenging Johnson Controls' fetal-protection policy as sex discrimination that violated Title VII of the Civil Rights Act of 1964 as amended. Among the individual plaintiffs were petitioners Mary Craig, who had chosen to be sterilized in order to avoid losing her job. . . .

III

The bias in Johnson Controls' policy is obvious. Fertile men, but not fertile women, are given a choice as to whether they wish to risk their reproductive health for a particular job. Section 703(a) of the Civil Rights Act of 1964 prohibits sex-based classifications in terms and conditions of employment, in hiring and discharging decisions, and in other employment decisions that adversely affect an employee's status. Respondent's fetal-protection policy explicitly discriminates against women on the basis of their sex. The policy excludes women with childbearing capacity from lead-exposed jobs and so creates a facial classification based on gender. Respondent assumes as much in its brief before this Court. Brief for Respondent.

---

89 U.S. 1215 (1991). Opinion delivered by Justice Blackmun.

Nevertheless, the Court of Appeals assumed, as did the two appellate courts who already had confronted the issue, that sex-specific fetal-protection policies do not involve facial discrimination. . . . The court assumed that because the asserted reason for the sex-based exclusion (protecting women's unconceived offspring) was ostensibly benign, the policy was not sex-based discrimination. That assumption, however, was incorrect.

First, Johnson Controls' policy classifies on the basis of gender and childbearing capacity, rather than fertility alone. Respondent does not seek to protect the unconceived children of all its employees. Despite evidence in the record about the debilitating effect of lead exposure on the male reproductive system, Johnson Controls is concerned only with the harms that may befall the unborn offspring of its female employees. . . . Johnson Controls' policy is facially discriminatory because it requires only a female employee to produce proof that she is not capable of reproducing.

Our conclusion is bolstered by the Pregnancy Discrimination Act of 1978, in which Congress explicitly provided that, for purposes of Title VII, discrimination "on the basis of sex" includes discrimination "because of or on the basis of pregnancy, childbirth, or related medical conditions." "The Pregnancy Discrimination Act has now made clear that, for all Title VII purposes, discrimination based on a woman's pregnancy is, on its face, discrimination because of her sex." *Newport News Shipbuilding & Dry Dock Co. v. EEOC.* In its use of the words "capable of bearing children" in the 1982 policy statement as the criterion for exclusion, Johnson Controls explicitly classifies on the basis of potential for pregnancy. Under the PDA, such a classification must be regarded, for Title VII purposes, in the same light as explicit sex discrimination. Respondent has chosen to treat all its female employees as potentially pregnant; that choice evinces discrimination on the basis of sex. . . .

The beneficence of an employer's purpose does not undermine the conclusion that an explicit gender-based policy is sex discrimination under § 703(a) and thus may be defended only as a BFOQ [bona fide occupational qualification].

The enforcement policy of the Equal Employment Opportunity Commission accords with this conclusion. On January 24, 1990, the EEOC issued a Policy Guidance in the light of the Seventh Circuit's decision in the present case. . . .

In sum, Johnson Controls' policy "does not pass the simple test of whether the evidence shows 'treatment of a person in a manner which but for that person's sex would be different.'" . . .

IV

Under Title VII, an employer may discriminate on the basis of "religion, sex, or national origin in those certain instances where religion, sex, or national origin is a bona fide occupational qualification reasonably necessary to the normal operation of that particular business or enterprise." We therefore turn to the question whether Johnson Controls' fetal-protection policy is one of those "certain instances" that come within the BFOQ exception. . . .

The PDA's amendment to Title VII contains a BFOQ standard of its own: unless pregnant employees differ from others "in their ability or inability to work," they must be "treated the same" as other employees "for all employment-related purposes." This language clearly sets forth Congress' remedy for discrimination on the basis of pregnancy and potential pregnancy. Women who are either pregnant or potentially pregnant must be treated like others "similar in their ability . . . to work." *Ibid.* In other words, women as capable of doing their jobs as their male counterparts may not be forced to choose between having a child and having a job. . . .

V

We have no difficulty concluding that Johnson Controls cannot establish a BFOQ. Fertile women, as far as appears in the record, participate in the manufacture of batteries as efficiently as anyone else. Johnson Controls' professed moral and ethical concerns about the welfare of the next generation do not suffice to establish a BFOQ of female sterility. Decisions about the welfare of future children must be left to the parents who conceive, bear, support, and raise them rather than to the employers who hire those parents. Congress has mandated this choice through Title VII, as amended by the Pregnancy Discrimination Act. Johnson Controls has attempted to exclude women because of their reproductive capacity. Title VII and the PDA simply do not allow a woman's dismissal because of her failure to submit to sterilization.

Nor can concerns about the welfare of the next generation be considered a part of the "essence" of Johnson Controls' business. . . .

Johnson Controls argues that it must exclude all fertile women because it is impossible to tell which women will become pregnant while working with lead. This argument is somewhat academic in light of our conclusion that the company may not exclude fertile women at all; it perhaps is worth noting, however, that Johnson Controls has shown no "factual basis for believing that all or substantially all women would be unable to perform safely and efficiently the duties of the job involved." *Weeks v. Southern Bell Tel. & Tel. Co.* Even on this sparse record, it is apparent that Johnson Controls is concerned about only a small minority of women. Of the eight pregnancies reported among the female employees, it has not been shown that any of the babies have birth defects or other abnormalities. The record does not reveal the birth rate for Johnson Controls' female workers but national statistics show that approximately nine percent of all fertile women become pregnant each year. The birthrate drops to two percent for blue collar workers over age 30. Johnson Controls' fear of prenatal injury, no matter how sincere, does not begin to show that substantially all of its fertile women employees are incapable of doing their jobs. . . .

It is no more appropriate for the courts than it is for individual employers to decide whether a woman's reproductive role is more important to herself and her family than her economic role. Congress has left this choice to the woman as hers to make.

The judgment of the Court of Appeals is reversed and the case is remanded for further proceedings consistent with this opinion.Study Questions

Study Questions

1. Was the fetal protection policy a form of sex discrimination against women?

2. How did Johnson Controls, Inc., treat men who were exposed to hazards? If a serious difference existed between how the corporation treated men and women facing hazards, does that show sexism?

3. Shouldn't women have reproductive freedom over their bodies? What moral principles would support such freedom? Does this freedom depend on whether the fetus is a person with all the rights any person has, including a right to life?

4. What would libertarianism say about the fetal protection policy? Do libertarians see the job as initially belonging to the employer or the employee? Would libertarianism allow the employer to put *any* conditions the employer wanted in the contract offered to an employee?

38

Has the Women's Movement Been Disastrous?: A *Firing Line* Debate

Resolved: The Women's Movement Has Been Disastrous

Moderator: Michael Kinsley

For the resolution:
William F. Buckley Jr.
Arianna Huffington
Elizabeth Fox-Genovese
Helen Alvare

Against the resolution:
Betty Friedan
Karen Burstein
Camille Paglia
Kathryn Kolbert

Mr. Kinsley: Good evening. From the Marvin Theater at the George Washington University in Washington, D.C., welcome to a special *Firing Line* debate on what used to be called "the woman question." The official wording of tonight's debate topic, composed by William F. Buckley for maximum fairness and balance, is "Resolved: The Women's Movement Has Been Disastrous." [applause]

It has been more than 30 years since Betty Friedan, who is captain of tonight's opposition team, published her seminal book, *The Feminine Mystique.* That book is widely credited or blamed for launching what became the modern feminist or women's movement. A generation later, has that movement been a success or a failure? On the one hand, opportunities for women have blossomed. Women now sit as governors, senators, members of the Supreme Court in numbers that were unimaginable in 1963. On the other hand, the American family is widely regarded as being in trouble, and some people blame attitudes promoted by the women's movement for that. So on

This is a transcript of the *Firing Line* program taped December 7, 1994, at George Washington University, Washington, D.C., aired on PBS December 23, 1994. *Firing Line* is produced and directed by Warren Steibel. Reprinted by permission.

the one hand, Ruth Bader Ginsburg; on the other hand, Roseanne. Those are the parameters of tonight's debate. Let's welcome tonight's debaters. [applause]

Captain of the affirmative team—and isn't it amazing that he is always on the affirmative side somehow? [laughter]—is William F. Buckley Jr., the patriarch, if I may call him that, of both *Firing Line* and *The National Review.* [applause] Something about Mr. Buckley sets him apart from the rest of tonight's debaters, but I can't quite put my finger on what that is. [laughter] Must be his tie is crooked. Perhaps that's it. Mr. Buckley, of course, has special insights on the thoughts and needs of women, being married to one, but I hope he won't press this advantage unfairly tonight.

Arianna Stassinopoulos Huffington honed her debating techniques as president of the Cambridge Union, the famous debating society at Cambridge University in England. She is the author of several books, including best-selling biographies of Maria Callas and Pablo Picasso. Her first book, *The Female Woman,* was an attack on feminist extremism. Since she is on the antifeminist side tonight, I guess it's okay to mention her husband. He is Republican congressman Michael Huffington of California who lost the Senate race last month to Dianne Feinstein. [laughter/applause] I don't know whether they're cheering Arianna or cheering that Michael lost the race. We'll find out.

Elizabeth Fox-Genovese is a professor at Emory University and founding director there of the Institute for Women's Studies. Her books include one entitled *Feminism without Illusion* and a new one to be published next year entitled *Revolt against Children,* and I take it that title is a description, not a recommendation. [laughter]

The final member of the affirmative team is Helen Alvare. Ms. Alvare is director of planning and information on pro-life activities for the National Conference of Catholic Bishops. She is also an attorney and has a masters degree in systematic theology, which should come in handy tonight. [applause] A profile of Ms. Alvare in *The New York Times* a few years ago said she has "a readiness to acknowledge a debt to feminism and liberal views." We'll see if that comes in handy tonight.

Captain of the opposition team tonight is Betty Friedan herself, the godmother of modern feminism. [applause] Not only is she the author of *The Feminine Mystique,* published in 1963, she is also the founder of the National Organization for Women and the National Women's Political Caucus. Oh, come on, no hissing. [applause] Her latest book, *The Fountain of Age*, addresses the role of older people in our society, a topic Mr. Buckley perhaps can relate to more than Ms. Friedan's writings on feminism. [laughter]

Judge Karen Burstein was the Democratic candidate for New York State attorney general in last month's election. She lost, so perhaps she and Arianna Huffington can console each other after the program. Before making that race, Ms. Burstein was family court judge in Brooklyn, she also served as auditor general of New York City and as president of the New York State Civil Service Commission. [applause]

Camille Paglia is—well, where to start? According to her latest book, entitled *Vamps and Tramps*, she is in her own words, "a parallel phenomenon to Rush Lim-baugh and Ross Perot, who suffers from raging egomania and a volatile comic persona." Sounds perfect for a *Firing Line* debate, wouldn't you say? Ms. Paglia is a writer and controversialist on almost any subject you can name and a professor at the University of the Arts in Philadelphia. She is neither a candidate nor married to a candidate for political office as far as we know. [laughter]

Finally on the opposition team is Kathryn Kolbert, probably America's best known leading attorney on abortion rights. She argued the most recent abortion case, *Planned Parenthood v. Casey*, in the Supreme Court a couple of years ago. Ms. Kolbert is founder and vice president of the Center for Reproductive Law and Policy. Before that she was for many years a reproductive freedom attorney for the American Civil Liberties Union. And I have to add, Kitty Kolbert and I went to high school together and I haven't seen her—never-mind since when. [applause]

Those are tonight's teams. My name is Mike Kinsley. Ordinarily I work at CNN's *Crossfire*, but tonight I wield the gavel in these more elevated surroundings. Gentlepersons, start your engines. I now call upon Mr. Buckley to propose tonight's motion. [applause]

Mr. Buckley: Mr. Chairman, ladies and gentlemen. Twenty-four years ago Germaine Greer was retained by the Cambridge Union to debate with me on some aspects of the women's movement. She insisted that I formulate the resolution, which I attempted to do from this side of the Atlantic, using what was then known as Western Union. The trouble was that she rejected my first three proposals on the grounds that they were, if I remember, stupid, asinine, something

similar for the third. The telephone call from the president of the union was now desperate. The BBC, which was filming the encounter, needed to know the resolution before noon the next day, when their guide went out to print. I sat down at the typewriter and typed out, "Resolved: Give Them an Inch and They'll Take a Mile." But thank God, I was smart enough to say no to myself. No, no, we don't play those games with Germaine Greer. So disconsolately I moved in the direction she had made it clear, however oblique her communication, she wanted to go. I gave her, "Resolved: The Women's Movement Is a Failure." She loved it. Absolutely certain that she would win any resolution so incautiously formulated. And I knew she should win it, not only because it is almost impossible to contend that the women's movement is a total failure, but because her considerable wit and learning would profitably scorn anyone who ventured, let alone argued, the opposite. Yet here we are contending with this distinguished panel on the resolution that the women's movement isn't a failure, but that it is a disaster. [applause] I will contend—and perhaps my colleagues will go along, that there is a difference: The women's movement has accomplished certain goals encouraged by sensible people, and yet at the same time it is a disaster, even as one might argue that the civil rights movement has accomplished a great deal, yet agree with such as Professor Sowell that from certain perspectives with crime, illegitimacy, ethnic hostility, is also a disaster. Well, how so? Inevitably one thinks of the most conspicuous symbols of a disaster. Such a symbol is, of course, political correctness. I have in my briefcase, Mr. Chairman, an article by Phyllis Schlafly. She is the godmother of the anti-feminist movement. We are careful tonight to identify the women's movement not with such as Clare Booth Luce, who was a feminist but despised the movement's excesses, but with such as my old friend Betty Friedan, the founder of the National Organization for Women, whose idea of a perfect culmination of feminism would be when the commandant of the Citadel announced a school holiday to celebrate her abortion. [laughter] But consider the far reaches of the women's movement and its effect on people as preternaturally normal as Mrs. Schlafly. In a published essay in *Current Events* last month, she used the following sentence: "Feminism has no happy role and can boast of almost no legislative victories. Its ideology is still and its spokespersons are bitter." Its what are bitter? Its spokespersons. Now if you are not disrupted by the word "spokesperson" used in place of the simple word "spokesman," denoting someone whether male or female who speaks for a collectivity, then the assault on your ear is nothing less than disastrous. But no one is more eloquent on the subject of PC than Professor Paglia. If the search for so-called gender-neutral language causes you to refer to first-year college students as "freshpersons" and to bridle at the sentence "Man is born to be free," then that is truly a disastrous turn against the laws of tradition and euphony. Yet it is so. Even in quarters that would squirm at the least liberty taken with the Bill of Rights, which no longer protects traditional usage, women should indeed and obviously be free to engage in any pursuit desired, but where did we get the conviction that to admit a woman into The Citadel is to augment freedom even as it denies to men the right to seek single-sex military education. Is the women's movement properly celebrating the first woman fighter pilot killed in a training accident on an aircraft carrier? Is the women's movement reduced to enthusiasm for the right to abort a fetus? The movement that in its devotion to choice refuses even to consider any possibility that the fetus deserves protection. I'm just about through. Subject ever so solemn, Mr. Chairman, but they're spoken in my case as the only male on the positive team, but I am not, so to speak, here as a former slaveholder feigning enthusiasm for the Emancipation Proclamation. In my lifetime in the company of my mother and my teachers and six sisters, the very idea that women should not have the freedoms of the free society simply did not occur to my father or my three brothers. Nothing else was even conceivable. But we did not think that parity should lead to the indistinction now everywhere urged, symbolized by the raw fear of using the word "spokesman" or "mankind" to denote thoughts entirely pure and free of sexual abuse. It is because of the excesses of the movement, Mr. Chairman, that we conclude that what began as the affirmation of rights became instead the nightmare we now designate as a disaster.

Kinsley: Thank you, Mr. Buckley. [applause] Ms. Friedan. [applause] Betty Friedan will now oppose the motion.

Ms. Friedan: Well, I cannot take the women's movement for equality as a joke. It has been perhaps the most life-affirming, life-opening development of modern democracy. It has been perhaps the most important movement that has changed people's lives for the better—women, men, and children—of this last half of the 20th century. I am not the godmother. I am sometimes called the mother of the women's movement. My book, *The Feminine Mystique*, in 1963 broke through the image of women that was absolutely the only image of women in those years after World War II. Women defined only in sexual relation to man, only as wife, mother, sex object, housewife, server of physical needs to husband, children, home. Never as a person defining herself by her own actions in society. And this image, fed to us by the mass media—television was beginning then—given new guise for old prejudices by Freudian thought that had hit these shores, bolstered by the return of the GIs from the war and women—Rosie the Riveter—left the jobs, and they were home making up for lost time in the Depression and the war, having the children. And war industry needed them as housewives to buy the appliances when they retooled out of war industry. But that image, which was obsolete, which did not enable women to take real control of their lives and use their possibilities in the last half of the 20th century in America, that image was so pervasive that it had blotted out of national memory 150 years of struggle for women's rights that ended with winning the vote the year before I was born. That image was so pervasive that I called it the problem that has no name when I heard from women—and if I was doing a group interview and they said the problem—and they said, "Well, I'm BJ's wife, I'm Junior and Janey's mommy, I'm a putter-on of diapers and server of meals, but who am I?" There was no name, though all sorts of things were blamed on women then, all sorts of problems. You know, not getting the kitchen sink clean enough, the husband's shirts ironed enough, the husband's ulcer, the children's bedwetting, her own lack of orgasms, but no word for a problem that had to do with woman as a person in society. And we had to break through that feminine mystique. And I feel awed that I was able to do that, with some combination of my good Smith education and my training in psychology and my experience as a journalist and my mother's frustration and the fact that I was fired from a newspaper job for being pregnant with my second child. But I really bought that feminine mystique—which I didn't call it back then—because it made women then feel guilty working outside the home, as if they were losing their femininity, undermining their husband's masculinity, neglecting the children. So I retreated to the housewife years and secretly, like secret drinking in the morning, freelanced for women's magazines, because I couldn't quite suppress the itch. But by putting a name to the problem and by saying women are people, no more and no less, and by figuring out how we had bought into this obsolete mystique, by taking women's experience seriously when it didn't fit the book, I was able with this little book—it wasn't so little then—I mean, to help women take their own experience seriously. And once we moved to the person-hood of women, which is what it was all about, then from that followed our claiming of our human and American birthright: equal opportunity in education and jobs, our own voice in the decisions of our destiny, in the decisions of society. [gavel] Oh dear, oh dear, oh dear. Well, in any event, it's not been a disaster. Look at the daughters today who have a whole world open to them that was not open to my generation. Look at the older women today, women in their 50s, 60s, 70s, their mental health used to decline precipitously every decade after 20, American women, and drastically after 40 compared to men. In my new book, *The Fountain of Age,* I give the evidence [gavel]—I give the evidence—that American women today, because they have more control over their lives and they have larger, more complex lives, their mental health is as good in their 50s and 60s as younger women in their 20s and 30s and this improvement has happened with women but not with men.

Kinsley: The producer's mental health is declining. Thank you very much. [applause] I think henceforth we will impose a rule: Only one book plug per speech. Arianna Huffington and Camille Paglia, please ascend the podium, and Arianna Huffington has a minute-and-a-half to make an opening remark.

Ms. Huffington: The last time I took part in a *Firing Line* debate was 24 years ago at the Cambridge Union. I was speaking on the side of Ken Galbraith against Bill Buckley. And ever since I have been praying to God to speak on the same side as Bill Buckley. [laughter] And finally tonight God has granted me— She has granted me this opportunity. [laughter] Thirty years ago Betty Friedan launched the women's movement with *The Feminine Mystique* at the same time that Lyndon Johnson launched the Great Society. Thirty years later we can look back and say that both the women's movement and the Great Society were spectacular disasters. [applause] They maintained the big lie that government, the federal father up in the sky, is going to take care of all social disputes and kiss away every economic boo-boo. They contributed to the breakup of the American family and they also contributed to the politicization of American life. Thirty years later to look around, the divorce rate has tripled, illegitimacy among teenagers has gone up 400 percent, violence against women,

rape, are worse than ever. So what has happened? What has happened to that marvelous social experiment that so completely failed? What has happened, as some might argue on this side of the aisle, is that somewhere along the way, the women's movement went wrong. Well, I am arguing that the women's movement was born wrong. It was born on the wrong side of the ideological tracks and it was born on the wrong side of history. It was born on the wrong side of history, as I argued in my first book, *The Female Woman,* 20 years ago, because it glamorized, it idealized the masculine realm. It idealized what it is like to have power, success, to make it in the world. And therefore it ignored what today we need more than ever—the feminine role of soul, spirit, compassion, heart, and empathy. [gavel] Thank you. [applause]

Kinsley: Don't go away. Thank you very much. Ms. Paglia. You have a minute-and-a-half to make an opening remark.

Ms. Paglia: I am very honored to be here in the presence of Betty Friedan, who indeed changed history. And I am known as someone who has many deep criticisms of the women's movement, but what I have constantly said is that if we could return to what Betty Friedan was saying at the beginning, we would be on the right track. I was born in 1947 into that horrible, repressive domestic era of the 1950s that Betty Friedan ended with her book *The Feminine Mystique,* and I feel that my generation of the '60s went through—there were many, many excesses that we committed—but essentially feminism remains one of the great progressive reform movements of the last 200 years. It is analogous to the abolition of slavery, to the abolition of child labor, and so on. Just as Mr. Buckley would not want to abolish Catholicism because of the excesses of certain fanatics, so must we not attribute to feminism the excesses of various neurotics and incompetents who have been swept into it underneath the table, as it were. For me, I believe that feminism is about equal opportunity for women and men in society, but I do agree that certain members of the movement have neglected areas outside the social realm, but this is simply part of what we must do to rectify feminism—a kind of narrow little steering thing to bring it back on track, but I remain 100 percent committed to this movement which has liberated women. Women will never go back in the closet again. [applause]

Kinsley: Thank you. Don't go away. Arianna Huffington, you now interrogate Camille Paglia.

Huffington: Camille, you have argued very eloquently that there are two realms in culture—the

Apollonian and the Dionysian, the rational and the intuitive, the spiritual, whatever word you want to apply to that. And yet, the women's movement has exclusively glorified the rational, the masculine. And whatever the result of that, however glorious that may have been in the past, wouldn't you consider the possibility that right now our culture needs more than anything to rediscover the spiritual, the intuitive, the emotional—all qualities that are very identified with the feminine?

Paglia: Well, Arianna, I totally agree with that, but you see, the women's movement is actually split. There is one part of the movement which glorifies achievement in the social realm, the woman with the attache case as the ultimate human person. I too have great disagreement with that. But there is another part of the movement, a separatist part, that glorifies the goddess and the irrational and the intuitive. So actually there is a kind of chaos, I think, in the movement for the last 15 years or so, and we need much more dialogue, we need much more discourse of a rational kind. But I agree with you, there are serious flaws in the current Western idolatry of the career woman.

Huffington: But even tonight, as Betty Friedan was giving her opening statement, she idealized work, she idealized the liberation of the woman from home as though what the woman was liberated into was this glamorous nine-to-five existence, and the idea of women not being as depressed as they were is absolutely pathetic. There are more women on Prozac, there are more women on Valium then there have ever been. [laughter] They may be less depressed because they are on so many drugs. [laughter/applause].

Paglia: Well, I agree with you, Arianna, that in point of fact, certain elements in the women's movement have gone too far and there has been a kind of denigration of the role of woman and mother. I agree with that. But feminism at its best is all about options. When I was growing up in the 1950s, I was the only young girl even dreaming of a career. It was assumed that you had to date, you had to marry. It was a horrible, repressive, totalitarian regime in America at that time. I think at that point you were in your native Greece and not in America. [laughter] But I remember—

Huffington: Which is a very liberated country, yes.

Paglia: Correct, and I am often saying that we need a little more of the sort of Mediterranean woman's moxie into the Anglo Saxon women's movement.

Huffington: Let's move to another subject for a minute. You have identified yourself as a Clinton Democrat. You were once in favor of the Clinton health care bill and you are proud of that—well, maybe less proud now than you were then, but nevertheless you are public about it. [laughter] The whole women's movement has been identified with this big government mentality. They do look to big government constantly to solve women's problems despite the amazing failures of big government. The definition of insanity is to keep doing the same thing again and again, expecting different results. I would say this is also a definitions of the women's movement, would you agree? [applause]

Paglia: Arianna, I agree with you that there has been an excessive partisanship on the part of many women in the feminist movement. I myself am a Clinton Democrat; I look forward to voting for Clinton again. However, despite all—[laughter/applause/boos] But I want George Stephanopolous fired immediately. I want the whole White House staff fired. [laughter/applause] But I do feel that there should be room in feminism for Republican women and for pro-life women as well, I agree. [applause] But those have been errors of the leadership. Again, we cannot dismiss the entire women's movement because of errors of the leadership.

Huffington: You have just demonstrated one of the main cornerstones of the women's movement, which is blame. Clinton is okay; his staff is at fault. You know, let's fire everybody at the White House; Clinton is okay. [laughter] The same thing, you know, the whole women's movement's mentality is always that somebody else is to blame. It's never the women themselves. If it's date rape, it's never anything the woman did, and you yourself have argued that brilliantly. [boos/applause] I would really like to ask you right now to do something which maybe has never happened before on *Firing Line,* but you always like to make news, and this is to cross over to our side. [laughter/applause] If nothing else, wouldn't you like to see the look on Michael Kinsley's face? [laughter]

Kinsley: I'd have to tear up my program here.

Paglia: Unfortunately I cannot because the resolution says "The women's movement has been a disaster," and I feel the women's movement, despite many errors, despite many excesses, is still an overwhelming success. [applause]

Kinsley: All right. On that note, if you're not going to cross over to the other side, you can start interrogating the other side.

Paglia: Arianna, I could ask you the same thing. Why aren't you on this side? Because in your book on Picasso you took a tack which I have been critical of the feminist leadership for taking, that is, you say that we cannot take Picasso seriously as a great artist because of the way he treated women in everyday life. That position seems so doctrinaire feminist; how can you defend that and yet be on that side.

Huffington: Well. I am sure you haven't read my book, because that is not exactly what I said. [laughter] What I said is much worse. [laughter] I said that Picasso, although a great genius, was not one of the greatest artists who ever lived, not just because of the way he treated women in life and in art, but because of the way he denied the existence of something transcendent, because of the way he was unable to give us a glimpse of the light through the darkness. And what I argued is that all great artists, whether Shakespeare or Mozart or anybody you would care to mention, even as they exposed the darkness, they were also able to give us a glimpse to the light. And that's really one of my problems with the women's movement as well, because it's a very secular movement. And I personally do not believe that there can be ultimately important, profound solutions to our problems without reconnecting with God, with the divine and with the spiritual element in our lives. [applause]

Paglia: But Arianna, there's an enormous part of the women's movement in America that is constantly talking about spiritual values. Unfortunately it's a big mess intellectually. It's one of the areas of feminism that I'm trying to clean up. To me it's often a big pile of manure. [laughter] But it is a whole wing— a very strong wing—associated with Mary Daly and so on. It is extraordinarily separatist. It involves often white witchcraft and worship of the goddess of nature and it is a kind of—

Huffington: White witchcraft is not my idea of spirituality, incidentally.

Paglia: Well, it is a vision of God as She. Surely you realize that a lot of these reforms of the language of the Bible, which I totally oppose on historical grounds, the rewriting of the language of the Bible so that there are gender-neutral phraseology and so on, that's coming from the spiritual wing of feminism. So I feel that you are blaming feminism for something—In fact this is one of the most dominant wings within it.

Huffington: Well, certainly not in my experience and certainly not in the way that the women's movement is perceived. You yourself have sort of described yourself as an atheist. I don't know whether you still have that option or not; I know your opinions tend

to change every week. [laughter] But what matters here for me is the recognition that what our culture is missing more than anything is that element of the spiritual. Because ultimately that's where our caring for each other comes from. When the Founding Fathers created this country, when the Constitution was first written, at the heart of it is that belief that there is a God, that there is something larger than ourselves, and that that's what ultimately unites us. And I believe that without rediscovering that force of caring for others, without moving beyond our own self-centeredness, which dominates the women's movement, we will never be able to solve the so-called women's problems, and even more importantly, we will never be able to solve the dramatic problems that we're facing in our culture. [applause]

Paglia: Well, Arianna, in saying that I change my ideas every week, you too have demonstrated that you have read nothing of my work, since *Sexual Personae* is all about the history of religion and argues in fact that art began as religion. And everywhere in my work I have argued, despite the fact that I am an atheist, that the true multiculturalism, the true reform of education, will be one based on comparative religion, on all the great religions of the world.

Kinsley: Is that a question?

Paglia: No, I'm just putting her in her place. [laughter]

Kinsley: All right. Keep on asking questions.

Paglia: Isn't she—I'm still asking her.

Kinsley: You're asking her, yes.

Paglia: All right. I would have to ask you, Arianna, what exactly is your direct or practical experiences of the American women's movement that enables you to make these judgments of it?

Huffington: I have lived in this country since 1980; before that for 12 years I lived in England. I wrote a book on the women's movement. And after I wrote that book in 1973, I decided I would never read or write another word about the women's movement for a very long time. Now this has given me the opportunity to revisit the women's movement and to also affirm the wisdom of my decision not to speak or write about it for over 20 years. [laughter] Because frankly, I don't believe that that movement, when you actually examine what is achieved, achieved things that are really fundamentally important to women. When you look at the way that so many pathetic women, like Gloria Steinem, are wandering around unhappy [laughter/applause/boos] depressed, trying to look 20 when they are over 60, unable to accept that they are older, [gavel] desperately trying to pretend they never wanted to marry a man who didn't want to marry them [gavel], desperately trying to pretend they never wanted a baby. You know, this is the kind of pathetic demonstration of the poster child of the feminist movement, still the same as it was 30 years ago. [gavel] [applause]

Kinsley: Thank you very much. Thank you very much, both of you. Your time is up. You're free. Thank you very much. Elizabeth Fox-Genovese, it's your chance to make an opening statement. [applause]

Ms. Fox-Genovese: It certainly is a measure of the complexity of what's going on with the women's movement these days that I find myself on the side I am in this debate. Let's start with the question: Which wom-en's movement and whose wom-en's movement? For years I have counted myself an unswerving supporter of the movement for women's formal equality in society. I have no desire to return to a world in which a married woman cannot get credit in her own name or a woman cannot get the same pay as a man for equal work. [applause] By the same token, I am not much interested in statist interventions to ensure that a woman gets the same pay as a man for different and unequal work. This is the problem we are confronting. If we were indeed talking about the movement that Betty Friedan had launched, I would be wholeheartedly on that side. That is not the movement we are talking about since it has been superseded by another women's movement, which means that it is the women's movement of today, not the women's movement of the past that I regard as a disaster and which has landed me on this side I am on. [applause]

Kinsley: Thank you very much. Does someone have a question for the professor?

Friedan: Professor, I have read some of your work on Southern women, and it's brilliant work. And I want to remind you that if there had not been a modern women's movement, the whole contribution of people like you, the whole study of women's history—women had been virtually blotted out of history, of the Civil War, of the history of the South, which is your specialty—and women like yourself, who are making enormous contributions now in every field—in every field—that has been made possible by the modern women's movement. Further, I think you would have to agree that the wom-en's movement for equality, which is in the society now—which is in the society now—which has made it possible for your students to aspire the way they do has enormous diversity you could not have now that the great majority of Americans identify with the gen-

eral movement to equality, even if they don't always call themselves feminists—you couldn't have a movement taking in so many women and have only one voice. The diversity of voices—My voice is still there, and the major thrust of the women's movement for equality as I helped organize it is still the basis of it. There are a lot of diverse new voices and they argue and they are opposed, and I am opposed to some of it, and I think some of it is silly and I think some of it is diversionary.

Kinsley: Okay.

Friedan: But the basic movement for equality—Wouldn't you agree? [laughter]

Kinsley: That is a question.

Fox-Genovese: That is a question. I do agree on the movement for formal equality. What I do not agree with is that the women's movement, having discovered that formal equality is not enough, is going to change the entire world in order to engineer a substantive equality. Furthermore, I would add on this score, elite women have done extremely well—upscale women. I have benefited inordinately, as have all of us. We are not typical. And as we have done better, other women have done worse. Today the typical working woman is a mother and the typical mother is a working woman, and the official feminist movement has nothing to say serious about the relation between taking care of children and enjoying and benefiting from work, the balancing—

Ms. Burstein: I—

Fox-Genovese: —of career, and—

Burstein: Don't you think that's tendentious? The truth of the matter is that it's the women's movement that has addressed itself in large measure to questions like: Do you share responsibility for raising children? What do you do in terms of providing for safe spaces for children when people have to work? It's the women's movement that said something is really desperately wrong when women are marginalized in our economy and therefore don't have the kinds of resources they need as they get older to be able to save themselves indignity. I mean, when I talk about the women's movement, I mean women like you and like me and the woman here and the women over there, who regardless of whether they belong to the National Organization for Women or some other, you know, some other organization of that kind, still speak out of their real experience. I mean that was the genius of Betty's book. What she said is, Look, you know—And Emma Goldman said it too. Equal rights and the right to vote are all very good in their way, but true emancipation begins in a woman's soul. And you don't believe what you're saying here about its being a disaster. What you believe is that some positions that have been taken by some parts of this movement are ill-founded, unwise, and ultimately counterproductive, but a lot has been done that's been important, and you've benefited from it and so have I. [applause]

Ms. Kolbert: I think it's time we make the invitation to come to this side of the table?

Fox-Genovese: The most successful dodge of the women's movement has been that each of us has our own opinion, that it doesn't really speak for any of us, that there are multiple feminisms and we all know that we all agree because we all benefit from it. Well, this is enough of that. There are a series of women's organizations that with the help of the media are invariably consulted on all important issues and are taken to be the women's movement. It is taken to be disrespectful, unsisterly, and frequently treasonous to challenge them in any way. Therefore, in private, Karen Burstein and Camille Paglia and all the rest of us have our own private modifications of the official line. When Felice Schwartz proposed *The Mommy Track* and when Betty Friedan wrote *The Second Stage*, they were trashed by the official women's movement. Shared parent-ing assumes you've got a father at home. Daycare assumes that we know that it is better for children to be out of their home than with one of their parents. The list could go on. I don't want to use up other people's time. But it simply is not honest to claim that the women's movement has seriously engaged the issues that are of most concern [gavel] to American women and men. These are all of our top priorities. [gavel] [applause]

Kinsley: Thank you very much. Judge Burstein. Judge Burstein. Judge Burstein, it's your turn. It's your turn. You have a chance to make an opening remark.

Burstein: How fortuitous.

Kinsley: It looks like you have something to say too.

Burstein: Well, what I really want to say is that this is not the most useful mechanism for exploring this issue—

Kinsley: That's out of bounds, I'm afraid. [laughter]

Burstein: I'm sorry, but I feel compelled to say what I think is the truth, which is that, you know, there isn't such a thing as a monolithic women's movement. I was thinking about preparing for this—and I said this to Helen before I came—and I decided I'd better not because I would have had to bring, you know, the Book of Esther and *Lysistrata* and some of the works of the early suffragists, and Betty's work, and the work of Elizabeth Fox-Genovese and—So I think we should start with the proposition that it is impossible to say that the women's movement has been a disaster because women are in movement and in a lot of ways what they have been able to do is experience themselves as full human beings, and they have been able to have a voice. And it becomes critical for them to have a voice because they are part of the human race, and unless their voice is able to—Unless that voice exists, what happens is that the dialogue is just too shrunken, it's too little, it doesn't get to these questions. And the truth is that these matters, for example—matters about what we will do with our children—these questions about how do we make relationships that are meaningful and continuing, and how do we connect in community? These are ideas that aren't better for the most part in this last period of time. I don't think it's a function of, you know, gender; I think it's a function of socialization, have been better addressed, more generally addressed by women. [gavel] And if there is something to be taken from this, it is in fact that absent that voice, there would be a deafening silence on these issues. [gavel]

Kinsley: Don't go away. Don't go away. [applause] Helen Alvare.

Ms. Alvare: You told me before that the women's movement is addressing the questions that actually do concern women today, such as how to combine the divergence of work of family at the same time. First I would agree with Professor Fox-Genovese, that there is such a thing as a women's movement that is most regularly consulted by the press, taken to be the women's movement. And they in fact ran a program on this at a Boston convention a few years ago and had 15 women show up. If it really was the case that addressing that central problem, what women really want to hear about today was being done, then why isn't the question that we have achieved abortion on demand for nine months for any reason as the law of the land and you still can't get child support if you are a woman who has custody of your children. [applause]

Burstein: Helen, I think the important thing is that we shouldn't confuse what the media determines, you know, constitutes a movement or an activity with what actually happens in people's lives and the kinds of questions that are addressed by people and the kinds of issues that are brought to consciousness as a function of their presence. And so let me tell you very concretely that when I was a legislator in 1972, three women for the first time sat in the New York State Senate—before this there had never been more than one. And when we came to the legislature—we were Democrats on the Senate side; on the assembly there were Republicans and conservative women—for the first time we had on the agenda child support enforcement legislation. For the first time we had full financial disclosure in divorce actions. For the first time we had some pregnancy disability coverage.

Alvare: But individual examples of this do not make the national trend. The national trend is opposite that.

Burstein: Helen, the fact is that the national trend is to the extent that women begin to enter these places of power—for example, the legislature or the Congress or even the United States Supreme Court—questions that otherwise were not even seen as critical ones begin in fact to be discussed. [applause] Now wait—

Alvare: That still doesn't—

Burstein: We don't have enough, Helen.

Alvare: —answer the question why we have all—

Burstein: We don't have enough, Helen.

Alvare: —of abortion and very little of child support—

Burstein: Helen.

Alvare: —in 26 years after—

Burstein: Helen.

Alvare: —NOW's founding.

Burstein: Helen. Helen, the fact of the matter is that there are very—You know, I said when we got into the legislature all of a sudden these issues got addressed. They didn't get solved, because there were only three of us out of 60. [laughter/applause]

Kinsley: Ms. Huffington. Ms. Huf-fington. Arianna, do you have any questions?

Huffington: Karen, I think it is incredible that you really still believe that all problems are going to be solved if only the correct legislation is passed. We have been passing the right legislation for years now, and every single cultural indicator has been getting worse, from violent crime to divorce statistics, to everything you want to look at. So on what is your faith in legislative solutions to social problems based? [applause]

Burstein: Well, it's a very good question. If that's what I'd said, you would really put me right up against the wall, Arianna. But the truth of the matter is, I didn't say that my belief is that everything should be resolved by legislation. I simply said to you that there were matters of the kind that Helen addressed

that got addressed in legislatures because women were there. I will say that legislation is sometimes necessary. I'm sure you would agree with me in that regard. Certainly—I know—I assume you're a citizen now and you like to vote. You wouldn't have been able to if we hadn't had a change in our Constitution. That came out of the women's movement. [applause]

Huffington: I'm not clear how my voting came out of the women's movement. I missed that. [laughter/boos]

Burstein: Arianna, this is the problem about coming to the country 14 years ago. [laughter/applause] You see, you didn't go to school with all of us and you didn't learn about the early suffragists and you didn't learn about the first World War and the impact that it had on women's self-perception, and the capacity that women then had—[hissinggovernmentgavel] [to audience] Now that's very productive.

Huffington: You know what is fascinating here? If she was a conservative making comments like that about somebody just because I am an immigrant, just because I am a naturalized American—[applause]

Burstein: Arianna—

Huffington: —there would have been—

Burstein: Arianna. Arianna. You know—

Huffington: No. No, one second. But because—

Burstein: Arianna, you know—

Huffington: But because she is liberal she can say anything. I've thought about this.

Friedan: [slams book on table] You—

Huffington: I'm sorry, Betty. Shut up, shut up. I'm talking. [laughter/applause]

Burstein: Arianna, Arianna. Arianna, let me add this.

Huffington: No, just one second. Just one second. I want you to let me finish.

Burstein: I will let you finish.

Huffington: Just because I was not born in this country, just because I went to school at Cambridge rather than here does not mean I have not studied. It does not mean that I have not—

Burstein: Well then—

Huffington: —learned about the women's movement, and to make that assumption is absolutely unbelievable, and you are only getting away with it just because you are a liberal. [laughter] If you were a conservative, you would not have gotten away with it. [laughter/applause]

Burstein: Arianna. Arianna, let me say something back to you. The truth is that I know that you are an extraordinarily intelligent person, and I know that you are also an extraordinarily educated person, so that when you said to me, I don't understand the relationship of the women's movement to the question of suffrage, I thought to myself: It can't be that she doesn't understand what is a historical fact. It must be that she doesn't know it. And therefore, rather than claim that it was a function of your not paying attention [laughter] to material that you could have learned, I thought I would give you a good excuse. [laughter/applause]

Kinsley: Thank you very much.

Burstein: Am I done?

Kinsley: You're all set. All right the only man here tonight on either side. Here is a chance for the four women on the opposing side to ask him a question. Kathryn Kolbert.

Kolbert: In your opening statement, you indicated that women participating in the military and women having the right to choose abortion were in some ways demeaning to them and therefore demonstrated that the movement was a disaster. But in fact, it is those very things—the fact that women can now equally participate with men in the military, have the same obligations and the same duties, as well as the same disadvantages as men that have led in many respects to changes in their ability to progress in other areas of the world. And similarly the right to choose abortion has meant that women have the ability to make child-bearing decisions both to choose abortion and—

Buckley: Is this a question about what I think?

Kolbert: —to choose family. The question I have for you is why can't—or why is it that real progress you denigrate and expect that change has to come so quickly that just because we haven't accomplished all of our goals—

Buckley: What's your question?

Kolbert: —it's been a disaster.

Kinsley: Her question is why do you assume that progress has to come right away and why do you denigrate all of their goals because not all of them have been achieved? That seems to be the question to me. [laughter/applause]

Kolbert: Yes, that's the question.

Buckley: Okay. That was a wonderful exercise in compression and I congratulate you on that.

Kinsley: I just repeated what she said.

Buckley: You of course transform—a favorite word of your movement—what I said. What I said was that so fanatical is the support for abortion in the women's

movement that no thought is permitted to be given to whether or not there might be certain rights that inhere in the fetus. I think it is at least a subject that can and ought to be discussed, but it isn't discussed. Nor in my judgment is serious attention given to whether it is appropriate for a woman to engage in trench warfare with bayonets and so on and so forth. Now it is considered an affront on the women's movement to suggest that a 19-year-old woman, or for that matter a 9-year-old woman to engage in jungle warfare using bayonets and—It makes me sound—God, Betty, are you that disgusted by what I am saying? [laughter] It makes me feel as if as though I am engaging in anti-feminist warfare to suggest that we should do the fighting and that you have enough responsibilities as it is. Now why is that not considered an open question by the women's movement? Why do you all want to go to The Citadel?

Kinsley: Betty Friedan.

Friedan: Well, you know, that women—I think very responsibly—when we demand equal rights and fight for equal rights and an equal voice, we have to accept equal responsibility and we cannot—My own position on that question was, I am very opposed, for instance,—

Buckley: This is a question?

Kinsley: Yes.

Friedan: —to nuclear warfare—

Buckley: These are the rules, aren't they?

Friedan: —or to women fighting—or men fighting—my sons or my daughter—in any unjust and unnecessary war—

Buckley: Oh, come on, come on.

Friedan: —which I think all war is today—

Buckley: We're not talking about whether—

Friedan: —but if there is such a thing—

Buckley: —this action is just or unjust.

Friedan: —as a just and necessary war—

Buckley: We're talking about whether—

Friedan: —women have the same responsibilities.

Buckley: —or not the women's movement has become so monolithic—

Friedan: We are not monolithic.

Buckley: —as not to permit serious questions on such matters as whether—

Burstein: Well, I'll—

Kinsley: Karen Burstein—

Burstein: —answer it. I mean, you know, I will tell you right now—

Buckley: You're not supposed to answer it.

Burstein: —I don't think a 90-year-old woman—

Buckley: You're supposed to ask a question.

Burstein: —should engage in trench warfare. [laughter/applause]

Kinsley: All right, Camille Paglia.

Burstein: I am pointing out to you, Bill. I know, I am going to ask you a question. The point is, Bill, if you make a straw person like that, I mean, obviously it becomes clear that it's entirely improper of anybody to, you know, believe what we believe, because it leads to the proposition that a 90 year old is going to be fighting in trench warfare. I want to go away from that for a moment. I want to ask you something that I thought was really interesting. Do you really think it's such a terrible thing to call a person a spokesperson? I understand it's offensive, but apparently Phyllis Schlafly has even adopted it. I got your point there. But do you really think that there is not a virtue in trying not to pretend that there is a generic in the English language for a species that has both men and women?

Kinsley: Okay.

Buckley: I think it is an index of a total perversion of taste and of a fanatical attention to details that are not only insignificant but absolutely unmusical in their consequences. [applause]

Kinsley: Camille Paglia. Let's get a question from Camille Paglia.

Buckley: A man sitting next to me in an airplane introduced himself to me—he was Haley Barbour—and he said—a liberal, by the way—he said—

Kinsley: Haley Barbour?

Buckley: "We used to refer to Congressperson Liz Holzperson." [laughter] It leads to that kind of—

Burstein: It should be Holtz-precipitous. You didn't even go—That's not what I asked you, Bill. What I asked you is: Is there no merit—Of course you can have an objection—

Kinsley: Quickly.

Burstein: —to particular words. But is there no merit, for example, to removing from us the assumption that every time you talk about a human being you should use the word "he"?

Kinsley: All right—

Burstein: Instead substitute for that the notion that occasionally you could use "she."

Buckley: No, what is objectionable is that you construe the use of "he" as offensive to women, in which case the entire English language [gavel] of the last thousand years becomes—[gavel]

Kinsley: No, I've got to cut you all off. [applause] Thank you very much. Betty Friedan, it's your turn to be interrogated by the affirmative team. You have to step into the torture chamber up here. [laughter] Elizabeth Fox-Genovese, would you like to ask a question of Betty Friedan?

Fox-Genovese: Oh, I would love to ask a question of Betty Friedan. The ones I'd really like to ask, however, I can't do in public. [laughter] No, because I wonder—very seriously I wonder—how you really feel about a movement that has moved so far from what you inaugurated? But I'll try another one.

Kinsley: I like that one.

Friedan: Yes, I'll answer. Every day I am stopped on the street by women of all ages, and often by men, in any town I go to in this country, and often in England as well, and they say, "It changed my life. It changed my whole life. And thank you." And I am very moved by that. And they mean by that not just my book *The Feminine Mystique*, but they mean the whole of the women's movement. And for me, the whole of the women's movement is what counts and what is open to my daughter and what will be open to my granddaughter if we are not pushed back, and what all these women are doing and what you are doing. And I have enormous awe almost that I have been able to be a part of that. Some of the derivatives that are going on today are silly—just silly. There can be a silliness about language. On the other hand, I mean, I can't believe that Bill Buckley, whom I have known since we were both kids, would try to claim that all of history has to be "he." There has been something added when Elizabeth Fox-Genovese adds a whole history of the Southern women that were ignored before in histories of the South. So how do I really feel? I feel proud and awed to have been a part of it. [laughter/applause]

Kinsley: Mr. Buckley.

Friedan: And I don't like the silliness. I don't like the silliness. I don't like the diversions.

Buckley: I would like to ask Betty how you react to the following sentence: "Our patriarchy requires violence or the subliminal threat of violence in order to maintain itself. The most dangerous situation for a woman is not an unknown man in the street or even the enemy, but a husband or lover in the isolation of their own home."

Friedan: Oh, please.

Buckley: That's Betty Friedan—not Betty Friedan.

Friedan: Not me. [Laughter]

Buckley: No, that's Gloria Steinem. Gloria Steinem.

Friedan: But I don't agree with everything Gloria Steinem says.

Buckley: Yes, but—

Friedan: She doesn't agree with everything I say. I don't like extremist statements like that.

Buckley: But she has—

Friedan: I think the relationship between woman and man—

Buckley: She is pretty universally acknowledged as a—

Friedan: —is much more complex than that.

Buckley: She is acknowledged as a leader in your movement.

Friedan: I happen to love a lot of men too well.

Buckley: Okay, so you disavow that sentiment.

Friedan: I don't disavow the contribution of Gloria Steinem. I don't approve of that kind of statement. These, you know, sort of excessive, "Oh, sexual intercourse between woman and man is oppression of women." No. That's not—That's MacKinnon. I absolutely disavow that.

Buckley: But what—

Kinsley: Helen Alvare.

Alvare: Did you want to continue?

Buckley: I just wanted to say when people reach for spokespersons [laughter] of the movement, they think in terms of Gloria Steinem, do they not, so I don't think—

Friedan: There are lots of spokespersons.

Buckley: Not exclusively of her, but they think of her as highly qualified.

Friedan: As one of them, absolutely. She is one of them.

Buckley: And yet she is capable of saying we are a patriarchy in which the principal danger to a woman is from her lover or her husband.

Friedan: I don't know when she said that. But it was a little excessive, let's face it.

Kinsley: Helen Alvare.

Alvare: You made reference to the women's movement as life-affirming.

Friedan: Yes.

Alvare: And in part, about parts of women, I could agree. Unfortunately, as you yourself acknowledged in many newspaper reports over time, abortion has almost threatened to take over every other issue in the movement. How can a movement that says that some have no right to be born based on dependency, size, stage of development, disability—and I might remind you some of your sisters say it's okay to have sex selection abortion—how can such a movement call itself life-affirming when the underlying principle is disaffirmed? [applause]

Friedan: The right of women to choose to have chil-

dren is enormously life-affirmative. It has moved—

Alvare: But not for the child.

Friedan: —motherhood to a choice rather than a martyrdom. And it is enormously important. And if we had better sex education in our schools and not what we have now in the reaction against it, I would hope that abortion wouldn't be necessary. I am not for abortion. I am for the right to choose. [applause]

Kinsley: Arianna Stassinopoulos. Ms. Huffington. Brief question, please.

Huffington: Betty, since sex education was introduced in schools and the distribution of condoms was made as available as it is now, abortions have gone dramatically up. So what kind of sex education do you have in mind? And you would consider the possibility of sex education that includes the connection between sexuality and ethics and morality and the connection also between sex and abstinence?

Kinsley: Okay. Go ahead.

Friedan: I don't know where your figures are, but again, the United States, you know, is not the best nation to look at for models here. We have very strange attitudes about sex in this country. We have a lot of conflicting—[gavel] There's prudishness and so on and so forth. And in many European countries [gavel] where they don't have such attitudes, you know, where sex is a fact of life, [gavel] they don't have all the problems of the teenage pregnancy. [gavel]

Kinsley: Thank you very much, Ms. Friedan. [applause] Helen Alvare, your opportunity to make an opening statement.

Alvare: Many women are waking up today in beds made with linens sold to them by the feminism of the '70s—and they are not warm and cozy. On the surface women are seeing improvement in the respect accorded them in some cases, and we are grateful. But beneath the surface lies a disastrous notion of the nature of freedom that was a guiding premise to the women's movement, a notion that has infected some of her healthier offspring. It envisions freedom as freedom from the other, not for. Freedom of will-ism or the license to do anything, not freedom as the capacity to do the good. Freedom as if objective reality's natural law limits didn't exist. Exercising this freedom hurt women and the whole culture's commitment to the common good. The most disastrous effects were produced in the name of freedom of choice, legal abortion—the most prominent cause and greatest pitfall of '70s feminism. Its sad fallout are legion. It reaffirms the old sexist canard that women's biology is a disability, one men don't have; that the women's movement doesn't mean its central tenet, one need only be a human to deserve human respect. It treats women and children as enemies, privatizes reproduction so as to invite irresponsible behavior toward women and children, stigmatizes the project for women as violent and oppressive. Since women are more pro-life than men, it chases many women from a unified women's movement. The abortion obsession leaves most issues of most concern to women completely unaddressed, such as easing a balancing act between home and work. In conclusion, a woman's movement is necessary, but only one that promotes authentic freedom [gavel] which includes a respect for life. Seventies-style feminism did not. [applause]

Kinsley: Thank you very much. Don't go away. Camille Paglia.

Paglia: I totally agree with you. I speak from the position of abortion advocacy, but I agree with you that the media—the firm media—again I think as a libertarian—the media's liberal bias has to emphasize the strains of feminism that insist on abortion rights and that media has totally neglected any other voices which are pro-life. So again, let's not just blame the women's movement, let's blame the cant, the conventionality of the media over 20 years.

Alvare: At some point some of the women's movement organizations have to take responsibility—

Paglia: Helen.

Alvare: —for what they are saying and some of their leaders. [applause]

Paglia: Helen.

Alvare: And I came tonight—let me just finish—with a list of quotes from those leaders of the women's movement, particularly NOW since its founding, which have said, "Abortion is the sum and substance of what we are about. It's the core."

Kolbert: No.

Alvare: The most prominent feminist book on this says this.

Kolbert: No. Absolutely not.

Kinsley: Ms. Kolbert.

Kolbert: No. I think of course we have to go toward the issues which are under the greatest attack. Frankly, if the Catholic Church hadn't put $100 million into fighting against abortion, I wouldn't have to spend my lifetime in the courtroom defending rights that we won in 1973. [applause]

Alvare: Oh, if my budget were only Planned Parenthood's, we wouldn't—

Kolbert: I would love to turn—

Alvare: If I only had a fourth of Planned Parenthood's budget.

Kolbert: The reality is that the issue of abortion gets to the core of equality for women, because without the ability to make decisions either to terminate a pregnancy or to carry a pregnancy to term, you have no ability to function as an equal participant in society.

Alvare: By endorsing abortion—

Kolbert: And it is the attacks—it is the attacks of your church, it is the attacks of the government that has led us to have to make that a premier fight—

Alvare: Let me respond to that by—

Kolbert: —and thousands and thousands—

Alvare: —saying that that is a good end.

Kolbert: —of people have fought for that.

Alvare: The end we likely very much agree on. It's the means that the leaders of the women's movement have used, and when you use a bad means, even for a good end, the handle is more dangerous than the sword.

Kolbert: Well—

Alvare: It has degraded women and—

Kinsley: Karen.

Alvare: —it has degraded their children in the long run.

Paglia: But my dear—My dear, you defend the killing of doctors—

Alvare: No.

Paglia: —and the killing of women we condemn to go into a clinic to exercise their right to choose?

Alvare: We condemn the killing of doctors—

Kinsley: All right, all right.

Alvare: —as strongly, probably more strongly than any group ever. [applause]

Kinsley: Karen Burstein.

Paglia: Helen, but your movement is divided on that question, isn't it?

Burstein: I want to ask you something. I want to ask you this as a very specific question. If a woman—and I had this case in my court—A 14-year-old girl was raped by her stepfather and she became pregnant. Is it your conviction, is it your belief, that it is in fact essential in order to be consistently life-affirming, that that child at 14 should have borne that fetus to term, should have given birth to a child?

Alvare: A couple points in response. First, it's very common that advocates for abortion use the rape-incest argument even though Planned Parenthood's own statistics show it's less than one-half of one percent—

Burstein: It doesn't matter.

Alvare: —to make the whole case.

Burstein: I'm asking you specifically.

Alvare: I want to make that point. Secondarily, it is our position that a child conceived crack-addicted, disable, in rape, in a non-loving marriage, no matter what, once you start to break down the wall and say some lives are less worthy than others, you have some trouble there. [applause] That is not to say, however, that you don't address the pain that the woman is feeling. I am proud to say that the Catholic Church is the largest provider of social services to—

Burstein: Helen, a 14—

Alvare: —born women in the entire United States.

Burstein: A 14-year-old girl's—

Alvare: So our objective is to address both—

Burstein: —life is involved here too.

Alvare: Exactly. And you can never cure that rape. So what's the best you can do? You try to address—

Burstein: You can give that—

Alvare: —both lives at stake.

Burstein: Just a minute. You're taking nine months—

Alvare: Speak to women whose lives have been destroyed by abortion after rape—

Burstein: Helen, you—

Alvare: —and you might have a different sense about it. [applause] There are two sides.

Burstein: Helen, you know, I was—I will say one thing. You have now actually answered the question that you originally set. You said why is the women's movement so obsessive about abortion? Why does it, you know, drown every other issue out? And you've said why and Bill Buckley has said why isn't it possible to discuss the rights that fetuses might have? But the truth of the matter is that your position is equally as—

Alvare: My position is a consistent one. I can only be for women because I am also for all human life. The bumper sticker, "Feminism is the surprising notion women are human beings"—if you hold that true, then you cannot be a movement [gavel] that endorses the abortion of the dependent and the vulnerable. Thank you. [applause]

Kinsley: Thank you very much. Kathryn Kolbert. Here's your opportunity to make an opening statement.

Kolbert: I would. We've all sat around this evening and talked about a simple vision of the feminist movement—that women and men must be equal, they must have equal duties and rights, and that they must have the right to dream and have the opportunity to make those dreams a reality. That vision is one that has captivated millions of Americans and

has palpably changed their lives through the last 30 years. The problem is that as we mature as a movement—like any movement for social justice, whether it be the civil rights movement or the gay rights movement—many, many voices are affirmed. And the ability to blame women for the very progress that we have made because we haven't gone far enough begins to adopt the view that all women's attitudes, just because they are different, are not worthy of exploration. We have to stop that blame, because the very resolution that the women's movement exists and has changed the lives of Americans means that it is worthy of debate and continuing attention. When I was 14 years old I was in France with my parents, and I met a woman who had worked very hard in the French Underground. And she said to me, as a 14 year old: I can't understand you Americans; you want change overnight. You want change to have happened yesterday. [gavel] You want your issues to be resolved in three-minute sound bites. [gavel] This is a long struggle. We've got a long way to go. But don't blame us for not getting there fast enough. [applause]

Kinsley: That was your minute-and-a-half sound bite, Kitty. Don't go away. Who has a question? Helen. Helen Alvare.

Alvare: Arianna was to start off.

Kinsley: Arianna, go ahead.

Huffington: We're not blaming you for not getting there faster. We're blaming you for going in the wrong direction. [applause]

Kolbert: Well, I don't believe—

Huffington: Let me ask you the question I want to ask you. We are blaming you for excluding the spiritual dimension out of life and yet calling your movement life-affirming. How do you feel about that?

Kolbert: Well, I think that you have a very limited view of millions of American women if you believe that spirituality isn't a very important part of their life. [applause] The important part of this is that our spirituality comes in many, many different forms. It comes in those people who practice spirituality in other forms. It comes in those people who practice religion in the Catholic Church and other people who practice spirituality in other forms. And the point of freedom is that Americans must respect the differing views, whatever they may be. And the women's movement does that. I think that the problem is that you take one voice—And again, frankly I can't tell given the discussion today which voice you seem to be identifying, because all of us at this table have been those spokespersons, if you like, and all of you at different points in your life have been those spokespersons, and we have all said different things. But the point is we are diverse and that diversity makes us strong and that diversity has led to major changes in the lives of women.

Kinsley: Helen Alvare.

Alvare: Following up on Arianna's theme that it is not a question of speed but of substance, how do you explain actions like the ACLU, who was I believe your former employer before the new group, going into states like Maine and New York and filing lawsuits against state programs providing prenatal care for poor women because those programs didn't provide equal money for abortions? How do you explain that?

Kolbert: Helen, I don't think you understand those lawsuits. I actually brought those lawsuits, and I think what we were saying is, in the same way we have said all along, people have a right to the full range of reproduction health information. We don't believe in gag rules, like the Catholic Church. [applause]

Alvare: So abortion—

Kolbert: We believe that all kinds of information—

Alvare: —is just on the same moral plane as bringing a child to term and it should be funded with the exact same dollars—

Kolbert: No. I think that—Let me finish.

Alvare: —even if those women were denied prenatal care because you wanted to shut down the whole program—

Kolbert: No, we didn't—

Alvare: —because it didn't include abortion.

Kolbert: —ask for shutting down the whole program. What we asked for is that if state dollars are going to provide services—In the same way as I believe if your church is going to provide services at your hospitals and you bring people in from the public and you subsidize child-bearing, then you ought to give people the full range of options whether that be sterilization, whether that be contraception, whether that be sexuality education, whether that be abortion. That is, if you are in the arena, you ought to be neutral in that arena and—

Kinsley: Elizabeth Fox-Genovese.

Kolbert: —not discriminate on the basis of your choice. [applause]

Fox-Genovese: It seems to me that what you've just said points to the core of one problem, and I am not going to argue spirituality, but—

Kinsley: Thank you.

Kolbert: Thank you. [laughter] I don't want to argue spirituality.

Fox-Genovese: Why hasn't the movement come out—

Kolbert: Let me just say why I disagree with you. The women's movement was there in Congress pushing for child care legislation. We were the leading backers of the parental leave legislation. We have been there fighting for children's services. Who is manning those domestic violence centers and those shelters for battered women? [applause] It is the women's movement and, therefore, it is just totally absurd for you to believe that we don't believe in children. It is like believing that all women have bouffant hairstyles or wear army boots. It's just crazy. All of us have differing views. We believe in children. I myself am a mother. I believe in giving my children rights and opportunities, and that's the critical point. I want my daughter as well as my son to have equal opportunity to advancement in this society. [gavel]

Kinsley: All right, thank you very much. [applause] Mr. Buckley and Judge Burstein. It's your chance to interrogate each other, and Mr. Buckley starts.

Buckley: Your Honor, with—[laughter] She was a judge until quite recently.

Burstein: And a fair one at that.

Buckley: Intending to pursue the question of who speaks for the movement that some people honor—as begun by Betty Friedan—dishonor as having gone in the wrong direction, as Ms. Huffington has said. Let me ask you to comment on three statements made by leaders of the movement. Deborah Louis, president of the National Women's Studies Association, said, "According to the last March of Dimes report, domestic violence against pregnant women is now responsible for more birth defects than all other causes combined." Asked to comment on that, the head of the Boston Children's Hospital said that although severe battery may occasionally cause miscarriage, he has never once heard of battery as a significant cause of birth defects.

Burstein: Well, you know—

Buckley: You're just sorry about that last.

Burstein: No, no, no. No, what I want to say is that you people make statements that sometimes can't be supported.

Buckley: Okay.

Burstein: I, for example, remember—excuse me?— Phyllis Schlafly saying that domestic violence shelters were R&R for irritated housewives.

Buckley: And what did Hitler say? I mean, are we discussing statements by people we don't approve of?

Burstein: No, no, I am simply saying that there are people who make statements—

Buckley: Okay, yes, but—

Burstein: —that represent—

Buckley: —I am talking about representatives of the movement. Now, you heard about—

Burstein: But I believe—

Buckley: —the great Super Bowl scoop in which it was maintained that "40 percent more women will be battered on the day of the Super Bowl than any other day of the year." This was a statement that alarmed a lot of people, including football enthusiasts. So people monitored movements to hospitals and so on, and it was found there was no difference whatsoever. Yet that statement was made and is very widely available in the literature. Does that embarrass you? Well, obviously it does. Yes, okay. All we— [laughter]

Burstein: No, it doesn't embarrass me. That people make mistaken statements on both sides of every issue seems to me to be terribly irrelevant to the discourse—

Buckley: No, no, it's not irrelevant. We're trying to—

Burstein: —we're engaging in at this moment. [applause]

Buckley: You are for or against a movement according to who is leading the movement, right?

Burstein: But who made that statement?

Buckley: And if Mr. X is leading the movement and we don't think he is doing a good job, then our views of the movement are affected.

Burstein: But—

Buckley: Gloria Steinem says, "In this country alone about 150,000 females die of anorexia each year." So physicians were asked about that and one of them says well, he has had 1400 patients which he has treated in 10 years, four have died who had anorexia and they committed suicide.

Kinsley: Is that a question?

Buckley: No, this is a part of the compilation which I am asking—

Burstein: Bill, you know perfectly well—

Buckley: —Judge Burstein to comment on—

Burstein: —if I were to take some of the statements that you've made—

Buckley: —as to whether or not she—

Burstein: —you know, *God and Man at Yale*, [laughter/applause] or any of the mystery books—which I've enjoyed a great deal, I must say—that you've written, I am sure you would be embarrassed also.

Buckley: Well—

Burstein: My point is that they are hardly representative of hereof. And I think it is ridiculous for you to find three statements—

Buckley: No, no, no—

Burstein: —one of which is ostensibly from an unnamed person who has now become a leader of the movement—

Buckley: A movement is—

Burstein: —and say that this should doom anybody's respect for the movement.

Buckley: Karen, a movement is known by its spokespeople.

Burstein: We're going to convert you, Bill. [laughter] Before he is through he is going to begin to think that that's euphonious, you know. [laughter]

Buckley: And a movement becomes contaminated if it is understood in the public perspective as a movement that is dominated—as has been charged here by Professor Fox-Genovese—by people who are taking it in a direction that is not congruent with its original purposes. As much happened in some people's position with the civil rights movement. Do quotas define the civil rights movement? Well, there are a lot of people who don't think so. But to the extent that people who dominate the megaphones in that movement say that it does, we have to ask: Do they speak from authority?

Burstein: But the women's movement is rooted in women's lives. I think that's the most important thing we have to remember. And the fact that at any particular time some phrase or some statistic becomes bandied about, either correctly or incorrectly, should not for one minute incline us to misunderstand the power of this movement. I can't underline it enough. The truth of the matter is that in every group, every organized activity of humankind, there are excesses. That's just the nature of human beings. But the reality is that what women strive for, which is to be full human beings, to be full participants in our society, that striving is going to go on no matter, you know, who speaks at any particular moment.

Kinsley: Okay. Here's—

Burstein: That striving will continue and will ultimately triumph.

Kinsley: Here's your—Don't go away. Here's your chance—

Burstein: I'm not going.

Kinsley: —to ask questions of Mr. Buckley.

Burstein: I'm kind of fascinated by your statement that you grew up in a home in which it would be inconceivable that women be not full participants. But I think you must be aware that for long periods of time our laws in fact did exclude women from participation in a number of things—in their own property and management of that property, in their

management of their children, in the custodianship
of th... ...u think really that none of the
...ly as a function of women's
...having presence in legisla-

...ical arena are bad?
...ut I do think that it has been
...perspectives do change and
...ties, that weren't open to
...sister worked for Betty
...paper have opened up. But
...tion has gone so far as to
...ntaminate the movement
...under the circumstances
...isavowals of people who

...repared to do the same
...your side?
...tely. I do it all the time.

...ou what. I am prepared
...nsible, but that doesn't
...resolve to continue to
...men. Of course, I also
...en because as that old

...want now?
...of the women is the

...estion, doesn't she?
...juage, you're still on the attack.

Burstein: Oh, what I want is a question. I'm sorry.
You asked me back a question. The question I guess
is—the last question is this: It seems to me that you
will now admit you were wrong when you took the
other position against Germaine Greer, right?

Buckley: Oh, I knew I was wrong when I took it. It
was simply a gymnastic exercise to—

Burstein: I see. So I am glad to say then that it is a
possibility that 10 years from now, from the vantage
point of all of our achievements between now and
then, that this proposition that the women's movement—

Buckley: I agree, 10 years from now—

Burstein: —has been—what? an abysmal failure?—
may in fact have been a mistake.

Buckley: Ten years from now the movement may
be reformed.

Kinsley: All right. Thank you very much. [ap-
plause] Now it's Arianna Huffington's turn to be interrogated by the opposition team. Who's—Camille

Paglia is itching to ask a question.

Paglia: Arianna, you gave a litany of the cultural
ills in America at the present time, most of which I
think we would not disagree with—it was sort of the
rising crime rate or anxiety over crime, and excessive divorce rate, and so on. Why do you blame this
on the women's movement per se? Would it not make
more sense to look to broader social and economic
changes, perhaps of 200 years in length, from the agricultural era into industrialization—you know, from
a manufacturing-based economy to a service-sector
economy, and so on.

Huffington: I am not blaming them on the women's
movement. The wom-en's movement is only a contributing factor. Most important though is the fact
that the women's movement has nothing important
to say about those problems. Take the important question of rebuilding our communities. You mentioned
it as something very important. Take the important
question of revitalizing our values. The women's
movement is totally silent on these issues unless it is
hostile towards them. There are constant writings,
not to mention speeches, on the fact that voluntarism
is part of the past. That is part of the way women
used to be when they didn't have important nine-to-
five jobs and they had to go out and volunteer and
do charity work. All of that is denigrated, and yet
again and again you see that the only way to rebuild
communities is to recognize that problems are local
and they are going to have local solutions only when
the whole community comes together and when everybody, men and women, give of themselves beyond
their own self-centered existence. In all this the movement has nothing important to say.

Kinsley: Kathryn Kolbert.

Kolbert: Don't you think it's a little exaggerated to
believe that the women's movement has not used volunteers to run institutions that we've built over the
last 20 years?

Huffington: This is not the point I am making.

Kolbert: The movement is thousands of women in
this country who are volunteering daily in rape crisis centers, in battered women's shelters, in homes
for—in orphanages, my God. [laughter]—the new
place—we do lots of wonderful work, and I think
that it is absolutely naive to believe—or you haven't
left California in a long time—to believe that the rest
of us are not contributing to our society in lots of different ways. The point is, is it not, that we have the
ability not only to do volunteer work, but also to work
or to go to school or to function as equals in society.

Huffington: Kathryn, what I said is very different,

and I would like you really to hear it because it is very important. What I said is that the women's movement has constantly looked to government, especially to Washington and to federal government to provide solutions. All the examples given here have to do with the Family Leave Act, with what Washington and the federal government did for child care. And what I am saying is that the solutions are not going to be found there. The solutions are going to be found in our neighborhoods, in our communities—

Kinsley: Betty.

Huffington: —when all of us reach out and find ways to solve these major social problems. [applause]

Kinsley: Betty Friedan.

Friedan: I have a problem with your somehow evasion of the reality of experience. I have been, am, and will be part of the women's movement. I am a spokesperson—

Huffington: Many of them don't like you. You know that.

Friedan: I helped—

Huffington: Many of them have spoken angrily against you.

Friedan: —and I keep helping the women's movement and the thought of the women's movement and feminism evolve, and I apply it to new questions, and I happen to believe today and have said so in all my lectures and so on, that a new vision of community that transcends polarization is the next stage. But I want you to be honest about your own experience. You were the first woman head of the Cambridge Union and—

Huffington: Actually I was the third.

Friedan: —you were the first woman head of the Cambridge Union—

Huffington: I was not. I was the third. [laughter]

Friedan: —in the 1970s, I believe, and you wouldn't have been the head of the Cambridge Union and wouldn't have had that easy route to a reputation that you got thereby if there had not been a women's movement. [applause] Furthermore—

Kinsley: No, no, we are running out of time.

Friedan: I know, I know. I have a question. The question is this: If you think politics, legislation, government, is so useless, why did you let your husband spend $80 million to try to buy a seat in the Senate? [laughter/applause]

Kinsley: We are out of time, but I am going to give you 30 seconds to answer that. Yes. [gavel] [gavel] Hold on, we're running out of time. [gavel] [gavel] Take a few seconds and answer that, even though we are out of time.

Huffington: Let me start by correcting all the inaccuracies in your statements. First of all, I was not the first woman president of the Cambridge Union; I was the third. And the first woman president of the Cambridge Union was there before *The Feminine Mystique* was written. [applause] And since you call yourself the mother of the movement, we are taking that as the beginning of the movement, to also answer your question, Karen, about my ignorance of the women's movement in relation to voting rights. The second point is that my husband is free to spend his money the way he wants. [laughter/applause] He doesn't ask me.

Kinsley: Okay, thank you.

Huffington: Let me continue. My husband could have spent $30 million—not $80 million, incidentally, another minor inaccuracy of $50 million in your calculations. He could have spent $30 million building a boat or buying a bad Picasso. [laughter] Instead he chose to spend it promoting some major ideas of importance to the whole country, including voluntarism, including replacing the welfare state, including things that I am sure you don't like just judging by your expression. [applause] [gavel]

Kinsley: Thank you very much. Thank you, Arianna. You're out of time. Camille Paglia. Your turn to be subjected to questioning from the affirmative team. Who wants to start?

Fox-Genovese: I'll start

Kinsley: Go ahead, Professor Fox-Genovese.

Fox-Genovese: Yes. I would like to ask Camille Paglia what she thinks of the Gender Equity in Education Act?

Paglia: Well, I am quite known for my opposition to the kinds of Rube Goldberg contraption. I am an equal opportunity feminist. I do not believe in these enormous bureaucratic special protections for women. I feel that that particular act is reactionary. But—

Kinsley: Take 15 seconds and tell them what it is.

Paglia: She asked the question. Let her define it. [laughter]

Kinsley: How do you know you're against it if you can't define it? [laughter]

Paglia: I know, I know. What I want to say—this has been a theme running through a lot of the comments on that side—is that again I must stress, all right, that there is a distorted voice it appears in feminism that is overemphasized by the media, that the media has given far too much attention to the present leaders of the movement who have promoted that particular act. The media does not give any voice, does not allow the kind of access to the talk shows and so on of people who would oppose that. So again I have to say—

Fox-Genovese: When do leaders of the women's movement ever challenge the media? When does someone defending abortion ever bring someone, a pro-life feminist, to a meeting with her? Why is it that most feminist groups will not tolerate pro-life feminists and will not allow them to use the word. [applause]

Paglia: This is true. You are correct.

Fox-Genovese: You can't blame the media.

Paglia: I speak as an expert in mass media. I teach mass media, so this is one of my areas of expertise. For 20 years dissident feminists like me have struggled to get heard, all right? There is an unholy marriage in this country between the liberal media on the East Coast, all right, in the Northeast, and these often self-appointed leaders of the movement. Now history will show that the moment the movement starting moving away from Betty Friedan, you started getting problems. I loved Gloria Steinem in the beginning, okay, but very soon she too became a prisoner of that cultural elite on the East Coast. We've got to go back to basics again. I agree with Betty Friedan on a lot of different issues and I still feel that her principles, you know, actually speak to every single thing that has been said on the opposite side, okay—her original writings speak to.

Kinsley: Okay. Helen Alvare. No, no. Mr. Buckley.

Buckley: Ms. Paglia, in your rather interesting, exciting book, *Vamps and Tramps*, you have an essay in which you describe the big freeze on you by the women's movement and also incidentally also by the gays and lesbians, who don't review your books even. At what point would you think that the leadership was excluding you and that therefore you should seek a different banner to march under?

Paglia: The leadership has been excluding me for 20 years. The point is, there are many women like me. We go all the way back to the late '60s. I belong to kind of an extinct strain—

Buckley: There are not many women like you. [laughter]

Paglia: I belong to a kind of extinct strain of a kind of a street-wise, streetsmart feminism. We believe in a personal responsibility and so on. Now another thing, the women's studies programs, okay? A lot of crap is coming out of them. I believe the whole thing should be demolished, all right? [laughter/applause] Do not confuse the women's studies program with the feminist movement, okay? The feminist movement is much larger than those horrible women on campus. [laughter/applause] And I blame, okay, not the women's movement but rather the servility of the administrators on campus and the self-castration of our American faculties that have permitted the creation of those cells of non-feminist women just for fanatics, doctrinaire, Orwellian women, who are indeed guilty of the perversion of language that you have so well spoken to. [laughter/applause] Is that it?

Kinsley: Yes. Thank you very much. Elizabeth Fox-Genovese, it's your turn to converse with Betty Friedan. Betty Friedan, ascend the podium please with Elizabeth Fox-Genovese. And Professor Fox-Genovese starts.

Fox-Genovese: Ms. Friedan, you went to, Smith, is that correct?

Friedan: Yes, sir.

Fox-Genovese: How do you feel about single-sex education?

Friedan: Well, I am very torn. I got a wonderful education at Smith, as did Bill's sisters. We were there together. I think that it is very important—you know, I don't think separate is equal—and I think it is very important that women learn how to be full people in the full society. And I deplore some of this new stuff that says, Oh, the girls can't speak up if they're in the class with boys. Then something should be done about the professors to make them treat the girls with equal respect to boys. I think it is regressive to return to single-sex education as the only way that women can be taught to have a full voice in society and full self-confidence. On the other hand, freedom of choice on education is part of the American ethos.

Fox-Genovese: Now just how do you expect to give people full self-confidence, much less competence and independence if the way you are going to handle the problem is to force the professors to behave one way or another? If you can't encourage people to internalize some sense of responsibility for themselves, aren't you facing problems? And if you go to telling professors how to behave at that level of micro-management, are you not moving into a serious abridgment of the freedoms of society as a whole in order to make women come out more equal—

Friedan: No.

Fox-Genovese: —than they would if things just took their course?

Friedan: I am not proposing anything of that sort. I am not proposing anything of that sort. If indeed there is a way that teachers—and I have seen it in studies in other countries, not just in the U.S.—that the teachers, for instance, call on the boys more often, then as a part of the education of the teachers, that kind of prejudice should be exposed. If indeed, as was the case in this country, black children were thought capable of nothing and therefore not given challenging assignments, then that kind of prejudice on the part of teachers needs to be dealt with educationally. I mean, we do progress, we do evolve. And I think it is a marvelous thing that women are now admitted to the law schools and the professional schools, and frankly, I would like to see women admitted to the Catholic priesthood. [applause]

Kinsley: Yes.

Friedan: I think that all of these educational opportunities are wonderful and they are wonderful not only for the women themselves, but for the dimension of experience, that—I mean, women are different from men, and I am a feminist and I've never denied that. And I think the different experience of women is necessary to have a full picture of history or of anything else, and you have made a contribution in that respect, and I want to ask you—

Kinsley: Good. And keep on asking. [laughter]

Friedan: —how can you deny the importance of the contribution to history that you yourself have made? I mean, the study that you have done of Southern women—and I can't claim I have read it all, but I have certainly read some of it—I mean, that wouldn't have been taken seriously 40 years ago.

Fox-Genovese: Well, I wanted—You give me an opportunity to make something very clear. I am not opposed to the women's movement you launched. What I am opposed to is what the women's movement is becoming. [applause] So the—

Friedan: But there is no "the" women's movement. You can say "the" women's movement in lower case, and that applies to all of the movement of women in this society. It applies to the caucuses that exist in academic associations, it applies to the networking that goes on in business. It applies to the different feminist organizations and to the League of Women Voters and the Junior League that are now—and AAUW—that are now of feminist orientation. But the women's movement applies to the whole of society, and the different voices that proclaim a kind of extreme version of feminism or political correctness—I mean, I am a feminist, but I am not politically correct [applause] and I hate that kind of rigidity. I hate the attempt to make a single doctrine, a single party line, whether it's feminism or anything else, but feminism has got to have diversity.

Kinsley: Don't forget you're asking questions.

Friedan: Let's see. What did I start to ask you? [laughter]

Fox-Genovese: That's all right. I can take that one as a question, because you talked earlier in your opening remarks about personhood and women's sense of themselves and the rest of it. And women's movement as a word is a little bit ambiguous because it does not capture only the change in women's situation and the importance of women's issues to our society. It's normally taken to be more or less synonymous with feminism. I would agree that the vast majority of women, and indeed men, in this country want fairness for women and regard women's issues as of the utmost importance. Yet the vast majority of women in this country say very firmly, Feminism is not a story about my life.

Friedan: No, that's— They do not.

Fox-Genovese: Yes, they do. [laughter]

Friedan: If you look at recent—

Fox-Genovese: Sorry, Ms. Friedan.

Friedan: If you look at recent polls you will see that the vast majority of women identify with the women's movement for equality. And there are women that do not use the word "feminist" and you find out why they don't use the word "feminist" and you find two things. You find that they equate feminism with some of this anti-man kind of thing, which I don't agree with and have always spoken out against [gavel]—my book *The Second Stage*, and I was attacked for that. But we have to have these differences [gavel] to evolve a larger truth. They also say, "I am not a feminist" because in the last 20 years [gavel] of, you know, Reagan and Bush leading to Newt Gingrich [gavel], we have made words like "liberalism," "feminism" dirty words. [gavel]

Kinsley: Thank you very much. Kathryn Kolbert and Helen Alvare. And Helen Alvare starts, questioning Kathryn Kolbert.

Alvare: Okay. Kathryn, polls when asked the direct question to women: Under what circumstances ought it to be legal, under what circumstances are moral? In other words a very straightforward question, have shown for 20 years—whether Gallup, Harris, *LA Times*, *Boston Globe*, you name it—that women are more pro-life than men. In fact, a woman of color is more pro-life than the non-Hispanic white woman, the poorer women are more pro-life than the rich, those with less education are more pro-life than those with more. In fact, the demographic of an abortion advocate is a white male with money and a lot of education. So how can a movement that puts abortion at its core ever claim to speak for women when it speaks so often about that? [applause]

Kolbert: Let me address that because I think it's a good question. And I think that we claim to speak for women because the vast majority of women and Americans believe that religious views shouldn't be imposed by government on all of us. We also believe that women need to have certain rights in order to be equal participants in society. And I think one of the problems with looking at polling data is that there is a poll for every point of view. And if you ask the questions—

Mr. Alvare: Some polls are more straightforward than others.

Kolbert: Well, except that if you ask the same question in a million different ways, you find very, very fine differences between points of view. And I think what it points up—and I think this is important—is that the question of abortion is one that people have very, very diverse views. And you can't capture ambiguity.

Alvare: Well, I am talking about—

Kolbert: You can't capture—

Alvare: —polls that have asked it in about 20 different ways.

Kolbert: Well, but—

Alvare: And so they managed to capture the same trend, no matter how they asked it over 20 years. And there is just no—there is no distinction. They always show that the demographic of the pro-abortion person is the male, not the female.

Kolbert: Well, I don't think the distinction is very large, but I think part of the reason that's true is for the most part that many people have very traditional views in the world, and so do many men, and I think you can't make—

Alvare: Well, that can't answer my question.

Kolbert: But the whole point here is that we don't want to draw distinctions or that we are trying to develop social policy not on gender alone. The point is we are fighting for a just cause. We are fighting for the right point of view. I will fight for rights of people—

Alvare: But the question was—

Kolbert: —even if there are only 20 of them in the world—

Alvare: —how when you're fighting—

Kolbert: —if that's the right point of view.

Alvare: —for that point of view can you simultaneously say you're for women? I wanted to move on to the next one. Today—

Kolbert: I think it's easy to believe when 100,000–200,000 wom-en march on Washington to support the right to choose that there are an awful lot of them that we're speaking for—

Alvare: That's just another evidence—

Kolbert: —and I am very, very happy to represent them. [applause]

Alvare: That's exactly the evidence I would have cited for NOW's obsession with abortion since the major marches they run are always for that cause. Tonight we have heard Betty Friedan say: I am not for abortion; I am for the right to choose. Kate Michelman has said abortion is a bad thing. Faye Wattleton: I've never had a woman approach me to say abortion would be a life-enriching experience. And in general, you will always hear no one is pro-abortion. If this is a "bad surgery," that women are not "pro," that it "does not enrich your life," why don't groups like yours, Planned Parenthood, and others spend money, litigation time, public face time, political time providing her ways to escape it instead of litigation money to promote it further when no one is for it? [applause]

Kolbert: Well, let me just say this: I would be happy to spend my time working to alleviate unwanted pregnancy, and I challenge the Catholic Church to join me, because the best way to do that is to provide sex education and contraceptives to millions of Americans, and those are the policies you oppose. [applause/boos]

Alvare: Of course that ignores the fact—that does ignore the facts. It ignores two facts: one, that Planned Parenthood shows that 50 percent of the women who were coming into their clinics were using contraceptive to get abortions; the other 50 percent weren't—abortion was their first backup. It also of course avoids the fact that contraception and rates of abortion have gone up simultaneously. What I'm saying is we spend our money—in fact we are the primary provider of social services to born women in poverty in the United States—trying to address the causes that lead them to abortion. Why doesn't your group, why doesn't Planned Parenthood, why doesn't NARAL spend its millions and millions and millions of dollars addressing that, since as they all say, it's a bad thing, it's not life-enriching, and we're not for it.

Kolbert: Well, frankly, if you gave me your budget I would be happy to work on the range of issues that you work on. But the reality is that the women's movement has grown and that the institutions we've developed are new. My organization is two-and-a-half years old. Planned Parenthood is a relatively new phenomenon.

Alvare: But don't you usually spend your money one way versus another, and that's really the point.

Kolbert: That's right, and the one way we choose to spend our money is frankly, to have the largest effect for the largest number of people and to make maximum change. It's the same issue we were talking about before. That is, if you are going to attack repressive policies, you go for first the things that are discriminatory in law that you can change because you can change the laws. You go for big changes. You then can work on maximizing a variety of other things as you go along.

Kinsley: Okay, now go on the offensive.

Kolbert: Well, you know, I think I already answered the question I was going to ask you, which is: If you really are into preventing or really if your goal is to prevent abortion—and I don't frankly disagree with the desire to eliminate unwanted pregnancy. I would like to eliminate rape; I would like to eliminate domestic violence. All of the causes of women's oppression I would like to eliminate. But if that's your goal, why does the Church take the consistent view opposing contraceptives that work prior to conception, and why does the Church take the point of view that sex education in our schools should not be taught and want to gag doctors from providing a range of information to all women?

Alvare: A couple of things. I'll start—since the last one you mentioned is prominent, what you call the gag rule. Title X, which provides abstinence education, was actually passed before abortion was legal. Those who argued that Title X must—not just did, but must—include advocacy—or I should say referrals—for abortion as part of it, were actually saying that a piece of legislation passed when abortion was criminal in the 50 states—

Kolbert: But you don't support Title X, do you?

Alvare: —ought to have required it. But I'm saying that it's a false argument.

Kolbert: But you're not there in Congress supporting Title X, are you?

Alvare: No—Yes, actually we do say that it should—We supported—We did not oppose Title X, first of all because we think contraception—Let me finish.

Kinsley: What is Title X?

Kolbert: Can I go to Newt Gingrich with you tomorrow—

Alvare: Title X is a program—

Kolbert: —and say the Catholic Church supports Title X?

Alvare: No.

Kolbert: Because we could reauthorize it tomorrow. [applause]

Alvare: Let me tell you where our position is.

Kinsley: The audience is begging you. Would one of you say that Title X is?

Alvare: Title X is a program founded in 1970 to provide family planning services to those who were poor. It was intended to be preventive. We do not take a position that contraception ought to be legal or illegal. It's a private, moral matter that we speak to people about. Abortion, of course, a public matter that destroys a life, ought to be a matter of public law. [applause] However, with regard to Title X, it was passed when abortion was criminal. It's silly to say that the lawmakers intended referral for a criminal act in the 50 states. With regard to the contraception and abortion link, your question has a false premise. If the last 20–25 years of increased availability and access to contraception had actually led to lower abortion rates, then your question would have some relevancy. But in fact, what we are seeing is the rate of use and availability of contraception, and the rate of abortion actually have gone up together. There is a variety of reasons for that. One is probably that when you get the notion instilled in the public mind that people have an absolute right—not just a hope or a wish, but a right—to control the timing and manner of their children, then in fact what you are going to end up with is people who are less disposed to put up with so-called errors. And so you see in other countries that when things like certain contraceptive modes are introduced and become prevalent, abortion rates actually go up.

Kolbert: But isn't it true that—

Alvare: So the premise to your whole question is flawed.

Kolbert: —in other countries where you provide a range of social services to women—Western Europe is the best example, when you have a national health care system that provides reproductive health care to all women at all stages of their lives, then you reduce unwanted pregnancy and—

Alvare: And that's a separate question.

Kolbert: —you increase the availability of contraception.

Alvare: And that's why the Catholic Church—

Kinsley: That's okay. You can answer it.

Alvare: Thank you. The Catholic Church was probably one of the most visible proponents of universal coverage in the most recent debate over that, at the same time taking the consistent position that it must not include abortion mandates. For us the consistent ethic of life requires that you not only preserve people's individual right to life, but also their right to a dignified life, access to health care being one of the most critical issues there.

Kolbert: Let me ask one question. You would agree, would you not, that you and I would never agree about the general view of when life begins, that you have a religious view and that I may have a religious view and those will differ.

Alvare: No. I would disagree first of all—

Kolbert: You would—

Alvare: —that this is a matter—I would not agree—

Kolbert: You think we are going to agree on this?

Alvare: I would not agree that your premises are correct. It is not a religious view. If you ever really sat down and read the Church's documents on this, it is based on the fact that all we can do is respect what science tells us about when life begins. [applause] And when that life begins, our only option is to respect—

Kolbert: That didn't answer my question. My question was, you would—

Alvare: It's not a religious view and therefore your—

Kolbert: Let's start though with the premise that you and I disagree.

Alvare: Well, you deny science.

Kolbert: Let me finish, if I can.

Alvare: I don't. That's really the issue. [applause]

Kolbert: Well, wait a second. I think that I look very pragmatically at science—at scientists, theologians, philosophers, religious leaders like yourself and religious leaders that I go to, which may be different from your religious view.

Alvare: But it's not a religious question.

Kolbert: They have no consistent view of when life begins.

Alvare: But that's because—

Kolbert: There is no consistent scientific—

Alvare: —some of them are denying science and some of them are not. There is a scientific consensus.

Kolbert: Well, see, your science and the scientists' sciences may be different.

Alvare: There is a difference in philosophical consensus about when someone is a person who should be valued—

Kolbert: I want to get to my question, please.

Alvare: But those people who haven't valued some who everyone acknowledges are human and alive have been referred to as things like bigots, racists and sexists. [gavel] What I say is that if it is human and alive, we respect it.

Ms. Kinsley: Thank you. It's time for closing arguments. No. No. You've both had a chance to interrogate each other. Am I right? Yes, yes, they have. Yes, you have. The producer was telling me I was wrong.

Kolbert: I'll be happy to ask her some more questions.

Kinsley: All right. Let me ask the producer, do they have a couple more minutes or should we proceed? No, I am afraid you are all through. Mr. Buckley and Ms. Friedan, it's time for closing arguments. First Betty Friedan.

Friedan: I can't find it amusing, a two-hour debate that begins, "The Women's Movement Has Been Disastrous"—not when there are so many women in this room, and men, that are benefitting from the 30 years of the women's movement for equality: from the ability of their mothers to choose to have children, from the ability of their mothers to earn so that at a time like this, when the corporate restructure of downsizing is really eroding men's sense of economic security, that they are not at least committing suicide the way men did in a depression when I was a child, because at least the wives are helping to share the burden. I cannot take lightly a statement that the women's movement has been disastrous when so many voices of women, including those at this table, are now being heard in every field, where only man's voice was heard before, and the interesting new questions that are being asked. But as a feminist—and I proudly call myself a feminist, and I proudly affirm the women's movement which I helped start, though I do not hesitate to attack positions with which I disagree—but I see myself now trying to give a vision for the women's movement to move beyond polarization, to face the need in this community, in this country of ours, in this democracy of ours, to transcend polarization, whether of gender, of race, of age, to make a reality of the American dream for all people, to see values and affirm values beyond the culture of greed, beyond, you know, the material profit that has been the only value that has been taken seriously in the last 10 years. And that women have their voice now and that women can use that voice politically may be an important part of our transcending what I feel a bad and dangerous period of American life that we are in now, where it is contemplated taking children away from their mothers and putting them in orphanages, where it is contemplated in the name of some new revolution destroying [gavel]—destroying any sense of responsibility to use the resources of this nation for all people, including the helpless and the poor. [gavel] [applause]

Kinsley: Thank you very much. You're all done. [applause] Closing arguments for the affirmative team, William F. Buckley Jr. [applause]

Buckley: Mr. Chairman, ladies and gentlemen, the trouble with taking a position different from Betty Friedan's is it does make you seem rather inhuman. [laughter] She speaks so endearingly about the plight of the women whom she rescued. That rescue actually was a continuing operation. As far as I am aware, there wasn't a single woman who voted in favor of the 19th Amendment, and yet it was the 19th Amendment that gave the vote to women. So something was happening along the line. But no, we sound as though we were reading from *Uncle Tom's Cabin* when we describe the plight of women. It's like Governor Cuomo talking about the GOP. He always sounds like he's reading from *The Grapes of Wrath.* [laughter] We speak about the 14-year-old girl who is impregnated by her stepfather. So I say, okay, you've got this person who is suffering terrible agony from cancer or whatever disease; so is it all right if I shoot him? Well, the answer is, of course, these points have to be made with some deliberation, which is what we have attempted. In 1923 Mussolini was welcomed by Winston Churchill and Lloyd George and by a lot of people, but seeds were sown of a movement that got out of hand. Now I think it's our point that this movement has in fact got out of hand. We have heard Ms. Paglia talk about neurotics, about incompetents, about people who have gone too far, about people being silly. But whenever any such point is raised to a level of generality—have they in fact made the movement simply a factionalist movement with a very narrow-minded agenda?—they sort of retreat. Then we hear even so robust and witty and resourceful voice as Camille Paglia saying, "Well, but nevertheless I am a member of that movement," but then she is capable of saying that she voted for Bill Clinton and "I look forward to voting for him again"—to which I can only recall the orator in North England, who said, "What's more, I was born an Englishman, I live an Englishman, and I hope to die an Englishman." And the voice from the back of the room said, "Man, have you no ambition?" [laughter/applause]

Kinsley: Thank you very much, Mr. Buckley. [applause] Well, I am not sure whether the past two hours have been Apollonian or Dionysian, to use Camille Paglia's distinction. I guess it was a little bit of both. We never found out what the Gender Equity in Education Act is. I guess we have to chalk that up to a failure. [laughter] We did find out what Title X is. I guess we have to chalk that up as a success. I did

hear Kathryn Kolbert use the phrase "manning the child abuse hotline," [laughter/applause] which showed that linguistically perhaps there is room for togetherness on at least that part of the issue.

At any rate I thank all of our panelists. This was a great debate. I thank the audience here at George Washington University and Producer Warren Steibel. For *Firing Line,* thank you very much. [applause]

Study Questions

1. Has there been one continuous women's movement, or a series of movements that support women or feminism?

*2. Have you ever taken a sick day from work when you weren't sick? If so, how did you justify your action to yourself the last time you did it? Would calling in sick in order to meet a parental responsibility for a sick or injured child be a good justification? Since society often holds mothers rather than fathers primarily responsible for the daily upbringing of children, don't such sex roles lead to more absenteeism for women and thus reinforce the sexist stereotype that women are not tough enough to succeed in business?

3. Is it fair for society to expect people generally to follow such sex roles in raising children? After all, none of us chooses which sex we are. (And it seems ridiculous to require someone to undergo a sex-change operation just to meet a socially assigned sex role.) Our sex is an accident of birth beyond our control, so why should society use that feature of us to determine our fates?

*4. If you knew you would never move beyond your current level of professional success, how would it alter your life? What if you knew your real income would remain just what it is now? What if you knew that although your income would steadily increase, at retirement you would still have the same job you do now? What if you knew all of this professional paralysis was because your bosses thought you deserved no better because you are a woman? Would you join and actively participate in the women's movement or feminist movement?

5. Speaker of the House of Representatives Newt Gingrich, a Republican, said in January of 1995: "There's a problem with women staying in a ditch for 30 days: they get infections." He also said: "Men are biologically driven to go out and hunt giraffes." Gingrich was teaching his course in American Civilization and trying to explain why he thought women

should not serve in combat but men should. Are Gingrich's comments sexist? Some worry that Gingrich is not only a sexist but also too sympathetic to racism. For example, the historian he wanted to hire for the House of Representatives stated that Nazi arguments should be taken more seriously and be presented more and reconsidered. Further, Gingrich has published a novel based on his fantasy that Nazi Germany won World War II. If anything should prevent President Clinton from serving out his term of office, Gingrich is next in line to become president after Vice President Al Gore. Do these statements by such a high-ranking official as Gingrich show that the women's movement is still greatly needed? Should women and ethnic minorities receive the same sort of protection from discrimination? Should women and ethnic minorities form an alliance to protect each other from discrimination?

39

Women's Work: Views from the History of Philosophy

Linda Nicholson

Editor's note: Nicholson surveys several views of major philosophers on women and work. The major philosophers she discusses are Aristotle, Plato, Locke, Rousseau, Mill, and Engels.

I. Introduction

When sex difference theorists talk about women having "feminine" psychological traits, they are usually referring to traits they consider to be either *characteristic* of women (i.e., traits they believe to be held by all, or at least most, women) or to traits they believe *proper* or desirable for women to have. At least four questions, therefore, arise in response to such ascriptions of "feminine" to psychological traits: (1) whether all or most women do, in fact, have such traits, (2) whether only women (and not men) do, (3) if only women do, whether this is due to some biological feature(s) that women have which men do not, and (4) if it is not the case that only women have such traits or that the cause is not biologically linked if they do, whether it is proper or desirable for women to develop these traits anyway.

But for the most part, sex difference theorists do not confine themselves to the ascription of the term "feminine" to psychological traits; they also quite liberally apply it to certain tasks such as childrearing and housekeeping. The difference in the ascription is that in calling certain tasks "feminine," the theorists are generally not interested in the questions

Reprinted from Linda Nicholson, "Women's Work: Views from the History of Philosophy," in Mary Vetterling-Braggin, ed., *"Femininity," "Masculinity," and "Androgeny,"* (Totowa, N.J.: Rowman & Littlefield, 1982), pp. 203–221. Reprinted by permission. The footnotes have been omitted.

whether all or most women, or only women and not men, perform such tasks. Rather they generally call such tasks "feminine" because they believe that it is either necessary or desirable that women do these jobs. Thus, in the ascription of "feminine" to certain tasks, a different set of questions arise: (1) whether such tasks must, in fact, be performed by all or most women (and no men), (2) if so, whether this is because all or most women have certain features, biological or other, that men do not have which directly or indirectly make it necessary that women, but not men, perform the tasks, and (3) if not, whether it is proper or desirable for women to perform these tasks anyway. Positive answers to questions (1) and (3) would entail that it is correct to apply the term "feminine" to certain types of labor. In this paper, I shall first try to show the different answers given to these questions by key philosophers of sex difference theory and secondly to determine whether there exists any explanatory pattern for the difference.

II. Aristotle

Deviating from chronology, I wish to begin with Aristotle and follow with Plato. Aristotle's arguments serve as a useful starting point for discussion in that they provide a clear example of a consistent justification of a sexual division of labor. In the following remarks Aristotle is saying what was widely held in the Greece of his time:

> .... the courage of a man is shown in commanding, of a woman in obeying. All classes must be deemed to have their special attributes; as the poet says of women.
>
> "Silence is a woman's glory," but this is not equally the glory of man.

For Aristotle, these 'oughts' follow from nature. A woman's very soul is different from that of a man:

> Now it is obvious that the same principle applies generally, and therefore almost all things rule and are ruled according to nature. But the kind of rule differs;—the freeman rules over the slave after another manner from that in which the male rules over the female, or the man over the child; although the parts of the soul are present in all of them, they are present in different degrees. For the slave has no deliberative faculty at all; the woman has, but it is without authority, and the child has, but it is immature.
>
> For although there may be exceptions to the order of nature, the male is by nature fitter for command

than the female, just as the elder and full-grown is superior to the younger and more immature.

As Christine Pierce has pointed out, there is no necessary connection between the "natural" and the "inevitable" or even "the good." Roaches, tornadoes, and bacteria are all "natural" phenomena. They are also phenomena which human beings attempt to eliminate. Thus even if one agreed with Aristotle that "the male is by nature fitter for command than the female," this does not lead to the conclusion that it is necessary or desirable that men command. One might, for example, want artificially to increase women's commanding abilities or diminish men's. Aristotle, however, believes in the desirability of the rule of those who are by nature "most fit" for rule:

> For that some should rule and others be ruled is a thing not only necessary, but expedient; from the hour of their birth, some are marked out for subjection, others for rule . . . . And it is clear that the rule of the soul over the body, and the mind and the rational element over the passionate, is natural and expedient; whereas the equality of the two or the rule of the inferior is always hurtful. The same holds good of animals in relation to men; for tame animals have a better nature than wild, and all tame animals are better off when they are ruled by man; for then they are preserved. Again, the male is by nature superior, and the female inferior; and the one rules, and the other is ruled; this principle, of necessity, extends to all mankind.

In sum, Aristotle supports the status quo by claiming not only that it is a manifestation of the "natural order of things," but also that this "natural order" is itself more desirable than any conceivable alternative. One can question this position on several grounds. First, it is obviously questionable whether women are "by nature" inferior to men. Even if it were the case in Aristotle's Greece that women did not possess the same abilities as men, Aristotle has provided no argument establishing any necessary connection between such a lack of capacities and "womanhood." As John Stuart Mill, a theorist I will discuss later, points out, since there is such overwhelming evidence of the social obstacles to women's development, a heavy burden of proof rests on the claim of women's "natural inferiority." Secondly, as I have already noted, what is "natural" is not necessarily inevitable or unchangeable. Even if it were the case that women were "naturally" less competent than men, we might still attempt to change this fact of nature by increased schooling for women (if we were interested, for example, in increasing the supply of competent people in the labor market).

Ultimately there is the question of social goals; in this case, it is the question of whether we believe social inequality to be desirable or not. From Aristotle's perspective (i.e., the perspective of the ruler) that "some are marked out for subjection, others for rule" is desirable, but this position is certainly questionable (particularly, although not exclusively, from the ruled's point of view).

III. Plato

For Plato, that which exists does not necessarily represent that which is desirable. The point of *The Republic* was to portray a society more desirable than that which Plato encountered. The ideal society which Plato constructed in that treatise allowed for women performing public roles unheard of in Plato's Greece. In Plato's Republic, the guardian class did contain women and thus they carried out the highest and most important functions of that society. Moreover, within the guardian class there was no sexual division of labor. What led Plato to adopt such a position? It is worthwhile to reproduce those passages in *The Republic* where he makes the argument justifying women as guardians:

> "Now," said I, "take the male and female sex; if either is found to be better as regards any art or other practice, we shall say that this ought to be assigned to it. But if we find that they differ only in one thing, that the male begets and the female bears the child, we shall not take that difference as having proved any more clearly that a woman differs from a man for what we are speaking of; but we shall still believe that our guardians and their wives should practice the same things." . . . .Then, my friend, no practice or calling in the life of the city belongs to woman as woman, or to man as man, but the various natures are dispersed among both sexes alike; by nature the woman has a share in all practices, and so has man, but in all, woman is rather weaker than man."

What is apparent from these passages is that Plato is *not* claiming that there are no differences between men and women. All that he is arguing is that the properties which do differentiate men and women are not relevant to the performance of those duties required of a member of the guardian class. What also should be stressed is that this argument does not commit Plato to a position on sexual equality. Plato did not believe that a woman's reproductive capacity, or that which distinguishes her as a woman, should determine her life activities. However, he did believe that women generally were inferior to men. The compatibility of these two positions can be illustrated in a contemporary argument for sexual equality in tryouts for professional basketball. While women are generally shorter than men, not all women are. Therefore, those women who are of the minimum height required for playing basketball on a given team ought to be allowed to play, other factors being equal. Similarly for Plato, while women generally are inferior to men and thus incapable of the tasks required of a guardian, this did not preclude the possibility of some women being equivalent in capacity and thus fully qualified.

What is interesting about the above argument is that it fits so well Plato's needs for his ideal society as a whole. Plato only abolishes a sexual division of labor among the guardian classes; among other classes the traditional division of labor between men and women is maintained. Thus if Plato required an argument which attacked the traditional division of labor only for one group within the society, he constructed the one most fitting. Susan Okin has argued that this perfect fit is not surprising, that Plato needed an argument to allow for the rejection of the conventional division of labor for the guardian class alone because of prior decisions concerning the way of life for the guardian class. In particular, Plato's prior abolition of private property and the family for members of the guardian class made necessary an abolishment of women's conventional roles within that class. Plato was aware of the danger of abolishing women's activities within the family without giving them alternative employment. That it was the abolition of the family which led Plato to emancipate female guardians and not vice versa, Okin argues, is evidenced in his maintenance of the traditional division of labor for other classes where the family is maintained but where the above arguments could also be applied. Finally, she notes that in *The Laws*, despite Plato's increasing conviction on the potential capabilities of the female sex, he is more conservative than in *The Republic* in maintaining traditional sex roles. This can be accounted for, she argues, by the reintroduction of the family and private property in that work.

Okin's argument is in accord with other recent theory which has argued for a historical connection between the nuclear family and a rigid sexual division of labor associated with female subordination. Marilyn Arthur, for example, has argued that the con-

trol of women which existed in fifth century B.C. Athens can in large part be accounted for by the transition in Greece in the eight and seventh centuries B.C. from a tribally/aristocratically organized society, where property was controlled and distributed through the extended kin, to a democracy, where property was transmitted through the more nuclear family residing in the individual oikos or household. This transition was accompanied by the emergence of the polis representing male heads of household qua heads of household. The oikos thus became an important political and economic entity. Maintaining its integrity and the legitimacy of its head's heirs became crucial. What developed was an increased control over women's sexuality and of her activities generally. Thus what Arthur points to is a historical connection between a concern for the integrity of the family and a control and limitation of women's activities, in particular, a restriction of women's activities to the household. Such a connection does appear borne out in the difference in Plato between activities appropriate for women of the guardian class who exist outside of a nuclear family and all other women. It might also explain the difference between Aristotle and Plato as the difference between a theorist endorsing the family and the activities of women associated with it and a theorist advocating the elimination of this institution for a small class of people.

In sum, Plato's position on women's capacities and tasks is quite problematic unless it is put in the context of a framework such as that provided by Okin. Plato argued that there was nothing in a woman's biology that prevented her from performing equivalent tasks to a man. He used this argument as a basis for allowing women to become guardians. If, however, biology is not destiny for a female guardian, then biology cannot be destiny for any other woman either. Even granting Plato's assumption that women were generally inferior to men, this does not justify a division of labor organized around gender; criteria of competence alone should suffice. Thus Plato's argument that the biological differences between men and women do not entail a gender-organized division of labor requires that he attack such a division of labor for everyone, not only for members of the guardian class. That he does not make this attack for those outside of the guardian class must therefore be explained by his commitment to family life for such people.

IV. Locke   *Libertarian*

There is a widespread, though not frequently articulated, theory that women's equality to men has gradually increased with the progress of time. In the cave, man ruled with a heavy, if not yet iron, club. The march of history, representing an overall march toward a greater enlightenment and equality for all, has been accompanied by greater equalization between the sexes. A different, more sophisticated theory would hold that while it is wrong to believe in any gradual increase in sexual equality, democracy, at least in its most recent manifestations, has contributed toward equalizing the sexes. Similarly, one might expect that exponents of modern democratic theory (who usually argue for an increase in human equality) would be highly sympathetic to increased equality between the sexes. I would now like to examine the work of two theorists, John Locke and Jean Jacques Rousseau, both major exponents of modern democracy, in order to explore this relation between democratic theory and sexual equality.

An initial examination of Locke's statements on women's place would tend to support the thesis that modern democracy represents an advance for women. Within the home, while Locke does place "ultimate authority" with the man, he also appears to argue for a high degree of equality between husband and wife in determining their own affairs and the affairs of their children

> 82. But the Husband and Wife, though they have but one common concern, yet having different understandings will unavoidably sometimes have different wills too; it therefore being necessary, that the last Determination, i.e., the Rule, should be placed somewhere it naturally falls to the Man's share, as the abler and the stronger. But this reaching out to the things of their common Interest and Property, leaves the Wife in the full and free possession of what by contract is her peculiar right, and gives the Husband no more power over her Life, than she has over his. *The Power of the Husband* being so far from that of an absolute Monarch, that the *Wife* has, in many cases, a Liberty to *separate* from him, where natural Right, or their Contract allows it, whether that Contract be made by themselves in the state of Nature, or by the Customs or Law of the Country they live in; and the Children upon such Separation fall to the Father or Mother's lot, as such Contract does determine.

> 52. It may perhaps be assured as an impertinent Criticism in a discourse of this nature, to find fault with words and names that have obtained in the World: And yet possibly it may not be amiss to offer new ones

when the old are apt to lead men into mistakes, as this of *Paternal Power* probably has done, which seems so to place the Power of Parents over their children wholly in the *Father*, as if the *Mother* had no share in it, whereas if we consult Reason or Revelation, we shall find that she hath an equal title.

What is noteworthy about these arguments is that the equality which Locke appears to grant women seems to follow directly from his democratic theory and particularly from his description of the family as a contractual unit:

> 78. *Conjugal Society* is made by a voluntary Compact between Man and Woman and tho' it consists chiefly in such a Communion and Right in one anothers Bodies, as is necessary to its chief End, Procreation; yet it draws with it mutual Support, and Assistance, and a Communion of Interest too, as necessary not only to unite their Care and Affection, but also necessary to their common off-spring, who have a right to be nourished and maintained by them, till they are able to provide for themselves.

Locke does argue that the conjugal unit has a biological basis, i.e., the dependency of a woman on the support of another person during the extended period of childrearing. However once these natural requirements are satisfied, there appears no reason for marriage not to be treated like any other contractual union.

> 81. But although these are Ties upon *Mankind* which make the Conjugal Bonds more firm and lasting in Man, than the other species of Animals; yet it would give one reason to enquire, why this *Compact*, where Procreation and Education are secured, and Inheritance taken care for, may not be made deternminable, either by consent, or upon a certain time, or upon certain conditions, as well as any other voluntary Compacts, there being no necessity in the nature of the thing, nor to the ends of it, that it should always be for life.

Lorenne Clark takes a skeptical position on such passages. She points out that Locke's belittling of the absolute power of the father and the husband is only undertaken where he wishes to undermine the concept of patriarchal government. Apart from those passages where Locke attacks a patriarchal model of the family as a justification for patriarchal government, he is quite conservative on the status of women. For example, there is the assumption throughout the *Treatises* that the natural place of women is in the family. Talk of single women does not appear in either work. We could supplement Clark's point here by noting that Locke's arguments justifying the existence of the family, that women need the protracted support of men during pregnancy and childrearing, would seem to imply that pregnancy is incapacitating and childrearing an all-consuming task.

Women's activity thus seems to Locke to be limited to those traditionally associated with the home and family. Moreover, once within the family, women appear to have rights different from those of men outside the family. Thus, as Clark also notes, whereas Locke does not assume that any natural differences between men mitigate against their equality "in respect of jurisdiction in dominion one over another," Locke uses the argument of women's "natural" inequality with respect to men to justify men's ultimate authority over women. Marxists have long criticized liberalism for not extending the notion of equality from the political sphere to the economic sphere. Similarly, feminists might argue that Lockean democratic theory stops at the door of the home.

V. Rousseau

One could argue that the failure of Locke's democratic theory with regard to women is mainly a failure of omission. True, Locke does speak of the ultimate authority of men in the home. True, Locke does seem to imply that most of a woman's life is necessarily spent producing and raising children in the confines of the family. On the other hand, Locke by and large does not speak very much of women concerning either their rights or their tasks. The same, however, cannot be said of Rousseau, who has a lot to say about what a woman ought to do:

> In the union of the sexes each contributes equally to the common aim, but not in the same way . . . . One ought to be active and strong, the other passive and weak. . . . Once this principle is established, it follows that woman is made specially to please man . . . . The first education of men depends on the care of women. Men's morals, their passions, their tastes, their pleasures, their very happiness also depend on women. Thus the whole education of women ought to relate to men. To please men, to be useful to them, to make herself loved and honored by them, to raise them when young, to care for them when grown, to counsel them, to console them, to make their lives agreeable and sweet—these are the duties of women at all times, and they ought to be taught from childhood.

In ministering to the needs of a man, a woman must be sure to satisfy what is for Rousseau a most crucial need, that a man be sure he is father to his wife's children.

> The strictness of the relative duties of the two sexes is not and cannot be the same. When woman complains on this score about unjust man-made inequality, she is wrong. This inequality is not a human institution—or, at least, it is not the result of mere prejudice but of reason. It is up to the sex that nature has charged with the bearing of children to be responsible for them to the other sex. Doubtless it is not permitted to anyone to violate his faith, and every unfaithful husband who deprives his wife of the only reward of the austere duties of her sex is an unjust and barbarous man. But the unfaithful woman does more; she dissolves the family and breaks all the bonds of nature. In giving the man children which are not his, she betrays both. She joins perfidy to infidelity. I have difficulty seeing what disorders and what crimes do not flow from this one. If there is a frightful condition in the world, it is that of an unhappy father who, lacking confidence in his wife, does not dare to yield to the sweetest sentiments of his heart, who wonders, in embracing his child, whether he is embracing another's, the token of his dishonor, the plunderer of his own children's property. What does the family become in such a situation if not a society of secret enemies whom a guilty woman arms against one another in forcing them to feign mutual love.

From the above we can see that for Rousseau the differences in duties between men and women follow from nature in conjunction with reason. The dictates of nature make woman the childbearer. Given this fact, social harmony in turn requires of the woman strict sexual fidelity in conjunction with other behavioral dictates:

> It is important then, not only that a woman be faithful but that she be judged to be faithful, by her husband, by those near her, by everyone. It is important that she be modest, attentive, reserved, and that she gives evidence of her virtue to the eyes of others as well as to her own conscience. If it is important that a father love his children, it is important that he esteems their mother. These are the reasons which put even appearances among the duties of women, and make honor and reputation no less indispensable to them than chastity. There follows from these principles, along with the moral difference of the sexes, a new motive of duty and propriety which prescribes especially to women the most scrupulous attention to their conduct, their manners, and their bearing. To maintain vaguely that the two sexes are equal and that their duties are the same, is to lose oneself in vain declaiming; it is to say nothing so long as one does not respond to these considerations.

The duties which Rousseau expects of a woman can be summarized in the overriding obligation that she keep the family together. Thus when Rousseau attacks Plato's elimination of a sexual division of labor among the guardian class, he notes that this elimination follows from Plato's elimination of the family.

> In his Republic, Plato gives women the same exercises as men. I can well believe it! Having removed private families from his regime and no longer knowing what to do with women, he found himself forced to make them men.

For Rousseau, Plato's elimination of the family was irrational even given Plato's end, the creation of a strong state. An elimination of the family, Rousseau says, harms rather than helps the state:

> . . . . as though there were no need for a natural base on which to form conventional ties; as though the love of one's nearest were not the principle of the love one owes the state; as though it were not by means of the small fatherland which is the family that the heart attaches itself to the large one; as though it were not the good son, the good husband, and the good father who make the good citizen.

What Rousseau is missing in his criticism of Plato is that the state constructed by Plato in *The Republic* was a very different kind of state from that endorsed by Rousseau himself. It was suggested earlier that there might be a connection between a democratically organized society based on representation by male heads of households and an importance and concern given to the integrity of the individual household unit. One manifestation of this concern would be a greater control over women's sexuality and activities than might be required in a more aristocratically organized society where property and power are distributed and transmitted through the line or extended kin network as opposed to the nuclear family. Thus, a political theorist who endorsed an aristocratically organized society might be more sympathetic to women's equality, at least for some women, than one might otherwise expect. This hypothesis was brought forth to help account for Plato's deviation from accepted Greek practice in his vision of the duties and position of women in the guardian class in his ideal society. Since Plato's ideal society was more aristocratic than democratic and since it did eliminate the family for the guardian class, this could explain the fact that some women in Plato's ideal society could be liberated from the position of citizen wife in the democracy of classical Athens. For the same reasons, a political philosopher whose theory was in other respects highly democratic might be less than sympathetic to women's equality. Thus one could at least account for the conjunction of Rousseau's democratic theory in the political realm and his position on sexual inequality within the family, an otherwise contradictory conjunction. I do not wish to suggest that there is any necessary connection between democratic theory and an espousal of a strong nuclear family and a subordinate position of women. The theorist whom I shall next consider, John Stuart Mill, could easily serve as a counterexample to such a thesis. Rather, all I wish to suggest is a compatibility between democratic theory and sexual inequality made understandable by the importance of the individual household unit in at least certain conceptions of, and perhaps certain historical exemplifications of, a democratic state.

VI. Mill   *utilitarian*

John Stuart Mill's position on women's work is light years away from that of Rousseau. Mill strongly argued against those laws which existed in nineteenth-century England (with similar counterparts in the United States) which made the wife a subordinate and unequal partner in the marriage relation, laws which denied a married woman rights of property and which denied her rights to control her children. More relevant to the concerns of this essay, he also strongly argued against those laws and social prohibitions which denied a woman entrance to any occupation she chose. Like Plato, he argued that the qualifications of any particular woman could not be deduced from the capabilities of women in general. Mill claimed that any decision over who was to fulfill a particular job should be decided by fair competition open to all regardless of sex. In this way, society would insure that any particular job was performed by the most qualified, guaranteeing social efficiency as well as satisfying the demands of social justice. Mill says,

> For if performance of the function is decided either by competition, or by any mode of choice which secures regard to the public interest, there need be no apprehension that any important employments will fall into the hands of women inferior to average men, or to the average of their male competitors . . . . Is there so great a superfluity of men fit for high duties, that society

can afford to reject the service of any competent person? Are we so certain of always finding a man made to our hands for any duty or function of social importance which falls vacant, that we lose nothing by putting a ban upon one half of mankind, and refusing beforehand to make their faculties available, however distinguished they may be? And even if we could do without them, would it be consistent with justice to refuse to them their fair share of honour and distinction, or to deny to them the equal moral right of all human beings to choose their occupation (short of injury to others) according to their own preferences, at their own risk?

Mill not only argued for free and open competition, but also that women's present capabilities might be a function of environmental factors and could thus possibly be changed in a differently ordered society. His position is even more radical than Plato's. Plato believed in free and open competition, but women in general were naturally inferior to men. Mill, on the contrary, argued that what women are "by nature" is impossible to say:

> I do not say, as they will continue to be; for as I have already said more than once, I consider it presumption in anyone to pretend to decide what women are or are not, can or cannot be, by natural constitution. They have always hitherto been kept, as far as regards spontaneous development, in so unnatural a state, that their nature cannot but have been greatly distorted and disguised; and no one can safely pronounce that if women's nature were let to choose its direction as freely as men's, and if no artificial bent were attempted to be given to it except that required by the conditions of human society, and given to both sexes alike, there would be any material difference, or perhaps any difference at all, in the character and capacities which would unfold themselves.

In spite of the above, Mill cannot be considered a feminist, at least by late twentieth-century standards. Mill believed a woman should be an equal partner with her husband in marriage. He also believed that a woman should be free to enter any occupation for which she was qualified. However, Mill did not believe that a woman, unlike a man, could choose both marriage and an occupation outside of marriage. Mill argued that for a married woman to take on an occupation in addition to marriage would inevitably result in poor child care and household management as there would be no one to relieve her of these tasks. Thus, he claimed that a woman's choice of marriage was equivalent to that of a man's choice of a profession, requiring the renunciation of many other activities.

Like a man when he chooses a profession, so, when a woman marries, it may in general be understood that she makes choice of the management of a household, and the bringing up of a family, as the first call upon her exertions, during as many years of her life as may be required for this purpose.

What Mill clearly could not see, as indeed could few others in the nineteenth century, was that child care and household management need be no more binding to a married woman than to a married man.

Mill's claim that married women ought to stay at home would seem to imply that many women ought to stay at home. If we can assume that Mill believed childbearing should take place within marriage and if he also believed that this was an activity necessarily engaging a high percentage of the female population, two widely held premises of his and our society, the consequence would be that many women, in Mill's view, should be homemakers. But this conclusion is in effect no different from Plato's. In other words, while Mill's views appeared to represent an advancement over Plato's, in actuality there may be no advancement at all. Mill, unlike Plato, allows for the possibility that all or many women could, in a well-ordered society, attain the capabilities required for the performance of occupations traditionally thought to be masculine. Thus it would appear that Mill allows for the possibility of the elimination of a sexual division of labor per se. On the other hand, he also accepts the traditional division of labor within the family which in addition carries the consequence of prohibiting married women from taking on jobs outside the family. The consequence, therefore, for the sexual division of labor, is in effect no different in Mill's ideal society than it was in Plato's. In both cases many women are to stay home managing the household and taking care of children. While some women could deviate from this assignment, they were exceptions. What is interesting is that for both Mill and Plato the exceptions are unmarried, with Mill their being "single women" and with Plato their existing with their male counterparts outside of a traditional family.

VII. Engels *Communy; Egalitarian*

One of the few pre-twentieth-century theorists to have critically examined the situation of women in light of women's roles within the family is Frederick Engels. Engels, in *The Origin of the Family, Private Prop-*

erty and the State, employed the anthropological work of Lewis Henry Morgan to argue for the existence of an early form of social organization where women enjoyed a certain supremacy. While there was a certain sexual division of labor such that men had principal responsibility for obtaining food and while there was a loose form of monogamy between men and women resulting in what Engels describes as the "pairing family," neither this division of labor nor this family form were, for Engels, comparable to the modern sexual division of labor nor to the modern monogamous family. The crucial difference was that the "pairing family" existed within a larger communistic type of household in which most or all of the women were related by blood. That this larger family unit, the 'gens,' was organized around the female line provided the material foundation for the supremacy of women and it was common in "primitive" times. This supremacy ended as a consequence of economic changes resulting from the transformation of the society from one based on hunting and gathering to one based on agriculture, the domestication of animals, and the breeding of herds. The transformation made possible a surplus of wealth or at least more than what was required for simple maintenance. That man's position in the division of labor grew in importance with this accumulation of wealth created tensions for the traditional form of inheritance:

> Thus on the one hand, in proportion as wealth increased it made the man's position in the family more important than the woman's, and on the other hand created an impulse to exploit this strengthened position in order to overthrow in favor of his children the traditional order of inheritance. This, however, was impossible so long as descent was reckoned according to mother right. Mother right, therefore, had to be overthrown, and overthrown it was . . . . The overthrow of mother right was the *world historical defeat of the female sex.* The man took command in the home also; the woman was degraded and reduced to servitude; she became the slave of his lust and a mere instrument for production of children.

From this transformation emerged the patriarchal family and its progeny, the modern monogamous family. Both, according to Engels, are characterized by a high degree of control of female sexuality and by a significant difference between the ways in which male and female labor is viewed:

> In the old communistic household, which comprised many couples and their children, the task entrusted to the women of managing the household was as much

a public, a socially necessary industry as the procuring of food by the men. With the patriarchal family and still more with the single monogamous family, a change came. Household management lost its public character. It no longer concerned society. It became a *private service;* the wife became the head servant, excluded from all participation in social production. Not until the coming of modern large-scale industry was the road to social production opened to her again— and then only to the proletarian wife. But it was opened in such a manner that, if she carries out her duties in the private service of her family, she remains excluded from public production and unable to earn; and if she wants to take part in public production and earn independently, she cannot carry out family duties.

Engels, unlike Mill, does not accept a division of labor which puts the woman in the home and the man in the social realm of industry. Such a division of labor contributes to the subordination of women to men and must be abolished for sexual equality:

> In the great majority of cases today, at least in the possessing classes, the husband is obliged to earn a living and support his family, and that in itself gives him a position of supremacy without any need for special legal titles and privileges. Within the family he is the bourgeois and the wife represents the proletariat . . . . And in the same way, the peculiar character of the supremacy of the husband over the wife in the modern family, the necessity of creating real social equality between them and the way to do it, will only be seen in the clear light of day when both possess legally complete equality of rights. Then it will be plain that the first condition for the liberation of the wife is to bring the whole female sex back into public industry and that this in turn demands that the characteristic of the monogamous family as the economic unit of society be abolished.

Thus, unlike Mill, Engels sees sexual inequality within the home as a consequence of a sexual division of labor which places women at home, outside of, and yet dependent upon, the monetary economy. Further, the elimination of this inequality requires an elimination of the sexual division of labor per se. Thus only when women work in the public realm with and alongside of men can women achieve any true form of equality. Moreover, also unlike Mill, Engels believes that a further necessary condition for such equality is the elimination of the monogamous family as an economic unit of society. This type of family, based on the transference of private property to the heirs of its male head, requires the control of female sexuality and consequently women's activities generally. Though Engels does not attack monogamy per se and indeed argues for the possibility of true "individual sex love" after property is socialized, he does believe in its incompatibility, when economically motivated, with sexual equality. In sum, in conjunction with Engels' attack on a sexual division of labor is his belief in the need to eliminate the monogamous family as an economic unit.

VIII. Conclusion

In comparing Plato and Aristotle, I introduced the thesis that Plato's rejection of a nuclear family for members of the guardian class might account for his rejection of the sexual division of labor for members of that class. Similarly, the endorsement of the nuclear family by both Locke and Rousseau seemed in both cases central to their acceptance of a sexual division of labor. Moreover, their beliefs in the necessity of a sexual division of labor and their beliefs in sexual inequality generally seemed compatible, rather than incompatible, with their democratic theory, given the importance of the family in certain forms of a democratic state. Finally, when I turned to Mill and Engels, the issue of the family again appeared the crucial variable in regard to both philosophers' positions on sexual division of labor. While Mill, like Plato, does allow for any woman to perform any job for which she is qualified, and even goes further than Plato in noting the probably social determinants of existing capabilities, he does not believe that a married woman, unlike a married man, can be both married and have an occupation outside of marriage. The consequence of this position seems to be that for Mill, as for Plato, there can be no conjunction of the family and an elimination of a sexual division of labor. Only Engels, who also attacks the monogamous family, at least when economically motivated, maintains an explicit rejection of a sexual division of labor per se. The glaring conclusion of these philosophers thus seems to be: where there is family, there women shall be.

The connection I am thus suggesting is between an endorsement of a sexual division of labor and an endorsement of the family, particularly in its nuclear form. This conclusion is broad, and should not obviate the important differences between the content of the sexual division of labor among even those theorists who endorse it in principle. That Locke believes that the appropriate place of married women is at home does not mean that he is thereby committed to the same pronouncements on the activities of a married woman as is Rousseau. Even Rousseau and Aristotle, who appear similarly conservative on the activities of women, must differ in giving content to such activities, if only because of the important economic differences between classical Athens and eighteenth-century France. That activity of raising children must inevitably be different in such different societies. Thus what I have examined in this essay has been the extent to which different theorists have been committed to the idea of a sexual division of labor per se. I have not explored in depth the differences which might, for example, exist between Aristotle and Rousseau on what specific tasks that women, as opposed to men, should perform. Also, I have employed a broad concept of a "nuclear family" thereby ignoring the differences which again must exist within this type of family. Lawrence Stone in his history of the English family from 1500 to 1800 notes important differences even within the modern English nuclear family in this period, particularly those between what he describes as the "Restricted Patriarchal Nuclear Family" and the "Closed Domesticated Nuclear Family," the latter being characterized by greater equality and autonomy of husband and wife. Nevertheless, though I have painted a conclusion in broad strokes, I believe it may prove helpful to further thought on this topic. That in the history of philosophy there appears a connection between an endorsement of a sexual division of labor and an endorsement of the family may indicate possible connections between these institutions as they have existed in practice.

Study Questions

1. Which of the various philosophers that Nicholson discusses has the best view of working women? *Engels*

2. Do you see any progress in the history of philosophical views about women and work? If you see some progress, has it been slow and steady progress, or has it been more inconsistent and dramatic?

40

Heelan v. Johns-Manville Corp.

United States District Court,
District of Colorado

Sherman G. Finesilver, District Judge

In this action under Title VII of the Civil Rights Act of 164,... Mary K. Heelan seeks damages against her former employer, Defendant Johns-Manville Corporation [JM]. She claims that her refusal to have sexual relations with her supervisor, Joseph Consigli, resulted in her employment termination.

Defendant denies any impropriety by Consigli or corporate liability. Defendant contends that plaintiff was terminated for insubordination, lack of application, and general inability to perform at the level required of her position.

We find that JM is guilty of sex discrimination under Title VII, and that the retention of plaintiff's job as a JM project director was conditioned on the acceptance of sexual relations with her supervisor, a company executive.

Facts and Conclusions

Much of the testimony is conflicting, not only in pivotal areas but in areas of marginal relevance as well. This case is based largely upon the court's view of the credibility of the witnesses, i.e., their worthiness of belief.

We have carefully scrutinized all testimony and the circumstances under which each witness has testified, and every matter in evidence which tends to show whether a witness is worthy of belief. For example, we have taken into account each witness' motive and state of mind, strength of memory and demeanor and manner while on the witness stand. We have considered factors which affect the witness'

Reprinted from United States District Court, District of Colorado, 1978.

recollection and his or her opportunity to observe and accurately relate to the matters discussed. We have considered whether a witness' testimony has been contradicted, and the bias, prejudice, and interest, if any, of each witness. In addition, we have considered any relation each witness may bear to either side of the case; the manner in which each witness might be affected by a decision in the case; and the extent to which, if at all, each witness is either supported or contradicted by other evidence.

With these factors in mind we find the following as facts and enter our conclusions of law.

I

In 1971, JM, an international corporation, commenced moving its world headquarters from New York to Colorado. The move necessitated temporary offices at Greenwood Plaza near Denver, and ultimately complete construction of a 55 million dollar building and amenities at the Ken Caryl Ranch, Jefferson County, Colorado.

Joseph Consigli of the New York home office, as Director of Facilities Planning, was transferred to Colorado to supervise a team to control and oversee the construction of the Colorado headquarters, obtain temporary office space, and assist relocation of 1,500 JM employees and their families to Colorado.

In August 1971, plaintiff was hired by JM as a senior secretary and assigned to Consigli. Her employment with JM continued until May 31, 1974, when she was terminated by Consigli.

The documentary evidence of plaintiff's work performance at JM shows her to be an outstanding employee. All her evaluations rated her consistently excellent. Statements by plaintiff's co-workers also found her to be a good employee and, from their standpoint, no work-related reason existed for her termination. The only person to question plaintiff's competence is her supervisor, and these criticisms do not appear in any of his formal written evaluations, but only in his oral statements and privately maintained notes.

Initially plaintiff's work was typical secretarial work and included assistance in relocation of employees. Her starting salary was $6,650 per year. Within a matter of months, plaintiff, under the direction of Consigli, was performing duties best characterized as a facilities planner. Consigli and staff had the responsibility of not only planning the world's headquarters but also the interior design of the Greenwood Plaza office. Thus, a major part of her responsibilities involved coordination with the Space Design Group, a New York design firm responsible for the interior work at Greenwood Plaza. Plaintiff's worth was clearly apparent to Consigli and in March 1972 he recommended plaintiff for a "twostep" raise, rather than the customary onestep advance. The pay recommendation form (Ex. 3) noted that the pay raise was a "special merit increase." Consigli rated plaintiff's work as "excellent" in the following five categories: (1) ability, (2) application, (3) job performance, (4) cooperativeness, and (5) capacity for growth. Because of the unusual two step pay raise Consigli felt constrained to attach a note to the recommendation form indicating his high regard for Mrs. Heelan's excellent employment record.

In November of 1972, plaintiff was promoted at Consigli's recommendation to the position of "associate facilities planner" and her salary increased from $7,500 to $10,000. Her new position carried with it considerable responsibility and attaining the associate position was a major accomplishment. The job description for the associate position provided that it would be filled by a person with a degree, or its equivalent, in architectural design supplemented by courses in business administration and management. Plaintiff had none of these qualifications. Plaintiff's performance in her more responsible position merited a raise in July 1973. The raise came, in part, as a result of her outstanding annual evaluation which was completed on May 23, 1973. The subjective portion of the evaluation indicated that plaintiff performed her duties as JM's "principal contact with design and planning professions and interior contractors . . . very well and exceeded most objectives." Consigli also noted that Mrs. Heelan's "greatest accomplishment and talent" was "[i]n solving problems and adjusting schedules to meet changing job conditions. Her rapport with the design and planning disciplines is a great asset to the company." In the objective portion of the appraisal, Consigli gave plaintiff the highest grades printed on the form.

Soon after the pay raise recommendation, Consigli recommended plaintiff for a JM "A" award. According to a JM President's Bulletin, the "A" award is given to employees

> who, through initiative, ability and wholehearted interest in the Company, perform with unusual merit and show extraordinary accomplishments. . . . [¶] Administration of "A" awards requires a high degree of managerial judgment. Selection and approval must be exercised with utmost care. . . .

Plaintiff received her "A" award on June 15, 1973, by letter from the president of JM, Dr. William Goodwin, and a monetary award of $1,000. Another raise to $12,000 followed in November. This raise was the result of a company wide upward adjustment of salary levels and included the following comments: "Mary's application to her work and often on her own initiative, and job performance has been excellent. She has excellent ability and capacity for growth."

In spring of 1973, JM began its construction efforts of the world headquarters at the Ken Caryl Ranch. The Architects' Collaborative [TAC] was selected as the architect; Turner Construction Company [Turner] was the construction manager; and Space Design was chosen to do the interior work. To assist him, Consigli hired Eric Dienstbach as project manager to work with the TAC to coordinate its efforts with the requirements of Turner and JM. Plaintiff, as associate of Facilities Planning, had the responsibility of working with Space Design to coordinate its efforts with the requirement of JM and Turner. In the Fall, plaintiff told Consigli that she felt that although she was doing the same type of work as the department's single project manager, Eric Dienstbach, she was paid less and held the lower title of "associate." Plaintiff claimed that this was a case of sex discrimination. She requested promotion to Project Director. Consigli conferred about plaintiff with his immediate supervisor Francis May, an executive vice president, and Richard Goodwin, then president of JM.

Although Heelan had an excellent performance record, serious reservations were expressed by top management about her attitude which was, at times, stated to be abrasive and arrogant. After several meetings with top management, Consigli recommended plaintiff's promotion to project manager which was approved in February 1974.

II

Mrs. Heelan articulated specific romantic advances made by Consigli beginning in April 1972, and extending through April 23, 1974, when she was informed of her termination. The sexual advances were occasioned as an integral part of her employment. The initial advances were made in April 1972. Consigli explained that the world headquarters duties would involve substantial travel responsibilities and family sacrifices. Plaintiff indicated her willingness to assume the duties and fulfill travel requirements. During the conversation Consigli put his arm around plaintiff and said that she really did not yet understand the job requirement but that she would in time. Explicit sexual invitations followed in late 1972, and continued on a regular basis through early 1974. All were refused.

In January 1973, Consigli had lunch with Space Design Group's Ronald Phillips. Although they had been discussing business Consigli began to talk about his affection for Mrs. Heelan. Consigli volunteered that he liked plaintiff very much but was not sure that he could have an affair with her as he was married. Phillips was surprised by the conversation and did not respond. Later that month Phillips was again brought into the situation, this time by plaintiff. On January 23, plaintiff, who had not worked with Phillips for over a year, told him that she was distressed about her relationship with Consigli. Plaintiff related that he had offered her an apartment if she would leave her husband and consent to an affair. Phillips apparently told no one about his discussions with Consigli and plaintiff.

During the last few months of her employment Consigli's sexual advances became more frequent, occurring as often as once a week. The final demand came on April 23, 1974. Plaintiff was called into her supervisor's office and told that she was to have an affair or be fired. Plaintiff refused any sexual relations with Consigli and was given notice that May 31, 1974, would be her last day of employment.

The evidence is in conflict as to whether plaintiff was offered another position at JM or extended an offer to return to her former position.

III

During the months of sexual harassment, plaintiff for the most part kept the matter to herself. On occasion, however, she discussed the matter with Eric Dienstbach, Ronald Phillips, Isabelle Dienstbach, and Francis May. On at least one occasion Consigli mentioned the possibility of an affair to Ronald Phillips.

Although plaintiff repeatedly refused any sexual relationship with Consigli, she did begin an affair with her co-worker, Eric Dienstbach, sometime in September or October. Plaintiff denied the liaison but the evidence contradicts her position. Both Consigli and Isabelle Dienstbach suspected the affair. Consigli asked Mrs. Dienstbach to question her son about the

matter. Eric denied having an affair when questioned by his mother. She testified that she did not believe this denial. Of more importance, however, is the fact that during the discussion Eric told his mother that Consigli was pressuring plaintiff to have an affair with him. Mrs. Dienstbach testified that she did not believe this statement either, but nonetheless questioned Consigli. He denied the charge and Mrs. Dienstbach did not pursue the matter. Just when this discussion occurred is in dispute—Eric saying it happened in February or March 1974 while Isabelle recalling the incident to have occurred earlier. Whatever the exact date, this discussion provided notice to top JM management that Consigli might have been making sexual advances toward Mrs. Heelan. It also alerted Consigli to the fact that others knew of those advances. At the earliest, the discussion would have taken place in late 1973 since, according to Eric Dienstbach his affair did not begin until September or October. This time period coincides with the time when, according to Consigli, plaintiff's work product seriously declined.

Some time in December 1973 or January 1974, plaintiff made an appointment to speak with Isabelle Dienstbach. Mrs. Dienstbach had for a long period served as a sounding board for many of the female employees at JM who had work-related problems. At the meeting, plaintiff told Mrs. Dienstbach about Consigli's sexual demands, that they were being made weekly, and that she did not know how to stop the incidents. This meeting was another instance when Isabelle Dienstbach was informed of Consigli's actions. During this period plaintiff again confided in Ronald Phillips of Space Design Group and Eric Dienstbach.

After plaintiff's notice of termination on April 23, she again sought out Isabelle Dienstbach. Plaintiff discussed the termination with her and was told to schedule a meeting with Francis May. Plaintiff met with May at the end of that month. She informed him, as she had informed Isabelle Dienstbach twice before, that Consigli had fired her not because of her work performance but because of her refusal to submit to her supervisor's sexual demands. May suggested that plaintiff discuss the matter with JM's personnel manager. Mrs. Heelan responded that May was the personnel manager's supervisor and that the personnel manager would in all probability not take action unless May ordered it. May agreed and declined to do anything at that time. After the meeting, May telephoned Consigli and asked him about plaintiff's charges. Consigli denied any wrongdoing and the matter was dropped. The law in this area is of recent vintage. Few trial courts have published pertinent opinions in the Federal Supplement. . . . In addition, only three Courts of Appeals have reviewed this issue. . . .

From these opinions a body of law is developing which, first and most importantly, recognizes that sexual harassment of female employees is gender-based discrimination which can violate Title VII. . . .

In order to recover on such a claim, however, the plaintiff must allege and establish that submission to the sexual suggestion constituted a term or condition of employment. A cause of action does not arise from an isolated incident or a mere flirtation. These may be more properly characterized as an attempt to establish personal relationships than an endeavor to tie employment to sexual submission. Title VII should not be interpreted as reaching into sexual relationships which may arise during the course of employment, but which do not have a substantial effect on that employment. In general, we would limit Title VII claims in this area, as suggested by one commentator, to "repeated, unwelcome sexual advances" which impact as a term or condition of employment . . .

It is not necessary for a plaintiff to prove a policy or practice of the employer endorsing sexual harassment. . . . To demand that a plaintiff prove a company-directed policy of sexual discrimination is merely to extend a claim for relief with one hand and take it away with the other. In no other area of employment discrimination do the courts require such proof. . . . The employer is responsible for the discriminatory acts of its agents. . . .

Thus, to present a *prima facie* case of sex discrimination by way of sexual harassment, a plaintiff must plead and prove that (1) submission to sexual advances of a supervisor was a term or condition of employment, (2) this fact substantially affected plaintiff's employment, and (3) employees of the opposite sex were not affected in the same way by these actions.

This, however, does not end the inquiry. Under certain circumstances the employer may be relieved from liability. As noted by the court in *Miller v. Bank of America*, supra, where the employer has no knowledge of the discrimination, liability may be avoided if the employer has a policy or history of discouraging sexual harassment of employees by supervisors and the employee has failed to present the matter to a publicized grievance board. If the employer is aware of the situation and rectifies it, the employer may not be held liable for the acts of its agents. . . .

This case can be determined on relatively narrow grounds. It is clear that the repeated sexual demands made on Mrs. Heelan by her supervisor over a twoyear period developed into a "term or condition" of employment. The facts here do not present a borderline case in which this court must decide whether the acts complained of substantially affected the terms of employment, or were nothing more than a personal flirtation unrelated to plaintiff's job. Here we have the paradigm of the repeated, unwelcome sexual advance. . . .

Nor in this case do we have the problem . . . concerning the liability of the employer for the unknown acts of its supervisor-employee. We have considered and reject JM's argument that plaintiff failed to take advantage of JM's internal grievance procedures. First, the evidence fails to establish the existence of any such procedure and second, during her tenure plaintiff advised top management of her allegations. We find that she did everything within her power to bring her charges to the attention of top management. Here, the employer through its highest officers knew of the charges of sexual harassment. In JM's organizational scheme Consigli answered to only two people: JM's president William Goodwin and its executive vice president Francis May. May was informed of plaintiff's claims after termination and did nothing more than call the "accused" for verification or denial. More importantly, the administrative assistant to the president had heard charges of impropriety from two sources prior to plaintiff's termination. Her investigation was no more thorough than May's. The depth and scope of these inquiries can hardly satisfy the corporation's obligation under Title VII.

The effect of the Civil Rights Act of 1964, and particularly of Title VII of that Act, has been to impose on employers certain duties which theretofore did not exist. No major employer in this nation can ignore the requirements of equal opportunity in hiring, promotion and general conditions of employment. What little legislative history that exists in the area of sex discrimination has convinced the courts that "Congress intended to strike at the entire spectrum of disparate treatment of men and women resulting from sex stereotypes." . . . This stereotype of the sexually accommodating secretary is well documented in popular novels, magazine cartoons and the theatre. As we have indicated, Title VII does not concern itself with sexual liaisons among men and women working for the same employer. Title VII does, however, become involved when acceptance of sexual advances is transformed into a condition of continued employment.

Under the facts of this case, the frequent sexual advances by a supervisor do not form the basis of the Title VII violation that we find to exist. Significantly, termination of plaintiff's employment when the advances were rejected is what makes the conduct legally objectionable. Receptivity of repeated sexual advances by a high level supervisor was inescapably a condition of the plaintiff's continued employment. The termination of plaintiff's employment as a retaliatory measure when advances were rejected are [sic] within the purview of Title VII. . . .

Plaintiff is entitled to damages in the form of back pay and lost employment benefits. Appropriate considerations include the difference between the salary plaintiff would have made had she remained in the JM organization and that which she actually made since her departure by way of unemployment compensation, wages, and the like. A determination of the proper amount of damages will be made in a separate order. In addition, plaintiff's attorneys are entitled to an award of reasonable attorneys' fees to be paid by defendant Johns-Manville Corporation.

Study Questions

1. Is sexual harassment sex discrimination?

*2. Should companies have training programs to try to prevent misunderstandings and sexual harassment? If so, should the company require all of its employees to be trained, or should it wait for the first complaint about a person before requiring that person to be trained about what constitutes sexual harassment?

*3. If you were single and began to feel strongly attracted to someone you saw regularly at work, would you be inclined to avoid or seek romantic involvement?

41

*Love in the Boardroom:
The Case of Mary Cunningham
and William Agee*

Michael Kinsley

"What you need now is to be mentored," said William Agee to Mary Cunningham. Then he lifted her gently in his strong, pinstriped arms, carried her to his executive desk, and mentored her till dawn.

No, no, not at all, says Cunningham in *Powerplay: What Really Happened at Bendix*. According to Cunningham, Agee did indeed utter the preposterous phrase, "What you need now is to be mentored." But this was the beginning of a *business* relationship. Only later did it bubble into love in the caldron of shared victimization by journalists and business rivals. Her story, written with Fran Schumer, is as follows:

She was a naive twenty-eight-year old Catholic girl when she arrived at Bendix in June 1979 fresh from Harvard Business School. "What I knew about the world and people I'd learned from reading Plato and Thomas Aquinas." Her only ambition was to do good. "I viewed myself as a latter-day Joan of Arc." Her saintly impulse had inclined her toward a career in investment banking. But then she met William Agee, the brilliant young chairman of Bendix. Agee enticed her to be his special assistant by appealing to her "missionary zeal." "He needs my help," she realized. After just one interview her stigmata were bleeding: "In the taxi on the way back to my hotel I was already shouldering the burdens of Bendix and getting a headache because of it."

Nevertheless, she wavered. Should it be investment banking after all? Nonsense, Agee said. "Just think of how it'll slow down your learning curve." Cunningham confesses: "That was the real killer. I was a sucker for steep learning curves." Soon they

were making beautiful business together. " 'So what's our opinion on this one, Cunningham?' he'd challenge me. 'Oh, I think it's full of prunes, Agee,' I'd say, and we'd both crack up."

Within a year she was promoted to vice president for corporate and public affairs, "the youngest female corporate vice president of a Fortune 500 company in America," as she tells us. She didn't really want the job, but Agee insisted. " 'If I can't appeal to you on the basis that I truly need you here (he knew he always could), let me appeal to you as your mentor,' he said."

But bliss was short-lived. People began spreading rumors that there was Something Going On between Agee and herself, both then married to others. " 'How dare they,' I said, my voice rising, the anger welling up inside me." (Elsewhere she complains about journalists presenting "my life as a soap opera.") She began suffering chest pains. The rumors continued. She told Agee that she couldn't take it anymore and—although "I'm not trying to downgrade the importance of my learning curve"—she wanted to quit. He dissuaded her. In fact, he promoted her to vice president for strategic planning.

Soon afterward their relationship came up at a meeting of Bendix employees, with reporters in attendance. Agee declared that Cunningham was "a very close friend of my family" but that her rapid rise was solely "because she's . . . . a very talented individual." Mary burst into tears and was comforted by one of Agee's secretaries (in the Zasu Pitts role): " 'Don't let it get to you. They're just jealous . . . . You're so young. So pretty. So bright. They're just being mean.' I thanked her and eventually ventured out the side door to the waiting limousine." But the rumors turned into newspaper headlines, and after a few more days of agony, on October 8, 1980, the Bendix board gave her $120,000 and forced her to resign. She felt like an aborted fetus. "Their solution: 'Get rid of the problem. Nice and clean.' "

She was desperate: she considered lobotomy, suicide, a visiting professorship at Harvard Business School. According to *Powerplay*, she had no contact with Agee during this period, until they were reconciled several weeks later with the help of a psychiatrist. But phone records obtained by Allan Sloan, author of *Three Plus One Equals Billions*, another Bendix book, show several long calls to Agee's office, home, and New York hotel suite.

As Thanksgiving approached, she felt she couldn't go home (although she had just been there) because "I had put my mother through so much grief, given her such cause for worry, that I couldn't bear the idea of bringing any more of my problems home." By coincidence Agee called soon after she reached this odd decision. Would she please come out to his retreat in Idaho to help nurse him through a case of mononucleosis? Naturally she was concerned about how this would look. But she was even more concerned that "this whole experience was starting to change me from a compassionate human being to a kind of unfeeling pragmatist." So she went to Idaho, where she stayed in Agee's guest room. (Agee told Allan Sloan that she'd stayed with friends.) They had long talks. Agee said he might quit Bendix, but she warned him—this was late November—of "what I'd learned about unemployment since October 8th." (By her own account, she'd spent most of the period at the La Costa resort in California and at the Waldorf in New York sorting through "more than 200 job queries.")

Back in New York she tried dating other men, but "I felt so removed from them all. I was laden with history." One day Agee showed up unexpectedly to help her move to a new apartment. They packed a few boxes, went out to dinner, and then—it's page 216—they kissed for the first time. "How natural and good it felt." Nevertheless, showing more patience than many readers will be able to muster, Agee slept in the den.

In June 1982 Mary Cunningham and William Agee were married in San Francisco. Visiting the church the day before, they discovered that Mother Teresa was about to speak. "I quickly turned to Bill. I couldn't believe she was speaking here exactly twenty-four hours before we were to be married at that very altar. The coincidence was too much. How many times had my life almost taken her path."

Is there a more audacious phony around than Mary Cunningham? Oh, who knows when she and Agee started canoodling. All we can say for sure is that since, by her own account, she was openly dating the guy by the spring of 1981, she might have the goodness to stop whining about how outrageous it was to suspect they were romantically linked the previous fall. Likewise, having sought publicity at every opportunity—from the Couples page of *People* magazine to this book—she might stop posing as St. Mary, Martyr of the Media. ("Which of the saints, I wondered, had ever lived through a mass-media event?") Cunningham seems to believe that all the job offers and speech invitations she brags about are due to her prowess at strategic planning.

Everything about Cunningham's story rings false. Taken at face value, though, as an accurate portrayal of two top executives in action at a major American corporation, her book is even more appalling.

For one thing, is American business actually this gullible? Cunningham describes recruiting dinners while at business school ("I was usually placed in the most desirable seat right next to the managing partner") at which she "delved into issues": "Do you feel investment bankers spend enough time thinking about their responsibilities to society at large?" She reports smugly, "This approach . . . . gave me a significant edge," resulting in many job offers. She attempts to gull her readers the same way. "I was ambitious for worldly success," she deadpans, "but only as a means to influence constructive change." Could anyone who meant this put it in such a stilted way?

For all the Mother Teresa talk, this book contains not one selfless word or deed. Quite the reverse: Cunningham comes off as an almost clinical egomaniac. Every other page contains a reference to her "excellent grades," praise from superiors (usually Agee), adoration from fans ("my speech was interrupted twelve times with applause"). Every facet of her life is canonization material. Even before business school, "I was already making a name for myself at Kass Goodkind Wechsler & Gerstein"—where she worked as a paralegal specializing in debt collection—because "I felt it was my special mission to help these people" pay their bills. Even the annulment of her first marriage, we learn, "was granted in almost record time." What a gal! The Church recognized immediately that it was "my orientation toward helping people" that had misled her into wedlock.

Powerplay, however, contains no examples of Cunningham "helping people," other than Agee and herself. Indeed her attitude toward others is distinctly uncharitable. Almost everyone at Bendix except for Agee is a boob, sycophant, sexist, and/or racist. The first Mrs. Agee is a scheming bitch. Cunningham's idea of a compliment is to say of her first husband, a black graduate of Exeter, Harvard College, and Harvard Business School: "He's a street fighter."

There is nothing in *Powerplay* to support Cunningham's contention that she is a business genius. Her chatter about learning curves and other B-school buzzwords seems infantile. What little discussion there is of actual business consists of genuflecting in front of a deity called The Strategy. The Strategy is what Mary and Bill were up to when nasty-minded people thought they were up to something else. Near as I can tell, it consisted of getting Bendix out of a lot of fuddy-duddy old-fashioned products and into glitzy high tech. What makes this a terribly ingenious idea, let alone a good one, she does not say. But she became very attached to it. "How's The Strategy going" she asked Agee the first time they met after her departure from Bendix. And at the book's emotional climax, as Agee realizes he's going to lose control of Bendix to Allied Corp., he says: " 'Of course, you know what this means? . . . The Strategy that we've worked on so hard'—and here he nodded at me—'won't be in our hands.'" And they cry.

Cunningham's breathless description of Agee's business skill calls her own into question. "For a long time," she writes at one point, "Agee had suspected that the company was losing its market share to foreign competition and even some U.S. companies in the manufacture of brakes." Suspected? How much brilliance does it take for a chairman to know his own company's market share? Elsewhere: "His sense of timing, as usual, was impeccable. Just at the time Bendix was buying, stock prices were going down and interest rates were going up. It was a perfect time to move out of cash and into stocks." It was? Well, what do I know about Strategy?

We don't really need to know about Cunningham's business acumen, or her sex life, to conclude that her rise in just one year from business school to, in essence, the No. 2 spot in a major industrial corporation was absurd. It cannot be explained (as she tries to explain it) as the inexorable result of "merit." Whether or not she was his lover, Cunningham was Agee's pet. As Cunningham describes it, gross favoritism is absolutely standard operating procedure in the business world. American capitalism is a veritable orgy of "mentoring." Agee himself had been "mentored" not once, but twice, and one of his mentors, Michael Blumenthal, also had a mentor, George Ball. And so on, I guess, back to Adam.

And talk about waste, fraud, and abuse! Where's Peter Grace when we need him? Unintentionally, Cunningham paints a picture of the corporate world as the Department of Energy with expense accounts. At Bendix under Agee, it appears, teams of executives spent days in preparation whenever the chairman had to give a speech, even a five-minute introduction. Official parties also sucked up huge chunks of executive energy, not to mention office politics. One of the most vital activities—assigned to Corporate V.P. Mary, natch—was opening the chairman's mail. (According to Allan Sloan's book, a corporate jet used to fly from Michigan to Idaho with Agee's mail during the long stretches when he was in residence there.) Meanwhile, you'd be hard put to learn from this book what exactly it is Bendix makes. Cunningham's offhand references to limousines and hotel suites (not to mention golden parachutes) make clear that millions were melting away in the care and feeding of the top birds. (Not that it turned her head, of course. In fact, toward the end at the Waldorf, "Just the sight of the silver cart sent me into the bathroom, retching.")

At their first meeting, Cunningham says, Agee listened to her for a while and then said, "Even I wasn't that sharp at your age." Today Agee and Cunningham are "doing strategy" together in their very own consulting and venture capital firm. They deserve each other.

Study Questions

1. Are Agee and Cunningham a couple of phonies?

2. Was Cunningham self-deceived, deliberately deceiving others, or telling the truth?

3. How often do you think such relationships occur in business? Is the Agee-Cunningham relationship symbolic of how women are treated in business?

4. Did any sexual harassment occur in this case?

5. Did Agee and Cunningham get what they deserved in the end: each other? Do they deserve any penalty? How much harm, if any, did they cause? If they harmed others, what was that harm?

42

Family Values: The Case of Parental Leave and the Business of Bringing Up Baby

Margaret E. Meiers

Editor's note: Meiers' essay, which surveyed key statistics, was prophetic. She predicted that parental leave was a coming policy and suggested that it was only a matter of time before federal legislation supported it. The Family Leave Act was one of the first major pieces of legislation President Clinton signed into law.

———————

Parental leave is here to stay. Whether federal legislation is enacted to enforce it this year or the next is not important. Already many states have parental leave requirements in place, and increasingly, corporations are developing programs to meet the needs particular to their workforce. Personnel managers are even using parental leave in the scramble to recruit and hold on to good workers as the labor pool shrinks.

Looking at parental leave from several different perspectives provides a clearer picture of the direction policies will take. The national picture reveals a burgeoning amount of pending federal and state legislation. Meanwhile, as indicated by Catalyst's National Study of Parental Leaves, conducted in 1986, corporate attitudes and policies are undergoing a transformation. From that information it is possible to set guidelines for developing and managing a progressive parental leave policy that managers can consider.

This article originally appeared as "Down with the Wait-and-See Approach," *Management Review* (January 1989), pp. 84–89. Copyright © 1989 by the American Management Association, New York. All rights reserved. Reprinted by permission.

The 1988 Family and Medical Leave Act was killed Congress this past October. It was combined with the ABC childcare bill and an antipornography amendment and died after the Senate failed to get enough votes to close off debate. The act will be reintroduced early this year and may move more quickly through this session of Congress.

The significance of the Family and Medical Leave Act does not lie so much in its passage but in its symbolization of a societal need. The status of the legislation will not affect this need. Employees need to be able to return to work after having babies. Thus they are turning to Congress, to state legislators, and to their companies to request responsive parental leave policies.

Many companies, however, are concentrating their efforts on fighting against parental leave legislation. This approach may be shortsighted. Eighty percent of women are expected to become pregnant at some point during their work lives. Two-thirds of the new entrants to the labor force over the next decade will be women. These statistics demonstrate that regardless of the legislation, the issue of parental leave will not go away, and companies must address it. Companies that do not provide parental leaves and have to find permanent replacements have a good chance of hiring other women who may also want to take a leave at some point.

On the state level, parental leave legislation is making steady progress. Thirty-three states introduced parental leave bills in the past year. Several states, including Connecticut, Oregon, Minnesota, and Rhode Island, passed parental leave laws, while others passed maternity leave bills. New York State has introduced parental leave bills for the past several years and will no doubt do so again in 1989.

Some companies that have offices in different regions of the country have responded to changing state laws by developing policies that are comprehensive and generous enough to go beyond the scope of the law in any given state. The process of tracking state laws and changing policy to accommodate them is cumbersome. One human resources executive I recently spoke with complained that following and complying with state parental leave laws was consuming a significant amount of time of the company's legal staff.

Some type of federal parental leave legislation most likely will pass in the next several years. In the meantime, companies have an opportunity to evaluate and revise their parental leave policies without having to respond to a mandate. One of the most interesting findings of Catalyst's National Study of Parental Leaves was that 88 percent of respondents had changed their parental leave policies in response to the 1978 Pregnancy Discrimination Act (PDA). The new law was their primary reason for changing their policies. The Pregnancy Discrimination Act requires that if a company provides a disability leave policy, it must treat pregnancy like any other disability. Some companies, in fact 23 percent, actually took away additional unpaid parental leave benefits they had offered prior to the PDA because they wanted their policies to comply with the letter of the law. These companies failed to see that a progressive leave policy could also serve as a retention tool. Companies are often reactive in changing their parental leave policies, responding to legislation rather than proactively developing innovative new policies.

The corporate response to the parental leave issue varies widely. Some companies have taken a wait-and-see stance and do not plan to develop policies until a new federal law requires them to do so. Other companies have modified their policies on a state-by-state basis. Still others have developed policies similar to and even more generous than the requirements of the Family and Medical Leave Act, so that they don't have to deal with the legal requirements at all.

In terms of corporate policy, Catalyst's National Study of Parental Leaves found:

- 95 percent of companies provided disability leave to pregnant employees. This leave is typically six to eight weeks.
- 52 percent of companies provide an additional, unpaid, job-protected leave to women. The average length of unpaid leave offered to women is one to three months.
- 37 percent of companies provide the same unpaid job protection to men.
- 60 percent of companies allow employees to return to work on a part-time basis.

The most universal corporate response has been concern over the cost of providing parental leave. For some companies, particularly smaller ones, this is a real and legitimate concern. But consider for a moment that the cost of *not* providing parental leave may be greater than the cost of providing it.

Most companies looking only at the cost of providing parental leave focus on two main elements:

- Maintaining benefits during the leave, and
- handling the work of someone on leave by either finding a temporary replacement or rerouting work to other employees.

Catalyst's study and a study conducted by the General Accounting Office found that companies typically reroute work to other employees rather than turn to outside replacements.

The cost of not providing parental leave is turnover and losing valuable employees. Turnover may also be the cost of providing leaves that are inadequate or inflexible. Turnover typically costs 93 percent of that employee's first-year salary. This cost includes the administrative costs associated with hiring a new employee, such as recruiting and interviewing time, and the new employee's learning-curve time. Companies invest time and money in training employees. When they lose an employee by not providing adequate parental leaves, they lose that investment. Consider the case of a woman who works for a company for five years, has a child and wants to take a three- or six-month parental leave. If her company refuses to provide her with that leave, it loses the time and money it has invested in training her. Six months later she may be working for a competitor while the first company is still looking for her replacement.

Many companies have assumed that women will not return to work, and consequently they haven't put much thought into their parental leave policies. This assumption may be rooted more in nostalgia than in reality. Today, most employees have to return to work, but parental leave policies haven't kept up with the times.

Recently media attention has focused on the perception that there is a trend that managerial women are dropping out of the workforce after having babies. This phenomenon may be a trend among certain groups of women, but statistics show that overall, more women than ever return to work quickly after having babies.

Companies may not be aware of this reality because they are not keeping statistics on how their policies are being used. When Catalyst conducted its National Study of Parental Leaves, one surprising discovery was that many companies had not kept records on things such as:

- The numbers of women taking leaves,
- The numbers of women returning or not returning to their jobs,
- The average length of leave,
- The numbers of women still with the company a year later, or

- The numbers of men requesting or taking leaves.

One company that conducted a cost analysis of its parental leave policy is Merck & Company, Incorporated of Rahway, New Jersey .... Merck compared the cost of offering a six-month parental leave with the cost of turnover and found that providing a six-month parental leave resulted in a $12,000 savings per employee.

The concept of family leave, the use of parental leave as a competitive recruitment strategy, and the provision of a part-time return from leave are three directions corporate policies are taking.

In the early 1980s, when Catalyst first started to study the issue of parental leave, many companies didn't know what was meant by that term. We had to call it maternity leave. The fact was that large numbers of men were not and still are not taking parental leaves. Now the term parental leave may become obsolete as a growing number of companies begin to provide "family leaves." In the past two years, Champion International, American Express, Campbell Soup, Aetna Life Insurance, and Kodak all have developed new family leave policies. American Express offers three months of unpaid, job-protected family leave to any employee to care for a newborn or newly adopted child or seriously ill family member.

The concept of family leave has developed as employers have realized that employees may have to take temporary leaves to care for elderly parents, sick children, as well as for newborn babies. The attention currently being given to leaves to care for the elderly has brought increased recognition to the issues of parental leave and childcare.

One human resources manager who did not have young children told me that he had always believed that companies should not become involved in providing work and family policies, such as parental leave and childcare. He viewed these policies as corporate intrusions into employees' lives and therefore inappropriate. In addition, he was concerned with the equity of providing special benefits to parents—benefits that would have no value to nonparent employees.

When his widowed mother became ill and he assumed responsibility for her care, the HR manager realized the difference that company flexibility and assistance could make in both his productivity and his personal stress level. Now he is a champion for work and family policies at his company.

Parental leave policies have become a competitive recruitment strategy. Five years ago, it would have been unheard of for a job applicant to inquire about parental leave policy during the interview process. Today, companies report that candidates regularly ask about these and other work and family policies. The question I am most frequently asked by human resource executives is what kinds of policies other companies in their industries are offering. These companies are concerned about providing policies that are competitive. Companies such as Ernst & Whinney and NCNB Corporation are two examples of companies using work and family policies as a recruitment tool. Some companies distribute parental leave kits as part of recruitment packages or even turn to their marketing departments to help them to communicate their work and family policies.

Another trend in corporate policy is offering a part-time return to work. Catalyst's National Study of Parental Leaves found that 60 percent of responding companies allowed some employees to return to work on a part-time basis. This was not usually a formal policy but was negotiated on a case-by-case basis. Human resources executives in some companies may not even be aware that these arrangements exist.

Corning Glass Works recently introduced a long-term, part-time policy that explicitly states that its intent is to enable employees with a dependent care situation to work part-time for several years, with the hope that they will return to full-time work when they are able. Because Corning believes that part-time work is the wave of the future, it is urging employees to use the new policy so that it will be an accepted business practice when the demand for part-time increases. Corning wants managers to adjust to the idea of alternative career tracks so that working part-time will not necessarily totally derail an employee's career.

What should be included in your company's leave policy? Following are seven general tips for developing and managing a parental leave policy:

1. Find out where you stand. Evaluate your current policy by collecting data on how it is being used. Look at your retention and turnover figures after parental leave.
2. Find out what kinds of policies other companies in your industry are offering. You may also want to investigate some of the cutting-edge parental leave policies to see what kinds of policies to expect in the future.
3. Know what current federal and state laws require, and assess the potential impact of

pending legislation.

4. Examine all possible policy components, and determine which best suit the needs of your employee population. Catalyst recommends that any parental leave policy include several basic elements:
   - A paid, job-protected disability leave for pregnant women;
   - An additional unpaid, job-protected family leave;
   - A part-time return to work; and
   - Reinstatement to the same or a comparable job at all stages of the leave.

5. Communicate your new policy to employees to let them know you recognize and support their responsibilities to their families as well as to their jobs.

6. Train supervisors to negotiate and arrange for a parental leave. If you offer flexibility, such as part-time work, encourage supervisors to provide that flexibility. A supervisor's reaction to an announcement of a pregnancy sets the tone for the entire leave process.

7. Develop strategies for handling work during a leave. Remember that parental leave is manageable and doesn't have to reduce productivity. Many companies treat a parental leave as a crisis despite the fact that there is plenty of time to plan in advance for a leave and develop strategies for handling work.

Whenever the topic of parental leave comes up, what I call "the Jane story" almost always follows. Everyone knows Jane. She is the dedicated career woman who decides to have a baby. Everyone believes that she will come back to work because she is so ambitious and devoted to her job. At the last minute, Jane surprises everyone by deciding not to return to work. Jane is the employee managers remember when they're developing a parental leave policy or negotiating a leave. Because of Jane, every other woman is suspect, no matter how much she insists she will return to work. All of the other women who do return from leave are forgotten while Jane will be remembered forever. It's time to move beyond the Jane story and address the real challenges of parental leave.

Study Questions

1. Do companies gain more loyalty from workers who know they can temporarily leave the company to care for their families and still get their old job back later? Wouldn't a family leave policy prevent more workers from merely playing out the string and going through the motions once they realize that they will have to leave their job to care for a family member? Wouldn't a family leave policy decrease stress and increase productivity for workers, since they would no longer face as many agonizing choices between continuing their careers and caring for their families? Would a family leave policy attract better workers in the first place? Would increases in loyalty, productivity, and quality of the workers outweigh the employer's cost of training workers to replace those on family leave? Aren't training costs inevitable for the employer anyway, since workers will almost always leave when they feel their families need them?

2. Will family leave save workers so much money on day care, nursing home care, etc., that the workers will be more willing to accept lower wages or even take pay cuts, making the company more productive and profitable?

3. Should family leave usually be with pay or without pay?

4. Would libertarianism oppose any federal legislation granting any workers any family leave no matter what the specifics of the legislation were? If so, is this too extreme to be justified?

5. Would utilitarianism support a family leave policy?

6. Germany, Japan, and other countries have more generous family leave policies than the United States does. For example, these policies usually provide for paid leave. Does the fact that America's main economic competitors have more generous policies on family leave show that America can have a family leave policy without any serious risk of becoming less competitive?

43

The Case of Comparable Worth

Judith Olans Brown
Phyllis Tropper Baumann
Elaine Millar Melnick

Editor's note: Comparable worth involves going beyond equal pay for equal work in order to combat sexism. The authors usefully define their key terms clearly and early. They survey three main arguments against comparable worth and try to rebut each: (1) discrimination doesn't cause the gap between wages for men and women; (2) comparable worth requires comparing incomparable jobs; and (3) comparable worth interferes too much with free-market economics.

A. Definitions: The Heart of the Debate

"Comparable worth" means that workers, regardless of their sex, should earn equal pay for work of comparable value to their common employer. Imprecise use of the phrase hinders meaningful discussion. Comparable worth is equated indiscriminately with comparable work, work of equal worth, work of equal value, or pay equity; however, these terms are not synonymous. Comparable worth theory addresses wage inequities that are associated with job segregation. The basic premise of comparable worth theory is that women should be able to substantiate a claim for equal wages by showing that their jobs and those of male workers are of equal value to their common employer. The doctrine allows comparison

of jobs which are different but which require comparable skills, effort, and responsibility.[1] In other words, this doctrine permits comparison of jobs which do not come within the ambit of the Equal Pay Act requirement of equal pay for jobs which are "substantially equal."

Opponents of comparable worth, however, focus on jobs that are not demonstrably equivalent and where a comparable worth claim is thus not present. Their rhetoric too often sacrifices accuracy to ideology.[2] In a popular but mistaken example, comparable worth opponents ask why such unrelated workers as nurses (not generally unionized) and truck drivers (highly unionized) should receive the same wages.[3] Opponents also ask why nurses and teamsters, who do not even work for the same employer, should receive the same pay. The response must emphasize that comparable worth cases always involve the same employer. The cases also always involve occupations which, according to a rational standard, are of comparable value to the employer.

The nurse/truck driver example implies that comparable worth requires equal pay for randomly selected job categories simply because the jobs being compared are ordinarily performed by members of one sex. What is really at issue, however, is equal pay for demonstrably equivalent jobs, as measured by either job content or a standard of experience, skill, or responsibility. An appropriate index against which to measure nurses' salaries might be the salaries of hospital sanitarians. Similarly, the appropriate comparable job for a truck driver is one which, although perhaps different in job content, is rated as equivalent in a job evaluation study, or which is capable of being so rated.[4]

Comparable worth doctrine differs from the Equal Pay Act formula in that it permits comparison of jobs which are not substantially similar in content. The Equal Pay Act of 1963 requires equal pay for work of equal skill, effort, and responsibility performed under similar working conditions. But the statute requires pay equality only for jobs which are *substantially equal.* If the jobs are relatively equivalent yet not sufficiently similar to meet that standard, no Equal Pay Act violation exists.

[In 1981 the Supreme Court] eliminated the requirement that Title VII plaintiffs prove the substantial equality of the jobs being compared.[5] . . . All Title VII plaintiffs alleging gender-based discrimination are comparing jobs which may have dissimilar functions but are of comparable value to the common employer.

The question for Title VII plaintiffs invoking comparable worth theory then becomes how to demonstrate that their jobs and those of male workers are of equal value to their common employer. [After the Court's 1981 decision] plaintiffs need not demonstrate job equivalency. Nor does a successful comparable worth claim require proof of undervaluation due to historical discrimination.[6] Instead, comparable worth requires proof that the employer's male and female workers perform work of comparable value and that the female workers are paid less. Such a demonstration necessarily depends upon the evaluation of jobs which are different in content.

B. Job Evaluation: The Red Herring of the Comparable Worth Debate

Job evaluation techniques provide a method for comparing jobs which are dissimilar in content. Job evaluation is a formal procedure which classifies a set of jobs on the basis of their relative value to the employer. Although the courts are uncomfortable with the concept of comparable worth, the technique of job evaluation has been familiar to American industry for decades.[7] Contrary to the claims of comparable worth critics, job evaluation does not require governmental participation. Evaluation merely eliminates resort to guesswork or unsubstantiated assertions of comparability. It provides a way of identifying situations in which wages remain artificially low because of sex, but where men and women are not performing identical or nearly identical operations.

Formal job evaluation originated in the late nineteenth century as part of a generalized expansion of organizational techniques and a restructuring of workplace control systems. Indeed, job evaluation was such a familiar method for comparing jobs that it provided the theoretical underpinning for the Equal Pay Act of 1963.[8] The various evaluation techniques all use similar methods to inject objectivity and equality into pay structures. The first stage requires a formal description of the duties, requirements, and working conditions of each job within the unit being evaluated. Next, jobs are evaluated in terms of "worth" to the organization. The outcome of these two processes is a ranking of all jobs in the valuation unit. The third stage involves setting wage rates for each job in accordance with the evaluation—the higher the ranking, the higher the wages. The job it-self, not the worker performing it, is the subject of evaluation.

Any attempt to raise wages on the basis of comparable worth turns on effective use of wage rate, job classification, promotion policy, and contractual data. Job evaluations assemble the relevant information in a form useful to employers, employees, and courts. Firmly grounded in existing industrial relations practice, job evaluation itself is hardly controversial. What is new is the use of this practice to address sex discrimination in wages.

Women in diverse occupations have begun to use job evaluation to demonstrate the discriminatory nature of their employers' male/female pay discrepancies.[9] The public rhetoric that characterizes job evaluation as an impossible task of comparing "apples and oranges" merely ignores the factual basis of the technique. The employer has already fashioned a wholly rational hierarchy of "apples and oranges" on the basis of relative worth to the employer. Unfortunately, the mistaken but popular notion of job evaluation has nonetheless prejudiced the courts against evaluation techniques that are essential to plaintiffs' cases.

C. Arguments against Comparable Worth: The Crux of the Rhetoric

Intense hostility has surrounded the idea of comparable worth. In order to understand this hostility, it is necessary to examine the arguments used by opponents of comparable worth. These arguments involve three related contentions: the male/female earnings gap results, at least in large part, from factors unrelated to discrimination by particular employers; comparable worth analysis is logistically impossible since there is no objective basis for establishing comparisons between different jobs; and, third, pay equity based on comparable worth would cripple the so-called free market.

1. The Non-Discriminatory Nature of the Wage Gap

The argument that the wage gap between men and women results from non-discriminatory factors is clearly expressed in a report by the U.S. Civil Rights Commission. In its findings, the Civil Rights Commission states that:

The wage gap between female and male earnings in America results, at least in significant part from a variety of things having nothing to do with discrimination by employers, including job expectations resulting from socialization beginning in the home; educational choices of women who anticipate performing child-bearing and child-rearing functions in the family and who wish to prepare for participation in the labor force in a manner which accommodates the performance of those functions, like the desire of women to work in the kinds of jobs which accommodate their family roles and the intermittency of women's labor force participation.

Essentially, one can reduce the Commission's argument to three basic propositions: women choose low-paying jobs because of their sociological predisposition; women make educational choices which lead to low-paying jobs; and the interrupted participation of women in the labor force leads to lower pay.

The first contention is misguided; comparable worth does not raise job *access* issues. Instead, it addresses situations where women who are already employed are paid less for jobs demonstrably similar to those of male co-workers. In comparable worth cases, women are not socialized to hold "easier" jobs; they are paid less for work of equivalent value. While the effect of socialization on job expectations is relevant to a woman's choice to become a nurse rather than a doctor, it does not address why female nurses are paid less than male orderlies or sanitarians at the same hospital. Comparable worth theory addresses inequities subsequent to access. The Commission simply misses the point in arguing that disadvantage results from the victim's choice, based on her own lower expectations.

The second and third contentions reflect the analytical framework used by human capital theorists to account for employment discrimination.[10] The touchstone of human capital theory as an explanation of wage differentials is productivity. Wages are viewed as a return on investments in human capital. The argument proceeds from the premise that individuals make investments in their productive capacity through education and training. These investments have costs, but they also produce returns in the form of higher wages. The male/female wage differential, therefore, merely reflects the different investments that men and women make.

Mincer and Polachek provide the classic formulation of the theory that women's lower wages merely reflect lower investments in human capital.[11] Productivity of men and women arguably differs . . . [due to] differences in education, training, or length of experience. [However] comparable worth theory does not rely on generalized statistical assertions; it requires a demonstration that in a particular case no other factor appears capable of explaining a proven disparity.

2. Comparing "Apples and Oranges"

The second major argument espoused by opponents of comparable worth is that no objective technique exists for comparing jobs that are not identical in content. The Civil Rights Commission contends that in comparable worth litigation job evaluations are inherently subjective and cannot establish jobs' intrinsic worth. Instead, the Commission claims that such studies function only "to establish rational pay-setting policies within an organization, satisfactory to the organization's employees and management."

This objection, though partially valid, goes too far. Although job evaluation is not absolutely objective, it is a well-established technique in American industry for determining relative wage levels. Representatives of business interests successfully sought to incorporate the concepts of job evaluation into the definition of equality in the Equal Pay Act of 1963. They argued that such a course was necessary because the use of job evaluation techniques was so widespread in industry. For example, E. G. Hester, the director of industrial relations research for Corning Glass, told the Senate Committee on Labor and Public Welfare of his company's concern over the proposed equality criteria. According to Mr. Hester, the proposed criteria would require equal pay "for equal work on jobs the performance of which requires equal skills." He asserted that his approach:

> . . . could give a great deal of difficulty to that large part of American industry and business which has relied upon systematic methods of job-evaluation for establishment of equitable rate relationships. Such job evaluation plans depend for their reliability upon other factors than skill alone.

Mr. Hester's statement to the Committee included evidence of the extent to which job evaluation was used. He argued that:

> With this general acceptance of job evaluation throughout industry on the part of both management and labor, we feel it most desirable that legislation related to the equal-pay principle incorporate in its language, recognition of job evaluation (or job classification) principles that have been developed, accepted, and are in general use.

In arguing for the incorporation of job evaluation principles, Mr. Hester conceded that job evaluation was "not a precise science governed by natural laws" but still lauded it as "a systematic approach to establish relative job order. . . ." He pointed out that industries using job evaluation principles had customarily constructed the hierarchy on the basis of "effort, skill, responsibility, and working conditions." The Equal Pay Act incorporates these same four factors.

Even a cursory examination of industrial relations practices demonstrates that business and industry have long used specific techniques to determine the relative wage rates of jobs which are dissimilar in content. While evaluation techniques are not absolutely objective, they are a logical starting point in any meaningful wage determination process. Comparable worth cases do not require an abstract showing of intrinsic value. Instead, plaintiffs' cases turn on proof that the employer's job worth determinations are gender-based. Since comparable worth cases always address alleged discrimination of a particular employer, they compare "pay-setting policies within an organization." The Commission itself admits that this use of job evaluation is "rational."

3. Laissez-Faire Economics and Antidiscrimination Law

The third argument commonly raised against comparable worth is that it requires an unwarranted intrusion into the market. Again, the Civil Rights Commission report provides an example. The Commission notes that: "The setting of wages is not and cannot be divorced from the forces of labor supply and demand. These factors heavily influence the setting of pay in many jobs and play an important role in setting wages for virtually all other jobs." The Commission then argues that there is nothing in the language or legislative history of Title VII to indicate that Congress intended to prevent employers from relying on the operation of the market in setting wages.

Courts have also made this assertion. However, any statute governing the employment relationship must by its very nature interfere with an employer's absolute freedom to determine wages by reference to the market. The enactment of Title VII Indicates congressional intent to intervene in the market to further significant policy interests.

Those who argue that comparable worth is an unwarranted interference insist that supply and de-

mand curves create the wage disparity at issue. Thus, comparable worth theory is not a legitimate response to discrimination but rather a specious definition of discrimination. If there is no impermissible discrimination, they argue, there is no social justification for judicial interference with market forces. A recent article called equal pay for work of comparable worth "a fallacious notion that apples are equal to oranges and that prices for both should be the same, even if that means overriding the law of supply and demand."[12] Market forces are the only relevant measure of value.

The argument's proponents would cloak impermissible sex-based discrimination in the putative legality of "market operation." Yet the argument sidesteps the contention of comparable worth proponents that, despite a pay differential, the jobs are equivalent according to a rational standard. Extolling the overriding authority of supply and demand is to ignore the possibility that the "law" conflicts with Title VII, which like other regulatory legislation necessarily interferes with a laissez-faire economy. The market-based argument against comparable worth is nonetheless instructive since it links criticisms of the allegedly spurious nature of comparable worth with antipathy to the remedy—interference with the market—that comparable worth purportedly implies. It is this connection which is critical to an understanding of judicial opinions in the comparable worth area, since judges often defer to the operation of the market.

Study Questions

1. Is the gap between wages for men and women due largely to discrimination? Affirmative action is intended to combat discrimination, and the gap between wages for men and women has closed from about 41 percent to about 29 percent since affirmative action for women began. Do these facts show that the gap probably was due largely to discrimination, especially given America's history of centuries of sexism against women? Why would women simply prefer to make less money for doing comparable work? Wouldn't that be irrational and masochistic?

2. Does comparable worth require comparing apples and oranges? Can't jobs be compared by such items as the number of employees supervised, the amount of money supervised, and the requirements listed in classified ads such as education and experience? Does comparable worth commit the fallacy of

false analogy by comparing things that are incomparable?

3. Would libertarianism allow the government to require comparable worth? Do libertarianism and egalitarianism clash here, or is there any way to reconcile them?

4. Should we completely trust the market to set wages? Since the market tries to satisfy the customer, what if many customers are sexists and prefer that women stay home rather than go to work?

Notes

1. See, e.g., Newman and Wilson, "Comparable Worth: A Job Inequity by Any Other Name," in *Manual on Pay Equality: Raising Wages for Women's Work* 54 (J. Grune, ed., undated) (on file with Harv. C.R.–C.L.L. Rev.).

2. President Reagan even dismissed comparable worth as a "cockamamie idea." Connant & Paine, "A Loss for Comparable Worth," *Newsweek* Sept. 16, 1985, 36.

3. See, e.g., Krucoff, "Money: The Question of Men, Women, and 'Comparable Worth,'" *Wash. Post*, Nov. 13, 1979, B5, col. 1.

4. The point is not to assert that equal pay *must* be based on similarity of job content, although it may be so based. Jobs which are quite different in content may properly be the basis for an equal pay claim if it can be demonstrated that they are of equal worth. A case brought under the British Equal Pay Act of 1970 provides an illustration. In *Hayward v. Cammell Laird Shipbuilders Ltd.*, IRLR 463 (1984), ICR 71 (1985), a female cook employed in the works cafeteria at the employer's shipyard sought equal pay with men employed as painters, thermal insulation engineers, and joiners. An independent expert appointed by the industrial tribunal hearing the claim assessed the various jobs under five factors: physical demands, environmental demands, planning and decisionmaking, skill and knowledge required, and responsibility involved. On the basis of this evaluation he found the jobs to be of equal value.

5. "Respondent's claims of discriminatory undercompensation are not barred by § 703(h) of Title VII merely because respondents do not perform work equal to that of male jail guards." *Gunther*, 452 U.S. at 181.

6. For a discussion of the historic undervaluation of women's jobs, see Blumrosen, "Wage Discrimination, Job Segregation, and Title VII of the Civil Rights Act of 1964,"

12 *U. Mich. J.L. Ref.* 397 (1979).

7. See, e.g., *Laffey v. Northwest Airlines*, 567 F.2d 429 (D.C. Cir. 1976), vacating and remanding in part, aff'g in pertinent part, 366 F. Supp. 763 (D.D.C. 1973), cert. denied, 434 U.S. 1080 (1978) (Court of Appeals agreeing with District Court judge who found, after testimony from expert witnesses on job evaluation presented by both plaintiff and defendant, that "pursers" and "stewardesses" performed substantially equal work even though jobs had different titles, descriptions, and responsibilities).

8. The "effort, skill, responsibility, and working conditions" criteria which the Equal Pay Act uses to determine whether jobs are equal were derived from then-current job evaluation systems.

9. See American Federation of State, County, and Municipal Employees, AFL-CIO (AFSCME), *Guide to Comparable Worth, in Pay Equity: A Union Issue for the 1980's*, 11–12 (1980). Unions representing women workers have begun to use evaluation techniques to demonstrate the extent to which women's work is undervalued and underpaid. AFSCME bargained for job evaluation studies in San Jose, California, Lane County, Oregon, and statewide in Minnesota, Wisconsin, and Michigan. *Manual on Pay Equality: Raising Wages for Women's Work* 152–53 (J. Grune, ed., undated) (on file with Harv. C.R.–C.L.L. Rev.). The trend has been especially pronounced in the public sector where 100 municipalities are now re-evaluating their job classification systems. See Noble, "Comparable Worth: How It's Figured," *New York Times*, Feb. 27, 1985, p. C7, Col. 1.

10. See Amsden, "Introduction," in *The Economics of Women and Work* 13–18 (A. Amsden, ed., 1980).

11. See Mincer and Polachek, "Family Investments in Human Capital: Earnings of Women," 82 *J. Pol. Econ.* 76 (1974) (supp.).

12. Smith, "The EEOC's Bold Foray into Job Evaluation," *Fortune*, Sept. 11, 1978, 58. The author goes on to talk of the "enormous inflationary effect" of comparable worth, which "at the extreme [would] raise the aggregate pay of the country's 27.3 million full-time working women high enough . . . [to] add a staggering $150 billion a year to civilian payrolls." *id.* at 59. The statement is typical of the hyperbole on which comparable worth arguments are often based. The author fails to acknowledge that no comparable worth advocate has suggested that all American working women will benefit from the implementation of the doctrine—only those doing work of demonstrably comparable value to that of a male worker of the same employer.

PART V

Privacy Challenges to Business as Usual: From Naked Consumers to the CIA

44

Introduction

Sterling Harwood

Statistics can help us paint an accurate portrait of the situation facing business here. Some are skeptical of statistics. Mark Twain said, "There are lies, damn lies, and then there are statistics." Another popular adage cautions, "You can prove anything with statistics." Even the Supreme Court—in *Croson* and other cases involving proof of racism, sexism, or the cause of pollution—seems skeptical of statistics. We would do well to remember, however, that statistics is a perfectly respectable field of scholarship. Ph.D.s are granted in statistics, for example. So, here are some statistics on privacy.

It takes only eight years for all the information stored in all the world's libraries and computers to double.[1] There is a voracious appetite for information, and privacy is often a casualty of this struggle to acquire more data. Eight consumer marketing studies are published every day in the United States.[2] David Burnham writes that of the 95 percent of Americans who do not work for themselves, "half are employed by large corporations that collect detailed information about the education, health, family and work habits of their employees." He also states, "Nine out of ten [Americans] are covered by health insurance plans. Insurance companies usually collect large amounts of information about their customers—revealing information such as whether they are seeing a psychiatrist, what drugs they use, and whether they have a drinking problem."[3] Employees rank the grapevine number one among the leading sources of information about their company.[4]

Of course, there is comparatively little privacy in prison. In 1994 it was widely reported that the U.S. prison population topped one million. In 1992 50 FBI agents were reassigned from counterintelligence to investigations of health-care fraud.[5] There is also not much privacy in the military. The U.S. military discharged 1,800 homosexuals from the armed forces in 1985.[6] President Clinton has acted to lessen the scrutiny or invasion of privacy of gays in the military. Of the information collected by U.S. agencies, 85 percent is acquired by technical means and 15 percent by agents.[7]

Despite the foregoing statistics indicating decreasing privacy, some studies and statistics do indicate areas where privacy is surprisingly high or is at least increasing. For example, a "study for the National Academy of Sciences . . . has demonstrated that, contrary to earlier beliefs, the great majority of organizations that have computerized their record-keeping systems have not significantly altered the data-collecting and data-sharing policies followed in earlier manual systems. In particular, computerized record-keeping is still expensive enough generally to deter excessive collection of personal information."[8] The federal government estimates the value of the untaxed U.S. underground economy to be $9 billion.[9] In 1980 there was a one in 15 chance that a tax return filed by a U.S. corporation would be audited, but in 1992 that chance was only one in 39.[10] Thirty-eight percent of Americans refuse to participate in market research surveys, and 55 percent of Americans say they would refuse a job if a lie detector test were required.[11] Some 496,000 Americans have required the removal of their names from direct-mail marketing lists.[12] Thirty-three percent of all newspaper stories quote an unnamed source.[13] The amount spent in the United States annually on private security forces is $21.7 billion.[14]

Notes

1. Lewis Lapham, Michael Pollan, and Eric Etheridge, eds., *The Harper's Index Book* (New York: Henry Holt, 1987), p. 73.

2. Ibid., p. 2.

3. David Burnham, *The Rise of the Computer State* (New York: Random House, 1983), p. 49.

4. Lapham, Pollan, and Etheridge, p. 60.

5. [Harper's Index, 1992?]

6. Lapham, Pollan, and Etheridge, p. 30.

7. Ibid., p. 60.

8. R. Turn and W. H. Ware, "Privacy and Security Issues in Information Systems," in *Ethical Issues in the Use of Computers*, ed. Deborah G. Johnson and John W. Snapper (Belmont, Calif.: Wadsworth, 1985), p. 135.

9. Lapham, Pollan, and Etheridge, p. 41.

10. [Harper's Index, 1992?]

11. Lapham, Pollan, and Etheridge, p. 41.

12. Ibid., p. 41.

13. Ibid., p. 11.

14. Ibid., p. 24.

45

Can Whistleblowing Be Fully Legitimated?

Natalie Dandekar

Whistleblowing as a phenomenon seems puzzling. The whistleblowing presumably acts to bring a wrongful practice to public attention so that those with power are enabled to correct the situation. Bok observes, "Given the indispensable services performed by so many whistleblowers, strong public support is often merited."[1] Yet Myron and Penina Glazer[2] report that in over two thirds of the sixty-four cases they documented whistleblowers suffered severe negative consequences.[3] When a social practice issues in consequences which marginalize or endanger the agent, when the agent may become a pariah for "committing the truth" it is impossible to claim that practice is regarded as fully legitimate. I am interested in exploring the paradox. Why, in the case of whistleblowing, does committing truth result in punitive sanctions? How might we, as a society, increase the probability that this virtue is rewarded rather than punished? Why have we been so slow to do just that?

To answer these questions, I consider all four topics Duska[4] considers central to a theoretical discussion of whistleblowing, (1) definition;[5] (2) whether and when whistleblowing is permissible; or (3) obligatory; and (4) appropriate mechanisms for institutionalizing whistleblowing, concluding that whistleblowing is a specific type of action: going public with privileged information about a legitimate organization in order to prevent non-trivial public harm. In Section 2, I explore the moral ambiguity inherent in whistleblowing and the complications this affords to Goldberg's persuasive case for seeing a case of potential whistleblowing as either inappropriate or obligatory.[6] In Section 3, citing studies which show that whistleblowers often suffer outrageous costs, I

From *Business and Professional Ethics Journal* 10, no. 1 (1990), 89–108. Reprinted by permission of the author.

explore legitimation factors which might safeguard the morally responsible whistleblower.

I. Whistleblowing Defined

Two recent books about whistleblowing differ in their definition of the term. For the Glazers, whistleblowing is defined by Norman Bowie's six ideal requirements:

B1. the act stems from appropriate moral motives of preventing unnecessary harm to others;

B2. the whistleblower uses all available internal procedures for rectifying the problematic behavior before public disclosure (except when special circumstances preclude this);

B3. the whistleblower has evidence that would persuade a reasonable person;

B4. the whistleblower acts in accordance with his or her responsibilities for avoiding/exposing moral violations; and

B6. the whistleblower's action has some reasonable chances of success.[7]

In contrast, Deborah Johnson, writing as a consultant for an NSF project on whistleblowing research,[8] concluded that a fully defined case of whistleblowing occurs when

J1. an individual performs an action or series of actions intended to make information public;

J2. the information is made a matter of public record;

J3. the information is about possible or actual nontrivial wrongdoing in an organization.[9]

As Heacock and McGee point out, managers define whistleblowing to include going outside the normal chain of command even if not actually going public with damaging information. Thus, whistleblowing can include internal reporting of wrongdoing in or by the organization.[10] Like Davis,[11] I am willing to see going outside the normal chain of command as a form of going public.[12]

The definitions offered by Johnson and Bowie differ with respect to whether a whistleblower's motivation should be included (B1), whether whistleblowing will succeed (B6), and whether the whistleblower is a member or former member of the organization (J4). Johnson's focus on action, exclusive of any reference to the whistleblower's motivation, seems preferable since, as Johnson observes,

> reasons for acting, the degree of certainty that the whistleblower has about the wrongdoing and whether or not the whistleblower has tried to remedy the wrongdoing by internal mechanisms . . . will bear on our understanding of when whistleblowing is permissible and when it is morally obligatory, but these factors should not be confused with definitional features.[13]

An additional reason for adopting Johnson's perspective arises when one considers a case of mixed motives. The *Wall Street Journal*[14] describes a former GE employee who spoke about time card fraud in a GE sponsored assertiveness training session. For six years afterward, Mr. Gravitt

> confronted executives with evidence . . . (until he) was fired (or laid off) . . . (He also) testified before the House subcommittee about mischarging as a way of life at GE.

Now he hopes to win a bountiful settlement, so "people will know they can do something to correct what isn't right."

Mr. Gravitt meets Johnson's definitional criteria though not those of Bowie. Since it seems wrong to dismiss his case simply because he might realize monetary gain, it seems appropriate to dismiss motivation as a definitional issue. The action—going public with possible or actual nontrivial wrongdoing—seems the more appropriate focus for definition.

There are however two points on which I think Johnson's definition could be improved. First, Johnson's stipulation that "whistleblowing always takes place in the context of an organization "[15] should be amended to include the point that the wrongdoers be persons of presumed respectability and the organization a legitimate one. This seems a little noted aspect of whistleblowing, but as with Gravitt's case where the reporter notes GE "prides itself on a favorable public image," presumptive organizational respectability consistently characterizes whistleblowers' self-reports. When they suspect wrongful practices, they feel surprise. Knowing the organization values its good reputation, the whistleblower sees the wrongful practice as a sign of deterioration but remediable.[16] Amazed that higher management avoids imposing remedies to restore reputable practice, the whistleblower is moved to protest.

Second, where Johnson stipulates the actor is a member or former member of the organization, I think the criterion should be broadened. The whistleblower must have privileged access and be trusted to maintain the confidentiality of this information. But not every privileged insider must be a member or former member of the organization. A rough survey of the ways whistleblowers have obtained incriminating information shows privileged access can result from six distinct relationships.[17]

Most often the whistleblower is a member / former member trusted with privileged information. Yet within the category of trusted employee, distinctions can be usefully drawn isolating four subcategories.

First, the whistleblower may have earned access to incriminating information through quite legal acts of loyalty. For example, when he brought charges against Senator Thomas Dodd, James Boyd was Dodd's chief aide and had worked devotedly on Senator Dodd's behalf for eleven years.

A second pattern involves a worker who colludes with the criminal practice. Thus, Dr. Arthur Console, medical director of Squibb, pressured by profit oriented superiors, pushed others to certify drugs they had not fully tested. After changing careers, he conscientiously reported the ongoing practice at Squibb.[18]

Third, a worker afraid to face reprisals may share data with a less obviously assailable colleague. A staff psychologist at the Veterans Administration Hospital in Leavenworth, Kansas, learned that a staff physician was conducting a drug-testing project using patients who could suffer harm from the drug's side effects. Believing the opinion of a trained physician would carry more weight with hospital administrators, he asked Dr. Mary McAnaw, then chief of surgery at the hospital, to accompany him when he discussed his concerns. In this way she learned of the hospital administration's complicity and eventually blew the whistle.[19]

Fourth, company arrogance may lead to information about wrongful practices being available to all employees, though the company hides these practices from the public. Karen Silkwood seems to have worked for such an arrogantly abusive corporation.

However, my rough survey also reveals two patterns by which a whistleblower may learn of an incriminating practice without being a member of an organization. Fifth, someone who is not a member of the organization may be given access to their records. Thus, Dr. Carl Johnson, a public health physician, established the probability of wrongful practices at the Rocky Flats nuclear weapons plants.[20] The company never gave him direct access to specifically incriminating information[21] but accepted that he had a right to acquire health-related data about their employees. In another such instance, Thomas Applegate, a private detective "hired by Cincinnati Gas and Electric to investigate timecard fraud among workers at the construction site of the Zimmer nuclear power plant in Ohio . . . inadvertently uncovered much more serious construction problems."[22] After utility officials ignored his warnings, he alerted the NRC. When no official body would pay attention, he sought help from GAP, a public interest watchdog group,[23] which forced additional investigations uncovering such gross violations the plant was cancelled.[24]

Sixth, the whistleblower may be a relative of the victim of wrongful practices, even if neither are members of the supposedly respectable organization. For example, in cases of nursing home abuse, drugged/senile patients are in no position to bring charges of wrongdoing. But some relatives have done so on their behalf. Mental patients too require someone else act e.g. to prevent fiscally wasteful practices, since testimony of the mentally deranged is unlikely to be believed trustworthy. Thus, a concerned relative may become a whistleblower on a wrongful organizational practice even when generally grateful for the care provided by the organization to the needy relative.

Gaining access to information, the whistleblower must be an insider in some sense, but it seems too restrictive to require the whistleblower be a member/former member of the organization accused of wrongdoing. Of the six distinct patterns of acquiring privileged information, two—the clue follower, who is not made directly privy to information about a wrongful practice but is given an opportunity to obtain clues, and the caring relative who, like the clue follower, discerns the outlines of a wrongful practice by observation—find themselves in possession of information because both have been trusted with privileged access though they are not members of the organization. Yet even these, when they go public, in some sense betray the trust which led to confidentiality.

II. The Moral Ambiguity of Whistleblowing

The whistleblower's act is intrinsically liable to moral ambiguity because whistleblowing (a) involves betrayal of confidentiality and (b) the organization is presumptively legitimate. Because the organization accused is legitimate and so presumably staffed by persons of at least ordinary moral probity, whistleblowing shares the moral ambiguity of insubordinate accusations which reject the judgment of a majority of normally competent individuals who find a dubious practice at least minimally acceptable.

In a case of price-fixing those charged include some "described as having high moral character. . . ."[25] A sympathetic analysis of their motivation showed these morally respectable perpetrators generally practiced some form of self-deception, excusing their wrongdoing as only trivially wrong, or offset by some non-trivial good. Knowing pricefixing to be illegal, some claimed that it helps stabilize the market, or serves the corporate good, ends which outweigh illegality. Others claimed the law was wrong, and pricefixing should not be illegal.[26] When respectable persons go along, their behavior suggests that the apparently wrongful practice is not thoroughly vicious. This undercuts the impetus to whistleblowing, and may also explain some of the anger that those who go along feel toward the whistleblower who won't.

The premise that private vices produce public goods, as in Adam Smith's theoretical conclusion that individual greed works through an Invisible Hand to produce the common welfare, may also promote hanging back in this respect. When respectable persons, obviously competent to engage in moral reasoning, have chosen to go along, an onlooker may wonder if this wrong nonetheless serves the common welfare in the long run, with whistleblowing morally compromised by that possibility.

Core elements of whistleblowing foster a condition of moral ambiguity. The whistleblower perceives the wrongful practice as a source of non-trivial public harm and the effort to bring the practice to public attention as serving the public interest. But from the perspective of ordinary citizens, the organization accused is respectable, so there is some doubt about the degree to which the wrongful practice will harm the public. Moreover, the person bringing the charge is betraying a trust on behalf of protecting the public interest. Paradoxically the one who betrays a trust claims to be more trustworthy than those who remain loyal to an apparently respectable corporation.

Apart from these sources of moral ambiguity, whistleblowing is liable to two other kinds of moral defect. The first stems from the motivation and character of the whistleblower.

(T)he disappointed, the incompetent, the malicious and the paranoid all too often leap to accusations in public . . . (while) ideological persecution throughout the world traditionally relies on insiders willing to inform on their colleagues or even on their family members.[27]

HUAC operated in an environment characterized by two factors: the communist party was illegal and ordinary citizens feared that communism might lead to society-wide harm. Thus those who chose to inform on communists acted in accordance with the definition of whistleblowing suggested above: bringing unlawful practices presumed harmful to the general public to the attention of those in a position to protect the public against the continuance of the practice. Even under Bowie's idealistic description of whistleblowing, the issue persists. For during that period of public hysteria, some testimony was motivated by a concern for preventing the spread of communism. However, the illegality reported and the harm feared seem less dangerous to the public than the practice of reporting and the climate thus engendered. Witchhunts illustrate the necessity to limit the powers of a wrongly aroused public opinion.

As Johnson noticed, once whistleblowing is defined, it remains worthwhile to discover under what circumstances it is permissible and when it is morally obligatory.[28] It may also be worth exploring the conditions under which whistleblowing is simply not the morally correct response to a situation. De George[29] suggests whistleblowing is *permissible* when

a. a practice or product does or will cause serious harm to individuals or society at large;
b. the charge of wrongdoing has been brought to the attention of immediate superiors; and
c. no appropriate action has been taken to remedy the wrongdoing.

If, in addition

d. there is documentation of the potentially harmful practice or defect; and
c. there is good reason to believe public disclosure will avoid the present or prevent similar future wrongdoing,

then according to De George whistleblowing becomes increasingly *obligatory*. But, since it is common knowledge that whistleblowers frequently suffer extreme retaliation, De George concludes that whistleblowing is to be understood as morally permissible, rather than obligatory.[30] Against this, Goldberg convincingly argues that if employees are to have a right, then they must be protected from reprisals in exercising the right. If conditions (a) through (e) are met and (d) and (e) are unavailable so too is the right.[31] It follows that some whistleblowing is obligatory. So, it is more than ever important to distinguish situations in which it does not pander to the wrongful arousal of public opinion or witchhunting. De George's conditions, unfortunately compatible with anti-communist witchhunts, need supplementation. Legitimate whistleblowing must be limited to cases where the wrongfulness ascribed is not the product of emotional distortion, rationalization, or prejudice.[32]

Whistleblowing is a morally ambiguous activity on a complex concatenation of grounds: it necessarily involves a betrayal of trust on behalf of a public interest which itself is on some occasions morally ambiguous; it indicts otherwise morally competent individuals and organizations concerned with being perceived as legitimate; sometimes it arouses public opinion, a frequently contaminated process. Understandably, whistleblowers are not always perceived as moral heroes.

Nonetheless when an outsider—an investigative reporter, or a political opponent, or a lawyer on behalf of a defendant—proves a corporation or government bureaucracy is wasting public funds, or endangering the lives of those who rely upon their integrity, the exposer reaps social rewards. Reporters enhance a valued reputation for sleuthing. Political opponents generally realize gains from making a case against corruption. Lawyers earn money and respect for success in prosecuting wrongdoing.

However, privileged insiders do best to serve as valuable but anonymous informants for outsiders. For if identified, they suffer outrageous costs. Once the charge becomes a threat to some superior, whistleblowers risk retaliation. Westin[33] suggests every whistleblower suffers loss of reputation. Supervisors redescribe them as disgruntled troublemakers, people who make an issue out of nothing, self-serving publicity seekers or troubled persons who distort and misinterpret situations due to their own psychological imbalance and irrationality.[34]

Yet character assassination barely begins to describe the consequences of submitting well-founded important alerts, serving to prevent harm in obvious ways. Some who work in private industry are fired, even black-listed so they cannot continue in their profession. Of sixty-four, the Glazers found forty-one lost their jobs; twenty-eight suffered long periods of idleness, and eighteen of these changed careers entirely. A ". . . career switch usually meant . . . a reduction in their standard of living . . . or a painful realization that closure was still beyond their farthest reach."[35] Others suffered transfer with prejudice, or demotion. Staff were transferred away. Letters of recommendation subtly or overtly mentioned the trouble caused by this employee's actions. When possible, the letter attacked professional competence and impugned professional judgment.

Even when evidence entirely supports the rightness of whistleblowing and the public benefit accruing therefrom, whistleblowers may find themselves unemployable in their chosen fields. Dr. Carl Johnson, after alerting the public to negligent practices at Rocky Flats nuclear weapons plants, had been "horribly mistreated and discredited" for many years, only finding rehabilitation after death.[36]

As mentioned earlier, other employees often feel that with respect to loyalty, they are morally superior. They are loyal. The whistleblower is disloyal. For this, other employees may shun, vilify, or physically attack whistleblowers.[37] Death threats may be aimed at the whistleblower and her family.[38]

Analysis shows whistleblowing is morally ambiguous. It is a betrayal of trust, and an accusation against a respectable person, corporate or natural. But when legitimate, it is also morally obligatory. So, the original puzzle remains: too often praiseworthy whistleblowing, deserving societal reward, results in severe social penalties for the whistleblower. As one writer put it, "It's a hell of a commentary on our contemporary society when you . . . become an insolvent pariah . . . to live up to your own ethical standards by 'committing the truth' and exercising your First Amendment rights."[39]

Where whistleblowing is a legitimate, responsible, morally obligatory action, this must be remedied. But how?

III. Safeguarding Legitimate Whistleblowing

In the early 1970s one who brought a charge of sexual harassment suffered character assassination and reprisals from more "loyal" employees, just as other whistleblowers of that period did. But, by the middle of the 1980s, one who brings a charge of sexual harassment is less likely to be perceived as a disloyal employee.[40] Her supervisor may even confront a harasser on her behalf.[41] Courts often support the legitimate complainant with continued job security and awards.

The difference in outcome can be related to several specific and to some extent imitable factors. First, the power imbalance between the one bringing the charge and the respectable institution is mitigated:

a. Because of consciousness raising techniques, those bringing charges of sexual harassment have a well-defined constituency willing to offer support;
b. sexual harassment offers a specific legal ground; and
c. organizations like the Women's Rights Litigation Clinic at Rutgers University Law School offer litigants well trained legal help, at a more affordable cost than is otherwise generally available.

Thus, the disparity of resources between the corporation and the claimant is made less overwhelming. Second, susceptible bureaucracies have established internal procedures for sensitizing employees to the issues that give rise to these complaints.[42] Two factors may be noted:

a. education about sexual harassment is mandated as part of the legal settlement for a proven sexual harassment case; and
b. sexual harassment is a "new" form of wrong.

By contrast, with respect to the power imbalance, only one organization correlates efforts on behalf of most whistleblowers

"organized . . . by a group of young attorneys to defend and investigate problems of national security resisters, such as Daniel Ellsberg. By the mid-1970s, their mission had expanded to . . . issues concerning waste and management . . . in large organizations (and) . . . gave whistleblowers an institutional home."[43]

Perhaps, in imitation of sexual harassment litigation, the Government Accountability Project (GAP) would do well to train lawyers in a variety of locations, and for a variety of specific purposes. The approach taken by GAP's Kohn in focussing on environmental whistleblowers suggests specificity is possible.[44]

A second potentially imitable factor pertaining to the protecting of whistleblowers relates to the law itself. While an employee who discovers criminal behavior is enjoined to blow the whistle or become personally liable to criminal penalties, only five states prohibit private employers from retaliating.[45] All but nine states have a public policy exception that limits an employer's right to fire at will.[46] Nevertheless, state by state exceptions limit the effectiveness of this tort. For example, Maryland law does not require any investigation into underlying charges of wrongdoing. California law protects whistleblowers who testify before special legislative committees[47] but those who give depositions may not be covered.[48]

Public sector employees under the Civil Service Reform Act of 1978 fall under language which seems to protect them for disclosures within a wide latitude. In addition to crimes, "an employee may now complain of mismanagement, gross waste of funds, abuse of authority or substantial and specific danger to public health and safety."[49] But those charged with protecting confidentiality of public sector employees apparently put whistleblowers at risk of reprisal, and "courts have struck an uneasy balance between the employee's First Amendment rights . . . vary from court to court."[50] Unions and professional societies generally fail to defend members who live up to professional codes of ethics by blowing the whistle.[51] Arbitrators, too, tend to see whistleblowing as an act of disloyalty which disrupts business and injures the employer's reputation.[52]

Unpredictability of legal protection may reflect the vagueness of the law enjoining that "possible acts of dishonest, improper actions or behavior, . . . should be reported."[53] MacKinnon found that when company policies were unspecific, cases alleging sexual harassment tended to be dismissed as personal rather than job related difficulties. This suggests that vague law might promote dismissive court responses. Thus, more specificity both of lawyers and laws might eventuate in a more protective environment for legitimate whistleblowing.

Another category of imitative practice might focus on educational sensitizing sessions, to establish some practices as no longer subject to social toleration. Educational procedures which create sensitivity about sexual harassment have been among the most productive means of fostering community tolerance. It therefore seems appropriate to suggest that the institution of procedures sensitizing and empowering employees to prevent other kinds of wrongful practices should be included among punishments meted out for corporate wrongdoers. It is important that others within the company be persuaded that loyalty to the company does not entail support of wrongful behavior.[54]

Another possibly imitable factor may be called "moral newness." As Calhoun[55] points out feminist moral critique begins in an abnormal moral context where moral ignorance is the norm and only a lim-

ited group are morally aware. Under these circumstances one need neither be morally defective nor morally corrupt to be at risk of wrongdoing. As public consensus emerges on the wrongness of the newly sensitive area, wrongdoers become the subject of reproach. Yet there is an excusatory element, an acknowledgment that at the level of social practice, the wrongdoer is part of an oppressive system. The complications of accommodating to a new consciousness allow for educational lapses. Normally ethical individuals might be ignorant; they occupy an abnormal moral context in process of being normalized. To realize a new level of moral behavior in the workplace, when presumably this level reflects new sensitivities, makes it easier for individuals to accept responsibility for change.

In 1974 when Catherine MacKinnon undertook to establish that sexual harassment fit the legal contours of discrimination she created a kind of moral newness as the draft copy of her book circulated. Courts came to agree with her analysis, so that by 1979, her published book cites favorable precedents establishing sexual harassment as a legal claim.[56] The very term, sexual harassment, is a neologism which "facilitate(s) . . . seeing moral issues where we had not previously and drawing connections between these and already acknowledged moral issues.[57]

Newness seems paradoxically to smooth the path for those bringing the charge. Where the accusation focuses upon a newly normalized moral context, the wrongdoer is accused more of ignorance than of vice, willful complicity, or self-deception. The wrongdoing is real, yet the wrongdoer is not ipso facto morally flawed. Rather, moral newness raises "the possibility of morally unflawed individuals committing serious wrongdoing."[58]

In pursuit of moral newness, perhaps the foolish sounding term whistleblowing should be replaced with a neologism of more apparent dignity. The Glazers suggest "ethical resistance." Other routes to moral newness, such as institutional ombuds or compliance officers, offer hope.[59] But they also pose risks since moral newness is endangered by familiarity/friendship within an organization. Bok warns that "many a patient representative in hospitals (experiences) . . . growing loyalty to co-workers and to the institution."[60] So the method for remedying defects within the corporate structure turns into a management tool, leaving the dissenter "little choice between submission and open revolt." Another risk involves what James Thomson calls domestication[61] co-opting the dissenter as the insider who might eventually persuade. Then the doubter's conscience is assuaged. But his position is made predictable. Hirschman concludes this predictability means a fatal loss of power with the dissenter left hoping even the tiniest influence is worth exerting.

Sensitivity to the need for remedy against deterioration can be blunted by the familiar and domesticated. As sexual harassment becomes a normal moral concept and newness thins, potential wrongdoers may practice techniques of self-deception. A colleague mentioned hearing an instance of sexual harassment that began with the offender saying "you will probably call this sexual harassment, but . . ." This demonstrates how fragile it is and yet how important it is to retain the lens of moral newness.

Re-inventing newness might serve as a means in restoring quality in legitimate organizations. One step to legitimating whistleblowing may be recognition that legitimate organizations suffer remediable deteriorations in quality. Perhaps eventually we could realize the ideal in which loyalty to an organization means loyal to ethical standards characteristic of the organization at its finest. But until then whistle-blowing deserves far greater legitimation than it evokes.

Conclusion

To answer the questions asked at the beginning of this paper, not all whistleblowing should be fully legitimated. The moral ambiguities of whistleblowing preclude any assumption that all whistleblowing is intrinsically virtuous. However, some whistle-blowing is morally justified and of indispensable service to society. Such whistleblowers should find legitimacy in new forms of social practice. At least they should be saved from suffering punitive sanctions. I argue two sorts of changes might promote such legitimation. The first requires redressing the power imbalance by means of specificity in laws and educational methods. The second, closely allied with the first, requires recognition that organizations suffer quality deterioration. Moral newness can serve to disintegrate misplaced familiarity and help repair quality deterioration within an organization by means of rhetorical neologisms, educational and legal consensus building techniques.

I should like to thank the anonymous readers and the editor for their helpful suggestions through several revisions.

Study Questions

1. Why do people so often call a whistleblower names such as tattletale, stoolie, traitor, snitch, ratfink, rat, or fink? Is it wrong to tell the truth? Do these common categories of criticism for whistleblowers show that the morality of most people is closer to perfectionism than to more abstract moralities such as utilitarianism and egalitarianism?

2. If whistleblowing is often disloyal, then do companies have a duty to cultivate loyalty by, for example, having parental leave policies, guarantees of lifetime employment, or excellent retirement benefits? If a company may fire a worker at any time, then why does the worker have any duty of loyalty to the company? Doesn't loyalty presuppose a longer-term relationship and not one where the loyal employee can be dismissed at will with little or no notice?

3. Since whistleblowing can be internal (up the chain of command in the firm) or alumni (after one leaves the firm), can whistleblowing avoid being disloyal quite easily?

4. Should the government promote truth, ethics, and law enforcement by passing more laws to protect whistleblowers from retaliation by their co-workers and bosses? Should this extend to anonymous whistleblowers whose identities are discovered?

Notes

1. Sissela Bok, "Whistleblowing and Professional Responsibility," *New York University Education Quarterly,* Vol. 11, #4 Summer 1980, p. 2.

2. Myron Peretz Glazer and Penina Migdal Glazer, *The Whistleblowers, Exposing Corruption in Government and Industry* (New York: Basic Books, 1989).

3. Glazer and Glazer, p. 206

4. Ronald Duska, "Whistleblowing and Employee Loyalty," in J. R. Des Jardins and J. J. McCall, *Contemporary Issues in Business Ethics* (Belmont, CA: Wadsworth, 1985), pp. 295–300.

5. A good summary of the recent literature of definition is provided by Marian V. Heacock and Gail W. McGee, "Whistleblowing: An Ethical Issue in Organizational and Human Behavior," *Business & Professional Ethics Journal,* Vol. 6 No. 4, pp. 35–45.

6. David Theo Goldberg, "Tuning in to Whistleblowing," *Business & Professional Ethics Journal,* Vol. 7, No. 2, pp. 85–94.

7. Norman Bowie, *Business Ethics* (Englewood Cliffs, N.J.: Prentice-Hall, 1982), p. 143, cited in Glazer and Glazer, p. 4.

8. Frederick Elliston, John Keenan, Paul Lockhart and Jane van Schaick, *Whistleblowing Research: Methodological and Moral Issues* (New York: Praeger, 1984), work conducted under a grant from NSF jointly sponsored by the National Endowment for the Humanities.

9. Elliston, et al., p. 15. (In the text, the authors attribute the definition to Dr. Johnson who worked as a consultant on the project. p. 23.)

10. However, with reference to the legitimation of the practice, Heacock and McGee suggest that the external whistleblower may suffer most. "External whistleblowing, in the absence of specific mechanisms to facilitate it, may be construed as a violation of the privilege of employment with a firm" (p. 37). Alternatively, Lee suggests that with respect to job loss in the private sector, the whistleblower is more fortunate than many in that all but nine states allow plaintiffs to use the law of personal injury in case of unjust discharge by private sector employers if and only if the employer discharges an employee without just cause and the employee can articulate a claim involving the public good. For discussion of these and related points, see Barbara A. Lee, "Something Akin to a Property Right: Protections for Employee Job Security" in *Business & Professional Ethics Journal*, Vol. 8, No. 3, pp. 63–82.

11. Davis appropriately notices that "taking the information out of channels to try to stop the organization from doing something he believes is morally wrong" is sufficient to cause organizational members to regard the informer as a whistleblower. Cf. Michael Davis, "Avoiding the Tragedy of Whistleblowing," *Business & Professional Ethics Journal*, Vol. 8, No. 3, pp. 3–20.

12. I think that Davis' observation can be accommodated to the claim that the whistleblower goes public by noticing the onionlike structure of the public-private distinction: what is private belongs on the inside of each enveloping segment, all the surrounding outer layers are perceived as public from that perspective.

13. Elliston, et al., p. 17.

14. Gregory Stricharchuk, "Bounty Hunter, Ex-Foreman May Win Millions for His Tale about Cheating at GE," *Wall Street Journal*, June 23, 1988, pp. 1 and 12.

15. Elliston, et al., p. 13.

16. Cf. Albert O. Hirschman's discussion of remediable flaws in deteriorating institutions growing out of an effort to connect economic and political theorizing. Albert O. Hirschman, *Exit, Voice and Loyalty, Responses to Decline in Firms, Organizations and States* (Cambridge, MA: Harvard University Press, 1970).

17. Ralph Nader, Peter J. Petkas and Kate Blackwell, eds., *Whistle Blowing* (New York: Bantam, 1972); Charles Peters and Taylor Branch, *Blowing the Whistle* (New York: Praeger, 1972); Allan Westin, ed., *Whistle Blowing! Loyalty and Dissent in the Corporation* (New York: McGraw-Hill, 1981); Greg Mitchell, *Truth . . . and Consequences* (New York: Dembner Books, 1981).

18. Glazer and Glazer, pp. 97ff.

19. Glazer and Glazer, pp. 85–85. This point may hold against one of Davis' suggestions about the way in which a conscientious employee may avoid the tragedy of whistleblowing by using some alternative informant to pass information. Cf. Davis, p. 14.

20. Pamela Reynolds, "Respect in Death, for Nuclear Safety He Took a Stand," *Boston Globe*, Jan. 11, 1989, p. 1.

21. Reynolds, p. 47.

22. Glazer and Glazer, pp. 30–31.

23. This is described more fully below.

24. Glazer and Glazer, p. 31.

25. Mike W. Martin, *Self-Deception and Morality* (Lawrence, Kansas: University Press of Kansas, 1986) p. 7.

26. Martin, p. 17.

27. Bok, p. 3.

28. In Elliston, et al., p. 17.

29. Richard De George, *Business Ethics* (New York: Macmillan, 1982).

30. Richard De George, "Ethical Responsibilities of Engineers in Large Organizations," *Business & Professional Ethics Journal*, Vol. 1, No. 1, pp. 1–14, and *Business Ethics* (New York: Macmillan, 1982), p. 161.

31. Goldberg, ibid.

32. Ronald Dworkin, "Should Homosexuality and Pornography Be Crimes?" *The Yale Law Journal*, Vol. 75, p. 986, reprinted in A. K. Bierman and James A. Gould, eds., *Philosophy for a New Generation* (New York: Macmillan, 1981), pp. 279–292.

33. Alan F. Westin, ibid.

34. Westin, pp. 22 ff, 34–35, 50 and 102; Elliston, et al., pp. 99 ff.

35. Glazer and Glazer, p. 210

36. Reynolds, p. 47.

37. Cf. Hirschman, Westin and Salisbury. Also, Albert Robbins, "Dissent in the Corporate World: When Does an Employee Have the Right to Speak Out?" *Civil Liberties Review 5*, (Sept./Oct. 1978), pp. 6–10, 15–17; Phillip I. Blumberg, "Corporate Responsibility and the Employee's Duty of Loyal and Obedience: A Preliminary Inquiry," *Oklahoma Law Rev. 24*, (Aug. 1971), pp. 197–318.

38. Glazer and Glazer, p. 160.

39. Cited in Glazer and Glazer, p. 207.

40. Natalie Dandekar, "Contrasting Consequences: Bringing Charges of Sexual Harassment Compared with Other Cases of Whistleblowing," *Journal of Business Ethics*, Vol. 9, No. 2 (1990), pp. 151–158.

41. Danielle Coviello, "Interviews with Students who Have Reported Sexual Harassment from Employers," unpublished paper, Bentley College.

42. Dandekar, p. 156.

43. Glazer and Glazer, p. 61.

44. Steven Kohn, *Protecting Environmental and Nuclear Whistleblowers: A Litigation Manual*, Nuclear Information and Resource Service, GAP, 1985.

45. David Lindorff, "How to Blow the Whistle—Safely," *Working Mother*, June, 1987, p. 25; John Conway,

"Protecting the Private Sector At-Will Employee Who `Blows the Whistle': A Cause of Action Based upon Determinants of Public Policy," *Wisconsin Law Review* 77 (1977), pp. 777–812; Alfred Feliu, "Discharge of Professional Employees: Protecting against Dismissal for Acts within a Professional Code of Ethics," *Columbia Human Rights Law Review* 11 (1980), pp. 149–187.

46. Stephen M. Kohn and Michael D. Kohn, "An Overview of Federal and State Whistleblower Protections," *Antioch Law Journal* (Summer, 1986), pp. 102–111.

47. Elliston, et al., p. 106.

48. Rosemary Chalk, "Making the World Safe for Whistle-blowers" *Technology Review*, Jan. 1988, pp. 48–58.

49. Elliston, et al., p. 109.

50. Elliston, p. 112.

51. Glazer and Glazer, pp. 97 ff.

52. Martin H. Marlin, "Current Status of Legal Protection for Whistleblowers," paper delivered at the Second Annual Conference on Ethics in Engineering, Illinois Institute of Technology, 1982, cited in Gene James, "In Defense of Whistle Blowing" in W. Michael Hoffman and Jennifer Mills Moore, eds., *Business Ethics, Readings and Cases in Corporate Morality* (New York: McGraw-Hill, 1984), pp. 249–252.

53. Bank of America policy as cited for *Miller v. Bank of America*, cited in MacKinnon, p. 62.

54. Michael Davis, whose interest coincides with mine in trying to support organizational change which would obviate the tragedies of whistleblowing suggests in addition that employees should receive training in how to present bad news effectively. I think there is merit in this suggestion, and I would like to see him explore the means by which this might actually be accomplished. (Davis, p. 15.) Perhaps Hirschman's conception of remediable defect in an organization also deserves more attention than those who discuss whistleblowing have yet given it. (Hirschman, pp. 33, 45–53, 59 and 77–106.)

55. Cheshire Calhoun, "Responsibility and Reproach," *Ethics* 99 (January 1989), p. 396.

56. Catherine A. MacKinnon, *Sexual Harassment of Working Women* (New Haven: Yale University Press, 1979), p. xi.

57. Calhoun, p. 397.

58. Calhoun, p. 389.

59. Cf. also, Monte Throdahl, "Anyone Can Whistle," describing the internal institutionalization of whistleblowing activities at Monsanto through the Environmental Policy Staff, in A. Pablo Iannone, ed. *Contemporary Moral Controversies in Business* (New York: Oxford University Press: 1989), pp. 219–220.

60. Bok, p. 8.

61. James C. Thomson, Jr., "How Could Vietnam Happen? An Autopsy," *Atlantic Monthly* (April 1968), pp. 45–57 cited in Hirschman, p. 115.

"YOU MUST HAVE FAITH IN THE CONFIDENTIALITY OF THIS OFFICE. NOTHING YOU SAY HERE WILL EVER GO BEYOND THE DATABANK."

© 1995 by Sidney Harris.

46

The Naked Consumer and the Trojan Teddy: How Business Knows Where You Live

Erik Larson

Editor's note: Larson gives a good sampling of the variety of ways in which our privacy is invaded by business on an everyday basis. He gives reasons to object to this practice even though it is business as usual. "Trojan Teddy" refers to the old military trick of the "Trojan Horse," where a gift of a huge wooden horse was actually a scheme to smuggle soldiers inside an enemy fort. Business wants to get into your home, and your home is your castle.

We can't tell you what they eat for dinner. But we can tell you where they live. And their phone number, who they live with, whether they have voted, and much, much more.

—Advertisement for Aristotle Industries, December 1991

Six days before my eldest daughter turned one she received the first birthday mail of her life, an eight-by-eleven envelope emblazoned with a big lavender teddy bear. Although addressed to my wife, the letter was deliberately timed to arrive for my daughter's initial birthday. It arrived, in fact, even before the birthday card sent by my daughter's godparents, who until then had been unsurpassed in their ability to mark every event in her short life with a promptly delivered card, gift, or telephone call. What interested me most, however, was that the teddy bear had been sent by a corporation. To me this letter marked a turning point in America's consumer culture, but then I take an unnatural interest in the commercial mail I

Reprinted from Erik Larson, *The Naked Consumer* (New York: Henry Holt and Co., Inc., 1992), pp. 3–15.

receive. I like to think that I read such mail the way Umberto Eco, the Italian semiotician and novelist, reads medieval texts. I collect the best, cleverest, and most alluring pieces and study them for signs of how far America's consumer marketers have come in figuring out what makes the American consumer, that insatiable engine of America's economy and culture, run.

By the time the big teddy arrived at my house I had begun seeing signs of an intelligence guiding a lot of the junk mail crowding my box, much the way I had begun seeing the first glimmerings of real cunning in my daughter. When you notice those first hints of intelligence in your children, your first instinct is to dismiss them as random events triggered by the chance entanglement of a couple of free-swinging neurons. By the time you realize that your child is indeed very smart—that the gagging cough that has brought you rushing to her crib at four A.M. every morning for the past week is a deliberate imitation of the real thing—you've already been caught in patterns of manipulation that you may need years to escape.

Someone out there was observing my little family and gauging its progress through time. But who? And how? The more I thought about it—and clearly you're not supposed to think about it, you're supposed to whip out your checkbook and start writing—the more intriguing the letter became. Somewhere a company not only had noticed the fact of my daughter's birth, but had made itself a little note to check back again in a year with a birthday letter chock full of consumer offerings, an accomplishment all the more impressive to me, who can't remember the birthdays of two children, let alone two million.

I opened the envelope. Inside I found a Sears flier containing twelve coupons for toddler-related clothing and supplies; a one-page coupon offer for Revlon baby mousse shampoo, featuring the ubiquitous Joan Lunden; and a sealed envelope that itself contained eight more special offers, including an invitation from the American Bronzing Company of Columbus, Ohio, to encase my daughter's first shoes in metal for just $7.99. I also found a pamphlet published by the Kimberly-Clark Corporation called "The Beginning Years: Your Baby at 12 Months." Inside was basic advice about toddlers in ten short segments: "First Steps," "First Shoes," "Keeping Your Toddler Safe," and so forth. Most were followed by a promotional blurb extolling some virtue of a Huggies diaper related to the topic at hand. A few of these paragraphs had to cast a good distance for the Huggies connection; a section called "Teething Continues" ended with this advice: "If your baby's teething is accompanied by loose stools, the last thing you want is a leaky diaper. Huggies diapers have cuddly-soft elastic at the legs and at the waist to help stop leaking." The pamphlet included a two-dollar coupon.

Something about all these companies joining forces under cover of a lavender teddy bear to cash in on my new kid began to irk me. I didn't know it then, but consumer theorists had a name for what I felt: commoditization—the conversion of important life events into trivial commercial moments. How did my guardian corporation (I'll reveal its name later) know that my wife and I even had a child? By what mechanism did this company remind itself to send us a birthday letter full of coupons? What else did the company know?

The Trojan teddy and a few other pieces of smart mail prompted me to embark on what soon became a rather spooky journey among a little-seen but hugely influential legion of marketers obsessed with capturing, quantifying, and ultimately distilling the soul of the American consumer. With a little help from their enthusiastic allies—census bureaucrats, demographers, postal officials, ex-military surveillance experts—the marketers have built a vast intelligence network containing the names, addresses, and personal records of virtually every consumer in America, all for the lofty goal of finding more irresistible ways to sell us more soaps, laxatives, and detergents.

The intelligence this network provides is the fuel that powers such consumer colossi as Procter & Gamble, General Motors, the national broadcasters, even Hollywood. What we eat, drink, drive, and smoke is determined in large part by what the consumer intelligence community decides we might like to eat, drink, drive, and smoke. Considered from this perspective, consumer espionage may be among the most influential industries in America. The annual allocation of $10 billion in network TV advertising, for example, is determined solely and directly by the numbers Nielsen Media Research produces each night from its ratings center in Dunedin, Florida.

With the costs of introducing and selling products now so high, companies believe they cannot afford to make mistakes and that every product has to be a best-seller. They have watched the comfortable mass market of the 1950s explode into smaller micromarkets of unfathomable consumers—blacks, Asians, empty-nesters, yuppies, dinks, and so forth—who don't play by the old rules. The marketers have

seen, too, how the rapid growth of cable television has eroded the power of the "Big Three" networks to reach the huge audiences they once commanded.

To make matters worse, the marketers now must wrestle with the aftereffects of their own excesses: pitch pollution—too many ads from too many places. In 1990 U.S. companies spent $238.7 billion on all forms of advertising and promotion, $23.6 billion on direct mail alone. The total is expected to rise to $331.2 billion by 1995, with roughly $10 billion of the increase due to spending on mail. Between 1965 and 1990 the number of network TV commercials shown in a year tripled to 5,400 distinct ads. The commercials, moreover, now arrive at twice the frequency allowing broadcasters to cram more ads into the same commercial time slots. In 1988, 38 percent of prime-time commercials were only fifteen seconds long, compared to 6 percent in 1984.

We not only encounter more advertising; we encounter it from more sources, some rather unorthodox. Airlines place ads on the backs of lavatory doors. Whittle Communications' Channel One broadcasts commercials directly into school classrooms. A telephone company tried inserting commercials between rings on outgoing phone calls. An Israeli company called Golden Eggs gingerly stamps advertising messages on the shells of eggs; a Chicago company puts them on hot dogs. Two dozen companies paid $30,000 each to buy space on a board game called It's Only Money. Commercials now appear on the videos we rent, spaced between the FBI warning and the movie. Buick, for example, jumped at the chance to place a leisurely commercial at the beginning of the video version of Rain Man, a bit redundant considering the praise co-stars Tom Cruise and Dustin Hoffman heap on the classic Buick convertible that appears throughout the film. Ads arrive unbidden on our fax machines; computerized jerks call us during dinner to pitch us home improvements and a better shot at the good life. In 1990, according to Congress, three hundred thousand telemarketers reached out to eighteen million of us every day and touched us for $435 billion worth of goods and services, four times the total sales of 1984.

In 1991 I found myself not just the target of junk mail, but the subject. Harper's magazine, in its own attempt to draw attention to its mailings, put the opening paragraphs of an article of mine on the envelope of a subscription offer mailed to fifty thousand households. The article was about junk mail. "We're excited about this package," the magazine's vice-president for corporate and public affairs wrote in a letter to me presenting the mailing. "We think it will break through junk-mail clutter. . . ."

Consumers also faced a torrent of look-alike, taste-alike products. In 1990, according to an annual count kept by *Gorman's New Product News*, 12,055 new products appeared on the shelves of America's drugstores and supermarkets, 60 percent more than in 1985. That comes to thirty-three new products a day. Meanwhile, the length of time an average shopper spends in the store has shrunk, forcing new and old products to compete more fiercely for the consumer's affection.

Once stable, faithful products have begun bearing offspring with rabbity proficiency. "Take something as simple as Coca-Cola," said Mark L. Capaldini, a vice-president at Claritas Corporation, an Alexandria, Virginia, company that pioneered the art and science of target marketing. "It's a great generic product, right? Well, in fact there are literally dozens of different combinations of packaging and even variations on the basic product. We've now got Coca-Cola and diet Coke and Caffeine-Free Coke and Caffeine-Free diet Coke. You can buy it in cans—six cans, twelve cans, or twenty-four cans. Then you can buy it in glass bottles, and the bottles come in different sizes, and then you can buy it in plastic bottles, and the plastic bottles come in different sizes. Here's an all-American product that's now available in all these different combinations, sizes, and flavors."

The combined force of all these pressures drives today's intrusive quest for the consumer. Companies dispatch their research battalions with orders to seek out any market advantage, the tiniest consumer twitch that could launch their products to stardom—even if to find it they have to hide cameras on store shelves or turn entire towns into electronically monitored consumption laboratories. The availability of new technologies, in particular huge amounts of cheap computing power, helped spur the campaign. So, too, did a fundamental science imperative, the continuing irresistible drive by marketers to transform what they do from pants-seat art to precision science and to reduce us all to "consuming units" for handy insertion into mathematical models of consumption.

The secrets prospectors are everywhere. You don't see them because so much of their probing is done from a distance through oblique means and because only a relative few of America's 250 million people are subjected to intense scrutiny at any one time (although for a while one project under way at Citicorp, the New York bank holding company, had the stated goal of creating a "census" data base that could monitor, model, and modify the consumption behavior of every upstanding American consumer).

But we continually betray secrets about ourselves, and the secrets are systematically collected by the marketers' intelligence network. Your telephone company can tell how often you travel by keeping track of how often and from what points on the globe you use your telephone calling card. (U.S. Sprint peddled such information to hotel companies and airlines.) When you register your car, you divulge an invaluable collection of socioeconomic clues, which your state motor vehicle department passes along to large data harvesters. The thirty-four states that offer this service provide the information at low cost on easy-to-use computer tapes. My motor vehicle department recently did a little marketing research of its own, mailing a survey that asked not only about the quality of department services, but about shopping at the malls in which the bureau's express offices were located. "If you did any shopping," the survey asked, "could you share with us how much money you spent?"

If you're a couple struggling with the pain and sorrow of not being able to have children, companies can know this or at least make a statistically reasonable guess. One hospital did so but made the mistake of including a *Washington Post* reporter on its mailing list. As I'll show, companies can also figure out whether or not you are gay, a nifty bit of intelligence that insurance companies find rather useful. Even the detailed answers you gave to the Census Bureau in 1990 will eventually find their way into the marketing intelligence network despite concerns within the bureau about the "less noble purposes" for which such data may be used.

Companies set clever little intelligence traps that trick us into shedding bits of information. One company adds a series of personal life-style questions to the guarantee cards that accompany TVs, stereo amplifiers, and backyard grills. The cards leave the impression that if you don't answer the questions, your warranty won't be valid. The Publishers Clearing House Sweepstakes is much more than just an offer of a chance to win a million bucks; it is also an intelligence feeler designed to help spot gullible consumers known in the trade as "opportunity seekers" and to build and update a massive data base of consumer names and addresses for its own internal use.

Some companies take the direct approach, but this can get expensive, Once, for example, my wife passed me an envelope marked discreetly with a return address on Lexington Avenue in New York. "Dear New Mother," the enclosed letter began. What really drew my attention, however, was the attached dollar bill. The envelope also contained a seventy-item consumer research questionnaire about the baby wipes we used and the television shows we watched, complete with forty little red-and-blue stickers to be stuck at various places on two inside pages. "The dollar is just a token of our appreciation—our way of saying thank you for your help," the letter said.

Competition for our secrets seems to be driving up the price we can charge. Recently a swank Boston Hotel offered me five bucks to answer a survey. In 1990 American Airlines, citing plummeting cooperation rates, gave survey respondents a $25 travel certificate. The price for more specialized intelligence is even higher. During annual meetings of the American Academy of Dermatology, pharmaceutical companies pay as much as fifty dollars to any doctor willing to stop by their booths and fill out a questionnaire. A dermatologist friend told me she walked away from one such encounter with an Orrefors crystal bowl.

Newsweek took a distinctly post-Reagan approach in a brief subscriber survey it mailed to my wife in October 1991, when it offered to contribute an unspecified amount of money to a charity of her choosing in return for her cooperation.

Corporate surveyors buttonhole consumers throughout the country, even the world. Every three months Coca-Cola conducts a monumental global survey, interviewing at least 1,000 people from almost every country where Coke is sold. In 1989, according to the Advertising Research Foundation, marketers conducted 70,000 focus groups and did one-on-one interviews with 130,000 individual consumers.

While strolling through your favorite store you may be captured secretly on videotape. Some day soon a video crew on the payroll of a New York advertising agency may invite itself into your home to film you in the revealing act of cleaning your sink. Agents of Arbitron may try to recruit you to use a household scanner to record the price and University Product Code of every single product you buy. Serpentlike infrared sensors may soon begin tracking you up and down the aisles of your local supermarket—in 1991 a handful of stores already had begun testing the technology.

We are the most heavily probed, surveyed, and categorized society since the dawn of human history. The intensity of this assault has changed us, both as individuals and as a culture.

How? Why? And at what cost?

Until the 1990s marketers were able to conduct their surveillance of America without attracting too much attention. As they got bolder and junk mail got smarter, a few newspapers and magazines began chronicling their efforts; privacy became for the marketers an inescapable and increasingly costly issue. Lotus Development Corporation became the most celebrated victim of growing privacy angst when, in January 1991, consumer pressure caused the company to cancel its introduction of Lotus Marketplace, a compact disc containing the names, addresses, income brackets, and life-style characteristics of some 120 million households. In announcing the cancellation, Jim Manzi, the company's chief executive officer, said, "Lotus cannot afford a prolonged battle over consumer privacy," and cited the "emotional firestorm" the product had created. The cost to Lotus of overlooking privacy was a cool $8 million.

While this is not a book about privacy, before we proceed a few words about privacy may be in order.

The most influential legal argument in support of a right to privacy appeared in the *Harvard Law Review* of December 15, 1890. The writers, Samuel D. Warren and Louis D. Brandeis (later a Supreme Court justice), described it as "a general right of the individual to be left alone." Sounds simple enough, yet legal scholars still debate whether such a right really exists. Federal Judge Robert H. Bork while a nominee for the Supreme Court argued there was no such thing; soon afterward a more successful nominee, David H. Souter, gave the right, as *The New York Times* put it, his "cautious endorsement."

What is private to one individual may not be private to his neighbor; what is considered private today may not be considered private tomorrow. Today, for example, an employee of the Census Bureau can go to jail—and one employee has—for disclosing addresses or personal data collected during the decennial census, yet over the bureau's first fifty years of operation all census information was considered public property. In fact, the federal census laws of those decades required that census takers display their information, names and all, "at two of the most public places" in their territories. Federal law now considers our tax returns to be private and confidential, but from time to time Congress has enacted laws forcing the public disclosure of tax information. The Revenue Act of 1924 required the public listing of taxpayers and their incomes. Two years later Congress withdrew the requirement. In 1934, however, Congress once again allowed limited disclosure and required taxpayers to file a separate tax form, the so-called pink slip, which the public could examine at the offices of their local tax collector. These slips included name, address, total gross income, total deductions, net income, total credit against net income, and tax payable—the stuff of a marketer's dream. This obligation, however, did not go over big with the American taxpayer, and Congress hurriedly rescinded the law, just in time for the 1935 tax-filing period when the act was to have taken effect.

What constitutes an invasion of privacy? And once your privacy is invaded, how do you prove you were harmed? Can you seek damages because your neighbor happened to peek at your tax form and saw how much you made last year? Suppose one of the many families receiving lavender teddy bears had lost its child before the letter's arrival—a direct-mail nightmare that a few parents in America probably did experience with this mailing, given the gloomy fact that ten of every one thousand American babies die before their first birthdays. Could the grieving parents sue Joan Lunden, Walt Disney Company, and Kimberly-Clark for invasion of privacy? Could they make a case for financial compensation?

"Would you want to go into court with a case like that?" asked Janlori Goldman, an attorney with the American Civil Liberties Union. The difficulty in proving invasion of privacy arises from what Goldman calls "the body-in-the-street syndrome."

Goldman, director of the ACLU's Privacy and Technology Project, is a prominent member of the small but earnest cadre of lawyers, scholars, and newsletter editors who worry about our privacy even when the rest of us do not. She is a tall, direct woman with a taste for rapid-fire conversation.

"With privacy issues, victims are not obvious. Harm is not identifiable. There's no blood, there's no body, no broken bones. The harm is not tangible, you can't point to it and say `You hurt me this way.' It's very hard to collect damages, it's very hard to make a legal case.

"It's very hard to explain to people why you just don't want to give out your Social Security number one more time; it's very hard to explain why when you get a targeted mailing you feel vulnerable; why you feel as though somebody knows something about you and you don't know why and you don't

know how. You don't even know what to do about it, because you have no recourse."

She believe harm does occur, however.

"It's the kind of harm that eats away at you," she told me. "It affects the choices you make, it affects the way you live, it affects your sense of being an individual, of being autonomous, of being able to live in the world without always being watched, without always being monitored. And that is a unique American quality. We believe we can live that way. But now it's starting to sink in that we don't."

Goldman contends the monitoring systems set up by America's marketing companies already have begun to influence the ebb and flow of our daily lives. After a Washington weekly newspaper ran an article on the films Judge Bork rented from his favorite video store, Goldman got a "flood" of calls from people concerned about the sanctity of their video habits. "People are afraid to go to the video store now and rent certain movies," she said. "They don't want to rent movies that are going to identify them as certain kinds of people. They don't want other people to make decisions about them or judgments about them based on the movies they watch. It feels *so* intrusive to them, so they make market decisions that they wouldn't otherwise have made. To me, *that's* the harm."

The new marketing technologies have greatly complicated the privacy issue. Sophisticated software developed in the 1980s and the ever-more powerful computers on which it runs allow marketers to collect huge amounts of information about each of us from courts and other public repositories and to combine it all into a single data base. Companies can further "enhance" this information with details about our credit card balances, bank accounts, subscriptions, store purchases, and a host of other personal data collected discretely by companies of all kinds and then widely, avidly, and aggressively marketed to anyone willing to pay for it. The result is a wholly new kind of information, what I call "recombinant information." Is the resulting electronic file a benign composite of humdrum data or something more threatening and intrusive, a dangerous mutation?

Technology has added yet another dimension to the collection of our personal statistics. Since the mid-1980s marketers have refined techniques that now give them the ability to track millions of consumers through time. By constantly updating their data bases they can monitor shifts in our financial and personal status on a monthly basis, soon perhaps on a daily basis, and thus hit us when we are most vulnerable.

They can pitch us mortgage life insurance just after we buy our homes, life insurance on the eve of child-birth.

The big marketing companies assure us they take the utmost precautions to protect our secrets. Consider, however, the findings of a study published in the *Journal of Business Ethics*, which found that today's marketing MBAs were far more likely "to engage in quasi-ethical (allowing the ends to justify the means) marketing research practices than their counterparts in the early 1980s." In particular, the study found these recent graduates to be far more willing to deceive the subjects of a marketing research poll in order to gain their cooperation. Studies done in 1981 and, appropriately, 1984 found that marketing research as a whole was rife with serious ethical abuse. "As the utilization of marketing research continues to increase," two marketing scholars wrote in 1988, "opportunities for the misuse of marketing research also increase."

If there is any doubt about the marketers' willingness to trample civil liberties, one need only read what they tell each other in their own publications and trade journals. The September 1990 issue of *Inside Strategy*, a newsletter produced by Strategy Research Corporation of Miami, printed a series of testimonials by customers who had used the company's new focus group center, where the company gathers consumers for conversations about products and other matters. It is customary during focus groups for marketers to observe consumers through one-way glass, but this center seems to have raised the practice to new heights. "State of the art!" exulted the vice-president of one client firm. "It was particularly interesting to me to be able to observe the respondents not only during the session, but before they started, in the waiting room."

Henry Johnson, while still chief executive of Spiegel Company, could barely contain his glee as he described in *Direct Marketing* magazine how computers and the new concept of psychographic marketing—an automated means of divining the attitudes of consumers—had given his company the power to see the "inner selves" of individuals.

"Through psychographics," he crowed, "we become the friend who knows them as well as—perhaps better than—they know themselves."

Such talk might have caused some marketers to worry about invading privacy. If so, they could have turned for comfort to a column by Robert J. Posch of Doubleday Book & Music Clubs, who reassuringly wrote: "There is *nothing* in the language of the Con-stitution that refers to any 'right of privacy' in the commercial context." (The emphasis is his.)

He went on, in fact, to chide those spineless members of his industry who cave in to criticism from privacy advocates. In particular he referred to a decision by a telephone company to drop its plan to rent lists of its customers. Posch wrote: "An industry that will voluntarily walk off its own economic plank deserves the consequences of the landing."

Some of his compatriots take a more thoughtful view. In a different issue of *Direct Marketing*, Pierre Passavant, a consultant, wrote the following: "At the risk of offending some of my colleagues in direct marketing, I must say that I have the impression that some list owners, brokers, and compilers are none too concerned with such esoteric subjects as rights to privacy and reasonable expectations of confidentiality."

He cited the case of a national medical laboratory that, for a time, rented the names of the patients whose tests it processed. "Is this the 1984 Big Brother viewing my activities via the telescreen? Or the 1984 thought police reading my mind? No, it's just my local friendly compiler. Working with my local friendly computer service bureau. To create a data base and interconnected data bases with information that would make Orwell smile. . . . If suddenly our personal lives become largely matters of public record, it will not be by government action, but due to our uncontrolled profit motives, also known as greed. We will have only ourselves to blame for the consequences."

My research for this book convinced me there are four universal laws governing the flow of data collected about individuals, which I call the "laws of data dynamics":

The First Law (also the "law of data coalescence"): Data *must* seek and merge with complementary data.

The Second Law: Data *always* will be used for purposes other than originally intended.

The Third Law: Data collected about individuals *will* be used to cause harm to one or more members of the group who provided the information or about whom it was collected, be it minor (the short-term aggravation of a "junk" call during dinner) or major (the sorrow of getting a free sample of formula just after your miscarriage).

The Fourth Law: Confidential information is confidential only until someone decides it's not.

The impact of mass surveillance reaches far beyond concerns about privacy. How companies use the secrets they discover causes subtle changes in our daily culture, the world we encounter every day on our way to work, in the grocery store, or when we watch television. Ours is a consumer subsociety—how could so much probing *not* change our lives?

What companies learn determines how they focus their advertisements and how precisely they can isolate our deep-seated vulnerabilities. The process takes place outside the public view. A product may suddenly disappear from the shelves of your local Safeway; even if you noticed its disappearance, you'd have no reason to imagine the complicated network of psychology and technology that led to it. You receive an offer for a new credit card, but the offer tells you nothing of the sophisticated technology that was brought to bear to pick you out of a hundred million American consumers and to exclude your friend, who happens to live in the wrong part of town. If you move and discover suddenly that your junk mail has caught up with you even faster than your friends have, you may be mildly fascinated or mildly annoyed, but you won't see any sign of the rather slavish degree to which the U.S. Postal Service has geared its technological resources to helping the likes of Lands' End and L. L. Bean keep abreast of our movements.

As consumers, we see Oz. We don't see the little man behind the curtain. We don't see how the marketers have eroded our civil rights; how by invoking the great god Efficiency they created an electronic caste system in which all of us reside and that reinforces class stereotypes and fosters a subtle new brand of discrimination based not on skin color, but on fiscal wherewithal. All this corporate probing, moreover, has produced a business culture that shies from true innovation and pays more attention to manipulating our needs, values, and shopping behavior than to giving us a better product. This dependence has grown so pervasive that it has crimped the national imagination and altered the way our product designers, directors, and politicians think.

How can you be truly creative if you're always looking over your shoulder for the approval of a panel of Baltimore housewives; if you know that any idea will be subjected to a battery of surveys, focus groups, or electronic ratings evaluations? Suppose God's product development team had first tried out His creations on a panel of average Americans—would the lobster and artichoke have made the convenience cut? Why, given all this poking and probing, are so many new products so disappointing? Ralph's Groceries, a West Coast chain, got so discouraged it considered charging "failure fees" to companies whose products took up valuable store space only to fail soon afterward. If all this snooping is so helpful, why *do* so many new products fail?

Study Questions

1. Do you object to corporations knowing so much about you?

2. Do innocent people have anything to hide from the prying eyes of business? Aren't there noncriminal but embarrassing things (for example, some spending habits and medical problems) that you have every moral right to keep secret from business?

3. Which of the business practices that Larson describes is hardest to justify morally? Which of them is easiest to justify morally?

47

Luedtke v.
Nabors Alaska Drilling, Inc.

Superior Court of Alaska

This case addresses one aspect of drug testing by employers. A private employer, Nabors Alaska Drilling, Inc. (Nabors), established a drug testing program for its employees. Two Nabors employees, Clarence Luedtke and Paul Luedtke, both of whom worked on drilling rigs on the North Slope, refused to submit to urinalysis screening for drug use as required by Nabors. As a result they were fired by Nabors. The Luedtkes challenge their discharge on the following grounds:

1. Nabors' drug testing program violates the Luedtkes' right to privacy guaranteed by article I, section 22 of the Alaska Constitution;
2. Nabors' demands violate the covenant of good faith and fair dealing implicit in all employment contracts;
3. Nabors' urinalysis requirement violates the public interest in personal privacy, giving the Luedtkes a cause of action for wrongful discharge; and
4. Nabors' actions give rise to a cause of action under the common law tort of invasion of privacy.

Nabors argues that the Luedtkes were "at will" employees whose employment relationship could be terminated at any time for any reason. Alternatively, even if termination had to be based on "just cause," such cause existed because the Luedtkes violated established company policy relating to employee safety by refusing to take the scheduled tests.

This case raises issues of first impression in Alaska law including: whether the constitutional right of privacy applies to private parties; some parameters of the tort of wrongful discharge; and the

768 P. 2d 1123 (1989). Opinion by Judge Compton.

extent to which certain employee drug testing by private employers can be controlled by courts.

Factual and Procedural Background

The Luedtkes' cases proceeded separately to judgment. Because they raised common legal issues, on Nabors' motion they were consolidated on appeal.

Paul's Case

Factual Background. Paul began working for Nabors, which operates drilling rigs on Alaska's North Slope, in February 1978. He began as a temporary employee, replacing a permanent employee on vacation for two weeks. During his two weeks of temporary work, a permanent position opened up on the rig on which he was working and he was hired to fill it. Paul began as a "floorman" and was eventually promoted to "driller." A driller oversees the work of an entire drilling crew.

Paul started work with Nabors as a union member, initially being hired from the union hall. During his tenure, however, Nabors "broke" the union. Paul continued to work without a union contract. Paul had no written contract with Nabors at the time of his discharge.

During his employment with Nabors, Paul was accused twice of violating the company's drug and alcohol policies. Once he was suspended for 90 days for taking alcohol to the North Slope. The other incident involved a search of the rig on which Paul worked. Aided by dogs trained to sniff out marijuana, the searchers found traces of marijuana in Paul's suitcase. Paul was allowed to continue working on the rig only after assuring his supervisors he did not use marijuana.

In October 1982, Paul scheduled a two-week vacation. Because his normal work schedule was two weeks of work on the North Slope followed by a week off, a two-week vacation amounted to 28 consecutive days away from work. Just prior to his vacation, Paul was instructed to arrange for a physical examination in Anchorage. He arranged for it to take place on October 19, during his vacation. It was at this examination that Nabors first tested Paul's urine for signs of drug use. The purpose of the physical, as understood by Paul, was to enable him to work on off-shore rigs should Nabors receive such contracts. Although Paul was told it would be a comprehensive physical he had no idea that a urinalysis screening test for drug use would be performed. He did voluntarily give a urine sample but assumed it would be tested only for "blood sugar, any kind of kidney failure [and] problems with bleeding." Nabors' policy of testing for drug use was not announced until November 1, 1982, almost two weeks after Paul's examination.

In early November 1982, Paul contacted Nabors regarding his flight to the North Slope to return to work. He was told at that time to report to the Nabors office in Anchorage. On November 5, Paul reported to the office where a Nabors representative informed him that he was suspended for "the use of alcohol or other illicit substances." No other information was forthcoming from Nabors until November 16 when Paul received a letter informing him that his urine had tested positive for cannabinoids. The letter informed him that he would be required to pass two subsequent urinalysis tests, one on November 30 and the other on December 30, before he would be allowed to return to work. In response Paul had delivered a letter drafted by his attorney to the Manager of Employee Relations for Nabors, explaining why he felt the testing and suspension were unfair. Paul did not take the urinalysis test on November 30 as requested by Nabors. On December 14, Nabors sent Paul a letter informing him he was discharged for refusing to take the November 30 test.

Procedural Background. Following his discharge, Paul applied for unemployment compensation benefits with the Alaska State Department of Labor (DOL). DOL initially denied Paul benefits for the period of December 12, 1982, through January 22, 1983, on the ground that his refusal to take the urinalysis test was misconduct under AS 23.30.379(a). Paul appealed that decision and on January 27, 1983, the DOL hearing officer concluded that the drug retest requirement was unreasonable. On that basis, the hearing officer held that Paul's dismissal was not for misconduct. Nabors appealed to the Commissioner of Labor, who sustained the decision of the appeals tribunal.

Paul initiated this civil action in November 1983. He asserted claims for wrongful dismissal, breach of contract, invasion of privacy, and defamation. Nabors moved for and was granted summary judgment on the invasion of privacy claim, on both the constitutional and common law tort theories. Prior to trial Paul voluntarily dismissed his defamation claim. The trial court, in a non-jury trial, held for Nabors on

Paul's wrongful dismissal and breach of contract claims.

Paul appeals the trial court's ruling with regard to his wrongful dismissal, breach of contract, and invasion of privacy claims.

Clarence's Case

Factual Background. Clarence has had seasonal employment with Nabors, working on drilling rigs, since the winter of 1977–78. Prior to beginning his first period of employment, he completed an employment application which provided for a probationary period.

In November 1982 Clarence became subject to the Nabors drug use and testing policy. In mid-November a list of persons scheduled for drug screening was posted at Clarence's rig. His name was on the list. The people listed were required to complete the test during their next "R & R" period. During that next "R & R" period Clarence decided he would not submit to the testing and informed Nabors of his decision.

Nabors offered to allow Clarence time to "clean up" but Clarence refused, insisting that he thought he could pass the test, but was refusing as "a matter of principle." At that point Nabors fired Clarence. The drug test that would have been performed on Clarence was the same as that performed on Paul.

Procedural Background. Following his discharge Clarence also sought unemployment compensation benefits with the DOL. Nabors objected because it believed his refusal to submit to the drug test was misconduct under AS 23.20.379(a). After a factual hearing and two appeals, the Commissioner of Labor found that "Nabors has not shown that there is any connection between off-the-job drug use and on-the-job performance." Thus, there was no showing that Nabors' test policy was related to job misconduct. Furthermore, the Commissioner adopted factual findings that 1) no evidence had been submitted by Nabors linking off-duty drug use with on-the-job accidents, and 2) Nabors was not alleging any drug use by Clarence.

Clarence filed his complaint in this case in November 1984. He alleged invasion of privacy, both at common law and under the Alaska Constitution, wrongful termination, breach of contract, and violation of the implied covenant of good faith and fair dealing. The trial court granted summary judgment in favor of Nabors on all of Clarence's claims. No opinion, findings of fact, or conclusions of law were entered.

Clarence appeals the award of summary judgment on all counts.

Discussion

The Right to Privacy

The right to privacy is a recent creation of American law. The inception of this right is generally credited to a law review article published in 1890 by Louis Brandeis and his law partner, Samuel Warren. Brandeis & Warren, *The Right to Privacy*, 4 *Harv. L.Rev.* 193 (1890). Brandeis and Warren observed that in a modern world with increasing population density and advancing technology, the number and types of matters theretofore easily concealed from public purview were rapidly decreasing. They wrote:

> Recent inventions and business methods call attention to the next step which must be taken for the protection of the person, and for securing to the individual what Judge Cooley calls the right "to be let alone." Instantaneous photographs and newspaper enterprise have invaded the sacred precincts of private and domestic life, and numerous mechanical devices threaten to make good the prediction that "what is whispered in the closet shall be proclaimed from the housetops."

Discussing the few precedential cases in tort law in which courts had afforded remedies for the publication of private letters or unauthorized photographs, Brandeis and Warren drew a common thread they called "privacy." They defined this right as the principle of "inviolate personality." *Id.* at 205.

While the legal grounds of this right were somewhat tenuous in the 1890's, American jurists found the logic of Brandeis and Warren's arguments compelling. The reporters of the first Restatement of Torts included a tort entitled "Interference with Privacy." By 1960, Professor Prosser could write that "the right of privacy, in one form or another, is declared to exist by the overwhelming majority of the American courts." . . . He cited cases in which private parties had been held liable in tort for eavesdropping on private conversations by means of wiretapping and microphones, or for peering into the windows of homes. In addition, while Brandeis and Warren were mainly concerned with the publication of private facts, Professor Prosser identified four different manifestations of the right to privacy: intrusion upon the

plaintiff's seclusion; public disclosure of embarrassing private facts; publicity which places the plaintiff in a false light; and appropriation, for the defendant's pecuniary advantage, of the plaintiff's name or likeness. Professor Prosser's categories form the framework of the expanded tort of invasion of privacy found in the Restatement (Second) of Torts.

Eventually the right to privacy attained sufficient recognition to be incorporated in several state constitutions. Alaska (adopted 1972); California (adopted 1972), Hawaii (adopted 1978); Montana (adopted 1972).

Interpreting the Constitution of the United States, the United States Supreme Court in 1965 held that a Connecticut statute banning the use of birth control devices by married couples was "repulsive to the notions of privacy surrounding the marriage relationship." . . . The Supreme Court wrote that "specific guarantees in the Bill of Rights have penumbras, formed by emanations from those guarantees that help give them life and substance. Various guarantees create zones of privacy." . . . Justice Goldberg's concurrence suggested that the right of marital privacy was fundamental to the concept of liberty. . . . Since *Griswold* the Supreme Court has found the federal constitutional right of privacy to apply to a number of other situations. . . .

In this case the plaintiffs seek to fit their cases within at least one of four legal frameworks in which the right to privacy has found expression: constitutional law, contract law, tort law, and the emerging mixture of theories known as the public policy exception to the at-will doctrine of employment law.

The Right to Privacy under the Alaska Constitution

The Alaska Constitution was amended in 1972 to add the following section:

> *Right of Privacy.* The right of the people to privacy is recognized and shall not be infringed. The legislature shall implement this section.

We observe initially that this provision, powerful as a constitutional statement of citizens' rights, contains no guidelines for its application. Nor does it appear that the legislature has exercised its power to apply the provision; the parties did not bring to our attention any statutes which "implement this section."

The Luedtkes argue that this court has never clearly answered the question of whether article I, section 22 applies only to state action or whether it also governs private action. The Luedtkes urge this court to hold that section 22 governs private action. This question was broached in *Allred v. State*. In *Allred* this court was faced with the question of whether a psychotherapist-patient privilege exists in Alaska. We found the privilege in the common law rather than under the constitutional right to privacy:

> Since it is apparent that [the psychotherapist] was not a police agent, we do not perceive any state action that would trigger the constitutional privacy guarantees.
> . . .

Our dictum in *Allred* comports with traditional constitutional analysis holding that the constitution serves as a check on the power of government: "That all lawful power derives from the people and must be held in check to preserve their freedom is the oldest and most central tenet of American constitutionalism." L. Tribe, *American Constitutional Law*. In the same vein, we have written in regard to Alaska's constitutional right to privacy: "[T]he primary purpose of these constitutional provisions is the protection of 'personal privacy and dignity against unwarranted intrusions by the State.'" . . .

The parties in the case at bar have failed to produce evidence that Alaska's constitutional right to privacy was intended to operate as a bar to private action, here Nabors' drug testing program. Absent a history demonstrating that the amendment was intended to proscribe private action, or a proscription of private action in the language of the amendment itself, we decline to extend the constitutional right to privacy to the actions of private parties.

Wrongful Termination

In *Mitford v. de LaSala*, this court held that at-will employment contracts in Alaska contain an implied covenant of good faith and fair dealing. In *Knight v. American Guard & Alert, Inc.*, we acknowledged that violation of a public policy could constitute a breach of that implied covenant. We wrote:

> The [plaintiff's] claim, concerning alleged termination in violation of public policy, is in accord with a theory of recovery accepted in many states. We have never rejected the public policy theory. Indeed, it seems that the public policy approach is largely encompassed within the implied covenant of good faith and fair dealing which we accepted in *Mitford*.

We conclude that there is a public policy supporting the protection of employee privacy. Violation of that policy by an employer may rise to the level of a breach of the implied covenant of good faith and fair dealing. However, the competing public concern for employee safety present in the case at bar leads us to hold that Nabors' actions did not breach the implied covenant.

The Luedtkes Were At-Will Employees. First, we address the Luedtkes' arguments, that they were not at-will employees, but rather that they could be fired only for good cause. The key difference between these two types of employment is whether the employment contract is for a determinable length of time. Employees hired on an at-will basis can be fired for any reason that does not violate the implied covenant of good faith and fair dealing. However, employees hired for a specific term may not be discharged before the expiration of the term except for good cause. Neither of the Luedtkes had any formal agreements for a specified term, so any such term, if it existed, must be implied.

In *Eales v. Tanana Valley Medical-Surgical Group, Inc.*, we held that where an employer promised employment that would last until the employee's retirement age, and that age was readily determinable, a contract for a definite duration would be implied. We also held that no additional consideration need be given the employee to create a contract for a definite term.

The Luedtkes' cases are distinguishable from that of the plaintiff in *Eales*. The Luedtkes received benefits, such as medical insurance and participation in a pension or profit sharing plan, which continued as long as they were employed. However, Nabors never gave an indication of a definite duration for their employment, nor a definite end-point to their employment. Instead, Nabors merely provided benefits consistent with modern employer/employee relations.

There Is a Public Policy Supporting Employee Privacy. The next question we address is whether a public policy exists protecting an employee's right to withhold certain "private" information from his employer. We believe such a policy does exist, and is evidenced in the common law, statutes and constitution of this state. . . .

Alaska law clearly evidences strong support for the public interest in employee privacy. First, state statutes support the policy that there are private sectors of employees' lives not subject to direct scrutiny by their employers. For example, employers may not require employees to take polygraph tests as a condition of employment. AS 23.10.037. In addition, AS

18.80.200(a) provides:

> It is determined and declared as a matter of legislative finding that discrimination against an inhabitant of the state because of race, religion, color, national origin, age, sex, marital status, changes in marital status, pregnancy, or parenthood is a matter of public concern and that this discrimination not only threatens the rights and privileges of the inhabitants of the state but also menaces the institutions of the state and threatens peace, order, health, safety and general welfare of the state and its inhabitants.

This policy is implemented by AS 18.80.220, which makes it unlawful for employers to inquire into such topics in connection with prospective employment. This statute demonstrates that in Alaska certain subjects are placed outside the consideration of employers in their relations with employees. The protections of AS 18.80.220 are extensive. This statute has been construed to be broader than federal anti-discrimination law. . . . We believe it evidences the legislature's intent to liberally protect employee rights.

Second, as previously noted, Alaska's constitution contains a right to privacy clause. While we have held, *supra*, that this clause does not proscribe the private action at issue, it can be viewed by this court as evidence of a public policy supporting privacy. . . .

Third, there exists a common law right to privacy. The Restatement (Second) of Torts provides:

> *Intrusion upon Seclusion* One who intentionally intrudes, physically or otherwise, upon the solitude or seclusion of another or his private affairs or concerns, is subject to liability to the other for invasion of his privacy, if the intrusion would be highly offensive to a reasonable person.

While we have not expressly considered the application of this tort in Alaska, we have recognized its existence.

Thus, the citizens' right to be protected against unwarranted intrusions into their private lives has been recognized in the law of Alaska. The constitution protects against governmental intrusion, statutes protect against employer intrusion, and the common law protects against intrusions by other private persons. As a result, there is sufficient evidence to support the conclusion that there exists a public policy protecting spheres of employee conduct into which employers may not intrude. The question then becomes whether employer monitoring of employee drug use outside the work place is such a prohibited intrusion.

The Public Policy Supporting Employee Privacy Must Be Balanced against the Public Policy Supporting Health and Safety. Since the recent advent of inexpensive urine tests for illicit drugs, most litigation regarding the use of these tests in the employment context has concerned government employees. The testing has been challenged under the proscriptions of federal fourth amendment search and seizure law. This body of law regulates only governmental activity, and as a result is of limited value to the case at bar, which involves private activity. However, the reasoning of the federal courts regarding the intrusiveness of urine testing can illuminate this court's consideration of the extent to which personal privacy is violated by these tests.

In *Capua v. City of Plainfield*, city firefighters sued to enjoin random urinalysis tests conducted by the fire department. The court wrote:

> Urine testing involves one of the most private of functions, a function traditionally performed in private, and indeed, usually prohibited in public. The proposed test, in order to ensure its reliability, requires the presence of another when the specimen is created and frequently reveals information about one's health unrelated to the use of drugs. If the tests are positive, it may affect one's employment status and even result in criminal prosecution.
>
> We would be appalled at the spectre of the police spying on employees during their free time and then reporting their activities to their employers. Drug testing is a form of surveillance, albeit a technological one. Nonetheless, it reports on a person's off-duty activities just as surely as someone had been present and watching. It is George Orwell's "Big Brother" Society come to life.

While there is a certain amount of hyperbole in this statement, it does portray the *potential* invasion that the technology of urinalysis makes possible. It is against this potential that the law must guard. Not all courts view urine testing with such skepticism, believing the intrusion justified in contemporary society.

Judge Patrick Higginbotham assumed a more cynical stance in *National Treasury Employees Union v. Von Raab*, observing that there is little difference between the intrusiveness of urine testing and the intrusiveness of other affronts to privacy regularly accepted by individuals today. He wrote:

> The precise privacy interest asserted is elusive, and the plaintiffs are, at best, inexact as to just what that privacy interest is. Finding an objectively reasonable expectation of privacy in urine, a waste product, contains inherent contradictions. The district court found

such a right of privacy, but, in fairness, plaintiffs do not rest there. Rather, it appears from the plaintiffs' brief that it is the manner of taking the samples that is said to invade a privacy, because outer garments in which a false sample might be hidden must be removed and a person of the same sex remains outside a stall while the applicant urinates. Yet, apart from the partial disrobing (apparently not independently challenged) persons using public toilet facilities experience a similar lack of privacy. The right must then be a perceived affront to personal identity by the presence in the same room of another while engaging in a private body function.

It is suggested that the testing program rests on a generalized lack of trust and not on a developed suspicion of an individual applicant. Necessarily there is a plain implication that an applicant is part of a group that, given the demands of the job, cannot be trusted to be truthful about drug use. The difficulty is that just such distrust, or equally accurate, care, is behind every background check and every security check; indeed the information gained in tests of urine is not different from that disclosed in medical records, for which consent to examine is a routine part of applications for many sensitive government posts. In short, given the practice of testing and background checks required for so many government jobs, whether any expectations of privacy by these job applicants were objectively reasonable is dubious at best. Certainly to ride with the cops one ought to expect inquiry, and by the surest means, into whether he is a robber.

. . . As Judge Higginbotham observes, society often tolerates intrusions into an individual's privacy under circumstances similar to those present in urinalysis. We find this persuasive. It appears, then, that it is the reason the urinalysis is conducted, and not the conduct of the test, that deserves analysis.

This court discussed, on the one hand, the reasons society protects privacy, and, on the other hand, the reasons society rightfully intrudes on personal privacy in *Ravin v. State. Ravin* addressed the issue of whether the state could prohibit the use of marijuana in the home. We held that it could not. We observed that "the right to privacy amendment to the Alaska Constitution cannot be read so as to make the possession or ingestion of marijuana itself a fundamental right." Rather, we "recognized the distinctive nature of the home as a place where the individual's privacy receives special protection." However, we recognized also that this "fundamental right" was limited to activity which remained in the home. We acknowledged that when an individual leaves his home and interacts with others, competing rights of others collectively and as individuals may take precedence:

Privacy in the home is a fundamental right, under both the federal and Alaska constitutions. We do not mean by this that a person may do anything at anytime as long as the activity takes place within a person's home. There are two important limitations on this facet of the right to privacy. First, we agree with the Supreme Court of the United States, which has strictly limited the *Stanley* guarantee to possession for purely private, noncommercial use in the home. And secondly, we think this right must yield when it interferes in a serious manner with the health, safety, rights and privileges of others or with the public welfare. No one has an absolute right to do things in the privacy of his own home which will affect himself or others adversely. Indeed, one aspect of a private matter is that it is private, that is, that it does not adversely affect persons beyond the actor, and hence is none of their business. When a matter does affect the public, directly or indirectly, it loses its wholly private character, and can be made to yield when an appropriate public need is demonstrated.

The *Ravin* analysis is analogous to the analysis that should be followed in cases construing the public policy exception to the at-will employment doctrine. That is, there is a sphere of activity in every person's life that is closed to scrutiny by others. The boundaries of that sphere are determined by balancing a person's right to privacy against other public policies, such as "the health, safety, rights and privileges of others." . . .

The Luedtkes claim that whether or not they use marijuana is information within that protected sphere into which their employer, Nabors, may not intrude. We disagree. As we have previously observed, marijuana can impair a person's ability to function normally:

> The short-term physiological effects are relatively undisputed. An immediate slight increase in the pulse, decrease in salivation, and a slight reddening of the eyes are usually noted. There is also impairment of psychomotor control. . . .

We also observe that work on an oil rig can be very dangerous. We have determined numerous cases involving serious injury or death resulting from accidents on oil drilling rigs. In addition, in Paul's case the trial court expressly considered the dangers of work on oil rigs. It found:

> 13. It is extremely important that the driller be drug free in the performance of his tasks in order to insure the immediate safety of the other personnel on the particular drill rig.

> 14. It is extremely important that the driller be drug free in the performance of his tasks in order to insure

the safety and protection of the oil field itself and the oil resource contained within it.

Where the public policy supporting the Luedtkes' privacy in off-duty activities conflicts with the public policy supporting the protection of the health and safety of other workers, and even the Luedtkes themselves, the health and safety concerns are paramount. As a result, Nabors is justified in determining whether the Luedtkes are possibly impaired on the job by drug usage off the job.

We observe, however, that the employer's prerogative does have limitations.

First, the drug test must be conducted at a time reasonably contemporaneous with the employee's work time. The employer's interest is in monitoring drug use that may directly affect employee performance. The employer's interest is not in the broader police function of discovering and controlling the use of illicit drugs in general society. In the context of this case, Nabors could have tested the Luedtkes immediately prior to their departure for the North Slope, or immediately upon their return from the North Slope when the test could be reasonably certain of detecting drugs consumed there. Further, given Nabors' need to control the oil rig community, Nabors could have tested the Luedtkes at any time they were on the North Slope.

Second, an employee must receive notice of the adoption of a drug testing program. By requiring a test, an employer introduces an additional term of employment. An employee should have notice of the additional term so that he may contest it, refuse to accept it and quit, seek to negotiate its conditions, or prepare for the test so that he will not fail it and thereby suffer sanctions.

These considerations do not apply with regard to the tests both Paul and Clarence refused to take. Paul was given notice of the future tests. He did not take the November 30 test. As a result, Nabors was justified in discharging Paul. Clarence had notice and the opportunity to schedule his test at a reasonable time. However, he refused to take any test. As a result, Nabors was justified in discharging Clarence. Neither discharge violated the implied covenant of good faith and fair dealing. . . .

Common Law Right to Privacy Claims

We recognize that "[t]he [common law] right to be free from harassment and constant intrusion into one's daily affairs is enjoyed by all persons."

Siggelkow v. State, ... As previously discussed, that law is delineated in the Restatement (Second) of Torts, entitled Intrusion upon Seclusion. That section provides: "One who intentionally intrudes . . . upon the solitude or seclusion of another or his private affairs or concerns, is subject to liability . . . if the intrusion would be highly offensive to a reasonable person."

It is true, as the Luedtkes contend, that publication of the facts obtained is not necessary. Instead, the liability is for the offensive intrusion. . . . However, courts have construed "offensive intrusion" to require either an unreasonable manner of intrusion, or intrusion for an unwarranted purpose. . . . Paul has failed to show either that the manner or reason for testing his urine was unreasonable. During his physical, he voluntarily gave a urine sample for the purpose of testing. Therefore, he cannot complain that urine testing is "highly offensive." . . . Paul can only complain about the purpose of the urine test, that is, to detect drug usage. However, we have held, *supra*, that Nabors was entitled to test its employees for drug usage. As a result, the intrusion was not unwarranted. Paul complains additionally that he was not aware his urine would be tested for drug usage. In this regard we observe that Paul was not aware of any of the tests being performed on his urine sample. Nor did he know the ramifications of those tests. But he did know that whatever the results were they would be reported to Nabors. Therefore, his complaint about a particular test is without merit. We conclude that for these reasons Paul could not maintain an action for invasion of privacy with regard to the urinalysis conducted October 19.

As to the urinalyses Paul and Clarence refused to take, we hold that no cause of action for invasion of privacy arises where the intrusion is prevented from taking place. . . .

Study Questions

1. If the court were deciding the case based only on the moral principles we have learned, what would the court's ruling be? Do all the moral principles agree on this case?

2. How would you vote to decide this case if you were a judge on the court and were trying to apply the moral principles we have learned? How would you justify your vote?

*3. Should companies require all employees to take randomly timed drug tests, or should they wait until the first complaint before requiring a drug test?

4. Aren't some jobs more important than others when it comes to drug testing? For example, wouldn't you be more concerned to do a drug test on an airline pilot than on a janitor? Where would you draw the line on which jobs should be tested, or would you always just let each company decide for itself?

5. Couldn't much of the controversy over drug tests be avoided by having a hand-eye coordination and mental alertness test administered routinely to all airline pilots, etc., before they start work each day? Wouldn't such tests keep unknown and hence private any cause for failing the tests, yet screen out many drug users at work?

48

Futurecraft v. Clary Corp.

Superior Court of California

This is an unfair competition action brought by Futurecraft Corporation (hereinafter referred to as Futurecraft) for an injunction, damages, and an accounting against a former employee, Roderick Koutnik (hereinafter referred to as Koutnik) and Koutnik's new employer, Clary Corporation (hereinafter referred to as Clary), for the wrongful use and disclosure of certain valve designs claimed to be confidential to and the trade secrets of Futurecraft. Futurecraft appeals from a judgment in favor of both defendants entered by the court below after a trial limited by that court to the following issue: "What, if any, trade secret, embraced within the issues as established by the pleadings, stipulations and pretrial order, *became entrusted to the defendant Roderick Koutnik while he was an employee of the plaintiff?*" . . . (Emphasis added)

The basis of plaintiff's claim for relief is, as set forth in the opening brief, "(1) that the various *design features* are protectible trade secrets, as such, and (2) that, at any rate, Koutnik had expressly agreed that he would not utilize these designs (and particularly the paragraph V design) in competition with Futurecraft." (Emphasis added.)

Futurecraft and Clary are, and since at least 1953 or early 1954 have been, competitors in the design, manufacture and sale of valves and valve components for guided missiles and rockets for the defense program of the United States. Koutnik was employed by Futurecraft during three separate periods (part-time from 1949 to 1951, and full-time from July 1, 1951, to April 25, 1952, and from January 31, 1953, to March 17, 1956) for the purpose of inventing, designing and developing such valves and valve components.

Koutnik had been employed by the California Institute of Technology at its Jet Propulsion Labora-

205 C.A.2d 279. Opinion by Judge J. Fourt.

tory from September 15, 1947, to May 11, 1951, and from April 28, 1952, to January 25, 1953.

The trial court stated in his memorandum of decision (footnote 1, par. IX) that when Koutnik entered the employ of Futurecraft, "he carried with him a good deal of knowledge concerning the art, science and mechanics of valve design and manufacture, and a good deal of skill in the application of that knowledge . . . [and that] [m]uch, probably most, of that knowledge had been acquired at the Jet Propulsion Laboratory of the California Institute of Technology. . . . "

The particular valve designs forming the subject matter of this action . . . consist of two types of valve mechanisms. . . . The information alleged by Futurecraft to be confidential to it consists of a number of specific design features of the respective valves. . . .

It is appropriately stated in appellant's opening brief:

". . . this Court will be presented with two basically divergent approaches, or view-points, on this definitional problem. The defendants successfully urged the trial court to adopt a rigidly narrow and absolutist view, based upon a concept that a trade secret must be 'an item of private property' and that one can have no 'property rights' in an idea if someone else—anyone else—knows about it.

"In contrast to defendants' property rights concept, plaintiff urged below and urges here a more realistic, equitable and common sense approach (which is widely accepted and applied in other jurisdictions), based upon the Restatement view that a trade secret may consist of anything which is '. . . used in one's business, and which gives him an opportunity to obtain an advantage over *competitors who do not know or use it*. . . .'" (Emphasis added)

[Ia] Before turning to the "definitional problem" of what constitutes a trade secret, it is well to mention a basic underlying problem, namely, the legal basis upon which plaintiff predicates its right to relief. This problem stems from the fact that ownership of a trade secret does not give the owner a monopoly in its use, but merely a proprietary right which equity protects against usurpation by unfair means. . . .

"'. . . The employer thus has the burden of showing two things: (1) a legally protectable trade secret; and (2) *a legal basis*, either a covenant or a confidential relationship, *upon which to predicate relief.*'" (Emphasis added.)

The case of *Wexler v. Greenberg, supra,* deals primarily with the "legal basis . . . upon which to predicate relief" problem. In many respects the *Wexler* case aptly illustrates the situation presented in the case at bar.

In *Wexler,* defendant Greenberg was a qualified chemist in the sanitation and maintenance field. In March of 1949 he was employed by plaintiff as its chief chemist and continued there for approximately eight years. In the performance of his duties he spent approximately half of his working time in plaintiff's laboratory where he would analyze and duplicate competitor's products and then use the resulting information to develop various new formulas. In August 1957 defendant Greenberg left plaintiff and went to work for defendant corporation. Plaintiff sought to enjoin the defendants from disclosing and using certain formulas and processes pertaining to manufacture of certain sanitation and maintenance chemicals which plaintiff claimed to be its trade secrets. The Chancellor found that the formulas constituted trade secrets and that their appropriation was in violation of the duty that Greenberg owed to plaintiff by virtue of his employment and the trust reposed in him.

The Supreme Court of Pennsylvania assumed that certain of the formulas were trade secrets of the plaintiff but reversed and stated in pertinent part as follows:

"We are initially concerned with the fact that the final formulations claimed to be trade secrets were not *disclosed to* Greenberg by the appellees during his service or because of his position. [Italics shown.] Rather, the fact is that these formulas had been developed by Greenberg himself, while in the pursuit of his duties as Buckingham's [i.e., plaintiff] chief chemist, or under Greenberg's direct supervision. We are thus faced with the problem of determining the extent to which a former employer, *without the aid of any express covenant* [italics shown], can restrict his ex-employee, a highly skilled chemist, in the uses to which this employee can put his knowledge of formulas and methods he himself developed during the course of his former employment because this employer claims these same formulas, as against the rest of the world, as his trade secrets. *This problem becomes particularly significant when one recognizes that Greenberg's situation is not uncommon. In this era of electronic, chemical, missile and atomic development, many skilled technicians and expert employers are concurrently in the process of developing potential trade secrets. Competition for personnel of this caliber is exceptionally keen, and the interchange of employment is commonplace.* One has but to reach for his daily newspaper to appreciate the current market for such skilled employees. *We must therefore be particularly mindful of any effect our decision in this case might have in disrupting this pattern of employee mobility, both in view of possible restraints upon an individual in the pursuit of his livelihood and the harm of the public in general in forestalling to any extent widespread technological advances.*" (Emphasis added.) . . .

"The usual situation involving misappropriation of trade secrets in violation of a confidential relationship is one in which an employer *discloses to his employee* a pre-existing trade secret (one already developed or formulated) so that the employee may duly perform his work. . . . In such a case the trust and confidence upon which legal relief is predicated stems from the instance of the employer's *turning over to the employee* the pre-existing trade secret. [Italics shown.] It is then that a pledge of secrecy is impliedly extracted from the employee, a pledge which he carries with him even beyond the ties of his employment relationship. Since it is conceptually impossible, however, to elicit an implied pledge of secrecy from the sole act of an employee turning over to his employer a trade secret which he, the employee, has developed, as occurred in the present case, the appellees must show a different manner in which the present circumstances support the permanent cloak of confidence cast upon Greenberg by the Chancellor. The only avenue open to the appellees is to show that the nature of the employment relationship itself gave rise to a duty of nondisclosure.

"The burden the appellees must thus meet brings to the fore a problem of accommodating competing policies in our law; the right of a businessman to be protected against unfair competition stemming from the usurpation of his trade secrets and the right of an individual to the unhampered pursuit of the occupations and livelihoods for which he is best suited. There are cogent socio-economic arguments in favor of either position. Society as a whole greatly benefits from technological improvements. Without some means of post-employment protection to assure that valuable developments or improvements are exclusively those of the employer, the businessman could not afford to subsidize research or improve current methods. In addition, it must be recognized that modern economic growth and development has pushed the business venture beyond the size of the one-man firm, forcing the businessman to a much greater degree to entrust confidential business information relating to technological development to appropriate employees. While recognizing the utility in the dispersion of responsibilities in larger firms, the optimum amount of "entrusting" will not occur unless the risk of loss to the businessman through a breach of trust can be held to a minimum.

"On the other hand, any form of post-employment restraint reduces the economic mobility of employees and limits their personal freedom to pursue a preferred course of livelihood. The employee's bargaining position is weakened because he is potentially shackled by the acquisition of alleged trade secrets; and thus, paradoxically, he is restrained, because of his increased expertise, from advancing further in the industry in which he is most productive. Moreover, as previously mentioned, society suffers because competition is diminished by slackening the dissemination of ideas, processes and methods."

The court concluded that Greenberg was privileged to disclose and use the formulas which he had developed—they being a part of the technical knowledge and skill that he had acquired by virtue of his employment. Therefore, even though the formulas were plaintiff's trade secrets, Greenberg was privileged to use them.

It is apparent that the trial judge in the case at bar did give careful consideration to the "legal basis . . . upon which to predicate relief" problem even though he ultimately held that there was no trade secret. This is evident from the trial court's framing of the issue to be: "What, if any, trade secret . . . became entrusted to the defendant Roderick Koutnik while he was an employee of the plaintiff" and by what was stated in paragraph IX of the notice of decision. . . .

Appellant asserts in its reply brief that the fact that Koutnik utilized knowledge and skill which he obtained at Jet Propulsion Laboratory in developing the Paragraph V valve design is immaterial. While it might well be immaterial on the "definitional problem" of what constitutes a trade secret, it is material on the "legal basis . . . upon which to predicate relief" phase of the problem. In other words, as illustrated by the *Wexler* case, plaintiff may well have a trade secret yet defendant Koutnik be privileged to use it by virtue of there being no covenant or breach of confidence. . . .

. . . The court cannot compel a man who changes employers to wipe clean the slate of his memory. . . . To grant plaintiff the relief prayed for would in ef-

fect restrain Koutnik from the pursuit of his profession. He would be deprived of the use of knowledge and skill which he gained which did not originate with plaintiff. . . .

Mr. Julian O. von Kalinowski in an excellent article entitled "Key Employees and Trade Secrets" in 47 *Virginia Law Review* 583 states in the conclusion of the article:

"Protection should be afforded when, and only when, the information in question has value in the sense that it affords the plaintiff [i.e., ex-employer] a competitive advantage over competitors who do not know of it [i.e., the trade secret], *and where the granting of such protection will not unduly hamstring the ex-employee in the practice of his occupation or profession.* This simple balancing process will invariably protect all of the pertinent interests—those of the former employer, of the former employee, and of the public. . . ." (Emphasis added)

The appellant's remaining contentions either have already been dealt with or are without merit.

For the reasons stated the judgment is affirmed.

Study Questions

*1. Have you ever cheated an employer by secretly spending time on personal projects while pretending to be working? What if one day you caught an employee of yours doing this?

*2. If a company invented and patented something that would greatly benefit society—for example, a device that dramatically reduced automobile emissions —and then decided to market it at an outlandish price, would you want the government to intervene in the public's interest?

*3. Whom at work do you trust enough to tell a secret that, if revealed, would cost you your job?

*4. If you discovered that your closest friend at work had for years forged records and stolen from the company, what would you do? What if you hardly knew the thief?

*5. If you hired a new employee and he refused to tell you some important confidential information about his previous employer, would you value him more or less? How long do your commitments and loyalties persist after a professional relationship ends? When there is conflict between your new and old loyalties, which generally takes precedence?

49

Shh!: Trade and Corporate Secrecy

Sissela Bok

Protection against Betrayal and Theft

> I believe I undertook amongst other things not to disclose any trade secrets. Well, I am not going to.
> —Joseph Conrad, *Heart of Darkness*

The evils exposed in *Heart of Darkness* were indeed no trade secrets, though they might have been kept secret and did concern trade, and though their disclosure might well have destroyed that trade. Except in an extended and sinister sense, they were far from the most widely cited legal definition of trade secret as

> any formula, pattern, device, or compilation of information which is used in one's business and which gives him an opportunity to obtain an advantage over competitors who do not know or use it.

Trade secrecy is the most frequent claim made by those who want to protect secrets in business—legitimate secrets as well as many forms of abuse and exploitation. To call something a trade secret is to invoke for it the protections due property, in particular that of keeping it hidden from others. Like property, trade secrets can be bought and sold, stolen and recaptured, even lost for good if their owner dies without passing them on. But unlike most property, trade secrets can also be betrayed. The great clandestine wars over trade secrecy have been fought with every means of seduction, bribery, and threat precisely in order to induce or prevent betrayal.

For an illustration of the different shadings of openness and secrecy in trade, and their effects on industry in all senses of that word, consider the evolution in Europe of the intricate art of porcelain-making. Long familiar to the Chinese, the products of this art astonished Europeans as traders began to bring them back from the East in the seventeenth century. The beauty of porcelain and the variety of its uses made many Europeans long to work with it, but they had no process for manufacturing it and knew that the Chinese methods were carefully protected against imitation. Over and over again European travelers and missionaries tried to discover the secret for making the mysterious substance. But the Chinese resisted, their suspicion heightened by the inquisitiveness of the foreigners.

Finally in 1712, a Jesuit father named Francis Xavier d'Entrecolles succeeded in unraveling the secret. He learned the complicated procedures used in the manufacture of porcelain, and obtained specimens of the different earths used in its composition. In a letter worded most cautiously, since he knew it might fall into the hands of persons who would wish to prevent the secret from being transmitted, he conveyed the information to a French friend, who promptly published it. Alas, the description was so abstract, and had been made on the basis of so little practical experience, that it could not be put to immediate use. But it did awaken the interest of scientists, among them an amateur experimenter, René-Antoine Ferchault de Réaumur. He set about a process of trial and error, using earth samples and broken pieces of Chinese porcelain. As he achieved new blends, he published his results. After many trials, the manufacture of porcelain was undertaken at Sèvres, and immediately shrouded in secrecy, for purposes that were now no longer scientific but commercial. The prospect of having sole control over the European manufacture of objects so highly prized was tantalizing.

Meanwhile, a German apothecary and alchemist, Johann Friedrich Böttger, had accidentally produced some porcelain while engaged in secret experiments to find the "philosopher's stone" in order to transmute common substances into gold. He recognized the value of his discovery as soon as he compared it with the Chinese specimens he could find. With this new process, he helped start the Dresden manufacture of porcelain; and in 1710, a factory was founded in nearby Meissen. Secrecy was second nature to Böttger with his alchemist's background; he carried it over with ease to the new trade. The secrecy stimulated the curiosity of outsiders, in turn increasing the need for even stricter measures to protect the secret techniques. A contemporary source describes them as follows:

> In order to preserve this art as much as possible a secret, the fabric at Meissen, which is near Dresden, is rendered impenetrable to any but those who are immediately employed about the work; and the secret of mixing and preparing the materials is known to very few of them. They are all confined as prisoners, and subject to be arrested if they go without the walls; and consequently a chapel, and everything necessary is provided within.

Keeping workers thus confined to protect the secrecy of what they are doing may seem extreme, or at least outdated. But the practice is far from unknown even today when it comes to trade secrets as well as military secrets. Both the German and the French porcelain factories became the focus of espionage as soon as their products began to be sold. Clandestine forces fought over the secrets in and around the factories. Surrounding villages were filled with spies and secret agents seeking to ferret out the correct techniques, and to sort out the claims by swindlers and others who hinted that they had secrets to sell. The French process was finally stolen by an English agent who had infiltrated one of the factories, helping England to begin its own manufacture at last.

Industrial espionage and counterespionage grew more common still in the nineteenth century. Companies warred over processes for manufacturing steel, chemicals, machinery of every kind. In order to protect against theft or disclosure of trade secrets, and to quell worker unrest, they employed private detective agencies such as Pinkerton's. By the time of World War II, military development in many countries such as Japan and Russia depended heavily on clandestine purchase or theft of foreign technological information and scarce materials. In the second half of this century, trade secrecy and assaults upon it have come to pervade entire industries and international conglomerates. More sophisticated means are used every year; batteries of lawyers employed by the larger firms take advantage of every subtlety of law and negotiation; and undercover means of both guarding and probing business information are the most fiercely protected trade secrets of all.

If Marx could witness this development, he might take it to be yet one more symptom of the ravages of the "wolfish hunger" for profit in capitalist society. And yet secrecy about industry and invention is often most coercively imposed in the societies farthest from capitalism; and neither socialism nor any other social structure seems to pose obstacles to participation in the international battles over industrial espionage and trade secrecy. Modern industrial societies, of whatever political persuasion, have doubtless brought these battles to their current intensity; but it is often those countries whose leaders see the greatest need to catch up industrially that go to the greatest lengths in industrial espionage—once again, quite independently of their political leanings.

In the United States, a growing number of states now impose criminal liability for the theft of industrial secrets. In 1980, one man was tried and sent to prison for four years, convicted of transferring trade secrets concerning the manufacture of specialized film for computers, satellites, and other uses, estimated as worth over $6 million, from the Celanese Corporation to purchasers in the Japanese Mitsubishi Corporation. And in 1982 an elaborate FBI undercover operation presented evidence that several Japanese firms had bought stolen documents containing IBM trade secrets. If a trade secret has been conveyed in confidence its revelation to others may be seen as a breach not only of trade secrecy but of confidentiality as well. Indeed, the law often punishes such breaches more in the name of respect for promises and contracts of confidentiality than out of concern for the secret itself.

The tension between secrecy and openness is intensified when economic well-being, at times even survival, seems to be at stake. Incentives are strong to be the sole beneficiary of a process unknown to competitors; so are the forces that press, from within and without, for openness.

A degree of openness is inherent in trade secrecy itself. In contrast to other secret property, hidden away from the world to be enjoyed in seclusion, all the applications resulting from the trade secret are out in the open and indeed pressed upon potential purchasers. Coca-Cola, for instance, aggressively merchandised all over the world, is hardly kept secret; the only thing secret about it is what imitators have failed to uncover for nearly one hundred years—how to reproduce it. Every effort to discover that secret has proved unsuccessful. Even chemical analysis has failed to sort out the sequence of steps used in its manufacture. The trade secret, then, safeguards the process; its products are anything but secret.

More open ways of protecting commercial property are often preferred if they can be counted on to do so. Copyrights, patents, and trademarks are means of protecting property and of achieving exclusivity without resort to secrecy. With a patent, a process or machine can be used openly, in principle, and treated as property for a set number of years. Many regard the patent system as a way for science and industry to avoid the drawbacks of secrecy. Thus Edwin Land contrasts it with the "horrible, unthinkable alternative,"

> a cesspool of secrecy, an industrial environment infiltrated by spies, an industrial environment where a true scientist would be embarrassed to participate because he could not speak freely of what he knew, and where he could not use freely what he had learned.

Yet the patent laws do not always secure protection from competition; when they do, they may be used unfairly by large companies against smaller ones, or by the most unscrupulous against all others. Patents may be sought on minute aspects of a technological process in order to block competition; terms such as "trap patents," "dragnet patents," and "fencing patents" point to the militant use of the patenting process to harm competitors. And large corporations may bring patent-infringement suits against smaller competitors simply to burden them with legal costs.

Moreover, many innovative ideas do not fall into categories that are eligible for patenting or satisfy the requisite criteria of novelty, utility, and nonobviousness. Thus new methods of doing business cannot be patented, nor can customer lists, ideas, or processes injurious to health or to the good of society. Finally, it is much less expensive to maintain trade secrecy than to seek a patent, and if there is litigation, it is more likely to succeed. About half of all lawsuits brought to defend trade secrets are decided in favor of the plaintiffs, but less than 30 percent of patent-infringement suits are decided in favor of the patent owners. As a result, companies are resorting more often to trade secrecy, even when patenting is a possibility.

The debate over trade secrecy is hesitant and conflicted. Articles analyzing it disagree even about what the law should protect: should it be ideas, property, or contracts? Should societies encourage or discourage practices of trade secrecy? These difficulties stem not just from the double function that rationales for secrecy always serve but also from special obstacles in delimiting and justifying trade secrecy itself. They are exacerbated by the growing international tensions and by pressures for increased commercial secrecy on national-security grounds.

Borrowed Finery

More than the rationales examined in other chapters, that of trade secrecy turns out to borrow its justifications from other practices of secrecy, achieving but indirect and at times groping endorsement. Those who argue for trade secrecy usually appeal, at least implicitly, to one or more of five premises: personal autonomy, property, confidentiality, incentives to invest, and national security. How persuasive are these arguments? And what are their limitations?

The appeal to *personal autonomy* is fundamental for the support of individual claims to control over trade secrets. It invokes the individual's legitimate claim to control over secrecy and openness about thoughts, ideas, inventions, and plans. Without such control, I have argued, personal identity might itself be threatened. Someone who cherishes a secret recipe or who is working in secret on a scientific formula or a new design for a machine may see its secrecy as of the highest personal importance, and efforts to discover the secret as invasive in the extreme. The invasiveness of such action is especially blatant when the secret exists in thought only. To try to wrench it loose by force or trickery is then an inroad not only on secrecy but on basic liberty. A society that condoned such inroads in pursuit of trade secrets—as of all others—would be intolerable.

The presumption is therefore strong against overriding such personal autonomy over secrets. But it is not absolute; with trade secrets as with others, concealment may present such dangers that outside pressure to reveal them becomes necessary. If, for instance, someone is known to keep secret the composition of a desperately needed drug that could save the lives of many, the presumption shifts, and the claim to personal autonomy over the secret loses its force.

The claim to personal autonomy over trade secrets, moreover, cannot simply be extrapolated to collective autonomy. Yet the two are often linked in arguments concerning trade secrecy. Thus Warren and Brandeis urged, in their 1890 article on privacy, that "the right to be let alone" should apply to trade secrets as well as to more personal matters. The authors may have been thinking primarily of the individual entrepreneur or inventor, rather than of large firms, and could perhaps not have foreseen trade secrecy on the scale now practiced by the multinational corporations. Other writers have suggested extending privacy law to cover even such conglomerates, but have so far failed to convince the courts to take such a step. Neither the concept of privacy nor that of personal autonomy can, by itself, easily be expanded to fit both the individual entrepreneur and the large corporation.

Does the second appeal, to *property*, provide the necessary further support for extensive trade secrecy? This argument asserts the right to guard one's property as one sees fit, through secrecy if need be. Many take the right to property to be so fundamental as to need no justification. Yet here again, the legitimacy of extrapolating from individual to collective ownership of trade secrets requires scrutiny. And no matter what one concludes in that regard, the connection of trade secrecy and property raises two further questions: Should secret knowledge necessarily count as property? And does owning something necessarily legitimate keeping it secret? Consider the relationship of secrecy, knowledge, and property in the following two cases, one hypothetical, the other recently decided in an American court:

> Suppose that, in a "state of nature," a group of people live near a river and subsist on fish, which they catch by hand, and berries. There is great difficulty in catching fish by hand. Berries are however fairly plentiful. There are bits of metal lying around and I discover how to make one of them into a fishhook. With this invention I quadruple my catch of fish. My neighbors cannot discover the knack and I decline to tell them. They press me to lend them the fishhook or to give them lessons in acquiring the technique. I have however acquired Western notions of property law. . . . I point out that I have just title to the fishhook. . . .

> A chemical company had developed a new process for making methanol, after extensive secret research. Expecting the new product to be highly profitable, company executives decided to build a plant for its manufacture. At one point during the construction, an unfinished roof exposed the interior design of the plant in such a way that a trained eye could detect the nature of the secret process. Spokesmen for the company later brought suit, claiming that a competitor had arranged to photograph the plant from an airplane at a time when the process was discernible. The spokesman alleged wrongful discovery of a trade secret. The court held the competitor culpable, and the company entitled to relief.

If asked, both the inventor of the fishhook and the guardians of the manufacturing process might argue that they are entitled to keep others from benefiting from their knowledge; that they have a property right in it, and therefore the right to refuse to hand it over to others or teach them its use, even a right, in the case of the chemical company, to prevent competitors from flying across the plant under construction. These arguments exhibit both the seeming naturalness of the trade secrecy rationale's appeal to property and its weaknesses.

The Western notions of property law mentioned in the first example presuppose a view of property expressed most forcefully by Locke: that individuals have a right to what they have made, joined their labor to, or worked to wrest from nature: "For this *Labour* being the unquestionable Property of the Labourer, no man but he can have a right to what this is once joyned to, at least where there is enough, and as good is left in common for others."

At the most personal level, say of the clothes one has made for oneself or the tools one has fashioned, Locke's theory has intuitive appeal. These can be claimed as belongings by right; and working to make them often creates the sense that one has put part of oneself into them. Such a personal sense of having invested part of oneself has given rise to a more general argument from desert: that one deserves to own what one has used one's labor to create. But beyond basic personal needs, the intuitive self-evidence of this argument diminishes. As many have pointed out, Locke's theory did not adequately consider what entitlements should ensue when, as is usually the case, one joins one's labor to something already owned or worked on by others, as in farming or industry. And it is especially difficult to stretch his argument so as to justify large-scale corporate ownership. Furthermore, Locke's limiting the right to conditions "where there is enough, and as good is left in common for others" makes his view inapplicable in the conditions of global scarcity we now acknowledge.

If it is difficult to extrapolate from a theory of individual property such as Locke's to one that suits large-scale state or industrial ownership, it is perhaps even harder to move in the opposite direction: to begin with a view justifying collective ownership or some form of communal control over inventions or resources, and to accept, nevertheless, an individual claim to separate property rights against the collectivity, as in the fishhook example.

Whatever one's view of property, the two examples raise a further question: Should knowledge about how to make fishhooks and how to plan industrial processes count as property in the first place? Is there not a difference, in this respect, between saying, No, you can't use my fishhook, and saying, No, I won't let you find out how to make one to use for yourself? Trade secrets are often odd aspirants to the status of property. They may or may not remain out of reach of the knowledge of others; but one cannot always claim, on grounds of ownership, to have some entitlement to keep them thus unknown. I have argued earlier that the claim to ownership of secrets is often spurious, no matter how legitimate one's actions in guarding them. Certainly company records of trade secrets or machinery embodying them constitute property. To purloin them is theft; but was it theft in the same sense to fly over and photograph the chemical plant?

Still another question remains, even for those who regard all such efforts at discovery as theft and all trade secrets as property: Do the rights that come with property go so far as to justify secrecy? Some have argued that the Lockean view of property establishes a moral right to exclude others from its use or benefit therefrom, that this right is transmissible from one person to another and from one generation to the next. This view of property rights as exclusive, permanent, and transmissible is by no means self-evident. Those who believe such a view ubiquitous or "natural" betray as limited a perspective as that of the many nineteenth-century thinkers who believed that all cultures once exhibited "primitive communism." Few laws concerning property guarantee exclusivity under all circumstances. Someone who turns out to have the only uncontaminated well in an epidemic will not be able to claim the right to exclude others from its use. But even if exclusivity were the rule, it would not automatically entail the right to secrecy for what one owns. For some kinds of property, secrecy would require intolerably high fences, or physical restraints on passers-by, or deceit of various kinds.

Why might secrecy nevertheless be claimed as an extension of exclusivity more often for trade secrets than for other kinds of property? The argument for doing so stems from the peculiar nature of trade secrets. Unlike most forms of property, trade secrets are of an ephemeral nature. They may be lost merely from being photographed or even seen; they may evaporate as the result of someone's facial expression at the moment one guesses at a formula. Controls over exclusivity, permanence, and transmissibility are more fragile for trade secrets than for other property; unusual secrecy is therefore needed to guard them. The special need for secrecy in such cases is clear, but the property argument does not suffice to justify it. This argument cannot easily accommodate both individual and collective trade secrecy; nor

does it establish all trade secrets *as* property; nor, finally, does it always legitimate the use of secrecy in the protection of trade secrets.

A third premise, that of *confidentiality*, is often brought in to shore up or even to replace the limited or indirect supports that claims to personal autonomy and property offer. It holds that trade secrets, once shared, should be kept by those who have promised to do so, simply because of the promise itself. The word "confidentiality" in this context can be confusing, for it refers both to promises about trade secrets and to the confidentiality owed employees concerning their personal files. In the first of these two uses, though not in the second, confidentiality has no extra binding force apart from that of promises in general. It is not premised on the personal nature of the information conveyed (except through some vast and sentimentalized identification between persons and their property). One does not confess to trade secrets as one might to personal ones; and the promise of secrecy about a formula or a design is different from that about illness or family rifts.

Confidentiality about trade secrets may bring into play loyalty of a different kind from that in professional relationships: loyalty to the company. Such loyalty may be entirely appropriate; but like all practices of secrecy it becomes morally problematic when it brings individuals into the secret who are thereby hampered, injured, or rendered less free. This can happen when employees, sometimes even without prior knowledge or consent, learn facts that make it more difficult for them to leave their place of employment; or when a condition of employment is that any inventions or innovations by the employee become the property of the employer. The workers held in confinement at the Meissen porcelain factory offer an extreme example; but when any important technological secret is shared, they risk bondage, not just bonds, especially since secrets, once learned, cannot easily be unlearned.

Consider, for example, a suit brought by the B. F. Goodrich Company against the former manager of its space-suit division, Donald Wohlgemuth, and heard by the Ohio Court of Appeals in 1963. Mr. Wohlgemuth had left the company to join a rival firm, International Latex, which had recently been awarded the major space-suit subcontract for the Apollo program. As one commentator relates:

> At the appeals court level, the Goodrich brief sought an injunction that would prevent Wohlgemuth from working in the space-suit field for *any* other company, prevent his disclosure of *any* information on space-

suit technology to *anyone*, prevent his consulting or conferring with *anyone* on Goodrich trade secrets, and finally, prevent *any* future contact he might seek with Goodrich employees.

These four broad measures were rejected by the Ohio Court of Appeals. . . . The court did provide an injunction restraining Wohlgemuth from disclosure of Goodrich trade secrets. In passing, the court noted that in the absence of any Goodrich employment contract restraining his employment with a competitor, Wohlgemuth could commence work with Latex.

A great many companies in Europe and the United States and elsewhere now ask employees to sign some agreement to protect patent and trade-secret rights. Employees may be asked not to accept work with competitors for a specified time after they leave the company, or not to use certain kinds of "know-how" they have acquired in the company, or not to disclose company secrets of a wide variety. And their mobility will be affected from the outset whenever potential employers fear that hiring persons who have signed such a contract may invite a lawsuit.

Confidentiality concerning trade secrets may also conceal dangerous aspects of a product. Under its shield, the side effects of certain drugs have been kept secret, as has the ineffectualness of others. For a number of years the United States Department of the Interior consented to protect as trade secrets all information received from industries about the amount and kinds of pollutants discharged into rivers and lakes from industrial plants. In such cases, trade secrecy is a means of shielding and covering up, much as medical confidentiality can conceal malpractice.

Even when confidentiality regarding trade secrets is not actually dangerous to the public, it may extend far beyond what are ordinarily regarded as trade secrets. Consider the following recommendations by a specialist in trade secrecy. He suggests that a company should post a statement on bulletin boards as part of its "trade-secret program" that should include this provision:

> Second, our trade secrets are Company assets. They were developed at great expense and only after long periods of experimentation. . . . if one of the Company's trade secrets is disclosed to a competitor or to the public, an asset of the Company will be destroyed and rendered useless to the Company.
> . . . The following information, although certainly not all-inclusive, is certainly to be considered *at all times* to be confidential:
>   a. Formulas for all products sold by the Company.
>   b. Research and development material.

>   c. Current sales data.
>   d. Advertising data.
>   e. Marketing data.
>   f. Customer information.
>   g. Purchasing, Pricing, and Profit data.
>   h. Personnel files.

In such statements—and parallels are to be found in a growing number of companies—vast amounts of information that are not strictly speaking trade secrets are grouped with them for protection. If taken literally, such injunctions would prohibit most work-related conversations. Because they are not taken literally, and because their excesses could never be enforced in court, they are routinely disregarded; as a result, the boundaries surrounding those few trade secrets that companies regard as indispensable grow even more blurred.

Trade secrecy vis-à-vis competitors is, in its strict sense, only one aspect of corporate secrecy, though many other aspects may be brought under its umbrella for protection. In addition, corporations conceal their activities and especially their plans from many others: from shareholders who might question investments and links to other companies; from the government, in order to avoid interference and the publicity that may surround information once it is given over into the government's hands; from consumers, in order not to lose business; and from employees about such matters as hidden dangers at the workplace, imminent relocation plans, and risks of bankruptcy.

In support of such general business secrecy as well as of trade secrecy, we encounter a fourth and fifth argument: the need to preserve incentives to innovate and to invest and the need to guard against foreign competition and industrial espionage. Because these arguments invoke no rights such as autonomy and property, they don't raise the same problems of extrapolation and application as the first three. They concern, rather, the benefits of secrecy to companies and indirectly to society.

The Scope of Corporate Secrecy

The fourth defense of secrecy in business concerns *incentives*. If corporate secrecy did not exist, this argument holds, it would have to be invented. No matter what our views about the inherent right to hold property or to keep secrets, societies need to allow a measure of commercial secrecy in order to preserve the incentive to make changes and to invest resources. Without such incentives, social stability and progress will be endangered. Thus Richard Posner argues that "some measure of privacy is necessary . . . to enable people, by concealing their ideas from other people, to appropriate the social benefits of their discoveries and inventions."

Up to a point, this argument is surely persuasive. To develop new processes and achieve new knowledge in industry takes time and often great resources; to copy them, very little. Why should a company use its stockholders' money and its own manpower and resources to develop, say, a new fertilizer, if other firms can wipe out its future profits by merely copying its final results? Without protection from competing firms, it would have no incentive to make the necessary outlays. In order to avoid the resulting stagnation and failure to innovate, a society must therefore protect some corporate secrecy as a matter of policy.

Arguments pointing to such benefits from secrecy nevertheless have two kinds of limit: the benefits may be overridden by moral considerations, or disputed on empirical grounds. First, the secrecy may concern practices so harmful or invasive that they ought to be revealed, no matter how much secrecy would increase business incentives. Certain kinds of knowledge are owed to the persons who might be adversely affected by what a firm does—to employees, for example, stockholders, customers, or persons living near its factories. Thus newspaper or airline executives may claim the need for secrecy regarding administrative decisions; but such a claim rings hollow when it is used to defend the failure to notify employees of an imminent bankruptcy, so that they find a notice pinned to the entrance door one morning announcing the bankruptcy, effective immediately. Likewise, research processes that present high risks to experimental subjects, or the dumping of toxic chemicals in woods and waterways, might well help firms remain competitive and stimulate investment, but that is hardly a sufficient argument for allowing such secrecy.

Second, even when there is no moral obligation to disclose information, the argument defending corporate secrecy on grounds of incentive has practical bounds. Because it posits benefits of secrecy and costs of openness, it becomes vulnerable as soon as these costs and benefits are in doubt—when secrecy appears counterproductive, so that it not only fails to foster competition and new ideas but helps to stifle them.

A current debate weighs precisely such costs and benefits of corporate secrecy. Some argue that the economy would benefit from greatly reduced secrecy. True, they admit, individual firms might suffer, but society would gain as the market came closer to the "perfect information" that encourages innovation and growth. Others hold, on the contrary, that businesses are now suffering from too much openness and probing into company affairs. They argue that the decline in productivity in the United States is in part traceable to the federal government's first demanding vast quantities of information from firms through innumerable regulations and then failing to keep the data confidential because of the requirements of the Freedom of Information Act. The act, these critics suggest, is increasingly used by businesses as a vehicle for mutual surveillance at the public's expense, to the disadvantage of all.

This debate illustrates the perspectives on secrecy and openness that we have encountered in so many guises. Both sides agree that neither "perfect information," with all that it implies in disclosure and surveillance, nor pervasive corporate secrecy is desirable. Their disagreement stems from differing evaluations of the costs of the various practices of secrecy and openness.

Some of the differences in view stem from the misapprehension that there are *no* costs associated either with secrecy or with openness. I have discussed the drawbacks of secrecy in business, and the disadvantages of full openness. But other costs, sometimes quite specific ones, are often overlooked, such as those of gathering and reproducing the data required for fiscal or other purposes, and the corresponding costs of storing, indexing, protecting, and retrieving the data thus obtained. For an example of the scope and intricacy of the conflicts generated by requirements of openness and secrecy, consider the prolonged controversy over trade secrecy between drug manufacturers and scientists working for the Food and Drug Administration (FDA).

In 1974, fourteen current and former employees of the FDA went before the United States Senate to denounce a number of abuses—among them what they held to be trade secrecy detrimental to the public interest. They charged that their efforts to investigate new drugs met with resistance and harassment, and that the drug industry applied inappropriate pressures to the drug review process. A panel set up to consider the various allegations found little evidence of inappropriate pressures from drug companies; but it held that the secrecy shrouding drug information posed serious problems. The public, kept in ignorance about matters of the highest importance, had no way of knowing about possible mistakes or fraud that might have grave consequences for health. The secret practices forced the public to take the decisions of the FDA on faith. No one other than chosen outsiders could question the data or compare alternative choices.

Equally serious was the danger to human subjects. The secrecy shrouding drug development meant that different companies, working to develop similar drugs, engaged in duplicating experimentation on human beings, placing many more at risk than if the information could have been shared.

Spokesmen for the drug industry replied that trade secrecy was needed in the testing and licensing of new drugs. Competition in the drug industry is fierce. Between two and seven million dollars are expended over several years in the development of the average new drug, and in proving it, to the FDA's satisfaction, sufficiently safe and efficacious to be put on the market. How can the FDA both demand to see the data and refuse the companies confidentiality? How can there be sufficient incentive for the companies to invest in the production of new drugs if "me-too" drugs can quickly be put on the market by competitors that have acquired all the necessary information? Without trade-secrecy protection, these spokesmen argued, there would be no profit in being first, to compensate for the great preliminary investments.

The controversy opposed the drug industry, with its immense investments and resources, to those who fear that secrecy conceals abuses, duplication, and risks to human subjects. To resolve the conflict, and diminish the risks of secrecy while protecting the drug companies' competitive advantage, some have suggested that all files be opened, but that no company be allowed to copy another firm's process for some period of time. In this way, both property and protection would be granted, without need for the secrecy that, in this case, carries so many disadvantages.

Such methods of enforcing disclosure while ensuring incentives to invest and to innovate seem preferable, and may be required increasingly as the effects of corporate secrecy on employees, customers, stockholders, and others come to be better known. It is possible that these solutions, combining accountability and protection, will be aided by the greater difficulty of permanent concealment, in industry as elsewhere; and by the growing realization that much

secrecy, unthinkingly applied, is counterproductive. It is also possible, however, that governments will choose to rely more and more on industry-generated information regarding the safety of new drugs or chemicals, rather than on independent sources of evaluation. To the extent that they do, corporate secrecy with all its drawbacks is likely to spread.

While some freedom from scrutiny is obviously necessary to preserve initiative, alternatives to secrecy are preferable whenever they can serve that purpose. For the same reason, patents are thought to be preferable to trade secrecy. Corporate secrecy differs in this respect from individual secrecy, where the burden of proof is on those who see reason to limit autonomy regarding personal information. Because all collective secrecy magnifies the risk of harm and increases imitation and retaliation, those who advocate more than a minimum must be required to show why additional secrecy is necessary and legitimate. Corporate secrecy differs, too, from those practices of professional confidentiality which concern such personal information (rather than, say, insurance fraud or medical malpractice).

This conclusion, however, is disputed by a last defense of business secrecy—one that is voiced ever more urgently in the 1980s. It is the cost-benefit argument writ large. Translated from national to international terms it warns of possible catastrophe for societies that do not guard commercial secrecy in the name of *national security*. The costs of industrial openness, or even slackness about security regulation, according to this argument, threaten not only individual firms but entire nations and defense alliances. Thus a spokesman for a company specializing in "security services" argued in 1981 that the United States "has become a soft target for industrial espionage that is costing the nation its technological superiority." The prime weakness, he held, is that the government has no consistent policies "to protect trade secrets and stop the flow of technology out of the country." He proposed tightening up the Freedom of Information Act, placing a total embargo "on information relating to research, technology, manufacturing, and marketing of all American products, military and consumer," and extending security checks to all persons who receive "information of a quasi-classified or highly classified type."

Underlying this argument are two assumptions. The first links economic well-being and strategic security. When societies fall behind economically, they are seen as more vulnerable militarily. According to the second, societies will fall behind unless they protect their industry, commerce, and scientific research from foreign surveillance and theft of secrets; conversely, they must do everything in their power to keep up with technological development abroad.

In evaluating these assumptions, the disadvantages of secrecy are often forgotten. It is easy to think of commercial secrecy in the interests of national security as purely beneficial or at least as inherently neutral—much like a blanket one can put on and remove at will. But a look at nations, such as China and the Soviet Union, where such secrecy is enforced hardly supports this bland view. In addition to the fundamental political dangers of government-sponsored secrecy, it increases the risks of industrial complacency and mismanagement. Heightened commercial secrecy, far from enhancing national security, may therefore have the reverse effect. President Paul E. Gray of the Massachusetts Institute of Technology has warned of such an outcome:

> There is growing concern in the Federal Government that the "leaking" of technical material and ideas to other nations imperils national security both by diminishing the ability of the U.S. to compete commercially and by reducing the country's edge in armaments. Yet specific efforts that have been initiated to control technology transfer in the university setting are themselves likely to weaken the U.S. position, and thus do not serve the national interest.

We must ask, finally, just how much information the new practices of secrecy will succeed in safeguarding. Such practices hardly guarantee *actual* secrecy—least of all in a world where the technology of detection and surveillance has been so assiduously pursued. Even from a strictly military point of view, extensive industrial secrecy may therefore be unwise. If implemented, it may offer yet another version of the Maginot Line: a set of fortifications erected at great human and commercial cost that gives a false sense of security even as newer practices of intelligence-gathering continue unabated, and satellites glide across it with ease.

Study Questions

1. Marx and Engels implied in section 2 of *The Communist Manifesto* that no significant trade secrets existed. Does Bok's essay clearly refute them?

*2. When a technological development arises independently several times, the advance is probably the natural outgrowth of what has gone before. If this is so, why should society greatly reward the people who happen to be first to claim it? If patents and copyrights lasted only half as long as they do now, do you think innovation would be significantly reduced? What about prices? Should there be any limit to the profits someone can extract from an invention, a book, or a song? Royalties are still paid whenever the familiar four-line ditty starting "Happy Birthday to You" is sung in a film or play. Do you think there is a point at which such creations become so embedded in our culture that they should belong to everyone?

"IT HAS TO BE UNDERSTANDABLE, HIGBE. A CODE OF ETHICS IS NOT ACTUALLY TO BE WRITTEN IN CODE."

50

Industrial Spies and the End of the Cold War: The CIA in Search of Something to Do

Doug Vaughan

Editor's note: Vaughan catalogs some of the CIA's dirty deeds over the years, and suggests that the CIA is especially dangerous now that it doesn't have the KGB to focus on as the major Cold War threat that it was. The CIA now has more time for you.

Last spring, as the incoming Clinton administration faced the challenge of economic decline in a global market and a new director of the CIA confronted the task of re-orienting the Agency to a much-changed world, a reporter got an envelope in the mail. Inside was a 21-page document, "Defense Confidential," which laid out assignments for French spies to steal technological secrets from U.S. firms. The document was authentic. The "news," however, was not: The resulting article reprised a plan, first revealed in 1990, in which the French government targeted 49 high-tech companies, 24 U.S. financial institutions, and six U.S. government agencies.[1] The "revelation" prompted a belated outcry in Congress and official protest,[2] the tenor of which was caught in a quote attributed to "a senior intelligence official":

"No more Mr. Nice Guy."[3]

The Clinton administration "is taking off the gloves," reported the Associated Press.[4] Henceforth,

the U.S. would no longer stand idly by, watching its secrets being stolen by ostensible allies and sold back in the form of cheap products that undercut U.S. companies and jobs.

Whether the CIA should become actively involved in what used to be called industrial espionage had become, in the words of the new director, "the hottest current topic in intelligence policy."[5] The problem, James Woolsey explained to his confirmation panel, is that "not everyone around the world plays the game we do."[6] Among the dirty players, the "cheaters," were the French, Japanese, Chinese, and Israeli intelligence services which actively gather intelligence on U.S.-based corporations and share it with private or state-owned companies.[7]

Even the most casual reading of the French document, however, shows that the main targets were aerospace and electronics companies with military technology, rather than commercial or strictly "economic" secrets. The leak of the three-year-old paper was clearly part of a coordinated campaign to draw out U.S. agencies to spy on economic competitors. The ensuing debate was stoked by the deterioration of those firms' competitive position—and by the intelligence agencies' need to redefine their missions in the post–Cold War era.

"They're Robbing Us Blind"

The corpse of the USSR was still warm when the clamor, fed by leaks and unnamed sources, rang out for the CIA and other agencies to put their resources to work for private business. In early 1989, the CIA, under William Webster, commissioned an in-house study on the viability of establishing one office to coordinate intelligence-gathering on the research and development efforts of foreign governments, research centers and businesses. The idea had percolated up from different sections of the bureaucracy and dripped back down as an internal policy review. In the end it evaporated for the usual reasons: Regional desks didn't want to give up operational turf in the face of impending budget cuts. Instead, a make-work project began, interrupted only for Operation Desert Storm.

One of the chief purveyors of this view is Peter Schweitzer. His book, *Friendly Spies: How America's Allies Are Using Economic Espionage to Steal Our Secrets*, and excerpted articles[8] rely heavily on former intelligence officials, many of whom now work as consultants to private business. "Our allies are rob-

This reading originally appeared as "The CIA in Search of Enemies." Copyright © *CovertAction Quarterly*, Number 46 (Fall 1993). Published since 1978, *CovertAction Quarterly* is a magazine that researches and carefully documents the role and activities of U.S. and allied intelligence agencies at home and abroad, and which examines other political and social ramifications of secret U.S. intervention. Address: 1500 Massachusetts Avenue, NW, Washington, DC 20005.

bing us blind," wrote Raymond Rocca, former Deputy Director, Counter-Intelligence Division, CIA.[9] "If you don't think we're being exploited by friends and enemies," lamented Walter Deeley, former Deputy Director, National Security Agency, "Buster, you're crazy."[10] "It has been known for some time that economic espionage takes place. But only now are people starting to talk about it. The real question is what to do about it,"[11] said former Director of Central Intelligence Richard Helms.

To characterize such sources as biased by their pocketbooks is perhaps too obvious.[12] These experts sounded a common theme relying heavily on use of the first person plural possessive. They presented a besieged and friendless America victimized because of its excessive benevolence and therefore justified in taking aggressive action against unscrupulous foreigners. Most of these intelligence veterans were caught off guard when the Berlin Wall fell in November 1989. They were still living in the world they had helped shape after 1945: a world divided into two competing camps. The policies of the Reagan-Bush era were geared toward confronting and defeating an enemy and the dust had barely settled before they conjured a new slew of demons.

The opening salvo was fired at the National Press Club by Sen. David Boren (D-Okla.), then chair of the Senate Select Committee on Intelligence. Citing anecdotes that would become familiar fodder over the next four years, he declaimed: "The spy race is heating up against commercial targets in the United States. More and more . . . [the goal of foreign intelligence agencies'] espionage is to steal our private commercial secrets for the sake of national economic purposes. . . . We are going to have to think about the role that we want our own intelligence service to play in terms of protecting America's commercial and economic interests around the world."[13] By focusing on the "alleged theft" of "our" secrets, Boren diverted attention from the CIA's transfer of lethal technology to such "friends" as the Afghan *Mujahadeen*, Iraq, and Iran.

The Press Club is a near-perfect forum for a policy-maker to float a trial balloon and for a politician to cultivate an image as a deep thinker.[14] Few in the obliging media stopped to ask, for example, whether IBM was "losing billions and billions" to international piracy, as one of its executives would soon claim,[15] or if incompetent management might at least be a co-culprit in Big Blue's fall from profitable grace.

Never mind. A campaign was under way, and the constant repetition of the theme was necessary for its success. There would be some hitches and glitches, of course: "once you've got the information," pondered a Boren aide, "who do you give it to? Ford, General Motors, Chevrolet or Oldsmobile?"[16]

There was also the sticky problem of distinguishing them from us. What about U.S. companies that are partially owned by foreigners? What about foreign-registered companies owned by U.S. citizens? Not to put it too crassly, a White House techno-wonk wondered, "How would it be disseminated without at the same time giving advantage to foreign competitors?"[17]

By 1991, the pressure had triggered the predictable policy review by the National Security Council at the direction of President Bush[18] which, in turn, prompted a new wave of articles on the foreign economic threat.[19] At the September 1991 hearings on the nomination of Robert Gates as Director of Central Intelligence (DCI), Sen. John Warner (R-Va.), who represents a state with a large stake in conversion from military to civilian production, returned to the theme: "We've got to focus more of our assets . . . on trying to give American industry, American traders, a competitive edge." Gates replied, predictably, that there should be better coordination between agencies. For example, more non-proprietary, unclassified information gathered by the agencies could be made available to business generally through the Commerce Department. Beyond that, however, he was noncommittal.[20]

When pressed to be more specific, Gates defined "three broad tasks for the CIA in economics. The first was to provide analyses of world economic trends, and intelligence on the negotiation positions and strategies of other countries. (None of the senators asked if this would require CIA operatives to bug the hotel rooms of foreign diplomats, as the French were accused of doing to former Under-secretary George Ball when he was in Paris for trade negotiations.) The second was to monitor trends in technological developments; and the third was to engage in counterespionage.[21] More of the same, but more of it.

The ongoing policy review would consider these tasks, Gates assured the senators, but once confirmed, he vetoed the idea of spying on economic competitors.[22] Henceforth, U.S. intelligence agencies would supply U.S. companies with general information to help them compete, but not with information that would be illegal if acquired in the United States. "We will not conduct—and have not conducted—industrial espionage" on their behalf, a CIA spokesperson declared.[23]

Congressional advocates fearful of foreign competition, however, were not assuaged. Rep. Jack Brooks (D-Texas), chair of the House Judiciary Committee, convened hearings the following spring before his Subcommittee on Economic and Commercial Law. A conga line of security experts danced to the witness table and sang the same song: Foreign governments were using advanced cryptographic methods to conceal sensitive communications, but could also break into commercial telephone, telex, fax, and other cable traffic, intercept microwave relays, and otherwise steal proprietary information from U.S.-based companies.[24] The French filched competing Soviet and U.S. firms' bids to supply India with fighter aircraft and the makers of the Mirage jet won the bidding. The Israelis slipped a contract for a top-secret airborne reconnaissance camera to an Israeli firm. Japanese government agencies were not directly engaged in such thievery, one official demurred; when pressed to come up with a suitably damning anecdote, he cited a company which pled guilty to transporting information stolen from IBM. (Of course, that was in 1983, but the point was made.)[25]

DCI Gates declined an invitation to appear at a public hearing and identify governments engaged in economic espionage against U.S.-based companies. "Some governments . . . nearly 20 governments overall—are involved in intelligence collection activities that are detrimental to our economic interests at some level.[26]

Gates was being diplomatic. Or perhaps deliberately vague to avoid compromising ongoing operations directed at foreign firms or counterintelligence efforts to stop foreign governments. Then again, maybe the anecdotal accounts, cited repeatedly in hearing after hearing, story after story, didn't amount to much.

Smart Weapons, Dumb Policies

The campaign for economic spying paused in 1991 while the campaign for the presidency roared by, but resumed with a vengeance as the Clinton-Gore crowd took office. At first, their nominee for Director of Central Intelligence appeared out of step with the administration's "it's the economy, stupid" marching song. In his pre-nomination declamations, Woolsey seemed stuck for a way to relate intelligence concerns back to the new administration's economic agenda. He drummed away on the message that the collapse of the Soviet Union, combined with the spread of advanced weaponry, had returned us to "a more lethal version of the world than existed before 1914."[27]

At his confirmation hearings, Woolsey waxed zoological: the Soviet dragon may have been slain but the world is still a dangerous place. "We live now in a jungle filled with a bewildering variety of poisonous snakes, and in many ways the dragon was easier to keep track of."[28] Slithering through the landscape were terrorism, nationalism, fundamentalist Islam, drug traffickers, and the usual reptilian leaders who threatened the picnic.

Woolsey would have to face, or cleverly avoid, a contradiction: The venom of U.S. enemies derives its power from the very process of research, development, and transfer of technology that capitalism is supposed to stimulate. For example, the development and export of semiconductors is highly profitable for U.S. corporations. The technology, however, can fit as neatly in smart bombs as in smart computers.

In his first public speech as DCI, however, Woolsey seemed to have gotten the message emanating from the White House. He put economics at the top of his list of priorities, and emphasized the need to analyze and predict the performance of the world economy, and various national economies. That implies, for example, the need to monitor international monetary flows, which means in turn (although he didn't mention it) more stringent and extensive regulatory requirements on financial institutions to report transactions. Hence, more intensive means of monitoring compliance. So, more and bigger, faster computers. But also, necessarily, expertise in unauthorized access—hacking—that is, stealing data about private transactions from private data banks.

Domestically, the implications for civil liberties are obvious. So, too, are the temptations to use such information to speculate in stock, commodity futures or currencies to benefit either individuals or the Agency itself. Internationally, the CIA has a long history of using economic information for economic sabotage, embargo, manipulation of markets, and creation of artificial shortages of critical commodities to provoke unrest.[29]

Woolsey was aware of the controversial foreign policy ramifications and worried publicly that the Agency would get embroiled in essentially private disputes that could compromise its mission. He took pains to distinguish between a simple extension of traditional intelligence—which has always sought to determine the economic capacity of potential adversaries—and CIA spying on friendly nations for the benefit of U.S. corporations. "I think down that path lies peril for the community," warned his predecessor, Gates.[30]

This wariness was shared by many in the Cold War generation of intelligence officers who were motivated, or so they say, by something more than mere lucre. When one false step could bring mass destruction, economic espionage seemed both unseemly and petty. "The fact that one of your allies was spying on one of your companies was deemed unimportant," recalls Colby.[31]

A station chief once reported to Admiral Stansfield Turner (DCI 1977–81) that a source had reported data on bids submitted by two foreign companies competing with a U.S. company for a foreign contract. Asked what he did with the tip, the station chief said, "I didn't do anything with it. We don't have a policy to deal with it."[32] Turner tried to remedy that by pushing the community to share counterintelligence with private companies. The other agencies resisted and the policy remained inchoate.

In the post–Cold War era, Sen. Dennis DeConcini (D-Ariz.), chair of the Senate Select Committee on Intelligence, actually wants the CIA to use its capabilities to mount covert operations against foreign business. "Every two or three years while I was in intelligence some turkey would come up with this idea," says the former director of NSA, William Odom. "I'd quash it."[33]

Not anymore. Republican lawmakers, especially, have been anxious to unleash the spooks on the competition. "Economic intelligence is going to be increasingly important to our country," says Sen. John Danforth (R-Mo.), also on the intelligence committee. If the CIA or NSA learns that foreign competitors are bribing customers, Danforth and others suggest, the Agency should notify the target.[34] No problem, but what if the U.S.-based company is the culprit, like Lockheed in the early 1970s? Should the spies tell the foreign target? Should they tell the foreign cops? Should they keep their mouths shut and blackmail Lockheed? How exactly does one go about defining an "American" company anyway?

Intelligence vs. Counterintelligence

Since most economic intelligence is gleaned from "open" sources (newspapers, magazines, books, reports of government agencies, universities and think-tanks) control over access is difficult to regulate. Increasingly, the sheer quantity of sources ensures that only those with the financial and technical ability to obtain and analyze the data will be able to put it to use. Like capital, information is being concentrated in fewer hands. News organizations, privately owned databases, electronic information utilities—all private enterprises—guard this information in order to maintain a competitive advantage, or sell it as a commodity for profit. How will the CIA fit into this? As just another customer for CompuServe?

"We don't have a workable policy to address this question in a meaningful manner," says Sen. Frank Murkowski (R-Alaska), one of those pushing for the CIA to get into business as a provider of economic intelligence.[35] Why, then, not privatize the operation and let the CIA support itself by selling intelligence to the highest bidder? Better yet, go all the way and make the Agency the manufacturer of the information and turn a profit.

Economic counterintelligence encompasses identifying foreign spies and preventing them from stealing proprietary information—trade secrets, intellectual property like patents, and technology itself, especially in commodities with potential military application. According to Woolsey, that mission is a legitimate function of the intelligence community. This position actually represents a shift in emphasis worth noting and watching: Before Stansfield Turner's tenure, it was considered bad policy to notify the target of foreign espionage. The revelation could compromise sources and methods. Now, the CIA's proposal to engage in economic counterintelligence has revived an old turf war with the FBI. Last summer, the FBI revised its list of threats posed to national security by foreign intelligence agencies. At the top, acquisition of sensitive technologies by hostile powers; next, "industrial proprietary information and technology."[36]

Consistent Abuse

The hubbub over industrial espionage—should we or shouldn't we—is a dissimulation to the extent that it suggests the CIA never did it and promises never to do it again. The CIA has always spied on foreign governments and corporations for the benefit of U.S.-based companies. More important, the "us versus them" rhetoric that pervades the debate helps to foment hostility and xenophobia: Who is this "we" they're talking about, anyway?

Woolsey need only remind himself of the CIA's early director, Allen Dulles, who came from a successful career as a Wall Street lawyer. His firm, Sullivan & Cromwell, held seats on the board of directors of United Fruit, among others. The firm virtually created the Republic of Panama at the turn of the century, and influenced policy in Latin America ever since.

When a liberal government in Guatemala threatened to redistribute United Fruit's uncultivated lands to the starving peasantry in 1954, the company made a few phone calls. The Secretary of State, John Foster Dulles, and his brother put together the CIA's first and most successful military *coup d'etat*. Old hands at Langley still tout the "Guat op" as a model for successful counterinsurgency: minimum resources expended for maximum results. What they don't mention is that, in direct consequence, at least 100,000 Guatemalans, mostly indigenous, have been slaughtered by successive U.S.-backed military dictatorships.

The world—and the CIA—have indeed changed since then, but not necessarily for the better. The main difference is that extension of superpower contention into remote backwaters of the international economy no longer can be supported by an anticommunist rationale. Whether "economic security" includes industrial espionage, therefore, is a red herring. The rationale—they're doing it to us, so we have to do it to them—is an echo of the reflexive justification of U.S. intervention as "self-defense" against Soviet "aggression," and with the same goal: to provide a pretext for otherwise inexcusable acts of piracy, theft and murder.

Study Questions

1. Is Senator Moynihan right that the CIA should be abolished now that the Cold War is over? Aren't there still so many foreign threats to the United States that it needs the CIA to spy on them? Is the terrorist bombing of the World Trade Center in New York only one of many such threats, or is it an isolated incident? Note: Woolsey no longer directs the CIA.

2. Is Mary McGrory, a columnist, right about the CIA? She argues that since the CIA overestimated Soviet strength so badly and failed to foresee the collapse of the USSR, since the CIA misjudged Iraq's strength in the Persian Gulf war, and since it has made other similar mistakes, we should give the CIA something else to do and end the CIA as we know it today.

3. Should the CIA help protect trade secrets of U.S. companies? Should the United States unleash the CIA against its foreign competitors in business? Should the CIA help uncover the trade secrets of foreign firms? Would utilitarianism make a distinction between protecting your own trade secrets and spying to obtain those of others? Would libertarianism make the same moral distinction? Where would you draw the line on industrial espionage by the CIA?

4. Does utilitarianism care who gets the happiness (Japanese, Germans, Americans, etc.) so long as the quantity of happiness overall stays the same? If not, would utilitarianism justify industrial espionage by one country against another?

5. Would libertarianism oppose using the CIA to do industrial espionage on the grounds that doing so interferes with the free market? Is libertarianism more nationalistic than utilitarianism, or are both internationalist because human happiness and markets are both international?

Notes

1. Frank Greve, "French Drafted Massive Spy Plan on U.S. Targets, Documents Show," Knight-Ridder Newspapers, April 16, 1993.

2. Susan Bennett, "U.S. Calls France on the Carpet," Knight-Ridder Newspapers, as reprinted in *Denver Post*, May 5, 1993, p. 19A.

3. Quoted by John Mintz, "CIA: French Targeted Secret of U.S. Firms," *Washington Post*, April 27, 1993, p. C1.

4. Ruth Sinai, "U.S. Prepares to Toughen Stance on Industrial Spying," Associated Press, *Denver Post*, May 1, 1993, p. D2.

5. Associated Press, *Hearing of the Senate Select Committee on Intelligence on the Nomination of R. James Woolsey to Become Director of Central Intelligence*, February 2, 1993, testimony of R. James Woolsey.

6. Ibid.

7. These episodes are recounted in Peter Schweitzer, *Friendly Spies: How America's Allies Are Using Economic Espionage to Steal Our Secrets* (New York: Atlantic Monthly Press, 1993), relying on intelligence sources; cf., the compendium, "Security Awareness in the 1980s," a collection

of feature articles from *Security Awareness Bulletin, 1981–1989*, Security Awareness Division, Educational Programs Department, Department of Defense Security Institute, Richmond, Va.

8. See Peter Schweitzer, "They're Stealing Our Secrets," *The American Legion*, Special Supplement, January 1993.

9. Schweitzer, on the dust jacket of *Friendly Spies*.

10. Ibid., p. 3.

11. Ibid., p. 283.

12. Aside from his government pension, for example, Helms derives income as president of the Washington, D.C.–based Safeer Company, a private security firm he started in 1977. He also chairs the advisory board of the Parvus Company, a consulting firm on national security issues based in Silver Spring, Maryland, and staffed by former intelligence professionals.

13. Boren, address to the National Press Club, Washington, D.C., April 3, 1990.

14. See for example, Jay Peterzell, "When Friends Become Moles," *Time*, May 20, 1990, p. 50.

15. Marshall C. Phelps, Jr., vice president of commercial and industrial relations, IBM, to hearings before the House Judiciary Committee, September 16, 1991, quoted in Robert H. Williams, "Economic Spying by Foes, Friends Gain Momentum," *Signal*, July 1992, pp. 57–58.

16. Ken Levit, of Boren's staff, quoted in Neil Munro, "U.S. Mulls Industrial Spy Role," *Defense News*, May 28, 1990, p. 35.

17. Michelle K. Van Cleave, Bush administration assistant director for national security affairs and general counsel, Office of Science and Technology Policy, quoted in Munro, op. cit.

18. *National Security Review*, "Intelligence Capabilities: 1992–2005." The policy review was initiated in March 1991.

19. See Richard A. Best, Jr., "The U.S. Intelligence Community: A Role in Supporting Economic Competitiveness?" *Congressional Research Service* (CRS), Library of Congress, December 7, 1990.

20. Hearings, op. cit., September 16, 1991.

21. Gates testimony, "Nomination of Robert Gates as Director of Central Intelligence," hearings before U.S. Senate Select Committee on Intelligence, September 17, 1991, Vol. 1, pp. 580–81.

22. Richard A. Best, "Intelligence Reorganization Proposals," *CRS*, December 18, 1992 (updated version).

23. Mike Mansfield, quoted in Neil Munro, "Intelligence Community Will Share Only Legal Data with U.S. Industry," *Defense News*, October 14, 1991, p. 28.

24. See testimony of Milton J. Socolar, special assistant to the Comptroller General, General Accounting Office, before Jack Brooks' (D-Texas) Subcommittee on Economic and Commercial Law, March 1992.

25. Ibid.

26. Ibid.

27. R. James Woolsey, "The End of the Cold War: Where Do We Go from Here?" remarks at the Smithsonian Institution Distinguished Speakers Program, Washington, D.C., March 11, 1993.

28. Intelligence Hearings, op. cit., February 2, 1993.

29. Cuba, 1961–present; Chile, 1970–73; Vietnam, 1965–present; and Iraq 1991–present are a few examples of U.S. use of economic weapons to destabilize uncooperative regimes.

30. Woolsey, op. cit.; Gates quoted from confirmation hearing, September 16, 1991.

31. Thomas Omestad, "Cloak and Dagger as R&D: The French Do It The Brits Do It but Corporate Spying May Not Be for Us," *Washington Post*, June 27, 1993, p. C2.

32. Gerald F. Seib, "Business Secrets: Some Urge CIA to Go Further in Gathering Economic Intelligence," *Wall Street Journal*, August 4, 1992, p. A1.

33. Omestad, op. cit.

34. Seib, op. cit.

35. Seib, op. cit.

36. Omestad, op. cit.

51

The Ethics of Genetic Screening in the Workplace

Joseph H. Kupfer

Author's abstract: This paper clarifies the nature of genetic screening and morally evaluates using it to deny people employment. Four sets of variables determine screening's ability to forecast disorder. The first two concern epistemological limitations: whether the gene itself has been located; whether knowledge of other family members is necessary. The latter two refer to genetic causality: whether the gene causes the disorder or just a susceptibility to it.

Considerations of privacy and justice warrant restricting screening to job-specific disorders, without prejudice to the worker. Screening is more of an invasion of privacy than most "searches" because our very selves are disclosed; serious stigmatizing can result. It is unjust to penalize someone for a *susceptibility* to a disorder. It is also unjust to use the genetic knowledge and technology, developed with public monies allocated for public good, against members of the public.

Today we are witnessing the onslaught of "testing" in the workplace. We test for personality, aptitude, competence, "truthfulness," drugs, and now genetic make-up. Clearly, some of this testing may well be warranted, but genetic "screening" as it's called raises some peculiar questions of its own—questions of meaning and questions of morality. In what follows, I shall spell out the nature of genetic screening, its possible purposes or values, and then raise some moral questions about it.

Reprinted from Joseph H. Kupfer, "The Ethics of Genetic Screening in the Workplace," *Business Ethics Quarterly* vol. 3, no. 1 (1993), pp. 17–25. Reprinted by permission.

The Issue and Its Background

Genetic research is one of those areas of science which has clear practical benefits. If we know that we are carrying a gene for an inheritable illness, such as Huntington's disease, we can make a more informed choice about procreation. Knowledge of our genetic disposition toward heart disease or high blood pressure can prompt us to change our patterns of eating and exercise. And once informed of our genetically-based vulnerability to lung disease, we are able to avoid threatening work conditions. Indeed, this was the first goal of genetic screening in the workplace: to enable the employee to steer clear of work situations which were liable to call forth a disabling condition or disease (henceforth, simply "disorder").

Obviously, businesses also had an interest in this goal. Fewer disabled workers means reduction in costs caused by illness, absenteeism, health insurance, workers' compensation, and turnover. In addition, the first work place screening was a response by business to 1970's legislation making business responsible for health in the workplace. DuPont, Dow Chemical and Johnson and Johnson were among the first companies to implement genetic screening.[1] The tests were voluntary and there was no threat of job loss, rather, "warning" and "relocating" to less hazardous conditions or functions were the procedure. Indeed, DuPont's testing for sickle cell trait was requested by its own black workers! So, at its inception, genetic screening of workers seemed to be a mutually agreed upon practice aimed at mutual benefits—workers and owners cooperating for the good of all.

If this were all there was to genetic screening in the workplace, obviously there would be little need for moral discussion. But, corporations have an interest in extending the purpose of screening beyond its original scope—to deny people work. What began as a benign program can be modified to serve only the interests of business. After all, relocating workers or modifying existing conditions so that they will be less hazardous takes time, effort, and money. It's just plain cheaper to fire or not hire a worker who is at "genetic risk." The facts of the matter, however, make the whole issue more complicated. They also point to moral difficulties with the use of genetic screening to exclude workers from jobs, what we shall consider "discriminatory genetic screening."

Before investigating the moral issues involved, we must get clear on the scientific ones concerning *how* genetic screening, in fact, works. There are serious limitations to what we can learn from genetic screening and they have moral implications. The limitations on the knowledge afforded by genetic screening are of two sorts—technical and causal. Technical limitations are determined by the level of sophistication of our techno-scientific understanding. Causal constraints depend upon how genes actually bring about disorders.

Each kind of limitation itself involves two sets of variables. Technical restrictions on genetic knowledge turn on (1) whether the gene itself has been located or simply correlated with other DNA material, and (2) whether knowledge of other family members is necessary to determine the presence of the affecting gene. Causal restrictions on genetic knowledge involve (1) whether the affecting gene requires other genes to produce the disorder, and (2) whether the gene causes the disorder with inevitability or just creates a vulnerability to it. We shall consider the two sorts of limitations on genetic knowledge by examining in order these sets of variables for their significance for the practice of genetic screening.

Technical Limitations

First is the question of whether the gene itself has been located. Hemophilia, Duchenne muscular dystrophy, and cystic fibrosis are among the few exceptions where the genetic test actually identifies the gene in question. What is more typical are DNA "probes" or "markers" which indicate the likelihood of the gene's presence. "Most of today's probes aren't capable of pinpointing a bad gene. They can only detect sequences of healthy genes called markers, that are usually found near a bad one."[2] When "restriction" enzymes are introduced into the chromosome material, DNA fragments are generated: specifically, strips of genetic material called restriction fragment length polymorphisms (RFLPs), whose patterns can be statistically associated with the occurrence of a particular disorder.[3] In the case of Huntington's disease, for example, the probe detects "a piece of DNA that is so close to the as yet unidentified Huntington's gene that it is inherited along with the gene."[4]

This technical limitation—inability to locate the particular gene in question—means that we are usually dealing with statistical correlations. The marker can be inherited without the defective gene; therefore, uncovering the marker must be treated with caution. Conversely, Marc Lappe warns,[5] failure to turn up the marker does not guarantee the gene's absence!

In order to establish the correlation between the marker and the disorder, collateral data may be needed. One kind, "linkage analysis," points to our second set of variables—whether or not reference to family members is needed. Linkage analysis is comparing a given individual's DNA pattern with both affected and unaffected family members. The marker for Huntington's disease, for example, is useless if there are no living family members *with* the disease. This is because what is needed is to identify the piece of DNA material *as* a marker for Huntington's disease. Its association with the disease must be ascertained by comparison with DNA fragments of surviving relatives.

This is obviously very time consuming and expensive, prohibitively so for workplace application. It also requires the consent of family members who may not be employed by the company (over whom the company can exert little leverage). In contrast, "direct markers" indicate a genetic connection with a disorder without linkage analysis. The marking of the genes for hemophilia, cystic fibrosis, and adult polycystic kidney disease can be ascertained directly. These are more feasible for workplace screening.

Causal Limitations

Our third set of variables concerns how the genetic material generates the disorder: whether the disorder is caused by one or several genes. When a disorder is coded for by more than a single gene, the gene is question must interact with these other genes in order to be expressed (as a disorder). For screening to have predictive value it must indicate the presence (or absence) of these auxiliary, "modifier" genes. For instance, in the case of Gaucher's disease, the gene marked by the DNA probe is associated with three forms of the disease. While one of the varieties of this neurological disorder is severe, the other two are fairly mild.[6] Without corroboration from modifier genes, which form of Gaucher's disease the individual will develop can't be determined.

One interesting combination of variables occurs in Huntington's disease. It is caused by a single gene; however, that gene has not yet been located. Therefore, it is identified by means of other DNA material, *and* correlation of the material with the disease requires linkage analysis. Because it is caused by a single gene, if that gene can be identified, then linkage analysis won't be needed. In addition, it will be known with virtual certainty that the individual will be afflicted. As with adult polycystic kidney disease, all carriers of the gene for Huntington's disease develop the disorder. The causal tie between the gene and the disorder is virtually absolute.

But this is the rare exception. The great majority of genes do not lead inevitably to the disorder. They create a susceptibility or vulnerability, not a certainty of expression. Our last set of variables concerns this—the nature of the gene's causal efficacy. Conditions such as high cholesterol levels and high blood pressure, and diseases such as Alzheimer's disease and diabetes, are determined by "contingency" genes. Certain contingencies must be met before these genes bring about their respective disorders.

One of these contingencies is the presence of other genes, as we have just noted. In addition, the expression of most genetically based disorders requires the influence of biological, social, or psychological factors. It is already common knowledge that diet and exercise (biological and social influences) can affect the onset of coronary artery disease and high blood pressure. The same also holds for diabetes and back arthritis.

What does it *mean* to say that the gene produces a disposition or susceptibility to a disorder? One fourth of the people with the genetic marker for "ankylosing spondylitis" develop this debilitating back arthritis. Put another way, someone with the marker is between forty and one hundred times more likely to develop ankylosing spondylitis than is someone without this genetic material.[7] Even in such "high odds" cases like this one, however, seventy-five percent of the people with the genetic marker do *not* develop the arthritis. Work and work conditions, for instance, contribute greatly to its onset. For many genetically determined disorders, the individual may have considerable control over whether and how severely the disorder occurs. Knowledge of our genetic constitution can be helpful in making practical decisions rather than simply forecasting our fate.

Considerations of Privacy

We come now to the moral questions of whether and to what extent genetic screening in the workplace is justified. Recall that we are talking about discriminatory screening which is designed to exclude workers from jobs, rather than to "warn and relocate." I shall argue that considerations of privacy and justice mitigate against screening or at least its untrammeled deployment.

Let's begin with considerations of privacy. When information is gathered about us our privacy may be infringed upon in varying degrees. Whether our privacy is violated depends on such things as whether we consent to the gathering of the information, the nature of the information, and what happens as a result of its gathering. What I would like to focus on here is the issue of control and autonomy. Many different sorts of information can be obtained, most of it valuable to the company. Some information concerns such things as credit ratings or religious affiliations, other involves ascertaining physical facts by monitoring drug use. Is genetic screening any different in principle from drug screening, polygraph tests, or surveillance? In at least one regard it seems to be. Although in most cases, we have some control over whether a gene is expressed as a disorder, we cannot control whether we *have* the gene in the first place. Whether we have the disposition, the vulnerability to the disorder, is out of our hands.

We have some say over our work, religion, credit rating, and most of us can choose to use drugs or not. But not so with genes. They are in and of us, forever. This lack of control is especially compounded in the workplace because of related lack of power in this context. First, most workers are not in a position to refuse to cooperate with demands for screening. When this is the case, they have no control over the gathering of information about which they also lack control. This lack of power is magnified by workers' overall status in the workplace. In spite of unionization, most workers have little say over working conditions, product manufacture, wages, promotions, and firing.

We need to see testing in general, and genetic screening in particular, within the context of the employer-employee relationship. Testing workers gives employers and managers still greater control over workers' lives. Screening of all sorts would be different, and experienced differently, in a context in which power were more equitably distributed in the workplace. This seems especially important in the area of testing for genetically-based disorders, precisely because we have no control over our genetic makeup.

This sense of powerlessness is critical to the special type of stigmatization associated with genetic defects. When screening uncovers a genetic abnormality, the individual can feel morally defective—cursed or damned. This could and has happened simply from acquiring genetic information under the most benign circumstances. Thus, Madeleine and Lenn Goodman found considerable stigmatization among Jewish people identified as carriers of Tay-Sachs disease even though no obvious disadvantages followed from such identification.[8] But when the information is used prejudicially, as in the workplace discrimination we are here considering, the likelihood and intensity of stigmatization increases. As Thomas Murray notes, diagnosing an illness as genetically caused may *label* the person as *constitutionally* weak, making finding another job difficult.[9]

All of these aspects of the situation help explain why the loss of privacy suffered in genetic screening in the workplace is serious. The screening is for properties over which the worker has no control and is not responsible; it occurs in a context of relative powerlessness; and it is likely to result in stigmatization with profound costs to his or her life-chances. The genetic screening as described here involves loss of privacy, but the stigmatization and its repercussions, as we shall see, are a matter of *injustice*. Loss or forfeiture of privacy is less defendable the less just the situation under which it occurs and the less just the purposes for which it is used.

The invasion of privacy is greater when the genetic screening is "across the board" rather than selective. When businesses screen for *any* potential disease or debilitating condition, it is like having the police come and search your house just to see what they'll turn up. In both cases, there is clearly an "interest" in uncovering the relevant danger. The state and employer reduce their respective risks. But such interests are not overriding, not in a society which claims to value the individual's autonomy and privacy. The employer has no more right to a total genetic profile than he has to information about one's sexual habits, recreational activities, or religious and political beliefs—even though knowledge of these and other details of our lives might well be of use to him.

Testing for job-specific susceptibilities is more warranted since directly connected to the work context and the employer's role in bringing about the disorder. It is more like searching someone's home for specific items, such as guns or counterfeit money. Presumably, there is a good reason for looking in both sorts of case. Since screening for just a *few*, job-related genetic dispositions, less of the self is being "searched." Therefore, there is probably less sense of

being violated or stigmatized. The individual is told that she is unfit to do this particular job, for example, heavy lifting because of the disposition to back arthritis. She is not labelled as constitutionally weak due to some general condition, such as vulnerability to heart disease.

Even here, however, another threat looms. It is all too likely that employers will tend to use such information to fire employees rather than improve workplace conditions. It's cheaper. But perhaps it's the employer's responsibility to make the workplace safe, even for those with susceptibilities to environmentally-triggered disorders. People who have a disposition to lung disease, for example, might be able to work in this particular factory at no increased risk *if* the employer provided better air ventilation and circulation. This issue seems to be a matter of justice: who should bear the burden of workplace danger?

Considerations of Justice

We turn now directly to considerations of justice. The first sort of consideration focuses on the individual and the nature of genetic causation. The second concerns these individuals as members of a paying public.

In the great majority of cases, genetic markers indicate merely a predisposition for a disorder, not the inevitability of its onset. (Even when inevitable, in many cases the degree of severity remains unpredictable.) It seems unjust to penalize an individual for something that has not yet come to pass and which may well be prevented by him. It is unjust to act as if the individual is already diseased or disabled, especially when he may run a lower risk than others without the marker because of healthful life-choices made on the basis of this information.

It is like treating someone as though guilty until proven innocent. In the case of genetically caused susceptibility to a disorder, it is worse because carrying the gene is beyond the person's control. Considerations of justice suggest that there is something wrong in penalizing people for conditions which are beyond their control. Of course, sometimes people are justly denied benefits or privileges on account of uncontrollable considerations. Thus, we don't allow blind people to drive or people who have slow reaction times to be air-traffic controllers. But this is not penalizing someone so much as finding them unqualified for performance of a task. Public safety certainly does and should operate as a constraint on opportunity. However, this kind of consideration is rare in the case of genetically based disorders; moreover, it should come into play only with the onset of the disabling condition, not with the mere discovery of a genetic propensity toward it. In a society proclaiming commitment to egalitarian principles, we shouldn't further handicap people who may become disabled by depriving them of work while they are still able to do the job.

The question of the justness of discriminatory genetic screening can also be posed from the larger, social perspective. It arises from the social nature and purpose of genetic research. Genetic research, including testing individuals and groups, was developed to help people. By diagnosing genetic predispositions, testing could enable people to make beneficial decisions concerning themselves, family members, and potential offspring. When individuals already manifested certain disorders, voluntary genetic counselling was designed to help provide diagnosis, prognosis, and information for vital decisions.

This is analogous to diagnostic reading tests conducted in the public schools. These are designed to help students get remedial help when needed. Instead, imagine a situation where such tests were used to "weed out" the weakest students so that they didn't clutter up the classroom and drain teaching resources. Surely we would find such a policy unjust, if not outrageous! This would be similar to the discriminatory use of genetic screening. Like individuals with contingency markers, slow readers often can *alter* their futures. In both cases, the diagnostic tests can be used to assist the individual deal with his problem and make life-enhancing choices. On the other hand, the tests can be used to exclude the individual from certain beneficial opportunities: jobs in the case of genetic screening, and instruction to improve reading skills in the case of the reading tests.

Each use of the diagnostic test can be viewed as part of a larger model. The "diagnostic-therapeutic" model takes as primary the interests of the individuals being tested. The "competition" model, however, takes as primary the interests of some other group or institution: the business in the case of genetic testing, the school or superior students in the case of reading diagnosis. On the competition model, the "defective" worker or student is displaced in favor of the competing interests.

My analogy between the school reading test and genetic screening being used against the diagnosed individuals faces the following objection. In the case of the reading test, public education is paid for by public monies; therefore, everybody has an equal right to instruction, including those with reading disabilities. But in the case of genetic screening, the employer is operating privately. She is under no obligation to serve the interests of the employee (or prospective employee). The parallel between people with reading disabilities and those genetically marked for disorders would then break down on the basis of the public/private distinction.

My reply is that genetic research and the procedures employed in genetic screening were developed with public monies. They were carried out by means of government grants and publicly financed facilities such as state universities. Even private universities and research institutes rely greatly on government monies for equipment and salaries, as well as the findings generated by the public institutions. Moreover, these public funds were allocated for the expressed purposes of increasing scientific knowledge and helping society's members. Promotion of these social goods was used to legitimate if not justify investing society's taxes in genetic research. For private businesses to use the knowledge and technology developed through this research in order to deny some of its members employment seems unjust. This is so even if private companies market instruments and procedures for the genetic screening; the technologies *these* private companies are selling could only have been developed on the shoulders of publicly financed (and publicly available) research.

This brings us to the importance of health. Health is unlike most other goods because it is a prerequisite for so many things we value. Without it, we are cut off from the joys of recreation, travel, the arts, work, socializing, sometimes even life itself. Depending on the degree of infirmity, even such simple, apparently available delights as reading, talking, or walking may be denied the individual. The economic benefits of work are usually needed for people to receive adequate long-term health care, so that depriving them of work is likely to be condemning people to lack of health.

Denying a person work on the basis of the *disposition* to develop a disorder may, ironically, increase its likelihood of occurrence. Prevention of its occurrence might require repeated diagnostic tests, treatment, or therapy; it might require the economic wherewithal for a particular health regimen, such as exercise. Even if the lack of work doesn't contribute to the onset of the genetically marked disorder through economic deprivation, it compounds the individual's plight. He not only suffers from the potential to develop this particular disorder, but is now unemployed (and probably uninsured) to boot. He is now economically unprotected against *other* misfortunes and subjected to the psychological stress which could foster other disorders.

What should we conclude from all this? It seems to me that these considerations of privacy and justice argue strongly against general, discriminatory genetic screening in the workplace. Thomas Murray has a list of requirements that a morally defensible exclusion policy must meet. Among them are two that especially turn on considerations of justice.[10] The policy must exclude workers from but a few jobs so that those affected stand a good chance of finding other employment. Otherwise, we'd be treating them unjustly by virtually denying them the opportunity to work at all. In addition, the exclusion shouldn't single out groups that have already been unjustly treated. This is important since genetic dispositions are often inherited along racial and ethnic lines such as the high black incidence of sickle cell anemia and the high Jewish incidence of Tay-Sachs. This, too, is a matter of justice. We shouldn't compound prior injustices with present ones.

I would qualify Murray's conditions with the following restrictions. Corporate screening should be confined to work-specific disorders, rather than probe for a general genetic profile. Moreover, the company should make it a policy to try to relocate the employee to a less hazardous work site or activity, just as the first companies engaged in screening did. This degree of constraint seems minimal in light of the importance of privacy and justice.

Study Questions

1. Would libertarianism allow employers in the private sector to require genetic screening before offering a job to an applicant?

2. Since your genetic defects, if any, are an accident of birth beyond your control, and hence not your fault, would egalitarianism allow someone's career to be ruined by genetic screening? Is there a question of merit here, apart from the question of fault?

3. Would utilitarianism require or even allow genetic screening?

Notes

1. William Pat Patterson, "Genetic Screening: How Much Should we Test Employees?," *Industry Week*, June 1, 1987, pp. 47–48.

2. Kathleen McAuliffe, "Predicting Diseases," *U.S. News and World Report*, May 25, 1987, p. 65.

3. Kathleen Nolan and Sara Swenson, "New Tools, New Dilemmas: Genetic Frontier," *The Hastings Center Report*, October/November, 1988, p. 65.

4. Gina Kolati, "Genetic Screening Raises Questions for Employers and Insurers," *Research News*, April 18, 1986, p. 317.

5. Marc Lappe, "The Limits of Genetic Inquiry," *The Hastings Center Report*, August, 1987, p. 7.

6. Ibid., p. 8.

7. Marc Lappe, *Genetic Politics* (New York: Simon and Schuster, 1979), p. 61.

8. Madeleine and Lenn Goodman, "The Overselling of Genetic Anxiety," *The Hastings Center Report*, October, 1982, p. 249. There was, however, fear of loss of marriage eligibility among many of the people tested. The Goodmans also cite a study of sickle cell trait in Greece, where "possession of sickle cell trait had become a socially stigmatized status, introducing new anxieties into this rural community," p. 26.

9. Thomas Murray, "Warning: Screening Workers for Genetic Risk," *The Hastings Center Report*, February, 1983.

10. Ibid., p. 8. Murray also includes the following: sound scientific basis linking anomaly to exposure to disease; risk should be very large and the disease should be severe and irreversible; and that the number of people excluded should be very small. This last stricture doesn't strike me as all that convincing. It isn't the number of people affected that *makes* a policy unjust. Although many suffering an injustice is worse than few suffering it, injustice done even to few is still injustice and weighs against the policy.

52

In the Closet?: The Politics of Homosexuality

Andrew Sullivan

Editor's note: Sullivan gives a poignant, personal, and political account of experiences and challenges many homosexuals have had. He discusses a wide range of topics from mass advertising explicitly catering to an openly gay audience to homosexual soldiers staying in the closet in order to keep their jobs in the military. Sullivan sees problems with gay radicalism and antigay conservatism. He tries to steer a middle course between these two extremes, and argues for a new beginning in thinking these things through.

Over the last four years I have been sent letters from strangers caught in doomed, desperate marriages because of repressed homosexuality and witnessed several thousand virtually naked, muscle-bound men dance for hours in the middle of New York City, in the middle of the day. I have lain down on top of a dying friend to restrain his hundred-pound body as it violently shook with the death-throes of AIDS and listened to soldiers equate the existence of homosexuals in the military with the dissolution of the meaning of the United States. I have openly discussed my sexuality on a television talk show and sat on the porch of an apartment building in downtown D.C. with an arm around a male friend and watched as a dozen cars in a half hour slowed to hurl abuse. I have seen mass advertising explicitly cater to an openly gay audience and watched my own father break down and weep at the declaration of his son's sexuality.

These different experiences of homosexuality are not new, of course. But that they can now be experienced within one life (and that you are now reading about them) is new. The cultural categories and social departments into which we once successfully consigned sexuality—departments that helped us avoid the anger and honesty with which we are now confronted—have begun to collapse. Where once there were patterns of discreet and discrete behavior to follow, there is now only an underlying confusion of roles and identities. Where once there was only the unmentionable, there are now only the unavoidable: gays, "queers," homosexuals, closet cases, bisexuals, the "out" and the "in," paraded for every heterosexual to see. As the straight world has been confronted with this, it has found itself reaching for a response: embarrassment, tolerance, fear, violence, oversensitivity, recognition. When Sam Nunn conducts hearings, he knows there is no common discourse in which he can now speak, that even the words he uses will betray worlds of conflicting experience and anxieties. Yet speak he must. In place of the silence that once encased the lives of homosexuals, there is now a loud argument. And there is no easy going back.

This fracturing of discourse is more than a cultural problem; it is a political problem. Without at least some common ground, no effective compromise to the homosexual question will be possible. Matters may be resolved, as they have been in the case of abortion, by a stand-off in the forces of cultural war. But unless we begin to discuss this subject with a degree of restraint and reason, the visceral unpleasantness that exploded earlier this year will dog the question of homosexuality for a long time to come, intensifying the anxieties that politics is supposed to relieve.

There are as many politics of homosexuality as there are words for it, and not all of them contain reason. And it is harder perhaps in this passionate area than in any other to separate a wish from an argument, a desire from a denial. Nevertheless, without such an effort, no true politics of sexuality can emerge. And besides, there are some discernible patterns, some sketches of political theory that have begun to emerge with clarity. I will discuss here only four, but four that encompass a reasonable span of possible arguments. Each has a separate analysis of sexuality and a distinct solution to the problem of gay-straight relations. Perhaps no person belongs in any single category; and they are by no means exclusive of one another. What follows is a brief description of each: why each is riven by internal and external conflict; and why none, finally, works.

I

The first I'll call, for the sake of argument, the conservative politics of sexuality. Its view of homosexuality is as dark as it is popular as it is unfashionable. It informs much of the opposition to allowing openly gay men and women to serve in the military and can be heard in living rooms, churches, bars and computer bulletin boards across America. It is found in most of the families in which homosexuals grow up and critically frames many homosexuals' view of their own identity. Its fundamental assertion is that homosexuality as such does not properly exist. Homosexual behavior is aberrant activity, either on the part of heterosexuals intent on subverting traditional society or by people who are prey to psychological, emotional or sexual dysfunction.

For adherents to the conservative politics of sexuality, therefore, the homosexual question concerns everyone. It cannot be dismissed merely as an affliction of the individual but is rather one that afflicts society at large. Since society depends on the rearing of a healthy future generation, the existence of homosexuals is a grave problem. People who would otherwise be living productive and socially beneficial lives are diverted by homosexuality into unhappiness and sterility and they may seek, in their bleak attempts at solace, to persuade others to join them. Two gerundives cling to this view of homosexuals: practicing and proselytizing. And both are habitually uttered with a mixture of pity and disgust.

The politics that springs out of this view of homosexuality has no essential parts: with the depraved, it must punish; with the sick, it must cure. There are, of course, degrees to which these two activities can be promoted. The recent practice in modern liberal democracies of imprisoning homosexuals or subjecting them to psychological or physiological "cures" is a good deal less repressive than the camps for homosexuals in Castro's Cuba, the spasmodic attempt at annihilation in Nazi Germany or the brutality of modern Islamic states. And the sporadic entrapment of gay men in public restrooms or parks is a good deal less repressive than the systematic hunting down and discharging of homosexuals that we require of our armed forces. But the differences are matters of

degree rather than of kind; and the essential characteristic of the conservative politics of homosexuality is that it pursues the logic of repression. Not for conservatives the hypocrisy of those who tolerate homosexuality in private and abhor it in public. They seek rather to grapple with the issue directly and to sustain the carapace of public condemnation and legal sanction that can keep the dark presence of homosexuality at bay.

This is not a distant politics. In twenty-four states sodomy is still illegal, and the constitutionality of these statutes was recently upheld by the Supreme Court. Much of the Republican Party supports this politics with varying degrees of sympathy for the victims of the affliction. The Houston convention was replete with jokes by speaker Patrick Buchanan that implicitly affirmed this view. Banners held aloft by delegates asserted "Family Rights For Ever, Gay Rights Never," implying a direct trade-off between tolerating homosexuals and maintaining the traditional family.

In its crudest and most politically dismissible forms, this politics invokes biblical revelation to make its civic claims. But in its subtler form, it draws strength from the natural law tradition, which, for all its failings, is a resilient pillar of Western thought. Following a Thomist argument conservatives argue that the natural function of sexuality is clearly procreative; and that all expressions of it outside procreation destroy human beings' potential for full and healthy development. Homosexuality—far from being natural—is clearly a perversion of, or turning away from, the legitimate and healthy growth of the human person.

Perhaps the least helpful element in the current debate is the assertion that this politics is simply bigotry. It isn't. Many bigots may, of course, support it, and by bigots I mean those whose "visceral recoil" from homosexuals (to quote Buchanan) expresses itself in thuggery and name-calling. But there are some who don't support anti-gay violence and who sincerely believe discouragement of homosexuality by law and "curing" homosexuals is in the best interest of everybody.

Nevertheless, this politics suffers from an increasingly acute internal contradiction and an irresistible external development. It is damaged, first, by the growing evidence that homosexuality does in fact exist as an identifiable and involuntary characteristic of some people, and that these people do not as a matter of course suffer from moral or psychological dysfunction; that it is, in other words, as close to "natural" as any human condition can be. New data about the possible genetic origins of homosexuality are only one part of this development. By far the most important element is the testimony of countless homosexuals. The number who say their orientation is a choice make up only a tiny minority; and the candor of those who say it isn't is overwhelming. To be sure, it is in the interests of gay people to affirm their lack of choice over the matter; but the consensus among homosexuals, the resilience of lesbian and gay minorities in the face of deep social disapproval and even a plague, suggests that homosexuality, whatever one would like to think, simply is not often chosen. A fundamental claim of natural law is that its truths are self-evident: across continents and centuries, homosexuality is a self-evident fact of life.

How large this population is does not matter. One percent or 10 percent: as long as a small but persistent part of the population is involuntarily gay, then the entire conservative politics of homosexuality rests on an unstable footing. It becomes simply a politics of denial or repression. Faced with a sizable and inextinguishable part of society, it can only pretend that it does not exist, or needn't be addressed, or can somehow be dismissed. This politics is less coherent than even the politics that opposed civil rights for blacks thirty years ago, because at least that had some answer to the question of the role of blacks in society, however subordinate. Today's conservatives have no role for homosexuals; they want them somehow to disappear, an option that was once illusory and is now impossible.

Some conservatives and conservative institutions have recognized this. They've even begun to use the term "homosexual," implicitly accepting the existence of a constitutive characteristic. Some have avoided it by the innovative term "homosexualist," but most cannot do so without a wry grin on their faces. The more serious opponents of equality for homosexuals finesse the problem by restricting their objections to "radical homosexuals," but the distinction doesn't help. They are still forced to confront the problem of unradical homosexuals, people whose sexuality is, presumably, constitutive. To make matters worse, the Roman Catholic Church—the firmest religious proponent of the conservative politics of homosexuality—has explicitly conceded the point. It declared in 1973 that homosexuality is indeed involuntary for many. In the recent Universal Catechism, the Church goes even further. Homosexuality is described as a "condition" of a "not negligible"

number of people who "do not choose" their sexuality and deserve to be treated with "respect, compassion and sensitivity." More critically, because of homosexuality's involuntary nature, it cannot of itself be morally culpable (although homosexual acts still are). The doctrine is thus no longer "hate the sin but love the sinner"; it's "hate the sin but accept the condition," a position unique in Catholic theology, and one that has already begun to creak under the strain of its own tortuousness.

But the loss of intellectual solidity isn't the only problem for the conservative politics of homosexuality. In a liberal policy, it has lost a good deal of its political coherence as well. When many people in a liberal society insist upon their validity as citizens and human beings, repression becomes a harder and harder task. It offends against fundamental notions of decency and civility to treat them as simple criminals or patients. To hunt them down, imprison them for private acts, subject government workers to surveillance and dismissal for reasons related to their deepest sense of personal identity becomes a policy not simply cruel but politically impossible in a civil order. For American society to return to the social norms around the question of homosexuality of a generation ago would require a renewed act of repression that not even many zealots could contemplate. What generations of inherited shame could not do, what AIDS could not accomplish, what the most decisive swing toward conservatism in the 1980s could not muster, must somehow be accomplished in the next few years. It simply cannot be done.

So even Patrick Buchanan is reduced to joke-telling; senators to professions of ignorance; military leaders to rationalizations of sheer discomfort. For those whose politics are a mere extension of religious faith, such impossibilism is part of the attraction (and spiritually, if not politically, defensible). But for conservatives who seek to act as citizens in a secular, civil order, the dilemma is terminal. An unremittingly hostile stance toward homosexuals runs the risk of sectarianism. At some point, not reached yet but fast approaching, their politics could become so estranged from the society in which it operates that it could cease to operate as a politics altogether.

II

The second politics of homosexuality shares with the first a conviction that homosexuality as an inherent and natural condition does not exist. Homosexuality, in this politics, is a cultural construction, a binary social conceit (along with heterosexuality) forced upon the sexually amorphous (all of us). This politics attempts to resist this oppressive construct, subverting it and subverting the society that allows it to fester. Where the first politics takes as its starting point the Thomist faith in nature, the second springs from the Nietzschean desire to surpass all natural necessities, to attack the construct of "nature" itself. Thus the pursuit of a homosexual existence is but one strategy of many to enlarge the possibility for human liberation.

Call this the radical politics of homosexuality. For the radicals, like the conservatives, homosexuality is definitely a choice: the choice to be a "queer," the choice to subvert oppressive institutions, the choice to be an activist. And it is a politics that, insofar as it finds its way from academic discourse into gay activism (and it does so fitfully), exercises a peculiar fascination for the adherents of the first politics. At times, indeed, both seem to exist in a bond of mutual contempt and admiration. That both prefer to use the word "queer," the one in private, the other in irony, is only one of many resemblances. They both react with disdain to those studies that seem to reflect a genetic source for homosexuality and they both favor, to some extent or other, the process of outing, because for both it is the flushing out of deviant behavior: for conservatives, of the morally impure, for radicals, of the politically incorrect. For conservatives, radical "queers" provide a frisson of cultural apocalypse and a steady stream of funding dollars. For radicals, the religious right can be tapped as an unreflective and easy justification for virtually any political impulse whatsoever.

Insofar as this radical politics is synonymous with a subcultural experience, it has stretched the limits of homosexual identity and expanded the cultural space in which some homosexuals can live. In the late 1980s the tactics of groups like Act-Up and Queer Nation did not merely shock and anger, but took the logic of shame-abandonment to a thrilling conclusion. To exist within their sudden energy was to be caught in a liberating rite of passage, which, when it did not transgress into political puritanism, exploded many of the cozy assumptions of closeted homosexual and liberal heterosexual alike.

This politics is as open-ended as the conservative politics is closed-minded. It seeks an end to all restrictions on homosexuality, but also the subversion of heterosexual norms, as taught in schools or

the media. By virtue of its intellectual origins, it affirms a close connection with every other minority group, whose cultural subversion of white, heterosexual, male norms is just as vital. It sees its crusades—now for an AIDS czar, now against the Catholic Church's abortion stance, now for the Rainbow Curriculum, now against the military ban—as a unified whole of protest, glorifying in its indiscriminateness as in its universality.

But like the conservative politics of homosexuality, which also provides a protective ghetto of liberation for its disciples, the radical politics of homosexuality now finds itself in an acute state of crisis. Its problem is twofold: its conception of homosexuality is so amorphous and indistinguishable from other minority concerns that it is doomed to be ultimately unfocused; and its relationship with the views of most homosexuals—let alone heterosexuals—is so tenuous that at moments of truth (like the military ban) it strains to have a viable politics at all.

The trouble with gay radicalism, in short, is the problem with subversive politics as a whole. It tends to subvert itself. Act-Up, for example, an AIDS group that began in the late 1980s as an activist group dedicated to finding a cure and better treatment for people with AIDS, soon found itself awash in a cacophony of internal division. Its belief that sexuality was only one of many oppressive constructions meant that it was constantly tempted to broaden its reach, to solve a whole range of gender and ethnic grievances. Similarly, each organizing committee in each state of this weekend's march on Washington was required to have a 50 percent "minority" composition. Even *Utah*. Although this universalist temptation was not always given in to, it exercised an enervating and dissipating effect on gay radicalism's political punch.

More important, the notion of sexuality as cultural subversion distanced it from the vast majority of gay people who not only accept the natural origin of their sexual orientation, but wish to be integrated into society as it is. For most gay people—the closet cases and barflies, the construction workers and investment bankers, the computer programmers and parents—a "queer" identity is precisely what they want to avoid. In this way, the radical politics of homosexuality, like the conservative politics of homosexuality, is caught in a political trap. The more it purifies its own belief about sexuality, the less able it is to engage the broader world as a whole. The more it acts upon its convictions, the less able it is to engage in politics at all.

For the "queer" fundamentalists, like the religious fundamentalists, this is no problem. Politics for both groups is essentially an exercise in theater and rhetoric, in which dialogue with one's opponent is an admission of defeat. It is no accident that Act-Up was founded by a playwright, since its politics was essentially theatrical, a fantastic display of rhetorical pique and visual brilliance. It became a national media hit, but eventually its lines became familiar and the audience's attention wavered. New shows have taken its place and will continue to do so, but they will always be constrained by their essential nature, which is performance, not persuasion.

The limits of this strategy can be seen in the politics of the military ban. Logically, there is no reason for radicals to support the ending of the ban: it means acceptance of presumably one of the most repressive institutions in American society. And, to be sure, no radical arguments have been made to end the ban. But in the last few months, "queers" have been appearing on television proclaiming that gay people are just like anybody else and defending the right of gay Midwestern Republicans to serve their country. In the pinch, "queer" politics was forced to abandon its theoretical essence if it was to advance its purported aims: the advancement of gay equality. The military ban illustrated the dilemma perfectly. As soon as radicalism was required actually to engage America, its politics disintegrated.

Similarly, "queer" radicalism's doctrine of cultural subversion and separatism has the effect of alienating those very gay Americans most in need of support and help: the young and teenagers. Separatism is even less of an option for gays than for any other minority, since each generation is literally umbilically connected to the majority. The young are permanently in the hands of the other. By creating a politics on a doctrine of separation and difference from the majority, "queer" politics ironically broke off dialogue with the heterosexual families whose cooperation is needed in every generation, if gay children are to be accorded a modicum of dignity and hope.

There's an argument, of course, that radicalism's politics is essentially instrumental; that by stretching the limits of what is acceptable it opens up space for more moderate types to negotiate; that without Act-Up and Queer Nation, no progress would have been made at all. But this both insults the theoretical integrity of the radical position (they surely do not see themselves as mere adjuncts to liberals) and underestimates the scope of the gay revolution that has been quietly taking place in America. Far more sub-versive than media-grabbing demonstrations on the evening news has been the slow effect of individual, private Americans becoming more open about their sexuality. The emergence of role models, the development of professional organizations and student groups, the growing influence of openly gay people in the media and the extraordinary impact of AIDS on families and friends have dwarfed radicalism's impact on the national consciousness. Likewise, the greatest public debate about homosexuality yet—the military debate—took place not because radicals besieged the Pentagon, but because of the ordinary and once-anonymous Americans within the military who simply refused to acquiesce in their own humiliation any longer. Their courage was illustrated not in taking to the streets in rage but in facing their families and colleagues with integrity.

And this presents the deepest problem for radicalism. As the closet slowly collapses, as gay people enter the mainstream, as suburban homosexuals and Republican homosexuals emerge blinking into the daylight, as the gay ghettos of the inner cities are diluted by the gay enclaves of the suburbs, the whole notion of a separate and homogeneous "queer identity" will become harder to defend. Far from redefining gay identity, "queer" radicalism may actually have to define itself in opposition to it. This is implicit in the punitive practice of "outing" and in the increasingly anti-gay politics of some "queer" radicals. But if "queer" politics is to survive, it will either have to be proved right about America's inherent hostility to gay people or become more insistent in its separatism. It will have to intensify its hatred of straights or its contempt for gays. Either path is likely to be as culturally creative as it is politically sterile.

III

Between these two cultural poles, an appealing alternative presents itself. You can hear it in the tone if not the substance of civilized columnists and embarrassed legislators, who are united most strongly by the desire that this awkward subject simply go away. It is the moderate politics of homosexuality. Unlike the conservatives and radicals, the moderates do believe that a small number of people are inherently homosexual, but they also believe that another group is susceptible to persuasion in that direction and should be dissuaded. These people do not want persecution of homosexuals, but they do not want overt approval either. They are most antsy when it comes to questions of the education of children but feel acute discomfort in supporting the likes of Patrick Buchanan and Pat Robertson.

Thus their politics has all the nuance and all the disingenuousness of classically conservative politics. They are not intolerant, but they oppose the presence of openly gay teachers in school; they have gay friends but hope that their child isn't homosexual; they are in favor of ending the military ban but would seek to do so either by reimposing the closet (ending discrimination in return for gay people never mentioning their sexuality) or by finding some other kind of solution, such as simply ending the witch hunts. If they support sodomy laws (*pour décourager les autres*), they prefer to see them unenforced. In either case, they do not regard the matter as very important. They are ambivalent about domestic partnership legislation but are offended by gay marriage. Above all, they prefer that the subject of homosexuality be discussed with delicacy and restraint, and are only likely to complain to their gay friends if they insist upon "bringing the subject up" too often.

This position too has a certain coherence. It insists that politics is a matter of custom as well as principle and that, in the words of Nunn, caution on the matter of sexuality is not so much a matter of prejudice as of prudence. It places a premium on discouraging the sexually ambivalent from resolving their ambiguity freely in the direction of homosexuality, because, society being as it is, such a life is more onerous than a heterosexual one. It sometimes exchanges this argument for the most honest one: that it wishes to promote procreation and the healthy rearing of the next generation and so wishes to create a cultural climate that promotes heterosexuality.

But this politics too has become somewhat unstable, if not as unstable as the first two. And this instability stems from an internal problem and a related external one. Being privately tolerant and publicly disapproving exacts something of a psychological cost on those who maintain it. In theory, it is not the same as hypocrisy; in practice, it comes perilously close. As the question of homosexuality refuses to disappear from public debate, explicit positions have to be taken. What once could be shrouded in discretion now has to be argued in public. For those who privately do not believe that homosexuality is inherently evil or always chosen, it has become increasingly difficult to pretend otherwise in public. Silence is an option—and numberless politicians are now

availing themselves of it—but increasingly a decision will have to be made. Are you in favor of or against allowing openly gay women and men to continue serving their country? Do you favor or oppose gay marriage? Do you support the idea of gay civil rights laws? Once those questions are asked, the gentle ambiguity of the moderates must be flushed out; they have to be forced either into the conservative camp or into formulating a new politics that does not depend on a code of discourse that is fast becoming defunct.

They cannot even rely upon their gay friends anymore. What ultimately sustained this politics was the complicity of the gay elites in it, their willingness to stay silent when a gay joke was made in their presence, their deference to the euphemisms—roommate, friend, companion—that denoted their lovers, husbands and wives, their support of the heterosexual assumptions of polite society. Now that complicity, if not vanished, has come under strain. There are fewer and fewer J. Edgar Hoovers and Roy Cohns, and the thousands of discreet gay executives and journalists, businessmen and politicians who long deferred to their sexual betters in matters of etiquette. AIDS rendered their balancing act finally absurd. Many people—gay and straight—were forced to have the public courage of their private convictions. They had to confront the fact that their delicacy was a way of disguising shame; that their silence was a means of hiding from themselves their intolerance. This is not an easy process; indeed, it can be a terrifying one for both gay and straight people alike. But there comes a point after which omissions become commissions; and that point, if not here yet, is coming. When it arrives, the moderate politics of homosexuality will be essentially over.

IV

The politics that is the most durable in our current attempt to deal with the homosexual question is the contemporary liberal politics of homosexuality. Like the moderates, the liberals accept that homosexuality exists, that it is involuntary for a proportion of society, that for a few more it is an option and that it need not be discouraged. Viewing the issue primarily through the prism of the civil rights movement, the liberals seek to extend to homosexuals the same protections they have granted to other minorities. The prime instrument for this is the regulation of private activities by heterosexuals, primarily in employment and housing, to guarantee non-discrimination against homosexuals.

Sometimes this strategy is echoed in the rhetoric of Edward Kennedy, who, in the hearings on the military gay ban, linked the gay rights agenda with the work of such disparate characters as John Kennedy, Cesar Chavez and Martin Luther King Jr. In other places it is reflected in the fact that sexual orientation is simply added to the end of a list of minority conditions, in formulaic civil rights legislation. And this strategy makes a certain sense. Homosexuals are clearly subject to private discrimination in the same way as many other minorities, and linking the causes helps defuse some of the trauma that the subject of homosexuality raises. Liberalism properly restricts itself to law—not culture—in addressing social problems; and by describing all homosexuals as a monolithic minority, it is able to avoid the complexities of the gay world as a whole, just as blanket civil rights legislation draws a veil over the varieties of black America by casting the question entirely in terms of non-black attitudes.

But this strategy is based on two assumptions: that sexuality is equivalent to race in terms of discrimination, and that the full equality of homosexuals can be accomplished by designating gay people as victims. Both are extremely dubious. And the consequence of these errors is to mistarget the good that liberals are trying to do.

Consider the first. Two truths (at least) profoundly alter the way the process of discrimination takes place against homosexuals and against racial minorities and distinguish the history of racial discrimination in this country from the history of homophobia. Race is always visible; sexuality can be hidden. Race is in no way behavioral; sexuality, though distinct from sexual activity, is profoundly linked to a settled pattern of behavior.

For lesbians and gay men, the option of self-concealment has always existed and still exists, an option that means that in a profound way, discrimination against them is linked to their own involvement, even acquiescence. Unlike blacks three decades ago, gay men and lesbians suffer no discernible communal economic deprivation and already operate at the highest levels of society: in boardrooms, governments, the media, the military, the law and industry. They may have advanced so far because they have not disclosed their sexuality, but their sexuality as such has not been an immediate cause for their dis-

advantage. In many cases, their sexuality is known, but it is disclosed at such a carefully calibrated level that it never actually works against them. At lower levels of society, the same pattern continues. As in the military, gay people are not uniformly discriminated against; *openly* gay people are.

Moreover, unlike blacks or other racial minorities, gay people are not subject to inherited patterns of discrimination. When generation after generation is discriminated against, a cumulative effect of deprivation may take place, where the gradual immiseration of a particular ethnic group may intensify with the years. A child born into a family subject to decades of accumulated poverty is clearly affected by a past history of discrimination in terms of his or her race. But homosexuality occurs randomly anew with every generation. No sociological pattern can be deduced from it. Each generation gets a completely fresh start in terms of the socioeconomic conditions inherited from the family unit.

This is not to say that the psychological toll of homosexuality is less problematic than that of race, but that it is different; in some ways better; in others, worse. Because the stigma is geared toward behavior, the level of shame and collapse of self-esteem may be more intractable. To reach puberty and find oneself falling in love with members of one's own sex is to experience a mixture of self-discovery and self-disgust that never leaves a human consciousness. If the stigma is attached not simply to an obviously random characteristic, such as skin pigmentation, but to the deepest desires of the human heart, then it can eat away at a person's sense of his own dignity with peculiar ferocity. When a young person confronts her sexuality, she is also completely alone. A young heterosexual black or Latino girl invariably has an existing network of people like her to interpret, support and explain the emotions she feels when confronting racial prejudice for the first time. But a gay child generally has no one. The very people she would most naturally turn to—the family—may be the very people she is most ashamed in front of.

The stigma attached to sexuality is also different than that attached to race because it attacks the very heart of what makes a human being human: her ability to love and be loved. Even the most vicious persecution of racial minorities allowed, in many cases, for the integrity of the marital bond or the emotional core of a human being. When it did not, when Nazism split husbands from wives, children from parents, when apartheid or slavery broke up familial bonds, it was clear that a particularly noxious form of repression was taking place. But the stigma attached to homosexuality *begins* with such a repression. It forbids, at a child's earliest stage of development, the possibility of the highest form of human happiness. It starts with emotional terror and ends with mild social disapproval. It's no accident that, later in life, when many gay people learn to reconnect the bonds of love and sex, they seek to do so in private, even protected from the knowledge of their family.

This unique combination of superficial privilege, acquiescence in repression and psychological pain is a human mix no politics can easily tackle. But it is the mix liberalism must address if it is to reach its goal of using politics to ease human suffering. The internal inconsistency of this politics is that by relying on the regulation of private activity, it misses this, its essential target—and may even make matters worse. In theory, a human rights statute sounds like an ideal solution, a way for straights to express their concern and homosexuals to legitimate their identity. But in practice, it misses the point. It might grant workers a greater sense of security were they to come out in the office; and it might, by the publicity it generates, allow for greater tolerance and approval of homosexuality generally. But the real terror of coming out is deeper than economic security, and is not resolved by it; it is related to emotional and interpersonal dignity. However effective or comprehensive antidiscrimination laws are, they cannot reach far enough to tackle this issue; it is one that can only be addressed person by person, life by life, heart by heart.

For these reasons, such legislation rarely touches the people most in need of it; those who live in communities where disapproval of homosexuality is so intense that the real obstacles to advancement remain impervious to legal remedy. And even in major urban areas, it can be largely irrelevant. (On average some 1 to 2 percent of anti-discrimination cases have to do with sexual orientation; in Wisconsin, which has had such a law in force for more than a decade and is the largest case study, the figure is 1.1 percent.) As with other civil rights legislation, those least in need of it may take fullest advantage: the most litigious and articulate homosexuals, who would likely brave the harsh winds of homophobia in any case.

Anti-discrimination laws scratch the privileged surface, while avoiding the problematic depths. Like too many drugs for AIDS, they treat the symptoms of the homosexual problem without being anything like a cure; they may buy some time, and it is a cruel doctor who, in the face of human needs, would refuse them. But they have about as much chance of tackling the deep roots of the gay-straight relationship as AZT has of curing AIDS. They want to substitute for the traumatic and difficult act of coming out the more formal and procedural act of legislation. But law cannot do the work of life. Even culture cannot do the work of life. Only life can do the work of life.

As the experience in Colorado and elsewhere shows, this strategy of using law to change private behavior also gives a fatal opening to the conservative politics of homosexuality. Civil rights laws essentially dictate the behavior of heterosexuals, in curtailing their ability to discriminate. They can, with justification, be portrayed as being an infringement of individual liberties. If the purpose of the liberal politics is to ensure the equality of homosexuals and their integration into society, it has thus achieved something quite peculiar. It has provided fuel for those who want to argue that homosexuals are actually seeking the infringement of heterosexuals' rights and the imposition of their values onto others. Much of this is propaganda, of course, and is fueled by fear and bigotry. But it works because it contains a germ of truth. Before most homosexuals have even come out of the closet, they are demanding concessions from the majority, including a clear curtailment of economic and social liberties, in order to ensure protections few of them will even avail themselves of. It is no wonder there is opposition, or that it seems to be growing. Nine states now have propositions to respond to what they see as the "special rights" onslaught.

In the process, the liberal politics of homosexuality has also reframed the position of gays in relation to straights. It has defined them in a permanent supplicant status, seeing gay freedom as dependent on straight enlightenment, achievable only by changing the behavior of heterosexuals. The valuable political insight of radicalism is that this is a fatal step. It could enshrine forever the notion that gay people are a vulnerable group in need of protection. By legislating homosexuals as victims, it sets up a psychological dynamic of supplication that too often only perpetuates cycles of inadequacy and self-doubt. Like blacks before them, gay people may grasp at what seems to be an escape from the prison of self-hatred, only to find it is another prison of patronized victimology. By seeking salvation in the hands of others, they may actually entrench in law and in their minds the notion that their equality is dependent on the goodwill of their betters. It isn't. This may have made a good deal of sense in the case of American blacks, with a clear and overwhelming history of accumulated discrimination and a social ghetto that seemed impossible to breach. But for gay people—already prosperous, independent and on the brink of real integration—that lesson should surely now be learned. To place our self-esteem in the benevolent hands of contemporary liberalism is more than a mistake. It is a historic error.

V

If there were no alternative to today's liberal politics of homosexuality, it should perhaps be embraced by default. But there is an alternative politics that is imaginable, which once too was called liberal. It begins with the view that for a small minority of people, homosexuality is an involuntary condition that can neither be denied or permanently repressed. It adheres to an understanding that there is a limit to what politics can achieve in such an area, and trains its focus not on the behavior of private heterosexual citizens but on the actions of the public and allegedly neutral state. While it eschews the use of law to legislate culture, it strongly believes that law can affect culture indirectly. Its goal would be full civil equality for those who, through no fault of their own, happen to be homosexual; and would not deny homosexuals, as the other four politics do, their existence, integrity, dignity or distinctness. It would attempt neither to patronize nor to exclude.

This liberal politics affirms a simple and limited criterion: that all *public* (as opposed to private) discrimination against homosexuals be ended and that every right and responsibility that heterosexuals enjoy by virtue of the state be extended to those who grow up different. And that is all. No cures or re-education; no wrenching civil litigation; no political imposition of tolerance; merely a political attempt to enshrine formal equality, in the hope that eventually, the private sphere will reflect this public civility. For these reasons, it is the only politics that actually tackles the core *political* problem of homosexuality and perhaps the only one that fully respects liberalism's public-private distinction. For these reasons, it has also the least chance of being adopted by gays and straights alike.

* * *

But is it impossible? By sheer circumstance, this politics has just been given its biggest boost since the beginning of the debate over the homosexual question. The military ban is by far the most egregious example of proactive government discrimination in this country. By conceding, as the military has done, the excellent service that many gay and lesbian soldiers have given to their country, the military has helped shatter a thousand stereotypes about their nature and competence. By focusing on the mere admission of homosexuality, the ban has purified the debate into a matter of the public enforcement of homophobia. Unlike anti-discrimination law, the campaign against the ban does not ask any private citizens to hire or fire anyone of whom they do not approve; it merely asks public servants to behave the same way with avowed homosexuals as with closeted ones.

Because of its timing, because of the way in which it has intersected with the coming of age of gay politics, the military debate has a chance of transforming the issue for good. Its real political power—and the real source of the resistance to it—comes from its symbolism. The acceptance of gay people at the heart of the state, at the core of the notion of patriotism, is anathema to those who wish to consign homosexuals to the margins of society. It offends conservatives by the simplicity of its demands, and radicals by the traditionalism of the gay people involved; it dismays moderates, who are forced publicly to discuss this issue for the first time; and it disorients liberals, who find it hard to fit the cause simply into the rubric of minority politics. For instead of seeking access, as other minorities have done, gays in the military are simply demanding recognition. They start not from the premise of suppliance, but of success, of proven ability and prowess in battle, of exemplary conduct and ability. This is a new kind of minority politics. It is less a matter of complaint than of pride; less about subversion than about the desire to contribute equally.

The military ban also forces our society to deal with the real issues at stake in dealing with homosexuals. The country has been forced to discuss sleeping arrangements, fears of sexual intimidation, the fraught emotional relations between gays and straights, the violent reaction to homosexuality among many young males, the hypocrisy involved in much condemnation of gays and the possible psychological and emotional syndromes that make homosexuals allegedly unfit for service. Like a family engaged in the first, angry steps toward dealing with a gay member, the country has been forced to debate a subject honestly—even calmly—in a way it never has before. This is a clear and enormous gain. Whatever the result of this process, it cannot be undone.

But the critical measure necessary for full gay equality is something deeper and more emotional perhaps than even the military. It is equal access to marriage. As with the military, this is a question of formal public discrimination. If the military ban deals with the heart of what it is to be a citizen, the marriage ban deals with the core of what it is to be a member of civil society. Marriage is not simply a private contract; it is a social and public recognition of a private commitment. As such it is the highest public recognition of our personal integrity. Denying it to gay people is the most public affront possible to their civil equality.

This issue may be the hardest for many heterosexuals to accept. Even those tolerant of homosexuals may find this institution so wedded to the notion of heterosexual commitment that to extend it would be to undo its very essence. And there may be religious reasons for resisting this that require far greater discussion than I can give them here. But *civilly* and *emotionally*, the case is compelling. The heterosexuality of marriage is civilly intrinsic only if it is understood to be inherently procreative; and that definition has long been abandoned in civil society. In contemporary America, marriage has become a way in which the state recognizes an emotional and economic commitment of two people to each other for life. No law requires children to consummate it. And within that definition, there is no civil way it can logically be denied homosexuals, except as a pure gesture of public disapproval. (I leave aside here the thorny issue of adoption rights, which I support in full. They are not the same as the right to marriage and can be legislated, or not, separately.)

In the same way, emotionally, marriage is characterized by a kind of commitment that is rare even among heterosexuals. Extending it to homosexuals need not dilute the special nature of that commitment, unless it is understood that gay people, by their very nature, are incapable of it. History and experience suggest the opposite. It is not necessary to prove that gay people are more or less able to form long-term relationships than straights for it to be clear that, at least, *some* are. Giving these people a right to affirm their commitment doesn't reduce the incentive for heterosexuals to do the same, and even provides a social incentive for lesbians and gay men to adopt socially beneficial relationships.

But for gay people, it would mean far more than simple civil equality. The vast majority of us—gay and straight—are brought up to understand that the apex of emotional life is found in the marital bond. It may not be something we achieve, or even ultimately desire, but its very existence premises the core of our emotional development. It is the architectonic institution that frames our emotional life. The marriages of others are a moment for celebration and self-affirmation; they are the way in which our families and friends reinforce us as human beings. Our parents consider our emotional lives to be more important than our professional ones, because they care about us at our core, not at our periphery. And it is not hard to see why the marriage of an offspring is often regarded as the high point of any parent's life.

Gay people always know this essential affirmation will be denied them. Thus their relationships are given no anchor, no endpoint, no way of integrating them fully into the network of family and friends that makes someone a full member of civil society. Even when those relationships become essentially the same—or even stronger—than straight relationships, they are never accorded the dignity of actual equality. Husbands remain "friends"; wives remain "partners." The very language sends a powerful signal of fault, a silent assumption of internal disorder or insufficiency. The euphemisms—and the brave attempt to pretend that gay people don't need marriage—do not successfully conceal the true emotional cost and psychological damage that this signal exacts. No true progress in the potential happiness of gay teenagers or in the stability of gay adults or in the full integration of gay and straight life is possible, or even imaginable, without it.

Those two measures—simple, direct, requiring no change in heterosexual behavior and no sacrifice from heterosexuals—represent a politics that tackles the heart of homophobia while leaving homophobes their freedom. It allows homosexuals to define their own future and their own identity and does not place it in the hands of the other. It makes a clear, public statement of equality, while leaving all the inequalities of emotion and passion to the private sphere, where they belong. It does not legislate prior tolerance, it declares public equality. It banishes the paradigm of victimology and replaces it with one of integrity. It requires one further step, of course, which is to say the continuing effort for honesty on the part of homosexuals themselves. This is not easily summed up in the crude phrase "coming out"; but it finds expression in the myriad ways in which gay men and lesbians talk, engage, explain, confront and seek out the other. Politics cannot substitute for this; heterosexuals cannot provide it. And, while it is not in some sense fair that homosexuals have to initiate the dialogue, it is a fact of life. Silence, if it does not equal death, equals the living equivalent.

It is not the least of the ironies of this politics that its objectives are in some sense not political at all. The family is prior to the liberal state; the military is coincident with it. Heterosexuals would not conceive of such rights as things to be won, but as things that predate modern political discussion. But it says something about the unique status of homosexuals in our society that we now have to be political in order to be prepolitical. Our battle is not for political victory but for personal integrity. Just as many of us had to leave our families in order to join them again, so now as citizens, we have to embrace politics, if only ultimately to be free of it. Our lives may have begun in simplicity; but they have not ended there. Our dream, perhaps, is that they might.

Study Questions

1. Should the military or other organizations spy on their employees to try to discover any homosexuality, with the intent of removing homosexuals from work?

2. How can we protect the privacy of all people, even those falsely accused of being homosexual, e.g., accused by someone who seeks revenge? Won't a policy of banning homosexuals inevitably degenerate or degenerate further into a witch hunt?

3. Would libertarianism allow any employer to ban all homosexuals from the workplace?

4. Would egalitarianism insist that all homosexuals be allowed to work so long as they have as much merit as anyone else who is allowed to work? In other words, would egalitarianism insist on equal opportunity for homosexuals?

5. In how many countries and American states is sodomy still illegal? Is it unethical for mass advertisers to cater to an audience that openly defies these laws? Are these laws themselves unethical? What would libertarianism conclude about these laws? Do these laws maximize utility for all in the long run? Are these laws unfair, especially if homosexual tendencies are genetically determined—an accident of birth at least initially beyond one's control?

PART VI

Political and Economic Challenges to Business as Usual:
From Class to Crass

53

Introduction:
Is Inheritance Immoral?

Sterling Harwood

Here are facts about American inequality and inheritance of the family fortune (hereinafter: inheritance). The combined value of all the currency and coins in circulation is $199 billion, while the combined net worth of the 400 richest Americans is at least $156 billion (*The Harpers Index Book*, Henry Holt & Co., 1987, p. 36, hereafter *HI*). 2% of families own 28% of net family wealth, and 10% own 57% (R. Avery, G. Elliehausen, G. Canner & T. Gustafson, "Survey of Consumer Finances, 1983: Second Report," 70 *Fed. Res. Bull.* 865 [1984]). The richest 20% own 80% of private wealth, while the poorest 20% own only .2% (Lester Thurow, "Tax Wealth, Not Income," *New York Times Magazine*, April 11, 1976, p. 33). 20% of families receive 57.3% of all family income, while the bottom 20% receives only 7.2% (Thurow, p. 33). 75% of unemployed Americans receive no unemployment benefits (*HI*, p. 51). 60% of families living below the poverty line have at least one member employed (*HI*, p. 51)

The average homeless person lives 7 years on the street (*HI*, p. 86). In 1987 Chrysler paid Lee Iacocca an hourly rate of $8,608, while 33% of American workers earning hourly wages made less than $5 an hour (*Harper's*, July 1988, p. 15). 15% of us under 65 have no health insurance (*HI*, p. 57). 40% of children in New York City live below the poverty line (*HI*, p. 3). Since 1980 the number of millionaires has increased 145% (*HI*, p.1). Before 1981 the average tax on an estate bequeathed was .2% including .8% for estates worth over $500,000 (D. W. Haslett, "Is Inheritance Justified?" 15 *Phil. & Pub. Affairs* 122–55 [1986], p. 124). The current law imposes no federal tax on any estate worth less than $600,000. And some prime states for retirement (e.g., Florida) have no inheritance tax.

The foregoing facts would be disturbing even if blacks and women were equally represented at each level of wealth. But they are not. 46.7% of black children live below the poverty line (*HI*, p. 14). 18.3% of black, but only 7.4% of white, high school graduates over 16 are unemployed (*U.S. Dept. of Commerce, Bureau of the Census, Statistical Abstract of the U.S. 1985*, pp. 407, hereafter: *Census*). 23.6% of black high school graduates, but only 16.3% of white high school dropouts, under 25 are unemployed (*HI*, p. 24). 97% of coronary bypass operations are performed on whites (*HI*, p. 10)

In 1983 median income for black families was 56% of that of white families, $14,506 for black families and $25,757 for white families (*Census*, p. 446). 32.4% of black families, and 9.7% of white families, are below the poverty level. S&Ls nationally reject black applicants for home loans twice as often as they reject whites (*Atlanta Journal-Constitution*, Jan. 22, 1989). 92.8% of the board members of the Fortune 1000 companies are white and male (*HI*, p. 15). The average working woman makes only about 61% of the average working man. A woman's average change in standard of living after divorce is a decrease of 73%, while a man's average change is an increase of 43% (*HI*, p. 16). 24% of mothers fail to receive their court-ordered child support (*HI*, p. 72). The market value of labor performed annually by the average housewife is over $40,000 (*HI*, p. 58). Given the inequality shown above, we should ask if we may do more. We have progressive income taxes, affirmative action, and welfare programs. But inequality persists even with these three types of redistributive programs, which are unreliable. First, loopholes notoriously riddle the progressivity of income taxes.

For example, 579 Americans declared over $200,000 in income in 1983 yet paid no taxes (*HI*, p. 9). Since 1977 the amount in federal taxes paid by the richest 1% of families decreased by $44,440, while the amount for the remaining 99% increased by $212 (*Harper's*, April 1989, p. 17). A family of four living at poverty level paid 1.9% in federal taxes in 1980, but 10.4% in 1986 (*Harper's*, March 1989, p. 11). Second, the Supreme Court is now putting severe limits on affirmative action. Third, welfare programs are inadequate. For example, in 1985 ($43.6 billion in federal tax revenues were lost in homeowner deductions (including those for second homes), while only $12.3 billion was spent in federal subsidies for housing the poor (*HI*, p. 24). So we have socialism for the rich, subsidizing homeowners more than providing shelter for the poor. And as we saw above, 75% of the unemployed have no benefits, and 15% of Americans have no health insurance, etc. So we need more.

I advocate reform of inheritance merely as one of many important and justified ways we could attack inequality. I urge reform rather than abolition of inheritance because parents do have a legitimate and admirable interest—even duty—in trying to ensure that their children enter society fully without unfair disadvantages compared to average children. So the tax should aim for that goal. Inheritance earmarked for education should be exempt from tax. And moderate amounts for each child's food, clothing and shelter should be exempt. But the current $600,000 federal exemption, regardless of how few will inherit, is too extreme to justify. And any state's unlimited exemption is maximally extreme and impossible to justify. Similarly, each spouse has an interest and duty in seeing that, upon his or her death, the other spouse is not plunged into poverty. So the government should exempt inheritance guaranteeing the national median income during a transition period (between death of the spouse and finding, if he or she does not already have, steady employment paying at least the national average). And all inheritance earmarked for medical expenses of the spouse and children should be exempt. Inheritance beyond that promoting the goal stated above should be taxed at nearly 100%. We will need details such as a legatee's right of first refusal to buy items to be taxed at 100%, and a savings clause to phase the system in gradually to avoid financial shocks. But we need no more details here to show my main point that we must make fundamental reforms. (For plausible and much more detailed reforms, see Haslett.)

What should the government do with the money? The spending should combat inequality. We could provide moderate health insurance for those now lacking it. We could guarantee tuition to qualified applicants who cannot afford it. Perhaps we could spend some on projects that benefit all citizens roughly equally (e.g., reducing pollution). But quite independently of how the money is spent, part of the goal of promoting equality will already have been served by simply taxing inheritances so they cannot perpetuate significant financial advantages based on irrelevancies such as parentage, race or sex.

I wish to consider three objections to my view. First, one may object that I seek equality of outcome in the name of equality of opportunity, and that equality of outcome will weaken incentives to produce and thus lower productivity. My first reply is that the two forms of equality are not as sharply distinct as many would have us believe. To the extent that you have inferior resources (lacking equality of the outcome so far), you will lack opportunities to compete equally in business. And the racist and sexist aspects in the foregoing statistics show that one's ability to compete is determined far too much by accidents of birth beyond one's control, such as which sex or race or parents one belongs to.

My second reply is that the objection underestimates greed and socialization. Ours is an acquisitive society, and those motivated or socialized to acquire so much cannot or will not just turn off their drives and personalities once they reach some tax bracket, especially when inheritance tax does not prevent them from enjoying their wealth at any time during their lives.

My third reply is that the objection simply assumes that those who turn off their drives and produce less will not be adequately replaced in a competitive market. There's no evidence for this assumption. And the government can use some revenue from my tax to subsidize small businesses to enhance competition and replacement. Finally, we can try the tax and end it if it causes production to decline too much.

Second, one may object that I seek egalitarian justice by violating meritocratic justice. One may argue that the rich deserve their wealth because they have been so meritorious in contributing to our society. But 67% of the wealth of the ultra-rich, which this objection implies are the most deserving and meritorious contributors, was itself unearned gain through inheritance (John A. Brittain, *Inheritance and the Inequality of National Wealth* [Brookings Institution, 1978, p. 99]). Having rich parents is hardly a social contribution meriting reward. Inheritance is determined by an accident of birth beyond one's control. Further, in capitalism there is, commonsensically, a strong tendency—if left unchecked by government—for the rich to get richer and the poor to get poorer. The rich use their superior resources (e.g., more efficient machines and better credit) to force their business rivals out of business. Superior resources allow the rich to weather bad periods (e.g., droughts and recessions) that cripple or bankrupt their competitors. So initial inheritances, however unearned, strongly tend to magnify one's wealth, which is less deserved than that of those who work harder with less to earn wealth.

Third, one may object that we can't get perfect equality, so we shouldn't even try to combat the inequality we now have. For example, some people are born, or naturally develop to become, more attractive than others. And it's not feasible to run around compensating people for having sub-par natural beauty. But this objection denies that half a loaf is better than none. We should take what equality we can get. We can't end all inequality, but we should rectify many of the most egregious and correctable inequalities. The objection wants us to quit prematurely in the fight against inequality.

I conclude that inheritance, as currently structured, is immoral. American inequality is too great, and too dependent on irrelevancies such as parentage, race and sex, to justify a complete federal tax exemption for estates under $600,000, much less a state tax exemption on all estates. But inheritance can be moral. Parents have a legitimate interest, even duty, to try to make at least moderate provisions for their children. And spouses have duties to provide for one another in the event of death. So I advocate fundamental reform, rather than abolition, of inheritance. Given the enormity—and racist and sexist nature—of American inequality, justice requires fundamental reforms in inheritance.

Capitalism versus Socialism

54

Father of Economics and Moral Philosopher: Adam Smith Was No Gordon Gekko

Sylvia Nasar

Author's abstract: The Scottish philosopher looks good to laissez-faire conservatives, but they may be seeing only what they want to see. To most Americans who have even heard of him, the 18th-century Scottish philosopher Adam Smith is simply the patron saint of conservative economics, the face on ties worn by Reagan aides, the name on the door of a libertarian think tank.

But to a growing and politically diverse fraternity of economists, historians, and philosophers, the popular image of Smith is little more than a caricature. To them he is the father of all economics, a brilliant observer of social institutions, the source of all current theories of how societies become prosperous.

"Smith has been misappropriated and misunderstood," said James Buchanan, a conservative economist and Nobel laureate at George Mason University. "He was certainly not an extreme advocate of laissez-faire."

And at a time when hundreds of millions of people in former Communist states are struggling to create viable economies, Smith admirers are urging more people to go back to the source.

Smith, a Scottish university professor, tutor to a duke, and, finally, customs official, lived from 1723 to 1790. A leading figure in the Scottish enlightenment, his two major books, *The Theory of Moral Sentiments* and *An Inquiry into the Nature and Causes of the Wealth of Nations* are to democratic capitalism what Marx's *Das Kapital* is to socialism.

Smith's cynicism toward government and devotion to individual liberty made him a symbol of conservatism within a century of his death. But his fundamental insight was that charity alone, while essential, would not suffice to create prosperity. "It is not from the benevolence of the butcher, the brewer, or the baker that we can expect our dinner, but from their regard to their own interest."

Smith's "invisible hand" is often misinterpreted as implying divine approval of greed. What Smith actually said is that self-interest, not charitable impulses, motivated butchers, brewers, and bakers to feed society. Every individual, he concluded, is "led by an invisible hand to, without intending it, without knowing it, advance the interest of society."

"Smith didn't say greed is good," said Robert Nozick, a conservative philosopher at Harvard, echoing Gordon Gekko's motto in the film *Wall Street*. He thought that a free-market economy was so structured that it led people pursuing their self-interest to end up serving the common good."

In his time, the philosopher was hardly a conservative. He thumbed his nose at church, university, and empire, and inspired French revolutionaries, American suffragists, and Japanese political reformers. "My Adam Smith isn't the guy on the ties," said Paul Samuelson of MIT, the liberal economist and Nobel laureate, who has argued that Smith's scientific genius was underrated. "He was for trade unions, he believed in public works, and he was very suspicious of businessmen."

Smith is also often thought of as being indifferent, even hostile, to the poor. On the contrary, he was not opposed as a matter of principle to redistributing income. He wanted to tax horse carriages so that the "indolence and vanity of the rich is made to contribute in a very easy manner to relief of the poor."

This champion of market forces is frequently misperceived as advocating no role for government. But Smith regarded national defense as a bigger priority than "national opulence" and supported pubic works.

In response to the new defenders of Smith's legacy, free-market advocates say they still prefer their emphasis on the conservative aspects of his thought. "We're trying to work out ways in which business can be conducted with less of a nanny state," said Dr. Eamonn Butler, director of the Adam Smith Institute in London. "What Adam Smith rails against is restraints on trade. That makes him extremely appropriate for us."

Though invoked as an authority by conservative governments around the world today, Smith in his own time was regarded with suspicion. Emma Rothschild, an economic historian at Cambridge University, reports that Scotland's leading newspaper devoted a mere dozen lines to Smith's obituary while allocating 65 lines to a "former quartermaster with an interest in barometers." She said British journalists were equally "disobliging," complaining that Smith tended to incite discussion of subjects that, as one obituary put it, "have become too popular in most countries of Europe."

The man himself is a far cry from the "simple Scottish professor" invoked by Victorian conservatives, said Ian S. Ross of the University of British Columbia and author of a forthcoming Smith biography. Smith adored Voltaire, was at ease in Parisian salons, and preferred the latest novels and plays to Greek philosophers. And though he was apparently homely and absent-minded, as the Victorians claimed, he was witty enough at dinner to cause a French countess to fall for him. Said Professor Rothschild, "All of us are just so fond of Smith. It's very nice to think he's being rescued."

Study Questions

1. Was Adam Smith a libertarian, a utilitarian, an egalitarian, or some mixture of these?

2. Can greed possibly be good? Isn't greed by definition bad, since greed involves wanting more than one's fair share or wanting one's fair share more desperately than one should? Don't egalitarianism and perfectionism condemn greed? What do libertarianism and utilitarianism imply about greed?

3. Is greed necessary for capitalism to work? Is greed the same as the profit motive?

55

Why the Rich Get Richer: Because the Fed Is Engineering a Recession for the Rest of Us

William Greider

Editor's note: William Greider explains the economics behind the old saying that the rich get richer and the poor get poorer. He examines the workings of an institution often neglected in business ethics, the Federal Reserve Board. Greider claims the Federal Reserve Board, or "the Fed" as it is often called, is undemocratic and essentially unaccountable by nature. The Fed decides on tradeoffs between higher inflation and higher unemployment by deciding what interest rates should be. Since so many economies are based largely on credit, interest rates are key statistics. Greider makes the issues of high finance interesting by focusing on the politics surrounding the Fed, and on how the Fed affects the middle class. Greider notes, for example, that about 85 percent of the net financial wealth held in the United States by individuals is owned by 10 percent of U.S. families. Greider rightly notes that statistics such as these are strangely neglected in politics. Greider also notes the peculiar orientation of economists. For example, a rise in wages, which helps middle-class workers, is called inflation, which is a negative term. But a rise in stock prices, which helps the upper class that owns 85 percent of all net financial wealth, is called a boom, which is a very positive term. The independence of the Fed is by design, in order to keep politicians from pursuing inflationary policies in order to win re-election by keeping voters happy. This was a key factor in the Mexican peso dropping 40 percent in value after the Mexi-

can elections. The Fed is designed to prevent that from happening in the United States. Greider sees some need for the Fed, but he thinks the Fed is tilted too far toward preventing inflation rather than keeping interest rates lower to help the economy and employment improve.

An associate of mine was puzzled by the stories in the financial pages. The government, he read, was trying to slow down the economy, concerned that unemployment had fallen too far and average wages might actually begin to rise. "How come they want to slow down the economy now that it's finally going again?" he asked. "Why is this happening?"

"Because the rich are running the country," I replied. My answer was a bit flip and grossly oversimplified but not essentially wrong.

The government, in this instance, is not Bill Clinton's White House or Newt Gingrich's Republican-controlled Congress but a set of obscure officials who are the real governors of the American economy: the Federal Reserve Board members, who deliberate in luxurious secrecy five blocks from the White House. By controlling the nation's supply of money and credit, the Fed—not the president—steers the economy. And the Fed has decided that it must pull on the reins and push interest rates higher and higher until the current boomlet subsides or maybe even collapses into a recession.

The Federal Reserve's decision making is politics posing as disinterested economics because the issue of monetary policy is always fundamentally about whose economic interests will be defended and whose will be sacrificed. The consequences are deeper than anything Clinton and Gingrich are now arguing over. Republicans and Democrats are competing to ingratiate themselves with the struggling middle class by proposing various tax cuts for families, but the actual effects of anything they do will be peanuts compared with what the Federal Reserve has already done to the same folks.

By raising the floor price of credit, the Fed has effectively enacted its own "tax increase" on all consumers and businesses, pushing monthly mortgage payments higher for homeowners, for instance, and raising the real sticker prices on everything from cars to credit-card purchases. To work its will, the Federal Reserve must inescapably pick winners and losers. The borrowers—the overwhelming majority in American society—lose while the relatively small group of influential big-money lenders wins, earning a higher price for their credit.

That such a policy should provoke puzzlement is well justified. After all, it really doesn't make sense that the government should be trying to hold back the economy just when people are finally beginning to recover a bit from the last drubbing. The expanding economy is now producing new jobs, unemployment is down, and capital investment is strong. But average wages are still declining in terms of purchasing power, consumers are still deeply in debt, and the median income of American families has still not improved in this recovery, as usually occurs during the upward phase of economic cycles.

So what is the Federal Reserve worried about? The specter of rising wages followed by rising prices. And that spells inflation. Fed chairman Alan Greenspan has reasoned that if the present boomlet continues, eventually labor markets will tighten, and both unions and individual workers will be able to demand higher pay. Businesses might then be compelled to raise prices to defend their profit margins, and eventually this could become a general pattern across the country. An escalating inflation, if it becomes ferocious, both debases the value of money and throws business decision making out of whack.

The disorienting experience of the late 1970s, when price inflation gained momentum year after year and became embedded in everyone's economic behavior, still haunts the Federal Reserve. It is determined to fight the last war and this time win. What's different now is that the central bank claims the right to make a preemptive strike—to hammer labor when job markets are still slack and the value of wages is falling, to battle price inflation before there is any tangible evidence that it even exists.

The Fed's argument is that once people expect price inflation, everyone from business managers to consumers begins to behave differently, and inflation then escalates and is very hard to stop. Therefore it must be stomped before it even happens. This is circular logic with dreadful consequences for the economy, but with a few honorable exceptions in Congress, no one prominent in politics has dared to challenge the concept.

The consumer price index was increasing last year at the quite moderate pace of 2.7 percent. Average wages in 1994, when discounted for inflation, held steady at around $7.40 an hour—compared with $7.64 an hour in 1989. But the language of economists is oddly skewed to favor certain sectors. If wages increase, that's called inflation. If stock and bond prices increase, that's called a boom.

To put the matter bluntly, the Fed is pursuing a strategy designed to ensure that average American wages continue to decline—despite occasional promises from politicians like Clinton that the government should work to reverse this long-running trend. Clinton has, nevertheless, stood by silently while the Fed does its thing. Perhaps he is afraid of being labeled an "irresponsible" liberal. Or maybe he agrees with the Fed's sense of priorities, even while publicly expressing deepest sympathy for the losers.

Yes, it is true that some pensioners on fixed incomes and some folks nurturing small savings accounts will benefit from the Fed's policies. But the financial wealth of America remains overwhelmingly concentrated among the very few: About 85 percent of the net financial wealth held by individuals is owned by 10 percent of the families. Those statistics are strangely neglected in the public debate. Financial editors assume that everyone has a stock portfolio, just like them.

If the Fed provokes a full-blown contraction and unemployment soars again, the financial economy will enjoy a new boom. Economic commentators will describe this experience in Calvinist terms—an unpleasant but necessary interlude where we all take our bad medicine to correct for past excesses. But only certain sectors have to take this bad medicine, and generally they are not the same folks who got to enjoy the excesses.

Nearly everyone suffers, to be sure, if price inflation really gets out of control, just as the Fed argues. But monetary policy is about choosing which risks to tolerate and which to avoid. Given the general deterioration of the American standard of living, the Fed ought to be tolerating the risks on the upside—letting economic growth continue unabated because that is what fosters the new capital investment that expands the nation's productive capacity and creates the new jobs and rising wages. When economic growth is thwarted, the new investment stops cold, and so do the prosperous results that flow from it.

Given Republican promises to enact major tax reduction for the wealthy owners of capital, 1995 may produce a weird replay of the damaging collisions of economic policies that occurred back in 1981 when Ronald Reagan pushed wholesale tax cuts while the Fed was simultaneously braking the economy by tightening the supply of credit. In theory tax cuts might stimulate a sagging economy, but not if the stimulus is canceled by higher interest rates from the Fed and from global bond investors. Sooner or later, investors will figure out the Republican game: Cut taxes first, then reduce federal spending later, preferably after the 1996 election. The result would be swelling federal deficits for 1996, and that would only heighten the investors' fear of inflation, prompting the Fed to stomp on the brakes even harder.

This scenario is like a game of chicken: Which side of the government will blink and back off? Except the last time it unfolded, neither side blinked. The result was not only the horrendous Reagan deficits that endure to the present day but also a punishing level of interest rates that sank the economy.

Bill Clinton has taken a lot of hits, but the worst may lie ahead: an economic recession. If a full-fledged shrinkage of economic activity unfolds during the presidential election year of 1996, then Clinton is doomed for sure.

The same event turned Jimmy Carter into a one-term president back in 1980 and did as much to George Bush in 1992. And like the Carter and Bush recessions, Clinton's will have been engineered by the Fed. The Fed governors raised short-term rates six times in 1994 and intend to continue to squeeze this year until they slow economic growth. If they overshoot this goal and tip the economy into a genuine recession, the Fed governors will shrug off responsibility: "Whoops, sorry about that." They will then serve up yards of woolly double talk about the complexities and uncertainties of making monetary policy.

"What we seek to avoid is an unnecessary and destructive recession," Greenspan told Congress in 1989. Instead, he promised, the Fed would engineer a soft landing: that is, merely subdue the unusual pressures for higher wages and prices. If Greenspan was sincere, the 1990 recession—with its horrendous fallout of bankruptcies, job losses and swelling welfare rolls—was his big mistake.

Maybe Greenspan will get it right this time, but don't count on it. The wondrous thing about the American economic system is that once this muscular engine gets rolling in all its diverse parts, as it is now, it's very hard to slow it down. That typically leads the Fed to keep pounding it over the head with higher and higher interest rates—like clubbing a stubborn mule until it finally falters.

At present a variety of authoritative analysts, from Albert Wojnilower of CS First Boston to J. P.

Morgan & Co., are predicting that one way or another, the mule will go to its knees. No one can say precisely when, but their calculations suggest that the business cycle will peak—and then turn downward—sometime in 1996.

If so, the timing will be perversely elegant for American politics. An electorate that is already anxious and angry about economic insecurities will have a brand-new reason to take out their anger on Mr. Bill. Perhaps voters will assign some blame to the new Republican majority in Congress, but it is always the chief executive who claims credit for the good news—as Clinton has done—and suffers most when things go wrong.

As I have been trying to suggest, the economic debate is really an argument about political power—the unaccountable power of the Federal Reserve to steer the economy in behalf of certain sectors and the cowardice of politicians from both parties who are afraid to challenge those decisions. If the Federal Reserve were reformed, opened up to public scrutiny and made more directly accountable to elected officials, neither the economic debate nor the hard choices would go away. But many more voices might be heard in the debate—especially those of the people who are most victimized by the present system.

The undemocratic nature of the Federal Reserve will become more visible later this year when the question of Alan Greenspan's reappointment as its chairman comes up. He is a conservative Republican (as are most Fed governors) who was first appointed by Reagan. Now his second four-year term is due to expire in early '96, and so Clinton will finally have a chance to pick his own chairman—but not until the last year of his own term, far too late to make any difference. This is wrong. A president gets the blame for the Fed's policies; he ought to have some authority over who runs it.

Clinton, given his general weakness, may well end up picking Greenspan anyway. Why? Because Republicans now own the Senate, which confirms new Fed governors, and they are sure to block any Clinton nominee who is not suitably conservative. Republicans can postpone confirmation until after the '96 elections in the hope that by then they will own the White House, too. In private conversations the president's key economic advisers already concede as much, calculating that Greenspan is probably the only safe choice that could win Republican clearance.

Thus a presidential election will be held in 1996, but the real government in Washington won't change—even if voters throw out Clinton. Cynical citizens who think elections are bogus events are not entirely mistaken. A simple reform that wouldn't threaten the Fed's independence could correct this: Congress should change the appointment calendar so that whoever gets elected president in 1996 can appoint a new Fed chairman within six months of taking office. That at least would give the White House an even start if it wants to persuade the central bank that its economic priorities are wrong.

A more fundamental program for reform—though very unlikely to happen, given present-day politics—will be needed to find genuine solutions to the economic dilemmas of inflation and growth, unemployment and falling wages. Monetary policy cannot by itself reverse the downward pressures on American wages from the global economy—but at least it shouldn't make things worse. The U.S. economy now functions in an utterly different world from the one that existed when the Fed's interest-rate levers were devised, yet the Fed sticks to its old familiar approach of smashing the overall economy. The global economy now provides powerful price competition that can foil any business or labor union that tries to inflate prices or wages, yet the Fed acts as if the United States still has a self-contained economy.

Furthermore, in theory at least, there are other ways the government might control price inflation, and discourage inflationary behavior that would not depend on raising interest rates or sinking house and auto purchases and the economy at large. Stabilizers could be built into the tax code, for instance, that automatically penalize firms from grabbing inflationary gains at everyone else's expense. Sectoral credit controls could be triggered to cool down certain industries that drive an inflationary spiral. Those alternative methods and others are never seriously explored by the technocrats, much less debated by politicians.

There is no debate because the powerful financial interests that always rally round the Fed—from commercial bankers to Wall Street investors—like the system the way it works now. The broad public of wage earners, meanwhile, simply doesn't understand who is doing this to them and why.

Study Questions

1. Is the Fed's policy too skewed toward favoring the rich? Is the Fed following trickle-down economics by looking after the rich first and then hoping that the money of the rich will somehow trickle down to the rest of us? Are you tired of being trickled on?

2. Isn't unemployment a much more serious problem than inflation? Doesn't unemployment cause an increase in crime and an increase in suicides as a result of so many people losing their jobs and self-esteem? Aren't these crimes and suicides matters of irreparable harm, whereas the harms of inflation can be repaired by cost of living adjustments and other selective subsidies and tax cuts?

3. Isn't class conflict inevitable concerning the Fed's policies, since the rich are by definition those who have enough money left over after everyday expenses to loan to others? Those who loan money have a clear interest in keeping inflation low if the money is loaned at a fixed interest rate, since inflation will lower the value of the money loaned by the time it is repaid. Those who borrow money, however, benefit from lower interest rates, since they are the ones paying the interest. So why shouldn't the vast majority of us who borrow money rather than loan it lobby in our democracy for a policy of lower interest rates? Lenders can simply loan money at adjustable interest rates (for example, the prime rate plus four percent) in order to protect against inflation, or they could index the loan to the inflation rate directly. Lenders could add one percent to the interest rate for every one percent increase in the inflation rate, and this could be part of the original loan agreement, couldn't it? So is the Fed serving to save the rich from making a bad deal with the middle class in the first place?

56

Out of Left Field: Socialism's Challenge to Capitalism

Bertell Ollman

A young reporter asked a leading capitalist how he made his fortune. "It was really quite simple," the capitalist answered. "I bought an apple for 5 cents, spent the evening polishing it, and sold it the next day for 10 cents. With this I bought two apples, spent the evening polishing them, and sold them for 20 cents. And so it went until I amassed 80 cents. It was at this point that my wife's father died and left us a million dollars." Is this true? Is it fair? What does it all mean? There are no more hotly contested questions in our society than why some are rich and others poor—and whether things have to be this way.

Karl Marx sought the answers to these questions by trying to understand how our capitalist society works (for whom it works better, for whom worse), how it arose out of feudalism and where it is likely to lead. Concentrating on the social and economic relations in which people earn their livings, Marx saw behind capitalism's law and order appearance a struggle of two main classes: the capitalists, who own the productive resources, and the workers or proletariat, who must work in order to survive. "Marxism" is essentially Marx's analysis of the complex and developing relations between these two classes.

1. Origins

The main theories that make up this analysis—the theory of alienation, the labor theory of value, and the materialist conception of history—must all be understood with this focus in mind. Even Marx's vision of socialism emerges from his study of capital-

A shortened version of this essay appeared in the *Academic American Encyclopedia* (Aretê Publishing Company, Princeton, N.J., 1981), and was republished in *Monthly Review* (New York, April, 1981).

ism, for socialism is the unrealized potential inherent in capitalism itself (something our great material wealth and advanced forms of organization makes possible) for a more just and democratic society in which everyone can develop his/her distinctively human qualities.

Some socialist ideas can be traced as far back as the Bible, but Marxism has its main intellectual origins in German philosophy, English political economy, and French utopian socialism. It is from the German philosopher, Hegel, that Marx learned a way of thinking about the world, in all its fluid complexity, that is called "dialectics." The British political economists, Adam Smith and David Ricardo, provided Marx with a first approximation of his labor theory of value. From the French utopians, especially Charles Fourier and the comte de Saint-Simon, Marx caught a glimpse of a happier future that lay beyond capitalism. Along with the paradox of an Industrial Revolution which produced as much poverty as it did wealth, these are the main ingredients that went into the formation of Marxism.

2. Marxist Philosophy

Marx's study of capitalism was grounded in a philosophy that is both dialectical and materialist. With dialectics, changes and interaction are brought into focus and emphasized by being viewed as essential parts of whatever institutions and processes are undergoing change and interaction. In this way, the system of capitalism, the wider context, is never lost sight of when studying any event within it, an election or an economic crisis for example; nor are its real past and future possibilities, the historical context, ever neglected when dealing with how something appears in the present. Whatever Marx's subject of the moment, his dialectical approach to it insures that his fuller subject is always capitalist society as it developed and is still developing. The actual changes that occur in history are seen here as the outcome of opposing tendencies, or "contradictions", which evolve in the ordinary functioning of society.

Unlike Hegel's dialectic, which operates solely on ideas, Marx's dialectic is materialist. Marx was primarily concerned with capitalism as lived rather than as thought about, but people's lives also involve consciousness. Whereas Hegel examined ideas apart from the people who held them, Marx's materialism puts ideas back into the heads of living people and treats both as parts of a world that is forever being remade through human activities, particularly in production. In this interaction, social condition and behavior are found to have a greater effect on the character and development of people's ideas than these ideas do on social conditions and behavior.

3. Alienation

Marx's specific theories are best understood as answers to his pointed questions about the nature and development of capitalism. *How do the ways in which people earn their living affect their bodies, minds and daily lives?* In the theory of alienation, Marx gives us his answer to this question. Workers in capitalist society do not own the means—machines, raw materials, factories—which they use in their work. These are owned by the capitalists to whom the workers must sell their "labor power", or ability to do work, in return for a wage.

This system of labor displays four relations that lie at the core of Marx's theory of alienation: 1) The worker is alienated (or cut off) from his or her productive activity, playing no part in deciding what to do or how to do it. Someone else, the capitalist, also sets the condition and speed of work and even decides if the worker is to be allowed to work or not, i.e. hires and fires him. 2) The worker is alienated from the product of that activity, having no control over what is made or what happens to it, often not even knowing what happens to it once it has left his hands. 3) The worker is alienated from other human beings, with competition and mutual indifference replacing most forms of cooperation. This applies not only to relations with the capitalists, who use their control over the worker's activity and product to further their own profit maximizing interests, but also to relations between individuals inside each class as everyone tries to survive as best he can. 4) Finally, the worker is alienated from the distinctive potential for creativity and community we all share just because we are human beings. Through labor which alienates them from their activity, product and other people, workers gradually lose their ability to develop the finer qualities which belong to them as members of the human species.

The cutting of these relationships in half leaves on one side a seriously diminished individual—physically weakened, mentally confused and mystified, isolated and virtually powerless. On the other side of this separation are the products and ties with other people, outside the control and lost to the understanding of the worker. Submitted to the mystification of the marketplace, the worker's products pass from one hand to another, changing form and names along the way—"value", "commodity", "capital", "interest", "rent", "wage"—depending chiefly on who has them and how they are used. Eventually, these same products—though no longer seen as such—reenter the worker's daily life as the landlord's house, the grocer's food, the banker's loan, the boss's factory, and the various laws and customs that prescribe his relations with other people.

Unknowingly, the worker has constructed the necessary conditions for reproducing his own alienation. The world that the worker has made and lost in alienated labor reappears as someone else's private property which he only has access to by selling his labor power and engaging in more alienated labor. Though Marx's main examples of alienation are drawn from the life of workers, other classes are also alienated to the degree that they share or are directly affected by these relations, and that includes the capitalists.

4. Theory of Value

What is the effect of the worker's alienated labor on its products, both on what they can do and what can be done with them? Smith and Ricardo used the labor theory of value to explain the cost of commodities. For them, the value of any commodity is the result of the amount of labor time that went into its production. Marx took this explanation more or less for granted. His labor theory of value, however, is primarily concerned with the more basic problem of why goods have prices of any kind. Only in capitalism does the distribution of what is produced take place through the medium of markets and prices. In slave society, the slave owner takes by force what his slaves produce, returning to them only what he wishes. While in feudalism, the lord claims as a feudal right some part of what is produced by his serfs, with the serfs consuming the rest of their output directly. In both societies, most of what is produced cannot be bought or sold, and therefore, does not have any price.

In accounting for the extraordinary fact that everything produced in capitalist society has a price, Marx emphasizes the separation of the worker from the means of production (whereas slaves and serfs are tied to their means of production) and the sale of his or her labor power that this separation makes necessary. To survive, the workers, who lack all means to produce, must sell their labor power. In selling their labor power, they give up all claims to the products of their labor. Hence these products become available for exchange in the market, indeed are produced with this exchange in mind, while workers are able to consume only that potion of their products which they can buy back in the market with the wages they are paid for their labor power.

"Value", then, is the most general effect of the worker's alienated labor on all its products; exchange—which is embodied in the fact that they all have a price—is what these products do and what can be done with them. Rather than a particular price, value stands for the whole set of conditions which are necessary for a commodity to have any price at all. It is in this sense that Marx calls value a product of capitalism. The ideal price ("exchanging value") of a commodity and the ways in which it is meant to be used ("use value") likewise exhibit in their different ways the distinctive relationships Marx uncovered between workers and their activities, products and other people in capitalist society.

"Exchange value" reflects a situation where the distinct human quality and variety of work has ceased to count. Through alienation, the relations between workers has been reduced to the quantity of labor that goes into their respective products. Only then can these products exchange for each other at a ratio which reflects these quantities. It is this which explains Smith's and Ricardo's finding that the value of a commodity is equal to the amount of labor time which has gone into its production. While in use value, the physical characteristics of commodities—planned obsolescence, the attention given to style over durability, the manufacture of individual and family as opposed to larger group units, etc.—give unmistakable evidence of the isolating and degraded quality of human relations found throughout capitalist society.

Surplus-value, the third aspect of value, is the difference between the amount of exchange and use value created by workers and the amount returned to them as wages. The capitalist buys the worker's labor power, as any other commodity, and puts it to work for eight or more hours a day. However, workers can make in, say, five hours products which are the equivalent of their wages. In the remaining three or more hours an amount of wealth is produced which remains in the hands of the capitalist. The capitalists' control over this surplus is the basis of their

power over the workers and the rest of society. Marx's labor theory of value also provides a detailed account of the struggle between capitalists and workers over the size of the surplus value, with the capitalists trying to extend the length of the working day, speed up the pace of work, etc., while the workers organize to protect themselves. Because of the competition among capitalists, workers are constantly being replaced by machinery, enabling and requiring capitalists to extract even greater amounts of surplus value from the workers who remain.

Paradoxically, the amount of surplus value is also the source of capitalism's greatest weakness. Because only part of their product is returned to them as wages, the workers cannot buy a large portion of the consumables that they produce. Under pressure from the constant growth of the total product, the capitalists periodically fail to find new markets to take up the slack. This leads to crises of "overproduction", capitalism's classic contradiction, in which people are forced to live on too little because they produce too much.

5. Historical Tendencies

How did capitalism originate, and where is it leading? Marx's materialist conception of history answers the first part of this question with an account of the transformation of feudalism into capitalism. He stresses the contradictions that arose through the growth of towns, population, technology and trade, which at a certain point burst asunder the feudal social and political forms in which production had been organized. Relations of lord to serf based on feudal rights and obligations had become a hindrance to the further development of these productive forces; over an extended period and after a series of political battles, they were replaced by the contractual relation of capitalists to workers. With capitalists free to pursue profits wherever they might take them and workers equally "free" to sell their labor power to the capitalists however they might use it, the productive potential inherent in the new forces of production, especially in technology and science, grew to unmeasured proportions.

However, if maximizing profits leads to rapid growth when rapid growth results in large profits, then growth is restricted as soon as it becomes unprofitable. The periodic crises which have plagued capitalism from about 1830 on are clear evidence of this. Since that time, the new forces of production which have come into being in capitalism, their growth and potential for producing wealth, have come increasingly into contradiction with the capitalist social relations in which production is organized. The capitalists put the factories, machines, raw materials, and labor power—all of which they own—into motion to produce goods only if they feel they can make a profit, no matter what the availability of these "factors of production", and no matter what the need of consumers for their products. The cost to society in wealth that is never produced (and in wealth which is produced but in forms that are anti-social in their character) continues to grow and with it the need for another, more efficient, more humane way of organizing production.

Within this framework the actual course of history is determined by class struggle. *According to Marx, each class is defined chiefly by its relation to the productive process and has objective interests rooted in that relation. The capitalists' interests lie in securing their power and expanding profits. Workers, on the other hand, have interests in higher wages, safe working conditions, shorter hours, job security, and—because it is required to realize other interests—a new distribution of power. The class struggle involves everything that these two major classes do to promote their incompatible interests at each other's expense.* In this battle, which rages throughout society, the capitalists are aided by their wealth, their control of the state, and their domination over other institutions—schools, media, churches—that guide and distort people's thinking. On the workers' side are their sheer numbers, their experience of cooperation—however alienated—while at work, trade unions, working class political parties (where they exist), and the contradictions within capitalism that make present conditions increasingly irrational.

In capitalism, the state is an instrument in the hands of the capitalists that is used to repress dangerous dissent and to help expand surplus value. This is done mainly by passing and enforcing anti-working class laws and by providing the capitalists with various economic subsides ("capitalist welfare"). Marx also views the state as a set of political structures interlocked with the economic structures of capitalism whose requirements—chiefly for accumulating capital (means of production used to produce value)—it must satisfy, if the whole system is not to go into a tailspin. And, finally, the state is an arena for class struggle where class and class factions contend for political advantage in an unfair fight that finds the capitalists holding all the most powerful weapons. An adequate understanding of the role of the capitalist state as a complex social relation requires that it be approached from each of these three angles: as an instrument of the capitalist class, as a structure of political offices and processes, and as an arena of class struggle.

In order to supplement the institutions of force, capitalism has given rise to an ideology, or way of thinking, which gets people to accept the status quo or, at least, confuses them as to the possibility of replacing it with something better. For the most part, the ideas and concepts which make up this ideology work by getting people to focus on the observable aspects of any event or institution, neglecting its history and potential for change as well as the broader context in which it resides. The result is a collection of partial, static, distorted, one-sided notions that reveal only what the capitalists would like everyone to think. For example, in capitalist ideology, consumers are considered sovereign, as if consumers actually determine what gets produced through the choices they make in the supermarket; and no effort is made to analyze how they develop their preferences (history) or who determines the range of available choices (larger system). Placing an event in its real historical and social context, which is to say studying it "dialectically," often leads (as in the case of "consumer sovereignty") to conclusions that are the direct opposite of those based on the narrow observations favored by ideological thinking. As the attempted separation of what cannot be separated without distortion, capitalist ideology reflects in thought the fractured lives of alienated people, while at the same time making it increasingly difficult for them to grasp their alienation.

As the contradictions of capitalism become greater, more intense, and less amenable to disguise, neither the state nor ideology can restrain the mass of workers, white and blue collar, from recognizing their interests (becoming "class conscious") and acting upon them. The overthrow of capitalism, when it comes, Marx believed, would proceed as quickly and democratically as the nature of capitalist opposition allowed. Out of the revolution would emerge a socialist society which would fully utilize and develop much further the productive potential inherited from capitalism. Through democratic planning, production would be directed to serving social needs instead of maximizing private profit. The final goal, toward which socialist society would constantly build, is the human one of abolishing alienation. Marx called the attainment of this goal "communism".

6. Marxism Today

Capitalism has obviously changed a lot in the hundred years since Marx wrote. In the basic relations and structures which distinguish capitalism from feudalism and socialism, however, it has changed very little, and these are the main features of capitalism addressed in Marx's theories. Workers, for example, may earn more money now than they did in the last century, but so do the capitalists. Consequently, the wealth and income gaps between the two classes is as great or greater than ever. The workers' relations to their labor, products and capitalists (which are traced in the theory of alienation and the labor theory of value) are basically unchanged from Marx's day. Probably the greatest difference between our capitalism and Marx's has to do with the more direct involvement of the state in the capitalist economy (primarily to bolster flagging profits) and, as a consequence of this, the expanded role of ideology to disguise the increasingly obvious ties between the agencies of the state and the capitalist class.

From its beginnings, Marxism has been under attack from all sides, but the major criticisms have been directed against claims that Marx never made. For example, some have mistakenly viewed Marx's materialism as evidence that he ignored the role of ideas in history and in people's lives. Viewed as an "economic determinism", Marxism has also been criticized for presenting politics, culture, religion, etc. as simple effects of a one-way economic cause. (This would be undialectical.) Viewed as a claim that labor is the only factor in determining prices (equated here with "value"), the labor theory of value has been wrongly attacked for ignoring the effect of competition on prices. And viewing what are projections of capitalism's tendencies into the future as inviolable predictions, Marx has been accused of making false predictions.

Some, finally, point to the anti-democratic practices of many Communist countries and claim that authoritarianism is inherent in Marxist doctrine. In fact, Marx's theories concentrate on advanced industrial capitalism with its imperfect but still functioning democratic institutions and he never thought that socialism could achieve its full promise in relatively poor, politically underdeveloped nations.

Marxism, as defined here, has had its main influence among workers and intellectuals in capitalist countries, especially in Europe, who have used it as a major tool in defining their problems and constructing political strategies. In the Western countries, even non-Marxist intellectuals, particularly sociologists and historians, have drawn considerable insights from Marx's writings. In the Third World, Marxism—considerably modified to deal with their special mixture of primitive and advanced capitalist conditions—has clarified the nature of the enemy for many liberation movements. In the Communist countries, selected doctrines of Marx have been frozen into abstract principles to serve as the official ideology of the regimes. The influence of these three varieties of Marxism is as different as their content.

In American capitalism's latest crisis, the combination of growing unemployment and worsening inflation has confounded all the usual experts. The most powerful nation in history cannot erase poverty, provide full employment, guarantee decent housing or an adequate diet or good health care to its people. Meanwhile, the rich get richer. *Only Marxism, as an account of the rational unfolding of a basically irrational capitalist system, makes sense of our current chaos. In class struggle, it also points the way out. The rest is up to us.*

Study Questions

1. What do you make of the first cartoon in this chapter? Is this switch of perspective a viable one? Does it accurately illustrate Ollman's views?

2. What do you make of the second cartoon in this chapter? Does it support Ollman's point that most of us should see ourselves as distinct from the ruling class?

3. Does Harwood's "Is Inheritance Immoral?" give any support to Ollman's initial point about inheritance?

4. Does the collapse of the Union of Soviet Socialist Republics (USSR), which was an economic collapse as well as a political and cultural one, mean that socialism has no merit and we should dismiss it without thinking further? Would it give you some second thoughts to realize that China, which is socialist, has a growth rate of over 13 percent (compared to the American growth rate of between 3 and 4 percent) and that China is scheduled by treaty to take possession of Hong Kong in 1997? Is socialism really dead, or is that wishful thinking on the part of many?

5. Which did more to undermine the Soviet Union, President Reagan or rock 'n' roll? Did Reagan's rhetoric or the cultural values of Americana embodied in rock 'n' roll music win over the hearts

and minds of so many Soviet citizens? Was it some combination of both together with all the rest of the Cold War, which was supported by Democrats and Republicans alike for decades? .

*6. Should there be a limit to the personal wealth one individual is allowed to amass? If so, how much is "too much"?

7. Is life for the living? If so, then should we allow a will to involve so much money that it lets the dead control the living by bequeathing money to people only if they do certain acts the will specifies (for example, get married, graduate from college, become a lawyer, or enter some other profession the will specifies)?

*8. Do you believe that wealth in our society is fairly apportioned according to what people contribute? If not, what is the most glaring inequity you know of?

*9. For how long should you (or your heirs) be allowed to receive fees and royalties from something you invent?

*10. Imagine that one day your widowed father, who is very wealthy and very old, tells you he is going to change his will and give all his money to charity. Assuming you know he is quite sane, and will not change his mind, would you consider trying to block your disinheritance by having him declared incompetent?

*11. If you could specify the philosophy the government used in raising money, would you choose an approach that falls more heavily on the wealthy (for example, progressive—that is, graduated—income, property, or inheritance taxes) or uniformly on all (for example, a flat income tax, uniform sales taxes, and usage fees)?

*12. If a wealthy uncle died and left everything to you, would you fight other relatives who threatened to contest the will unless you shared the estate with them? Assume you think they have no reasonable claim but may create a bitter enough legal battle to use up most of the inheritance.

Select Bibliography

Marx, Karl, *Wage Labor and Capital.*
Engels, Friedrich, *Socialism: Utopian and Scientific.*
Marx/Engels, *Communist Manifesto.*
Marx/Engels, *German Ideology, Part I.*
Heilbroner, Robert, *Marxism: For and Against* (1980).
McLellan, David, *The Thought of Karl Marx* (1971).
Miliband, Ralph, *Marxism and Politics* (1977).
Ollman, Bertell, *Alienation: Marx's Conception of Man in Capitalist Society* (1976).
Popper, Karl, *Open Society and Its Enemies* (1963).
Rader, Melvin, *Marx's Materialist Interpretation of History* (1979).
Rius, *CAPITAL for Beginners* (1981).
Sweezy, Paul, *The Theory of Capitalist Development* (1963).
Tressell, Robert, *The Ragged Trousered Philanthropist* (1980).

Reprinted from Bertell Ollman, *What Is Marxism? A Bird's-Eye View* (New York: Red Hot Publications, 1982).

Reprinted from Bertell Ollman, *What Is Marxism? A Bird's-Eye View* (New York: Red Hot Publications, 1982).

57

Income Comparisons by State, Including the District of Columbia

Commerce Department

How do you compare? The Department of Commerce calculated the 1993 per capita income for each state and percentage of gain from 1992.

	Income	% Gain
Alabama	$18,010	5.1
Alaska	$23,788	3.1
Arizona	$19,001	5.1
Arkansas	$16,888	5.6
California	$22,493	2.7
Colorado	$22,333	3.9
Connecticut	$29,402	4.4
Delaware	$22,828	4.5
District of Columbia	$31,136	5.5
Florida	$21,677	5.0
Georgia	$20,251	5.2
Hawaii	$24,057	2.4
Idaho	$18,231	4.1
Illinois	$23,784	5.4
Indiana	$20,378	6.1
Iowa	$20,265	10.9
Kansas	$20,896	5.3
Kentucky	$17,807	5.4
Louisiana	$17,651	6.3
Maine	$19,663	4.7
Maryland	$24,933	4.3
Massachusetts	$25,616	4.9
Michigan	$22,333	8.5
Minnesota	$22,453	7.0
Mississippi	$15,838	7.4
Missouri	$20,717	5.9
Montana	$17,865	2.8
Nebraska	$20,488	4.1
Nevada	$24,023	4.9

	Income	% Gain
New Hampshire	$23,434	4.8
New Jersey	$28,038	4.3
New Mexico	$17,106	4.6
New York	$25,999	4.7
North Carolina	$19,669	5.4
North Dakota	$18,546	8.6
Ohio	$20,928	6.3
Oklahoma	$17,744	4.2
Oregon	$20,419	5.1
Pennsylvania	$22,324	4.9
Rhode Island	$22,251	4.7
South Carolina	$17,695	4.9
South Dakota	$19,577	9.5
Tennessee	$19,482	5.7
Texas	$19,857	3.7
Utah	$17,043	5.6
Vermont	$20,224	4.0
Virginia	$22,594	4.3
Washington	$22,610	3.8
West Virginia	$17,208	6.4
Wisconsin	$21,019	6.1
Wyoming	$20,436	3.6

Study Questions

1. Do you see the significance of the difference between "How Do You Compare?" and "How Does Your Income Compare?" Does measuring the value of a person based on his or her income make any sense? Is it degrading or overly materialistic?

2. Do you compare?!

*3. What would you do if you found out that a recently hired co-worker was making a third more than you for the same job you were doing?

*4. If a casual acquaintance asked you how much your salary was, would you reveal it? What about a friend who asked you for the same information? If not, why not?

*5. How much additional income would you need to meaningfully change your day-to-day life?

*6. If what you earned were to fairly reflect what you contribute, how much would you be paid? Do you think others would agree with you? Where you work, who—if anyone—makes a lot more or less than they deserve?

58

A Critique of Socialism: Problems with Marxism

Leslie Stevenson

Editor's note: Leslie Stevenson details Marx's life and work, theory of human nature, theory of the universe, and recommendations. Stevenson also gives several interesting criticisms of Marxism.

In this [selection] I would like to go a little deeper by giving an introduction to Marx's life and work, followed by a critical analysis of his theory of history, theory of man, diagnosis, and prescription. I shall not attempt to define or discuss the many subsequent varieties of Marxism and communism; I concentrate on the ideas of Karl Marx himself. (Although Marx and Engels wrote some works in collaboration, there is no doubt that Engels's contribution was relatively minor.)

Life and Work

Karl Marx was born in 1818 in the German Rhineland, of a Jewish family who became Christian; he was brought up as a Protestant, but soon abandoned religion. He displayed his intellectual ability early, and in 1836 he entered the University of Berlin as a student in the faculty of Law. The dominant intellectual influence in Germany at that time was the philosophy of Hegel, and Marx very soon became immersed in reading and discussing Hegel's ideas, so much so that he abandoned his legal studies and devoted himself completely to philosophy. The leading idea of

Reprinted from Leslie Stevenson, *Seven Theories of Human Nature* (Oxford: Oxford University Press, 1987), pp. 53–67.

Hegel's work was that of historical development. He held that each period in the history of each culture or nation has a character of its own, as a stage in the development from what proceeded it to what will succeed it. Such development, according to Hegel, proceeds by laws which are fundamentally mental or spiritual; a culture or nation has a kind of personality of its own, and its development is to be explained in terms of its own character. Hegel took this personification even further and applied it to the whole world. He identified the whole of reality with what he called 'the Absolute,' or world-self, or God (this is of course a pantheist rather than a Christian concept of God), and interpreted the whole of human history as the progressive self-realization of this Absolute Spirit. 'Self-realization' is thus seen as the fundamental spiritual progress behind all history. It is the overcoming of what Hegel called 'alienation,' in which the knowing person (the subject) is confronted with something other than or alien to himself (an object); somehow this distinction between subject and object is to be merged in the process of Spirit realizing itself in the world.

The followers of Hegel split into two camps over the question of how his ideas applied to politics. The 'Right' Hegelians held that the process of historical development automatically led to the best possible results. So they saw the contemporary Prussian State as the ideal culmination of preceding history. Accordingly, they had conservative political views, and tended to emphasize the religious elements in Hegel's thought. The 'Left' or 'Young' Hegelians thought that the ideal had yet to be realized, that the nation-states of the time were very far from ideal, and that it was the duty of men to help change the old order and assist the development of the next stage of human history. Accordingly, they held radical political views, and tended to identify God with man, thus taking a fundamental atheist view. One of the most important thinkers in this direction was Feuerbach, whose *Essence of Christianity* was published in 1841. Feuerbach held that Hegel had got everything upside-down, that far from God progressively realizing Himself in history, the situation is really that the ideas of religion are produced by men as a pale reflection of this world, which is the only reality. It is because men are dissatisfied or 'alienated' in their practical life that they need to believe in illusory ideas. Accordingly, metaphysics is just 'esoteric psychology,' the expression of feelings within ourselves rather than truth about the universe. Religion is the expression of alienation, from which men must be freed by realizing their purely human destiny in this world. Feuerbach, is, then, one of the most important sources of humanist thought.

This was the intellectual atmosphere of Marx's formative years. His reading of Feuerbach broke the spell that Hegel had cast on him, but what remained was the idea that in Hegel's writings the truth about human nature and society was concealed in a kind of inverted form. As we shall see, the notions of historical development and of alienation play a crucial role in Marx's thought. He wrote a critique of Hegel's *Philosophy of Right* in 1842–3, and at the same time became editor of a radical journal of politics and economics called the *Rheinische Zeitung*. This journal was soon suppressed by the Prussian government, so Marx emigrated to Paris in 1843. In the next two years there he encountered the other great intellectual influences of his life, and began to formulate his own distinctive theories. His wide reading included the British economist Adam Smith and the French socialist Saint-Simon. He met other socialist and communist thinkers such as Proudhon, Bakunin, and Engels. (This was the beginning of his lifelong friendship and collaboration with Engels.) In 1845 he was expelled from Paris, and he moved to Brussels.

In these years in Paris and Brussels Marx formulated his so-called 'Materialist Theory of History.' By inverting Hegel's view as Feuerbach had suggested, Marx came to see the driving force of historical change as not spiritual but material in character. Not in men's *ideas*, but in the *economic* conditions of men's life, lay the key to all history. Alienation is neither metaphysical nor religious, but really social and economic. Under the capitalist system labour is something external and alien to the labourer; he does not work for himself but for someone else—the capitalist—who owns the product as private property. This diagnosis of alienation is to be found in the 'Economic and Philosophical Manuscripts' which Marx wrote in Paris in 1844, but which did not become generally available in English until the 1950s. The materialist conception of history is to be found in other works of this period—*The Holy Family* of 1845, *The German Ideology* of 1846 (written with Engels), and *The Poverty of Philosophy* of 1847.

In Brussels Marx became involved with the practical organization of the socialist and communist movement, a task which occupied much of the rest of his life. For he saw the main purpose of his work as 'not just to interpret the world, but to change it' (as he put it in his *Theses on Feuerbach* in 1845). Convinced that history was moving towards the revolution by which capitalism would give way to communism, he tried to educate and organize the 'proletariat'—the class of workers to whom he thought victory would go in the imminent struggle. He was commissioned to write a definitive statement of the aims of the international communist movement, and together with Engels, he produced the famous *Manifesto of the Communist Party*, which was published early in 1848. Soon afterwards in that year (although hardly as a result of the *Manifesto!*) there were abortive revolutions in several of the major European countries. After their failure Marx found himself expelled from Belgium, France, and Germany, so in 1849 he went into exile in London, where he remained for the rest of his life.

In London Marx endured a life of poverty, existing on occasional journalism and gifts from Engels. He began daily research in the British Museum and continued to organize the international communist movement. In 1857–8 he wrote another series of manuscripts called *Grundrisse*, sketching a plan of his total theory of history and society. Not until 1973 has the complete text of these been available in English. In 1859 he published his *Critique of Political Economy*, and in 1867 the first volume of his most substantial work, *Das Kapital*. These last two works contain much detailed economic and social history, reflecting the results of Marx's labours in the British Museum. Although there is less evidence of Hegelian philosophical ideas such as alienation, Marx was still trying to apply his materialist interpretation of history to prove the inevitability of the downfall of capitalism.

It is these later works, from the *Communist Manifesto* onwards, that have been best known and have formed the basis of much communist theory and practice. In them we find German philosophy, French socialism, and British political economy, the three main influences on Marx, integrated into an all-embracing theory of history, economics, and politics. This is what Engels came to call 'scientific socialism'; for Marx and Engels thought they had discovered the correct *scientific* method for the study of history, and hence the truth about the present and future development of the society of their time. But the recent publication of the earlier works, particularly the Paris Manuscripts of 1844, has shown us much about the origin of Marx's thought in Hegelian philosophy, and has revealed the more philosophical nature of his early ideas. So the question has been raised whether there were two distinct periods in his thought—an early phase which has been called humanist or even existentialist, giving way to the later and more austere 'scientific socialist.' I think it is fair to say that the consensus of opinion is that there is a continuity between the two phases, that the theme of alienation is buried but still there in the later work; the contents of the *Grundrisse* of 857-8 seem to confirm this. My discussion of Marx will therefore be based on the assumption that his thought is not discontinuous. My page references in what follows are to the Pelican book *Karl Marx: Selected Writings in Sociology and Social Philosophy*, which is perhaps the most useful of the many volumes of selected readings from Marx and Engels, containing as it does selections from both the early and late phases. (Page references to the American paperback edition are supplied at the end of the chapter.)

Theory of the Universe

Let us now begin our critical analysis of Marx's main theory. He was of course an atheist, but this is not peculiar to him. What is distinctive of his understanding of the world as a whole is his interpretation of history. He claimed to have found the *scientific* method for studying the history of human societies, and looked forward to the day when there would be a single science, including the science of man along with natural science (p. 85). Accordingly, he held that there are universal *laws* behind historical change, and that the future large-scale course of history can be *predicted* from knowledge of these laws (just as astronomy predicts eclipses). In the preface to the first edition of *Capital*, Marx compared his method to that of the physicist and said 'the ultimate aim of this work is to lay bare the economic law of motion of modern society'; he also talked of the natural laws of capitalist production 'working with iron necessity towards inevitable results.' He agreed with Hegel that each period in each culture has a character of its own, so that the only truly universal laws in history could be those concerned with the processes of *development* by which one stage gives rise to the next. He divided history roughly into the Asiatic, the ancient, the feudal, and the 'bourgeois' or capitalist phases, and held that each had to give way to the next when conditions were ripe (p. 68). Capitalism was expected to give way, just as inevitably, to communism (pp. 150–1).

However, there are strong reasons for questioning the concept of laws of history. Certainly, history is an *empirical* study in that its propositions can and must be tested by evidence of what has actually hap-

pened. But it does not follow that it has the other main feature of a *science*, that it tries to arrive at *laws*, that is, generalizations of unrestricted universality. For history is after all the study of what has happened on one particular planet in a finite period of time. The subject matter is wide, but it is one *particular* series of events; we know of no similar series of events elsewhere in the universe, so human history is unique. Now for any particular series of events, even an apparently simple one like the fall of an apple from a tree, there is no clear limit to the number of different scientific laws that may be involved—the laws of gravity and mechanics, of wind pressure, of elasticity of twigs, of decay of wood, etc. If there is no one law governing the fall of an apple, then how much more implausible it is to postulate a general law of development behind the whole of human history.

The idea that the course of history is predetermined, so that one main function of historical study is large-scale prophecy, is at least as questionable. Certainly there may be some long-term and large-scale *trends* to be found, for instance the increase of human population since the Middle Ages. But a trend is not a *law*; its continuation is not inevitable but may depend on conditions which can change. (It is obvious that population cannot increase indefinitely, indeed its growth might be quite suddenly reversed by nuclear war or widespread famine.)

The other main feature of Marx's view of history is what is called his materialist conception of history. This is the theory that the supposed laws of history are *economic* in nature, that 'the mode of production of material life determines the general character of the social, political, and spiritual processes of life' (p. 67, cf. pp. 70, 90, 111–12, etc.). The economic structure is supposed to be the real basis by which everything else about a society is determined. Now it is undeniable that economic factors are hugely important, and that no serious study of history or social science can ignore them. Marx can take some of the credit for the fact that we now recognize this so readily. But he himself is committed to the more dubious assertion that the economic structure of a society *determines* its 'superstructures.'

This proposition is difficult to interpret, for it is not clear where the dividing line between basis and superstructure should run. Marx talks of 'the material powers of production' (p. 67) which presumably would cover land and mineral resources, tools and machines, plus perhaps the knowledge and skills of men. But he also talks of the economic structure as including 'relations of production,' which presumably means the way in which work is organized (e.g., division of labour and certain hierarchies of authority); yet the description of such organization must surely use concepts like property and money, which seem to be the kind of legal concepts that Marx would wish to put into the superstructure. If the basis includes only the material powers of production, then Marx is committed to a rather implausible 'technological determinism'; but if it includes also the relations of production, then the distinction between basis and superstructure is blurred.

From his general theory of history Marx derived a very specific prediction about the future of capitalism. He confidently expected that it would become more and more unstable economically, that the class struggle between bourgeois and proletariat would increase, with proletariat getting both poorer and larger in number, until in a major social revolution the workers would take power and institute the new communist phase of history (pp. 79–80, 147–52, 194, 207, 236–8). Now the huge and simple fact is that this has not happened in the main capitalist countries—Britain, France, Germany, and the United States. On the contrary, the economic system of capitalism has become more stable, conditions of life for most people have improved vastly on what they were in Marx's time, and class-divisions have been blurred rather than intensified (consider the large numbers of 'white-collar' workers—office staff, civil servants, teachers, etc., who are neither industrial labourers nor industrial owners). Where communist revolutions *have* taken place, they were in countries which had little or no capitalist development at the time—Russia in 1917, Yugoslavia in 1945, China in 1949. This must surely constitute the major falsification of Marx's theory. It cannot really be explained away by saying that the proletariat have been 'bought off' by concessions of higher wages—for Marx predicted their lot would get worse. Nor is it plausible to say that colonies have formed the proletariat vis-à-vis the industrialized countries—for some, such as Scandinavia, have had no colonies, and even in the colonies conditions did improve, however slightly. To maintain Marx's theory as he stated it, in the face of such counter-evidence, makes it into a matter of blind faith, a closed system, rather than the scientific theory he claimed it to be.

Theory of Human Nature

Except perhaps when he read Hegel's philosophy as a young man, Marx was not interested in questions of 'pure' or academic philosophy, which he would dismiss as mere speculation compared to the vital task of changing the world (p. 82). So when he is called a materialist, this refers to his materialist theory of history and not to a theory about the relation of mind to body. Certainly, he would dismiss belief in life after death as one of the illusory ideas of religion, and would emphasize that everything about the individual person (including his consciousness) is determined by the material conditions of his life (pp. 69, 85). But this could well be an 'epiphenomenalist' view—that consciousness is something non-material but entirely determined by material events—rather than a strictly materialist view that consciousness is itself material.

His view on the metaphysical question of determinism is rather ambiguous too. Of course his general view sounds determinist, with his theory of the inevitable progress of history through economic stages and his referring of all change to economic causes. And yet, just as with the Augustinian-Pelagian controversy within Christianity, there seems to be an irreducible element of free will too. For Marxists constantly appeal to their readers and hearers to realize the direction in which history is moving, and to *act* accordingly—to help bring about the communist revolution. Within Marxism there has been controversy between those who emphasize the need to wait for the appropriate stage of historical development before expecting the revolution, and those who emphasize the need to act to bring it about. But perhaps there is no ultimate contradiction here, for Marx can say that although the revolution will inevitably occur sooner or later, it is possible for individuals and groups to assist its coming and ease its birth pangs, acting as the midwives of history. Further inquiry into determinism and free will would probably be condemned as useless speculation.

What is most distinctive of Marx's concept of man is his view of our essentially *social* nature: 'the real nature of man is the totality of social relations'; (p. 83). Apart from a few obvious biological facts such as the need to eat, Marx would tend to say that there is no such thing as individual human nature—what is true (and even universally true) of men in one society or period is not necessarily true of them in another place or time. Whatever a person does is an essentially social act, which presupposes the existence of other people standing in certain relations to (pp. 91–2, 251). Even the ways in which we eat, sleep, copulate, and defecate are socially learned. This is true above all of every activity of production, for the production of our means of subsistence is typically a social activity in that it requires the cooperation of men in some way or other (p. 77). It is not that society is an abstract entity which affects the individual (p. 91), but rather that what kind of individual one is and what kind of things one does are determined by what kind of society one lives in. What seems instinctual in one society—for example, a certain role for women—may be quite different in another society. In one of Marx's typical aphorisms: 'it is not the consciousness of men that determines their being, but, on the contrary, their social being determines their consciousness' (p. 67). In modern terms, we can summarize this crucial point by saying that sociology is not reducible to psychology, that is, it is not the case that everything about men can be explained in terms of facts about individuals; the kind of society they live in must be considered too. This methodological point is one of Marx's most distinctive contributions, and one of the most widely accepted. For this reason alone, he must be recognized as one of the founding fathers of sociology. And the *method* can of course be accepted whether or not one agrees with the particular *conclusions* Marx came to about economics and politics.

But there does seem to be at least one universal generalization that Marx is prepared to make about human nature. This is that man is an *active*, productive being, who distinguishes himself from the other animals by the fact that he *produces* his means of subsistence (p. 69). It is natural for men to work for their living. No doubt there is an empirical truth here, but it seems that Marx also draws a value-judgement out of this, namely that the kind of life which is *right* for men is one of productive activity. As we shall see, this is implicit in his diagnosis of alienation as a lack of fulfillment in industrial labour (p. 177), and in his prescription for future communist society in which everyone can be free to cultivate their own talents in every direction (p. 253). No doubt it is because of this point, which is clearest in his early writings, that Marx has been called a humanist.

Diagnosis

Marx's theory of what is wrong with man and society involves his concept of alienation, which, as we have seen, is a descendant of the concept used by Hegel and Feuerbach. For Marx, alienation sums up what is wrong with capitalism; the concept rolls up together both a description of certain features of capitalist society and a value-judgement that they are fundamentally wrong. But the trouble with the notion of alienation is that it is so vague that we hardly know *which* feature of capitalism Marx is condemning. Logically, alienation is a relation, that is, it must be *from* somebody or something; one cannot just be alienated any more than one can kill without killing something. Marx says that alienation is from man himself and from Nature (p. 177). But this does not help us very much, for it is not clear how one can be alienated from oneself; and the concept of Nature involved here has obscure Hegelian roots in the distinction between subject and supposedly alien object. For Marx, Nature means the man-created world, so we can take him as saying that men are not what they should be because they are alienated from the objects and social relations that they create. The general idea that emerges from this rather mystifying terminology is that capitalist society is in some respects not in accordance with basic human nature. But it still remains to be seen what those respects are.

Sometimes it seems that private property is what Marx primarily blames for alienation, for he says that the abolition of private property is the abolition of alienation (p. 250). But elsewhere he says that 'although private property appears to be the basis and cause of alienated labour, it is rather a consequence of the latter' (p. 176). He describes this alienation of labour as consisting in the fact that the work is not part of the worker's nature, he does not fulfill himself in his work, but feels miserable, physically exhausted, and mentally debased. His work is forced on him as a means for satisfying other needs, and at work he does not belong to himself but to another person. Even the objects he produces are alien to him, because they are owned by someone else (pp. 177–8). Sometimes Marx seems to be blaming alienation on the institution of money, as a means of exchange which reduces social relationships to a common commercial denominator (pp. 179–81). Elsewhere he says that the division of labour makes man's work into an alien power opposed to him, preventing him from switching from one activity to another at will (which Marx improbably alleges will be possible in communist society; pp. 110–11). And in another passage, Marx locates the basis of social evils and the general explanation of them in the principle of the State itself (p. 223).

What then *is* Marx diagnosing as the basic cause of alienation? It may be hard to believe that anyone would seriously advocate the abolition of money (a return to a system of barter?), the disappearance of all specialization in work, or the nationalization of all property (even tooth-brushes, shirts, books, etc.?). It is the private ownership of industry—the means of production and exchange—that is usually taken as the defining feature of capitalism. And the main points in the programme of the *Communist Manifesto* are the nationalization of land, factories, transport, and banks. But it is not at all clear that such institutional changes could cure the alienation of labour which Marx describes in such psychological terms (in the early works referred to in my previous paragraph). And if the State is the basis of social evils, nationalization would make things worse, by increasing the power of the State.

It looks as if we must understand Marx as saying, at least in his early phase, that alienation consists in a lack of *community*, so that people cannot see their work as contributing to a group of which they are members, since the State is not a real community (p. 226). Such a diagnosis would suggest a prescription not of nationalization but of decentralization into genuine communities or 'communes' (in which the abolition of money, specialization, and private property might begin to look more realistic).

If this is contentious, there is a more general diagnosis implicit in Marx, which would perhaps command universal assent. This is that it is always wrong to treat any human being as only a means to an economic end. This is just what did happen in the unrestrained capitalism of the early nineteenth century, when children worked long hours in filthy conditions and died early deaths after miserable lives. Industry is made for man, not man for industry—and 'man' here must mean *all* the human beings involved. But it is of course more difficult to agree on how to give effect to this very general value-judgement.

Prescription

'If man is formed by circumstances, these circumstances must be humanly formed' (p. 249). If alienation is a social problem caused by the nature of the capitalist economic system, then the solution is to abolish that system and replace it by a better one. And we have already seen that Marx thinks that this is bound to happen anyway, for capitalism will burst asunder because of its inner contradictions, and the communist revolution will usher in the new order of things in which alienation will disappear and man will be regenerated in his true nature. Just as Christianity claims that salvation has already been enacted

for us, so Marx claims that the resolution of the problems of capitalism is already on the way in the movement of history.

But Marx holds that only a complete revolution of the economic system will do. There is no point in trying to achieve limited reform such as higher wages, shorter hours, etc., for these do not alter the evil nature of the basic system, and only distract attention from the real task, which is to overthrow it. Hence the radical difference between the programme of the Communist Party and that of most trade unions and social democratic parties. This doctrine of 'the impotence of politics' follows from Marx's premises in his materialist theory of history—for if all legal and political institutions are really determined by the underlying economic system, then they cannot be used to change the economic system. However, this doctrine flies in the face of the facts of the development of capitalism since Marx's time. Legal and other institutions *have* modified the economic system of capitalism very considerably, beginning with the Factory Acts of the nineteenth century which limited the worst excesses of exploitation of workers, continuing with National Insurance, unemployment benefit, National Health Services, and steady progress by trade unions in increasing real wages and decreasing working hours. In fact, many of the specific measures proposed in the *Communist Manifesto* have come into effect in the so-called capitalist countries—graduated income tax, centralization of much economic control in the hands of the State, nationalization of several major industries including transport, free education for all children in state schools. The unrestrained capitalist system as Marx knew it in the nineteenth century has everywhere ceased to exist, and this has happened by step-by-step reform, not by once-for-all revolution. This is not to say that the existing system is perfect—far from it. But it is to suggest that Marx's rejection of any idea of gradual reform is radically mistaken; and reflection on the suffering and violence involved in real revolutions may confirm this.

Like Christianity, Marx envisages a total regeneration of man, but he expects it entirely within this secular world. Communism is 'the solution to the riddle of history' (p. 250), for the abolition of private property is supposed to ensure the disappearance of alienation and the coming of a genuinely classless society. Marx is very vague on how all this will be achieved, but he suggests that there will be an intermediate period during which the transition will take place, and that this will require 'the dictatorship of the proletariat' for its accomplishment (p. 261). But in the higher phase of communist society, the State will wither away, and the true realm of freedom will begin. Then human potentiality can develop for its own sake (p. 260), and the guiding principle can be: 'From each according to his ability, to each according to his needs' (p. 263).

Some of this utopian vision must surely be judged wildly unrealistic. Marx gives us no good reason to believe that communist society will be genuinely classless, that those who exercise the dictatorship of the proletariat will not form a new governing class with many opportunities to abuse their power, as the history of Russia since the revolution obviously suggests. There is no ground for expecting any set of economic changes to eliminate *all* conflicts of interest forever. The State, far from withering away, has become ever more powerful in communist countries (perhaps the very nature of modern industry and technology makes this inevitable).

Yet with other elements in Marx's vision, we cannot but agree. The idea of a decentralized society in which men cooperate in communities for the common good, the application of science and technology to produce enough for all, the shortening of the working day so that men can increasingly choose to spend their leisure time in the free development of their potential, the idea of a society in balance with nature—all these are ideals which almost everyone will share, even though it is not clear that they are compatible. No doubt, it is because Marxism offers this kind of hopeful vision of the future that it can still win and retain the allegiance of so many people. For despite the obvious defects of life in the existing communist countries, many of their inhabitants maintain a genuine belief in Marxist theory. And despite the reforms that have already altered the face of capitalism, many people in the West see the need for a further transformation of the existing socioeconomic system and look to Marx for inspiration for such a change.

Like Christianity, Marxism is more than a theory, and the disputability of many of its theoretical assertions does not make it lie down and die. It contains a recipe for social salvation and offers a critique of any existing society. However, Marx's emphasis on social and economic factors directs our attention to one, but only one, of the obstacles in the way of human progress. We must look elsewhere, for instance to Freud, for more about the nature and problems of human *individuals*.

Study Questions

1. Is Marx seriously underrated or even too casually dismissed in America? Consider the following quotation from American historian Charles A. Beard:

> It may be appropriate to remind those who may be inclined to treat Marx as a mere revolutionary or hot partisan that he was more than that. He was a doctor of philosophy from a German university, possessing the hallmark of the scholar. He was a student of Greek and Latin learning. He read, besides German, his native tongue, Greek, Latin, French, English, Italian, and Russian. He was widely read in contemporary history and economic thought. Hence however one may dislike Marx's personal views, one cannot deny to him wide and deep knowledge—and a fearless and sacrificial life. He not only interpreted history, as everyone does who writes any history, but he helped to make history. Possibly he may have known something.[1]

2. Is there any way to reconcile Marxism with utilitarianism?

3. Marx is often criticized for being too materialistic, but is capitalism any less materialistic? Don't Marx and capitalism both stress material gains rather than spiritual ones?

4. Isn't capitalism more inefficient than it should be, since capitalism pays wages based on performance and not mere need, which means that those who are needy, poor, and less talented will try to hold down several jobs while the more talented who perform well will probably be well paid, content to do only one job, and prone to retire early? Isn't the upshot that more work is done by people with less talent, and thus the consumer gets lower quality than he or she would otherwise?

5. Isn't capitalism more inefficient than it should be, since people are promoted for doing good work, but then rise to their level of incompetence by finally reaching a position in which they don't do good work and so don't get promoted? After promoting these people for years, isn't it impractical to demote them back down to the level where they did good work?

6. Some leading business ethicists, such as Lisa Newton, suggest that "no other prophets of the time had any more luck with prognostications about the twentieth century."[2] That a leading business ethicist such as Newton would imply that Marx is a prophet is quite telling. Does Newton's suggestion that Marx's success in prediction is unsurpassed by his contemporaries in economics make you more skeptical of economics, which is sometimes called the dismal science?

Notes

1. *American Historical Review*, 1935.
2. Lisa Newton and Maureen Ford, *Taking Sides: Clashing Views on Controversial Views in Business Ethics and Society*, 3rd ed. (1993), p. xviii.

© 1995 by Sidney Harris.

59

Madisonian Democracy and Marxist Analysis: Ryder on the Constitution

Sterling Harwood

With
Without
And who'll deny
It's what the fighting's all about.
—Roger Waters*

I shall consider two main problems raised by Professor John Ryder's thought-provoking paper. First, is Ryder's interpretation of Madison's "Federalist No. 10" correct? Second, is the Constitution, as Ryder claims, an obstacle to social progress?[1] I focus on "Federalist No. 10," rather than on Madison's account of the Constitutional Convention, on which Ryder also relies, since *The Federalist* is simply much more reliable. As Stephen Macedo observes:

> [N]o official record of the closed proceedings in Philadelphia was ever published, an incomprehensible oversight if it had been expected that future interpreters would be guided by the Framers' intentions. . . . Madison's unofficial account of the convention, reconstructed from his notes, was published posthumously in 1840, after everyone who had attended the convention was dead [and thus unable to corroborate it].[2]

Some scholars charge "that Madison altered his notes in later life in order to support the partisan political positions he then espoused."[3] But even those who most convincingly rebut this charge admit that "the words Madison recorded could not, at a generous estimate, have amounted to more than ten percent of what was spoken."[4]

Interpreting "Federalist No. 10"

Ryder says "the Founders persistently and consistently employed a class analysis of society in general and of the proper ends of government."[5] I see, however, no persuasive evidence of class bias in "Federalist No. 10." And Charles Beard's book which purports to show the Founders' class bias, and which devotes an entire chapter to *The Federalist*, does not even once cite "Federalist No. 10."[6] I deny that, as Ryder says, the Founders *took for granted* that propertied interests should prevail over unpropertied interests.[7] Taking that for granted does not follow even if, as Ryder claims, the Founders deny that each faction's interests are equally legitimate. For the inferior interest may still be legitimate and crucial. After all, the Founders rejected all proposals to make ownership of property a constitutional requirement for the right to vote. And any inequality of the legitimacy of the interests may be entirely explained by the Founders' view, which Ryder admits is admirable, that the superior, propertied interests were, compared to the unpropertied interests, more in the interest of the common good.

Further, since Madison repeatedly expresses much concern for the common good, he cannot *consistently* take protection of property for granted, unless, perhaps, he takes for granted that protecting property is for the common good, which would not be a class bias. Ryder's interpretation imputes a major *inconsistency* to Madison, which violates the interpretive principle of charity. Since Madison values the common good, which includes the interests of the unpropertied, he is *committed* to refusing to dismiss the interests of the unpropertied. Ryder says that the most striking example of misunderstanding caused by neglecting the Founders' class analysis is thinking that the Founders believe "government is essentially an arena in which a plurality of interests and pursuits interact, and that such interaction should lead, if government is properly constituted, to the greater good of the society as a whole."[8] But I will argue that this striking example is an interpretation superior to Ryder's.

A major fear that democratic government is especially unstable and perishable pervades "Federalist No. 10." Madison apparently thought the collapse of the new American democracy would be contrary to the greater good of the society as a whole, that is, contrary to the common good. I agree with Ryder that there is a class analysis in No. 10, since Madison discusses factions, which are classes. But as we shall

---

From Sterling Harwood in Christopher B. Gray, ed., *Philosophical Reflections on the United States Constitution* (Lewiston, N.Y.: Edwin Mellen Press, 1989), pp. 29–36.

see, factions include many significant non-economic classes (e.g., religious factions). So Madison's class analysis is not exclusively, or even primarily, an economic class analysis. Further, since I see Madison's analysis primarily as the means intended to further the end of promoting the common good, I do not see the class analysis as a class bias. I agree with Ryder that it is a mistake to try to show a class bias by simply trying to ascribe to the Founders the individualized motives of narrow, financial self-interest.[9] Claiming that the Founders favored the propertied simply because the Founders were propertied is an *ad hominem* argument attacking the messengers rather than any class-biased message.[10]

Here is the textual evidence for my interpretation that Madison was concerned at least as much with the common or public good as he was with private property rights. Also, note that Madison was concerned with the non-economic classes as well as economic classes when he said:

> zeal for different opinions concerning religion, concerning government, and many other points . . .; an attachment to different leaders ambitiously contending for pre-eminence and power; or to persons of other descriptions whose fortunes have been interested to the human passions, have, in turn, divided mankind into parties, inflamed them with mutual animosity, and rendered them much more disposed to vex and oppress each other than to co-operate for their *common good*.[11]

Madison also says:

> It is vain to say that enlightened statesmen will be able to adjust these clashing interests, and render them all subservient to *the public good*. Enlightened statesmen will not always be at the helm. Nor, in many cases, can such an adjustment be made at all without taking into view indirect and remote considerations, which will rarely prevail over the immediate interest which one party may find in disregarding the rights of another or the *good of the whole*.[12]

As Ryder notes, Madison said: "To secure the *public good* and private rights against the danger of [a majority] faction, and at the same time to preserve the spirit and the form of popular government, is then the great object to which our inquiries are directed."[13] Madison prominently considers the public good. And private rights are not limited to property rights, since they include rights to freedom of religious worship, and so forth. Further, Madison begins by claiming that his arguments are in the interest of *any* "friend of popular governments," since the "instability, injustice, and confusion introduced" by factions have

"been the mortal disease under which popular governments have everywhere perished . . ."[14] Madison tries to show how democratic government can control factions, and he assumes that the perishing of American democratic government is contrary to the common good. Madison's concern for the common good is evident even in his definition of a faction:

> a number of citizens, whether amounting to a majority or minority of the whole, who are united and actuated by some common impulse of passion, or of interest, adverse to the rights of other citizens, *or to the permanent and aggregate interests of the community*.[15]

Again, communal or common interests get equal time in Madison's considerations.

Madison is, of course, *also* concerned with rights to private property. But such a concern need not be a class bias. Far from it, for as Ryder notes, the Founders' "principles of economic liberalism which allowed the release of the extraordinary power of private capital . . . was to be admired."[16] It seems clearly in the common interest of people in a new, growing country to release this extraordinary power to propel growth and promote the country's development and maturation. The common good would converge with the alleged class bias for the propertied. So the common good, along with respect for Lockean property rights, both seem to motivate Madison even when he may seem to have a class bias, as when he said a "rage for . . . equal division of property" is an "improper or wicked project."[17] One need not have a class bias, or a Lockean theory of property, to condemn dividing property equally, regardless of how hard people have worked to get it. Sufficient for such a condemnation are (1) the unfair surprise of pulling the rug out from under people by taking their life's savings, and (2) the deterring of the release of the extraordinary power of private capital to raise standards of living generally. Madison's consideration of classes is best explained not by a motive of class bias, but by the understandably urgent motive of forming a union, a nation, of many classes, including economic and non-economic classes. The nation's motto even then was *E pluribus unum*—out of many, one.

Is the Constitution an Obstacle to Social Progress?

Ryder says the principles that informed the Constitution at its inception continue to inform the Constitution in many crucial respects, and form a significant obstacle to social progress and democratic government. Is this so? Before answering "yes," Ryder must solve two problems.

First, Ryder admits his thesis that the Founders used a class analysis is:

> a minority view, and the fact that most of the literature which deals with the Constitution and the events and issues related to it has failed to appreciate and employ the founders' own class analysis had led to serious misunderstandings of the Founders' intentions and of the new form of government they created.[18]

But if Ryder is right, why has not this great failure and misunderstanding prevented the Founders' class principles from crucially informing the Constitution and from forming a significant obstacle to social progress, as Ryder claims? Ryder seems inconsistent. Further, why should the Founders' principles crucially inform the Constitution, since, as we saw above, Macedo argues that the Founders would have kept better, official records were their original intentions and principles to be crucial?

Second, Ryder must rebut Frank Michelman's arguments that, on the contrary, the Constitution is an important source of social progress toward democratic participation and welfare rights, rights the poor have to food, shelter, clothing, education and health. The gist of Michelman's argument is: to will the Founders' end, democratic participation, is to will the necessary means to that end, welfare rights. Michelman argues:

> Without basic education—without the literacy, fluency, and elementary understanding of politics and markets that are hard to obtain without it—what hope is there of effective participation in the last-resort political system? On just this basis, it seems, the Supreme Court itself has expressly allowed that "some identifiable quantum of education" may be a constitutional right. But if so, then what about life itself, health and vigor, presentable attire, or shelter not only from the onslaughts of social debilitation? Are not these interests the universal, rock-bottom prerequisites of effective participation in democratic representation—even paramount in importance to education and, certainly, to the niceties of apportionment, districting, and ballot access . . .? How can there be those sophisticated rights to a formally unbiased majoritarian system, but no rights to the indispensable means of effective participation in that system?[19]

Thus the Constitution, properly interpreted, promises to be a compelling force for progressive change.[20]

Study Questions

*1. What does "freedom" mean to you? Is it important to you to have freedoms you are unable to exercise? What freedoms do you value most: the freedom to choose your occupation? to marry whomever you wish? to live where you want? to speak freely? to travel anywhere?

2. Is Harwood wrong to put so much emphasis on the people rather than on the Constitution alone?

*3. Do you resent having to pay taxes? If so, why? What responsibilities do you feel toward other people in our society? What—if anything—do you do to increase the general good rather than that of yourself and your family? Our society offers us some measure of personal safety, political freedom, economic opportunity, health care, education, transportation, and other benefits; what do you think are the two most important services our *government* provides you personally? Would you be willing to give them up if it meant you would pay no taxes?

*4. Do you pay too much in taxes? If so, what do you think would be a fair amount for you to pay? Would you voluntarily pay twice the taxes you do now if it would confer your standard of living on all who are poorer than you?

*5. What is the biggest effort you have ever made to influence public policy? If you decided you had to do something about the public issue you feel most strongly about, what could you do that would have the most impact?

Notes

1. John Ryder, "Private Property and the U.S. Constitution," p. 25.

2. Stephen Macedo, *The New Right v. the Constitution.* (CATO Institute, 1986), p. 10. See also Winton U. Solberg, *The Federal Convention and the Formation of the Union of American States* (Bobbs-Merrill Co., 1976), pp. 67–70.

3. Edmund S. Morgan, "Popular Fiction," *The New Republic*, June 29, 1987, p. 28.

4. Ibid.

5. Ryder, p. 17.

6. Charles A. Beard, *An Economic Interpretation of the Constitution of the United States* (Macmillan, 1935, originally 1913), esp. Ch. 6. Note that Beard is quite cynical about the general good, saying: "Of course it may be shown that the 'general good' is the ostensible object of any particular act; but the general good is a passive force, and unless we know who are the several individuals that benefit in its name, it has no meaning." Ibid., p. 155. But we have no reason to assume that the general good is always—or even usually—

reducible to the good of only the *special* class of individuals who actively promoted the so-called *general* good. For a general convergence of interests, and even altruism, are often known to motivate actions.

Further, note the argument that Forrest McDonald exhaustively analyzed the economic interests not only of the members of the Philadelphia convention but also of every member of every state ratifying convention. The result was a highly complex picture that served to discredit and replace Charles Beard's simplistic *Economic Interpretation of the Constitution*.

Morgan, p. 30. See also Forrest McDonald, *We the People: The Economic Origins of the Constitution* (University of Chicago, 1958).

7. Ryder, p. 24.

8. Ibid., p. 17

9. Ibid., p. 19.

10. I call this the *ad hominem* fallacy, but others call it the genetic fallacy. See Richard W. Miller, *Analyzing Marx* (Princeton, 1984), pp. 48f. Frederick Engels is a striking counterexample to the arguments committing these fallacies. Engels was a member of a bourgeois family. His father was a manufacturer and Engels served in a commercial firm owned by his father. But Engels had no class bias for the bourgeoisie. On the contrary, he had a class bias for the proletariat. See V.I. Lenin, "Frederick Engels," in *Karl Marx & Frederick Engels: Selected Works* (International Publishers, 1968), pp. 16–17.

11. James Madison, *The Federalist Papers,* No. 10, paragraph 7, emphasis added.

12. Ibid., paragraph 9, emphasis added.

13. Ryder, p. 22, quoting Madison.

14. Madison, paragraph 1.

15. Ibid., paragraph 2, emphasis added.

16. Ryder, p. 25.

17. Madison, penultimate paragraph.

18. Ryder, p. 17. One explanation of why Ryder's is the minority view is the persuasiveness of the work of Forrest McDonald. See note 6, above.

19. Frank I. Michelman, "Welfare Rights in a Constitutional Democracy," *Washington University Law Quarterly* 659 (1979), p. 677.

20. Ryder gives little or no support for his claims, near the end of his paper, about the Constitution's allegedly unhelpful role in foreign policy. Of course, many invoked the Constitution to criticize those in the Iran/Contra scandal. For example, some used the metaphor of Oliver North shredding the Constitution. And there are, for example, at least plausible arguments for the unconstitutionality of America's undeclared war in Vietnam. See, e.g., Ronald Dworkin, *Taking Rights Seriously* (Harvard University Press, 1977), Ch. 8. The Constitution democratically leaves much power to the people. Ryder fails to show that the Constitution, moreso than the popular electorate, is to blame for allowing abuses of power.

60

Why Have Labor Unions?

AFL-CIO

Editor's note: The AFL-CIO states its reasons for being. AFL stands for American Federation of Labor. CIO stands for Congress of Industrial Organizations. Their merger created one of the strongest labor unions ever. Labor unions, however, are on the decline in America. Union membership is down, and so is the influence labor has on policy. For example, many labor unions opposed NAFTA, the North American Free Trade Agreement, but the agreement became law. Members of labor unions make more money on average than nonunion workers in the same industry. Labor unions also collectively bargain for safer working conditions, more job security, and impartial procedures for resolving disputes about individual workers. Marx thought labor unions would unite the workers of the world to battle the capitalist class internationally. Others think labor unions prevent violent revolution by providing a peaceful method of bargaining for more gradual reform rather than radical revolution.

Why Unions?

Ever walk into your local chain department store and ask to see the president? Or into your local telephone office and ask for an appointment with the chairman of the board?

Or maybe you are a high school student or one of the millions of college students in America. How many times have you talked with the principal or president of the college or university? For that mat-

Excerpts from a pamphlet, *Why Unions?*, published by the American Federation of Labor and Congress of Industrial Organizations. Reprinted by permission.

ter, how many times have you personally talked to your professor in that large auditorium-packed lecture course, "Humanities 1," or something similar?

Now suppose you are out in the world working for a living as an engineer or technician or administrative and clerical worker in an aerospace, electronics, or insurance firm. Or in one of the big companies in the basic industries such as steel, auto, or food processing. Or as a skilled building trades worker. You need a day off to move to a new home, or to look after things at home because your spouse is ill. Or maybe you unexpectedly come down with sickness. Do you call your supervisor or department head and ask for time off? What if the supervisor says "No"? What do you do then? Go to the chairman of the board?

Or maybe you've been a loyal, productive worker for the past year or two. You know the company is doing well and making money. So you want a raise and figure you're worth more than you're earning. Do you ask your boss? What if the boss says "No" or offers a few pennies?

What do you do then?

Or assume you've been a loyal dedicated employee for 17 years. You've got a husband or wife, kids in high school hoping to go to college, equity in the house and stature in the community. You are over 40 but retirement is a long way off yet. Then one day your company is merged with or acquired by another one. New management moves in and decides you're through. They want younger employees; it's new company policy. Or they want more efficient production and are installing some new automated equipment that eliminates the need for your job—and you.

What do you do then and who do you talk to about finding a new job or taking another job in the same company through job retraining? How are you going to pull up roots in your community?

In each of these cases, what can you as an individual do to protect yourself and your livelihood? Who has the final word if you disagree with your employer's decision?

Now consider that there are millions of other wages and salary earners, just like you, working for a living in organizations or firms that are apt to be very large, fluid and impersonal.

Some people say you can't fight city hall or buck the boss. In a democracy this isn't true. You can. And this is what unions are for. To establish industrial democracy in our private enterprise and corporate-oriented economy. To represent the individual's interest when the company's interest conflicts with it or fails, even, to consider it. To represent the public or government employee as he seeks to apply industrial democracy to his job and working conditions.

Look at it this way. Without collective bargaining, the individual employee has no voice, but is subject to every arbitrary decision the employer makes. Some minimum legal standards excepted, the employer sets hours of work, level of wages and salaries. He determines job assignments, production quotas, and when promotions are involved, he can reward his favorites and ignore qualified workers of longer service. He can lay off or fire whomever he chooses—for any reason or even for no reason. He can manipulate the organization chart and demote or shunt aside.

He can, in fact, be a dictator, answerable to no one but himself. Neither democracy nor human dignity has any place in this scheme of things.

In a nation, the benevolent dictator, trying to look out for the best interests of his subjects, is no substitute for democratically structured employee organizations and collective bargaining.

Where there is collective bargaining in industry, the individual worker has a voice and is not subject to arbitrary decision. That worker shares with other employees and with the employer the responsibility for establishing orderly procedures for determining wages, hours of work, rates of production, promotion and layoff policies, and just penalties for the violation of necessary work rules.

As part of a union, you have the strength that comes from numbers and through your union, the ability to hire able staff people—negotiators, lawyers, research specialists, and others who are skilled in the arts of collective bargaining.

Only as part of a group do you have the economic strength that permits bargaining with the employer on a basis approaching equality.

You may not find all the answers to your job problems by becoming a union member. But you will be free to present your problems and have them considered. This is the function of shop and department stewards, grievance committees and business agents. If you don't like the job they're doing, you have an opportunity to do something about it. They're not appointed. They're elected—by you and your fellow employees. The same goes for the other union officers. They're democratically elected and the members do the nominating.

The policies and conduct of the union are determined by its constitution and by-laws and these, too, are subject to amendment and change by the membership.

What Unions Want

. . . Collective bargaining is a rational, democratic and peaceful way to resolve conflict. In recent years, some 150,000 collective bargaining agreements have been made. Only two percent of them were affected by strikes. So in 98 percent of all cases, collective bargaining was successful. Not a bad record.

Back around the turn of the century, things were different. There were not very many unions then, and those that existed had a tough time of it. Employer resistance to collective bargaining was fierce and many times violent. There was no National Labor Relations Act then to give workers the right to organize and to promote collective bargaining. But workers persisted and the fledgling unions survived. Collective bargaining became the accepted way of regulating employer-employee disputes.

It took a lot of nerve for employees to stand up for their rights in those days. There were no job safety standards, paid vacations, sick leaves or retirement plans. Hiring and firing, promotion and layoff policies were under the exclusive control of employers.

But they did it, and today we are enjoying the results. You can't put a price tag on the human dignity individual workers feel when they stand up for their rights, either.

It hasn't changed today. Every time the union-negotiated contract expires, the members have to assess the situation again. They look at their wages and compare them with current price levels; look at company profits; determine if pensions, health and medical care plans are adequate. These are the quantitative factors that go into wages and salaries at collective bargaining time.

There are qualitative factors, too. Things like work rules, work speeds, occupational safety and health, time off for vacations and holidays, and promotion policies.

Put them all together and you have a package of wages, benefits, and work rules that become the subject of contract negotiations. Employers—large or small—don't just hand out this package. The employees have to stick together, send their elected representatives into the negotiating room with employers or their representatives, and through a process of fact finding, discussion, argument and debate, make an agreement on just what the package will contain. Then the membership has to ratify or reject it.

We call it collective bargaining, and it has played a vital part in lifting the living standards of the American worker to the highest level in the world.

Think about this next time you hear a company official say, "Here's what we give our employees." Even if that company doesn't have a union or the employees he is talking about aren't part of the union in the firm, do you really think they would give these wages and benefits if there were no unions? Maybe. But it isn't likely unless a pattern of union-won gains is in existence.

But even then, the employee has no voice in matters affecting the job. Where's the dignity in that system? Or security?

About Strikes

Unions negotiate for agreements—not strikes. No union wants a strike. Strikes develop only when both sides—labor and management—can in no other way reach an agreement.

To a union member, a strike means sacrifice for himself and his family. And he will not vote to go on a strike unless the issues involved are so great they are worth the sacrifice.

Remember, strikes are not called or ordered by union leaders. They are voted by the union membership—to take strike action or not to take it—and the majority rules.

We've already said 98 percent of all contacts negotiated result in agreements achieved without a strike. In fact, the work time lost because of strikes in recent years has been less than three days for every four work years. The common cold causes more lost time than strikes.

But strikes are controversial and controversy makes news. This, no doubt, is why many people think strikes are the rule rather than the exception.

Management can trigger a strike simply by refusing to bargain or to yield on a point of contention. But the union has to take the first overt action and the strike is the first visible sign of dispute. This probably accounts for the public blaming unions for strikes in many cases.

But the right to strike—or right to withhold one's labor in unison and agreement with fellow workers—is paramount to maintaining democracy. In totalitarian countries the right to strike is prohibited along with all other freedoms. Put in proper perspective, then, the right to strike is a matter of freedom, and a democracy cannot function without freedom.

Study Questions

*1. If you went to a store and found it was being peacefully picketed by striking employees, would you be more likely to go elsewhere or to shop there anyway? Why?

2. Which purposes listed for labor unions do you think are valuable, if any?

3. What is the best alternative to labor unions?

4. Was it the success of labor unions that undermined so many of Marx's predictions? With the decline of labor unions recently should we keep an eye on Marx's old predictions, to see if more of them might come true?

*5. Do you expect people who are working under your direction to work harder or put in longer hours than you yourself do?

*6. If you had to fire a problem employee, would you be more inclined to give the minimum or the maximum notice possible? Why?

*7. If a person with whom you were negotiating a lucrative business arrangement lost his temper and started insulting you, would you be likely to pull out of the deal?

*8. Would you rather your work were more or less of a team effort than it is now?

*9. If restoring this country's economic competitiveness meant tightening your belt and saving 20 percent of your earnings during the coming decade, would you be willing to do so?

*10 If you had to choose between a satisfying job with little security and a secure job with little satisfaction, which would you take? Has your attitude about this changed over time?

61

American Textile Manufacturers
Institute, Inc., v. Raymond J.
Donovan, Secretary of Labor

Supreme Court of the United States

. . . Congress enacted the Occupational Safety and Health Act of 1970 (the Act) "to assure so far as possible every working man and woman in the Nation safe and healthful working conditions. . . ." The Act authorizes the Secretary of Labor to establish, after notice and opportunity to comment, mandatory nationwide standards governing health and safety in the workplace. In 1978, the Secretary, acting through the Occupational Safety and Health Administration (OSHA), promulgated a standard limiting occupational exposure to cotton dust, an airborne particle byproduct of the preparation and manufacture of cotton products, exposure to which induces a "constellation of respiratory effects" known as "byssinosis." This disease was one of the expressly recognized health hazards that led to passage of the Occupational Safety and Health Act of 1970.

Petitioners in these consolidated cases, representing the interests of the cotton industry, challenged the validity of the "Cotton Dust Standard" in the Court of Appeals for the District of Columbia Circuit pursuant to § 6 (f) of the Act, 29 U.S.C. § 655 (f). They contend in this Court, as they did below, that the Act requires OSHA to demonstrate that its Standard reflects a reasonable relationship between the costs and benefits associated with the Standard. Respondents, the Secretary of Labor and two labor organizations, counter that Congress balanced the costs and benefits in the Act itself, and that the Act should therefore be construed not to require OSHA to do so. They interpret the Act as mandating that OSHA enact the most protective standard possible to eliminate a significant risk of material health impairment, subject to the constraints of economic and techno-

452 U.S. 490 (1981). Majority opinion by Justice William J. Brennan.

logical feasibility. The Court of Appeals held that the Act did not require OSHA to compare costs and benefits. . . .

I

. . . In enacting the Cotton Dust Standard, OSHA interpreted the Act to require adoption of the most stringent standards to protect against material health impairment, bounded only by technological and economic feasibility. OSHA therefore rejected the industry's alternative proposal for a PEL of 500 µg/ m^2 in yard manufacturing, a proposal which would produce a 25% prevalence of at least Grade $\frac{1}{2}$ byssinosis. The agency expressly found the Standard to be both technologically and economically feasible based on the evidence in the record as a whole. Although recognizing that permitted levels of exposure to cotton dust would still cause some byssinosis, OSHA nevertheless rejected the union proposal for a 100 µg/m^2 PEL because it was not within the "technological capabilities of the industry." Similarly, OSHA set PELS for some segments of the cotton industry at 500 µg/m^2 in part because of limitations of technological feasibility. Finally, the Secretary found that "engineering dust controls in weaving may not be feasible even with massive expenditures by the industry," and for that and other reasons adopted a less stringent PEL of 750 µg/m^2 for weaving and slashing.

The Court of Appeals upheld the Standard in all major respects. The court rejected the industry's claim that OSHA failed to consider its proposed alternative or give sufficient reasons for failing to adopt it. The court also held that the Standard was "reasonably necessary and appropriate" within the meaning of the Act, because of the risk of material health impairment caused by exposure to cotton dust. Rejecting the industry position that OSHA must demonstrate that the benefits of the Standard are proportionate to its costs, the court instead agreed with OSHA's interpretation that the Standard must protect employees against material health impairment subject only to the limits of technological and economic feasibility. The court held that "Congress itself struck the balance between costs and benefits in the mandate to the agency" under § 6 of the Act, and that OSHA is powerless to circumvent that judgment by adopting less than the most protective feasible standard. Finally, the court held that the agency's determination of technological and economic feasibility was supported by substantial evidence in the record as a whole.

We affirm in part, and vacate in part.

II

The principal question presented in this case is whether the Occupational Safety and Health Act requires the Secretary, in promulgating a standard pursuant to § 6 of the Act, to determine that the costs of the standard bear a reasonable relationship to its benefits. Relying on §§ 6 (b) (5), and 3 (8) of the Act, petitioners urge not only that OSHA must show that a standard addresses a significant risk of material health impairment, but also that OSHA must demonstrate that the reduction in risk of material health impairment is significant in light of the costs of attaining that reduction. Respondents on the other hand contend that the Act requires OSHA to promulgate standards that eliminate or reduce such risks "to the extent such protection is technologically and economically feasible." To resolve this debate, we must turn to the language, structure, and legislative history of the Occupational Safety and Health Act. . . .

The legislative history of the Act, while concededly not crystal clear, provides general support for respondents' interpretation of the Act. The congressional reports and debates certainly confirm that Congress meant "feasible" and nothing else in using that term. Congress was concerned that the Act might be thought to require achievement of absolute safety, an impossible standard, and therefore insisted that health and safety goals be capable of economic and technological accomplishment. Perhaps most telling is the absence of any indication whatsoever that Congress intended OSHA to conduct its own cost-benefit analysis before promulgating a toxic material or harmful physical agent standard. The legislative history demonstrates conclusively that Congress was fully aware that the Act would impose real and substantial costs of compliance on industry, and believed that such costs were part of the cost of doing business. . . .

Not only does the legislative history confirm that Congress meant "feasible" rather than "cost-benefit" when it used the former term, but it also shows that Congress understood that the Act would create substantial costs for employers, yet intended to impose such costs when necessary to create a safe and healthful working environment. Congress viewed the costs of health and safety as a cost of doing business. Sena-

tor Yarborough, a cosponsor of the Williams bill, stated: "We know the costs would be put into consumer goods but that is the price we should pay for the 80 million workers in America." He asked:

> One may well ask too expensive for whom? Is it too expensive for the company who for lack of proper safety equipment loses the services of its skilled employees? Is it too expensive for the employee who loses his hand or leg or eyesight? Is it too expensive for the widow trying to raise her children on meager allowance under workmen's compensation and social security? And what about the man—a good hardworking man—tied to a wheel chair or hospital bed for the rest of his life? That is what we are dealing with when we talk about industrial safety. . . . We are talking about people's lives, not the indifference of some cost accountants.

Senator Eagleton commented that "[t]he costs that will be incurred by employers in meeting the standards of health and safety to be established under this bill are, in my view, *reasonable and necessary costs of doing business.*"

Other Members of Congress voiced similar views. Nowhere is there any indication that Congress contemplated a different balancing by OSHA of the benefits of worker health and safety against the costs of achieving them. Indeed Congress thought that the *financial costs* of health and safety problems in the workplace were as large or larger than the *financial costs* of eliminating these problems. In its statement of findings and declaration of purpose encompassed in the Act itself, Congress announced that "personal injuries and illnesses arising out of work situations impose a substantial burden upon, and are a hindrance to, interstate commerce in terms of lost production, wage loss, medical expenses, and disability compensation payment." The Senate was well aware of the magnitude of these costs:

> [T]he economic impact of industrial deaths and disability is staggering. Over $1.5 billion is wasted in lost wages, and the annual loss to the Gross National Product is estimated to be over $8 billion. Vast resources that could be available for productive use are siphoned off to pay workmen's compensation benefits and medical expenses. . . .

V

When Congress passed the Occupational Safety and Health Act in 1970, it chose to place pre-eminent value on assuring employees a safe and healthful working environment, limited only by the feasibility of achieving such an environment. We must measure the validity of the Secretary's actions against the requirements of that Act. For "[t]he judicial function does not extend to substantive revision of regulatory policy. That function lies elsewhere—in Congressional and Executive oversight or amendatory legislation."

Accordingly, the judgment of the Court of Appeals is affirmed in all respects except to the extent of its approval of the Secretary's application of the wage guarantee provision of the Cotton Dust Standard. To that extent, the judgment of the Court of Appeals is vacated and the case remanded with directions to remand to the Secretary for further proceedings consistent with this opinion. . . .

Study Questions

1. Did the court reach a decision that is more morally justifiable than any of the alternatives?

2. Did the court uphold stricter or looser standards for OSHA to apply?

3. Should the standards for a healthy environment for workers be national or local? Leaving it to local standards would allow for experimentation with different levels of risk to health, but should workers be guinea pigs? Wouldn't the federal government be able to hire the best medical experts to set the right standard while some local governments could not or would be corrupted by lobbyists to lower standards to help companies meet all standards? Wouldn't it be easier to prevent corruption by focusing on one national source subject to the spotlight of national media rather than over 50 local sources with varying degrees of scrutiny by the media?

4. In 1985 the average penalty OSHA imposed for a "serious" violation of safety regulation was only $195.[1] Is this amount high enough to make business take OSHA's safety regulations seriously?

Note

1. Lewis H. Lapham, Michael Pollan, and Eric Etheridge, eds., *The Harper's Index Book* (Henry Holt, 1987), p. 9.

62

What's Left and Who's Right?

Mark Green

Laissez (Isn't) Faire

"The only thing we have to fear is government itself." "Ask not what you can do for your country; ask what you can do for yourself."

Such are the words of FDR and JFK, as Ronald Reagan might have delivered them. For based on his volume of abuse of government and praise of business, President Reagan apparently believes that the private sector is invariably good and the public sector invariably bad, or at best a tolerable nuisance. Hence, the less government, the better.

The theory behind this viewpoint is that of *laissez-faire* capitalism: competing firms can maximize output, spur innovation, and minimize price, without government interference. The problem is that this pristine model of the "free market" often conflicts with the practice of corporate enterprise in the real world, requiring the government to police abuse.

· Market theory doesn't account for *compulsory consumption*, or what economists call "externalities." Automakers produce cars that consumers voluntarily buy, but they also produce exhaust fumes that the neighbors of auto consumers involuntarily inhale; airlines carry willing passengers, but also produce jet noise that communities around airports unwillingly hear; coal companies produce coal, and black lung disease in their miners. As K. William Kapp argued in his prescient 1950 book, *The Social Costs of Private Enterprise*, GNP and production data usually "leave out important social costs of production borne by third parties and future generations.... The institutionalized system of

decision-making in a system of business enterprise has a built-in tendency to disregard those negative effects on the environment that are 'external' to the decision-making unit."

· The market can inspire short-run efficiency, but often ignore long-run costs. The theory of supply and demand easily establishes the price of, say a pair of sneakers, but not the price of nuclear power, many of whose costs will be borne by future generations in the form of waste disposal and low-level radiation—generations who are not around now to "vote with their dollars" against nuclear power.

· The market assumes that competitors compete freely within certain rules of the game—no deceptive advertising, no price-fixing, no false labeling. So government agencies act as cops on the business beat to protect law-abiding businesses and innocent consumers from fraudulent companies. When one discovers that 70 percent of supermarkets in one Tennessee survey "short-weighted" meat at the check-out counter, that half of all auto dealers in a Long Island study performed inadequate or unnecessary work, and that price-fixing is a "prevalent" business practice, according to Antitrust Division officials, such corporate law enforcement is necessary.

· While free market theory assumes that companies are Ma and Pa groceries, Edmund Burke's observation that the large companies of his time were "states disguised as merchants" is more relevant today. Exxon alone has greater sales than each of the GNPs of Austria, Denmark, and South Africa. General Motors employs more people than are employed by the states of California, New York, Pennsylvania, and Michigan combined. When U.S. Steel decides to close down a major facility in a small community, or to raise prices substantially in the face of slackening demand, knowing that other firms will follow suit, the influence on the abandoned community or on prices can be far more influential than any government activity.

The laissez-faire capitalism advocated by conservative Republicans today is another reminder why nostalgia should be a thing of the past. For it assumes that only isolated individuals and huge corporations in the economic marketplace can legitimately shape society, while individuals coordinated in the political process cannot. Wealth, however, is not created by 240 million Robinson Crusoes. All of us are part of the political and economic community that permits each of us to work, earn, and produce. Laissez-faire in the 1980s is a throwback not so much to Adam Smith as to a combination, cinematically, of Cash McCall, Judd Rink, and J. R. Ewing, to a philosophy of isolated individualism which defends the private at the sake of the public, and self-interest over community interest. The 1980 election did not mean that *public* welfare is the responsibility of *private* sector. The "General Welfare" clause of the Constitution establishes that responsibility in government generally, not General Motors, General Mills, *or* General Haig. As one businessman observed in Leonard Silk and David Vogel's *Ethics and Profits,* "Government without business is tyranny. But business without government is piracy."

Reagan, Inc.

There can be no doubt that Ronald Reagan sincerely and devoutly believes in getting government off the backs of business—and there is also no doubt that the kitchen cabinet of wealthy California businessmen that enabled him to be a success in politics believes so as well. Verne Orr, Governor Reagan's director of finance and now his secretary of the Air Force, once candidly described the role of such key supporters. "It is natural that the type of special interest group that puts you there [in office] is the one that you're going to listen to more closely. In our case it was the conservative groups, the business groups, that put this administration in. They are our constituency."

They certainly have acted like his "constituency." Back in 1966, Holmes Tuttle acknowledged that "He [Reagan] asked us to fill thirty-five or forty of the top jobs. We met for 10 hours a day, for weeks, and with the help of other people we looked for the best people we could find and made the recommendations to Ron. He didn't have to accept them, but I'll say this, in all but one or two cases, he did." Fourteen years later, banker and old Reagan friend Charles Z. Wick said, "We won the election. We don't intend to lose the government." Added department store magnate and Reagan intimate Alfred Bloomingdale, "We're surrounding Ronnie with the best people— the ones we'd hire for our own business. . . . Running the government is like running General Motors. It's twice General Motors or three times General Motors, but it's General Motors.

Charles Z. Wick can stop worrying about "losing the government." For President Reagan has invariably selected people for business-sensitive posts who either represented the regulated industry previously or who are philosophically opposed to the regulatory mission entrusted to them, or both. A former OSHA violator runs OSHA. A former Exxon lawyer is the general counsel of the EPA. A cattleman runs the Bureau of Land Management.

This pattern of selections, says a White House advisor, "reflects the belief that an election occurred in November, and that the president was selected with a clear promise that he would appoint people in the regulatory and environmental areas that favor less regulation." Another key Reagan advisor adds, "It's not unlike putting Carol Foreman in the consumer affairs division at the Agriculture Department."

Consumer advocate Carol Foreman, though, had a *harmony,* not a *conflict,* of interest in her position. She believed in her mission to be a consumer overseer of the food industry. Reagan's appointees, on the other hand, simply don't believe in what taxpayers are paying them a salary to do. But allowing business to police itself, like making prisoners wardens or hookers the heads of the vice squads, makes no sense—unless one wants to repeal legislation without bothering to go back to the legislature. The Reagan "mandate" did not include merging Washington and Wall Street.

Not only have Reagan's appointments been weighted to his business constituency, but his policy decisions have been almost exactly what it has desired:

- For the oil industry, the Administration wants to hasten oil decontrol and allow more oil and gas exploration on more federal land. It also reduced the Department of Energy's enforcement unit by two-thirds and imposed a twelve-month deadline on it to complete pending audits and lawsuits involving $11 billion against thirty-four oil companies. Said outgoing deputy energy counsel Paul Bloom, "What that amounts to is amnesty for the oil industry under the guise of budget-cutting."
- After five years of deliberations, OSHA proposed its landmark Access Rule, allowing workers and their union representatives access to company medical records. Secretary of Labor Ray Donovan withdrew the standard from consideration following complaints from the Chemical Manufacturers Association.

- After American companies marketing baby formula abroad complained to the White House about a proposed voluntary code against the deceptive marketing of infant formula abroad, the Reagan White House overruled the Reagan State Department to cast the only vote in the World Health Organization against the code.
- Speaking for the Administration, Trade Administrator Bill Brock urged a significant relaxation of the ban on business bribery abroad, arguing that the law made it harder for American firms to compete overseas. When Senator William Proxmire (D-Wisc.) asked him to provide a single example of commerce lost due to the law, Brock couldn't, perhaps because there had been a doubling of U.S. trade in the years since the anti-bribery legislation in 1977.
- As subsequent chapters describe in more detail, the Administration has pulled back the throttle on antitrust law enforcement and reduced corporate income taxes by nearly half.

Periodically, Ronald Reagan has shown he understands the peril of being too closely linked to a big business community which is as unpopular in America as big government. "The new Republican party I envision," he told biographer Frank Van Der Linder, "will not, and cannot, be limited to the country club–Big Business image that it is burdened with. . . . It is going to have to make room for the men and women in the factories." Yet he will almost invariably, if not automatically, support the position of the corporate interests that for so long had supported him.

The point is not that such corporate positions are always or usually wrong, but rather that they're not *always* right, as Reagan's uncritical policies imply. And as his speeches imply. He has rarely if ever uttered any recognition of or sympathy for the victims of business discrimination, pollution, oligopoly, payoffs, corruption, or fraud. His is a world full of anecdotes about governmental bungling, where flammable Pintos, exploding Firestone 500s, and cancerous toxic waste dumps simply don't exist. This is bad policy, and bad politics. A survey even in *Fortune* reveals that 51 percent of Americans with incomes *over* $25,000 believe that "big business is becoming a threat to the American way of life." Such skepticism will not forever condone a give-big-business-everything program.

Cowboy Capitalism Is a Rope of Sand

If there is one issue that elevated Republicans in 1980, it was "the economic mess." Instead of the Keynesian manipulation of consumer demand as the lever to move the economy, the new conservative administration advocated "supply-side" economics. If government policy stimulated greater supplies of goods and services, inflation would ease and more jobs would be produced. At this level of abstraction, who can disagree? Economic growth is essential to economic well-being.

But when the Administration got into detail *why* the economy was in trouble and *how* supply-side economics would work, the shakiness of the approach became clear. For example, consider a few of the factual predicates of what could be called Cowboy Capitalism:

- *Federal Deficits Cause Inflation.* "Inflation results from all that deficit spending," said President Reagan in his first economic address to the Congress. Yet the cumulative governmental budget—federal, state, and local combined— has been in rough balance for years. Of seven leading industrial countries, the United States had the lowest ratio of government deficits as a percentage of GNP—one percent in 1977–79, compared with three percent in West Germany and six percent in Japan. And while the federal deficit alone was over 100 percent of the GNP in 1946, it declined to only 27 percent in 1980.
- *America Has a Capital and Investment Shortage.* OMB Director David Stockman said the United States is "on the dangerous path of consuming its own capital and living off its own savings." He made this remark in 1980, a year when *The New York Times* ran an article with the headline, "American Industry Heads toward Record Year for New Financing" (Sept. 3, 1980). Total investment (apart from housing) has risen from 9.5 percent of GNP in 1950 to 9.6 percent in 1960, 10.5 percent in 1970, and 11.3 percent in 1980. In 1978 *Business Week* reported that "the 400 largest U.S. companies together have more than $60 billion in cash—almost triple the amount they had at the beginning of the 1970s."
- *Individual Taxes Are Too High.* Even before the legislated tax cut in 1981, America ranked eleventh of twelve major industrial nations in the share of personal income taken by the tax col-

lector. In this country it is 29 percent; in France, 39 percent; in West Germany and Britain, 37 percent; and in the Netherlands, 46 percent.

- *Corporate Taxes Are Too High.* Receipts from federal corporate income taxes accounted for 33.6 percent of all federal revenue in 1944, about 20 percent under Eisenhower in the 1950s. They were only 12 percent by the late 1970s—before the Reagan tax plan cut them in half. A survey by the International Monetary Fund reported that in 1980 the U.S. provided the second most generous tax subsidy on new investment of any non-communist country; Great Britain was the most generous, and Japan and West Germany the least.
- *Federal Regulation Is a Tax on Business.* According to the Organization for Economic Cooperation and Development (OECD), the country which spends the largest share of its GNP on environmental protection is not the U.S., but Japan. President Reagan alleged that federal regulation increases the price of a car by $666. Yet when a federal agency asked car manufacturers how much price would fall if all existing regulations were revoked, the answer was $80 a car. Murray Weidenbaum, his top economist, estimates that environmental and consumer regulation costs $32 billion—which is one percent of GNP and $5.7 billion less than the benefits of such regulation, according to a Public Citizen study.
- *We're Worse Off.* President Reagan in his first economics address to the nation argued that "we're very much worse off" in 1980 than 1960. And in their overheated "Economic Dunkirk" memorandum to the president-elect in late 1980, David Stockman and Jack Kemp painted a picture of economic calamity in America. But real per capita income after taxes *rose* 80 percent from 1960 to 1980 (in constant 1972 dollars), from $2,709 to $4,567.

Not only are the factual premises of Reagan's Cowboy Capitalism faulty, but its theoretical underpinning seems pretty speculative. Supply-side economics stresses that an excessively high level of taxation creates a disincentive to work or invest, because the marginal return is simply not worth it. Therefore, we must grossly cut individual and corporate income taxes, for, as Andrew Mellon once bluntly observed, "the prosperity of the middle and lower classes depends on the good fortune and light taxes of the rich."

Not only are we nowhere near such a confiscatory level of taxation, as noted above, but there is also no guarantee that the new tax breaks will be productively reinvested, as opposed to "invested" in mergers, acquisitions, gold speculation, or third homes. Lower taxes might lead to more profits rather than more supply. They may well induce taxpayers to substitute leisure for work rather than incite more work. For example, the Government Accounting Office concluded that $19 billion of investment tax credits in 1978 had little effect on investment decision; and a study by the Treasury's Office of Tax Analysis found that big investment tax credits "buy little or no additional equipment." Such refutations of supply-side theory logically flow from the way business works in the real world: business invests if there is a profit to be made, not necessarily because one of its costs is reduced.

Supply-siders go on to argue that tax cuts will lead the wealthy to shun non-productive tax shelters for productive investment, and can counterbalance the way the government subsidizes consumption and penalizes production. But why slash spending and taxes to accomplish indirectly what could be done directly? Why not simply close unproductive tax shelters; why not end the deductibility of interest payments on credit charges and end the tax-free status of many mergers, moves that would be anticonsumption and pro-production? And how can you reconcile a stimulative fiscal policy of tax cuts with an anti-stimulative policy of tight money, which author Hazel Henderson remarked was comparable to driving a car with your feet simultaneously on the accelerator and brake? The answer is that these two contradictory policies cannot be reconciled.

A successful economic policy cannot flow from such myopia and confusion, as many leading economists, even Republican economists, have recognized. Henry Kaufman, chief economist at Salomon Bros., predicted that huge tax cuts and increases in military spending would lead to double-digit inflation and higher interest rates. Herbert Stein, former chairman of the Council of Economic Advisors, said that supply-side economics might work, just as there might be life on Mars, "but I wouldn't invest much in a McDonald's franchise on that planet, and I wouldn't bet a nation's economic policy on the assumption that the tax cut will increase that revenue." And who can forget how Vice-President George Bush, before he joined Reagan on the Republican ticket, called this approach "voodoo economics" during the Republican primaries?

Although the factual and theoretical underpinnings of Reaganomics turn out to be a house of cards, the president appears eager to play poker with the only economy we have. It turns out, however, that the Reagan Administration has one final ace up its economic sleeve—faith. It has attempted to apply Coleridge's standard for poetry—"the willing suspension of disbelief"—to economic Peter-Panism, that things will work if you will them to work.

President Reagan told a joint session of Congress, "All we need to have is faith, and that dream will come true." He later added to a congressional reception that his economic program would unleash "an 'X factor' in human affairs—a confidence or a spirit that makes men and women dream and dare and take greater risks. . . . The can-do spirit that made this country an industrial and economic giant."

This is not optimism, but ecstasy. Yet with little empirical or analytic support for his economic program, Ronald Reagan had no choice other than such bravado. Irving Kristol, the leading neo-conservative writer, put the best face on a dubious proposition: "A skeptic might inquire: what if this new conservative political economy doesn't work? To which one can only reply, it had better work. It is the last, best hope of democratic capitalism in America and if it fails—well, then conservatives can concentrate on nostalgic poetry and forget all about political economy. Someone else will be in charge of that."

A generation of nostalgic conservative poets may be in the offing. For within a year of taking office, Reaganomics had accomplished the following:

- promised it would produce "13 million jobs in the next five years," but instead produced a severe recession and 100,000 fewer people working in December of 1981 than the year before;
- promised a balanced budget by 1984, but instead threatened a record level of deficits, $423.4 billion between 1982 and 1984 according to the Administration's Office of Management and Budget;
- promised that the mere "expectation" of their program going into effect would spur the stock and bond markets, and lower interest rates, but instead the stock and bond markets fell (interest rates did settle down into the mid-teens, due to the recession);

- promised that huge tax cuts would stimulate new investment which would more than offset any loss in tax revenues, but instead of new investment there was a surge of new mergers, and a McGraw Hill survey indicated that business did not plan any "real" increase in capital expenditures the next year.

Yes, acknowledged columnist and Reaganite Patrick Buchanan, "supply-side economics has been oversold." And yes, admitted David Stockman, "None of us really understands what's going on with all these numbers . . . I've never believed that just cutting taxes alone will cause output and employment to expand." President Reagan, in the bold language that has become almost a trademark, told the nation that the government would "stiffen its spine and not throw in the towel." But his seconds, and the economic indicators, already had.

The Problem with Business, Says Business, Is Business

A fundamental premise of Cowboy Capitalism has been that if we cut businessmen loose from government regulation, slash their taxes, and free more money for them to borrow, they will produce an abundance of wealth and jobs. This is supposed to create "the rising tide which lifts all boats." But, judging by the growing criticism *of* business *by* business and its supporters, we shouldn't count on too large a trickle down, much less a rising tide, from such lavish corporate subsidies.

In a widely discussed article in the *Harvard Business Review* in 1980, for example, professors Robert Hayes and William Abernathy conclude that we are "managing our way to economic decline." Reginald Jones, until recently the head of General Electric, blames the low quality of American goods on "management malaise." Businessman and former Commerce Department Undersecretary Howard Samuels believes that "inefficient management may be the factor economists have underestimated in attempting to analyze our productivity failure." According to a *Wall Street Journal* report, 80 percent of the top managers at 221 companies cite "poor management" as a major reason for lackluster productivity. And Lewis Young, editor-in-chief of *Business Week*, charges that executives "are building corporate hierarchies and bureaucracies that are every bit as lethargic, obstructive and nonproductive as those in government about which business people complain so bitterly."

Contrary to the conservative mythology, top American executives are no longer so much risk-taking entrepreneurs as they are money managers who juggle accounting statements and acquisitions to show short-run paper profits. For example, Robert Reich, the former director of policy planning at the Federal Trade Commission, has decried what he calls "the rise of the paper entrepreneurs. . . . An ever larger portion of our economic activity is focused on rearranging industrial assets rather than increasing their size. Instead of enlarging the economic pie, we are busy reassigning the slices." Former Securities and Exchange Commission Chairman Harold Williams lectures business audiences against acquiring companies they "don't have the time to understand." A major study of why firms succeed, by the management company of McKinsey & Co., concludes that the most successful ones were more single-industry than conglomerate enterprises—companies such as 3M, Procter & Gamble, and Johnson & Johnson.

This merger activity contributes to a growing and measurable decline in American innovation. U.S. companies in 1979, for example, spent more for acquisitions than for research and development. In fact, R&D expenditures in this country in noninflated dollars peaked in the mid-1960s, both in absolute terms and as a percentage of GNP. Perhaps that's why we have something of a "balance of patents" problem today, as more patents are granted here to Japanese and West German companies than to U.S. firms in those countries. While small American firms pioneered in xerography and instant photography a couple of decades ago, today our corporate research factories come up too often with feminine hygiene sprays and "me-too" drugs.

No government regulator told American industry not to market radial tires, small cars, small motorcycles, and small TV sets—markets which Michelin, Toyota, Wang, and Sony succeeded in serving. The fault, here as elsewhere, has been more with self-immolating managers than with over-regulating federal bureaucrats. Indeed, in the May, 1981 *Fortune*, management consultant Jewell Westerman reported that the costs of "the bureaucracy of business management itself" are "far larger" than costs stemming from government bureaucracy. Westerman raises the neglected issue of waste, which the Reagan Administration somehow sees everywhere in big govern-

ment but nowhere in big business. The bigger the firm, the bigger the costs of bureaucracy; excessive paperwork; committees reviewing committees; undetected sloth; institutional caution and delay; and the Parkinson's Law effect of superiors creating more subordinates. Economist F. M. Scherer concludes that "the unit costs of management, including the hidden losses due to delayed or faulty decisions and weakened or distorted incentives . . . do tend to rise with the organizational size. How typical it is for firms insulated from competition to operate with copious layers of fat can only be guessed. My own belief is that padding as high as 10 percent of costs is not at all uncommon."

This chronicle of business "waste, fraud, and abuse," documented by businessmen themselves, should produce the rallying cry, "get the corporate bureaucrats off our backs."

Study Questions

1. Is Mark Green too pessimistic about Reaganomics, the economic philosophy of President Reagan?

2. What is Green's best argument that laissez-faire capitalism, which he also calls Cowboy Capitalism, is unfair?

3. What is Green's weakest argument? Is there any way to strengthen it?

4. Green's analysis is unusually interesting since he cites the criticisms that businesspeople have of businesspeople. Are these criticisms sound? Are they based on solid business experience?

5. Which moral principles would give the most support to Green's views? Which moral principles would be most critical of his views? Explain your answers in detail.

6. Has capitalism lost its bearings? Does the fact that Britain's Barings Bank, which was hundreds of years old, bankrupted itself in 1995 through speculative trading by a 28-year-old employee in Singapore—Nicholas Leeson—show that capitalism concentrates too much power in the hands of some individuals? Leeson lost a billion dollars on his own authority. Do you believe Lord H. B. Acton's famous saying "Power tends to corrupt and absolute power corrupts absolutely"? Must capitalism lead to corruption—too much corruption? How can corruption best be prevented? Through government regulation?

63

The American Paradox of Poverty amid Plenty: Morally Evaluating the Welfare State

Sterling Harwood

Author's abstract: The trailblazing sociologist William Graham Sumner stated in 1881 that "the human race has never done anything else but struggle with the problem of social welfare." Longstanding issues of social justice drive the development of the welfare state. Below we examine how welfare is often evaluated by four moral views: egalitarianism, libertarianism, utilitarianism, and perfectionism. We also briefly examine criticisms of the history of welfare programs and look at current proposals and criticisms.

Egalitarianism, perfectionism, libertarianism, and utilitarianism are the main moral principles most often used to evaluate welfare.

Because so many people are poor through no fault of their own, elementary justice requires a fair amount of welfare to promote equality of opportunity. Egalitarianism gives strong yet significantly limited support for welfare. The egalitarian principle that we should prevent innocent people from suffering through no fault of their own supports welfare. But the emphasis on innocence and the egalitarian principles that no one should profit from his or her own wrong do not support welfare for those whose need is due to their own laziness or hostility. Further, egalitarianism's commitment to rewarding merit also limits welfare to an amount less than what meritorious workers earn. Thus the question of welfare must be considered together with the question of how high the minimum wage, if any, should be. Egalitarians include a variety of political positions from welfare-state liberals to democratic socialists (or social demo-crats) to more radical Marxists or revolutionary socialists. But, surprisingly, revolutionary egalitarians and conservatives become strange bedfellows by joining to condemn welfare, because the revolutionaries see welfare as merely treating symptoms of capitalism and putting off the day of reckoning when the revolution will give capitalism "the full treatment" and cure the underlying problems. As Walter I. Trattner writes, during the 1970s the debate over welfare was "dominated by critics from the left, those who advocate the so-called social control thesis—the argument that the middle and upper classes have devised and used the nation's welfare institutions and agencies not to help but to control the needy in order to safeguard the existing class system, perpetuate capitalism, and serve their own interests."

Perfectionism believes that we should all try to perfect our characters by developing excellence in our personalities. This is usually put in terms of virtues and vices. Industriousness is a virtue. So welfare payments should not be so high as to undermine the work ethic of industriousness, the willingness to work. Further, laziness is a vice. But perfectionism supports welfare, because it is only with some significant financial resources that the poor can have any realistic hope of developing virtuous characters. The coarsening and corrupting influences of poverty must be counteracted by encouraging education or vocational training. If realistic opportunities for jobs do not exist, then the real opportunities of a life of crime will inevitably tempt many into lawlessness and vice.

Libertarianism takes a very different view. What many would call vice—for example, prostitution, drug abuse, and gambling—libertarians would not criminalize or morally forbid at all. These are so-called victimless crimes if they involve only consenting adults, and libertarianism morally permits anything between consenting adults. Furthermore, libertarianism puts an absolute or almost absolute value on private property rights. So libertarianism objects to compulsory taxation just to pay for welfare. Libertarianism has no commitment to equality of opportunity. The rich may use their property to get richer, even if the poor get poorer, because libertarians value proceeding by voluntary transactions rather than achieving any particular substantive results. Critics of libertarianism charge that it exalts legalistic, procedural form over moral substance and results. Libertarianism is not only a moral principle but also a political party. It was the third most influential political party in the United States from the mid 1970s until multibillionaire Ross Perot's United

We Stand America became a force to be reckoned with in 1992. Libertarians want to minimize the power of the state. They endorse Thomas Jefferson's view that the government that governs best governs least.

Noam Chomsky's criticism of the "welfare/warfare state" nicely illustrates how radical egalitarianism can overlap with anarchistic libertarianism, because it is unclear which label best describes Chomsky's view. His view, however, has been shared somewhat by mainstream politicians as diverse as former President Dwight Eisenhower, who coined the phrase "the military-industrial complex" in criticizing it in his farewell address, and the Clinton administration's Secretary of Labor, Robert Reich, who criticized the corporate welfare of hundreds of billions of dollars of government subsidies to multinational and other enormously wealthy corporations, many of which are part of the military-industrial complex. The huge size of the military budget even after the end of the Cold War is a testament to the extent of this corporate welfare.

Utilitarianism is the moral principle that requires each of us to maximize net expected happiness for all in the long run. Its slogans include "Promote the greatest happiness for the greatest number of people" and "Each to count for one and only one in calculating the greatest good." Utilitarianism supports welfare based on the economic law of the diminishing marginal utility of wealth. This law states that, all other things being equal, the poor will get more happiness from transfers of wealth at the margin than the rich will. This is so because people tend to be rational in spending wealth, and because it is rational to spend money first on the basics, such as food, medicine, and shelter, that bring the most happiness. The rich have already secured these basics, but the poor have not yet been financially able to do so. So welfare money, obtained from progressive taxation for example, maximizes happiness, because it transfers some wealth from the rich to the poor. Welfare enables the poor to meet their previously unmet basic needs, which are generally greater in number than those of the rich. But utilitarianism is not at all nationalistic, because each person from whatever country counts the same in calculating the greatest good, and so it gives no priority to domestic welfare over humanitarian aid to foreigners, for example. The upshot would be to spread resources to the needy all over the world. Thus, under utilitarianism, the domestic welfare state might actually be reduced by this thinner spreading of resources.

After former President Richard Nixon devalued the dollar twice within about six months, the purchasing power of the average American's wages has steadily declined since 1973. This decline is often blamed on the welfare state. More and more families need two full-time breadwinners to live in the style to which their parents were accustomed with only one full-time breadwinner. But foreign competition is reducing the American standard of living much more than welfare is. For example, *Harper's Index* reported in March of 1995 that the average American taxpayer pays only $26 a year to fund welfare programs. But foreign competition, as Germany and Japan have recovered economically from World War II, has reduced the power of labor unions and cut jobs from key American industries such as automobiles and steel. Labor unions have traditionally sought higher wages and more job security for workers.

Critics of the welfare state argue that the heart of the problem is subsidizing "babies making babies" without the financial support of husbands. But even Republican Representative Jim Talent of Missouri, an opponent of welfare, admits that only four percent of the welfare caseload involves unwed mothers under age 18. Statistics debunk such stereotypes, which hamper progress toward welfare reform. For example, the average welfare mother has the same number of children as the average mother not on welfare. Charles Murray claims that welfare causes the high rate of out-of-wedlock births. But such births rose even when welfare benefits were stagnant or declining. Further, such births increased for the middle class without welfare. The stereotype that average welfare recipients are blacks of lesser intelligence, a view fostered largely by Charles Murray and Richard Herrnstein, is debunked by two statistics. First, most welfare recipients are whites, and most blacks are not welfare recipients. Second, the *San Jose Mercury News* reports that the average difference in IQ scores between identical twins is 15 percent and that this matches the average difference between the IQ scores of blacks and whites, which is also 15 percent. These matching statistics indicate that blacks are not genetically less intelligent than whites, because identical twins are genetic equals and show the same 15 percent difference due to environmental factors such as poverty. Many refuse to take poverty as a serious environmental factor that creates a need for welfare because they assume American poverty is not as bad as poverty elsewhere in the world. But statistics show, for example, that the average life expectancy in Harlem is lower than in Bangladesh, and that the leading cause of death is not crime but cardiovascular disease, primarily due to an unhealthy diet.

The poverty rate, by at least one measure, is slightly higher now than when former President Lyndon B. Johnson launched his Great Society programs to enhance the New Deal's welfare state created by former President Franklin Roosevelt to combat the Great Depression. But even conservatives like financier Lawrence Kudlow admit the poverty rate statistic is poorly understood even by experts and is far from a decisive point. Critics of the welfare state cite some economic setbacks as late as 1937 as evidence that the welfare state did not help America out of the Great Depression. But these critics overlook the fact that only in 1937 did the Supreme Court make the famous "switch in time that saved nine," when by supporting the constitutionality of the New Deal the Court ended Roosevelt's threat to pack the Court with New Deal supporters. It was only after this switch in 1937 that the New Deal had its full force.

In 1995 a consensus developed that serious welfare reform was necessary, but no consensus was reached on what reforms to make. President Clinton campaigned for "an end to welfare as we know it." Some proposals included job training after two years on welfare and then a government job as a work requirement for continued payments. Others—like Republican Senator Richard Lugar of Indiana, who in 1995 declared himself a presidential candidate—proposed eliminating all welfare to save money. Democratic Senator Daniel Patrick Moynihan of New York, who has served in both Democratic and Republic administrations, has joined those claiming that no alternative to welfare seems any cheaper, all things considered.

Study Questions

1. Is the laissez-faire capitalism that all libertarians support morally superior to the welfare-state capitalism that so many liberals, egalitarians, and utilitarians support? If so, why? If not, why not?

2. Using the *prima facie* moral principles described in Chapter 2, what is the best evaluation of the welfare state? 4

3. Isn't it wrong to criticize people for acting rationally? Is the behavior of those on welfare rational? Even if the stereotype of welfare recipients driving Cadillacs is true, wouldn't it be rational for these people to drive Cadillacs? Don't Cadillacs retain more of their value for resale than ordinary cars? Don't Cadillacs have more room for larger families—another stereotype regarding welfare? Because poor people living in crowded quarters often can't entertain very well in their homes or afford stereo systems, would it make sense to entertain in a Cadillac equipped with a tape deck, CD player, or AM/FM radio? Would owning a Cadillac impress a potential landlord when one is trying to rent an apartment after being evicted from another apartment, as so many poor people are? Would a large car like a Cadillac be safer to drive in?

4. Studies show that poor people and ordinary people have the same desire to work. Do you believe these studies, based on your personal experience? Is your personal experience of poor people too limited to base a sound argument against the studies? Don't many poor people show their willingness to work by taking menial jobs, standing in long lines in the cold to accept free cheese from the government or to apply for low-level jobs in hotels in Chicago, for example? Wouldn't raising many children, as the stereotype claims welfare mothers do, also involve a lot of drudgery?

Bibliography

Anderson, Martin, *Welfare* (Hoover Institution, 1978).

Brown, Peter G., Conrad Johnson, and Paul Vernier, eds, *Income Support: Conceptual and Policy Issues* (Totowa, N.J.: Rowman & Littlefield, 1981).

Burke, Vincent, and Vee Burke, *Nixon's Good Deed: Welfare Reform* (New York: Columbia University Press, 1974).

Galbraith, John Kenneth, *The Affluent Society* (New York: Mentor Books, 1958).

Gronbjerg, Kirsten, *Mass Society and the Extension of Welfare 1960–1970* (Chicago: University of Chicago Press, 1977).

Harrington, Michael, *The Other America: Poverty in the United States* (New York: Penguin Books 1962).

Herrnstein, Richard J., and Charles Murray, *The Bell Curve: Intelligence and Class Structure in American Life* (New York: The Free Press, 1994).

Katz, Michael B., *The Undeserving Poor: From the War on Poverty to the War on Welfare* (New York: Pantheon, 1989).

Kipnis, Kenneth, and Diana T. Meyers, eds., *Economic Justice: Private Rights and Public Responsibilities* (Totowa, N.J.: Rowman and Allanheld, 1985).

Kozol, Jonathan, *Savage Inequalities: Children in America's Schools* (New York: Crown, 1991).

Lynn, Lawrence H., and David DeF. Whitman, *The President as Policymaker: Jimmy Carter and Welfare Reform* (Philadelphia: Temple University Press, 1981).

MacDonald, Maurice, *Food Stamps and Income Maintenance* (Academic Press, 1977).

Moynihan, Daniel P., *The Politics of a Guaranteed Income: The Nixon Administration and the Family Assistance Plan* (New York: Vintage Books, 1973).

_____, *Family and Nation* (New York: Harcourt Brace Jovanovich, 1986).

Murray, Charles, *Losing Ground: American Social Policy 1950–1980* (New York: Basic Books, 1984).

Piven, Frances F., and Richard A. Cloward, *The New Class War: Reagan's Attack on the Welfare State and its Consequences* (New York: Pantheon Books, 1982).

President's Commission on Income Maintenance Programs, *Poverty amid Plenty: The American Paradox* (Washington, D.C.: Government Printing Office, 1969).

Review of *The Bell Curve*, *San Jose Mercury News*, October 23, 1994, p. 12A.

Trattner, Walter I., *From Poor Law to Welfare State: A History of Social Welfare in America*, 3rd ed. (New York: The Free Press, 1984).

Marketing and Morality

The Case of the Professor's Free and Well-Read Textbook

Franklin B. Krohn

During the recent past, increasing attention has been focused on the ethical dimensions of modern marketing practices such as frequent flyer and hotel club bonuses, entertainment provided by sales representatives, gifts given and received by business associates, and free samples provided to potential buyers (Bellizzi and Hite, 1989; Bragg, 1987; Comer, 1991; Dubinsky and Loken, 1989; Ferrell, Greshan, and Fraedrich, 1989; Nielson, 1989; O'Reilly, 1989; Stern and Eovaldi, 1984; Trawick and Swan, 1988; and Trawick, Swan, and Rink, 1989).

One type of professional employee who is not commonly thought of as having to make ethical decisions concerning marketing is the college professor. However, over the past decade a new business has developed that has forced professors to make ethical decisions regularly. The new business makes its presence known through the door-to-door complimentary textbook buyer.

Briefly, complimentary textbooks (commonly referred to as "comp" or examination copies), are new textbooks given to professors by book publishers to solicit the professors' adoption of the book that students must subsequently purchase. It is not unusual

Reprinted from Franklin B. Krohn, "Marketing Ethics and the Complimentary Textbook 'Problem,'" *Business and Professional Ethics Journal,* vol. 10, no. 4, pp. 99–108. Reprinted by permission.

for professors, especially those teaching large enrollment classes, to regularly receive a new textbook from nearly every major textbook publisher. These new books are distributed with clearly no expectation of return to the publisher.

In the recent past, a proliferation of buyers of comp books has come about. As the number of buyers increased, an increase in the number of comp books has occurred in the used book market. Consequently, the sale of new textbooks has decreased. It is estimated that at least one out of nine textbooks purchased by students was originally a comp copy. The publishing industry disseminates stories about authors of brand new textbooks discovering a large percentage of their students using "used" textbooks when none should have been available. Obviously, the used books were comp books sold by other professors resulting in no profit for the publisher or royalties for the author (DeYoung, 1988).

The publishing industry claims lost sales of $80 million per year because of comp book selling and has launched a campaign emphasizing the unethical nature of such sales (Veliotes, 1987; Ladd, 1988). This paper will first attempt to explore the dimensions of the comp book "problem" from the perspective of the participants: (1) authors; (2) middlemen-buyers of comp books; (3) student purchasers; (4) professors; and (5) textbook publishers. Then, a summary and conclusions will be presented and several recommendations will be made.

Perspective of the Participants

Authors

It has been claimed that selling comp books is unfair to authors because "every sample book that is sold is one less copy for which authors receive royalties" (Ladd, 1989). While textbook authors may privately express their regret over lost royalties, few declare that regret publicly. When authors state their reasons for writing a book, the most common reasons seem to be a perception of an educational need, a desire to improve upon what is presently available on the topic, and the wish to perpetuate the teaching of beloved mentors.

The failure to publicly express a desire for royalties might be attributed to avoidance of the appearance of crassness, custom, or the simple fact that the authors may be less motivated by money than the publishers believe. On the other hand, textbook authors have formed a Textbook Authors Association (TAA) whose prime concerns are "the problems of complimentary copies and used books, and the effects of each on the textbook industry. . . ." (*College Store Executive*, 1988). At least the 1,000 members of TAA are willing to express their discontent over lost royalties through collective action. However, at least one author places the blame for the problem on the publishers. According to Lee (1989):

> The promiscuity with which publishers ship out texts is unbelievable to me. If the publishers want to give away texts which have not been requested, that is their right. If I want to sell those texts that is my right. This is strongly supported by the Federal Trade Commission's ruling on the shipping of unordered merchandise (p. 2).

Lee thus argues that there is a critical distinction between textbooks that professors request as comp copies and those that are sent unsolicited.

It has been contended that textbook authors will be less likely to write textbooks because of lower anticipated royalties. However, most academicians engage in writing not for direct financial remuneration but for other rewards such as recognition in the field, sense of accomplishment, promotions and salary increases, and the various reasons cited in their prefaces. Few persons enter the professoriate with the intention of earning large amounts of money. In fact, most professors who do publish do so in scholarly journals where they are not paid directly for their efforts, and there seems to be no shortage of articles submitted to the ever-growing number of academic journals devoted to scholarly topics.

Middlemen-Buyers of Comp Books

The buyers of comp books are modern extensions of the long-established used textbook business. College bookstores have participated in the used textbook business as both buyers and sellers for many years. The advent of widespread sales of comp books has added a new and difficult dimension to bookstore management (Sipes, 1987). The legal, economic, and ethical problems produced by comp book sales have engendered heated debates among professors (particularly those who are also authors) and college bookstore owners (*The College Store Journal*, 1987).

However, college bookstores are not the major channel for buying and selling of comp books. The number of independent buyers has grown dramatically over the years. These buyers come directly to the offices of professors and inquire about any books for sale. As with any other form of entrepreneurism, some buyers are paragons of courtesy; others are pushy and demanding. The price they pay for comp copies, often one-sixth or less of the retail price, is usually determined by a catalog provided by large wholesale buyers to whom they sell. The buyers can usually double their investment when reselling the books into a used book distribution chain where the eventual retail purchasers (students) will pay 80% of the list price of a new textbook.

As would be expected, the comp book buyers care little about publishers' admonitions against resale, as long as the book has ready resale value. The book buyers contend that they are merely independent businesspeople making an initial contact in what will be a chain of middlemen, each of whom will extract their profit for handling the textbooks. Eventually, the final consumer will pay less than the cost of a new textbook. Thus, they contend, they are performing a vital entrepreneurial service in the free enterprise economy.

Consequently, while the individual book buyers argue that their activities are a service to professors, students, and the free enterprise system, publishers argue that they are the instigators of a pernicious system of devious and unethical behavior. The book buyers reason that their activities are perfectly legal and that ethical allegations against them are unwarranted.

Student Purchasers

Students generally seem to be unaware of the controversy raging about comp book sales. Their aim seems to be to purchase required textbooks at the lowest possible price regardless of source. No published information could be found concerning student opinions about the comp book problem.

The publishers contend that the textbooks cost students more than they should because of the sale of comp books by professors. Their position is that the comp books add to their cost of doing business to such an extent that retail prices for textbooks invariably rise. On the other hand, they readily admit that students pay approximately 20% less for used textbooks, comp copies or otherwise. Thus, students are able to purchase used and comp books at less cost than new ones, unless the resale of comp books increases the list price by more than 20%.

In the absence of precise proprietary financial data, it is impossible to ascertain the authenticity of the claims of the publishers. The publishers believe "that the prices of hard-bound college textbooks have not risen unreasonably" during a 27-year period up to 1980 (Addison, 1980). However, in more recent years, the prices of textbooks do appear to have risen more so than many other consumer goods, such as food, household appliances, and private college tuition and fees, perhaps partly because of the sale of comp books ("Selling Your Complimentary Books? Five Points to Consider," undated).

Students seem unaware of the reasons why textbooks are so costly, but they generally believe that they suffer the greatest consequences of anything that increases the costs to them.

Professors

Professors are the prime target of the publishers' allegations of unethical behavior. Yet, many professors believe that they have a right to dispose of comp books as they see fit. For instance, Bauerle (1985) contends that:

> The publisher who exploits the teacher to make money, and then condemns the teacher for selling the examination copy to make money, follows a double standard.

Still other professors make a distinction between textbooks that they request as comp copies and those that are sent to them unsolicited. Some side with the publishers and refuse to sell any comp copies (Laughton, 1986).

Viewing the comp book resale issue from a business perspective, it would appear that professors act as agents for the students and receive the comp copies as samples. There are few other, if any, situations where the value of a sample is as great as in the textbook business. Samples are commonly used in marketing to familiarize prospective buyers with the benefits of the product by freely providing small quanti-

ties in the expectation that larger quantities will be purchased in the future. Some providers of samples require their return if no future purchase is to be made. But few publishers desire to take back their comp books for several reasons: (1) inconvenience, (2) tax purposes, and (3) a hope that the professor will eventually adopt the book thus requiring its purchase by students.

College bookstore managers appear to reflect the diversity of professorial views on the comp book problem. In a survey conducted by *The College Store Journal* (1987), a full range of attitudes was expressed. Some bookstore managers believed that once a book is sent, a professor is completely free to do with it as he or she wishes. Others refused to accept comp copies as used books; some stated unequivocally that "selling desk copies is unethical." Some bookstore managers also made the distinction between solicited and unsolicited copies, or considered the intent of the professor when soliciting the book. Most commonly, the publishers themselves were held responsible for the practice (*The College Store Journal*, 1987). Thus, there does not appear to be any single accepted opinion among college bookstore managers.

Textbook Publishers

Within recent years, textbook publishers have engaged in a variety of common marketing techniques. Contests, sweepstakes, games, specialty advertising items, and gifts for adopting specific textbooks have been added to the traditional business communication of brochures, mailings, advertisements in professional publications, and direct sales calls.

One of the first to use creative marketing and imaginative business communication was PWS-Kent Publishing Company (1987) who developed a complete campaign requiring professors to examine one of their textbooks before being able to play a sweepstakes game for a free trip to Hawaii. South-Western (1987) promoted one of their college editions with a military-motif campaign complete with a "survival kit" for professors containing aspirin, candy, and other samples needed for "survival." Free Cross pens were given by Harcourt Brace Jovanovich, Inc. (1988) to those professors lucky enough to rub off a coated area on a winning game card promoting a particular college text. According to their literature, only one in fifty could win. Random House (1988) offered free books from a list of their popular business titles to professors who adopted one of their college titles.

More recently, Prentice-Hall (1989) gave professors a free videocassette copy of the Paramount film, "Tucker: The Man and His Dream," for adopting certain business titles. However, creative marketing/unique business communication is the exception in the industry that seems to prefer to do business unimaginatively, e.g., by use of brochures and comp copies.

Publishers have tried aversive techniques to discourage the sale of comp copies, such as drilling holes through the comp copy, stamping or otherwise permanently imprinting words such as "Complimentary Copy—Not for Sale," omitting entire chapters, and more recently, combining the instructor's edition with the copy of the book. Publishers have also tried to discourage comp book sales with a public relations campaign directed at professors, college bookstore managers, and college administrators, using a variety of rhetorical devices to persuade them that selling comp books is unethical.

The publishers suggest that professors donate their unwanted books to college libraries, prisons, department libraries, or anywhere else where the books will not find their way into the used book distribution system. Ostensibly, textbook publishers will take back unwanted comp books but tax disadvantages for them discourage such repossession.

Summary and Conclusions

The intention of the publishers and professors are not clear. The publishers claim they oppose comp book sales because loss of income leads to higher textbook prices. But in a profit-oriented society, legitimate questions can be raised concerning whether eliminating sales of comp books will significantly reduce prices or simply increase profits to publishers. Thus, their intentions in raising the issue may be more for self-interest and less for the college-student ultimate consumer.

Legitimate questions, too, can be asked of professors. Those who deliberately request comp books with the sole intention of selling them probably violate ethical standards. However, professors who request comp books intending serious consideration of adoption, and those who receive unsolicited comp books, and then sell them, seem to be functioning within ethical guidelines.

There can be little doubt that when a major industry is confronting $80 million in lost sales a serious problem exists. Furthermore, when that problem may be a consequence of possibly unethical behavior on the part of some participants, it is an issue of even greater magnitude. But if the "problem" is seen as a very expensive marketing strategy with questionable effectiveness, the ethical issues are less clear.

The comp textbook problem originates with the publishers and they appear to be the ones most negatively affected by it. They will unlikely resolve the problem by attempting to label professors as unethical in what is essentially a free enterprise situation. There is a serious question about the wisdom of the publishing industry in attempting to divide professors on the question of ethical behavior. Professors are their natural allies in a system that requires individual students to pay hundreds of dollars each semester for textbooks not of their own choosing. (Insofar as the students have no voice in the selection of their textbooks, they are more the victims of the system than are the publishers.)

The publishers are not helpless in this situation. Their complaints that they are victims of profit-seeking professors tend to appear as self-serving, as there are a number of actions that they could take to protect themselves. For example, they could

1. require that all comp books be solicited, and not send out any comp books that have not been requested by the professor or department.
2. include a license agreement with every comp book.
3. accompany each comp book with a postage-paid return mailer.
4. develop more creative business communication and marketing methods to promote textbooks.

The textbook publishers should attempt to develop more effective communication between themselves and professors. Their present attempts appear to be oriented towards increasing revenue rather than conveying a genuine interest in serving as partners in education. When they start to recognize that professors should be acknowledged as performing vital services for them, and act accordingly, the comp book "problem" will be resolved. The question is possibly much more one of ineffective business practices than unethical behavior on the part of college professors.

Study Questions

1. Publishers argue that selling exam copies increases textbook prices, but doesn't it also lower costs for the students who can find used books?

*2. When you spend money, do you consider who is profiting from your purchases? Should you generally pay more attention to who profits?

3. Is it immoral to buy used textbooks? Is it immoral for a professor to sell exam copies that are unsolicited or not given on condition that they remain unsold? If these practices are immoral, which moral principles do they violate?

References

Addison, H. J. (1980). *Books and Bucks: The Business of Textbook Publishing.* New York: Association of American Publishers, Inc.

Bauerle, R. (1985). My Say, *Publishers Weekly*, Oct. 4.

Bellizzi, Joseph A. and Robert E. Hite (1989). Supervising Unethical Salesforce Behavior, *Journal of Marketing*, April, pp. 36–47.

Bragg, Arthur (1987). Ethics in Selling Honest! *Sales and Marketing Management*, 9, 2, Summer, pp. 31–38.

College Store Executive (1988). Textbook Authors Take On Problems of Complimentary Copies and Used Books. March, 49.

College Store Journal (1987). The Controversial Issue of Selling Comps: A College Store Journal Survey. December-January, 59–61, 102.

Comer, James M. (1991). *Sales Management.* Boston: Allyn and Bacon.

DeYoung, M. (1988). We're all involved in the comp copy problem, *The College Store Journal*, Feb.-March, 77–78.

Dubinsky, Alan J. and Barbara Loken (1989). Analyzing Ethical Decision Making in Marketing, *Journal of Business Research*, September.

Ferrell, O. C., Larry G. Greshan, and John Fraedrich (1989). A Synthesis of Ethical Decision Making Models for Marketing, *Journal of Macromarketing*, Fall, pp. 55–64.

Harcourt Brace Jovanovich, Inc. (1988). Promotional brochure, *Marketing Plan to Shed New Light on the Subject.* Chicago, Ill.: Harcourt Brace Jovanovich.

Laczniak, G. R. (1983). Frameworks for Analyzing Marketing Ethics, *Journal of Macromarketing*, Spring, 7–18.

Ladd, P. (1988). Memo sent to presidents of faculty councils and managers of college bookstores, Sept. 30.

Ladd, P. (1989). Selling Ourselves Short: Integrity of Higher Education Is Compromised by "Used-book" Practices, *Marketing Educator*, 8, 1, Winter, 1 and 6.

Laughton, C. D. (1986). The Cost of Free Texts, *Publishers Weekly*, April 26, 92.

Lee, S. M. (1989). Publishers Must Share the Blame, *Marketing Educator*, 8, 2, Spring, p. 2.

Nielson, Richard P. (1989). Changing Unethical Organizational Behavior, *The Academy of Management Executive*, May, pp. 123–130.

O'Reilly, Charles (1989). Corporations, Culture and Commitment: Motivation and Social Control in Organizations, *California Management Review*, Summer, pp. 9–25.

Prentice-Hall, Inc. (1989). Promotional brochure, *Who Says You Can't Mix Business with Pleasure?* Spring. Englewood Cliffs, N.J.: Prentice-Hall, Inc.

PWS-Kent Publishing Co. (1987). Promotional package, *You Need the Book to Play the Game.* Boston: PWS-Kent Publishing.

Random House, Inc. (1988). Promotional brochure, *Make Random House Your Library for Business.* New York: Random House, Inc.

Selling Your Complimentary Books? Five Points to Consider. Association of American Publishers, Inc., College Division, One Park Avenue, New York, New York 10016. Brochure (undated).

Sipes, D. (1987). The Resale of Complimentary Textbooks: Legal and Economic Perspectives, *The College Store Journal*, December-January, 63–64.

South-Western Publishing (1987). Promotional brochure, *Mission: Marketing Survival: Do Your "Troops" Have What It Takes?* Cincinnati, Ohio: South-Western Publishing.

Stern, Louis W. and Thomas L. Eovaldi (1984). *Legal Aspects of Marketing Strategy: Antitrust and Consumer Protection Issues.* Englewood Cliffs, N.J.: Prentice-Hall, Inc.

Trawick, Jr., I. Fredrick, John E. Swan, and David Rink (1989). Industrial Buyer Evaluation of the Ethics of Salesperson Gift Giving: Value of the Gift and Customer vs. Prospect Status, *The Journal of Personal Selling and Sales Management*, Summer, pp. 31–37.

Veliotes, N. A. (1987). Association of American Publishers, letters sent to college presidents and administrators, February and August. New York: Association of American Publishers.

65

The Nicotine War

Frontline

Editor's note: Frontline discusses evidence that smoking is highly addictive, that some manufacturers spiked cigarettes to hook people on smoking, and that government tests were cheated on or bypassed so often that they became inaccurate in measuring the danger of cigarettes.

Announcer: Tonight on *Frontline*—there has been a political revolution.

Speaker: The "ayes" have it.

Announcer: And dramatic change has been promised. How different will America become?

Rep. Newt Gingrich, (R), Georgia: There will be no compromise.

Announcer: As the new Republican Congress takes power, *Frontline* examines how the first and most dramatic upheaval will come in the battle over cigarettes. Tonight on *Frontline*, "The Nicotine War."

Narrator: On April 14th, 1994, for the first time ever, the chief executives of the seven U.S. tobacco companies appeared before Congress.

Committee Chairman: If you raise your right hand? Do you swear that the testimony you are about to give is the—

Narrator: Viewers watched as the CEOs, who represented a $54 billion enterprise with 50 million customers, struggled to defend themselves against a barrage of attacks.

Rep. Ron Wyden, (D), Oregon: The preponderance of medical experts in our country say nicotine is addicting and that there is solid, indisputable proof that smoking causes lung cancer.

Andrew Tisch, CEO, Lorillard Tobacco Co.: Well, we—we have looked at the data and the data that

we have been able to see has all been statistical data that has not convinced me that smoking causes death.

James W. Johnston, CEO, R.J. Reynolds Tobacco Co.: It's my understanding of how that number is derived—

Rep. Henry Waxman, (D), California: If you don't agree with the number, then give us your number. How many smokers die each year from smoking cigarettes?

Johnston: I will—I will explain—

Waxman: No, I want you to answer.

Johnston: —fully—

Waxman: We have a limited time.

Johnston: I do not know how many—

Narrator: This tense melodrama was only a small part of a story that would mix together science, politics, the fate of thousands of agricultural and industrial jobs and the public health of the nation.

Waxman: Do you or do you not agree with the surgeon general's estimate of over 400,000 smokers dying each year?

Johnston: I do not agree.

Waxman: Okay.

Narrator: And it all hinged on a single substance, a natural chemical present in the tobacco plant called nicotine.

Wyden: Do you believe nicotine is not addictive?

1st CEO: I believe nicotine is not addictive, yes.

Wyden: Mr. Johnston?

Johnston: Congressman, cigarettes and nicotine clearly do not meet the classic definitions of addiction. There is no—

Wyden: All right.

Johnston: —intoxicating—

Wyden: We'll take that as a "no."

2nd CEO: I don't believe that nicotine or our products are addictive.

Wyden: All right.

Tisch: I believe nicotine is not addictive.

3rd CEO: I believe that nicotine is not addictive.

4th CEO: I believe that nicotine is not addictive.

5th CEO: And I, too, believe that nicotine is not addictive.

Wyden: All right.

Narrator: The story had begun more than two years before inside the Food and Drug Administration when Commissioner Dr. David Kessler had discreetly began to examine the possibility of regulating tobacco. A former pediatrician, Kessler felt passionately that a way had to be found to stop the next generation of kids from taking up smoking. The more

---

Frontline Show #1306. Air date: January 3, 1995.

Kessler and his FDA colleagues studied the tobacco industry, the more convinced they became that cigarettes were not a habit, like coffee. According to many scientists, the nicotine in cigarettes was a powerful addicting drug and drugs were what the FDA regulated.

On February 25th, 1994, Kessler decided to act. He released a letter in which he wrote, "Evidence brought to our attention is accumulating that suggests that cigarette manufacturers may intend that their products contain nicotine to satisfy an addiction on the part of some of their customers."

While polite in tone, the letter's message was shocking. Kessler was implying that the FDA might have the authority to treat the tobacco industry as being in the drug business and, in principle, shut them down. Congress immediately wanted to hear more.

David Kessler, M.D., Commissioner, Food and Drug Administration: The cigarette industry has attempted to frame the debate on smoking as the right of each American to choose. The question we must ask is whether smokers really have that choice. Consider these facts. Two thirds of adults who smoke say they wish they could quit.

After surgery for lung cancer, almost half of smokers resume smoking. Even when a smoker has his or her larynx removed, 40 percent try smoking again. The nicotine delivered by tobacco products is highly addictive.

Narrator: What Kessler had done was unprecedented. Simply stated, if nicotine was legally a drug, he had a duty to regulate products that contained it, like cigarettes.

The FDA regulates the substances and devices we consume, from the efficacy of drugs and vitamins to the purity of the food we eat. It assures the safety and reliability of everything from the strength of condoms to the durability of breast implants. The FDA had not regulated tobacco because, traditionally, it had been defined as an agricultural product.

It's true that tobacco starts out as an agricultural plant that is grown, harvested, cured and sold in much the same way it has been for hundreds of years. But this rustic image disguises the technology that now goes into manufacturing cigarettes. While cigarettes originally were made from dried tobacco leaves chopped and rolled in paper, today the manufacture of cigarettes is a highly sophisticated process involving the removal and addition of hundreds of ingredients in highly controlled ways.

If the tobacco companies were controlling nico-tine content in cigarettes with the intention of keeping their customers hooked, then, Kessler reasoned, he had a legal basis for regulating cigarettes as drugs. Cigarette companies would not be selling an agricultural product, but a drug—nicotine—and should be subject, like all drug manufacturers, to the Food, Drug and Cosmetic Act, which the FDA was compelled by law to enforce.

Within days of Kessler's letter, an ABC *Day One* report brought the industry more bad news. It claimed to have hard evidence the industry was manipulating nicotine levels in cigarettes.

Forrest Sawyer, ABC News: *"Day One"* There's something tobacco companies don't want you to know.

Reporter: Why are you artificially spiking your cigarettes with nicotine?

Tobacco Company Representative: We are not in any way doing that.

Sawyer: Cigarettes—they'll hook you fast and it's not just an accident of nature.

Narrator: Philip Morris hit back with a $10 billion lawsuit against ABC.

Philip Morris Spokesman: These allegations are not true and ABC knows that they are not true. Philip Morris does not in any way, shape or form spike its cigarettes with nicotine.

Narrator: Then the industry's public relations organization, the Tobacco Institute, took the offensive.

Brennan Dawson, V.P., Tobacco Institute: So there is no process that adds nicotine to the cigarette. Nicotine is not added during the manufacturing process. It is that simple.

Narrator: The scene was set for a showdown in Washington. While traditionally the tobacco industry had great influence in Congress, in the spring of 1994 there was a powerful group of anti-tobacco Congressmen, including Democrats Henry Waxman of California, the chairman of the key subcommittee overseeing tobacco, Mike Synar of Oklahoma and Ron Wyden of Oregon.

The tobacco industry still had many strong supporters: Republicans Thomas Bliley of Virginia, Alex McMillan from North Carolina and Dennis Hastert of Illinois. And so when on April 14th, 1994, the seven CEOs appeared before Waxman's committee, they realized it was vital they challenge Kessler's contention that nicotine was a highly addictive drug, like heroin or cocaine.

William Campbell, CEO, Philip Morris U.S.A.: Commissioner Kessler and members of the subcommittee contended that nicotine is an addictive drug and therefore smokers are drug addicts. I strenuously object to that premise. I strenuously object to that conclusion. Smoking is not intoxicating. No one gets drunk from cigarettes. No one is likely to be arrested for driving under the influence of cigarettes. Our consumers smoke for many reasons. Smokers are not drug users or drug addicts and we do not appreciate or accept being characterized as such because, yes, Mr. Chairman, I am one of the 50 million smokers in this country.

Johnston: Would you rather board a plane with a pilot who just smoked a cigarette or one with a pilot who just had a couple of beers or snorted cocaine or shot heroin or popped some pills? Dr. Kessler's definition of addiction would classify most coffee, cola and tea drinkers as addicts. If cigarettes were addictive, could almost 43 million American have quit smoking, almost all of them on their own without any outside help?

Congressman: I'm struck by what I think is a calculated attempt to trivialize the devastating health impact—

Narrator: Among the people watching the hearings were Mrs. Eleanor Ross and her family. Eleanor Ross has smoked for almost 60 years. She has inoperable lung cancer, emphysema, has suffered two heart attacks and a stroke. Still, she hasn't been able to stop smoking.

Ross: I've quite a thousand times.

1st Family Member: You quit one time there for—

2nd Family Member: During a chemo. During your chemo you stopped, which was good.

1st Family Member: Yeah, and before that, didn't you stop for about two years?

2nd Family Member: I don't know.

1st Family Member: A year and a half *crosstalk*

Ross: No, one time I did stop, yeah. Come to think of it, I did stop, and I gained 12 pounds. I couldn't get out of my own weight.

2nd Family Member: There you go.

1st Family Member: You went to the *unintelligible*

Ross: No, no, no.

Narrator: You would think if anyone would be motivated to quit smoking it would be Mrs. Eleanor Ross.

Ross: My husband smoked three to four packages of cigarettes a day for a great many years and he did die of lung cancer. And last year, I was very ill. I was there for a whole month with—I believe it was double pneumonia and congestive heart failure and they didn't have much hope. They thought that I would

have to go into a rehabilitation home and it looked like I was going to come home with some oxygen and so forth. But I—I persevered and, fortunately, I didn't have to.

I've gone the patches route three times, I believe, and I've been to hypnotists and—and I've been to that bio-energy person and I've been to non-smoking things and no way can I stop smoking. I would try very hard.

Narrator: Why, then, does she continue to smoke? Is she addicted to nicotine or simply too weak-willed to quit?

Ross: I don't know. I don't know. Just no self-control, perhaps. Maybe that's where I don't have self-control.

Narrator: Dr. Neal Benowitz has seen many cases like Eleanor Ross. He has studied the effects of nicotine on humans for more than 15 years.

Neal Benowitz, M.D., U.C. San Francisco: The issue for addiction is to what degree does the drug control your behavior? The drug, meaning a substance that is not food and is not required for life, because obviously, air controls your behavior, yet we don't think of air as an addiction. People need air to live. They need food to live. No one needs nicotine to live, but once they become regular smokers, they don't function very well without nicotine. About 6 to 12 milligrams of nicotine are contained within most commercial cigarettes. When the cigarette is burned, the nicotine is boiled off. Those droplets are breathed into the lung and then rapidly get transported in the bloodstream to the heart and then to the brain and other body tissues. When you're smoking cigarettes throughout the day, levels of nicotine built up over six to eight hours of smoking and then they persist at a constant level throughout most of the day, while you're smoking, and then they fall overnight. Some smokers are so addicted that they wake up at night. They can't even sleep through the whole night without smoking.

Narrator: Scientists at the National Institute on Drug Abuse have long argued that nicotine was a powerful addictive drug. Pharmacologist Jack Henningfield:

Jack E. Henningfield, Ph.D., Addiction Research Center: A lot of times, when people say that nicotine isn't like drugs like cocaine, they're talking about social consequences and issues that have to do with availability and whether or not the drug is legal or not. They're not talking about the basic biology. When you take a hit of nicotine, it sets up a biological chain reaction in the brain in much the same way that taking a hit of cocaine sets up a biological chain reaction.

A lot of this pleasure of smoking is due to the receptors in the brain, not just the taste in the mouth. And we know this because we can give drugs that block the receptors in the brain and then we ask people how their cigarettes are and they say they don't taste as good. "I don't get any taste from them." Well, they're—they're getting all the taste that they used to get from the tobacco. They just not affecting the receptors in the brain.

Narrator: The tobacco industry, however, argues that smokers like Mrs. Eleanor Ross are not nicotine addicts. They have a bad habit. *Frontline* invited the tobacco companies and the Tobacco Institute to participate in this program, but they declined to be interviewed, saying their position was already on record. So we have drawn their arguments about nicotine from different sources.

Dawson: If you look at the definition of addiction, there are two different ones. We talk about people being "news junkies." We talk about "chocaholics." We talk about being "hooked" on exercise. That's a very loose, jargon word that we have all somehow seemed to adopt into our lexicon. Then there's a classical definition of addiction, which talks about withdrawal symptoms, that puts you in the hospital, that talks about intoxication, that talks about ruining your lifestyle, you know, resorting to crime in order to get a drug. None of those things fit nicotine or smoking. That's why you can smoke a cigarette and drive a car. That's why people who quit smoking, and there are as many people in the United States who have quit smoking as now currently smoke—that's why people who've quit smoking are walking down the street. They are not in rehab centers, for goodness sakes.

Henningfield: When you look at the features of addicting drugs, you can look at a different feature and put different drugs at the top of the list. If all you're looking at is reinforcement in animals, then you put cocaine at the top of the list. If you're looking for severity of the withdrawal, from a life-threatening perspective, well, then you've got alcohol at the top and the short-acting barbiturates. If you're talking about tolerance, well, you put nicotine right up there with heroin, as far as remarkable level of tolerance that that body develops. If you're looking at intoxication, you put alcohol back up at the top, as the drug that produces the most pronounced intoxication, even in people that have

used it for years. When you look at the constellation of features of addicting drugs, you see that nicotine is right in the top tier with cocaine, heroin and alcohol. The tobacco industry likes to focus on intoxication because that is about the only consequence that is sometimes associated with addicting drugs on which nicotine comes out very low.

Narrator: But if smoking were addictive, how could so many people have quit?

Henningfield: We know that with help, people can beat addictions and we know that many people beat their addictions on their own. Over the last 30 years, more than 40 million people have quit smoking. That amounts to lots of lives saved. The bad news is that that only amounts to about 2.5 percent—2.5 percent only that have been able to quit smoking per year, on average. That is a lousy rate of quitting by oneself, when we compare that to what we know about heroin addiction, cocaine addiction and alcoholism.

Physician: Does that hurt you back here at all when I tap?

Ross: Not particularly, no.

Narrator: Mrs. Ross's doctor, Dr. Sylvestri of Boston's Deaconess Hospital, like the vast majority of physicians, wishes his patients wouldn't smoke. There are more than 50,000 studies linking smoking and disease and a virtual consensus among doctors and scientists that nicotine is a highly addictive drug.

Building on this consensus, Kessler now needed to prove that the tobacco industry was deliberately manipulating nicotine with the intention of keeping smokers like Mrs. Ross hooked.

Tour Guide: So if this machine's down, that one can keep on running. Cigarettes are fed down—seven, six and seven.

Narrator: You don't hear much about nicotine on the tours R.J. Reynolds offers to the public. Whatever the scientific community says, their official position is that nicotine is a naturally occurring ingredient of tobacco that is crucial to the taste of cigarettes. As in the past, they are ready to fight for the future of their industry.

Despite warning labels and advertising restrictions, the tobacco industry has been very successful at repelling attempts to fully regulate cigarettes, gaining exemptions from all key consumer legislation—the Consumer Product Safety Act—

Reader: The term "consumer product" does not include tobacco and tobacco products.

Narrator: —the Fair Packaging and Labeling Act—

Reader: "Consumer commodity" does not include any tobacco or tobacco product.

Narrator: —the Federal Hazardous Substances Act—

Reader: The term "Hazardous substance" shall not apply to tobacco and tobacco products.

Narrator: —the Toxic Substances Control Act.

Reader: The term "chemical substance" does not include tobacco or any tobacco product.

Michael Pertschuk, Advocacy Institute: If you want to look at how they've been able to hold back the tide of public health opinion for so many decades, you begin with a very strong and rather traditional political base of support, the tobacco farmers, in a very concentrated part of the country.

Narrator: Michael Pertschuk, former commissioner of the Federal Trade Commission, has made a career of studying the politics of tobacco and analyzing where its political power lies.

Pertschuk: One of the gauges of political power, or of power in the legislative process, is not just numbers. I mean, the poll results have always shown a majority of Americans, large majorities, for example, for banning cigarette advertising and other restrictions. But intensity, the intensity with which a group focuses on an issue and the intensity with which the members of Congress who represent that group focus on that issue is critical, in terms of the political power. I mean, they're willing to say on health care, "We don't give a damn if the citizens of Kentucky go without health care, we're not going to give an inch on—and we're not going to support any health care plan unless you keep that cigarette excise tax down." That's the kind of intensity of commitment that creates political power inside Congress. It also creates it outside, with constituents.

Rep. Thomas Bliley, (R), Virginia: I am proud to represent thousands of honest, hard-working men and women who earn their livelihood producing this legal product and I'll be damned if they ought to be sacrificed on the altar of political correctness. Mr. Johnston, I want to be absolutely certain of this because there's been a lot of interest in this subject and at least one of your competitors has sued ABC over it. Once and for all, does your company spike its cigarettes with nicotine?

Johnston: No, Mr. Congressman, we do not spike our products with nicotine.

Bliley: Mr. Camp-bell?

Campbell: Mr. Bliley, we do not spike our cigarettes and we have sued the ABC company for its accusing of us of doing so.

Bliley: Mr. Tisch?

Tisch: No, sir, we do not spike our cigarettes with nicotine.

Bliley: Mr. Horri-gan?

1st CEO: At Liggett, we do not spike our cigarettes with nicotine.

Bliley: Mr. Sandefur?

Thomas E. Sandefur, Jr., CEO, Brown & Williamson: We do not add nicotine to our cigarettes. No, sir.

Bliley: Mr. Johnson?

3rd CEO: We do not spike our cigarettes at all.

Bliley: Thank you. Thank you, Mr. Chairman, for your indulgence.

Narrator: The industry protested that, far from adding nicotine, up to a quarter of the nicotine present in the leaf was lost during manufacture. Kessler and others, they said, had misunderstood the manufacturing process. It is, indeed, rather complex, as this Philip Morris film shows.

Philip Morris Video: —then mixed with ammonium hydroxide and water to release the pectin, a naturally occurring carbohydrate in plants. When heated, pectin forms a gel-like material that binds the particles together. Flavorings and preservatives are added and the mixture is cast onto a moving belt. Never at any point in the processing of these components has any additional nicotine been added.

Narrator: But Kessler maintained that adding nicotine wasn't the issue. He had not spoken of nicotine spiking, but of nicotine manipulation. It made little difference to Kessler whether the industry was adding additional nicotine to cigarettes or manipulating the naturally occurring nicotine in the leaf. The issue was whether they were intentionally delivering precisely controlled addictive doses of nicotine to smokers.

Under oath before Congress, the CEOs denied they manipulated nicotine, claiming they didn't even measure it during manufacture. The amount of nicotine in any cigarette, they argued, was a side effect of the level of tar, the key ingredient for taste.

Campbell: We design cigarettes according to tar and that's why it's very difficult for all of us to express it as nicotine. We design—we design in the early stages for nicotine—for tar. Excuse me.

If you would join us, like the FDA experts did, you would find that we actually only ever measure nicotine in two places: one, before the tobacco enters the factory and then, 18 months later, after it's a finished product.

Narrator: And in those finished products, they went on to claim, the nicotine delivered to smokers has gone down dramatically over the years as the companies offered low-tar and -nicotine brands to health-conscious smokers. According to the figures written on many cigarette packs, some brands deliver tiny amounts of nicotine to smokers, as little as a tenth of a milligram. But critics say these numbers aren't what they seem.

Benowitz: What you need to know about these cigarettes is the tobacco in the lowest-yield cigarettes and the highest-yield cigarettes are the same tobacco with the same amount of nicotine or even more in the low-yield cigarettes. So—so it's only the machine testing which makes the yields differently.

Narrator: For several decades, nicotine and tar yields have been generated by a special test monitored by the Federal Trade Commission. In this test, measured machine puffs of smoke are analyzed to get the official FTC nicotine yields. But, critics say, many cigarettes have been specially designed to beat the machines. Ventilation holds in the filter are specially positioned to suck in air. Some cigarettes even have long channels running along the length of the filter, all designed, critics charge, to dilute the smoke going into the machines.

Benowitz: The machine puffs from the very tip, doesn't block any of the holes, and therefore you can get as much as 90 percent mixture of fresh air plus tobacco smoke. However, a smoker, when they smoke this sort of a cigarette, finds that it's like smoking air. The draw characteristics are not good. The taste is not good. And what they learn is, one, that if they hold the cigarette in a certain way—say they hold it like this—then without even knowing they're doing it, they're blocking the ventilation holes and the draw characteristics and taste gets better. Or they can take it and put it in the mouth a little further, like this. If they put it in the mouth like this, then their lips are blocking the ventilation holes. The draw and taste is better. And it's been well shown, even on smoking machines, if you tape up those holes, it becomes a regular cigarette.

Narrator: The tobacco industry disagrees.

Johnston: Think of an FTC number as an EPA gas mileage number. If I drive my car fast, I get less gas mileage than what the sticker says. I drive it easy, I get more. So it is with—with the FTC tar numbers. If—I may smoke one cigarette differently from another. Within a cigarette, I will get different tar and nicotine per puff—

Bliley: Are you—

Johnston: —depending on how I—

Bliley: Are you saying you could get different levels of nicotine from two cigarettes from the same pack?

Johnston: Depending on how I smoke it. If I'm under stress—wait'll you see the cigarette I light up after this hearing. It's probably going to—

Narrator: Agricultural product or drug delivery device? It depended on the intent of the cigarette manufacturers and that, in turn, depended on what they knew about the addictive properties of nicotine and when they knew it. To answer these questions, Kessler and his FDA staff began to look for ex-industry employees willing to talk about the tobacco companies' highly secretive practices.

One man they were interested in was Dr.

DeNoble: Recruited to work at Philip Morris in 1979, he set up a lab to find a substitute for nicotine that was equally reinforcing, but avoided its cardiovascular side effects.

DeNoble: Nicotine wasn't studied very heavily, at that time. It was only just becoming under investigation by the National Institute of Drug Abuse. So it became a real challenge. I saw it as a real positive way to make something come back to the—from the scientific community to the public.

Narrator: Working with his colleague, Paul Melle, DeNoble set out to model nicotine's reinforcing properties in animals. Using techniques developed at the National Institute on Drug Abuse, he showed that a rat could be made to self-administer intravenous nicotine by pushing a level in much the same way as happens with heroin and cocaine. While this doesn't by itself prove a substance is addictive in humans, it is a hallmark of addiction. He then used this model to test nicotine substitutes to see if the rats found them equally reinforcing. After getting Philip Morris's permission, he wrote up the research for publication, but before the article made it into print, he got a visit from the company's lawyers.

DeNoble: They had told us that there was some litigation against the tobacco industry—they didn't specifically say Philip Morris. We didn't find out that until much later—and that they wanted to look through our files because the data that we were generating may, in fact, be involved in that litigation. And they proceeded to spend several weeks understanding what we did in the laboratory, actually coming in the lab and viewing the animals. One of the Philip Morris attorneys told us that the work we were doing looked—made them look like a drug company and they just couldn't afford to do that work.

Narrator: After a series of meetings, including a visit from the CEO of Philip Morris, DeNoble was told that he could not publish the research or talk about it publicly, for the time being. Disappointed, DeNoble continued quietly with other work. Then, on April 5th, 1984, his supervisor, Jim Charles, asked to see him.

DeNoble: Jim went into a dialogue of how—how wonderful a job I had done for the company and—with the reinforcing effects and the analog programs and, quite frankly, I thought I was being promoted. I had just been promoted the year before. Paul was promoted the year before that. And I said, "Gee, this is great. I'm getting another promotion." And about 10 minutes into the conversation, he said, "but as of 3:00 o'clock today"—and it's 10 after 3:00—"we're no longer doing any behavioral pharmacology. Shut off your experiments. Kill your animals. Turn over your files." That was it.

About a week after this happened, they brought me back into the building to open up the safe and, literally, the lab was gone. I mean, the computers were gone. The cages were gone. The animals were gone. The wires were gone. The benches were gone. The surgery tables were gone. Everything was gone. It was like there was a vacant room.

Narrator: Told they had no future at Philip Morris, DeNoble and Melle left the company. DeNoble made one more attempt, in 1986, to publish, but after Philip Morris's legal counsel threatened action, he gave it up and got on with his life.

There things stood until one day in April, 1994, he got a call from an FDA investigator asking him if he'd be willing to talk. It took the powers of Congress to free DeNoble from his confidentiality agreement with Philip Morris, but his story raised the question of whether some of the tobacco executives had been completely open with Congress and, if not, what had been the cost to the American people?

Wyden: If your studies had gotten out at the time that they were written, at a minimum, at a bare minimum, other scientists would have followed up on the research that you had done and then, clearly, the American people could have made a more informed choice about smoking. Would you agree with that, Dr. DeNoble?

DeNoble: Yes, I do agree with that. It was the reason that—that Paul and I took the risk in '86 to try to publish this material and present it. The scientific community had the right to look at this research and to confirm or dis-confirm it.

Narrator: Philip Morris was quick to respond.

Steven Parrish, General Counsel, Philip Morris U.S.A.: The American people deserve better than

innuendo, leaked documents, conveniently changed opinions and scientific sensationalism.

Reporter: ?; What about the suppression of the findings of their work? Now, they said that—they said that it was suppressed and they said it had nothing to do with proprietary reasons and they found that unusual.

Parrish: Well, that's one of the things that the subcommittee has asked us to investigate and provide them documents. We're going to do that. As soon as we have all the documents and we know what the facts are, we'll—we'll tell you what they are.

Narrator: For Kessler and his team, DeNoble's story showed that Philip Morris had clear knowledge of the reinforcing properties of nicotine in 1983 and had synthesized and tested drugs as possible nicotine substitutes. But to build a solid case against all the technology companies, Kessler needed more evidence. In May, 1994, a series of internal memos and letters purported to be tobacco industry communications began appearing in the media. These documents indicated that high-ranking employees in Brown & Williamson and other tobacco companies had knowledge of nicotine addiction in the early 1960s.

1st Reader: We are, then, in the business of selling nicotine, an addictive drug effective in the release of stress mechanisms. Addison Yeaman, general counsel, July, 1963.

2nd Reader: Nicotine is not only a very fine drug, but the techniques of administration by smoking have distinct psychological advantages. Smoking is a habit of addiction. Sir Charles Ellis, scientific adviser to British American Tobacco Company, 1962.

3rd Reader: Think of the cigarette pack as a storage container for a day's supply of nicotine. Think of the cigarette as a dispenser for a dose unit of nicotine. Tobacco industry internal memo, 1972.

Narrator: The industry argued that these statements, if genuine, did not prove the tobacco companies knew nicotine was addictive, only that some of their employees held these views. Meanwhile, Kessler and his team at the FDA were methodically continuing their investigation.

Mitch Zeller, a special assistant to Kessler, was interested in the possibility that some companies might be breeding tobacco plants high in nicotine as a way of manipulating nicotine levels in cigarettes. One day, Zeller got a tip that if he checked the patents, he might find something interesting. He instigated an extensive search of national and international patents, looking for anything about high-nicotine tobacco plants. And, finally, he came up with this: a Brazilian patent written in Portuguese. The patent spoke of a type of tobacco with a 6 percent concentration of nicotine, more than twice the usual amount. And the owner of the patent was the Brown & Williamson Tobacco Corporation.

Mitchell Zeller, Special Assistant for Policy, FDA: We saw that Brown & Williamson had at least patented a variety of flue-cured tobacco that was double the nicotine content of the average flue-cured tobacco and that they had done this overseas in Brazil. Well, that piqued our interest. We wanted to know a lot more about this, and so we simply tried to track down the names of the people who were identified as the patent holders and took the investigation from there.

Narrator: Why, Zeller wondered, would Brown & Williamson be involved in developing a high-nicotine tobacco plant? Bit by bit, Zeller pieced together the story of a specially-bred high-nicotine tobacco plant called "Y1." Brown & Williamson had developed Y1 and tested it on an experimental farm in Wilson, North Carolina. The tobacco was shipped to New Jersey, where the seeds were processed by a biotechnology company and exported to southern Brazil, to the farming region of Rio Grande do Sol. There, Zeller learned, Brown & Williamson had grown quantities of Y1 tobacco. Growing Y1 abroad was one thing. But had they reimported the Y1 into the United States for use in commercial cigarettes? Zeller dispatched investigators to ports like Charleston, South Carolina, where tobacco is imported, to find out.

Zeller: We had somebody painstakingly go through millions of invoices to see if there were any references to this thing called "Y1" tobacco and it really was like looking for a needle in a haystack.

Narrator: But eventually, they found a Brown & Williamson invoice referring to a shipment of a half million pounds of tobacco, variety Y1. Within days, Brown & Williamson admitted to Zeller that they had, in fact, imported four million pounds of Y1 and put it in these brands of cigarettes. Y1, they told Zeller, enabled them to produce a low-tar cigarette with a moderate level of nicotine. For Zeller, this was hard evidence that Brown & Williamson was independently manipulating nicotine.

Zeller: Publicly, the cigarette companies have said that they do not design for nicotine when they design and manufacture cigarettes, that if they design for anything, they design for tar. The significance of the Y1 story is it shows that, in fact, they are manipulating and controlling nicotine levels. Brown & Williamson admitted to us they wanted to lower the tar content of cigarettes and maintain the nicotine content. If that's not a perfect example of manipulation and control of nicotine in cigarettes, I don't know what is.

Narrator: Kessler and Zeller's aggressive investigation had made them extremely unpopular with the tobacco industry and its political supporters. When they appeared before Congress to give details of the Y1 story, they faced tough questioning from tobacco Congressmen, who wanted them to reveal the private sources that had helped them break the Y1 affair.

Kessler: I am not prepared, at this point, to make investigative files—I mean, I'm not prepared to make those investigative files that could jeopardize either an investigation or jeopardize certain confidential informants—that's why we have, Congressman, established procedures and I'm willing to follow those established procedures.

Rep. J. Dennis Hastert, (R), Illinois: Dr. Kessler, I'm listening to this and I—kind of surreal here. Are you saying that you don't—I mean, you think that Congress, members of Congress, this subcommittee, the whole committee, have to make intelligent decisions, right? But you're going to give us or spoon feed us only that information that you want to spoon feed us, that you're not going to give us all the information that's available to you, but you don't think we should have that information because you don't trust us? That's contempt. I think that's contempt of Congress, sir.

Kessler: Congressman, there are established procedures and we will follow—

Hastert: Well, what are—

Kessler: —those established procedures.

Hastert: —those—tell me what those established procedures are.

Kessler: I'd be happy—

Hastert: Tell them right now! Here's the members of Congress. What are the established procedures?

Kessler: We have—

Hastert: Tell me!

Kessler: Congressman—

Hastert: What are they? You—you're telling mumbo jumbo!

Sandefur: This is nothing more than grandstanding. If Dr. Kessler had been sincere or sincerely interested in getting the facts, all he had to do was ask Brown & Williamson.

Narrator: Two days later, Tommy Sandefur, CEO of Brown & Williamson, got a similar grilling.

Rep. Mike Synar, (D), Oklahoma: How did you manage to grow and ship millions pounds of Y1 if the USDA permits only experimental quantities of seed to leave the country in the first place?

Sandefur: That's a good question. I don't know.

Synar: Is there any additional Y1 being stored anywhere in the world under your control?

Sandefur: Under my control?

Synar: Ownership.

Sandefur: Under my ownership? Not that I know of.

Synar: Sister corporations or anything else?

Sandefur: There may be some sister corporations that have some Y1, yes.

Synar: Will you provide that information to the record, also?

Sandefur: Yes, I will.

Narrator: Sandefur maintained he knew few of the details of Y1 and promised to hand over documents to Congress.

Wyden: I think you all are going to get more and more marginalized. You will become more and more irrelevant in this debate. And it just seems to me there's a better way to do business. Mr. Chairman, thank you.

Sandefur: Well, Congressman, it's hard for me to envision becoming more of an outcast than I already feel that I am.

Narrator: The political troubles of the tobacco industry had not gone unnoticed by attorneys like the New Orleans lawyer Wendell Gautier. Gautier had been seriously thinking about litigation against the tobacco industry ever since his best friend, Pete Castano, had died of lung cancer in 1993. Following the funeral, Pete's widow, Diane, had come to see him.

Diane Castano: Shortly after Peter died, I received the death certificate and the primary cause of death was cancer and the second one was cigarette smoking. And obviously, it was something that I got very upset about, got very angered about, and I contacted Wendell, at which time he informed me that there was really nothing we could do, that, you know, everything that's been brought against a tobacco company—or almost everything up until then—it was a losing battle and that there was really nothing we could do about it.

Narrator: But the events of 1994, especially Kessler's focus on nicotine addiction, changed Gautier's mind.

Gautier: Addiction appears nowhere on the warning label and I, the manufacturer, stand before Congress and the world and swear that it's not addicting. Now, if I were a smoker, which I am not—but if I were, I have a right to rely on the manufacturer, who knows more about his product than anyone else. If he says it's not addicting, I should be entitled to believe that it's not addicting. He made it.

Narrator: A successful and wealthy attorney, Gautier knew the risks of taking on the tobacco industry. After all, they had never lost a personal injury case.

Gautier: The reason they've won before is they outman the plaintiff attorney. They outspent the plaintiff attorney. And, consequently, they outlasted him, all the way through the supreme courts, making litigation that should have been two-, three-year litigation eight-, twelve-year litigation. This time, they will not outman. They will not outspend and they will not outlast. We're here for the duration.

Narrator: Now the tobacco industry will have to deal with a group of 50 of the top law firms in the country, experts in corporate litigation from asbestos to breast implants. With Gautier at the helm, they plan to take on the ultimate legal foe. Gautier has some heavy hitters on his team. Elizabeth Cabraser won a $4.2 billion global settlement against breast implant manufacturers. Ron Motley won over $500 million in asbestos litigation. Diane Nast won a $458 million settlement against six major airlines.

Gautier has gathered the cream of the country's personal injury lawyers in New Orleans to plan tactics in a billion-dollar federal class action lawsuit on behalf of 40 million current, former and deceased nicotine-dependent smokers, all done in the name of Diane Castano. Each firm has put up $100,000 towards a $5 million yearly war chest and they say they are ready to continue as long as is necessary.

Gautier: In their other cases, what they have successfully urged is, "Listen, this country is based on freedom of choice and on assumption of the risk. If you freely want to assume a risk, that should be your right in the United States." And you know what? I agree with that. They are completely right. But for you to make a free choice, you have to have all of the information. They deceived you and concealed the information about addiction that they knew of and they ask you to choose without information, so you didn't make an intelligent choice.

Narrator: While Gautier's group is the biggest, dozens of other legal actions against the tobacco companies are under way. In one ground-breaking case, the state of Minnesota, in collaboration with Blue Cross–Blue Shield, is suing the tobacco industry for cigarette-related health costs.

Hubert H. Humphrey, 3rd, Minnesota Attorney General: *August 17, 1994* This morning we filed a historic lawsuit charging the tobacco cartel with conspiracy, consumer fraud and anti-trust violations, and demanding that tobacco companies, not Minnesota taxpayers, pay the staggering health care costs caused by the company's deception and violations of law.

Narrator: The companies deny nicotine is addictive and deny concealing important health information from the public, but in court their lawyers will have to deal with witnesses like **DeNoble:**.

DeNoble: I left the company in 1984. The company was years and years and years ahead of anybody else out there. We knew more about tobacco, tobacco products, by-products and nicotine than any government or federal institution.

Narrator: Did Philip Morris, for example, know that smokers were blocking the ventilation holes?

DeNoble: Absolutely. yes. There's no doubt about that. In fact, there was a project which this psychology group at Philip Morris actually filmed people smoking, to determine where filter and dilution holes should be placed so that the fingers would cover them up.

Ray Suarez, Host: *"Talk of the Nation," National Public Radio* The commissioner of the Food and Drug Administration, Dr. David Kessler, is with me here in studio 3-A in Washington for this hour of "Talk of the Nation." Welcome to the program, Doctor.

Kessler: It's great being here, Ray.

Narrator: In a few short months, David Kess-ler had changed the debate over cigarettes. Now tobacco was spoken of in the same way as illegal drugs like heroin and cocaine.

Suarez: Thomas, welcome to the program.

1st Caller: Hi. Many years ago, I was addicted to cocaine for about two or three years. When I realized what I was doing to myself, I stopped and I stopped cold turkey. I'm still smoking. I've been smoking since I'm 16. I'm 52 years old and I can't stop smoking. I smoke about a pack, a pack and a half of cigarettes a day.

Kessler: And it was harder to stop—it's harder to stop smoking?

1st Caller: Yes.

Kessler: I mean, ask smokers whether the nicotine is addictive in cigarettes. And I think—just listening to smokers—I mean, they tell you unequivocally how addictive it is.

Narrator: Kessler didn't plan to ban tobacco, but as a former pediatrician, he did want to find a way to stop the next generation of children from taking up smoking.

Suarez: —and tightening up the access, that we could get fewer kids to stop smoking sic or are they going to get the cigarettes anyway?

2nd Caller: Well, it depends on which way you look at it. I know kids my age that can just walk into the convenience store and, boom, they got the cigarettes in their hand.

Kessler: Let me ask you a question. If we just cut down on cigarette vending machines, would that help?

2nd Caller: No.

Kessler: Not help at all?

2nd Caller: No. That's just—that's just a way to—you know.

Kessler: What else would you do besides cigarette vending machines?

2nd Caller: Well, you'd have—you definitely have to put more enforcement on the—on the subject. You have to—

Kessler: On who's selling.

2nd Caller: You have to put as much enforcement on cigarettes as you do on beer and alcohol

Narrator: Smoking is a habit that starts in childhood. Two thirds of all smokers start smoking before the age of 16. By age 18, that figure rises to nearly 90 percent. People who don't start smoking before the age of 20 probably never will. Kessler had many options, from reducing the nicotine content of cigarettes to banning advertising critics say is aimed at children, like Joe Camel. Ironically, on October 10th, as if symbolizing the terrible year tobacco had faced, Joe Camel was taken down from his place in Times Square, to be replaced with a public health warning not to eat fat. Smoking was now banned in places from McDonald's to the Pentagon, from Amtrak to the airlines. Nervous shareholders were urging Philip Morris and R.J. Reynolds to split off their tobacco divisions from the main business. It looked to some observers like the tobacco industry was finished.

Announcer: From ABC, this is "World News Tonight" with Peter Jennings.

Peter Jennings, ABC News: Republicans are now the majority party, both in the Congress and in the governors' mansions across the nation. The only power base the Democrats still have is the one that was not at stake yesterday, the presidency itself.

Narrator: Within 24 hours of the election, it was clear that the political fortunes of tobacco had been transformed. Henry Waxman lost the chairmanship of the subcommittee on health and environment. Gone altogether from the new Congress will be Mike Synar of Oklahoma. This January, Republican Thomas Bliley of Virginia will be sitting in the chair and he wasted no time in announcing his intentions.

Bliley: What's the purpose of continuing the hearings and dragging these company executives before the committee and, in effect, beating up on them? I don't—I don't think that's necessary.

Narrator: Bliley went on to say he would try to block any attempts by the Food and Drug Administration to regulate tobacco. Despite the setbacks, Kessler can continue if Bill Clinton supports him. But can a weakened president afford to back Kessler's bold plan?

Pres. Bill Clinton: —too much partisan conflict, too little reform—

Pertschuk: There will be people inside the White House and close to the White House who will go to Clinton and say, "If you support what Kessler's proposing to do, you will put the final nail in the coffin of the Democratic Party in the South." It's a powerful argument. On the other hand, I can't think of a better issue to challenge the Republicans on than the issue of children and tobacco and the issue of the cigarette companies and their exploitation of vulnerable children. I think that's a strong issue, a strong issue politically for him, and one that he may see the virtue of standing firm on.

Narrator: Tomorrow the new Congress begins. With the Republicans in charge, there probably won't be any investigation of the tobacco industry. Incoming speaker Newt Gingrich has characterized Dr. Kessler as—quote—"a bully and a thug." Might the new Congress turn the tables on Kessler and now choose to investigate him and the activities of the FDA?

Inside the FDA, things are tense. A few days after the election, Kessler canceled an interview for this program that had been arranged for over a month. So it's not clear what Kessler will do next. Will he finish what he started or will his initiative to regulate tobacco meet the same fate as other reform efforts and be smothered by the political realities of Washington?

Study Questions

1. Should the law treat cigarettes as a highly addictive drug? Are heavy smokers drug addicts?

2. Should cigarettes be banned? Could cigarettes be effectively banned? Remember the failure of Prohibition to effectively ban alcohol.

3. Does the evidence presented show that some companies probably spiked their cigarettes with nicotine? If they did spike, would this be immoral? If spiking is immoral, which moral principles does it violate?

4. What is libertarianism's approach to the manufacture and sale of cigarettes? Can you reconcile libertarianism with utilitarianism in this case?

5. If second-hand smoke were a serious danger to health, would that be enough, in addition to all the rest we know, to make banning smoking in all public places morally acceptable?

*6. What, if anything, is more important for a business than making a profit?

*7. Suppose you disapproved of tobacco companies. If you knew you could double your money in two years by investing in a company whose activities you strongly disapproved of, would you do it?

*8. Would you like every product to be taxed so that its price includes payment for what it indirectly costs society? For example, should the price of cigarettes be raised so that smokers pay for the added medical costs they incur? Would this make the smokers pay the price twice, and thus be unfair? Or would it fairly compensate society for costs to its members? Would it discourage smokers from smoking more and thus harming their health more?

*9. If you could stop all cigarette smoking by releasing a virus that would destroy every tobacco plant in the world, would you? Note: ABC apologized for its claim about spiking.

66

Temptation

Sterling Harwood

Type of Ethics: Personal and social ethics

Date: Coined 1340

Definition: Feeling inclined to act in some unethical or questionable way, or trying to make another person feel so inclined.

Significance: Many people argue that the central task of ethics is to lead people to resist temptation to perform unethical acts.

Oscar Wilde's witty descriptions of temptation help to demonstrate the tremendous power of temptation over the human will. He said: "I can resist everything except temptation" and "The only way to get rid of a temptation is to yield to it."

Temptation is closely linked conceptually to the phenomenon of the weakness of human will. Paradoxically, although stories of weakness of will are found as early as in the biblical story of Adam and Eve, many philosophers have insisted that weakness of will does not exist. Weakness of will is usually defined as action that is contrary to one's better judgment. Some people have argued that it is impossible for a rational agent to act voluntarily while simultaneously realizing that his or her best judgment condemns that very act. Others have argued that since the acts in question are voluntary, the best evidence of what an agent wanted most strongly is the act itself. Therefore, they argue, it is impossible to know that weakness of will has been involved in any observed act.

Such arguments fly in the face of ordinary human experience, but the plausibility of the arguments does make the temptation involved in weakness of will seem paradoxical. Some thinkers (such as Ster-

ling Harwood and David McNaughton) suggest that weakness of will should be defined not as action contrary to one's better judgment but as a disposition to act against one's higher-order desires. Lower-order desires include hunger, thirst, and lust. Higher-order desires are desires that have to do with desires such as a dieter's desire for a suppressed appetite. This is one possible way to resolve the paradox, for it allows one to define the temptation in weakness of will as an unusually strong disposition to do the tempting act, whether or not one in fact succumbs to the temptation by performing that act. This conception of temptation seem to fit the hard data of human experience, which show (Fingarette, 1988) that even those who are professionally treated for alcoholism indulge their craving for drink about as often as those who are left untreated, and also show that smoking tobacco is roughly as addictive as heroin.

Study Questions

1. Is temptation in advertising usually a form of exploitation that egalitarianism would condemn? Exploitation is taking unfair advantage of an innocent person's predicament.

2. What is the strongest temptation you usually resist in deciding how to spend your money?

3. Consider the usual cases of weakness of will: (a) smoking more than you really want; (b) drinking more alcohol than you really want; (c) overeating; and (d) oversleeping. Is weakness of will usually a character flaw or a compulsion involving a loss of freedom for which the person is not morally responsible?

Bibliography

Fingarette, Herbert. *Heavy Drinking: The Myth of Alcoholism as a Disease.* Berkeley: University of California Press, 1988.

Harwood, Sterling. "For an Amoral, Dispositional Account of Weakness of Will." *Auslegung* 18 (1992): 27–38.

Kruschwitz, Robert B., and Robert C. Roberts, eds. *The Virtues: Contemporary Essays on Moral Character.* Belmont, Calif.: Wadsworth, 1987.

McNaughton, David. *Moral Vision: An Introduction to Ethics.* New York: Basil Blackwell, 1988.

Mele, Alfred R. *Irrationality: An Essay on Akrasia, Self-deception, and Self-control.* New York: Oxford University Press, 1987.

Mortimore, Geoffrey. *Weakness of Will.* New York: St. Martin's Press, 1971.

Plato. *Protagoras.* Translated by C. C. W. Taylor, Oxford, England: Clarendon Press, 1976.

Reprinted from Sterling Harwood, "Temptation," in *Ready Reference: Ethics* (Pasadena, Calif.: Salem Press, 1994). Reprinted by permission.

67

An Amoral, Dispositional Account of Weakness of Will

Sterling Harwood

§1 Introduction

The topic of weakness of will (WOW) has attracted a significant amount of philosophical analysis within the last decade or so.[1] But a standard approach is still to analyze WOW as basically some kind of action contrary to one's better judgment (ACBJ, for short). I shall argue that WOW need not involve, and often is not, ACBJ, and thus should not be defined as such conduct. My argument is twofold. First, in §2, I will argue for WOW *without conduct* (i.e., merely dispositional WOW). Second, in §3, I will argue against the normative standards in Robert Audi's conception of WOW, and for an amoral conception of WOW. Further, I shall argue that WOW is a particular kind of disposition to fail to act in accord with one's highest order desire (e.g., one's second order desires about first order desires such as hunger and thirst). Our topic, after all, is weakness of *will*. So I want to avoid assuming, as ACBJ does, that WOW fundamentally concerns judgment, which is identified with the *intellect* as distinct from the will. I want to avoid assuming the conflation of conative states (which involve desires, dispositions and the will) with cognitive states (which concern beliefs, judgments, and the intellect).

§2 Dispositional WOW

In this section I shall argue for merely dispositional WOW. If WOW can be merely dispositional, WOW need not involve action, and so *a fortiori* WOW need not involve *action contrary* to one's *better judgment*

This article originally appeared as "For an Amoral, Dispositional Account of Weakness of Will," in *Auslegung* 27 (38) (1992).

(ACBJ, for short). ACBJ is the definition of WOW which many (e.g., Donald Davidson) defend, and which Audi and I attack (though Audi uses ACBJ as a part of his definition of WOW).

ACBJ is misleading from the start. ACBJ is a misnomer for WOW, since "better judgment" suggests there must be two judgments, one better than the other. But WOW does not require more than one judgment (even counting all prior judgments about whatever option is in question). Audi recognizes this when he says:

> Whether one's will is weak at a given time should be determined in relation to the practical judgments one holds *at the time*. It does not depend on which of one's judgments about a given option is better, nor does it ever depend simply on what decisions one has made (and not abandoned) prior to the time in question.[2]

Audi's quoted view follows his general strategy of developing a conception of WOW that preserves the distinction between "vacillation of intellect" and WOW.[3] I agree with Audi that WOW essentially involves something other than merely changing one's beliefs. All I have read who advocate ACBJ agree with Audi here. So we should beware of interpreting ACBJ as classifying the following case as one of WOW. Al wholeheartedly acts in accordance with his present evaluative judgment about his options. But Al changed his judgment prior to his act and his prior judgment was better than his later judgment with which his acts accorded. ACBJ does not say Al's act was WOW, regardless of how his previous judgment was better (e.g., better accuracy, better information, better deliberation, better morally, or better prudentially).

The other distinctions Audi wants his conception of WOW to preserve are the distinctions between: 1) WOW and irresolution (he says irresolution does not imply WOW); 2) acting contrary to one's better judgment and acting inconsistently with one's better judgment (only the former requires awareness of one's judgment when acting); 3) WOW and imprudence; and 4) WOW and compulsion (or coerced action), since he says an unfree will cannot be weak.[4] I cannot discuss all these distinctions here, but it may help interpretation of our views to note them and note that I fully agree with only 2). In §3 I discuss 4). Finally, note that ACBJ means WOW is action contrary to one's *present* judgment, of which one is *aware*, as to what option is better than all other options.

Audi and I reject ACBJ and advocate a merely dispositional conception of WOW. Audi argues:

Suppose S judges that he should not take a drink and quite consciously tried to resist doing so. He may still form the intention to take one. May he not have *thereby* exhibited weakness of will? Even if he is not able to take one because the bottle is empty, he has already *failed* in the *kind* of inner struggle that often precedes incontinent action [i.e., action manifesting WOW]. Similarly, if S makes the judgment at *t* that it would be better to do A than anything incompatible with doing it, then provided he believes he can do it, his *failure* to form, at (approximately) t, an intention to do A, would manifest weakness of will . . . the same kind of failure of will.[5]

I advocate Audi's description here of WOW as failure of will, an inefficacy of will. The failure can be manifested in *inaction* and hence ACBJ is inaccurate. One may object that S's forming the intention to take the drink is an act, and so Audi's example comports with ACBJ. I grant that there are mental acts (e.g., mathematical calculations) and that one can form an intention through the mental act of deliberation. But reducing ACBJ to such acts is still a major refinement of WOW which Audi achieves, having shown that WOW need not involve overt acts. Moreover, Audi's example of manifesting WOW by *failing* to form an intention shows that *inaction* can manifest WOW. And one cannot rebut the point by saying that the so-called inaction was really the action of refraining or deciding not to act overtly. For the inaction was, by hypothesis, due to *not* forming an intention rather than forming an intention to refrain from acting. And the failure did not involve deciding to refrain because, by hypothesis, S makes the judgment (i.e., decision) that it would be better to do A (which is the act S failed to form the intention to do).

And I would take Audi's analysis further. One might not *completely* fail to form the intention to do A; one may form it but only after too much of a delay or too much of what Audi calls an inner struggle. "Too much of a struggle" means that even though the result of the struggle conforms to S's better judgment, the struggle was more agonizing, involved stronger desires (on the losing side of the conflict) than those that would have been involved had there been no WOW (i.e., than if one had followed one's highest order desire, as we shall see). This is what Audi means by the *kind* of inner struggle that normally precedes incontinent action. The struggle (which manifests WOW) can occur even though incontinent action does not. In other words, in WOW the struggle is not *always* won by the desires conflict-

ing with one's better judgment (or higher order desire, as we shall see).

Audi's view, which I endorse on these points, does not say that acting without WOW requires *wholehearted* action. Only a certain *kind* of motivational struggle constitutes WOW. Not just any struggle constitutes WOW. He says:

> [I]t is not reasonable to regard as incontinent just any want of S's that is at odds with his practical judgment. S's want to do A may be too weak to be at all likely to bring him to do or even intend to do it; hence, even if doing A is against S's practical judgment, his wanting to do it does not imply that his will has failed in its function [which is making one's second order of desires *effective* (i.e., cause action aimed at fulfilling the second-order desire)]. But what if the want, though not predominant, is "strong" . . . We do not and should not assume *that one ought not to* want, even strongly, things whose realization is against one's practical judgment. For . . . we regard it as quite natural to want, even strongly, things which we judge we ought not to have, e.g., sweets.[6]

So Audi does not require wholeheartedness to avoid WOW. The strong-willed person can still be tempted to eat sweets. And at least in more serious matters one can even face an agonizing choice. Given some sets of desires, some choices just *are* agonizing. WOW occurs only when some desires have more strength or influence over you than they would if you were prudent.[7] For the desires competing against them are *weaker* than they would be if one fulfilled one's second-order desire (i.e., one's desire about how strong one's first-order desires, e.g., hunger and thirst, are). This *weakness* is WOW.

In the immediately foregoing quotation Audi introduces the ideas of what we "ought not to want" and what is "natural to want" and what is "reasonable to regard as" a failure.[8] These are normative concepts I wish to avoid using; for I advocate a non-moral conception of WOW. I shall present and criticize Audi's overly normative conception of WOW in the next section. The foregoing arguments show how WOW is often merely dispositional, and so show the error of defining WOW as *action* contrary to one's better judgment.

Consider a final example. Suppose Al is a guard with a weakness for women in that Al could not bring himself knowingly to shoot an attacking woman, even if he had a second-order desire to shoot her, and believed doing so would be prudent and morally required. Fortunately, no woman ever attacks Al. So his WOW never manifests itself in any struggle, or any action or inaction. Still, Al is weak-willed, since he is disposed to act incontinently under certain circumstances. This advances Audi's analysis a step further, showing that the disposition that is WOW need not even involve a struggle.

§3 Against Audi's Normative Standards for WOW

In this section we reach deeper and more important issues. I now argue against the normative standards in Audi's conception of WOW, and for an *amoral* conception of WOW. Audi holds a conception of WOW which has moral or normative implications. Audi makes a moral—or at least a normative—argument for his view that WOW never involves succumbing to an irresistible impulse. He says:

> Weakness of will is surely a normative phenomenon in at least this sense: if S does A incontinently [i.e., due to WOW] then S is in some way criticizable for doing A . . . whether morally, prudentially, or in some other way(s) . . . Now suppose we add the widely believed premise that if S does A under compulsion, he is *not* criticizable for doing it. It would follow that incontinent actions are never compelled.[9]

I am willing to grant the widely believed premise, which seems to be a special case of "'ought' implies 'can,'" though the premise has increasingly come under attack in recent years, especially concerning the insanity defense. An irresistible impulse (or compulsion) cannot be resisted, and so, based on "'ought' implies 'can,'" I am willing to grant here that one cannot correctly criticize someone for failing to resist such an impulse. Still, I think that it is at least sometimes a motivational failure, and hence that it can correctly be called a *weakness* of one's will. But, instead of adopting Audi's view, we can simply conclude that WOW is not always correctly criticizable. This seems a much simpler and better solution. And since not all cases of WOW involve compulsion, the simpler solution preserves Audi's distinction between compelled action and WOW, which is the rationale for his argument.[10]

On whether WOW is always criticizable, and whether WOW is a moral concept, I side with Davidson, who sees WOW as a metaphysical concept in the theory of action, independent of ethics.[11] WOW is more useful as a metaphysical concept free of moral baggage and entanglements. For psychologists could then use the concept of WOW without

venturing into an area where they may consider themselves somewhat less qualified, moral philosophy. And an amoral conception of WOW will help moral theory and action theory, since we could then use the concept of WOW without begging moral questions. I shall defend a somewhat normative, but amoral, conception of WOW. Since the norm I use is *prudence*, and since I deny that all WOW is (even prudentially) criticizable, psychologists and psychiatrists can use the concept of WOW with less danger of imposing values upon a client that are not the client's own.

Further, Thalberg gives an initially plausible argument against a moral conception of WOW, saying:

> "He shouldn't have done Y" . . . cannot always [be said] of a person who had better [subjective] reasons to do X instead. Otherwise you would be endorsing the dubious principle that everyone including Nero, Genghis Khan, Torquemada and Hitler, ought to do what he judges best . . . The point is that we often hold that some action, which another person believes he ought to perform is wrong or inadvisable in some way. If he fails to perform, then we would be inconsistent if we maintained our disapproval of the action he was contemplating, but condemned him for failing to carry it out. Only when we share the agent's belief that he ought to do X is it logically possible for us [consistently and correctly] to decry his failure [as such].[12]

But I must disagree with Thalberg. For we can consistently and correctly condemn Jim Bakker or Jimmy Swaggart for their hypocrisy even if we scarcely share their beliefs about what they ought to do. Specifically, a libertarian or liberal might claim that Bakker and Swaggart are wrong to condemn prostitution among consenting adults, but that *if* they are going to condemn prostitution anyway, at least *they* should not pay prostitutes for sex. One can correctly decry *their* paying for sex even if one thinks prostitution per se is morally permissible.

But we need an amoral conception of WOW, for in at least some cases of WOW we should even praise the would-be Hitler for his WOW. Here is the first of the two main examples in this paper that I wish my reader to focus on. Suppose young Hans is indoctrinated by Nazis and is months later ordered to kill a group of Jews. Hans believes he ought to kill them, but his humanity "gets the better of him." He has lingering, unarticulated feelings about what he ought to do. Still, he believes he ought to kill them, and that it is highly probable that his Nazi teachers and superiors have been right all along. Hans is not a squeamish person. And he has a second-order desire to kill them according to his orders. But come time to pull the trigger, his humanity and sympathetic feelings for the Jews lead Hans to let them escape, even though he has not changed his mind, and is acutely aware of his motivational failing. Further, suppose Hans is prudent to let them escape because Hans has been trusted to kill them, by himself, in an area bordering enemy lines (and far from other Nazis or Nazi-sympathizers) and to dispose of their bodies completely. We can suppose that firing his gun so close to enemy lines (or taking time to dispose of the bodies completely) is imprudent. I see no sound, normative criticism of Hans' act of letting the Jews escape.

The counterargument that we can always criticize someone for acting against his better judgment just because it is against his better judgment (i.e., just on grounds of internal inconsistency) trivializes the thesis. First, the counterargument begs the question against arguments that sympathy should sometimes take priority over conscience.[13] Second, I argued above that WOW need not involve inconsistency between superior and inferior judgments. Third, foolish consistency is the hobgoblin of little minds; not *all* internal inconsistencies are *normatively* criticizable, but some are—as the cases of Bakker and Swaggart show. Simply saying that all internal inconsistencies are criticizable as *such* trivializes the thesis, and begs the question by failing to give any further or independent rationale for the criticism. Moreover, this objection would require fanaticism (Nazi massacre) to avoid criticizable WOW, which is absurd. Hans *should* have conflicting feelings, given his circumstances. Further, even if there is an undiscovered, normative criticism of Hans, we can tell Hans' case is one of WOW even before discovering any criticism. So it is highly misleading and unnecessary to go out on a limb and say WOW *must* be normatively criticizable and include that as one of the very defining characteristics of WOW.

One may object that I owe an explanation for how the WOW of Hans is not criticizable even though the WOW of Bakker and Swaggart is criticizable. The distinction between the cases is that Hans is young and (understandably) confused whereas Bakker and Swaggart are older (old enough to know better) and hypocritical.

Perhaps all Audi means by saying WOW is always criticizable is that WOW always involves a case where the agent is morally responsible and *could* have refrained from doing the incontinent act. That is,

WOW is always criticizable because *were* the incontinent act wrong, the actor could be correctly criticized for doing the act, since the stricture "'ought' implies 'can'" is met in all cases of WOW. I consider this to be too watered down to be Audi's view. But if it is his view, then I differ only on case of compulsion (e.g., irresistible impulses). Audi's argument for distinguishing compulsion from WOW is that WOW is essentially a normative concept.

There is another reason, besides Hans' case, to avoid Audi's normative analysis of WOW. Audi classifies the (voluntary) knowing pursuit of evil as WOW, saying: "S exhibits [WOW] . . . if . . . S forms the intention or a predominant want to do A, where doing A is against his better judgment . . ."[14] The knowing pursuit of evil is, I grant, acting against one's better judgment. But here is the second of the two main examples I wish my reader to focus on. Surely an evil person, call him Cecil the devil worshipper, can even do research on what the morally right thing to do would be, and then, based on this research, deliberately and painstakingly do what is evil. Cecil can be moved by prudential considerations (e.g., he can safely steal undetected) and his desire to act on evil desires and do evil (as such). *Moreover*, suppose knowingly doing evil fulfills Cecil's second-order desire to do evil as such. Audi would say Cecil exhibits WOW because, by hypothesis, Cecil's moral judgment is that Cecil ought not do the evil. Because Cecil acts wholeheartedly, without motivational conflict and in accordance with his second-order desire to do things based on evil desires, I claim he does not act incontinently. I grant that Cecil acts against his better judgment, but I claim this is irrelevant given that he acts in accord with his second-order desire (i.e., his desire about his other desires).

One may object that Cecil must have some sort of overall judgment that it is really best to do what is evil, since to *worship* the devil is to *believe* that the devil's way (evil) is best. Thus, one may object, Cecil's case fails to fit ACBJ, and thus cannot be a counterexample to ACBJ. But this objection conflates conative and cognitive states. Cecil, as a purely intellectual matter, identifies the evil and the good acts to do. Cecil can even intellectually accept a Kantian view that obeying morality is what is more important overall. Yet Cecil can have absolutely no desire to obey morality. He *can* have a desire to do evil, as such, instead. If Cecil's case is too strange to see this clearly at first, compare the following more mundane case. Pat acknowledges the soundness of arguments concluding that he should give at least something to charity to relieve hunger. But Pat is unmoved, having no desire to do so. Pat asks "What's in it for me?" Pat is apathetic toward morality. Similarly, Cecil is unmoved to obey morality. He can say "What's in it for me? I desire to do evil as such, and prudence does not go against the sort of evil I have in mind." But in the cases of Pat and Cecil where is the motivational weakness required for WOW? They act exactly as they want, and they act wholeheartedly without any motivational conflict. So I conclude that there is no WOW in their cases.

Those who object to my view here have the burden of showing the motivational weakness in Cecil's wholehearted actions. One may object that the motivational weakness is simply the absence of motivation to do the right thing. But this simple view would prove too much. Since nobody is perfect, we would all be weak of will virtually all the time. I cannot defend a particular morality here. But morality seems demanding enough to make this objection classify too much of us as weak of will too much of the time. Further, the objection fails to see how WOW involves a conflict *within* the agent's psychology. Recall Audi's view about WOW as an *inner struggle*. A case of wholehearted yet incontinent action seems incoherent.

One may object that I am taking "better judgment" to mean "judgment as to what is morally best" and that this is not the way it would be taken by anyone inclined to accept the definition of WOW as acting against one's better judgment. The objection clearly fails, for I do not so take "better judgment." I mean it just as Audi, Davidson, and Thalberg mean it, namely as a judgment as to what one ought to do, *all things considered*.[15] The point in Cecil's case is that this judgment about what is best, all things considered, is a purely intellectual judgment that the moral act is best, and that the judgment involves no motivation to do the moral act.

But the ambiguity in the use of "better judgment" by Audi does create some important ground where my view and Audi's might be reconciled. Audi might mean by "better judgment" one's *decision*, all things considered, about what one *will* do. The judgment here is the occurrent, present decision to start *willing* the act in question (i.e., to issue the relevant volition). It is not a mere prediction about what one is about to do. I agree that if one acted contrary to one's better judgment (in this sense), then one could act incontinently. And to the degree that one was *disposed* to act contrary to such *decisions* one would have WOW. One

can have conflicting second-order desires A only, and desires to have a set of desires B only, yet know that the two sets are incompatible because the sets contain different elements (desires). But in such cases the decision one acts against must be *present* at the time of action, since I agree with Audi that WOW is distinct from mere intellectual vacillation. If one failed to form the intent to do the act decided upon, one has WOW. Such a failure would occur if one formed instead an intent to do another act (or no act). All decisions, in the sense used here, are accompanied by first-order and second-order desires to do the act decided upon (or, in the case of conflicting second-order desires, a third-order desire—i.e., a desire about one's second-order desires, particularly a desire about how the conflict between the second-order desires will be resolved). For one is deciding which of one's first- and second-order desires to fulfill. Harry Frankfurt details the role second-order desires play in self-reflection, self-evaluation, and in the issuance of volitions.[16] And I at least roughly follow Frankfurt here.

Consider another case. Audi might mean that in some cases the better judgment is one's judgment about what act all prudential factors favor. One could be not incontinent yet act against such a judgment based on a first-order desire (e.g., an imprudent impulse) or even based on a second-order desire rather than on a lack of certain first-order desires. Since prudence is calculated by considering *all* desires of the agent, even the first-order desires that one has a second-order desire to end, one's second-order desire can conflict with one's prudential judgment. (For simplification, I assume they conflict in a case where the agent knows that moral considerations and other nonprudential considerations favor neither option considered by the agent.) Such a conflicting second-order desire can be, for example, the desire to do an act that will thereby make one a different sort of person than one is. But *given* that one is not that sort of person, prudence dictates refraining from doing an act, A, to fulfill the second-order desire, and to do instead another act, B, which prudently satisfies the vast bulk of one's desires, but which fails to satisfy one's second-order desire. If one had a conflicting second-order desire to do B, then I think knowingly doing A instead would be incontinent. But if the second-order desire to do A were one's only second-order desire (and there were no even higher order desires), then I suspect that knowingly doing A would hardly be incontinent. For, on the contrary, the case seems to involve *strength* of will, where one *becomes* what one really wants to be (and has a second-order desire to be) through sheer *force of will*, even though becoming such a person is imprudent. The very fact that one overcame all the other desires that made doing B prudent shows how strong one's will was. So such cases fit what I conclude must be the best definition of WOW, namely, that WOW is the disposition to fail to act in accord with one's highest order desire. As Robert Roberts argues:

> Why do we tend to think a moral achievement greater if more difficult? . . . [M]orally difficult actions display . . . the virtues of will power. But . . . a deeper basis for our feeling here is that the greater the moral obstacles (that is, contrary indications) a person has overcome in doing something, the more his action seems to be his own *achievement*, his own *choice*, and thus to reflect credit on him as an *agent*. It seems to show his action is *his* in a special way.[17]

The agent should get metaphysical credit for the strength of this effort.

§4 Conclusion

I conclude that not all WOW is criticizable, since Hans' case is a counterexample to Audi's view. And using Cecil as a counterexample I argued against Audi's classification of the knowing pursuit of evil as WOW. Those who object to my view have the burden of showing 1) what is immoral in Hans' action of letting the Jews escape, and 2) what is motivationally weak in Cecil's wholehearted actions. My main conclusion is that WOW is having a *disposition* (to fail to act in accord with one's highest order desire) that is greater than such a disposition would be (at least typically) if one were completely *prudent*. One may object that my view leaves no rational, motivational role for *morality*. But prudence is at least normative, and thus my conception of WOW, although amoral, is normative and hence partially reconciled with Audi's view. Moreover, as I said earlier, I mean prudence in the sense of maximizing the satisfaction of *all* of one's desires, *including* one's desires about doing the *moral* thing as such. So I leave room for a rational, motivational role for morality, since I preserve the distinction between prudence and egoism (by including in prudence any desires to do the morally right thing as such). But while my conception of WOW is somewhat normative, it is still an amoral conception of WOW, because I showed how morality is irrelevant to the definition of WOW. My con-

ception of WOW is only somewhat normative, since I conclude, based on my example of Hans, that nothing criticizable or imprudent is a necessary condition of WOW. But I conclude that following the norm of prudence, except in the case at the end of §3, which involves willing to become a new sort of person, is a sufficient condition for strength of will.[18]

Study Questions

1. Is a wholehearted person weak of will just because he or she does an act contrary to his or her better judgment? Consider the case of Cecil in the reading above.

2. Is weakness of will always a moral character flaw? Consider the case of Hans in the reading above.

3. Are the usual cases of weakness of will—for example, overeating, oversleeping, drinking, smoking too much—moral weaknesses or moral errors? Is perfectionism right to classify succumbing to temptation as a vice, for example, classifying overeating as the vice of gluttony?

Notes

1. For a good survey of this work, see Arthur F. Walker, "The Problem of Weakness of Will," *Nous* 23 (1989), pp. 653–76, which has a bibliography of 56 recent works concerning WOW. My paper here concerns incontinent action (i.e., action manifesting WOW). For work on a doxastic analogue of incontinent action, see Alfred R. Mele, "Incontinent Believing," *Philosophical Quarterly* 36 (1986), pp. 212–22.

2. Robert Audi, "Weakness of Will and Practical Judgment," *Nous* 13 (1979), p. 178. See also Audi's "Intending, Intentional Action, and Desire," in Joel Marks, ed., *The Ways of Desire* (Precedent, 1986), 17–38, though §4 seems too kind to internalism, which I discuss later concerning the wholehearted pursuit of evil, and "Acting for Reasons," *Philosophical Review*, 95 (1986), pp. 511–46. All references to Audi below are to his essay in *Nous*.

3. Audi, p. 178.

4. Ibid, pp. 176f.

5. Ibid., p. 181 (emphasis added, except for 'failure').

6. Ibid., p. 183. As we will see, my view leads me to say "that the strong-willed person does not want" instead of *"one ought not to want."*

7. Quantifying the motivational strength of desires may initially seem somewhat problematic, but commonsense clearly accepts ordinal rankings of preferences. Indeed, the concept of *preferring* one thing to another

implies an ordinal ranking. So we need not try to develop a cardinal ranking of preferences to continue to use the metaphorical concept of motivational *strength* (which is a quantifiable concept). One may object that motivational strength is so metaphorical that it is not an empirically testable concept, especially considering the lack of cardinal rankings of preferences. And since psychology is an empirical science, one might conclude that motivational strength is psychologically unhelpful, explaining little or nothing about the psychological phenomenon of WOW. But Santas, citing two psychological studies, shows how motivational strength has empirically testable significance. See Gerasimos Xenophon Santas, *Socrates: Philosophy in Plato's Early Dialogues* (New York: RKP, 1979), pp. 213–14.

8. Audi, p. 183.

9. Ibid., p. 179. Audi actually rejects this formulation of the argument. He rejects the second premise formulated as "if S does A under compulsion, S is not criticizable for doing A." But Audi has reservations about this argument only because he advances a group of counterexamples which he admits includes *no* cases of WOW. Thus, we can easily save the second premise from Audi's reservation, which is irrelevant to WOW, by reformulating the second premise as "if S does A under compulsion and if A is a case of WOW, then S is not criticizable for doing A." Audi admits that the originally formulated argument is valid. My revision of the second premise does not change that.

My revision merely makes clearer what the original context was—cases of WOW. And Audi accepts the first premise (i.e., "if S does A incontinently, then S is in some way criticizable for doing A") and the conclusion (i.e., "incontinent actions are never compelled") of the argument. On all this, see ibid, pp. 179–80.

10. Ibid., p. 180.

11. Donald Davidson, "How Is Weakness of the Will Possible?" in *Essays on Actions & Events* (Oxford: Oxford University Press, 1980).

12. Irving Thalberg, "Acting against One's Better Judgment," in *Weakness of Will*, ed. Geoffrey Mortimer (New York: RKP, 1979), p. 244.

13. See, e.g., "The Conscience of Huckleberry Finn," *Philosophy* 49 (1974), pp. 123–134.

14. Audi, pp. 180f.

15. Ibid., p. 177, Davidson, p. 21, and Thalberg, p. 234.

16. See Harry G. Frankfurt, "Freedom of the Will and the Concept of a Person," *Journal of Philosophy* 68 (1971), especially §11.

17. Robert C. Roberts, "Will Power and the Virtues," in Robert C. Roberts and Robert B. Kroschwitz, eds., *The Virtues: Contemporary Essays on Moral Character* (Belmont, Calif.: Wadsworth, 1987), pp. 125 (emphasis in original).

18. I wish to thank the following for their comments: Carl Ginet, Gordon Graham, John Heil, Alfred Mele, William Rottschaefer, Natalie Vania and Burt Warner.

68

The Ethics of Psychoactive Ads

Michael R. Hyman
Richard Tansey

Author's abstract: Many of today's ads work by arousing the viewer's emotions. Although emotion-arousing ads are widely used and are commonly thought to be effective, their careless use produces a side-effect: the *psychoactive ad*. A psychoactive ad is any emotion-arousing ad that can cause a meaningful, well-defined group of viewers to feel extremely anxious, to feel hostile towards others, or to feel a loss of self-esteem. We argue that, because some ill-conceived psychoactive ads can cause harm, ethical issues must arise during their production. Current pretesting methods cannot identify the potentially psychoactive ads; therefore, we offer some tentative guidelines for reducing the number of viewers harmed by psychoactive ads.

No professional, be he doctor, lawyer, or manager, can promise that he will indeed do good for his client. All he can do is try. But he can promise that he will not knowingly do harm. . . .
                    —Peter F. Drucker, *Management*

. . . [C]oncern for consumer welfare includes an obligation to critically evaluate all marketing techniques that have indeterminate psychological effects.
                    —Spence and Moinpour, 1972, p. 43

Consider the following three ads:

- An announcer first holds up a raw egg and asks the viewer to pretend that this egg is the viewer's brain. He then performs a demonstration: he breaks the egg and drops it into a hot frying pan, saying that this is what drugs do to brains.
- A boy had graduated from high school, and his father had wanted him to attend college. Instead, the boy had joined the Army. After a year, the son now returns home to visit his family. Dad now realizes that the Army has "turned his boy into a man," and therefore accepts his son's decision with a warm welcome.
- A young black stands beside a rural road, awaiting a bus—the one that will take him to college. It arrives; the driver opens the door; the young man stays beside the road as the bus leaves. The voice-over implies that the young man's family cannot afford to send him to college.

The goal of the first ad, which is a public service announcement, is to discourage teen-agers and adults from using drugs; the goal of the second ad is to encourage young men and women to enlist in the U.S. Army; the goal of the third ad is to solicit funds for the United Negro College Fund (UNCF). Each goal seems laudable. We assume that advertisers show these ads because they think them effective in furthering these goals by evoking an emotional response from viewers.

Unfortunately, each of these ads may also evoke an extreme, unintended, emotional response from a meaningful, well-defined group of viewers.

- The anti-drug ad employs a high fear-appeal theme to "scare casual users and non-users straight." However, such an appeal can surely cause great anxiety in many addicted viewers; as a result, some may become suicidal and kill themselves.
- The recruiting ad for the U.S. Army employs a common, unambiguous stereotype to portray conditional love and acceptance; the stereotype of the strong father-figure. However, the depth psychologies of Freud, Jung, and Adler suggest that viewing such a figure could so anger some persons, who have a negative image of father, that they would lash out against their friends and family.
- The UNCF ad may anger some blacks: the ad implies that (1) blacks do not or cannot work their way through college, and (2) black parents do not or cannot save for their children's education. Thus, by ignoring the efforts of many proud, independent blacks, the ad could cause some blacks to feel a loss of self-esteem.[1]

Reprinted from Michael R. Hyman and Richard Tansey, "The Ethics of Psychoactive Drugs," *Journal of Business Ethics* 9 (1990), pp. 105–114. Reprinted by permission of Kluwer Academic Publishers.

These seemingly innocent bits of imagery need, we suggest, more thought than may at first seem necessary.

What Are Psychoactive Ads?

There is a widely-used tool of advertising, the full consequences of which are unknown: the emotion-arousing ad. It may be used by sponsors seeking a specific result, such as the election of a certain politician, or higher sales for their products, or less lung cancer, or more people seeking psychological counseling. Whatever it promotes, it does so by reaching out, grabbing its viewers, and demanding attention. It need not amuse the viewer: it can annoy; it can anger; it can alarm; it can sadden.

One type of emotion-arousing ad is what we call a *psychoactive ad*. A psychoactive ad is any emotion-arousing ad that causes a meaningful, well-defined group of viewers to feel extremely anxious, to feel hostile toward others, or to feel a loss of self-esteem.

Though all psychoactive ads cause viewers to respond emotionally, all ads that cause viewers to respond emotionally are not psychoactive ads. Neither upbeat ads nor warm ads are psychoactive. Upbeat ads are ads that cause viewers to feel alive, cheerful, happy, light-hearted, care-free, and so forth (Edell and Burke, 1987, p. 424). Warm ads are ads that cause viewers to feel a "... positive, mild, volatile emotion involving physiological arousal and precipitated by experiencing directly or vicariously a love, family, or friendship relationship" (Aaker *et al.*, 1986, p. 366).

Table 68-1 describes psychoactive ads, defined and organized by type. On this view, ads that can cause extreme anxiety rely on appeals using pathos, tragedy or heroism, or fear; ads that can cause hostility toward others rely on appeals that incite Freudian, Jungian, or Adlerian complexes, cater to unfashionable value systems, or promise hatred or contempt of others; ads that can cause a loss of self-esteem employ some myth contrary to the viewer's self-image. The value of this speculative schema is presently under empirical study by the authors.

Our discussion of psychoactive ads proceeds as follows. First, we discuss the reasons that emotion-arousing ads are widely-used. Then, we argue that a type of emotion-arousing ad, the psychoactive ad, can cause harm. Next, we discuss why current pretesting methods cannot help advertisers distinguish between merely emotion-arousing ads and psychoactive ads. Finally, we propose some common-

sense ways to reduce the number of viewers harmed by psychoactive ads.

Emotion-Arousing Ads: Current Practice and Theory

Today's advertiser has to work hard for the attention of viewers: viewers are generally inattentive to ads in the first place, they are besieged by many competing ads, and they use VCRs and remote controls to avoid TV ads. Increasingly, advertisers try to grab a viewer's attention by provoking an emotional response.

Advertisers try to arouse emotions for three distinct purposes (Mizerski and White, 1986; Zeitlin and Westwood, 1986):

1. emotions per se can be an important benefit derived from a product or brand;
2. emotions can sometimes help communicate the benefits of a product or brand; and
3. emotions can directly influence attitudes.

Each of these purposes help advertisers sell goods and services.

Many advertising researchers now recommend using emotion-arousing ads. After years of analyzing consumers in terms of information processing, these researchers have begun to acknowledge the importance of emotion-arousing ads.

> For the marketing company, emotion should be considered as an integral, possibly central, aspect of the communication activity (Zeitlin and Westwood, 1986, p. 35).

Furthermore, Mizerski and White (1986) suggest that:

> Emotions might be profitably used to teach consumers to purchase the brand when they find themselves in emotional states they wish to alter or extend (p. 67).

One increasingly common type of emotion-arousing ad, the so-called fear-appeal ad, seems to be highly effective, under some circumstances, on certain demographic and sociopsychological market segments (Stuteville, 1970; Burnett and Wilkes, 1980; Zeitlin and Westwood, 1986). Empirical studies by Thorson and Friestad indicate that subjects better remember and more frequently recall ads that portray fear than they do warm or upbeat ads or ads with no emotional content (as reported in *Psychology Today*, 1985). LaTour and Zahra (1989) indicate that viewers hold more positive attitudes toward fear-appeal ads, when such ads cause them to feel ener-

Table 68-1 Psychoactive Ads: Types, Definitions, and Examples.

Category	Definition	Advertising Examples
Pathos	An ad that shows a helpless person, usually a woman or child, crushed by forces beyond her control. This type of ad does not seek viewer identification, only viewer sympathy.	Some ads about drunk driving (MADD), poverty, child abuse, life insurance, and political candidates (e.g., the 1964 Johnson Atomic Daisy ad).
Tragedy or heroism	An ad that shows a noble person crushed is tragic; one that shows the person overcoming opposition is heroic. These ads often imply that the person's fate is in the viewer's hands.	United Negro College Fund; Save the Children; outreach programs; an ad portraying a desperate wife and child trapped in a bleak situation without cash (American Express ad for MoneyGram).
Fear	An ad that arouses fear in the viewer regarding the effect of the viewer's suboptimal lifestyle.	Anti-smoking ads by the American Cancer Society; anti-cavity toothpaste (Crest); breath-freshening mouthwash (Scope); deodorant soap ("Aren't you glad you use Dial?").
Freudian, Jungian, or Adlerian complexes	An ad that sets up a scene which illustrates one of the neuroses identified by these psychologists.	A man who needs a long-distance phone service because he can't leave his mother (AT&T—Freudian Oedipus complex); a father handing down a tradition to his son (Chivas Regal—Jungian Senex/Puer complex); a coffee-spilling nerd who is pushed aside (AT&T—Adlerian Power complex).
Unfashionable value systems	An ad that says, "when the rest of society condemns you for liking this product, it is just sour grapes." This ad is used to fight popular trends.	A man sneering at vegetables on cheeseburgers (Jack in the Box); "75 years and still smoking" (Camel); "for people who like to smoke" (Benson & Hedges).
Hatred or contempt	An ad that assumes a derogatory or chauvinist stereotype. These ads are often tucked away in specialty magazines.	Love 'em and leave 'em (Playboy ad for "Scotch" cologne); NBA basketball star (Michael Jordan) shows contempt for small, intellectual male (Spike Lee) by dunking a basketball in the intellectual's face (Air Jordan sports shoes).
Myth	An ad that ties a product to a mythical figure or lifestyle.	Rough, two-fisted woodsmen (Jack Daniels); party till you drop (some tequilas): "Marlboro country" (Marlboro); pictures of bloodied lineman in football ad with headline, "*You think your* day was tough (ESPN);" Jolly Green Giant; Tony the Tiger (Frosted Flakes).

gized, rather than tense. (Aaker, *et al.*, 1986; Burke and Edell, 1989; and Edell and Burke, 1987, claim that a positive attitude toward an ad enhances any already favorable attitude toward the brand and increases the intention to buy the brand.)

Because advertisers and advertising researchers consider fear-appeal and other emotion-arousing ads to be effective ads, we see such ads frequently. However, some advertisers try to create emotion-arous-ing ads that work "psychoactively." As Freedman (1988) reports:

> Advertisers have long known that commercials that make you feel good are likely to make you feel good about the product. But, more recent research indicates that advertisers might be able to do even better with ads that evoke unpleasant feelings. If getting you to suffer will boost sales, don't expect advertisers to shrink from the task (Freedman, 1988, p. 6).

Thus, emotion-arousing ads are widely used because advertisers believe such ads are effective. However, many emotion-arousing ads are also psychoactive ads. Because we believe psychoactive ads can cause harm, we now argue that it is unethical to carelessly or ruthlessly produce such ads.

The Argument

Consider the following hypothetical example: Boris, a misguided social scientist, believes that frequent exposure to emotion-arousing television ads about the horrors of child abuse causes some postpartum depressive mothers to commit infanticide. To test his belief, Boris conducts an experiment. First, he develops the following null hypothesis:

> H_0 The probability that a mother, suffering from postpartum depression, will commit infanticide is independent of her exposure to emotion-arousing television ads about child abuse.

Boris then produces several 60-second emotion-arousing ads about the horrors of child abuse. Next, he infiltrates the offices of several local hospitals and the TV-Tyme Cable Company. (The TV-Tyme Cable Company operates a sophisticated, uniquely addressable split-cable system with subscriber-monitoring capabilities.) From stolen patient lists and subscriber lists, Boris selects 200 households, each one with (1) a new mother who suffers from postpartum depression, and (2) a subscription to TV-Tyme Cable. He assigns 100 of these households to a control group, and 100 of these households to an experimental group. Next, for one month, he manipulates all advertising televised to each household in the experimental group as follows: for each viewing session, 60 seconds of Boris' child abuse ads replace the first 60 seconds of scheduled advertising. In the homes of the control group, a neutral ad replaces any televised ad against child abuse. After one month, Boris finds, as he expects, that the number of infanticides is significantly higher in the experimental group than in the control group. Thus, Boris rejects his null hypothesis.

We are morally offended by such an experiment, one which would not be performed by any reputable social scientist. What are the reasons for calling Boris' experiment immoral? First, we already know that women who suffer from postpartum depression are prone to infanticide (O'Hara, 1986). Common sense tells us that subjecting them to such disturbing images and violent thoughts would ensure that at least some of them would hurt themselves or their infants. Second, because we feel certain that any intelligent person could see the danger of such an "experiment," we condemn Boris for his actions. In short, Boris is unethical because he does harm, and because he knew, or should have known, that he was doing harm.

Now consider the following realistic situation. The policy of television superstation KABC is to regularly broadcast emotion-arousing public service announcements designed to reduce child abuse. Many postpartum depressives across American who subscribe to a television cable service do in fact see many of these ads. For these postpartum depressives, such ads are psychoactive ads; such ads may cause them to feel hostile toward their newborn children. Because far more than a hundred postpartum depressive mothers regularly view such ads, KABC's management thoughtlessly replicates Boris' unethical experiment almost every day.

Thus, the argument suggests that the management of superstation KABC is acting at least as unethically as Boris, the misguided scientist.

Is the Argument Reasonable?

Somehow, the parallel between the noble efforts of KABC's management and Boris' highly unethical experiment may seem weak. The argument might seem unfair for any of the following reasons:

- The intentions are different. The public service announcements aim at preventing child abuse, and thus saving children's lives, whereas Boris' experiment invites murder.
- Any ad could provoke some well-defined group of people. Thus, if the argument is taken to its logical conclusion, all advertising would be immoral. The legal implications would be staggering; advertising as we know it would disappear simply from the prohibitive costs of product liability insurance.
- The argument uses scare tactics; it preys on the reader's pity by using images of women and children. It relies on sentimentality, apparently to muddy the issue, rather than clarify it.

We will examine these objections one at a time.

Scare Tactics

To object to the argument because it uses scare tactics is to object to scare tactics, whether we use them or advertisers use them. Thus, the objection concedes the argument.

Scare tactics are often used by people who have non-substantive arguments. But people who have good arguments also use them to make their point memorable. The presence of scare tactics does not invalidate an argument.

Put aside the image, for a moment, and look at the structure of the argument. The structure is simple and clear:

· Many groups of people are known to be hurt or offended by exposure to certain images.
· Hurting or offending people is wrong.

· Therefore, to show these images publicly, knowing that members of these groups cannot help but see them and be hurt or offended, is wrong.

To circumvent the scare-tactic objection, simply pick another group of highly sensitive people plus an appropriate, but disturbing image. Then restate the argument in those terms. Some possibilities would be: people who have just lost a spouse, plus a "keep in touch" ad; recent amputees plus a "be all that you can be" ad; and so forth. Pick one that does not seem unfair, yet fits the argument outlined above.

Intended Results

Let us strengthen the example. Suppose that the televising of emotion-arousing child abuse ads by KABC caused five more infanticides that would have occurred without the televising. Suppose also that fifty more child-beaters sought professional help than otherwise would have; as a result, ten fewer children died from abuse. The net results of televising the ads would then be that five more children lived than would otherwise have lived. The management of KABC can therefore claim a net benefit to society, whereas Boris has no such defense. How can we say the cases are parallel?

This objection might look powerful on a casual glance, were it not that saving some lives is always a poor excuse for taking others. The objection ignores the issue of whether it is right to expose a person against his or her will to harmful or seriously offen-

sive images. One must suspect that a thoughtful management of KABC could have found a way of doing good without also doing harm. In failing to look for a solution, these managers were not malicious, as was Boris, but negligent.

Taken to Its Logical Conclusion, All Advertising Is Immoral

If any ad could trigger an anti-social response from a group of vulnerable viewers, why wouldn't all ads be dangerous? What would keep the courts from being inundated with complaints about injuries caused by broadcasted or printed ads? Surely ads are not so sinister, surely the argument with such an absurd outcome must be absurd.

Consider the following seemingly parallel example. Bathtubs are dangerous; many people slip and seriously injure themselves in bathtub accidents. Any ad that *increases* the number of baths also increases the number of accidents. The argument seems to lead to the absurd conclusion that advertising bath products is immoral. Aren't the arguments parallel?

No, the cases are very different. A person chooses to take a bath, but emotional responses to psychoactive ads are not freely chosen. Thus, the real issue is not one of producing bad consequences, but of preying on vulnerable innocents.

Furthermore, the bath product company could act morally to reduce the number of bathtub accidents. In fact, the problem of bathtub accidents, if recognized, could even become a marketing opportunity. The ethically-minded bath product company could choose to run this special promotion: mail in five proofs-of-purchase of their product and receive a free bath safety mat. Thus, even the conclusion of the bath argument is not as absurd as it sounded at first. Advertising any dangerous product, whether it be bathtubs, beer, or blasting caps, may be done more or less responsibly.

Protecting Viewers from Psychoactive Ads

Viewers cannot expect government to regulate the use of emotion-arousing ads.

> If the advertising industry gets any better at employing subtle psychological strategies . . . it may become

nearly impossible [for viewers] to figure out the ways in which commercials are hitting home. That may be a little frightening, but it's not illegal—so don't expect the government to protect . . . [viewers] from high-tech advertising, at least not in today's climate of deregulation. In the end, it's strictly viewer beware (Freedman, 1988, p. 7).

Thus, the community of advertisers is morally responsible for vulnerable viewers. Perhaps this is just as well; free markets prefer self-regulation to government intervention, *ceteris paribus*.

How should advertisers protect vulnerable viewers from psychoactive ads? An obvious suggestion would be to pretest each emotion-arousing ad. If a pretest suggests that a well-defined, meaningful group of viewers will psychoactively respond to an ad, that ad should not be shown to that group. If it is impossible, even through careful media targeting, to protect these viewers from that ad, then that ad should be discarded.

LaTour and Zahra (1989) advocate using such pretests to identify unethical (i.e., tension-producing) fear-appeal ads.

> Each ad, even those with a supposed "low level" fear appeal, should be evaluated. . . . Extensive pretests of each ad should be performed to ensure effective balance between the message and associated levels of tension (p. 68).

One common pretesting method involves showing an ad to a group and then asking them about it. Unfortunately, such a procedure is problematic.

> The mental or cognitive activity prompted by the advertising may often operate at a level below conscious awareness. In other words, the cognitive activity initiated by the emotional cues in an advertisement may occur so rapidly that the individual cannot observe and report on the process as it happens. This has significant implications on the choice of copytesting procedures. Because of the unconscious mental activity, data gathering techniques based on verbal self-reports may be totally ineffective for gauging the intensity of type of emotional experience(s) developed after exposure to the ad (Mizerski and White, 1986, p. 62).

Because viewers may be unable to report psychoactive responses to an ad, such pretests are not the complete answer.

Along similar lines, advertisers could pretest their emotion-arousing ads by exposing them, in a controlled setting, to hundreds of subjects hooked to psychophysiological apparatuses. Unfortunately, these apparatuses only measure a subject's level of activation; they do not identify the activated emotions, nor do they suggest the potential consequences of these emotions. Furthermore, marketing researchers suggest that our present knowledge of psychophysiological responses is too primitive for us to apply them practically (Rothschild *et al*, 1986; Stewart and Furst, 1982). Therefore, such pretests are not the full answer either.

LaTour and Zahra (1989) suggest another alternative in their discussion of fear-appeal ads:

> To minimize abuse of fear appeals, some effective, functional and practical ethical guidelines need to be adopted by firms sponsoring such advertising (p. 68).

Thus, we propose that advertisers adopt the following simple practices whenever they design and place an emotion-arousing ad.

Three Simple Practices

Carefully Target the Medium as Well as the Market

Obviously, to guard against every possible negative side-effect of an ad would be impossible. First, psychotics cannot be outguessed; because they will interpret even the dullest images to fit their delusions, no amount of care taken over an ad will remove all chances of its doing harm to these people. Second, if a person named Spuds MacKenzie were to die in a freak yachting accident, his bereaved wife might be upset by some recent Budweiser commercials; Anheuser Busch cannot and should not plan for these circumstances.

Instead of worrying over unique psychoses or strange coincidences, advertisers should use common sense and psychological theory to identify large groups of people whose members are prone to be hurt by the images used in emotion-arousing ads.

Advertisers will easily recognize some groups. For example, common sense (as well as psychological research) suggests that the following groups may respond psychoactively to emotion-arousing ads:

1. AIDS victims (Atkinson *et al.* [1988] report that many are deeply psychologically disturbed);
2. Vietnam combat veterans (Pitman *et al.* [1987] report that these veterans are highly susceptible to combat-reminding imagery);
3. young women (Gould [1987] and Regier *et al.* [1988] suggest that many [i.e., 10%] have anxi-

ety disorders because they are prone to be publicly self-conscious and socially anxious);

4. young men (Caprara *et al.* [1987] report that young males who first viewed aggressive ads then acted more aggressively toward other males); and

5. compulsive gamblers (Roy *et al.* [1988] report that compulsive gamblers are attracted to sensation-seeking events).

It will be more difficult for advertisers to recognize other groups. One not-so-obvious group is non-institutionalized adults with affective disorders or anxiety disorders. (A survey by the National Institute of Mental Health [Regier *et al.*, 1988] found that, of non-institutionalized adults, 5.1% had affective disorders and 7.3% had anxiety disorders.) Persons with affective or anxiety disorders have high levels of *negative affectivity*. Negative affectivity (NA) reflects pervasive individual differences in negative emotionality and in self-concept: high-NA individuals tend toward distress, aggression (sadistic or masochistic), and negative self-image (Watson and Clark, 1984). Relative to low-NAs, high-NAs are more likely to (1) identify with any aggressive, anti-social behavior shown in ads, (2) read negative things into ads, and (3) dwell on threats and loss of self-esteem posed by ads (Watson and Clark, 1984). Thus, high-NAs are more likely to respond "psychoactively" to emotion-arousing ads.

This leads us to our first recommended practice: *Advertisers should carefully target the medium as well as the market.*

Because the ad rates charged by broadcasters and publishers are based largely on audience size, advertisers have long recognized the economic reasons for advertising in just the media viewed, heard, or read by their current and likely customers. But now, it seems that there are also ethical reasons for targeting.

For example, specialized magazines, such as *Field & Stream, Ebony, American Baby, Soldier of Fortune, Millionaire,* and *Hustler,* to name but a few, have special, fairly well-defined audiences. A reader of one of these magazines comes to expect certain types of ads and certain types of thematic emotional appeals. By recognizing the acceptable appeals for the readers of these magazines, advertisers can create appropriate ads. Such a precaution will not only reduce one source of unwanted side-effects, but it would also cost the advertiser less than the less responsible approach

Clearly Label Psychoactive Ads

A general rule of thumb for designing emotion-arousing ad is: Give the viewer a fair chance to avoid the climax of the ad. This rule is based on two assumptions: (1) viewers know best which images they can tolerate and which they cannot, and (2) viewers threatened by an image used in an ad will actively avoid it *if they are given a fair chance to do so.* As Caprara *et al.* (1987) suggest,

> [I]n the case of programmes such as movies, cartoons, and championship fights, the audience is always free to select and therefore, to a certain extent, be prepared to see what is portrayed on the screen . . . [I]n the case of commercials, because of their unexpectedness, their effects are usually out of the viewer's control. . . . [In] television advertising one has the impression that the viewer is often left to the mercy of the advertising agent (Caprara *et al.,* 1987, p. 24).

This rule does not cover every possibility, but it does offer a useful guide for most normal cases.

Thus, our second recommended practice is: *Advertisers should introduce their emotion-arousing ads with an announcement.*

If viewers know of the strong nature of the imagery or themes prior to their onset, they have ample time to decide whether to see or avoid the ad. Advertisers could place brief warnings, in advance of a video or radio ad, or at the heading of printed copy, about the nature of the ad, much as warnings often precede the airings of movies or political announcements. For example,

> Due to its emotional subject matter, the following pro-abortion message may be offensive to some people.

This practice requires that the advertiser keeps the element of choice in mind while considering the ethics of a proposed course of action. If the viewer of a visual image has consciously chosen, on the basis of accurate information, to see it, responsibility for the consequences is shared by the maker and the viewer of the image. Many people will not willingly watch a movie which they suspect contains intolerable images. Nonetheless, these same people, in watching an ad, may find themselves besieged by the same images, held off until the last few seconds. People consciously censor what they view, and it is not the legitimate prerogative of an advertiser to override these efforts at psychological self-protection.

On the other hand, such warnings could do no harm. By taking the trouble to warn the audience about the content of a commercial, advertisers could actually draw more attention to their ads—attention, that is, from those people who are the proper targets.

Advertisers should note that content-specific warnings, i.e., warnings that refer to specific ad content, may actually sensitize viewers, and thus increase the negative effects of psychoactive ads. In studying the effect of forewarning on a viewer's emotional response to horror films, Cantor, Ziemke, and Clark (1984) found that the more explicit the forewarning about the graphic nature of the film, the greater the viewer's fright and upset. Thus, advertisers should be careful, even in their forewarning, to use only the most general warning messages.

Avoid Trick Endings

Trick endings appear often in ads that rely on appeals using pathos, tragedy or heroism, or fear. A trick ending is an unexpected plot twist, such as a MADD ad in which a little girl, happily playing along the side of a road, is suddenly killed by an intoxicated truck driver.

Clearly, such ads are designed to shock viewers into modifying inappropriate attitudes (e.g., it is acceptable to first imbibe, and then drive) and behaviors (e.g., driving when intoxicated). Though shocking ads may save some lives, such ads will also cause many viewers to feel tense (LaTour and Zahra, 1989). When these ads cause many susceptible viewers to feel extreme anxiety, these ads become psychoactive ads. Thus, advertisers should refrain, for ethical reasons, from showing such ads.

If the ending is really a trick, viewers have no chance to avoid it. Although a clever twist may be amusing when used for humor, it should never be used for a powerful, emotion-arousing message.

Thus, our third recommended practice, which also follows from our rule of thumb, is: *Advertisers should avoid trick endings in their ads.* This practice should minimize the abusive use of fear appeals.

Conclusion

Advertisers often use emotion-arousing ads to promote goods, services, and ideas. We have argued that, because emotion-arousing ads are often psychoactive, advertisers should take care when they deploy them.

We therefore propose some simple rules for a more responsible use of emotion-arousing ads. These rules would neither hobble such ads nor greatly increase their cost.

Study Questions

*1. If there were a subliminal advertising technique so effective it could induce people to make purchases they would otherwise resist, would you want to ban it? What about an equally effective technique that wasn't subliminal but was just a great pitch strongly appealing to people's hopes and fears?

*2. If you were a salesperson working on commission, might you sometimes misrepresent a product to sell it? Is such a deceptive salesperson any worse than a similarly deceptive psychoactive ad?

*3. Does it offend you when you are misled with half-truths in a business deal? What do you see as the ethical distinction between lying and intentionally leading people astray by cleverly omitting key parts of a story?

Note

1. In a pretest designed to help us select the psychoactive ads we would use in a subsequent empirical study, one of the authors received such responses from a large number of black subjects.

References

Aaker, David A, Douglas M. Stayman, and Michael R. Hagerty: 1986, "Warmth in Advertising: Measurement, Impact, and Sequence Effects", *Journal of Consumer Research* 12, 365–381.

Atkinson, J. Hampton, Igor Grant, Caroline J. Kennedy, Douglas D. Richman, Stephen A. Spector, and J. Allen McCutchan: 1988, "Prevalence of Psychiatric Disorders among Men Infected with Human Immunodeficiency Virus", *Archives of General Psychiatry* 45, 859–864.

Burke, Marian Chapman, and Julie A. Edell: 1989, "The Impact of Feelings on Ad-Based Affect and Cognition", *Journal of Marketing Research* 26, 69–83.

Burnett, John J., and Robert E. Wilkes: 1980, "Fear Appeals to Segments Only", *Journal of Advertising Research* 20, 21–24.

Cantor, Joanne, Dean Ziemke, and Glenn G. Sparks: 1984, "Effect of Forewarning on Emotional Responses to a Horror Film", *Journal of Broadcasting* 28, 21–31.

Caprara, G. V., G. D'Imperio, A. Gentilomo, A. Mammucari, P. Renzi, and G. Travaglia: 1987, "The Intrusive Commercial: Influence of Aggressive TV Commercials on Aggression", *European Journal of Social Psychology* 17 (1), 23–31.

Drucker, Peter: 1973, *Management: Tasks, Responsibilities, Practices* (Harper and Row, New York).

Edell, Julie A., and Marian Chapman Burke: 1987, "The Power of Feelings in Understanding Advertising Effects", *Journal of Consumer Research* 14, 421–433.

Freedman, David H.: 1988, "Why We Watch Certain Commercials", *TV Guide* 36 (8), 4–7.

Gould, Stephen J.: "Gender Differences in Advertising Response and Self-Consciousness Variables," *Sex Roles* 16, 215–225.

LaTour, Michael S., and Shaker A. Zahra: 1989, "Fear Appeals as Advertising Strategy: Should They Be Used?", *The Journal of Consumer Marketing* 6 (2), 61–70.

Mizerski, Richard W., and J. Dennis White: 1986, "Understanding and Using Emotions in Advertising", *The Journal of Consumer Marketing* 3 (3), 57–69.

O'Hara, Michael W.: 1986, "Social Support, Life Events, and Depression during Pregnancy and the Puerperium", *Archives of General Psychiatry* 43, 569–573.

Pitman, Roger K., Scott P. Orr, Dennis F. Forgue, Jacob B. deJong, and James M. Claiborn: 1987, "Psychophysiologic Assessment of Posttraumatic Stress Disorder Imagery in Vietnam Combat Veterans", *Archives of General Psychiatry* 44, 970–975.

Psychology Today: 1985, "Advertising: Sold on Emotion", 19 (3), 9.

Regier, Darrel A., Jeffrey H. Boyd, Jack D. Burke, Donald S. Rae, Jerome K. Myers, Morton Kramer, Lee N. Robins, Linda K. George, Marvin Karno, and Ben Z. Locke: 1988, "One-Month Prevalence of Mental Disorders in the United States", *Archives of General Psychiatry* 45, 977–986.

Rothschild, Michael L., Ester Thorson, Byron Reeves, Judith E. Hirsch, and Robert Goldstein: 1986, "EEG Activity and the Processing of Television Commercials", *Communication Research* 13, 182–220.

Roy, Alex, Byron Adinoff, Laurie Roehrich, Danuta Lamparski, Robert Custer, Valerie Lorenz, Maria Barbaccia, Alessandro Guidotti, Erminio Costa, and Markku Linnoila: 1988, "Pathological Gambling", *Archives of General Psychiatry* 45, 369–373.

Spence, Homer E., and Resa Moinpour: 1972, "Fear Appeals in Marketing: A Social Perspective", *Journal of Marketing* 36 (3), 39–43.

Stewart, David W., and David H. Furse: 1982, "Applying Psychophysiological Measures to Marketing and Advertising Research Problems", in *Current Issues and Research in Advertising*, James H. Leigh and Claude R. Martin, editors (University of Michigan, Ann Arbor, MI), 1–38.

Stuteville, John R.: 1970, "Psychic Defenses against High Fear Appeals: A Key Marketing Variable", *Journal of Marketing* 34, 39–45.

Watson, David, and Lee Anna Clark: 1984, "Negative Affectivity: The Disposition to Experience Aversive Emotional States", *Psychological Bulletin* 96, 465–490.

Zeitlin, David M., and Richard A. Westwood: 1986, "Measuring Emotional Response", *Journal of Advertising Research* 26, 34–44.

"THIS RESUMÉ IS ONE OF THE MOST BOASTFUL, DECEPTIVE PIECES OF FRAUD I'VE EVER SEEN. YOU'RE HIRED."

© 1995 by Sidney Harris.

69

Fraud

Sterling Harwood

Type of Ethics: Legal and judicial ethics

Date: Coined 1330

Definition: Intentional deception intended to give one some advantage in a transaction

Significance: Ethicists believe that fraud is one of the fundamental kinds of unethical acts

---

The long history of ethical condemnation of deception helps to show fraud's significance to ethics; in the Judeo-Christian tradition, for example, one of the Ten Commandments is "Thou shalt not bear false witness." This commandment is broad enough to cover fraud.

The famous English Statute of Frauds, which was passed in 1677 and has now been adopted in one form or another in almost every part of the United States, requires that one must "get it in writing" before one can sue to recover more than a specific monetary amount (for example, $500) or to enforce a contract that extends beyond a certain period of time (for example, one year). The statute's point was to reduce the number of claims regarding purported fraud. Leaving important matters to memories of oral statements resulted too often in cases that pitted one person's word against another's.

Good faith precludes fraud even when honest mistakes are made. The classic slogan defining good faith is "white heart and empty head," which refers to having good intentions but being stupid. Stupid mistakes are not fraud.

Reprinted from Sterling Harwood, "Fraud," in *Ready Reference: Ethics* (Pasadena, Calif.: Salem Press, 1994). Reprinted by permission.

Deceptive advertising is a matter of degree, but at some point, exaggeration becomes fraud. This is especially true of intentionally false quantitative claims. Qualitative claims are difficult to classify as fraud, since quality is characteristically a matter of opinion rather than fact. Therefore, U.S. law recognizes "puffing" as nonfraudulent falsehood. Puffing is, essentially, an overstatement of the quality of something that is being sold. An example of puffing is a cologne maker's claim that Cologne X makes one as "mysterious as the wind." Furthermore, if the falsehood is so obvious that no reasonable person would be deceived by it, then stating that falsehood does not constitute fraud. (For example, one brand of toothpaste was sold with the claim that it would straighten teeth!)

Fraud can be committed by either commission or omission. A fraud of commission involves lying or making some other type of material misrepresentation. A fraud of omission involves the failure to disclose some significant fact that the law requires to be disclosed. Libertarianism, and ethical principle that has been politically influential, endorses the idea of *caveat emptor* ("Let the buyer beware") rather than the idea that some bureaucracy should interfere with the free market by legally requiring disclosures. Libertarianism supports laissez-faire capitalism with only minimal government and opposes the welfare state that began with President Franklin Delano Roosevelt's New Deal. Libertarianism condemns fraud but defines it narrowly, requiring that a lie be committed for fraud to exist.

Egalitarianism, by contrast, is an ethical principle that allows the mere withholding of information to be considered fraud. Egalitarians condemn exploitation, which involves taking advantage of an innocent person's predicament. Therefore, egalitarians support laws defining fraud so as to include the failure to disclose key facts. Libertarians do not recognize the applicability of the concept of exploitation in its ethically pejorative sense. They view charging whatever the market will bear, for example, not as exploitation but as entrepreneurship, which they see as a virtue. The two approaches of libertarianism and egalitarianism correspond at least roughly to actual fraud and constructive fraud, respectively. Actual fraud involves some active deception or lie. Constructive fraud includes any act of commission or omission that is contrary to law or fair play.

As Richard Whately has said, "All frauds, like the wall daubed with untempered mortar . . . always tend to the decay of what they are devised to support." The law tries to enhance this ethical tendency by punishing fraud.

Study Questions

1. Libertarianism condemns fraud and allows the government to assume a role in detecting and punishing it. But given libertarianism's endorsement of caveat emptor, let the buyer beware, and its insistence on having minimal government, why does libertarianism make an exception for fraud? Is libertarianism inconsistent here?

2. Does fraud always involve lying? Can the truth be so misleading that telling the truth would be fraud?

Bibliography

Beringer, Johann Bartholomans. *The Lying Stones of Dr. Johan Bartholomans Adam Beringer*. Berkeley, Calif.: University of California Press, 1963.

Bok, Sissela. *Lying: Moral Choice in Public and Private Life*. New York: Pantheon Books, 1978.

_____. *Secrets*. New York: Pantheon Books, 1982.

Broad, William, and Nicholas Wade. *Betrayers of the Truth*. New York: Simon & Schuster, 1982.

Cahn, Steven M. *Saints and Scamps: Ethics in Academia*. Totowa, N.J.: Rowman & Littlefield, 1986.

Gould, Stephen Jay. *The Mismeasure of Man*. New York: W. W. Norton, 1981.

Kant, Immanuel. *Critique of Practical Reason and Other Writings in Moral Philosophy*. Edited and translated by Lewis White Beck. Chicago: University of Chicago Press, 1949.

Magnuson, Warren G., and Jean Carper. *The Dark Side of the Marketplace: The Plight of the American Consumer*. Englewood Cliffs, N.J.: Prentice-Hall, 1968.

Newman, John Henry Cardinal. *Apologia Pro Vita Sua: Being a History of His Religious Opinions*. New York: Modern Library, 1950.

Plato, *Republic*. 2d rev. ed. Harmondsworth, England: Penguin Books, 1986.

Rawlins, Dennis. *Peary at the North Pole: Fact or Fiction?* Washington, D.C.: Robert B. Luce, 1973.

Weiner, J. S. *The Piltdown Forgery*. London: Oxford University Press, 1955.

70

The Oil Seller

Lu Tung Pin

Editor's note: Scholars consider Lu Tung Pin to be one of the three most popular of the Eight Immortals of Taoism. The moral of this story concerns the surprising benefits of honesty in business.

Lu Tung Pin liked to travel about in disguise to test the honesty of people on earth. It was always his job to give to those who were honest the understanding of the Tao and the chance of immortality.

One day he decided to become an oil seller. Dressing himself up and carrying his barrels of oil, he set off to find anyone who would accept his measure of oil for a fixed and just price.

At first he was very hopeful and journeyed to the nearby city to sell his wares. The first house he went up to was a very grand place so he knocked at the main door. The doorman opened it and scowled at Lu Tung Pin.

"What do you want?" he demanded.

"To sell you a little oil," replied Lu Tung Pin.

"Then get round to the back door. Only gentlemen come through this door." And so saying he suddenly lashed out with his boot and kicked Lu Tung Pin down the stairs.

Picking himself up, Lu Tung Pin trudged round to the back door. But he got little encouragement there. The doorman had already told the kitchen staff about the oil seller who had come to the front door. When Lu Tung Pin knocked, he was treated as a joke and the rubbish was tipped over him. Filled with anger, Lu Tung Pin was tempted to strike the whole

house down. But he decided to leave them to their own foolish ways.

Over the next few days, he tried to sell his oil in the market place. Everyone wanted to barter with him but when he told them that the price was fixed, noone would believe him. They were sure that he must be trying to trick them, so they would not buy.

Lu Tung Pin soon tired of the city and thought that he might be better off in a smaller place. So he travelled to the nearby town and approached the smartest house. Remembering his painful experience in the city, he knocked at the back door. A friendly young woman opened the door and asked what he was selling. He told her he was selling oil. Suddenly a gruff voice sounded from within the house. "Who is at the door?" The young woman looked frightened and said it was an oil seller. "Tell him to come in," said the gruff voice.

When Lu Tung Pin came inside the biggest man he had ever seen was seated at a table. "How much are you charging for your oil?" asked the man. When he heard what Lu Tung Pin was charging, he frowned and said, "I'll give you half your price." When Lu Tung Pin refused, he said, "Then I will take it anyway," and he rose to his feet with a menacing look on his face.

Lu Tung Pin was not sure what to do. He could see the woman was very frightened, so he decided to face up to this bully. Lu Tung Pin whisked his fly whisk out and waved it in the giant's direction. There was a loud bang and the giant disappeared. Bowing politely to the terrified woman, he made his way out of the house and decided that perhaps the town was not the right place for him either. So he went to the local village.

But he fared no better in the village. People tried to trick him or simply ignored him. Eventually, after weeks of wandering and trying, he came at last to an isolated country lane. As he passed a tiny, tumbledown farm, a woman ran out to him. "Please can I buy some oil from you, for I have almost none left?" Lu Tung Pin hesitated. He did not want to say yes, because he was afraid that the woman would not have enough money to pay the fair price. But he had to stick to what he had agreed with himself. So he named his price. To his astonishment and delight, the woman agreed and ran back to get the money.

Lu Tung Pin followed her and saw the poverty of her house and little farm. As the woman was finding the coins, Lu Tung Pin took a few grains of rice and threw them into the well. Then he turned and received the money and gave the woman her oil. With that he wished her well and went on his way. It was not until later that day that the woman went to draw water from the well. Imagine her astonishment when she found the well did not give her water, but wine! She drew another bucket full. More wine! She soon discovered that whenever she drew water, it was wine.

Within weeks she opened a wine shop. People came from miles around to buy her wine, for it had a most wonderful taste. Within a very short time she was able to rebuild her farm and within a year or two, she was one of the wealthiest people in the area and much sought after by the eligible bachelors of the area. And all this came about because she had been honest.

Study Questions

1. Is this just a story, or does it make a more general point applicable to many other cases?

2. If we try to generalize from just this one story, will we be committing the fallacy of hasty generalization?

"IT WON'T BOTHER US IF WE'RE NOT ALLOWED TO AIM OUR ADS AT THE KIDS. THE ADULTS ARE EASIER TO FOOL ANYWAY."

71

Federal Trade Commission v. Colgate-Palmolive Co. et al.

Supreme Court of the United States

The basic question before us is whether it is a deceptive trade practice, prohibited by § 5 of the Federal Trade Commission Act, to represent falsely that a televised test, experiment, or demonstration provides a viewer with visual proof of a product claim, regardless of whether the product claim is itself true. The case arises out of an attempt by respondent Colgate-Palmolive Company to prove to the television public that its shaving cream, "Rapid Shave," outshaves them all. Respondent Ted Bates & Company, Inc., an advertising agency, prepared for Colgate three one-minute commercials designed to show that Rapid Shave could soften even the toughness of sandpaper. Each of the commercials contained the same "sandpaper test." The announcer informed the audience that, "To prove RAPID SHAVE'S super-moisturizing power, we put it right from the can onto this tough, dry sandpaper. It was apply . . . soak . . . and off in a stroke." While the announcer was speaking, Rapid Shave was applied to a substance that appeared to be sandpaper, and immediately thereafter a razor was shown shaving the substance clean.

The Federal Trade Commission issued a complaint against respondents Colgate and Bates charging that the commercials were false and deceptive. The evidence before the hearing examiner disclosed that sandpaper of the type depicted in the commercials could not be shaved immediately following the application of Rapid Shave, but required a substantial soaking period of approximately 80 minutes. The evidence also showed that the substance resembling sandpaper was in fact a simulated prop, or "mockup" made of plexiglass, to which sand had been applied. However, the examiner found that Rapid Shave could shave sandpaper, even though not in the short time

*380 U.S. 374 (1964), 85 S. Ct. 1035, 13 L. Ed. 2nd 904. Opinion by Chief Justice Earl Warren. The footnotes have been omitted.

represented by the commercials, and that if real sandpaper had been used in the commercials the inadequacies of television transmission would have made it appear to viewers to be nothing more than plain colored paper. The examiner dismissed the complaint because neither misrepresentation—concerning the actual moistening time or the identity of the shaved substance—was in his opinion a material one that would mislead the public.

The Commission, in 1961, reversed the hearing examiner. It found that since Rapid Shave could not shave sandpaper within the time depicted in the commercials, respondents had misrepresented the product's moisturizing power. Moreover, the Commission found that the undisclosed use of a plexiglass substitute for sandpaper was an additional material misrepresentation that was a deceptive act separate and distinct from the misrepresentation concerning Rapid Shave's underlying qualities. Even if the sandpaper could be shaved just as depicted in the commercials, the Commission found that viewers had been misled into believing they had seen it done with their own eyes. As a result of these findings, the Commission entered a cease-and-desist order against the respondents.

An appeal was taken to the Court of Appeals for the First Circuit which rendered an opinion on November 20, 1962. That court sustained the Commission's conclusion that respondents had misrepresented the qualities of Rapid Shave, but it would not accept the order forbidding the future use of undisclosed simulations in television commercials. It set aside the Commission's order and directed that a new order be entered. On May 7, 1963, the Commission, over the protest of respondents, issued a new order narrowing and clarifying its original order to comply with the court's mandate. The Court of Appeals again found unsatisfactory that portion of the order dealing with simulated props and refused to enforce it. We . . . consider this aspect of the case and do not have before us any question concerning the misrepresentation that Rapid Shave could shave sandpaper immediately after application, that being conceded. . . .

We are not concerned in this case with the clear misrepresentation in the commercials concerning the speed with which Rapid Shave could shave sandpaper, since the Court of Appeals upheld the Commission's finding on that matter and the respondents have not challenged the finding here. We granted certiorari to consider the Commission's conclusion that even if an advertiser has himself conducted a test, experiment or demonstration which he honestly believes will prove a certain product claim, he may not convey to television viewers the false impression that they are seeing the test, experiment or demonstration for themselves, when they are not because of the undisclosed use of mock-ups.

We accept the commission's determination that the commercials involved in this case contained three representations to the public: (1) that sandpaper could be shaved by Rapid Shave; (2) that an experiment had been conducted which verified this claim; and (3) that the viewer was seeing this experiment for himself. Respondents admit that the first two representations were made, but deny that the third was. The Commission, however, found to the contrary, and, since this is a matter of fact resting on an inference that could reasonably be drawn from the commercials themselves, the Commission's finding should be sustained. For the purposes of our review, we can assume that the first two representations were true; the focus of our consideration is on the third, which was clearly false. The parties agree that § 5 prohibits the intentional misrepresentation of any fact which would constitute a material factor in a purchaser's decision whether to buy. They differ, however, in their conception of what "facts" constitute a "material factor" in a purchaser's decision to buy. Respondents submit, in effect, that the only material facts are those which deal with the substantive qualities of a product. The Commission, on the other hand, submits that the misrepresentation of *any* fact so long as it materially induces a purchaser's decision to buy is a deception prohibited by § 5.

The Commission's interpretation of what is a deceptive practice seems more in line with the decided cases than that of respondents. This Court said in *Federal Trade Comm'n v. Algoma Lumber Co.*: "[T]he public is entitled to get what it chooses, though the choice may be dictated by caprice or by fashion or perhaps by ignorance." It has long been considered a deceptive practice to state falsely that a product ordinarily sells for an inflated price but that it is being offered at a special reduced price, even if the offered price represents the actual value of the product and the purchaser is receiving his money's worth. Applying respondents' arguments to these cases, it would appear that so long as buyers paid no more than the product was actually worth and the product contained the qualities advertised, the misstatement of an inflated original price was immaterial.

It had also been held a violation of § 5 for a seller to misrepresent to the public that he is in a certain line of business, even though the misstatement in no way affects the qualities of the product. As was said in *Federal Trade Comm'n v. Royal Milling Co.*:

> If consumers or dealers prefer to purchase a given article because it was made by a particular manufacturer or class of manufacturers, they have a right to do so, and this right cannot be satisfied by imposing upon them an exactly similar article, or one equally as good, but having a different origin.

The courts of appeals have applied this reasoning to the merchandising of reprocessed products that are as good as new, without a disclosure that they are in fact reprocessed. And it has also been held that it is a deceptive practice to misappropriate the trade name of another.

Respondents claim that all these cases are irrelevant to our decision because they involve misrepresentations related to the product itself and not merely to the manner in which an advertising message is communicated. This distinction misses the mark for two reasons. In the first place, the present case is not concerned with a mode of communication, but with a misrepresentation that viewers have objective proof of a seller's product claim over and above the seller's word. Secondly, all of the above cases, like the present case, deal with methods designed to get a consumer to purchase a product, not with whether the product, when purchased, will perform up to expectations. We find an especially strong similarity between the present case and those cases in which a seller induces the public to purchase an arguably good product by misrepresenting his line of business, by concealing the fact that the product is reprocessed, or by misappropriating another's trademark. In each the seller has used a misrepresentation to break down what he regards to be an annoying or irrational habit of the buying public—the preference for particular manufacturers or known brands regardless of a product's actual qualities, the prejudice against reprocessed goods, and the desire for verification of a product claim. In each case the seller reasons that when the habit is broken the buyer will be satisfied with the performance of the product he receives. Yet, a misrepresentation has been used to break the habit and, as was stated in *Algoma Lumber*, a misrepresentation for such an end is not permitted.

We need not limit ourselves to the cases already mentioned because there are other situations which also illustrate the correctness of the Commission's finding in the present case. It is generally accepted that it is a deceptive practice to state falsely that a product has received a testimonial from a respected source. In addition, the Commission has consistently acted to prevent sellers from falsely stating that their product claims have been "certified." We find these situations to be indistinguishable from the present case. We can assume that in each the underlying product claim is true and in each the seller actually conducted an experiment sufficient to prove to himself the truth of the claim. But in each the seller has told the public that it could rely on something other than his word concerning both the truth of the claim and the validity of his experiment. We find it an immaterial difference that in one case the viewer is told to rely on the word of a celebrity or authority he respects, in another on the word of a testing agency, and in the present case on his own perception of an undisclosed simulation.

Respondents again insist that the present case is not like any of the above, but is more like a case in which a celebrity or independent testing agency has in fact submitted a written verification of an experiment actually observed, but, because of the inability of the camera to transmit accurately an impression of the paper on which the testimonial is written, the seller reproduces it on another substance so that it can be seen by the viewing audience. This analogy ignores the finding of the Commission that in the present case the seller misrepresented to the public that it was being given objective proof of a product claim. In respondents' hypothetical the objective proof of the product claim that is offered, the word of the celebrity or agency that the experiment was actually conducted, does exist; while in the case before us the objective proof offered, the viewer's own perception of an actual experiment, does not exist. Thus, in respondents' hypothetical, unlike the present case, the use of the undisclosed mock-up does not conflict with the seller's claim that there is objective proof.

We agree with the Commission, therefore, that the undisclosed use of plexiglass in the present commercials was a material deceptive practice independent and separate from the other misrepresentations found. . . .

We turn our attention now to the order issued by the Commission. . . . The Court of Appeals has criticized the reference in the Commission's order to "test, experiment or demonstration" as not capable of practical interpretation. It could find no difference between the Rapid Shave commercial and a commer-

cial which extolled the goodness of ice cream while giving viewers a picture of a scoop of mashed potatoes appearing to be ice cream. We do not understand this difficulty. In the ice cream case the mashed potato prop is not being used for additional proof of the product claim, while the purpose of the Rapid Shave commercial is to give the viewer objective proof of the claims made. If in the ice cream hypothetical the focus of the commercial becomes the undisclosed potato prop and the viewer is invited, explicitly or by implication, to see for himself the truth of the claims about the ice cream's rich texture and full color, and perhaps compare it to a "rival product," then the commercial has become similar to the one now before us. Clearly, however, a commercial which depicts happy actors delightedly eating ice cream that is in fact mashed potatoes or drinking a product appearing to be coffee but which is in fact some other substance is not covered by the present order.

The crucial terms of the present order—"test, experiment or demonstration . . . represented . . . as actual proof of a claim"—are as specific as the circumstances will permit. If respondents in their subsequent commercials attempt to come as close to the line of misrepresentation as the Commission's order permits, they may without specifically intending to do so cross into the area proscribed by this order. However, it does not seem "unfair to require that one who deliberately goes perilously close to an area of proscribed conduct shall take the risk that he may cross the line." *Boyce Motor Lines, Inc. v. United States* . . . In commercials where the emphasis is on the seller's word, and not on the viewer's own perception, the respondents need not fear that an undisclosed use of props is prohibited by the present order. On the other hand, when the commercial not only makes a claim, but also invites the viewer to rely on his own perception for demonstrative proof of the claim, the respondents will be aware that the use of undisclosed props in strategic places might be a material deception. We believe that respondents will have no difficulty applying the Commission's order to the vast majority of their contemplated future commercials. If, however, a situation arises in which respondents are sincerely unable to determine whether a proposed course of action would violate the present order, they can, by complying with the Commission's rules, oblige the Commission to give them definitive advice as to whether their proposed action, if pursued, would constitute compliance with the order.

Study Questions

1. Were the ads in this case deceptive? Were they unethical?

2. Did the court reach the decision that is most morally defensible?

"...NO, HE CAN'T REALLY FLY.. NO, THE BAD GUYS REALLY DON'T HAVE A RAY GUN... NO, THIS CEREAL REALLY ISN'T THE BEST FOOD IN THE WHOLE WORLD... NO, IT WON'T REALLY MAKE YOU AS STRONG AS A GIANT..."

72

I'm Dancing as Fast as I Can!: The Case of Snevellicci v. Arthur Murray, Inc.*

District Court of Appeals of Florida

Pierce, Judge. This is an appeal by Sally Snevellicci, plaintiff below, from a final order dismissing . . . for failure to state a cause of action, her . . . complaint.

Plaintiff Mrs. Sally Snevellicci, a widow of 51 years and without family, had a yen to be "an accomplished dancer" with the hopes of finding "new interest in life." So on February 10, 1961, a dubious fate, with the assist of a motivated acquaintance, procured her to attend a "dance party" at Davenport's "School of Dancing" where she whiled away the pleasant hours, sometimes in a private room, absorbing [Davenport's] accomplished sales technique, during which her grace and poise were elaborated upon and her rosy future as "an excellent dancer" was painted for her in vivid and glowing colors. As an incident to this interlude, [Davenport] sold her eight half-hour dance lessons to be utilized within one calendar month therefrom, for the sum of $14.50 cash in hand paid, obviously a baited "come-on."

Thus she embarked upon an almost endless pursuit of the terpsichorean art during which, over a period of less than sixteen months, she was sold fourteen "dance courses" totaling in the aggregate 2302 hours of dancing lessons for a total cash outlay of $31,090.45, all at [Davenport's] dance emporium. All of these fourteen courses were evidenced by execution of a written "Enrollment Agreement—Arthur Murray's School of Dancing" with the addendum in heavy black print, "No one will be informed that you are taking dancing lessons. Your relations with us are held in strict confidence," setting forth the number of "dancing lessons" and the "lessons in rhythm sessions" currently sold to her from time to time, and

*A fictitious name.
Reprinted from District Court of Appeals of Florida, 1968.

always of course accompanied by payment of cash of the realm.

These dance lesson contracts and the monetary consideration therefor of over $31,000 were procured from her by means and methods of Davenport and his associates which went beyond the unsavory, yet legally permissible, perimeter of "sales puffing" and intruded well into the forbidden area of undue influence, the suggestion of falsehood, the suppression of truth, and the free exercise of rational judgment, if what plaintiff alleged in her complaint was true. From the time of her first contact with the dancing school in February 1961, she was influenced unwittingly by a constant and continuous barrage of flattery, false praise, excessive compliments, and panegyric encomiums, to such extent that it would be not only inequitable, but unconscionable, for a Court exercising inherent chancery power to allow such contracts to stand.

She was incessantly subjected to overreaching blandishment and cajolery. She was assured she had "grace and poise"; that she was "rapidly improving and developing in her dancing skill"; that the additional lessons would "make her a beautiful dancer, capable of dancing with the most accomplished dancers"; that she was "rapidly progressing in the development of her dancing skill and gracefulness," etc., etc. She was given "dance aptitute tests" for the ostensible purpose of "determining" the number of remaining hours instructions needed by her from time to time. . . .

In fact she did not develop in her dancing ability, she had no "dance aptitude," and in fact had difficulty in "hearing the musical beat." The complaint alleged that such representations to her "were in fact false and known by the defendant to be false and contrary to the plaintiff's true ability, the truth of plaintiff's ability being fully known to the defendants, but withheld from the plaintiff for the sole and specific intent to deceive and defraud the plaintiff and to induce her in the purchasing of additional hours of dance lessons." It was averred that the lessons were sold to her "in total disregard to the true physical, rhythm, and mental ability of the plaintiff." In other words, while she first exulted that she was entering the "spring of her life," she finally was awakened to the fact there was "spring" neither in her life nor in her feet.

The complaint prayed that the Court decree the dance contracts to be null and void and to be canceled, that an accounting be had, and judgment entered against the defendants "for that portion of the

$31,090.45 not charged against specific hours of instruction given to the plaintiff." The Court held the complaint not to state a cause of action and dismissed it with prejudice. We disagree and reverse.

The material allegations of the complaint must, of course, be accepted as true for the purpose of testing its legal sufficiency. Defendants contend that contracts can only be rescinded for fraud or misrepresentation as to a material fact, rather than an opinion, prediction or expectation, and that the statements and representations set forth at length in the complaint were in the category of "trade puffing," within its legal orbit.

It is true that "generally a misrepresentation, to be actionable, must be one of fact rather than of opinion." . . . But this rule has significant qualifications, applicable here. It does not apply where there is a fiduciary relationship between the parties, or where there has been some artifice or trick employed by the representor, or where the parties do not in general deal at "arm's length" as we understand the phrase, or where the representee does not have equal opportunity to become apprised of the truth or falsity of the fact represented. . . .

It could be reasonably supposed here that defendants had "superior knowledge" as to whether plaintiff had "dance potential" and as to whether she was noticeably improving in the art of terpsichore. . . .

Even in contractural situations where a party to a transaction owes no duty to disclose facts within his knowledge or to answer inquiries respecting such facts, the law is if he undertakes to do so he must disclose the *whole truth*.

We repeat that where parties are dealing on a contractual basis at arm's length with no inequities or inherently unfair practices employed, the Courts will in general "leave the parties where they find themselves." But in the case sub judice . . . from the showing made in her complaint, plaintiff is entitled to her day in Court.

Study Questions

1. Did the court reach the decision that is most morally defensible?

2. Was the plaintiff tricked here?

3. Were the two parties at arm's length in bargaining, though they literally had their arms around each other dancing?

4. Were the plaintiff's loneliness and hearing inability exploited even if she was not deceived? How would egalitarianism decide this case?

73

Libel

Sterling Harwood

Type of Ethics: Media ethics

Date: Coined 1631

Definition: The defamation of a person or group by means of writing or visual images

Significance: Libel is a rare exception to the legal protection of freedom of speech in the United States, a freedom that many ethicists consider essential for democracy and ethical government.

———————

Libel is often confused with slander, which is oral defamation rather than written or visual defamation. One's good reputation is usually among one's most valuable possessions. Since libel, by definition, damages the reputation of another, it does serious harm and thus is clearly unethical. Criminal libel is the malicious publishing of durable defamation. In common law and under most modern criminal statutes, criminal libel is a misdemeanor (an infraction usually punishable by a year or less in prison) rather than a felony (a more serious infraction punishable by more than a year in prison). Libel is also a tort, a noncontractual and noncriminal wrongdoing. Libel is thus grounds for a civil lawsuit in which one may seek to recover money to compensate for the damage that the libel has caused to one's reputation. Truth, however, is a defense against libel, and even if the damage is caused by a false claim, if the damaged person is a public figure, then one must show malice (intent to harm) or a reckless disregard for the truth in order to prove libel. Honest mistakes do not constitute libel against public figures. (Civil lawsuits against libel and punishment for criminal libel are both limited by the First Amendment of the Constitution.) This was the upshot of the landmark Supreme Court case *New York Times Co. v. Sullivan* (1964) and its progeny. This landmark case was designed to preserve the vigor and variety of public debate in a democracy, balancing democracy against serious harms to reputations in order to avoid a chilling effect on the exercise of the constitutional right of free speech.

Study Questions

1. Should freedom of speech include the freedom to libel another person?

2. Is freedom of expression protected enough by the legal rule that truth is a defense to a charge of libel? Should there be some freedom to make false claims that damage others' reputations?

3. Should there be a higher standard for proving libel of a politician or leading personality in the news? Won't a higher standard protect freedom of speech, allowing people to have peace of mind as they criticize politicians, cultural icons, etc.?

4. Should the higher standard for public figures being libeled be malice or reckless disregard for the truth by the person alleged to have committed libel? Are there any better standards? If so, what are they? If not, why not?

———————

Reprinted from Sterling Harwood, "Libel," in *Ready Reference: Ethics* (Pasadena, Calif.: Salem Press, 1994). Reprinted by permission.

"SURE I'M A STRONG DEFENDER OF THE FIRST AMENDMENT AND ALL ITS RAMIFICATIONS, BUT IT'S VERY CLEAR THAT IF HE CALLED US A BUNCH OF JERKS, THAT'S LIBEL."

© 1995 by Sidney Harris.

74

The Case of the Disappearing Reference in Marketing Your Skills: Even Good Employees Can't Get Raves

Pat Butler

Editor's note: Pat Butler briefly chronicles a new reluctance among employers to give more than minimal references for their employees seeking work elsewhere. The main problem seems to be legal liability. Employers wish to avoid lawsuits claiming that they have libeled or defamed the reputations of their employees or former employees. This problem creates a dynamic tension in the workplace, since more than ever before, it seems, employees must move from employer to employer rather than settle in with one employer for a lifelong career. But such dramatic moves from job to job and career to career require informative references that go beyond the bare minimum.

Your job performance has been stellar. Your evaluations read like nominations for the Nobel Peace Prize. Your boss has confided that she wishes she could clone you and fire the rest of the staff.

So now that you're considering a new job, why will she tell your prospective employer nothing more than your job title and length of service?

The reason: The fear of lawsuits is increasingly driving employers to divulge nothing about former or current workers other than "name, rank and serial number." Even the most exceptional employees get no more than a neutral reference.

This article originally appeared as "References Becoming Thing of the Past," *The State* (1994).

"We are finding it more difficult to do reference checks. And yes, we are giving out less information" when other companies do reference checks, said Emily Metzger, supervisor of human resources at Allied Fibers in Irmo. "So we're our own worst enemy."

Like many companies, Allied gives out nothing more than what a worker did at the plant and how long he did it. That's because of the potential for lawsuits from employees who believe they've been libeled or slandered by their former bosses, Metzger said.

But ironically, that trend is putting employers at risk of another kind of lawsuit: They are frequently being sued for the misdeeds of employees they would never have hired had they made a thorough background check.

As a result, companies are becoming more and more zealous in gathering information about potential employees even as the sources of the information are drying up.

"The trend is toward suits against employers who didn't consider hires carefully enough," said Rick Morgan, an employment attorney with McNair & Sanford. Because of that, "I think the business community needs to rethink how we do reference checks."

There are two victims of the widespread practice: the exceptional workers who get the same neutral references as poor workers, and the employers who are unable to gain crucial information in the hiring process. But experts say both victims can get around the neutral reference—with some work.

"Most of the time, we are able to get a reference—probably 75 percent of the time. It depends on how hard you dig," said Joel Watts, a human resource specialist at Lexington Medical Center who, like Metzger, admitted that he tries to get detailed references on applicants despite his business's refusal to give them.

In a nationwide survey conducted last year, more than two-thirds of companies said they were finding it harder to do reference checks than three years previously. And in the same survey, conducted by personnel service Robert Half International, three-fourths of companies said they were providing less information on checks.

They're reluctant because employees who receive a bad reference are increasingly likely to sue—and win. A California jury awarded a fired Lockheed employee almost $1 million because the company provided defamatory job references to prospective employers.

On the other and, businesses also are at risk of losing lawsuits because they didn't check into a worker's background well enough before hiring. For example, a fast-food restaurant in California had to pay over $200,000 in damages to the family of a 3-year-old boy who was sexually assaulted by an employee; and a Georgia apartment maintenance company paid $600,000 to a woman raped by one of its employees.

In both cases, the employee had a history of criminal behavior that wasn't revealed during the reference checking process, according to the Society for Human Resource Management, which publishes the "Reference Checking Handbook."

Given that dilemma, how much information should an employer give out in references?

Lawyers who counsel employers give different advice. Ted Speth, managing partner of the Columbia law firm Haynsworth Baldwin Johnson and Greaves, advises employers to continue giving neutral references.

Recent court rulings have led Speth to believe that workers who sue an employer for giving them a bad reference are unlikely to win unless they can prove malice. But fighting such a suit would be risky and expensive even if won, Speth said.

On the other hand, Ken Childs, partner in the Childs and Duff firm, believes the "fear of suits resulting from bad references is probably exaggerated," as long as employers are careful about the kind of information they give out.

Morgan said that any information given out should be factual and job-related, such as: "He was frequently tardy" or "She didn't meet quality requirements." Avoid references based on opinion or innuendo, such as: "He had a bad attitude" or "We suspected she was taking things on the side."

"Unless you actually know, you better not say it," Morgan said.

There also are steps employers who are hiring can take to get around the neutral reference. While a company's official policy may be to give only neutral references, a worker's immediate supervisor or colleagues often will say more.

"When you talk to the human resources department, you'll get the official policy: 'Yes, he or she worked at the company as a project engineer,'" said Lee Trimble, technical recruiter with Howett Personnel Associates. "But sometimes managers or individuals in the company are interested in providing a positive reference."

If all else fails, an employer who has made a thorough attempt to check out references is reasonably protected from lawsuit, Speth said.

Strategies for the Worker

Most experts said that neutral references don't hurt the employee's chances of being hired.

"It's no longer a shock when you do a reference check," said Larry Parker, Columbia area director for Job Service. "It doesn't have near the adverse impact that it did at one time."

But that's little consolation to the worker whose job performance has been outstanding but can't get anyone to say so. There are steps such workers can take to better their chances of being hired.

First, they should save any material, such as glowing job reviews or commendations, that shows they were highly regarded. Second, they should ask for a written reference when leaving a job.

Workers also should ask supervisors and co-workers to put in a good word if a prospective employer contacts them. But too many people make the mistake of listing someone as a reference without knowing what that person will say, Parker said.

Trimble remembers one client who made that mistake. A company was on the verge of making an offer to the client but decided to check one of the references provided by him.

That person told the company that "the man's performance had been aboveboard and positive ever since he finished his alcoholic detoxification program," Trimble said.

The company decided not to make an offer.

Study Questions

1. Would egalitarianism require employers to give a meritorious worker a good reference when the worker leaves to take another job?

2. Would libertarianism require employers to give a good worker a good reference when the worker wants to leave for another job, even when that job is not with a competitor? If not, is that a counterexample that shows libertarianism is false?

75

Ford Pintos, GM Trucks, and Media Distortions

Peter Hadreas

Editor's note: Hadreas explores the eerie similarities between the Ford Pinto and some General Motors (GM) trucks, concentrating on some distortions in the media and in business ethics textbooks. President Clinton's administration recently settled the case of the GM trucks by taking $51.4 million from GM to pay for federal auto safety programs instead of forcing GM to recall thousands of older pickup trucks that might be fire hazards.

The U.S. style of life in the 1960s centered around the family car. And, up until the 1960s, automobiles made in the United States had uncontested dominance of the market. But in the 1960s U.S. preeminence in car manufacturing began to erode. Subcompacts, especially the German-made Volkswagen, were slowly claiming more and more of the U.S. market share. Lee Iacocca, then president of Ford, answered the new competition with an American-made subcompact that he hoped would restore Ford's dwindling market share. Iacocca conceived of a car that would weigh no more than 2,000 pounds and cost no more than $2,000. Robert Alexander, Ford's vice president of car engineering, completed a feasibility study, and Ford decided to go ahead with the car. Ford would call it the Pinto and would introduce it as "a carefree little American car." Although the time to bring a car to market, from preproduction designing and testing to manufacturing, was normally 43 months, Ford brought the Pinto to the showroom in only 38 months by putting together a special team of engineers who devoted their efforts wholly to the Pinto.

The Pinto was clearly a commercial success. After its introduction in September of 1970, sales continued to climb for six years. In fact, by 1976, two million Pintos were on the road, making it one of the company's all-time best-selling automobiles. And the Pinto played a large role in stabilizing Ford's market position in relation to GM and Chrysler.[1]

The success of the Pinto came in spite of problems confronted early on in the positioning of the gas tank. The car's engineers had debated early in its production where to put the gas tank. They opted for a strap-on tank behind the rear axle. Although at that time almost every American car had a gas tank in just the same place, matters were different for the Pinto. Since the car's weight was so reduced, the standard positioning of the gas tank actually was much more open to rear impact than in heavier cars.

The governmental agency that proposed safety standards at this time was the newly organized National Traffic Highway Safety Administration (NHTSA), a regulatory agency in the Department of Transportation. The NHTSA was hampered through this period by the lack of a data base of reliable statistical information about how cars withstood various types of rear impact. In January 1969, NHTSA proposed its first fuel system integrity standard. The proposed standard, which was not passed into law, required that, after being hit by a 4,000-pound barrier moving at 20 mph, an automobile must leak less than one ounce of fuel per minute. Four tests were conducted with prototypes of the Pinto. In three of the tests, the prototypes slightly exceeded the standard. In a fourth test the fuel tank split at the seams. After these tests, Ford altered the fuel tank design and the Pinto with the revised fuel tank design was introduced to the American public.[2]

Although the NHTSA proposed many fuel system integrity standards between 1969 and 1976—a 20 mph moving-barrier standard, a 20 mph fixed-barrier standard, and finally a 30 mph moving-barrier standard—a NHTSA standard was not passed into law until 1977. By then the Pinto's capacity to leak gas on rear impact was already being treated as a scandal in the media.

Human Tragedy and Overstated Corporate Villainy

In August of 1977, one could pick up on newsstands the self-avowed radical magazine *Mother Jones* and read Mark Dowie's article "Pinto Madness." The article claimed, citing as evidence "secret documents," that Ford had known for eight years that the Pinto was a "firetrap." The article concluded: "By conservative estimates, Pinto crashes have caused 500 burn deaths to people who would not have been seriously injured if the car had not burst into flames."[3] To make the picture of Ford even more condemnable, an episode of *60 Minutes* entitled "Is Your Car Safe?"[4] opened with an interview of teenager Richard Grimshaw. Richard Grimshaw was the victim of a Pinto rear-impact crash and fire explosion.

On May 28, 1972, Richard Grimshaw was riding in the car with Lily Gray. Gray was driving a six-month-old Pinto and was for many a truly admirable human being. She had adopted two girls, worked 40 hours a week (earning $20,000 a year), was "den-mother" for all the teenagers in the neighborhood, sold refreshments at the Bobby Sox games, and had maintained a happy marriage of 22 years.

Mrs. Gray, after stopping in San Bernardino, California, for gasoline, returned to Interstate 15, the main highway that traverses San Bernardino. Changing lanes, her Pinto suddenly stalled and then coasted to a halt. The car traveling immediately behind Mrs. Gray was able to swerve and avoid hitting her. The driver of a 1962 Ford Galaxie, the second car behind Mrs. Gray, could not do so. It was later determined that when the Galaxie driver collided with Mrs. Gray's Pinto, it was going only between 28 and 37 miles per hour. Even so, at the moment of the impact, the Pinto caught fire and its interior burst into flames. The crash had driven the gas tank forward, puncturing it on the differential housing and thereby spraying fuel into the passenger compartment. The fuel immediately caught fire. By the time the Pinto came to a rest, both occupants had third-degree burns. When they were taken from the Pinto, their clothes were almost completely burned off. Mrs. Gray died a few days later. Although badly disfigured, Grimshaw survived with severe burns over 90 percent of his body. Grimshaw, presented to the U.S. public in the *60 Minutes* episode, subsequently underwent over 70 operations and skin grafts. He would undergo additional surgeries in the next ten years. He lost portions of several fingers and portions of his left ear; his face required many skin grafts from various parts of his body.[5]

The defense attorney for Richard Grimshaw explained on the *60 Minutes* segment that documents had been discovered that proved that Ford had understood in detail the likelihood of such fatal and near-fatal crashes. Even so, Ford had refused to in-

stall a relatively inexpensive device that would correct the problem. (The cost of the device was usually listed as $11, although, according to Dowie in the *Mother Jones* article, Ford had successfully employed a rubber bladder inside the gas tank that sopped up gas leakage for only $5.08.[6]) Grimshaw's attorney explained that Ford conducted a cost-benefit analysis and determined that it would be cheaper to pay death benefits and the medical costs of burn victims than to install a corrective device in the Pinto that would prevent such accidents. Grimshaw's attorney cited a Grush and Saundby report,[7] which revealed the cost comparison presented below.

Cost to Society for Burn Deaths, Injuries, and Vehicle Loss

Units lost: 180 burn deaths, 180 serious burn injuries, 2,100 burned vehicles

Unit cost: $200,000 per death, $67,000 per injury, $700 per vehicle.

Total Cost: 180 × ($200,000) +
180 × ($67,000) +
2100 × ($700)   = $49.15 million.

Cost to Repair Ford Motor Cars

Number of Units: 11 million cars, 1.5 million trucks

Unit cost: $11 per car, $11 per truck

Total Cost: 11,000,000 × ($11) +
1,500,000 × ($11) = $137 million

Ford's estimate of the number of burn deaths, injuries, and lost vehicles as a result of fires from fuel leakage was based on statistical studies. The $200,000 value attributed to the loss of life was based on a study of the NHTSA. It broke down the estimated social costs of death as follows:

Detailing the Costs of Death

Component	1971 Costs
Future Productivity Losses	
Direct	$132,000
Indirect	41,300
Medical Costs	
Hospital	700
Other	425
Property Damage	1,500
Insurance Administration	4,700

Component	1971 Costs
Legal and Court	3,000
Employer Losses	1,000
Victim's Pain and Suffering	10,000
Funeral	900
Assets (Lost Consumption)	5,000
Miscellaneous Accident Cost	200
Total per Fatality:	$200,725

This report was offered in the *60 Minutes* program as the rationale by which Ford executives decided not to repair the defective gas tank. It was also reprinted in the *Mother Jones* article cited above. Indeed, it has come to epitomize misguided business practices that are monstrously blind to everything but "the bottom line." It is quoted in nearly all business ethics textbooks as part of the procedure by which Ford decided not to recall the Pinto.[8]

But these accounts misrepresent the role of this cost-benefit analysis. As in many business ethics cases, there is no question of villains and victims but of organizations that poorly handle the policy changes that new products demand and of leaders who narrowly focus on short-term goals. In fact the Grush-Saundby report was not about recalling Pintos. In 1973, at the same time the NHTSA was proposing rear-end crash standards, it also proposed fuel system integrity standards applicable to *rollover* accidents. In the case of the rollover standard, cars were tested on the amount of fuel leaked when a car was turned upside down in an accident. This was actually a more complicated design problem for Ford engineers to solve, because in an accident where there is a rollover, gasoline may leak from the carburetor and fuel vents as well as from the gas cap hole. Ford personnel without design responsibilities attempted to lobby against this rollover standard by proposing this cost-benefit analysis. It was this analysis that became known as the Grush-Saundby Report and would be the basis for countless media indictments, including the *Mother Jones* article and the *60 Minutes* segment, "Is Your Car Safe?" But if one looks more closely at the report, one can see that it cannot apply to the Pinto. The computation in the Grush-Saundby Report in the table above, "Costs to Repair Ford Motor Cars," applied to all Ford vehicles on the road. As the table indicates, a total of 11 million Ford cars and 1.5 million Ford trucks were taken into account.

But there had been roughly 2 million Pintos sold by 1976. The cost-benefit analysis could not apply to Pintos. If it did, it would have been cheaper by far to recall the Pintos than to pay insurance costs!

The imposition of a villain/victim scenario upon this case by the media and by reprints of this report in ethics textbooks, in fact, only serves to hide the actual areas of Ford's negligence. What is at issue is not villainous and inhuman Ford executives let loose upon a credulous public. Rather, two forces played heavily into Ford's mistakes. First, the breakneck speed at which Ford rushed to recover a failing market share by a new kind of car, a subcompact, helped to make design responsibilities a low priority. And second, the failure of the NHTSA to set a standard of safety for rear-impact collisions made older and lower standards of safety appear adequate. This of course does not excuse Ford for mishandling its design responsibilities. But it makes clearer the forces that led Ford to lose sight of the welfare of its customers *as well as* its own financial well-being.

History Repeats Itself

Severe accidents caused by the misplaced Pinto gas tank in models of Pintos from 1971 to 1976 resulted in 27 fatalities and 24 nonfatal burns.[9] In February 1978 a California jury handed down a verdict that awarded $125 million in punitive damages to Richard Grimshaw. This was the largest amount of punitive damages ever awarded for such a suit in U.S. history. A judge later reduced the amount to $3.5 million. Even so, we find a similar story befalling General Motors (GM) in the late 1980s and continuing right up into the 1990s regarding the company's handling of misplaced gas tanks in 4.7 million of its full-sized and medium-sized trucks. GM's mismanagement of gas tank design involves an eerie return to the Ford tragedy.

In February 1993, a jury awarded a total of $105.2 million in damages to an Atlanta couple, $101 million in punitive damages and $4.2 million in compensatory damages, finding that GM was negligent in its placement of the gas tank. From 1973 to 1987, GM trucks were designed to provide a greater amount of fuel storage through the attachment of two side-mounted gas tanks.[10] These tanks were positioned under the body of the truck, beneath the passenger compartment but still outside the steel frame of the truck. So positioned, the tanks carry as much as 40 gallons of gas. This capacity to tote a hefty load of gas was a selling point to many of its buyers. But according to the 12-member jury in Fulton County (Georgia) State Court, this selling point was also deadly. According to the Fulton County jury, it was this faulty design that was responsible for the death of Shannon Mosely, Thomas and Elaine Mosely's 17-year-old son.

In 1985 Shannon Mosely died in a fiery crash when his 1985 GMC pickup was hit broadside by a drunken driver at an intersection. The Moselys contended, and the Fulton County jury agreed, that Shannon's death was caused by a rupture in the gas tank. Since the gas tanks in the GMC truck are outside the truck frame, they are protected only by the thin wall of the truck cab. They are particularly exposed in a broadside collision. In fact, GMC models manufactured since 1987 have a corrected design. The gas tank has been reduced in capacity from 40 gallons to 34, and placed well under and inside the car frame. Design safety activists claim that this design flaw in GM trucks before 1987 has caused 300 deaths. The auto maker, not surprisingly, argues that the design is safe. GM claims that the Mosely case is only the fourth in which the jury found in favor of the plaintiff. The auto maker contends that it has won three cases and that a number of others have been settled out of court.[11]

An analogy can be drawn between the media coverage of the Ford Pintos and the GM trucks. *Dateline NBC*, an NBC-affiliated TV news magazine, in a segment aired on November 17, 1992, attempted to graphically communicate to the U.S. public just how unsafe GMC trucks were. It threw the U.S. public a similar red herring as "Pinto Madness" and the *60 Minutes* segment had done 15 years before. The 1977 *Mother Jones* article, "Pinto Madness," and the *60 Minutes* segment, "Is Your Car Safe?," had overdramatized the Pinto's safety hazards by casting Ford executives as villains. In 1992, *Dateline NBC* producers overdramatized the crashes, making the trucks into even more of an inferno than they might have been in life. In the production of 58 seconds of footage, presumed by viewers to be an undoctored record of a GMC truck crash, *Dateline NBC* producers hid toy rocket engines in the truck, ensuring that the GM truck would burst into flame on cue, used a truck whose gas tank didn't fit, employed multiple camera angles that would depict a larger and more threatening fire, and failed to inform the public that the fire went out on its own in 15 seconds. But the breach of journalistic ethics had complicated consequences. The "media scandal" that ensued led the public to

overlook that the TV news program had in fact made a strong case for how GMC trucks were safety hazards by means of its undoctored news material. Leaving out the 58-second phony simulation, the rest of the segment included the following:

1. Interviews with the parents of Shannon Mosely.
2. An examination of the Mosely truck and an explanation of how the gas tank burst into flames upon the broadside collision.
3. Interviews with a police officer and an attorney who reconstructed Shannon Mosely's death.
4. A woman painfully recounting the accident that killed her two daughters, which involved the bursting of the gas tank of a GM truck. Her lawyer explained how without the fire everyone would have survived.
5. Conflicting GM surveys about the comparative safety of trucks.
6. A GM engineer's memo saying that merely moving the gas tank "might eliminate most of these potential leakers."
7. A GM film of side-impact crash tests. One showed a shower of liquid spraying from a ruptured experimental fuel tank. Another showed the gas tank of a 1984 model that leaked and that was subject to hazardous combustion..[12]

None of these aspects of the news show were simulated. The nonsimulated parts of this *Dateline NBC* broadcast would by themselves have made a strong case for recalling GM trucks from 1973 to 1987. To be sure, the breach in journalistic ethics had serious consequences for the producers of *Dateline NBC*. The show's executive producer, Jeff Diamond, was forced to resign, along with senior producer David Rummel and Robert Read, who produced the GM story. NBC News settled a lawsuit with GM and issued an on-air apology in February 1993.[13] As for the trucks themselves, they are still on the road and plans to recall them are at a standstill.[14]

Study Questions

1. The NHTSA did not enact safety standards for rear-end collisions until 1977. What effect did this delay have on Ford's failure to recall Pintos before 1978?

2. What ethical theories should have been brought to bear on this case by Ford designers? Why do you think the designers failed to apply them?

3. In terms of the "bottom line," would Ford have been better off recalling Pintos in 1973?

4. How did the media play a positive role in bringing about a recall of the Pinto? To what extent did it play a negative role?

5. It was suggested in the case that in its design of trucks from 1973 to 1987 GM failed to learn a lesson from the history of the Pinto. What lesson did GM fail to learn? Do you agree with the philosopher George Santayana, who said, "Those who cannot remember the past are condemned to repeat it"?

6. How serious do you think the breach of journalistic ethics by *Dateline NBC* in its November 17, 1992, segment on GM trucks is in comparison to the issue of safety of GM trucks in broadside collisions? Are there two ethical considerations in conflict here?

Notes

1. The 1973–1974 Arab oil embargo hit Ford's major competitors, GM and Chrysler, particularly hard because neither had much to offer in the way of small fuel-efficient cars. In 1975 Congress set mandatory fuel economy targets that would encourage auto makers to develop smaller cars. GM responded with a massive downsizing program that helped it to become small-car-oriented. Chrysler, in financial difficulty, belatedly followed. Even so, the Pinto continued to outsell most competitive offerings in its size category. See the detailed account of the competitive environment in which the Pinto was developed in Kenneth E. Goodpaster, "Managing Product Safety: The Ford Pinto," in Kenneth E. Goodpaster, ed., *Ethics in Management* (Boston: Harvard Business School, 1984), pp. 112–114.

2. Ford Motor Company Crash Tests 1137, 1138, 1214; memorandum, H. P. Freers to T. J. Feaheny, January 31, 1969.

3. Mark Dowie, "Pinto Madness," *Mother Jones* (September/October 1977, p. 18.

4. The *60 Minutes* segment "Is Your Car Safe?" was produced by CBS News and was first broadcast in 1978.

5. All the facts in this and the preceding paragraph are from *Grimshaw v. Ford Motor Co.*, App., 174 Cal. Rptr. 348, pp. 359–70.

6. Dowie, "Pinto Madness," pp. 28—29.

7. E. S. Grush and C. S. Saundby, "Fatalities Associated with Crash-Induced Fuel Leakage and Fires," Ford Motor Company (September 19, 1973).

8. In "Pinto Madness," Mark Dowie writes: "Ford waited eight years because its internal 'cost-benefit analysis,' which places a dollar value on human life, said it wasn't profitable to make the changes sooner." Op. cit., pp. 18 and 20. Dowie clearly implies that the cost-benefit analy-

sis known as the Grush-Saundby Report was used to keep the Pintos on the road.

Regarding the presentation of the cost-benefit analysis as it appears in business ethics textbooks, Thomas Donaldson, for example, in *Case Studies in Business Ethics* (Englewood Cliffs, N.J.: Prentice Hall, Inc., 1984), p. 151, states: "This study [the cost-benefit analysis in question, "Fatalities Associated with Crash-Induced Fuel Leakage and Fires"] apparently convinced Ford and was intended to convince the federal government that a technological improvement costing $11 per car which would have prevented gas tanks from rupturing so easily was not cost-effective for society." Although Donaldson questions soberly many of the claims made by Dowie in his *Mother Jones* article, he never doubts that the cost-benefit analysis was applicable to recalling Pintos.

Solomon and Hanson in *It's Good Business* (New York: Atheneum, 1985), p. 78, reprint the cost-benefit analysis as quoted above. In citing the title of the study, they have added the parenthetical phrase "in the Ford Pinto." Readers meet the following citation: "Fatalities Associated with Crash-Induced Fuel Leakage and Fires (in the Ford Pinto)." Solomon and Hanson seem to have thought that the cost-benefit analysis was so much about Pintos that they might as well save time and put "Pintos" into its official title.

Even Manuel G. Velasquez, who usually scrupulously attends to facts, seems to have missed the mark here. In *Business Ethics, Concepts and Cases*, 2nd ed. (Englewood Cliffs, N.J.: Prentice Hall, 1988), p. 120, Velasquez takes pains to point out that the Grush-Saundby Report, released by J. C. Echold, was "a later Ford company study." Even so, he states that the study was designed "to counter the prospect of stiffer government regulations on gasoline tank design." In fact, the study was about gasoline leakage rollovers. As indicated above, leakage could come from the carburetor, fuel vents, or the gas cap hole. By erroneously suggesting that this study applied to gas tank problems, Velasquez makes the study appear to be about Pintos when it was about all Ford motor cars on the road when the study was done.

9. "U.S. Agency Suggests Ford Pintos Have a Fuel Safety Defect," *New York Times* (May 9, 1978), p. 22.

10. "GM Assessed $105 Million in Truck Death," *San Francisco Chronicle* (February 5, 1993), page A21, col 1.

11. All the facts in this paragraph are taken from the *San Francisco Chronicle*, "GM Assessed $105 Million in Truck Death," cited above.

12. Description of the segments of the November 17, 1992, broadcast of *Dateline NBC* is taken from *The Washington Post*, "TV News: The Pickup Trucks" (March 7, 1993).

13. "NBC-Sponsored Inquiry Calls GM Crash on News Program a Lapse in Judgment," *The Wall Street Journal* (March 23, 1994).

14. I would surely be remiss if I did not thank, even if in an endnote, Prof. Sterling Harwood, who read over an earlier draft of this essay and made many helpful suggestions.

76

Closing Arguments to the Jury in the Classic Ford Pinto Case

Ford Motor Company

Editor's note: This is Mr. Neal's closing argument to the jury that found Ford not guilty of criminal homicide. The case is the same one Hadreas discusses in the previous selection.

If it please the Court, Counsel, ladies and gentlemen:

Not too many years ago our broad American Industry straddled the world like a giant.

It provided us with the highest standards of living ever known to man.

It was ended, eliminated, no more. Now it is an Industry weakened by deteriorating plants and equipment, weakened by lack of products, weakened by lack of manpower, weakened by inadequate capital, weakened by massive Government controls, weakened by demands on foreign oil and reeling from competition from foreign manufacturers.

I stand here today to defend a segment of that tattered Industry.

One company that saw the influx of foreign, small-made cars in 1967 and '68 and tried to do something about it, tried to build a small car with American labor that would compete with foreign imports, that would keep Americans employed, that would keep American money in America.

As State's witness, Mr. Copp, admitted, Ford Motor Company would have made more profit sticking to the bigger cars where the profit is.

That would have been the easiest way.

It was not the way Ford Motor Company took.

It made the Ford to compete. And this is no easy effort, members of the jury.

From *State of Indiana v. Ford Motor Company.* U.S. District Court, South Bend, Indiana. January 15, 1980.

As even Mr. Copp admitted, the Automobile Industry is extremely regulated.

It has to comply with the Clean Air Act, the Safety Act, the Emissions Control Act, the Corporate Average Fuel Economy Act, the Safety Act, and OSHA as well as a myriad of Statutes and Regulations applicable to large and small businesses generally, and again, as Mr. Copp admitted, it now takes twice as many Engineers to make a car as it did before all the massive Government controls.

Nevertheless, Ford Motor Company undertook the effort to build a subcompact, to take on the imports, to save jobs for Americans and to make a profit for its stockholders.

This rather admirable effort has a sad ending.

On August 10, 1978, a young man gets into a van weighing over 4,000 pounds and heads towards Elkhart, Indiana, on a bad highway called "U.S. 33."

He has a couple of open beer bottles in his van, together with his marijuana which he may or may not have been smoking. . . .

As he was cruising along on an open stretch of highway in broad daylight at at least 50 to 55 miles per hour, he drops his "smoke," ignores his driving and the road, and fails to see a little Pinto with its emergency flashers on stopped on the highway ahead.

He plows into the rear of the Pinto with enormous force and three young girls are killed.

Not the young man, but Ford Motor Company is charged with reckless homicide and arraigned before you.

I stand here to defend Ford Motor Company, and to tell you that we are not killers. . . .

Mr. Cosentino gave you the definition of "reckless homicide" as "plain, conscious and unjustifiable disregard of harm, which conduct involves substantial deviation from acceptable standards of conduct."

This case and the elements of this case, strictly speaking, involve 40 days, July 1, 1978 to August 10, 1978, and the issue is whether, during that period of time, Ford Motor Company recklessly, as that term is defined, omitted to warn of a danger and repair, and that reckless omission caused the deaths involved. . . .

[I]n my opening statement, I asked you to remember nine points, and I asked you to judge me, my client, by how well or how poorly we supported those nine points.

Let me run through briefly and just tick them off, the nine points, with you, and then let me get down to discussing the evidence and record with respect to those nine points.

One, I said this was a badly-designed highway, with curbs so high the girls couldn't get off when they had to stop their car in an emergency.

Two, I said the girls stopped there with their emergency flashers on, and this boy in a van weighing more than 4,000 pounds, with his eyes off the road, looking down trying to find the "smoke," rammed into the rear of that Pinto at at least 50 miles an hour, closing speed.

And by "closing speed," I mean the differential speed.

That is Points 1 and 2.

Point 3, I said the 1973 Pinto met every fuel-system integrity standard of any Federal, State or Local Government.

Point No. 4, I said, Ford Motor Company adopted a mandatory standard dealing with fuel-system integrity on rear-impact of 20 miles per hour moving-barrier, 4,000 pound moving-barrier, and I said that no other manufacturer in the world had adopted any standard, only Ford Motor Company.

Five, I said that the Pinto, it is not comparable to a Lincoln Continental, a Cadillac, a Mercedes Benz or that Ascona, or whatever that exotic car was that Mr. Bloch called—but I did say No. 5, it is comparable to other 1973 subcompacts.

No. 6, I said that . . . we would bring in the Engineers who designed and manufactured the Pinto, and I brought them from the stand, and they would tell you that they thought the Pinto was a good, safe car, and they bought it for themselves, their wives and their children to drive.

No. 7, I told you that we would bring in the statistics that indicated to us as to our state of mind that the Pinto performed as well or better than other subcompacts.

And, No. 8, I said we would nevertheless tell you that we decided to recall the Pinto in June of 1978, and having made that decision for the reasons that I—that I told you I would explain, we did everything in our power to recall that Pinto as quickly as possible, that there was nothing we could have done between July 1, 1978 and 8-10-1978, to recall the Pinto any faster.

And finally, No. 9, I said we would demonstrate that any car, any subcompact, any small car, and even some larger cars, sitting out there on Highway 33 in the late afternoon of August 10, 1978 and watching that van roar down that highway with the boy looking for his "smoke"—any car would have suffered the same consequences.

Those are the nine points I ask you to judge me by, and let me touch on the evidence, now, with re-spect to those nine points. . . .

The van driver, Duggar, took his eyes off the road and off driving to look around the floor of the van for a "smoke."

Duggar had two open beer bottles in the car and a quantity of marijuana.

Duggar was not prosecuted for reckless homicide or for the possession of marijuana, even though his prior record of conviction was:

November, '73, failure to yield right-of-way;

April, '76, speeding 65 miles an hour in a 45 mile an hour zone;

July, '76, running stop sign;

June '77, speeding 45 in a 25 zone;

August, '77, driver's license suspended;

September, '77, driving with suspended license;

December, '77, license suspended again.

Mr. Cosentino, you got up in front of this jury and you cried.

Well, I cry, too, because Mr. Duggar is driving, and you didn't do anything about him with a record like that except say, "Come in and help me convict Ford Motor Company, and I will help you get probation."

We all cry.

But crying doesn't do any good, and it doesn't help this jury.

The big disputed fact in this case regarding the accident, ladies and gentlemen, is the closing speed. The differential speed, the difference between the speed the Pinto was going, if any, and the speed the van was going.

That is the big disputed fact in regard to this accident.

And whether the Pinto was stopped or not is relevant only as it affects closing speed. . . .

Mr. Duggar testified—I guess he is great about speed, because while he's looking down there for his "smoke," he knows he is going 50 miles per hour in the van.

But he said he was going 50 miles per hour at the time of impact, and he said the Pinto was going 15.

But here is the same man who admitted he was going at least 50 miles per hour and looking around down "on a clear day," trying to find the "smoke" and looked up only to see the Pinto ten feet ahead of him.

Here is a witness willing to say under oath that the Pinto was going 15 miles per hour, even though he had one-sixth of a second—one-sixth of a second to make the judgment on the speed.

Here is a witness who says he had the time to

calculate the speed of the Pinto but had no time even to try to apply brakes because there were no skid marks.

And here is a witness who told Dr. Galen Miller, who testified here, that—told him right after the accident that in fact the Pinto was stopped.

And here was a witness who made a deal with the State.

And here was a witness who's not prosecuted for recklessness.

And here is a witness who is not prosecuted for possession of marijuana.

So the State's proof from Mr. Alfred Clark through Mr. Duggar is kind of a smorgasbord or a buffet—you can go in and take your choice.

You can pick 15—5 miles per hour, if you want to as to differential speed, or you can take 35 miles per hour.

And the State, with the burden of proof says, "Here," "Here," "Here. I will give you a lot of choice."

"You want choices? I will give you choices. Here. Take 5. Take 15. 10, 15, 20, 25, 30, 35."

Because, ladies and gentlemen of the jury—and I'm sure you are—the alternatives the State offers you are closing speeds of anywhere from 5 miles—on the low side—to 35 miles on the high side as a differential speed in this accident. . . .

Mr. Toms, the former National Highway Traffic Safety Administrator, told you that in his opinion the 20 mile per hour rear-impact moving-barrier was a reasonable and acceptable standard of conduct for 1973 vehicles.

Why didn't Ford adopt a higher standard?

Mr. MacDonald, a man even Mr. Copp—do you remember this? Mr. MacDonald sitting on the stand, the father of the Pinto, as Mr. Cosentino called him—and he didn't deny it.

He says, "Yes, it is my car."

Mr. MacDonald, a man even Mr. Copp—on cross examination I asked him, I said:

"Q Mr. Copp, isn't it a fact that you consider Harold MacDonald an extremely safety-conscious Engineer?"

And he said:

"A Yes, sir."

Mr. MacDonald, that extremely safety-conscious Engineer, told you he did not believe a higher standard could be met for 1973 cars without greater problems, such as handling, where more accidents and death occur.

Mr. Copp, let's take the State's witness, Copp.

Mr. Copp admitted that even today, seven years later, the Federal Government Standards is only 30 miles per hour, 10 miles higher than what Ford adopted—voluntarily adopted for itself for 1973.

And Mr. Copp further testified that a 30 mile an hour would be equivalent only to a 31.5 or 32 mile car-to-car.

So, ladies and gentlemen of the jury, Mr. Cosentino tells you about, "Oh, isn't it terrible to put these cars out there, wasn't it awful—did you know?"

Well, do you know that today, the—today, 1980 model cars are required to meet only a 30 mile an hour rear-impact moving-barrier standard? 1980 cars.

And that that is equivalent to a 32 mile an hour car-to-car, and yet Ford Motor Company, the only company in the world, imposed upon itself a standard and made a car in 1973, seven years ago that would meet 26 to 28 miles an hour, within 5, 6 or 7 miles of what the cars are required by law to meet today.

Mr. Cosentino will tell you, frankly, the cars today, in his judgment, are defective and he will prosecute.

What a chaos would evolve if the Government set the standard for automobiles and says, "That is reasonable," and then Local Prosecutors in the fifty states around the country start saying, "I am not satisfied, and I am going to prosecute the manufacturer."

Well, Mr. Cosentino may say that the standard should be 40.

The Prosecutor in Alabama may say, "No, it should be 50."

The Prosecutor in Alaska may say, "No, it should be 60."

And the Prosecutor in Tennessee—they say—you know, "I am satisfied—I am satisfied with 30," or, "I think it should be 70."

How can our companies survive?

Point 5, the 1973 Pinto was comparable in design and manufacture to other 1973 subcompacts.

I say again, ladies and gentlemen, we don't compare the Pinto with Lincolns, Cadillacs, Mercedes Benz—we ask you to compare the Pinto with the other three subcompacts.

Let's take the State's witnesses on this point first.

Mr. Bloch—Mr. Cosentino didn't mention Mr. Bloch, but I don't want him to be forgotten.

Mr. Bloch and Mr. Copp complain about the Pinto, and that is easy.

Let's descend to the particulars. Let's see what they really said.

Well, they complain about the metal, the gauge of the metal in the fuel tank; you remember that?

And then on cross examination it was brought out that the general range of metal in fuel tanks ranged between twenty-three-thousands of an inch and forty-thousandths of an inch.

That is the general range. Twenty-three-thousandths on the low to forty-thousandths on the high, and lo and behold, what is the gauge of metal in the Pinto tank?

Thirty-five thousandths.

And Mr. Bloch admits that it is in the upper third of the general range.

And they complain about the bumper on the Pinto.

And, remember, I said we would show that the Pinto was comparable to other '73 subcompacts.

They complain about the bumper, but then they admit on cross examination the Vega, the Gremlin, the Colt, the Pinto and the Toyota had about the same bumper.

And they complain of a lack of a protective shield between the tank and the axle, but they admitted on cross examination that no other 1973 car had such a shield, and Mr. Copp admits that there was no significant puncture in the 1973—in the Ulrich accident caused by the axle, and you remember I had him get up here and say, "Point out where this protective shield would have done something, where this puncture source we are talking about—" and you remember, it is so small—I can't find it now.

So much for the protective shield.

And then they complained about the insufficient rear structure in the Pinto but they both admit that the Pinto had left side rail hat section and that the Vega had none, nothing on either side, that the Pinto had shear plates, these plates in the trunk, and that neither the Vega, the Gremlin or the Colt or Toyota had any of these.

And the Vega used the coil-spring suspension, when the Pinto had a leaf-spring, and that was additional structure. . . .

They talked about puncture sources, there is a puncture source there, puncture source here, but on cross examination, they end up by admitting that the puncture sources on all subcompacts have about the same—and in about the same space. . . .

Mr. MacDonald testified, "Yes, I thought the Pinto was a reasonably safe car. I think the '73 Pinto is still a reasonably safe car, and I bought one, I drove it for years for myself.

Mr. Olsen—you remember little Mr. Frank Olsen?

He came in here, had his little eighteen-year-old daughter—he said, "I am an Engineer responsible for the Pinto. I think it is a safe car. I bought one for my little eighteen-year-old daughter, and she drove it for several years."

And Mr. Freers, the man who Mr. Cosentino objected to going over the fact that he was from Rose-Hullman, and on the Board of Trustees there—Mr. Freers said, "I like the Pinto. I am an Engineer responsible for the Pinto, and I bought a '73 Pinto for my young son and he drove it several years."

And then Mr. Feaheny says, "I am one of the Engineers responsible for the Pinto, and I bought one for my wife, the mother of my six children, and she drove it for several years."

Now, when Mr. Cosentino tried to say there was something phoney about that—he brought out their salaries.

And I—I don't know to deal with the salary question.

It just seems to me to be so irrelevant, like some other things I am going to talk about in a minute that I am just going to simply say, "It is irrelevant," and go on.

But he said to these people—he suggested to you, suggested to these people, "Well, you make a lot of money, you can afford better than a Pinto."

Like, "You don't really mean you had a Pinto?"

And Mr. Feaheny says, "Yes, I could afford a more expensive car, but, you know, I—all of us, we have been fighting, we come out with something we thought would fight the imports, and we were proud of it, and our families were proud of it."

Do you think, ladies and gentlemen of the jury, that Mr. MacDonald was indifferent, reckless, when he bought and drove the Pinto?

He drives on the same roads, he has the—subject to the same reckless people that Mr. Cosentino didn't prosecute.

Do you think that Mr. Olsen was reckless and indifferent when he gave a Pinto to his eighteen-year-old daughter, a '73 Pinto?

Do you think that Mr. Freers was reckless when he gave one to his young son? . . .

Point No. 8: Notwithstanding all I have said, Ford Motor Company decided on June 8th, 1978, to recall the Pintos to improve fuel systems, and did everything in its power to recall it as quickly as possible.

This is really what this case, I guess, is all about, because that period of time involved is July 1, 1978 until August 10, 1978.

And the Court will charge you, as I said the elements are whether we recklessly failed to warn and repair during that period of time.

And whether that reckless omission, if any, caused the deaths.

And you may ask—and I think it is fair to ask—why recall the Pinto, the '73 Pinto, if it is comparable to other subcompacts, if statistics say it is performing as well as other '73 subcompacts?

And if Ford had a standard for '73 that no other manufacturer had?

And Feaheny and Mr. Misch told you why.

The Federal Government started an investigation. The publicity was hurting the Company.

They thought the Government was wrong, but they said, "You can't fight City Hall."

"We could fight and fight and we could go to Court and we could fight, but it's not going to get us anywhere. If we can improve it, let's do it and let's don't fight the Federal Government."

Maybe the Company should not have recalled the '73 Pinto.

Douglas Toms did not think, as he told you on the stand under oath, that the '73 Pinto should have been recalled.

He had information that the Pinto did as well as other cars;

That Pinto fire accidents equaled the total Pinto population or equaled the percentage of Pinto population to all car population.

And Mr. Bloch, on the other hand, says, "All of them should be recalled."

He said, "The Pinto should have been recalled."

He said, "The Vega should have been recalled."

He said, "The Gremlin should be recalled."

And he didn't know about the Dodge Colt.

Nevertheless, the Company did decide to recall the Pinto. And they issued widely-disseminated Press Releases on June 9, 1978.

It was in the newspapers, TV, radio, according to the proof in this case.

And thereafter the Government regulated what they did in the recall.

That is what Mr. Misch told you.

He said, "From the time we started—June 9, 1978—to August 10, Mr.—the Federal Government regulated what we did."

Now, Mr. Cosentino is prosecuting us.

And the Federal Government has regulated us.

Mr. Misch said, "The Federal Government reviewed what kind of Press Releases we should issue, what kind of Recall Letter we should issue, what kind of a Modification Kit that they would approve.

Even so—it is undisputed, absolutely undisputed that we did everything in our power to recall as fast as possible—nights, days, weekends.

And notwithstanding all of that, the first kit—the first complete kit was assembled August 1, 1978.

And on August 9, 1978, there were only 20,000 kits available for 1,600,000 cars.

And this was not Ford's fault. Ford was pushing the suppliers, the people who were outside the Company doing work for them.

And Mr. Vasher testified that he got the names of the current owners from R. L. Polk on July 17;

That the Ulrich name was not among them;

That he sent the Recall Letter in August to the original owner because he had no Ulrich name.

Now,—and he said he couldn't have gotten the Ulrich name by August 10.

Now, Mr. Cosentino said, "Well, the Ulrich Registration was on file with the State of Indiana and it is open to the public."

Well, Ford Motor Company doesn't know where these 1,600,000 cars are. It has to use R. L. Polk because they collect the information by the VIN Numbers.

If Ford Motor Company went to each state, they would go to fifty states and they would have each of the fifty states run through its files 1,600,000 VIN Numbers.

And Mr. Vasher, who is the expert in there, said it would take months and months to do that.

And, finally, ladies and gentlemen, the Government didn't approve the Modification Kit until August 15, 1978.

But the State says that we should have warned—we should have warned 1973 Pinto owners not to drive the car.

But the Government never suggested that.

Based on our information, and confirmed by the Toms testimony, our cars were performing as well—or better than—other '73 subcompacts.

As Mr. Misch so succinctly stated, "We would have been telling the Pinto owners to park their Pintos and get into another car no safer—and perhaps even less safe—than the Pinto." . . .

Well, we submit that the physical facts, the placement of the—the placement of the gasoline cap, where it is found, the testimony of Levi Woodard, and Nancy Fogo—demonstrate the closing speed in this case was at least 50 to 60 miles per hour.

Mr. Copp, the State's witness, testified that no small car made in America in 1973 would withstand 40 to 50 miles per hour—40 to 50 rear-impact. No small car made in America in 1973 would withstand a 40-plus mile per hour rear-impact.

The Dodge Colt would not have; the Vega could not have; the Gremlin would not have; and certainly even the Toyota would not have.

Mr. Habberstad told you that no small car—and some big cars—would have withstood this crash.

And he established by the crash-tests you have seen that the Vega could not withstand 50;

That the Gremlin could not withstand 50;

That the Toyota Corolla with the tank over the axle could not withstand 50;

And that even a full-sized Chevrolet Impala cannot withstand 50 miles per hour.

If it made no difference what kind of car was out there, members of the jury, how can Ford Motor Company have caused the deaths? . . .

I am not here to tell you that the 1973 Pinto was the strongest car ever built.

I'm not here to tell you it is equal to a Lincoln, a Cadillac, a Mercedes—that funny car that Mr. Bloch mentioned.

I'm not here to tell you a stronger car couldn't be built.

Most of us, however, learn early in life that there is "no Santa Claus," and "There's no such thing as a free lunch."

If the public wanted it, and could pay for it, and we had the gasoline to drive it, Detroit could build a tank of a car—a car that would withstand practically anything, a car that would float if a careless driver drove it into the water.

A car that would be invulnerable even to the "Duggars" of the world.

But, members of the jury, only the rich could afford it and they would have to stop at every other gasoline station for a refill.

I am here to tell you that the 1973 Pinto is comparable to other '73 subcompacts, including that Toyota, that Corolla with the tank over the axle.

I am here to tell you it was not designed by some mysterious figure you have never seen.

It was designed and manufactured by Harold MacDonald, Frank Olsen and Howard Freers.

I am here to tell you these are the decent men doing an honorable job and trying to do a decent job.

I am here to tell you that Harold MacDonald, Frank Olsen, and Howard Freers are not reckless killers.

Harold MacDonald is the same man, State's witness, Copp, called an "extremely safety-conscious individual."

Frank Olsen is the same "Frank Olsen" Mr. Copp said was a "good Engineer."

And Howard Freers is the same "Howard Freers" Mr. Copp said was a "man of honesty and integrity."

I am here to tell you that these men honestly believe and honestly believed that the 1973 Pinto was—and is—a reasonably safe car—so safe they bought it for their daughters, sons and family.

Do you think that Frank Olsen believed he was acting in plain, conscious, unjustifiable disregard of harm?

When he bought a '73 Pinto for his eighteen-year-old daughter?

Or Howard Freers, when he bought one for his young son?

I am here to tell you that the design and manufacture of an automobile is not an easy task;

That it takes time to know whether a change in one part of the 14,000 parts of a car will or will not cause greater problems elsewhere in the car or its performance.

I am here to tell you that safety is a matter of degree;

That no one can say that a car that will meet a 26 to 28 mile per hour rear-impact is unsafe and one that will meet a 30 to 32 impact is safe.

I am here to tell you that if this country is to survive economically, it is really time to stop blaming Industry or Business, large or small, for our own sins.

I am here to tell you that no car is now or ever can be safe when reckless drivers are on the road.

I am here to tell you that Ford Motor Company may not be perfect, but it is not guilty of reckless homicide.

Thank you, members of the jury.

And God bless you in your deliberations.

Study Questions

1. Do you think Ford was guilty as charged?

2. Do you think it was a key fact that some of the Pinto's engineers bought Pintos for some of their relatives? Was it just a gimmick? Don't we need to know when the engineers bought the cars, since they could have bought them just to look better in the trial? Does Neal say when the engineers bought the cars for their relatives? Even if they bought the cars right away, couldn't they have had court appearances in mind?

3. Does Neal pose a false dilemma by suggesting that finding the Pinto unacceptable would require companies to build a car like a military tank?

"WHAT I FOUND WORSE THAN THE CONVICTION WAS THAT TWO WINOS, A DELIVERY BOY, THREE RECEPTIONISTS, A CUSTODIAN, A TICKET TAKER, A ZIPPER TESTER, TWO FILE CLERKS AND A FEATHER SALESMAN WERE CONSIDERED A JURY OF MY PEERS."

© 1995 by Sidney Harris.

77

Jury System

Sterling Harwood

Type of Ethics: Legal and judicial ethics

Date: Established constitutionally in the United States in 1783; term coined 1188

Definition: An institution consisting of groups of persons selected by law to decide specific questions based on the evidence presented

Significance: The jury system is one of the most fundamental checks and balances in law, allowing a commonsense working of justice in a particular case that would not otherwise occur, because of the general nature of laws.

Some hard historical data show how important a well-functioning jury system is to the encouraging of ethical behavior. The verdict in the famous Los Angeles, California, police brutality case involving the videotaped beating of black motorist Rodney King sparked an explosion of riots that lasted five days and set new records in terms of the number of casualties and the amount of damage; there were 60 dead, 2,383 injured, at least $1 billion in damage to property, and at least 20,000 residents lost jobs as a result of the business closings that followed. Some people argue that the riots were a rebellion that was akin to the Boston Tea Party and that it was unethical neglect of the problems of the underclass in Los Angeles that provided the powder keg that was ignited by the spark of the jury's verdict. The tragic riots focused much more attention on these problems.

Law is often complex and abstract. The jury system serves to forestall the potential injustice of a large or remote government. A jury of one's peers, to which U.S. citizens are constitutionally entitled, often prevents the law from running roughshod over people in situations that could not have been foreseen by the legislators who, often decades earlier, created the law. At the point of application of law, the jury can work justice in the particular case. Jury nullification is the jury's refusal to apply an unethical law. A jury can see people in court and adjust its views based on the equities it observes.

A major ethical issue surrounding the jury system is how representative of the larger community a jury should be. Many people believe that the verdict leading to the riots in the King case was the result of the facts that no African Americans were on that jury and that King was African American. During the *voir dire*, lawyers for each side have a limited power to prevent some people from serving on the jury without even showing why they may not serve. Lawyers have the right to remove any juror by showing cause (for example, that a juror is related to the accused). Lawyers use many psychological profiles involving stereotypes to remove potential jurors without cause. This may be unethical, because some discriminatory stereotypes are used in this process.

Jurors are drawn from ordinary life. Therefore, the jury system is also a check and balance against unethical elitism in a democracy. This is why some states make jurors with extraordinary qualifications (such as a law degree) ineligible for jury duty. The jury system is used in both criminal prosecutions and civil suits. Usually, a unanimous verdict is needed to avoid a hung jury, but some states have allowed a nearly unanimous verdict to be decisive in some civil suits. The jury system is part of an adversary system in which two sides clash and thereby, according to theory, provide the best picture of the whole truth by presenting both sides of the issue. Some countries use an inquisitorial system that uses judges or panels of authorities as investigators. The adversary system is often emotional and messy, but it provides a powerful incentive for each side to present its story. With this greater incentive comes a greater chance for the jury to hear the whole truth.

Study Questions

1. Does the jury system make the American legal system more democratic?

2. Jurors are often paid as little as $5 a day and must spend weeks or even months away from any other job. Does this make the jury system similar to

Reprinted from Sterling Harwood, "Jury System," in *Ready Reference: Ethics* (Pasadena, Calif.: Salem Press, 1994). Reprinted by permission.

affirmative action, since it is disproportionately minorities and women who can afford to be jurors?

3. Is the jury system illogical, since it allows lawyers to sway the jury based on emotional appeals rather than having impartial or heartless bureaucrats decide what should happen? Or is allowing some significant role for the emotions of ordinary people reasonable and logical after all?

"REMEMBER US? THE JURY YOU
BRIBED TO LET YOU OFF..."

© 1995 by Sidney Harris.

78

Henningsen v. Bloomfield Motors, Inc. and Chrysler Corporation

Supreme Court of New Jersey

Claus H. Henningsen purchased a Plymouth automobile, manufactured by defendant Chrysler Corporation, from defendant Bloomfield Motors, Inc. His wife, plaintiff Helen Henningsen, was injured while driving it and instituted suit against both defendants to recover damages on account of her injuries. Her husband joined in the action seeking compensation for his consequential losses. The complaint was predicated upon breach of express and implied warranties and upon negligence. At the trial the negligence counts were dismissed by the court and the case was submitted to the jury for determination solely on the issues of implied warranty of merchantability. Verdicts were returned against both defendants and in favor of the plaintiffs. Defendants appealed and plaintiffs cross-appealed from the dismissal of their negligence claim. . . .

. . . The particular car selected was described as a 1955 Plymouth, Plaza "6," Club Sedan. The type used in the printed parts of the form became smaller in size, different in style, and less readable toward the bottom where the line for the purchaser's signature was placed. The smallest type on the page appears in the two paragraphs, one of two and one-quarter lines and the second of one and one-half lines, on which great stress is laid by the defense in the case. These two paragraphs are the least legible and the most difficult to read in the instrument, but they are most important in the evaluation of the rights of the contesting parties. They do not attract attention and there is nothing about the format which would draw the reader's eye to them. In fact, a studied and concentrated effort would have to be made to read them. De-emphasis seems the motive rather than emphasis. . . . The two paragraphs are:

"The front and back of this Order comprise the entire agreement affecting this purchase and no other agreement or understanding of any nature concerning same has been made or entered into, or will be recognized. I hereby certify that no credit has been extended to me for the purchase of this motor vehicle except as appears in writing on the face of this agreement.

"I have read the matter printed on the back hereof and agree to it as a part of this order the same as if it were printed above my signature. . . . "

The testimony of Claus Henningsen justifies the conclusion that he did not read the two fine print paragraphs referring to the back of the purchase contract. And it is uncontradicted that no one made any reference to them, or called them to his attention. With respect to the matter appearing on the back, it is likewise uncontradicted that he did not read it and that no one called it to his attention.

. . . The warranty, which is the focal point of the case, is set forth [on the reverse side of the page]. It is as follows:

"It is expressly agreed that there are no warranties, express or implied, *made* by either the dealer or the manufacturer on the motor vehicle, chassis, or parts furnished hereunder except as follows.

"The manufacturer warrants each new motor vehicle (including original equipment placed thereon by the manufacturer except tires), chassis or parts manufactured by it to be free from defects in material or workmanship under normal use and service. Its obligation under this warranty being limited to making good at its factory any part or parts thereof which shall, within ninety (90) days after delivery of such vehicle *to the original purchaser* or before such vehicle has been driven 4,000 miles, whichever event shall first occur, be returned to it with transportation charges prepaid and which its examination shall disclose to its satisfaction to have been thus defective: This warranty being expressly in lieu of all other warranties expressed or implied, and all other obligations or liabilities on its part, and it neither assumes nor authorizes any other person to assume for it any other liability in connection with the sale of its vehicles. . . .'"

The new Plymouth was turned over to the Henningsens on May 9, 1955. No proof was adduced by the dealer to show precisely what was done in the way of mechanical or road testing beyond testimony that the manufacturer's instructions were probably followed. Mr. Henningsen drove it from the dealer's place of business in Bloomfield to their home in

Reprinted from Supreme Court of New Jersey, 161 A2d 69 (1960).

Keansburg. On the trip nothing unusual appeared in the way in which it operated. Thereafter, it was used for short trips on paved streets about the town. It had no servicing and no mishaps of any kind before the event of May 19. That day, Mrs. Henningsen drove to Asbury Park [New Jersey]. On the way down and in returning the car performed in normal fashion until the accident occurred. She was proceeding north on Route 36 in Highlands, New Jersey, at 20–22 miles per hour. The highway was paved and smooth, and contained two lanes for northbound travel. She was riding in the right-hand lane. Suddenly she heard a loud noise "from the bottom, by the hood." It "felt as if something cracked." The steering wheel spun in her hands; the car veered sharply to the right and crashed into a highway sign and a brick wall. No other vehicle was in any way involved. A bus operator driving in the left-hand lane testified that he observed plaintiff's car approaching in normal fashion in the opposite direction; "all of a sudden [it] veered at 90 degrees . . . and right into this wall." As a result of the impact, the front of the car was so badly damaged that it was impossible to determine if any of the parts of the steering wheel mechanism or workmanship or assembly were defective or improper prior to the accident. The condition was such that the collision insurance carrier, after inspection, declared the vehicle a total loss. It had 468 miles on the speedometer at the time. . . .

The terms of the warranty are a sad commentary upon the automobile manufacturers' marketing practices. Warranties developed in the law in the interest of and to protect the ordinary consumer who cannot be expected to have the knowledge or capacity or even the opportunity to make adequate inspection of mechanical instrumentalities, like automobiles, and to decide for himself whether they are reasonably fit for the designed purpose. . . . But the ingenuity of the Automobile Manufacturers Association, by means of its standardized form, has metamorphosed the warranty into a device to limit the maker's liability. To call it an "equivocal" agreement, as the Minnesota Supreme Court did, is the least that can be said in criticism of it.

The manufacturer agrees to replace defective parts for 90 days after the sale or until the car has been driven 4,000 miles, whichever is first to occur, *if the part is sent to the factory, transportation charges prepaid, and if examination discloses to its satisfaction that the part is defective.* . . .

Chrysler points out that an implied warranty of merchantability is an incident of a contract of sale. It concedes, of course, the making of the original sale to Bloomfield Motors, Inc., but maintains that this transaction marked the terminal point of its contractual connection with the car. Then Chrysler urges that since it was not a party to the sale by the dealer to Henningsen, there is no privity of contract between it and the plaintiffs, and the absence of this privity eliminates any such implied warranty.

There is no doubt that under early common-law concepts of contractual liability only those persons who were parties to the bargain could sue for a breach of it. In more recent times a noticeable disposition has appeared in a number of jurisdictions to break through the narrow barrier of privity when dealing with sales of goods in order to give realistic recognition to a universally accepted fact. The fact is that the dealer and the ordinary buyer do not, and are not expected to, buy goods, whether they be foodstuffs or automobiles, exclusively for their own consumption or use. Makers and manufacturers know this and advertise and market their products on that assumption; witness the "family" car, the baby foods, etc. The limitations of privity in contracts for the sale of goods developed their place in the law when marketing conditions were simple, when maker and buyer frequently met face to face on an equal bargaining plane and when many of the products were relatively uncomplicated and conducive to inspection by a buyer competent to evaluate their quality. With the advent of mass marketing, the manufacturer became remote from the purchaser, sales were accomplished through intermediaries, and the demand for the product was created by advertising media. In such an economy it became obvious that the consumer was the person being cultivated. Manifestly, the connotation of "consumer" was broader than that of "buyer." He signified such a person who, in the reasonable contemplation of the parties to the sale, might be expected to use the product. Thus, where the commodities sold are such that if defectively manufactured they will be dangerous to life or limb, then society's interests can only be protected by eliminating the requirement of privity between the maker and his dealers and the reasonably expected ultimate consumer. In that way the burden of losses consequent upon use of defective articles is borne by those who are in a position to either control the danger or make an equitable distribution of the losses when they do occur. . . .

Under modern conditions the ordinary layman, on responding to the importuning of colorful advertising, has neither the opportunity nor the capacity to inspect or to determine the fitness of an automobile for use; he must rely on the manufacturer who has control of its construction, and to some degree on the dealer who, to the limited extent called for by the manufacturer's instructions, inspects and services it before delivery. In such a marketing milieu his remedies and those of persons who properly claim through him should not depend "upon the intricacies of the law of sales. The obligation of the manufacturer should not be based alone on privity of contract. It should rest, as was once said, upon 'the demands of social justice.'" . . .

In a society such as ours, where the automobile is a common and necessary adjunct of daily life, and where its use is so fraught with danger to the driver, passengers, and the public, the manufacturer is under a special obligation in connection with the construction, promotion, and sale of his cars. Consequently, the courts must examine purchase agreements closely to see if consumer and public interests are treated fairly. . . .

What influence should these circumstances have on the restrictive effect of Chrysler's express warranty in the framework of the purchase contract? As we have said, warranties originated in the law to safeguard the buyer and not to limit the liability of the seller or manufacturer. It seems obvious in this instance that the motive was to avoid the warranty obligations which are normally incidental to such sales. The language gave little and withdrew much. In return for the delusive remedy of replacement of defective parts at the factory, the buyer is said to have accepted the exclusion of the maker's liability for personal injuries arising from the breach of the warranty, and to have agreed to the elimination of any other express or implied warranty. An instinctively felt sense of justice cries out against such a sharp bargain. But does the doctrine that a person is bound by his signed agreement, in the absence of fraud, stand in the way of any relief? . . .

The warranty before us is a standardized form designed for mass use. It is imposed upon the automobile consumer. He takes it or leaves it, and he must take it to buy an automobile. No bargaining is engaged in with respect to it. In fact, the dealer through whom it comes to the buyer is without authority to alter it; his function is ministerial—simply to deliver it. The form warranty is not only standard with Chrysler but, as mentioned above, it is the uniform warranty of the Automobile Manufacturers Association. . . . Of these companies, the "Big Three" (General Motors, Ford, and Chrysler) represented 93.5% of the passenger-car production for 1958 and the independents 6.5%. And for the same year the "Big Three" had 86.72% of the total passenger vehicle registrations. . . .

In the context of this warranty, only the abandonment of all sense of justice would permit us to hold that, as a matter of law, the phrase "its obligation under this warranty being limited to making good at its factory any part or parts thereof" signifies to an ordinary reasonable person that he is relinquishing any personal injury claim that might flow from the use of a defective automobile. Such claims are nowhere mentioned. . . .

In the matter of warranties on the sale of their products, the Automobile Manufacturers Association has enabled them to present a united front. From the standpoint of the purchaser, there can be no arms length negotiating on the subject. Because his capacity for bargaining is so grossly unequal, the inexorable conclusion which follows is that he is not permitted to bargain at all. He must take or leave the automobile on the warranty terms dictated by the maker. He cannot turn to a competitor for better security.

Public policy is a term not easily defined. Its significance varies as the habits and needs of a people may vary. It is not static and the field of application is an ever increasing one. A contract, or a particular provision therein, valid in one era may be wholly opposed to the public policy of another. Courts keep in mind the principle that the best interests of society demand that persons should not be unnecessarily restricted in their freedom to contract. But they do not hesitate to declare void as against public policy contractual provisions which clearly tend to the injury of the public in some way. . . .

In the framework of this case, illuminated as it is by the facts and the many decisions noted, we are of the opinion that Chrysler's attempted disclaimer of an implied warranty of the merchantability and of the obligations arising therefrom is so inimical to the public good as to compel an adjudication of its invalidity. . . .

The principles that have been expounded as to the obligation of the manufacturer apply with equal force to the separate express warranty of the dealer. This is so, irrespective of the absence of the relationship of principle and agent between these defendants, because the manufacturer and the Association establish the warranty policy for the industry. The bargaining position of the dealer is inextricably bound by practice to that of the maker and the purchaser must take or leave the automobile, accompanied and encumbered as it is by the uniform warranty. . . .

Under all of the circumstances outlined above, the judgments in favor of the plaintiffs and against the defendants are affirmed.

Study Questions

1. Did the court reach the decision that is most morally justifiable?

2. Would libertarianism support the court's decision? If so, why? If not, why not? If you were not privy (that is, party) to a contract with the manufacturer, then would libertarianism require the manufacturer to guarantee that the car manufactured would not malfunction and hurt you?

3. Would egalitarianism support the court's decision? If so, why? If not, why not?

79

Road Kill

Toronto Sun

These are real statements—by real people. The following quotes were taken from insurance forms and were eventually published in the *Toronto Sun*, July 26, 1977. They'll just kill you.

Coming home, I drove in the wrong house and collided with a tree I don't have.

The other car collided with mine without giving warning of its intentions.

I thought my window was down, but I found out it was up when I put my hand through it.

I collided with a stationary truck coming the other way.

A truck backed through my windshield into my wife's face.

A pedestrian hit me and went under my car.

The guy was all over the road. I had to swerve a number of times before I hit him.

I pulled away from the side of the road, glanced at my mother-in-law and headed over the embankment.

In my attempt to kill a fly, I drove into a telephone pole.

I had been shopping for plants all day and was on my way home. As I reached the intersection, a hedge sprang up obscuring my vision. I did not see the other car.

I had been driving my car for forty years when I fell asleep at the wheel and had an accident.

I was on my way to the doctor's office with rear-end trouble when my universal joint gave way causing me to have an accident.

To avoid hitting the bumper of the car in front, I struck the pedestrian.

As I approached the intersection, a stop sign suddenly appeared in a place where no stop sign had ever appeared before. I was unable to stop in time to avoid the accident.

My car was legally parked as it backed into the other vehicle.

An invisible car came out of nowhere, struck my vehicle and vanished.

I told the police that I was not injured but on removing my hat, I found that I had a skull fracture.

The pedestrian had no idea which direction to go, so I ran over him.

The indirect cause of this accident was a little guy in a small car with a big mouth.

I was thrown from my car as it left the road. I was later found in a ditch by some stray cows.

The telephone pole was approaching fast. I was attempting to swerve out of its path when it struck my front end.

I was unable to stop in time and my car crashed into the vehicle. The driver and passenger then left immediately for a vacation with injuries.

I saw the slow-moving, sad-faced, old gentleman as he bounced off the hood of my car.

I was sure the old fellow would never make it to the other side of the roadway when I struck him.

Copy courtesy of: Northfield License Bureau, Northfield, Ohio, Dorothy Davis, Deputy Registrar.

80

Food and Welfare State Capitalism: A Success Story

Farmers for an Orderly Market

Editor's note: Many business ethics textbooks neglect agriculture. But these farmers make six key arguments for using marketing orders from the federal government and farmers to regulate agriculture. First, the farmers argue that marketing orders keep citrus flowing to the stores in a steady supply year-round, and have kept prices significantly more stable. Second, citrus fruit has the unusual trait of storing well on the tree, and this natural trait, combined with the growers' self-regulation, produces a steady supply of freshly picked, high-quality fruit for consumers to enjoy year-round. Third, agriculture is the only industry that cannot control its supply of raw material, and that fact of nature is the realistic foundation for using marketing orders. Fourth, many opponents of citrus marketing orders are companies whose primary economic interest is in something other than farm income. Fifth, many groups benefit from marketing orders because of the interweaving of interests in an advanced economy. Sixth, marketing orders are programs of self-regulation that farmers adopt through a democratic process to solve agricultural problems. They are not subsidies. They do not use tax dollars.

Marketing orders keep citrus flowing to the supermarkets and other outlets in steady supply year-round, and, over the years, have kept prices in a relatively stable range.

From Farmers for an Orderly Market, *Democratic Self-Determination: An Alternative to Subsidies* (Sunkist Growers, Inc., 1984, reissued 1991). Reprinted by permission.

Federal marketing orders for fruit and vegetables, enabled under the Agricultural Marketing Agreement Act of 1937, allow farmers to develop and implement self-help programs to regulate the marketing of certain specialty crops.

There are many types of marketing orders because each program is specifically designed to meet the needs of a particular commodity. For example, there are size and grade orders which remove undesirable sizes and qualities of fruit from the marketplace. Marketing orders covering commodities that are harvested once a year and then preserved for use at a later time, such as raisins, almonds and prunes, rely on set-aside or reserve-pool provisions which allow the surplus portion of a crop to be stored for sale later.

The citrus industry utilizes a flow-to-market feature or prorate provision that works like this: An industry committee, nominated by the growers and appointed by the Secretary of Agriculture, determines the amount of fruit that can be absorbed into the domestic market *each week* without glutting or shorting the market. (Fruit for export channels and the juice market is exempt.)

This has the effect of spreading both the harvesting and marketing of the crop in an orderly fashion over its full life cycle. By tying harvesting to market demand, consumers get a continuing supply of fresh fruit each week of the season while warehouse storage of citrus is kept to an absolute minimum. Uncontrolled glutting of the market with a perishable product like oranges would cause consumers to receive unappealing, aged fruit out of storage until the supply returns to normal.

It should be clearly understood that while the marketing order authorizes volume regulations, it does not establish the price. The price of an orange is, for example, established in the overall marketplace on the basis of supply and demand.

The marketing order does not diminish the need for a grower to compete efficiently. Nor does it guarantee a sale. It is still the grower's responsibility to grow a quality product, package it properly and market it aggressively. He will not survive if he produces something that is not acceptable to the consumer.

Under the prorate provisions in 1982, when there was a normal production of navel oranges, the California-Arizona citrus industry was able to move 38 million cartons. Conversely, in 1983, a year with an enormous crop of navels, the industry moved 49 million cartons. The price, however, was $1.13 less per carton than it had been the previous year. So the laws of supply and demand continue to work under the marketing order system.

In no way can the prorate system constitute what one critic has called "a hidden tax on consumers." This would be true only if the effect were to maintain consumer prices consistently higher than the free market. However, in fact and by design, the effect is to cut price troughs relative to price peaks. Thus, the week-by-week determination of market demand ensures stability in the price of citrus and keeps price fluctuations within a narrow range of slightly higher prices during some parts of the season and lower prices at others.

Citrus fruit has the unusual characteristic of storing well on the tree; this natural gift, combined with self-regulation by the growers themselves, accounts for the steady supply of freshly picked, quality fruit consumers enjoy year-round.

Without the mechanisms for the orderly marketing of citrus, the general structure of the fresh food distribution system and, indeed, the dietary pattern of the U.S. consumer would be quite different.

The importance of fresh fruit in the diet is universally accepted and the availability of such products is considered a routine accomplishment. What is ignored is the fact that there are only three fruits that are widely accepted by consumers and available on a daily basis at reasonable prices throughout the year. These fruits are oranges, apples and bananas; all other available fruits are seasonal in nature and subject to a high degree of variability in price, quantity and quality.

Through the influx of South American fruit in the last few years, some fruit has been made available for a longer period of time. However, price and quality still fluctuate greatly.

Of the three basics, bananas are mostly imported and thus supplies are largely dependent on economic and political conditions in those areas.

The second, apples, have become available on a 12-month basis because of technological developments with controlled atmosphere (CA) storage. The use of CA technology has had only limited value with other fresh fruits and vegetables; with citrus it has proven to be completely unworkable.

Oranges, the third of the basic three, have remained important in the diet because of the development of a marketing strategy in California and Arizona that has turned a seasonal fruit into a year-round staple. (Florida oranges are used mostly for

processing, whereas Western oranges are largely marketed fresh.) Oranges have a unique characteristic—they can be stored on the tree for up to several months. Unlike other tree crops, which must be picked immediately upon ripening or else rot on the tree, oranges can remain on the tree for a reasonable time until the market demand calls for them to be picked. This is the basis on which the orange marketing orders were established.

The removal of the orderly marketing system could result in the "dependable" orange becoming a seasonal specialty.

Agriculture is the only industry that cannot control its supply of raw material; that fact of nature is the realistic foundation for instituting market orders.

Weather occurrences—hail, frost, wind, storms and drought—along with inexplicable vagaries of nature, cause crop harvests to fluctuate tremendously. In the citrus industry, for example, crop sizes can easily vary 50 percent up or down from one year to the next.

Agriculturists have long realized that in order to produce to the point of normal demand, it is necessary to plant deliberately to the point of surplus. This is because in two out of five years, crops are small, causing the supply to be barely enough to satisfy the needs of our domestic and export markets. Had farmers not planted to abundance, however, those years would have seen severe shortages of food. This means that for the other three years, or 60 percent of the time, production will be excessive.

While the years of abundant production protect the consumer, they can force farmers into bankruptcy because production beyond consumer demand forces prices below the farmer's costs. Therefore, a major part of our national agricultural policy is designed to protect our farmers who, in turn, are responsible for protecting our food supply. Some protective measures are in the form of direct subsidies paid for by taxpayers, e.g., target price systems, parity programs and government purchase of surplus. These allow the farmer to continue producing abundant food supplies.

Others—and these include federal marketing orders such as those for citrus—likewise allow the farmer to produce abundant supplies, but with no subsidy paid by the taxpayer to the grower.

Volume controls, as permitted under the citrus marketing orders, are not rigid. As mentioned above, there are no limits on the amounts that can be exported or marketed as processed products. In addition, donations to charity, direct sales to consumers and parcel post sales are not regulated by volume restrictions. Further flexibility is provided by the automatic lifting of limits when 85 percent of the crop has been harvested. In addition, each handler is permitted to overship his allotment by up to 10 percent each week, subject to repayment in subsequent weeks; the borrowing and lending of prorate within the same district are also permitted.

All in all, even in years of record production, such as the 1980–81 season, virtually the entire crop is used. That year was also characterized by a very large number of undersized and poor quality fruit, which are not highly prized by the consumer. Despite the difficulties in moving such a large crop with a disproportionate number of small fruit, 92 percent of it did reach the consumer as fresh fruit or orange juice in the U.S. and abroad. Included in that amount were donations to charitable organizations of 2.4 million pounds of navel oranges.

When the juice processing plants could not handle the excess amounts available, the overflow of undersized or damaged fruit was marketed to cattle feeding operations where the oranges were dried by solar heat and ground into livestock feed. Agricultural commodities, such as apples, carrots, potatoes and beets, are regularly used as livestock feed when the cost of other uses is higher than the return to the farmer. This provides additional income to the agricultural producer and is an inexpensive feed source for livestock and poultry. This should ultimately benefit the consumer by making meat, poultry and dairy products available at lower prices.

"Large surpluses contribute to the economic turmoil that is driving family farmers out of business and forcing a dramatic restructuring of agriculture, America's largest industry."—Larry Green, Los Angeles Times *Staff Writer, in a feature entitled* Agriculture in Turmoil, *May 13, 1985. The above quote is true—except for California and Arizona citrus.*

Thus, at a point when most of the United States farmers' livelihoods are being undercut by spiraling production costs and declining market prices, the California and Arizona citrus farmer is thriving. The Farmers for an Orderly Market group believes the economic stability stems from the implementation of marketing orders.

Many of the opponents of citrus marketing orders are companies whose primary economic interest is in something other than farm income.

For several years now we have heard a small, but vocal minority claim that our federal marketing orders are unfair. Who are these opponents to marketing orders? Most entered the industry only recently. Some are huge conglomerate corporations and large "real estate syndicators" who calculate their yields in terms of tax shelters and asset appreciation rather than in oranges.

We are forced, for example, to wonder how Belridge Farms, an opponent of marketing orders, can make an issue of "fairness." Belridge is wholly owned by the Shell Oil Company of the United States, which is, in turn, controlled by Shell Petroleum N.V. of the Netherlands. Is it fair for a foreign oil company to try to dictate marketing policies for American farmers?

Shell Oil, like the majority of opponents to marketing orders, consists of people who do not rely on regular farm income for economic survival.

On the other hand, Farmers for an Orderly Market, fighting to protect the marketing order system, presents a different profile. Records of a typical marketing organization show that four out of five growers live on or near their farms. They are not absentee owners. They are not in the orange business as a tax shelter. The range of motivations of circumstances under which they became and are orange producers is very wide. For some it represents their entire subsistence. For others—retired couples, business people with small enterprises, farmers with other farming interests nearby—growing oranges serves to supplement their limited incomes and is vital to their well-being. For example, a check of the zip codes of Sunkist's 6,000 member growers confirms the basic fact that 80 percent are family farmers who live on or near their farms.

It is these real farmers, most of whom rely on farming for economic survival, who are represented by Farmers for an Orderly Market. They recognize the responsibility for self-regulation as well as the benefits to society flowing from these programs. The 1981 referendum demonstrated the support of these farmers. Ninety-one percent voted in favor of maintaining the order.

As reason for this support, an economist testifying at a recent hearing stated that without the marketing order, the instability created could result in 20 to 30 percent of the production being forced out of the orange industry. All things being equal, this means the smaller farmers. If these farms go out of business, we could project one of two scenarios (or a mix):

- If they were sold to developers, that would severely reduce production and threaten the current system of planting to abundance in order to prevent shortages.
- If the farms were gobbled up by large corporate growers, they in turn might develop the land and take it out of production, or if they continued in the business, the industry could tend toward monopoly, with the consequences we have learned to expect from monopolies with respect to maximizing profits at the expense of consumers.

In either case, there is only one conclusion: In the long run, there would be less fruit reaching the consumer and at higher prices.

Despite everything said above, it would be a distortion of the Farmers for an Orderly Market position to interpret it as solely defending small farmers against large. Proponents of marketing orders include both large and small farmers. As is more fully discussed later, marketing orders prevent over-concentration of supply in the hands of a few large farmers and allow both large and small growers to sell their produce on an equal footing.

Many groups benefit from marketing orders because of the interweaving of interests in an advanced economy.

The marketing order system for citrus has proven its value over more than three decades. Today the Western citrus industry is one of the strongest in all agriculture, while much of the rest of U.S. agriculture is depressed. It is obvious that Western citrus has not only avoided the calamities experienced by most of American agriculture, but the economic outlook for the future looks very good. The industry has achieved this by democratic self-determination, not government regulation.

Despite this beneficial result, it is wrong to focus so much attention on the first section of the policy— that is, the establishing and maintaining of orderly market conditions for the benefit of the farmer—to the point of overlooking the second portion of the Congressional intent,". . . to protect the interest of the consumer . . . ." Indeed, this function of protecting the consumer's food supply has been accomplished so well that it has become a basic part of the national food distribution system and is largely taken for granted. If citrus fruit is available in steady supply year-round, it is because of the marketing order and the sensible way it is carried out by the shippers.

With marketing orders, shippers do not sit back and wait for their prices to rise before shipping oranges to market. If they did, they would lose their allotment. The opponents of marketing orders have another point of view. One such packer, in a published interview, said, "Without prorate we can sit back and wait for the market to go up. If the market is there, pick oranges. If it isn't, wait."

Who loses? The consumer who has to wait until the price goes up before he can buy a fresh orange.

That is not the pattern under marketing orders. Both availability—so important to the customer—and reasonable price—even more crucial on a day-to-day basis—are satisfied. In spite of all the difficulties and costs involved in the production and distribution of fresh oranges, oranges are consistently lower priced at retail than other fruit, according to USDA studies, and are often a better retail buy than many other staples.

Stabilizing the flow of food is in the best interest of everyone. The entire distribution chain operates more efficiently. Supermarkets and produce wholesalers can count on a steady supply throughout the season, knowing that when they place an order, it will be filled. Transportation companies can plan when and where to have equipment available. Warehouses can plan for optimum storage space utilization.

The labor force benefits because the marketing order stretches the citrus consuming season, thus assuring longer periods of employment. Steady supply means steady employment. In most instances, farm laborers no longer need to be transient. Surveys have shown that because of these stable working conditions, California and Arizona citrus workers are among the most highly paid and enjoy some of the best benefits in agriculture.

And, finally, the grower benefits from stability of prices and has his proportional opportunity to market his fruit, no matter how small he might be.

Marketing orders are programs of self-regulation adopted by farmers through a democratic process to solve agricultural problems. They are not subsidies. They do not use tax dollars.

Although the Secretary of Agriculture has the authority to administer marketing order programs for various commodities for the purpose of stabilizing the market, these programs are not ordered by the government, but rather are voted into existence by a referendum of growers themselves, and then paid for by the growers. Since the marketing orders were established, they have been amended by growers' votes several times in recognition of changes within the industry.

Some critics of marketing orders have spread confusing information about barriers to entry, suggesting they were applicable to navel and valencia oranges. It is true that some marketing orders, for reasons particular to these industries, do limit the entry of new growers. However, *there are no imposed limits on becoming a navel orange or valencia orange farmer*—all claims to the contrary notwithstanding.

Recently, critics of the orange marketing orders have complained about the composition of the Administrative Committees that implement the orders. As they well know, the composition is provided for in the marketing orders themselves: six growers, four marketers and one consumer. The United States Department of Agriculture is now entertaining suggestions from several sources as to how that composition might be changed.

Marketing orders are supported by grower-paid assessments and are virtually without cost to the U.S. government. Commodities regulated by marketing orders, such as citrus, have not sought or received costly assistance of government subsidies. Farmers operating under marketing orders believe that a better way to address the problems facing agriculture is to focus on marketing crops, not removing them from production. They continue to support responsible self-regulation rather than expensive subsidy programs.

When marketing orders are suspended, the result can be an adverse effect on orange growers without any benefit to consumers.

Early this year, the Secretary of Agriculture, noting the Florida freeze, also observed that the price of oranges had risen. Apparently, he assumed that the increase in the price of oranges was related to the shortage caused by the freeze. So, without consulting or communicating with the citrus growers, he suspended the flow-to-market provisions of the navel orange marketing order.

However, California/Arizona eating oranges and the juice oranges of Florida are marketed differently. In the case observed by the Secretary of Agriculture, the improved prices for navel oranges were actually the result primarily of a smaller navel orange crop. Because 90 percent of Florida oranges are made into juice products, the freeze may have substantially raised orange juice prices but it had little effect on navel oranges. Navel oranges have excel-

lent fresh eating qualities, and consequently their prices are determined by what is happening in the fresh fruit market, not the processed fruit market.

The suspension of the navel orange marketing order had an immediate negative effect on the market. Produce industry buyers expected—correctly, as it turned out—a temporary oversupply and a consequent drop in the price they would have to pay to farmers. And indeed, the average price to growers decreased from over $6.00 per carton to about $4.30 within five weeks. As of mid-March 1985, the growers had lost over $10 million. While this was occurring, there was little or no change in the consumer's price for navel oranges.

When critics attack marketing orders in the name of buzz words like "deregulation" and "free enterprise," they ignore some basic truths with respect to farming and the free market.

The free enterprise system is based on the premise that the law of supply and demand will keep the economic activities of producers in balance with the needs of consumers—that the former will increase or decrease production as demand increases or decreases. If current producers do not respond quickly enough, thus causing prices to rise inordinately, then new producers will come in to meet the need.

This economic model comes largely from the industrial and service sectors. Agriculture—and tree crops, especially—cannot respond quickly to the need for more produce. The trees, which are the raw material, require, in the case of citrus, some six years to come into production. A manufacturing concern can relatively quickly increase production in response to market demand by ordering more raw material and putting on another shift. So can a professional service firm—only its raw material is people.

Farmers cannot suddenly make more citrus come into existence. So they plant a generous number of trees, six years in advance, knowing that in some years they will have crops that are more than the domestic market can absorb as fresh fruit, but also knowing that in poor years the consumer will not be deprived.

Farmers have no control over production. But the need for a balance between supply and demand remains. Consumers still want a steady supply of fresh fruit at reasonable prices. Marketing orders do what is practical: control the rate at which fruit enters the market; this takes the place of the needed—but impossible—control over production. It replaces something nature does not permit with something that is within the farmer's control—as long as it is applied universally to the total supply. The universal application assures that there will be no discrimination between large and small farmers—shipments are prorated according to crop size and everyone ships his fair share.

This is the justification for limited government intervention: it is the only way to make the program universal, practical and fair. Marketing orders, established by government, free the citrus industry to regulate itself through joint action. The Secretary of Agriculture appoints members of the Administrative Committee from nominees of the industry. The members decide the amount of fruit that should be shipped each week. The USDA holds referenda among farmers as to whether they wish to continue the marketing orders. Farmers rely on self-assessments for the money needed to carry out the work necessitated by the marketing orders, so they are not a burden to the taxpayers. This self-reliance is consonant with their basic position as fiscal conservatives.

The prorate system protects small farmers against monetary losses occurring during times of surplus. Farmers want and need rules—not economic anarchy—so they can stay in business and practice the free enterprise they believe in.

American agriculture is a twentieth-century miracle.

It is indeed a miracle that 3 percent of the people of America produce enough food for all their fellow countrymen plus 150 million others in foreign lands. The American farmer is the most productive human being on earth. While improved technology has contributed greatly to increased production, another major factor is an outstanding national agriculture policy that has been in place for many years.

Federal marketing orders, which permit farmers in democratic elections to use self-control rather than tax dollars to solve their problems, represent an appropriate and efficient part of agriculture in this country.

Study Questions

1. Would libertarians allow federal marketing orders? Is agriculture a major counterexample to the libertarian claim that government has a reverse Midas touch, meaning that government ruins everything it touches? Isn't American agriculture, which is heavily subsidized and regulated by government, the best in the world? Americans spend less of their income on food than do citizens of any other country. And the quality and quantity of food in America speak for themselves. Is agriculture an isolated area of great government programs? Which, if any, of the following areas regulated or subsidized heavily by the U.S. government would you add to the list of major counterexamples to this libertarian claim: (1) the military; (2) the space program; (3) the airlines (even with deregulation, many federal regulations remain on safety, etc.); (4) colleges and universities; and (5) medicine? Note that even one counterexample to a claim is enough to show that the claim is false.

2. Would utilitarians support a stable market? Would a stable market facilitate planning and budgeting, and therefore promote more happiness?

3. Wouldn't egalitarians support a stable market to prevent arbitrary price fluctuations from hurting innocent individual consumers who have no control over the prices?

81

African Philosophy and Agribusiness

Leo Apostel

Editor's note: Apostel explains an approach to agriculture based on African philosophy, including African ethics. He explains many key terms in African philosophy, which far too many business ethics textbooks neglect.

Let us now consider African philosophy. Procreation is the aim of human life. It is thus normal that the woman-man complementarity should determine everything else. The woman is the visible instrument of procreation. It is thus normal that to her should belong the complete set of instruments and field types; that the man should be an incomplete atomic social part and yet the ruler of the family molecule is not, as far as we can see, derivable from African philosophy. The complete sense of autarchy, the tendency toward self-sufficiency, stands, however, almost certainly in relation to this philosophy. It could perhaps even be said that here, in the economy of the subsistence level in the wet belt of Central Africa, we find one of the roots of the philosophy we have been studying. Proof of this conjecture is, however, not at our disposal.

We shall find still other economical explanations of the adoption of the African worldview, but to the present agronomical situation, we may add, as possible causes, the following: (a) the demographic emptiness of this large continent; and (b) the extreme frequency of long-range migration. *Pluralistic energetism could also be connected with African history.* We surmise that nowhere is a philosophy adopted, except as a specific reaction to the past destiny of the group that

Reprinted from *African Philosophy* (Gent, Belgium: E. Story Scientia, 1981), pp. 273–274, 276–279, 294–297, and 320–323.

adopts it. For future research, we recommend the study of the influence of African history on African philosophy.

* * *

In African philosophy plants and crops are *kintu*, beings whose life force is subordinate to that of man and can be used by the life force of the *muntu*. We are here confronted with the problem of the organization of subordinate life forces in order to save superior life forces. The question we have to answer is: will the principles according to which this happens be related or not to the central Bantu philosophy? The major crop of the Zande is eleusine, finger millet, a specific type of cereal, strongly adaptable and stable. The three basic types of fields are as follows: (a) an eleusine field that either follows noncultivated land or another eleusine field; (b) an eleusine field that follows a grass field; and (c) an eleusine field that follows a groundnut field. We can interpret the eleusine, quite speculatively, as the main life preserver of the Zande and should thus be able, if our philosophical concept is of any use, to say something about its cultivation from this point of view.

The main eleusine type, the *oti-moru*, is treated as follows:

a. by hoeing the field is cleared, and in the case of a *ngasu* (clearing in the forest) the trees are felt;
b. 20 days later the clearing is burnt;
c. nearly simultaneously maize is sown;
d. two to seven weeks later the eleusine seeds are sown, which requires great skill because one needs a position of eleusine neither too close nor too open;
e. two or three days after sowing, eleusine germinates, and a few days later, seeds are eliminated;
f. with early eleusines, sesame and hyptis are sown; with late eleusine, sorghum;
g. three months later the dense eleusine fields are hand-weeded. Dynamistic beliefs are attached to the practice.

Our attempt to relate these *functionally* agricultural practices to African philosophy will take the following form:

1. man has to establish his domination over the environment first by a weak attack: with the *ax* he clears the main branches of the trees;
2. then he burns the part of the forest selected, in a strong attack using fire in order to obtain *space* and the fertilizing effect of the *ashes*;
3. finally by means of the *hoe*, the region is cleaned up.

Even though the Zande are by no means the best farmers of Africa, and not forgetting the nonrepresentative character of their customs, we still can try to relate their practice to the African worldview. This philosophico-religious explanation is naturally (as always) compatible with a purely utilitarian and functional interpretation.

There should be a time lag between the three attacks because the underlying life forces should accept the symbolic domination. The central life-preserving plant, symbol of man himself, should not be introduced alone but together with others in an agricultural society that resembles the human society. The independence of the *kintu* (eleusine) should be preserved as much as possible, and associations of *kintu* under the domination of *muntu* should be formed (the hand-weeding). The fact that neither too dense nor too sparse fields should be realized is an expression of the same dialectics of autonomy and communication that characterizes the whole African philosophy. The eleusine field type does not need constant oversight and can be interpreted as an independent field of man-dominated *kintu*.

Note: Once and for all, we apologize for using terms, borrowed from the *kinyarwanda* used as a foundation by Kagame, to describe situations occurring in regions where completely different languages are spoken. The reader should understand their use as an attempt to remind him of the basic categories of African philosophy, as described by Kagame.

The African mode of production shows thus clearly a variety of contradictions, only a few of which are pointed out by Suret-Canale and Coquery-Vidrovitch, though these authors give all the information necessary to point them out.

1. The basic contradiction pointed out by Coquery-Vidrovitch is the contradiction between the commercial life giving rise to the unstable state (due to the instability of the market, and the instability of the exposed routes) and the agricultural life giving rise to the stable village community. Situations may have existed in which both sources of power (chieftainship and control of commerce) coincided; other situations may have them separated, and in a third type of situation either the market controller may seize power in a village or the village chieftain may seize the control of a commercial route. None of these possibilities are really stable.

2. Within the central state, however, the contradiction between the king and the oligarchy, over which the king has to preserve supremacy by large presents, is a constant source of instability.

3. Within the village one may discern (though here the instability is much less):
   a. the opposition between the family on the one side and the group of families that is the village as a whole on the other side;
   b. the opposition between the collective property and the functional authority of the master of soil or water;
   c. the opposition between the work on collective and individual land.

In any Marxist economy the development of a form of production must derive from the contradictions proper to it. In the last part of this paper we shall have to come back briefly to this topic.

For our present purposes however, we must, having explained as succinctly as possible, following mainly Coquery-Vidrovitch and sometimes Suret-Canale, the typically African mode of production, come back to our main purpose: what is the relation between the pluralistic energetism of African philosophy and this type of economical organization?

1. The basic fact that there cannot exist any private property of the soil must imply that the type of individual independence and isolation typical for the western mind is excluded in a traditional African society. Property and individuality are related as to their forms. For this very reason an ontology in which a person is only what he is in virtue of his relations would be probable in Africa.

2. The basic fact of continuous migration on the one hand and of long-distance commerce on the other hand could explain partly:
   a. the feeling of independence and autonomy of the African personality, and
   b. most interestingly, the importance of the word, the symbol, the means of communication. The king is the controller of trade, i.e., of communication; it would seem probable that the association of power and word would exist in such a society. Even if this situation is clearest in West Africa, it is not absent elsewhere.

3. The society is basically egalitarian and democratic; all power is counterbalanced by counterpower. Dualistic forms, opposition of forces, and unstable balances should be widely used in understanding the world if the world is understood as analogous to the economic

and political structure of the society.

4. Economically the correspondent of the adage "Being is force" could be "Possession is gift" or "Prestige and power is gift and contribution," but essentially "Being is struggle against counterforce."

5. The strong stress on individuality, joined to the equally strong stress on collectivity, finds its counterpart in the coexistence of individually and collectively worked land.

6. According to Coquery-Vidrovitch, the basic contradiction of the African mode of production, the contradiction between the traditionally reigned village and the more progressive but unstable kingdoms, finds its counterpart in the mythical and immovable reign of the ancestor (the actuality is the future of the past, Ziegler told us in a striking paradox) and the movable changing actuality of commerce.

Let us first stress the fact that if every being is force and every force is individual then there can be no universal standard of value and no unlimited medium of exchange.

The impossibility of the existence of money follows from pluralistic energetism.

If it is, however, also true that the aim of human life is to acquire the maximum of force, then it is necessary to exhibit this force by means of a gift, establishing the existence of one's power in a visible form, in relation to other conscious persons. These gifts should extend themselves over as wide spaces as possible. The large distances covered by African external exchange is the economical image of the force net covering the visible universe.

Every being occupying, however, a given specific place in this net, it is natural that the gift giving should be limited in quality of goods and in space.

Power being essentially power over other human beings, the aims of the universe, the power aimed at could not be a means of production of a set of lifeless objects but only a means of conspicuous consumption with the aim of establishing social assertion.

The person being only the intersection of a net of force relations, no obligation could concern one person alone.

It thus appears that we have established as concomitants (effects or causes) of pluralistic energetism most aspects of African economy. Only the function of middlemen tribes appears to us in contradiction with the ontology we are studying. Ideologically they would correspond to the nonspecific "mana" force whose presence in African philosophy we have so often strongly denied. However, is this contradiction (as Dr. Rossie suggests) not solved if one observes that frequently forces act on each other by means of intermediaries? One could mention the function of *kintu*, of so-called fetishes, and of mediums used by healers. The slave trade, present before colonial influences gave it such an enormous and destructive importance, can be understood from the point of view of African philosophy (man is the highest wealth that can be possessed and man can be possessed because his personality is multiple and open) but is obviously in radical contradiction with the cosmic humanism also so deeply a part of African philosophy.

We come to the conclusion that we do not reach a complete correspondence between the exchange economy we encounter and the philosophy we study. We do, however, obtain a strong partial correspondence.

Summarizing this part of our paper we repeat:

1. We agree with our Marxist sources that a specific type of African production exists, and we show the correspondence between this type of production and African philosophy.

2. When we study one of the dialectical poles of this production mode, the village community, then the African agrarian production types again correspond with African philosophy.

3. A large variety of historically and spatially different variants of the African type of production must be noted, and we can at least already offer some suggestions as to the internal variants of an ideological nature they introduce in the general African philosophy we discover everywhere in the continent.

4. When we study the other dialectical pole of the African production type, the exchange economy, we discover not a complete but nevertheless a very strong correspondence between the forms of this exchange and African philosophy.

Study Questions

1. Do you see why Apostel claims African philosophy has a tendency towards self-sufficiency? Is Apostel's claim reconcilable with the African proverb "To raise a child it takes a whole village"?

2. Does Apostel note any contradictions in the African mode of production? Can you resolve or explain away any apparent contradictions?

3. What influences from Marxism does Apostel note?

82

Food and Third World "Economic Miracles": An Interview with Noam Chomsky

Talk about the political economy of food, its production and distribution, particularly within the framework of IMF and World Bank policies. These institutions extend loans under very strict conditions to the nations of the South: they have to promote the market economy, pay back the loans in hard currency and increase exports—like coffee, so that we can drink cappuccino, or beef, so that we can eat hamburgers—at the expense of indigenous agriculture.

You've described the basic picture. It's also interesting to have a close look at the individual cases. Take Bolivia. It was in trouble. There'd been brutal, highly repressive dictators, huge debt—the whole business.

The West went in—Jeffrey Sachs, a leading Harvard expert, was the advisor—with the IMF rules: stabilize the currency, increase agro-export, cut down production for domestic needs, etc. It worked. The figures, the macroeconomic statistics, looked quite good. The currency has been stabilized. The debt has been reduced. The GNP has been increasing.

But there are a few flies in the ointment. Poverty has rapidly increased. Malnutrition has increased. The educational system has collapsed. But the most interesting thing is what's stabilized the economy—exporting coca [*the plant from which cocaine is made*]. It now accounts for about two-thirds of Bolivian exports, by some estimates.

The reason is obvious. Take a peasant farmer somewhere and flood his area with US-subsidized agriculture—maybe through a Food for Peace program—so he can't produce or compete. Set up a situation in which he can only function as an agricul-

tural exporter. He's not an idiot. He's going to turn to the most profitable crop, which happens to be coca.

The peasants, of course, don't get much money out of this, and they also get guns and DEA [*the US Drug Enforcement Agency*] helicopters. But at least they can survive. And the world gets a flood of coca exports.

The profits mostly go to big syndicates or, for that matter, to New York banks. Nobody knows how many billions of dollars of cocaine profits pass through New York banks or their offshore affiliates, but it's undoubtedly plenty.

Plenty of it also goes to US-based chemical companies which, as is well known, are exporting the chemicals used in cocaine production to Latin America. So there's plenty of profit. It's probably giving a shot in the arm to the US economy as well. And it's contributing nicely to the international drug epidemic, including here in the US.

That's the economic miracle in Bolivia. And that's not the only case. Take a look at Chile. There's another big economic miracle. The poverty level has increased from about 20% during the Allende years [*Salvador Allende, a democratically elected Socialist president of Chile, was assassinated in a US-backed military coup in 1973*] up to about 40% now, after the great miracle. And that's true in country after country.

These are the kinds of consequences that will follow from what has properly been called "IMF fundamentalism." It's having a disastrous effect everywhere it's applied.

But from the point of view of the perpetrators, it's quite successful. As you sell off public assets, there's lots of money to be made, so much of the capital that fled Latin America is now back. The stock markets are doing nicely. The professionals and businessmen are very happy with it. And they're the ones who make the plans, write the articles, etc.

And now the same methods are being applied in Eastern Europe. In fact, the same people are going. After Sachs carried through the economic miracle in Bolivia, he went off to Poland and Russia to teach them the same rules.

Between 1985 and 1992, Americans suffering from hunger rose from twenty to thirty million. Yet novelist Tom Wolfe described the 1980s as one of the "great golden moments that humanity has ever experienced."

A couple of years ago Boston City Hospital—that's the hospital for the poor and the general public in Boston, not the fancy Harvard teaching hospital—had to institute a malnutrition clinic, because

---

Reprinted from Noam Chomsky, *The Prosperous Few and the Restless Many* (Tucson, Ariz.: Odonian Press, 1993), pp. 25–29. Reprinted by permission.

they were seeing it at Third World levels.

Most of the deep starvation and malnutrition in the US had pretty well been eliminated by the Great Society programs in the 1960s. But by the early 1980s it was beginning to creep up again, and now the latest estimates are thirty million or so in deep hunger.

It gets much worse over the winter because parents have to make an agonizing decision between heat and food, and children die because they're not getting water with some rice in it.

The group World Watch says that one of the solutions to the shortage of food is control of population. Do you support efforts to limit population?

First of all, there's no shortage of food. There are serious problems of distribution. That aside, I think there should be efforts to control population. There's a well-known way to do it—increase the economic level.

Population is declining very sharply in industrial societies. Many of them are barely reproducing their own population. Take Italy, which is a late industrializing country. The birth rate now doesn't reproduce the population. That's a standard phenomenon.

Coupled with Education?

Coupled with education and, of course, the means for birth control. The United States has had a terrible role. It won't even help fund international efforts to provide education about birth control.

Study Questions

1. Is Chomsky right to claim that there is no shortage of food?

2. If there is no shortage of food, then why do about 40,000 people worldwide die each day from starvation or malnutrition?

3. If there is a shortage of food, is that a sound basis on which to criticize the current system of producing food? Does the blame for any shortage of food lie primarily with population policies? Or is there enough blame to go around, both on the issue of food production and the issue of reproduction?

4. Which moral principles would give the most support to Chomsky's views? Which moral principles would be most critical of his views? Explain your answers in detail.

Tough, Hard-Boiled Corporate Types and Their Financial Empires

83

Strongmen

Michael Kinsley

Editor's note: Kinsley explains why Iacocca and Ueberroth have enjoyed such good reputations in politics but also why they are not likely to be riding high for long.

A manly clenched fist fills the page. In the background, the American flag. Four words in block type: "THE PRIDE IS BACK." It's the front of a four-page foldout Chrysler ad now running in various magazines. Inside is a patriotic collage: The Statue of Liberty (of course), fireworks, a victorious runner in a "USA" T-shirt, another flag, and so on, plus a couple of cars and Chrysler's new slogan, "BORN IN AMERICA."

This should not be confused with the title of Peter Ueberroth's new book, *Made in America*—also, as it happens, what Chrysler chairman Lee Iacocca calls the first section of his own recent book. That book is titled simply *Iacocca*. Both books are examples of a genre best described as autohagiography. Iacocca's has sold more than 2 million hardcover copies.

Ueberroth's publisher had 200,000 in print even before publication date. Iacocca and Ueberroth are exhibits A and B of that amazing recent development, the emergence of the businessman as hero and patriotic icon.

Both men get talked about for President. The talk usually is of one of the other riding to the rescue of the Democratic Party, although both are nominal Republicans. A recent poll shows Iacocca second only to President Reagan in eliciting positive feelings from the electorate, second only to Ted Kennedy as a favorite for the Democratic nomination, and triumphing over either George Bush or Jack Kemp in a general election.

Ueberroth shot to fame as head of the 1984 "private enterprise" Los Angeles Olympics. Now he is Commissioner of Baseball. Iacocca essentially purchased his national reputation at the expense of Chrysler shareholders and the taxpayers through years of television commercials starring himself as the feisty carmaker leading the charge to make America great again. Lately he has draped himself around the Statue of Liberty, as the well-publicized chairman of the corporate extravaganza raising money to refurbish the monument.

Ueberroth has not expressed many political views. His book doesn't get beyond patriotic boilerplate: "The United States of America is the greatest country in the world," and so forth. Iacocca, by contrast, has a clear political agenda. He stands for trade barriers and national economic planning through an alliance of business and government, beliefs he promotes in apocalyptic and xenophobic language. "America is losing its *ability* and maybe even its *will* to compete," he warns. While we look the other way, the Japanese are "taking over the backyard." He says, "When you're getting mugged . . . you should really look at who in the hell's mugging you." Iacocca favors quotas and taxes on imports, setting interest rates by law, and an industrial policy modeled on our present farm policy of price and production controls and subsidies. "Adam Smith went out of style decades ago," he declares.

Iacocca insists he doesn't want to be President. Indeed, he devotes an entire chapter of his book to insisting. But this is the usual stance of the businessman/hero: he does not seek challenges, they seek him out. He is at first reluctant . . . the challenge is beyond all human capability . . . but he succumbs to entreaties . . . he soon discovers it's even worse than he imagined . . . but in the end, with strong leadership, devoted followers, and a loving family . . . *Iacocca* and *Made in America* both follow this leitmotiv. In any event, the interesting question isn't whether Iacocca and Ueberroth want to run for President. It's why so many other people want them to run.

The hunger for a leader who is "above politics" reminds some of the Eisenhower era. But Eisenhower's appeal was as a caretaker who wouldn't bother people much. People today look to Iacocca or Ueberroth as a savior who'll take bold action. It's the difference between a kindly uncle and a strong father. As political heroes, Iacocca and Ueberroth radiate a rather austere kind of charisma. It's not the personal warmth projected by successful modern American politicians from FDR through Ike to Ronald Reagan. It's more like the mystical ability to command that is the original meaning of "charisma."

As culture heroes, too, Iacocca and Ueberroth are a novelty. The American hero used to be a loner who rode off into the sunset. These corporate heroes sit atop large organizations and, in fact, are admired in part for their organizational skills. Even as business heroes, they are different from the entrepreneurs and inventors of the past, the Henry Fords and Thomas Edisons. They are salesmen, not engineers. Marketing, public relations, and lobbying are the keys to their success.

There used to be a name for the political philosophy of a strong charismatic leader, a Darwinian struggle among nations, and a privately owned but centrally planned economy, with a heavy emphasis on heroic images and pageantry. That name was fascism. Iacocca and Ueberroth are not fascists, of course, even in the clinical sense that Mussolini and Hitler made obsolete. But the flavor is definitely there. And it's a bit scary how appealing many find it.

Iacocca's vision of an economy managed by tripartite boards of government, business, and labor leaders is the classic corporate state of fascist ideology. It is capitalism without free enterprise, socialism without social justice, a deeply conservative and disastrous arrangement that would freeze the economy in place for the benefit of current property owners. His talk of Japanese "mugging" (which consists of selling people goods they wish to buy at prices they wish to pay) and of America's loss of "will" is straight out of fascist rhetoric about dynamic nations triumphing over complacent ones.

Ueberroth's Los Angeles Olympics were a tiny model of the corporate state. They may have been "private" in the sense that corporations financed and ran them, but almost nothing truly private or spontaneous was permitted to happen. Everything was planned and organized down to the tiniest detail. The mammoth security apparatus, the strict standardization of uniforms and decorations, the vast cheering crowds, the endless marching and singing in unison and standing at attention, demonstrated that even the world's freest city can be turned into an authoritarian fantasy world under the right kind of leadership.

Time made Ueberroth its "Man of the Year." The photos—gazing upward at him from a point about six inches off the ground, with some grandiose marble pile in the background—would have made Leni Riefenstahl proud. And America swooned. But the romance won't last. These guys aren't really our type.

Study Questions

1. Kinsley raises the issue of fascism, and offers a definition of it. Do you see any relevant similarities between the rallies associated with the Olympics (which Ueberroth organized) or the nationalistic fanfare surrounding the Statue of Liberty (which Iacocca organized) and the fascists' use of large, nationalistic rallies in Nazi Germany?

2. What have Iacocca and Ueberroth done lately? Are they still in the news? If not, has Kinsley's prediction of fading glory for these two men come true?

84

Machiavelli's Prince as CEO

Kendall D'Andrade

Author's abstract: The Machiavellian model is often praised as a realistic description of modern corporate life. My analysis of *The Prince* follows Rousseau in arguing that the prince can survive and prosper most easily by creating an environment in which almost all the citizens prosper. Far from licensing unrestrained self-aggrandizement, in this model success only comes from providing real value to almost every citizen for the entire period of one's leadership.

Translation from the early sixteenth to the late twentieth century is far from simple: for example, the CEO is in many ways far less powerful than a Medici prince. The closest approximation is a far less bureaucratic organization with very small units possessing maximum autonomy. Also, deciding who is, and who is not, a citizen is not nearly as straightforward as it was for Machiavelli; it probably includes every stakeholder on whom the corporation has a major impact.

Given the sorry state of Machiavelli's reputation, anyone recommending his picture of the prince as an appropriate role model for a CEO should expect to be lumped with those who proclaim that "Only cream and SOBs rise to the top." Well, at least we've hit a popular cliche: the view that crooks have the advantage over honest men. Nor is this a terribly recent insight, since it's traceable back at least to Plato, and he disclaims any originality for the position, noting that others had been advocating lack of moral restraint as a means of gaining advantage for at least two generations before he wrote the *Republic*. Not that

Reprinted from *Business Ethics Quarterly*, vol. 3, no. 4 (1993), pp. 395–405. Reprinted by permission.

every situation can be better exploited by dishonest conduct, only that occasionally an immoral choice is decidedly more profitable than any morally acceptable alternative. If we think of morality as limiting our range of action by forbidding us to make certain choices, then the person who is not constrained by moral scruples will always have a wider range of alternatives than the moral man. If sometimes the difference in payoff is huge, then the judicious addition of immoral action to your arsenal will bring both those payoffs themselves and the advantages stemming from the legitimate use of those larger resources.[1] Perhaps it is also desirable to be thought an honest person while enjoying the fruits of the occasional dishonest act—Plato at least appears to believe this—perhaps not. It depends on whether the reputation for dishonesty discourages people from dealing with you more than the belief in your greater power makes them anxious to ally themselves with you. Machiavelli can be interpreted as holding the second position. Even if he is right, this is not a second advantage to be derived from immoral conduct, merely a way to leverage the first advantage—a significantly expanded range of options.

I

One common way to misread Machiavelli is to take the views of the previous paragraph as a prescription for how to climb to the top. Although those ideas alone are not sufficient to generate the conclusion that a smart person can, and therefore should, use any means available to advance his career, we might not notice the lack because the additional premises needed are so obvious. Machiavelli certainly seems to argue that successful direction of an enterprise virtually requires one to step outside the bounds imposed by morality once in a while; he even criticizes the failure to brutally repress some opposition, therefore allowing it to grow into a full rebellion that required a great deal more trouble to suppress than if it had been dealt with properly in its early stages. He never objects to seizing a kingdom; his only criterion is that the person be able to hold what he has seized. He even encourages princes to enlarge their domains through judicious invasions; here too, his sole interests are the long-term success of the annexation and the cost-benefit balance of the move. What he doesn't say is that it is reasonable to want to improve one's situation whenever feasible, or that anyone is entitled to use any effective means to advance his own position. In fact he denies both of these propositions.

So much of Machiavelli's discussion focuses on the prince and his relation to the common people that a casual reader might equate these two groups with ruler and ruled, then infer that this was the whole society. But there is a third class, both in Machiavelli's world and our own. He calls them nobles; their contemporary analogue is senior, and sometimes also middle, management. Machiavelli quite correctly notices that many from this class aspire to supplant the prince, an ambition which is at least as evident in their modern counterparts. Since the prince and the nobles both rule, and the CEO and many managers each head up their own domains, it is tempting to think of the prince or CEO as simply the currently most successful of his class. In our society both the political and corporate leaders succeed to their positions after occupying a place on the organizational chart relatively near the top; often we think this is where they hone their skills and display their abilities. On this view, the major difference between the person at the top and those just under him is the extent of their domain, which is merely a difference in amount rather than the more fundamental difference in kind. In many cases the head of the organization is simply the most successful of the major leaders. Although Machiavelli found this in his time as well, he believes it a too-frequent mistake. Perhaps we can tolerate greedy nobles, though Machiavelli urges the prince to keep them in check as much as possible. But we cannot allow greedy princes because their pursuit of private goals, whether economic or political, will weaken the state too much, and may end in the overthrow of the prince as well. And while Machiavelli wastes no tears on fallen leaders, he understands as few others do the costs to the state of the deterioration that led to rebellion as well as the costs all segments of society must bear in adjusting to a new head.

Every change has its price, but we are more willing to consider change than was Machiavelli because we hope to improve our lot, whether as a result of the change or because we are smart enough to pick up some advantage during the turmoil while the change is in progress. Maybe some are even sufficiently anxious for advancement that they will choose almost any random change as a means of "shaking up" the system, perhaps in the belief that they can profit from these times of uncertainty. Such people were around in Machiavelli's time as well, but he rightly saw that they were manipulating the system for their own advantage. And though that may sound to us like what the prince does, in Machiavelli's view, there's a world of difference. Although the prince is no more motivated by what we might call the higher motives (acting morally just because that act is the morally correct choice, or preferring the greater good of the many over one's own personal good, perhaps even thinking that the many deserve a better life) than any corporate raider today, the prince realizes that he must consider the good of his subjects or face ouster; and in 1513 ouster from rule meant not hanging from a golden parachute but more often simply hanging, giving the prince a much stronger interest in lifetime appointment.

How can the prince best insure his survival, both administratively and biologically? Machiavelli's answer is as simple as it is unusual, in either the Sixteenth Century or the end of the Twentieth: actually provide the best possible environment for all the citizens. This insistence on providing real value, avoiding tricks and short-cuts of any kind, including PR manipulation, may well mark the greatest difference between the Machiavellian prince and the modern head of almost any organization.

II

A contemporary reader might wonder how the prince can provide the best value for all since in each case the value given to one person must first be extracted from another, then the administrative costs skimmed off, and then the administrator's view of what will be desired provided. Only when what is provided is tolerably close to what is really wanted is the recipient satisfied, even for the moment. OK, if that's the best deal possible then the prince provides the second best environment, which is still pretty good. Further, the putative best is not a realistic option, so the prince must take special care to regularly remind the people of that fact so they will not be seduced by impossible promises.

Let's see why this allegedly best deal is really an impossible dream. Presumably the recipients of the prince's favor lack the power to force the rest of society to contribute to their welfare, otherwise they would not have bothered waiting for the prince to give them anything. But if they are less powerful than those who are being forced to contribute to them, the prince has no reason to continue supporting them at the price of alienating the contributors since he is weakening his own support, both numerically and in terms of aggregate power. Perhaps he would even take this risk out of gratitude to those who helped him gain power, or even because he believed it morally appropriate. But continuing to funnel resources from the stronger to the weaker for his entire reign is just asking for trouble. After 20 or 30 years, most everybody's patience runs out. Those who pay for the prince's largesse will at the very least begin looking around for alternatives; they will surely be sympathetic to any contenders who approach them offering just to restore neutrality. Nor can the prince count on the favored group to lend him much support since they will long since have become so accustomed to their perks they will treat these favors as simply their due. A smart ruler realizes this and avoids favoring one group or person at the expense of many others just because he wants to minimize opposition to his rule.

Perhaps a really clever prince might be able to avoid this trap by rotating the advantage among many different groups, all the while promising everyone who was currently paying instead of receiving that their turn would come soon. Perhaps that is even what we see today. Machiavelli's objections to this approach are legion. It's inefficient; first you set up one system, then tear it down and set up another. It's not particularly helpful to anybody, not even to those who spend a fair amount of time being benefitted. Since the only constant is change, no one can make rational plans for the future. That's also inefficient since we must all invest some of our resources in some form of insurance, or at least some form of defensive preparation for whatever changes we can anticipate, perhaps with the hope of at least delaying them and/or reducing their negative impact. We would all be better off if we could keep the larger share of what we have.

We've all heard this slogan before, though few have been won over, because it's generally nothing more than a very shallow cover for a preference to continue enjoying a relatively privileged position without having to even listen to, let alone evaluate, the legitimacy of others' claims. But that's not true of Machiavelli's use of this conclusion because there is very little inequality in his ideal state. Almost everyone is part of the producer class as a participant in a very small business. Although there may be some distinction between the owners and the employees, many employees are part of the extended family, and none are regarded as temporaries who can be furloughed or dismissed as a cost-cutting measure. Like almost everything else in the prince's society, employment relations are incredibly stable. And lest we try a Nozick-style argument to show that even if the society were set up optimally, the sum of many independent free choices would quickly destabilize it,[2] Machiavelli had his reply already written. In effect, it is a denial that many would have an interest in creating these destabilizing situations, and that those few who do could almost always be controlled, at least to the extent of limiting the ripple effect of their activities.

On our current theory of human nature, people always want to improve their standard of living, most approaches go so far as to incorporate this wish for improvement into the very meaning of rationality. At least that way when someone clearly chooses not to pursue a self-interested course of action we can label any behavior not fitting our pattern as irrational and dismiss it. Machiavelli starts from the other direction; he looks at how people behave, then tries to fashion a society that supports this behavior. Far from having boundless ambitions, Machiavelli finds that most people only wish for moderate success, but they want the highest possible assurance that that level of success will continue throughout their lives. Look at the average worker, even the average lower-level manager, and you will find a fundamentally risk-averse person. If we try to imagine him without the various cultural pressures that "support" an acquisitive life-style, we may imagine that he will be content with the satisfaction of only his basic needs and a few of his most important interests. If such a person occasionally indulges in fantasies of enjoying far greater wealth, he quickly realizes that he's not prepared to earn that wealth for himself. On the other hand, there is a lot about this job he would gladly change: uncertainty, far too little control over his own future, and all those parts of his job which seem to have plenty to do with actually doing a useful job.

Although we praise the worker whose ambition drove him to "make something of himself," the real reason we want to nourish that myth that continual striving to do better can lead to a much better life is the hope that we'll get far more work than we pay for out of such a work force. Since jobs are organized in a roughly pyramidal fashion, there are always many more people available for promotion than places to promote them to. But if many are in some sense competing for those few promotions just one level up, using the additional work done in the present job as evidence of worthiness for promotion, then many must be working harder than is necessary to keep the present job but not well enough to receive any substantial reward for that extra productivity. If it worked, this system would be the most productive one imaginable. Sadly, many people apparently still believe in it, adapting it only slightly to fit the times. Nowadays there seems to be a hope that fear of losing one's job will drive workers to greater productivity, with that increase going to the company, to the shareholders, and probably to a few top managers as well. This newest version of an old theory combines the worst of two strands: that most are driven by ambition, and that fear is a powerful motivator. The second view can claim some support in Machiavelli's text, but only by elevating one aspect of the prince's method of governing into the primary instrument for achieving his aims.

Machiavelli does advise the prince to rule through fear, quite regularly in fact. But he does not mean the kind of fear which induces insecurity, for that would go exactly counter to one of the prince's major aims. The prince aims for maximal stability because it simplifies the citizens' lives. Fear that at any moment the prince might impose some punishment, some sanction, even some new policy affecting me would divert resources from my work and enjoyment into various forms of self-protection, creating an unnecessary inefficiency, and so an unnecessary cost which I could easily come to resent. The prince does not even seek to create fear of himself, or fear of being in his presence, or fear of being observed by him or his agents. In Machiavelli's ideal realm you can face the ruler quite confidently so long as you know that you have scrupulously followed his rules. Since he would like everyone to face him this way, his rules must also be simple, both to understand and to obey. That means they must state goals rather than means of getting to those goals, and they must demand and forbid very general types of conduct.

The prince can now safely leave working out the details to the individual, confident that his self-interest will motivate him as the prince would wish were he to take the time to learn about the citizen's particular situation and his range of options. Of course, that approach doesn't work in our society, and it only works in Machiavelli's because the prince creates a quite different set of habits and expectations. Because the prince is an absolute dictator, he need not worry about niceties of proof, or even intricacies of interpretation. He is also very efficient in discovering opposition to his policies. In one sense that's the hardest part of his job, and Machiavelli is very

clear that there is no magic formula for accomplishing it. Quite the opposite. He advises the prince to look far ahead so that he may distinguish problems which will grow into critical difficulties from minor annoyances which will disappear of themselves; once the ruler has discovered what will later be obvious to all he must then devise a way to address that budding problem without creating further problems. We might put that advice into slogan form: be farsighted and clever! Not very helpful; but that's one reason why it's so very hard to be a successful prince.

Swift and certain punishment is neither a particularly new idea nor is it by itself sufficient to create nearly universal cooperation with the prince's plans. Instead the prince must reinforce a culture in which law-breaking is simply not a live option. For Machiavelli, that always means appealing to the person's self-interest, which is equivalent to showing the person that he is really better off living as the prince wishes than he would be living any other way, at least while he remains inside the prince's domain. Then he will live as the laws dictate without needing to consult them; in that sense the laws simply prescribe what he would do anyway, so he does not literally obey the law in the sense of having the law influence his conduct.

If we believe that most people prefer a smaller but much more secure income to the chance to try for much more, then greed alone will not drive many people to seek ways to evade the law, or the prince. If they see that others have no luck with legalistic, technical defenses, they will not feel safe getting too close to the boundary between legal and illegal action. Additionally, the prince reverses the burden of proof in our society and requires the person charged to demonstrate that he has not gone against the prince's intent. For a risk-averse person, the only safe course is clear obedience to both letter and spirit; since the prince's laws are nothing but an announcement of the spirit, there is no conflict of interpretations to worry over. If the laws are all public, individually simple, and not very numerous then not only are they easy to obey, the person who would prefer to obey need not worry about someone cleverer or more favorably placed than himself turning some technicality of the law against him;[3] so envy of the successful lawbreaker will not incite many to attempt to imitate their successes. Add to this the force of habit and tradition, for the prince remains in office for at least a generation, often two, all the while maintaining a very consistent set of policies. For practical purposes, in the prince's domain there is but a single model for success: obeying the law while creating some thing, or service, clearly desired by a few steady customers.

Though we might carelessly say that the prince makes good citizenship pay, he does not; it is the individual who makes his own good citizenship pay. "All" the prince does is render bad citizenship spectacularly unprofitable, including most antisocial acts directed against me. Not only does he enforce the laws effectively, he designs them so that there are no loopholes for the powerful to use to rob me. Thus the prince's laws and my own naive, nonacquisitive sense of fairness coincide. To insure this fit, even in a pluralistic society, the prince concentrates on "negative" laws, leaving positive policy choices to individuals and groups quite independent of him. From our perspective, he would provide very little of what we apparently demand from our politicians under the heading of leadership. He would have few causes (or grand plans, if a fancier description is wanted) because almost every program would be a personal choice that would in effect favor some against others, thereby inviting everyone to look again for someone who would favor them, if only by favoring some of their pet projects.

In Machiavelli's view, self-interest and our own measure of personal success have a strong economic component. Almost by definition, long term success is a persistent motivating interest in our lives. But it rarely engages our passions at a very high level, except perhaps when its continuation seems threatened. Other events can trigger much more intense reactions; Machiavelli refers to this class as acts which give offense. It is easy to get people morally outraged at some injustice, often one that does not even affect their other interests directly. At such a time many a person will temporarily forget about his long-term interests, even act in ways which compromise them seriously. But we also see that this level of emotion is rarely sustained, almost never for more than a month or two. Now if we identify our "real" interests with our long-term interests, then we are foolishly short-sighted to compromise those interests for much shorter-term interests. Notice that Machiavelli is not claiming that these sharply peaking emotions do not also represent real interests, only that those interests are less important to us than the long-term interests which get forgotten for a while. A wise prince minimizes these distractions, then depends on his citizens to look back after a number of years and recognize that he has helped them concentrate on their most important goals.

III

Large modern corporations have much in common with many modern political entities. These corporations are quite powerful, are the focus of many of its citizens' lives, even have their own independent policies; and on one view of competition, they are also continually at war. Such parallels have not gone unnoticed, especially by those who believe that modern business is and/or should be conducted by the same "rules" that governed sixteenth century principalities. One commentator even translated *The Prince* under the title *To: The Boss, From: Mack*.[4] Since his was a translation from one setting to another, rather than one language to another (unless you think of cultures as language games), some parts went smoothly because the parallels were so striking. For example, neither head of organization should be bound by promises except as they affect his reputation, both should be careful to interpret advice, not just solicit it, etc. But often the translation is a little rougher.

Machiavelli advises the prince to simply kill rebels; the CEO can only exile them.[5] The prince is literally the only law in his realm, the CEO is constrained by the society of which his corporation is only a part. So the comparison will work best when both the CEO and the corporation he heads are not at odds with the political entity in which they are operating, however they managed to gain that permission. The prince's freedom of action is limited only by the power of others to restrain him, and by his own sense of what will alienate too many of his citizens; the CEO must at least take cognizance of many more potentially hostile major (external) powers in framing his policies. So I don't think we get very far treating the prince and the CEO as just two of a kind, then using Machiavelli's advice to the prince to justify what we take to be similar recommendations for the CEO. We certainly need more than the claim that the prince is independent of ordinary moral constraints and should be. In fact these extraordinary powers should be used very much more sparingly than is commonly supposed, and then only as a means of promoting a better society. Since Machiavelli's vision of a good life is so different from the contemporary view, we need to be even more than ordinarily careful in assuring ourselves that the approach of *The Prince* actually supports our proposals. Given that Machiavelli preferred very small business at a time when big business was a lot smaller than today, we should expect him to do all he could to break up large corporations, resist mergers, and try to encourage people to start their own family businesses. So he would hardly endorse giving corporate CEOs the same freedoms as he urged on the prince.

So rather than looking for how much the CEO is allowed to do, let me focus instead on how he can change the modern corporation to approximate the Machiavellian state. The most obvious change is organizational. Far too much direction comes from the top, and it filters through far too many bureaucratic layers. Technological complexity makes it unlikely we can totally recreate a "nation" of small family enterprises, but how close can we come? One radical suggestion is to transform the corporation into a shell to handle financing and represent its citizens in dealings with other corporate giants. Virtually all the employees would become independent contractors, organized into groups of ten to fifty people around a logical unit of work. A more modest approach is to reorganize the production employees into these same small groups, then give them as much autonomy as possible consistent with producing a saleable product. Such a shop would look a lot more like a series of quality circles where each employee did relatively complex tasks than a traditional assembly line where each task was broken into its smallest parts, then each of these parts assigned to a different worker, or even group of workers. Individual workers would no longer be seen as interchangeable parts because they would not function like them. For example, in different parts of the shop, one group might handle major assembly and another painting, while elsewhere a single group did both. Recall that the Machiavellian goal is enabling each group to have as much control over its future as possible. So the little bit of management that remained would lose the power to assign individuals to groups; each group would select its own members who would then work more like a cooperative than a division.

Because the groups would be much more self-directing, there is much less need for supervisory personnel. This only works in a corporate culture where employees fully understand what they are doing and wish to do it well. The rewards of success are the continuing motivators, and when they work properly, there is no need to even be aware of the threat of punishment for failure. In such a corporate setting, one of the major management perks disappears: the right to inspect the employee's work at any time at any level of completion, with the unstated but obvious intention of catching them doing some-

thing they are not supposed to do. Doubtless quality will shoot up after these hassles disappear. After all, when do you work best? When your every move is scrutinized or when you are left alone with only a deadline to meet? While it's true that in a Machiavellian corporation there are no contests between labor and management, each trying to get more and give less, that is in large measure due to the virtual disappearance of management.

Deciding on how the corporation would compete is a little more difficult. On the most literal reading of *The Prince* competition would be fiercer than it is now because nothing but the possibility of failure would restrain it. Just as Machiavelli advises the prince to look around for weaker states to absorb or dismember, so the corporate "state" would feel free to undermine competitors in any way it could, including industrial espionage, luring away key personnel, sabotaging the competitors' plants or products, undermining their reputations with customers, forming strategic partnerships (alliances) which weakened and isolated a competitor, and hostile takeovers (war). Product development, brand differentiation and brand loyalty, and advertising of every kind would be legitimate weapons in the fight against competitors. This view licenses consumer fraud of the most blatant kind, all for the good of the corporation. But that only works when you identify the corporate state with some limited, usually legal, version of the corporation. For Machiavelli, this could not be just the shareholders, for they would be identified with the nobles, who form less than 5% of the state. So we must include the employees as well, since they directly produce the corporation's products and deliver its services. That view still legitimizes corporate warfare, only now it's for the good of both shareholders and employees, not just the "owners." But even this "state" is not very close to Machiavelli's; for example, customers and suppliers were generally fellow citizens, not outsiders. Once we start including everyone in the corporate state with a counterpart in the sixteenth century principality, we will have a stakeholder corporation. Under that interpretation, the CEO becomes responsible for seeing that no stakeholder cheats any other stakeholder, which includes restraining the corporation itself. Multiple citizenship, almost unknown in Machiavelli's time, has become the norm today.

Machiavelli advises the prince to demonstrate to his citizens that they cannot do better under any other ruler, and will likely fare much worse. This is how the prince appeals to his subjects' self-interest. Since they will have a very long time to observe him, and since the prince's job is difficult enough without adding extra problems, Machiavelli wants the prince to actually deliver on this promise. For all his differences with Plato, Machiavelli would agree that it is just easier to rely on the truth, assuming of course that the truth favors your position, for then there is nothing you need to conceal, no one who can threaten you with exposure, etc. If the CEO follows this advice, he will try to ensure that every citizen gives and receives fair value for real value produced. He will always prefer substance over style, though he will have no simple test to distinguish one from the other. And he will be modest about the extent of his contribution to the prospering of the people within the organization he heads, realizing that his greatest contribution was in eliminating the problems people might have unnecessarily caused each other.

IV

From this extended examination of Machiavelli, both as political philosopher and business ethicist, you might conclude that I was recommending this version of the Machiavellian model as the ideal CEO. But I am not. I believe this is only the second best way to run an enterprise, though second best is still very far ahead of what we're doing now. Although the Machiavellian corporation would be responsive to the claims of all stakeholders, the decisions would still be imposed from above rather than generated by the stakeholders themselves. But with our current preoccupation with top-down models of corporate control and the derivation of authority, a Machiavellian CEO would do the best job possible for all those in whose lives that corporation looms so large.[6]

Study Questions

1. Does Machiavelli deserve his reputation as a deceptive, ruthless, scheming manipulator of other people?

2. Which of the quotations from Machiavelli do you think are hardest to defend morally or are the cause of Machiavelli's bad reputation?

Notes

1. While not denying the validity of the standard interpretation of the Ring of Gyges story in Book II, I suggest that this extended parable also supports my interpretation.

2. The famous Wilt Chamberlain example in *Anarchy, State and Utopia*.

3. A pleasant interpretation of Hegel's view in *The Philosophy of Right*.

4. With a descriptive subtitle just to be sure we don't miss the connection. *A Contemporary Rendering of the Prince*. By W. T. Brahmstedt, ETC Publications, 1986.

5. Thus neither *The Solid Gold Cadillac* nor *Wall Street* are really orthodox. To be faithful to this aspect of his thought we need something more melodramatic, *The China Syndrome*, for instance.

6. My thanks to the Society for Business Ethics for picking this as one of the two best papers on their 1992 program, and for the Editor's invitation to publish it here. Substantially the same version was presented to the Midwest Academy of Legal Studies in March of '92. Various revisions/extensions were presented at the October, 1992 meeting of the West Virginia Philosophical Society and the March, '93 meeting of the Midwest Academy of Legal Studies. And my students have been hearing various versions over the last four years.

85

Selected Quotations from Machiavelli

1. "[O]ne must either pamper or do away with men, because they will avenge themselves for minor offenses while for more serious ones they cannot; so that any harm done to a man must be the kind that removes any fear of revenge." *The Portable Machiavelli*, edited and translated by Peter Bondanella and Mark Musa (Penguin Books, 1979), abbreviated as PM, below, p. 83.

2. "The desire to acquire is truly a very natural and normal thing; and when men can do so, they will always be praised and not condemned; but when they cannot and wish to do so at any cost, herein lies the error and the blame." PM, p. 86.

3. "[O]ne can derive a general rule which rarely, if ever, fails: that anyone who is the cause of another's becoming powerful comes to ruin himself, because that power is the result either of diligence or of force, and both of these two qualities are suspect to the one who has become powerful." PM, p. 88.

4. "[M]en almost always tread the paths made by others and proceed in their affairs by imitation, although they are not completely able to stay on the path of others nor reach the skill of those they imitate, a prudent man should always enter those paths taken by great men and imitate those who have been most excellent, so that if one's own skill does not match theirs, at least it will have the smell of it . . ." PM, p. 92

5. "[T]here is nothing more difficult to execute, nor more dubious of success, nor more damaging to administer than to introduce a new system of things: for he who introduces it has all those who profit from the old system as his enemies, and he has only lukewarm allies in all those who might profit from the new system. This lukewarmness partly stems from fear of their adversaries who have the law on their side, and partly from the skepticism of men who do not truly believe in new things unless they have actually had personal experience of them." PM, p. 94.

6. "[P]eople are fickle by nature; and it is simple to convince them of something but difficult to hold them in that conviction; and, therefore, affairs should be managed in such a way that when they no longer believe, they can be made to believe by force." PM, p. 95.

7. "Still, it cannot be called skill to kill one's fellow citizens, to betray friends, to be without faith, without mercy, without religion; by these means one can acquire power but not glory." PM, p. 104.

8. "Injuries, therefore, should be inflicted all at the same time, for the less they are tasted, the less they offend; and benefits should be distributed a bit at a time in order that they may be savored fully." PM, p. 107.

9. "Moreover, one cannot honestly satisfy the nobles without harming others, but the common people can surely be satisfied: their desire is more honest than that of the nobles—the former wishing not to be oppressed and the latter wishing to oppress. Moreover, a prince can never make himself secure when the people are his enemy because they are so many; he can make himself secure against the nobles because they are so few." PM, p. 108.

10. "[A] wise prince should think of a method by which his citizens, at all times and in every circumstance, will need the assistance of the state and of himself; and then they will always be loyal to him." PM, p. 110.

11. "And it was always the opinion and belief of wise men that 'nothing is so unhealthy or unstable as the reputation for power that is not based upon one's own power.'" PM, p. 123.

12. "[T]here is such a gap between how one lives and how one ought to live that anyone who abandons what is done for

what ought to be done learns his ruin rather than his preservation: for a man who wishes to make a vocation of being good at all times will come to ruin among so many who are not good. Hence it is necessary for a prince who wishes to maintain his position to learn how not to be good, and to use this knowledge or not to use it according to necessity." PM, p. 127.

13. "[E]very prince must desire to be considered merciful and not cruel." PM, p. 130.

14. "[On] whether it is better to be loved than to be feared, or the contrary, I reply that one should like to be both one and the other; but since it is difficult to join them together, it is much safer to be feared than to be loved when one of the two must be lacking. For one can generally say this about men: that they are ungrateful, fickle, simulators and deceivers, avoiders of danger, greedy for gain . . ." PM, p. 131.

15. "[F]riendships that are acquired by a price and not by greatness and nobility of character are purchased but are not owned, and at the proper moment they cannot be spent. And men are less hesitant about harming someone who makes himself loved than one who makes himself feared because love is held together by a chain of obligation which, since men are a sorry lot, is broken on every occasion in which their own self-interest is concerned; but fear is held together by a dread of punishment which will never abandon you." PM, p. 131.

16. "[T]o be feared and not to be hated can very well be combined; and this will always be so when he [the prince] keeps his hands off the property and the women of his citizens and his subjects. . . . [A]bove all, he should avoid the property of others; for men forget more quickly the death of their father than the loss of their patrimony." PM, p. 132.

17. "How praiseworthy it is for a prince to keep his word and to live by integrity and not by deceit everyone knows; nevertheless, one sees from the experience of our times that the princes who have accomplished great deeds are those who have

cared little for keeping their promises and who have known how to manipulate the minds of men by shrewdness; and in the end they have surpassed those who laid their foundations upon honesty." PM, p. 133.

18. "[S]ince men are a sorry lot and will not keep their promises to you, you likewise need not keep yours to them." PM, p. 134.

19. "[I]n order to maintain the state he [the prince] is often obliged to act against his promise, against charity, against humanity, and against religion. And therefore, it is necessary that he have a mind ready to turn . . . [A]s long as possible, he should not stray from the good, but he should know how to enter into evil when necessity commands." PM, p. 135.

20. "[W]here there is no impartial arbiter, one must consider the final result." PM, p. 135. Bondanella and Musa note that this passage "has often been mistranslated as 'the ends justify the means,' something Machiavelli never wrote." PM, p. 135, note 1. Compare quotations 20 and 21 here.

21. "[N]or will a wise mind ever reproach anyone for some extraordinary action performed in order to found a kingdom or to institute a republic. It is, indeed, fitting that while the action accuses him, the result excuses him; and when this result is good . . . it will always excuse him: for one should reproach a man who is violent in order to destroy, not one who is violent in order to mend things." PM, pp. 200–201.

22. "[H]atred is acquired just as much by means of good actions as by bad ones . . ." PM, p. 141.

23. "[P]rudence consists in knowing how to recognize the nature of disadvantages and how to choose the least bad as good." PM, p. 153.

24. "[H]e [the prince] should act [so] that a man is not afraid to increase his goods for fear that they will be taken away from him, while another will not be afraid to engage in commerce for fear of taxes; instead, he must set up rewards for those who wish to do these things, and for anyone who seeks in any way to aggrandize his city or state. He should, besides this, at the appropriate

times of the year, keep the populace occupied with festivals and spectacles." PM, p. 153.

25. "[A] wise prince should take a third course, choosing wise men for his state and giving only those free rein to speak the truth to him, and only on those matters as he inquires about and not on others. But he should ask them about everything and should hear their opinions . . ." PM, p. 155.

26. "[M]en always turn out badly for you unless some necessity makes them good." PM, p. 157.

27. "[N]ever having thought in peaceful times that things might change (which is a common defect in men, not to consider in good weather the possibility of a tempest), when adverse times finally arrived they thought about running away and not about defending themselves . . ." PM, p. 158.

28. "I am certainly convinced of this: that it is better to be impetuous than cautious, because Fortune is a woman, and it is necessary, in order to keep her down, to beat her and to struggle with her. And it is seen that she more often allows herself to be taken over by men who are impetuous than by those who make cold advances; and then, being a woman, she is always the friend of young men, for they are less cautious, more aggressive, and they command her with more audacity." PM, p. 162.

86

The Day the American Empire Ran Out of Gas

Gore Vidal

Editor's note: Vidal was prophetic in his prediction of an alliance between the United States and Russia.

On September 16, 1985, when the Commerce Department announced that the United States had become a debtor nation, the American Empire died. The empire was seventy-one years old and had been in ill health since 1968. Like most modern empires, ours rested not so much on military prowess as on economic primacy.[1]

After the French Revolution, the world money power shifted from Paris to London. For three generations, the British had maintained an old-fashioned colonial empire, as well as a modern empire based on London's primacy in the money markets. Then, in 1914, New York replaced London as the world's financial capital.

Before 1914, the United States had been a developing country, dependent on outside investment. But with the shift of the money power from Old World to New, what had been a debtor nation became a creditor nation and central motor to the world's economy.

All in all, the English were well pleased to have us take their place. They were too few in number for so big a task. As early as the turn of the century, they were eager for us not only to help them out financially but to continue, in their behalf, the destiny of the Anglo-Saxon race: to bear with courage the white man's burden, as Rudyard Kipling not so tactfully put it.

Were we not—English and Americans—all Anglo-Saxons, united by common blood, laws, language? Well, no, we were not. But our differences were not so apparent then. In any case, we took on the job. We would supervise and civilize the lesser breeds. We would make money.

By the end of the Second World War, we were the most powerful and least damaged of the great nations. We also had most of the money. America's hegemony lasted exactly five years. Then the cold and hot wars began.

Our masters would have us believe that all our problems are the fault of the Evil Empire of the East, with its satanic and atheistic religion, ever ready to destroy us in the night. This nonsense began at a time when we had atomic weapons and the Russians did not. They had lost twenty million of their people in the war, thanks to their neoconservative Mongolian political system. Most important, there was never any chance, then or now, of the money power shifting from New York to Moscow.

What was—and is—the reason for the big scare? Well, the Second War made prosperous the United States, which had been undergoing a depression for a dozen years, and made very rich those magnates and their managers who govern the republic, with many a wink, in the people's name. In order to maintain a general prosperity (and enormous wealth for the few), they decided that we would become the world's policeman, perennial shield against the Mongol hordes.

We shall have an arms race, said one of the high priests, John Foster Dulles, and we shall win it because the Russians will go broke first. We were then put on a permanent wartime economy, which is why close to 90% of the government's revenues are constantly being siphoned off to pay for what is euphemistically called defense. As early as 1950, Albert Einstein understood the nature of the rip-off. He said, "The men who possess real power in this country have no intention of ending the cold war." Thirty-five years later, they are still at it, making money while the nation itself declines to eleventh place in world per capita income, to forty-sixth in literacy and so on, until last summer [1985] (not suddenly, I fear), we found ourselves close to two trillion dollars in debt. (Now [in 1992] the debt is $4 trillion, with a Bullet, as they say in *Billboard*.)

Then, in the fall, the money power shifted from New York to Tokyo, and that was the end of our empire. Now the long-feared Asiatic colossus takes its turn as world leader, and we—the white race—have become the yellow man's burden. Let us hope

Reprinted from *The Decline and Fall of the American Empire* (Berkeley, Calif.: Odonian Press, 1993). Reprinted by permission. This article originally appeared in *The Nation* (1986).

that he will treat us more kindly than we treated him.[2]

In any case, if the foreseeable future is not nuclear, it will be Asiatic, some combination of Japan's advanced technology with China's resourceful landmass. Europe and the United States will then be, simply, irrelevant to the world that matters, and so we come full circle: Europe began as the relatively empty uncivilized Wild West of Asia; then the Western Hemisphere became the Wild West of Europe. Now the sun has set in our West and risen once more in the East.

The British used to say that their empire was obtained in a fit of absentmindedness. They exaggerate, of course. On the other hand, our modern empire was carefully thought out by four men. In 1890, a US Navy captain, Alfred Thayer Mahan, wrote the blue-print for the American imperium, *The Influence of Sea Power upon History, 1660–1783*.

Then Mahan's friend, the historian-geopolitician Brooks Adams, younger brother of Henry, came up with the following formula: "All civilization is centralization. All centralization is economy." He applied the formula in the following syllogism: "Under economical centralization, Asia is cheaper than Europe. The world tends to economic centralization. Therefore, Asia tends to survive and Europe to perish." Ultimately, *that* is why we were in Vietnam.

The amateur historian and professional politician Theodore Roosevelt was much under the influence of Adams and Mahan; he was also their political instrument, most active not so much during his presidency as during the crucial war with Spain, where he can take a good deal of credit for our seizure of the Philippines, which made us a world empire. Finally, Senator Henry Cabot Lodge, Roosevelt's closest friend, kept in line a Congress that had a tendency to forget our holy mission—our manifest destiny—and ask, rather wistfully, for internal improvements.

From the beginning of our republic we have had imperial longings. We took care—as we continue to take care—of the indigenous population. We maintained slavery a bit too long even by a cynical world's tolerant standards. Then, in 1846, we produced our first conquistador, President James K. Polk.

After acquiring Texas, Polk deliberately started a war with Mexico because, as he later told the historian George Bancroft, we had to acquire California. Thanks to Polk, we did. And that is why to this day the Mexicans refer to our southwestern states as "the occupied lands," which Hispanics are now, quite sensibly, filling up.

The case against empire began as early as 1847. Representative Abraham Lincoln did not think much

of Polk's war, while Lieutenant Ulysses S. Grant, who fought at Veracruz, said in his memoirs, "The war was an instance of a republic following the bad example of European monarchies, in not considering justice in their desire to acquire additional territory."

He went on to make a causal link, something not usual in our politics then and completely unknown now: "The Southern rebellion was largely the outgrowth of the Mexican War. Nations, like individuals, are punished for their transgressions. We got our punishment in the most sanguinary and expensive war of modern times."

But the empire has always had more supporters than opponents. By 1895 we had filled up our section of North America. We had tried twice—and failed—to conquer Canada.[3] We had taken everything that we wanted from Mexico. Where next? Well, there was the Caribbean at our front door and the vast Pacific at our back. Enter the Four Horsemen—Mahan, Adams, Roosevelt and Lodge.

The original republic was thought out carefully, and openly, in *The Federalist Papers*: We were not going to have a monarchy, and we were not going to have a democracy. And to this day we have had neither. For two hundred years we have had an oligarchical system in which men of property can do well and the others are on their own.

Or, as Brooks Adams put it, the sole problem of our ruling class is whether to coerce or to bribe the powerless majority. The so-called Great Society bribed; today coercion is very much in the air. Happily, our neoconservatives favor only authoritarian and never totalitarian means of coercion.

Unlike the republic, the empire was worked out largely in secret. Captain Mahan, in a series of lectures delivered at the Naval War College, compared the United States with England. Each was essentially an island state that could prevail in the world only through sea power.

England had already proved his thesis. Now the United States must do the same. We must build a great navy in order to acquire overseas possessions. Since great navies are expensive, the wealth of new colonies must be used to pay for our fleets. In fact, the more colonies acquired, the more ships; the more ships, the more empire.

Mahan's thesis is agreeably circular. He showed how small England had ended up with most of Africa and all of southern Asia, thanks to sea power. He thought that we should do the same. The Caribbean was our first and easiest target. Then on to the Pacific Ocean, with all its islands. And, finally, to China, which was breaking up as a political entity.

Theodore Roosevelt and Brooks Adams were tremendously excited by this prospect. At the time Roosevelt was a mere police commissioner in New York City, but he had dreams of imperial glory. "He wants to be," snarled Henry Adams, "our Dutch-American Napoleon."

Roosevelt began to maneuver his way toward the heart of power, sea power. With Lodge's help, he got himself appointed assistant secretary of the navy, under a weak secretary and a mild president. Now he was in place to modernize the fleet and to acquire colonies.

Hawaii was annexed. Then a part of Samoa. Finally, colonial Cuba, somehow, had to be liberated from Spain's tyranny. At the Naval War College, Roosevelt declared, "To prepare for war is the most effectual means to promote peace."

How familiar that sounds! But since the United States had no enemies as of June 1897, a contemporary might have remarked that since we were already at peace with everybody, why prepare for war?

Today, of course, we are what he dreamed we would be, a nation armed to the teeth and hostile to everyone. But what with Roosevelt was a design to acquire an empire is for us a means to transfer money from the Treasury to the various defense industries, which in turn pay for the elections of Congress and president.

Our turn-of-the-century imperialists may have been wrong, and I think they were. But they were intelligent men with a plan, and the plan worked. Aided by Lodge in the Senate, Brooks Adams in the press, Admiral Mahan at the Naval War College, the young assistant secretary of the navy began to build up a fleet and look for enemies. After all, as Brooks Adams proclaimed, "war is the solvent." But war with whom? And for what? And where?

At one point England seemed a likely enemy. There was a boundary dispute over Venezuela, which meant that we could invoke the all-purpose Monroe Doctrine (the invention of John Quincy Adams, Brooks' grandfather). But as we might have lost such a war, nothing happened. Nevertheless, Roosevelt kept on beating his drum: "No triumph of peace," he shouted, "can equal the armed triumph of war." Also: "We must take Hawaii in the interests of the white race."

Even Henry Adams, who found T.R. tiresome and Brooks, his own brother, brilliant but mad, suddenly declared, "In another fifty years . . . the white race will have to reconquer the tropics by war and nomadic invasion, or be shut up north of the 50th parallel." And so at century's end, our most distinguished ancestral voices were not prophesying but praying for war.

An American warship, the *Maine*, blew up in Havana harbor. We held Spain responsible; thus, we got what John Hay called "a splendid little war." We would liberate Cuba, drive Spain from the Caribbean. As for the Pacific, even before the *Maine* was sunk, Roosevelt had ordered Commodore Dewey and his fleet to the Spanish Philippines—just in case. Spain promptly collapsed, and we inherited its Pacific and Caribbean colonies. Admiral Mahan's plan was working triumphantly.

In time we allowed Cuba the appearance of freedom while holding on to Puerto Rico. Then President William McKinley, after an in-depth talk with God, decided that we should also keep the Philippines, in order, he said, to Christianize them. When reminded that the Filipinos were Roman Catholics, the president said, "Exactly. We must Christianize them."

Although Philippine nationalists had been our allies against Spain, we promptly betrayed them and their leader, Emilio Aguinaldo. As a result it took us several years to conquer the Philippines, and tens of thousands of Filipinos died that our empire might grow.

The war was the making of Theodore Roosevelt. Surrounded by the flower of the American press, he led a group of so-called Rough Riders up a very small hill in Cuba. As a result of this proto–photo opportunity he became a national hero, governor of New York, McKinley's running mate and, when McKinley was killed in 1901, president.

Not everyone liked the new empire. After Manila, Mark Twain thought that the stars and bars of the American flag should be replaced by a skull and crossbones. He also said, "We cannot maintain an empire in the Orient and maintain a republic in America." He was right, of course. But as he was only a writer who said funny things, he was ignored.

The compulsively vigorous Roosevelt defended our war against the Philippine population, and he attacked the likes of Twain. "Every argument that can be made for the Filipinos could be made for the Apaches," he explained, with his lovely gift for analogy. "And every word that can be said for Aguinaldo could be said for Sitting Bull. As peace, order and prosperity followed our expansion over the land of the Indians, so they'll follow us in the Philippines."

Despite the criticism of the few, the Four Horsemen had pulled it off. The United States was a world empire. And one of the horsemen not only got to be president, but for his pious meddling in the Russo-Japanese conflict, our greatest apostle of war was awarded the Nobel Peace Prize. One must never underestimate Scandinavian wit.

Empires are restless organisms. They must constantly renew themselves; should an empire start leaking energy, it will die. Not for nothing were the Adams brothers fascinated by entropy. By energy. By force.

Brooks Adams, as usual, said the unsayable. "Laws are a necessity," he declared. "Laws are made by the strongest, and they must and shall be obeyed." Oliver Wendell Holmes, Jr., thought this a wonderful observation, while the philosopher William James came to a similar conclusion, which can also be detected, like an invisible dynamo, at the heart of the novels of his brother Henry.

According to Brooks Adams, "The most difficult problem of modern times is unquestionably how to protect property under popular governments." The Four Horsemen fretted a lot about this. They need not have.

We have never had a popular government in the sense that they feared, nor are we in any danger now. Our only political party has two right wings, one called Republican, the other Democratic. But Henry Adams figured all that out back in the 1890s. "We have a single system," he wrote, and "in that system the only question is the price at which the proletariat is to be bought and sold, the bread and circuses."

But none of this was for public consumption. Publicly, the Four Horsemen and their outriders spoke of the American mission to bring to all the world freedom and peace, through slavery and war if necessary. Privately, their constant fear was that the weak masses might combine one day against the strong few, their natural leaders, and take away their money.

As early as the election of 1876, socialism had been targeted as a vast evil that must never be allowed to corrupt simple American persons. When Christianity was invoked as the natural enemy of those who might limit the rich and their games, the combination of cross and dollar sign proved—and proves—irresistible.

During the first decade of our disagreeable century, the great world fact was the internal collapse of China. Who could pick up the pieces? Britain grabbed Kowloon; Russia was busy in the north; the Kaiser's fleet prowled the China coast; Japan was modernizing itself and biding its time.

Although Theodore Roosevelt lived and died a dedicated racist, the Japanese puzzled him. After they sank the Russian fleet, Roosevelt decided that they were to be respected and feared even though they were our racial inferiors. For those Americans who served in the Second World War, it was an article of faith—as of 1941 anyway—that the Japanese could never win a modern war. Because of their slant eyes, they would not be able to master aircraft. Then they sank our fleet in Pearl Harbor.

Jingoism aside, Brooks Adams was a good analyst. In the 1890s he wrote: "Russia, to survive, must undergo a social revolution internally and/or expand externally. She will try to move into Shansi Province, the richest prize in the world. Should Russia and Germany combine . . ." That was the nightmare of the Four Horsemen.

At a time when simpler folk feared the rise of Germany alone, Brooks Adams saw the world ultimately polarized between Russia and the United States, with China as the common prize. American maritime power versus Russia's landmass. That is why, quite seriously, he wanted to extend the Monroe Doctrine to the Pacific Ocean. For him, "war [was] the ultimate form of economic competition."

We are now at the end of the twentieth century. England, France and Germany have all disappeared from the imperial stage. China is now reassembling itself, and Confucius, greatest of political thinkers, is again at the center of the Middle Kingdom. Japan has the world money power and wants a landmass; China now seems ready to go into business with its ancient enemy.

Wars of the sort that the Four Horsemen enjoyed are, if no longer possible, no longer practical. Today's conquests are shifts of currency by computer and the manufacture of those things that people everywhere are willing to buy.

I have said very little about writers because writers have figured very little in our imperial story. The founders of both republic and empire wrote well: Jefferson and Hamilton, Lincoln and Grant, T.R. and the Adamses. Today public figures can no longer write their own speeches or books, and there is some evidence that they can't read them either.

Yet at the dawn of empire, for a brief instant, our *professional* writers tried to make a difference. Upton Sinclair and company attacked the excesses of the ruling class. Theodore Roosevelt coined the word "muckraking" to describe what they were doing. He did not mean the word as praise.

Since then a few of our writers have written on public themes, but as they were not taken seriously, they have ended by not taking themselves seriously, at least as citizens of a republic. After all, most writers are paid by universities, and it is not wise to be thought critical of a garrison state which spends so much money on so many campuses.

When Confucius was asked what would be the first thing that he would do if he were to lead the state—his never-to-be-fulfilled dream—he said *rectify the language*. This is wise. This is subtle. As societies grow decadent, the language grows decadent too.

Words are used to disguise, not to illuminate, action: You liberate a city by destroying it. Words are used to confuse, so that at election time people will solemnly vote against their own interests. Finally, words must be so twisted as to justify an empire that has now ceased to exist, much less make sense.

Is rectification of our system possible for us? Henry Adams thought not. In 1910 he wrote: "The whole fabric of society will go to wrack if we really lay hands of reform on our rotten institutions." Then he added, "From top to bottom the whole system is a fraud, all of us know it, laborers and capitalists alike, and all of us are consenting parties to it." Since then, consent has grown frayed; and we have become poor, and our people sullen.

To maintain a thirty-five-year arms race it is necessary to have a fearsome enemy. Not since the invention of the Wizard of Oz have American publicists created anything quite so demented as the idea that the Soviet Union is a monolithic, omnipotent empire with tentacles everywhere on earth, intent on our destruction, which will surely take place unless we constantly imitate it with our war machine and its secret services.[4]

In actual fact, the Soviet Union is a Second World country with First World military capacity. Frighten the Russians sufficiently and they might blow us up.

By the same token, as our republic now begins to crack under the vast expense of maintaining a mindless imperial force, we might try to blow them up. Particularly if we had a president who really was a twice-born Christian and believed that the good folks would all go to heaven (where they were headed anyway), and the bad folks would go where *they* belong. Fortunately, to date, we have had only hypocrites in the White House. But you never can tell.

Even worse than the not-very-likely prospect of nuclear war—deliberate or by accident—is the economic collapse of our society because too many of our resources have been wasted on the military. The Pentagon is like a black hole; what goes in is forever lost to us, and no new wealth is created. Hence, our cities, whose centers are unlivable; our crime rate, the highest in the Western world; a public education system that has given up . . . you know the litany.

There is only one way out. The time has come for the United States to make common cause with the Soviet Union. The bringing together of the Soviet landmass (with all its natural resources) would be of great benefit to each society, not to mention the world.

Also, to recall the wisdom of the Four Horsemen who gave us our empire, the Soviet Union and our section of North America combined would be a match, industrially and technologically, for the Sino-Japanese axis that will dominate the future just as Japan dominates world trade today. But where the horsemen thought of war as the supreme solvent, we now know that war is worse than useless. Therefore, the alliance of the two great powers of the Northern Hemisphere will double the strength of each and give us, working together, an opportunity to survive, economically, in a highly centralized Asiatic world.[5]

Study Questions

1. Are Vidal's views about the Japanese true?
2. Given the North American Free Trade Agreement (NAFTA), will the United States have closer trading relations with Mexico than with Russia? If so, does this undercut Vidal's analysis? Does the recent collapse of the Mexican peso by about 40 percent against the U.S. dollar help Vidal's analysis?

Notes

1. In *The Guardian* Frank Kermode wrote: "I happened to hear Vidal expound this thesis in a New York theater, to a highly ribald and incredulous, though doubtless very ignorant audience . . ." Since then, my thesis has been repeated by others so many times that it is now conventional wisdom.
2. Believe it or not, this plain observation was interpreted as a racist invocation of "the Yellow Peril"!
3. When the British occupied Boston in 1775, Washington struck not at Boston but at Montreal. In 1812, a year before the British burned the White House, we again invaded, unsuccessfully, Canada.
4. Now that the Soviet has collapsed, the lies that our secret police and media told us for so many years are

coming to light. Remember how, in the 1970s, the CIA was reporting the Soviets' astonishing economic surge.

5. The suggestion that the United States and the USSR join forces set alarm bells ringing in Freedom's Land. I was denounced as a Communist. Now, six years later, as I predicted, the Russian states are working out partnerships with us.

87

The Diamond Empire

Frontline

Announcer: Last year Americans spent more than $10 billion on diamond jewelry.

Herbert Chao Gunther, Marketing Consultant: Nobody's aware that diamonds and all the associations we have with diamonds is a product of a marketing strategy. It's completely invisible, transparent. If you measure it in terms of how all the myths associated with this advertising campaign have been deeply inculcated in people—it's reached deeply into the popular imagination—this is probably the most successful campaign in history.

Announcer: Tonight on *Frontline*—

Party Guest: Diamonds? Aren't they a girl's best friend? Did something change?

Announcer: —are diamonds what we think they are, precious and rare?

Edward Epstein, Author, "The Rise and Fall of Diamonds": I wound up discovering it was just the opposite. Everywhere there's carbon, which is everywhere, you find diamonds.

Announcer: *Frontline* examines the cartel that controls the diamond trade—the supply, the price and the myth.

Thomas Helsby, Kroll Associates, Corporate Investigators: What makes this cartel different is it's controlled by a single company.

Announcer: Tonight, "The Diamond Empire."

Narrator: In the spring of 1992, more than 100 wealthy benefactors from around the world were invited to the Hotel Pierre in New York City, to a fundraiser for AIDS research. Elizabeth Taylor, the high priestess of the mystique of diamonds, had invited them personally to an auction of fine jewelry that raised more than a half million dollars. The evening itself was a glittering tribute to the allure of diamonds.

1st Party Guest: I'm wearing the diamonds because my sweetheart has given them to me and it means love and it means forever.

2nd Party Guest: Diamonds? Aren't they a girl's best friend? Did something change?

3rd Party Guest: Diamonds? Diamonds! They're a woman's best friend.

Narrator: But what we think about diamonds is, in fact, a myth. At the center of that myth is an illusion, that diamonds are valuable because they are rare. When writer Edward Epstein set out to investigate the diamond trade, he discovered that diamonds aren't rare at all.

Epstein: Well, what I learned was that the diamond business wasn't a business of extracting, as I originally expected, something of enormous value and then simply seeing how much of this object you could get out of the ground and selling it. That was what the business appeared to be when I started my venture. But their real business was restricting what came out of the ground, restricting what was discovered, restricting what got cut, restricting what actually found its way into the retail market and, at the same time, through movies, through advertising, through Hollywood, through the manipulation of perceptions, creating the idea that there was this enormous demand for these shiny little objects that they seemed to have in abundant supply. So I wound up on this voyage of discovery starting off with the idea that there was this object of great value, and it was just a question of how many could you get out, and I wound up discovering it was just the opposite.

Narrator: This is the story of how that grand illusion was created, and the story of how one family gained control of the world's diamond trade and for nearly a century has maintained its hold on an empire that defines the very idea of what diamonds really are.

New York is the center of the world's richest diamond jewelry market. It's a $10.8 billion industry. Around 74th Street there are 25,000 people buying, selling, cutting, polishing and marketing diamonds, from the most glamorous jewelry to cheap mail-order.

Very few in the diamond business will talk freely about what they do. There is a great deal of money at stake. There is also a great deal of uncertainty, but that's something top dealers like William Goldberg take in their stride.

William Goldberg, William Goldberg Diamond Corp.: It's amazing that a lot of men that I know that are 10 years younger than I am can't wait to retire and I can't wait to get here in the morning at 8:00

Frontline Show #1209, Air date: February 1, 1994.

o'clock to produce these beautiful works—you know, these beautiful pieces of art from what looks like a pebble on the beach. And then to nurse it through all its stages and then to finally come up with some of these wonderful things is just a joy.

Narrator: Goldberg is one of the elite dealers who specialize in rare and precious stones. He has a team of cutters working just off 5th Avenue. Some of the diamonds they handle will sell to royalty and movie stars for a million dollars or more.

Goldberg: This stone took us one of the longest ever, eight or nine months. It was—it was the most impossible task we—every time, we had new surprises. Nature is very funny when it comes to these things. You know, there are new hidden imperfections, which we didn't think existed before, which always seemed to sneak in. And we paid in excess of $10 million for this diamond.

Robert Bogel, William Goldberg Diamond Corp.: Everyone here is a very highly skilled technician and some of them have very specific jobs to do. This man, for example, he's cutting the 85-carat stone. Right now, it's around 36-and-a-half carats and he's putting the finishing facets on the bottom of the stone. The man behind him brillianteered—put the finishing facets on the top of the stone. These gentlemen are very skilled and they do—they bring out the final fire in the diamond, the brillianteering.

This stone's going to be a gem. This stone started out 38 carats. It's down to 21 now?

Cutter: It's around 21, yeah.

Bogel: Harvey's working the stone out. There's a lot of problems. There's a lot of balancing to do. It's coming out nice. You can see the shape. It's going to be a gorgeous marquis. Moishe's shaping the stone, using a diamond that's attached to this stick and another diamond that's rotating on the spindle, and he's shaping both at the same time.

Narrator: They measure diamonds by weight, in carats, five to the gram. Their value depends on color, clarity and cut. Flawless stones which are pink, blue or yellow bring the highest prices. The best can top $100,000 a carat. This stone will sell for a million dollars. Diamond is among the hardest known substances, but many carats must often be ground away to cut a rough stone into a traditional marquis or brilliant. The smallest mistake is inordinately expensive. It calls for expert planning from a rough designer.

Bogel: I will try and find the largest, most pure stone in here. Matter of fact, this stone will probably end up being three different stones because of the imperfections that I can find. For example, I do see a

pear shape and I do see an emerald cut and I do see an oval. The most important thing is bringing out the beauty.

Television Commercial: De Beers is very proud to continue the diamond decade by presenting its program for 1992.

Narrator: Most of the world's rough gem diamonds come through organizations run by the South African company De Beers, known in the United States by its famous advertising slogan, "A diamond is forever." Fewer than 200 diamond merchants qualify for a sight, the privilege of buying directly from De Beers. Everyone else must buy, in turn, from them.

Goldberg: We're sight-holders. We get a sight every five weeks from De Beers. If you can come up with a huge sum of money, it would not—would—certainly would not qualify you to be a sight-holder. It's rather the man that started 25 years ago with very little, with one or two cutters, who has 15 or 20 now here and who is constantly on the scene, buying and—and who—and he's the man who means to stay here, with his children to follow him. He's the man that qualifies to be a sight-holder. It's like being admitted to a club.

Narrator: The headquarters of that club is London. Because it is a virtual monopoly, De Beers cannot operate legally in the United States. All sight-holders must travel here to buy their rough gems, to a building known only as 17 Charterhouse Street. This is a fortress, where 80 percent of the world's gem diamonds are sorted, graded and sold.

A sight-holder sends his request for the grade of diamonds he needs, but there are no guarantees. It is De Beers that decides whether or not he gets them. It's a decision that can make or break his business.

De Beers Employee: This is your sight for October.

Epstein: In this shoebox is basically the diamonds that they're going to cut that month. And in this mixture of diamonds, there are large diamonds, there are small diamonds, there are colored diamonds. There's what De Beers wants to be on the market. So they distribute to the cutters what is in short supply and withhold from the cutters what is in abundance, so they control the market through this and there are all sorts of hidden signals in this box, like if, suddenly, the sight-holder, as the person's called, gets many diamonds worth hundreds of thousands of dollars, he'll know he did a special favor and he's being rewarded for that favor. The other hand, if he finds he's been given a large number of uneconomical diamonds to cut, he'll realize he's fallen out of favor.

Narrator: Even the world's top dealers are at the mercy of De Beers's central selling organization. William Goldberg usually has special requests alongside the ordinary stones, but even he does not know what to expect.

De Beers Employee: Here are the regular goods and two boxes of specials. So, see you later.

Goldberg: Fine. Thank you very much.

De Beers Employee: Okay.

Goldberg: See you later.

Goldberg: A-ha! See, this is very interesting. These are greens that come from Botswana and this is a regular, cut-and-dried and bread-and-butter item. And quite often, these are—these are priced in such a way that there's very little profit to be made on these goods. For whatever reason, at any given moment, they make a policy decision. I've been very angry and cussed a lot and been very upset, but that's—that's how the cookie crumbles. I have no—I have no options.

Interviewer: What can you do when that happens?

Goldberg: Just cuss and fret and look forward to the next—that things will change at the next sight.

Interviewer: Can you leave all that on the table and say, "I'm just—I'm not interested, I'm not going to make a profit this month"? Can you do that?

Goldberg: I—I told you on the way over here, we can leave some of the specials, but it's just—it's not in the—we just don't leave the regular goods. Somehow, it's—it's—it doesn't work that way.

Narrator: On a hill in Johannesburg, South Africa, is the private estate of the family that controls the diamond empire. These are the Oppen-heimers. In two generations they have built one of the most powerful industrial cartels of the 20th century.

Helsby: The diamond cartel has lasted 70 years and shows no sign of weakening. What makes this cartel different is it's controlled by a single company, a single commercial organization, and that's De Beers. And De Beers itself is controlled by another South African company, Anglo American. Interestingly, Anglo American is controlled by De Beers and that interlocking ownership is what allows one small family, E. Oppenheimer's & Sons, who own just a small shareholding in Anglo American, to control the whole edifice.

Narrator: The diamond mines of southern Africa are the heart of the diamond empire. Diamonds are crystals of carbon, formed in the heat and pressure, 1,200 miles below ground. Where volcanoes have brought them to the surface, they can be dug out of the rock. But many have been washed down rivers to the sea and these, the alluvial diamonds, can be picked up along the riverbeds and shorelines.

Sand and gravel are brushed out of the crevices, or scooped in huge quantities out of the hillside, and the rough diamonds are simply sorted out from the rest. There are extinct volcanoes throughout Africa, Asia, Russia, Australia and America and they are littered with diamonds. For a commodity which sells at thousands of dollars a carat, the supply seems truly staggering. Diamonds can even be picked out of these shallow waters along the African coast.

John Gurney, Offshore Mining Executive: You can go to other coastlines and expect to find a few diamonds, but I think you can't build up a scenario that's as optimistic as one can build up for the west coast of South Africa. If you look at what's on the land—and there's three or four raised beaches on land that have produced more than 100 million carats of diamonds. In one of our concessions alone—and it's not one of the bigger concessions—we have mapped 22 beach levels, so you're again going to come out to a number which is of the order of a billion carats or in excess of that.

Narrator: Because diamonds are so plentiful, it makes De Beers's virtual monopoly an astonishing feat. Its history begins at Kimberley, South Africa, in 1871. Until that year, mines had been few and diamonds truly rare, mostly from India and Brazil. But the Kimberley find was huge. Among those who rushed to make their fortunes were two young Englishmen.

John Rudd, Former Director, De Beers Industrial Diamonds: Charles Darnel Rudd, my great-grandfather, and Cecil Rhodes met here in October, 1871. They were early in the rush here and they would have found an ant-hill, a mining camp, and as Rhodes described it, as Stilton cheese as the claim holders dug down into this enormous diamondiferous Kimberlite pipe. But their eyes were more towards De Beers's mine, which is about a mile over the horizon there, and that's where they dealt with the farmer De Beer and they bought that farm out for 6,000 pounds. The thoughts of Rhodes immediately began to concentrate on the amalgamation of all these individual claim-holders. And by 1880, he had amalgamated all the claim-holders on his mine, the De Beers mine, and that began the amalgamation of all the diamond mines and the formation of De Beers Consolidated Mines began in 1888.

Narrator: What Cecil Rhodes launched was a diamond cartel. It was based on an earlier French scheme to monopolize copper—buying up mines, restricting supply and raising prices. From its first headquarters in Kimberley, De Beers bought out almost every other large mine in South Africa. But shortly before the First World War, diamonds were found over the border, to the north, in German southwest Africa. A young German-born diamond dealer in South Africa went there to investigate. His name was Ernest Oppenheimer.

Albert Alletzhauser, Oppenheimer Biographer: Ernest Oppenheimer, in 1914, two months before the outbreak of war, went there to survey the territory and came back with a report that was mind-boggling and subsequently hidden from the public, the fact that this was the richest diamond field in the history of the world. It was an alluvial field, meaning diamonds were on the surface. You could go pick them up. And, in fact, they put what they termed back then "natives," black natives—each put a tin can around their neck and they lined them up and they got on their hands and knees and they just— "Pink! Pink! Pink!"—put the diamonds into the tin cans as they walked on their hands and knees. This is how rich the fields were.

Narrator: Oppenheimer saw an opportunity and seized it. The German land-owners, afraid of expropriation as World War I came to an end, agreed to merge their companies with his. Because both British investors and American financier J. P. Morgan had stock in his venture, Oppenheimer called his company the Anglo American Corporation. Within a few years, it was clear that he had landed a supply of diamonds to rival even the mines owned by De Beers.

Alletzhauser: Coming into the 1920s, Ernest Oppenheimer then said to De Beers, who controlled, for the most part, the diamond syndicate, diamond cartel—he said to them, "Listen, I am going to flood the world market unless you make me chairman of the company." And in 1929, he was made chairman of De Beers. That is the basis of the Oppen-heimer fortune.

Narrator: Oppenheimer's mine, a private estate three times the size of New Jersey, became an exclusive territory known as the "forbidden zone." It was the bedrock of a world-wide De Beers diamond empire, which the Oppenheimers began to build.

Epstein: The true genius of diamonds came through the Oppenheimer family and came even with Harry Oppenheimer, who is running it today, where they realized that diamonds, as originally conceived, coming from only three or four mines, was wrong, that diamonds existed everywhere in the world. Every-

where where there's carbon, which is everywhere, you find diamonds.

Newsreel: Most every famous diamond in the world is represented in this case. They are worth many millions of dollars and trails of blood—

Narrator: While the public continued to imagine that diamonds were rare and romantic, De Beers was mining enormous quantities. Ernest Oppenheimer saw that more huge finds might force prices to go plummeting downwards. In 1930, a De Beers mining engineer warned, "The diamond market is dependent for its smooth function on the maintenance of the illusion in the minds of the general public that the diamond is a rare and valuable stone." A De Beers director agreed, "For goodness sake, keep out of the newspapers and parliament the quantity of diamonds that can be produced and put on the market."

But as the colonies developed, diamonds began turning up all over Africa. Local people knew where to find them. Eddy Fortune is one of the small-claim miners in South Africa.

Eddy Fortune: In the year 1931, in the morning, I used to leave Kimberley 3:00 o'clock by bicycle and then I used to ride about 31 miles out to a little shack out on the diggings and I used to work there. I didn't have trouble selling diamonds because my quality was very good. There was very big demand. But I never found a big diamond. The biggest I found was 38 carats. But small diamonds and medium-sized— 10s, 12s, 14s—plenty of them.

Narrator: To keep control, De Beers had to prevent the little mines from putting too many diamonds on the market. The simplest answer was to buy them up.

Fortune: Certain companies came and they bought up the small diggers, you see. That's how they developed and became the big company, De Beers— bought out everything.

Narrator: But alluvial diamonds washed up along the riverbanks were much more difficult to control. A film inspired by De Beers in the 1950s portrayed its adventurous young traders setting up buying offices in the jungle.

Alletzhauser: These young graduates, Oxford graduates—basically, a buying office was them, a bunch of porters with food on their head, and a cash box on their head, and they'd put a box down in the middle of a clearing and they'd start buying diamonds in the local currency. So they'd ship in all these guys to do this, to prevent smuggling.

Fouad Kamil, Former Diamond Detective, Anglo

American: There is always a competition between the Anglo American–De Beers group and other dealers all over the world for a bigger slice of the world diamond markets. And this did not suit Anglo American. They wanted the whole plate for themselves.

Narrator: Fouad Kamil claims he contracted to work as a detective for the cartel in the 1950s and '60s, investigating unlicensed diamond dealing and smuggling from its mines.

Kamil: Diamonds going out of Sierra Leone and the other African diamond markets were going to what Anglo American described as "black markets," that is, Antwerp, Amsterdam, Germany, some parts of the United States and Israel. Now, these people were labeled "black markets" by Anglo American, but in their own countries, they were respectable diamond dealers.

Narrator: To get information, Kamil says he broke the law and even kidnaped people who fell under suspicion.

Kamil: And those that had diamonds, I took them as prisoners. I interrogated them, got information from them. I kept them as long as I wanted, week to week, some of them months, and released them when I wanted.

There was beatings. There was punishments without food. We did everything we could to extort the information from them. There was a stage when no one dared to pass from there, diamonds or no diamonds. So to put it bluntly, we were a terrorist group. That's what it amounts to.

Narrator: The cartel denies that Kamil worked for either De Beers or Anglo American and says his accusations are part of a vendetta against them.

By the 1950s the diamond cartel had amassed enormous power, taking control of diamonds at the source, making deals with colonial powers, building its network mine by mine, country by country.

Newsreel: Thirtieth of June, 1960. This was a city of radiant joy, as the people celebrated Congo independence day, a happy occasion full of bright hope.

Narrator: In the 1960s, the rise of African nationalism presented new challenges to the cartel.

Newsreel: The army of the young republic marches by.

Narrator: The Congo's first democratically elected leader, Patrice Lumumba, was critical of the colonial mining arrangements and the local Belgian mining companies supported army actions against him.

Newsreel: A new chapter begins in the dark and tragic history of the Congo.

Narrator: The coup against the leftist leader was backed by the CIA and it ended in Lumumba's murder.

Newsreel: —Colonel Mobutu. Taken to Mobutu's headquarters—

Narrator: Mobutu Sese Seko emerged as the dictator of what became Zaire. At first, he, too, sounded like an African nationalist.

Steve Askin, Writer, "Diamond Registry Bulletin": Mobutu had made what seemed like very left-wing, radical statements, talking about the "colonial exploiters," threatening to nationalize all sorts of foreign mining property. And in flies American businessman Maurice Tempelsman.

Narrator: Maurice Tempelsman is an independent diamond dealer and a key intermediary for De Beers.

Askin: In a matter of, oh, 10 days, Maurice Tempelsman holds consultations in Brussels with key officials. He meets with the U.S. embassy in Kinshasa, has consultations with the U.S. State Department, speaks with Mobutu, flies on to go meet with Mr. Oppenheimer of De Beers in South Africa in what, according to—what is certainly shown by a number of declassified U.S. State Department documents to be an attempt to stitch together a relationship between the De Beers empire and the Mobutu regime. So it's very clear from the very beginning of the Mobutu regime Tempelsman had an important role in, to put it most charitably, advising and guiding Mobutu on how to deal with companies like De Beers.

Narrator: The Oppenheimers, through Tempelsman, arranged to have the exclusive supply of diamonds shipped to their offices in London. De Beers has done well on Zaire's diamonds. So has President Mobutu.

Askin: For many years, there was a pattern and a practice whereby, at regular intervals, Mobutu would send some of his agents to Miba, the diamond company, to take a look at the most recent production and to select out the best gem-quality stones to be flown off, presumably to be sold for his account in Antwerp.

Narrator: Madame Mobutu also has an eye for diamonds.

Askin: This is somebody who's traveled on a diplomatic passport, who just gets whisked right through Customs, doesn't get stopped. However, there was one occasion a few years ago when Madame Mobutu went off to Belgium and she forgot some of her luggage. She sent her secretary, apparently, back to Kinshasa or back to Gbadolite, where Mobutu has his main palace, to get the luggage. The secretary went into Customs, didn't show the right kind of documents, was stopped and inspected. And, according to the Belgian reports, was found carrying $6 million worth of diamonds.

You just need one word. The word is "kleptocracy." I'm not the person who invented the word. I wish I did. But it's been used by political scientists to describe governments whose fundamental organizing principle is one of theft.

Narrator: Mobutu spends huge sums on an army to keep himself in power. He himself is one of the richest men in Africa, while his people are among the poorest.

Stephen Cohen, Former U.S. Human Rights Official: Zaire has substantial diamond resources, as well as other mineral resources, and the revenues generated from those resources could have gone to benefit the Zairean people and they haven't. The revenues have gone for two purposes. They've either been siphoned off to Mobutu's private bank accounts or they've been used to provide benefits for foreign governments or foreign companies, in the hope that those foreign governments and foreign companies will then be supportive of Mobutu and help him remain in power. I mean, essentially, Mobutu's used the wealth of Zaire for two purposes: to enrich himself and to enrich his foreign supporters.

Narrator: Despite De Beers's deal with Zaire, some mines in the country are beyond its control. These wildcat miners are fighting over a new claim. The diamonds they find will likely be smuggled out of the country to the few markets the cartel still doesn't control.

Askin: You're talking about a country which is certainly one of the two largest diamond producers in the world, where you have this Wild West atmosphere, and looking at it from the outside, I would guess that this is the most difficult relationship over the years that a company like De Beers could have with an African government.

Narrator: In neighboring Angola, regulated diamond mining is a casualty of its devastating civil war. In 1992, wildcat miners there swarmed the diamond-rich dry riverbeds, picking up small fortunes in alluvial diamonds. De Beers has spent an estimated half billion dollars to keep them from flooding the market and depressing prices.

Each time diamonds are found in an inconvenient place, they begin, the diamond cartel, through intermediaries, through law firms they hire, ways to think, "How can we prevent these diamonds from reaching the market?" And declaring something a national park, tying things up in litigation—these are just the methods and there's an infinite number of different methods you could use, once you understand what the objective is. The objective is to prevent mines from being developed that are outside their control.

Narrator: Murfreesboro in southwest Arkansas is the home of America's only diamond mine. At the inauguration, Hillary Clinton wore a diamond found in this mine, which was discovered at the turn of the century. But today the 100-acre site is mined only by tourists and amateur prospectors. Commercial mining was abandoned here in the 1920s, even though geological surveys showed the mine had great promise. The Justice Department investigated allegations that Ernest Oppenheimer had illegally influenced the closing of the mine to keep its diamonds off the market.

John Henderson, Historian: According to the Justice Department records, Sam Rayburn and other principals of the Arkansas Diamond Corporation, met in the office of J. P. Morgan. In attendance at that meeting was Sir Ernest Oppenheimer. As a result of that meeting—and what transpired is unknown, but the mine superintendent was telegrammed to shut the mine down and prepare it for a sustained closure. And as a result, major operations never resumed at the Arkansas diamond mining plant.

Narrator: The Justice Department was unable to determine whether the mine had been closed illegally or simply because it was unprofitable, but in 1992 a new preliminary geological study indicated the mine may, in fact, have commercial potential. Like most deposits, it will produce few gem stones, but many smaller stones could be found. They are important because they're used in cutting tools. Industrial diamonds are a multi-billion-dollar business in their own right.

1st Prospector: Got one! Got one, Mr. Fred.

2nd Prospector: What?

1st Prospector: Got one. It's yellow, light yellow—light yellow. *crosstalk*

2nd Prospector: Triangular in shape.

1st Prospector: Yeah.

2nd Prospector: I'm going to dig a hole right here, right next to—

1st Prospector: All right. All right.

Narrator: Industrial diamonds have a strategic importance because they're used in the making of weapons. After the Arkansas mine closed, it meant that the U.S. military depended, like everyone else, on De Beers in London. When the Second World War started and Britain was faced with Nazi occupation, American strategists wanted to transfer a stockpile of diamonds to this side of the Atlantic, but De Beers hesitated.

Walter Adams, Professor of Economics, Michigan State University: The story of the De Beers during World War II was truly shameful when they denied the United States, which was an ally of Great Britain and an ally of South Africa in prosecuting the war—when it denied the U.S. free access to required quantities of industrial diamonds.

  Newsreel: Defense production in factory and arsenal begins far behind the assembly line.

Narrator: Apparently fearful that diamond prices would fall if a military stockpile were sold off after the war, the Oppenheimers refused to allow any diamonds out of their control. De Beers claims it was only following the advice of the British government, but the cartel's actions were criticized by the U.S. Justice Department.

Adams: Only after complicated arrangements, where De Beers insisted on retaining control of those industrial diamonds by placing the supply organization in Canada, was some accommodation reached so that the United States could obtain the quantities of industrial diamonds needed for the war effort on its own behalf and the behalf of its allies.

Helsby: Meanwhile, however, the Nazis did appear to be getting a steady supply of diamonds and the Americans were very concerned to find out where they came from. We were able to get documents, secret documents, declassified from the National Archives in Washington that describe the investigation that they mounted into smuggling of diamonds out of the Congo.

Narrator: A U.S. intelligence officer, Henry Lee Staples, led the American investigation into the smuggling. Before he died, he worked with his son on a memoir of those days.

Henry Staples, Jr.: He had assigned an agent—"Teton" was his code name, and he had, through whatever means those agents have, determined that the largest source of leakage was the Forminier mine and the diamonds from the—that were leaked from the Forminier mine went to various points in Africa and from there were, by various routes, smuggled into Germany. Belgian Red Cross parcels were loaded with illegal diamonds and then sent to Switzerland, and from Switzerland to Belgium, which was, of course, occupied by the German forces.

Narrator: The Allies knew that without the Congo stones, Hitler had only an eight-month supply of industrial diamonds, but their hardest task still lay ahead. How could the smuggling be stopped?

Helsby: The Forminier mine is, of course, one of the producers that is signed up in the cartel. Its production is exclusively marketed through the cartel and, indeed, the company which controls the mine, Sobeca, had, as one of its principal share-holders, Ernest Oppenheimer.

Epstein: So that as De Beers—they were faced with the problem of either shutting down their mines entirely so there'd be no leakage or operating their mines and making profits and leakage would be inevitable. And as they were a business, they elected to continue in the diamond business even though it meant, inevitably, no matter what they did—and I'm not sure they did that much, but no matter what they did, diamonds would get through. It was impossible to stop diamonds from getting to Hitler. And what the diamond cartel then tried to do is prevent any investigation which would have revealed the very embarrassing reality that diamonds were getting to Hitler.

Helsby: The investigation was terminated and the agent, Teton, was convinced the investigation was terminated as the result of influence by the cartel on the British government. We were able to obtain declassified documents in Washington showing his cables complaining that his investigation had been aborted early.

Narrator: In its extensive investigation of the cartel's behavior during World War II, the Justice Department also concluded De Beers had overcharged the United States for the industrial diamonds it did supply. One U.S. official complained, "This form of profiteering is the more obnoxious because it has been accompanied by pious public professions of sacrifice and patriotic foregoing of profit."

  And De Beers's wartime advertising did appeal to American patriotism. "Buy our gems," the ads said, "because they pay for mining which produces the industrial diamonds America needs to win the war."

  Television Commercial: I was born three billion years ago of fire and light.

Narrator: Cornering the world's supply of diamonds was a stunning achievement. No less extraordinary was the cartel's success in creating a demand for its huge stockpile of diamonds.

  Television Commercial: Who am I? The eternal gift of love between man and woman. I am a diamond. I am forever.

Gunther: The De Beers campaign is probably one of the most successful campaigns—I mean, you measure it in terms of—of the growth in the market—in the 1930s, they were selling a rather insignificant amount of diamonds to America. By the early '80s, they were selling close to $2 billion worth.

Narrator: De Beers first targeted American consumers through the movies.

Epstein: And they opened a Hollywood office and in the Hollywood office, they would give out diamonds to producers, in return for them putting the diamonds in the film in a way that was considered favorable. Now, what was considered favorable was very simple: surprise. If a woman was brought in on the decision, she might have a lot of ideas of what she wanted, so what they wanted to do was create the idea that the man had to surprise the woman and present her with a diamond.

Actor: *Men on Her Mind,* 1994 And now for the important question I wanted to ask you.

Actress: Well, it's about time. I'm dying of curiosity.

Actor: You know I'm madly in love with you. I want you to marry me, Lily. You're in love with me, too, aren't you?

Actress: Well, if I'm not, then I'm afraid I don't know what love is.

Actor: Here's your engagement ring, darling.

Actress: Oh, Jeffrey, it's beautiful.

Actor: Oh, that's Milo.

Actress: Milo?

Actor: Yes. He's wondering what's taking us so long.

Actress: Wouldn't he be surprised if he knew!

Actor: I doubt if he'd be surprised at anything.

Gunther: Not only are we talking about what is a familiar process today of planting products in films—I mean, we've all heard of the product endorsements and that sort of thing—but we're talking about Hollywood in its golden age, where entire movies were created. They identified the biggest stars, actresses of that period, and they never appeared in public without their De Beers diamonds.

Narrator: Claudette Colbert and Merle Oberon were given special scenes to show off their De Beers diamonds. *Diamonds Are Dangerous* was conveniently retitled *Adventure in Diamonds*. But De Beers aimed even higher than Hollywood.

Epstein: The British royal family was another idea of what, in the American mind, represented the ultimate in how you should behave and how you should behave aristocratically and well. And, of course, the British royal family was more than willing to go along because diamonds came from British colonies.

Newsreel: From this, the largest man-made hole in the world, over 100 million pounds worth of diamonds have been recovered. In the De Beers sorting room, three million pounds worth of rough diamonds are on view.

Gunther: The royal family was lobbied heavily, and successfully so, so that the English royalty—Queen Elizabeth started wearing diamonds, you know, and she basically left all of her other gems off. That's a tremendous coup for a public relations agent, to get the royal family to essentially become sales agents.

Newsreel: Caskets made of Kimberley blueground embossed with coronets contained a six-carat stone for Princess Elizabeth and a four-and-a-half-carat diamond for Princess Margaret.

Television Commercial: You must travel back in time one billion years to witness its birth.

Narrator: De Beers advertising set its diamonds in worlds of glamour and royalty, but it's best-known slogan arose out of the fear that sales would be undercut if people began putting second-hand jewelry on the market.

Epstein: So they had to create the idea that, one, you should never sell a diamond, even though its value would only increase and, secondly, that people should store and hoard these diamonds. So the whole idea that a diamond is forever is really their desperate hope that people will hold diamonds forever.

Television Commercial: It is love and its only promise is forever.

Narrator: In its message to dealers, De Beers reveals its key marketing strategy is to convince consumers to buy diamonds for every romantic milestone.

De Beers Promotional Video: Let's start with your bread and butter, the support behind the "rites of passage"—the diamond engagement ring, diamond anniversary band and the 25th anniversary diamond. Our goal is to make diamonds a cultural imperative for all these important occasions in a woman's life. That's why we are continuing to support these segments, so that your products, like the diamond anniversary band and the 25th anniversary diamond, will become as obligatory as the diamond engagement ring, bringing your customers back again and again.

Gunther: Nobody's aware that diamonds and all the associations we have with diamonds is the product of marketing strategy. It's completely invisible, transparent. If you measure it in terms of how all the myths associated with this advertising campaign have been deeply inculcated in people—it's reached deeply into the popular imagination—this is probably the most successful campaign in history.

De Beers Promotional Video: That's what we're here for, to respond to your requests and to help you sell more diamonds.

Narrator: De Beers's control of African stones and American consumers made it one of the most successful cartels in history, but it would face new challenges as diamond mines were discovered around the world. In the 1950s diamonds were found in a place where neither South Africans nor Americans could easily do business, in Siberia.

Newsreel: In 1947, geological prospecting parties entered the Yakutian taiga. Would this daring hypothesis be confirmed or not? The answer was given after seven years of persevering research: Yakut diamonds.

Narrator: If the Russians dumped their diamonds on the market, it might have put an end to the cartel, but in 1957, while De Beers was very publicly opening a new building for its central selling organization in London, the Oppenheimers were very privately beginning to do business with the Russians.

Newsreel: The workers gaze with pride at what they have accomplished.

Helsby: Russian diamond production was a problem for the cartel. Russia, the communists, were anathema to the South Africans. Equally, the South Africans were an anathema to the Russians. This created a problem for the cartel because they couldn't be seen to be dealing with the Soviet diamond production. The cartel is an operation that's well used to cloaking their business operations in mystery. They simply set up a separate operation owned by a U.K merchant bank across the street from their offices. The diamonds would appear to have found their way into the central selling organization without a problem.

Narrator: By the 1980s, Russian diamonds were pouring quietly through London, into the market. Harry Oppenheimer's son-in-law was seen at the Bolshoi. Officially coming from South Africa, he could not even have had an entry visa.

Reporter: Could I ask you—

Son-in-Law: No. *crosstalk*

Reporter: I'd like to ask you—

Son-in-Law: No.

Reporter: —what you were doing in Moscow.

Son-in-Law: No. Now, just go away. You're being thoroughly unreasonable. You spoke to me politely and I said no. I have nothing to say. Thank you very much.

Reporter: You don't think it's interesting that—

Son-in-Law: I have nothing to say.

Reporter: Were you just there for the ballet?

Helsby: The other interesting feature of the Russian diamond production was that there was an extraordinarily large proportion of medium-sized stones in the quarter- to half-carat size. De Beers then came up with perhaps one of the great new product inventions in jewelry history, the "eternity ring," a ring that was designed to use up this excessive production of low-size stones. And it is perhaps amusing to think that, at the height of the cold war, the eternity ring that was being so successfully marketed in America was filled with stones from Siberia.

Narrator: As the Soviet Union became an important source of small stones, the problem for the diamond industry became finding cutters willing to work for low enough wages to make these stones profitable. India soon developed into the world's greatest cutting center. There are 750,000 cutters in workshops around Surat, perhaps 100,000 of them children under 13. They place 58 exact cuts on a diamond less than half a carat, smaller than a broken pencil lead. Many children work a 12-hour day, six days a week. They earn 4 cents a stone.

Dale Bearman, Jewelry Manufacturer: The Indian diamonds have made it possible to make a low-priced jewelry that looks like a lot. It's called "more flash for less cash." This is the expression that's used in the industry, and this seems to be the trend. We perceive popular retail price points to top out at about $500—this is what most of our customers are demanding now—and starting as low as $75, $80. We just got in some new samples today. These are examples. Here's a ring that sells for $70. There is $2 worth of diamond in this ring. But the fact that we can market it as an article with a genuine diamond makes it more salable. Here's another ring. This is a $90 ring. There's a $1 diamond in here. It's a white finish that makes it appear like diamonds. There's only one diamond in the center.

Narrator: When diamonds were discovered in 1979 at Australia's Ashton mine, the cartel machinery mobilized once again to bring this new find, the largest ever, into the fold. Until then, the cartel had co-opted diamond sources largely in Russia and African countries. Could they repeat the success in a country that was modern and democratic?

Neville Legg, Pan African Congress, Australia/ Asia: The Ashton project certainly had huge reserves which, if it had gone into independent hands, would certainly have challenged De Beers's monopoly. Now, I know that the Indian government had made representations to Australia to take over the marketing. I, myself, met with one independent diamond trader who was visiting from London and he was also putting in his bid and trying to persuade the Australian government that, in fact, as said, there were enormous benefits for Australia and it was not in the interest to further reinforce a monopoly.

Narrator: But De Beers pressured Australia by threatening to reduce diamond prices in the categories of stones the new mine would produce. At the same time, the Oppenheimers bought stock in key Australian companies. De Beers chairman, Henry Oppenheimer, flew in to cement alliances and the cartel began to lobby the government and mold public opinion.

Legg: Many Australian journalists were invited to South Africa, sponsored by De Beers, to go on, I suppose, tours which were meant to promote De Beers's image and soften the impact of De Beers's penetration into the Australian economy. And soon after these tours took place, it became quite evident in the Australian media, mainly through the newspapers, that there was a very pro-CSO approach being adopted by the media. So I think De Beers's strategy worked quite well in that they'd softened up the Australian media and the media reciprocated by promoting very favorable stories to the De Beers takeover of the Ashton project.

Narrator: After a major political battle, the cartel scored a crucial victory. The bulk of Australia's output, mainly industrial-grade and small gem stones, would flow through the cartel's central selling organization in London. A small number of rare gem stones, known as the "Argyle pinks," were Australia's own to market independently.

Charles Devenish, Perth Diamond Dealer: They produce a variety of colors, which is very unique to this mine. And out of the 36 million carats come some of the rarest diamonds in the world. The extraordinary thing is nature's thrown up these freaks, which are just unique and special and, you know, they're—they're something that we're all madly trying to get hold of, can't get enough.

If you look at this small, very intense pink from Argyle—and it's only—I think it's about 18 points—and then you compare it against this two-carater from Argyle, the two-carater is worth about $22,000. Now, if we could superimpose that color on that small pink into that two-carater, that two-carater would be worth at least a million dollars in today's market. Now, Argyle only gets maybe three, four or five of those stones a year, maximum, out of, remember, 35, 36 million carats of diamonds.

Helsby: The De Beers operation is essentially the control of the production of diamonds. They control the chain of supply of diamonds and that's the way in which they control the diamond market. If somebody were to try to go around the cartel, the concern that they would have to have is how long it would last, because of course, De Beers, in the past, has been very successful at bringing all the producers into the cartel.

Narrator: Today, a century after it began, the diamond cartel still controls the production, the marketing and the pricing of rough diamonds around the world. But that world is changing and there are new threats to the Oppenheimers' dominance of the diamond trade.

In its largest market, the United States, the cartel cannot operate openly. Its monopolistic control of the worldwide diamond trade violates U.S. anti-trust laws.

Adams: Section 1 of the Sherman Act says, "Every contract combination or conspiracy in restraint of trade is hereby declared to be unlawful." The Sherman Act, in effect, says that as long as you have enough competitors and as long as they act independently, the public interest will be protected, but once you have conspiracy among them, the public interest will be undermined.

Narrator: Four times since the 1940s the U.S. government has investigated De Beers and its associates under the Sherman Act, but bringing a South African company to American justice has proved almost impossible.

Joel Davidow, Former U.S. Justice Department Attorney: We hired a South African solicitor to serve a notice on De Beers in South Africa. It took a while to get any South African lawyer who was willing to even serve the paper. Eventually, one agreed and he wrote us an affidavit of his experience, which was that he took the court paper and took it to De Beers and the De Beers representative took the paper, ripped it into small shreds, threw it on the ground and stamped on it, and then basically threw him out.

Narrator: And the cartel has successfully kept its executives beyond the reach of American justice.

Alletzhauser: I'll tell you, when the red flag goes up from their lawyers, these guys are not allowed to set foot in the U.S. The name goes on a computer—beep, beep, beep, beep, beep! "I'm sorry, sir. We have to subpoena you." And under a subpoena in the U.S., you have no rights. You have to tell everything. You cannot lie. You cannot plead irrelevance. It's for them to decide what's irrelevance. It's not like a court, where you have certain rights. And so on occasion, when I interview these guys, they always tell me, "Al! Al! The best exit from the U.S. is always Chicago's O'Hare airport. That's where we're ordered to go immediately, because they're the laxest in terms of immigration. We can get right out of the country."

Narrator: While a subsidiary once paid a nominal fine, De Beers has avoided prosecution in the U.S. Not only has the Justice Department found it impossible to touch the Oppen-heimers in South Africa, it has been unable to penetrate the cartel's respectable London operation.

Carl Schwartz, Former U.S. Justice Department Attorney: It's well known that the British government has historically been vigorously opposed to any U.S. enforcement of anti-trust laws against activity that takes place in Great Britain. And, as we know, a great deal of what De Beers does takes place in Great Britain.

Epstein: Now, the United States has been extending its reach outside its boundaries, sort of as we have done by seizing General Noriega in Panama and prosecuting him with American laws. We've been doing this more and more. And I don't think it's inconceivable that, at a certain point, the fiction that the American diamond industry—the stores that sell—the merchants that sell the diamonds and sell most of the diamonds in the world and sell them to American customers—the idea that De Beers is not acting in cahoots with them in America by putting rules on them in London, then I think that fairly soon the Department of Justice will come to the idea that even though the diamonds are handed over in London, they're handed over with rules and stipulations which mean that De Beers is operating in the American market. And De Beers could be tried if they came to that decision, which I think is—eventually they will.

Narrator: And the Justice Department may now be closing in on one alleged De Beers operation.

Synthetic diamonds were developed long ago for use in industry. De Beers has its own factory in Ireland. Its biggest international rival is General Electric. The Sherman Act strictly limits how two giants like De Beers and G.E. can work together, but the relationship they developed in the '80s has been brought into question.

Edward Russell, Former G.E. Executive: G.E. developed this process for making a pure C-12 diamond and I was widely quoted in the international press that this would be a several-hundred-million-dollar opportunity for us, but to do it, we'd have to go to gem stones. And we started a process for growing gem stones and after a short period of time, we were making gem stones, 3 to 4 carats, flawless E's, which is a very high grade of diamonds, and because we were growing them synthetically, we had a number of advantages. We could make them all the same size and you could color them. You can make them blues, so it's very easy to grow a 3- or 4-carat blue diamond. Once having established our technical capability to do that, we decided to look at the $4 billion gem stone market.

Narrator: But as soon as Ed Russell began to edge beyond industrials and towards the valuable market for gems, he ran into resistance within G.E., from his own immediate boss.

Russell: Glenn Heiner, who is, at this time, meeting with De Beers on a regular basis and having phone calls and what have you, simply killed the project and said, "We will not compete with De Beers," period.

Narrator: Soon afterwards, Ed Russell was fired. He's now suing G.E. for wrongful discharge and alleging it is involved in a cartel with De Beers.

Russell: What happened after I was terminated, a price increase on all industrial diamond products was put in by G.E. and De Beers. They followed each other with identical prices that were—were implemented.

Narrator: In his lawsuit, Russell claims G.E. fired him for blowing the whistle about its dealings with De Beers. The Justice Department has investigated and for more than a year, a federal grand jury has been hearing evidence on the price-fixing allegation. General Electric denies any wrongdoing, saying it met with De Beers only to discuss exchanging technology and fired Russell because of his poor job performance.

Back in South Africa, still the center of its power, the diamond cartel is also dealing with a political earthquake. What impact will the dismantling of apartheid have on the De Beers monopoly? Harry Oppenheimer, the man who ran the cartel for 25 years, has been a long-time critic of the South African government's apartheid policy.

Henry Oppenheimer: —more peaceful conditions in South Africa as a whole. We have to believe, and by our practice demonstrate, that the pursuit of business efficiency and the search for a free and just society are, in fact, two aspects of the same thing, two sides of one coin.

Duncan Innes, Author, "Anglo American and the Rise of Modern South Africa": He himself has publicly come out against apartheid on many occasions and continues to do so. I think the problem is—

and this is where he's been criticized in the past. The problem is that the mining houses that he controlled made use of the migrant labor system. They made use of the compound system. They made use of the pass laws. They made use of all the institutions which, in fact, created apartheid. So in that sense, people question why, on the one hand, does this man oppose apartheid, but on the other hand, he makes money out of apartheid.

Narrator: A hundred years ago, De Beers's founder, Cecil Rhodes, laid the groundwork for the cartel's success in South Africa.

Newsreel: Ironically, the famous empire builder, in his commercial activities, turning the early diamond rush into a vast industry, sowed the seeds of apartheid.

Mr. Innes: Particularly after they discovered the diamond mines, what they were looking for was to try and create a workforce for those mines. And the problem was that they needed unskilled workers, but the problem was that most of the available potential labor force were black people living on the land. And in order to get them into the mines, they had to find ways of forcing them off the land. And one of the mechanisms they adopted was passing various taxes, such as a poll tax, hut tax, even a dog tax, which forced people living on the land to pay cash to the government and they didn't have cash because they were not part of a cash economy. So they therefore had to go into the mines to earn the money to pay the taxes.

Narrator: In order to pay their taxes, many Africans had to leave their families behind and walk hundreds of miles to work in the mines. Once inside, a miner could not leave until his contract was over. De Beers's closed compounds became the model for the entire mining industry in South Africa. By the 1960s, these compounds had expanded into enormous complexes housing thousands of men.

Gordon Brown, Former De Beers Employee: When I arrived in the mine in 1968, I was quite appalled by the conditions for the migrant laborers. The working hours were long. It was a 60-hour week. The conditions under which they worked—they—well, they were out in the open, very little protection against the cold and the wind. They weren't given much to eat. They were given half a loaf of brown bread and a flask of cold tea to last them throughout that 10-hour shift. Conditions in the hostels were not much better. There were no decent dining facilities. They had to eat in their rooms out of aluminum buckets. There was no real privacy. The hostels themselves were not very nice places to be in—single-sex hostels, 20 people to a room, in some instances.

Narrator: Many black miners still live in segregated compounds away from their families. In a country in which it is illegal to pick a diamond up off the ground and keep it, the miners union claims workers can be dismissed merely on suspicion of stealing diamonds. But today, De Beers says, everybody gets a proper hearing.

Mene Dipico, National Union of Mineworkers: Any employee who could literally buy a new car is being investigated and people were dismissed summarily because they were suspected of dealing with diamonds. How can they buy a new car? So people were dismissed without a hearing, not a proper hearing, without an inquiry whatsoever. People were dismissed and the reasons given, which was there on paper, was "security reason" and that cannot be followed up, in terms of an appeal, and so on. And our people were very—were very afraid to take De Beers at a higher level because in our country, De Beers is an empire.

Narrator: Ironically, the revulsion of the world to the brutality of the apartheid government contributed to the growth of the Oppenheimers' power inside South Africa.

Mr. Innes: When, in 1960, we had the Sharpeville massacre, a number of international companies in South Africa decided to get out of the country and the—and many investors also withdrew. Overseas investors withdrew their investments from the stock exchange. Companies like Anglo American and other large corporations then bought up the shares on the stock exchange in order to prevent the exchange from collapsing, which would have generated a financial crisis. Instead of possibly allowing a financial crisis, which would have then forced the government into more difficulties and perhaps brought about an earlier end to apartheid, they actively supported the economy, and therefore gave the government a base from which it could protect itself.

Narrator: Companies in the Oppenheimer empire include breweries, paper mills, chemicals, farms and businesses of every description. Today the empire's interests represent up to 40 percent of the total value of the Johannesburg stock exchange.

But as his empire grew, Harry Oppenheimer tried to separate his reputation from that of the pariah government in South Africa. This 1979 De Beers film showed Oppen-heimer the reformer.

Oppenheimer: —in a decision taken by the De Beers company to move away, so far as it was possible to do so, and as quickly as possible, from the system of migrant labor. We are moving away from that system and we are making a great effort, and I think a very successful effort, to replace it by a system by which the workers in the mines will be permanently resident and will not be going backwards and forwards between the mines and their homes in quite different parts of the country.

Narrator: In spite of Oppenheimer's reforms, his early support of black labor unions and other liberal causes, he says he's been hesitant to use his business clout to influence the government's policies. He explained why in an interview with South African television.

> **Oppenheimer:** I think one's got to put this in two ways. I mean, there's my own position, as an individual. I have never believed that the government's policies are right, particularly in the racial field. But I also would think it quite wrong, in my capacity as chairman of the Anglo American Corporation, to use that position in order to try to press the government into views which I believe in, but they don't believe in.

Narrator: In a few months, Nelson Mandela will lead the black majority to power in South Africa. But as the election nears, the ANC is sending out strong signals that it needs the support of the white business community. So what will the new South Africa mean for the diamond empire?

Mr. Innes: Until there is legislation preventing the existence of these cartels, or until there's a major crack in the market, the cartel will survive. I do know that the ANC is thinking about anti-trust legislation in South Africa for the future, but whether they would include a company like De Beers in that or not is an open question, simply because De Beers is too powerful. If they were to include De Beers in that and De Beers were to stop producing diamonds, it would be very serious for our economy.

Narrator: Another challenge to the cartel's power is the political unrest in the former Soviet Union. Boris Yeltsin is unhappy with the terms of a five-year De Beers contract signed by Mikhail Gorbachev. In 1992, the Russian parliament investigated an allegation that De Beers had undervalued Russian diamonds.

Mendy Kaszirer, Former De Beers Sight-Holder I think it's difficult to estimate how much they lost, actually, with De Beers. Could have very, very well been possible that if they would have sold the goods to somebody else, that they would have made also only the same price. There just wasn't anybody else

who could get in. That's the difference and that's why we go back to the monopoly.

Narrator: Yevgeny Bishkopf oversees the country's diamond stockpiles.

Yevgeny Bishkopf: *through interpreter* It's in Russia's interests to get a good price and sell the goods in order to cover the expenses of mining and making a profit. And we're going to negotiate with De Beers about reducing this quota. Let us hope that a mutually beneficial solution will be found. Let us not approach these issues from the point of view of, "What if they say no?"

Narrator: Russia has more leverage than other producers. Its diamond production is greater than South Africa's. Its deposits in the ground are immense and its stockpiles may exceed even those of De Beers.

Russia's instability and desperate need for hard currency are potentially devastating to De Beers. These millions of carats of diamonds, if suddenly dumped onto the market, could destroy the cartel.

Two years ago, the Oppen-heimers opened an office in Moscow. They seemed to spare no effort to cement friendships and influence people in the government circles, trying to keep the Russians inside the cartel.

Despite all the forces that threaten the diamond empire, the cartel seems to approach these latest challenges with a serene confidence.

> **Oppenheimer:** I think you carry on with where you find yourself in life. I chose my father with discretion and I found myself in a certain position and, I mean, like the prayer book says, I have sought to do my duty in the station in which it pleases the Lord to call me.

Narrator: After a century of maneuvers to control the supply and price of diamonds, the cartel's greatest accomplishment may be that it has transformed the illusion that diamonds are valuable into a hard reality. And the future of the diamond empire may now rest with the complicity of millions of consumers, all invested in the myth that diamonds will be valuable forever.

Television Commercial: Give her what her heart wants most—a diamond.

Epstein: People feel that a diamond is only desirable because it's a symbol of great sacrifice. A man will make a great sacrifice to a woman and take a portion of his wealth and buy a diamond.

Actor: *TV commercial* I know. You shouldn't have waited 10 years for this.

Epstein: If a diamond cost relatively nothing—say,

$5 or $10, what a breakfast costs—it would have the same esthetic value, but not the same value in the imagination that it has. So people like spending a lot of money on diamonds.

Actor: *TV commercial*—that I waited 25 years to give you this.

Announcer: *TV commercial* The 25th anniversary diamond—a brilliant celebration of the loving marriage.

Actress: *TV commercial* I've got goose bumps!

Epstein: So like all deception, the person who's deceived plays a part in the deception, as well as the deceiver. It's not a one-person act. It's two people, the deceiver and the deceived, acting in collaboration.

Announcer: *TV commercial* More profound than words—diamonds.

De Beers, Anglo American and the Oppenheimer family all declined to be interviewed for this program.

Study Questions

1. Are cartels inherently unstable, since there is so much money to be gained by selling more of the item in question at the high price inflated by the cartel's agreement? What has kept this cartel so stable?

2. Is libertarianism undercut because so much of the economy is not really free to begin with? The Organization of Petroleum Exporting Countries (OPEC) is an oil cartel, and some are concerned that aluminum or other important metals are almost subject to a monopoly or oligarchy. For many food items in America the top three brands account for about 90 percent of all sales.

3. Is a monopoly on a luxury item morally more acceptable than a monopoly on a basic necessity? If so, why? Isn't the basic principle of freedom the same? If not, why not? Are diamonds mere luxuries, given the monopoly on industrial diamonds? What is the property of a diamond that makes it so valuable as a tool of industry rather than as luxurious jewelry?

88

Jettison the Policy of Human Rights

Alan Tonelson

President Bill Clinton's team-up with the Haitian military and his acknowledgment last summer that trade sanctions would not hasten democracy's development in China are only the latest signs that America's human rights policy has collapsed. The signs of America's failure to achieve the policy's objectives appear everywhere: from the halls of power in defiant Beijing to the streets of Port-au-Prince, from the mountains of Bosnia to the tenant farms of rebellious Chiapas in southern Mexico. At least as important, the policy has antagonized or simply turned off numerous democratic countries, as well as endangered a broad range of U.S. strategic and economic interests in key regions around the world.

No one can fairly blame U.S. policy for the world's continuing—and in many respects worsening—human rights situation. But Washington has been so ineffective in combating human rights violations in so many places for so long, and so many of its efforts at promoting democracy—especially their unilateral elements—have entailed such high costs, that the usual explanations seem inadequate.

Rather than blame Secretary of State Warren Christopher's alleged incompetence and Clinton's allegedly naive campaign promises, or struggle to better "balance" human rights concerns with other major U.S. interests, Americans might instead begin asking a fundamental question: Does any government-centered human rights policy make sense in the post–Cold War era? All the evidence indicates that such policies, however morally compelling, are obsolete—swamped, ironically, by the very forces that only yesterday inspired such bipartisan optimism in a new age of human rights progress. The immense tides of information, technology, goods, and capital that now flow so effortlessly across borders have turned Washington's efforts into Cold War relics, as antiquated as fallout shelters—and, in their own way, as falsely comforting.

Since the Cold War spawned U.S. human rights policy, its post–Cold War collapse should come as no surprise. American leaders have spoken out against oppression abroad throughout U.S. history, and the American people fought two global hot wars as well as a cold war against imperialist adversaries. But a systematic, dedicated policy to promote greater respect worldwide for human rights dates back only to the 1970s. Unfortunately, the policy was never rooted in a rigorous critique of prevailing American approaches to world affairs, or in a careful search for alternatives, but in a politically inspired temper tantrum by foreign policy professionals of the Left and Right.

Of course, as left-of-center human rights advocates argued, Washington's Cold War alliances with anticommunist dictators sometimes backfired. Of course, as right-of-center human rights advocates argued, American leaders episodically kept quiet about communist oppression whenever they pursued detente-like policies. And, of course, there was much heartfelt concern at the grassroots level about the moral tone and impact of American foreign policy. But the high-profile politicians and activists across the political spectrum who created and debated official human rights policies were, at bottom, simply venting frustrations over the compromises with evil that no foreign policy in an imperfect, anarchic world can avoid, and using human rights debates to push broader, more questionable agendas.

Liberals and other left-wing opponents of the Vietnam War used the human rights issue to push the broader view that millennial change was sweeping over world affairs, and that the United States could abandon the use of force and power-politicking altogether. They asserted that America's essential foreign policy objectives could be secured with more morally and aesthetically pleasing tools like foreign aid, diplomacy, and acceding to the (usually legitimate) interests of even hostile powers. The political Right used the human rights issue to attack detente with the Soviet Union and the larger belief that peaceful coexistence with other nuclear superpowers not only was necessary, but also could improve national security by reducing tensions and even produce mutually beneficial agreements.

Not surprisingly, given such political and polemical origins, human rights policy rarely advanced U.S. national interests in the 1970s. Relations with both

Reprinted from Alan Tonelson, "Jettison the Policy," *Foreign Policy*, Number 97, Winter 1994–95, pp. 121–132.

allies and adversaries worsened (including West European countries that criticized the policy's heavy-handed treatment of the former Soviet Union), dictatorial friends were often weakened without generating better replacements (as in Iran and Nicaragua), and equally dictatorial foes remained securely in power (throughout the communist bloc and much of the developing world).

More surprisingly, prominent human rights advocates rarely sounded troubled when their policies failed to significantly improve human rights practices worldwide. Did U.S. policy simply help replace a friendly autocrat with an equally ruthless and hostile successor, as in Iran and Nicaragua? Did American initiatives lead a target regime to crack down on dissenters or aspiring emigrants, as in the Soviet Union? Was America aiming at countries where it had no influence at all, as in Vietnam or Ethiopia?

When advocates did try to answer such questions, their responses spoke volumes about their real priorities. Symbolism was critical. Consistency was essential—never mind that the objects of human rights policy were countries that differed completely in their level of social and economic development, their significance to the United States, and their political relations with America. The United States had to go on record. Americans had to do "what they could"—implying, of course, that salving American consciences was the main point.

For those reasons, moderate critics of the policies were missing the point entirely when they labored mightily to reconcile human rights positions with American strategic and economic interests. U.S. efforts did score limited successes—securing the release of numerous political prisoners during the 1970s (especially in Latin America) and joining in rare global economic sanctions that did advance the cause of reform in South Africa—although how those successes made the United States appreciably more secure or more prosperous was never explained. But human rights activism was never primarily about enhancing national security and welfare, or even alleviating suffering abroad. It was an exercise in therapy. The bottom line, as Jimmy Carter made clear, was to give Americans a foreign policy they could feel good about.

By the early 1980s, human rights policy became bogged down in sterile debates over the relative merits of left- and right-wing dictators, or the relative importance of the more traditional political rights such as free expression and the vote versus social and economic rights (to a job or education). Advancing

the national interest or achieving concrete results receded further into the background. Pushing one's left- or right-wing sympathies and elegantly rationalizing them became higher priorities.

Human Rights in the Age of Clinton

The end of the Cold War generated broad optimism that human rights would take center stage, not only in U.S. foreign policy, but in world politics as a whole. Economic and trade issues aside, human rights dominated Clinton's intermittent foreign policy rhetoric during the 1992 campaign, as he and other Democrats repeatedly blasted George Bush's alleged indifference to human rights horrors in Tiananmen Square, Iraq, and the former Yugoslavia.

And so far—again, leaving economics aside—human rights issues have dominated Clinton's intermittent foreign policy making as president. His inaugural address promised to use American power if necessary whenever "the will and conscience of the international community is defied." His national security adviser Anthony Lake has made the "enlargement" of the world's roster of democratic countries one of America's top foreign policy priorities. And human rights considerations permeate the U.S. foreign policy agenda from Russia to China to Somalia to Bosnia to Haiti.

Clinton's priorities clearly reflected a rapidly emerging bipartisan conventional wisdom. The reasons for optimism were obvious to conservatives and liberals alike—although they disagreed sharply on what some of them were. Both were thrilled by the prospect of an America no longer forced to back dictators for anti-Soviet reasons. Both expected the collapse of Soviet power and Soviet stooges around the world to bring the blessings of national self-determination to numerous captive peoples. And both assumed that the global revolutions in communications and commerce would inevitably carry democratic political ideas and liberal economic practices to even the most repressive and backward societies.

But conservatives were more taken with the role that America, as the last superpower, could play unilaterally in fostering democracy and capitalism. Some even urged the United States to launch a global crusade to help the process along and create a worldwide Pax Democratica shaped by American political principles and Reaganomics.

Liberals focused on multilateral approaches, churning out blueprints for creating a U.N. that could oust repressive regimes through sanctions or force of arms. As demonstrated most dramatically in 1991 by the establishment of safe havens for Iraq's Kurds, the international community, they argued, was acquiring the right to intervene in sovereign states' internal affairs when rights violations threatened international security or passed some unspecified threshold of savagery.

Yet none of the countries that the president or the world community has focused on have become significantly freer or more democratic places since Clinton's inauguration or since the Soviet Union's demise. In other areas of American concern, notably Russia and its "Near Abroad," the situation has arguably worsened in recent months. Bleaker still is the human rights outlook in those regions that have so far eluded either the administration's or the media's focus—from sub-Saharan Africa to suddenly shaky Mexico to the Arab world.

Even in Western Europe, democracy is deeply troubled as high unemployment and burgeoning immigrant populations have strengthened xenophobic politicians in many countries. And writers such as Jean-Francois Revel argue convincingly that the rampant corruption of social democratic systems in Italy and France has undermined the public trust in government that is crucial to the survival of democracy.

However, success stories are by no means unknown. So far, they include Taiwan, South Korea, and Chile, and even economically troubled countries such as Argentina, the Czech Republic, and the Baltic states. Nor can prospects for near-term improvement be written off completely in Russia and Mexico.

Still, one of the most comprehensive annual studies of the global human rights picture—the traditionally optimistic Freedom House's *Comparative Survey of Freedom*—concluded at the end of last year that "freedom around the world is in retreat while violence, repression and state control are on the increase." Of course, recent U.S. policy is not exclusively, largely, or even significantly responsible for that. But it is not apparent that official efforts have achieved many durable gains, either.

Even more disturbing has been the global reaction to U.S. human rights policies, especially their unilateral elements. Not a single major power, for example, emulated Washington's linkage of trade relations with human rights progress in China. Some of America's staunchest regional allies, such as Ja-

pan and Australia, openly criticized that strategy from the start. Other allies, principally the West Europeans, quietly worked overtime to cut deals with a booming economy that is already the world's third largest.

Furthermore, many East Asian governments—and many Asian voices outside government—have openly challenged U.S. human rights initiatives as arrogant efforts to impose Western values on proud, ancient societies that are doing quite well economically and socially, thank you. Similar resentments are widely expressed in the Arab world and other Islamic countries.

But the best evidence of failure is the administration's zig-zag record on numerous human rights fronts. Human rights issues are a large part of the president's most embarrassing retreats from campaign promises. Clinton has decided to follow the Bush administration's approach to China, finally agreeing that continued economic engagement is the best way to advance America's human rights and broader agendas with the world's most populous country. Even before his inauguration, the president had to endorse his predecessor's policy of returning Haiti's boat people, and in September 1994 he acquiesced in an agreement negotiated mainly by former president Jimmy Carter for joint U.S. administration of Haiti's democratic transition with the very military leaders he had condemned as murderers and rapists the week before. Moreover, bitter experiences in Somalia and Haiti in 1993 have so far led to a lowering of America's peacekeeping goals.

Decline in Public Support

In part, U.S. human rights policies are failing because their consistently shaky strategic foundations have crumbled. During the Cold War, a plausible case could be made for denying an ideologically hostile rival superpower targets of opportunity by fostering democratic practices abroad. But in the absence of such a rival, the state of human rights around the world does not have, and has never had, any demonstrable effect on U.S. national security. America's rise to global prominence occurred primarily in periods when democracies were few and far between, and a combination of geography, power, wealth, and social cohesion will continue to be the country's best guarantees of security in a turbulent world. In the wake of the Cold War, both liberal and conservative human rights advocates (including the president) have argued that democracies rarely fight each other—hence the more there are, the merrier and safer America will be. Yet the jury is still out: Significant numbers of democracies have existed together only in the last 50 years. Furthermore, U.S. leaders obviously have never bought the argument themselves—otherwise, they would not continue to be terrified by the prospect of democratic Germany and Japan carrying out independent foreign policies or going nuclear.

Moreover, strong domestic support for an active human rights policy has been difficult to detect. Although Americans often endorse vigorous human rights policies when talking with pollsters, they have not recently acted or voted as if they cared much about them. Carter made human rights a top foreign policy priority and was rewarded with early retirement—because he let the economy deteriorate and seemed ineffective in dealing with the Soviets. His 1980 opponent, Ronald Reagan, promised to uphold American values against an evil Soviet empire, but his most politically popular foreign policy position was his stand against the military threat he saw emanating from Moscow. And what happened when the greatest White House communicator since Franklin Roosevelt tried to mobilize public support for his Reagan Doctrine policies of arming "freedom fighters" combating pro-Soviet Third World regimes? He failed everywhere except Afghanistan, where the Soviet occupation arguably threatened the oil-rich Persian Gulf.

What politicians and pundits do not understand—and may not want to understand—is that unlike their leaders, the American people evidently have learned from past mistakes. The Iran hostage crisis happened. As the 1992 election and its aftermath showed, when voters care deeply about issues—from the economy to Zoe Baird's nanny problem—they are not shy about making their feelings known. And just as they never filled the streets or flooded Washington's phone banks protesting oppression around the world during the 1970s and 1980s, they have not been demanding the denial of tariff breaks to China or intervention in basket-case countries in the 1990s. If the American people retain any significant missionary impulse, or much optimism that the world craves American guidance on human rights issues, they are hiding their feelings well.

To a depressing degree, however, U.S. human rights policy grinds on along the same well-worn tracks. Despite the China trade decision, another China-like struggle over linking trade relations with human rights practices may be unfolding with Indonesia, and yet another looms with Vietnam. Both controversies have scary implications for America's economic position in rapidly growing Asia (where establishing long-term relationships and, consequently, a reputation for reliability are keys to business success) and other emerging markets.

And as during the 1970s and 1980s, today's human rights skeptics unwittingly play along, accepting the basic assumptions driving human rights policy but pleading for moderation, perspective, and "balancing" human rights considerations with America's strategic and economic objectives.

In the process, critics have periodically aired stronger objections, calling human rights policy arrogant, naive, inconsistent—a juvenile protest against life's built-in imperfections. They are largely correct. Yet two even greater obstacles to a successful government-led U.S. human rights policy are embedded in the very nature of the post–Cold War world.

The first concerns the phenomenon of failed states that has been exposed by the retreat of Soviet power in Eastern Europe and by the end of Cold War confrontation in much of the Third World—in Bosnia, Georgia, Haiti, Somalia, Rwanda, and elsewhere. The often horrendous general conditions and specific outrages that have resulted from the breakdown of governments in those regions are usually described as "human rights violations," but the phrase trivializes the problem. At worst, they are endemic features of deep-rooted ethnic conflicts. At best, they are symptoms of a monumental struggle over issues not of liberalization or democratization, but of minimal coherence or further fragmentation. Welcome to the dark side of national self-determination, as Colonel E. M. House warned Woodrow Wilson nearly 75 years ago.

Outside Western Europe, North America, and East Asia, most "countries" around the world simply do not deserve that label. They may have the trappings of statehood—postage stamps, U.N. membership—but their populations lack a sense of mutual loyalty and obligation, and their politics lack strong institutions, a commitment to the rule of law, and even a tradition of public service as anything more than an opportunity for theft and vengeance. They are straining to reach minimal viability not even as nation-states but as societies. The conceit behind the idea that even the best designed policies, or a few billion dollars' worth of foreign aid, or "how to" democracy courses can make a real difference is, to put it kindly, immense.

As for U.S. human rights policies toward more advanced repressive countries, they are swamped by a similar problem—by the very global economic and cultural interaction responsible for much of the optimism of human rights advocates. Precisely because ideas and capital and technology—and, to a somewhat lesser extent, people—can cross borders so easily, official rhetoric and even sanctions get lost in the shuffle. Government words and deeds form merely one small breeze in the gales of commerce and culture blowing around the world today. Western and American values will not be the only seeds dropped by those winds. But if we consider their spread and growth to be essential, then we are better advised to lead from strength—to energetically add to America's already vast commercial, cultural, and ideological influence around the world, rather than seek to replace it with legislation or executive orders or official oratory.

Leave aside for the moment the op-ed level arguments that dominated the China most-favored-nation debate—for example, over which country has the most leverage, over whether economic relations with America strengthen the Chinese government's economic base and help pacify the population, over whether other countries will rush in to replace American suppliers and investors. Say Americans were to start from scratch on an imaginary campaign to reform China. What would the most promising tools be? "Sense of the Congress" resolutions? Cut-backs in the numbers of American companies that the Chinese can work for or do business with, and that pay Chinese employees higher wages and provide safer working conditions than do China's state-owned enterprises? Or would America send as many businesspeople to China as quickly as it could? The answer should be obvious even to those who do not believe in business-created utopias.

The China issue, however, along with last year's controversy over the North American Free Trade Agreement, does bring up one bona fide human rights issue where more effective U.S. government action is needed: the question of how most of America's workforce can benefit from trade with countries that repress labor rights. American workers are already exposed to strong competition from hundreds of millions of workers in developing countries who are highly educated, highly productive, and organized by the world's leading multinational cor-porations, but who are paid a fraction of what their U.S. counterparts earn and who are systematically denied the right to form independent unions and bargain collectively for wages that bear some relationship to productivity increases, for decent workplaces, and for nonwage benefits—rights and conditions until recently taken for granted in North America and Western Europe. Many more such workers will soon be coming into the world economy from China's interior (as opposed to its already booming coastal regions), from South and Southeast Asia, and, farther down the road, from Russia and Eastern Europe.

Even if all of them work for politically and socially progressive American companies, which they will not, the capacity of those workers to export will exceed by orders of magnitude their capacity to consume. Lack of labor rights is hardly the only reason, but it can create major competitive advantages. As Labor Secretary Robert Reich noted in an April 1994 speech, the problem is part and parcel of the inherent difficulties of commerce between countries at greatly differing levels of economic and social development in an age of highly mobile capital and technology.

Unlike other human rights issues, moreover, labor rights controversies and their resolutions are already having concrete effects on the lives of millions of Americans. But they are best seen not as human rights issues at all, but as challenges in managing interdependence—in ensuring that the great integrative forces shaping the world economy work for the long-term benefit of the great majority of the American people, not against it.

Nor can labor rights controversies be successfully resolved by acting out the stylized morality plays that make up human rights policy today—by issuing the same threats and voluminous reports, by trotting out the same dissidents in front of the press, by fasting, or by any other attempts to dictate the social and economic priorities of other countries. Instead, labor rights problems require a raft of new trade, technology, foreign investment, and other policies designed to increase America's economic power.

A vibrant industrial base that creates millions of new high-wage jobs can give America the economic leverage needed to negotiate beneficial economic agreements with the rest of the world. A prosperous America can generate enough markets, capital, and technology to give other countries powerful incentives to conform to U.S. labor, environmental, and other standards voluntarily—not as acknowledgments of American moral superiority or as acts of surrender, but simply as the price of access.

As Americans will discover in many foreign policy fields, crusades to bring about utopian change around the world will rarely achieve their goals. The best bets lie in measures that enable the country to survive, flourish, and bargain successfully in the deeply flawed world that we will remain stuck with for many decades. Americans wishing their government to act in moral ways might consider focusing on their own country—which suffers its share of problems and moral outrages, but is also blessed with the institutions and social cohesion to make serious reform more than a pipe dream.

Study Questions

1. Are Tonelson's criticisms of President Clinton's policies correct? If so, why? If not, why not?

2. Should we follow Tonelson's recommendation and jettison President Clinton's policy of trying to protect human rights around the world?

3. What is the answer to this question posed by Tonelson: "Does any government-centered human rights policy make sense in a post–Cold War era?"

4. Tonelson expresses surprise that prominent human rights advocates rarely sounded troubled when their policies failed to significantly improve human rights practices worldwide. Should Tonelson have been so surprised? Isn't the point that we should at least try to protect and promote human rights globally, even if success is elusive? Were these human rights advocates merely being realistic when they were not troubled by a lack of success? Isn't there some significant consolation and peace of mind in knowing that you have tried your best to improve human rights practices, come what may?

89

Rally 'round Human Rights

Michael Posner

Alan Tonelson has written a provocative but premature obituary to international human rights. He asserts that the tragedies in Bosnia, Somalia, and Haiti prove that it is no longer useful or productive for the U.S. government to challenge state-sponsored murder and torture in other countries and to emphasize human rights as an element of its foreign policy.

Tonelson's postmortem is flawed in at least four basic assumptions: In a relatively short space, he manages to misrepresent the origins of human rights, its scope and objectives, reasonable measures to judge the effectiveness of U.S. human rights policy, and the view of key U.S. allies with respect to this policy.

According to Tonelson, the emphasis on human rights was a product of the Cold War, designed principally to challenge the Soviet Union. From his perspective, the starting point for the discussion was the 1970s. He is wrong, both about the purpose and timing. Contrary to Tonelson's narrow world view, attention to international human rights has evolved steadily over the last five decades.

The international community in fact began to focus on human rights immediately after World War II. Shaken by the Holocaust and determined to make amends for their slow and inadequate response to the murder of millions of innocent victims, the United States and its allies sought to take steps to prevent similar future occurrences. The United Nations Charter, adopted in 1945, made human rights a central purpose of that new organization. Governments pledge to take joint and separate actions to encourage a more just, humane world.

A year later, the U.N. created its own Commission on Human Rights, with former first lady Eleanor Roosevelt serving as its first chair. Under her stew-

ardship, the commission moved quickly to draft a body of human rights principles—the Universal Declaration of Human Rights, adopted by the U.N. General Assembly in 1948. Working closely with the U.S. Department of State, Roosevelt helped develop two other key treaties, the International Covenant on Civil and Political Rights and the International Covenant on Economic, Social and Cultural Rights. Many other countries participated in those early developments and many more, including virtually all key American allies, now view the treaties as the basis for international consideration of those rights.

Official U.S. attention to those issues increased significantly in the 1970s with congressional efforts like the Jackson-Vanik Amendment, which linked trade with the Soviet Union to its willingness to allow emigration by Soviet Jews. As president, Jimmy Carter greatly expanded U.S. initiatives in the area and gave human rights a much higher profile.

Nongovernmental organizations also came of age at that time. Amnesty International was awarded the 1977 Nobel Peace Prize in recognition of its unique rule in human rights advocacy. Several key U.S.-based human rights organizations, including Helsinki Watch (now part of Human Rights Watch) and the Lawyers Committee for Human Rights, were also founded during that period. Thus, over the past 50 years, significant progress has been made in developing human rights law and in setting practical objectives for its implementation.

Scope and Objectives

Tonelson offers a confusing and sometimes contradictory view of the scope and objectives of U.S. human rights policy. On one hand, he criticizes politicians and activists for using human rights "to push broader, more questionable agendas." On the other hand, he urges that we pursue labor rights, not because it is the right thing to do, but to protect the economic well-being of "millions of Americans."

Tonelson also builds straw men, only to tear them down. He refers repeatedly to "human rights advocates," a term he never defines. Using that broad rubric he notes that conservatives are using human rights to foster "democracy and capitalism." He then accuses liberals of using human rights to advocate using U.N. sanctions or military force "to oust repressive regimes." While some have indeed used the language of human rights to pursue these broad politi-

Reprinted from "Rally Round Human Rights," *Foreign Policy*, no. 97 (Winter 1994–1995), pp. 133–139.

cal objectives, in doing so they are going beyond the core meaning of human rights, which is to challenge governments when they mistreat their own people.

Human rights advocates such as Amnesty International and hundreds of national rights advocacy groups around the world rely on international human rights standards that set minimum requirements for governments. States that ratify international treaties make a pledge to abide by these core legal principles, which include commitments not to torture their own people, subject them to slavery, or engage in political murder. Tonelson blithely dismisses efforts by human rights groups and others to challenge such violations as "an exercise in therapy." On the contrary, human rights advocacy has evolved into a worldwide movement aimed at exposing and combating official misconduct and alleviating suffering. There is now ample evidence that by exposing violations and challenging the violators, lives are being saved.

The international treaties provide a foundation for such efforts, but set forth only broad basic principles. The civil and political covenant, for example, requires governments to allow for a free press, for the right to hold public meetings, and for the right to speak freely. It also requires popular participation in choosing a government. But it neither spells out how that should be accomplished, nor suggests a specific political structure or system. Those who seek to wrap broader economic and political agendas in the flag of human rights, including some in the Clinton administration, are overloading the system.

The treaties are also silent on the sanctions that may be imposed on governments that systematically violate basic human rights. Although there is nothing to prevent the U.N. Security Council from invoking the language of human rights to help justify military action, there is nothing in the treaties that compels it, or even suggests that it should do so.

Some governments, including that of the United States, have linked their provision of bilateral aid and trade privileges to human rights. In the last 20 years, the United States has occasionally withheld or delayed the provision of bilateral aid—particularly military aid—in situations where a sustained pattern of violations was occurring. The connection to military aid is the most direct, given the possibility that the weapons provided will be used to commit further violations.

It is much more difficult to impose trade sanctions, in part because there is much less agreement on the usefulness of trade restrictions as an instru-

ment of leverage. The Jackson-Vanik Amendment, which restricted trade to the former Soviet Union, was an exception for two reasons: U.S. economic opportunities in the USSR were limited, and such sanctions had bipartisan support in the broader effort to challenge Soviet influence worldwide.

The recent controversy over the linkage between trade and human rights in China was not surprising, given the economic opportunities at stake. Yet the Clinton administration's decision to de-link the two issues by renewing China's most-favored-nation trading status does not mean that future human rights initiatives should be avoided, or that long-term international pressure on the human rights front will be ineffective.

Measures of Effectiveness

Tonelson's sole criterion for measuring human rights progress appears to be whether U.S. strategic interests are being advanced. While governments that respect human rights are likely to be more stable and reliable strategic allies, the protection and promotion of basic rights worldwide is important in itself. Consistent with our values and traditions, the U.S. government should promote international initiatives designed to alleviate suffering and to challenge governments that deny basic freedoms to their own people.

Tonelson argues that since human rights are being violated all around the world, the human rights policy must be failing, and therefore should be abandoned. That is akin to arguing that since thousands of businesses go bankrupt each year, we must abandon the free market system. While progress on human rights cannot be evaluated with the precision of a profit and loss statement, there are several useful measures of effectiveness.

The first measure is public attention to and awareness of human rights issues. Twenty years ago it was rare to see any reference to international human rights in the news media. By contrast, in any newspaper today one is likely to see several articles, often including one or more front-page stories, where human rights issues are featured prominently. While growing awareness does not automatically lead to greater respect for human rights, it is an important step toward that goal. Most governments are surprisingly thin-skinned on those issues and will go out of their way to avoid being stigmatized by a broad public spotlight.

A second measure of progress is the extent to which indigenous human rights activists are raising the issue in their own countries. Apparently Tonelson does not see such activists from his perch in Washington, since he makes no reference to the proliferation of national advocates and organizations. In the 1970s there were perhaps a few dozen human rights organizations around the world. Today, there are hundreds of such organizations operating in countries throughout the world. Every day the groups are busy documenting abuses, filing lawsuits, and challenging their own governments when they violate basic human rights. Most of the groups are underfunded and work in very difficult circumstances. Those who participate in such activism frequently do so at personal risk. But they carry on, often relying on international diplomatic pressure from the U.S. government and influential parties to protect them and help reinforce the legitimacy of their efforts.

Many of the Asian governments, like those of China and Singapore, that are most critical of U.S. human rights policy and seek to characterize it as Western-based and culturally biased are among the declining number of regimes that absolutely prevent any independent human rights groups from operating. Their claims of cultural relativism can only be sustained if they can continue to prevent their own people from raising human rights issues. But they are fighting a losing battle. Recent experience in countries as diverse as Chile, Kuwait, Nigeria, South Africa, and Sri Lanka leave no doubt that where people are allowed to organize and advocate their own human rights, they will do so. The common denominators in this area are much stronger than the cultural divisions.

Finally, look around the world and note that progress continues to be made on human rights issues. Contrast the Latin America today with the one 15 years ago. Tonelson's own criteria also lead him to assert that none of the countries on which Washington has focused its attention since 1991 have become any freer or more democratic. On that he is simply wrong. A great majority of South Africans, among others, would undoubtedly disagree with him.

Even in the many places where governments do continue to commit serious violations, Tonelson offers no viable alternative to challenging the violators. His suggestion that the United States abandon ship rather than risk the embarrassment of future failure adds little more than a rhetorical flourish to his argument.

The fourth broad mistake in Tonelson's analysis is his assertion that U.S. human rights policy is a failure because it has "antagonized or simply turned off numerous democratic countries." To support his proposition, he notes that not a single "major power" followed the Clinton administration's lead in linking human rights and trade in China. He also notes that some of America's strongest allies in the region, such as Australia and Japan, were openly critical of the policy.

While Tonelson is correct in identifying discomfort and in some cases opposition to the U.S. approach, his analysis is incomplete and therefore misleading. A number of key U.S. allies—Canada, Great Britain, the Netherlands, Sweden, Australia—include human rights as a component in their own foreign policies. But they often prefer to pursue those concerns on a multilateral rather than a bilateral basis. Historically, the U.S. government has disdained multilateral institutions, viewing U.N. debates as an exercise in damage control. In the 1980s, U.S. representatives to the U.N. repeatedly opposed resolutions that called for the appointment of special experts to investigate and report on situations in Guatemala, Haiti, and El Salvador, among others—preferring to address those situations in a less-confrontational manner.

Tonelson also misses another important point, which is the declining U.S. ability to act unilaterally. During the Cold War, the United States invested billions of dollars in bilateral military and economic aid. Most of the money went to the support of strategic allies in the geopolitical confrontation with the Soviet bloc. A number of governments, such as those in El Salvador, Haiti, Indonesia, Liberia, the Philippines, and Zaire, were committing serious human rights violations. In those situations, the United States had enormous influence and could threaten to cut off aid as a means of ultimate leverage. Following the collapse of the Soviet Union, however, Congress drastically reduced foreign aid—particularly military aid—and, concomitantly, U.S. influence and ability to act unilaterally.

To date, both the Clinton administration and the human rights community have been slow to accept the new reality. The real failure of Clinton's China policy was not that he tried to link trade and human rights, but that he tried to do it alone. American companies quickly mobilized when they realized that not only would they be shut out of a huge market, but that their overseas competitors would jump in to fill the void. So while it remains an open question whether linking trade to human rights is a politically viable option for advancing the cause of human rights, in China or elsewhere, it is clear that whatever America's tactical approach is, it can no longer act alone if it is going to be effective.

Concern for human rights is far from obsolete— either as a set of U.N. principles or as an element of U.S. foreign policy. In looking to the future, these issues are likely to loom more prominently than ever before, particularly in those societies that are in transition, such as China, India, Mexico, Nigeria, and Russia. To be effective, U.S. policymakers and activists need to rethink strategies while working more in concert with others who regard human rights as a vital international concern.

Study Questions

1. Who has the better of this debate, Tonelson or Posner? Why?

2. Which single argument, by either Tonelson or Posner, is most persuasive? Why?

3. What was Posner's most unconvincing point? Why was it so unconvincing? In light of Posner's rebuttal, what was Tonelson's most unconvincing point? Why was Tonelson's point so unconvincing?

4. Should we follow Posner's recommendation and rally 'round human rights? If so, why? If not, why not?

5. Aren't the Holocaust and World War II examples that show that no nation can afford to ignore the issue of human rights? Is there a slippery slope, as violating one group's human rights leads to further violations of the human rights of other groups? Does "Divide and conquer" apply here?

"LET'S GET THIS STRAIGHT. THE BUSINESS RUNS ITSELF. YOU GO TO A BOARD MEETING ONCE A MONTH. WHAT DO YOU WANT TO RETIRE <u>FROM</u>?"

© 1995 by Sidney Harris.

90

In Praise of Idleness

Bertrand Russell

Editor's note: Russell, who won the Nobel Prize for literature, is one of the greatest philosophers in the Western tradition. His surprising praise of idleness, in the face of his culture's work ethic, is characteristically clear. For example, he defines the key term "work" clearly and early. He bases his analysis on his concern for history and happiness. He explains why so many are misled into believing in the work ethic.

Like most of my generation I was brought up on the saying: "Satan finds some mischief still for idle hands to do." Being a highly virtuous child, I believed all that I was told, and acquired a conscience which has kept me working hard down to the present moment. But although my conscience has controlled my *actions*, my *opinions* have undergone a revolution. I think that there is far too much work done in the world, that immense harm is caused by the belief that work is virtuous, and that what needs to be preached in modern industrial countries is quite different from what always has been preached. Everyone knows the story of the traveler in Naples who saw twelve beggars lying in the sun (it was before the days of Mussolini) and offered a lira to the laziest of them. Eleven of them jumped up to claim it, so he gave it to the twelfth. This traveler was on the right lines. But in countries which do not enjoy Mediterranean sunshine idleness is more difficult, and a great public propaganda will be required to inaugurate it. I hope that, after reading the following pages, the leaders of the Y.M.C.A. will start a campaign to induce good young men to do nothing. If so, I shall not have lived in vain.

Before advancing my own arguments for laziness, I must dispose of one which I cannot accept. Whenever a person who already has enough to live on proposes to engage in some everyday kind of job, such as schoolteaching or typing, he or she is told that such conduct takes the bread out of other people's mouths, and is therefore wicked. If this argument were valid, it would only be necessary for us all to be idle in order that we should all have our mouths full of bread. What people who say such things forget is that what a man earns he usually spends, and in spending he gives employment. As long as a man spends his income, he puts just as much bread into people's mouths in spending as he takes out of other people's mouths in earning. The real villain, from this point of view, is the man who saves. If he merely puts his savings in a stocking, like the proverbial French peasant, it is obvious that they do not give employment. If he invests his savings, the matter is less obvious, and different cases arise.

One of the commonest things to do with savings is to lend them to some Government. In view of the fact that the bulk of the public expenditure of most civilized Governments consists in payment for past wars or preparation for future wars, the man who lends his money to a Government is in the same position as the bad men in Shakespeare who hire murderers. The net result of the man's economical habits is to increase the armed forces of the State to which he lends his savings. Obviously it would be better if he spent the money, even if he spent it in drink or gambling.

But, I shall be told, the case is quite different when savings are invested in industrial enterprises. When such enterprises succeed, and produce something useful, this may be conceded. In these days, however, no one will deny that most enterprises fail. That means that a large amount of human labor, which might have been devoted to producing something that could be enjoyed, was expended on producing machines which, when produced, lay idle and did no good to anyone. The man who invests his savings in a concern that goes bankrupt is therefore injuring others as well as himself. If he spent his money, say, in giving parties for his friends, they (we may hope) would get pleasure, and so would all those upon whom he spent money, such as the butcher, the baker, and the bootlegger. But if he spends it (let us say) upon laying down rails for surface cars in some place where surface cars turn out to be not wanted, he has diverted a mass of labor into channels where it gives pleasure to no one. Nevertheless, when he becomes poor through the failure of his investment he will be regarded as a victim of undeserved misfortune, whereas the gay spendthrift, who has spent his money philanthropically, will be despised as a fool and a frivolous person.

All this is only preliminary. I want to say, in all seriousness, that a great deal of harm is being done in the modern world by belief in the virtuousness of *work*, and that the road to happiness and prosperity lies in an organized diminution of work.

First of all: what is work? Work is of two kinds: first, altering the position of matter at or near the earth's surface relatively to other such matter; second, telling other people to do so. The first kind is unpleasant and ill paid; the second is pleasant and highly paid. The second kind is capable of indefinite extension: there are not only those who give orders, but those who give advice as to what orders should be given. Usually two opposite kinds of advice are given simultaneously by two organized bodies of men; this is called politics. The skill required for this kind of work is not knowledge of the subjects as to which advice is given, but knowledge of the art of persuasive speaking and writing, i.e., of advertising.

Throughout Europe, though not in America, there is a third class of men, more respected than either of the classes of workers. There are men who, through ownership of land, are able to make others pay for the privilege of being allowed to exist and to work. These landowners are idle, and I might therefore be expected to praise them. Unfortunately, their idleness is only rendered possible by the industry of others; indeed their desire for comfortable idleness is historically the source of the whole gospel of work. The last thing they have ever wished is that others should follow their example.

From the beginning of civilization until the Industrial Revolution, a man could, as a rule, produce by hard work little more than was required for the subsistence of himself and his family, although his wife worked at least as hard as he did, and his children added their labor as soon as they were old enough to do so. The small surplus above bare necessaries was not left to those who produced it, but was appropriated by warriors and priests. In times of famine there was no surplus; the warriors and priests, however, still secured as much as at other times, with the result that many of the workers died of hunger. This system persisted in Russia until 1917, and still persists in the East: in England, in spite of the Industrial Revolution, it remained in full force throughout the Napoleonic Wars, and until a hundred years ago, when the new class of manufacturers acquired power. In America, the system came to

an end with the Revolution, except in the South, where it persisted until the Civil War. A system which lasted so long and ended so recently has naturally left a profound impress upon men's thoughts and opinions. Much that we take for granted about the desirability of work is derived from this system, and, being pre-industrial, is not adapted to the modern world. Modern technique has made it possible for leisure, within limits, to be not the prerogative of small privileged classes, but a right evenly distributed throughout the community. The morality of work is the morality of slaves, and the modern world has no need of slavery.

It is obvious that, in primitive communities, peasants, left to themselves, would not have parted with the slender surplus upon which the warriors and priests subsisted, but would have either produced less or consumed more. At first, sheer force compelled them to produce and part with the surplus. Gradually, however, it was found possible to induce many of them to accept an ethic according to which it was their duty to work hard, although part of their work went to support others in idleness. By this means the amount of compulsion required was lessened, and the expenses of government were diminished. To this day, 99 per cent of British wage-earners would be genuinely shocked if it were proposed that the King should not have a larger income than a workingman. The conception of duty, speaking historically, has been a means used by the holders of power to induce others to live for the interests of their masters rather than for their own. Of course the holders of power conceal this fact from themselves by managing to believe that their interests are identical with the larger interests of humanity. Sometimes this is true; Athenian slaveowners, for instance, employed part of their leisure in making a permanent contribution to civilization which would have been impossible under a just economic system. Leisure is essential to civilization, and in former times leisure for the few was only rendered possible by the labors of the many. But their labors were valuable, not because work is good, but because leisure is good. And with modern technique it would be possible to distribute leisure justly without injury to civilization.

Modern technique has made it possible to diminish enormously the amount of labor required to secure the necessaries of life for everyone. This was made obvious during the war. At that time all the men in the armed forces, all the men and women engaged in the production of munitions, all the men and women engaged in spying, war propaganda, or

Government offices connected with the war, were withdrawn from productive occupations. In spite of this, the general level of physical well-being among unskilled wage-earners on the side of the Allies was higher than before or since. The significance of this fact was concealed by finance: borrowing made it appear as if the future was nourishing the present. But that, of course, would have been impossible; a man cannot eat a loaf of bread that does not yet exist. The war showed conclusively that, by the scientific organization of production, it is possible to keep modern populations in fair comfort on a small part of the working capacity of the modern world. If, at the end of the war the scientific organization which had been created in order to liberate men for fighting and munition work, had been preserved, and the hours of work had been cut down to four, all would have been well. Instead of that the old chaos was restored, those whose work was demanded were made to work long hours, and the rest were left to starve as unemployed. Why? Because work is a duty, and a man should not receive wages in proportion to what he has produced, but in proportion to his virtue as exemplified by his industry.

This is the morality of the Slave State, applied in circumstances totally unlike those in which it arose. No wonder the result has been disastrous. Let us take an illustration. Suppose that, at a given moment, a certain number of people are engaged in the manufacture of pins. They make as many pins as the world needs, working (say) eight hours a day. Someone makes an invention by which the same number of men can make twice as many pins as before. But the world does not need twice as many pins: pins are already so cheap that hardly any more will be bought at a lower price. In a sensible world, everybody concerned in the manufacture of pins would take to working four hours instead of eight, and everything else would go on as before. But in the actual world this would be thought demoralizing. The men still work eight hours, there are too many pins, some employers go bankrupt, and half the men previously concerned in making pins are thrown out of work. There is, in the end, just as much leisure as on the other plan, but half the men are totally idle while half are still overworked. In this way, it is insured that the unavoidable leisure shall cause misery all round instead of being a universal source of happiness. Can anything more insane be imagined?

The idea that the poor should have leisure has always been shocking to the rich. In England, in the early nineteenth century, fifteen hours was the ordinary day's work for a man; children sometimes did as much, and very commonly did twelve hours a day. When meddlesome busybodies suggested that perhaps these hours were rather long, they were told that work kept adults from drink and children from mischief. When I was a child, shortly after urban workingmen had acquired the vote, certain public holidays were established by law, to the great indignation of the upper classes. I remember hearing an old Duchess say: "What do the poor want with holidays? They ought to work." People nowadays are less frank, but the sentiment persists, and is the source of much of our economic confusion.

Let us, for a moment, consider the ethics of work frankly, without superstition. Every human being, of necessity, consumes, in the course of his life, a certain amount of the produce of human labor. Assuming, as we may, that labor is on the whole disagreeable, it is unjust that a man should consume more than he produces. Of course he may provide services rather than commodities, like a medical man, for example; but he should provide something in return for his board and lodging. To this extent, the duty of work must be admitted, but to this extent only.

I shall not dwell upon the fact that, in all modern societies outside the USSR, many people escape even this minimum amount of work, namely all those who inherit money and all those who marry money. I do not think the fact that these people are allowed to be idle is nearly so harmful as the fact that wage-earners are expected to overwork or starve.

If the ordinary wage-earner worked four hours a day, there would be enough for everybody, and no unemployment—assuming a certain very moderate amount of sensible organization. This idea shocks the well-to-do, because they are convinced that the poor would not know how to use so much leisure. In America, men often work long hours even when they are already well off; such men, naturally, are indignant at the idea of leisure for wage-earners, except as the grim punishment of unemployment; in fact, they dislike leisure even for their sons. Oddly enough, while they wish their sons to work so hard as to have no time to be civilized, they do not mind their wives and daughters having no work at all. The snobbish admiration of uselessness, which, in an aristocratic society, extends to both sexes is, under a plutocracy, confined to women; this, however, does not make it any more in agreement with common sense.

The wise use of leisure, it must be conceded, is a product of civilization and education. A man who has worked long hours all his life will be bored if he becomes suddenly idle. But without a considerable amount of leisure a man is cut off from many of the best things. There is no longer any reason why the bulk of the population should suffer this deprivation; only a foolish asceticism, usually vicarious, makes us continue to insist on work in excessive quantities now that the need no longer exists.

In the new creed which controls the government of Russia, while there is much that is very different from the traditional teaching of the West, there are some things that are quite unchanged. The attitude of the governing classes, and especially of those who conduct educational propaganda, on the subject of dignity of labor, is almost exactly that which the governing classes of the world have always preached to what were called the "honest poor." Industry, sobriety, willingness to work long hours for distant advantages, even submissiveness to authority, all these reappear; moreover authority still represents the will of the Ruler of the Universe, who, however, is now called by a new name, Dialectical Materialism.

The victory of the proletariat in Russia has some points in common with the victory of the feminists in some other countries. For ages, men had conceded the superior saintliness of women, and had consoled women for their inferiority by maintaining that saintliness is more desirable than power. At last the feminists decided that they would have both, since the pioneers among them believed all that the men had told them about the desirability of virtue, but not what they had told them about the worthlessness of political power. A similar thing has happened in Russia as regards manual work. For ages, the rich and their sycophants have written in praise of "honest toil," have praised the simple life, have professed a religion which teaches that the poor are much more likely to go to heaven than the rich, and in general have tried to make manual workers believe that there is some special nobility about altering the position of matter in space, just as men tried to make women believe that they derived some special nobility from their sexual enslavement. In Russia, all this teaching about the excellence of manual work has been taken seriously, with the result that the manual worker is more honored than anyone else. What are, in essence, revivalist appeals are made, but not for the old purposes: they are made to secure shock workers for special tasks. Manual work is the ideal which is held before the young, and is the basis of all ethical teaching.

For the present, possibly, this is all to the good. A large country, full of natural resources, awaits development, and has to be developed with very little use of credit. In these circumstances, hard work is necessary, and is likely to bring a great reward. But what will happen when the point has been reached where everybody could be comfortable without working long hours?

In the West, we have various ways of dealing with this problem. We have no attempt at economic justice, so that a large proportion of the total produce goes to a small minority of the population, many of whom do no work at all. Owing to the absence of any central control over production, we produce hosts of things that are not wanted. We keep a large percentage of the working population idle, because we can dispense with their labor by making the others overwork. When all these methods prove inadequate, we have a war: we cause a number of people to manufacture high explosives, and a number of others to explode them, as if we were children who had just discovered fireworks. By a combination of all these devices we manage, though with difficulty, to keep alive the notion that a great deal of severe manual work must be the lot of the average man.

In Russia, owing to more economic justice and central control over production, the problem will have to be differently solved. The rational solution would be, as soon as the necessaries and elementary comforts can be provided for all, to reduce the hours of labor gradually, allowing a popular vote to decide, at each stage, whether more leisure or more goods were to be preferred. But, having taught the supreme virtue of hard work, it is difficult to see how the authorities can aim at a paradise in which there will be much leisure and little work. It seems more likely that they will find continually fresh schemes, by which present leisure is to be sacrificed to future productivity. I read recently of an ingenious plan put forward by Russian engineers, for making the White Sea and the northern coasts of Siberia warm, by putting a dam across the Kara Sea. An admirable project, but liable to postpone proletarian comfort for a generation, while the nobility of toil is being displayed amid the ice fields and snowstorms of the Arctic Ocean. This sort of thing, if it happens, will be the result of regarding the virtue of hard work as an end in itself, rather than as a means to a state of affairs in which it is no longer needed.

The fact is that moving matter about, while a certain amount of it is necessary to our existence, is emphatically not one of the ends of human life. If it were, we should have to consider every navvy superior to Shakespeare. We have been misled in this matter by two causes. One is the necessity of keeping the poor contented, which has led the rich, for thousands of years, to preach the dignity of labor, while taking care themselves to remain undignified in this respect. The other is the new pleasure in mechanism, which makes us delight in the astonishingly clever changes that we can produce on the earth's surface. Neither of these motives makes any great appeal to the actual worker. If you ask him what he thinks the best part of his life, he is not likely to say: "I enjoy manual work because it makes me feel that I am fulfilling man's noblest tasks, and because I like to think how much man can transform his planet. It is true that my body demands periods of rest, which I have to fill in as best I may, but I am never so happy as when the morning comes and I can return to the toil from which my contentment springs." I have never heard workingmen say this sort of thing. They consider work, as it should be considered, a necessary means to a livelihood, and it is from their leisure hours that they derive whatever happiness they may enjoy.

It will be said that, while a little leisure is pleasant, men would not know how to fill their days if they had only four hours of work out of the twenty-four. In so far as this is true in the modern world, it is a condemnation of our civilization; it would not have been true at any earlier period. There was formerly a capacity for lightheartedness and play which has been to some extent inhibited by the cult of efficiency. The modern man thinks that everything ought to be done for the sake of something else, and never for its own sake. Serious-minded persons, for example, are continually condemning the habit of going to the cinema, and telling us that it leads the young into crime. But all the work that goes to producing a cinema is respectable, because it is work, and because it brings a money profit. The notion that the desirable activities are those that bring a profit has made everything topsy-turvy. The butcher who provides you with meat and the baker who provides you with bread are praiseworthy, because they are making money; but when you enjoy the food they have provided, you are merely frivolous, unless you eat only to get strength for your work. Broadly speaking, it is held that getting money is good and spending money is bad. Seeing that they are two sides of one transaction, this is absurd; one might as well maintain that keys are good, but keyholes are bad. Whatever merit there may be in the production of goods must be entirely derivative from the advantage to be obtained by consuming them. The individual, in our society, works for profit; but the social purpose of his work lies in the consumption of what he produces. It is this divorce between the individual and the social purpose of production that makes it so difficult for men to think clearly in a world in which profit-making is the incentive to industry. We think too much of production, and too little of consumption. One result is that we attach too little importance to enjoyment and simple happiness, and that we do not judge production by the pleasure that it gives to the consumer.

When I suggest that working hours should be reduced to four, I am not meaning to imply that all the remaining time should necessarily be spent in pure frivolity. I mean that four hours' work a day should entitle a man to the necessities and elementary comforts of life, and that the rest of his time should be his to use as he might see fit. It is an essential part of any such social system that education should be carried further than it usually is at present, and should aim, in part, at providing tastes which would enable a man to use leisure intelligently. I am not thinking mainly of the sort of things that would be considered "highbrow." Peasant dances have died out except in remote rural areas, but the impulses which caused them to be cultivated must still exist in human nature. The pleasures of urban populations have become mainly passive: seeing cinemas, watching football matches, listening to the radio, and so on. This results from the fact that their active energies are fully taken up with work; if they had more leisure, they would again enjoy pleasures in which they took an active part.

In the past, there was a small leisure class and a larger working class. The leisure class enjoyed advantages for which there was no basis in social justice; this necessarily made it oppressive, limited its sympathies, and caused it to invent theories by which to justify its privileges. These facts greatly diminished its excellence, but in spite of this drawback it contributed nearly the whole of what we call civilization. It cultivated the arts and discovered the sciences; it wrote the books, invented the philosophies, and refined social relations. Even the liberation of the oppressed has usually been inaugurated from above. Without the leisure class, mankind would never have emerged from barbarism.

The method of a hereditary leisure class without duties was, however, extraordinarily wasteful. None of the members of the class had been taught to be industrious, and the class as a whole was not exceptionally intelligent. The class might produce one

Darwin, but against him had to be set tens of thousands of country gentlemen who never thought of anything more intelligent than fox-hunting and punishing poachers. At present, the universities are supposed to provide, in a more systematic way, what the leisure class provided accidentally and as a byproduct. This is a great improvement, but it has certain drawbacks. University life is so different from life in the world at large that men who live in an academic *milieu* tend to be unaware of the preoccupations and problems of ordinary men and women; moreover their ways of expressing themselves are usually such as to rob their opinions of the influence that they ought to have upon the general public. Another disadvantage is that in universities studies are organized, and the man who thinks of some original line of research is likely to be discouraged. Academic institutions, therefore, useful as they are, are not adequate guardians of the interests of civilization in a world where everyone outside their walls is too busy for unutilitarian pursuits.

In a world where no one is compelled to work more than four hours a day, every person possessed of scientific curiosity will be able to indulge it, and every painter will be able to paint without starving, however excellent his pictures may be. Young writers will not be obliged to draw attention to themselves by sensational potboilers, with a view to acquiring the economic independence needed for monumental works, for which, when the time at last comes, they will have lost the taste and the capacity. Men who, in their professional work, have become interested in some phase of economics or government, will be able to develop their ideas without the academic detachment that makes the work of university economists often seem lacking in reality. Medical men will have time to learn about the progress of medicine, teachers will not be exasperatedly struggling to teach by routine methods things which they learned in their youth, which may, in the interval, have been proved to be untrue.

Above all there will be happiness and joy of life, instead of frayed nerves, weariness, and dyspepsia. The work exacted will be enough to make leisure delightful, but not enough to produce exhaustion. Since men will not be tired in their spare time, they will not demand only such amusements as are passive and vapid. At least 1 per cent will probably devote the time not spent in professional work to pursuits of some public importance, and, since they will not depend upon these pursuits for their livelihood, their originality will be unhampered, and there will be no need to conform to the standards set by elderly pundits. But it is not only in these exceptional cases that the advantages of leisure will appear. Ordinary men and women, having the opportunity of a happy life, will become more kindly and less persecuting and less inclined to view others with suspicion. The taste for war will die out, partly for this reason, and partly because it will involve long and severe work for all. Good nature is, of all moral qualities, the one that the world needs most, and good nature is the result of ease and security, not of a life of arduous struggle. Modern methods of production have given us the possibility of ease and security for all; we have chosen, instead, to have overwork for some and starvation for the others. Hitherto we have continued to be as energetic as we were before there were machines; in this we have been foolish, but there is no reason to go on being foolish for ever.

Study Questions

1. Is the work ethic a plot to keep the poor down?
2. G. A. Cohen argues that capitalism unreasonably supports production at the expense of losing too much leisure. He says there are no "leisure ads," meaning ads for leisure rather than ads, for example, to consume some product.[1] But can't you think of some ads for leisure? Don't some ads promote the idea of retiring early and other ads promote taking a vacation and doing little or nothing? Aren't there services advertised to help people relax?

Note

1. G. A. Cohen, *Karl Marx's Theory of History: A Defense* (Princeton, N.J.: Princeton University Press, 1978), pp. 303–320.

91

Head to Head

Lester Thurow

Editor's note: Lester Thurow, a very well-known economist at MIT, argues that America and Japan are on a collision course economically. This impending head-on collision pits two different versions of capitalism against each other. The Japanese version uses an element of socialism, centralized planning by way of a national industrial policy targeting certain industries and markets. Japan's prime minister is a socialist, and the ruling coalition in Japan is formed from the Socialist and other parties. The American version of capitalism is closer to laissez-faire capitalism, though it still counts as welfare state capitalism. The American version has much less centralized planning of the economy. The other elements of socialism, besides centralized planning, are (1) government ownership of the means of production (for example, factories, farms, and universities); (2) emphasis on cooperation over competition; and (3) emphasis on patriotic or ideological motives over the profit motive. Japan and Thurow's article raise the possibility of a mixed economy, using the best elements of each major economic system.

Consider the comments of Ichiro Fujiwara, former vice-minister of the Japanese Ministry of International Trade and Industry (MITI), on national strategies:

> Let's take the case of the mainframe computer as an example. After the war, Japanese business firms had to start from scratch. To survive, they had to struggle

with outmoded technology and meager capital to fend off foreign competitors armed with computerized manufacturing systems and management. No responsible government leaders, faced with such a situation, would have sat on their hands and watched domestic industries crushed under the juggernaut of foreign competition. We had to help the domestic computer industry to get on its feet. Government leaders of other countries have done, and are still doing, the same thing.

A wide variety of techniques were used to develop the Japanese mainframe computer industry. To set up a wholly owned subsidiary in 1960, IBM had to make its basic patents available to Japanese manufacturers. A government-financed computer-leasing company made it cheaper and less risky to buy Japanese computers. Directly and indirectly, large government investments were made in establishing a successful computer industry in Japan.

The Japanese government has never picked winners and losers. Their strategies have always been bottom-up, industry-led strategies, where government was a participant but never a dictator. Companies could, and do, reject government initiatives. The auto manufacturers' rejection of a consolidation plan in the 1960s is only the most dramatic of many such examples.

In developing national strategies, the Japanese goal is to focus on those industries with high income elasticities of demand, high rates of growth in productivity, and high value added per employee. High value added means that high wages can be paid. When productivity has a high rate of growth, wages can go up rapidly even as product prices are going down. With falling prices and a high income elasticity of demand, markets will be expanding rapidly as consumer incomes grow, and labor won't need to be fired. Those trained and added to the work force can remain as permanent employees. In the 1990s there are believed to be seven industries that meet these criteria—microelectronics, the new materials-science industries, biotechnology, telecommunications, civilian aircraft manufacturing, robots plus machine tools, computers plus software.

Business firms are believed to be too risk-averse when it comes to projects that require large investments. Rationally, private firms see a riskless project with a payout of $1 billion as much better than a project with a $2.4 billion expected payoff but a 50 percent risk of failure. What is rational for business firms is, however, irrational for nations. Nations can average out their risks across many such projects. Government support encourages private industries to make the *right* market choices—like getting into aircraft manufacturing in the 1990s.

Similarly, private time horizons are believed to be too short. Private hurdle rates used in business-investment calculations are always far above the economy's long-term rate of return on assets. In the United States the private hurdle rate is 15 to 20 percent, while the historical rate of return on business assets is 7 percent. Banks such as the Japanese Development Bank or the Long-Term Credit Bank are designed to finance the long-term investments that normal banks and firms avoid.

Private firms invest too little in research and development (R&D) and don't want to diffuse the fruits of such activities fast enough. All empirical studies show that the social rate of return on R&D is far above the private rate of return. This occurs because new technologies often prove to be of most use to a company other than the one that paid to develop them. As a result, firms invest too little in R&D.

Those who invest in private R&D also want a monopoly on their ideas, so that they can earn the largest possible rate of return on their investments. To encourage R&D investment, monopolistic patent rights are given. Yet any society is much better off if the ideas developed within its jurisdictions are diffused to every producer as fast as possible. What is needed to stimulate R&D investments (patents) reduces their payoff (diffusion). Joint, partly government financed, cooperative R&D projects such as those found in the Japanese Key Technologies Center are one way to simultaneously get more investment and more diffusion. The former head of R&D at Nippon Electric Corporation notes that "R&D resources in the world are scarce; even big companies scream for these resources. If we don't collaborate, we can't advance. It's too expensive even for NEC. MITI is the third party needed to coordinate industry."

Certain industries are seen as key industries with linkages (externalities) affecting other industries. Strengthen them, and other industries get stronger. Machine tools and key component suppliers, such as semiconductor chip manufacturers, are seen as linkage industries. A stronger machine-tool industry and a stronger semiconductor industry allows Japan to be more competitive in automobiles and consumer electronics. As a result, the total return to these investments is higher than the returns that show up in machine tools or semiconductor manufacturing alone.

Above all, government has an important role to play in accelerating economic growth. This means raising investments in plant and equipment, skills, infrastructure, and R&D above the levels that would occur in unfettered markets. Market participants are believed to have too much interest in the present. Government essentially represents the interest of the future in the present. It works to speed up markets and to encourage firms to go down their learning curves faster than they would if they were on their own.

As an illustration, the Japanese Development Bank provided funds for the Japanese semiconductor firms to continue building production facilities during recessions when their American competitors would stop construction. This gave the Japanese the capacity to service demands that could not be met by the Americans during the next cyclical boom. A government-financed short-term robot-leasing company persuaded firms to use robots faster than they otherwise would have. As a result, the market for robots grew far faster and became far larger in Japan than elsewhere in the industrial world. With larger and faster-growing markets, Japan's robotics firms could go down their learning curves faster and get a cost advantage over the rest of the world.

If Japanese firms are not yet prepared to compete, foreign firms are held at bay. Satellite television is such an industry at the moment. To give the domestic industry time to get organized, the Ministry of Post and Telecommunications prohibits Japanese citizens from having the dishes necessary to receive satellite signals from foreign broadcasters.

Over time the instruments used to implement national strategies have changed. The foreign-exchange controls of the 1950s were replaced with capital allocation in the income-doubling decade of the 1960s. Today the focus is on research support, as in the case of the Japanese Key Technology Center, where government and private funds are commingled to lower private risk.

MITI's vision for the 1990s calls for securing the foundations for long-term economic growth. A flexible industrial infrastructure is to be combined with a better public infrastructure and improved capital and human resources. Despite the shift to services, manufacturing continues to be seen as crucial to technological innovation and growth. Basic science is to be strengthened, and the country is to make whatever efforts are necessary to stay at the forefront of the information revolution.

These strategies create a problem for nations that do not believe in national strategies. How are countries without national strategies to compete? Japan recently announced a national strategy for capturing 10 percent of civilian aircraft manufacturing by the year 2000. A 10 percent market share must be dislodged from one of three competitors—Airbus Industries in Europe, Boeing in the United States, or McDonnell Douglas in the United States. Since McDonnell Douglas is the weakest of the three, its market share will probably go to the Japanese.

Historically, Americans have never had comprehensive civilian economic strategies. Only in wartime have such efforts occurred. Until recently, Anglo-Saxon economics denied the validity of national strategies. Economies of scale were exhausted, and diseconomies of scale set in long before any one supplier could capture an industry. If economies of scale were not exhausted, monopolies emerged, and these had to be broken up with antitrust laws to maintain a competitive market. No industries were believed to have externalities that were important to the existence of other industries. One could always buy one's supplies on the same basis as any other buyer—even if the seller were foreign. Profit-maximizing sellers do not discriminate, since to do so is to fail to maximize profits. Yet according to the U.S. General Accounting Office, American firms seem to find that when supplies are scarce, they don't get their equipment as fast from Japanese suppliers as the Japanese firms who belong to the same business group.

In Anglo-Saxon economics there are no intrinsically high value-added industries. High-wage industries only look like high-wage industries because they use more skills. Higher wages are merely compensation for the costs of creating those skills. Once returns on human capital investments are subtracted, wages—the bribe for sacrificing leisure—are the same in every industry.

Even if national strategies could be made to work theoretically, many Americans argue that they cannot work practically. Sometimes this argument is narrowed still further to state that even if national strategies are shown to work abroad, they could not work in the United States because of its brand of special-interest-group politics.

Others argue that Americans should just accept the below-cost (subsidized) goods that they are getting as a result of these foreign strategies and withdraw from the businesses that are being targeted by others. If foreigners raise their prices when there are no American producers left, Americans will simply get back onto those businesses. This argument ignores what happens when an American industry is driven out of business. The Japanese business firm is not in the business of making permanent gifts to Americans. American competitors do not come back into business because of the high transition costs of going in and out of business and because they know that if they were willing to come back into business, those fat Japanese profit margins would promptly disappear.

Abstractly, firms based upon the motivation of value added or market-share maximization and those based upon the motivation of profit maximization would each seem to have advantages. The strategic-conquest firm is willing to work for a lower rate of return and can use this ability to force profit-maximizing firms to drop out of an industry. It simply accepts a rate of return below the minimum thresholds of the profit-maximizing firm.

From the perspective of Anglo-Saxon economics, however, the profit-maximizing firms should win. They should be better cost minimizers. They are both more concerned about lowering costs and more willing to do it (i.e., fire workers), and this advantage should be large enough to allow them to meet their rate of return on investments targets and still sell products at prices equal to, or lower than, that of empire-building firms. Empire-building firms may not have a high demanded rate of return on investment, but they do have a profit constraint. They cannot grow unless their profits are positive. If profit-maximizing firms' costs are low enough, they can defeat empire-building firms by forcing consistent losses upon them.

Recent empirical evidence would also seem to favor the long-run success of the empire-building firms. Firms based on the principle of producer economics are clearly on the offensive in international markets, while those based upon profit maximizing are on the defensive. But perhaps this is just the ebb and flow of economic battle. In the 1950s and 1960s the profit-maximizing firms of the United States put their competitors on the defensive.

Which of the two is to triumph will depend in the long run upon the extent to which the problems of growth (economic dynamics) are different from those of competition in a static environment (comparative statics). The theoretical advantages of profit maximization were in fact mathematically derived under the assumptions of what economists call "comparative statics." In comparative statics, a stable no-growth environment, firms prove their effectiveness by becoming efficient (moving from inside the production-possibilities curve to a place on the maximum production-possibilities curve). The cost minimizer wins. In getting onto that maximum production-possibility curve, Japanese lifetime employment and seniority wages should, for example, be a handicap. Labor is not paid in accordance with its individual marginal productivity. It is not laid off when it should be laid off. It is not paid the wages it should be paid.

In economic dynamics the central problem is rapid growth (getting the production-possibility curve to move to the right as rapidly as possible). Being on the curve, being the most efficient at any moment in time, is unimportant.

In reaching this growth goal, many of the cost-cutting advantages of comparative statics may be liabilities. Reducing wages and firing people may allow the firm to cut costs, but it lowers the willingness of the work force to accept new technologies, leads to a less well trained labor force, and eliminates loyalty—the willingness to make short-run self-sacrifices for the good of the firm. Similarly, the Anglo-Saxon willingness to reduce R&D spending, investment, and training in recessions may similarly be a short-run static advantage that turns out to be a long-run dynamic handicap.

By reducing the individual's risks with lifetime employment and seniority wage systems, the Japanese firm handicaps itself in the world of comparative statics. It cannot efficiently cut costs. But if the name of the game is dynamic growth, lifetime employment means that no one will become unemployed if new technologies reduce the demand for labor. Workers will be retrained if new technologies come along and make one's skills obsolete. With seniority wages, whatever happens, one's wages will not be reduced. Producer economics forces investments in skills and creates motivation that may offset its static inefficiencies. It has what Ronald Dore, an MIT Japanologist, calls "flexible rigidities."

The economic risks of change are the same in the two systems, but in one system the risks of economic change are carried by the individual, and in the other, by the group. When the risks are carried by the group, individuals lose their rational incentive to fight technical change. What is good for the group is automatically good for the individual. In contrast, in the American system, what is good for the group—

higher productivity from new technologies—is often bad for particular individuals.

In the long run history will tell us which theory is right. An empirical experiment is now under way. The profit-maximizing firms of the Untied States have faced off against the empire-building firms of Japan. Individualistic capitalism meets communitarian capitalism. Eventually, the winners will be known. In the end the winner will force the losers to change and play by the winner's rules. . . .

It is the official American position that it does not need to worry about the national strategies of other countries. Foreign national strategies simply won't work. But this is a belief that looks increasingly untenable if one looks at the industries that have been lost, such as robots, or industries under threat, such as aircraft manufacturing. It also confronts a world of man-made comparative advantage where the brainpower industries of the future will exist in those places where institutions organize to capture them.

The rest of the world is not cheating when it employs national strategies. That is just the way those nations play economic football. Americans can respond in one of three ways:

1. True believers in the American way can argue that we Americans have got it right and that the Germans and the Japanese have got it wrong. In the end their national strategies will hurt them more than they help. Keep the faith!
2. The agnostics can argue for change in American laws to permit American firms to get together if they wish. Try a few experiments with national industrial policies. Let a thousand flowers bloom!
3. The converts (heretics?) can argue for an aggressive American effort to counter foreign national strategies with American strategies. Fight fire with fire!

Benchmarking reveals a variety of foreign models. The Japanese Ministry of International Trade and Industry . . . orchestrates the development of a game plan in Japan. In Germany the large industrial banks, among them, the Deutsche Bank, are the conductors of the economic orchestra. Government-owned firms play a key role in France. But none of these foreign systems could easily be grafted onto the U.S. system. America is going to have to find a uniquely American way to develop a game plan.

The nature of the problems are neatly encapsulated in America's experience with amorphous metals—metals made by rapidly quenching alloys of iron, boron, and silicon to give them a glasslike consistency that has exceptional electrical and magnetic properties. Amorphous metals were developed by a New Jersey–based firm, in the early 1970s. Much of the market for the products it makes is in Japan. If the Japanese engineers had used amorphous metals, they would have saved one billion dollars per year in electricity costs alone. But Japanese officials intervened to delay patent approval for eleven years, which left very little time to use the product before the original patents expired. Japanese companies were also persuaded not to use amorphous metals until the American patents expired. As the end of the patents approached (1993), MITI announced a catch-up program involving thirty-four Japanese companies in an effort to learn how to make amorphous metals themselves so that no time would be lost when the patents expired. What should have been a market of over one hundred million dollars per year has never been a market of more than a few million.

What should Americans do when other nations target an industry where they have a technical lead? Screams and protests do very little good. After intensive negotiations with the American trade representative, the Japanese agreed to buy thirty-two thousand amorphous-metal transformers (0.5 percent of the market) before the patents run out in 1993—essentially nothing. Allied-Signal has been accused by security analysts of having spent too much money on research and development. If it cannot make its R&D pay off by selling its products, it should do no R&D. On one level, the stock-market analysts are right. If products cannot be sold, they should not be invented.

To be successful, American firms have to be able to build dominant market shares when they have technological leadership. If this is prohibited by foreign industrial policies, others will effectively compete in the U.S. market when they have technical superiority, but American firms will not be able to compete effectively in foreign markets when Americans have technological superiority.

The key difference between the United States and the rest of the industrial world is not the existence of protection. About 25 percent of all U.S. imports, double the amount of two decades ago, are now affected by nontariff trade barriers. International businessmen see Japan as the world's most unfair trading nation, but they see the United States as the third most unfair after Korea and Japan. The European Community has published a book listing hundreds of American violations of free trade.

If industrial policies are defined as trade protection, American industrial policies are as extensive as those in either Germany or Japan. But as the Japanese say, it is a "loser-driven" industrial policy—the product of random political lobbying power to gain protection for dying industries. The rest of the world's industrial policies involve strategic thinking and are "winner-driven." The Japanese protect amorphous metals; the Americans protect low-tech steel. While Americans are afraid to use the term *industrial policy*, the Europeans are proudly designing pan-European industrial policies.

The results show. Although a big decline in the value of the dollar succeeded in reducing the Japanese-U.S. deficit, the high-tech, high-wage part of the trade deficit is expanding. America is increasingly depending on low-wage, low-tech commodity exports to balance its trading accounts. Any country can be competitive as a low-wage country. Any country can reduce its wage level by reducing the value of its currency. The issue is not balancing trading accounts but being competitive while paying high wages.

At some point Washington will have to come to grips with foreign industrial policies. What does one do when other nations target an industry? The American solution to Airbus is to try to stop European funds from going into Airbus Industries by getting GATT [General Agreement on Tariffs and Trade] to rule that their activities are illegal. As in amorphous metals, America will fail. It does not have the power to force the rest of the world to abandon national strategies. Airbus subsidies won't be ruled illegal by GATT; if ruled illegal, the ruling would simply be ignored by the Europeans.

In 1989 and 1990 the Bush administration was engaged in an internal intellectual debate revolving around the high-definition television (HDTV): Should the Defense Department subsidize research on HDTV? Sadly, the debate remained an abstract ideological debate about the merits of government interference in the market rather than a real debate over whether HDTV was the place to jump back into consumer electronics, and if so, how? The ideological crusaders in the White House, a troika composed of John Sununu, Richard Darman and Michael Boskin, beat the advocates of government research subsidies in the Commerce and Defense departments, but it is also clear that their victory was temporary.

The issue will continue to reappear.

It is of course possible to argue that the American system is uniquely unsuited to formulating strategic policies. A recent article by Pietro S. Nivola in the *Brookings Review* provides a good example of the argument. In outline, the argument is as follows:

1. America has a "closet industrial policy" hidden in the Defense Department.
2. Target industries in the rest of the world haven't earned high or even normal rates of return.
   a. Scholars argue over whether Japanese industrial policies have helped or hurt.
3. Industry-led industrial policies could become self-serving to the firms that participated.
   a. It is hard to figure out "who is us" when American firms manufacture abroad and foreign firms manufacture in the United States.
   b. [National industrial policy] might result.
4. Americans would not be very good in defensive "tit-for-tat" industrial policies, since American government institutions aren't very flexible.
   a. Random interventions aren't always bad.

Because of our own incompetence, we may be able to do nothing better than do nothing. No one can prove with complete certainty that this argument is wrong. But what we do know for certain is that the American system as it is now formulated isn't working. That is what falling real wages, stagnant productivity growth, and a growing high-wage trade deficit mean. America may try something new, and it may fail, but nothing will have been lost—the old ways aren't working anyway.

In the real world of the twenty-first century, defensive industrial polices are unavoidable. To have any chance, America's corporations at least need a defensive strategic-trade policy in the United States. Such a policy is not designed to help American corporations (there is the problem of who is us), it is simply part of a federal strategic-growth policy designed to help the American people. Public investments made to gain sustainable advantages should be limited to investments that will stay in America, such as investments in skills or domestic infrastructure.

Beyond such home investments, the search for strategic advantage abroad now revolves around process R&D investments. In Japan, MITI has shifted from the foreign-exchange and capital-locations strategies of earlier decades to a strategy of pushing key technologies. The Europeans have set up an alphabet soup of cooperative R&D projects—Esprit, Jessi, Eureka—designed to do the same for European firms. While the details differ as to how it is done on the other sides of the Atlantic and Pacific oceans, the basic organizational structures are similar.

As George Lodge, a Harvard Business School professor, has described in detail in his recent book, *Perestroika for America*, strategies are industry-led when groups of companies, not government civil servants, propose the technologies that should be pushed. Governments never provide more than 50 percent of the total funding. If companies don't think that projects are worth risking some of their own money, the projects simply aren't done. Companies have to put together consortia, so that the government is not subsidizing a special favorite. More than one company has to think that the technology is important. In Europe the consortia have to come from more than one country. In the United States they could be required to come from more than one region. The idea is to magnify private funds with public funds, not to publicly finance research and development. The projects must have finite lifetimes with clearly stated objectives. No project is publicly funded forever. The purpose of a project must never be to advance knowledge for the sake of advancing knowledge. Other institutions, such as the National Science Foundation, have that task. The bureaucracy that makes the funding decisions can be very small, since business firms are making the basic go–no-go decisions when they decide whether they are willing to risk their own money.

Economic analysis shows that there are gains to be made with strategic trade policies, especially in industries with increasing returns, and this advantage will get bigger in a world of man-made comparative advantage and trading blocks. If government aid drives technology faster, everyone is a winner in the long run. More funds go into important areas that will raise long-run living standards, and no region of the world is going to be able to keep any key technology secret for more than short period of time. A twenty-first-century civilian R&D race for supremacy among the economic superpowers is far better than a twentieth-century military R&D race for supremacy among the military superpowers.

Ideally, a new GATT for quasi trading blocks would limit government aid to R&D subsidies. But in a world without clearly defined rules that determine what governments can permissibly do to aid their strategic industries, America's game plan has to go beyond an R&D policy. Like American companies that advertise they will not knowingly be undersold, the United States should announce that it will duplicate any policies put in place in the rest of the world. Foreign industrial policies in wealthy countries will be matched dollar for dollar. Any subsidy going to Airbus Industries in Europe will be matched by an equivalent subsidy to the American airframe-manufacturing industry. Any delay in permitting an American telecommunication device to be used abroad, such as the delays Motorola experienced in Japan with its cellular telephones, will be matched with delays for advanced Japanese equipment in the United States. Americans are no longer in a position to force the rest of the world to play the economic game by its rules but Americans can play the game by their rules. If they want to play hardball, we'll play hardball.

Change is blowing in the winds. Listen to the words of two prominent economists that used to argue regularly against industrial policies:

> Unlike the United States, both Japan and Europe have had extensive programs aimed at improving commercial performance. . . . As long as Japan and other nations helped companies that produced goods that the United States imported, such as textiles and steel, the United States was likely to gain. But the United States was hurt as countries started to subsidize products that competed with U.S. exports, such as aircraft, satellites, and computers. Targeting by foreign countries must be taken more seriously as they become competitive with the United States.
>
> —Robert Lawrence, Brookings economist

> My own proposal is that we adopt an explicit, but limited, US industrial policy. That is, the US government should make a decision to frankly subsidize a few sectors, especially in the high technology area, that may plausibly be described as "strategic.". . . One of the main purposes of this proposal is precisely to provide an alternative to managed trade. . . . Viewed from the right perspective, then, limited US industrial policies could be a relatively cheap way to cope with the stresses produced by the relative US decline and the special problem of dealing with Japan.
>
> —Paul Krugman, MIT economist

A decade ago it was possible to argue that instead of experimenting with strategic-growth policies to stimulate investments (physical and human), business groups, and national strategic planning,

America could solve its problems by moving to a more vigorous form of traditional Anglo-Saxon capitalism. Both [former prime minister] Mrs. Thatcher of Great Britain and Mr. Reagan in the United States were elected on such platforms. Both advocated a return to "ancient virtues"—that is, they emphasized the role of the individual in economic performance, the stress on the Anglo-Saxon *I*. Government enterprises were privatized in Great Britain. American personal income taxes were dramatically lowered. Both experiments are now more than a decade old. Neither succeeded.

In the United Kingdom unemployment is higher than it was when Mrs. Thatcher came into office (7.3 percent versus 5.8 percent), and the UK continues its slow drift down the list of the world's richest countries. In the United States productivity growth was negative in the two years before Reagan took office and in the two years after he left office. What was a small trade surplus became a large trade deficit.

Empirical experimentation revealed that a return to ancient Anglo-Saxon virtues is not the answer.

Japan and Germany, the countries that are outperforming America in international trade, do not have less government or more motivated individuals. They are countries noted for their careful organization of teams—teams that involve workers and managers, teams that involve government and business.

There is nothing antithetical in American history, culture, or traditions to teamwork. Teams were important in America's history—wagon trains conquered the West, men working together on the assembly line in American industry conquered the world, a successful national strategy and a lot of teamwork put an American on the moon first (and thus far, last). But American mythology extols only the individual—the Lone Ranger or Rambo. In America halls of fame exist for almost every conceivable activity, but nowhere do Americans raise monuments in praise of teamwork. Only national mythology stands between Americans and the construction of successful economic teams. To say this is not, however, to say that change is easy. History is littered with the wrecks of countries whose mythologies were more important than reality.

Systematic benchmarking reveals that the United States does not have to undergo a period of blood, sweat, and tears to regain its productive edge. Much of what has to be done, such as improving the K–12 education system, would make America a better place to live. With clear goals, schools would be more fun—not less. If spread out over time, even changes that would require a reduction in short-term American standards of living, such as a shift from consumption to investment, would be barely noticeable. Consumption, both public and private, just has to grow more slowly than the GNP [gross national product]. It doesn't have to fall.

While the necessary solutions would impose small burdens on the present, the failure to adopt these small solutions will impose major burdens on the future. We and our children will not have a world-class standard of living, and some of the chances for the good life that Americans have come to expect, such as heading major corporations, will diminish. Not doing anything is far worse than doing something.

The American problem does not lie in the severity of the necessary solutions. America's tough problem is realizing that there are problems that must be solved. Without that realization, nothing can be done.

Minor problems that remain unsolvable in the present will create major problems that are difficult to solve in the future.

Study Questions

1. Which moral principles would give the most support to Thurow's views? Which moral principles would criticize Thurow's views most?

2. Which arguments are Thurow's best? Which argument is his weakest? Is there any way to strengthen it?

3. Is it realistically possible to combine the best elements of socialism and capitalism? Would this be a way to cancel out the harshest effects of capitalism (for example, the Great Depression and massive worldwide starvation)?

4. Who will win the economic battle between Japan and America? Why? Is there any way that both can lose?

92

Free Trade and the Decline of Democracy

Ralph Nader

Citizens beware: An unprecedented corporate power grab is underway in global negotiations over international trade.

Operating under the deceptive banner of "free" trade, multinational corporations are working hard to expand their control over the international economy and to undo vital health, safety, and environmental protections won by citizen movements across the globe in recent decades.

The megacorporations are not expecting these victories to be gained in town halls, state offices, the U.S. Capitol, or even at the United Nations. They are looking to circumvent the democratic process altogether, in a bold and brazen drive to achieve an autocratic far-reaching agenda through two trade agreements, the U.S.-Mexico-Canada free trade deal (formally known as NAFTA, the North American Free Trade Agreement) and an expansion of the General Agreement on Tariffs and Trade (GATT), called the Uruguay Round.

The Fortune 200's GATT and NAFTA agenda would make the air you breathe dirtier and the water you drink more polluted. It would cost jobs, depress wage levels, and make workplaces less safe. It would destroy family farms and undermine consumer protections such as those ensuring that the food you eat is not compromised by unsanitary conditions or higher levels of pesticides and preservatives.

And that's only for the industrialized countries. The large global companies have an even more ambitious set of goals for the Third World. They hope to use GATT and NAFTA to capitalize on the poverty of Third World countries and exploit their generally low environmental, safety, and wage standards. At the same time, these corporations plan to displace locally owned businesses and solidify their control over developing countries' economies and natural resources.

It is only recently that corporations developed the notion of using trade agreements to establish autocratic governance over many modestly democratic countries. The world community founded GATT after World War II as an institution to peacefully regulate world trade. At present, more than 100 nations responsible for more than four-fifths of world trade belong to it. In its first 40 years of existence, GATT concerned itself primarily with tariffs and related matters; periodically, the GATT signatories would meet and negotiate lower tariffs on imported goods. In 1986, however, when the current Uruguay Round of GATT negotiations began, things changed. Multinational corporations thrust an expanded set of concerns on GATT that went far beyond traditional trade matters. They demanded that they be free to invest anywhere in the world with no restrictions; that environmental and safety standards be "harmonized" (made the same everywhere)—with the practical result that they would be pulled down toward a lowest common international denominator level; and that monopoly rights governing ownership of intellectual property (patents, copyrights, and trademarks) enforced throughout the world be entrenched. They also asked that food, agriculture, and services (banking, insurance, shipping, etc.) be brought under GATT disciplines. Finally, they crafted a new structure called the Multilateral Trade Organization to enhance GATT's power over each participating country. In short these companies sought to expand GATT's reach and elevate its importance as a means of undermining the ability of local, state, or national governments to impose any sort of controls on business.

In 1990, George Bush announced his proposal for a U.S.-Mexico-Canada free trade pact. NAFTA is basically a mini-GATT, except that NAFTA offers even greater privileges to business and allows for fewer restrictions on corporate operations in the three countries.

American Express, Cargill, Imperial Chemical and their allies have managed to turn trade talks into a debate over whether nations may retain their sovereign right to protect their citizens from harm. Global commerce without commensurate democratic global law may be the dream of corporate chief executive officers, but it would be a disaster for the rest

Reprinted from *The Case against Free Trade* (Earth Island Press, 1993), pp. 1–12. Reprinted by permission.

of the world with its ratcheting downwards of workers, consumer, and environmental standards.

The Uruguay Round expansion of GATT and NAFTA would establish a world economic government dominated by giant corporations, but they do not propose a democratic rule of law to hold this economic government accountable. It is bad enough to have the U.S. Fortune 200 along with European and Japanese corporations effectively ruling the Seven Seas of the marketplace, which affects workers, the environment, and consumers. But it is a level of magnitude worse for this rule to be formally expanded over entire political economies without any democratic accountability to the people.

Thieves in the Night

Secrecy, abstruseness, and unaccountability: these are the watchwords of global trade policy-making. Every element of the negotiation, adoption, and implementation of the trade agreements is designed to foreclose citizen participation or even awareness.

The process by which a policy is developed and enacted often yields insights into who stands to benefit from its enactment. Narrow, private interests inevitably prefer secrecy; in the halls of the U.S. Congress, for example, corporate lobbyists roam the corridors before a budget or tax package is to be voted on, hoping to insert a special tax exemption or subsidy in the dark of night and have it voted on before the public (or even most Congressional representatives) knows it exists. By contrast, citizen-based initiatives generally succeed only if they generate public debate and receive widespread support.

One can be properly suspicious of the intent of these trade agreements given the process by which they have been negotiated.

Negotiations over the Uruguay Round expansion of GATT—different from those over NAFTA only in that they involve more than 100 countries rather than just three—are taking place behind closed doors in Geneva, Switzerland, between unelected and largely unaccountable government agents who are mainly representing business interests. The provisions decided there, if approved by Congress, could undermine existing U.S. domestic laws and limit future action, not only in the direct regulation of commerce, but in areas ranging from food and auto safety to patent laws.

In a virtual self-parody, on the order of the old television show "Get Smart," secrecy predominates even within the GATT negotiating process itself. Small cliques of powerful nations regularly retreat to "green rooms" to cut deals that will then be forced on a take it or tough luck basis on other GATT signatory countries as "consensus" positions. The process would be hilarious were the consequences not so serious.

Corporate lobbyists, cruising in the halls outside the negotiating rooms, have been able to exert tremendous influence over the negotiations. Citizen groups have not been able to play a parallel role; with few exceptions, citizen organizations do not have the resources nor the contacts to post lobbyists in Geneva.

As if the advantage in resources were not enough, the corporate lobbying function has been institutionalized in the United States in a set of official trade advisory committees to the U.S. trade negotiators. Appointed by the President, the advisory committees are composed of over 800 business executives and consultants, with token labor representation, five representatives of environmental groups who were supportive or neutral on Bush's trade policy, and no consumer or health representatives.

On occasion, business groups are even willing to admit their influence over the process. The business coalition calling itself the Intellectual Property Committee (IPC)—its members include IBM, Du Pont, General Electric, Merck and Pfizer—has bragged in its own literature that its "close association with the U.S. Trade Representative and [the Department of] Commerce has permitted the IPC to shape the U.S. proposals and negotiating positions during the course of the [GATT] negotiations."

This sort of candor is atypical, however. The general rule is secrecy and mystification. Proponents of the trade agreements are so afraid of the consequences of public understanding of the pacts' implications that they believe it is not enough merely for the agreements to be negotiated behind closed doors. Once the agreements are completed—or on those rare occasions when the negotiators deign to make drafts of the agreements public—any person who wants to figure out what the agreements say faces a herculean task.

The first step is to obtain a copy of the agreement. This is not always possible. When then-President Bush announced that he had come to a final agreement with Mexico and Canada in August 1992, he gave an optimistic spin to the deal—but he did not make the text of the agreement available to the news media or to the American people so they could judge for themselves how beneficial the agreement might actually be. An unofficial text of the agreement was not available for over a month after its official conclusion. Once the official NAFTA text was finally made available through the Government Printing Office after President Bush left office, the government imposed a new barrier to access: it is charging citizens interested in receiving a copy of the two-volume, 1000+ page document $41.

Suppose a person decides to pay $41. The next obstacle they face is decoding the agreement's meaning. The agreement is very complex. It is written in arcane, almost impenetrable technical jargon that bears only a passing resemblance to the English language. Only those with a passing knowledge of GATTese or NAFTAese can comprehend what the trade jargon means for their jobs, food, or environment.

This difficulty in obtaining and understanding the actual agreements is not an accident; it reflects a purposeful effort by government negotiators to conceal the terms and effect of the agreements from the public, the news media, and even Congress. They would rather have citizens read a sanitized summary suitably interpreted by the agreements' boosters.

In the United States, Congress has limited the effectiveness of its own role in the trade agreement negotiation process by deciding that it will consider the agreements according to a uniquely anti-democratic procedure. Called "fast track," the special rule for Congressional consideration of trade agreements allows Congress to avoid its responsibilities by assuring that the agreements will not be subject to the full scrutiny they deserve. Under fast track, Congress must vote up or down on the agreements—with no amendments permitted—within a brief 60 to 90 days of the President's submission of the agreement, and must limit its debate on the agreements to not more than 20 hours in either the House or Senate! Congress must agree to deal with completed trade agreements in this fashion before the President even begins to negotiate.

With citizens shut out of the process at every turn, it is no surprise that these trade agreements pose such a threat to the procedural gains of citizen movements in numerous countries in recent decades, to their potential to rein in multinational corporations, and to both Third World and industrialized countries' ability to maintain control over their economies through some measure of feasible self-sufficiency. On procedural grounds alone, the authoritarian exclusion of citizen participation condemns the GATT and NAFTA operations. Are people to struggle for such rights as freedom of information, openness, and access in their domestic countries only to lose these rights in closed international negotiations dominated by corporate interests and their bureaucratic allies?

The Modern, Global "Race to the Bottom"

U.S. corporations long ago learned how to pit states against each other in "a race to the bottom"—to profit from the lower wages, pollution standards, and taxes. Now, through their NAFTA and GATT campaigns, multinational corporations are directing their efforts to the international arena, where desperately poor countries are willing and able to offer standards at 19th century American levels and below.

It's an old game: when fifty years ago the textile workers of Massachusetts demanded higher wages and safer working conditions, the industry moved its factories to the Carolinas and Georgia. If California considers enacting environmental standards in order to make it safer for people to breathe, business threatens to shut down and move to another state.

The trade agreements are crafted to enable corporations to play this game at the global level, to pit country against country in a race to see who can set the lowest wage levels, the lowest environmental standards, the lowest consumer safety standards. It is a tragic "incentives" lure that has its winners and losers determined before it even gets underway: workers, consumers, and communities in all countries lose; short-term profits soar and big business "wins."

We have already seen the results of "free" trade. California improves its workplace and pollution standards; the furniture industry migrates from Southern California to Mexico. Reeling from decades of underinvestment in quality and safety, U.S. automakers look to regain their "competitiveness" by moving their plants to Mexico, where the wages are far lower and pollution and workplace safety standards are inferior. The free trade deals are designed to make it even easier for business to play the game by harmonizing matters downwards.

Enactment of the free trade deals virtually ensures that any local, state, or even national effort in the United States to demand that corporations pay their fair share of taxes, provide a decent standard of living to their employees, or limit their pollution of the air, water, and land will be met with the refrain, "You can't burden us like that. If you do, we won't be able to compete. We'll have to close down and move to a country that offers us a more hospitable business climate." This sort of threat is extremely powerful—communities already devastated by plant closures and a declining manufacturing base are desperate not to lose more jobs, and they know all too well from experience that threats of this sort are often carried out.

Want a small-scale preview of the post-GATT and NAFTA free trade world? Check out the U.S.-Mexico border region, where hundreds of U.S. companies have opened up shop during the last two decades in a special free trade zone made up of factories known as *maquiladoras*. When U.S. factories have closed down and moved to Mexico, this is where they have gone. The attraction is simple: a workforce that earns as little as four to five dollars a day and does not have the means to defend itself against employer aggression because it is effectively denied the right to organize, and environmental and workplace standards are either lax or largely unenforced.

Don't make the mistake of thinking the *maquiladora* system is benefitting the Mexican people; they have to live in the polluted areas and accept the low wages and dangerous work. Here are some examples of the conditions that prevail in the U.S.-Mexico border region:

- In Brownsville, Texas, just across the border from Matamoros, a *maquiladora* town, babies are being born without brains in record numbers; public health officials in the area believe there is a link between anencephaly (the name of this horrendous birth defect) and exposure of pregnant women to certain toxic chemicals dumped in streams and on the ground in the *maquiladoras* across the border. Imagine the effect on fetal health in Matamoros itself.
- U.S. companies in Mexico dump xylene, an industrial solvent, at levels up to 50,000 times what is allowed in the United States, and some companies dump methylene chloride at levels up to 215,000 times the U.S. standards, according to test results of a U.S. Environmental Protection Agency–certified laboratory.

- Both U.S. and Mexican-owned factories in the *maquiladora* zone engage in widespread violations of Mexican environmental laws, according to the U.S. General Accounting Office. Moreover, a 1993 random examination of twelve U.S.-owned *maquila* plants showed not one was in compliance with Mexican environmental law. An Arizona-based environmental group, The Border Ecology Project, found that *maquiladoras* are unable to account for 95 percent of the waste they generated between 1969 and 1989.
- Working conditions inside the *maquiladora* plants are deplorable. The National Safe Workplace Institute reports that "most experts are in agreement that *maquila* workers suffer much higher levels of injuries than U.S. workers," and notes that "an alarming number of mentally retarded infants have been born to mothers who worked in *maquila* plants during pregnancies."

In many instances, large corporations are already forcing U.S. workers and communities to compete against this Dickensian industrialization—but the situation will become much worse with NAFTA and the Uruguay Round expansion of GATT. This is the case because the agreements will lock in rules for countries' treatment of multinational companies and capital that will make it even less risky for U.S. and other foreign companies to open factories in Mexico and other impoverished countries. Further, GATT and NAFTA set out rules limiting countries' ability to exclude imports on the basis of labor, human rights, or environmental conditions in the country of production.

Worst of all, the corporate-induced race to the bottom is a game that no country or community can win. There is always some place in the world that is a little worse off, where the living conditions are a little bit more wretched. Look at the electronics industry, where dozens of assembly and other factories, in search of ever lower production costs, have migrated from California to Korea to Malaysia. Many of those businesses are now contemplating moving on to China, where wages and workplace and environmental standards are still lower. The game of countries bidding against each other causes a downward spiral.

The most important tool countries have to combat this corporate blackmail is to say, "Go abroad. Only you are not going to be able to sell back in this country if you play that game." But the Uruguay Round expansion of GATT and NAFTA would take this power out of the hands of national governments. The trade pacts label such efforts to protect national standards "non-tariff trade barriers," and they outlaw them.

Dirty Milk, Dangerous Cars, and Dying Dolphins

"Non-tariff trade barriers," in fact, has become a code phrase to undermine all sorts of citizen-protection standards and regulations. Literally, the term means any measure that is not a tariff and that inhibits trade—for instance restrictions on trade in food containing too much pesticide residue or products that don't meet safety standards. Corporate interests focus on a safety, health, or environmental regulation that they don't like, develop an argument about how it violates the rules of a trade agreement, and then demand that the regulation be revoked. Several examples illustrate how insidious this concept of non-tariff trade barriers can be.

In 1991, Puerto Rico, a U.S. territory, upgraded the quality of its milk supply by instituting the Pasteurized Milk Ordinance, a tougher system of regulation than it previously had in place. Ultra-high temperature (UHT) milk from Canada was unable to meet the island's new, more rigorous standard. Puerto Rico subsequently banned the sale of Canadian UHT milk.

Canada is now challenging Puerto Rico's consumer safety measure as a non-tariff trade barrier under the existing U.S.-Canada free trade agreement. A panel of five trade bureaucrats—three from Canada, two from the United States—will hear the case. (The ratio was decided by a coin toss.) If Canada wins its challenge, Puerto Rico will either have to allow the Canadian milk in or face economic sanctions.

Most Americans probably find this unbelievable; after all, they would suppose, the United States can surely impose whatever standards it wants on products made or consumed in this country without being second-guessed by anonymous trade bureaucrats. But in signing the U.S.-Canada trade agreement, the United States surrendered such laws to the review of trade bureaucrats, and the United States will do so on a much larger and more significant scale if it signs GATT or NAFTA and Congress approves the agreements.

Consider what would have happened to current auto safety developments if these trade agreements had already been in operation. To push for airbags in cars, auto safety advocates had to convince the federal government to *mandate* the equivalent of airbag protection in cars.

If the trade agreements had been in place at the time, the auto companies and their political allies in Washington, D.C. would have said, "Oh no. You can't have airbags because the international standard only provides for three-point seatbelts. And if we require cars produced or imported into the United States to have airbags, that is really a disguised way to keep foreign car imports from coming into the United States, and then they won't let our cars into their markets. That's a non-tariff trade barrier and therefore a violation of the trade agreement."

The milk and airbag examples are only the tip of the iceberg. Already, a Dutch and several U.S. states' recycling programs, the U.S. asbestos ban, the U.S. Delaney clause prohibiting carcinogenic additives to food, a Canadian reforestation program, U.S., Indonesian, and other countries' restrictions on exports of unprocessed logs, CAFE standards, the gas guzzler tax, driftnet fishing and whaling restrictions, U.S. laws designed to protect dolphins, smoking and smokeless tobacco restrictions, and a European ban on beef tainted with growth hormones have either been attacked as non-tariff barriers under existing free trade agreements or threatened with future challenges under the Uruguay Round when it is completed. The most recent version of the European Community's list of alleged U.S. non-tariff trade barriers includes the Consumer Nutrition and Education labeling act, state recycling laws, dolphin protection laws, and fuel efficiency regulations for motor vehicles.

U.S. citizen groups already have enough problems dealing in Washington with corporate lobbyists and indentured politicians without being told that decisions are going to be made in other countries, by other officials, and by other lobbies that have no accountability or disclosure requirements in this country. The problem is exactly the same for citizen organizations in other nations, already struggling against the entrenched monied interests (including foreign subsidiaries) in their own countries.

To compound the autocracy, disputes about non-tariff trade barriers are decided not by elected officials or their appointees, but by secretive panels of foreign trade bureaucrats. Only national government representatives are allowed to participate in the trade agreement dispute resolution; citizen organizations are locked out. The European press reported that the Bush Administration had "thrown" a case brought by Mexico attacking the Marine Mammal Protection Act of 1972 as an illegal trade barrier. The Administration had long opposed the law, yet under GATT they were the law's only defender behind closed doors. The GATT panel ruled in Mexico's favor. Imagine if the Uruguay Round expansion of GATT had been completed, so that Japan had been able to use it to challenge the mandatory air bag rule in 1991. The Bush administration, which, in keeping with the Reagan administration, had long opposed the air bag requirement, would then have been its only theoretical defender—the auto safety advocates who pressed on the Bush administration to adopt it would be locked out. Moreover, under the Uruguay Round expansion of GATT the burden of proof is on the defending country; thus once a challenge is lodged, a law is considered GATT-illegal unless proved innocent.

It is hard enough when people in local communities have to defer to the state government, or when the state government has to defer to the federal government. But it is quite another order of democratic surrender to defer to trade agreement bureaucracies, where the decisions are made by unaccountable members of tribunals in Geneva, Rome, or elsewhere.

GATT and NAFTA: Headed in the Wrong Direction

As the world prepares to enter the twenty-first century, GATT and NAFTA would lead the planet in exactly the wrong direction.

One of the clearest lessons that emerges from a study of industrialized societies is that the centralization of the power of commerce is environmentally and democratically unsound. No one denies the usefulness of international trade and commerce. But societies need to focus their attention on fostering community-oriented production. Such smaller-scale operations are most flexible and adaptable to local needs and environmentally sustainable production methods, and more susceptible to democratic controls. They are less likely to threaten to migrate, and they may perceive their interests as more overlapping with general community interests.

Similarly, allocating power to lower level governmental bodies tends to increase citizen power.

Concentrating power in international organizations, as the trade pacts do, tends to remove critical decisions from citizen influence—it's a lot easier to get ahold of your city council representative than international trade bureaucrats.

All over this country—and indeed all over the world—there is a bubbling up of citizen activity dealing with consumer rights, the environment, and public health. People want safe and healthy food, products, and services. They want solar energy instead of fossil fuels; they want recycling; they want to contain soil erosion and to clean up toxic waste dumps; they want safer, environmentally benign material instead of others that happen to be sold in greater numbers worldwide. And if local or state governments can make decisions to help achieve these goals, then people can really make a difference. But if local and state standards can be jeopardized by a foreign country's mere accusation that the standards are a non-tariff trade barrier, if countries must pay a bribe in trade sanctions to maintain laws ruled to be trade barriers by foreign tribunals, if a company's claim that the burden the standard would impose is so great that they would have to pick up their stakes and move elsewhere, then the evolution of health and safety standards worldwide will be stalled. For it is rare that regulatory breakthroughs occur at the national, let alone international, level. Usually, a smaller jurisdiction—a town, city, or state—experiments with a standard, other cities and states copy it and, eventually, national governments and international governments, lagging behind, follow their lead. This percolating-up process will be squelched by GATT and NAFTA, with top-down mercantile dictates replacing bottom-up democratic impulses.

Study Questions

1. Which moral principles support Nader's views the most? Which moral principles are most critical of Nader's views? Explain your answers in detail.

2. What are Nader's best arguments? What is Nader's weakest argument? Can it be strengthened? Explain your answers in detail.

3. Has NAFTA been a success so far? Has the collapse of the value of the Mexican peso shown that NAFTA has been a disaster?

4. Will average wages increase or decrease under NAFTA? Why?

5. Will the cost of government red tape increase or decrease under NAFTA? Why?

6. Will environmental standards in America be lowered under NAFTA to make the standards in North America uniform? Will the standards in Mexico be raised? What will be the net effect, an overall raising or lowering of standards? Why?

PART VII

Environmental Challenges to Business as Usual:
From the Greenbacks to the Greens and from
the Greenhouse Effect to the Green Revolution

93

Introduction

Sterling Harwood

The sky is falling, or so it seems to many scholars. A part of the ozone layer in the atmosphere has dropped out, leaving a hole through which radiation passes unfiltered to cause cancer and cataracts. Something else is wrong with the sky. Some trends in temperature indicate that global warming is underway. A third major problem is acid rain. From the sky falls acid that creates dead lakes, in which no fish can live. The main sources of acid rain seem to be emissions from electric power plants and smokestacks that lack expensive scrubbers to reduce emissions of sulfur. Unfortunately, environmental problems are hardly confined to the air, because pollution of the land and water are also major problems. As we shall see in one reading below, there is an ozone problem near the ground as well: too much ozone!

Again I wish to introduce a chapter by using statistics to paint a portrait of the landscape. The landscape of environmental ethics overlaps greatly with business ethics, since many businesses pollute or damage the environment in other ways.

In 1972 the federal government created the Environmental Protection Agency (EPA) and the Clean Water Act. Due to budget cutbacks or bureaucratic inertia, or both, the EPA has examined only a small percentage of pesticides to determine their safety. The *Washington Post*, Rachel Carson, and other authorities have cited pesticides as one of the greatest environmental crises, if not the greatest.

Some business ethicists emphasize that:

> The National Academy of Science estimates that 15,000 deaths a year and 7 million sick days are traceable to air pollution. And according to EPA figures, about $9 billion a year is spent on health costs incurred for air-related ailments, such as lung cancer and emphysema. The EPA also estimates that air pollution causes $8 billion a year in property losses and $7.6 billion in destruction of vegetation.[1]

Some textbooks fail to notice the large discrepancy between some key statistics here. The National Academy of Science's estimate seems low, since the *San Jose Mercury News* reports that soot alone is a big killer in America, killing between 50,000 to 60,000 people each year.[2]

There are still a lot of people of course, perhaps too many for the planet to sustain in health (not that being killed would be preferable, obviously!). Vice President Al Gore notes that "in 422 years, from the time of Christopher Columbus until 1914, world population tripled, to 1.6 billion. In the last 75 years it has tripled again to 5.2 billion. We are told [by scholars] that in the next 75 years it will double and perhaps even triple once more."[3] The world economy produces $21 trillion annually.[4] Gore reports that each year America now produces half a ton of synthetic organic chemicals (for example, pesticides) per American. One incident, the Exxon Valdez oil spill, poured 11 million gallons of oil into the environment. And that oil spill was not clearly the largest of all time, because another one of similar size occurred in the Atlantic several years before. How much of this mistreatment can the earth's habitats withstand?

Gore emphasizes that "we are causing living species to be destroyed at a rate 1,000 times greater than at any time in the last 65 million years." But Louis P. Pojman reports the 98 percent of all species ever known to exist are now extinct.[5] Indeed, *Harper's Index* suggests the percentage is even higher than that. It states that only 0.01 percent of all life forms known to have existed exist today.[6] And yet the earth is still very much full of life. Pojman claims that "Earth is the only planet that is a home."[7] Given the incredible enormity of the universe and the amazing number of stars it contains, Pojman is probably overstating his point. The odds are that the universe is teeming with life. But even if life on earth is not alone in the universe, Pojman gives us the right emphasis by suggesting that the stakes in treating the environment ethically surely are high. Much life in the universe is located right here on earth, too much life to protect as poorly as we have so far.

Despite the gloom and doom you might feel from the statistics above, there are some major success stories in environmental ethics. The bald eagle was removed from the endangered species list, a symbolic victory as well as a substantive one. Government restrictions on leaded gasoline have decreased the amount of lead in the air by almost 90 percent.[8] These success stories fly in the face of libertarian charges that government has a reverse Midas touch, spoiling all it touches. People have a record of repairing and preventing significant damage to the environment. Indeed, people created at least one political party, the Green Party, to deal primarily with environmental issues. Even libertarians, who might seem to have a do-nothing approach to environmental crises, imply that people can solve environmental problems through so-called free-market solutions. For example, many people prefer buying recycled or other "green products" that help limit the damage done to the environment. Business has an incentive to satisfy such consumer preferences. But whether this incentive is as great as the incentives to pollute, etc., is very much an open question. People, however, can use laws (for example, taxes, regulations, and criminal punishments) to try to get the incentives balanced enough to protect the environment. So there is significant cause for you to feel optimism as you read about the environmental threats detailed in this chapter.

Notes

1. Vincent Barry and William Harry Shaw, eds., "Moral Issues in Business," 6th ed. (Belmont, Calif.: Wadsworth, 1995), p. 529.

2. July 19, 1993, p. 4A.

3. *The New Republic*, 25th anniversary issue, 1989.

4. Paul Hawken, *The Ecology of Commerce: A Declaration of Sustainability* (New York: Harpe-Business, 1993), p. 1.

5. Louis P. Pojman, ed., *Environmental Ethics: Readings in Theory and Application* (Boston: Jones and Bartlett, 1994), p. xv.

6. Lewis H. Lapham, Michael Pollan, and Eric Etheridge, eds., *The Harper's Index Book* (New York: Henry Holt, 1987), p. 72.

7. Pojman, p. xv.

8. Barry and Shaw, p. 529.

94

Mass Extinction: We Lose 50 to 150 Species Every Day

Norman Myers

Editor's note: This brief essay documents vast destruction. Myers calls for us to recognize that for decades we have been practicing triage on many species. He argues that, since we cannot save all species, wisdom requires selecting the surviving species by choice rather than by chance.

No doubt about it, we are facing a mass extinction of species. According to several analyses, we are losing between 50 and 150 species every day. Our conservation resources—funds, scientific skills, etc.—are insufficient thus far to save more than a small proportion of the several million species at risk of eventual extinction. How shall we ensure that we are getting the optimal use of every scarce dollar spent on conservation?

We must come to grips with the facts: having goofed at playing Noah, we now find ourselves playing God. We are effectively deciding that certain of our fellow species are more deserving of a place on Earth than others. Through our deployment of conservation efforts, we are saying that species A, B, C and so on are worthy of our support, and hence that species R, S, and T through Z are going to have to do without our support and thus are doomed.

Since we are committed, willy-nilly, to consigning large numbers of species to extinction, let us do it with all the selective wisdom we can muster. We could, for instance, abandon the Mauritius kestrel to its all-but-inevitable fate, and use our funds to support many of the hundreds of other threatened bird

Reprinted from Norman Myers, "Noah's Choice," *Earthwatch* (July/August 1991), pp. 20–21.

species that are more likely to survive. In short, certain species would disappear through human design. As agonizing a prospect as this is, is it not better than allowing species to disappear by default?

An approach along these lines would amount to a "triage strategy" for species. The term derives from the French medical practice in World War I, when battlefield doctors had more wounded than they could treat. So they assigned each soldier to one of three categories: first, those who would die without medical attention but would survive with it; second, those who could probably survive without attention; and third, those who were likely to die no matter how much attention they received. The first category absorbed all the medical services available, and the other two categories were ignored. A biological triage program would be systematic rather than haphazard, and would enable us to make maximum use of conservation funds.

But under such a system, how shall we determine which species shall be allowed to become extinct so that we can concentrate our limited conservation efforts on "better" species? If the biological variety were as clear-cut as the battlefield form, many of the so-called charismatic megavertebrates we're now spending millions trying to save—the panda, black rhino, tiger, California condor, blue whale—might not merit nearly so much support as we now supply them; in other words, one could argue that these species are less "deserving" of our support, insofar as the same funds could certainly save many more species such as plants and insects, albeit species with less public appeal. But for biological triage to function properly, we must weigh many factors.

First, we must consider ecological attributes. Species are necessary components of healthy ecosystems, just as healthy ecosystems underpin the biosphere's capacity to support life of all kinds, including human life. We need to ask: Which species contribute more than others? Are certain species essential to the survival of their ecosystems, while others are by comparison superfluous? While the disappearance of a species must constitute an impoverishment for its ecosystem, the loss can range from regrettable but marginal to critical, if not worse.

One way these questions can be broached is through the concept of energy flow, which serves as a measure of a species' relative importance. If all bird species in a temperate-zone ecosystem amount to, say, 0.5 percent of animal biomass, and their contribution to energy flow can be measured only at several places to the right of the decimal point, how is their role in that ecosystem's healthy functioning to be evaluated in comparison with that of arthropod species that amount to, say, 10 percent of the biomass, thereby contributing an even larger proportion of energy flow? Similarly, do some species contribute more than others by virtue of their numbers rather than their biomass? Or by their status in the food pyramids? Losing half of all mammal species would be appalling, but not as ecologically drastic as losing half of all insect species.

We should also contemplate the question of taxonomic uniqueness. When a species is a sole extant representative of a taxonomic grouping such as a genus or a family, there is a *prima facie* case that it deserves a ranking above another species that shares a genus with tens if not hundreds of other species. Thus preference should be accorded to monotypic groups such as solenodons, aardvarks, hoatzins, the aye-aye, and the tuatara. But then what is the value, for instance, of the po'o-uli, a bird recently discovered in Hawaii and assigned to an entirely new genus, compared to—and in conservation competition with—the solenodon?

Triage strategists should also look at factors that make some species more susceptible to extinction than others. Island species, for example, are particularly prone to extinction; only about 20 percent of bird species are island dwellers, yet about 90 percent of extinct birds have been island species. Many large mammals are vulnerable because they direct less energy to producing many offspring and more to caring for them. These include the whales, rhinos, great apes, many large predators such as the mountain lion, cheetah, tiger, and polar bear, and several large birds, including seven crane species.

Such species have received special attention from conservationists not only because of their status as likely losers but because of their public appeal as charismatic megavertebrates. But should our overriding aim be to preserve particular species? Or should it be to safeguard those evolutionary processes that will most help to repair the damage when the biotic holocaust is over?

The main mode of generating new species, natural selection, operates best when there is a large stock of genetic material for it to work on. The more individuals from which evolution can select the fittest for survival, the more the "fit" genes will be passed on and spread around—leading steadily to new races, sub-species, and ultimately, species. The categories

of species most capable of fostering speciation are insects and other invertebrates. Many such species produce dozens of generations within a single season, throwing off progeny totaling 10 million billion billion and supplying abundant raw material for natural selection. But whereas the time-scale for insects to speciate could be merely dozens of years, large mammals such as the whales, rhinos, and great apes take many thousands if not millions. Furthermore, insects, with their quick-response adaptability, are better suited than most species to survive the environmental upheavals of humans' activities. Together with plants, they will be the main evolutionary resource in the wake of the present episode of mass extinction. In comparison, the whales, rhinos, and the rest constitute something close to evolutionary dead-ends.

This is *not* to say that triage would necessarily pull the rug from beneath the whales and the rest. But it does say that we should look more carefully at the economic tradeoffs involved. We should also weigh political and social concerns. The Bengal tiger requires vast living space in a part of the world that is crowded with human beings, but it could stimulate more public support for conservation of its ecosystem—and thereby help save many other species—than could a less charismatic creature as a crab.

Bottom-line conclusion: we have been practicing triage for decades, so let us recognize this fact of life and deploy utmost wisdom from *all* standpoints. Above all, let us recognize the urgent necessity of making choices *now* among threatened species.

Study Questions

1. Can humans afford to lose so many species a day? Aren't irreplaceable and valuable resources going to waste?

2. Should we consider an extinct species gone forever, or will gene-splicing and other technologies enable us to replace some someday, as in the film *Jurassic Park*?

3. Do humans have a right "to play God," as many would call it, by selecting which species will become extinct? Wouldn't it be irresponsible and bad faith to put our heads in the sand and refuse to make intelligent choices, leaving such massive death and destruction to sheer luck?

95

Scientists and Shamans:
The Case of Tropical Rainforests

Aubrey Wallace

Editor's note: This case, documented on the Public Broadcasting Service (PBS), shows an innovative way to help deal with the problems of acquiring medical knowledge, conserving the tropical rainforests, and interacting in a mutually profitable way with some Third World cultures. A mutually beneficial exchange of medical information results. This helps lead to a longer-term, sustainable economy in the rainforest, reducing the need to destroy the rainforest for short-term benefits.

The richest ecosystems in the world, the tropical rainforests, occur where there are the poorest populations—the Third World. The tropical rainforests contain half the world's gene pool, and yet, in Brazil, where one-third of the world's rainforest grows, biological riches don't always mean economic success. Some twenty-five million children and young adults—the country's future—live below the poverty level. Poor and developing countries exploit their forests in desperate (and unsuccessful) attempts to earn the money they need. Every second of every day a tropical forest the size of a football field is destroyed; that destruction affects the entire planet, because the rainforests act as the lungs of the earth. In addition, the destruction of rainforests shrinks the habitat of animal species and contributes to their extinction.

Developed countries have also plundered the rainforests. But some have become increasingly aware of the importance of preserving these rich areas. The most potent argument for saving the tropi-

Reprinted by permission from *Green Means: Living Gently on the Planet* by Aubrey Wallace, published by KQED Books, 1994.

cal rainforests—the argument that appeals best to human self-interest—is their pharmaceutical richness. Prescription drugs that treat eighty percent of humanity and sell for tens of billions of dollars each year contain compounds from rainforest plants. One-fourth of the prescription drugs in the United States contain at least one ingredient taken from plants. New miracle drugs may be living in the forests, not yet discovered, because experts estimate that as few as one percent of the more than 250,000 flowering plant species have been examined for medicinal uses. Examined by scientists, that is. Some of their medicinal uses are already known to many of the forty million human beings who live in the world's forests. Traditional healers in the Amazon rainforests alone use some six thousand different plants to treat and cure a wide range of disease and discomfort, according to *Newsweek* magazine.

Their knowledge is as threatened as their ecosystem. As development invades their lands and traditions, indigenous knowledge disappears. "There's so much knowledge and tradition passed on by word of mouth, from generation to generation," says Lisa Conte, chief executive officer and cofounder of Shaman Pharmaceuticals, which describes itself as the first drug company to research and develop natural, botanical pharmaceuticals based on traditional usage by indigenous people. "As those cultures get wiped out or are fiercely influenced by what we call civilization, all of a sudden they want aspirin and Michael Jackson. They don't want their own traditions. And there's going to be nobody left who remembers. We're going to lose them forever."

In 1900, Brazil was known to have 270 Indian tribes. Today, ninety of them have completely disappeared. Scattered and assimilated into other populations, they have abandoned their ways or lost their land. One of the most obvious signs of the loss of traditional ways is the population explosion that results when people have lost traditional methods of birth control. In some tribes, women who used to bear an average of five or six children now often have more than ten.

Shaman (the word means medicine man in northeast Asian cultures) Pharmaceuticals works with traditional healers in tropical rainforest–dwelling communities to find and develop new plant-based painkillers and medicines for viral and fungal diseases. At the same time, the company is dedicated to supporting the biological and cultural diversity that produced the plants and knowledge of them. The unique approach of the company relies on ethnobotany, an interdisciplinary study of human relationships to plants that combines anthropology, botany, ecology, economics, and medicine. The field of ethnobotany was only recently developed by Harvard professor Richard Schultes, who confers his intellectual blessing on Shaman Pharmaceuticals. The company has assembled a staff that includes most of the small number of ethnobotanists in the world. The firm also hired Steven King, formerly chief botanist for Latin America at the Nature Conservancy, to head the Ethnobotany and Conservation division of the company.

The discovery process at Shaman Pharmaceuticals begins with the knowledge of traditional healers—shamans, midwives, elders, and witch doctors—to pre-select potential new drugs. "The biggest reason why products fall out of clinical trials is that they have adverse side effects that you don't want to face," says Conte. "We feel we're more likely to get successfully through the clinical trial process because the starting material has been used by people for thousands and thousands of years."

A Shaman team that includes an ethnobotanist, a Western physician, and a local contact who speaks the language makes an expedition into the deep forests of a country such as Ecuador, for example, where people live in houses on wooden stilts, with palm-thatched roofs.

The scientists come prepared to work. Already well-versed in regional diseases, they know something about the local remedies, as well as the kinds of plants found in the area, and they bring pictures of disease symptoms to show the healer. Pictures accurately depict specific symptoms, such as certain skin lesions that might elude translation. They meet with the town leader and the shaman. As the shaman studies the pictures, the scientists, trained in observation methods, carefully avoid steering the healer in one direction or another. Slowly, the shaman tells them what plants he or she uses for such maladies. They find out from the shaman which part of the plant—the leaf, bark, root, or twig—is used to prepare the potion or poultice, and how the preparation is concocted. Later, the scientists will collate this information with similar tips from medical experts in other tropical countries, such as West Africa, Papua New Guinea, and Peru. Before they leave the village, the team collects specimens to take back to California with them. Also before they leave, the physician visits patients the shaman hasn't been able to help. Occasionally, the physician can dispense some knowledge or potion from his or her own country that cures the patients or eases their symptoms.

The scientists take their plants back to the Shaman Pharmaceuticals lab, a modern facility that adheres strictly to regulatory procedures laid down by the Food and Drug Administration (FDA). In its first, dazzling success the lab identified the pure compound of a medicinal preparation that the company put through preclinical development and soon had in clinical trials. The product, called Provir™, is an oral medicine to treat respiratory viruses, including one that attacks young children. The discovery has significance in a broader sense because modern medicine currently has few drugs to treat viruses. Antibiotics treat bacteria and are sometimes used on viruses but with little effect. Shaman soon followed the first success with a second product, called Virend™, a topical agent for herpes. Herpes afflicts more than thirty million people in the United States, with another half million new cases diagnosed annually.

"In the first two years of operation we had two products in clinical trials, which is the fastest timeframe for any startup pharmaceutical or biotech company," explains Conte. "It was a strong validation that we had developed a company, not just around one or two products, but around a process that can continue."

The company carefully studies the availability of supplies and the environmental impact of extracting them. Both of their first potential drug products are based on "a tree in the Croton genus. It's like a weed, sort of a pest in the rainforest. These products are probably the most highly valued nontimber rainforest-harvested products out there," says Conte. "We've also looked into putting the tree on plantations as a backup, but it's not our intention to do that right now. We have estimated that if we produce a successful product, we would use less than one-tenth of one percent of what is naturally occurring in the rainforest." The world market for the two drugs Shaman has in clinical trials is estimated to be worth $500 million a year when the products hit the market in 1998.

The company, founded in 1989, has not generated one penny of revenue yet, but its prospects look so good that it has raised twenty-seven million dollars in venture-capital financing and funds from a corporate partner. The initial public offering of shares in 1993 brought in another forty-two million dollars. This is despite the fact that major investors and mutual fund managers thought at first that going down and talking to witch doctors had to be a joke.

Revenue, though, is still a long way off. "We're five and a half years old, and we've never made a cent. Yet, we just built into the cost of doing business returning something to society, reciprocity, and sustainable harvesting, the whole green aspect of our business. If we can do that, certainly other companies—that make money—can do that."

Green businesses such as Shaman Pharmaceuticals are cheered on by environmental activists who hope that sustainable enterprises will lead governments and individuals away from destructive industry, such as logging and cattle ranching, the two most lucrative commercial enterprises in the economy of most developing forest countries. Studies in Peru and Belize show that sustainable harvesting of resins, oils, fruits, and medicinal plants—which can be collected without bulldozers or chainsaws—could bring in two or three times more money than farming on cleared land. In Tanzania, the export of honey from forest bees is several times more valuable than the timber produced in the country's forests. One environmental group has estimated that within twenty years the retail market for the nuts, resins, oils, and medicinal plants of the Amazon rainforest alone could total fifteen billion dollars a year.

Linking rainforest conservation to commerce presents special concerns, though. If conservation focuses on profitable forms of nature, perhaps those will be the only forms preserved. The value of biodiversity lies in the great variety of animals and plants and their unique relationships that create an ecosystem.

The two most immediate concerns center around how best to extract products from the ecologically complex rainforests—which we know we do not understand—and how to deal ethically with native people who may be unaccustomed to northern countries' concepts of materialism and property rights. The Brazil-nut business, for example, which generated great hope as a sustainable industry, developed and boomed seemingly overnight. Now, though, observers are beginning to see an absence of Brazil-nut seedlings and saplings, which may be a result of overharvesting, or may be a natural cycle that was never noticed before. We also do not know what part the missing nuts play in the food chain of the birds, mammals, fish, and insects that live there. Neither the forest dwellers, with extensive knowledge of their local ecosystems, nor modern biologists have experience in devising sustainable systems for Brazil nuts, or for anything else in the tropical rainforests. Nor do we have ethical systems established for compensating the local people. Exploitation occurs. Brazil-

nut gatherers, for example, are paid about four cents per pound, about one percent of the retail value of the product, by the three companies owned by three cousins that control seventy-five percent of the market.

Despite these serious philosophical and practical questions about harvesting the rainforests, the fact remains that poverty and environmental degradation are moving faster than even the most concerned activists. The world cannot wait for long-term ecological studies. Enlisting the local people and assuring them a fair economic incentive currently appears to be the only real hope for preserving both the biological and cultural diversity of the rainforests. By concentrating efforts on products that bring very high prices for very small quantities, such as fragrances and drugs, some of the abuses associated with extractive industry may be minimized. One study estimates that the full development of medicinal plants from tropical countries could earn their economies some nine hundred billion dollars a year. Third World researchers, however, are unable to pursue commercial plant remedies, because their poverty prevents them from competing with multibillion-dollar international corporations.

Shaman Pharmaceuticals was founded with noble goals. Lisa Conte says her company is "a conservationist's dream come true." Shaman takes a low-tech approach in a high-tech industry and is committed to passing up endangered plants, paying sizable royalties from drug revenue to local communities where they work—and providing compensation just for the privilege of being able to conduct research. Each expedition's budget includes a contribution for a project requested by the local people, such as potable water systems, regular dental visits, or training for apprentice shamans. The company is not afraid to take a political stand, either. At the 1992 Earth Summit in Rio de Janeiro, when President Bush's administration refused to sign the biodiversity treaty designed to stem the loss of animal and plant species, most biotech and pharmaceutical companies backed the stand. Shaman officials criticized it as shortsighted.

Conte started Shaman Pharmaceuticals with money borrowed from credit cards. "It's really wonderful. This is the only country in the world where you can do that." At the time, she had an undergraduate degree in biochemistry, a master's in pharmacology, an M.B.A., and was vice president of a venture capital firm specializing in the medical and biotechnology industry.

One morning while waiting for a meeting, she leafed through magazines about drug development. To find the one hit product, most drug companies use high-tech spectroscopy, powerful computers, and robots that can quickly scan tens of thousands of samples. The chemical makeup of a single plant may include five hundred or six hundred compounds, and each compound may have fifty or sixty different biological activities. Using enzymes, instead of laboratory animals, a company can test as many as 150,000 samples in a year—hundreds of times more than was possible by conventional testing. Though this sort of hit-or-miss testing will result in only one compound in ten thousand that gets to market, the random screening method allows such huge numbers to be studied that the scientists are likely to find something useful.

While Conte was waiting and reading, the receptionist brought in a new stack of magazines. Conte saw a cover article on the destruction of rainforests. "A little light bulb went off at that moment," she says. "Why not use plants that have been used for thousands of years and are therefore more likely to be safe and active?" The next day she quit her job and began living on credit cards. She spent four months investigating the opportunity to start such a company. Soon convinced she was on to something, she raised a quarter of a million dollars to begin tracking down the small supply of ethnobotanists in universities around the country. By May 1990, the company had raised $3.8 million and was officially founded. It targeted drugs to treat viral and fungal diseases and diabetes.

Shamans are best at treating conditions with obvious symptoms; they don't know much about complex pathology such as cancer. The virus we call herpes is thought of by some local healers as a kind of skin wound. Nomenclature aside, they have found plants that are used for modern cures. A rosy periwinkle used for various ailments by healers in Madagascar has been transformed into a drug called vinblastine that successfully treats some forms of a disease we call cancer. The local healers and communities received no compensation for the drug company's (not Shaman) priceless, profitable "discovery." The plant is now commercially cultivated in Texas.

Other drug companies are rushing into the Third World to collect plants. The National Cancer Insti- tute has mounted perhaps the most extensive search. Since 1986, it has collected 23,000 samples from 7,000 species in tropical areas. From this collection, the institute has three compounds in preclinical tests.

Developing countries have begun to catch on to the value of their resources. Brazil and Mexico recently curtailed exports of plants, and other countries are tightening regulations. Costa Rica, one of the most diverse plant environments in the world, containing five percent of all plant and animal species, is negotiating with drug firms to allow plant collecting in exchange for royalties and technology. Meanwhile, good news is filtering up from Brazil: deforestation rates have been declining steadily since their 1987 peak.

Study Questions

*1. What legacies would you like our society to leave to distant future generations? What sacrifices would you be willing to make to help this happen? Would you sacrifice all the fast-food burger restaurants in order to preserve the tropical rainforests for our grandchildren and beyond?

*2. Would you like our government to pay for its programs by raising money primarily from those who will benefit from those programs? If so, how should it handle the many situations where those who will benefit can't afford to pay—for example, care for the aged or the poor? How did Shaman Pharmaceutical handle similar situations? Did they share the wealth even with those who didn't produce it or benefit from it before?

3. The famous television and film series *Star Trek* has a principle called the Prime Directive, which requires that many characters in the series not interfere with the ordinary development of other cultures they encounter. This makes for a bit of a paradox. Those on *Star Trek* pledge to *boldly* go where no one has gone before then to *timidly* avoid any interference with whatever they find once they finally get there! It sounds like astronauts serving as high-tech voyeurs. Still, does the Prime Directive make good moral sense? Do those from the First World in this case do well enough at avoiding excessive interference with the indigenous cultures they encounter?

96

Animal Rights: The Case of Selling Out Pets to Science

Judith Reitman

Editor's note: One way humans have tried to master much of our environment is to domesticate many animals. This case involves shocking crimes of stealing hundreds or thousands of pets for profit, at the emotional expense of hundreds of families.

———————

In a small outbuilding nestled in the emerald-green hills of Virginia horse country, Mary Warner waited for a phone call from the San Fernando Courthouse. The interior of her office was chaotic with documents and photos accumulated over the course of 30 years. As Mary waited, she played back dozens of phone messages.

"We figure it's a ring of about fifteen people in Kentucky and Indiana, Mary." Mary recognized Sue K.'s voice. "They're packin' Huskies, Shepherds, 150 big dogs per trip in three pickups and bringin' them to the South Carolina flatlands." A ring of poachers was stealing dogs to stake out for alligator bait in the swamps. "They promise to shoot and burn out people if they rat on them."

Patty in Texas called: "We found the source of the bait for the dog-fighting rings, Mary. A buncher consortium. Dope and dogs."

But the bulk of messages that flooded Mary's answering machine were from front-line fighters tracking the dealer/research circuit for Action 81, Mary's pet-theft tracking network. "Mary," Linda Elliot drawled, "I got Deputy Sheriff Tyler over to

that buncher camp. The place stinks. I think they're eatin' what they ain't sellin'." Mary smiled as she thought of Linda, a tough gal who looked like a beauty queen. Linda had singlehandedly busted the buncher encampment of an Arkansas kingpin.

Dwayne Reitz called to report his group's vigilant surveillance had paid off. The warehouses on the New York/Pennsylvania border were dealer waystations. "We were right. One of the drivers said they're supplying New York labs. A couple of people here found their missing dogs in the shed, but they're too afraid to prosecute. Can you blame them?" Dwayne and his family had been plagued by death threats. "These people don't fool around," he once told her.

Debby in Missouri left a message about "a run on big-chested dogs. We figure the call is out from cardiovascular researchers. We're getting two hundred calls a week for the past three weeks, people missing big dogs—Labs, Shepherds, Huskies. Animal Control's taking the dogs right out of people's yards. Have you got a contact in Arkansas for us?"

Pound managers were on the take, and with those kind of numbers, so was the local law.

The schemes and numbers did not shock Mary Warner. Few horror stories shocked her anymore. The ever-growing list of casualties tacked on her wall was a tragic reminder that nothing had really changed: over 10,000 dogs missing in Rochester, New York, within six months in 1983; seven hundred dogs missing in eleven months in Orlando, Florida, in 1985; 985 dogs and cats missing within eleven months in 1987 in Concord, North Carolina; over 1,000 dogs and cats reported missing in Indianapolis in one month in 1989. In 1990, in Columbus, Georgia, 2,500 dogs and cats had been reported missing: 5,000 in two consecutive years.

Many of the owners of these pets had learned the painful truth about their destinations: Mayo Clinic, Harvard, Yale, University of California at Los Angeles, Washington University in St. Louis, University of Missouri, University of Virginia, University of Minnesota, University of Washington in Seattle, Gore Labs, Letterman Army Institute, University of California at Davis, 3M Corporation. . . .

The men and women who delivered these family pets into laboratories were licensed to do so by the United States Department of Agriculture. For as little as $40 plus a $10 application fee, virtually anyone could become a USDA-licensed purveyor of stolen pets for sale to medical research, and make a small fortune in the process. Fact was, as buncher Ralf

Jacobsen had known, a license was not even really needed.

In Los Angeles, 140 pet owners had only recently discovered the horrifying reality that dogs and cats in laboratories are stolen pets. But why did it take such tragedy before the public, which pays for this research, was allowed to look behind the laboratory doors?

Mary had been asking that question for nearly thirty years.

The sun glittered gold and amber over the Shenandoah River as Mary jotted down the last of her messages. It was nearly 6:30 P.M.; 3:30 LA time. On this sultry summer evening, when the scent of newly mown grass rose from the moist fields and the honeysuckle hung heavy on the bushes, Mary was waiting for far more than a verdict in the Ruggiero case. She waited for a vindication of thousands of front-line fighters who were risking their lives battling the Dog Mafia.

Mary Warner would settle for nothing less than an indictment of the U.S. government on charges of conspiracy.

Study Questions

1. Do you treat any of your pets as members of your family? Wouldn't you be heartbroken or outraged if someone took away a member of your family, a favorite pet, to sell for scientific experiments?

2. Couldn't computerized organization of animal pounds prevent the demand for animals from getting so large as to encourage theft? Aren't there so many abandoned dogs and cats that science could get all it needed if only a centralized computer record of abandoned pets were available?

3. Should the thieves and their corrupt accomplices in dog pounds and local law enforcement receive strict punishment, or should this be treated as a minor crime of petty theft of property?

4. Why should we treat our pets (dogs, cats, rabbits, etc.) so much better than we treat livestock or wild animals? Isn't our preference for certain animals a form of speciesism, a form of discrimination analogous to racism or sexism? Should an animal's species alone determine its fate and determine how much we care about it?

97

The Threat of Global Warming

Claudine Schneider

Last summer, American farms suffered multibillion-dollar crop losses from a devastating drought. Thousands of square miles of dry forests went up in smoke as fires raged uncontrollably. Entire communities were left homeless and destitute in the wake of hurricanes Gilbert and Helene. And smog blanketed many cities as a mass of hot air hovered over the country. "It must be the greenhouse effect," was the comment made over and over again by members of Congress. Media coverage had sensitized most Americans to the peril imposed by the unchecked growth of greenhouse gas emissions, and the unpleasant weather seemed to be a preview of what we can expect if global climate models are accurate in their predictions.

As scientists debate the validity of these climate models, policymakers must decide what to do. Two opposing schools of thought are emerging: One school promotes adaptation, the other prevention.

Advocates of the adaptation approach argue that we should wait until more scientific evidence is in, which will allow us to take more targeted actions. They worry that premature efforts to cut greenhouse gases may needlessly disrupt the world economy. But by the time we are sure that the greenhouse effect is with us, it will be too late to reverse it; the only recourse will be adaptation. To my mind, this approach is too much like the crisis management tactic of "Let's wait until the ship hits the sand, then figure out what to do" so prevalent in public policymaking today.

Reprinted from Claudine Schneider, "Preventing Climate Change," *Issues in Science and Technology*, vol. 5, no. 4 (Summer 1989). Copyright © 1989 by the National Academy of Sciences, Washington, D.C.

Luckily, many conclude that inaction with respect to global warming is foolhardy. When symptoms of an illness appear, they say, a remedy should be sought. Thus there is growing support for a preventive strategy, which means reducing the emissions of greenhouse gases—primarily carbon dioxide (CO_2), but also chlorofluorocarbons (CFCs) and methane. For example, the recommendations of the 1988 Toronto Conference on the Changing Atmosphere include a call for at least a 20 percent reduction in global CO_2 emissions below the 1987 level by the year 2005, and a 50 percent reduction by the year 2015. This goal has been endorsed by the Prime Ministers of Canada and Norway. The Global Warming Prevention Act . . . and . . . National Energy Policy Act seek a 20 percent reduction by the end of the century.

Noting that society is at risk from the threat of global warming, the National Academy of Sciences recently called on President Bush to take a leadership role in gaining international consensus on this difficult issue and urged the president to adopt "prudent" policies to slow the pace of global climate change. Prudence dictates reducing our dependency on fossil fuels, which are the primary source of CO_2; phasing out most ozone-depleting chlorofluorocarbons and other halocarbons, which are also destroying the ozone layer; halting deforestation and promoting reforestation (trees remove CO_2 from the air whereas burning them releases it); and adopting agricultural and livestock practices that minimize forest conversion and reduce methane emission. Slowing population growth will also have a profound impact.

Securing these changes will not be easy. Altering the ways of 240 million Americans, let alone 5 billion human beings worldwide, poses a formidable challenge. Confronting the vested economic interests adamantly opposed to change is an equally daunting task for political leaders. Moreover, the greenhouse peril must compete with other serious, and more immediate, environmental problems such as acid rain, urban ozone, indoor air pollution, the cleanup of contaminated nuclear weapons production facilities, and the disposal of toxic wastes.

The slow pace of climate change breeds complacency, but we must remember that the climate will also be slow to respond to after-the-fact solutions. We must begin now to adopt the good stewardship practices that will reduce the likelihood of human-induced climate disruption. Fortunately, congressional testimony received over the past several years indicates a wide range of actions to reduce greenhouse gases that are already cost-effective and many others that could be, given sufficient research and development. Rapid progress has already begun on reducing CFC emissions, and many of the suggestions for minimizing other threats to the climate have been incorporated into legislative proposals.

The path to pursue is one that not only reduces emissions of greenhouse gases but that makes economic sense as well. Each choice we make should spur multiple benefits. Stephen Schneider, a climate expert at the National Center for Atmospheric Research, calls this the "tie-in" strategy: Take those actions that reduce the trade deficit, free up capital, save consumers money, and enhance the competitiveness of U.S. industry, as well as reduce greenhouse gases.

In this spirit, the Global Warming Prevention Act builds upon existing federal programs and newly proposed legislation that can help slow climate change as well as achieve these multiple purposes. By linking these disparate efforts in a coordinated program and adding a few initiatives focused primarily on climate change, we can increase the likelihood that Congress will approve a plan sufficiently comprehensive to alter the conditions that threaten to disrupt the climate. In spite of the global nature of the problem, the emphasis is on domestic policy because the United States is the major producer of greenhouse gases—contributing approximately 20 percent of the total—and the place where we as Americans have the ability to take immediate action. In addition, we cannot expect other countries to listen to our advice until we lead by example.

The most impressive tie-in advantages result from improving energy efficiency. We have already witnessed the power of this approach in responding to the energy crisis of the 1970s. Seeking to reduce oil imports and energy costs, scientists and engineers spawned a veritable revolution in product design and manufacturing techniques. The result was the emergence of an enormous new energy "resource." One can now "produce" energy by using light bulbs that are four times as efficient as conventional models or by living in a superinsulated home that requires only one-tenth as much energy for heating as a typical home.

Such innovations still await widespread adoption. But so far, even the modest improvements that have been made in America's stock of buildings, vehicles, factories, and appliances have secured dramatic results. Since 1973, energy efficiency gains have displaced the equivalent of 14 million barrels of oil

per day, saving Americans more than $150 billion per year. In addition, CO_2 emissions are 50 percent lower than they otherwise would have been. Foreign oil imports are less than half of what they would have been, lowering the annual trade deficit by more than $50 billion. Efficiency gains worldwide have been instrumental in spawning a global oil glut, collapsing world oil prices, curtailing OPEC's power, and reducing inflation rates fanned by high energy costs.

How much efficiency is possible? A staggering amount, according to a study by the Global End-Use Oriented Energy Project based in part at Princeton University's Center for Energy and the Environment. For example, the international research team's 5-year energy scenario, based on extensive (but far from exhaustive) use of efficiency improvements, projects that it would be technologically feasible and economically compelling to hold energy use constant and reduce CO_2 emissions over the next half century even as world population doubled and gross world product quadrupled. . . .

The potential for energy savings is reflected in the success of the federally mandated Northwest Electric Power and Conservation Plan. Begun in 1980 when it became clear that the region had exhausted the supply of cheap federally produced hydropower, the plan established a rigorous least-cost planning process for Washington, Oregon, Idaho, and Montana. By focusing on low-cost energy efficiency measures, these states were able to indefinitely defer the need for all 16 planned generating plants, preventing the expenditure of billions of dollars in construction costs and keeping electric rates low. . . .

Transportation, particularly automobiles and light trucks, is responsible for almost one-third of U.S. carbon emissions, as well as a large fraction of tropospheric ozone and acid rain pollutants. Market forces are not sufficient to spur optimal efficiency because the cost of gasoline comprises only about 20 percent of the total cost of operating a car. Even doubling the price of gasoline, as many countries have done, would not give consumers enough incentive to demand cars that get more than 35 miles per gallon (mpg).

Several policies to reduce fuel use in transportation are already in effect. Since 1975, the Corporate Average Fuel Economy (CAFE) standards have required U.S. manufacturers to achieve a minimum average efficiency among all new cars sold. The fuel economy of new U.S. cars doubled between 1974 and 1985 as the standard rose gradually to 27.5 mpg.

Under pressure from manufacturers, the standard was relaxed to 26 mpg in 1986, 1987, and 1988. President Bush recently announced that the standard will be raised to 27.5 mpg in 1990. We should continue gradually increasing the standard over the next decade to 45 mpg for cars and 35 mpg for light trucks, thereby eliminating the need for 15 billion barrels of oil.

Some manufacturers argue that more demanding standards will make it impossible to produce the big cars consumers want and to provide adequate safety for drivers. But Department of Transportation studies indicate that the use of technologies such as continuously variable transmissions, multivalve engines, and advanced lightweight materials will make it possible to achieve 48 mpg in large cars. A few four- and five-passenger prototypes have done much better. As for safety, design is more important than weight. Chevrolet's 4,100-pound 1985 Astro minivan, for example, was one of the worst performers in crash tests; the high-mileage 2,600-pound Chevy Nova had the best crash test rating of any of the new cars tested that year.

Volvo's prototype mid-sized passenger sedan, the LCP 2000, indicates what is technologically feasible. Road tested at a combined city/highway mileage of 75 mpg, the car exceeds EPA's stringent safety standards, accelerates to 60 mph in 11 seconds, and is expected to cost no more than current models.

One drawback of the CAFE standards is that a manufacturer cannot force consumers to choose its more efficient models and therefore cannot guarantee that it will meet the specified average for all cars sold. Congress, therefore, should reinforce the efficiency mandate by strengthening the existing gas guzzler tax, which is levied on any car that gets less than 22 mpg and rises as the mileage falls. I propose increasing the amount of the tax, gradually increasing the kick-in mileage to 32 mpg by 2004, and extending it to light trucks, which are currently exempt. In addition, I propose a "gas-sippers" rebate of up to $2,000 on the purchase of the most fuel-efficient vehicles.

Industry should not have to bear the entire research burden for developing more efficient cars. The Department of Energy (DOE) spends a piddling $50 million per year on all transportation R&D, while the nation is spending $100 billion a year on gasoline. DOE needs to increase its research on auto efficiency, particularly in areas that will have near-term commercial application. To ensure that the money is spent wisely, Congress should ask the National Academy of Sciences to do a thorough review of fuel economy R&D opportunities and recommend priorities for the DOE program.

Underpinning all of these efforts must be a stable federal research and development effort, working jointly with private industry. A 50 percent cut since 1980 in the federal energy efficiency R&D budget has meant that there have been no new research projects begun this decade. These budget cuts seem particularly shortsighted in light of the spectacular success of federal energy-efficiency R&D. According to a 1987 analysis by the American Council for an Energy Efficient Economy, the $16 million that DOE spent on cooperative projects with industry to develop heat pumps, more efficient refrigerators, new ballasts to improve the efficiency of fluorescent lights, and glass coatings that control heat loss and gain through windows will help save the country billions of dollars through energy savings.

Federal R&D can be especially productive in the areas of building design and industrial processes. The annual utility bill for the nation's buildings is $160 billion, but the fragmented building industry spends almost nothing on energy efficiency R&D. The federal government can coordinate research with the 28,000 homebuilders and 150,000 special trade contractors to tap energy savings in virtually every part of the building, from the foundation to the roof and from the heating and cooling system to the windows.

Similar savings can be found in industry. Generic research in industrial process efficiency can lead to significant savings across many industries, but no individual company will reap sufficient benefit to justify funding the research itself. The Global Warming Prevention Act therefore calls for the creation of a number of industrial research centers to conduct joint projects with industry to improve the efficiency of manufacturing processes. This effort will not only reduce greenhouse gases and other pollutants but will enhance industrial competitiveness by cutting production costs.

Efficiency improvements alone will not be enough, but they will buy us time to develop renewable energy sources that do not produce greenhouse gases. The world's renewable resource base is enormous. According to a 1985 report by the DOE, a 25-year research and development effort could make it possible to economically extract 85 quads of renewable energy in the United States. Combined with efficiency improvements, this amount could conceivably meet virtually the entire U.S. energy demand in the year 2010. But the necessary work is not being done. The federal R&D budget for renewable energy has fallen from more than $800 million in 1979 to a proposed $130 million in 1990—less than one percent of DOE's total budget.

With such a vast potential available and opinion polls reporting a high public regard for solar energy, why has there been so little progress? There are several reasons. In part, the outstanding success of energy efficiency has eclipsed the promise of sun power. In the wake of an oil glut and collapsed energy prices, the market for renewable energy technology virtually disappeared. Moreover, ill-conceived public policies did little to advance the infant solar industry toward maturity. R&D efforts were misplaced, emphasizing giant centralized projects, rather than capitalizing on the inherently dispersed and diffuse nature of solar energy flows. Tax incentives, while well-intentioned, were in some ways counterproductive. Pegged to a system cost rather than energy production, the solar tax credits favored expensive "gold-plate" systems over low-cost options such as passive solar design.

Although some solar technologies will require more R&D before they are economically competitive, many untapped opportunities are now available. For example, large scale use of solar-generated electricity may still be a decade away, but the use of daylight in buildings is feasible now—and lighting accounts for 25 percent of all U.S. electricity use. DOE's Solar Energy Research Institute estimates that designing buildings to take advantage of daylight could provide one-fourth of lighting requirements. Daylighting should therefore be an integral part of all least-cost utility planning programs.

Several other renewable energy technologies are also in widespread practice or ready for use. Passive solar space heating has become an essential part of energy efficient building practice in northern climates, and solar water heating is being used in hundreds of thousands of buildings throughout the country. Although very cost-effective, these technologies are not being used to their full potential because many consumers lack information about their value, because renters have no incentive to invest in their homes, and because builders compete on home price rather than on operating costs. Least-cost planning programs need to include financial incentives or building standards that promote use of these established renewable-energy technologies.

Photovoltaic cells and high-temperature solar thermal systems offer economically attractive ways

of meeting utility peak power demands during summer, and wind power offers the same potential during cold weather. Biomass-derived ethanol is already in use in blends of gasoline, and biogas from waste could be used to fuel new, highly efficient aircraft-derived gas turbines. In fact, Sweden plans to use biogas-fired turbines as one of the replacements for nuclear power, which it is phasing out over the coming decade.

Renewable energy sources, primarily hydropower and biomass, supply close to 10 percent of total U.S. energy needs. To tap the full potential of renewable energy, the federal government must reverse the decline in R&D funding. Government spending still reflects pre-greenhouse thinking. DOE will spend $1 billion on fossil fuel research this year, seven times what it will spend on all renewable energy technologies combined. At a time when we should be exploring every opportunity for replacing fossil fuels, this simply makes no sense.

In addition, the government itself can make a concerted effort to use renewable energy. Federal buildings, military bases, and public housing continue to ignore cost-effective investments in solar technology and energy-saving measures. Federal procurement guidelines should be made more stringent in requiring this use.

Likewise, national and multinational assistance to developing countries should include more attention to renewable energy technologies. For example, the World Bank, which currently underwrites the cost of diesel water pumps, should also subsidize solar-powered pumps, which are just as cost-effective, more reliable and also useful for operating filters to remove waterborne parasites. Stimulating use of photovoltaic cells would also enable the industry to reduce prices by scaling up production processes.

Between 10 and 20 percent of greenhouse gas emissions are due to the deforestation of some 11 million hectares annually. One "Yellowstone Park" is disappearing every month; a forested area the size of Pennsylvania is ravaged every year. Reforesting efforts are pathetically weak, with just one tree replanted for every 10 cut down. At the current rate of deforestation nearly half the world's remaining forests will be lost within the next several generations. . . .

Nevertheless, we cannot forget that preserving the tropical forests, which contain more than three-fourths of the world's biological diversity, has obvious tie-in appeal. The world relies heavily on the forests for a wide variety of products, including many important medicines. But as the forests disappear, plant and animal species are becoming extinct at a rate not witnessed since the demise of the dinosaurs 65 million years ago. We are in danger of losing an irreplaceable natural resource just as advances in molecular biology and genetic engineering are enhancing our ability to use it.

The importance of the tropical forests makes it incumbent on the United States to find a way to encourage their preservation. Self-righteous—and self-serving—homilies will not do. But through policy analysis, technological assistance, and financial aid, the United States can show Brazil and others how current practices are unsound and how alternatives can benefit them economically as well as environmentally. . . .

The developing countries will act to preserve the forests when they are convinced that it is in their best interest to do so. The rural poor in developing countries need to grow food to survive, and the countries need to produce products for export. Cleared tropical forest land can be farmed (though only for a few years), and timber is a valuable export product. To reduce the incentive to destroy the forests, it is necessary to improve the productivity of agriculture on already cleared land and to find a way to generate wealth from the forests without destroying them.

The United States should expand on the pioneering work by the Agency for International Development (AID) to develop agroforestry, the nondestructive use of forest land to produce food and other products. For example, since 1965, AID forester Michael Benge has been demonstrating the advantages of leucena, a fast-growing, nitrogen-fixing species that enriches the soil while serving as live fencing and producing forage for livestock and fuel wood. The National Academy of Sciences has published a series of handbooks on multiuse species for agroforestry in developing countries, and these could readily serve as the foundation for an expanded effort by AID and other development organizations.

Finally, we cannot forget that a rapidly growing population increases the pressure to burn fossil fuels and to use forests to produce energy and provide new land for farms and ranches. The United States pioneered family planning efforts to stabilize population growth several decades ago, long before most developing countries with high birth rates saw any need. Ironically, now that these same developing countries have reversed their positions and recognized the need to step up such efforts, the United States is steadily reducing its funding commitment to international family planning assistance.

Efforts to reduce CO_2 emissions through improving energy efficiency and tapping renewable energy sources can be overwhelmed by the increased energy needs that will accompany a growing world population. Every three years the world is adding a population the size of the United States, 95 percent of it in developing countries. Improving the standard of living in developing countries without increasing energy use is difficult enough without having to deal with the increased needs of a growing population. As a first step, the United States needs to double its international family planning funds. Developing countries need the means to control population growth—for their economic well-being and for the health of the planet.

The prevention approach to global climate change clearly entails an ambitious public policy agenda. Can we justify such a program with a few computer models? No, but we don't have to. Government initiatives to use energy more efficiently, to develop safe renewable alternatives to fossil fuels, to preserve tropical forests, and to slow population growth make economic and environmental sense even if climate disruption was not a danger.

If further research increases the certainty that we face rapid global warming, we will have to consider more dramatic measures. What I have proposed requires no sacrifice, and by setting in motion efforts that will steadily reduce CO_2 emissions, it will reduce the severity of measures needed if we find that the climate is changing more quickly than predicted.

Study Questions

1. Even if global warming is not currently a serious threat, can we afford to take many chances with such a devastating problem? If we cannot, then wouldn't it be wise to act as if global warming is a serious problem as long as there is reasonable doubt about it?

2. What approach would utilitarianism take to the problem of global warming?

3. Would libertarianism allow strong government action and cooperation with other governments if that were necessary to stop global warming? Or would libertarianism leave even such worldwide problems to be solved by economic markets?

*4. Would your enjoyment of life be significantly diminished if you could only own one small car or not use air-conditioning? If you were forced to sharply cut your material consumption, what would be the least painful way for you to do so?

*5. If the only way to avoid disastrous global warming were to halve our current consumption of energy, would you do so voluntarily or only under duress (that is, compulsion)?

98

Errors of Environmentalism

Rush Limbaugh III

Editor's note: Limbaugh, a conservative member of the media who is heard on over 600 radio stations and seen on his own show on TV every weeknight, claims environmentalists overstate their case on a number of key issues.

[T]o appreciate how radical, how out of the mainstream *Algore* truly is, you have to listen to what he says about the environment. Until now, that meant you had to read his book. Fortunately, I am going to save you some money, some time, and a good deal of boredom by highlighting it for you.

It's called *Earth in the Balance: Ecology and the Human Spirit*. *Algore's* collaborator was Environmental Protection Agency chief Carol Browner. If *Earth in the Balance* accomplishes anything, it should be to discredit both of them from any serious participation in our nation's debate over the environment. It is nothing more than a hysterical, pseudo-scientific tract designed to cut off calm, reasoned discussion of environmental issues and simply push the nation toward irrational, irreversible, misguided (not to mention expensive) public policies.

Algore's book is full of calculated disinformation. For instance, he claims that 98 percent of scientists believe global warming is taking place. However, a Gallup poll of scientists involved in global climate research shows that 53 percent do not believe that global warming has occurred, 30 percent say they don't know, and only 17 percent are devotees of this

dubious theory. During the summer of 1993 it was reported that *Algore* actually suggested that the record flooding that occurred along the Mississippi River in the Midwest might have resulted from global warming. Don't forget folks: This guy's not really Taxula's lab assistant; he's the vice-president of the United States.

He claims that agriculture in America is threatened because of topsoil erosion. Yet, according to the Soil Conservation Service, thanks to technological breakthroughs, fewer acres have been suffering severe erosion in the United States.

He takes a gratuitous swipe at DDT, which he calls "a symbol of how carelessly our civilization could do harm to the world." Harm to the world? DDT has saved the lives of tens of millions of people! For instance, in 1951, 75 million people in India suffered from malaria. Thanks to DDT, that number was down to 50,000 in 1961. When India stopped using DDT, malaria came back strong, resulting in illness and deaths for millions. In 1977, the number of cases ranged between 30 million and 50 million.

In his book, obviously written before the budget deficit became his cause celebre, *Algore* calls for America to embark on a "Global Marshall Plan," at a cost of $100 billion, to protect the environment. He has some ideas on how to raise that money: a tax on carbon, a virgin-materials tax, a higher tax on fossil fuels. This guy's got more taxes up his sleeve than Congress does. As part of this master plan, *Algore* would turn over authority for administering international environmental agreements to a U.N. Stewardship Council, modeled after the Security Council. This is no laughing matter, my friends. We're talking here about forfeiting U.S. sovereignty to a bunch of Third World America-bashers.

There is something intrinsically anti-American about the way *Algore* flagellates the U.S. over its environmental policies. He writes that cultures are like families and "our civilization must be considered in some way dysfunctional. . . . We consume the Earth and its resources as a way to distract ourselves from the pain. . . ." He draws comparisons to other dysfunctional families—like Nazi Germany and Mussolini's Italy. This, from a guy who gets lost hiking in a park with the Secret Service!

But the guiding theme throughout this master literary work is that solely because of our technological advances and our destruction of the environment, we are headed for the apocalypse. Doomsday is rapidly approaching. Environmental Armageddon is right around the corner. If you think I'm exaggerat-

Reprinted from *See, I Told You So* (New York: Pocket Books, 1993), pp. 162–165 and 171–184.

ing, read his own words: "Now warnings of a differ-ent sort signal an environmental holocaust without precedent. . . . Today the evidence of an ecological Kristallnacht is as clear as the sound of glass shatter-ing in Berlin." Hey, Al, maybe that was Tipper throw-ing out your crystals.

What's the answer? If you can't convince the elec-torate that government should be expanded for eco-nomic reasons, fabricate a crisis of another sort. But it's got to be grave enough to justify a massive aug-mentation of government. Over and over again, *Algore* makes it clear that he believes the threat to the environment is so severe that we need to resort to the kind of Draconian central planning that has failed so miserably in every place it has been tried: "Adopt-ing a central organizing principle . . . means embark-ing on an all-out effort to use every policy and pro-gram, every law and institution . . . to halt the de-struction of the environment." That is his solution. Let's consolidate all of our legal, political, and gov-ernmental resources (never mind the cost, never mind the proper purposes of these resources and the ad-verse consequences that would surely ensue from their diversion) to launch our assault on Western civi-lization, capitalism, and our very way of life. Let's give the federal government lots more money so it can solve our environmental problems just as it has solved so many other problems—poverty, illiteracy, homelessness, drug abuse, crime; you name it. What a track record big government has!

To listen to *Algore*, you would think that the rea-son we have environmental problems is that the fed-eral government doesn't have enough money and enough authority to intervene in our lives. If only he were technology czar, he could make the right deci-sions for American businesses (such as paralyzing them) and we'd all be a lot better off.

Part of the problem, he says, is that our back-ward business community has placed too much em-phasis on technologies "associated more with males than females . . . [and] ways to dominate nature re-ceive more attention than ways to work with nature." If you can translate that non sequitur, you're a better man—uh, excuse me; person—than I. In typical psychobabble fashion, he suggests that "part of the solution for the environmental crisis may well lie in our ability to achieve a better balance between the sexes, leavening the dominant male perspective with a healthier respect for female ways of experiencing the world." Would someone please tell me what in the he— this has to do with the environment?

* * *

I have been proved right about so many things since my first book was published that *See, I Told You So* could easily have filled several volumes by sim-ply cataloging such validations. But on no issue has the evidence of my foresight and keen political in-stincts been more compelling than that of the envi-ronment.

What did I tell you? What have I been saying and writing that flies in the face of so-called "con-ventional wisdom"? How many times do I have the right to say "Nya-nya-nya-nya-nya-nya!" because of my uncanny calls on this subject? Come, let us count the ways:

· Despite the hysterics of a few pseudo-scientists, there is no reason to believe in global warming.
· Mankind is not responsible for depleting the ozone layer.
· The Earth's ecosystem is not fragile, and humans are not capable of destroying it.
· The real enemies of the radical environmen-tal leadership are capitalism and the Ameri-can way of life.
· There are more acres of forest land in America today than when Columbus discov-ered the continent in 1492.
· Less-developed cultures are not necessarily more pure or kinder to nature than techno-logically sophisticated civilizations. In fact, the reverse more often is true.
· Big-government regulation is not the best way to protect the environment.
· Many environmental groups have adopted their cause with all the fervor and enthusi-asm of a religious crusade, abandoning reason and accepting many faulty premises on faith.
· Mankind is part of nature and not necessarily its enemy.

But, perhaps most important, what have I told you about the environmental movement? What have I said it's really about? What have I told you over and over and over again? If you have listened to my radio program, seen my television show, subscribed to my newsletter, or read my first book, you know how I have characterized this movement.

It's about panic. It's about fear. It's about instill-ing the American populace with terror, dread, and apprehension about the future. It's all about making you think that your way of life is "destroying the world." America is the root of all evil in the world, according to the environmentalist wackos. You, the citizens of the United States, are ruining everything. Unless the industrialized, civilized world is willing to make tremendous sacrifices with respect to people's personal lives, this planet is soon going to be uninhabitable, they say.

Now let's look at some recent developments. On May 30, 1993, *The New York Times Magazine* contained an article that proves so much of what I have been saying. Titled "Is Humanity Suicidal?," it was written by Edward O. Wilson, a professor of sociobiology at Harvard University.

The premise of the piece was laughable, but then you have to catch yourself, because, after all, it is being published by *The New York Times*, our nation's newspaper of record. The article asks us to imagine that there is a civilization far more intelligent than mankind, perhaps on Ganymede, the icy moon of Jupiter, waiting for us to destroy Earth. They are wise creatures, of course, and never interfere with inhabited planets. But when civilizations destroy their own world, this noble and highly advanced race moves in and takes over. They're waiting, Professor Wilson suggests, for what could be called "The Moment." That's the time when the forests shrink back to a certain point, carbon dioxide levels reach a critical stage, ozone holes open at the poles, and oil fires rage around the Persian Gulf.

These other beings, of course, are all-knowing and morally superior. However, to this Harvard professor, the rest of humanity is nothing more than a bunch of boobs bent on self-destruction.

"Darwin's dice may have rolled badly for Earth," Wilson writes. "It was a misfortune for the living world in particular, many scientists believe, that a carnivorous primate and not some more benign form of animal made the breakthrough. Our species retains hereditary traits that add greatly to our destructive impact. We are tribal and aggressively territorial, intent on private space beyond minimal requirements and oriented by selfish sexual and reproductive drives. Cooperation beyond the family and tribal levels comes hard." Sounds a bit like Michael Lerner, wouldn't you say?

Do you get this? It's just the worst luck for all living things that we humans are the ones who took dominion over the Earth. If only the dolphins had been the ones to make the leap, everything would be all right for planet Earth.

Humans, the good professor writes, are an environmental abnormality. Except for allusions to the Earth Goddess Gaia, there is no mention of a supreme being or a Creator in this story. This, my friends, is what they're teaching your kid at Harvard. If you ever doubted me when I said that the militant environmentalists were anti-people New Age mystics, this article should prove my case.

It also illustrated the profound gulf between people of theology and many in the scientific community. No allowances are made here at all for God. This is why modern, politicized science offends so many people. To take God's most perfect creation and debase it like this is insulting not only to humans, but to God. And this type of writing fits so well into the liberal policy agenda. Liberal institutions love to fund this kind of wacky, anti-people theory. Liberal publishers love to support it. The liberal media love to publicize it.

Nevertheless, the truth continues to leak out. Even the liberal media cannot contain it any longer. Myths are being shattered. Real science is overshadowing pseudo-science. It turns out, after all, that advanced technology may not be the archenemy of nature. White males may not be the only ones in history who have used Earth's natural resources.

On March 30, 1993, *The New York Times* published a fascinating science-section story headlined: "An Eden in Ancient America? Not Really." Allow me to quote: "Contrary to widespread belief, evidence is mounting that pre-Columbian America was not a pristine wilderness inhabited by people who lived in such harmony with nature that they left it unmarked. Instead, many scientists now say, the original Americans powerfully transformed their landscape in ways both destructive and benign—just like modern people."

Oh, really? You mean the Indians were just like us, huh? They weren't perfect? This is about as startling a revelation as the discovery that males and females are indeed born with different traits. This, my friends, is why I tell you I am on the cutting edge of societal evolution. What have I been telling you? The environmental radicals have been holding up as a model for us to follow the agricultural techniques of the Native American people. Now we find out the truth. Their techniques were more abusive of the environment than our modern farming methods are. But do you think the radicals will revise their stories accordingly? Don't hold your breath.

The story goes on to explain that British researchers have analyzed soil samples in the highlands of central Mexico and discovered that ancient farming techniques caused a "staggeringly high" rate of erosion. What do you have to say about that, *Algore*?

"It is becoming abundantly clear to geographers, ecologists, and archaeologists that, whether for good or ill, ancient people had a heavy and widespread impact on their environment," the article by William K. Stevens continued. "Some scientists are convinced that a number of early civilizations were brought down by environmental degradation of the land. The brilliant cultural centers of ancient Mesopotamia, for instance, are widely thought to have collapsed because of over-irrigation, which forced water tables to rise and carry salt to the surface, where it made land unfit for farming. And some scientists suggest that erosion brought about by over-clearing of forests undermined the Maya of Central America."

But as corrupting as any civilization may be to the environment, Earth is remarkably adept at healing itself. And this may come as a real shock to the eco-fanatics: Man can actually play a significant redemptive role in managing nature. Now, the real shocker: Human beings, operating freely in a capitalistic system, are better equipped to solve their own environmental problems, to clean up their own messes, than any other species operating under any other economic system. In other words, free markets and technology are not incompatible with, but essential to, environmental health.

Would it surprise you to learn, for instance, that America's forests are much healthier today in the 1990s than they were at the turn of the century? In fact, you could say that in the last seventy years America's forests have been reborn. There are 730 million acres of forest land in our country today, and the growth on those acres is denser than at any time, with about 230 billion trees—or 900 for every American.

According to a study by Jonathan Adler, an environmental policy analyst at the Competitive Enterprise Institute, New England has more forested acres than it did in the mid-1800s. Vermont is twice as forested as it was then. Almost half of the densely populated northeastern United States is covered by forest. Why? How could this be? If we are ravaging our land, as the environmentalists suggest, why are there more trees around—more forests?

There are several reasons that are important to our discussion. For one thing, technological breakthroughs have drastically reduced our need for lumber. Wood preservatives, for instance, mean that timber products have a much longer life. The automobile, so cursed by *Algore*, has reduced the heavy need for timber required by the rail industry. Our agriculture industry, thanks to chemical fertilizers and pes-

ticides, is more efficient and requires less land to grow even greater quantities of food. Most of the planting done—about 80 percent, in fact—is done on private land because there is a financial incentive to grow trees.

But there's an even bigger reason why we have larger, healthier forests today than 100 years ago. It's the simple fact that we know better how to put out forest fires today than was known at the turn of the century. Back then, 50 million acres of forest were destroyed by fire every year. That's an area representing the size of West Virginia, Virginia, or Maryland, for instance. In modern times, wildfires have consumed annually less than one-tenth of that amount of timberland.

"But wait!" you say. "How can that be? I thought man was evil and only destroyed the pristine wilderness. You mean, Rush, that humans have actually saved trees?"

Well, yes, until now, that is. Because if we leave forest-management policy up to Bill Clinton, *Algore*, and their environmentalist wacko friends, what's to prevent us from returning to the days of rapidly spreading wildfires that destroy 50 million acres or more a year? Remember back a few years ago when Yellowstone National Park was literally ablaze? Ultimately about 1.2 million acres were destroyed, $120 million of damage was done, and three people were killed. Why? Because, believe it or not, those managing the park made a conscious decision to let it burn.

The goal of the environmentalists—and this has been adopted by the current administration—is to create in our national parks and all land under federal and state control what they call "a vignette of primitive America." They want to set up "ecosystems" that are free of any contamination by man. You should understand that in their lexicon, "contamination by man" means "interaction with man other than those wearing Earth shoes." In these systems, whatever happens naturally happens. Man, not being a part of nature, cannot interfere. If lightning strikes and causes a fire, it should be allowed to burn, no matter how much damage it does. This is the thinking behind our current forest-management techniques. It doesn't take a Rhodes scholar to figure out that it won't be long before we're right back where we were at the turn of the century—wondering why all the forest land is disappearing.

Conservationist Alston Chase calls this ecosystem philosophy a "quasi-mystical idea," and he's right. There's no logic behind it. There is no good reason for it. What the environmentalists are saying, in effect, is that some trees are better than others. Trees that have been planted by man are not as worthy or valuable as those that grow in "virgin" forests. What is a virgin forest anyway? Most trees live for only a couple of hundred years and then die. No tree lives forever. Nothing on Earth remains unchanged. So what are virgin forests? Are they made up of trees that have never had sex?

Nevertheless, the Clinton administration is determined to protect virgin forests. (Ironically, our government has little interest in promoting the virginity and innocence of our young people.) It is also establishing a policy to protect more ecosystems and has even signed the international biodiversity treaty that calls for setting them up around the world. This is just the latest technique to stop development and halt the timber industry. The trouble is, this time it's on a global level.

This policy is shortsighted, to say the least. To the environmentalists, it's a tragedy if a man drops a cigarette butt that starts a forest fire that destroys 100,000 acres. But if a lightning bolt does it, it's no problem. So, many environmentalists and the politicians they keep on a leash simply ignore reality and common sense. It reminds me of the researchers who recently ventured into the forests in California. Do you know what they found? No, not *Algore*. They found spotted owls. It seems the place is teeming with spotted owls—even though they're supposed to be an endangered species.

Once again, folks, all I can say is SITYS. But how many of you believed it when you were told that the spotted owl was one logger away from extinction? I was right yesterday, I am right today, and I will be right tomorrow. But you still won't hear about any of this from the major media.

There are other things I have warned you about. I mentioned earlier that widespread use of pesticides, along with chemical fertilizers, has—gasp—actually resulted in more trees being grown in the United States. Again, this flies in the face of conventional wisdom. Every day we're told how evil these things are—how we've got to reduce our reliance on them. Hogwash! Pesticides and chemical fertilizers have provided us with an unprecedented abundance of safer food than ever before. And, according to a recent report in *Investor's Business Daily*, the anti-pesticide, pro-organic campaign may actually be hazardous to the health of the nation.

Think about it. Everybody in America today can afford to buy fresh produce in his or her local market. Even the poorest Americans have access to healthy fruits and vegetables because of our ability to raise these crops economically. However, if America's farmers turned strictly to organic, pesticide-free techniques, you would see a dramatic drop in the amount and quality of produce available.

That's why it's laughable that the anti-pesticide, pro-organic lobby claims to be interested in improving America's health. Don't believe this baloney! Nothing would do more harm to the nation's health than to reduce the food supply, diminish its quality, and raise the prices of produce. Listen to the scientists—the experts in their field—not the crackpots who preach doom and gloom in furtherance of some far-out political agenda.

Perhaps the biggest environmental frauds perpetuated on us in recent years are the notions that Earth is heating up and that the ozone layer is disappearing because of man's abuse of the environment. I've been telling you for years that there is little scientific evidence behind either of these theories, and what I have been saying is being validated by virtually every new study being done, with the exception of those using solely computer models.

Let's just use our heads for a minute. Let's employ a little common sense. Scientists say a supernova 340,000 years ago disrupted 10 percent to 20 percent of the ozone layer, causing sunburn in prehistoric man. Wait a minute—I thought only man could destroy the ozone. I thought only modern technological innovation and the horrible products of human progress were lethal enough to damage the planet.

Has anything man has ever done even approximated the radiation and explosive force of a supernova? And if prehistoric man merely got a sunburn, how is it that we are going to destroy the ozone layer with our air conditioners and underarm deodorants and cause everybody to get cancer?

Obviously, we're not . . . and we can't . . . and it's a hoax. Evidence is mounting all the time that ozone depletion, if occurring at all, is not doing so at an alarming rate. Even *The Washington Post*—that haven of liberal mythology—published a front-page story on April 15, 1993, that dismissed most of the fears about the so-called ozone hole.

For years the media have been calling for immediate action and writing hysterical, alarmist editorials about the imminent threat that the ozone hole poses for humanity. Now, very quietly, they have begun whispering, Gilda Radner's "Saturday Night

Live"–character Emily Latella–style, "Never mind." No apology, mind you. No *mea culpa*. Just "Never mind."

For example, here's what *The Washington Post* said in an editorial on February 5, 1992: "Once again, it turns out that the protective ozone layer in the sky is being destroyed faster than even the pessimists had expected. Until now, the disappearance of ozone had seemed to be limited to the polar regions. But the new data . . . warn that an ozone hole may open up later this winter over the temperate Northern Hemisphere with its dense population."

Then, on April 15, 1993, a front-page story had this to say: "In fact, researchers say the problem appears to be heading toward solution before they can find any solid evidence that serious harm was or is being done."

A few days later, the authoritative journal *Science* published a story headlined "Ozone Takes Nose Dive After the Eruption of Mt. Pinatubo." It pointed out that the ozone layer should show significant signs of recovery by 1994. But have you heard *Algore* or any other ozone alarmist step up and admit that he or she perpetuated a fraud on the American people? Have you even heard any of them admit they were dead wrong? No problem, I'll say it for them—and more articulately than they ever could.

That brings us to global warming. Even though quite a few scientists are now backtracking on their once-dire predictions of melting ice caps and worldwide flooding, *Algore* and a few hard-line doomsayers are sticking to their thermostats. *Algore* told the *Washington Times* on May 19, 1993: "That increased accumulations of greenhouse gases, particularly CO_2, cause global warming, there is no longer any serious debate. There are a few naysayers far outside the consensus who try to dispute that. They are not really taken seriously by the mainstream scientific community."

Yet we see in the last chapter that there is nothing resembling a consensus on this issue among scientists who have some expertise in the area. In fact, a majority does not believe global warming has occurred. A fact you never hear the environmentalist wacko crowd acknowledge is that 96 percent of the so-called "greenhouse" gases are not created by man, but by nature.

Panic, fear, dread, doom and gloom—that's what the environmental movement is about. When the ozone-hole theory is discarded, the wacko environmentalists will come up with some new crisis—cellular phones cause brain cancer, power lines cause leukemia, irradiation of food will nuke us. There is never any shortage of techno-phobic scenarios. How many have we heard already? Do the following eco-hysterics sound familiar?

- In ten years city dwellers will need gas masks to breathe.
- In a decade, America's mighty rivers will have reached the boiling point.
- In ten years all important animal life in the sea will be extinct. Large areas of coastline will have to be evacuated because of the stench of dead fish.
- Five years is all we have left if we are going to preserve any kind of quality in the world.

We hear wild claims like this every day from environmental wackos, right? Trouble is, these notable predictions weren't even made last week or last month or even last year. All of them were made more than twenty years ago. Believe it or not, their author is not Ted Danson. In fact, each of these doomsday forecasts were made on or before the very first Earth Day in 1970!

It was *Life* magazine that claimed our air would be so polluted by 1980 that we would need to wear gas masks. It was commentator Edwin Newman who was predicting boiling rivers. And it was the godfather of the modern environmental movement himself, Paul Ehrlich, who was responsible for the last two false prophecies. It's amazing that this movement has any credibility left after nearly a quarter-century of forecasting an imminent apocalypse and having nothing to show for it.

But when you examine the track record closely, it gets even worse. For example, back at the time of the first Earth Day, the big concern wasn't global warming, it was global cooling.

"If present trends continue, the world will be about four degrees colder for the global mean temperature in 1990, but eleven degrees colder by the year 2000," University of California professor Kenneth E. F. Watt told the assembled multitudes. "This is about twice what it would take to put us in an ice age."

This comment reflected the view of most environmentalists for years afterward. The winter of 1976–77 was one of the coldest in a century, so the environmentalists then were demanding immediate action to head off the coming ice age. We are now told that the exact same pollution they were blaming for the imminent ice age is about to cause the melting of the polar ice caps and a horrific global warming.

Yesterday it was an impending ice age, today it's the greenhouse effect. It doesn't really make any difference to the environmentalists as long as they have a crisis to push.

Former senator Tim Wirth, now undersecretary for global affairs and one of President Clinton's top advisers on environmental issues, explained it best to a newspaper reporter a few years ago when he said: "We've got to ride the global-warming issue. Even if the theory is wrong, we will be doing the right thing in terms of economic and environmental policy."

To Paul Ehrlich, even back in 1970, America was the problem. He called the American people "a cancer on the planet." Later, in 1990, he wrote an article published in the Environmental Media Association's newsletter, *EMA News,* titled simply: "Too Many Rich Folks." The problem with the environment worldwide, according to Ehrlich, is the Western way of life: capitalism, consumption, industry, and technology. If we would all just live like simple peasants, we might have a chance of restoring the Earth to its pristine state. Ehrlich's essay, which argues that the industrialized nations of the world—and particularly the United States—are destroying the Earth through exploitation and environmental degradation, is nothing short of a declaration of war on the rich.

"It is the rich who dump most of the carbon dioxide and chlorofluorocarbons into the atmosphere," he wrote. "It is the rich who generate acid rain. And the rich [who] are 'strip-mining' the seas and pushing the world toward a gigantic fisheries collapse. The oil staining the shores of Prince William Sound was intended for the gas-guzzling cars of North America. The agricultural technology of the rich is destroying soils and draining supplies of underground water around the globe. And the rich are wood-chipping many tropical forests in order to make cardboard to wrap around their electronic products."

Perhaps the most ironic part of this story is the fact that it appeared in the publication of an organization founded by Norman Lear to encourage the incorporation of anti-pollution themes in television programs and movies. For some reason, all this bashing of the rich goes over big with the folks in Beverly Hills and Bel Air. They don't take it personally in Hollywood. Hypocrisy has so totally enveloped the

Hollywood culture that they unconsciously exempt themselves from self-scrutiny.

To Ehrlich, meanwhile, a man who prophesied more than twenty years ago that all important sea-animal life would be extinct in ten years, the way to save humanity from pollution and death is to force mankind to live in abject poverty.

"Poor people don't use much energy, so they don't contribute much to the damage caused by mobilizing it," he writes. "The average Bangladeshi is not surrounded by plastic gadgets, the average Bolivian doesn't fly in jet aircraft, the average Kenyan farmer doesn't have a tractor or a pickup, the average Chinese does not have air conditioning or central heating in his apartment."

Mind you, none of these notions has persuaded Ehrlich himself to move to Bangladesh, Bolivia, Kenya, or China. In fact, Ehrlich has not even adopted the lifestyle of an average Bangladeshi, Bolivian, Kenyan, or Chinese. By all accounts, he lives quite comfortably in a very large air-conditioned house in the United States. He still flies in jet aircraft, rides in automobiles, and feeds himself with the fruits and vegetables harvested by American tractors.

No, it's not Paul Ehrlich's lifestyle that needs changing, you see, but that of all the rest of us greedy Westerners. You and I are the problem. Get this, for instance: "Based upon per-capita commercial energy use, a baby born in the United States represents twice the disaster for Earth as one born in Sweden or the USSR, three times one born in Italy, thirteen times one born in Brazil, thirty-five times one in India, 140 times one in Bangladesh or Kenya, and 280 times one in Chad, Rwanda, Haiti or Nepal. . . ." So, what are we supposed to do? Pack up our babies and move to Haiti? The last time I checked, Haiti's entire population was manufacturing cheap boats from the roofs of their homes to they could get the heck out of Haiti. Maybe they don't know what a valiant contribution they are making to the salvation of the world by staying. Also note his phraseology: Babies, the epitome of innocence and harmlessness, represent disaster. And they tell us they are for family values.

But the silliness continues even further.

"There are more than three times as many Indians as Americans, so, as a rough estimate, the United States contributes about ten times as much to the deterioration of Earth's life-support systems as does India," explains Ehrlich. "By the same standard, the United States has 300 times the negative impact on the world's environment and resources as

Bangladesh, and Sweden is twenty-five times more dangerous to our future than Kenya."

Ehrlich doesn't mention how all those environmentally correct Bangladeshis would survive without receiving care packages from the "dangerous" United States. But, then again, he probably doesn't care. People are the problem, as far as the environmental wackos are concerned. In their world, starvation, plagues, and death are blessings that simply buy more time for planet Earth. I've warned you before about the worldview of environmentalists. They are pantheistic; their God is an impersonal god, who resides passively in every fiber of the universe; to them, to destroy a plant is to destroy their god; to decimate the quality of human life, on the other hand, is of no concern, because humanity represents the greatest danger to the rest of creation.

How could so many people be fooled so badly? Only with the active complicity of a willing media or the stunning ignorance of a media blinded by political indoctrination and the scandalous misuse of our educational system. The environmentalists have even been allowed to set the terms of the debate by creating a new lexicon. They say "global" instead of "world." Why? Because "global" sounds smaller. You can visualize a globe in your hands. It's a much more finite term. They also prefer "planet" to "world." After all, we have all seen planets pictured in the pages of astronomy books. Again, it is a much more finite term. It's a little sphere. But "world" sounds

much bigger. It's a tougher sell to convince people that the world is going to be destroyed. Plus, "planet" reduces Earth to the level of all other planets in this solar system and others. Earth is to be given no extra points for housing human life.

Study Questions

1. If Limbaugh is right, why have some companies put so much effort into developing substitutes for CFCs, which deplete the ozone layer? Shouldn't we trust the free market, as he does, to indicate that there must be some problem that is worth this effort?

2. Why should we trust the free market any more or less than we trust democracy? If people democratically decide to focus heavily on some potential environmental hazards, why not respect that choice as much as we respect choices in the marketplace?

3. Is Limbaugh right to say that the ecosystem of the earth is not fragile? Recent studies show that many frogs are dying from ultraviolet radiation formerly screened by the ozone layer. Frog eggs that are unprotected from the sun's rays die at a 25 percent higher rate than protected eggs. Won't the shortfall of frogs cause ripple effects throughout the ecosystem, throwing it out of balance, e.g., by causing a huge increase in the number of insects that frogs eat?

99

The Threat of Acid Rain and the Ozone Hole

George Reiger

Editor's note: Reiger claims that all major environmental crises have four stages: (1) discovery; (2) acknowledgment of the crisis by a majority of the scientific community; (3) the press plays an increasingly important role by publishing each new scientific finding and each new example of environmental degradation; and (4) the public is persuaded that it will cost society far more to continue ignoring the problem than it will to try to do something about it. Reiger discusses the stages of acid rain and of ozone depletion.

All major environmental crises seem to go through four stages. The first is one of discovery. A research team or a solitary worker perceives a problem and begins accumulating data about its causes and effects. Acid rain historian Robert H. Boyle writes that "acid rain as such was first described as a local phenomenon in England in 1852 by Robert Angus Smith, who did his research in and around the city of Manchester. Smith blamed the sulfuric acid in the city air for the rusting of metals and the fading of colors in dyed goods."

The next stage occurs when the problem is acknowledged by a majority of the scientific community. In the case of acid rain, this took more than a century after Smith's initial work, but today's research has come to involve everyone from meteorologists to microbiologists.

As early as 1895, Norwegian observers began documenting a decline in fish populations in the southern lakes of their country, and as early as 1905, trout had vanished completely from several lakes where they had flourished before the industrial revolution. However, it wasn't until after World War II that Swedish soil, forestry, and meteorological scientists proved the connection between industrialization, acid rain, and the resulting deterioration of "downstream" air and water.

Still, as Bob Boyle writes, "a thundering silence" greeted the evidence. Additional findings in the 1950s and 1960s on both sides of the North Atlantic did little to alter public apathy. Most people seem to feel that since our modern economy depends on an ever-increasing human population educated from birth to be better consumers than citizens, and that since a visionary has not yet shown us how we can satisfy both our appetite for more things and our need for a healthy environment, we'll simply put off worrying about our need while catering to our appetite.

As long as pollution is reckoned to be a part of the cost of upward mobility and national security, people seem to display an amazing tolerance for degraded land, air, and water, even though scientists warn of the dangers of complacency.

It is at this stage in the evolution of the environmental crisis that the press begins to play an increasingly important role by publicizing each new scientific finding and each new example of environmental degradation. In the case of the present acid rain crisis, now in this third phase of development, concerned technicians and economists are placing increasing emphasis on the overall social cost of worsening air quality. Their understanding of the problem has moved many of them from positions of "scientific objectivity" to partisan commitment, and it is from such concerned scientists that we journalists get much of our information.

Actually, this third stage was entered a few years ago as more and more agricultural publications featured articles about the harm that acid rain causes plant life; architectural magazines began to concentrate on the damage inflicted by acid rain on buildings and historic monuments; and outdoor journals such as *Field & Stream* focused on the subtle harm of acid rain to gamefish fry, which need to feed on microorganisms and invertebrates that can no longer live in acidified watersheds. More recently, the equally harmful effects of acid rain on waterfowl production has also been recognized as a major cause in the decline of species that breed in areas hard hit by the high acidity.

At this stage, a businessman who is also a sportsman may not *want* to think about acid rain in his workaday existence, but he is increasingly *forced* to face the issue because of his interest in sport. He may tell himself for a while that the decline of black ducks and Atlantic salmon, for example, is due to many factors. But as we better regulate the commercial harvest of salmon or eliminate the incidental mortality of black ducks due to lead shot ingestion and still see these species declining, it becomes increasingly evident that acid rain is a major stumbling block to the restoration of any sport linked to productive fresh water. No matter how much money a businessman has, there is no place left in the Northern Hemisphere where he can find recreation that is not impacted to one degree or another by acid rain.

The final phase in the evolution of an environmental crisis comes about when the public is finally persuaded that it will cost society far more to continue ignoring the problem that it will to try to do something about it. We should be entering this phase now, except that first our political leaders and press must convince the public that something *can* be done about the problem. Unfortunately, so far as acid rain is concerned, the public is not yet convinced.

It does no good for conservationists to point to the partial restoration of the Great Lakes as an example of what can be done through a large-scale regional effort. The partial restoration of the Great Lakes was largely a matter of cleaning up point sources of pollution in selected areas of a relatively few states and provinces.

By contrast, although most sources of acid rain can also be pinpointed, they include petroleum-powered vehicles, coal-fired power plants, and Freon-associated refrigerators and air-conditioners. Unfortunately, every modern economy is based on a growing demand for transportation, refrigeration, and electricity. As the dream of safe and inexpensive nuclear power fades, and as the cost of oil again begins to climb, most nations will find themselves burning more coal which, with our presently inadequate anti-pollution devices, will mean more acid rain.

There is no longer any doubt that since the advent of the industrial age, carbon dioxide levels have risen everywhere in the world. The only question is how long it will take (or has it already occurred?) for the increasing levels of CO_2 to affect global climate, possibly causing polar ice caps to melt and flooding *billions* of people presently living on the coastal plains.

Likewise, there is no longer any doubt that ozone, which helps screen the earth from excessive solar radiation but which also damages many forms of life, is decreasing where it is most needed (in the stratosphere) and increasing where it is least wanted (in the troposphere, the lower reaches of the atmosphere). The only debate among scientists is whether the growing "ozone hole" above Antarctica is a result of industrial pollution or whether it is caused by a changing climate, perhaps resulting from the CO_2-inspired "greenhouse effect."

This debate seems as irrelevant as asking which came first, the chicken or the egg, since the point is that both chickens and eggs exist as well as, unfortunately, increasing CO_2 and decreasing atmospheric ozone.

Until recently, acid rain was perceived as exclusively a product of industrial smokestacks and vehicular exhaust pipes. Today, however, many atmospheric chemists suggest that acid rain is only one effect of a global alteration of the air we breathe.

"We see about a 2 percent increase in smog ozone from a 1 percent decrease in stratospheric ozone," says Gary Z. Whitten of Systems Applications Inc. of San Raphael, California. This suggests that the risks to plants, fish, wildlife, and human health from acid rain may be growing much faster than what is implied by the gradual increase of sulfur dioxide, nitrogen oxides, and other chemical pollutants in the atmosphere.

It also suggests that the escalating increase in the atmospheric production of hydrogen peroxide due to the increase of smog ozone will lead to dramatically increased acid rain over the next quarter century. Our children may look back on our presently poor air quality as a standard to which they aspire in their efforts to restore the environment.

Michael Gery, also with Systems Applications Inc., reports that there might be as much as "an 80 percent increase in hydrogen peroxide production for each 1 percent decrease in stratospheric ozone." If this is so, most other researchers have grossly underestimated not only the extent of our smog and acid rain dilemma, but the eventual cost of rehabilitation.

Indeed, much of the damage currently assumed to be the work of regional acid rain may actually be the result of stratospheric ozone depletion. Researchers at the Yale School of Forestry and at Michigan Technological University discovered a 16 to 19 percent stunting in growth of several key species of trees exposed to outdoor ozone levels well within the current federal air-quality limit. Such stunting is alarming to foresters around the world, not only because, as Deane Wang of the University of Washington's Center for Urban Horticulture in Seattle notes, ozone and acid-rain-damaged trees have less capacity than "normal" trees to resist stress—be it in the form of harsh weather, insects, or disease.

Although some people still insist that the entire acid rain issue is inconsequential—Dixy Lee Ray, former chairperson of the Atomic Energy Commission and former Governor of Washington State, recently wrote that "rainwater is *always acidic*, or if you like, acid rain is normal"—most scientists and engineers now argue over what can be done to alleviate the problem. So far, the consensus seems to be "not very much" as long as we continue with "business as usual."

What does this mean? Basically, the same thing it has meant for years. We must stop talking and begin to do what we can to eliminate sources of acid rain where we can. We must reduce the emission of acid rain precursors at smokestacks and exhaust pipes. However, this is not going to be easy.

Two years ago, David C. Pierce of Rome, New York, sent a letter to *Field & Stream*'s *Cheers & Jeers* pointing out that the electrostatic precipitators promoted by utility companies and the federal government as the surest way to reduce air pollution were actually contributing to greater unseen air pollution by removing the soot and fly ash that had formerly helped neutralize much of the acid-forming oxides generated by coal burning.

When this letter was brought to the attention of the Environmental Protection Agency, administrators indicated that they were officially skeptical about the existence of acid rain and felt cleaning up the visible problems of soot and ash was sufficient. This Administration continues to trickle a few million dollars a year into "more research" on whether or not there is a problem in order to avoid spending the billions of dollars that an increasing army of scientists feels must eventually be spent to correct the rapidly escalating problem of air pollution. . . . For example, the U.S. Forest Service provided a grant, which could eventually amount to $1.7 million, to Penn State University to study the effects of acid rain on Pennsylvanian forests over the next four years.

We don't need any more redundant research designed to muzzle scientists and placate critics. And we don't need any more cosmetic solutions like electrostatic precipitators. Had we spent as much time studying the viability of space exploration as we have in reconfirming what researchers understood about acid rain half a century ago, we would still be contemplating a mission to the moon!

Surely a nation that has sent space probes to the farthest reaches of the solar system can come up with an effective way to remove the oxides of sulfur and nitrogen from industrial exhausts. And surely a nation that is now planning manned missions to Mars can find some substitute for Freon in refrigerators and air conditioners.

Of course, we must demand greater knowledge and better conscience from our politicians and journalists about what's at stake. So long as our opinion makers do not question the traditional parameters of Gross National Production, we will go on thinking that paving more farm fields for more roads for more cars and clearing more woods and filling more swamps for more housing is our only proper course when it is now abundantly clear that short-term profit and convenience lead to long-term environmental decay and human disease.

Can something be done about atmospheric pollution and acid rain?

Yes, but not so long as we keep on spending our research dollars on studies of the problem rather than searches for some solutions, and imagining that there is no middle road between mindless mass production and economic stagnation.

Obviously, we cannot return to a "state of nature," free of cars, power plants, air conditioners, and the like. Our entire society is built around these technological entities. But we must recognize the damage being done by the residues of this technology, and put all our intelligence and resources to work finding less harmful substitutes or remedies.

First, however, it must be acknowledged that a problem exists, and that a "middle road" solution can be sought. Judging by the amount of official foot-dragging that has been going on for years, getting any real movement on this issue will be difficult. Yet with enough pressure from ordinary citizens it can be done. The sooner all of us move into the final stage of environmental awareness, the sooner the job of rehabilitating our fragile atmospheric envelope can begin.

Study Questions

*1. Would you like every product to be taxed so that its price included payment for what it indirectly costs society? For example, should the price of cigarettes be raised so that smokers pay for the added medical costs they incur? Should gasoline taxes be increased so that motorists bear the costs of pollution and acid rain?

2. Why do the media not seem to cover the problem of acid rain as much today as they did several years ago? Is it because more pressing or more recently recognized problems such as ozone depletion and global warming are more newsworthy? What do you think our most serious environmental problem is?

100

State Department of Environmental Protection v. Ventron Corp.

Supreme Court of New Jersey

This appeal concerns the responsibility of various corporations for the cost of the cleanup and removal of mercury pollution seeping from a 40-acre tract of land into Berry's Creek, a tidal estuary of the Hackensack River that flows through the Meadowlands. The plaintiff is the State of New Jersey, Department of Environmental Protection (DEP); the primary defendants are Velsicol Chemical Corporation (Velsicol), its former subsidiary, Wood Ridge Chemical Corporation (Wood Ridge), and Ventron Corporation (Ventron), into which Wood Ridge was merged. . . .

Beneath its surface, the tract is saturated by an estimated 268 tons of toxic waste, primarily mercury. For a stretch of several thousand feet, the concentration of mercury in Berry's Creek is the highest found in fresh water sediments in the world. The waters of the creek are contaminated by the compound methyl mercury, which continues to be released as the mercury interacts with other elements. Due to depleted oxygen levels, fish no longer inhabit Berry's Creek, but are present only when swept in by the tide and, thus, irreversibly toxified.

The contamination at Berry's Creek results from mercury processing operations carried on at the site for almost fifty years. In March, 1976, DEP filled a complaint against Ventron, Wood Ridge, Velsicol, Berk, and the Wolfs, charging them with violating the "New Jersey Water Quality Improvement Act of 1971," and further, with creating or maintaining a nuisance. . . .

After a fifty-five-day trial, the trial court determined that Berk and Wood Ridge were jointly liable for the cleanup and removal of the mercury;

[and] that Velsicol and Ventron were severally liable for half of the costs; . . .

The Appellate Division substantially affirmed the judgment, but modified it in several respects, including the imposition of joint and several liability on Ventron and Velsicol for all costs incurred in the cleanup and removal of the mercury pollution in Berry's Creek. . . . We modify and affirm the judgment of the Appellate Division.

I

From 1929 to 1960, first as lessee and then as owner of the entire forty-acre tract, Berk operated a mercury processing plant, dumping untreated waste material and allowing mercury-laden effluent to drain on the tract. Berk continued uninterrupted operations until 1960, at which time it sold its assets to Wood Ridge and ceased its corporate existence.

In 1960, Velsicol formed Wood Ridge as a wholly-owned subsidiary for the sole purpose of purchasing Berk's assets and operating the mercury processing plant. . . . Wood Ridge continued to operate the processing plant on the 7.1-acre tract from 1960 to 1968, when Velsicol sold Wood Ridge to Ventron. . . .

In 1968, Velsicol sold 100% of the Wood Ridge stock to Ventron, which began to consider a course of treatment for plant wastes. Until this time, the waste had been allowed to course over the land through open drainage ditches. In March 1968, Ventron engaged the firm of Metcalf & Eddy to study the effects of mercury on the land, and three months later, Ventron constructed a weir to aid in monitoring the effluent. . . .

In 1970, the contamination at Berry's Creek came to the attention of the United States Environmental Protection Agency (EPA), which conducted a test of Wood Ridge's waste water. The tests indicated that the effluent carried two to four pounds of mercury into Berry's Creek each day. . . .

On February 5, 1974, Wood Ridge granted to Robert Wolf, a commercial real estate developer, an option to purchase the 7.1-acre tract on which the plant was located, and on May 20, 1974, Ventron conveyed the tract to the Wolfs. The Wolfs planned to demolish the plant and construct a warehousing facility. In the course of the demolition, mercury-contaminated water was used to wet down the structures and allowed to run into the creek. The problem

94 N.J. 473 (1983). Opinion presented by Justice J. Pollock.

came to the attention of DEP, which ordered a halt to the demolition, pending adequate removal or containment of the contamination. DEP proposed a containment plan, but the Wolfs implemented another plan and proceeded with their project. DEP then instituted this action. . . .

The trial court concluded that the entire tract and Berry's Creek are polluted and that additional mercury from the tract has reached, and may continue to reach, the creek via ground and surface waters. Every operator of the mercury processing plant contributed to the pollution; while the plant was in operation, the discharge of effluent resulted in a dangerous and hazardous mercurial content in Berry's Creek. The trial court found that from 1960–74 the dangers of mercury were becoming better known and that Berk, Wood Ridge, Velsicol, and Ventron knew of those dangers. . . .

II

The lower courts imposed strict liability on Wood Ridge under common-law principles for causing a public nuisance and for "unleashing a dangerous substance during nonnatural use of the land." . . .

Twenty-one years ago, without referring to either *Marshall v. Welwood* or *Rylands v. Fletcher*, this Court adopted the proposition that "an ultrahazardous activity which introduces an unusual danger into the community . . . should pay its own way in the event it actually causes damage to others." *Berg v. Reaction Motors Div., Thiokol Chem. Corp.,* . . . (1962). . . .

We believe it is time to recognize expressly that the law of liability has evolved so that a landowner is strictly liable to others for harm caused by toxic wastes that are stored on his property and flow onto the property of others. Therefore, we . . . adopt the principle of liability originally declared in *Rylands v. Fletcher*. The net result is that those who use, or permit others to use, land for the conduct of abnormally dangerous activities are strictly liable for resultant damages. . . .

Under the *Restatement [(Second) of Torts]* analysis, whether an activity is abnormally dangerous is to be determined on a case-by-case basis, taking all relevant circumstances into consideration. As set forth in the *Restatement*:

> In determining whether an activity is abnormally dangerous, the following factors are to be considered:

a. existence of a high degree of risk of some harm to the person, land or chattels of others;
b. likelihood that the harm that results from it will be great;
c. inability to eliminate the risk by the exercise of reasonable care;
d. extent to which the activity is not a matter of common usage;
e. inappropriateness of the activity to the place where it is carried on; and
f. extent to which its value to the community is outweighed by its dangerous attributes.

Pollution from toxic wastes that seeps onto the land of others and into streams necessarily harms the environment. . . . The lower courts found that each of those hazards was present as a result of the contamination of the entire tract. . . . With respect to the ability to eliminate the risks involved in disposing of hazardous wastes by the exercise of reasonable care, no safe way exists to dispose of mercury by simply dumping it onto land or into water. . . .

Even if they did not intend to pollute or adhered to the standards of the time, all of these parties remain liable. Those who poison the land must pay for its cure.

We approve the trial court's finding that Berk, Wood Ridge, Velsicol, and Ventron are liable under common-law principles for the abatement of the resulting nuisance and damage. . . .

III

We agree with the trial court's finding that both Berk and Wood Ridge violated the statute by intentionally permitting mercury-laden effluent to escape onto the land surrounding Berry's Creek. . . .

In an appropriate exercise of its original jurisdiction under R. 2:10–5, the Appellate Division found that the record overwhelmingly supported the conclusion that the mercury pollution in Berry's Creek and the surrounding area presented a substantial and imminent threat to the environment, thus satisfying the requirement for a retroactive application of the act. Our independent analysis leads us to the same conclusion. Thus, we find Berk, Wood Ridge, and Velsicol liable under the Spill Act. Ventron is liable because it expressly assumed the liabilities of Wood Ridge in their merger. . . .

As amended, the Spill Act provides: "Any person who has discharged a hazardous substance or is in any way responsible for any hazardous substance

... shall be strictly liable, jointly and severally, without regard to fault, for all clean up and removal costs." ... g(c) (emphasis added). ...

From 1967 to 1974, and thereafter, Velsicol could have controlled the dumping of mercury onto its own thirty-three-acre tract. By permitting Wood Ridge, even after it became a Ventron subsidiary in 1968, to use that tract as a mercury dump, Velsicol made possible the seepage of hazardous wastes into Berry's Creek. Furthermore, from 1960 to 1968, Velsicol was the sole shareholder of Wood Ridge and all members of the Wood Ridge Board of Directors were Velsicol employees. Velsicol personnel, officers, and directors were involved in the day-to-day operation of Wood Ridge. In addition to constant involvement in Wood Ridge's activities, Velsicol permitted the dumping of waste material on the thirty-three-acre tract. When viewed together, those facts compel a finding that Velsicol was "responsible" within the meaning of the Spill Act for the pollution that occurred from 1960 to 1968. ...

Through the merger of Wood Ridge into Ventron, the latter corporation assumed all of Wood Ridge's liabilities, including those arising out of the pollution of Berry's Creek. ... Ventron, however, did not assume Velsicol's liability.

Pursuant to the mandate of the Spill Act, ... Berk, Wood Ridge, Velsicol, and Ventron are jointly and severally liable without regard to fault. Only Ventron and Velsicol remain in existence and we affirm that portion of the Appellate Division judgment that holds them jointly and severally liable for the cleanup and removal of mercury from the Berry's Creek area.

IV

... As modified, the judgment of the Appellate Division is affirmed.

Study Questions

*1. If a powerful corporation thwarted all your legal efforts to stop it from dumping toxic chemicals into a stream near your home, would you be more likely to sell your home, try to live with the situation, or do something else?

2. Did the court reach a decision that is most morally acceptable? Which moral principles would support the court's decision and which would oppose it? Why?

101

The Case of the Exxon Valdez Oil Spill

Associated Press

Exxon's $1 billion penalty settlement for the 1989 oil spill in Alaska's Prince William Sound has—at least until recently—been squandered, with little lasting benefit to the public, according to a federal government study being released today.

Nearly 15 percent of the money has been spent to reimburse government agencies and Exxon itself for expenses, the General Accounting Office reported.

"The report documents that the past (Bush) administration failed to assure that the Exxon Valdez funds were used wisely to protect natural resources that were affected by the oil spill. Instead, the bureaucrats gave top priority to feathering their own nests with reimbursements and gold-plated studies of questionable merit," said Rep. George Miller, D-Pleasant Hill, chairman of the House Interior Committee.

Over the objections of environmentalists, the fishing industry, and Eskimos and other native people of Alaska, the governments of Alaska and the United States agreed in October 1991 to settle damages with Exxon for $900 million in civil penalties and $126 million in criminal fines. The money, which will be paid out over 11 years, is administered by government trustees supposedly to restore the coastal waters of south-central Alaska.

As of December 1992, the GAO reported, $107 million was paid out to government agencies as reimbursement for spill-related activities. About $40 million more was offset against Exxon's fines to cover cleanup costs incurred by the oil company in 1991, as provided in the terms of the settlement. And $19 million more was spent for various government administrative costs and damage assessments.

These expenditures have been reported previously. But the GAO report and Miller's harsh critique will no doubt add to the already noisy clamor over how to spend the remaining money.

In a written statement prepared to accompany release of the report, Miller acknowledged that the trustees themselves, including Alaska Attorney General Charles Cole and representatives of the Clinton administration recently have taken steps to "improve management" of the funds.

In particular, Cole has joined with coastal residents and environmentalists and pushed to spend more of the money to acquire lands in Prince William Sound to prevent further degradation from logging or development.

So far this year, $39 million has been appropriated for land acquisition in an area known as Seal Bay on Afognak Island, and $7 million more for land near Homer that was threatened by logging.

Interior Secretary Bruce Babbitt and other top officials are in Alaska and are scheduled to attend a meeting today of the trustee council. Environmentalists said they expect a strong expression of support for land acquisition.

In a related development, the Associated Press reported that fishermen agreed Sunday in Anchorage to lift a blockade keeping oil tankers from the trans-Alaska pipeline terminal. They called off the blockade after Babbitt promised more help for the oil-spill recovery effort.

Study Questions

*1. If a foreign nation refused to stop dumping dangerous wastes into the ocean, what—if all else failed—would be the most drastic or dramatic step you would favor taking to stop them?

2. Since Exxon is a multinational corporation with assets greater than those of most countries, should Exxon be treated any more gingerly than the foreign nation in the immediately preceding question?

102

The Case of the Killer Smog of 1952: In Four Days 4,000 Died in London

William Wise

". . . the London fog of December, 1952, was no strange new phenomenon. It was no acute epidemic caused by a hitherto unrecognized virus nor was it a visitation of some known pathogen against which we had no defence. It was simply the occurrence of a well known meteorological phenomenon in an area where the toxic products of combustion are vomited in excess into the air . . ."

—The Medical Officer, February 14, 1953

One blustery morning in late November, 1966, I found myself at London Airport, boarding a plane for the United States and home. I'd been in England a number of weeks, a writer gathering information about the notorious London smog of December, 1952. Most of the people I'd interviewed had been patient and helpful. A few had also been openly skeptical.

Why, the doubters had wanted to know, was I investigating London's "Killer Smog" of a decade-and-a-half before? Would the story of that landmark disaster be likely to prove very meaningful to an American audience? Was smog of much concern to my fellow countrymen? They were only asking me because—well, surely in the States, with the exception of Los Angeles, of course—we Americans didn't really *have* any smog, did we?

The doubters should have been aboard my plane later in the day. Approaching Kennedy Airport, in New York, we were told there would be a half-hour's delay in landing. Puzzled, I raised the plastic window shade and peered out.

We were flying at about two thousand feet, through a curiously greasy-looking and pervasive haze. The ground could just be made out below—cars, roads, houses, all dim but visible.

Then we began to climb. In less than a minute the ground had vanished. Cars, roads, houses, the very earth itself had been blotted out. We were circling in bright sunlight, above an apparently limitless bank of opaque, polluted air. The smog extended to the horizon in every direction. At a distance, the slanting rays of the sun gave it a coppery, rather handsome appearance. Nearer at hand it merely looked yellow and ugly, like nothing so much as a vast and unappetizing sea of chicken soup.

Such was the air which the people of New York, Connecticut, and New Jersey were compelled to breathe for three consecutive days and nights during Thanksgiving weekend, 1966. Newly born infants, the old, the infirm—all were subjected to a poisoned atmosphere which at one measuring station contained five times the "normal" level of sulfur dioxide. At the same station smoke and deadly carbon monoxide were recorded in amounts above the "danger" level.

Nor was this the first acute air pollution episode the area's inhabitants had experienced. In 1953, an estimated 240 people had been killed in New York City alone by a similar mass of stagnant, filthy air; a decade later more than 400 excess deaths were reported in the city during a five-day smog. In neither instance was there any way of calculating how many additional victims had been killed in other communities along America's East Coast or how many thousands, from Washington, D.C., in the south, to Massachusetts in the north, had been made severely ill.

Was smog of much concern to my fellow countrymen . . .? Eight months prior to New York's Thanksgiving Smog of 1966, Dr. Walter Orr Roberts, director of America's National Center for Atmospheric Research, had spoken of the imminent likelihood of an air pollution disaster taking place somewhere in the world which would kill as many as ten thousand people. Almost any large industrial center, the doctor had said, might well provide the setting for such a deadly smog. Particularly vulnerable foreign cities included London; Hamburg, Germany; and Santiago, Chile; in the United States, Los Angeles and New York were the most obvious candidates.

Shortly before the Thanksgiving smog, Dr. Roberts was asked whether he believed that *many* of America's cities were vulnerable to a disaster similar to London's great killer smog of 1952. "Yes," he replied, "I have been worried . . . that we might wake

Reprinted from *Killer Smog* (New York: Ballantine Books, 1968), pp. 2–5.

up some morning in some major city to an unusual meteorological situation . . . that prevented the air from circulating . . . and that we might find thousands of people dead as the result of the air they were forced to breathe in that smog situation."

Why, the doubters had wanted to know, was I investigating London's killer smog of a decade-and-a-half before? Surely in the States, we Americans didn't really have any smog, did we . . . ?

Anyone aboard a plane arriving in New York on the twenty-third of November would have been able to answer for himself.

Study Questions

*1. Who would you punish more harshly: someone who knowingly dumped chemicals likely to cause a number of cancer deaths, or someone who fatally shot a person in a brawl?

2. Whom do you think our society actually punishes more harshly per death, the white-collar polluter or the blue-collar mugger?

3. Why have the media been so quiet about this tragedy from 1952? Have you ever seen any news footage of this disaster?

103

We All Live in Bhopal: The Case of Union Carbide and More

David Watson

Editor's note: Watson gives many statistics to paint a portrait of many toxic hazards. He focuses on the large-scale tragedy of Union Carbide's plant in Bhopal. About 3,000 people were killed and another 20,000 people were permanently blinded or otherwise permanently disabled by Union Carbide's industrial plant. Watson goes on to argue that the Green Revolution, which led many Third World countries to become self-sufficient in food, is actually a nightmare except for dictators and the rich.

The cinders of the funeral pyres at Bhopal were still warm, and the mass graves still fresh, but the media prostitutes of the corporations have already begun their homilies in defense of industrialism and its uncounted horrors. Some 3,000 people were slaughtered in the wake of the deadly gas cloud, and 20,000 will remain permanently disabled. The poison gas left a 25 square mile swath of dead and dying, people and animals, as it drifted southeast away from the Union Carbide factory. "We thought it was a plague," said one victim. Indeed it was: a chemical plague, an *industrial plague.*

Ashes, ashes, all fall down!

A terrible, unfortunate, "accident," we are reassured by the propaganda apparatus for Progress, for History, for "Our Modern Way of Life." A price, of course, has to be paid—since the risks are necessary to ensure a higher Standard of Living, a Better Way of Life.

Reprinted from *The Fifth Estate* (Winter 1985), pp. 1, 7. Reprinted by permission. This reading originally appeared under the pen name George Bradford.

The *Wall Street Journal*, tribune of the bourgeoisie, editorialized, "It is worthwhile to remember that the Union Carbide insecticide plant and the people surrounding it were where they were for compelling reasons. India's agriculture is thriving, bringing a better life to millions of rural people, and partly because of the use of modern agricultural technology that includes applications of insect killers." The indisputable fact of life, according to this sermon, is that universal recognition that India, like everyone else, "needs" technology. Calcutta-style scenes of human deprivation can be replaced as fast as the country imports the benefits of the West's industrial revolution and market economics." So, despite whatever dangers are involved, "the benefits outweigh the costs." (Dec. 13, 1984)

The *Journal* was certainly right in one regard—the reasons for the plant and the people's presence there were certainly compelling: capitalist market relations and technological invasion are as compelling as a hurricane to the small communities from which these people were uprooted. It conveniently failed to notice, however, that countries like India do not import the *benefits* of industrial capitalism; those benefits are *exported* in the form of loan repayments to fill the coffers of the bankers and corporate vampires who read the *Wall Street Journal* for the latest news of their investments. The Indians only take the risks and pay the costs; in fact, for them, as for the immiserated masses of people living in shantytowns of the Third World, there are no risks, only certain hunger and disease, only the certainty of death squad revenge for criticizing the state of things as they are.

Green Revolution a Nightmare

In fact, the Calcutta-style misery is the result of Third World industrialization and the so-called industrial "Green Revolution" in agriculture. The Green Revolution, which was to revolutionize agriculture in the "backward" countries and produce greater crop yields, has only been a miracle for the banks, corporations and military dictatorships who defend them. The influx of fertilizers, technology, insecticides and bureaucratic administration exploded millennia-old rural economies based on subsistence farming, creating a class of wealthier farmers dependent upon western technologies to produce cash crops such as coffee, cotton and wheat for export, while the vast majority of farming communities were destroyed by capitalist market competition and sent like refugees into the growing cities. These victims, paralleling the destroyed peasantry of Europe's Industrial Revolution several hundred years before, joined either the permanent underclass of unemployed and underemployed slumdwellers eking out a survival on the tenuous margins of civilization, or became proletariat fodder in the Bhopals, Sao Paulos and Djakartas of an industrializing world—an industrializing process, like all industrialization in history, paid for by the pillage of nature and human beings in the countryside.

Food production goes up in some cases, of course, because the measure is only quantitative—some foods disappear while others are produced year round, even for export. *But subsistence is destroyed.* Not only does the rural landscape begin to suffer the consequences of constant crop production and use of chemicals, but the masses of people—laborers on the land and in the teeming hovels growing around the industrial plants—go hungrier in a vicious cycle of exploitation, while the wheat goes abroad to buy absurd commodities and weapons.

But subsistence is culture as well: culture is destroyed with subsistence, and people are further trapped in the technological labyrinth. The ideology of progress is there, blared louder than ever by those with something to hide, a cover-up for plunder and murder on levels never before witnessed.

Industrialization of the Third World

The industrialization of the Third World is a story familiar to anyone who takes even a glance at what is occurring. The colonial countries are nothing but a dumping ground and a pool of cheap labor for capitalist corporations. Obsolete technology is shipped there along with the production of chemicals, medicines and other products banned in the developed world. Labor is cheap, there are few if any safety standards, and *costs are cut.* But the formula of cost-benefit still stands: the costs are simply borne by others, by the victims of Union Carbide, Dow, and Standard Oil.

Chemicals found to be dangerous and banned in the US and Europe are produced instead overseas—DDT is a well-known example of an enormous number of such products, such as the unregistered pesticide Leptophos exported by the Velsicol Corporation to Egypt which killed and injured many Egyptian farmers in the mid-1970s. Other products are simply dumped on Third World markets, like the mercury-tainted wheat which led to the death of as many as 5,000 Iraqis in 1972, wheat which had been imported from the US. Another example was the wanton contamination of Nicaragua's Lake Managua by a chlorine and caustic soda factory owned by Pennwalt Corporation and other investors, which caused a major outbreak of mercury poisoning in a primary source of fish for people living in Managua.

Union Carbide's plant at Bhopal did not even meet US safety standards according to its own safety inspector, but a UN expert on international corporate behavior told the *New York Times*, "A whole list of factors is not in place to insure adequate industrial safety" throughout the Third World. "Carbide is not very different from any other chemical company in this regard." According to the *Times*, "In a Union Carbide battery plant in Jakarta, Indonesia, more than half the workers had kidney damage from mercury exposure. In an asbestos cement factory owned by the Manville Corporation 200 miles west of Bhopal, workers in 1981 were routinely covered with asbestos dust, a practice that would never be tolerated here." (12/9/84)

Some 22,500 people are killed every year by exposure to insecticides—a much higher percentage of them in the Third World than use of such chemicals would suggest. Many experts decried the lack of an "industrial culture" in the "underdeveloped" countries as a major cause of accidents and contamination. But where an "industrial culture" thrives, is the situation really much better?

Industrial Culture and Industrial Plague

In the advanced industrial nations an "industrial culture" (and little other) exists. Have such disasters been avoided as the claims of these experts would lead us to believe?

Another event of such mammoth proportions as those of Bhopal would suggest otherwise—in that case, industrial pollution killed some 4,000 people in a large population center. That was London, in 1952, when several days of "normal" pollution accumulated in the stagnant air to kill and permanently injure thousands of Britons.

Then there are the disasters closer to home or to memory, for example, the Love Canal (still leaking into the Great Lakes water system), or the massive dioxin contaminations at Seveso, Italy, and Times

Creek, Missouri, where thousands of residents had to be permanently evacuated. And there is the Berlin and Farro dump at Swartz Creek, Michigan, where C-56 (a pesticide by-product of Love Canal fame) hydrochloric acid and cyanide from Flint auto plants had accumulated. "They think we're not scientists and not even educated," said one enraged resident, "but anyone who's been in high school knows that cyanide and hydrochloric acid is what they mixed to kill the people in the concentration camps."

A powerful image: industrial civilization as one vast, stinking extermination camp. We all live in Bhopal, some closer to the gas chambers and to the mass graves, but all of us close enough to be victims. And Union Carbide is obviously not a fluke—the poisons are vented into the air and water, dumped in rivers, ponds and streams, fed to animals going to market, sprayed on lawns and roadways, sprayed on food crops, every day, everywhere. The result may not be as dramatic as Bhopal (which then almost comes to serve as a *diversion*, a deterrence machine to take our minds off the pervasive reality which Bhopal truly represents), but it is as deadly. When ABC News asked University of Chicago professor of public health and author of *The Politics of Cancer*, Jason Epstein, if he thought a Bhopal-style disaster could occur in the US, he replied: "I think what we're seeing in America is far more slow—not such large accidental occurrences, but a slow, gradual leakage with the result that you have excess cancers or reproductive abnormalities."

In fact, birth defects have doubled in the last 25 years. And cancer is on the rise. In an interview with the *Guardian*, Hunter College professor David Kotelchuck described the "Cancer Atlas" maps published in 1975 by the Department of Health, Education and Welfare. "Show me a red spot on these maps and I'll show you an industrial center of the US," he said. "There aren't any place names on the maps but you can easily pick out concentrations of industry. See, it's not Pennsylvania that's red it's just Philadelphia, Erie and Pittsburgh. Look at West Virginia here, there's only two red spots, the Kanawha Valley, where there are nine chemical plants including Union Carbide's, and this industrialized stretch of the Ohio River. It's the same story wherever you look."

There are 50,000 toxic waste dumps in the United States. The EPA admits that *ninety per cent* of the 90 billion pounds of toxic waste produced annually by US industry (70 per cent of it by chemical companies) is disposed of "improperly" (although we wonder what they would consider "proper" disposal).

These deadly products of industrial civilization—arsenic, mercury, dioxin, cyanide, and many others—are simply dumped, "legally" and "illegally," wherever convenient to industry. Some 66,000 different compounds are used in industry. Nearly a billion tons of pesticides and herbicides comprising 225 different chemicals were produced in the US last year, and an additional 79 million pounds were imported. Some two per cent of chemical compounds have been tested for side effects. There are 15,000 chemical plants in the United States, daily manufacturing mass death.

All of the dumped chemicals are leaching into our water. Some three to four thousand wells, depending on which government agency you ask, are contaminated or closed in the US. In Michigan alone, 24 municipal water systems have been contaminated, and a thousand sites have suffered major contamination. According to the Detroit *Free Press*, "The final toll could be as many as 10,000 sites" in Michigan's "water wonderland" alone (April 15, 1984).

And the coverups go unabated here as in the Third World. One example is that of dioxin; during the proceedings around Agent Orange investigations, it came out that Dow Chemical had lied all along about the effects of dioxin. Despite research findings that dioxin is "exceptionally toxic" with "a tremendous potential for producing chlor-acne and systemic injury," Dow's top toxicologist, V. K. Rowe, wrote in 1965, "We are not in any way attempting to hide our problems under a heap of sand. But we certainly do not want to have any situations arise which will cause the regulatory agencies to become restrictive."

Now Vietnam suffers a liver cancer epidemic and a host of cancers and health problems caused by the massive use of Agent Orange there during the genocidal war waged by the US. The sufferings of the US veterans are only a drop in the bucket. And dioxin is appearing everywhere in our environment as well, in the form of recently discovered "dioxin rain."

Going to the Village

When the Indian authorities and Union Carbide began to process the remaining gases in the Bhopal plant, thousands of residents fled, despite the reassurances of the authorities. The *New York Times* quoted one old man who said, "They are not believing the scientists or the state government or anybody.

They only want to save their lives."

The same reporter wrote that one man had gone to the train station with his goats, "hoping that he could take them with him—anywhere, as long as it was away from Bhopal" (Dec. 14, 1984). The same old man quoted above told the reporter, "All the public has gone to the village." The reporter explained that "going to the village" is what Indians do when trouble comes.

A wise and age-old strategy for survival by which little communities always renewed themselves when bronze, iron and golden empires with clay feet fell to their ruin. But subsistence has been and is everywhere being destroyed, and with it, culture. What are we to do when there is no village to go to? When we all live in Bhopal, and Bhopal is everywhere? The comments of two women, one a refugee from Times Creek, Missouri, and another from Bhopal, come to mind. The first woman said of her former home, "This was a nice place once. Now we have to bury it." The other woman said, "Life cannot come back. Can the government pay for the lives? Can you bring those people back?"

The corporate vampires are guilty of greed, plunder, murder, slavery, extermination and devastation. And we should avoid any pang of sentimentalism when the time comes for them to pay for their crimes against humanity and the natural world. But we will have to go beyond them, to ourselves: subsistence, and with it culture, has been destroyed. We have to find our way back to the village, out of industrial civilization, out of this exterminist system.

The Union Carbides, the Warren Andersons, the "optimistic experts" and the lying propagandists all must go, but with them must go the pesticides, the herbicides, the chemical factories and the chemical way of life which is nothing but death.

Because this is Bhopal, and it is all we've got. This "once nice place" can't be simply buried for us to move on to another pristine beginning. The empire is collapsing. We must find our way back to the village, or as the North American natives say, "back to the blanket," and we must do this not by trying to save an industrial civilization which is doomed, but in the renewal of life which must take place in its ruin. By throwing off this Modern Way of Life, we won't be "giving things up" or sacrificing, but throwing off a terrible burden. Let us do so soon before we are crushed by it.

Study Questions

1. Does the "Killer Smog" discussed in the previous essay reinforce Watson's point that we all live in Bhopal?

2. Do we, in any meaningful sense, all live in Bhopal?

*3. After testing for radon, you discover your home is too hazardous to live in; furthermore, since your insurance doesn't cover such a thing, the house will become worthless as soon as the contamination is revealed. If you knew you could destroy the test results and sell the house without anyone ever knowing what had occurred, would you do so?

4. Is the Green Revolution really a nightmare except for dictators and the rich?

5. How can you protect yourself and those you care about from a large cloud of poison gas drifting over your home town? Isn't it too late once such a cloud is released? Is the best protection to engage yourself in politics and elections in order to support environmental protection agencies and stronger laws?

104

The High Cost of High Tech:
The Dark Side of the Chip

Lenny Siegel
John Markoff

The belt of industrial communities at the southern edge of San Francisco Bay universally symbolizes the promise of the microelectronics era. It was first called Silicon Valley in the early 1970s, when manufacturers of silicon chips became the Santa Clara Valley's major employers. The Valley is home to the greatest concentration of high-tech professionals and enterprises in the world. It is land where the information-rich, particularly those trained in science and technology, can make both their mark and their millions.

Though Silicon Valley is in many ways unique, planners, officials, and commercial interests throughout the country see the area as a model for industrial growth in the information age. While few other areas can hope to rival the Valley, many have already attracted their share of high-tech facilities. As high tech grows, they will learn the harsh truth behind the legends of Silicon Valley.

Many of the Valley's problems are directly caused by high tech. Others are found elsewhere, but they are significant merely because the residents of would-be Silicon Valleys have been told that the electronics industry has no serious problems. If they study the lessons of the Valley, they can avoid many of the pitfalls of high-tech growth.

"Maria," a 26-year-old political refugee from Argentina, found work in Silicon Valley, but she did not strike gold. She quit her $4.10 an hour production job at Memorex to have her first baby. For two years, she illegally stuffed and soldered thousands of printed circuit (PC) boards in her home. Her employer, a middle-aged woman she calls "Lady," sub-

Reprinted from *Clinton Quarterly* (Fall 1985), pp. 8–9. Reprinted by permission.

contracted assembly work from big firms—so Maria was told—like Apple and Memorex.

Maria gladly accepted the low piece-rate work because child care would have eaten up most of her after-tax earnings at a full-time job. She quit, however, when Lady asked her to wash her assembled boards by dipping them into a panful of solvent, heated on her kitchen stove. Maria, unlike most Silicon Valley cottage workers, had studied chemistry before immigrating into the US and she knew that the hydrocarbon fumes could make her young son, crawling around on the kitchen floor, seriously ill.

Lady contracts with about a hundred minority women, primarily immigrants and refugees from Latin America, Korea, and Indochina. Although semiconductor chips are fabricated with precise machinery in super-clean rooms, they can be attached by hand, anywhere, to the printed circuit boards that form the heart of most computer equipment.

Silicon Valley's workforce is sharply stratified. In the electronics industry, pay, status, and responsibility are primarily a function of education. The professionals who make the Valley unique sit at the top of the occupational ladder; they are paid well, and the ambitious among them can make millions. Most are white men, but Japanese-Americans and ethnic Chinese are over-represented as well.

The world of Silicon Valley's managers and professionals is centered in northern Santa Clara County, near Stanford University and the historical center of the Valley's high-tech industry. Unlike the white-collar workers who commute to America's established downtown areas, Silicon Valley's affluent have chosen to live near their place of work. Other new, high-tech centers appear to be developing along a remarkably similar pattern.

Since Stanford University established its Industrial Park in 1951, high-tech companies have clustered near the university. The Industrial Park, on Stanford-owned land just a mile from the academic campus, established standards for industrial development in Silicon Valley, and it is still considered a model throughout North America. For three decades, its low-slung buildings, innovative architecture, and expanses of green landscape perpetuated the belief that high tech was a clean industry and a good neighbor. The suburbs around Stanford have long been known for their attractive living environment and good schools; and commuting, even before the 1973 rise in oil prices, was uncomfortable, costly, and time-consuming. So professional workers generally bought homes or rented as close to work as possible.

As the Valley boomed, its industrial core spread, but until the 1980s this core was for the most part confined to the northern, suburban portion. Like their predecessors, the engineers, scientists, and managers who came to the Valley from all over the world settled near their jobs. This influx of high-income families drove up the cost of housing. By the 1970s, rents and prices in the Valley were among the highest in the nation.

By and large, the unemployed, the service workers, and the Valley's low-paid production workers—who have always earned a fraction of the professionals' salaries—were driven from the centers of employment. San Jose, the county's traditional urban center and home to half its residents, became a bedroom community for the production workforce.

Palo Alto, which receives property and sales tax revenues from the Stanford Industrial Park, easily provides municipal services to its relatively affluent citizens. San Jose, on the other hand, has a much smaller tax base from which it must serve the county's poor residents. Production workers from San Jose spend their days in the north county, generating wealth for electronics companies to pay into suburban treasuries. They then return to homes protected by San Jose's underfunded police and fire departments and streets poorly maintained by its public works department.

Nowhere are the two worlds of Silicon Valley further apart than in education. Palo Alto's public school system is considered among the best in the nation. In fact, that is a major reason why high-tech professionals move to the area. In 1983, however, the San Jose Unified School District, the largest of several districts in the city, became the first American school system since 1943 to declare bankruptcy.

A few years back, several women on the morning shift at Verbatim, a Silicon Valley manufacturer of memory disks for computers, complained of dizziness, shortness of breath, and weakness. Some even reported seeing a haze in the factory air. More than 100 people were quickly evacuated from the building, and the company sent 35 of them to a nearby industrial clinic.

Hours later, inspectors from the California Occupational Safety and Health Administration could not find fumes intense enough to explain the complaints, and they termed the episode "mass psychogenic illness," also known as assembly-line hysteria. In the stressful world of high-volume electronics assembly, hysteria is not unknown. But chances are high that the Verbatim workers' bodies

had detected the presence of toxic chemicals at a level below the threshold recognized by health officials.

High-tech industry's environmentally controlled "clean rooms," in which electronics workers must wear surgical gowns and gloves, are not designed to protect the workers; they are built to protect microelectronic products against particulate contamination. Despite the protective clothing, equipment, and vents found at a typical semiconductor plant, in the pressure to meet production quotas many Silicon Valley workers are frequently exposed to hazardous liquids and fumes.

The hazardous materials used in semi-conductor production include acids, cyanide compounds, organic solvents, and silicon tetrachloride, which turns into hydrochloric acid when its fumes are inhaled into the lungs. Arsine gas, a lethal form of arsenic, can cause serious damage to the liver, heart, and blood cells, even when inhaled in small quantities. It has been used extensively for years in the production of silicon chips. Now, as the Pentagon is promoting the development and production of chips based upon gallium arsenide instead of silicon, the likelihood of workers being exposed to arsenic is growing.

It is possible that communities and regions which study the lessons of Silicon Valley can substantially reduce the risk high-tech production poses to the environment and public health. Unfortunately, high tech's environmental record has not leaked out to the rest of the country. Officials who promote high tech as a solution to local or regional economic ills paint a picture of the industry as shiny as the surface of a silicon wafer. They call high tech a "sunrise industry," clean and light in contrast to "smokestack" industries like steel and auto production, known for their drab, monstrous factories and ever present plumes of vapor and smoke.

It isn't hard to see where high tech got its reputation. Electronic products—chips, computers, switchboards, and so on—don't breathe exhaust or drip oil. The factories are rambling, well-landscaped buildings, resembling modern college libraries; no smokestacks protrude above their facades. Many production steps take place in so-called clean rooms, where the air is fanatically filtered and production workers wear surgical gowns. But the industry's vast investment in cleanliness is designed principally to protect microelectronic components from the dust particles that could prevent them from functioning properly. It does not protect high-tech's workers nor the residents who live in the communities that surround the plants, from the toxic chemicals and metals essential to high-tech manufacturing.

One of the greatest ironies of micro-electronics technology is that the transformation of America into an information society relies, at its core, upon a technology from the industrial era: chemical processing. The manufacture of chips, printed circuit boards, magnetic media, and other high-tech products uses some of the most dangerous materials known to humanity. And the accidental release of those toxins into the air, the ground, and bodies of water poses a significant threat to public health.

High-tech pollution is a fact of life wherever the industry has operated for any length of time, from Malaysia to Massachusetts. Yet nowhere has the growing threat that electronics production poses to public health been clearer than in Silicon Valley, where the concentration of high-tech production has greatly magnified the industry's environmental problems.

The hazards of high tech have become increasingly clear during the past few years, but it may be decades before the full impact on public health is known. The electronics industry uses thousands of different toxic materials, yet the volume is small compared to chemical-intensive industries such as petroleum and pesticide production. Still, a Bhopal-like incident, in which hundreds of people are killed immediately from a single leak, is a serious possibility.

Even without such a catastrophic accident, however, the long-term toll from high-tech pollution may be enormous. High-tech toxics have been slowly entering the environment of Silicon Valley for decades. Though widely used chemicals such as hydrocarbon solvents are known to cause ailments ranging from headaches to birth defects to cancer, it is difficult to demonstrate that any particular person is a victim of a particular leak or spill. But there is no doubt that industrial chemicals are affecting the health of growing numbers of people.

San Jose attorney Amanda Hawes is one of a handful of Silicon Valley activists who warned for years that high tech was indeed a hazardous industry. She has built up her reputation by representing electronics workers injured by chemicals on the job. Today she also represents residents of the Los Paseos neighborhood in southern San Jose. A new, comfortable, working-class suburb typical of Silicon Valley, Los Paseos is distinguished by the presence of a chip manufacturing factory built by Fairchild Semiconductor in 1975.

Hawes carries with her a large zoning map of the area surrounding the Fairchild plant. On every block in the surrounding neighborhood there are several colored pins and flags. Each triangular red flag represents a child born with heart anomalies; each blue pin marks a miscarriage; each yellow flag signals a cancer case. Black flags, superimposed on the other markers, note recent deaths. Hawes also carries with her a supply of pins, and she must frequently add one to the display. She charges that Fairchild is responsible for the area's high incidence of disease.

Most of Hawes's clients believed that electronics was a pollution-free industry until January 1982. At that time, officials disclosed that six weeks earlier they had shut down a drinking water well operated by the Great Oaks Water Co., just 2,000 feet from an underground storage tank, including suspected carcinogens trichloroethane and dichloroethylene, had entered the water supply. When residents learned of the leak, they quickly concluded that the company was to blame for the area's alarmingly high incidence of birth defects and miscarriages.

Since then, Fairchild spent at least $15 million to reduce the concentration of solvents in the aquifer, but the water will never be as clean as it was before Fairchild set up shop there. Now the factory stands empty, a monument to the dying myth of high tech as a clean, light industry.

The Fairchild leak exploded onto the local front pages and six o'clock news, breaking through a longstanding barrier of silence on high-tech pollution. The Bay Area press, public officials, and electronics corporations themselves have all been forced to investigate environmental hazards that nobody wanted to believe existed.

Today, scarcely a week passes without the revelation of a new leaking storage tank, poisoned well, or pollution law violation. As soon as the extent of the Fairchild leak was known, other companies started to test the ground water around their underground chemical tanks, and the Bay Area's Regional Water Quality Control Board ordered a comprehensive testing program. Most of the Valley's large production sites were checked—and most came up dirty. Even firms with a reputation for environmental concern, like Hewlett-Packard, had been leaking dangerous toxics used in their manufacturing process.

Leaks were found at scores of industrial locations within Santa Clara County, but many small facilities have still not been tested.

Nineteen high-tech sites have been placed on the Environmental Protection Agency's "Superfund" list. Nine public and more than sixty private wells have been shut down; many others contain legally allowed levels of contamination. Luckily, Silicon Valley residents have thus far been spared an outright environmental disaster. The Valley's largest source of drinking water is protected by a 200-foot layer of clay, which separates polluted ground water from deep aquifers.

Though Fairchild and nearby IBM began the task of clean-up soon after pollution from their facilities was discovered, many Valley electronics firms have not done much more than sink test wells to determine the extent of their leaks. Pools of hazardous chemicals still drift around underground, poisoning shallow private wells and possibly finding a route—for example, via an abandoned agricultural well—to the public water supply. Unless the toxic chemicals are removed or neutralized before they percolate through the clay, the primary water supply of several hundred thousand people will be permanently poisoned. Silicon Valley is sitting on a toxic time bomb. No one knows when it is set to go off; certainly, not enough is being done to defuse it.

Study Questions

1. What is the libertarian approach to stop pollution? Would they allow the government to have a role big enough to help solve the problem of pollution?

2. Should we be generally optimistic that there will be a technological fix to help us solve our environmental problems, or should we be more pessimistic and conclude that technology is more part of the problem than part of the solution?

105

The Case of Nuclear Power

Denis Hayes

Arguments against nuclear power are rooted in a simple paradox. Commercial nuclear power is viable only under social conditions of absolute stability and predictability. Yet the mere existence of fissile materials undermines the security that nuclear technology requires.

A commitment to nuclear fission is uncompromising and unending. This power source cannot brook natural disasters or serious mechanical failures, human mistakes or willful malevolence. It demands an unprecedented vigilance of our social institutions and demands it for a quarter million years. At the same time, the use of commercial nuclear power dramatically increases the fragility of the human civilization. Acceptance of nuclear technology amounts to acceptance of the inevitable spread of nuclear weapons from nation to nation, and the near-certainty that some nuclear bombs will end up in terrorist hands. The debate is not whether nuclear power will lead to nuclear weapons; it is beyond question. What is unknown is who will control these bombs, how they will be used, and what their use will portend for even the most stable environments.

The weapons proliferation question ranks above all others. But a swarm of auxiliary problems, many of which have received more scrutiny in some countries than in others, deserves attention. If the world is indeed to "go nuclear," all will be legitimate matters of international concern. The entire case against commercial nuclear power deserves broad scrutiny *before* we become irreversibly committed to a nuclear future....

Global nuclear development was initially spurred by the belief that fission would provide a cheap, clean, safe source of power for rich and poor alike. However, the dream of "electricity too cheap to meter" has foundered under a heavy burden of technical, economic, and moral problems—some of which appear to be inherently unsolvable. A growing body of analysis suggests that the total costs of nuclear power far outweigh the total benefits....

Early nuclear critics tended to be gadflies, pointing out flaws in reactor designs and calling for immediate remedies. With the passage of years, many of these reformers became outright opponents, convinced that the problems with nuclear technology were so intractable that commercial fission should be bypassed as a major energy source. In early 1976, three high-level officials resigned from the U.S. General Electric Company in order to work full-time on behalf of the Nuclear Safeguards Initiative in California. Antinuclear sentiment is now coalescing into an international movement with a rapidly growing base of political support....

Although fission was at one time viewed as a "clean" source of energy, it is now opposed by almost every major environmental organization in the world. Nonetheless, nuclear proponents continue to argue that nuclear power is ecologically benign.

The environmental argument is almost always framed in terms of the relative environmental costs of nuclear power and coal. Moreover, the environmental effects of a perfectly functioning nuclear fuel cycle are usually measured against the American experience with coal *before* the passage of the landmark Coal Mine Safety Act and *before* the implementation of the Clean Air Act of 1970. Coal mine accidents in the United States have decreased steadily over the last few years, and improvements in mining conditions will result in a dramatic decrease in the incidence of black lung disease. When electric utilities are finally compelled to meet the terms of the Clean Air Act, airborne emissions (which in the past have been a major health menace, causing widespread premature death among the elderly and people suffering from respiratory ailments) will be significantly reduced.

Moreover, comparisons between coal and nuclear power plants are irrelevant to the great majority of nations without significant coal reserves. Thus, if environmental comparisons are to be made, they ought to focus on the relative impacts of nuclear power and renewable sources (solar power, wind power, wood and other organic sources, etc.) that are available to all countries.

At present, thermal pollution and radiation are the principal environmental dangers spawned by the nuclear fuel cycle. Other threats may be unleashed. Should nuclear power grow to the point where massive amounts of low-grade ore were being processed for fuel, environmental repercussions would surely be felt. If nuclear power were to survive until mankind stumbled into a nuclear war, the environmental consequences would be of an altogether different magnitude.

All mechanical processes that generate electricity also generate thermal pollution. But nuclear power plants cast off more waste heat per unit of electricity produced than does any other commercial technology. This heat must be dissipated, either through the use of cooling towers or through direct discharge into a body of water. Since cooling towers are exceedingly expensive, most reactors planned around the world will inject heat directly into lakes and streams. If a power plant operates constantly, the local habitat would undergo a massive transformation and a new ecosystem that could thrive at the higher temperatures would develop. However, reactors must be shut down regularly for fuel changes, and irregularly for various other reasons. Thus, the consequent erratic temperature changes make it difficult for any stable ecological community to survive.

Many of the problems associated with a nuclear reactor would be multiplied manyfold with the coming of a proposed pattern of intensive nuclear development misleadingly called a "nuclear park." The park would contain uranium enrichment facilities, a fuel fabrication plant, a large number (10 to 40) individual reactors, and a fuel reprocessing plant. The thermal burden associated with such a development could be sufficient to alter the local climate and, possibly, to generate a continuous cloud cover. Yet Dr. Chauncey Starr, President of the Electric Power Research Institute, considers such parks the "inevitable result of the growth of the nuclear power industry."

The environmental threats posed by the nuclear power cycle cannot be fully measured without an understanding of the effects of radiation on life at the molecular level—an understanding that is at present far from complete. The radiation associated with nuclear power is emitted through the spontaneous decay of reactor-produced radioactive materials. (In addition to its 100 tons of uranium oxide fuel, one large modern reactor contains about two tons of various radioactive isotopes—one thousand times as much radioactive material as the Hiroshima bomb produced.) Each radioactive isotope has a pre-cisely measurable half-life (time during which half the atoms in any piece of that radioactive material will decay) that ranges from less than a second to more than a million years. The half-life of plutonium-239, the most controversial isotope associated with nuclear power, is 24,400 years. . . .

The effects of "ionizing radiation" have been studied in many experiments performed on hamsters, guinea pigs, and beagles. Some clear statistical correlations have emerged—especially in experiments involving high dosages of radiation. But we have almost no knowledge of the cancer-causing and mutation-causing mechanisms at the molecular level. We know that radiation causes cancer, but we don't know *how* it causes cancer.

Information on the effects of radiation on human beings is sketchier than that on radiation-exposed laboratory animals. The debate over the effects of atmospheric nuclear bomb tests, sparked by two-time Nobel Prize winner Linus Pauling, has never been resolved (although a large and growing body of evidence seems to support Pauling's claims.) A U.S. medical data bank, established in 1968 to monitor nuclear workers, has been handicapped by the refusal of some private nuclear companies to cooperate. Moreover, this "Transuranium Registry" has been unable to track down many exposed workers from the early years of the nuclear era—a severe research handicap since many radiation-induced effects have very long lag times before symptoms appear.

Because we lack a scientific understanding of how ionizing radiation actually affects discrete biological processes, the link between cause and effect is necessarily speculative (much as is the case with cigarette smoking). This inductive leap leaves the experts divided. The Natural Resources Defense Council, an environmental group, is petitioning U.S. authorities to lower the permissible concentration of plutonium aerosols by 115,000 times.

Many radiation disputes revolve around linear concepts, around the probability of an ill-effect increasing in direct proportion to the amount of radiation received. Will even very low dosages cause some cancers, or is there a threshold below which exposure to radiation is harmless? If a minuscule amount of lung tissue is subjected to a very high dosage of radiation, should the likelihood of cancer be derived from the high intensity in the physically affected area or from the low intensity in relation to the whole lung?

We don't understand the molecular biology of radiation-induced cancer, so our policies are necessarily based upon statistical inferences. But radiation statistics are particularly ambiguous because (1) routine radiation from nuclear power is in addition to inescapable radiation from other sources and considerable variation exists in the amount of natural background radiation and medical radiation that people are subjected to; (2) interrelationships between different types of cancers and different types of radiation are extremely confusing; (3) the public is exposed to many carcinogens other than radiation that cannot be controlled in large-scale epidemiological surveys; and (4) because of the lag time, many potential radiation victims die from other causes before radiation-induced effects appear.

The low levels of radioactive isotopes routinely emitted through a perfectly functioning nuclear fuel cycle, or from a leaking low-level waste repository, have not been "proven" either safe or unsafe. In several developed countries, reactor emission standards have been dramatically tightened in recent years, although not enough to satisfy many critics. Other countries have no standards whatsoever—even though radionuclides can become concentrated up to several thousand times as they move up a food chain, so dilute emissions may be in a more dangerous form when ingested by people at the top of the food chain. . . .

Every major energy transition brings with it profound social change. The substitution of coal for wood and wind ushered in the industrial revolution. The petroleum era revolutionized mankind's approach to movement—restructuring our cities and shrinking our world. Now, at the twilight of the petroleum age, we face another energy transition in the certain knowledge that it will radically alter tomorrow's society. Each of the many energy options available to us today carries with it far-reaching social implications.

Nuclear power is highly centralized, technically complex, capital intensive, and fraught with long-term dangers. It produces electricity, a form of energy that is difficult to store and that can be transported only along expensive, vulnerable corridors. Some of the consequences of the widespread use of nuclear power can be easily anticipated.

Increased deployment of nuclear power must lead to a more authoritarian society. Reliance upon nuclear power as the principal source of energy is probably possible only in a totalitarian state. Nobel Prize winning physicist Hannes Alfven has described the requirements of a stable nuclear state in striking terms:

> Fission energy is safe only if a number of critical devices work as they should, if a number of people in key positions follow all of their instructions, if there is no sabotage, no hijacking of transports, if no reactor fuel processing plant or waste repository anywhere in the world is situated in a region of riots or guerrilla activity, and no revolution or war—even a "conventional one"—takes place in these regions. The enormous quantities of extremely dangerous material must not get into the hands of ignorant people or desperados. No acts of God can be permitted.

The existence of highly centralized facilities and their frail transmission tendrils will foster a garrison mentality in those responsible for their security. Such systems are vulnerable to sabotage, and a coordinated attack could immobilize even a large country, since storing a substantial volume of "reserve" electricity is so difficult. Moreover, 100,000 shipments of plutonium each year would saddle societies with risks that have no peace-time parallel.

Nuclear power is viable only under conditions of absolute stability. The nuclear option requires guaranteed quiescence—internationally and in perpetuity. Widespread surveillance and police infiltration of all dissident organizations will become social imperatives, as will deployment of a paramilitary nuclear police force to safeguard every facet of the massive and labyrinthine fissile fuel cycle.

Broad nuclear development could, of course, be attempted with precautions no more elaborate or oppressive than those that have characterized nuclear efforts to date. Such a course would assure a nuclear tragedy, after which public opinion would demand authoritarian measures of great severity. Orwellian abrogations of civil liberties would be tolerated if they were deemed necessary to prevent nuclear terrorism.

Guarding long-lived toxic radioactive waste will require not just the sworn vigilance of centuries; it will require an eternal commitment. Thoughtful nuclear supporters are suggesting the creation of a nuclear "priesthood" to assume the burden of perpetual surveillance. Since the nuclear wastes now being created will remain toxic for 100 times longer than all recorded human history, an approach with quasi-religious overtones is only fitting.

The capital-intensive nature of nuclear development will foreclose other options. As governments channel massive streams of capital into directions in which they would not naturally flow, investment opportunities in industry, agriculture, transportation, and housing—not to mention those investments in more energy-efficient technologies and alternative energy sources—will be bypassed. The U.S. Project Independence effort would require one trillion dollars by 1985, four-fifths of which would be earmarked for new rather than replacement facilities. Under such a scenario, new energy plants would require two-thirds of all net capital investment during that period. If Project Independence were more exclusively nuclear, the figure would be even higher.

With such a large portion of its capital tied up in nuclear investments, a nation will have no option but to continue to use this power source, come what may. Already it has become extremely difficult for many countries to turn away from their nuclear commitments. If current nuclear projections hold true for the next few years, it will be too late. Already there have been frightening examples of falsified reports filed by nuclear owners seeking to avoid expensive shutdowns. When vast sums are tied up in initial capital investments, every idle moment is extremely costly. After some level of investment, the abandonment of a technology becomes unthinkable.

In a world where money is power, these same large investments will cause inordinate power to accrue to the managers of nuclear energy.

These managers will be a highly trained, remote, technocratic elite, making decisions for an alienated society on technical grounds beyond the public ken. C. S. Lewis has written that "what we call Man's power over Nature turns out to be a power exercised by some men over others with nature as its instrument." As nations grow increasingly reliant upon exotic technologies, the authority of the technological bureaucracies will necessarily become more complete. Energy planners now project that by the year 2000 most countries will be building the equivalent of their total 1975 energy facilities *every three years*. Although central planners may have no difficulty locating such a mass of energy facilities on their maps, they will face tremendous difficulties siting them in the actual countryside of a democratic state. . . .

The nations of the world must together make an end-of-an-epoch decision. As the finite remaining supply of petroleum fuels continues to shrink, the need for a fundamental transition becomes increasingly urgent. The nuclear Siren is presently attracting much interest, but hopefully her appeal will be short-lived. Alternatives are abundant.

Coal can play an important role in the immediate future. The energy context of the world's remaining coal far exceeds that of the remaining oil, and recent advances in mining and combustion will allow much of this resource to be tapped without imposing unacceptable environmental costs.

A wide range of solar devices is becoming available. Systems to capture low-grade heat to warm buildings and water—uses which constitute more than 25 percent of current energy needed in all countries—are now on the market at competitive prices. Photovoltaics, thermalelectric systems, bioconversion processes, windpower, and other benign, renewable options promise large amounts of relatively low-cost, reliable, high-quality energy with less effort than would be required by the new generation of breeder reactors. Solar options can be decentralized, simple, adapted to indigenous materials, and dependent only upon a country's energy "income" from the sun. They produce no toxic wastes and no potential bomb materials.

Finally, it is of critical importance that greater attention be paid to opportunities for energy conservation. The United States could, according to several analyses, eliminate about half of its fuel budget without significant alterations in its economic system or its way of life. Even greater reductions might be accompanied by improvements in public health and the general quality of life. Sweden and West Germany manage to achieve an excellent standard of living on about half the U.S. per capita level of fuel consumption. Enormous savings can be made throughout much of the industrialized world, where for the last several decades cheap energy has been systematically substituted for labor, capital, and materials. Even in poor countries, the replacement of open fires with cheap, efficient stoves, the use of inexpensive pressure cookers instead of pots, etc., would allow significant energy savings. Moreover, such countries should employ anticipatory conservation measures in their development plans, taking care to avoid the sloppiness and wastefulness that characterize those nations that industrialized in the era of cheap oil.

It is already too late to halt entirely the widespread dissemination of the scientific principles underlying nuclear power. What *can* still be sought, however, is the international renunciation of this technology and all the grave threats it entails. Although the nuclear debate has been dominated by technical issues, the real points of controversy fall in the realm of values and ethics. No person, regardless of technical skill, has a right to impose a personal moral judgment on society. No country, regardless of strength, will be able to make the nuclear decision for the world. But if increasing numbers of people and countries begin independently and actively to oppose nuclear power, the world may follow.

Study Questions

1. Is nuclear power worth the long-term risks involved? What are your reasons for your answer?

2. Do Chernobyl and the Challenger disaster give you serious doubts about the reliability of technology in general and nuclear power in particular?

*3. What would you do if you found out that you had been working unknowingly with dangerous carcinogens for several years while your company's management hid the dangers from you?

4. Does the profit motive give nuclear power plants too much of an incentive to skimp on safety? Isn't it amazingly expensive for a nuclear power plant to "go off line" (shut down) even for a day or two?

*5. NIMBY is a severe problem with nuclear power, since the radioactive waste nuclear power produces remains toxic for so long. NIMBY stands for "not in my backyard." If everyone in your community would be paid $5,000 to allow a disposal site for toxic chemicals or wastes to be located nearby, would you support or oppose its construction? Assume the plant design was certified by the government and industry as absolutely safe.

APPENDICES

Appendix A

Guidelines for Writing Papers in Business Ethics

Concentrate primarily on guidelines 1 through 6 when writing your first draft, but follow *all* 18 guidelines before submitting your paper. Points with an asterisk (*) are especially important. The numerical order does not indicate any order of importance.

1. Number *all* your pages (except the title page) and *don't* use any covers for your paper. Just staple your paper in the upper left-hand corner. Create an imaginative title for your paper that clearly indicates your paper's main question and that summarizes your answer to that question.

*2. Announce in your first paragraph what conclusion you will argue for in your paper and what moral principles you will use to support your conclusion. State your moral evaluations of each morally questionable action in your case clearly and early in your first paragraph on page 1. You must argue from at least one moral principle. Clearly identify which arguments are yours. Take a stand on the main issues early on, and continue to take stands on issues throughout your paper.

*3. Anticipate and fully present all significant counterarguments to your view, and respond to them. You may respond by modifying your position or by arguing against them. In your first paragraph on page 1 announce what moral principles your opponents will use. You will find counterarguments in the assigned readings. The better the argument, whether it favors your side or not, the more space you should devote to it in your paper.

*4. Avoid extreme moral relativism and extreme moral skepticism.

*5. Show that you have read and mastered all the assigned readings. You must always use endnotes to indicate what readings you are discussing. See guideline no. 15. Carefully present and evaluate *all* the arguments in the assigned readings that are relevant to your paper topic. *Don't* view the paper as a mere exercise that must be completed; the paper is one of the few chances you will have to show what

you know. View the paper as a great opportunity to show *all* of the *relevant* information you know. Your paper should be an analytical paper rather than a research paper. You might find some outside research helpful *after* mastering and analyzing the readings assigned. But you *must* document *any* factual claims you make that are not obvious. If you have any doubt about whether your factual claims are obvious, document them. See guideline no. 15. Philosophy papers are not history or psychology papers. Morally evaluate and argue; don't just describe.

*6. Give the *full* and *complete* definition of any principle or concept when you first use it. After you have given the definition, you should just repeat the element in the definition that you intend to apply to evaluate an action in your case. Since this course involves applying principles and concepts, define your terms and then *show how* they *apply* to the case or argument in question. Show, *by argument*, that the moral principles make the facts of the case morally relevant. Argue that the facts favor one side rather than the other(s). The more principles you can use (without distorting the moral principles or the facts of your case) to support your moral evaluations, the better your paper will be.

7. Use topic sentences. Use words to show the relationships between sentences in your arguments (e.g., "In other words," "That is," "For example," "But," "However," "Still," "And," "Besides," "Indeed," "So," "Therefore," "Further," "Furthermore," "Moreover," "Similarly," "Likewise," "Contrariwise," "On the contrary," "Rather," "Instead," "In sum," "Finally," " In conclusion").

*8. Minimize assumptions, especially key, controversial, or unstated assumptions. *Clearly* and *explicitly argue* for every moral evaluation you make. Morally evaluate every morally questionable action in your case. The number will vary from case to case.

*9. Be specific.

*10. Use *extreme* words (e.g., "any," "all," "always," "whenever," "never," "no," "none," "every," "solely," "only," "must," "absolutely," "unquestionable") only with *extreme caution*. Avoid hyperbole. Don't overstate arguments. Avoid slanted rhetoric.

11. Avoid using rhetorical questions as substitutes for arguments. Try to answer any questions you pose in your paper. Consider the following exchange from Gore Vidal's novel *Lincoln*:

> Seward: "Never end a speech with a question."
> Lincoln smiled, "For fear you'll get the wrong answer?"
> Seward nodded, "People are perverse."

12. Be brief. Eliminate unnecessary words, but use any words needed to make your argument clear and forceful.

*13. If a paragraph consists of only one or two brief sentences, check to see whether the paragraph is best incorporated into another paragraph of your paper. If a paragraph runs for much over a page, check to see that you are neither rambling, merely drifting down a stream of consciousness, nor being verbose.

14. Avoid using scarequotes (i.e., inverted commas).

*15. Use an endnote precisely citing the *page* and the source to credit others whenever you use their ideas. Follow the same method of using endnotes that is used in one of your required books. Avoid quote-quilting (that is, overusing others' arguments and merely weaving them together into a position).

*16. Avoid understating your point. Probabili-ties are usually crucial. Showing a mere possibility is helpful only when rebutting a claim that something is impossible.

*17. Expose the commission of any fallacies others commit, but don't oversimplify or distort others' views or the definitions of fallacies just to rebut your opponents. Don't commit any fallacies yourself.

*18. *Proofread your paper carefully*! At best, typographical or grammatical errors distract your reader; and dividing your reader's attention risks misinterpretation. At worst, such errors obscure thoughts you wish to convey, and convince your reader that his or her wisdom is no match for your ignorance. Here are some words often misspelled or misused: (1) it's "argument," not "arguement"; (2) "it's" means "it is"; (3) "its" is the possessive of "it"; (4) "criterion" is singular and "criteria" is plural; (5) it's "solely," not "soley" or "soly"; (6) "occurrence," not "occurence"; (7) "likelihood," not "likelyhood."

Appendix B

Conventional Wisdom Is Self-contradictory: Why Is Common Sense So Nonsensical?

Isn't morality, after all, just a matter of common sense? But bits of conventional wisdom in commonsense proverbs seem to cancel each other out and thus fail to provide specific or reliable guidance. Moral principles sometimes conflict but often have enough complexity and specificity to allow rational argument to end the conflict. Here are examples of prescriptions and observations in commonsense adages that cancel each other out and provide little or no basis for rational argument instead of sloganeering.

1. "Birds of a feather flock together" versus "Opposites attract."
2. "Two heads are better than one" versus "Too many cooks spoil the broth."
3. "Too many cooks spoil the broth" versus "Many hands make light work."
4. "Knowledge is power" versus "Ignorance is bliss."
5. "Ignorance is bliss" versus "Look before you leap."
6. "Look before you leap" versus "He who hesitates is lost."
7. "He who hesitates is lost" versus "Haste makes waste."
8. "Haste makes waste" versus "Opportunity knocks just once."
9. "Opportunity knocks just once" versus "Look before you leap."
10. "Look before you leap" versus "What you don't know can't hurt you."
11. "What you don't know can't hurt you" versus "Knowledge is power."
12. "Knowledge is power" versus "Curiosity killed the cat."
13. "Curiosity killed the cat" versus "Look before you leap."
14. "There's no such thing as a free lunch" versus "Don't look a gift horse in the mouth."
15. "The squeaky wheel gets the grease" versus "Silence is golden."
16. "Silence is golden" versus "Money talks."
17. "Money talks" (and "Money doesn't grow on trees") versus "Talk is cheap."
18. "Absence makes the heart grow fonder" versus "Out of sight, out of mind."
19. "Misery loves company" versus "Familiarity breeds contempt."
20. "Charity begins at home" versus "Familiarity breeds contempt."
21. "Familiarity breeds contempt" versus "Home is where the heart is."
22. "Familiarity breeds contempt" versus "Every frog likes to croak about its own pond."
23. "Every frog likes to croak about its own pond" versus "The grass is always greener on the other side."
24. "The grass is always greener on the other side" versus "A rolling stone gathers no moss."
25. "A rolling stone gathers no moss" versus "Nothing ventured, nothing gained."
26. "A rolling stone gathers no moss" versus "There's no substitute for experience."
27. "There's no substitute for experience" versus "Violence begets violence."
29. "Seeing is believing" versus "All that glitters is not gold."

Appendix C

Selected Bibliography of over 300 Works on Affirmative Action

Compiled by Sterling Harwood and Tracy Russ

Abrahms, Kathryn, "Gender Discrimination and the Transformation of Workplace Norms," *Vanderbilt Law Review* 42 (1989): 1183.

Abrams, Charles, Foreword to *Equality*, by Robert Carter. (New York: Pantheon, 1965), pp. i–xiv.

Abrams, Eliot, "The Quota Commission," *Commentary* 50 (October 1972).

Adelson, Joseph, "Living with Quotas," *Commentary* 65 (May 1987): 23–29.

Alevy v. Downstate Med. Center, N.Y.S. Court of Appeals, Apr. 8, 1976.

Alexander, George J., "Symposium—*Bakke v. Board of Regents*: Foreword," *Santa Clara Law Review* 17 (1977): 271–278.

Amdur, Robert, "Compensatory Justice: The Question of Costs," *Political Theory* 7 (May 1979): 229–244.

America, Richard, "A New Rationale for Income Redistribution," *The Review of Black Political Economy* 2 (1972).

"Are Sex-Based Classifications Constitutionally Suspect?" *Northwestern Law Review* 66 (1971).

Astin, Helen, *The Woman Doctorate in America* (New York: Russell Sage Foundation, 1969).

Auer, Andreas, "Public School Desegregation and the Color-Blind Constitution." *Southwestern Law Journal* 27 (August 1973): 454–489.

Axelsen, Diana, "With All Deliberate Delay: On Justifying Preferential Policies in Education and Employment," *Philosophical Forum* 9 (Winter-Spring 1977–1978): 264–288.

Babcock, Barbara, Ann Freedman, Eleanor Norton, and Susan Ross, *Sex Discrimination and the Law: Causes and Remedies* (Boston: Little, Brown and Company, 1975).

Baker, C. E., "Outcome Equality or Equality of Respect: The Substantive Content of Equal Protection," *University of Pennsylvania Law Review* 131 (1983): 933.

Balabkins, Nicholas, *West German Reparations to Israel* (New Brunswick, N. J.: Rutgers University Press, 1971).

Barasch, Frances, "H.E.W., the Universities, and Women," *Dissent* 20 (Summer 1973): 332–40.

Bard, Bernard, "College for All: Dream or Disaster?," *Phi Delta Kappan* 56 (1975).

Barnett, Marguerite Ross, "A Theoretical Perspective on American Racial Policy," in *Public Policy for the Black Community: Strategies and Perspectives*, ed. Marguerite Ross Barnett and James A. Hefner (Port Washington, N.Y.: Alfred Publishing Company, 1976), pp. 1–54.

Bates, F. L. "A Conceptual Analysis of Group Structure," *Social Forces* 36 (1957): 103–11.

Bayles, Michael D., "Compensatory Reverse Discrimination in Hiring," *Social Theory and Practice* 2 (Spring 1973): 301–312.

_____, "Reparations to Wronged Groups," *Analysis* (June 1973): 182–184, reprinted in *Reverse Discrimination*, Barry R. Gross ed., (Buffalo, N.Y.: Prometheus Books, 1977).

Becker, Gary S., *The Economic Approach to Human Behavior* (Chicago: University of Chicago Press, 1976).

_____, "The Economics of Discrimination" (Chicago: University of Chicago Press, 1957).

Bedau, Hugo Adam, "Compensatory Justice and the Black Manifesto," *The Monist* 56 (January 1972): 20–42.

Bell, Derrick A., Jr., "Bakke, Minority Admissions, and the Usual Price of Racial Remedies," *California Law Review* 67 (January 1979): 3–19.

_____, "Black Students in White Law Schools: The Ordeal and the Opportunity," *Toledo Law Review* (1970): 539.

_____, "Book Review: *Affirmative Discrimination: Ethnic Inequality and Public Policy*, by Nathan Glazer," *Emory Law Journal* 25 (Fall 1976): 879–898.

_____, "In Defense of Minority Admissions Programs: A Reply to Professor Graglia," *University of Pennsylvania Law Review* 119 (1970): 264.

_____, "Introduction: Awakening after *Bakke*," *Harvard Civil Rights–Civil Liberties Law Review* 14 (Spring 1979): 1–6.

_____, "Racial Remediation: A Historical Perspective on Current Conditions," *Notre Dame Lawyer* 52 (October 1976): 5–29.

_____, "Racism in American Courts: Cause for Black Disruption or Despair?," *California Law Review* 61 (1973): 165.

Benhabib, Seyla, *Critique, Norm and Utopia: A Study of the Foundations of Critical Theory* (New York: Columbia University Press, 1986).

Benn, S. I., and R. S. Peters, *The Principles of Political Thought* (New York: Free Press, 1965).

Bennett, Robert W., "Objectivity in Constitutional Law," *University of Pennsylvania Law Review* 132 (1984): 445.

Bennett, William J., and Terry Eastland. "Why Bakke Won't End Reverse Discrimination," *Commentary* 66 (September 1978): 29–35.

Benson, Robert S., and Harold Wolmen, eds. *Counterbudget: A Blueprint for Changing National Priorities 1971–1976* (New York: Praeger, 1971).

Berger, Raoul, *Government by Judiciary: The Transformation of the Fourteenth Amendment* (Cambridge: Harvard University Press, 1977).

Bertrand, A. L., *Basic Sociology* (New York: Appleton-Century-Crofts, 1967).

Bickel, A., "The Original Understanding and the Segregation Decision," *Harvard Law Review* 69 (1955): 1.

Binder, Guyora, "Mastery, Slavery and Emancipation," *Cardozo Law Review* 10 (1989): 1435.

Bittker, Boris I. *The Case for Black Reparations* (New York, Vintage Books, 1973).

_____ , "The Case of the Checker-Board Ordinance: An Experiment in Race Relations," *Yale Law Journal* 71 (1962): 1887.

Black, Virginia, "The Erosion of Legal Principles in Creation of Legal Policies," *Ethics* 84 (January 1974): 93–115.

Blackstone, William T., "An Assessment of the Ethical Pros and Cons of Reverse Discrimination," in *Philosophy and Public Policy*, ed. Donnie J. Self (Norfolk, Va.: Teagle and Little, Inc., 1977), pp. 53–67.

_____ , "Compensatory Justice and Affirmative Action," *Proceedings of the American Catholic Philosophical Association* 69 (1975): 218–229.

_____ , "Reverse Discrimination and Compensatory Justice," *Social Theory and Practice* 3 (Spring 1975): 253–288.

Blackstone, William T., and Robert Heslep, eds., *Social Justice and Preferential Treatment* (Athens, Ga.: University of Georgia Press, 1977).

Blasi, Vincent, "Bakke as Precedent: Does Mr. Justice Powell Have a Theory?" *California Law Review* 67 (January 1979): 21–69.

Block, N. J., and Gerald Dworkin, eds., *The I.Q. Controversy* (New York: Pantheon Books, 1976).

Blumenrosen, Alfred, *Black Employment and the Law* (New York: Rutgers University Press, 1971).

_____ , "The Crossroads for Equal Employment Opportunity: Incisive Administration or Indecisive Bureaucracy?" *Notre Dame Law* 49 (1973): 46.

_____ , "Quotas, Common Sense, and Law in Labor Relations: Three Dimensions of Equal Opportunity," *Rutgers Law Review* 27 (Spring 1974): 675–703.

_____ , "Strangers in Paradise: *Griggs v. Duke Power Co.* and the Concept of Employment Discrimination," *Michigan Law Review* 71 (1975): 59.

Boxhill, Bernard, *Blacks and Social Justice*, rev. ed. (Totowa, N.J.: Rowman and Littlefield, 1993).

_____ , "The Morality of Preferential Hiring," *Philosophy and Public Affairs* 7 (Spring 1978): 246–268.

_____ , "The Morality of Reparations," *Social Theory and Practice* 2 (1972): 113–24; reprinted in *Today's Moral Problems*, ed. Richard Wasserstrom (New York: Macmillan Publishing Company, 1975), pp. 209–217.

Bracy, Warren, "The Questionable Legality of Affirmative Action: A Response," *Journal of Urban Law* 51 (February 1974): 421–431.

_____ , "The Questionable Legality of Affirmative Action: A Response to Rejoinder," *Journal of Urban Law* 52 (November 1974): 273–276.

Brest, Paul, "The Supreme Court 1975 Term Forward: In Defense of the Antidiscrimination Principle," *Harvard Law Review* 90 (1976): 1.

Brown, Dee, *Bury My Heart at Wounded Knee* (New York: Bantam, 1971).

Brown, Robert A., "The Economic Basis for Reparations to Black America," *The Review of Black Political Economy* 2 (1972).

Cadei, Raymond M., "Hiring Goals, California State Government, and Title VII: Is This Numbers Game Legal?" *Pacific Law Journal* 8 (January 1977): 49–72.

Calabresi, Guido, "*Bakke* as Pseudo-Tragedy," *Catholic University Law Review* 28 (Spring 1979): 427–444.

Campbell, T. D., "Equal of Opportunity," *Proceedings of the Aristotelian Society* 75 (1974–75): 51–68.

Carnegie Commission on Higher Education, *Making Affirmative Action Work* (San Francisco: Jossey-Bass, 1975).

Carter, Robert L., *Equality* (New York: Pantheon, 1965).

Carter, Stephen L., *Reflections of an Affirmative Action Baby* (New York: Basic Books, 1991).

Choper, Jesse H., "The Constitutionality of Affirmative Action: Views from the Supreme Court," *Kentucky Law Journal* 79 (1981–82): 1.

_____ , "Continued Uncertainty as to the Constitutionality of Remedial Racial Classifications: Identifying the Pieces of the Puzzle," *Iowa Law Review* 72 (1987): 255.

Cohen, Carl, "The DeFunis Case: Race and Constitution," *The Nation* (February 8, 1975): 135–145.

_____ , "Why Racial Preference is Illegal and Immoral," *Commentary* 67 (June 1979): 40–52.

Cohen, Marshall, Thomas Nagel, and Thomas Scanlon, eds. *Equality and Preferential Treatment* (Princeton, N.J.: Princeton University Press, 1977).

Coleman, Jules L., "Justice and Preferential Hiring," *Journal of Critical Analysis* 5 (July-October 1973): 27–30.

_____ , "Moral Theories of Torts: Their Scope and Limits, Part II," *Law and Philosophy* 2 (1983): 3.

Cooper, G., and R. B. Sobol, "Seniority and Testing under Fair Employment Laws: A General Approach to Objective Criteria of Hiring and Promotion," *Harvard Law Review* 82 (1969): 1598.

Copp, David, "Collective Actions and Secondary Actions," *American Philosophical Quarterly* 16 (July 1979): 177–186.

Coser, Rose Laub, "Affirmative Action: Letter to a Worried Colleague," *Dissent* 22 (Fall 1975): 366–369.

Countryman, Vern, ed. *Discrimination and the Law* (Chicago: University of Chicago Press, 1965).

Cowan, L. J. "Group Interests," *Virginia Law Review* 44 (1958).

Cowan, J. L. "Inverse Discrimination," *Analysis* 33 (October 1972): 10–12.

Cox, Archibald, "Foreword: Constitutional Adjudication and the Promotion of Human Rights," *Harvard Law*

Review 80 (November 1966): 91–122.

_____, *The Role of the Supreme Court in American Government* (New York: Oxford University Press, 1976).

Crandel, John C., "Affirmative Action: Goals and Consequences," *Philosophical Exchange* 1 (Summer 1974).

Crenshaw, Kirberle, "Race, Reform and Retrenchment: Transformation and Legitimation in Antidiscrimination Law," *Harvard Law Review* 101 (1988): 1331.

Crocker, Lad, "Preferential Treatment: An Approach to the Topics," *UCLA Law Review* 24 (February 1977): 581–622.

"DeFunis," Columbia Law Review 75 (1975): 483.

Ezorsky, Gertrude, ed., *Moral Rights in the Workplace* (Albany, N.Y.: State University of New York Press, 1987). Chapter 7 of this book is called "Discrimination and Affirmative Action" and is composed of five essays and four legal cases.

Ford, Maureen, and Lisa H. Newton, eds., *Taking Sides: Clashing Views on Controversial Issues in Business Ethics and Society* (Guilford, Conn.: Dushkin Publishing, 1992).

Fullinwider, Robert K., *The Reverse Discrimination Controversy: A Moral and Legal Analysis* (Totowa, N.J.: Rowman and Littlefield, 1980).

Fullinwider, Robert K., and Claudia Mills, *The Moral Foundations of Civil Rights* (Totowa, N.J.: Rowman and Littlefield, 1986).

Goldman, Alan H., *Justice and Reverse Discrimination* (Princeton, N.J.: Princeton University Press, 1979).

Greenawalt, Kent, ed. *Discrimination and Reverse Discrimination* (New York: Alfred A. Knopf, 1983).

Gross, Barry R., *Discrimination in Reverse: Is Turnabout Fair Play?* (New York: New York University Press, 1978).

_____, Review of O'Neill, *Discrimination against Discrimination*, and Glazer, *Affirmative Discrimination*, in *The Humanist* (November-December, 1976).

_____, "Is Turnabout Fair Play?," *The Journal of Critical Analysis* 5 (1975): 4.

_____, Letter, *The New York Times* (April 1975): 12.

_____, *Reverse Discrimination* (Buffalo, N.Y.: Prometheus Press, 1977).

Gruner, Rolf, "On the Action of Social Groups," *Inquiry* 19 (Winter 1976): 443–454.

Guinier, Ewart, "Review: *The Case for Black Reparations* by Boris I. Bittker," *Yale Law Journal* 82 (July 1973): 1719–1724.

Guinier, Lani, "Don't Scapegoat the Gerrymander," *The New York Times Magazine* (January 8, 1995): 36–37.

Gunther, Gerald, *Constitutional Law*, 11th ed. (Mineola, N.Y.: Foundation Press, 1985).

_____, "Foreword: In Search of Evolving Doctrine on a Changing Court: A Model for a Newer Equal Protection, The Supreme Court, 1971 Term," *Harvard Law Review* 86 (1972): 1.

Gutmann, Amy, *Liberal Equality* (Cambridge: Cambridge University Press, 1980).

Hadreas, Peter, "Foucault and Affirmative Action," *Praxis International* 11 (2) (July 1991): 214–226.

Hall, James H., Jr. "A Case for Reverse Discrimination," in *Philosophy and Public Policy*, ed. Donnie J. Self (Norfolk, Va.: Teagle and Little, 1977), pp. 68–73.

Harder, Martha B., "How They Get Us with Subtle Discrimination," *Context* 12 (Spring 1978): 21–23.

Hare, R. M., "What Is Wrong With Slavery?," *Philosophy and Public Affairs* (1979).

Harwood, Sterling, "Affirmative Action Is Justified: A Reply to Newton," *Contemporary Philosophy* 13 (2) (March/April 1990): 14–17.

_____, "Against MacIntyre's Relativistic Communitarianism," in *Liberalism and Community*, ed. R. Moffat, C. Murphy and N. Reynolds (New York: New York University Press, forthcoming, 1995).

_____, "The Justice of Affirmative Action," in Yeager Hudson and Creighton Peden, eds., *The Bill of Rights: Bicentennial Reflections* (Lewiston, N.Y.: Edwin Mellen Press, 1993), pp. 77–89.

Henkin, Louis, "*DeFunis*: An Introduction," *Columbia Law Review* 75 (April 1975): 481–494.

_____, "What of the Right to Practice a Profession?" *California Law Review* 67 (January 1979): 131–141.

Hill, Herbert, , "The New Judicial Perception of Employment Discrimination: Litigation under Title VII of the Civil Rights Act of 1964," *University of Colorado Law Review* 43 (March 1972): 243–268.

Hill, James, "What Justice Requires: Some Comments on Professor Schoeman's Views on Compensatory Justice," *Personalist* 56 (Winter 1975): 96–103.

Hook, Sidney, "The Bias in Anti-Bias Regulations" (review of Lester, below), *Measure* (Summer 1974).

_____, "Discrimination, Color Blindness, and the Quota System," *Measure* (October 1971).

_____, "Discrimination, Color Blindness, and the Quota System," in *Reverse Discrimination*, ed. Barry Gross (Buffalo, N.Y.: Prometheus Books, 1977), 84–87.

_____, "H.E.W. Regulations—A New Threat to Educational Integrity," *Freedom at Issue* 10 (1971).

_____, "A Quota Is a Quota" (op-ed), *The New York Times* (November 1974), 13.

_____, "The Road to a University Quota System," *Freedom at Issue* (March-April 1972).

Hooks, Benjamin L., "Affirmative Action: A Needed Remedy," *Georgia Law Review* 21 (1987): 1043.

Horowitz, Donald L. "Are the Courts Going Too Far?" *Commentary* 63 (January 1977): 37–44.

Jacobson, Julius, "Notes on the Bakkelash," *New Politics* 12 (3) (Winter 1978): 66–68.

Jaggar, Alison, "Relaxing the Limits of Preferential Treatment," *Social Theory and Practice* 4 (Spring 1977): 227–235.

Johnson, Sheila K., "It's Action, But Is It Affirmative?" *The New York Times Magazine* (May 1975): 11.

Jones, Hardy, "Fairness, Meritocracy, and Reverse Discrimination," *Social Theory and Practice* 4 (Spring 1977): 211–226.

Jones, J. E., "The Bugaboo of Employment Quotas," *Wisconsin Law Review (1970): 341.

———, "Federal-Contract Compliance in Phase II—The Dawning of the Age of Enforcement of Equal Employment Obligations," *Georgia Law Review* 4 (1970): 756.

Kahn v. Shevin, 416 U.S. 351 (1974), Brennan, J., dissenting.

Kain, J. F., *Race and Poverty: The Economics of Discrimination* (Englewood Cliffs, N.J.: Prentice-Hall, 1969).

Karst, Kenneth L., "Foreword: Equal Citizenship under the Fourteenth Amendment," *Harvard Law Review* 91 (November 1977): 1–68.

Karst, Kenneth L., and Harold W. Horowitz, "Affirmative Action and Equal Protection," *Virginia Law Review* 60 (October 1974): 955–974.

———, "The *Bakke* Opinions and Equal Protection Doctrine," *Harvard Civil Rights-Civil Liberties Law Review* 14 (Spring 1979): 7–29.

Katzner, Louis, "Is the Favoring of Women and Blacks in Employment and Educational Opportunities Justified?" in *Philosophy of Law*, 4th ed., ed. Joel Feinberg and Hyman Gross (Belmont, Calif.: Wadsworth, 1991), pp. 468–473.

Kohlberg, Lawrence, *The Philosophy of Moral Development: Moral Stages and the Idea of Justice* (New York: Harper and Row, 1981).

Kurland, P., "Egalitarianism and the Warren Court," *Michigan Law Review* 68 (1970): 629.

———, *Politics, the Constitution, and the Warren Court* (Chicago: University of Chicago Press, 1971).

Kuttner, Bob, "White Males and Jews Need Not Apply," *The Village Voice* (August 31, 1972).

Lavinsky, Larry M., "*DeFunis v. Odegaard*: The 'Non-Decision' with a Message," *Columbia Law Review* 75 (April 1975): 520–533.

Lester, Richard, *Anti-Bias Regulation of Universities* (New York: McGraw-Hill, 1974).

Levin, Betsy, and Willis D. Hawley, eds. *The Courts, Social Science, and School Desegregation* (New Brunswick, N.J.: Transaction Books, 1977).

Levine, D. M., and M. J. Bane, eds., "The 'Inequality' Controversy: School after DeFunis—Filling the Constitutional Vacuum," *University of Florida Law Review* 27 (1975): 315.

Lichtman, Richard, "The Ethics of Compensatory Justice," *Law in Transition Quarterly* 1 (1964): 76.

Livingston, John C., *Fair Game?: Inequality and Affirmative Action* (San Francisco: W. H. Freeman and Co., 1979).

Longwood, Merle, "Justice and Reparations: The Black Manifesto Reconsidered," *Lutheran Quarterly* 27 (August 1975): 203–213.

Lorch, Barbara R., "Reverse Discrimination in Hiring in Sociology Departments: A Preliminary Report," *American Sociologist* 8 (August 1973): 116–170.

Lucas, John, *On Justice* (Oxford: Clarendon Press, 1980).

Lukes, Stephen, *Individualism* (New York: Harper and Row, 1973).

Lyliffs, N.J.: Prentice-Hall, Inc., 1975. Held focuses on two questions: How long is it reasonable to expect the victims of past discrimination to wait for a redress of their wrongs? What reasonable rate of progress would not involve a lass of self-respect?

Lyon, Catherine D., and Terry Saario, "Woman in Educational Administration," *UCEA Review* (September 1974).

Lyons, David, "Rights, Utility, and Racial Discrimination," in *Philosophical Law*, ed. Richard Bronaugh (Westport, Conn.: Greenwood Press, 1978), pp. 74–83.

MacGuigan, Mark R., "Reverse Discrimination Reversed, " in *Philosophical Law*, ed. Richard Bronaugh (Westport, Conn.: Greenwood Press, 1978), pp. 84–92.

MacIntyre, Alasdair, "Utilitarianism and Cost-Benefit Analysis: An Essay on the Relevance of Moral Philosophy to Bureaucratic Theory," in *Values in the Electric Power Industry*, ed. K. Sayre (Notre Dame, Ind.: University of Notre Dame Press, 1977).

———, *After Virtue*, 2nd ed. (Notre Dame, Ind.: University of Notre Dame Press, 1981).

———, *Whose Justice? Which Rationality?* (Notre Dame, Ind.: University of Notre Dame Press, 1988).

MacKinnon, Catherine, *Feminism Unmodified: Discourses on Life and Law* (Cambridge: Harvard University Press, 1987).

Maguire, Daniel C., "The Triumph of Unequal Justice," *Christian Century* 95 (1978): 882.

Marcuse, P., "Benign Quotas Re-examined," *Journal of Intergroup Relations* 3 (1962).

Marketti, Jim, "Black Equity in the Slave Industry," *The Review of Black Political Economy* 2 (1972).

Martin, Michael, "Pedagogical Arguments for Preferential Hiring and Tenuring of Women Teachers in the University," *Philosophical Forum* 5 (Fall-Winter 1973–1974).

Martinez, Suzanne, "Affirmative Action and Public Education: Some Preliminary Issues and Questions," *Youth Law Center* (September 1975).

Murray, Charles, and Richard Herrnstein, *The Bell Curve: Intelligence and Class Structure in American Life* (New York: Free Press, 1994).

Nagel, Thomas, "Equal Treatment and Compensatory Discrimination," *Philosophy and Public Affairs* 2 (4) (Summer 1973): reprinted in *Ethics and Public Policy* ed. Tom Beauchamp (Englewood Cliffs, N.J.: Prentice Hall, Inc., 1975).

Navasky, Victor, "The Greening of Griffen Bell," *The New York Times Magazine* (February 27, 1977), pp. 41–44, 50.

Newton, Lisa H., "Reverse Discrimination as Unjustified," *Ethics* (1973): 308–312; reprinted in *Today's Moral Problems*, ed. Richard Wasserstrom (New York: Macmillan Publishing Co., 1975), pp. 204–209; *Reverse Discrimination*, ed. Barry R. Gross (Buffalo, N.Y.: Prometheus Books, 1977), pp. 373–378; *Philosophical Issues in Law*, ed. Kenneth Kipnis (Englewood Cliffs, N.J.: Prentice Hall, 1977), pp. 240–245; *Social Ethics: Morality and Social Policy*, ed. Thomas A. Mappes and Jane Zembaty (New York: McGraw-Hill, 1977), pp. 173–177; *Personal and Social Ethics: Moral Problems with Integrated Theory,* ed. Vincent Barry (Belmont, Calif.: Wadsworth, 1978), pp. 339–343; *Moral Issues*, ed. Jan Narveson (New York: Oxford University Press, 1983), pp. 388–392; *The Philosophy of Law*, 3rd ed., ed. Joel Feinberg and Hyman Gross (Belmont, Calif: Wadsworth, 1986), pp. 346–458; *Ethics and the Professions*, ed. David Appelbaum and Sarah Verone Lawton (Englewood Cliffs, N.J.: Prentice Hall 1990), pp. 178–181; *Contemporary Issues in Business Ethics*, 2nd ed., ed. Joseph R. DesJardins and John J. McCall (Belmont, Calif.: Wadsworth, 1990), pp. 384–387; *Taking Sides: Clashing Views on Controversial Moral Issues*, 2nd ed., ed. Stephen Satris (Guilford, Conn.: Dushkin, 199), pp. 262–266; reprinted as "Against Affirmative Action" in *Ethics for Modern Life*, 4th ed., ed. Raziel Abelson and Marie-Louise Friquegnon (New York: St. Martin's Press, 1991), pp. 271–275; *Applying Ethics: A Text with Readings*, 4th ed., ed. Jeffrey Olen and Vincent Barry (Belmont, Calif.: Wadsworth, 1992), pp. 326–329; and *Taking Sides: Clashing Views on Controversial Issues in Business Ethics and Society*, 2nd ed., ed. Lisa H. Newton and Maureen M. Ford (Guilford, Conn.: Dushkin Publishing, 1992), pp. 70–74.

_____, "Bakke and Davis: Justice, American Style," *National Forum* 53 (1978): 22–23; reprinted in *Social Ethics: Morality and Social Policy*, 2nd ed., ed. Thomas A. Mappes and Jane S. Zembaty (New York: McGraw-Hill, 1982), pp. 185–186.

_____, "Corruption of Thought, Word and Deed: Reflections on Affirmative Action and Its Current Defenders," *Contemporary Philosophy* 13 (7) (January/February 1991): 14–16.

Newton, Lisa H., and Maureen M. Ford, "Postscript: Are Programs of Preferential Treatment Unjustifiable?," in *Taking Sides: Clashing Views on Controversial Issues in Business Ethics and Society*, 2nd ed., ed. Lisa H. Newton and Maureen M. Ford (Guilford, Conn.: Dushkin Publishing, 1992), p. 81.

Nickel, James W., "Discrimination and Morally Relevant Characteristics," *Analysis* 32 (March 1972): 113–114.

_____, Review of Boris Bittiker, *The Case for Black Reparations*, in *Ethics* 84 (1974): 2.

_____, "Should Reparations Be to Individuals or to Groups?" *Analysis* 34 (April 1974): 154–160.

_____, "Preferential Policies in Hiring and Admissions: A Jurisprudential Approach," *Columbia Law Review* 75 (April 1975): 534–559.

_____, Review of Robert M. O'Neil, *Discriminating against Discrimination*, in *The Chronicle of Higher Education*, forthcoming.

Noonan, Richard D., "Semantics of Equality of Educational Opportunity," *Teachers College Record* 76 (September 1974): 63–88.

"Note: Constitutional Law and Reverse Discrimination," *Cincinnati Law Review* 41 (1972): 250.

"Note: Constitutionality of Remedial Minority Preferences in Employment," *Minnesota Law Review* 56 (1972): 56.

"Note: Decline and Fall of the New Equal Protection: A Polemical Approach," *Virginia Law Review* 58 (1972): 1489.

"Note: Racial Bias and the LSAT: A New Approach to the Defense of Preferential Admissions," *Buffalo Law Review* 24 (1975): 439.

Novak, J., R. Rotunda, and J. Yound, *Constitutional Law* 2nd ed. (St. Paul, Minn.: West Publishing, 1983).

Nunn, William A., "Reverse Discrimination," *Analysis* 34 (April 1974): 151–154.

O'Fallon, James, "Adjudication and Contested Concepts: The Case of Equal Protection," *New York University Law Review* 54 (1979): 189.

O'Krueger, Anne, "The Economics of Discrimination," *Journal of Political Economy* 72 (1963).

O'Neil, Robert M., *Bakke* in Balance: Some Preliminary Thoughts," *California Law Review* 67 (January 1979): 143–170.

_____, *Discriminating against Discrimination: Preferential Admissions and the DeFunis Case* (Bloomington, Ind.: Indiana University Press, 1975).

_____, "Preferential Admissions: Equalizing Access to Legal Education," *Toledo Law Review* (1970): 281.

_____, "Preferential Admissions: Equalizing the Access of Minority Groups to Higher Education," *Yale Law Journal* 80 (1971): 699.

_____, "Racial Preference and Higher Education: The Larger Context," *Virginia Law Review* 60 (October 1974): 60.

_____, "Comparative Evaluation of Forums," *Washington Law Review* 46 (1971): 455.

O'Neill, Onora, "How Do We Know When Opportunities Are Equal?," in *Feminism and Philosophy*, ed. Mary Vetterling-Braggin, Frederick A. Ellison, and Jane English (Totowa, N.J.: Littlefield, Adams and Co., 1981), pp. 177–189.

Pelikan, Jaroslav, "Quality and Equality," *The New York Times* (March 29, 1976).

Pemberton, John de, Jr. ed., *Equal Employment Opportunity—Responsibilities, Rights, Remedies* (New York: Practicing Law Institute, 1975).

Perelman, Chaim, *The Idea of Justice and the Problem of Argument* (London: Routledge & Kegan Paul, 1963).

Perry, Michael J., "Modern Equal Protection: A Conceptualization and Appraisal," *Columbia Law Review* 79 (1979): 1023.

Pettit, Philip, *Judging Justice: An Introduction to Contemporary Political Philosophy* (London: Routledge & Kegan Paul, 1980).

Plamenatz, John, "Equality of Opportunity," in *Aspects of Human Equality*, ed. Lyman Bryson et al. (New York: Harper, 1956).

Plessy v. Ferguson, 163 U.S. 537 (1896), Harlan, J., dissenting.

Pollack, Louise H., "*DeFunis* Non Est Disputantum," *Columbia Law Review* 75 (April 1975): 495–511.

Pollit, D. H., "Racial Discrimination in Employment: Proposals for Corrective Action," *Buffalo Law Review* 13 (1963): 59.

Pollock, Mordeca Jane, "On Academic Quotas" (op-ed), *The New York Times* (March 4, 1975).

Poplin, Caroline, "Fair Employment in a Depressed Economy: The Layoff Problem" *UCLA Law Review* 23 (December 1975): 177–234.

Posner, Richard A., "The *Bakke* Case and the Future of 'Affirmative Action,'" *California Law Review* 67 (January 1979): 171–189.

———, "The *DeFunis* Case and the Constitutionality of Preferential Treatment of Racial Minorities," in *The Supreme Court Review*, ed. Philip Kurland (Chicago: University of Chicago Press, 1975), pp. 1–32.

Pottinger, Stanley, "The Drive toward Equality," in *Sex Discrimination and the Law*, ed. Barbara Babcock et al. (Boston: Little, Brown and Company, 1975), pp. 514–518.

"Preferential Treatment and Other Improper Procedures ..." pamphlet submitted to the secretary of H.E.W. by six Jewish organizations, April 8, 1972.

"Proportional Representation by Race: The Constitutionality of Benign Racial Redistricting," *Michigan Law Review* 74 (March 1976): 820–841.

Rae, D., D. Yates, J. Hochschild, J. Morone, and C. Fessler, *Equalities* (Cambridge: Harvard University Press, 1981).

Raphael, D. D., "Equality and Equity," *Philosophy* 21 (1946).

Rawls, John, "Justice as Fairness," *Philosophical Review* (April 1958): 164–194.

———, *A Theory of Justice* (Cambridge: Harvard University Press, 1971).

Raz, Joseph, "Principles of Equality," *Mind* 88 (July 1978): 321–342.

Redish, Martin H., "Preferential Law School Admissions and the Equal Protection Clause: An Analysis of the Competing Arguments," *UCLA Law Review* 22 (December 1974): 343–400.

"Report of the AAUP Committee on Discrimination," *AAUP Bulletin* (June 1973).

Rescher, Nicolas, *Distributive Justice* (Indianapolis, Ind: Bobbs-Merrill, 1976).

Reynolds, William Bradford, "An Equal Opportunity Scorecard," *Georgia Law Review* 21 (1987): 1007.

Richards, David A. J., "Equal Opportunity and School Financing: Towards a Moral Theory of Constitutional Adjudication," *University of Chicago Law Review* 41 (Fall 1973): 32–71.

———, *The Moral Criticism of the Law* (Encino, Calif: Dickenson Publishing Company, 1977).

———, *Toleration and the Constitution* (New York: Oxford University Press, 1986).

Richardson, Henry J., III, "Black People, Technocracy and Legal Process: Thoughts, Fears, and Goals," in *Public Policy for the Black Community: Strategies and Perspectives*, ed. Marguerite Ross Barnett and James A. Hefner (Port Washington, N.Y.: Alfred Publishing Company, 1976), pp. 157–190.

Rosenfeld, Michel, "Contract and Justice: The Relation between Classical Contract Law and Social Contract Theory," *Iowa Law Review* 70 (1985): 69.

———, "Affirmative Action, Justice, and Equalities: A Philosophical and Constitutional Appraisal," *Ohio State Law Journal* 46 (1985): 845.

———, "Substantive Equality and Equal Opportunity: A Jurisprudential Appraisal," *California Law Review* 74 (1986): 1687.

———, "Hegel and the Dialectics of Contract," *Cardozo Law Review* 10 (1989): 1199.

———, "Decoding *Richmond*: Affirmative Action and the Elusive Meaning of Constitutional Equality," *Michigan Law Review* 87 (1989): 1729.

———, *Affirmative Action and Justice: A Philosophical and Constitutional Inquiry* (New Haven, Conn.: Yale University Press, 1991).

Ross, Alf, *On Law and Justice* (London: Stevens & Sons, 1958).

Rossum, Ralph A., "Ameliorative Racial Preference and the Fourteenth Amendment: Some Constitutional Problems," *Journal of Politics* 38 (May 1976): 346–366.

Rothbard, Murray, "The Quota System, in Short, Must Be Repudiated Immediately," *Intellectual Digest* (February 1973).

St. Antoine, Theodore, "Affirmative Action, A 'Heroic' Measure" (op-ed), *The New York Times* (November 26, 1976).

———, "Affirmative Action: Hypocritical Euphemism or Noble Mandate?," *University of Michigan Journal of Law Reform* 10 (Fall 1976): 28–43.

Samford, Frank P., "Towards a Constitutional Definition of Racial Discrimination," *Emory Law Journal* 25 (Summer 1976): 509–578.

San Antonio Independent School District v. Rodriguez, 411 U.S. 1 (1973).

Sandler, Bernice, Letter, *Commentary* 53 (1972): 14–16.

Sandlow, Terrance, "Judicial Protection of Minorities," *Michigan Law Review* (April-May 1977): 1162–1195.

———, "Racial Preferences in Higher Education: Political Responsibility and the Judicial Role," *University of Chicago Law Review* 42 (Summer 1975): 653–703.

Sasseen, Robert F., "Affirmative Action and the Principle of Equality," *Studies in Philosophy and Education* 9 (Spring 1976): 275–295.

Scales, Ann, "The Emergence of Feminist Jurisprudence: An Essay," *Yale Law Journal* 95 (1986): 1373.

Schaar, John, "Equality of Opportunity and Beyond," In *Nomos IX: Equality*, ed. J. Roland Pennock and John W. Chapman (New York: Atherton, 1967).

Schlafly, Phyllis, *The Power of the Positive Woman* (New Rochelle, N.Y.: Arlington House, 1977).

Schneider, Elizabeth M., and Nadine Taub, "Perspective on Women's Subordination and the Role of Law," in *The Politics of Law: A Progressive Critique*, ed. David Kairys (New York: Pantheon, 1982).

Shoeman, Ferdinand, "When Is It Just to Discriminate?"

Personalist 56 (Spring 1975): 170–177.

Schucter, Arnold, *Reparations* (Philadelphia: Lippincott, 1970).

Schwartz, Herman, "The 1986 and 1987 Affirmative Action Cases: It's All Over but the Shouting," *Michigan Law Review* 86 (1987): 524.

Schwerin, Kurt, "German Compensation for Victims of Nazi Persecution," *Northwestern University Law Review* 67 (September-October 1972): 479–527.

Scott, Jongeward, *Affirmative Action for Women: A Practical Guide for Women and Management* (Addison-Wesley Publishing Co., 1975).

Seabury, Paul, "H.E.W. and the Universities," *Commentary* 53 (February 1972): 38–44.

Sedler, Robert Allen, "Beyond *Bakke*: The Constitution and Redressing the Social History of Racism," *Harvard Civil Rights-Civil Liberties Law Review* 14 (Spring 1979): 133–171.

_____ , "Racial Preference, Reality, and the Constitution: *Bakke v. Regents of University of California*," *Santa Clara Law Review* 17 (1977): 329–384.

Seligman, Daniel, "How 'Equal Opportunity' Turned into Employment Quotas," *Fortune* 87 (March 1973): 160–174.

Sher, George, "Justifying Reverse Discrimination in Employment," *Philosophy and Public Affairs* 4 (Winter 1975): 159–170; reprinted in *Equality and Preferential Treatment* ed. Marshall Cohen, Thomas Nagel, and Thomas Scanlon (Princeton, N.J.: Princeton University Press, 1977).

_____ , "Groups and Justice," *Ethics* 87 (January 1977): 174–181; reprinted in *Moral Rights in the Workplace*, ed. Gertrude Ezorsky (Albany, N.Y.: State University of New York Press, 1987), pp. 253–258.

_____ , "Reverse Discrimination, the Future and the Past," *Ethics* 90 (1979): 81–87.

Sherain, Howard, "The Questionable Legality of Affirmative Action," *Journal of Urban Law* 51 (August 1973): 25–47.

_____ , "The Questionable Legality of Affirmative Action: A Rejoinder," *Journal of Urban Law* 52 (November 1974): 267–271.

Sherman, Malcolm J., "Affirmative Action and the AAUP," *AAUP Bulletin* 61 (Winter 1975): 293–303.

_____ , "Anti-Intellectualism and Civil Rights," *Change* 8 (Winter 1976): 34–40.

Sherry, Suzanna, "Selective Judicial Activism in the Equal Protection Context: Democracy, Distrust, and Deconstruction," *Georgetown Law Journal* 73 (1984): 89.

Shiner, Roger A., "Individuals, Groups and Inverse Discrimination," *Analysis* 33 (June 1973): 185–187.

Silvestri, Philip, "The Justification of Inverse Discrimination," *Analysis* 34 (October 1973): 31–32.

Simon, Robert L., "Preferential Hiring: A Reply to Judith Jarvis Thomson," *Philosophy and Public Affairs* 3 (Spring 1974): 312–320.

_____ , "Equality, Merit, and the Determination of Our Gifts," *Social Research* 41 (Autumn 1974): 492–514.

_____ , "Statistical Justification of Discrimination," *Analysis* 38 (January 1978): 37–42.

_____ , "Individual Rights and 'Benign' Discrimination," *Ethics* 90 (1979): 88–97.

Simpson, Evan, "Discrimination as an Example of Moral Irrationality," in *Fact, Value and Perception: Essays in Honor of Charles A. Baylis,* ed. Paul Welsh (Durham, N.C.: Duke University Press, 1975), pp. 107–122.

Sindler, Allan P., "The Court's Three Decisions," *Regulation* 2 (September-October 1978): 15–23.

Soloman, Lewis D., and Judith S. Heeter, "Affirmative Action in Higher Education: Towards a Rationale for Preference," *Notre Dame Lawyer* 52 (October 1976): 41–76.

Sowell, Thomas, *Black Education: Myths and Tragedies* (New York: McKay, 1974).

_____ , *Affirmative Action Reconsidered* (pamphlet), (American Enterprise Institute for Public Policy Research, 1975).

_____ , "'Affirmative Action' Reconsidered," *Public Interest* 42 (Winter 1976): 47–65; reprinted in *Reverse Discrimination,* ed. Barry R. Gross (Buffalo, N.Y.: Prometheus Books, 1977), pp. 113–131. This is a shorter version of his pamphlet from 1975.

_____ , "A Black Conservative Dissents," *The New York Times Magazine* (August 8, 1976).

_____ , *Civil Rights: Rhetoric or Reality?* (New York: William Morrow, 1984).

Steele, Claude, and Stephen Greer, "Affirmative Action and Academic Hiring: A Case Study of a Value Conflict," *Journal of Higher Education* 47 (July-August 1976): 413–435.

Steele, Shelby, *The Content of Our Character: A New Vision of Race in America* (New York: St. Martin's Press, 1990).

Steinbach, Sheldon, "Fighting Campus Job Discrimination in Higher Education," *Change* 5 (November 1973).

Sterba, James P., "Justice as Desert," *Social Theory and Practice* 3 (1974): 101–116.

Stewart, M. A., ed., *Law, Morality and Rights* (Boston: D. Reidel Publishing Co., 1979), pp. 259–332. Part V of this book is called "Reverse Discrimination" and is composed of essays by Richard, H. S. Tur, Elizabeth H. Wolgast, and Jenny Teichman.

Stone, Julius, "Justice Not Equality," in *Justice* ed. Eugene Kamenka and Alice Erh-Soon Tay (New York: St. Martin's Press, 1980).

Streibergh, Fred, "Troubled Times with A.A." *Yale Alumni Magazine* (April 1973).

Strike, Kenneth A., "Justice and Reverse Discrimination," *University of Chicago School Review* 84 (August 1976): 516–537.

Sullivan, Kathleen M., "Sins of Discrimination: Last Term's Affirmative Action Cases," *Harvard Law Review* 100 (1986): 78.

Summers, Robert Samuel, "Preferential Admissions: An Unreal Solution to a Real Problem," *Toledo Law Review* (1970): 377.

Swann v. Charlotte-Mecklenburg Board of Education, 402 U.S. 1 (1971).

Sweatt v. Painter, 339 U.S. 629 (1950).

Taylor, Paul, "Reverse Discrimination and Compensatory Justice," *Analysis* 33 (June 1973): 177–182.

tenBroek, Jacobus, *Equal under Law* (New York: Collier, 1969).

Tenzer, Morton J., and Rose Laub Coser, "A Debate on Affirmative Action," *Dissent* 23 (Spring 1976): 208–210.

Thalberg, Irving, "Justifications of Institutional Racism," *Philosophical Forum* (1971–1972).

_____ , "Reverse Discrimination and the Future," *Philosophical Forum* 5 (Fall-Winter 1973–1974); reprinted in *Women and Philosophy: Toward a Theory of Liberation,* ed. Carol C. Gould and Marx W. Wartofsky (New York: Perigee Books, 1976), pp. 294–308.

_____ , "Themes in the Reverse Discrimination Debate," *Ethics* 91 (1980): 138–50.

U.S. Commission on Civil Rights, 1977; excerpt reprinted in *Moral Rights in the Workplace,* ed. Gertrude Ezorsky (Albany: State University of New York Press, 1987), pp. 283–286.

Vetterling, Mary K., "Some Common Sense Notes on Preferential Hiring," *Philosophical Forum* 5 (Fall-Winter, 1973–1974); reprinted in *Women and Philosophy* ed. Carol C. Gould and Marx Wartofsky (New York: Perigee Books, 1976), pp. 320–324.

Vetterling-Braggin, Mary, Frederick Elliston, and Jane English, eds., *Feminism and Philosophy* (Totowa, N.J.: Littlefield, Adams and Co., 1977).

Vieira, Norman, "Racial Imbalance, Black Separatism and Permissible Classification by Race," *Michigan Law Review* 67 (1969): 1553.

Vulcan Pioneers v. N.J. Dept. of Civil Service, excerpt reprinted in *Moral Rights in the Workplace,* ed. Gertrude Ezorsky (Albany: State University of New York Press, 1987), pp. 278–281.

Wade, Francis C., "Preferential Treatment of Blacks," *Social Theory and Practice* 4 (Spring 1978): 445–470.

Walzer, Michael, *Spheres of Justice: A Defense of Pluralism and Equality* (New York: Basic Books, 1983).

Warren, Mary Anne, "Secondary Sexism and Quota Hiring," *Philosophy and Public Affairs* 6 (Spring 1977): 240–261.

Wasserstrom, Richard A., "The University and the Case for Preferential Treatment," *American Philosophical Quarterly* 13 (April 1976): 165–170.

_____ , "A Defense of Programs of Preferential Treatment," National Forum, *The Phi Kappa Phi Journal;* reprinted in *Taking Sides: Clashing Views on Controversial Issues in Business Ethics and Society,* 2nd ed., ed. Lisa H. Newton and Maureen M. Ford (Guilford, Conn.: Dushkin Publishing, 1992), pp. 75–80.

Weaver, Robert, "Integration in Public Housing," *Annals* 86 (1956).

"*Weber v. Kaiser Aluminum & Chemical Corp.*: The Challenge to Voluntary Compliance under Title VII," *Columbia Journal of Law and Social Problems* 14 (1978): 123–187.

Weinrib, Ernest, "Toward a Moral Theory of Negligence Law," *Law and Philosophy* 2 (1983): 37.

Welch, Finis, "Employment Quotas for Minorities," *Journal of Political Economy* 84 (August 1976): 5105–5139.

Wellman, Carl, *Morals and Ethics* (Glenview, Ill.: Scott, Foresman, 1975).

Westen, Peter, "The Empty Idea of Equality," *Harvard Law Review* 95 (1982): 537.

_____ , "The Concept of Equal Opportunity," *Ethics* 95 (1985): 837.

"What Do You People Want?," *Harvard Business Review* (March-April 1969).

"Where We Stand: Quotas and Goals," pamphlet from the American Jewish Congress (May 12, 1972).

White, Stephen K., *The Recent Work of Jurgen Habermas* (Cambridge: Cambridge University Press).

INDEX

Baltimore, Maryland 267
Bancroft, George 455
Bangladesh 359, 532–533
bankruptcy 55
Bantu 437–439
Barbach, Lonnie 186
Barbour, Haley 207
Barings Bank 356
baseball 36–37, 40, 64, 442–443
Bastiat, Frederic 67
Baumann, Phyllis Tropper 243–247
Beard, Charles 338, 341
Beardsley, Monroe 73
Beatles, the 158–159
Beauchamp, Tom L. 42
beauty 3, 7, 39. *See also* art; aesthetics; taste
Beethoven, Ludwig von 162
Bendix, William 236–238
beneficence 25, 55, 85, 195
    distinguished from benevolence 25
benevolence 25
    distinguished from beneficence 25
Benn, Stanley I. 73
Bennett, Jonathan 16
Bentham, Jeremy 36, 74, 76–77, 79
Berlin 527
Bernhard, Prince 135, 142
BFOQ (bona fide occupational qualification) 195
Bhopal, India 544–547
bias 44, 73. *See also* bigotry; chauvinism; discrimination; racism; sexism
Bible 158, 323
    Bible belt 158
Bickel, Alexander 9
bigotry 42–43. *See also* bias; discrimination; racism; sexism
biology 220
birth control 441
Bishkopf, Yevgeny 472
blacks 48, 81–82, 135. *See also* affirmative action
Blaine, James 137
Bloom, Allan 13
Bloom, Paul 352
Blumenthal, Michael 238
Bogel, Robert 461
Bok, Sissela 279–287
Bolivia 440, 532
Bondanella, Peter 451–453
Book of the Dead, The 134, 137
books 361–365
Boskin, Michael 495
Bosnia 84, 475, 480
Boston 211, 423, 440–441
Boston Tea Party 423
Bostonians, The (Henry James) 28
boycott 171

Boyle, Robert H. 534
Bradbury, Ray 158
Brazil 513–516
breast enlargement 173–174
breastfeeding 171–172
Brennan, Justice William J. 348–350
bribes 133–147, 425
Bridge, Robert 161
Brock, Bill 353
Brooke, Rupert 161
Brooks, James 137
Brown, Judith Olans 243–247
Browner, Carol 526
Buber, Martin 84
Buchanan, James 317
Buchanan, Pat 158–159, 355
Buck, Pearl 177
Buckley, William F., Jr. 166, 197–221
Buddhism 5, 149
Buffalo Springfield, the 43
Buffett, Warren 121
bureaucrats 54, 356, 504, 541
    corporate 356
    international 504
Burke, Edmund 9
Burstein, Karen 197–221
Bush, George Herbert Walker 216, 321, 442, 475, 495, 499–500, 504, 515, 519, 521, 541
Butler, Eamonn 318
Butler, Pat 409–410

Cadillac 359
CAFE (corporate average fuel economy) 503, 520–521
Calderone, Mary 177
California 38, 50, 135, 139, 197, 213, 351, 409, 413, 423, 431–436, 442–443, 455, 501–502, 530, 535, 548–552
Callas, Maria 197
Calvinism 320
Campbell soup 241
Cambridge University 197, 205, 214, 318
Canada 455, 482, 499–505
cannibalism 140
capital 50, 478. *See also* capitalism; money
capital punishment 68
capitalism 52–53, 57, 67, 134, 154, 317–360, 527
    defined 52
    distinguished from democracy 67
    laissez-faire 351f.
care ethics 84
Cargill 499
Caribbean 455
Caro 137
Carpenter, Karen 166
Carritt, E. F. 73
Carson, Rachel 509
cartels 461–473

morality, purpose of 64. *See also* egalitarianism; libertarianism; prima facie principles; utilitarianism; virtue

moral and ethical 2–10, 14–17
relativity, theory of 3, 7
religion 137, 556
    quasi-religious 556
remedies 29
reparation 25
Republic (Plato) 224
Republican Party (GOP) 47, 197, 220, 319–321, 328, 351, 359, 366, 376
Rescher, Nicholas 85
resources 65
responsibilities 48, 190, 243
resumes 394
retirement 484
retribution 26
Revel, Jean-François 476
reverse discrimination. *See* affirmative action
Rhodes, Cecil 471
Ricardo, David 323–324
Richmond v. Croson 113–117
Rickey, Branch 40
Riefenstahl, Leni 443
Riggs v. Palmer 160
rights 29, 49, 58–59, 62–64, 68, 154–156, 191, 193–194, 199, 203, 208, 210, 219, 239, 325, 340, 474–483
    Bill of 199
    civil 194, 210, 239
    equal 203
    feudal 325
    gay 210
    human 474–483
    in personam 59
    in rem 58
    individual 219
    natural 59
    negative 58–59, 62
    positive 59
    right to privacy. *See* privacy
Ringle, Ken 167
Rio de Janeiro 515
risk 121, 131
Robert Half International 409
Roberts, Robert C. 383
Rockefeller, Nelson 142
role models 110
Romans 134, 137, 183–184
Rome 504
Roosevelt, Eleanor 480
Roosevelt, Franklin Delano 28, 351, 359, 395, 443, 477
Roosevelt, Theodore 134, 455–457
Rose, Axl 160
Rosenberg, Isaac 161
Ross, Ian S. 318
Ross, William David 84
Rothbard, Murray 56
Rothschild, Emma 318
Rousseau, Jean-Jacques 79, 226–227, 230

Rowe, V. K. 546
rudeness 26
rules 35, 41–42, 43, 56
Rummel, David 414
Rushton, Philippe 76
Russ, Tracy 561–568
Russell, Bertrand 485–490
Russia 440, 462, 468, 472, 475–476, 478, 486–488. *See also* Union of Soviet Socialist Republics (USSR)
Rwanda 477, 532
Ryder, John 341–344

Sachs, Jeffrey 440
sacrifice 37, 59
sadism 42–43
safety 56. *See also* Occupational Safety and Health Administration (OSHA)
Sagan, Carl 187
Salomon Brothers 120–132
Samuels, Howard 355
Samuels, Myron 130
Samuelson, Paul 317
San Francisco, California 135, 139, 548–551
San Jose, California 548–551
Sandel, Michael 5, 79
Santa Clara County, California 548–551
Sartre, Jean-Paul 84
SAT (Scholastic Aptitude Test) 110
Saudi Arabia 136, 139
Scandanavia 457
scepticism. *See* skepticism
Schaeffer, Nicholas 158–159
Scherer, F. M. 356
Scheer, Robert 173–174
Schlafly, Phyllis 198, 207
Schneider, Claudine 519–524
Schneider, Stephen 520
Schultes, Richard 514
Schumer, Fran 236
Schwartz, Felice 204
science 7, 183, 185, 219, 513–518, 531
Scotland 8, 317–318
Searle, John 7
Sears 53
secrecy 141–143, 279–287, 500. *See also* privacy
Securities and Exchange Commission (SEC) 139, 356
self-discipline 183
self-interest 178, 352
selfishness 54–55, 183, 528
self-respect 80
semiotics 7
sex 3, 26, 39, 137–145, 176, 202, 208, 234, 236–238, 410, 528. *See also* pornography
    sexual dimorphism 176
sexism 3, 39, 167
Shakespeare, William 80, 134, 141, 202
shame 26, 145, 154